Hangingout.
in
ITALY

(H)anging out™ in ITaly

First Edition

Hungry Minds™

Best-Selling Books • Digital Downloads • e-Books • Answer Networks
e-Newsletters • Branded Web Sites • e-Learning

New York, NY ♦ Cleveland, OH ♦ Indianapolis, IN

Project Editors: Kristen Couse and Liz Barrett
Production Managers: Maria Fernandez, Mike Walters
Production Editors: Paul Paddock, Simon Sullivan
Cartographers: Elizabeth Puhl, Roberta Stockwell, Doris Kreisler
Line Editors: Alix McNamara, Kevin McLain, Dana Terebelski
Copy Editors: Corey Alstom, Craig Colligan, Allison Devers,
Rebecca Wolff
Proofreaders: Shoshanna Wingate, Joshua Mehigan
Associate Editor: Nathaniel Knaebel
Editorial Intern: Emily Reid

Published by
Hungry Minds, Inc.
909 Third Avenue
New York, NY 10022

ISBN: 0-7645-6243-6
ISSN: 1531-1562

Book design: Sue Canavan and Mike Walters

Special Sales: For general information on Hungry Minds' products and
services please contact our Customer Care Department within the U.S. at
800-762-2974, outside the U.S. at 317-572-3993 or fax 317-572-4002.

For sales inquires and reseller information, including discounts, premium
and bulk quantity sales, and foreign-language translations, please contact
our Customer Care Department at 1-800-434-3422 or fax 317-572-
4002.

Hanging Out is a trademark or registered trademark of Hungry Minds,
Inc. All other trademarks are the property of their respective owners.

Manufactured in the United States of America

5   4   3   2   1

CONTENTS

ITALY

contents

ITALY

maps

a disclaimer

Please note that prices fluctuate in the course of time, and travel information changes under the impact of the many factors that influence the travel industry. We therefore suggest that you write or call ahead for confirmation when making your travel plans. Every effort has been made to ensure the accuracy of information throughout this book and the contents of this publication are believed correct at the time of printing. Nevertheless, the publishers cannot accept responsibility for errors or omissions or for changes in details given in this guide or for the consequences of any reliance on the information provided by the same. Assessments of attractions and so forth are based upon the author's own experience and therefore, descriptions given in this guide necessarily contain an element of subjective opinion, which may not reflect the publisher's opinion or dictate a reader's own experience on another occasion. Readers are invited to write the publisher with ideas, comments, and suggestions for future editions.

Your safety is important to us, however, so we encourage you to stay alert and be aware of your surroundings. Keep a close eye on cameras, purse, and wallets, all favorite targets of thieves and pickpockets.

foreword

most of us have had the experience of going to a new school or moving to a new neighborhood and not knowing a soul there, not knowing the laws of the land, feeling lost and uncool. But if you're lucky, someone comes along who invites you in and shows you where the action is. The same can be said for travel—unless you're committed to seeing Europe through the moving tinted window of a tour bus, pretty soon you're going to want to get past the initial strangeness and get with it. And to really be able to do that, you need someone or something to help you along, so that what could have been just another cute postcard turns into a new chapter in your life. We created the *Hanging Out* guides to be that thing.

Going to Europe is infinitely more complicated—and ultimately more rewarding—than just going on your standard road trip. Without some help, you may repeatedly find yourself surrounded by a numbed-out tour group, scratching your head and wondering what all the fuss is about. We sent out our team of 15 writers with just that in mind. Go to where the action is, we instructed them, and tell us how to find it.

Of course we tell you how to see all the cultural and historical goodies you've read about in art history class and heard about from your folks, but we also tell you where to find the party, shake your butt, and make friends with the locals. We've tried to find the hottest scenes in Europe—where traditions are being reinvented daily—and make this guide into the equivalent of a hip friend to show you the ropes.

So, welcome to the new Europe, on the verge of mighty unification. The European Union (EU)—and the euro's arrival as a common currency—is already making many happy, others nervous, and setting the entire continent abuzz with a different kind of energy. As the Grand Tour of Europe meets the Info Age, the old ways are having to adjust to a faster tempo.

But even as the globe is shrinking to the size of a dot com, Europe remains a vast vast place with enough history and art and monuments to fill endless guides—so we had to make a choice. We wanted the Hanging Out Guides to live up to their title, so we decided to specialize and not only show you the best spots to eat, shop, sightsee, party, and crash, but also give you a real feeling for each place, and unique but do-able ways to get to know it better. So we don't cover every single European city—instead, we picked what we felt were the best and served them up with plenty of detail. We felt it was crucial to have the room to go deeper, and to tip you off as to how to do the same, so that after you see the sights, you'll almost certainly end up in a place where you'll get to know the secret to the best travel—the locals.

Aside from the basics—neighborhoods, eats, crashing, stuff (shopping), culture zoo (sightseeing stuff), and need to know (the essentials)—we cover the bar scene, the live music scene, the club scene, the gay scene, the visual arts scene, and the performing arts scene, always giving you the scoop on where to chill out and where to get wild. We take you on some beautiful walks and show you great places to hang (sometimes for no money). "Things to Talk to a Local About" actually gives you some fun conversation openers. "Fashion" tells you what people are wearing. "Wired" lists websites for each city—some general, some cool, some out-of-the-way—so you can start checking things out immediately; it also takes you to the best cybercafes in each place. "Rules of the Game" lays out local liquor and substance laws and also gives you the vibe on the street. "Five-0" does a quick sketch of cops in each city. "Boy Meets Girl" dares to speculate on that most mysterious of travel adventures. And "Festivals & Events" lists just that.

Our adventurous team of writers (average age, 24) and editors lets you in on the ongoing party. We want to make sure that your time abroad is punctuated by moments when you've sunk deep enough into the mix (or danced long enough to it), so that you suddenly get it, you have that flash of knowing what it's like to actually be somewhere else, to live there—to hang out in Europe.

INTRODUCTION

Somewhere in Italy, right now, someone is popping open a bottle of wine in a medieval piazza. Someone else is lying on the beach, sand between their toes, daydreaming about the hottie that just walked by. Someone is sitting at an outdoor cafe, sipping their third cappuccino and zoning out on the Renaissance church facade across the street. Someone is window-shopping. Someone is rock-climbing. Someone is sitting around a table with friends after a long meal, deciding whether to go dancing or to bar hop. And someone and a certain someone else they just met are toasting the fine Italian art of *dolce far niente*: the sweetness of doing nothing.

You think you know how to kick back and enjoy the ride? Well, prepare to learn a thing or two from the Italians. Hanging out is an art form here—not just as a way to deal with *"lo stress"* of life, but the point of life itself. More than any other people on the planet, Italians live and revel in the moment, infusing even the most mundane activity with good-hearted conversation and cheer. As Viv Savage said in *This is Spinal Tap:* "Have a good time, all the time." No one rushes anywhere—there's no such thing as an appointment that can't be broken, no excuse for not stopping and talking with a friend, no reason to eat and run. Italians live to have fun, which is why you'll want to hang out here for a good long while.

So when in Rome, do as the Romans (and the Sicilians, and the Venetians, and everyone on this magnificent Mediterranean peninsula) do—chill. Too many agenda-toting travelers miss out on the pleasures of downshifting to the local pace because they're too busy running from Michelangelo's this to Da Vinci's that. Of course, Italy *is* the most culturally and artistically stimulating country in the world: that explains all the tour buses and fanny packs, and is probably why you're here, too. Florence's Renaissance Cathedral, topped by Brunelleschi's dome and flanked by Giotto's tower; Venice's pastiche of eastern and western ornamentation in Piazza San Marco; Rome's ancient survivors, the Pantheon and Coliseum; Ravenna's glittering mosaic-covered churches—these are all unmissable and unforgettable. Museums like Florence's Uffizi, Rome's Sistine Chapel and Vatican museums, and Venice's Accademia together contain the world's best collection of Classical and Renaissance art. But it's easy to miss the best of Italy by trying to see all the best things in it.

The Ghost of Italy Past may have the best PR machine, but the Ghosts of Italy Present and Future have all the fun. The same artistic spirit that fueled both the Renaissance and the swinging '60s of Fellini's films now shines through in the contemporary arts scene, music clubs, and dance parties all over the country. Whether you're looking for your kind of crowd in the anarcho-punk clubs around Bologna, gallery openings in Rome, trendy fashion events in Milan, smoky cafes in Trieste, all-night outdoor parties in Tuscany, Neapolitan wine bars, or seaside dance clubs in Rimini, you'll find willing partners in crime somewhere in this diverse country.

Geography quiz, class: What does the Italian peninsula most resemble? That's right, a boot. On a large scale, you can think of the cowboy footwear that is Italy as broken up into Northeast, Northwest, Central, and South Boot. But hop-scotching through the 20 regions in these areas is like visiting 20 completely different countries, each with its own geography, dialect, foods, fashion sense, and party tactics.

It wasn't until 1861 that Vittorio Emanuel II unified Italy for the first time since the Roman Empire, bringing together an ethnically varied group into one republic. Even today, residents identify themselves first as being from a specific town, second from the region, and third as Italian. This *campanalismo*, which translates into "patriotism for the area within the sound of a town's church bells," make Italians a proud and provincial lot. We've all heard the generalizations that lump all U.S. Southerners together as soft-spoken, gracious, and polite, and all U.S. Northerners as ruthless, fast-talking money-grubbers—similar stereotypes are at work in Italy as well. Everyone knows that Florentines have a great sense of style, and Sicilians are fast-talking charmers, but did you know that the Modenese are known for their business acumen, the Sulmonese for their hospitality, the Perugini for their impulse to throw rocks at their neighbors? Did you know that natives of Alto Adige, on the Austrian border, speak German, and that Slovene is heard just as often as Italian in the farther reaches of Friuli-Venezia Giulia?

Cultural ancestry and linguistic dialects are factors that definitely shape a region's identity, but none so much as culinary inclinations. In Italy, you literally are what you eat, because *what* you eat is determined by where you come from. Each region has its own specialties, and this sort of culinary *campanalismo* means that you'll rarely see dishes or items outside of their region of origin—and when you do, they never taste as good. It also explains why Italian food in America—heavy-sauced spaghetti, pizza, cannoli—isn't on every menu in Italy. This cuisine came from the south, like most Italian immigrants. After tourism, agriculture is Italy's leading industry, so the country's collective appetite is finely tuned to the season's bounty and what grows best in each region. Each town's local food market is a lesson in local produce, cheeses, meats and wine, and furnishes the finest makings of a picnic dinner.

There are just as many types of eateries in Italy as there are food cravings, and lucky for us, you don't have to shell out a load of lire to eat like Italian royalty. *Pizza a Taglio* (by the slice) to *Ristorante free-flows* (self-service) are all over, but you'll still eat best at down to earth *osterie*, casual, rustic looking places with communal tables that serve local wines and regional favorites. *Trattorie* are a bit more polished, and *ristoranti* are down-right fancy. You'll spend a lot of time at the Bar or Caffe—usually a nondescript, fluorescent-lit place serving up coffee, pastries, and *panini* (sandwiches), with outside tables when the weather's nice. No matter what kind of eatery, sitting down at a table means you'll have to shell out a few extra thousand lire per person. This *coperto* is always listed on the menu, and in bars, the Lista dei Prezzi hanging on the wall outlines prices for standing up and sitting down.

And, no, lifting your fork does not count as exercise. From Alpine slopes, to the sea-sprayed coasts on all sides, to subtropical islands, to Italy's version on the Appalachian trail, the Sentiero d'Italia, to national parks, Italy is a dream for both tree-hugging naturalists and lycra-clad adrenalin junkies. Even if you're not planning on hang-gliding off the cliffs of Trieste, or snowboarding in the Dolomites, plan on visiting at least one sleepy village and one gorgeous nature spot, like the Cinque Terre on the Ligurian coast near Genoa or volcanic Mt. Etna on Sicily. The weather in Italy can be anything from desert-like in the South, London foggy in Milan, to snow-capped and crisp in the Alps, so it's a must to pack for various climates if you're covering a lot of ground. The best time to see Italy is anytime but summer, when most of the country gets sticky-hot and all city-dwellers get outta Dodge to the beach or mountain houses. Add the fact that more people travel to Italy in this "high season," and you'll be spending way too much of your trip in line for museums and surrounded by sweaty tourists and pickpockets with no locals in sight. And some of Italy's many vivacious college towns, like Bologna and Perugia, turn into ghost towns during the long breaks around Christmas, Easter, and in the summers.

Italy can take some getting used to, and some great tips are hard to pick up on the first few trips—so listen up. If you plan to do a lot of moving around and you don't have an unlimited Eurail, buy a "kilometric ticket" *(Biglietto Chilometrico)*. This handy little item will allow you to travel 3,000km (or 20 trips, whichever comes first) anywhere in

Italy for one very reasonable price. Just write down the name of the next town you are going to before you get on the train, and have someone at the station ticket counter stamp it. There'll be a supplemental ticket for express trains, but it's still a great bargain. Stamp these supplements and any normal train tickets in the orange boxes on the train platforms before boarding the train, or you'll catch an earful from the conductors. Also, pick up an ARCI card if you are traveling through college towns or planning on hanging out with the locals in big cities. These members-only "social centers" are the heart of the alternative bar and club scene in Italy. You can buy a year-membership in most of they member clubs, which grants you access to all ARCIs in the country, and they usually don't cost more than 20,000L. And as far as bus tickets go, you buy them in tobacco-shops newsstands and stamp them in the little orange boxes on the bus. Even though no one seems to care if you don't, the one time you try to get away with it will be when the *polizia* does a spot-check.

One of Italy's most time-honored traditions, like in other Southern European countries, is the midday siesta. This trend gets stronger as you head toward the Mediterranean. Don't plan to get much sightseeing or re-supplying done between 12:30 and 3:30 PM when, traditionally, everyone closes up shop and heads home for lunch, naps, and maybe a quickie. And you wondered why everyone was always so crazy laid-back.

It's a good thing that the siesta exists. The flip side of *dolce far niente* is that trying to get anything done in Italy can be so exhausting that a nap or a stiff drink is required by noon. ATMs draw money only from your checking account, but never let you know that. Railroad workers are always on strike. There is no way to buy tickets on the bus. Traffic gets so snarled that you dodge cars on the sidewalk.

Take a deep breath and relax—Italy is worth the occasional headache. Keep a paperback in your bag for all the time that you'll spend waiting in lines, and try not to get stressed out by the little old Signora who appears to be cutting in front. You'll get there eventually, and have plenty of time left to enjoy the wine, the piazzas, the beaches, the slopes, the cafes, the clubs, the scenes, or just the dolce far niente.

And when you do, you'll know what the Italians have known forever: it's not about who gets there fastest, but who has the most fun along the way.

Buon viaggio, ragazzi!

the best of ITaly

party spots

Umbrian Jazz Festival [Perugia]: If you can visit Perugia when the jazz men (and women) come to town for 10 days every July, you're in for a treat. It's one of the most important jazz festivals in Europe and the most popular event of the year. The party atmosphere in Perugia is at its peak during the festival when the streets, squares, and concert halls are packed for the concerts that rock the city morning, noon, and night.

Contrapunto [Perugia]: If you can't make it for the Jazz Festival (above), you can take solace in Contrapunto, one of the most popular jazz bars in town. There's live music just about every night during the summer, and they often host well-known national and international bands.

Piazza del Campo [Siena]: This famously pinkish and sea shell–shaped piazza is the geographic, political, social, and party center of Siena. It's always filled with gobs of tourists and locals who are eager to meet other travelers.

Cagliostro [Pisa]: Come to this trendy and stylishly elegant restaurant/bar to mingle with the super stylish Italians.

Meccano [Florence]: The city's best-known nightclub is also its coolest. It has everything that a good nightspot needs: girls dancing on tables, guys doing Chippendales renditions, good cocktails, and many dance floors.

Piazza Santo Spirito [Florence]: If hanging out in piazzas is your thing, this may be your Mecca. It's *the place* to come late at night with a bottle of wine.

Trastevere [Rome]: This neighborhood is by far the best place to go for a night on the town in Rome, maybe in the whole country. Find a great restaurant (there are tons of them), wander from pub to pub until you've had enough, and top the night off by hanging out in Piazza di Santa Maria.

Alpheus [Rome]: Every kind of clubber you could imagine comes here to Alpheus, one of the city's biggest clubs. Why? Easy: It hosts the best parties, hands down.

Rimini: Rimini is to Italy what Daytona Beach is to the U.S. Come for the Spring Break-esque beach party, which lasts from June until August, and stay for the professional-league Eurotrash club scene. Sun-deprived partiers, from Swedes to Slovaks, descend upon this coco-butter-scented club-fest every summer. With city buses that take you from club to club, you'll feel like mindless excess is your civic duty.

Bologna: This lefty college town is packed with more bohemian bars and alterno music spots and coffee houses than a 16 year-old Iowa punk's vision of San Francisco. You might find yourself at a bar at 4am saying, "I forget what I was talking about, but I'm pretty sure it had something to do with Marx."

Trieste: Italians in other cities might not have heard much about this scene, but Trieste is just a few magazine articles away from being Italy's Next Big Thing. Home to the country's only sizeable Mod scene, as well as creative parties thrown by even more creative DJs, Trieste's under-the-radar nightlife may be a little harder to track down than in some places, but you'll be able to say, "I was in Trieste before the hype."

Corso Porta Ticinese [Milan]: The slammin'-est strip in a city that knows no end to nightlife. Chic lounges, bass-booming clubs and English pubs draw the young masses every night of the week till sun-up.

Il Bottigliere [Turino]: With over a hundred bars to choose from, this is the niehgborhood where you'll come closest to finding the local watering hole. If a local isn't persuading you to try his or her favorite wine, one of the young bartenders will be throwing free glasses of whatever your way. You can't go wrong with a place that has corkscrews for their business cards that read "Life is too short to drink bad wine."

the outdoors

Assisi: This historical center is surrounded by forests filled with pastures, fields, hills, and many unusual types of plants and animals. Get out there!

Mura Rinascimentali (Ramparts) [Lucca's]: This 4.2km (2.5 mile) tree-lined promenade runs along the top of Lucca's city walls, and is a great place for cycling, biking, jogging and walking.

Cortina: Brave souls who have skied all their lives quiver in fear at the tops of the twisty, tree-lined expert slopes in the Ampezzo valley around Cortina. The downhills here make hot doggers on North American ski resorts look like bunny-slopers. If skiing's not your bag, you'll still appreciate the Alpine beauty and the Alpine beauties.

Natisone Valley: Italy's version of the Appalachian trail, Sentiero d'Italia, curves up and around the picturesque city of Cividale di Friuli, offering great views, adrenalin-pumping inclines, and relaxing mountain refuges where you can rest your weary soul. Grab a map and a bag full of GORP (Good Ole Risotto and Peanuts) and hit the trails.

Merano: Europeans have been soaking up *la dolce vita* in this Dolomite spa town for centuries. The curative "grape juice" and therapeutic waters are reason alone to come to this high-altitude town, but the little former Austrian villages like Dorf Tirol, accessible by footpaths, make this an almost un-Italian side-trip.

Domaso: Howling thermal winds and crystal waters draw Europe's most addicted windsurfers year round, especially for the handful of windsurfing championships held here over the summer.

Courmayeur: Skiiers, bow your poles—this is the Mecca. 5,000 craggy vertical feet spanning three mountains, consistent snow dumpings and one raging river make for northern Italy's best extreme sports. With heliskiing, ice-climbing and some of the purest hiking the country has to offer, Courmayeur is a must-do.

CULTURE

Basilica di San Francesco [Assisi]: Undoubtedly the Umbria region's biggest tourist attraction, and for good reason. The Basilica is one of the world's primary Christian shrines, and one of Italy's greatest artistic treasures. Be sure to see Giotto's cycle of frescoes depicting important scenes in St. Francis' life in the upper church.

Fontana Maggiore (Grand Fountain) [Perugia]: The 25 incredibly detailed reliefs and statues on the base of this fountain were carved by Nicola Pisano and his son Giovanni. The lower basin depicts the months of the year and their corresponding zodiac signs; the statuettes around the upper basin are of saints, bible characters, and 13th-century local officials.

Basilica di San Pietro (St. Peter's Basilica) [Rome]: Come get in line. The Vatican holds thousands of Italy's greatest works of art, and much of St. Peter's itself was designed by the greatest Renaissance artists. The Basilica sits on one of the great architectural creations in the world, Piazza San Pietro, which was designed by Lorenzo Bernini and consists of pillared colonnades that curve around the square and reach toward the Basilica.

Vatican Museums/Sistine Chapel [Rome]: Undoubtedly the best art collection in the world, with works by all of the top Renaissance artists like Botticelli, Raphael, Ghirlandaio, Perugino, Signorelli, and Michelangelo.

Pantheon [Rome]: This is the only ancient building in Rome that remains perfectly preserved. It's architecturally unique because of its perfect proportions. The walls of the Pantheon are now lined with tombs of famous Italian artists and heroes such as Raphael and King Vittorio Emanuele II.

Galleria degli Uffizi (Uffizi Galleries) [Florence]: This place vies with Saint Peter's for the title of Heavyweight Art Champion of the World. Unless you're more sheltered than we'd like to think about, the Renaissance and Classical art here will look familiar to you. Botticellis, Da Vincis, Michelangelos—come 'n' get 'em!

Galleria dell' Accademia (Academy Gallery) [Florence]: You've just gotta see Michaelangelo's colossal David statue, the Master's masterpiece. The Museum also contains many other famous Michelangelo works like *St. Matthew* and *The Four Prisoners.*

Cathedral of Santa Maria del Fiore (Il Duomo) [Florence]: Sick of Florence yet? Too bad—we've got just one more must-see for you: The Duomo is the most important monument in town, and its enormous dome dominates the entire city. At least give it a walk-by.

Duomo [Siena]: This is Florence's Duomo's competition. The Romanesque-Gothic building took almost 200 years to complete and is one of the most impressive in the country.

National Gallery of the Marches [Urbino]: Located inside of the spectacular Palazzo Ducale, this gallery contains much of the best art which has come out of the entire region of the Marches, and particularly of the city's most famous son: Raphael.

Campo dei Miracoli [Pisa]: All of the city's main sights, including the Romanesque **Leaning Tower,** are on this square. Also in the Campo dei Miracoli are the **Cattedrale,** the Battistero, the Museo delle Sinopie, Museo dell' Opera del Duomo, and the Camposanto.

San Michele in Foro [Lucca]: This pink and white marble, multi-tiered church is just one of Lucca's many, but it is also the most beautiful. The Pisan-Romanesque facade is incredibly ornate and extravagant, with scenes depicting wild animals and hunters on horseback, swirling columns, and a big figure of St. Michael slaying a dragon with two angels standing on the pediment.

Venice: A bazillion tourists a year can't be wrong—well, they can be, but not in this case. Venice is one of the world's most-visited cities for a very good reason. The Accademia and Peggy Guggenheim Museums, Saint Mark's Basilica, and the hundreds of canal-side churches brimming with artistic treasures make this town an unparalleled cultural experience.

Ravenna: The glittering mosaics of the Byzantine empire's western outpost is an overwhelming introduction to the kind of post-Roman art found in ancient sites from Istanbul to Jerusalem.

Padova's Scrovengi Chapel: Giotto's finest works outside of Assisi decorate every square inch of the walls of this small Renaissance church. Don't let the size fool you, this is one of European painting's greatest triumphs. It's one of the few places that can hold its own with the Sistine Chapel in a staring contest.

Duomo [Milan]: A true appreciation of the detail and the cathedral's design can be found on the roof. If you can muster the energy to walk up the thirtysomething flights of stairs, the Duomo's roof reveals the ornate detail of the hundreds of statues that cover the cathedral as well as a spectacular view of the city.

Isola Bella [Barromean Islands]: The tiny cobbled streets and Baroque Palace on this little island on Lago Maggiore will put you in Italian bliss. Take a stroll through the palace's gardens, grab a slice of thin-crusted homemade pizza and take in the serenity of the lake.

weird and bizarre

Eurochocolate [Perugia]: This week-long festival, held every October, is a Mecca for chocolate lovers from around the world. The entire city is transformed into an open air chocolate shop.

Museum of Confetti [Sulmona's]: No, not the ripped-up paper. This museum is a monument to what the city is most famous for: the brightly colored, sugar-coated almonds which are thrown at happy couples on the wedding day, called *canfetti*.

Museo della Tortura (Museum of Torture) [San Gimignano]: Yes, these "museums" are all over the place. But this one is a class above. It has more than 100 original instruments used for causing pain, torture, or death and makes an interesting compliment to all the churches you've probably been visiting.

Archeological Museum [Bolzano]: If seeing a 5,300-year-old mummy in a stainless steel tomb through a Plexiglas window doesn't strike you as odd, then maybe you don't need a vacation. Actually, this is one of Italy's most interesting museums, with exhibits from the Paleolithic age through to the Roman conquest, and handy audio guides and multi-lingual brochures. The star attraction is Ötzi, a perfectly preserved Ice Age hunter found in 1991, loin-cloth and all.

San Marino: If Walt Disney ran Vatican City, it would be like San Marino, the world's smallest free-standing republic. This place comes complete with storybook fortresses, its own money, and lots of kitschy souvenir shops. The mitigating factors of this day-tripper's pilgrimage are the proud and feisty history of this independent mountaintop republic, the winding cobblestoned alleys, and the wonderful views of Italy in all directions.

Keith Herring's "Tutto Mundo" Mural [Pisa]: It's the last thing you expect to see on the side of a 500 year old church.... You can check out the mural on the northwest corner of Piazza Vittorio Emanuele II; crack a bottle of Chianti and take it in.

Portello-Castello Elevator [Genoa]: Take a ride on one of the most bizarre forms of public transportation you'll ever see. Situated right on the water, the views from atop this oversized mushroom are one of a kind.

rome &
lazio

ROME & LAZIO

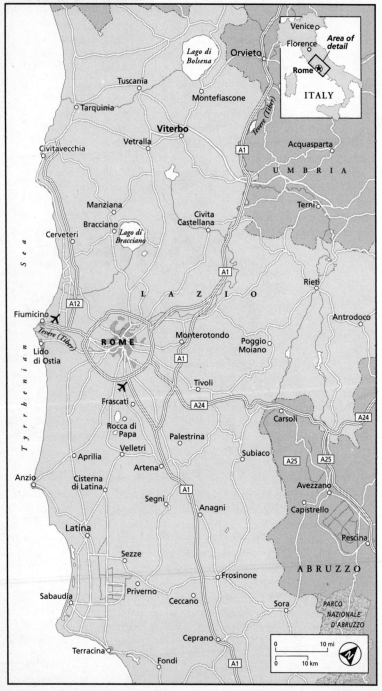

Area of detail

Venice
Florence
Rome
ITALY

Lago di Bolsena
Orvieto
Tuscania
Montefiascone
Tarquinia
Viterbo
Civitavecchia
Vetralla
Tevere (Tiber)
A1
Acquasparta

U M B R I A

Manziana
Bracciano
Lago di Bracciano
Civita Castellana
Terni
Cerveteri

S e a

L A Z I O
A1
Rieti
Antrodoco

A12
Fiumicino
Tevere (Tiber)
ROME
Monterotondo
Poggio Moiano

Lido di Ostia
A1

T y r r h e n i a n
Tivoli
A24
Frascati
Carsoli
A24
Rocca di Papa
Palestrina
A25
A25
Aprilia
Velletri
Subiaco
Anzio
Artena
Avezzano
Cisterna di Latina
Segni
Capistrello
Anagni
A1
Latina
Pescina
Sezze
A B R U Z Z O
Frosinone
Sabaudia
Priverno
Sora
Ceccano
PARCO NAZIONALE D'ABRUZZO
Ceprano
Terracina
Fondi
A1

0   10 mi
0   10 km

ask any traveler in **Rome** what they think of Lazio, and the answer will most likely be "What? Who?" Italy's capital city—with its amazing nightlife, restaurants, cafes, fashions, art, architecture, and general rep as one of the coolest cities on the planet—completely dominates the Lazio region. The scene in Rome is everything you imagined it would be: Vespas whizzing past the Coliseum, portrait painters on the Spanish Steps, and the Pope waving to massive crowds in Vatican City from time to time.

But there's much more to the Lazio region than Rome (other than, of course, the city's nonstop nightlife, which is unmatched anywhere else in Italy). What makes the rest of Lazio, which stretches from the Apennine Mountains to the Tyrrhenian Sea, such a great place to visit is the beaches, lakes, and miles of pristine hiking paths in the hills—all of which is unknown to most other tourists. And within this incredibly scenic environment, there are beautiful little medieval towns like **Viterbo,** where the laid-back scene is perfect for curing a hangover or taking a break between megadoses of Rome's deep party scene.

But back to Rome, which is the real reason you're here, right? The city is looking better than ever, thanks to a trillion-lira restoration effort in 2000 for the Papal Jubilee. There are spectacular sights on nearly every corner, many of which you'll recognize even if this is your first time here, like the Pantheon, the Coliseum, and St. Peter's. The bustling city has some of the most famous Renaissance works for art lovers, bars and clubs for night owls, Roman ruins for archeology buffs, shops from Italy's most famous fashion designers for clothes addicts, excellent restaurants and charming sidewalk cafes for chow hounds, and green parks for when the cultural overload hits (and it will).

Throughout its history, Rome has attracted Italy's best thinkers, artists, and architects, all of whom helped make it one of Europe's great cities. And the environment they created is still one of the coolest anywhere. Don't let all the ancient ruins and art treasures keep you from checking out the contemporary arts scene; gallery-hopping is a major pastime in the city.

Modern Rome is dominated by a hip urban edge, much like New York. Locals often look like *Vogue* inventions in their dark black sunglasses and tight clothes. They're used to the millions of tourists who visit their city, and they seem to actually like to give directions, recommend

art + architecture

Even if you slept through Art History 101, Rome's artistic treasures will seem familiar to you. "The Eternal City" was once the center of Western civilization and needed to look the part, so it's a no-brainer that its artistic heritage eclipses that of the entire region, if not the country. There are examples of nearly every architectural style: a brisk walk will tour you past Egyptian obelisks, ancient Roman triumphal arches, Renaissance churches, Medieval basilicas, and Baroque palazzos. The Coliseum and Pantheon are perhaps the most studied and admired structures on earth. Some of the world's greatest paintings and sculptures live here: Michelangelo's *Moses,* the Sistine Chapel frescoes by Michelangelo, Raphael's frescoes in the Vatican Museum, sculptures by Bernini, and much more. Walking through Rome will touch all of your senses, but your aesthetic sense kicks into overdrive here. The experience can be overwhelming, and a short trip to one of Lazio's smaller towns, where the art and architecture delights on a smaller scale, is just what the doctor ordered.

The once-Etruscan town of Viterbo was home of the papacy for a short period during the Middle Ages, and its Palazzo Papale is one of the gems of the region. Viterbo is also Lazio's best-preserved medieval town, and wandering the streets of its historic San Pellegrino quarter will reveal how art and architecture are woven into daily life. The people living around these cobblestoned streets, with laundry hanging from house to house over ancient fountains and reliefs, seem unaware of the beauty that surrounds them. Delicious smells drift from open kitchen windows while kids play in the streets and old men talk politics at their favorite tables of their favorite cafes.

cool places to go, or just hang out and talk—even when they don't speak much English.

Viterbo, just 71 kilometers north of the capital, is a great place to experience Life Outside Rome. Few tourists make it out here to see the ancient San Pellegrino quarter with its medieval towers and arches, pleasant little cafes, antique stores, great regional restaurants, and fun piazza parties. Viterbo is close enough to be a day-trip from Rome, but diverse enough to keep you occupied for a few days. The locals are provincial, warm, and friendly—and about as far away from Rome's fashion sense as possible.

The delicious food in Lazio is a big contrast to the cuisine of the neighboring regions. Peasant cooking developed over the centuries in Rome and has spread to the rest of the region. Romans love meat, and you'll find nearly every animal part on Roman menus—ask before you order if you're not an adventurous eater. Some specialties of Lazio include artichokes, *Saltimbocca alla Romana* (veal topped with prosciutto, cheese, and sage), *spaghetti alla carbonara* (pasta with ham in a light egg, cream and cheese sauce—perfect for a hangover), and rich, creamy *gelato* (ice cream), some of the best of which can be found on the streets of Rome.

The Etruscans were one of the first major civilizations to inhabit the area, in the 7th century B.C. They were mainly concentrated in the northern part of the region, while the Latins, Ernici, and Volsci tribes controlled the south. The Roman Empire steadily grew, and took control in the 4th century B.C.—we all know what happened for the next 800 years. After the fall of the Roman Empire, Lazio and Rome became increasingly tied to the Papacy until the unification of Italy in 1870. During the Renaissance, when Rome, as well as most other towns in the country, underwent a building boom, artists like Michelangelo, Raphael, and Bernini were enlisted to design and decorate the city's new structures.

getting around the region

Rome is the transportation hub for the southern half of the country, with two international airports (Fiumicino and Ciampino), and a train and bus station that connects to Italian and other European cities. Florence is less than 300 kilometers away and can be reached easily by train or bus. **Viterbo** is just 71 kilometers north of Rome, and can be reached by train in about an hour; by bus in about and hour and a half. Traveling between smaller towns can be a bit more difficult, however, because of infrequent bus and train connections. But traveling between towns that lie on the same route is usually quick, simple, and hassle-free. Trains are usually quicker, and more comfortable than buses.

Rome is the best base, because it has a huge selection of hotels, restaurants, and bars. Daytrips from here are a breeze. For visiting the region's small towns, Viterbo is a good place to base yourself for a few days—hotels rarely book up, and it's well-served by transportation.

rome

In *Fellini's Roma*—a lesser-known '70s must-see by the *La Dolce Vita* man himself—horrific modern traffic jams and ancient ruins play together in a way that just nails the spirit of this multi-layered city. So multi-layered, in fact, that when you party (or do anything else) here, you'll rarely lose sight of the fact that you're doing it on top of 3,000 years of history—much of which is still staring you in the face. The dichotomies here keep coming at you: ubiquitous cell phones and the Coliseum; the old-school ladies in black cardigans who think Madonna is the devil and the kids shooting by on their Vespas; the sophisticated international clerical community that runs Vatican City and the hedonistic club-goers who pile into Alpheus every Saturday night. The center of Rome is a near-inbred Mediterranean beehive of a town, yet it's also one of the most international and cosmopolitan spots on earth, and the hub of a huge exurban sprawl. During the day the city is teeming with people, local and tourist alike, but if you walk here at night you can let the watery echo of the fountains lead you from one beautiful, empty piazza to the next. In other words, just when you think you've got this place down, well, try again.

It helps that in general temperament, Romans are not unlike New Yorkers: They like to hear themselves talk, they can be a bit gruff and imposing at first glance—and underneath it all they're much nicer and more welcoming than you could have guessed. In other words, don't be surprised if at one point while you're in Rome, some drunken local grabs you in the bathroom of a bar and demands: "American?! Ah, New York? San Francisco? Los Angeles?" and invites you to come hang out with him and his friends. Go to Rome with this in mind: You are welcome here.

This really is a city that is ready and willing to grant you plenty of conversation, drink, dancing, and great meals.

Young Italians in general—and, it seems, Romans in particular—really like their pleasures, and like them most nights of the week. And the concept of "recreational" drug use actually exists in Rome. While the law is sort of wishy-washy [see *rules of the game,* below], for the most part it doesn't paint dabblers as criminals. Also, romance (read: sex) is treated with a bit more levity and less hysteria than, for example, the American there-is-no-such-thing-as-safe-sex! cultural message. And while Rome's gay and lesbian scene may not be as in-your-face (or even as visible) as the scene in, say, San Francisco or New York's Chelsea, it is also sophisticated and offers a lot of variety.

Rome could be the poster-child city for this book—it is truly one of the easier cities in which to instantly gain access to a memorably good time. Roman pop/party culture has its own flavor and style—it is energetic, outgoing, and, for the most part, lacks the nastiness and random exclusivity that a lot of big city scenes are laced with. Why? Maybe it's 'cause clubs and party promoters show a lot of talent for mixing it up, bringing in influences from all over, and constantly throwing out a variety of new themes and ideas that keep staleness and cliqueishness at bay. Maybe it's because there are a bunch of active and productive politically/socially based groups run by young partying kinds of people in Rome. Here, the Young Democrats Club isn't a bunch of aggressive yuppies, but rather a group of fun twentysomethings who sponsor clubs that promote their political views. And we're not talking debate clubs, or some geeked-out function with chips and dip and hard plastic chairs—we're talking *nightclubs.* Their attitude seems to be, hey, we'd like to have a party and go a little crazy so we might as well benefit a good cause while we're doing it. It's pretty doubtful that the crowd at **Brancaleone** or any of the other activist-minded social clubs [see *club scene,* below] has a *complete* grasp on the status of the latest UN peace talks, but hell, they'll throw in a little donation and give a shout out to the refugees of war (and so should you!). Their hearts are in the right place, and it makes a big difference.

And if you think other European cities are great for people-spying and general ogling, forget about it, Rome wins hands down. There are an inordinate number of attractive people here, blessed with good looks *and* great clothes and style. Unless you want to feel really unhip while in Rome, leave the sweatpants, ratty sweaters, and backpack at the hostel, and don't feel shy about slapping on some cool, dark sunglasses like you know you want to.

And before you arrive, try to get at least a little experience on a motorbike (not a Harley—think less power and chrome) so that you can do like the Romans do for a while. Nothing can compare with the rush of driving a motorbike when in Rome (the bus sure can't). You can zoom around these streets, pretending to race other people (*pretending*), coming up on beautiful white palaces and the glimmering water of the Tiber (Tevere) River at night...*aaahh.* The cost is actually not so bad if

12 hours in rome

1. Eat a pizza—the kind made out of two pieces of focaccia with different stuff in between, like artichokes and tuna in a creamy sauce or sun-dried tomatoes and prosciutto. You'll never even look at nasty Domino's again.
2. If it's nighttime, go for a walk along the Tevere River, cross the bridges, stroll, get lost.
3. If it's daytime, get a motorbike, look around for a mountain, ride to the top, and get a view of the whole city.
4. Eat gelato, and lots of it. Try every kind you can in small portions—amaretto, pistachio, hazelnut—and try them at different places so you can compare.
5. Go to the **Pantheon** [see *culture zoo,* below]; feel your mind expand.
6. Wander around **Vatican City** [see *Vatican Museum* in *culture zoo,* below]. No matter who your god is, it's a trip—and truly beautiful.
7. Go to **Campo de' Fiori** [see *neighborhoods,* below] at night, drink red wine until you feel really relaxed, and ask one of the strolling musicians to play you a bawdy love song.
8. Go have a sword fight with one of the gladiators at the **Foro Romano** *(Metro Line B to Colosseo).* You can get your picture taken with them, and if you're a girl, they'll tell you your mama made you better than Michelangelo could have.
9. Make like Audrey Hepburn: Eat a chocolate bread and drink coffee while spying the display windows of all the super-beautiful, outlandishly expensive clothing stores.
10. Hang out at a cafe: Drink espresso, try to decipher the newspaper, watch couples have heated arguments at neighboring tables (*always* interesting), listen to a soccer match on the radio....

you get a cheap bike (you don't need the shiny, spanking-new Vespa) [see *need to know,* below]. Every young Italian person knows that motorbikes are really the best way to get around the city, so it's also a great way to check people out, get checked out, flirt at the gas station, etc. Gas is fairly cheap, and, being so light, scooters get good mileage. Feel free to ask the attendant for help if you need it—don't laugh, scooters are tricky little buggers. Plus the good clubs and bars are all spaced pretty far apart, so if you want the freedom to really get around at night, a bike can be key. Oh, and apparently there are actual traffic laws in Rome, although to the untrained eye it looks like total freakin' chaos. Everyone seems to be doing whatever he or she wants—weaving in between cars, driving the wrong way down one-way streets. Still, keep an eye out for cops. If a bike's not in the budget, or just not your thing, the next-best way to get around is, obviously, to walk—and for those out-of-the-way clubs, the subway is a great, reliable way to go.

Most people here don't speak fluent English—many speak or at least understand a moderate amount, but a lot speak absolutely none, so there's going to be confusion or at least some challenge if you speak no Italian. But folks are real nice about it and they won't make you feel stupid if you try, even if your accent tears the hell out of their beautiful language *and* they have no clue what you're trying to say. Most people genuinely appreciate the fact that you're making an attempt—especially if you smile while you're doing it. In places like the hospital, police station, or the AMEX office, there's always somebody who speaks English, so don't freak out if you have a serious problem.

There are a few local magazine/newspaper-type things that you can check to see what's up if you're gonna be shy about it and not just ask around. They're all in Italian, but hey, "Can you translate this for me?" is a great opening pickup line.... **Roma C'e** is a good one to try. Another is **Il Manifesto,** the official daily of the Italian Communist Party. Its weekly supplement, **Alias,** which you can get at most newspaper stands, contains kind of modern arty/intellectual stuff, i.e., articles about Van Gogh right

only here

Okay, so you want to see something really amazing that you can't see anywhere else in the world? This is something out of a fairy tale, a perfect, beautiful view of St. Peter's Basilica, through a keyhole. But I'm not giving it away: If you want to see this one you've got to go work for it—ask around, you'll find someone who knows where it is. If it's given away, everyone would go, and then it wouldn't be so special....

Then there's the *piazzardone,* the last of his kind in Rome. He stands on a little circle platform in the middle of a crazy intersection in front of Piazza Venezia directing traffic. Wearing a big black coat, pristine white gloves, and a little white cap, and twirling his arms and hands all around, he kind of looks like Mickey Mouse in *Fantasia.*

next to an in-depth analysis on the theoretical significance of hip-hop. *Trova Roma,* the weekly supplement to the paper *La Repùbblica,* is another source for art shows and music performances, film festivals, dinner places, and various other entertaining whatnots. These papers can be helpful, but remember, results may vary. The "hot" party you read about may end up being nothing but weak music and a couple of stiffs; the "cutting-edge" modern art exhibit might be some guy in body paint spanking himself.

If you want to avoid flocks of tourists, schedule your trip in a non-summer month, when there are fewer tourists and better rates for hotels. The last two weeks of August are an especially bad time to be here—aside from being incredibly hot and crowded, it's also when most Romans take off for their own vacations.

No matter when you come, there's one Roman tradition you have to follow: You've got to throw a penny into a fountain (traditionally the Trevi, but your own pick will do just fine). You're supposed to stand with your back to the fountain and chuck it over your shoulder. There are about six gazillion fountains in Rome—which may actually shock you on your first couple of nights here just by being so awfully pretty—so it's not exactly a difficult tradition to carry out. Supposedly once you do this, it's guaranteed that you'll return to the city one day before you die. Lucky you.

neighborhoods

In a nutshell, you've got a city surrounded by what used to be a big wall (most has crumbled at this point), the Great Aurelian Wall, and divided by a big river, the **Tiber River** (Fiume Tevere). On the west side, you've got **Vatican City** and all of its great museums [see *culture zoo,* below], and, southeast of all that, a working-class city neighborhood called **Trastevere** that's fun to hang out in, with great bars and music spots and a generally laid-back vibe. Over on the east side of the river is where most of the action, as well as most of **ancient Rome,** lies. **Vía del Corso,** or Il Corso, which runs north-south from the **Piazza del Popolo** to the Victor Emmanuel monument, should be your main point of reference. Starting from the Vittorio Emanuele monument, the major road going west is Corso Vittorio Emanuele. To the east of the monument, running toward the **Coliseum,** is Vía dei Fori Imperiale. Vía Nazionale runs from in front of the monument toward the **Termini** (train station), out on the eastern edge of the city, where you'll find a bunch of late-night spots, especially around the **Piazza della Repùbblica.** The **Spanish Steps** and the big shopping streets that surround it are at the north end of the city, a few blocks southeast of Piazza del Popolo. Ancient Rome is down at the south end of the city, starting a few blocks after Vía del Corso ends. **Campo de' Fiori** [see *hanging out,* below], where fun young locals come to hang out, is west of Vía del Corso, northwest of ancient Rome. At its north end is Piazza Navona, a great lounging and people-watching spot, and a few blocks east of that is the **Pantheon** [see *culture zoo,* below]. At the south end of ancient Rome is the **Piramide** area, where you'll find many clubs and bars. At the west end of Campo de' Fiori is the old Jewish ghetto.

Rome is a big, modern city, and while random crime is not a huge problem, and the weapons laws and regulations are some of the toughest, it does happen. The common sense that applies to hanging out in all cities applies here: Walk with friends or take a cab at night, and if someplace gives you an unsafe feeling, get out of there. The buses and Metro system are okay—they're not that hard to figure out, and there are night buses that keep running on the main roads *all* night [see *need to know*, below].

hanging out

Rome is host to a seemingly infinite number of hang-out spots, which makes meeting people just a matter of getting out and exploring. And it's great for your travel budget too—hanging out in a square won't cost you anything. Clubs, bars and such, on the other hand, while not exorbitant, can be a bit pricey, especially once you start drinking.

After the airport, the train, the bus, the hotel, yadda-yadda, you'll probably need a drink or six. A nice, relaxed-yet-lively, non-intimidating area for your first night is **Campo de' Fiori.** The crowd is mainly 25- to 35-year-olds, and everyone is drinking (beer or wine or coffee) and

five things to talk to a local about

1. **Movies:** Go educate yourself at a video store before you go: *8 1/2, Umberto D.* (get ready to cut your wrists, but still incredible), and *Big Deal on Madonna Street* are all good places to start.
2. **Politics:** Anything but Italian issues, which no one seems willing to discuss other than to say that every politician in Italy is corrupt.
3. **Soccer:** Try to feel out what team they're for before you make any keen observations about the season.
4. **How beautiful their country is:** Italians already know it, but they really like talking about it, recommending places to go, things you must experience, delicious things to eat that you can only get in Rome, etc.
5. **Learn some Italian:** Give it a shot! It's not like you can learn the language in a single conversation, but you can pick up some funny phrases that you won't find in books, like a special saying for good luck, something about a wolf's mouth, I think....

talking. This is a popular place for locals to meet up in smallish groups to mingle on the cobblestones before or after going to a club or party or to a friend's house. To whom it may concern: Skinny heels are not recommended here. (Actually that's a good note for the whole city—there are cobblestones everywhere, even in random bathrooms(!), so unless you want to break your ass in public, wear thick heels or platforms.) The majority of people are young, white-collar professionals who are younger, trendier, and more easy-outgoing than the kind of person that comes to mind when you hear "young white-collar professional" in other cities. If you're a club kid or have some unresolved angst, you'll still like it here, and you'll find people like yourself to hang out with. There's always at least a couple of little crews of visor-wearing kids in elephant pants, chicks with fit-and-flares and pink lipstick, and punk-rockers and squatters. Even if you don't find the Italian version of your hometown posse, it's a great place to just bliss out, talk with friends, and get loaded. There are a few wine bars, which sound fancier than they are, with some indoor seating, really crowded standing room, and outdoor seating for about 40—plus you can take your wine out into the square and soak up the fresh air.

If you're still goin' strong at 7am, stop by **Café Renault** [see *bar scene,* below] near ancient Rome. It's a great after-after spot, with DJ Pierandrea the Professor spinning everything from jazz to house at the bar. And if you're finally ready to feed your body something solid, you can grab a small breakfast of pastry, fresh orange juice, and espresso at the cafe.

Also good for lolling around at night is the Trastevere's **Piazza di Santa Maria.** It's really crowded during the day, especially in summer, but can be mellow and relaxing at night, with lots of little cafes around and a mix of people young, old, and in between. Also, people love flopping on the Spanish Steps at all hours—during the day it's completely glutted with tourists; at night it's a bit more chilled-out and quiet, with lots of teenagers and early-twenties people just hanging out, flitting around. **Piazza San Lorenzo,** in the heart of the city, is another good spot, with some really good cafes and plenty of room to just kick it, the occasional chick strumming a guitar, circles of kids hacking—you get the idea.

bar scene

No beer funnels, brawling, or throwing your bra at the bartender here—generally bars in Rome are pretty mellow. That is, unless one of the local football teams just won a really important game, and even then only if the bar is overrun with fans. Sometimes you get singing, shouting, big toasts, the occasional argument...but not often. The vibe is largely social but not cruisy, most folks relaxing with whomever they came in with or else striking up conversations with people at nearby tables, and the bartenders tend to be non-snotty.

Café Renault (*Via Nazionale 183 B; Tel 06/47-82-44-52, 06/47-82-45-48; Metro Line A to Repùbblica; 7am-2am daily; www.cafere-*

fIVE-O

There are two breeds of cops here: the *polizia*, who have light-blue-and-white cars and uniforms, and the *carabinieri*, who wear black uniforms with white sashes, carry machine guns (so that you know *they* mean business), and are actually kind of spooky-looking. In the opinion of most Italians, both are decently mannered, helpful on occasion, and not too much of an impediment to fun. Once I was riding a motorbike (slowly) through a small piazza and a *carabiniere* motioned me over, so I hopped off and walked the bike—no ticket, no attitude, nothing.

nault.com, info@caferenault.com; No credit cards) is housed in what used to be a Renault car dealership (a few blocks north of ancient Rome), which explains the car in the cafe part downstairs. The wide-open and well-lit space has a polished, modern look, with high ceilings, glass surfaces, lots of black and steel/chrome detail, which is refreshing if you've been exploring Rome's more traditional bars and restaurants and are craving something modern. There's a bar, a cafe, and, at the top of a twisty metal staircase, a restaurant; all are a bit pricey but not outrageous. It's great for people-spying late at night, when the crowd is kind of trendy and appealing, and you can sip a drink and space out on the little objects "floating" in your table. Is it your eyes or the table playing tricks? That should keep you busy until you get your order.

If you've managed to get a wink of sleep and are ready to get started early, or need to break up that day of sightseeing, go have a couple midday drinks at the rooftop restaurant at **Hotel Forum** *(Via Tor De' Conti 25, Fori Imperiali; Tel 06/679-24-46; Metro Line B to Colosseo; 12:30pm-3pm/7:30pm-1am Mon-Sat; 25,000-60,000L per entree; forum@venere.it; AE, V, MC, DC).* Sitting at a shaded table with a cool breeze blowing, a perfect view of the Foro Romano (Roman Forum) in front of you, and people zipping by on Vía dei Fori Imperiali, it's kind of hard to leave. And who cares-it's even more gorgeous at sunset.

If you just want a nice drink before bed, try **Bar del Fico** *(Piazza del Fico; Tel 06/686-52-05; Metro Line A or Bus 95, 490, 495 to Flaminio; 9-2am Mon-Sat, noon-2am Sun; No credit cards),* set on a quiet little street near the Piazza del Popolo, which manages to be active yet somehow still calming and comfy. Take all the time you like to drink a good glass of wine (5,000-12,000L) and soak up the night under the canopy of trees at one of the several small outdoor tables. Inside is cozy too, with marble, brass, candles, a nice, well-stocked bar, and a few tables. All kinds of people come and go from this place—young couples, families, friends—and the staff is very relaxed and sweet.

A great spot for that calming first drink in a new city—it's not intimidating, because all the employees speak your language—is the Campo de' Fiori's **St. Andrew's Pub** *(Via della Cancelleria 36; Tel 06/683-26-38; Bus 116; 7pm-3am daily; No credit cards)*, a lively, casual pub in the Scottish tradition that's a popular local hang. They serve pretty standard pub food—burgers and such—but also some simple Roman dishes like panini and other starters, plus tasty crêpes...a good place to check out if you start to tire of Italian food. The prices are fair, from 3,500L for some small fried-fish dish to 12,000L for a good-size burger. The crowd ranges in age and is mostly locals and expats or traveling Americans, Scots, and Irish.

Another good place to hang if you long to hear a language you understand is **The Drunken Ship** *(Campo de' Fiori 20-21; Tel 06/68-30-05-35; Bus 60, 64, 116; 5pm-2am daily, happy hour 5-9pm; www.drunkenship.com; V, MC, AE)*, in the Campo de' Fiori. Active—no, *packed*—at night, this place has a friendly bar staff and a gregarious crowd that spills outside on nice nights. They play American music, have drink specials every night, and offer student discounts (bust out that unflattering ID card!). Stays pretty happening until about 2am.

LIVE MUSIC SCENE

Although live music in Rome is generally not terribly original or exciting (that's the consensus even among Romans), some venues do manage to bring in cool acts. Trastevere is a good neighborhood for strolling around looking for random bars and places with live music, or the kind of combination places that play music but are really about conversation, meeting, and hanging out. Besides the places listed below, you can also intermittently find great live music at several clubs, like **Radio Londra** and **Brancaleone** [see *club scene,* below, for both].

Among the best of the live-music venues is Trastevere's **Big Mama** *(Vicolo San Francesco a Ripa 18; Tel 06/581-25-51; Tram 8 to Viale Trastevere; 9:30pm-1:30am daily Oct-June; Usually free or 20,000-30,000L cover for biggish shows, plus 20,000L membership card; www.nexus.it/bigmama; No credit cards)*, a down-to-earth place frequented by a more mature (late-twenties to mid-thirties) but very hospitable crowd. Blues, jazz, and some funk comes to this dimly lit club—they play really good music of all sorts between live sets, too. Lots of tables are cluttered in front of the stage, plus a few more spread out off to the sides in case you want to breathe. A popular place, well liked by the locals. Feel comfortable to dress up or down. Call or go by and get a schedule for show times.

Near the Piazza del Popolo, **Il Locale** *(Vicolo del Fico 3; Tel 06/687-90-75; Metro Line A to Flaminio; 10pm-3am daily, closed June-Sept 15; 10,000L cover; www.il-locale.com; No credit cards)* hosts what are considered the best local bands and is almost exclusively full of people who actually live in Rome ("Romans" sounds like history class). Think American rock 'n' roll bar, only not so predictable—there's pop/rock, grunge/alternative, funk, disco, electronica, riot grrrl rock, dance/house, and every other modern music mutation you can think of. Sometimes in English, sometimes Italian,

ragazzo meets piccola

We've all seen it in the movies: Some young, slightly bumbling, would-be Casanova falls for a gorgeous, dark-eyed Italian beauty. Picture it—he sees her leaving the marketplace, his heart leaps, he must pursue! He trails her for blocks through winding cobblestone streets struggling to think of something to say. It starts to rain—he's got an umbrella—she doesn't—there *is* a God! They walk, they talk, she smiles, bliss, bliss, bliss! Yeah, well, that's why movies are movies and real men take Viagra. But don't let these modern times get you down. Romance is alive and well in Rome, though it's a bit more low-key than you might think based on the standard image of Italians as *the* lovers of this world. Actually, things seem to be getting on like they do elsewhere in the world: Girls ignore the occasional moron who loudly calls out what he thinks is a compliment; eye contact is made (and pretended not to be made) at coffeeshops, newspaper stands, and bakeries; people drink and kiss and grope each other on the way home. Life is good. Guys, any old notions/fears/stereotypes you might have of the ultra-protective older Italian brother are *justified*—I saw some guy get his ass beat by, like, five of 'em, just for looking at a girl too long. And women, if you're worried about that old notion/fear/stereotype of Italian guys as charming players full of pretty lies, well, you're smart enough to spot the fakes. Send them off to buy you roses, then tell them you've got an incurable VD.

depends on the band. The crowd ranges all over; club kids, divas, army-fatigue-ripped-T-shirt-wearing-unshavens, tomboy lesbians—wear whatever you want and feel welcome. Almost all of the gigs that show up are good—it probably helps that they're playing for an appreciative crowd. Half-price cocktails at happy hour, which ends at 11pm.

Vatican City's chilled-out jazz club **Alexanderplatz** (*Via Ostia 9; Tel 06/39-74-21-71; Metro Line A to Ottaviano; 9pm-2am Mon-Sat, live music starts about 10pm; 12,000L membership, good for 2 months; V, MC, AE, DC*), is much beloved by the mid- to late- twenties, stylish/bohemian/casual crowd. The full menu lists all kinds of really random, tasty Italian, Asian, and American dishes. Dress a little bit nicer—clean, unripped, unwrinkled clothes are appropriate.

club scene

Clubs offer the kind of impersonal charm that some people hate; they're too dark to see exactly who's doing what, too loud to have an actual conversation, and people don't give a crap if you're breathing their second-

Rules of the game

While there's no drinking age in Rome, a 12-year-old *would* get laughed out of a bar. The legal age to buy is 18, but no one enforces it, and anyone who seems to be reasonably past puberty can drink. The drug laws here are kind of peculiar. Technically speaking, the use of drugs is tolerated under criminal law, although use in public might be viewed as an "offense to the public order." Realistically speaking, small amounts of certain drugs (marijuana, hashish) are accepted. The law goes something like this: You're not permitted to buy, sell, grow, or collect these kinds of drugs for buying, selling, or growing, and if you are caught doing these things you can be prosecuted. If you have on your person only what you are consuming right then and there you might face "administrative sanctions," like having your driver's license taken away for six months or having to undergo a social reintegration program, but it seems really, really unlikely that smoking a little doob on the street is going to get anybody in any trouble, as long as they keep things discreet—while the *carabinieri* (cops) are considered morons by most Romans, they *will* bust you for flagrant behavior.

hand smoke. But these are also the best elements of a club: You can disappear, then reappear, get lost in a crowd of strangers, you never know who's lurking in there, you're free of the obligation of carrying on bullshit talk when you'd really rather be scamming on that guy/girl over there. Clubs are fun, don't be old and crusty! Even if you didn't always get out and get down back home, you're away now, and the general vibe of clubs in Italy is mellow, eclectic, and non-snotty, so get your booty on the dance floor. There's enough variety and selection that you can get two or more very different kinds of parties in one night, and it's not so crazy expensive that you'll feel forced to stay someplace you don't like. Most all door policies are fine (as always, it's easier for women to get in than men), the people who work there are normal, helpful even, and the crowds are outgoing, not clique-y. It's a good idea to call ahead about a guest list, which often works if it's not a too-special occasion *and* you get someone on the phone who speaks English (which is a 50/50 chance). Get dressed around 10, find your friends, do what you gotta do to get in a good dancing mood, get there around midnight to 12:30, and try not to have any expectations—that's when good things happen.

South of ancient Rome, **Alpheus** *(Via del Commercio 36; Tel 06/541-39-85; Bus 23, 702 or Metro Line B to Pyramide; Call for information about specific parties, 10pm-4:30am Tue-Sun; 10,000-20,000L cover; AE),* one of the biggest clubs in Rome, hosts hip-hop or gay-themed parties on Friday nights. The music varies: house, '80s, commercial. There are three large rooms for dancing, connected to several other largish rooms for hanging-out and cooling off, and an area with small tables and chairs and large windows with steps leading outdoors. The crowd is mixed—gay and straight, trendy club girls with baby barrettes, lanky guys in jeans and sweaters, baby dykes in corduroys and white pocket tees, gay guys with no shirts vogueing—and very energetic. On most nights the door simply requires some patience—on Fridays and for other big parties it takes a *lot* of patience. If you're lucky you'll see a performance by the party's host, Vladimir, Rome's most celebrated guy-in-a-dress-with-better-legs-than-a-lot-of-girls. Despite the smart layout, at certain points it just gets too packed.

When the crowd has reached that critical mass, say 2 or 3am, or if you're looking for a slightly more earthy, less pop/commercial kind of place, **Goa** *(Via Libetta 13; Tel 06/574-82-77; Metro Line B to Garbatella; 10pm-5am Thur-Tue, closed May-Aug; 15,000-30,000L cover; goaclub@mclink.it; No credit cards)* has a lot of energy and an appealing tribal/Pacific Islands look going on, and (unfortunately) very expensive drinks. In the southern end of the city, the exterior is especially cool, with a section of thatched roof and burning torches. The door is a little picky but not ridiculous—wear something nice, a little bit sexy is cool, no need to go crazy. The crowd is mostly early twenties, hip, and good-looking, trendy but not hostile, with young hot things climbing onto raised levels to dance—basically a little bit more grown-up-looking/acting than the scene at Alpheus, but not *too* serious. Most important, the music is great. Claudio Coccoluto spins house, tribal, and drum 'n' bass on Thursdays, Stefano Gamma does house, funk, and groove on Fridays, Luis Radio spins American house on Saturdays, and Chicco Messina puts out funk, jungle, and house on Sundays. The bartenders actually look like they're having a good time, bopping around the well-run and well-stocked bar between drinks. The club is closed in the summer, but that's only because the club's owner is busy organizing open-air parties—call for dates and locations.

Even farther south of ancient Rome, **Ex Magazzini** *(Via dei Magazzini Generali 8; Tel 06/575-80-40; Bus 23, 702 or Metro Line B to Pyramide; Hours, days vary; Most parties free w/cash bar; No credit cards)* puts together a lot of '70s disco-revival-type stuff, like the *Velvet Goldmine Party*—think men in lipstick, tight nylon pants, and electric guitars—hosted by DJs Al Casey, Pier, and MDF. While not strictly a gay place, it's definitely gay-friendly—many of their invites note that homophobia is not admitted at the door.

B-side *(Via dei Funari 21a; Tel 06/68-80-05-24; Bus 46, 87; 11pm-4am Tue-Fri, till 6am Sat, Sun, closed July-Aug; 10,000-15,000L cover; No credit cards)*, in the old Jewish ghetto, is an excellent place for dancing to new hip-hop, R&B, and house—or easing out and watching everyone else grind. The big circular dance floor usually gets packed, the whole place is lit with glowing blue light...it's all kind of sexy. The generally mid-twenties crowd dresses pretty nice—lots of fitted things and stretch

rome bars clubs and culture zoo

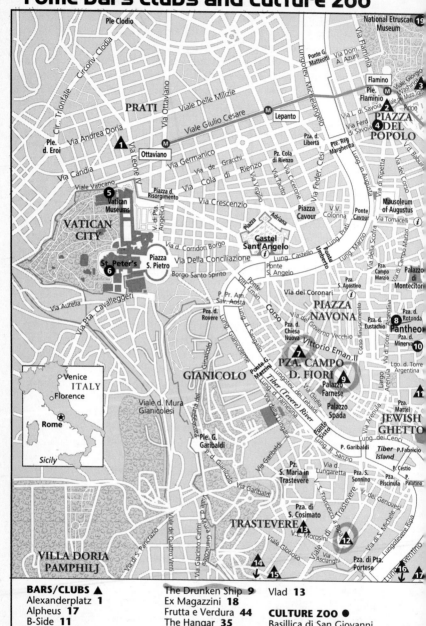

BARS/CLUBS ▲

Alexanderplatz **1**
Alpheus **17**
B-Side **11**
Bar Del Fico **3**
Big Mama **12**
Café Renault **28**
Circolo degli Artisti **16**
Discoteca Teatriz Baccara **26**

The Drunken Ship **9**
Ex Magazzini **18**
Frutta e Verdura **44**
The Hangar **35**
Hotel Forum **29**
Il Locale **2**
Marani **34**
Radio Landra **15**
St. Andrews Pub **7**

Vlad **13**

CULTURE ZOO ●

Basillica di San Giovanni
  in Laterano **43**
Basillica di Santa Maria Maggiore **3**
Capitoline Museum and Palazzo
  dei Conservatori **39**
Castel Sant'Angelo **21**

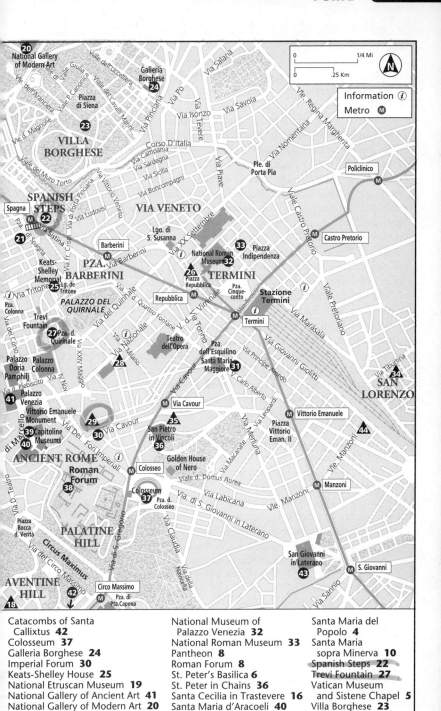

fabrics on women and button-down shirts and leather shoes on guys—
and you should too, or you'll wait outside for a looong time. Occasionally live rappers or R&B acts show up. Listen for Italian hip-hop like
Articulo 31, kind of like a cross between Black Sheep and House of Pain,
but totally different than either, 'cause they're Italian. Hang around for
the good after-hours on weekends.

If you're looking for something more tripped-out, call up and find out
what kind of party is in the works from **Discoteca Teatriz Baccara'**
*(Via Provinciale Felicisio 108; Tel 054/526-120; Bus A14 to Ravenna;
Hours, cover vary; No credit cards)*—or better yet, ask someone who speaks
Italian to do it for you, like the guy at the hotel desk, who'll comply if you
smile and ask nice. They produce big, rave-like fiestas featuring DJs from
Italy, the U.S., and the UK, spinning big beat, trance, jungle, and ambient
that draws club kids with glow-in-the-dark tongue toys from surrounding
towns and suburbs.

On a different tip, south of ancient Rome is **Radio Londra** *(Via Monte
Testaccio; Metro line B to Pyramide; Tel 06/575-00-44; L15,000 cover weekends includes first drink, 5,000L membership weekdays; Club 11:30am-4am
Wed-Mon, bar and pizzeria 9pm-3am Wed-Mon, till 4am Sat; No credit
cards),* which is kind of cave-like, and looks like an old war bunker. Fortunately, it lacks that "more punk rock than you" attitude—anyone who
wants to hear some loud, cranky, Brit-inspired garage, underground punk,
or hardcore and work out some heartfelt angst through slam-dancing will
feel right at home. The crowd isn't particularly outgoing, but it's not intimidating either, and it's definitely not violent (aw bollocks!). While there are
a lot of safety-pin-covered, wallet-chain-wearing, spiked-with-white-glue-
haired people around, not everyone sports the uniform of nonconformity,
and you can feel free to dress in casual travel clothes. Obviously, you might
feel a tad out of place if you show up in an Izod shirt and wing-tips (if you
do, let's *hope* somebody kicks your ass). There's a lot of crossover with the
gay crowd from L'Alibi [see *gay scene,* below] right next door (which is very
straight-friendly). Live bands (mostly Italian) play occasionally, although
the quality is kind of inconsistent and many just do covers, so call to see
who's playing and then try to ask around. There's a patio outside where you
can let your sweat dry, and, believe it or not, the pub food is really good.
The weekday membership card is good for three months, although the
cover thing seems kind of flexible if you arrive late.

Along similar lines is Trastevere's **Vlad** *(Piazza San Cosimato 39; Tel
06/580-08-98; Bus 44, 75, 8; About 10pm-4am, days vary; Usually no
cover; No credit cards).* Specializing in new wave, electro, goth, industrial,
and post-punk—this is about as hardcore as Rome gets. Think black lipstick, Marilyn Manson, the Cure, and melancholy, angry, disillusioned
youth. There's a big, dark dance floor downstairs where DJs spin to an
active crowd, and a pub on the ground floor. Occasional live punk/goth
bands, call and ask (again, finding an English speaker is iffy, ask your
hotel desk guy to call) about shows. The crowd ranges from late teens to
mid-twenties, and is nice enough, if just a bit cliqueish.

Something quite common in Rome that's completely bizarre to most travelers are the *centri sociali* (social clubs). Politically slanted, leftist, late-teens and twentysomethings form these clubs and use them for hanging out, holding concerts, throwing parties, showing films, etc. The less active clubs are less inviting for non-locals (they're mostly for people who all know each other, clustered in little groups talking about *their* stuff)—it's the ones that throw biggish open parties and show movies that are more fun for visitors, like **Brancaleone** *(Via Levanna 11; Tel 06/82-00-09-59; Bus 36, 37, 60, 366 to Piazza Sempione; 10:30pm-5am Thur-Sun; Cover varies; No credit cards).* Friday is the best night here, and, although it officially closes at 4am, the festivities go later on the weekends. The music fluctuates: from DJs spinning drum 'n' bass, slinky lounge, and house, to live alterna-rock bands. Call for info on events. There's a mess-hall kind of barroom, with a smaller adjoining bar that also serves coffee, which is convenient if you're dragging but don't want to call it a night. This all empties outside, where there's some tables in a pretty seedy-looking courtyard, which is actually totally safe. After a little walk out, you'll pass into another building with a musty dirt floor and tripped-out black and white strobe lighting, where there's more dancing, less talking. The crowd is mainly straight, early twenties, some squatter-looking types, but mainly college-educated, left-leaning people who like to go out and party. On a recent Friday, the young people here were actually talking about UN bombings—between flirting outrageously and getting tanked, of course. Someone told me that some of these joints register as a social center instead of a nightclub just so they can legally be open after-hours.

Another *centro sociale* with a welcoming vibe is **Circolo degli Artisti** *(Via Casilina Vecchia 42; Tel 06/70-30-56-84; Bus to Via Casilina; 9pm-3am Tue-Sun; 7,000L membership good for 3 months, cover varies; No credit cards),* near the Termini in an old milk-production center, a good-sized place with a bar, a video room, and two theaters. The music varies—although hip-hop and jungle are in abundance—as does what's going on: live performances, movie screenings, DJs.... The crowd is generally early twenties, some ghetto-brat types, hip-hop kids, and guys with no shirts *and* pierced septums. No one who answers the phone here is completely with it, so the best way to get information about a particular show is to call Mondo Radio 90.9 FM *(Tel 06/207-32-32, 06/70-30-56-84)* for the pertinent details; they speak English. Oh, good note: You can find an excellent hip-hop set on that same station, called Zulu Nation *(9-10:30pm Mon-Sat; 6-8pm Sun).*

after-hours scene

After-hours in Rome is lots of fun: The city is really empty except for the other half-wits careening around the streets and some old ladies, like, getting bread or something, so you can enjoy the splendor of the rosy glow spreading across the sky and dappling the stone of the spectacular buildings without endangering too many other people.

Frutta e Verdura (*Via Principe Umberto, Piazza Vittorio 36; Tel 0347/879-70-63; Bus 105 or Metro Line A to Vittorio Emanuele; Hours, days vary; 15,000L plus 5,000L membership; No credit cards*) consistently provides a packed and energetic party east of the city center, near the Termini. On Fridays things really get started at about 5am and go strong until at least 9am; Saturday things start a bit later, about 7am, and end around 9. Not a huge place, but big enough to make it comfortable and provide cool, dark places to slip away to. The crowd is mixed gay and straight with some trannies milling around, and a bit more sophisticated than at the *centri sociali,* but not obnoxiously so. The prompt and active bar definitely helps keep the crowd going. Once you descend the stairs to the club, it's hard to get a sense of the place, what with all the gyrating bodies and flashing lights—with stone walls and arched entries into darkened rooms where people keep on disappearing and reappearing; the main impression is of a comfortable dungeon somewhere. While the crowd is definitely not running on adrenaline alone, it's *nothing* like those nightmare sketchy after-hours scenes with depressing-looking people flopping around doing drugs. Music is mainly electronic house, with some commercial thrown in. The line to get in is a bit long, but moves fairly quickly; dressing a little bit nice—something with a little grown-up style—is appropriate. Guys, it's unfair, but it really helps to be with at least *a* girl....

If at about 7am you're feeling kind of hungry, having danced off those 5 million saturated-fat calories that you consumed at lunch, go by **Marani** (*Via dei Volsci 47; Bus 71, 492, 19, 30b; No phone; 7am-9pm daily; V, MC, AE*), a great place to grab that milky cappuccino Italians say is good for you to drink *right* before you go to sleep (ha!) and devour fresh, flaky pastries. There's a nice little patio with tables and chairs outside where you can chill out and watch the day break in peace. A nice stop to make before you go home and pass out. Also near the Termini.

ARTS SCENE

Okay, so most people think art died when Marcel Duchamp put a signed urinal in a gallery, but believe it or not, people are still painting—with paint and brushes! On canvas! Holy crap, does Bill Gates know about this? Maybe some things never really change; there's still a whole lot of bad artists out there and a handful of interesting ones. Just think—out of the zillions of would-be greats through the centuries we've gotten, what? a couple thousand artists, if that, who can be taken seriously. The same applies to the modern art scene in Rome, although, to its credit, it's active and not very prefab or living room color coordinated.

▶▶VISUAL ARTS
Among the most interesting private art galleries is **Stefania Miscetti** (*Via delle Mantellate 14; Tel 06/68-80-58-80; Bus 23, 280; 4-8pm Tue-Fri, closed July-Sept*), southeast of Vatican City, where Yoko Ono had work—sure, our parents still think she broke up the Beatles, but get over it. Her artwork is totally bizarre and creative and ahead of its

time—and so is the work of many of the young, new sculptors who show their work here.

Also worth a look is **Galleria Emanuela Oddi Baglioni** (*Via Gregoriana 34; Tel 06/679-79-06; Metro Line A to Spagna; 10am-1pm/4-7:30pm, Mon-Fri, closed Aug*). Near the Spanish Steps in the city center, the main attraction here is abstract sculpture, from big names like Marina Abramovic.

Galleria Gian Enzo Sperone (*Via di Pallacorda 15; Tel 06/689-35-25; Bus 52, 53, 56, 58b; 4-8pm Mon, 10am-1pm/4-8pm Tue-Sat, closed Aug*) tends to have wilder, more experimental exhibits—it was one of the first Italian galleries to promote pop artists like Warhol and Lichtenstein.

Another good one is the **Studio d'Arte Contemporànea Pino Casagande** (*Via Degli Ausoni 7a; Tel 06/446-34-80; Bus 19, 30b; 5-8pm Mon-Fri, closed Aug*), exhibiting often bizarre and original sculpture and mixed-media stuff near the Termini. It walks that fine line of being almost too trendy for its own good—the work being featured becomes irrelevant at the wine, cheese, and who-is-*that*-over-your-shoulder!? party.

Near the Spanish Steps, the **Associazióne Culturale Valentina Moncada** (*Via Margutta 54; Tel 06/320-79-56; Metro Line A to Spagna; 4-8pm Mon-Fri, closed Aug*) is actually a series of garden-surrounded artists' studios. Well, we can't see those, but the gallery downstairs is open to the public. The work is generally semi-challenging painting and sculpture, a bit more difficult, less refined, and more intriguing than most of what's around right now.

Artists like to sit for hours and have coffee at the centrally located, quasi-trendy **Antico Caffè della Pace** (*Via dell Pace 3-4-5-7; Tel 06/686-12-16; Bus 87, 280, 492; 11am-11:30pm Tue-Sun; V, MC, AE*).

A bit more discreet and charming is **Cafe Notegen** [see *eats*, below], which is also just an all-around great place for lunch. It's a favorite of the older generation of local painters and poets, the kind who come every day, read the paper, and know the waitress. They have reasonably priced sandwiches, pastries, and coffees, but the real draw is the comfortable, homey atmosphere.

▶▶PERFORMING ARTS

The performing arts scene in Rome boasts a great ballet, the Rome Opera Ballet, which performs at the Teatro dell'Opera, as well as a highly praised orchestra, the RAI Symphony Orchestra, which usually performs in Vatican City at the **Academy of St. Cecilia** (*Via Concillazione 4; Bus 23, 34, 64*). The best bet for getting information about their shows, as well as other well-established performers', is via a ticket agent like Termini-area Orbis (*Piazza Esquilino 37; Tel 06/474-47-76; Bus 4, 9, 16, 74; Box office 9:30am-1pm/4-7:30pm; MC, V, AE, DC*)—you can usually get an English-speaker on the phone. The periodicals mentioned earlier for clubs and live-music happenings (*Trova Roma, Alias,* or *Roma C'e*), are definitely convenient for spotting something interesting, although again, quality-wise, it's hit-or-miss—look for reviews and trust word of mouth.

North of the city center, **Teatro Argentina** (*Largo Argentina; Tel 06/68-80-46-01; Tickets at Vía Barbieri 21; Tel 06/68-40-00-11; Box office open 10am-2pm/3-7pm Mon-Sat, performances 9pm Mon-Wed, Fri, Sat, 5pm Thur, Sat, Oct-June; V, MC, AE*), run by the Teatro di Roma group, is the oldest theater in Rome. It used to be led by Luigi Ronconi, a big name in Italian theater, till he left for the bigger scene in Milan. Luckily he has a young, very talented replacement in Mario Martone, who is also known for his film work, but has remained true to his theater roots. Left-leaning and politically correct like Ronconi, but less famous and more humble, he takes on more challenging work.

Martone is also one of the many influential folks who opened the very new and rightfully hyped **Teatro India** (*Lungoteverie dei Papareschi; Buy tickets at Vía Barbieri 21; Tel 06/686-56-69; No credit cards*). It's out of the center of the city (south of Trastevere, on the west side of the Tiber), not just in location but in general feel—young, more experimental. Right now it's hosting plays and also exhibitions, shows, and various multimedia performances.

Teatro di Roma also manages the smaller **Sala 1** (*10 Piazza di Porto San Giovanni; Tel 06/670-93-29*), which hosts dance performances, theater, poetry readings—anything that needs a more intimate space than the Argentina.

Teatro Quirino (*Vía Marco Minghetti 7; Tel 06/679-06-16, 678-30-42, 678-58-02; Buy tickets at Vía Minghetti; Tel 06/679-45-85; To theater, take Bus 81, 62, 85, 60; Box office 10am-1pm/3-7pm Tue-Sat, 10am-1pm/3:30-5pm Sun, performances 9pm Tue, Fri, Sat, 5pm Wed, Thur, Sun; Tickets 11,500-44,000L; V, MC, DC, AE*), near the Via del Corso, is consistently lauded, hosting diverse music, dance, spoken word, and theater performances. It often presents the work of Carmelo Bene, who was once considered a great of Italian theater but now has gotten kind of tired.

During the balmier months of spring and summer, Rome hosts many beautiful open-air performances in places like the **Terme di Caracalla** (*Tickets and info: 06/481-70-03, 06/488-34-69; No credit cards*), the very impressive, huge, and beautiful ruins of baths built by Emperor Caracalla, not far from the Forum. A lot of these are live musical performances, but there is also a good dose of drama: Italian playwrights (maybe not too amusing if you don't speak Italian) for the most part, but also some American and others. There's often some Eugene O'Neill, Shakespeare (of course), or Tennessee Williams, so look around for details in the aforementioned periodicals.

For really big concerts, look out at **Teatro Olímpico** (*Piazza Gentile da Fabriano 17; Tel 06/326-59-91; Bus 48, 280, 910; Box office 11am-7pm daily, performances 9pm daily Oct-May; Tickets 20,000-85,000L*), northeast of the city center, on the eastern bank of the Tiber. Anything from string quartets to pop, rock, or alternative shows up here.

It's actually pretty easy to get cheap tickets to the opera (20,000L for decent seats or standing room in the back), which has helped to attract a younger audience in Rome. Unfortunately, the people who really know opera, the older crowd, think it sucks right now and only mention it to complain or compare it to the *Scala* in Milan. **Teatro dell'Opera di Roma** *(Via firenze 72; Tel 06/481-601; Bus 75, 170, 64, 640; Box office 9am-5pm Mon-Sat, 9am-1:30pm Sun; Tickets 20,000-260,000L; No credit cards),* east of the city center, is the place to go if you'd like to give it a shot anyhow.

At **Pasquino Cínema** *(Vicolo de Peide 19, just off Piazza Santa Maria in Trastevere; Tel 06/580-36-22; Bus 23; 12,000L; No credit cards),* you can catch either a very slightly dated new American movie or a screening of a great old classic. Most are in English with Italian subtitles (great if you're trying to learn the language). There's also a small bookstore, a cafe, and a bar that shows independent flicks on video. It's nice, comfy, air-conditioned, and usually brimming with youngish people, including lots of Italian and foreign students.

gay scene

In general, the gay scene is not exclusive *or* cut off from Rome's straight party scene. Big clubs like **Alpheus** [see *club scene*, above] regularly throw gay-friendly parties with themes like gay pride, drag divas, and AIDS awareness. Check in any of the entertainment guides to see when they're going on.

Pretty packed most nights, **The Hangar** *(Via in Selci 69; Tel 06/488-13-97; Metro Line B to Via Cavour; 10:30pm-2:30am Wed-Mon; No cover, 5,000L membership; No credit cards),* near the Coliseum, is mainly for men. Two very active and prompt bars, great music-mixed '80s like the Stray Cats and the Cure—and several screens flashing clips of music videos and stills keep the senses stimulated and thereby distracted from the squeeze of so many people in a not-huge space. Kind of half-dark, half-light, with lots of blind corners, it's a good place to check people out, invisibly or openly. Lots of cute, social twenty- and thirtysomething guys.

Women will feel more comfortable at **L'Alibi** *(Via Monte Testaccio 44; Tel 06/574-34-48; Bus 95, 673; 11pm-5am Wed-Sun; 20,000L cover; No credit cards),* where the crowd is more mixed—boys and girls, tourists and locals. One prompt bar, one big, lively dance floor, and mainly commercial dance/pop and techno-type house keep things goin'. As it's right next to Radio Londra [see *club scene*, above], south of the city center, there's a good deal of crossover crowd-wise, which keeps the people-watching pretty interesting.

A more strictly girl-oriented spot is **Joli Coeur** *(Via Sirte 5; Tel 06/86-21-62-40; Bus 38, 38b, 58, 58b; 10:30pm-2am Sat, Sun; 20,000L cover; No credit cards),* definitely the most popular and active club for women in the city. Some mixture in the crowd, but really a place for those of us who use tampons. Out in the northwest corner of the city.

CULTURE ZOO

Even the most jaded can't help being floored by Rome. Rome can seem almost unreal, something from a book of legends we had as kids. If your curiosity isn't piqued, even a little, to go romp around the ruins, and if

festivals and events

La Festa Di Noiantri *(July)*: Basically a great big feast in Trastevere where all the local restaurants fill the streets with tables, musicians play, and everybody stuffs themselves silly and gets drunk. It gets pretty hectic but avoids being congested to the point of suffocation.

Sagra dell'Uva *(beginning of Sept)*: The celebration of the grape! It's at the Basilica of Maxentius in the Foro Romano *(Metro Line B to Colosseo)* and the perfect setting to see grown men in skirts (ancient Roman garb). Lots of cheap, delicious grapes, and music to boot.

Carnival in Piazza Navona *(on or around Jan 5)*: We're talking games, junk food, performances, juggling, and the occasional fire-eater.

Festa della Primavera *(sometime in Apr)*: A celebration of the changing seasons, when the Spanish Steps are loaded with flowers and classical concerts are presented. Not a rockin' good time, but pretty and relaxing.

Go to the **Ente Provinciale per il Turismo** [see *need to know*, below] for details on all of these events.

the high point of centuries of art just leaves you blank, head cocked to one side saying, "Huh? I don't get it," well, at least you can tell them back home that you tried.

Basilica di San Pietro (St. Peter's Basilica) *(Vatican City, Piazza San Pietro; Tel 06/69-88-44-66 or 06/69-88-53-18; Metro Line A to Ottaviano/San Pietro, Bus 46; Basilica: 7am-7pm daily Apr-Sept, until 6pm Oct-Mar; Dome: 8am-6pm daily Apr-Sept, until 5pm Oct-Mar; Basilica: free, Dome: 4,000L without lift, 5,000L with lift):* The Basilica sits on one of the great architectural creations in the world, Piazza San Pietro, designed by Lorenzo Bernini. Statues of 140 saints sit on top of the 284 columns in the majestic colonnade, which curves around the square and reaches toward the Basilica. The church you'll see was built in the early 16th century, when the previous one was torn down to make way for something bigger and better. The interior of the Basilica is a testament to how enormously wealthy the Catholic church once was; one of the first treasures you'll see as you enter is Michelangelo's Pietá, which is one of his greatest works. But the most eye-catching monument in the Basilica is Bernini's huge *baldacchino,* an elaborate Baroque brass canopy. You get fantastic views of Rome and the Vatican gardens from the top of the 448 ft dome.

Vatican Museums and Sistine Chapel *(Vatican City; Viale Vaticano; Tel 06/69-88-33-33; Metro Line A to Ottaviano/San Pietro or Bus 64,*

280 to Piazza del Risorgimento; 8:45am-4:45pm Mon-Fri, 8:45am-1:45pm Sat, mid-March to late Oct and last Sun of each month; 8:45am-1:45pm Mon-Sat rest of year; www.christusrex.org/www1/vaticano/0-Musei.html; 18,000L admission, free last Sun of each month): The entrance to what is commonly regarded as the best art collection in the world is on Viale Vaticano, which is a long walk around the Vatican walls, north of the entrance to St. Peter's. If you're coming during the summer be prepared for a long, long—but worthwhile—wait. The palace that houses the museums was originally built as the residence for popes, and it is a vast, never-ending maze. All halls lead to the best part: The Sistine Chapel. It took Michelangelo four years to complete his most famous work: 33 panels depict the Creation of the World and the Fall of Man, surrounded by characters and scenes from the Old and New Testaments. Some of the scenes on the Sistine's ceiling are the most recognizable of Michelangelo's works, and it's quite a shock to see how small and detailed they actually are. Bring along a small mirror, and you won't have to hurt your neck to enjoy the show. The walls of the Sistine Chapel were also painted by some of the top Renaissance artists like Botticelli, Ghirlandaio, Perugino, and Signorelli. But it was also Michelangelo who painted the most famous wall fresco: *The Last Judgment.* It took the artist seven years to complete that fresco, which is on the wall behind the altar.

The next-greatest gems of the Vatican's collection are the *Raphael Rooms,* which were the apartments of Pope Julius II. Raphael worked for 16 years on these frescos, and died before they were finished. The Room of the Segnatura contains one of Raphael's most famous works, *The School of Athens,* which depicts some of his fellow painters, like Michelangelo, Da Vinci, and Bramante, as philosophers. Others rooms are more straightforward in their purpose—to illustrate the power of the papacy. *L'Appartamento Borgia* **(The Borgia Room)** was frescoed with a series of biblical, classical, and religious scenes by Pinturicchio and his assistants, and is where the Borgia Pope, Alexander VI once lived. The *Pinacoteca* **(Picture Gallery)** holds paintings and tapestries from the 11th to 19th centuries from great artists such as Raphael, Giotto, Da Vinci, Bellini, Fra Angelico, Titian, Caravaggio, Bernardo Daddi, as well as works by Dutch and French painters. The huge **"Collection of Modern Religious Art"** contains the only works by American artists in the whole place. The *Museo Gregoriano Egizio* **(The Egyptian Museum)** displays pieces that were found in 19th- and 20th-century digs in Egypt, and a few artifacts found in Italy. The *Museo Gregorio-Etrusco* **(The Etruscan Museum)** contains a good collection of Greek, Roman, and Etruscan art. The highlight of this collection is the contents of the Regolini-Galassi Tomb from 650 B.C.: lots of gold jewelry, bronze furniture, a bed, and other treasures. The *Museo Chiaramonti* holds a huge collection of Roman sculpture and many ancient copies of Greek originals. The *Museo Pio Clementino* is one of the world's largest (and best) collections of Greek and Roman sculptures, which were greatly admired by Renaissance artists, like Michelangelo, during their quest to portray the human body accurately.

Some of the best-known works in this collection are: the *Belvedere Torso, Apollo Belvedere*, the *Apollo Sauroctonos,* and the *Laocoö*. The **Galleria delle Carte Geografiche** holds maps illustrating the Catholic church's territories, most of which were drawn up by a Perugian cartographer. The **Biblioteca Apostolica Vaticana (The Vatican Library)** is one of the most valuable libraries in the world, with over a million documents, including many handwritten Medieval manuscripts. The library is frescoed with elaborate Mannerist paintings.

Castel Sant'Angelo *(Lungotevere Castello 50; Tel 06/687-50-36; Metro Line A to Ottaviano or Bus 23, 46, 49, 62, 87, 98, 280, 910, to San Pietro or Lapanta; 9am-3pm daily, closed last Tues of each month; L8,000 admission):* This huge fortress, which is just over the Ponte S. Angelo, was

by foot

Trastevere is great for rambling around. It's not so bustling and full of tourists as other parts of the city; it's more just a normal neighborhood where people come and go about their regular lives—hence, great people-watching. Get a big bag of fresh fruit at a good price here to snack on while wandering around **Piazza di Sa Cosimato** *(Bus 44, 75, 8)*. From here make your way east, enjoying the wide-open stroll on Viale di Trastevere for a bit, and then continue over to the previously mentioned **Santa Cecilia** in Trastevere (on Piazza Mercanti) [see *culture zoo*, above]. Right around here are several cafes with outdoor seating where you can kick back for a while with a Coke or a gelato. From here continue east until you hit Porto di Ripa Grande, then make your way north and west along the Tiber. As you approach the second bridge, **Ponte Fabricio,** you'll see a small island, Tiber Island (*Isula Tiburtina*). There's a semi-interesting church here and a hospital, but mainly it's fun just because it's a strange and kind of beautiful little island in the middle of a huge city—a nice stop if you've got the energy and the time. From here you can cross back into Trastevere and mosey over to the monument to **Santa Maria della Scala** (*Via della Scala*), which has works by Caravaggio inside and an old-style pharmacy with herbal remedies and weird potions in glass jars from the 1700s—unfortunately, you can't get samples. And just south of there, down Vía della Scala, is **Piazza di Santa Maria** in Trastevere. Although annoyingly packed during summer days, in the evening and in quieter seasons, it's great; there's a couple of fine neighboring cafes, a beautiful fountain, and a steady trickle of passersby.

built in the 2nd century A.D. as a tomb for the Emperor Hadrian. It's connected to the Vatican by an underground tunnel, which was used by the popes many times when they were forced to flee the Vatican due to political reasons. The museum—which consists of cells used for torture, extravagant apartments, and art galleries—is well worth a visit.

Santa Cecilia in Trastevere *(Piazza di Santa Cecilia; Tel 06/589-92-89; Bus 44, 75; 10am-noon/4pm-6pm daily, frescoes 10am-11:30am Tues, Thur; Church free, 2,000L admission to excavations):* In the cool Trastevere area, to the south of Vatican City, this is the site where St. Cecilia, an aristocrat who left the life of leisure for religious pursuits, was martyred in 230 A.D. Be sure to see Pietro Cavallini's 13th-century fresco of the *Last Judgment,* which once covered the whole church. It can be reached through the adjoining convent.

Pantheon *(Piazza della Rotunda; Tel 06/68-30-02-30; Bus 70, 81, 119, 170; 9am-6pm Mon-Sat; Free admission):* The Pantheon is the only ancient building in Rome that remains perfectly preserved. It's probably the most studied building in the world, and is architecturally unique because of its perfect proportions: the radius of its hemispherical dome is equal to the height of the cylinder—in other words, it's 142 feet wide and 142 feet high. This Roman temple of the Gods was built in 27 B.C. and rebuilt by Hadrian in the 2nd century A.D. The 18-foot opening in the center of the building is its only source of light, and when animals were once sacrificed inside, it acted as a chimney. The walls of the Pantheon are 25 feet thick, and are now lined with tombs of famous Italian artists and heroes, such as Raphael and King Vittorio Emanuele II.

Galleria Nazionale d'Arte Moderna (National Gallery of Modern Art) *(Viale delle Belle Arte 131; Tel 06/322-981; Bus 52, 53, 56, 910; 9am-10pm Tues-Sun; 8,000L admission):* This museum makes for a nice change from gold-tinted *Madonna col Bambino* paintings. With over 75 rooms, this is one of Italy's largest collections of modern Italian art. Marini, Burri, De Chirico, Fontana, and many artists from the Ialian Futurist movement are represented. The gallery, which is just north of Villa Borghese, also has a nice collection of works by foreign moderns like Cézanne, Klimt, Kandinsky, Miró, Pollock, Degas, Monet, Van Gogh, Klee, Ernst, and Rodin.

Fontana dei Trevi (Trevi Fountain) *(Piazza di Trevi; Metro Line A to Barberini)* A few blocks east of the Pantheon, this is Rome's largest fountain, made famous by the movie *Three Coins In The Fountain.* Completed in 1762, it depicts a huge Neptune in his chariot being led by two Tritons. It sits on the site of the ancient Aqua Virgo Aqueduct, which was built in 19 B.C. to bring water to Rome's bathhouses. You'll be lucky if you're able to get up close to the fountain, which is almost always completely surrounded by tourists tossing in coins to assure their return to Rome someday.

Santa Maria del Popolo *(Piazza del Popolo 12; Tel 06/361-08-36; Metro Line A to Flaminio or Bus 90, 90B, 95, 490, 495; 7am-12:30pm/4pm-7pm daily; Free admission):* Right off Piazza del Popolo, this is one of Rome's greatest Renaissance churches. Two of the chapels—the first and the third—are frescoed by Pinturicchio. The apse, also painted by Pinturicchio, was built by Bramante. The Chigi Chapel was designed by Raphael, who died before it was completed, and was finished by Bernini. In the chapel to the left of the altar there are two beautiful works by Caravaggio, *Conversion of St. Peter* and *Crucifixion of St. Peter.*

Foro Romano (Roman Forum) *(Via del Fori Imperiali; Metro Colosseo or Bus 27, 81, 85, 87, 186; 9am-6pm Mon-Sat and 9am-1pm Sun, Apr-Sept, 9am-sunset Mon-Sat, Oct-Mar, last admission 1 hour before closing; Free admission):* Although there are only fragments and big pieces of stone here today, the Roman Forum, just east behind Capitoline Hill, was once the center of ancient Roman life. Like many old Roman buildings, much of the stone that was once in the Forum was quarried off and used in the construction of the city's other buildings during the Renaissance building boom. Get a map from the entrance and see for yourself where the ancient temples and buildings were once located. The Temple of Saturn is where one of Ancient Rome's biggest annual festivals was held. The Arch of Septimus Severus is the best-preserved monument in the Forum and has marble reliefs depicting Rome's military victories. The Temple of Vesta is one of the most sacred sites and holds the House of the Vestal Virgins which was an enormous complex where the women who looked after the flame in the Temple of Vesta lived. The Basilica of Constantine was once an enormous building, which Michelangelo is said to have studied while drawing up his plans for St. Peter's.

Fori Imperiali (Imperial Forums) *(Via de Fori Imperiali; Metro Colosseo or Bus 27, 81, 85, 87, 186; 9am-6pm Mon-Sat and 9am-1pm Sun, Apr-Sept, 9am-sunset Mon-Sat, Oct-Mar, last admission 1 hour before closing; Free admission):* When the Fori Imperiali, which are just north of the Roman Forum, were built by Julius Caesar, they took the Fori Romano's place as the center of ancient Rome. The buildings were bigger, grander, and more elaborate than those in the Foro Romano. Not that you can tell—this area is preserved even less than the Foro Romano. Of particular interest are the Forum of Augustus, the Forum of Trajan, the Tower of the Milizi (which can be climbed for a great view), Trajan's Column, the Forum of Julius Caesar, and Trajan's Market.

Museo Capitolino (Capitoline Museum) and **Palazzo dei Conservatori** *(Piazza del Campidoglio; Tel 06/67-10-20-71; Bus 44, 89, 92, 94, 716; 9am-7pm, Closed Mon; 10,000L for both):* Capitoline Hill, or *Campidoglio,* is one of Rome's most ancient and sacred hills and was the center of the Roman world. In the 16th century Michelangelo designed Piazza del Campidoglio and the Cordonata, which is the wide flight of stairs you have to climb to get there. Piazza del Campidoglio, which is just south of the Victor Emmanuele II Monument, is laid out in perfect geometric proportions. The equestrian statue that stands in the center is of Emperor Marcus Aurelius (it's a copy—the original is inside the museum). Around the piazza are Palazzo Nuovo and Palazzo dei Conservatori, both of which house the Capitoline collection. The Capitoline Museum, which was the first modern public museum in the world, holds one of the best collections of ancient art and classical sculpture. Highlights to look out for include *The Dying Gaul* and *The Capitoline Venus* (both Roman copies of 3rd century B.C. Greek works), *Discobolus* (part of a Greek discus thrower, which was transformed to a wounded warrior in the 18th century), Pietro da Cortona's painting *The Rape of the Sabine Women*, *Spinario* (a famous 1st century B.C. sculpture of a boy removing a thorn from his foot), *Mosaic of the Doves* (which once decorated Hadrian's villa), and Caravaggio's *John the Baptist* and *Fortune Teller*. Also worth seeking out is the Hall of the Philosophers, which consists of two rooms full of busts of emperors and philosophers. The expressions on some of the faces are priceless.

Coliseum *(Piazzale del Colosseo, Via del Fori Imperiali; Tel 06/700-42-61; Metro Colosseo; 9am-7pm Mon, Tues, Thur-Sat, 9am-1pm Sun, Wed Apr-Sept; 9am-3pm Mon, Tues, Thur-Sat, 9am-1pm Sun, Wed, Oct-Mar; Street level free, upper levels 8,000L admission):* Built in 72 A.D., this amphitheater could once hold 55,000 people. Cruel, savage gladiatorial fights took place in the arena, and thousands of animals were often slaughtered in a single night. It ceased to be used for many centuries, and during the Renaissance, artists who admired its Doric, Ionic, and Corinthian tiers pilfered much of the building and used its stones and marble to build other buildings and churches. The arch that stands next to the Coliseum is **The Arch of Constantine,** which he built in 315 A.D. after defeating a group of Pagans. It was then that he converted to Christianity and ended the persecution of the Christians.

Santa Maria d'Aracoeli *(Piazza d'Aracoeli; Tel 06/679-81-55; 6:30am-5pm daily; Bus 44, 46, 75; Free admission):* This church, which is across from Piazza del Campidoglio and up a flight of stairs, was built in the 13th century on what was once the site of the Temple of Juno. The highlight of the church is the Bufalini Chapel, which is frescoed with scenes from the life of San Bernardino by Pinturicchio. There is also a painting by him of St. Francis receiving the stigmata.

Museo Nazionale dei Palazzo di Venezia (National Museum of Palazzo Venezia) *(Via del Plebiscito 118; Tel 06/679-88-65; Bus 57, 65, 70, 75; 9am-2pm, Closed Mon; 8,000L admission):* Palazzo Venezia, which is just east of Termini station, was once the home of Mussolini, who used to give speeches from one of its balconies. The museum isn't one of Rome's best and doesn't contain any well-known masterpieces, but it's pleasant and worth a visit. Most of the stuff on exhibit is medieval decorative art, but there's an eclectic collection of tapestries, antiques, paintings, porcelain, frescoes, and more *Madonna col Bambinos* than you can count.

Basilica di San Giovanni in Laterano *(Piazza San Giovanni in Laterano 4; Tel 06/69-88-64-33; Metro San Giovanni or Bus 4, 16, 30, 85, 87, 174; 7am-6:45pm daily summer, till 6pm low-season; Basilica free, Cloisters 4,000L):* San Giovanni, and not the Vatican, is actually Rome's Cathedral, since St. Peter's is in Vatican City, which is technically its own country. In the southeastern part of the city (from the Colosseum take Via di S. Giovanni in Laterno east), the Basilica was founded by Emperor

Constantine in 314 A.D. and was one of the first churches to be built in Rome. But almost nothing remains of the original church since it has been rebuilt so many times over the years. The facade, built in the 18th century, is decorated with 15 huge statues of the saints, Christ, and the Apostles. The last major renovation of the interior of the cathedral was in the 17th century, when Boromini did some re-decorating and may have destroyed many frescoes by Giotto. In the apse, however, there are some remaining fragments of frescoes, which are attributed to Giotto, as well as a 13th-century mosaic. The Baptistery is the oldest part of the church, and contains several 5th-century mosaics. Be sure to take a look in the 13th-century cloisters, which have twisted double columns and marble mosaics. On the eastside of Piazza San Giovanni, Palazzo Laterano was the papal residence before the Papacy moved to Avignon in the 14th century.

San Pietro in Vincoli (St. Peter in Chains) *(Piazza San Pietro in Vincoli 4A; Tel 06/488-28-65; Metro V. Cavour; Bus 11, 27, 81 to Colosseo; 7am-12:30pm and 3:30pm-7pm daily, Spring and Summer, till 6pm Winter and Fall; Free admission):* This church, a few blocks north of the Colosseum, was built to house the chains which were used to bind St. Peter in prison in Jerusalem. But the real attraction of this church is Michelangelo's *Moses,* which is one of his most famous sculptures, commissioned for the tomb of Pope Julius II. Michelangelo was supposed to have carved 44 figures for the tomb, but he was called away to paint the Sistine Chapel and left the tomb unfinished. The *Dying Slaves* [see **Florence**] were also meant to be part of the tomb. St. Peter's chains are displayed in a glass case below the altar and are taken out every year on August 1st.

Santa Maria Sopra Minerva *(Piazza della Minerva 42; Tel 06/679-39-26; Bus 64, 119; 7am-noon/4pm-7pm daily; Free admission):* Just east of the Pantheon, this is one of Rome's few Gothic churches, which was built on the site of an ancient temple to Minerva, and contains a great collection of Renaissance paintings by Filippino Lippi and Fra Angelico. There is also a bust and a sculpted elephant with an obelisk, carved by Bernini, and a *Risen Christ* by Michelangelo, to which a bronze loincloth was later added to cover Christ's genitals. St. Catherine of Siena is buried under the main altar, Fra Angelico is buried in the chapel on the left side of the altar, and two 16th-century popes are buried in the Aldobrandini chapel.

Scalinata di Spagna (Spanish Steps) *(Piazza di Spagna; Metro Spagna):* So, you're probably thinking, why the heck are there *Spanish* steps in Rome? Easy answer: The famed Steps and the piazza below them, Piazza di Spagna, were named for the Spanish Embassy, which was once located there. And your second question is probably: Why would I want to spend my time checking out some statirs? Another easy answer: They're breathtaking. They curve gracefully up the hill, ending dramatically at the **Trinità dei Monte** church. At the foot of the Steps is a boat-shaped fountain, which was designed by Giovanni Lorenzo Bernini and his pops, Pietro Bernini. The Steps are at their best during the spring and the summer when they are lined with pots of pink azaleas. Of course, you may not be able to see all of their beauty through the masses of tourists and Italian teenagers who are constantly sprawled over the steps.

Keats-Shelley House *(Piazza di Spagna 26; Tel 06/678-42-35; Metro Spagna; 9am-1pm/3pm-6pm Mon-Fri, 10am-1pm/3pm-6pm Sat, May-Sept; 5,000L admission):* Fans of the Romantics should pay a visit this house at the bottom of the Spanish Steps where John Keats died at the age of 25. Shelley doesn't have much of a connection to the house, besides the fact that he visited Rome once and died in a nearby town. The 18th-century house contains a variety of memorabilia related to Keats, Shelley, Byron, and other Romantic poets. Some of it is interesting, but much of it isn't.

Galleria Nazionale d'Arte Antica (National Gallery of Ancient Art) *(Via Quattro Fontane 113; Tel 06/481-44-30; Bus 23, 65, 280; Metro Barberini; 10am-2pm Mon-Fri, 9am-7pm Sat, 9am-1pm Sun; 10,000L admission):* Housed in the Baroque Palazzo Barberini, just off of Piazza Barberini, a few steps from the Victor Emanuelle monument, this collection of antiques and household objects is worth seeking out. The gallery contains many excellent paintings by artists such as Filippino Lippi, Simone Martini, Il Sodoma, Raphael, Titian, Tintoretto, Caravaggio, and El Greco.

Villa Borghese is one of Europe's finest parks, occupying 3 1/2 miles in the very center of Rome. You can enter the park on all sides—it's always open. The beautifully landscaped park and villa were designed in 1605 for Cardinal Scipione Borghese, a nephew of the pope. You could spend days wandering around the park, discovering its fountains, statues, secluded gardens, and green piazzas. Bring a picnic and hang out for a while.

Galleria Borghese *(Piazza Scipione Borghese; Tel 06/841-76-45; Bus 56, 910; 9am-10pm Tues-Sat, 9am-8pm Sun; 12,000L admission):* Cardinal Scipione Borghese once lived in this villa, which now houses one of Rome's most impressive art collections, which he single-handedly amassed. The highlight is the collection of Bernini scuptures, for which Borghese had a particular fondness. Many of the Berninis in the collection are from early in his career, and are still considered his greatest works. Look out for *The Rape of Prosperine, Apollo and Daphne,* and *David.* One of the Borghese's best-known works is Canova's half-nude sculpture of Pauline Borghese as *Venus Victrix,* which was kept locked away for many years by her husband. It was during Pauline's time that the collection was greatly reduced when she sold off much of the collection, mostly to the Louvre. The museum also contains some great works by Raphael, Titian, and Caravaggio. The gallery was closed for many years for restoration and was just recently re-opened, so it can be quite busy at times.

Museo Nazionale di Villa Giulia (National Etruscan Museum) *(Piazzale di Villa Giulia 9; Tel 06/320-1951; Bus 30b, 926; Metro Flaminio; 9am-7pm Tues-Sat, 9am-2pm Sun; 8,000L admission):* Housed in a palace built for Pope Julius III in the 16th century, this is one of

Rome's best museums. Villa Giulia itself, with its pretty gardens and fountains, is impressive enough, but the collection, which contains mostly Etruscan art and artifacts found in Etruscan tombs around Central Italy, is the reason to come. The black and red painted vases, decorated with scenes from Etruscan daily life, give us a general idea about their culture. There are many cases of jewelry, detailed bronze sculptures, mini terracotta vases, statues, and fragments of furniture and buildings. One of the highlights of the museum, which is north of Piazza del Popolo, is the Husband and Wife Sarcophagus from the 6th century B.C. in room 9.

Basilica di Santa Maria Maggiore *(Piazza di Santa Maria Maggiore; Tel 06/488-10-94; Metro Termini; 7am-7pm daily; Free admission):* After seeing the simple facade, the interior of Santa Maria Maggiore is surprisingly lavish. A few steps away from Termini station, this is one of Rome's largest and most important churches. Founded in 420 A.D. and then rebuilt and added upon from the 14th through the 18th centuries, Santa Maria is famous for its great mosaics, some of which date back to the 5th century (in the nave). The coffered ceiling is said to have been made with gold brought over from America. Highlights of the church include the 13th-century *Coronation of the Virgin* mosaic in the apse, the *Cappella Paolina* (designed by the architect who built Villa Borghese), and the *Cappella Sistena* (built with ancient marble, Pope Sixus V is buried here). Bernini, one of Italy's most important sculptors/architects, is also buried here in a simple tomb near the altar.

Museo Nazionale Romano (National Roman Museum) *(Via Enrico de Nicola 79; Tel 06/488-08-56; Metro Repubblica; 9am-2pm Tues-Sat, 9am-1pm Sun; 12,000L admission):* Housed in a section of the 3rd-century Baths of Diocletian, which were once the largest baths in Ancient Rome, this museum holds one of the greatest collections of Greek and Roman antiquities in the world. The courtyard of the building, just north of Termini station, was designed by Michelangelo, and is filled with many statues and ancient fragments. The museum's collection includes mosaics, sarcophagi, sculptures, Roman inscriptions and writings, and tomb reliefs. Highlights include the *Ludovisi Throne*, a Greek relief from 460 B.C. that shows the birth of Aphrodite, and a one-armed Greek statue of Apollo. Recently much of the collection was moved to **Palazza Massimo alle Terme** *(Largo di Villa Peretti 67; Tel 06/48-90-35-00; 9am-2pm Tues-Sat, 9am-1pm Sun),* which is also included in the ticket price.

Catacombs of Santa Callixtus *(Via Appia Antica 110; Tel 06/513-67-25; Bus 218 to Fose Ardeatine; 8:30am-noon/2:30pm-5pm, till 5:30pm during Summer, Thur-Tues; 8,000L admission):* This underground cemetery, which is southeast of the city and reachable by bus, was Christian Rome's first cemetery. It's huge, stretching 12 miles over five levels. The hundreds of thousands of tombs contain 16 popes and several saints. If the thought of being surrounded by thousands of dead bodies doesn't deter you, the catacombs, which contain sculptures, paintings, and drawings on the wall, are worth the trek.

modification

So you're in love with a *bello Italiano* and you want his name tattooed on your arm. **Tattooing Demon Studio** *(Via dei Farnesi 72; Tel 06/687-32-06, 06/686-89-04; Bus 81 or Metro Line A to Lepanto; 1-8pm Mon-Sat, closed Sun; V, MC, AE),* near the Campo de' Fiori, can do the honors, and they also do piercing of all kinds of delicate parts. Everything's nice and sanitary and fresh and crispy out of new plastic packages (whew!). This is supposed to be the best place, with the best tattoo artists in all of Rome, so if you're gonna do it....

great outdoors

Even though Rome is a distinctly urban place, it's relatively easy to escape the city vibe and wiggle your toes in the grass. At the **Villa Borghese** [see *culture zoo,* above] you can take a relaxing walk, go jogging, take a bike ride, rollerblade, or make a picnic among its sloping green lawns.

forza italia

Don't be scared, there aren't *usually* riots....

Okay, Italians really love soccer, big surprise. So, predictably, a soccer match in Italy is something to see. First of all, everybody else seems to know exactly what's going on—when to sing a supportive song to the home team, when to hiss at the small section of visiting fans and make obscene hand gestures toward them as they chuck coins, plastic bottles, etc. over the Plexiglas dividers and light smoke bombs while riot police with batons and helmets keep them in check.... No, really, it's a lot of fun, even if you're not a sports fan; by the second half, you'll be riveted. Rome has two major teams, Roma and Lazio. Roma is the really popular, more successful team, while Lazio is the beloved underdog that hasn't been Number One in about three decades but is getting it together these days (think Yankees and Mets). If you're in Rome between September and May, you can probably get tickets to a game; they're on Sundays at the **Stadio Olímpico** *(Foro Italico dei Gladitori; Tel 06/368-51; Bus 32, 48, 391).* Unless it's a big game, you can usually get tickets at the stadium (go about three hours before). Otherwise go to **Lazio Point** *(Via Farini 24; Tel 06/482-66-88; Metro Line A, B to Termini or Bus 4, 9, 14, 16).* Tickets will run you about 42,000L, more or less, depending on the game. The scalpers here are definitely to be avoided.

There's plenty of other folks lolling around, but it's not crowded, except on the occasional *very* beautiful Saturday or Sunday, so you can get a little solitude, meditate, do your tai chi, whatever. Almost every kind of person in the city is here, from young families to athletes to slackers to old men reading the paper.

Horseback riding is another random stay-fit thing you could give a go while in Rome. With riding grounds conveniently located in the Villa Borghese, the **Associazione Sportiva Villa Borghese** *(Vía del Galoppatoio 25; Tel 06/320-04-87; Bus 95, 490, 495; Rates and hours vary, call for schedules and non-member rates)* can provide you with a decent horse and English tack if you already know how to ride—or, if you're a novice, a glue-factory candidate or a pony and a guy to lead you around comfortingly while you cling for dear life to the poor animal....

After that little adventure, you could hobble next door to the open-to-the-public **Roman Sport Center** *(Vía del Galoppatoio 33; Tel 06/320-16-67; Bus 95, 490, 495; Call for times and non-member rates)* and lick your wounds in one of the saunas, go swim in one of the two great big year-round swimming pools (be warned, I hear it's packed with teeny-boppers and bed-wetters in the summer months), whack a ball around in one of the squash courts, or work out at the pumping-iron-style gym.

STUFF

Rome is definitely a good place to get a fashion fix. While it's not the ultra-trendy scene that Milan is and doesn't generally target big-label bar-gain-hunters, that just makes it all the more appealing for those who can't afford, and wouldn't wear, but like to look at, what's coming out in haute couture and ready-to-wear. The major streets to spy or shop for clothing and accessories from houses like Armani, Valentino, Donna Karan, Versace, Gianfranco Ferré, Givenchy, Max Mara, Missoni, etc., are Vía Condotti, Vía Borgognona, Vía Frattina, and, generally, all around the blocks at the foot of the Spanish Steps. Especially beautiful are the windows at Valentino; especially sexy, Missoni. A better area to check out if you actu-ally want to *buy* something is around Vía del Govèrno Vècchio, where there are a bundle of used-clothing shops hawking old cords, fuzzy sweaters of uncertain colors, peasant skirts, beat-up leather jackets and pants, vintage T-shirts printed with obscure messages, plus a number of less-expensive shops that sell ready-to-wear stuff, mainly from European designers.

As far as picking up some random cool souvenirs, you can get some great kitsch stuff in any number of the Catholic accessory shops near the Vatican, like plastic glow-in-the-dark rosaries or even the full priest vest-ments (you never know when *that* could come in handy).

▶▶**HOT COUTURE**
Josephine de Huertas & Co. *(Vía del Govèrno Vècchio 68; Tel 06/687-65-86; Bus 46, 62, 64; 10am-8pm Mon-Sat; V, MC, AE)* is a small shop selling prêt-à-porter designs from Anna Sui, Bella Freud, Alberto Biani, Montana Blu, Liviana Conti, and some very sexy swimsuits (in season)

from Capucine Puerari. A good selection of both funky and classic-looking stuff and not outrageously priced.

The style of **Arsenale** *(Vía del Govèrno Vècchio 64; Tel 06/686-13-80; Bus 46, 62, 64; 3:30-7:30pm Mon, 10am-7:30pm Tue-Sat; V, MC, AE, DC)* is what you could call orphan industrial: men's wear in dark wool, beautiful scarves, elegant and sexy but comfortable-looking shoes, and funky jewelry made of plastic tubing, wire, beads, stone, glass, etc., all in a black-walled, metal-shelved store with big velvet seats.

Along the same route you can check out **Mado** *(Vía del Govèrno Vècchio 89a; No phone; Bus 46, 62, 64; 11am-1pm/4-8pm, Mon-Sat; www.madonet.com; V, MC, DC, AE)*, a small but packed place with lots of glam clothes like silk kimonos; high-necked, full-length embroidered

fashion

Some people would argue that it's the French who really know fashion. Sure, they're masters at creating outlandish outfits that manage to look elegant and not ridiculous and tacky. But who wears that stuff to, say, the supermarket? When it comes to casual, it's Americans who rule, right? They invented the patched jeans/T-shirt look and the Converse-with-a-dress look, and no one seems to wear it more naturally. It's between these two extremes that the Italians have it together. For the most part, urbanized Italian people really do know how to dress well and, more important, seem to know what works on them and what doesn't. You just don't see really overweight people wearing spandex in Italy, nor do you see women with hair-sprayed poof-wing things or boys with one wind pant-leg rolled up to their calf. Nor does everyone from 12 to 35 jump on any trend, no matter how ridiculous, that shows up on models or in Hollywood. And thank god for that! While you do get the occasional 14-year-old girl who thinks she's a sex goddess in her Hello Kitty wear, or your standard shirt-unbuttoned-down-to-here-pinky-ring-wearing stud who thinks you want a real good look at his big ol' hairy belly, for the most part, people tend to wear simple, classic clothes, sometimes a little bit sexy but rarely in a look-at-me kind of way. It's really refreshing to be reminded that what is relaxed and subtle can still be extremely attractive and appealing. The only big exceptions are in clubland, where some people just go crazy—Hilfiger head-to-toe, tube tops, zebra-print bustiers—but even so, it depends on the club.

dresses; great accessories; big, floppy feather fans; animal-shaped brooches; and dramatic hats with gauze veils. In other words, all of the cool stuff your grandmother has in tissue paper in the back of her closet because she doesn't go work it anymore. Also great shoes and menswear.

▶▶VINTAGE

Around the corner is **Distané** *(Via della Chièsa Nuòva 17; Tel 06/683-33-63; Bus 46, 62, 64; 10am-8pm Mon-Sat; MC, V)*, another teeny-but-stocked place with great racks to dig through. You can find crazy lace-front bells, leather pants, every color hoodie, and great catch-all bags. Directly across from Distané is a small church and square. The church steps are a great spot for people-watching on a nice day, and there are usually a couple of people kicking around a soccer ball on the square, in case you need to catch your breath or sit and have a think.

▶▶TUNES

Locals say the only real places to go for CDs are the two branches of **Disfunzioni Musicaii,** one for new stuff *(Via Degli Etruschi 4-14; Tel 06/446-19-84; Bus 71, 492; 10:30am-7:30pm Mon-Sat; AE, MC, V, DC)* and the other for used and rare items *(Via deo Marruccini 1; Tel 06/445-42-63; Bus 71, 492; 10:30am-7:30pm Mon-Sat; AE, MC, V, DC)*. The new stuff branch has all of the latest in dance, house, techno, hip-hop, trance, etc., as well as a solid selection from the past. The used-and-rare store has great deals, especially on vinyl, and between the two, they either carry or can order just about anything you ask for. Both branches have helpful, knowledgeable staffs, who will do their best in English or help you muddle through in Italian.

Goody Music *(Via C. Beccaria 2; Tel 06/361-09-59; Metro Line A to Flaminio; 9:30am-2pm/3:30-8pm Mon-Sat, closed 2 weeks in Aug; www.goodymusic.it; MC, V, AE, DC)* caters more to the DJ set with an especially excellent selection of new hip-hop and import mixes. They also have several tables set up where you can sample. Despite its professional vibe, this shop is not snotty at all and has a great, helpful staff some; English is spoken here.

▶▶BOUND

If you want to pick up something to read while you pass the hours in a cafe or park, try Il Manifesto *(Via Tomacelli 144; Tel 06/68-80-81-60; Bus 81, 628; 9am-7pm Mon-Sat; md2511@mclink.it; V, MC, AE)* for a good selection of all kinds of books in Italian and a decent selection in English. They also have attractive gift books, magazines, maps, etc.

Al Ferro di Cavallo *(Via di Ripetta 67; Tel 06/322-73-03; Bus 628, 926; 9am-1pm/3-7pm Mon-Sat; V, MC, AE, DC)* is a great one for really big, glossy, beautiful books on art, photography, fashion, architecture, history, and so on. A small but well-stocked place where you can feel comfortable browsing for a while. Both located near the Via del Corso.

EATS

The Italian meal plan seems to be something like this: dessert and coffee for breakfast, pasta/carbohydrate-energy and coffee for lunch, and a fairly big, carefully selected, balanced dinner, with coffee. Most people have cappuccino or latte (both of which are usually just warm, not scalding hot) just for breakfast, but some have these later in the day or before bed—they don't keep you up as much as a straight espresso. It's not necessary to tip your waitperson in most restaurants, cafes, bars, etc., as the tip is already figured as part of the price. Still, a small tip (500-1,000L) is nice. There's excellent food to be had at very fair prices in Rome, so don't settle for mediocre meals just to fill yourself up. If the pastries look waxy or the place is completely empty, move on. And don't be intimidated if the menu is all in Italian—what you can't figure out you can ask about, or you can always just smack your hands together and lick your chops while pointing at someone else's food.

First of all, it's good to know where to get some staples. A few suggestions:

Good fruits and vegetables: **Campo de' Fiori** in the morning. From about 9am until around 1pm Monday through Saturday, it's packed with vendors selling good produce at fair—if not dirt-cheap—prices. This is where all the old people go to pick out perfect tomatoes. You can also find flowers, fish, herbs, and lots more.

Good bread: **Antico Fórno** *(Campo de' Fiori; Tel 06/68-80-66-62; Bus 42, 62, 64; 7:30am-2pm/4:45-8pm daily; No credit cards)* has all kinds of great twists of Italian, semolina, focaccia, and peasant bread with a nice, thick, crackly crust. Everything is freshly baked and consistently delicious.

Good meat: An excellent butcher is **Antica Norcineria** *(Via Campo de' Fiori; Tel 06/68-80-61-14; Bus 42, 62, 64; 7:30am-1:30pm/4:30-8pm daily; No credit cards)*. They've got just about everything here— prosciutto, salami, ham, beef, you name it. All the best quality, great cuts, and reasonably priced. The counter people are friendly and helpful, and won't get huffy if you ask for small amounts of lots of different things to get a good sampling.

Good wine: **Buccone** *(Via Ripetta 19; Tel 06/361-21-54; Bus 628, 926; 9am-8pm daily; V, MC, AE)* is a trusty place with fair prices. The staff will be glad to help you choose a good bottle in your price range.

▶▶**CHEAP**

The city is covered with small "bars" that sell different pastries, as well as coffee (that means espresso, cappuccino, etc.). These are also the best places to go for all three meals if you're on a really tight budget; you can get some sandwiches, maybe two or three, and a soda for under L10,000.

According to locals, **Teichner** *(Piazza San Lorenzo in Lucina 15; Bus 81, 628, 492, 70, 80; No phone; 7:30am-9pm daily; V, MC, AE, DC)* has the best coffee in the city for the best price (1,000L), as well as cheap and delicious pastries, sandwiches, candies, chocolates, and a large selection of cheeses, meats, olives, and dairy products. It's a perfect place to grab some snack supplies for later. There are also several outdoor tables and one or two inside. Directly across the piazza is **Ciampini** *(Piazza San Lorenzo 'n Lucina 33; Tel 06/687-63-04; Bus 81, 628, 492, 70, 80; 7:30am-9pm Thur-Tue, closed Wed; V, MC, AE)*, which also has very good

down and out

There's plenty of stuff you can do in Rome even if you are totally, unequivocally broke, especially in the summertime. When it's warm, most of the good stuff in Rome is to be had outdoors: concerts galore, theater, art shows, and impromptu soccer games. Just look around for signs (they're *everywhere*); you can always go linger around, lie on the grass, and enjoy. All year-round, Piazza Navona is great for kicking around and people-watching; same for **Campo de' Fiori** [see *hanging out*, above]. They're old hat to locals, but for visitors, especially first-timers, the city's zillion fountains at night are truly gorgeous. With their lights making tangled, glowing reflections on the moving water and the gently bubbling sounds—which you can actually appreciate now that the noise of the city has hushed up—well, it's kind of tough not to be dumbstruck. Some dazzling ones: Bernini's Fountain at Piazza Navona, the Trevi Fountain at Piazza di Trevi [see *culture zoo*, above], the Fontana del Tritone at Piazza Barberini, the Naiads at Piazza della Repùbblica. The very top of the Spanish Steps, although really touristy during the day, is an amazing place to watch the sun come up.

Another fine way to live the high life on next to nothing is sneaking into private gallery openings and partaking of the wine and cheese until someone catches on, at which point you beeline for the door [see *arts scene*, above].

coffees, sandwiches, pastries, many kinds of tasty gelati, and indoor and outdoor seating. A bit more pricey and less intimate, but still a fine place for a simple, portable, and quick meal.

Don't ignore **Cafe Notegen** (*Via del Babuino 159; Tel 06/320-08-55; Metro Line A to Spagna; 7am-midnight Mon-Sat, 10am-midnight Sun; MC, V, DC*) just because of its location—even though it's only a few minutes' walk from the touristy Spanish Steps, it has successfully retained its charm and authenticity with dark wooden booths and old pictures on the walls. You can get a steaming, delicious *pizza margherita*—no, it's not some bizzare mozzarella cocktail (ew!), it's a straight-up pizza with sauce and cheese—for a mere 8,000L.

Valzani (*Via del Moro 37 A/B; Tel 06/580-37-92; Bus 23, 280; 9am-8:30pm daily; V, MC*) has been around since 1925, so they've got all the best old-school sweet stuff: *torróne, tiramisù, pangiallo,* as well as about a hundred other homemade specialties that you can't find correctly made outside Italy. There are smaller, bite-size versions of most things for 2,000L to 3,500L, if you can't decide between them.

▶▶DO-ABLE

For a terrific meal that's light but satisfying and delicious, particularly for lunch, try **ëGusto** *(Piazza Augusto Imperatore 9; Tel 06/322-62-73; Bus 628, 926, 81, 492; Noon-2am Tue-Sun; 14,000-45,000L per person; AE, DC, MC, V)* near the Piazza dei Popolo. There's a pizzeria that serves piping-hot thin-crust pizzas with all kinds of great toppings like artichokes, chicken, and sun-dried tomatoes, but even better is the lunch buffet with about 20 different dishes—pasta and rice salads, vegetables, cheeses, breads, baked quiches—all very fresh and very good. Scarf as much as you like for 14,000L including tax; you can't go wrong. Big rooms with high ceilings with modern/rustic/industrial-looking details are filled with small tables that the staff will gladly push together for groups. There's also a classy little wine and cigar bar, full lunch and dinner menus, and occasionally live, light, lounge-y music at night, when it's also a bit more trendy and formal.

Despite its discreet Vatican City location, most nights around dinnertime there are a bunch of people lined up at **Trattoria da Augusto** *(Piazza de Renzi 15; Tel 06/580-37-98; 12:30-3:30pm/8-11pm Mon-Fri, 12:30-3pm Sat, closed mid-Aug to Sept; No credit cards)* for plates of perfectly turned-out lamb or mouth-watering gnocchi in tomato sauce. Just point at the menu—even if they get it wrong, you'll get something really delicious. The proprieter is brisk but welcoming, and you'll feel right at home when he writes out your check on the paper tablecloth. Somewhat nice clothing, nothing dribbled with gelato, is great. Sometimes there are gypsies wandering in with organettos or selling lighters shaped like bird cages or kissing pixies. Simple, pleasant, and comfortable, with tables inside and out.

Another place that just screams "You're in Italy!" is centrally located **Ristorante Cartoccio d'Abruzzo** *(Largo Febo; Tel 06/67-70-24-27; Bus 70, 81, 87; 12:30-3pm/7:30-10:30pm Tue-Sun, closed Mon; 8,000-22,000L per entree; MC, V, DC)*. Its raised patio, outlined by two pretty, quiet streets and sheltered by some wrought-iron fencing that's twined with plants and flowers, is made even more lovely at night when they light the lanterns hanging from the overhanging trees. (There's cozy indoor seating too, but why?) The menu is filled with traditional Roman and Italian dishes: tender meats like lamb and veal in savory vegetable or cream-based sauces, as well as really delicious gelato. The all-male wait staff has that white shirt/black tie thing going on. No need to go crazy, but nicer clothing is more appropriate.

The truly mellow **Surya Mahal** *(Via di Ponte Sisto 67; Tel 06/589-45-54; Bus 23, 280; 12:30-3pm/7:30-11:30pm daily; 15,000-40,000L per entree; MC, AE, V)* is set up beside a fountain in the city center with outdoor tables on gravel with standing gas torch/lamps, simple indoor bamboo wicker tables and chairs, jeweled elephants, and bowls of floating flower petals and candles. Very good, light Indian food, a selection of fruit- and yogurt-based special Indian drinks (a meal in themselves— maybe save it for dessert), tender meats, and tasty appetizers like fried

rome eats and crashing

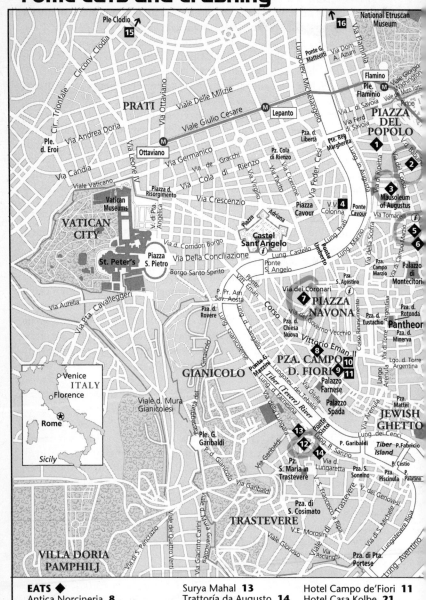

EATS ◆
Antica Norcineria **8**
Antico Fórno **9**
Buccone **1**
Cafe Notegen **2**
Ciampini **6**
ëGusto **3**
Otello alla Concordia **18**
Ristorante Cartoccio d'Abruzzo **7**

Surya Mahal **13**
Trattoría da Augusto **14**
Teichner **5**
Valzani **12**
Vècchia Roma **22**

CRASHING ■
Albergo del Sole **10**
Flaminio **16**

Hotel Campo de'Fiori **11**
Hotel Casa Kolbe **21**
Hotel Delle Muse **17**
Hotel Forum **20**
Marta Guest House **4**
Ostello Del Foro (HI) **15**
Pensione Papá
  Germano **19**

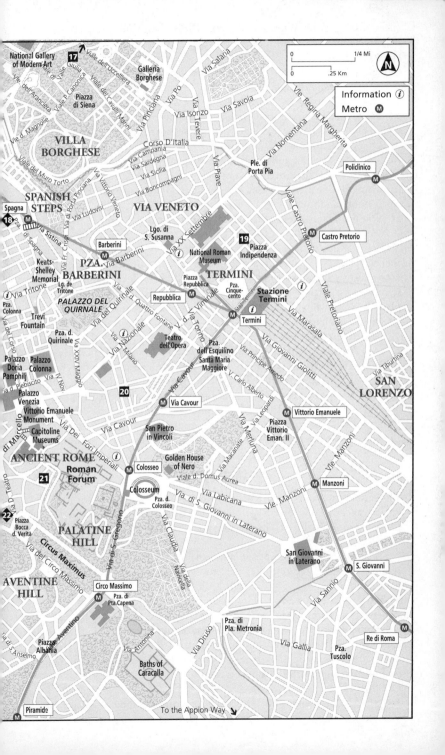

National Gallery of Modern Art

17 Viale dell'Uccelliera

Galleria Borghese

Piazza di Siena

VILLA BORGHESE

Corso D'Italia

Ple. di Porta Pia

Policlinico

SPANISH STEPS

Spagna

18

VIA VENETO

Lgo. di S. Susanna

Barberini

National Roman Museum

19 Piazza Indipendenza

Castro Pretorio

Keats-Shelley Memorial

PZA. BARBERINI

Piazza Repubblica

TERMINI

Pza. Cinque-cento

Stazione Termini

Via Tritone

Pza. Colonna

PALAZZO DEL QUIRINALE

Republica

Trevi Fountain

Termini

Via Marasala

Pza. d. Quirinale

Teatro dell'Opera

Pza. dell'Esquilino Santa Maria Maggiore

Via Giovanni Giolitti

SAN LORENZO

Palazzo Doria Pamphilj

Palazzo Colonna

20

Via Cavour

Vittorio Emanuele

Piazza Vittorio Eman. II

Palazzo Venezia

Vittorio Emanuele Monument

Capitoline Museums

San Pietro in Vincoli

Manzoni

ANCIENT ROME

Roman Forum

21

Colosseo

Golden House of Nero

Viale d. Domus Aurea

22 Piazza Bocca d. Verità

Colosseum

Pza. d. Colosseo

Via di S. Giovanni in Laterano

PALATINE HILL

San Giovanni in Laterano

S. Giovanni

Circus Maximus

AVENTINE HILL

Circo Massimo

Pza. di Pta.Capena

Re di Roma

Piazza Albania

Pza. di Pla. Metronia

Via Gallia

Pza. Tuscolo

Baths of Caracalla

Piramide

To the Appion Way

Information (i)
Metro (M)

0 ———— 1/4 Mi
0 ———— .25 Km

cheese-fish-spice mixtures. Ask the waiter to recommend a good Indian beer to complement your meal.

▶▶**SPLURGE**

The antipasti at the comfortable and centrally located **Vècchia Roma** *(Via della Tribuna di Campitelli 18, Piazza Campitelli; Tel 06/68-64-66-04; Bus 44, 95, 160, 715, 716; 20,000-30,000L main courses; 1-3:30pm/8-11pm Thur-Tue; AE)* are good enough to be dinner all by themselves, but it's no excuse to miss out on the perfectly seasoned, super-tender meat dishes and delicious pastas. While eating outside at the little tables with freshly pressed tablecloths and flowers is just fine, especially at night when the candles have been lit, it's the inside of Vècchia Roma that's so surprising: a seemingly endless number of little rooms separated by drapes and a bubbling fountain.

Near the Spanish Steps, **Otello alla Concordia** *(Via della Croce 81; Tel 06/679-11-78; Metro Line A to Spagna; 12:30-3pm/7:30-11pm Mon-Sat; 12,000-28,000L main courses; AE, MC, DC, V)* serves super-tender veal that makes any qualms you had about their cruel upbringing and tragic end fly out the window, but the real draw is the possibility that some celebrity icon will show up for dinner. Also, it's an awfully pretty place at night, when the arbor and raised patio outside make it resemble a fairy-tale garden.

La Dolceroma *(Via del Portico D'Ottavia 20B; Tel 06/689-21-96; Bus 8, 44, 170, 81; 7:30am-1:30pm/4-8pm Tue-Sat, 10am-1pm Sun, closed Mon; V, MC, AE, DC)* is a bakery in the southern end of the city center that serves up American specialties, including really great chocolate-chip cookies, carrot cake, cheesecake, and brownies, as well as Austrian concoctions like apple strudel, marzipan, and yogurt-flavored cake. Everything is high quality and often made from organic ingredients. It's particularly nice in the late afternoon, when it's quiet and you can take your time to contemplate/resist trying all the cookies *(L2,000-5,000 each)*.

crashing

Three things to know about hotels in Rome:

1. You can check the back of your door to make sure you're not getting ripped off—the maximum that they can charge for the room is posted there.

2. If you get really desperate and can find nothing, go to a tourist booth [see *need to know, below*] and grovel; they'll usually be able to find you *something*.

3. When it comes to sneaking extra people into your room, it really depends on the reception situation. Sometimes it's possible if you're coming in during the wee hours and the receptionist has taken off to get some sleep or conked out at the desk. More often than not, it's tough to do and really not appreciated if you get caught. But hey, make friends with the manager and see what you can do.

Oh, and one last thing: Regardless of how desperate you get, it's a *really* bad idea to crash outside on some steps or something. It's illegal, so you could possibly get arrested; moreover, while Rome is a fairly safe city, it's not *that* safe. Drink coffee and sleep during the day.

While not as expensive as, say, Manhattan, Rome is not a budgeter's dream as far as accommodations go. Most places in the city center are wildly overpriced. But don't be too freaked-out—there are some good deals and even some dirt-cheap deals. In all of the inexpensive and mid-range places it's often possible to ask for and get a reduction in rate, especially if you're there in the off-season or there's some weird hole in their bookings. It's worth a shot....

▶▶CHEAP

Marta Guest House *(Vía Marrianna Dionigi 17; Tel 06/323-01-84; Metro Line A to Ottaviano; 95,000L single w/o bath, 130,000L double w/bath; No credit cards)*, right near the Spanish Steps on the second floor of an apartment building. The fact that the rooms all have high ceilings is their saving grace.

OK, so the neighborhood is not exactly stellar, but no place near the train station is. Nevertheless, **Pensione Papá Germano** *(Vía Calatafimi 14A; Tel 06/486-919; Metro Line A, B to Termini; 65,000L double w/o bath, 100,000L triple w/bath, phone; AE, V, MC)* is clean and decent and even kind of fun, filled with mostly young, social, college-age backpackers from all over.

Aside from these types of pension deals, the only lower-cost option in Rome is the youth hostel. It's crowded, and you get a bunk, a locker with no lock, almost no privacy, a three-day-max stay, and funky smells—hey, *that* sounds like fun, doesn't it?! The big one in Rome is the **Ostello del Foro Italico (HI)** *(Viale delle Olimpiadi 61; Tel 06/323-62-67; Metro Line A to Ottaviano; 25,000L with HI card, 30,000L for sale at the desk; Midnight curfew, 9am-2pm lockout, reception noon-11pm; No credit cards)*, well north of Vatican City. No way around it, the curfew just sucks; so does the lockout. Don't these people realize those are key sleeping hours?! It may be best to just accept the fact that you won't make curfew most nights and that your internal clock is screwed. The sunny side of the hostel thing is: You get a shower (no curtain! woo-hoo!), a place to ditch your stuff so you don't have to carry it, breakfast, and, most important, a lot of outgoing bunkmates of all varieties from all over the world (think ages 18 to 25, slanting downward) who want to hang out, get loaded, have fun, etc. Reservations are a very good idea; they've got 300-plus beds, and they still get booked out.

One more low-cost option if you're really desperate, or you just like Phish: camping! No, really, it's a perfectly fun and realistic option in the late spring through summer months. **Flaminio** *(Vía Flaminia Nuòva 821; Tel 06/333-14-31; Bus 910 from Termini to Piazza Mancini, then Bus 200 to Vía Flaminia Nuòva; 13,000L/person per night, 8,000L/per tent, bungalows 38,000-128,000L; Mar-Oct; No credit cards)* isn't exactly the garden at Versailles, but the grounds are well-kept, clean, and green, and they have a clean swimming pool, a little grocery, a cafe, and a bar. The only tough thing is that it's about 5 miles north of city center, so you've got to figure out transportation—renting a bike is a good way to go.

▶▶DO-ABLE

Hotel Casa Kolbe *(Via S. Teodoro 44; 06/679-49-74, Tel 06/679-497; Bus 81, 160, 628, 810; 105,000L single, 135,000L double, 170,000L triple, 190,000L quad, breakfast 7,000L; V, MC, AE)* has a lot going for it. First, it's right in the center of ancient Rome, which is beautiful night and day, but it's tucked away on a cozy little street. Second, lots of young people stay here, so it's really conducive to meeting small groups of people to kick around with. The rooms are simple and on the small side but comfortable, all have private baths and daily housekeeping, and many look down onto a nice garden with great big palm trees. The staff is welcoming, helpful, and largely English-speaking.

The beautiful little **Albergo del Sole** *(Via del Biscione 76; Tel 06/68-80-68-73; Bus 46, 62, 64; 100,000L single w/o bath, 200,000L double w/bath; AE, MC, DC, V)* is located literally right next door to Campo de' Fiori, close to a lot of great stuff, yet not so close that you can't get any sleep. While the check-in staff isn't the most warm and welcoming, they're not awful, and there's a really great marble sitting room and a classy little garden out back, complete with naked statues, where you can hang out and drink and even bring non-guest friends. The rooms are A-OK, nothing to write home about, but neat, clean, and comfortable. Mostly youngish twenty- to thirtysomethingish people. Breakfast not included.

Right across the street is **Hotel Campo de' Fiori** *(Via del Biscione 6; Tel 06/68-80-68-65 or 06/68-30-90-36; Bus 46, 62, 64; 150,000L single w/o bath, 180,000L single w/bath, 180,000L double w/o bath, 230,000L double w/bath, continental breakfast included; V, MC).* The nicest part about this hotel, aside from its convenient location, is the fact that it has a very cool sun roof with terra cotta tiles, lounge chairs, a garden, and a great view of St. Pete's. Again, the rooms are fine, kind of on the dark side, but hell, if you're doing most of your sleeping during the day, that's what you want. Beware, this place looks like it attracts young families, which can mean rug rats.

Hotel Delle Muse *(Via Tommaso Salvini 18; Tel 06/808-57-49; Bus 360 to Piazza dell Muse, Bus 53; 150,000L single w/bath, 260,000L triple w/bath, continental breakfast included; www.hoteldellemuse.com; info@hoteldellemuse.co; V, MC, AE, DC),* in the northern part of Rome, is a bit out of the way (about 2 miles north of the Termini), but a good spot just the same. There's a large open garden/restaurant of the same name around back that's open in the summer, and a decent, large restaurant inside serving standard Italian fare: pasta, meat, fish, chicken, and desserts; entrees between 15,000L and 45,000L. There's also a bar that closes at 10:30pm. The rooms are neat and clean, and many have little porches. Seems to attract a lot of backpackers and college students. Oh, and if you're still torn out of the frame from last night, or just plain old lazy, you can get the sweet and accommodating staff to bring your breakfast to your room for 3,000L.

▶▶SPLURGE

Ancient Rome's **Hotel Forum** *(Via Tor Dé Conti 25, Fori Imperiali; Tel 06/679-24-46; Bus 27, 81, 85, 87, 186; 390,000-520,000L/double,*

550,000L/triple, 630,000L/suite, all including breakfast; forum@venere.it; AE, V, MC, DC), mentioned earlier for its stellar rooftop bar, is another swank-ass place in an easy-access location. For your money you get air-conditioning, private bath, radio, satellite TV, a continuous music system in all rooms (which, thankfully, can be shut off), garage, private parking, direct-dial phones, a bar, the roof garden, a restaurant, in-room massage, etc. The furnishings are traditional, ornate Italian/French provincial, but tasteful and not intimidating. While this hotel isn't exactly a slamming good time, there are a lot of youngish people around, especially young couples.

need to know

Currency Exchange The local currency is the **lira (L).** *Cambio* means money change, so look for signs. The best places to change money are definitely the banks, some of which now have ATM machines outside that change bills. There's a **Banca Nazionale delle Communicazióni** right in the train station.

Tourist Information There's an information desk in the airport *(Tel 06/65-95-60-74)* where you can get a general map; for more info, contact **Ente Provinciale per il Turismo** *(Via Parigi 11; Tel 06/48-89-92-53; Metro Line A to Repùbblica),* across the street from the train station.

Public Transportation Rome's got the *Metropolitana* **(Metro),** which is pretty fast and not too confusing. There are two underground lines, A and B; entrances have signs with big red M's. Tickets are 1,500L and can be bought at vending machines at the stations, or you can get books of tickets at places that sell cigs, which is really the easiest thing to do if you're going to ride a lot. Trains run from 6:30am-11:30pm. The bus company is **Azienda Tramvie e Autobus del Commune di Roma** *(Via Volturno 65; Tel 06/46-95-44-44; Bus 3, 4, 16, 36).* The bus is also 1,500L, and there are free transfers for an hour and a quarter after you use your ticket. Night buses-marked with a big ol' N before their number-run from midnight till 6am, on the main routes only. Good, clear maps for both the Metro and the buses can be gotten for free at Metro station booths or bought at the Stazione Termini. If it's late and you're too retarded to get yourself home on the bus, call 06/6645, 06/3570, or 06/4994 for a cab.

Motorbike Rental Romarent *(Vicolo dei Bovari 7a; Tel 06/689-65-55; Bus 46, 62, 64; 8:30am-7pm daily; MC, V, AE, DC)* has good package deals for several-day rentals; they also rent cars and video. An inexpensive bike will run you 100,000L for three days, and that includes tax, helmets, and insurance. Or go to **Bichi & Bachi** *(Via dei Viminale 5; Tel 06/48-28-84-43; Bus 70; 8am-7pm daily; V, MC, AE, DC).* An inexpensive bike here is about 40,000L per day, with all of the above also included.

American Express AMEX *(Piazza di Spagna 38; Tel 06/676-41; Metro Line A to Spagna; Travel service and tour desk 9am-5:30pm Mon-Fri, till 12:30pm Sat Nov-Apr, plus 2-2:30pm Sat May-Oct; Financial and* mail services 9am-5pm Mon-Fri, till noon Sat), near the Spanish Steps, will save your ass in so many lousy situations—they deal with money wiring, traveler's checks, and cash advances on your credit card.

Health and Emergency Emergencies: *112;* State police with an English interpreter: *113;* police hotline (for, say, a violent crime in progress): *21-21-21.* The **U.S. Embassy** has a list of English-speaking doctors, call them at *06/434-71.* All the big hospitals have 24-hour emergency rooms: **Ospedale S. Giovanni-Addolorata** *(Vía dell'Amba Aradam 9; Operator 06/770-51; Emergencies 06/77-05-56-61),* **Ospedale Fatebenefratelli** *(Piazza Fatebenefratelli 2 (on the Tiburna Island); Operator 06/668-371; Emergencies 118).*

Pharmacies **Farmacia Internazionale** *(Piazza Barberini 49; Tel 06/679-46-80; Metro Line A to Barberini)* is dependable, well-stocked, and open all day and night a few blocks north of ancient Rome. Most pharmacies are open only from 8:30am-1pm/4-7:30pm and are on a rotation system, with a list posted outside of the pharmacies saying which one is open all night that night.

Telephone Country code: *39;* city code: *06.* There are orange pay phones all over the city. Local calls are 200L. You can pay in coins, but phone cards are more convenient. You can get them at most places

wired

Fight it if you will; it is undeniable that computer networking, if not taking over the world, is at least popping up all over it. Rome is no exception, with cybercafes and Internet hookup joints abounding. If you need to get an Internet porn fix, or just feel like checking your e-mail to see if your friends have noticed you're not around lately, you can go by **Internet Cafe** *(Via dei Marrucini 12; Tel 06/445-49-53; Bus 11, 71, 204, 492; 9am-2am Mon-Fri, 5pm-2am Sat-Sun; www.internetcafe.it; AE, V, MC).* The place has everything a good work station should: air conditioning and a full bar. The rates are reasonable, between 8,000-10,000L per hour, cheaper before 9pm.

The **Net Gate** *(Piazza Firenze 25; Tel 06/689-34-45; Bus 116, 70, 87; 10:30am-10:30pm Mon-Sat June-Aug, 10:40am-8:30pm Mon-Sat Sept-May; www.netgate.it; V, MC)* has AC, but no bar. This place is a little bit bigger, so you'll probably never have to wait around for a computer, and they've got good package deals if you think you're going to need a couple of hours. These aren't the most happening places, but people seem nice enough. Both are located in the city center.

that sell cigarettes in 5,000L, 10,000L or 15,000L denominations: Break the corner off and follow the directions clearly marked on the phone, in Italian and English, with pictures. For collect calls, deposit a refundable 200L and dial 170 for an English-speaking operator. To use a calling card, deposit the same 200L, and dial your card's number. **AT&T:** *172-10-11;* **MCI:** *172-10-22;* **Sprint:** *172-18-77.*

Airports Leonardo da Vinci International Airport *(Tel 06/659-51, 06/65-95-36-40 for info),* which the locals call *Fiumincino,* handles most flights. (Charter flights arrive at **Ciampino:** *06/794-941).* The airport is about 18 unexceptional miles from the heart of the city. Follow the signs that say TRENI for the shuttle service directly to **Stazione Termini** *(arriving Track 22; 6:50am-9:20pm; about 16,000L one-way).* If you're really strapped, get a local train (7,000L and change), running every hour to **Tiburtina Station,** and from there get the **Linea B** of the local underground for 1,000L. A taxi from the airport is at least 73,000L, and if you hit any traffic it can quickly go as high as 106,500L.

Airlines TWA *(800/221-20-00; www.twa.com);* **Delta** *(800/241-41-41; www.delta-air.com);* **United Airlines** *(800/538-29-29; www.ual.com);* **US Airways** *(800/428-43-22; www.usairways.com).*

Trains Stazione Termini *(Piazza Cinquecento; Tel 1478/880-881),* smack-dab in the city center, is the one and only big station in the city. If you want the Metro, follow the red M signs. To get a bus, go straight through the outer hall of the Termini and enter the bus lot of Piazza dei Cinquecento. You can also get a taxi here, and there's an information booth in the hall with info about trips to the rest of Italy.

Bus Lines Out of the City Depending on where you're going, check out a Metro map for the bus, underground, or combination of the two that will take you away. Buses to nearby (30 minutes to an hour away) popular excursion points run between 10,000-20,000L. The bus lot is right in front of the **Stazione Termini** at Piazza dei Cinquecento *(Tel 06/465-91; Booth open 7:30am-7:30pm).*

Laundry OndaBlu *(Via Milazzo 8; Bus 492, 9, 310; 9am-10pm daily; 12,000L/load, wash and dry),* a block northeast of the train station.

Viterbo

Since few visitors to Lazio venture outside of Rome, little Viterbo (population 60,000) has been spared the crush of tourism. And though the locals seem to really value those who make their way here, they haven't turned their town into a theme park. Inside the ancient stone walls that encircle the city, the narrow streets are filled with ancient arches, medieval fountains, quiet piazzas, and crumbling stone buildings. The unmistakable imprint of Viterbo's historical background is always there, but the town lives in the present—and protects the future by not exploiting its ancient sites. It's by far the region's most well-preserved city.

There's not one particular attraction that stands out—the most pleasant thing to do here is to wander around, making your own discoveries and immersing yourself in the daily rhythms of small-town life. The locals are warm and friendly, with the possible exception of Italian soldiers who blow into town on their nights off (there's a base nearby). The nightlife, as you might expect, is pretty quiet—have a few bottles of wine over a long dinner and call it a night.

Viterbo was once an ancient Etruscan village, until the Romans came in and conquered it in the 4th century B.C. The town's biggest claim to fame is that it was the seat of the Papacy between 1257 and 1281, which was the most prosperous point in its long history. The Gothic **Palazzo Papale** [see *culture zoo,* below], the town's most famous site, was the site of the papal elections. During World War II many parts of town were badly destroyed, but they have been meticulously restored.

neighborhoods and hanging out

All of the cool sights are within walking distance of each other inside the city's gray stone walls. There's no public transportation, except for a few taxis, but you don't really need it—even the train stations are just a ten-minute walk from the center of town (one to the southwest, one to the north). The rectangular **Piazza Plebiscito,** home of the **Palazzo dei Priori** [see *culture zoo,* below] with its lovely courtyard and medieval fountain, is the geographical and social center of the town.

Corso Italia, the city's main shopping street, runs north from the piazza and ends at **Piazza Guiseppe Verdi,** up near the city wall, where you'll find the **Teatro Comunale dell'Unione** [see *arts scene,* below] and the church of **Santa Rosa** [see *culture zoo,* below]. **Via F. Ascenzi**—another shopping street—runs northwest from Piazza del Plebiscito to the round **Piazza dei Caduti,** where you'll find tourist info [see *need to know,* below]. Continue northwest out the other end of the piazza on **Via Cairoli** to get to the pretty **Piazza San Faustino** with its big, medieval fountain.

Via Cavour runs southeast from Piazza Plebiscito, and the narrow **Via San Lorenzo** runs south to the oldest section of the city, the well-preserved medieval **Quartiere San Pellegrino** neighborhood. It's really fun to get lost down here in the maze of tiny piazzas, narrow streets with laundry strung from house to house, and arches that stand tall over the cobblestoned alleys. The narrow streets are full of interesting little junk stores and restaurants to peek into. At **Piazza di Morte**—which marks the western edge of Quartiere San Pelligrino—Via San Lorenzo veers west and ends up at **Piazza San Lorenza,** where the Cattedrale and the **Palazzo Papale** preside [see *culture zoo,* below, for both].

Locals spend afternoons and evenings hanging out by the fountains in Viterbo's many pretty medieval piazzas.

Since Piazza Plebiscito isn't closed to traffic, Piazza dei Caduti, Piazza Giuseppe Verdi, and Piazza S. Faustino are the best ones for meeting people or just chilling with a bottle of wine or a beer. Piazza-hopping isn't restricted to the young, hip Viterbese—old men gravitate here to talk politics, young mothers bring their babies in strollers, and middle-aged couples come on romantic strolls. Warning: Most of the soldiers stick to the bars, but occasionally one or two stagger into the piazzas to make their presence known. They're nothing to be afraid of; they're just loud and obnoxious.

bar, club, and live music scene

Viterbo's piazzas and restaurants—which often stay open till midnight— and deliver what its bars don't: a cool laid-back scene where conversations pour out as freely as the beer and wine. If you prefer to hit one of the bars, be prepared to be the only tourist in a room full of guys with crew cuts.

Andrew's Pub *(Viale Francesco Baracca 13; Tel 0761/304-876; 8pm-2am, closed Mon)* has happy hour every day from 8 to 10pm. All your drinks are 20 percent off, though you'd almost pay extra for a little elbow room.

Other almost-indistinguishable choices around town include **Bel & Crow** *(Via Marconi 41; 0761/340-003; 8pm-2am, closed Mon)*, **Toto's**

festivals and events

Viterbo's biggest party happens each year on the third of September, when the town celebrates the **Feast of Santa Rosa.** One hundred men parade a five-ton, 30-meter tall tower with a statue of the saint on top, around town. The day before the festival, there's a procession through the city where all of the residents dress in period costumes from the Middle Ages and the Renaissance. Why do they do this? You're just going to have to visit the **Museo della Macchina di Santa Rosa** [see *culture zoo,* above] to find out for yourself.

viterbo

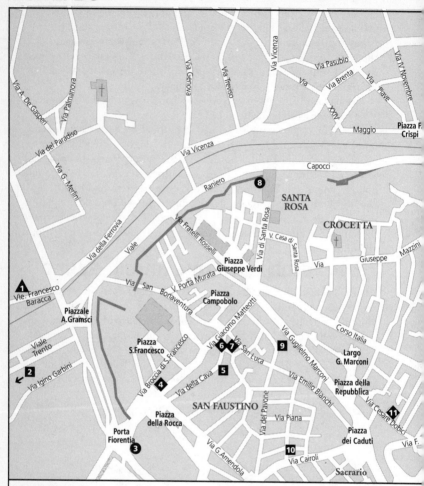

BARS/CLUBS▲
Andrew's Pub **1**

CULTURE ZOO ●
Cattedrale di San Lorenzo **16**
Museo Civico **12**
Museo della Ceramica **14**
Museo della Macchina di Santa Rosa **8**
National Archaeology Museum **3**
Palazzo dei Priori **13**
Palazzo Papale **15**

EATS ◆
Bar Rodolfo **11**
Il Grottino **6**

Il Monastero **17**
La Taverna de Cardinale **19**
L'Incontro **4**
Ristorante Il Portico **18**
Ristorante la Pentolaccia **20**
Taverna del Padrino **7**
Trattoria Porta Romana **21**

CRASHING ■
Balleti Palace Hotel **2**
Hotel Roma **5**
Hotel Tuscia **10**
Hotel Venzia Residence **9**

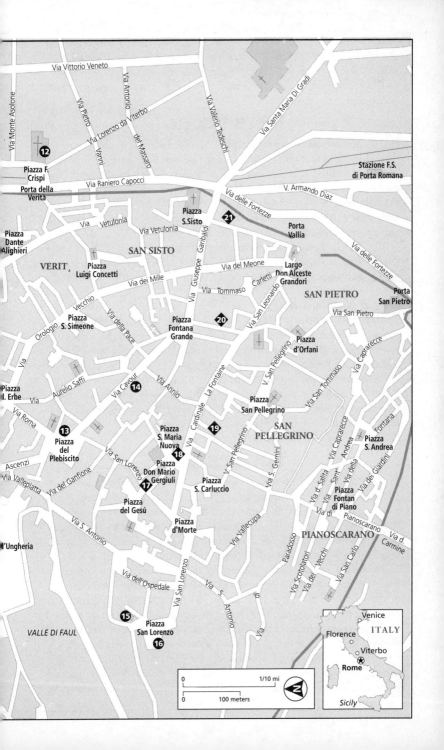

Via Vittorio Veneto

Via Monte Asolone

Via Pietro

Via Antonio

Via Lorenzo da Viterbo

Vanni

del Massaro

Via Valerio Tedeschi

Via Santa Maria Di Gradi

Stazione F.S.
di Porta Romana

12

Piazza F.
Crispi

**Porta della
Verità**

Via Raniero Capocci

Via delle Fortezze

V. Armando Diaz

Via Vetulonia

Piazza
S.Sisto

21

Porta
Vallia

Via delle Fortezze

**Piazza
Dante
Alighieri**

Via Vetulonia

SAN SISTO

Via del Meone

Largo
Don Alceste
Grandori

VERIT

Piazza
Luigi Concetti

Via dei Mille

Via Giuseppe Garibaldi

Via Tommaso

Carletti

Via San Leonardo

SAN PIETRO

**Porta
San Pietro**

Vecchio

Piazza
S. Simeone

Via della Pace

Piazza
Fontana
Grande

20

Via San Pietro

Via San Pellegrino

Piazza
d'Orfani

Via Caprarecce

Orologio

Via

Aurelio Saffi

Via Cavour

Via Annio

La Fontaine

V. San Pellegrino

Via San Tommaso

**Piazza
I. Erbe**

Via

Via Roma

14

Piazza
San Pellegrino

**SAN
PELLEGRINO**

Fontana

Piazza
S. Andrea

13

Piazza
del
Plebiscito

Via San Lorenzo

Via Cardinale

Piazza
S. Maria
Nuova

19

Via San Pellegrino

Via S. Gemini

Via Caprarecce

Sant' Andrea

Via dei Giardini

Via della

Ascenzi

Via del Ganfione

18

Piazza
Don Mario
Gergiuli

Piazza
S. Carluccio

Via d. Salita

Piazza
Fontan
di Piano

Via Vallepiatta

17

Piazza
del Gesú

Piazza
S. Antonio

Piazza
d'Morte

Via Vallecupa

Via di

Pianoscarano

Via d.
Carmine

PIANOSCARANO

d'Ungheria

Via S. Antonio

Via dell'Ospedale

Via San Lorenzo

Via S. Antonio

di

Paiadosso

Via Scopolatori

Via del Vecchi

Via San Carlo

VALLE DI FAUL

15

Piazza
San Lorenzo

16

0   1/10 mi

0   100 meters

N

Venice

ITALY

Florence

Viterbo

Rome

Sicily

(Via Genova 32; 0761/347-339; 8pm-2am, closed Mon), **Sand Glass**
(Viale Trieste 159; 0761/325-407; 8pm-2am, closed Mon), **Tikaldi** *(Piazza
delle Erbe 12; 0761/326-87; 8pm-2am, closed Mon)*, and **Van Dyck**
(Piazza della Trinitá; 0761/345-070; 8pm-2am, closed Mon).

But really, trust us—sticking to the piazzas and restaurants is a much
better plan.

arts scene

Since Viterbo is so close to the capital city, the locals seem content to get
their dose of contemporary arts there. The city does have two theaters
that hold limited schedules of musical concerts, theatrical events, and
dance performances. Tickets and schedules for city events are available at
Promo Tuscia *(Piazza dei Caduti; Tel 0761/307-284 or 0761/304-603;
9am-1pm/1:30pm-3:30pm Mon-Fri, 9am-1pm Sat; info@promotuscia.it;
www.promotuscia.it)* and **Camillo Sound** *(Via Cavour 69; Tel 0761/305-
947)*. During the summer there are often concerts at the 13th-century
Gothic Palazzo Papale [see *culture zoo,* below], which are worth attending
just to get a glimpse of the inside of the building, which is normally
closed to the public.

▶▶PERFORMING ARTS

Teatro San Leonardo *(Via Cavour 9; Tel/Fax 0761/341-893)*, located
just east of Piazza del Plebiscito on Via Cavour, is the smaller of the city's
two theaters and hosts mainly musical events. If you've never seen Cats in
Italian, now's your chance.

Viterbo's main theater, **Comunale dell'Unione** *(Piazza G. Verdi;
Tel 0761/340-170; Box office open from 10am-1pm Tues-Sat; www.
teatrounione.spettacolo-online.it; Tickets from 20,000-50,000L)* hosts
mostly Italian theater, dance, and musical concerts. It's just north of
Piazza Giuseppe Verdi near the Chiesa Santa Rosa.

culture zoo

Your cultural tour begins with the medieval buildings, the Piazzas, and
the well-preserved Gothic streets. There are few museums here, but if
time is a consideration, skip them and wander around the city gaping at
the architecture instead. The Palazzo dei Priori is one of the city's loveliest
buildings, the Palazzo Papale, one of its most important. All the sights are
within the city walls, just a short walk from each other.

Museo Civico *(Piazza Crispi; Tel 0761/348-275; 9am-7pm daily,
Summer; 9am-6pm daily, Winter; 6,000L Adults):* Inside the former convent
of the Chiesa di S. Maria della Verità, the Civic Museum holds mostly
ancient art and fragments. The cloister holds sarcophagi, funerary art, and
fragments found inside the tombs, as well as two rooms full of Etruscan and
Roman stuff. On the first floor there's a small section of paintings, highlighted by two works by Sebastiano del Piombo, *La Pietà* and *La Flagel-
lazione.* There are also a bunch of 14th- and 15th- century frescoes that were
taken from Viterbese churches and palazzos and placed here for safekeeping.

Museo della Macchina di Santa Rosa *(Via San Pellegrino 60; Tel 0761/345-157; 10am-1pm/4pm-7pm Fri-Sun, Winter; 10am-1pm/4pm-8pm Wed-Sun, Summer; Free entrance):* Every year on September 3rd Viterbo celebrates the feast of Santa Rosa [see *festivals and events,* below] by parading a 30-meter high, five-ton tower around the city's streets, stopping at sites that were sacred to Santa Rosa. This museum documents past festivals of the *Transporto della Macchina di Santa Rosa* (Transport of the Tower of Santa Rosa), and holds drawings, photos, posters, and other mementos from Viterbo's most important festival. It's cool, but you're better off just trying to be in town for the real thing....

Cattedrale di San Lorenzo *(Piazza San Lorenzo):* This 12th-century cathedral has been greatly amended and rebuilt over the centuries. The spacious interior holds many frescoes and paintings worth seeking out, such as the Byzantine painting of *Madonna della Carbonara* in the left aisle, the nearby fragments of 13th-century frescoes, and the 14th-century frescoes near the tomb of Pope John XXI who died in Viterbo in 1277. The facade was added in the 16th century, and the black- and white-striped Gothic bell tower was built in 1368.

Museo Nazionale Archeologico *(Piazza della Rocca; Tel 0761/325-929; 9am-7pm, Closed Mon; 4,000L Adults):* The Museo Nazionale is housed in the Rocca Albornoz, which was heavily damaged by bombs in World War II and has since been completely rebuilt. The enormous building was first designed in the 14th century, and wasn't completed until a century later. Besides the Archeology Museum, which contains a mediocre collection of Etruscan artifacts and reconstructions of Etruscan life, the building also houses courtyards with fountains, and the former private apartments of the Pope.

Palazzo dei Priori *(Piazza del Plebiscito; Tel 0761/340-729; 9am-1pm/3pm-6:30pm weekdays, 10am-1pm/3:30-7:30 Sat-Sun; Free admission):* This lavishly decorated Palazzo is one of Viterbo's star sights. Parts of the building date back to 1263, although most of it was built in the 15th century. Once the seat of the government, it contains many beautiful, well-preserved frescoes, and lots of quiet nooks worth seeking out. The courtyard behind the Palazzo is one of the nicest in the city, with a Baroque fountain (Fontana del Palazzo dei Priori), remnants of Etruscan sarcophagi, and a gorgeous view over the city. Inside the Palazzo, Sala del Consiglio has 16th-century frescoes by Teodoro Siciliano depicting the Emperors of Constantinople. The Sala Regia is one of the most beautiful rooms in the Palazzo, with its 16th-century frescoes covering every inch of the walls, depicting mythological and historical persons involved in Viterbo's history.

Palazzo Papale *(Piazza San Lorenzo; Tel 0761/321-124; Open only for concerts, special events, and by appointment):* Construction began on Viterbo's pride and joy in 1255, and was completed in 1267, after Pope Alexander IV had already arrived. The loggia, which is one of the prettiest sights in Viterbo, is on nearly every postcard of the city. The ornate finely carved loggia was originally a double one, but half of it collapsed from the weight soon after it was built.

CITY SPORTS

Though Viterbo doesn't have much green space, its southern section is full of hilly streets that'll elevate your heart rate in no time if you walk at a good pace. If you'd rather work out inside, head to the gym with the rest of the city's athletes for a workout and a peek at all those buff bodies. **Fitness Gym** *(Via Garbini 76/B; Tel 0338/872-8211)* has lots of exercise equipment along with a full lineup of classes: aerobics, step aerobics, circuit training, bodybuilding, karate, boxing, and Latin dancing. You can pop in and take a single class no problem. There's even a solarium where you can catch a tan.

GREAT OUTDOORS

The best place to dive in to the Lazio wilderness is the **Riserva Naturale del Lago di Vico,** a nature preserve in a gorgeous valley centered around Lago di Vico, about 10km south of Viterbo. Legend has it that the lake was formed by Hercules when the tribe of giants who ruled this area dared to challenge his strength. To shut the non-believers up, he drove a huge club into the ground like it was nothing. When he pulled it out, water began to gush up out of the spot where the trunk hit, filling up the hole it left behind and forming the lake. Back here in reality, the story of Lago di Vico is a little less exciting: the lake started out as a crater formed from the collapse of a volcano, and slowly filled up with water from underground springs over a few centuries' time. In the 16th century, the water level was lowered, making way for the beautiful lush land that surrounds the lake—some of the first trees that sprung up at this time are still around today. Beyond these woods are the **Cimini mountains,** which form a ring that semi-enclose the valley.

Well-marked trails make it easy to explore the reserve on your own, but if you want some guidance—or to do something that requires renting some equipment—get in touch with **Camping Natura** *(Tel/Fax 0761/612-347; www.camping-natura.com; 145,000L/half-day guided hiking tour, 250,000L/half-day Land Rover tour for 4-16 people, 80,000L/day sailboat rental, 25,000L/day bike rental, 25,000L/half-day canoe rental, 25,000L/2 hour horseback ride),* whose main office is in Caprarola, the nearest village to the reserve. They can give you guided tours by foot or in a Land Rover, rent you canoes, mountain bikes, or small sailboats, or match you up with a nice horse to carry your butt around for a couple hours (they'll even give lessons to equestrian novices). You can also spend the night in their campsite, right in the heart of the reserve. Don't worry if you don't have a tent—you can rent one, or take the more comfortable road and stay in one of their bungalows *(Camping 10,000L/person, 4-person bungalow 85,000L, tent rental 8,000L).*

When you're done romping around and want to soothe those tired muscles, head for the very cool **Terme dei Papi** *(Tel 0761/3501; City* *bus 2 from Piazza Martiri d'Ungheria)* natural sulpher baths. They're just about 3km to the west of Viterbo, a short bus ride away.

STUFF

Walk along Viterbo's main shopping street, Corso Italia, and you'll soon realize that locals probably head to Rome for their shopping sprees. There are some funky junk stores worth checking out in the medieval **San Pellegrino district,** where you can haggle for an antique souvenir or two.

EATS

The cuisine here is a combination of Roman, Tuscan, and Umbrian tastes, and it really works—the restaurants here are excellent. For a small town, there's a great selection of cheap eats and cozy, typical trattorias. Local specialties to keep an eye out for are *Giubba e Calzoni* (lamb soup with artichokes, potatoes, and vegetables), *Minestrone Viterbese, Pignattaccia* (stewed beef and pork with vegetables), and any dish with rabbit. Oddly, many restaurants in Viterbo keep their pizza ovens off during the day and only serve their pies at night.

▶▶CHEAP

If you haven't yet tried the hot chocolate in Italy, try it at **Bar Rodolfo** *(Via C. Dobici 11; No phone; 8am-9pm daily; 1,500L cappucino; No credit cards)*...you'll never crave Swiss Miss again. It's a good place to come for breakfast or for your afternoon caffeine fix. Sit in the room off the main bar—it has cool copper chairs and a TV.

Il Monastero *(Via Fattungheri 10; Tel 0761/324-346; 12:30-2:30pm/7:30-10:30pm, closed Wed; Pizza 10,000-15,000L; V, MC, AE, EC),* just off Piazza Don Mario Gargioli, has great cheap pizza and a delicious selection of pastas and other main courses. With its vaulted ceiling and brick walls, the place looks like it could have been a monastery in a former life.

Taverna del Padrino *(Via della Cava 22-24; Tel/Fax 0761/342-743; 12:30-2:30pm/7:30-10:30pm; Avg meal 30,000L; No credit cards)* is a

TO MARKET

Grande Spesa *(Via G. Marconi 36; Tel 0761/321-232; 9am-1pm/3:30-7:30pm)* is a big supermarket that sells just about anything you'll need. **Casa Italia** *(Strada Cimina 14; Tel 0761/324-172; Fax 0761/227-414; 9am-1pm/3:30-7:30pm)* is a smaller food store with a huge variety of Italian salamis and sausages.

friendly, family-run place, also a favorite with soldiers on their nights off (watch out, ladies). The home-style comfort food served in this friendly, no-frills dining room has a cultish following, and it's tempting to eat all your meals in Viterbo here. The portions are big and all the pasta dishes are excellent, particularly the hearty spaghetti carbonara and the linguini with *porcini* mushrooms. Save room for the home made desserts. The same family owns the Hotel Venezia Residence [see *crashing,* below] around the corner, and usually gives their hotel guests discounts on their meals.

In the San Pellegrino area, **La Taverna del Cardinale** *(Via San Vito 10; Tel 0761/345-361, closed Mon; 30,000-40,000L average meal)* serves good pizza and other simple dishes for nice prices. With red and white tablecloths, old copperware hanging on the walls, and exposed bricks popping out from under the white paint in places, this tavern has a real homey feel. It's full of locals who come here to enjoy homemade pastas and great local wine.

▶▶**DO-ABLE**

L'Incontro *(Via G. Matteotti 67; Tel 0761/227-293; 9am-midnight, closed Sat; Pizza 14,000L, tourist menu 18,000L, lunch buffet 11,000L; V, MC, AE, DC, EC),* a few steps from the Museo Nazionale, has an outdoor patio where you can enjoy long, leisurely meals in the sun when it's warm. At lunch time there's a self-service buffet (11,000L) for those on tight budgets. They only serve pizza at night, but with specialties like *pizza contadina con pomodorini vesuviani* (pizza with Vesuvian cherry-tomatoes), it's worth the wait. Try the homemade pasta dishes like cannelloni and lasagna.

The small and simple **Trattoria Porta Romana** *(Via della Bontá 12; Tel 0761/307-118; Closed Sun and month of Aug; No credit cards),* near the Porta Romana, serves great classic dishes that the locals eat with gusto. The place is cozy, with pink tablecloths and wood-paneled walls. The specialties of the house revolve around the hearty meat dishes for which Viterbo is known. And it all tastes better with a carafe of inexpensive local wine.

Between Via Garibaldi and Via Monastero, **Ristorante la Pentolaccia** *(Via delle Fabbriche 20-22; Tel 0761/342-775; Average meal 40,000L; V, MC, AE, EC)* feels like your typical Central Italian restaurant with its earthen tile floors, Mediterranean color scheme, and bare decor. It serves simple, regional meat dishes and homemade pastas that will blow you away.

▶▶**SPLURGE**

For a cozy Mediterranean feel, head to **Ristorante Il Portico** *(Piazza Don Marco Gargiuli 11; Tel 0761/328-021 or 0761/321-143; Average meal 60,000L; V, MC, AE, EC)* with its warm colors, hanging plants, and antique furniture. The menu is creative, using all fresh, locally-grown ingredients. There's a daily specials menu which the helpful waitstaff will try to translate—be sure to try the pumpkin ravioli if it happens to be on the menu. The desserts are some of the best in town.

crashing

Since Viterbo isn't a top tourist destination (most folks just come on day trips from Rome), there isn't a huge selection of hotels. But even during

wired

Just about the only place in town to surf the Web is the **Internet Bar** *(Vicolo Macel Gattesco 35; Tel 0761/333-085; Closed Sun; 10,000L per hour)*, around the corner from S. Giovanni Battista degli Almadiani. It's a small, friendly place, but with just three computers most people come here to drink coffee, eat pastries, and chat with the friendly matron. For information on Viterbo on the Web check out ***http://www.viterboonline.com.***

the high season it's not hard to find accommodation, even if you arrive without reservations. Most hotels in Viterbo are affordable, and are right in the city center. **Promo Tuscia** [see *need to know,* below] can help you find a hotel, and also has listings of private rooms for rent.

▶▶**CHEAP**

The 14 rooms at the family-run **Hotel Venezia Residence** *(Via del Pavone 23; Tel 0761/303-409, Fax 0761/309-848; Singles 65,000-100,000L, Doubles 80,000-150,000L; V, MC)* are simple and nondescript, but it's one of the most pleasant places in town. The friendly staff will go out of their way to help you enjoy your stay. Prices tend to vary, so it's worth asking for a discount. All rooms have TVs and mini-bars, and most have showers instead of bathtubs. The owners of the hotel also run the **Taverna del Padrino** [see *eats,* above] around the corner. Try to eat there at least once—the proprietors tend to get offended if you don't. A breakfast of coffee, croissants, and pastries is included in the price.

A comfortable, family-run hotel, **Hotel Roma** *(Via della Cava 26; Tel 0761/227-274 or 0761/226-474; Fax 0761/305-507; Singles with baths 50,000-70,000L, doubles with baths 70,000-100,000L, Full board 85,000-170,000L, half board 70,000-140,000L; AE, V, MC, DC, EC)* has spacious rooms, each with TV and private baths.

▶▶**DO-ABLE**

With 105 modern, classy rooms, all with private baths, even in the high season it's not hard to get a room at **Balletti Palace Hotel** *(Via F. Molini 8; Tel 0761/344-777, Fax 0761/345-060; Singles 80,000-105,000L, doubles 125,000-165,000L; V, MC, AE)*. All rooms have TVs, phones, and mini bars, and there's a bar and a few common areas where you can hang out with other guests.

Although the slightly tacky decor at **Hotel Tuscia** *(Via Cairoli 41; Tel 0761/344-400; Fax 0761/345-976; Singles with baths 85,000-100,000L, doubles with baths 130,000-160,000L; V, AE, EC)* makes you feel like you're on a cruise ship, all 39 rooms are clean, spacious, and have private baths and TVs. Skip breakfast in the dark and gloomy dining room and head to a cafe instead.

need to know

Currency Exchange The best place to change money in Viterbo is at the **banks** (most of which have ATMs), which are open from 8:30am to 1:30pm and between 2:45pm and 3:45pm. There is a **Banca d'Italia** at Via G. Marconi 26 and a **Banca del Cimino** on Piazza Martiri d'Ungheria.

Tourist Info The tourist office, **Promo Tuscia** *(Piazza dei Caduti; Tel 0761/304-643 or 0761/307-284; Fax 0761/308-480; 9am-1pm/1:30pm-3:30pm Mon-Fri, 9am-1pm Sat; info@promotuscia.it; www.promotuscia.it)* is located inside what used to be Chiesa Almadiani. The staff is helpful, and they will assist you with hotel reservations. There's another tourist office, **Porto del Parco di Viterbo,** around the corner *(Via Ascenzi 4; Tel/Fax 0761/325-992; portavt/isa.it; Same hours).*

Public Transportation Inside Viterbo's walls there's no need to take the bus since everything is within walking distance. There's a **taxi stand** *(Tel 0761/340-777 or 0761/40-811)* at Piazzale Gramsci, just outside Porta Fiorentina.

Health and Emergency Emergencies: *113;* Police emergencies: *112;* Ambulance service: *0761/33-91;* Medical emergencies: *118.* There's a **police station** *(Via Monte Cervino; Tel 0761/228-383 or 0761/348-549)* in the center. **Hospital Belcolle** is on Strada Sammartinese *(Tel 0761/33-91).*

Pharmacies There are **pharmacies** at Corso Italia 37 *(Tel 0761/304-613)* and Via Cairoli 14 *(Tel 0761/304-034),* which post signs for the rotating 24-hour pharmacies in town.

Telephone City code: *0761.* There are Telecom Italia calling centers at Corso Cavour 33, Via Matteotti, Via Calabresi, and Via Nazario Sauro. They're all open from 9am-10pm.

Trains Station Porta Fiorentina *(Viale Trento; Tel 0761/3161, 0761/316-550, or 0761/316-358),* just north of the city walls, is a ten-minute walk from the town center. Viterbo lies on the Florence-Rome line, less than an hour from Rome, but you've got to change at Orte-Viterbo to a local train. **Station Porta Romana** *(Via Romiti; Tel 0761/303-429)* is about a ten-minute walk southeast of the city.

Bus Lines Out of the City The **bus station** is inconveniently located in Riello, a few kilometers away from Viterbo, and buses are infrequent. For bus information call 0761/324-914 or 0761/308-837.

Postal The main **post office** *(Via ascenzi 9; Tel 0761/304-806; 8:30am-1:30pm Mon-Fri; 8:10am-noon Sat and the last day of each month)* is right in the center of town. You can stick your postcards in the red post boxes throughout the city.

Internet See *wired,* above.

umbria

umbria

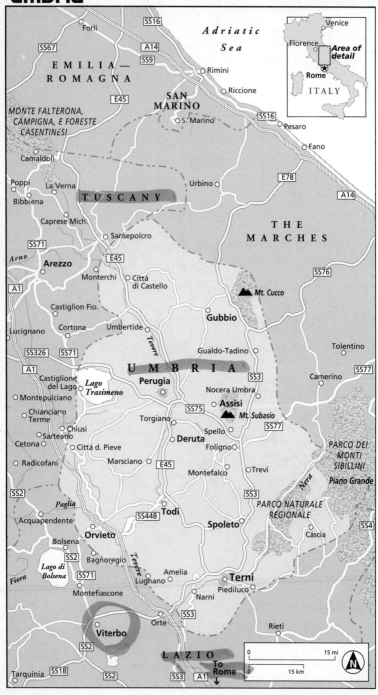

Smack in the center of Italy, little-known Umbria is graced with good looks and lots of personality. The wild nightlife and cultural scene that revolves around its capital, **Perugia,** rivals that of Italy's largest cities. Its landscape is lush and green, with rolling hills, sunflower fields, olive groves, vineyards, and remarkably well-preserved medieval towns like **Assisi** and teeny **Todi.**

So with all that snapshot-fodder, you'd think that this place would be crawling with tourists, right? Amazingly, it's not. Visitors often overlook landlocked Umbria in favor of fashion-conscious Florence and trendy Tuscany to the north, ancient Rome to the south, and sandy Le Marche to the east, so it's all yours, relatively speaking. Extensive damage done to the region by earthquakes in 1997—which claimed the lives of 11 people and shook some of Giotto's famous Assisi frescoes beyond repair—doesn't exactly help lure the tour buses either.

What savvy travelers are clued in to is the 3,000 years worth of artistic, architectural, and religious masterpieces to be found in even the smallest towns. Assisi, one of the country's finest art centers, is also the region's biggest tourist hotspot. It has attracted thousands of religious pilgrims each year since the 13th century, when Assisi's most beloved resident, St. Francis, died, and a basilica was built to house his mortal remains. Finished in 1228, it's one of the world's greatest Christian shrines. Unfortunately, it's kinda overshadowed by the stands surrounding it selling "I St. Francis" key chains....

But being ancient doesn't automatically mean being dull—there is serious nightlife in some of these little hamlets. Perugia, a pretty medieval hill town with a penchant for partying, is by far the region's liveliest scene, with loads of pubs, clubs, summer parties, and dark underground venues for live music.

The whole area is also a major outdoor playground. Regional parks like Mount Subasio have thousands of kilometers of marked paths for hiking, cross-country skiing, and cycling. And the labyrinthine, pedestrian-only streets of Assisi and Perugia—which often include some serious steps—offer better exercise than a Stairmaster.

Umbria's history dates back to the 8th century B.C., when this area was inhabited by a tribe called the Umbrian. The Etruscans settled here shortly thereafter, and many of their architectural contributions remain standing—Perugia's Etruscan Arch (aka Arco di Augusto) is perhaps the

arт + arcнiтecтure

Within the many walled towns in Umbria you will find monasteries, churches, towers, cathedrals, basilicas, town halls, museums, abbeys, piazzas, and crumbling Medieval houses—any of which alone would be worth a visit. Together they make Umbria feel like a living, breathing museum. Most of the cathedrals and architectural sightswere built in the 11th and 12th centuries, during a great rebirth of the region. Since the towns' treasures were erected inside the protection of the city walls, there has been no room for modern urban expansion, and venturing inside these Medieval centers today is like walking onto a magical stage set. The greatest display of Umbrian art is in the **Galleria Nazionale dell' Umbria** in Perugia (one of Italy's most renowned museums), which contains 13th- to 18th-century paintings by "local artists" such as Piero della Francesca, Fra Angelico, and Perugino. The pride of the region, however, is undoubtedly Assisi's **Basilica di San Francesco.** The early frescoes by Giotto, Cimabue, Pietro Lorenzeti, and Simone Martini are treasures of art history.

most impressive example. The Romans eventually colonized the land—built roads, founded settlements, drained marshes—and are partly responsible for its present-day look. Umbria was controlled by the Lombards during the Middle Ages, but by St. Francis's time, mostly consisted of independent townships, of which the Vatican eventually took control.

Agriculture remains one of Umbria's main industries, especially around Lake Trasimeno and along the banks of the Tiber River, which cuts across the entire region. And where there are farms, there's great fresh food on restaurant tables. Some of Italy's most prized delicacies are rooted in Umbria's culinary traditions: Orvieto wine, olive oil, truffles, lentils, cured hams, sausages, and salamis. Umbria's regional cooking is rich with game, like pheasant, hare, and cingale (wild boar), which is made into rich sauces and dried sausages. Handmade pastas, like stringozzi and strangolopreti, are served with seasonal specialties, such as fall truffles, winter pumpkin, and spring asparagus. But the most well-known and well-loved specialty is the bite-sized baci, Italy's equivalent to the Hershey's Kiss. Made by Perugia's Perugino chocolate empire (now owned by Nestle), these foil-wrapped candies are the pride of the region.

Umbria has been a cultural crossroads throughout history, and Perugia continues that melting-pot tradition today by welcoming large numbers of immigrants and students. Even in the smallest towns, cosmopolitan sophistication has a mind-opening effect on what might otherwise be just your typical rural provincialism. It also brings with it a strong fashion sense: Women get all decked out to go to the grocery store; men get dressed up to take their evening walk. But, thankfully for those of us in sneakers and wrinkled jeans, that's just part of the story: the predominant style in Umbria is laid-back and casual.

getting around the region

Traveling between **Assisi** and **Perugia,** the two most-visited towns in Umbria, is a simple 25-minute train ride. But traveling between other towns (particularly to small towns in other regions) without the luxury of a car can be much more time-consuming. If you're relying on trains and buses, and don't check the connections ahead of time, a 100km trip could turn into a half-day ordeal. Trains in the region are usually more comfortable, more frequent, and better connected than buses, and the views are stunning.

Perugia and Assisi make excellent bases for exploring the region, as they're both on the Foligno-Terontola train line. (For Florence, change at Terontola, and for Rome, change at Foligno.) Most folks opt to base themselves in lively Perugia, but if small-town life is more your thing, stay in Assisi and day-trip from there. From either city, visiting other picturesque little villages in the region like **Todi** is simply a matter of knowing when to hop off the train. When en route to Florence or Rome (or whatever your next destination may be), taking a bus or a train is a good way to see both the towns and a bit of the countryside at the same time.

Travel Times

All times by train.

	Assisi	Perugia	Todi
Assisi	-	:25	1:00
Perugia	:25	-	:45
Todi	1:00	:45	-

perugia

The first thing you' may notice about Perugia, one of Italy's best pre-served medieval towns, is that it has a more diverse population than most small Italian cities. The **University of Perugia** attracts Italians from all over the country, but the **Universitá per Stranieri** [see *too cool for school?*, below] is the most respected university in Italy for foreigners, hosting students from Africa, Asia, Europe, and North America all year round. These students, plus an increasing number of immigrants from African and Arabic countries, come to Perugia every year. This adds up to a city where the old naturally mixes with the new, where you'll find African groceries next to Italian butchers, and where the locals enthusias-tically welcome students and tourists. And style here is just as varied as nationality. Women wear everything from Gucci to torn and faded Jor-dache. Guys here range from grungy chain-wearing punks to preps in ties to fashion victims decked out in Armani.

Sunrise or sunset, the winding, cobblestone streets retain a provincial, postcard-perfect atmosphere. But the city—with its many bars, cafes, bookstores, movie theaters, arts spaces and boutiques—is far more cos-mopolitan than its ancient surface suggests. The booming technology and industrial economy helps out, bringing in cash and a sizeable popu-lation of young twentysomething professionals.

Perugians pride themselves on their artistic legacy. The vibrant art scene dates back to the Umbrian school of painting, whose luminaries were Pietro Vannucci (aka Perugino) (1446-1523), Pinturicchio (1454-1513), and Raphael (1483-1520). The **Galleria Nazionale dell' Umbria** [see *culture zoo*, below] contains the best collection of this period's masterpieces. Music is everywhere in Perugia, echoing under the arches strung precipitously over the narrow streets. **The Umbria Jazz Festival** [see *festivals and events,* below], the largest of its kind in the world, rivals only **Eurochocolate** [see *only here,* below] for the town's coolest happening.

Fierce individuality is a hallmark of the Perugians, who have spent much of the past millennium conquering nearby towns, and resisting papal rule. The story starts in the 6th century B.C., when the town was home to the Etruscans, a tribe whose culture and language eludes archaeologists today. They built the city walls and gates in the 2nd century B.C., as well as the base upon which the massive **Arco di Augusto** site [see *neighborhoods,* below] rests. The entire city was then burned to the ground in 40 B.C., rebuilt by Augustus, and passed between various bloodthirsty families throughout the Middle Ages. Pope Paul III, who finally overthrew the bloody ruling Baglioni family in the 16th century and claimed Perugia in the name of the Holy Roman Empire, was no lamb, either. He built the **Rocca Paolino** fortress [see *culture zoo,* below] to protect himself from the townsfolk, who were protesting his salt tax. It took a few hundred years, but in 1860, the locals finally managed to tear down this symbol of papal domination and build the lovely **Piazza Italia** [see *neighborhoods,* below] right on top of its remains. What's left of the actual Rocca Paolina has recently been renovated to house a public gallery, a cafe, and a few shops—though the dark, arched eeriness remains.

neighborhoods

It's easy to get lost wandering through Perugia's winding streets and alleyways, which sometimes feel like a maze. Streets often suddenly change names or directions, turn into torturously steep hills, or become completely deserted. There are no cars allowed in most of the center, but there is a system of **escalators** [see *need to know,* below] that connects some of the highest points in town with some of the lowest. Know the escalators, love the escalators—they are your friends. These high-tech innovations (in place since 1983) go from **Piazza Partigiani,** where the bus station for out-of-town travel is, just outside the city walls to the south, up to **Piazza Italia,** the central square of the **centro storico** (historic center).

Everything you'll want to see—the college town, the piazzas, the churches and museums—are in the *centro storico,* on top of the hill that is Perugia. The train station is located a few kilometers southwest and downhill from here. Piazza Italia is a half-hour uphill hike or a 10-minute bus ride [see *need to know,* below] from the train station.

The city's main drag is **Corso Vannucci,** an exceptionally wide pedestrian street that runs from **Piazza IV Novembre** and **Piazza Danti,** which flank the **Duomo** [see *culture zoo,* below] at the northern end, through **Piazza della Repubblica,** and ends up at **Piazza Italia** to the south. The benches in Piazza Italia offer great views of the rolling green Umbrian countryside, Mount Subasio, and Assisi. The busy **Piazza Matteotti** lies one block east of Corso Vannucci on **Via Mazzini,** which runs

perugia bars clubs and culture zoo

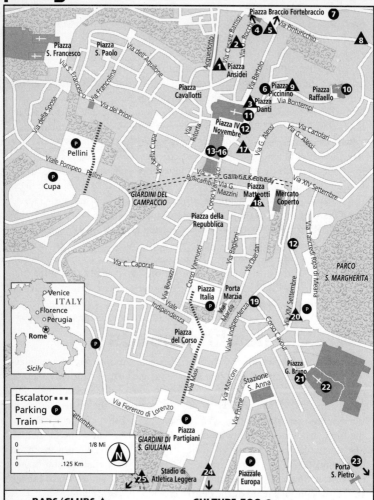

BARS/CLUBS ▲
Celebrate Café Pub **9**
Contrapunto **5**
Crazy Bull Café **24**
Enoteca Provencale di Perugia **2**
Hogan's Bar and Grill **18**
Il Dollaro **25**
Il Settimo Sigillo **1**
La Lumera Osteria **8**
Merlin Pub **17**
Shamrock Pub **3**
Sullivan's Irish Restaurant **20**

CULTURE ZOO ●
Archaeology Museum **22**
Arco di Augusto **7**
Cappella di S. Severo **10**
Chiesa di San Domenico **21**
Chiesa di San Pietro **23**
Chiesa di Sant'Angelo **4**
Chiesa di Sant'Ercolano **19**
Collegia della Mercanzia **15**
Collegio del Cambio **14**
Duomo **11**
Etruscan Wall **6**
Galleria Nazionale dell'Umbria **13**
Grand Fountain **12**
Hall of the Notaries **16**

too cool for school

Not this one. The **Universita per Stranieri** *(Piazza Fortebraccio 4; Tel 075/57461, Fax 075/573-20-14; www. unistrapg.it/inglese.htm)* teaches as many as 5,000 international students a year (all year round) in the beautiful Palazzo Gallenga, and it's *the* reason that Perugia has such a multicultural flavor. This is not some chichi language school. Founded in the 1920s, and supported by the Italian government, it will provide you with the most linguistic bang for your buck. Intense, month-long classes only cost around $280 for about 100 hours, and the learning is total-immersion style—you may be the only English-speaker in the class. The university will also help you find a short-term apartment, which is a great way to get to know Perugia. Arrangements can be made beforehand; however, you'll still be in good shape if you show up a few days before classes start. Check out the website for schedules and fees.

perpendicular to Vannucci. Mazzini houses the city's coolest bars, clubs, and restaurants. Most of Perugia's major sights, such as the **Museo Civico, Fontana Maggiore, Comune,** and **Duomo** [see *culture zoo,* below] are concentrated around Piazza IV Novembre, Perugia's grandest square. The tourist info office [see *need to know,* below] is also here.

hanging out

Corso Vannucci is packed with Italians and foreigners—young and old, dressed-up and casual—day and night. Between 6 and 9pm, it's practically elbow to elbow for the evening *la passeggiata,* when the town gets gussied up to stroll n' socialize. The steps of the **Duomo** are always full of kids sipping cans of beer, tourists poring over maps, and old ladies feeding the pigeons at the Fontana Maggiore. At the other end of Corso Vannucci, at Piazza Italia, there's a little park, with benches under the trees, that's perfect for picnicking. And a few steps south of that, past **Viale Indepenzia,** there's another little park where Italian couples come in the evenings to gaze out at the panoramic view of the countryside. Most bars, pubs, and restaurants are conveniently within a few blocks of this area.

To steer clear of the tourists and meet some local students, your best bet is the **Giardini Università** and the **Piazza Università,** about four blocks west of **Piazza Fortebraccio,** up in the university quarter. **Corso Giuseppe Garibaldi** is where many students live, and the wide lawn that

wired

Since Perugia is full of students, finding Internet access here is *nessun problema* (no prob). If you're low on money, several places in town offer free Internet access. **EPNET** *(Via Cartolari 18; Tel/Fax 075/572-2707 or 075/573-3167; 10am-11:30pm Mon-Sat, 1:30-11:30pm Sun; V,MC)*, **Infotourist Point** *(Piazza Partigiani; Tel 075/572-7218; 9am-1pm/2-7pm, closed Sun)*, and **Horusbird** *(Via Adamo Rossi 14; Tel 075/572-5038; 3:30-11pm daily; V,MC)* will let you check your e-mail for free, but only for 10 minutes, once a day—otherwise, they charge 4,500L an hour (still the cheapest in town). **Cafe Concerto** [see *eats,* above] also has a computer with free Internet access in the basement. **Internet Point** *(Via Ulisse Rocchi 4; Tel 0339/269-1728; 10am-10pm Mon-Fri, 10am-8:30pm Sat, 4-8pm Sun, V, MC)*, is the most conveniently located, right behind the Duomo. They charge 7,000L/hour, but have "happy hour" specials from 10:30am to 1pm and 8 to 10pm when they charge only 5,000L/hour. The smaller **Internet Train** *(Via Ulisse Rocchi 30; Tel 075/573-45555 or 0349/649-8820; info@internettrain.it, www.internettrain.it; V, MC)* is farther down the street and has similar prices. For information on the web about Perugia, check out ***www.umbria2000.it,*** ***www.umbria.org,*** ***www.bellaumbria.net,*** or ***www.perugiaonline.com.***

surrounds the **Tempio San Angelo** [see *culture zoo,* below] is a popular spot for picnicking and partying.

cafe scene

Between classes, after meals, and pretty much all weekend, Perugia's cafes are packed with caffeine-guzzlers, pastry-eaters, and social butterflies. When warm weather hits, the scene moves outside to the cafe tables that line the streets.

It's hard to decide whether the glass cases of Perugina chocolate or the elaborate cakes and pastries in the front window are more tempting at **Sandri Pasticceria** *(Corso Vannucci 52; Tel 075/572-4112; Seasonal hours, generally 8am-10pm; Cappuccino 2,600L; No credit cards).* You won't linger too long with your cappuccino here, unless you can handle the "can you leave now?" stares from the Perugians continuously pouring through the door of Perugia's oldest and most elegant cafe. The waiters (wearing long white aprons, red tuxedo jackets, bow ties...and jeans) can recommend the freshest pastries, and whip up mean cappuccinos and hot chocolates. Sit inside under the frescoes of landscapes, or outside for some prime people-watching.

Between Corso Vannucci and Piazza Matteotti, **Cafe Concerto** *(Via Mazzini 19; Tel 075/572-38-63; No credit cards)* serves great coffee, crepes, gelato, and light meals. The tables outside are always packed, and there's free Internet access inside the dim dining room.

bar scene

Perugia's bar scene is a blast—the energy of the college crowd fills the town's many pubs, nightspots, and piazzas, and keeps on keepin' on into the wee hours of the morn. Though there's a wide variety of watering holes to choose from, American-themed bars and restaurants—particularly Tex/Mex—are favorites. Don't worry too much about prettying yourself up for a night on the town here—most of the local students don't bother. Pulling your wrinkled jeans out of your backpack will do, especially when it comes to the BYOB party that goes on in Piazza IV Novembre every night. The steps of the Duomo double as a meeting ground for folks "between bars." During the summer there are huge rave-like parties lasting from Friday to Sunday in some of the small villages in the area around Assisi and Perugia. For information about the parties, which are called *sangre,* pick up a copy of *Viva Perugia* (1,000L) from the tourist office or a newsstand, or keep your eyes open for posters explaining where to catch a bus out to the party. Piazza Fortebraccio is a common departure point, where buses pick up and drop off busloads of scenesters.

The walls of **Hogan's Bar & Grill** *(Piazza Matteotti 20; Tel 075/393-22-59; 12:30-3:30pm/7:30pm-2am daily; V, MC),* a hugely popular restaurant/bar, are covered with football and hockey jerseys, baseball souvenirs, flags, and pictures of Popeye and other American icons. Come here if you're dying for some good ol' American grub or want to meet some American-loving, beer-drinking Perugians. Suds are the libation of choice, and the music is loud and—surprise—American. Hogan's food is a fave of the student crowd [see *eats,* below].

The **Crazy Bull Café** *(Via Palermo 21/b; Tel 075/573-07-83 or 075/35-346; 12:30-3pm/7:30pm-2am Mon-Sat, closed Aug 10-20; Avg. drink 4,000L; Avg. bar food 7,000L; V, MC, DC, EC)* is popular with locals *and* tourists. If you're homesick for chips and salsa to go with your beer, this is the place to be—especially after 10pm, when it turns into one of the most happening spots in town. American music plays on the stereo, live bands occasionally drop in, the bar food is great, and the crowd is mixed and laid-back. It's a tricky walk, just south of the city walls: from Piazzale Europa, just south of the train station, head south on Via dei Filosofi, turn west on Via della Pallotta, and then south again on Via Palermo.

Il Dollaro *(Via Piccolopasso 2; Tel 075/505-78-57; Noon-2:30pm/7:30pm-2am daily; Closed Mon night and Aug 10-20; Avg. drink 4,000L; V, MC, DC, EC),* situated four blocks west of the train station, sports a Cowboys-and-Indians theme. Each room of this highly decorated, always-packed nightspot houses lively pockets of conversation. There's music and dancing every night—disco parties (Thursday and Saturday) and '80s nights (Friday and Sunday) are extra-packed. The restaurant serves Tex/Mex classics, but the bar-food and beer are more popular.

Il Settimo Sigillo *(Via Ulisse Rocchi 1; Tel 075/572-43-06; Varying opening hours-2am, Tue-Sun; V, MC, AE)*, just north of Piazza Danti, calls itself a "traditional medieval pub" (whatever that means). The clientele is a bit reserved, the atmosphere is sedate, and the music is low—the whole effect is very grown-up and mellow. Come here to try some of the region's great wine and snack from a daily-changing menu of traditional Umbrian specialties.

The **Merlin Pub** *(Via Forno 19; Tel 075/572-27-08; 8pm-2am daily; V, MC, AE)*, advertises itself as an "English-speaking pub," and has been a favorite with backpackers for decades. Located at the end of a small, dark, alley-like street called Via Fani, between Piazza Matteotti and Corso Vannucci, it's little, smoky, and, in the summer, a bit sweaty. Come here to rub elbows and trade tales with your fellow travelers and local students. Don't show up until about 11pm, when the commercial Italian pop starts blasting and the beer really gets flowing.

Shamrock Pub *(Piazza Danti 18; Tel 075/573-66-25; 6pm-2am daily; No cover; V, MC)*, just north of the Duomo, is the most popular of Perugia's many Irish pubs, and is busiest late-night (or early in the morning, however you want to look at it). Gaelic paraphernalia and artifacts hang on the walls of the front bar and two large sitting rooms, where all kinds of beer-drinkers cluster around games of darts and in big booths. Guiness is the brew of choice, though the high-brow crowd makes good use of an extensive whisky selection.

If wine sampling is more your thing, come to **Enoteca Provencale di Perugia** *(Via Ulisse Rocchi 18; Tel 075/572-48-24; 4:30-8:30pm Mon, 10:30am-2:30pm/4:30-10pm Tue-Sat; V, MC, AE, DC)*, just north of Piazza Danti, for a before- or after-dinner drink. Sit at one of the wooden tables inside and order a glass oflocal Umbrian wine—they have a huge selection. Try one of the 20 different types of *bruschetta* (toast topped with local cheese and vegetables). The crowd is an unpretentious mix of young and old.

La Lumera Osteria *(Largo Cacciatori delle Alpi 3/b; Tel 075/572-72-18, Fax 075/572-72-35; Noon-3pm/7pm-2am, closed Tue; V, MC, AE)* may be more of a restaurant than a bar [see *eats,* below], but it's open just as late as all the pubs, and is a great place to catch a midnight snack while getting directions to the next party. A few blocks north of the **Cappella di S. Severo**[see *culture zoo,* below], it's a scene in itself, with plenty of glasses lifted high.

LIVE MUSIC SCENE

Blame it on the college kids, but in Perugia you can't escape music, be it buskers in the piazza or guitar players on the Duomo steps. Berklee College of Music (in Boston) has an exchange program here, and every year the students kick off the world-renowned Umbria Jazz Festival in July [see *festivals and events,* below]. The rest of the season, many of them play

fEStivals and EVENts

The **Umbria Jazz Festival** swings into town for 10 days every July, and is the pride of the region. It has become one of the most important jazz festivals in Europe and hosts many of the best musicians around the world. The streets, squares, and concert halls are packed for concerts that rock the city morning, noon, and night. Tickets cost 15,000 to 60,000L, but the music played out on the street is free of charge. For more information, or to purchase tickets, contact the **Associazione Umbria Jazz** *(Piazza Danti 28; Tel 075/573-24-32, Fax 075/572-26-56; umbriajazz@tin.it, www.umbriajazz.com).*

If church music is more your thing, stay in town for the **Umbrian Festival of Sacred Music**, which takes place in late August, and promotes sacred music, new and old, in Italy.

gigs in local bars. **Musica Musica** [see *stuff*, below] can give you info and sell you tickets.

Contrapunto *(Via Scortici 4/a; Tel 075/573-36-67; 7pm-2am daily; Drinks 5,000-7,000L; No cover; V, MC, AE)*, just one block east of Piazza Fortebraccio, is the center of Perugia's jazz scene, with live shows every night in the summer. The bar is cozy, if a bit smoky (there's a pretty outdoor terrace when it gets thick), with lots of wooden tables and chairs surrounding the small stage where local and national acts perform. You might feel a bit out of place in denim cutoffs—grab something black and artsy and you'll fit right in. Pizzas and other hearty fare are served during the show, though the food alone isn't reason enough to come.

Sullivan's Irish Restaurant *(Via Bovaro 2; Tel 075/572-43-81; 7pm-2am daily; Drinks 4-8,000L; No cover; V, MC)*, one block east of Sant' Ercolano, northeast of Piazza Italia, has different types of live music several times a week. During the Umbria Jazz Festival [see *festivals/cool annual events,* below] the Berklee kids play here, but the stools along the enormous bar are packed with a mixed bag of imbibers year round. The generally reserved crowd perks up when there's a band—get there by 8pm to snag a seat. The pub grub is pretty good, and the beer selection, extensive.

Celebrate Café Pub *(Via Bontempi 15/a; Tel 0338/913-92-11; 12:30-3pm/7pm-2am, closed Sun; Drinks 4-8,000L; No cover; V, MC, AE)*, a few blocks north of Piazza IV Novembre, is one of the best choices if you're looking to nod your head to good live music while sipping a cold beer or a glass of Chianti. Tuesdays it's live jazz, Thursdays, the blues, and on nights when there's no band lined up, DJs spin from 7pm 'til 2am. Students and twenty- and thirtysomethings cram into the small tables around the darkly lit stage area. From the north side of Piazza Danti, head to the connecting Piazza Piccinino, which leads into via Bontempi on the northeast side.

arts scene

Like most Italians, Perugians tend to bask in the glory of old masters rather than discovering new ones. Contemporary art lovers in search of cutting-edge exhibits have only a few options. Performing arts, especially concerts, are more frequent. Jazz is enormously popular here, and while there are often live jazz shows at pubs [see *live music scene*, above], more formal venues also pack them in. The **Sala dei Notari,** the **Duomo,** and the **Basilica di San Pietro** are beautiful spots to hear music [see *culture zoo*, below, for all three]. Check out *Viva Perugia*, a 'zine available at tourist info and local newsstands, for up-to-date listings. The Association of Music, **Amici della Musica** *(Corso Vannucci 63; Tel 075/572-52-64, Fax 075/572-22-71; amicimusicapg@edisons.it, www.amicimusicapg.it)*, can also provide detailed listings of events in the city. Drop by **Musica Musica** [see *stuff*, below] to pick up tickets for local rock concerts and peruse the abundance of flyers advertising parties and DJ nights. Or ask around at **Locanda degli Artisti** [see *eats*, below], an artists' hangout that doubles as a gallery.

▶▶VISUAL ARTS

Ipso Art Gallery *(Via Bonazzi 41; No phone; 4:30-7:30pm daily; Free admission)* shows off contemporary paintings and photographs. Located just east of Piazza Italia, it's one of the few venues that make room for modern art.

Spazio Arte *(Via della Nespola 8/a; Tel 075/572-00-41; 4:30-7:30pm; Free admission)*, just east of Via Ulisse Rocchi, often hosts contemporary international artists who work in mixed mediums.

▶▶PERFORMING ARTS

Teatro Morlacchi *(Piazza Morlacchi 11; Tel 075/572-25-55 or 075/575-421, Fax 075/572-9039; tsu@krenet.it, www.teatrostabile.umbria.it; Tickets 13,000-79,000L; V, MC)*, a few blocks north of the Duomo, is the main venue for performing arts, from opera to modern dance. Tickets can be purchased up to an hour before the show.

Teatro Zenith *(Via Bonfigli 11; Tel 075/572-85-88)* and **Sala Cutu** *(Piazza G.Bruno; Tel 075/584-77-31)* are smaller theaters in the city center that occasionally have performances by visiting theater groups. Check with tourist info for current events, prices, and times.

Accademia del Teatro Pavone *(Piazza della Repubblica 67; Tel 075/572-81-53)* hosts many of the Umbria Jazz Festival concerts as well as other musical events throughout the year. Tourist info publicizes all the events, which vary widely in price.

There are many cinemas in town, but unless you're fluent in Italian be sure to ask if the movie you want to see is in the *lingua originale* (original language) before you shell out 10,000L. **Cinema Modernissimo** *(Via del Carmine 4; Tel 075/573-66-16)*, in the university district, shows English-language movies (with subtitles in Italian—maybe you'll learn a thing or two!) once a week. **Cinema Teatro del Pavone** (*Corso Vannucci; Tel 075/572-49-11*), near Piazza della Repubblica, **Cinema Teatro Turreno** (*Piazza Danti 13; Tel 075/572-21-10*), one block north of the Duomo, and **Cinema Teatro Zenith** (*Via Bonfigli 11; Tel 075/572-85-88*), just north of the Basilica di San Pietro, are always crowded with students.

gay scene

Though Perugia is a liberal college town, the gay scene isn't as out as you'd expect. Check with **ArciGay** (*Via A. Fratti 18; Tel 075/572-31-75 or 075/573-10-74*), two blocks west of the Duomo, for info on events and current hotspots.

CuLTure zOO

If you only have a few hours to spend sightseeing in Perugia, don't stress—the main sights are in spitting distance of one another. Palazzo dei Priori (Town Hall) is right across from the Duomo (Cathedral of San Lorenzo) and the Fontana Maggiore in Piazza IV Novembre. The Palazzo was built in the 13th century, enlarged in the 15th century, restored in the 19th and 20th centuries, and is still in use today. With its long, curved facade, the Palazzo stands out above all buildings along Corso Vannucci and has rightly been called "the most beautiful town hall in Italy." The Palazzo houses the Galleria Nazionale dell'Umbria (National Gallery of Umbria), the Collegio del Cambio (Exchange Guild), the Collegia della Mercanzia (Merchant's Guild), and the Sala dei Notari (Notaries Hall).

    Galleria Nazionale dell'Umbria (*Corso Vannucci 19; Tel 075/574-1247; 8:30am-7:30pm (ticket office closes at 7pm) daily, closed the first Mon of every month; 12,000L Adults, 6,000L 18-25 years; No credit cards*): From the 12th to the 15th century, Perugia was the center of the Umbrian school of painting. The best examples of this era—including the works of hometown boy Pietro Vannucci, better known as Perugino—are housed in this museum, up on the third floor of the Palazzo dei Priori. Perugino's students included local luminaries Raphael and Pinturicchio. Highlights of Perugino's work in the Gallery include his Adoration of the Magi and Pietà. Other highlights include an altarpiece, Polyptych of Sant'Antonio, by Piero della Francesca, which was painted for a monastery in Perugia in the 15th century, and the Miracles of St. Bernadine of Siena, a series of eight panels whose attribution is still being debated.

    Collegio del Cambio (*Corso Vannucci 25, Palazzo dei Priori; Tel 075/572-8599; 9am-noon/2:30-5:30pm daily, 9am-12:30pm holidays; 8am-2pm Tue-Sat 11/1-12/19 and 1/7-2/28; 9am-12:30pm Sat, Sun 11/1-12/19 and 1/7-2/28; 5,000L admission, combined ticket with the Collegio della Mercanzia is 6,000L*): This building once played a key role in the financial administration of the city of Perugia; now it's just another museum. It doesn't take long to walk through, but it's worth a visit to see Perugino's frescoes in the *Sala di Udienza* (Hall of the Audience), completed in 1500. These extremely well-preserved Renaissance representations of the planets, classical figures, a self-portrait, and the

Daniel—which is thought to be modeled after Raphael—are regarded as the artist's best works.

Collegia della Mercanzia *(Corso Vannucci 15, Palazzo dei Priori; Tel 075/573-0366; 9am-1pm/2:30-5:30pm Mon-Sat, 9am-1pm holidays; 2,000L admission, combined ticket with Collegio del Cambio is 6,000L):* Unless you're a big fan of 15th-century carved-wood walls, the Merchant's Guild isn't terribly exciting, but hey, it's included in your combined ticket price! The walls, with their strong Northern European influence, are incredibly ornate.

Sala dei Notari (Hall of the Notaries) *(Palazzo dei Priori, entrance on Piazza IV Novembre; Tel 075/577-2339; 9am-1pm/3-7pm, closed Mon; Free admission):* Climb the flight of stairs above the tourist office to enter a huge, vaulted, late-13th-century room covered with brightly colored frescoes of Old Testament scenes. The most eye-catching are the illustrations of fables. The room is sometimes used for concerts and other events—stop in during the day to enjoy it without the crowds.

Fontana Maggiore (Grand Fountain) *(Piazza IV Novembre):* You could spend hours, walking in circles, gazing in awe at this fountain. One of the most important monuments of its time, it was designed in the late 13th century by a Perugian monk, and the incredibly detailed reliefs and statues were carved by Nicola Pisano and his son Giovanni. The lower basin consists of 25 reliefs depicting the months of the year and their corresponding zodiac signs, as well as symbols of Perugia and of the Liberal Arts, Old Testament scenes, and a few of Aesop's fables. For years, the fountain was obscured by scaffolding, but a recent restoration has left it dazzling.

Duomo (Cattedrale di S. Lorenzo) *(Piazza IV Novembre; Tel 075/572-3832 or 075/988-0143; 7am-12:30pm/3:30-6:45pm daily; Free admission):* The facade of the church on Piazza Danti was left unfinished, but side facing the Piazza IV Novembre shows off the Gothic style in all its glory. The pulpit inside was built for San Bernardino in 1425. Besides the mystery of the Virgin Mary's supposed wedding ring—stored in the Cappella del Santo Anello inside 15 concentric boxes, with 15 locks—the darkly lit Duomo isn't very interesting. Unless, that is, you're around on July 29th and 30th, when, every year, they unveil the ring.

Chiesa di Sant' Ercolano *(Scalette di Sant Ercolano; Tel 075/572-22-97):* This small church is a few blocks northeast of Piazza Italia, down the steep, cobblestone Scalette di Sant Ercolano. The early-14th-century, polygon-shaped church is worth checking out for a few minutes if only for the unique frescoes that look like marble arches.

Museo Archeologico Nazionale dell'Umbria *(Piazza G. Bruno 10; 8:30am-7:30pm daily, ticket office closes at 7pm; 4,000L Adults, 2,000L 18-25 years):* From Sant' Ercolano, take Corso Cavour south for a few blocks to reach this museum, which is housed in what used to be the convent of San Domenico. The museum holds Etruscan/Roman artifacts, but is better known for its prehistoric collection, which is said to be one of the best in Italy. Even if archaeology isn't your bag, this collection is worth it.

Chiesa di San Domenico *(Piazza G. Bruno; Tel 075/573-1568; Free admission):* Situated right next door to the Museo Archeologico, Perugia's largest church is surprisingly bare inside. It was built in 1305— and rebuilt in 1632 after the vault collapsed. The sheer size of the church and its enormous stained glass windows are reason enough to check it out.

Chiesa di San Pietro *(Borgo XX Giugno; Tel 075/573-47-70; Free admission):* The Gothic bell tower of this extraordinary 10th-century church can be spotted from miles away. From San Domenico, follow Corso Cavour, which will change names to Borgo XX Giugno and bring you to the courtyard of the church (a 15-minute walk) beyond the city walls. After your eyes adjust to the darkness, you'll notice an incredibly detailed interior, full of ancient marble columns and paintings so old and dirty that it's difficult to make them out. The many highlights include: the wooden choir, a *pietá* by Perugino, and a *pietá* by Sebastiano del Piombo in the Chapel of St. Joseph. A door behind the altar leads to a terrace, from which there's a beautiful view of the countryside.

Cappella di S. Severo *(Piazza Raffaello; Tel 075/573-3864; 10am-1:30pm/2:30-6:30pm daily; 3,500L Adults for Pozzo Etrusca and the Cappella):* What is thought to be Raphael's first fresco—a 1505 representation of the Holy Trinity, restored in 1976—is housed here. The chapel also holds some paintings by Perugino, but the *Pozzo Etrusco* (Etruscan Well), between Piazza Dante and Piazza Piccinino, is the other highlight. Built in the 3rd century B.C. by the Etruscans, it can still hold enough water for all Perugians. But truth be told, unless you're an avid Raphael fan, or an Etruscan well-lover, don't feel bad about skipping this one.

Arco di Augusto *(Piazza Fortebraccio):* At the end of via Ulisse Rocchi stands the Arco di Augusto (aka Arco Etrusco), one of the ancient city gates and a perfect representation of the layers of history that have shaped Perugia. The Etruscan base was built in the 2nd or 3rd century B.C., the upper section is Roman and was built around 40 B.C., and the towers and loggia date back to the 16th century.

Chiesa di Sant'Angelo *(Via del Tempio):* From the Arco di Augusto, walk northwest along Corso Giuseppe Garibaldi, which leads directly to Perugia's oldest house of worship. This round church is said to stand on the site of an ancient pagan temple—it's always open, and virtually empty inside, but the cool marble and quiet serenity makes it one of the most spiritual spots in Perugia. The view from the surrounding garden is unforgettable.

modification

One block west of Piazza Italia, **Jean Louis David** *(Via Bonazzi 51-53; Tel 075/573-0227; 9am-7pm daily; V, MC, AE)* can shampoo, cut, and blow-dry your hair for 52,000L. This is the same inexpensive chain you know from the states, but you won't feel rushed in and out here.

city sports

Because of its small, crowded, often death-defyingly steep streets, Perugia is not the best place for biking, jogging, or roller-blading. If you're interested in hiking, the tourist office has free maps and information for nearby trails.

There's nothing like a little horseback-riding through the Umbrian lanscapes just outside the city walls—the trail rides are all picture-perfect view after picture-perfect view. There are a few year-round riding schools that offer such tours: **Associazione Ippica San Martino** *(Strasa Montebello 2, Ponte Pattoli; Tel/Fax 075/694-897),* **Centro Ippico II Covone** *(Strada della Fratticiola 2, Ponte Pattoli; Tel 075594-6008),* and **Club Ippico Santa Sabina** *(Loc. Sodi do Santa Sabina; Tel 0335/816-7953).*

Students here stay fit by enrolling in every kind of athletic class available, and you can too! These places don't mind if you just pop in for one class. The aerobic dance and hip-hop classes at Rosano and Alessandro's **Dance Gallery** *(Via XIV Settembre 64; Tel/Fax 075/572-77-17),* a few blocks east of Piazza Matteotti, are super-popular with students. Stop by on Mondays, Tuesdays, and Fridays from 1 to 2:30pm, and just try to get in. Various types of yoga, dance, and stretching courses are offered at the **Associazione Culturale** *(Piazza Alfani 4/c; Tel 075/572-15-93 or 075/500-09-44),* a few blocks north of Piazza Danti.

CKA *(Via Piccolopasso 11-13; Tel 075/691-96-00; fulvi@cka.it, www.cka.it),* four blocks south of the train station, offers Kung Fu and Tai Chi lessons.

STUff

Perugia revolves around its student population, as you'll learn when it comes time to do some shopping. The main commercial street, Corso Vannucci, is full of window-shoppers all day long. The side streets off Corso Vannucci that lead to Piazza Matteotti (between Piazza IV Novembre and Piazza Italia) are full of smaller boutiques, popular Italian clothing store chains, and gourmet stores. From the southern end of Piazza Matteotti, Via Guglielmo Oberdan, which leads to **Sant Ercolano** [see *culture zoo,* above], holds a slew of top-dollar boutiques and shoe stores. Many Italian chains, including **Benetton** *(Via Fani 12; Tel 075/572049-95; V, MC)* are in this area.

▶▶**DUDS**

At the department store **Coin** *(Corso Vannucci 84; Tel 075/573-5341; 9:30am-1pm/4-8pm Mon-Sat; V, MC, AE),* you can find anything you need—clothes, shoes, accessories, lingerie, perfume, cosmetics—at bargain prices.

Il Bandito *(Via Cavour 42; Tel 075/573-56-54; 9:30am-1pm/4-8pm Mon-Sat; V, MC, AE)* has a good selection of stylish Italian fashions for men and women. Prices are somewhere between cheap and do-able.

The sprawling **Andrei** *(Corso Vannucci 46-52; Tel 075/572-89-27; 9:30am-1pm/4-pm8 Mon-Sat; V, MC, AE)* has it all—clothes, shoes, accessories, bags, backpacks, hats, and lots of other cool stuff.

Try not to drool upon entering **Buonumori Boutique** *(Corso Vannucci 55; Tel 075/573-52-84; 9:30am-1pm/4-8pm Mon-Sat; No credit*

only here

Probably no other city in the world caters to chocoholics better than Perugia. Home to Perugina chocolate, the Perugini go *pazzo* for the little, bite-sized hazelnut and chocolate "kisses," known as "baci," each of which come with a multilingual, amorous quote. The **Eurochocolate** *(Tel 075/573-2670; cpc@chocolate.perugia.it www.chocolate.perugia.it)* festival, which takes place every October, pays homage to chocolates of every size, shape, and flavor. Chocolatiers from Italy and all over the world come to Perugia for this week-long festival, and if you're lucky enough to be here, you can forget about dieting. The entire city center is transformed into an open-air chocolate shop where you can learn more than you ever wanted to know about the "food of the gods", as Perugians call it. Explore chocolate-making workshops; chocolate tastings; three-course meals with all-chocolate menus; hotel rooms decorated in chocolate motifs; games; concerts; and sculptures carved from 1000kg blocks of chocolate. The festival comes to its sweet conclusion with an open-air chocolate breakfast for all those who can still stand the smell of the stuff. If you miss Eurochocolate, you can always hit **Perugina** *(Corso Vannucci 101; Tel 075/573-6677; V, MC, AE)* to satisfy your sweet tooth year-round.

cards), which is packed with Prada, Dolce & Gabbana, and other Italian high fashions. Just make sure your wallet is full, or that you know how to say "just looking" in Italian.

▶▶CLUB GEAR
Planet Cyberg *(Via Calderni 18; Tel 075/572-47-18; 9:30am-1pm/4-8pm Mon-Sat; No credit cards)*, between Piazza Matteotti and Piazza IV Novembre, sells inexpensive club clothes. It's also a great place to stock up on haute couture knockoffs.

▶▶USED AND BRUISED
The small but stocked **Medialuz** *(Via Cartolari 42; Tel 075/572-0820; 10am-8pm daily; No credit cards)*, one block north of Piazza Matteotti, sells not only secondhand clothes and vintage suede jackets, but also a small selection of new, handmade clothes that are worth checking out. The owner sits by the door and sews them all day.

▶▶TUNES
Just east of Piazza Matteotti, walk upstairs to get to **Musica Musica** *(Via G. Oberdan 51; Tel 075/572-093; 9:30am-1pm/4-8pm daily; V, MC,*

AE), which has the best selection of music in town. There's a **box office** *(Tel 075/572-09-23)* that sells tickets for big concerts, and a slew of flyers for smaller shows and dance parties.

Tarpani *(Piazza Matteotti 30; Tel 075/572-4151; 9:30am-1pm/4-8pm daily; V, MC, AE)* is expert in be-bop, fusion, swing, and avant-garde, offering by far the best selection of jazz CDs in town. It also features a pretty good classic rock section.

▶▶BOUND

Perugia has scores of bookstores, but very few carrying English-language titles. **Libreria C. Betti** *(Corso Vannucci 107; Tel 075/573-1667; 9:30am-1pm/4-8pm daily; No credit cards)* offers the best selection of English-language books—classics, pulp fiction, and best-sellers—as well as an entire shelf of guide books right by the entrance. A few doors down, **Libreria Simonelli** *(Corso Vannucci 82; 075/5572-37-44; 9:30am-1pm/4-8pm daily; V, MC)* has a random sampling of English-language titles, with Danielle Steele and Stephen King taking precedence. **La Libreria** *(Via G. Oberdan 52; Tel 075/573-5057; 9:30am-1pm/4-8pm daily; V, MC)* has just a few books in English, a huge Italian section, and some great postcards.

▶▶HOW BAZAAR

Perugia's **flea market** is held on Tuesdays and Saturdays on Via Ercolano, near the Chiesa Sant' Ercolano. As at any great flea market, you never know what you're going to find—old books and antiques, new housewares, and local pottery are regulars.

There's a **permanent market** housed in the scenic overlook area just behind Piazza Matteotti. Inexpensive shoes, clothing, and accessories are for sale in these wooden stalls from 10am-7pm, Monday to Saturday.

The nearby town of Deruta is known for its colorful and heavy terracotta pottery, and you can get a good bargain if you haggle with the artists that set up and sell their work on the steps of the Duomo. There's no set schedule.

▶▶FOOT FETISH

The **Bata** *(Corso Vannucci 22; Tel 049/899-1111; 9:30am-1pm/4-8pm daily; www.bata.it; V, MC, AE)* chain has an excellent selection of reasonably priced shoes, boots, sneakers, handbags, and leather jackets.

Need new walking shoes? **Docksteps Store** *(Piazza della Republica 79; Tel 075/572-39-69; 9:30am-1pm/4-8pm daily)* sells shoes made for comfort—a factor valued by international jet-setters like you.

▶▶SMELLS

Il Chiostro delle Erbe *(Via Cavour 106; Tel 075/572-98-23; 9:30am-1pm/4-8pm daily; V, MC, AE),* a few doors away from the Archaeology Museum, is the best-smelling store in town. They sell aromatherapy stuff, healing herbs, incense, and candles—all made from natural products.

L'Orchidea Profumerie *(Corso Vannucci 65; Tel 075/572-11-45; V, MC)* sells the most delicious brands of Italian perfume. Take a bottle of *Ricette Meditterannee* (25,000L) home to remind you of your trip.

▶▶GIFTS
Need something for mom? **Il Telaio** *(Via Ulisse Rocchi 19; Tel 075/57266-03; 9:30am-1pm/4-8pm Mon-Sat)* sells pretty, handmade tablecloths, ceramics, lace, and folk art.

EATS

As the capital of the region, Perugia trumpets its reputation as the best place to sample Umbria's delicacies. But as a student town, there are tons of budget haunts to balance out the pricey options. Local olive oil sits on most tables, and in the fall, Umbria's famous *tartufi* (black truffles from the town of Norcia) and *porcini* mushrooms find their way onto every menu. The preferred method of cooking is over a fire—roasted pig, lamb, wild boar, and rabbit are popular main dishes. *Strangolopreti*, the name for a handmade twisted-pasta dish traditionally served with meat sauce, translates to "priest-stranglers"—just another reminder of the town's historical resistance to church-rule. Try the crisp white Orvieto Classico wine, and try not to develop an addiction to *baci* [see *only here,* below].

▶▶CHEAP
Caffé del Sopamuro *(Piazza Matteotti 24; Tel 075/572-26-96; Noon-10:30pm daily; Avg. meal 10,000L; V, MC)* serves cheap pizza, whole and by the slice, and has tables on the sidewalk that are perfect for people-watching in one of Perugia's most popular piazzas. If you don't have time (or money) for a full meal, come join the rest of the starving artists who make this place their second home.

Near the university area, **Pizzeria Etrusca** *(Via Ulisse Rocchi 29-31; Tel 075/572-0762; 11:30am-10:30pm daily (later on weekends); 2,500-4,000L a slice; No credit cards)* is, predictably, overrun with students. The sliced pizza, calzones, and stuffed pizzas are delicious, filling, and cheap. Eat at a table, or take it to the steps of the Duomo.

TO THE MARKET

Right next to the Archaeology museum, **Ortofrutta** *(Via Cavour 96; Tel 075/573-57-55; No credit cards)* offers a great selection of fresh fruit. Push your way into **Giuliano** *(Via Danzetta 1)*, which is between Piazza Matteotti and Corso Vannucci, for artisanal cheeses and meats, and pre-made stuff for take-out. **Casa del Parmigiano** *(Via Ercolano 36; Tel 075/1233)*, across from the Chiesa di Sant' Ercolano, sells a huge selection of cheese and good fresh bread.

perugia eats and crashing

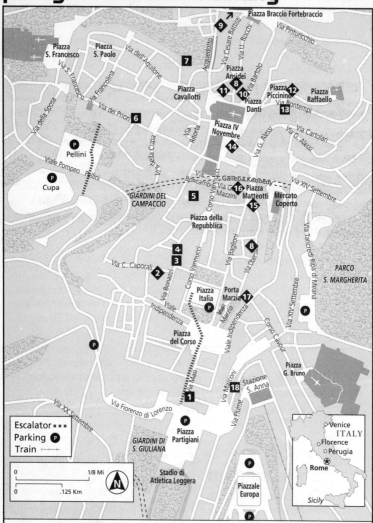

EATS ◆

Cafe Concerto 16
Caffé del Sopamuro 15
Garibaldi Osteria 2
La Botte 12
La Lanterna 8
La Locanda degli Artisti 17
Osteria de Bartolo 10
Pizzeria Etrusca 11
Restaurant Milano 9
Sandri Pasticceria 14

CRASHING ■

Centro Internazionale
  per la Gioventú 13
Hotel Anna 6
Hotel Fortuna 4
Hotel Iris 18
Hotel San Sebastiano 7
Hotel Umbria 5
Piccolo Hotel 3
Sangallo Palace Hotel 1

The friendly **La Botte** *(Via Volte della Pace 33; Tel/Fax 075/572-61-04; Noon-3pm/7:30-10:30pm, closed Sun; Pizzas 5,000-15,000L, avg. meal 30,000L, tourist meal 15,000L; V, MC, AE, DC, EC)* serves great pizzas baked in wood-burning ovens, and full meals at very nice prices. The medieval decor and exposed brick walls make for a comfortable and unpretentious space, which is packed with families, tourists, and students day in and day out. It's just off the eastern side of Piazza Piccinino, in the northern part of town,

Restaurant Milano *(Via Fabbretti 7; Tel/Fax 075/572-48-83; Noon-3:30pm, closed Sun; Main dishes 3,500-10,000L; V, MC, AE, DC, EC)*, just off Piazza Fortebraccio, is a savior if you're really hungry and really broke. The three self-service counters offer a huge selection of surprisingly delicious and fresh vegetables, salads, pastas, meat dishes, and cheeses, and lead into a spacious, comfortable dining room that's packed with students and business folks. Located in the heart of the student district, Milano also runs a bakery around the corner *(Corso Garibaldi 2; 6:30am-8pm, closed Sunday)*.

▶▶**DO-ABLE**

Hogan's Bar and Grill [see *bar scene,* above] the favorite American-themed bar/restaurant, serves just what you'd expect—big cheeseburgers, greasy fries, and other American classics *(Avg. meal 15,000L)*. The scene is lively and loud, and there's plenty of beer to be had with your meal.

Crazy Bull Café *(Via Palermo 21/b; Tel 075/573-07-83 or 075/35-346; 12:30-3pm/7:30pm-2am Mon-Sat, closed Aug 10-20; Avg. bar food 7,000L; Avg. meal 15,000L; V, MC, DC, EC)*, also popular with the kids, serves two different menus. For lunch, it's hearty Italian fare with pastas and roasted meats, but for dinner they break out the Tex/Mex; not exactly authentic, but the fajitas, chili, and bottomless bowls of chips and salsa will curb any cravings for food diversity. Get there early for dinner, before the bar crowd moves in [see *bar scene,* above].

The little, family-run **Garibaldi Osteria** *(Via C. Caporali 12; Tel 075/572-77-88; 6:30pm-12:30am Mon, Wed, Fri, 12:30-3:30pm/6:30pm-12:30am Sat, Sun, closed Tue; Avg. meal with wine 40,000L; V, MC)* is hidden away from the tourist track on a quiet street a few blocks west of Piazza Italia. The menu is tiny, but the quality of the food and good house wine make up for limited choices. The sweet, mostly English-speaking father and daughter who run the place are happy to answer questions about their unusual menu. For starters, try the *antipasta della casa* (six types of grilled and sautéed vegetables), and the *cavetelli* (homemade round pasta) served with white beans in a soup-like broth. This spacious restaurant is popular with locals, who evidently appreciate the red-checkered tablecloths and the Italian New-Age music.

If you missed dinner, or happen to want a steak to go with your drinks, try **La Lumera Osteria** *(Corso Bersaglieri 22; Tel 075/572-61-81; Noon-3pm/7pm-2am, closed Tue; Avg. meal 25-30,000L; V, MC, AE)*, which is open just as late as the pubs are. Hordes of scenesters come here for hearty Umbrian pastas and meats, and a huge selection of wine, all at decent prices. The candlelit tables are perfect for a quiet late-night meal or nightcap. From the north side of Piazza Danti, head to connecting Piazza Piccinino, which leads into Via Bontempi. This road changes to Via del Roscetto, which ends up at Corso Bersaglieri.

Next to Sant' Ercolano, **La Locanda degli Artisti** *(Via Campo Battaglia 10; Tel 075/573-58-51; 12:30-2:30pm/7:30-10:30pm, closed Tue; Pizzas avg. 18,000L; Avg. meal with wine 40,000L; V, MC, AE, DC, EC)* serves simple Umbrian classics, great pies, and daily house specials. What's unique about this place is that it's also an art gallery, with walls full of cool paintings by local artists, and the seats are packed with Perugia's art crowd. Try the chef's innovative pasta dishes—*gnocchetti* (little potato dumplings) with arugula, *cappelletti* (similar to tortellini) with walnuts, or ravioli with nettles. Heartier dishes, like pork chops with radicchio, are also stupendous. Be sure to top off your meal with their homemade *tiramisù*.

Behind the Duomo, **La Lanterna** *(Via Ulisse Rocchi 6; Tel 075/572-63-97; 12:30-3pm/7:30-10:30pm, closed Wed; Avg. meal 40,000L; V, MC, AE, DC, EC)* is a maze of pretty little rooms with vaulted brick ceilings illuminated by candles and sconces. Try the local game here; thankfully they print their menu in English, in case you don't know what *struzzo* means (it's ostrich). The wine list is kinda expensive, unless you stick with house carafes.

▶▶**SPLURGE**

If you go out for one expensive meal in Perugia, **Osteria del Bartolo** *(Via Bartolo 30; Tel/Fax 075/573-15-61; 1-2:30pm/8-10:30pm, closed Sun; Main courses 25-40,000L; V, MC, AE, DC, EC)*, in a grand palazzo near Piazza Danti, should be the place. The chef is one of Italy's most famous (he has a TV show, of course), with an outstanding reputation for his creativity in the kitchen. Specialties include sheep's-milk cheese baked in puff pastry and topped with a sauce of black truffles, shrimp, and lobster with fresh herbs; quail egg pasta with cherry tomatoes; and panna cotta for dessert. The simple dining room is dimly lit, with vaulted ceilings and tables set with white tablecloths, flowers, and candles. Break out the slacks or little black dress for this occasion—and borrow an iron.

crashing

Luckily, most of the budget hotels here are in the *centro storico,* right in the thick of things. You shouldn't have a problem finding a place to stay, except during the Umbria Jazz Festival and Eurochocolate [see *festivals and events,* below], but it's always a good idea to reserve a room in advance if you can. The tourist office won't help you, but they do provide detailed lists of hotels. If you're really stuck (or really trying to save money), there are several religious institutions and private homes which rent out rooms—ask for the list at tourist info [see *need to know,* below].

▶▶**CHEAP**

Centro Internazionale per la Gioventú *(Via Bontempi 13; Tel 075/572-46-23, Fax 075/573-87-00; 9:30am-4pm lockout, midnight* *curfew, closed Dec 14-Jan 15; 20,000L beds, 2,000L sheets; No credit cards),* a few blocks north of the Duomo, is Perugia's non-HI youth hostel. There are 23 rooms of various sizes, accommodating 133 beds in all. Despite its dormitory feel, the building is beautiful, and has a terrace with a gorgeous view. The large kitchen and TV room are packed with backpackers from all over.

Even though it's in a historic mansion with a nice patio, **Hotel Iris** *(Via Marconi 37; Tel 075/573-6882, Fax 075/572-0259; 50-75,000L singles without private baths, 70-80,000L singles with baths, 100,000L doubles without private baths, 120,000L doubles with private baths; V, MC),* southwest of Corso Cavour, is a bit shabby and past its heyday. But it's cheap, the rooms are clean, and the staff is ultra-friendly. If you opt for a room without a bathroom, the shared shower isn't the greatest, but at least it has a shower curtain, unlike many hotel bathrooms in Italy. The rooms have TVs, but no English-language channels.

The huge terrace at **Hotel San Sebastiano** *(Via San Sebastiano 4; Tel 075/573-20-06, Fax 075/572-70-16; 40-65,000L singles without private baths, 55-80,000L singles with private baths, 75-110,000L doubles without private baths, breakfast 5,000L extra; V, MC, AE)* is a great spot for winding down from sightseeing overload. Not all rooms have TVs and hairdryers, but they're all clean, comfortable, and have phones. There's a bar and a common TV room for hanging out.

Hotel Umbria *(Via Boncambi 37; Tel 075/572-12-03, Fax 075/573-79-52; 40-50,000L singles without private baths, 65-80,000L singles with private baths, 85-120,000L doubles with private baths; No credit cards)* is centrally located two blocks west of Piazza Italia. All 18 rooms are simple, clean, and have phones and TV's. The little bar is a great place to take your first cappuccino of the day, but there's no breakfast served.

From the Duomo end of Corso Vannucci, take Via dei Priori west to reach **Hotel Anna** *(Via dei Priori 48; Tel/Fax 075/573-63-04; 50,000L singles without baths, 70,000L singles with baths, 80,000L doubles without baths, 100,000L doubles with baths; V, MC),* one of the best values in the city. This small *albergo,* a few floors up in an old *palazzo,* is run by a sweet elderly couple who will make you feel like their long-lost grandchild. The rooms don't have TVs, but they do have phones, and are generally very large. The sitting room is furnished with lovely antiques, old trophies, and lithographs of Perugia in the old days.

Just south of Piazza della Republica, **Piccolo Hotel** *(Via Bonazzi 25; Tel 075/572-29-87; 60,000L doubles without private baths, 75,000L doubles with private baths; No credit cards)* has just 10 very simple rooms, a few of which have private balconies. Since there's nothing here to keep you occupied (no TVs, bar, or phones), you'll have no choice but to soak up culture during the day and sample pubs at night.

▶▶DO-ABLE

Hotel Fortuna *(Via Bonazzi 19; Tel 075/572-28-45, Fax 075/573-50-40; 60-130,000L singles without private baths, 60-138,000L singles with baths, 80-180,000L doubles without private baths, 90-256,000L doubles* *with baths, breakfast included; V, MC, AE, DI),* a few doors down from Piccolo Hotel in a 14th-century *palazzo,* is one of the swankiest spots in town, but outside of the summer season, their rates are reasonable. The rooms are big and comfortable, tastefully decorated with lots of contemporary art posters and photos of Italy, and have TVs and mini bars. Ask for a room with a balcony and be sure to have coffee up on the rooftop terrace.

▸▸**SPLURGE**

From outside, the **Sangallo Palace Hotel** *(Via Masi 9; Tel 075/573-0202, Fax 075/573-00-68; hotel@sangallo.it; www.sangallo.it; 115-157,000L per person, breakfast included; V, MC, AE)* doesn't look anything like a palace. In fact, it looks quite modestly modern. But once you get inside, it's old-school luxurious—lay on the huge beds, take a swim in the indoor pool, work out in the fitness center, or pamper yourself in one of the deluxe bathrooms. Every room has a tub, TV, phone, minibar, hairdryer, and even speakers in the bathroom so you can hear the TV while you're soaking in the tub. The Sangallo Palace is just below Piazza Italia, via the escalator through the Rocca Paolina.

need to know

Currency Exchange Banks with *ATMs* are scattered throughout the city, particularly on **Corso Vannucci.** If you need to change hard currency, stop in at any bank 8:30am-1:30pm and 2:45-3:45pm, Monday through Friday. The **post office** also has an exchange window. After hours, **B.N.L.** and **Banca Toscana** (both on Piazza Italia) and **Banca dell'Umbria** (Corso Vannucci 39) have automatic money exchange machines. The **train station** also has an exchange window, open daily 7am-8pm.

Tourist Information The **iat** office *(Piazza iv novembre 3; Tel 075/573-6458; 8:30am-6:30pm Mon-Fri, 8:30am-1:30pm Sat)* won't book rooms for you, but they're a great info source. It's across from the Fontana Maggiore on the ground level, next to the flight of stairs that leads up to the **Sala dei Notari** [see *culture zoo,* above].

Public Transportation All **buses** leave from Piazza Italia, but besides getting to and from the train station, a bus really isn't necessary since all of the sights are a short walk from the center. Perugia's bus company, **APM** *(Pian di Massiano 1; Tel 075/501-14-34)* sells several types of tickets: *Tipo Giallo* (yellow) is valid for 20 minutes and costs 1,200L; *Tipo Verde* (green) is valid for 40 minutes and costs 1,400L; *Tipo Azzurro* (blue) is valid for 70 minutes and costs 1,700L; the light gray is valid for 24 hours and costs 5,000L; and the dark gray is valid for 48 hours and costs 7,500L. Tickets can be bought at the APM ticket counter in Piazza Partigiani, at any *tabacchi,* or onboard.

You might be stuck with a long walk back to your hotel if you're out too late: the free **escalator** from Piazza Partigiani to Piazza Italia is open 6:15am-2am, the one from Via Pellini to Via dei Priori is open

6:45am-2am, and the one that goes down to Piazzale Europa is open 7am-10pm.

Health and Emergency Emergency health service: *118;* Police emergency line: *113;* Perugia police station (non-emergency line): *075/50-621;* Red Cross ambulance: *075/572-1111, 075/572-5090;* Ospedale Riuniti-Policlinico *(Viale Bonacci Brunamonti; Tel 075/5781);* Doctor Service: *075/34-024 (weekdays), 075/36-584 (weekends).*

Pharmacies Pharmacies are open 9am-1pm and 4-8pm Monday to Friday, and 9am-1pm on Saturdays. They work on a rotating system, so one pharmacy in town is always open continuously 9am-10pm, and one is open for night service, 8pm-9am—look for signs posted on pharmacy doors. There are several pharmacies in the center, such as **Andreoli** *(Corso Vannucci 27; Tel 075/572-0915; 9am-1pm/4-8pm Mon-Fri, 9am-1pm Sat; V, MC, AE)* and **Tarpani** *(Piazza Matteotti; Tel 075/572-0925; 9am-1pm/4-8pm Mon-Fri, 9am-1pm Sat; V, MC).*

Telephone City code: *075.* There's a Telecom Italia calling center at Corso Vannucci 76.

Trains The **Fontivegge** train station at Piazza Vittorio Veneto, the only Perugia station, is a few kilometers southwest of the town center, and a 10-minute bus ride from the heart of the *centro storico* (buses 6,7,9,11, and 12 end up at Piazza Italia). There are a few daily direct trains between Rome and Florence; otherwise trains from Florence connect in Terontola and trains from Rome connect in Foligno. For train info call 075/500-7467 or 075/506-7891.

Bus Lines Out of the City The **bus station** is in Piazza Partigiani, which is a short walk or escalator ride from Piazza Italia. Regular buses go to Assisi and Rome; one bus a day heads to Florence, at 7:30am; one goes to Pompei, at 2:30pm. For bus info call 075/30-799 or 075/506-7894.

Bike/Moped Rental Mountain bikes can be rented at **Ciclismo Sport** *(Via Settevalli 195; Tel/Fax 075/505-25-31),* located on the street that runs south from the piazza in front of the train station.

Laundry Lava & Lava *(Via M. Angeloni 32 A/6 and Via A. Vecchi 5; No phone; 8am-10pm daily; No credit cards)* is a self-service, coin-operated Laundromat.

Postal The main **post office** is in piazza matteotti *(Tel 075/572-0395; 8:10am-5:30pm Mon-Sat; Closes at noon on the last day of each month.)*

Internet See *wired,* above.

everywhere else

assisi

If any town is going to inspire you to give up on worldly possessions and get in touch with your spiritual side, it probably wouldn't be modern-day Assisi. The tiny hilltop village, with its winding, steep medieval streets and green, mountainous scenery, is jammed with tacky souvenir shops and other assorted tourist traps set up to make a buck off tourists like you and religious pilgrims who come to honor St. Francis (1181-1226). Assisi's patron saint was the son of a wealthy merchant before he tossed off that life to become a humble monk (he's also the patron saint of San Francisco, that American city where thousands of hippies once converged to give it all away). Francis heard the voice of God telling him to "Rebuild my Church," (no, it's not the Catholic version of Field of Dreams), so he founded the Franciscan Order. Their tenets of obedience, chastity, and poverty remain the basis of the worldwide monastic order today.

Ever since the monumental Basilica di San Francesco [see *culture zoo,* below] was constructed to house St. Francis's remains, in the process creating some of the finest frescoes of the Renaissance, Assisi has become one of the world's most important pilgrimage sites, hosting millions of visitors a year. And most of them don't leave home without their credit cards, judging by the glut of souvenir stands. Tourism is tiny Assisi's only industry, and its 3,000 permanent residents thrive on peddling religious trinkets like wooden cross necklaces and drunk-monk figurines. The streets around the main sites feel like St. Francis Land at Disney World, but instead of Mickey and Goofy, you get brown-robed friars and nuns.

Most of the kids head out to Perugia in the evening, as there aren't many places to get your groove on in Assisi [see *need to know,* below, for info on transportation to Perugia]. But during the day, you can have fun romping around the back streets, which open out to fantastic panoramic views of the Umbrian valleys. Assisi is located halfway up the slopes of **Mount Subasio** [see *city sports,* below], under cover of the **Rocca**

festivals and annual events

Most events in Assisi revolve around the church (of course). The **Festa di San Francesco** (on October 3 and 4), **Easter Week,** and **Christmas Week** are celebrated with solemn rites and processions through the city. The **Festa di Calendimaggio,** celebrated on the first Thursday, Friday, and Saturday of May, is the liveliest celebration. This Medieval-Renaissance festival divides the city into two parts, with residents wearing colorful costumes, to reenact ancient duels and traditions. Theatrical, musical, and vocal performances, archery contests, and lots of street food make this a real extravaganza.

Maggiore [see *culture zoo,* below], a 14th-century fortress that's an easy hike from the center of town.

Why are all the main streets filled with scaffolding and hammer-wielding construction workers, you ask? They're trying to repair the heavy damage from 1997's earthquakes, which crumbled some of history's most significant art and architecture, and they won't be done any time soon. Repairs have been swift on the Basilica (perhaps papal influence had something to do with it), but hundreds of residents still live in temporary housing, and many municipal buildings are closed for repairs.

neighborhoods and hanging out

Assisi's train station is southwest of the city center, in the shadow of Mount Subasio. The town is traversed by a twice-hourly shuttle bus, which ends up at **Piazza Matteotti** to the east and **Porta San Pietro** to the west, both a 15-minute walk from **Piazza del Comune,** the geographic and social center of Assisi. Comune was built on the site of an ancient Roman forum, and several of the major sights, such as the **Pinacoteca Comunale** and the **Temple Minerva,** are located here [see *culture zoo,* below, for both]. The town's main streets branch off from this square: **Via San Rufino** runs southeast and leads to the **Cattedrale di San Rufino**; **Corso Mazzini** runs southeast and leads to the **Basilica di Santa Chiara**; and **Via San Paolo** runs northwest. **Via Portica,** which runs parallel to San Paolo out of Piazza Comune, turns into **Via del Seminario** and then **Via San Francesco** as it leads you to the enormous **Basilica di San Francesco** in the far northwestern corner of town—it's about a ten-minute walk from Comune to the Basilica. The **Rocco Maggiore** fortress, a 25-minute uphill walk from the Piazza del Comune, lies along the northern wall of the town.

If you're feeling too lazy to venture out into the surrounding forests and mountain trails [see *city sports,* below], head to **Parco Regina**

assisi bars clubs and culture zoo

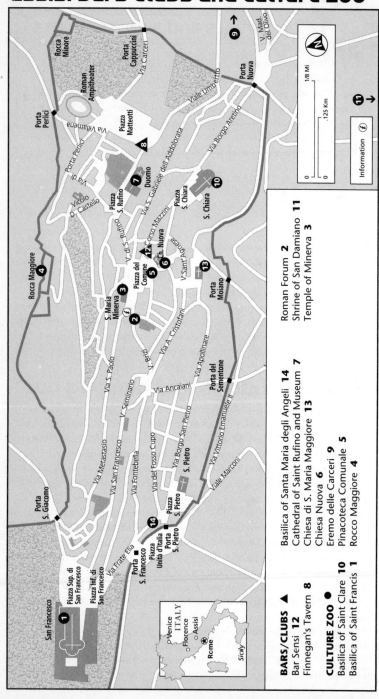

BARS/CLUBS ▲
Bar Sensi **12**
Finnegan's Tavern **8**

CULTURE ZOO ●
Basilica of Saint Clare **10**
Basilica of Saint Francis **1**

Basilica of Santa Maria degli Angeli **14**
Cathedral of Saint Rufino and Museum **7**
Chiesa di S. Maria Maggiore **13**
Chiesa Nuova **6**
Eremo delle Carceri **9**
Pinacoteca Comunale **5**
Rocco Maggiore **4**

Roman Forum **2**
Shrine of San Damiano **11**
Temple of Minerva **3**

Information ⓘ

1/8 Mi
.125 Km

ITALY
Venice
Florence
Assisi
Rome
Sicily

fashion

You certainly won't be tempted to spend your vacation funds on clothes here. Unlike most Italian towns, where style and fashion rule, Assisi is the land of zero-fashion-sense, partly because nuns, monks, and priests are far more common than "civilians." Most locals run around town in sweats and ratty sneakers. And other than not wearing the huge wooden St. Francis crosses that seem to be required tourist accessories, you'll never have to worry about being underdressed.

Margherita, just behind Piazza Matteotti). The small park is immaculately landscaped with cedar and elm trees—a great place to hang out, plop your feet up on the benches, and chill, away from the crowds for a while. Other than that, hanging-out choices are rather limited, especially as night falls. If you decide to pass on evening choral recitals and organ concerts, then there's no choice but to hit the piazzas. Spend a night enjoying the town's tranquil atmosphere in Piazza del Comune with a bottle of wine and some new friends, or for a more solitary piazza experience, head to either **Piazza Santa Chiara** or **Piazza San Rufino** (both just a minute's walk southeast of Comune).

You won't get lost—the town is too small. So just ramble around a little. Every pretty little building, scents of tomato sauce and garlic drifting from its kitchen window, every tiny church hiding a group of singing nuns, and every little neatly planned piazza will make you feel like you're discovering Italy for the first time (especially if you are). And despite the crass commercialism, you can't help but feel a tiny bit more spiritual in Assisi, as the sound of church bells accompanies you wherever you go.

café scene

With so many culture-seekers en route to their next epiphany, it's no wonder the cafe scene is lively in Assisi. Piazza del Comune is the center of it all, and come warm weather, the tables are brought outside and gelato beats out caffeine as the preferred pick-me-up.

The best gelato in town can be found at **Café Central de Bocchini** (*Piazza del Comune 47; Tel 075/812-464; 2,000L per scoop; No credit cards*), where the *stracciatella* and hazelnut varieties take top prize.

Gran Caffé (*Corso Mazzini 16; Tel 075/815-5144; Cappuccino 5,000L; V, MC, AE*), just a few steps east of Piazza del Comune, is the classiest cafe in Assisi, and the priciest (coffee is about double what it is at the other cafes here). Vaulted brick ceilings, champagne bottles behind the bar, frescoes of little naked angels, gold-trimmed tables, and pastries galore...this is what traveling in Italy should always be like.

bar scene

Assisi's few bars—and we do mean few—are packed morning, noon, and night with a mixed crowd of locals and tourists. But don't expect to meet anyone under 30 after the sun sets—they all flee to Perugia. During the summer there are huge rave-like parties lasting from Friday to Sunday in some of the small villages in the area. For information about the parties, which are called *sangre,* pick up a copy of *Viva Perugia* (1,000L) at the tourist office or from newsstands in Perugia, or keep your eyes open for posters and flyers telling you where to catch the bus out to them.

Finnegan's Tavern *(Via Torrione 7; Tel 075/816-873; 8pm-late, closed Mon; No credit cards),* which is just off the southwestern corner of Piazza Matteotti, is your typical Irish pub in Italy, complete with pop music blasting. There are tons of tourists here in the summer, but usually it's young locals and people from nearby villages who come to catch up with friends over pints of Guiness. There's nothing very special about Finnegan's, except for the fact that it's the only pub in town. Light food—pastas, appetizers, sandwiches—is served here until closing time.

During the day, **Bar Sensi** *(Corso Mazzini 14; Tel 075/812-529; 4-8,000L drinks; No credit cards),* just a few steps east of Piazza del Comune, is packed with people gulping down espressos and devouring croissants. Come afternoon, the sandwich case empties out and the stack of ice cream cones disappears as the brightly-lit place starts filling up with locals chatting over glasses of wine digestive. The crowd is younger at night, though the old men standing around the bar drinking spirits seem to be permanent fixtures.

arts scene

There's nothing cutting-edge about Assisi's art scene, unless you consider kitsch a new art form. Most contemporary arts in Assisi revolve around religious themes. There are choral and orchestral concerts in the town's churches almost nightly; most are free and worth checking out. The fine folks at tourist info [see *need to know,* below] hand out weekly listings of such events.

▶▶PERFORMING ARTS

The **Lyrick Theater** *(Via Gabriele D'Annunzio, S.M. Angeli; Tel 075/804-4352; Box office 10am-1pm/3:30-7pm, Show times 9pm Tue-Sat, 3pm matinees Fri, Sun; 50-60,000L),* which is 4km away, in Santa Maria degli Angeli (near the train station), is in an old factory that was recently renovated by an American producer specifically for the performance of Francesco il Musical. This production of the life of St. Francis, set to modern music in six languages, is tourist trash times 10—so how can you resist? Tickets are available at any location that displays a "Francesco il Musical" poster.

Box Office Assisi *(Biblioteca Comunale, Via San Francesco 12; Tel 0335/641-1211; 10am-1pm/3:30-7pm; V, MC, AE, EC),* a short walk east of the Basilica di San Francesco, and **Box Office Umbria** *(Inside of the Agenzia Viaggi Stoppini, Corso Mazzini 31; Tel 075/812-597; Fax 075/816-730; V, MC, AE, EC)*, located between Piazza del Comune and Piazza Santa Chiara, sell tickets to all music and theater performances in the region. There is one cinema, **Metastasio** *(Piazzetta Verdi; Tel 075/813-796)*, which rarely shows films in English.

CULTURE ZOO

Assisi has a tremendous number of artistic and architectural masterpieces within its city walls, but one full day is still enough to explore in depth. Combination tickets for the Rocco Maggiore, the Foro Romano, and the Pinacoteca Comunale are 10,000L full price, and 7,000L for under-25ers, and can be purchased at any of the three locations.

Basilica di San Francesco (Basilica of St. Francis) *(Piazza San Francesco; Tel 075/819-00-84 or 075/819-001; Fax 075/075/819-00-35; 6:30am-7pm Easter-Nov, 6:30am-6pm Dec-Easter; Closed Sun mornings; assisisanfrancesco@krenet.it; No credit cards)*: It's Assisi's, and possibly all of Umbria's, biggest tourist attraction, and one of the holiest spots in Christendom. The building itself was badly damaged during the earthquakes in '97, which took the lives of two monks and two inspectors when the ceiling crashed to the floor. Entire sections of the ceiling frescoes were beyond repair, but the rest of the reconstruction has been successful. The church consists of two parts: the lower church, which was built in 1228, two years after St. Francis's death, and the upper church, which didn't get started until 1230. Both house frescoes painted by the leading artists of the day, and which are considered to be some of the best in the country. The highlight of the upper church, which you enter from either a staircase inside the lower church or from Piazza Superiore di San Francesco is the cycle of frescoes by Giotto and his collaborators, depicting important scenes in St.

MUST SEE TV

Saint Clara, the leader of the Poor Clares and St. Francis's disciple, saw a vision on her deathbed of a mass being given by St. Francis. For this reason, she's been named the **patron saint of television.** St. Clara rabbit ears (for better reception on your tube), tiny TV sets where you can change the channel to see different scenes from her life, and mini-statues to stick on top of your set are just a few of the souvenirs that can only be found here.

Francis's life. You can pick up a pamphlet that will explain all the scenes to you, or you could just ask one of the super-friendly monks to walk you through it. The facade-less lower church is darkly lit—its vaulted ceilings are relatively low, there are numerous stained glass windows, and nearly the entire place is covered in frescoes by Cesare Sermai, Simone Martini, Giotto, Pietro Lorenzetti, and many others. St. Francis's tomb is downstairs in the crypt, elevated over an altar. The tomb was hidden for many centuries, out of fear of theft, and then re-discovered in 1818. In the chapel, several of St. Francis's relics, like his robe, sandals, and chalice, are on view.

Tesora (Treasury) and the Collezione Perkins (Perkins Collection) *(In the Basilica; Tel 075/819-001; 9:30am-noon/2:30-6pm, closed Sundays and from Nov-Mar; 3,000L for both):* The treasury, which resides in a few rooms off the lower church, houses an interesting collection of paintings, religious treasures, and tapestries belonging to the Franciscans. The Perkins Collection of painting was left to the Franciscans by an art collector in 1955, and though it consists mostly of unknown paintings, there are also works by important Italian artists. It's a worthy visit for art history lovers and Franciscan-o-philes.

Basilica di Santa Chiara (Basilica of St. Clare) *(Piazza S. Chiara; Tel 075/812-282; 7am-noon/2-7pm, closed during services; Free entrance):* From Piazza del Comune, follow Corso Mazzini through the Portello di San Giorgio to this Gothic pink and white church. This important monument to Saint Clare—St. Francis's first disciple, who founded the Poor Clares order—was also heavily damaged during the earthquake, and both the facade and the interior were still being repaired at the time of this writing. Most of the frescoes inside the basilica have disintegrated and the walls are now almost completely bare, save the ornately frescoed ceiling. One of the most sacred relics here is the crucifix that is said to have told St. Francis to rebuild the church. Down the marble staircase, the Sanctuary of St. Clare (which contains the saint's tomb) escaped earthquake damage. Once outside, check out the amazing views of the countryside and red-tiled rooftops from the wall that encloses the piazza.

Cattedrale di San Rufino (Cathedral of St. Rufino) *(Piazza S. Rufino; Tel 075/816-016 or 071/812-283; 7am-noon/2-7pm, closed during services; Free entrance):,* From Piazza del Comune, walk uphill along Via San Ruffino to this church, where yet another saint is buried. The Cathedral was built in 1140 and remodeled in the 16th century, but legend says that a chapel was originally built on the site in the 5th century to honor St. Rufino, the first bishop of Assisi. The Cathedral still contains the baptismal font where St. Francis, St. Clare, and Emperor Frederick II were baptized. Visit the Cappella del Sacramento, which holds a few magnificent paintings.

Museo Capitolare della Cattedrale *(Piazza San Rufino; Tel 075/912-283; 10am-12am/3pm-6pm daily, closed Mon-Fri Nov 5 -March 1; 3,000L):* This museumcan be entered through the Cattedrale di San Rufino, and contains frescoes that have been detached from the Cathedral as well as other paintings that once hung inside. The **crypt** *(Piazza San Rufino; Tel 075/912-283; 10am-12:30pm/3pm-6pm; 3,000L Adults, 2,000L Students)*, which you enter from Piazza San Rufino on the right side of the cathedral, has a few frescoes, but otherwise can be skipped.

Foro Romano (Roman Forum) *(Via Portica; Tel 075/813-053; 10am-1pm/3pm-7pm Mar 16-Oct 15, 10am-1pm/2pm-5pm Oct 16-March 15; 4,000L adults, 3,000L under 25):* Escape from the crowds to the Roman Forum, or Civic Museum, which holds the original base of the Temple of Minerva, Roman artifacts found in and around Assisi, and ancient Etruscan artifacts. Ask for the free English-language pamphlet. The entrance to the museum is just west of Piazza del Comune—skip it if archeology isn't your thing.

Tempio di Minerva (Temple of Minerva) *(Piazza del Comune; Tel 075/812-268; 7:15am-7pm; Free admission):* The remains of this Roman temple, that once hovered over the northwest corner of the piazza, dates back to the 1st century B.C., and was re-christened Santa Maria della Minerva in the 16th century. The six Corinthian columns along the facade, however, are reminders of its pagan history.

Pinacoteca Comunale *(Palazzo dei Priori, Piazza del Comune; Tel 075/815-292; 10am-1pm/3pm-7pm daily March 16-Oct 15, 10am-1pm/2pm-5pm Oct 16-March 15; L5,000 Adults, L3,500 Under 25):* Only recently re-opened after heavy earthquake damage, this museum is well worth a visit for its great collection of Umbrian Renaissance and Medieval art, much of which has been removed from churches in the area.

Chiesa Nuova *(Piazza Chiesa Nuova; Tel 075/812-339; 6:30am-noon/2:30-6pm, closed during services; Free entrance):* On the southern side of the Piazza del Comune, walk through the Arco dei Priori, down the tiny Via Arco dei Priori, to reach the site of St. Francis's childhood home. A church was built here in 1615, but it still contains a tiny cell in which St. Francis is said to have been held by his father after sharing his plans to renounce his wealth. Notice the particularly graphic paintings behind the altar depicting Franciscan brothers being stabbed and disemboweled—it's martyrdom at its most gruesome.

Chiesa di S. Maria Maggiore *(Piazza Vescovado; Tel 075/813-085; 8am-7pm Easter-Nov, 8am-5pm Nov-Easter; Free entrance):* Assisi's first cathedral is a few blocks south of Piazza del Comune. Most of the walls in this small church are now empty, save a few remnants of frescoes. The pink-and-white checkered facade features a 12th-century rose window, and the simple interior contains little more than the 9th-century crypt and high wooden rafters.

Rocco Maggiore *(Tel 075/815-292; 10am-sunset Sept-June, 9am-sunset July, Aug; 5,000L adults, 3,500L under 25):* The 14th-century fortress which is along the northern wall of the city, dominates Assisi's skyline. Trek up the steep hill for views of the countryside and the Basilica. Since the Fortress itself isn't that thrilling inside, there are plans to use the space as an art gallery. The walk takes 15 minutes—from Piazza San Rufino, walk northeast along via Porta Perlici for a block and then turn north on vicolo di Castello, which will take you to via della Rocca and the Fortress. Sorry, no buses.

▶▶**OUTSIDE THE CITY WALLS**

Shrine of San Damiano *(Via San Damiano; Tel 075/812-273; 10am-6pm; Free admission):* One and a half kilometers south of Assisi, a nice half-hour walk through the countryside from Porta Nuova along Via S. Damiano, is where it all went down: St. Francis heard the word from the cross here, and St. Clare died here in 1205. Alongside the shrine are a convent and a monastery.

Eremo delle Carceri *(Via Eremo delle Carceri; Tel 075/812-301; 6:30am-7:15pm, Easter-Nov, 6:30am-5:30pm, Nov-Easter; Free admission):* These are the caves in which St. Francis and his followers came to live after having sworn to a life of pious poverty. From Porta Cappuccini, follow Via Eremo delle Careceri for 4km along the slopes of **Mt. Subasio** [see *city sports,* below] to reach the secluded forest entrance to Eremo delle Careceri—or shell out around 25,000L for a cab from the center of town. During Francis's time, only a small chapel existed here. In the 15th century, St. Bernardine of Siena built the church of St. Maria delle Carceri and its convent around St. Francis's chapel. Walk through the woods to see the caves of the hermits, now inhabited by white doves and a few devout Franciscans. A beautiful, serene spot for a visit, no matter which god you worship.

   The Basilica of Santa Maria degli Angeli *(Piazza Garibaldi; Tel 075/80-511; Bus from Piazza Matteotti; 6:30am-8pm daily Sept-July, 6:30am-8pm/9-11pm daily Aug; Free admission):* This is one of the largest Christian churches in the world—so much for Franciscan simplicity. The church was built in the 16th century around Porziuncola, the chapel given to St. Francis by the Benedictine monks of Mt. Subasio. St. Francis died in the tiny Cappella del Transito (Chapel of Death), inside the Basilica. One of the highlights of the church is the unique Fontana dei Pellegrini (Pilgrims' Fountain), which has 26 spouts and was a gift from the Medicis in 1610. Walk around the lovely rose garden, the convent, and the Cappella del Roseto (Rose Chapel). The Basilica is 4km southwest of the city, near the train station and on the bus route.

CITY SPORTS

Unless you've got legs of steel, you might find jogging along Assisi's steep streets a bit difficult. The only green space within the city walls, **Parco Regina Margherita** [see *neighborhoods and hanging out,* above] is really too small for jogging. But nature lovers and hikers will have plenty to do outside the city limits. The 1290m high **Mt. Subasio Park** *(Infoline Tel 075/815-181, Fax 075/815-307)* dominates the Umbrian valley—Assisi actually lies within the park and was built out of the mountain's rocks. For an introduction to the park, and a fairly easy hike, walk the 4km from Assisi to St. Francis' hideout at **Eremo delle Carceri** [see *culture zoo,* above]. The forests of Mt. Subasio are broken up by pastures and full of all kinds of trees—olive, turkey oak, minor oak, hornbeam, flowering ash, maple, beech and ilex, to name a few. Unfortunately, many animal species, such as the royal eagle and the quail, have been hunted nearly out of existence. But you can still see gray partridges, wild cats, wood pigeons, magpies, jays, hedgehogs, badgers, weasels, and the occasional wild boar (which are a popular Umbrian delicacy). The Assisi tourist office offers detailed hiking maps of the park for free. Several horseback riding schools operate in the outlying areas, including **Centro Equitazione Ranch Allegro** *(Loc. Beviglie; Tel 075/816-893)* and **Centro Ippico Assisi** *(Loc. Santa Maria Maddalena, S.S. 75, Rivotorto; Tel 075/804-2997)*. The thousands of kilometers of marked trails in the park are perfect for riding or biking [see *need to know*, below, for bike rentals].

STUFF

Assisi's shopping scene is short on the basics, but when it comes to souvenirs and local folk crafts, there's a ton to spend your money on.

▶▶BOUND

Libreria Fonteviva *(Via S. Paolo 37/c; Tel 075/812-467; 8am-8pm Tue-Sun, 3-4pm Mon)*, just east of Piazza del Comune, specializes in art and religion books with pretty pictures, but none are in English.

Zubboli Maurizio *(Piazza del Comune 5; Tel 075/812-381; 8am-8pm Tue-Sun, 3-4pm Mon)* has a small selection of English-language books and lots of Italian art books.

▶▶DUDS

Lisa Assisi *(Corso Mazzini 27/a; Tel 075/816-622; 8am-8pm Tue-Sun, 3-4pm Mon; V, MC, AE)*, on Corso Mazzini between Piazza del Comune and Piazza Santa Chiara, is one of the few clothing stores in town. It offers a strange mixture of Moschino pants and Assisi T-shirts, but the huge 50-percent-off bin in the basement makes it all worthwhile.

▶▶HOW BAZAAR

You'll find a market every Saturday, at Via San Gabriele dell' Addolorata and Via Alessi, which run off from the northeast corner of Piazza del Comune. Expect your usual smattering o' household stuff, with some cool, inexpensive clothes and shoes. Folks start setting up around 9am, and shut down when the sun sets.

▶▶LEATHER

Mauro Cenci makes and sells everything at **Il Tapiro** *(Via San Rufino 6/b; Tel 075/816-773; 8am-8pm Tue-Sun, 3-4pm Mon; V, MC)*, just east of Piazza del Comune. Although the price tags may look a little high, he's known to give "special prices," which can be up to half off what the tag says. The handmade bags here (80,000L up to 300,000L) are especially nice.

▶▶ARTSY STUFF & SOUVENIRS

The two owners of **Stedav** *(Via San Rufino 15; Tel 075/815-375; 8am-8pm Tue-Sun, 3-4pm Mon; V, MC)* make all the cool ceramics and jewelry for sale in their store. Nearly everything is painted with moons and suns, and the funky copper, gold, and silver jewelry is guaranteed to be a conversation starter.

In his small shop, **Enrico Marrani** *(Via S. Agnese 13/b; Tel 075/592-81-08 or 0338/233-66-68, Fax 075/692-01-95; 8am-8pm Tue-Sun, 3-4pm Mon)* sells handmade ceramics, which are mostly religious in theme.

The sweet smell of wood and beeswax will draw you into **Tutto Arte** *(Via Portica 18; Tel 075/813-185; 8am-8pm Tue-Sun, 3-4pm Mon)*, just east of Piazza del Comune, and **Poiesis** *(Corso Mazzini 14/d; Tel 075/816-565; 8am-8pm Tue-Sun, 3-4pm Mon)*, between Piazza del Comune and Piazza Santa Chiara. Everything in both stores is handmade out of beautiful, sweet-smelling olive wood. If you have to buy one of those wooden crosses all the tourists wear, at least do it in one of these shops.

Buonumore *(Via San Rufino 25; Tel 075/812-530; 8am-8pm Tue-Sun, 3-4pm Mon; V, MC)* sells beautiful hand-painted candles, candle-holders, books, stationary, jewelry, and scarves. It's on via San Rufino, northeast of Piazza del Comune. This is a great place to pick up a few reasonably priced pieces for friends back home.

EATS

From cheap pizza to upscale meals, Assisi offers a good range of restaurants—just watch out for the overpriced tourist traps on Piazza del Comune. Tourist menus in other towns are generally a good value, and give you the chance to try several different house specialties, but here you should check first to make sure that something you want to eat is offered on the limited menu. Assisi's Umbrian specialties—wild game, truffles, porcini mushrooms—should not be missed. And it all goes better with a *quartino* (quarter liter) of Orvieto, the local white wine.

▶▶CHEAP

Il Menestrello *(Vicolo S. Gregorio 1/a; Tel 075/812-334; Fax 075816-499; Noon-3:30pm/7-10pm, closed Mon; Pizza 9,000-16,000L; V, MC, AE)*, on a small side street running south from via Portico, serves great food and wine at super-cheap prices. The downside is that it's always packed with students and families—good luck scoring a table. The subterranean, cellar-like dining room, with its exposed stone walls and candlelight, is the perfect spot to linger for a few hours over a bottle of wine.

Pizzeria Otello *(Piazzetta Chiesa Nuova; Tel 075/812-415; Noon-3:30pm/7-10pm, closed Sun; 10,000L for a pizza; V, MC)*, has tables on a patio overlooking Chiesa Nuovo—a very desirable spot at any time of day. Inside, it's cozy, casual, and fun—make friends with the people seated next to you at the long wooden tables. The food is simple and delicious, though pizzas are a tad on the small side.

The decor is bland at **Il Pozzo Romano** *(Via S. Agnese 10; Tel 075/813-057; Noon-3:30pm/7-10pm, closed Thurs; 20,000L tourist menu, 8,000L pizzas; V, MC, AE)*, but it is one of the cheapest places in town, and that's why everyone—and we mean *everyone*—comes here. The food is surprisingly good and portions are generous. The restaurant is a few steps away from Piazza Santa Chiara, where Via S. Agnese meets Via S. Chiara.

TO MARKET

Budget travelers and gourmet hounds alike will love Assisi's tiny food markets with their fantastic selections of Umbrian specialties, fresh baked pastries, and local wines. A meal of groceries from one of these shops, eaten out in a medieval piazza, is an inexpensive and delicious option. **Il Mercantino** *(Piazzetta Garibaldi 2-3; Tel 075/816-026; 8am-1pm/4:30-7:30pm Mon-Sat, closed Sun and Thur evening; No credit cards)*, in a small piazza one block south of the Teatro Metastasio, sells a variety of gourmet foods from their deli cases. The folks at **Gambacorta, Bottega del Bongustaio** *(Via San Gabriele 17; Tel 075/812-454; Fax 075/813-186; 8am-1pm/4:30-7:30pm Mon-Sat, closed Sun and Thur evening; geo@umbrars; V, MC, AE)*, on Via San Gabriele, just east of Piazza del Comune, have been written up in numerous Italian travel and gourmet magazines. This is one of the biggest food markets in Assisi, selling all types of regional specialties like cheese, salami, wild boar, truffles, olive oils, wines, and loads of other delicacies. **Vendita Carni Fresche** *(Via San Rufino 45/a; No phone; 8am-1pm/4:30-7:30pm Mon-Sat, closed Sun and Thur evening; No credit cards)* specializes in meat and cold cuts. **La Bottega del Pasticcere** *(Via Portico 9; No phone; 8am-10pm, closed Tue; No credit cards)*, a few steps west of Piazza del Comune, has the most mouthwatering pastries. Try the pistachio candies and the *rocciata umbra,* a delicious nut pastry. If you're anything like the Italians (you love truffles), check out **Fortunati Alfonso** *(Via Filippo da Campello 67; Tel 0743/521-548, Fax 0743/521-124; 8am-1pm/4:30-7:30pm Mon-Sat, closed Sun and Thur evening)*, where everything is truffle-flavored, even the grappa.

Next to the Cathedral, **Pizza al Taglio** *(Via San Rufino 26; No phone; Noon-3:30pm/7-10pm daily; No credit cards)* sells pizza by the slice, as well as good *panini* (sandwiches). Pizza is sold by weight, coming to around 3,000-5,000L per slice, depending on how heavy your toppings are. No tables, so take your pizza outside and admire the Cathedral.

The **Forro Romano** *(Via Portica 23; Tel 075/815-370; Noon-10pm daily; Avg. meal 15,000L; No credit cards)* is a popular self-service restaurant just east of Piazza del Comune. The fact that it's open throughout the day is a plus, but the food is a little bland. Big counters serve up many different varieties of pastas, meat dishes, salads, and desserts in a huge, industrial-looking dining room.

assisi eats and crashing

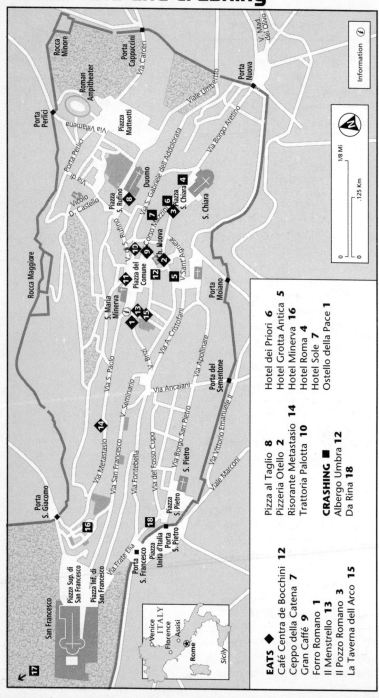

EATS ◆

Café Centra de Bocchini **12**
Ceppo della Catena **7**
Gran Caffé **9**
Forro Romano **1**
Il Menstrello **13**
Il Pozzo Romano **3**
La Taverna dell Arco **15**

Pizza al Taglio **8**
Pizzeria Otello **2**
Risorante Metastasio **14**
Trattoria Palotta **10**

CRASHING ■

Albergo Umbra **12**
Da Rina **18**

Hotel dei Priori **6**
Hotel Grotta Antica **5**
Hotel Minerva **16**
Hotel Roma **4**
Hotel Sole **7**
Ostello della Pace **1**

▶▶DO-ABLE
La Taverna dell Arco *(Via S. Gregorio 8; Tel 075/812-383; Fax 075/815-340; Noon-3:30pm/7-10pm, closed Mon; Avg. meal 30,000L; No credit cards)*, a family-style restaurant on a small street off the southern side of Piazza del Comune, should not be skipped. The dining room is tiny and cozy, with candles on the tables and knick-knacks decorating the walls. The food is just as homey, with traditional fresh pasta dishes, roasted meats, and vegetables.

Normally it's best to stay as far away as possible from restaurants attached to cheap hotels, but **Ceppo della Catena** *(Corso Mazzini 35; Tel 075/812-378; Fax 075/813-706; Noon-3:30pm/7-10pm, closed Wed; 25,000L tourist menu; AE, DC, MC, V)*, the restaurant at **Hotel Sole** [see *crashing*, below], is the exception. Run by a family with generations of restaurant experience and a fondness for old copperware and antique weapons, this cozy restaurant, between Piazza del Comune and Piazza Santa Chiara, serves extraordinarily simple, but extremely flavorful, traditional food. Be sure to try the homemade *minestrone* and *bruschetta*. Well loved by the locals, it's unfortunately often full of huge American groups staying at the hotel. If you come with a few people, the waitress—who happens to be the owner's wife—will serve your meal family-style on huge serving plates.

▶▶SPLURGE
Trattoria Pallotta *(Via San Rufino 4; Tel 075/812-649; Closed Tue; Avg. meal with wine 50,000L; V, MC, AE, DC)*, just a few steps northeast of Piazza del Comune, is one of the best restaurants in Assisi. Beautifully set tables, an appetizing menu with daily specials, and an expert staff make a meal here mandatory if you can swing the tab.

Ristorante Metastasio *(Via Metastasio 9; Tel 075/816-525; Noon-3:30pm/7-10pm; Avg. meal 50,000L; AE, DC, MC, V)*, about a two-minute walk west of Piazza del Comune down Via San Paolo to via Metastasio, is another memorable dining experience. The view is magnificent, the food, first-rate—come here with someone special and spoil yourself with a bottle of fine local wine with your meal.

crashing

Overflowing with reasonably priced hotels, Assisi makes a good base for exploring the region. During the peak season—from April to October, and especially around Easter, when there are lots of holy festivities—it's a good idea to book in advance. Many religious institutions rent rooms, and if you find yourself stuck without a place to sleep (which can happen between January and March, when many of the town's hotels close), about 40 families with rooms for rent are listed with the tourism office.

▶▶CHEAP
The HI youth hostel, **Ostello della Pace** *(Via di Valecchie 171; Tel/Fax 075/ 816-767; Check-in 7am, lockout 10am-3:30pm, curfew 11:30pm; Sheets provided; No credit cards)* is open from March to mid-January. The hostel is about a 20-minute walk from the Basilica di San Francesco, but

wired

It's not easy to find Internet access in Assisi, and the few places that have it have extremely slow connections. **Unipol Assicurazioni** *(Via Borgo Aeration 5/a; Tel 075/819-82-31; 9am-12:30pm/4-7pm Mon-Fri, 9am-12:30pm Sat, closed Sun)*, at the southern end of Borgo Aeration (near Porta Nuova) has a few hooked-up computers available for 10,000L an hour. **Bar del Corso** *(Via Richard Francalancia 2; Tel 075/812-989; 8am-10pm daily; esservice@edisons.it)*, between Piazza del Comune and Piazza Santa Chiara, has one computer and charges 5,000L for 15 minutes, but it's hardly worth it at this speed. For Assisi info on the Internet check out *www.comune.assisi.pg.it, www.umbria2000.it, www.umbria.org, www.assisi.com,* and *www.assisionline.com.*

is close to the Porta San Pietro bus stop. It offers pay phones, a yard, and several common rooms, which are all spotless. Otherwise, it's your typical, institutional hostel experience.

The pretty and tastefully decorated **Hotel Da Rina** *(Piaggia San Pietro 22; Tel 075/812-817; Fax 075/816-824; 70-100,000L singles with private baths, 80-120,000L doubles with baths, 5,000L breakfast, 15,000L meals; V, MC)* is conveniently located within sight of the Porta San Pietro bus stop, and features tons of extras: free Internet access, common rooms with TVs, laundry, a garden, bicycles for guests to borrow, and a small library. All nine of the small, cozy rooms have phones and TVs, and there's a small bar and restaurant. Take the bus from the train station to Porto San Pietro, then walk southeast on Viale G. Marconi, which turns into Via di Valecchie.

Hotel Grotta Antica *(Via Macelli Vecchi 1; Tel 075/813-467; 40-50,000L singles with private baths, 70-75,000L doubles with private baths; No credit cards)*, on a small street behind Piazza del Comune, is clean and simple, if a bit dreary. But at these prices, and with TVs in every room, who's complaining? The bathrooms technically have showers, but they're those cheap tricky showers in the center of the bathroom with no curtain. There's no reception desk here—either ring the doorbell or walk downstairs to the hotel's attached pizzeria. You're on your own for breakfast.

The comfy, family-run **Hotel Minerva** *(Piazzetta Bonghi 7; Tel 075/812-416; Fax 075/813-770; 60-80,000L singles, 80-100,000L doubles, 12,000L breakfast; V, MC)* is said to be built on ancient medieval remains. Located south of the Basilica of San Francesco, many of its rooms have panoramic views of the Umbrian countryside. The rooms are sparsely, yet tastefully decorated, and all have TVs, bathrooms, and phones.

The 19 rooms at **Hotel Sole** *(Corso Mazzini 20; Tel 075/812-373; Fax 075/813-706; 30-45,000L singles without private baths, 50-75,000L singles with private baths, 50-75,000L doubles without private baths, 110,000L doubles with private baths, 10,000L breakfast, 85,000L per person full board; V, MC, AE)* are usually full of American tour groups. But if you're lucky enough to get one, go ahead and shell out the few extra lire for half board or full board—the restaurant is fantastic [see *eats*, above]. Although not every room has its own TV, the marble staircases, exposed stone walls, and helpful, friendly staff make this a great budget hotel. Located between Piazza del Comune and Piazza Santa Chiara.

▶▶**DO-ABLE**

The family-run **Albergo Umbra** *(Via degli Archi 6; Tel 075/812-240; Fax 075/813-653; 120,000-150,000L singles with private baths, 160,000-180,000L doubles with private baths, extra beds 50,000L; V, MC, AE),* just off Piazza del Comune, has large rooms (all decorated with posters of St. Francis), and plenty of terraces and sitting areas with lovely countryside views. All rooms have phones, TVs, and mini bars, and most have bathtubs and hairdryers. Breakfast is included, but it's better to skip the watered-down coffee and Tang-like orange juice and head to a cafe instead.

Hotel Roma *(Piazza Santa Chiara 13-15; Tel 075/812-390 or 075/816-745; Fax 075/816-74; 70,000L singles with baths, 120,000L doubles with baths; V, MC)* is right across the street from the Basilica di Santa Chiara. All rooms have bathrooms, TVs, and phones, but even though it's clean and friendly, the only stand-out about this hotel is its location.

▶▶**SPLURGE**

Right in the center of town, between Piazza del Comune and Piazza Santa Chiara, is **Hotel dei Priori** *(Corso Mazzini 15; Tel 075/812-237; Fax 075/816-804; 75-155,000L singles with private baths, 100-290,000L doubles with private baths, breakfast included; V, MC, AE),* set in a romantic, 16th-century Palazzo. All 34 rooms have bathrooms, TVs, phones, mini bars, and air conditioning. The rooms are pretty, with antique oriental rugs; the dining room, with its vaulted ceiling, is a pleasant place to eat breakfast, and the marble staircases make you feel elegant.

need to know

Currency Exchange Exchange your money at **banks** for the best rate, from 8:20am-1:20pm/2:30-3:30pm Mon-Fri. There are banks with **ATMs** at **Porta San Francesco, Piazza Santa Chiara,** and **Piazza San Pietro.** There's an **exchange office** at Assisi's **Stazione S. Maria degli Angeli** *(Tel 075/804-02-72; 6:10am-7:30pm daily).* Money can also be changed at the post office from 8:10am-1:30pm Mon-Fri and at the **Ufficio di Cambio Interchange** *(Via S. Francesco 20/D; 075/816-220; 9:30am-5:30pm daily Nov-Mar, 9:30am-8pm daily Apr-Oct).* In case of an emergency, the **Tabaccheria Capitanucci** *(Piazza Garibaldi 2; Tel 075/812-403)* can send faxes and receive money via Western Union.

Tourist Information The **IAT** *(Piazza del Comune 12; Tel 075/812-534 or 075/812-923, Fax 075/813-727; 8am-2pm/3:30-6:30pm Mon-Fri, 9am-1pm/3:30-6:30pm Sat, 9am-1pm Sun; aptas@krenet.it or info@iat.assisi.pg.it, www.umbria2000.it)* won't make hotel reservations for you, but they do have extensive lists of hotels, religious institutions, and private families that rent rooms.

Public Transportation A **bus,** which leaves from the front of the train station every half an hour, connects the station with Assisi's Piazza Matteotti and Porta San Pietro, which are each a 15-minute walk from Piazza del Comune. Tickets for the 20-minute journey can be bought on the bus (2,000L), but to save a few lira, buy them from a *tabacchi* shop (1,400L). There are **Posteggitaxi** taxi stands at **Piazza San Francesco** *(Tel 075/812-606)*, **Piazza Santa Chiara** *(Tel 075/812-600)*, and **Piazza del Comune** *(Tel 075/813-193)*.

Health and Emergency Emergencies: *118;* Emergency room of Assisi hospital: *075/812-824* or *075/813-92-27*. Physician on call: *075/36-584;* Ambulance: *075/804-35-00;* Police: *113*. The Police station is on Piazza Santa Chiara *(Tel 075/812-215)*.

Pharmacies **Farmacia Antica dei Caldari** *(Via S. Gabriele dell' Addolorata 4; Tel 075/812-552; 8am-8pm daily)*, just east of Piazza del Comune, is a convenient and well-stocked pharmacy.

Telephone City code: *075*. There are pay phones on Piazza del Comune.

Trains Assisi's train station, **Stazione Santa Maria Degli Angelli** *(Piazza Dante Alighieri 5, Santa Maria degli Angeli; Tel 075/804-02-72 or 1478/88-088)*, which is also labeled "Assisi," is 4km away from the center of town—the best way into town is to catch one of the buses that are always out front. Assisi is on the Foligno-Terontola line. For Florence, change at Terontola, and for Rome, change at Foligno. There are a few daily direct trains to Rome and to Florence. There are also frequent trains connecting Perugia and Assisi, which run all night. **Left Luggage** *(Tel 0339/372-45-92; 6:30am-6:30pm)* will store your bags for 5,000L per piece for up to 12 hours.

Bus Lines Out of the City Assisi isn't very well-connected by bus, except to Perugia. **ASP** buses leave from the bus station at Piazza Matteotti. During the week there is one bus daily to Florence, leaving at 6:50am and arriving at 9:30am. Every day there are buses to Rome at 1:45pm (arriving at 4:55pm) and 4:45pm (arriving at 7:45pm). There are seven buses to Perugia (5,000L) each weekday, and two daily buses on weekends.

Bike/Moped Rental **Bartolucci Bruno** *(Tel 0368/431-758 or 0330/882-762)* rents bikes and mopeds, and will deliver them to your hotel.

Postal Red post boxes can be found all over the city. There is also a **post office** just inside of Porta S. Pietro *(Piazza S. Pietro 4; Tel 075/815-178; 8am-6pm Mon-Fri)*.

Internet See *wired*, above.

TODI

We hate to use the word "quaint", but you really can't talk about Todi without it. It's the picture-perfect little hill town, plastered on posters and perpetually invaded by film crews making period pieces. The narrow medieval streets twist and turn and plunge down hills with no warning, and its central square is known as one of the most pristine in all of Italy. It makes a perfect day-trip from Rome or Perugia.

Todi doesn't have any great Renaissance art treasures, amazing regional delicacies, or any bar scene to speak of. People come here to wander the streets, gape at the buildings, take in the views, and generally kick back. Trust us—the atmosphere and architecture make up for anything else that's lacking.

You may notice lots of luxury cars purring through town—these belong to the Italian businesspeople who have moved out to the country, set up camp in Todi's medieval *palazzi,* and now commute back to Rome from here. They're easy to ignore, especially if you come here on a weekday (hint, hint). English-speaking tourists are just picking up on this place, and the crowds are generally thin, except around the **Todi Festival** [see *festivals and events,* below].

The best thing to do here is just take a nice long walk around town. The bus from the train station will drop you off in the **Piazza del Popolo,** so why don't you start there? This is, as we said, one of the most amazing piazzas in the country. The squat brick-and-marble **Palazzo dei Priori** sits on its south side—it's the one with the big bronze eagle on top. Legend has it that some picnicking Umbrians (or Etruscans, depending on who's telling the story) founded Todi after an eagle nicked their picnic basket and dropped it on this very hill. True or not, the eagle is now the official symbol of the town. The two Gothic structures linked by the big staircase on the east side of the piazza are the **Palazzo del Popolo** and the **Palazzo del Capitano,** both built in the 13th century. The rose window of the **Duomo** shines down on the north side of the Piazza. None of the buildings on the Piazza are really worth venturing

festivals and events

The classy **Todi Festival** *(late August; Tel 075/894-3611)* moves into town every summer and blasts the town with theater, music, and ballet. Some of it is surprisingly cutting edge for this old-fashioned little hill town.

in to—the facades are the best part. North of the Duomo the town takes a nose dive into the adjacent valley—head down only if your calves need a workout.

On the opposite side of the Piazza del Priori, behind and to the right of the Palazzo dei Priori, you'll come upon the massive **shrine of San Fortunato.** It was begun in 1291, but construction dragged on till 1459. The carvings on the central doorway are why you're here—they show a Gothic tangle of religious, symbolic, and just plain naked figures climbing on vines or just hanging out under some Greek canopies. The *Annunciation* statues that flank the door are stunning as well.

To the right of San Fortunato is a path that leads up to the little public park, where you'll get the best views in town of the surrounding valleys and countryside. Take the path at the other end of the park down to Todi's High Renaissance masterpiece, the **Temple of Santa Maria della Consolazione.** It's a mathematically correct interpretation of a classic Greek temple that took 90 years to complete. Today its quiet, serious massiveness is still shockingly impressive. You can walk back into town from here on Viale della Consolazione, which will be on your left as you head away from the temple (don't get mixed up with the SS79 highway!).

eats

There aren't really any cheap places to eat in these parts—your best bet is to bring a lunch with you from wherever you're day-tripping from. But if you want to sit down and be waited on, **Umbria** (*Via S. Bonaventura 13; Tel 075/894-2390; 12:30-2:30pm/7:30-10:30pm Wed-Mon; 10-18,000L first course, 10-25,000L second course; V, ME, AE, DC*) won't entirely break the bank—plus you'll get some incredible views with your lunch if you reserve a table out on the terrace. In the colder months you can cozy up to the huge fireplace in the wood-beamed dining room. The food is typical Umbiran home cookin', done well. The *spaghetti alla boscaiola* (with asparagus, egg, and bacon sauce) or *polenta con fungi e tartufo nero* (corn meal with mushrooms and truffle shavings) are both creamy and delicious. Or tear into one of the big steaks that they grill over and open flame. Whatever you do, make reservations.

crashing

We'd recommend just day-tripping it here—there's not a lot of choices (this tiny town couldn't hold a lot of choices). The rooms at **Villa Luisa** (*Via A. Cortesi 147; Tel 075/894-8571, Fax 075/894-8472; Bus from train station will drop you here if you ask; 100-140,000L double, 180,000L suite, breakfast 10,000L; V, MC, AE, DC*) don't have the kind of charm you might expect from a hotel in these parts, but they're clean, and pleasant enough in a chain-hotel kinda way. There's a big tree-filled park behind the hotel for strolling and napping. It's situated 2km outside of town, toward the train station, but the bus goes by all day long. Call ahead and reserve, it's a popular little joint.

need to know

Currency Exchange There is an exchange in the train station.

Tourist Information The central **tourist office** *(Tel 075/894-3062; 9am-1pm/3:30-6:30pm Mon-Sat, 9:30am-12:30pm Sun)* is under the arches of the Palazzo del Popolo. There are also two local **APT** offices at Piazza Umberto I6 *(Tel 075/894-3395)* and *(Tel 075/894-3867)*.

Trains Todi is on the private FCU line, not the state-run FS rail routes. There are about a dozen trains a day from **Perugia;** from **Rome** you have to take the FS train to **Terni** and transfer to an FCU train. When you get to Todi, get out at the **Ponte Rio station** *(Tel 075/894-2092)* (not the Ponte Naia station), where you can grab the bus that's always waiting out front to take you the three miles uphill into town.

Bus Lines Out of the City There are two **bus terminals** in town: From Piazza della Consolazione, there are four—-eight runs daily to and from **Perugia.** From Piazza Jacapone, one bus runs daily to and from Rome and the Fiumicino airpost (21/2 hours away).

florence &
Tuscany

for many travelers, Tuscany *is* Italy. It's Michelangelo's David; it's big, frothy cappuccinos; it's olive groves, vineyards, and villas the color of honey; it's late nights in the piazza, great shopping, and more museums than you can count. Oh, and it's also the Renaissance. **Florence**—along with the rest of Tuscany—was a canvas for medieval as well as Renaissance masters in the 15th and 16th centuries, and the results are still here for you to enjoy: Siena's seashell-pink piazza, **Lucca's** Renaissance city walls, **San Gimignano's** towers, **Cortona's** quiet churches, and **Pisa's** infamous leaning tower are just a few reasons to come here. Natural beauty is another—generations of expats have poured in by the plane-load, bought and restored old farmhouses and villas, and are living *la dolce vita* (the sweet life).

Despite daily swarms of tourists arriving in the region's cities (it's one of the most visited areas in Italy), the Tuscan countryside remains largely unspoiled due to the continuing economic importance of agriculture. The breathtaking landscape, with its rolling grassy plains, fields of sunflowers, and brown hills, looks like a patchwork quilt when seen from up in the hills of one of Tuscany's many small walled towns, like Cortona or San Gimignano. Tuscany's vineyards produce some of the best wine in the country, and its olive groves turn out some of the best oil.

Tuscan food is hearty yet simple—quintessential peasant food. There's nothing tastier than a *bistecca alla Fiorentina* (a large, tender steak grilled over an open fire, seasoned with olive oil and herbs) accompanied by a glass of local Chianti. Tomatoes, olive oil, beans, salami, ham, and mushrooms are in every kitchen pantry in the region. Typically, meals in Tuscany begin with *antipasti* (starters); *crostini*—small pieces of toast drizzled with warm olive oil and topped with, for example, olive paste and chopped tomato—are a great way to get a feel for the variety of the region. A *primi* (first course) usually consists of pasta, rice, soup, or polenta. Next comes the *secondi* (main course), which traditionally revolves around a big piece of fish or meat, or a pot of stew. One typical Tuscan dessert is *cantucci* (almond-flavored biscuits), which are dipped in *vino santo* (sweet dessert wine).

You will find fantastic food throughout the region, but for nightlife, no other Tuscan city can match Florence. Florence stays up later, parties harder, and has clubs and bars to match every style and budget. Pisa's large student population translates into lots of cool places to hang out. Siena and Lucca both have vibrant scenes. And in the smaller towns like

FLORENCE & TUSCANY

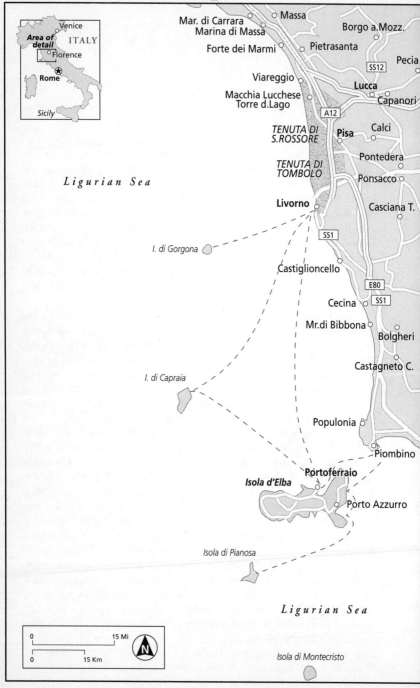

Area of detail
ITALY
Venice
Florence
Rome
Sicily

Mar. di Carrara
Marina di Massa
Massa
Borgo a.Mozz.
Forte dei Marmi
Pietrasanta
Pecia
SS12
Viareggio
Lucca
Macchia Lucchese
Torre d.Lago
Capanori
A12
TENUTA DI
S.ROSSORE
Pisa
Calci
TENUTA DI
TOMBOLO
Pontedera
Ponsacco

Ligurian Sea

Livorno
SS1
I. di Gorgona
Castiglioncello
E80
Cecina
SS1
Mr.di Bibbona
Bolgheri
Castagneto C.
I. di Capraia
Populonia
Piombino
Portoferraio
Isola d'Elba
Porto Azzurro
Isola di Pianosa

Ligurian Sea

0   15 Mi
0   15 Km

N

Isola di Montecristo

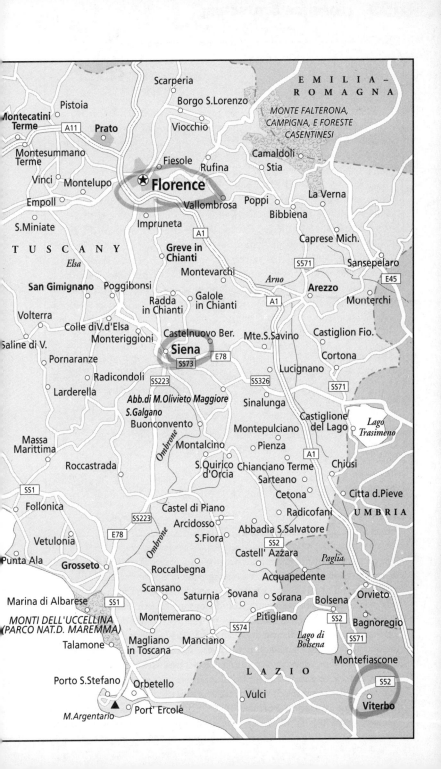

art + architecture

Look at any piece of art created in the past four centuries and you can pretty much guarantee that its creator was influenced in some way by the art that spewed forth from the Tuscany region during the Renaissance. We could go on and on (lord knows thousands of people before us have), but the heart of the matter, the thing you have to keep in mind while you're traipsing through the overstuffed museums and glorious piazza, is this: The men (and women! there were some women!) who worked in this region in the 15th and 16th centuries completely revolutionized the way the world looks at, thinks about, and makes art.

Of course, they didn't start from scratch. The artistic revolution of the Renaissance was inspired by Classical Roman art; Renaissance artists used math, science, and linear perspective to portray the human body more realistically, as artists had in Ancient Rome. Renaissance sculptors and painters wanted to stage a "rebirth" of Classical ideas, and the church and Tuscany's wealthy families, especially those Medicis you hear so much about, were huge supporters. The greatest collections of Renaissance art are housed in Florence's **Uffizi Gallery, Academy Gallery, Bargello Museum,** and **Museo San Marco,** as well as in Siena's **Pinoteca Nazionale,** but churches and cathedrals in even the smallest towns have impressive collections.

Mannerism took over from the Renaissance phase in the 16th century. Mannerist artists used brighter colors, and often elongated or otherwise distorted the human body, which was usually depicted in some kind of complicated pose. Michelangelo's *Holy Family,* in the Uffizi Gallery, is one of the best examples of the dramatic Mannerist style.

Cortona and San Gimignano, the gorgeous piazzas, where locals and tourists alike pass long summer evenings, make up for the lack of bars.

The first Tuscans were Etruscans, and their heritage is still visible today. The Etruscans touched ground here in the 9th century B.C., and Florence's Museo Archeologico and Cortona's Museo dell' Accademia Etrusca have outstanding collections of Etruscan artifacts. By the 4th century B.C., the Romans had taken over. Medieval Tuscany consisted of numerous independent (and feuding) city-states. Around 1000 A.D., the idea of democracy developed as merchants became wealthier and used that wealth to grab power from the fading feudal system, set up *communi,* or independent town governments. Of course, like most government takeovers, this wasn't an entirely peaceful process—there was feuding between the *communi* and the old nobility (who wanted to go back to the good ol' days of feudalism), as well as inter-*communi* feuding. But the guilds won out in the end, gathering up more and more wealth along the way, and by the 13th century, Tuscany was a wealthy region. It was during the 13th century that some of its most significant buildings were erected: Pisa's **Leaning Tower** and **Duomo,** Florence's **Duomo,** and Siena's **Town Hall.**

The 14th century brought tragedy in the form of the Black Death, which killed off half of Tuscany's population. But by the time the Renaissance arrived in the 15th century, Tuscany—and especially Florence—had rebounded. The rest of Europe realized that there was something incredible going on down here, and Florence became the cultural and artistic focal point of the continent. Between the mid-15th century and the mid-18th century, the enormously wealthy Medici family controlled Florence, and they commissioned many of the masterpieces we know and love today. The 16th century passed rather quietly—more Medicis, more art, not as many masterpieces. In 1860 Italy became a country and chose Florence as its capital in 1865, which didn't have the best results: The medieval walls and the Jewish ghetto were torn down to make room for more modern structures (kinda like when cities refurbish their waterfronts when they win the bid to hold the Olympics...). Luckily power shifted to Rome in 1871, before they could make too many more "improvements".

Tuscany was stomped all over by the retreating Nazi troops in World War II, and Florence was hit hard by bombs—all of its bridges, except the Ponte Vecchio, were blown away. They had barely had time to recover when they were hit again, this time by massive flooding from the Arno river, in 1966. Much of the city was covered in up to 20 feet of sludge and water (gross!), and thousands of works of art and literature were destroyed or severely damaged—8,000 paintings alone in the basement of the Uffizi were beyond help. Things have been fairly calm since then—no natural disasters, no manmade disasters, no government takeovers. Just tourists. Lots and lots of tourists.

getting around the region

Florence is the most sensible starting point for a trip to Tuscany. It's easy to get just about anywhere in the country from Florence, plus it has tons of hotels, great nightlife, amazing restaurants, and good train and bus connections throughout the region.

If you're looking for cheaper accommodations and restaurants, both Pisa and Siena are smart options. Fewer travelers choose quiet Lucca as their base. It doesn't have as much art or as many attractions as the more touristy Tuscan towns, but its peaceful, provincial, and friendly atmosphere is authentically Tuscan, and day trips, using Lucca as a base, are just as easy to orchestrate.

Tuscany is best navigated by car if you want to stop and enjoy the churches, vineyards, and views along the country roads, but you can see plenty by train or bus as well. The region has extremely good connections, and train and bus are both comfortable; and offer great views (though trains generally run more frequently).

At least three days in Florence is a must. Lucca, Pisa, and Siena can each be done in a day if you're rushing through—two days would be better. Cortona and San Gimignano can be done as day trips, but you'll miss out on their prime time—nighttime, when all the other tourists leave. Cortona and San Gimignano can only be reached by bus.

TRAVEL TIMES

All times by train.

	Cortona	San	Gimignano	Siena	Lucca
Florence	1:20	1:15	1:40	1:30	1:15
Cortona	-	2:45	2:00	3:30	3:00
San Gimignano	2:45	-	:30	2:30	1:30
Siena	2:00	:30	-	3:00	2:00
Lucca	3:30	2:30	3:00	-	:30

fLORENCE

Florence is a tightly packed, hectic, scooter-crazy hub of modern northern Italian life, simultaneously creating and smashing stereotypes. The masses that come here to bask in the glow of the city's Renaissance grandeur find its beauty matched, if not surpassed, by the lively and animated locals.

Yeah, we've heard it before, but the perpetually bronzed residents *do* look better in their clothes than the rest of us. What's worse, they love to flaunt it. Second only to Milan in fashion sense—and often more put-together, thanks to a less harried city life—person for person, Florentines make great eye candy. Men, women, gay, straight, no matter, you will have a field day falling into superficial love with so many beautiful Mediterranean people about. Girls, you may have trouble keeping your boyfriends from staring putty-jawed, 'cause the Italian women love to show skin, but there's no need to be prudish, with so many hunky Giorgios, Giannis, and Fabios around. In fact, while Italian girls rarely give the white-skinned Teva-wearing tourist boys the time of day, the salivating Latin macho men are hard-wired to shower foreign women with heavenly praise. They'll do anything to get you to stop and talk so they can look and talk.

Traditional elegance aside, there's also a scrap of attitude here. Many of Florence's MTV-influenced disaffected youth have wholeheartedly embraced the spirit of grunge chic. Though not as large as Bologna's or Rome's, Florence's large T-shirt-clad university population is *unmistakably* present, especially at **Cabiria Cafe** [see *bar scene,* below] in Piazza Santo Spirito, or scattered around nearby. While this is good news for the budget traveler in dirty cutoffs and sandals, there's definitely enough Gucci and Prada around to give anyone a complex. But have no fear, the abundance of cute boutiques along vias del Corso, Magazzini, and Tournabuoni and in piazzas della Republica and Signoría give you ample opportunity to upgrade your "wardrobe." The daily outdoor market at Piazza San Lorenzo is a must for bargain hunters and hagglers.

The city is also home to a seemingly endless list of foreign university programs (mostly American), and many centrally located hangouts are almost exclusively patronized by students from abroad. That, combined with the influx of family vacationers and package-tour sightseers, sometimes makes summer in Florence (particularly June through August) feel like an eerie burlesque, where you'll hear as many regional dialects of American English (not to mention Irish, British, and Australian) in one day as you might the rest of your life. If you want to avoid the throngs, plan on visiting in March or April or during the fall. Fewer visitors mean shorter lines, cheaper and more available rooms, and a generally mellower vibe. Cooler spring and fall temperatures are also a lot easier on the body, as the mercury during the humid summer months often hits 95° Fahrenheit and sometimes rises to 100°.

neighborhoods

Since the city itself isn't very big, and most tourist attractions are packed around **Piazza del Duomo** and the **River Arno**—which cuts the city into northern and southern areas, the latter known as **Oltrarno**—all can be easily and quickly reached on foot. While the major concentrations of popular sites such as **Santa Croce,** the **Uffizi,** and **Accademía** [see *culture zoo,* below, for all three] are huddled in *centro storico,* the "historic center," to the north of the river, the Oltrarno features the grandiose **Palazzo Pitti** [see *culture zoo,* below] and an array of cheap *trattorie.* Besides **Santo Spirito,** most piazza hangout areas are in the historic center. Though residential, venturing north on **Via San Zanobi** and west on **Via Palazzuolo** will lead you to some good cheap fare [see *eats,* below]. The **Ponte Vècchio,** lined with overhanging jewelry shops and packed tight with tourists, is the most famous and celebrated of Florence's eight bridges.

Finding an address in Florence can be a little tricky. The wacky Florentines use two separate street-numbering systems: one red, the other blue or black. Red is for shops and restaurants, and blue or black are for offices, hotels, and apartments and houses. In this chapter, the red addresses are noted by an "r" following the building number. It's really best to try to get a cross street or landmark if you're looking for an address that's on a long boulevard.

Though the bright orange public transportation ATC buses have extensive routes in the city center, it's best to use them for sights located outside the center such as **Piazzale Michelangelo** [see *great outdoors,* below]. That way you can save your money for the things that really count: gelati, beer, and cheap Chianti.

hanging out

Cheap nighttime—or *any*time—fun can be had chilling out in one of the city's many lovely squares. Piazzas surrounding the Duomo, Uffizi/Palazzo Vècchio, Santa Croce, and Santo Spirito are the most popular. Here you can spend hours nursing a drink with scores of locals and tourists, young and old alike. The piazza drinking scene is chatty and friendly, and if you want to speak English, you should have no problem talking with locals (keep in mind that Florentines are overexposed to the average tourist, so be fresh, dammit!). Florentines don't have the carousing spirit of the Brits or Germans, and even when the wine-drinking piazza crowds get rowdy, it's usually just harmless teenage hipsters on their scooters. In the most popular piazzas (Santo Spirito, Santa Croce, della Signoría, della Repùbblica), the flocks peter out around 3 or 4am most summer nights, and happy boozy people walk home through the deserted narrow streets—just as they've been doing for hundreds of years. With more than 20 statues, including a replica of Michelangelo's famous stud, *David,* the classic **Piazza della Signoría** *(3 minutes' walk south of the Duomo)* is a clear favorite for loafing. At all hours, swarms of sightseers snack on gelati, snap photographs, write postcards, and plan their next stop. During the day and early evening, **Piazza del Duomo** has pretty much the same crowd, but it clears out at night. Both piazzas are not bad for striking up conversations with locals. The restaurants, cafes, and endless stream of guitar and accordion serenaders found in the gray-stone **Piazza della Repùbblica** *(2 minutes southwest of the Duomo)* and the multicolored trade shops of the small **Piazza di Mercato Centrale** *(4 minutes east of the train station)* offer maximum relaxation, as do the steps of the **San Lorenzo** and **Santa Croce.** Via Tournabuoni, Via del Corso, and the bustling area around the mustard-yellow **Ponte Vècchio** contain hundreds of shops hawking everything from shoes, ties, underwear, posters/postcards, Duomo and Virgin Mary replicas, and Asian-made jewelry to cheesy Renaissance-style marble rip-offs. Some shops, such as **Giulio Giannini e Figlio** [see *stuff,* below], have been open for over a hundred years, and many have been in the same family for three and four generations. The **Oltrarno** is the area of Florence on the southern side of the river, where there are a number of good congregating spots led by **Piazzale Michelangelo,** which offers wonderful views of the north and west sides of the city, including the Duomo, Santa Croce, and the Ponte Vècchio. From this height you can also see **Piazza Santo Spirito,** the unanimous nighttime choice for Florentine hippie youth. With over a half a dozen outdoor restaurants and bars and perfect church steps that invite buskers, bongo players, hacky-sackers, and backpack-wielding students, this is *the* locals' evening and late-night choice for chilling, swilling, and debating. Take a relaxing stroll along either side of the Arno and enjoy wonderful views of the city and Ponte Vècchio from the Ponte San Trinità or Ponte Carraia. Located just a few minutes' walk from the Duomo, Volta di San Piero, Borgo Albizi, Via Pandolfini, and Via Faenza

five things to talk to a local about

Though friendly and helpful, Italians have a flair for making conversation that is reverential and deprecating at the same time.

1. **American Politics**—Since the U.S. alternately bombed and then saved Italy during WWII, Italians have been obsessed with the American system of politicking. The Clinton/Lewinsky thing didn't help matters; the Florida ballot debacle just made things worse.

2. **Stately Vespas vs. Moto Guzzi Crotch-Rockets**—Is it better to ride through the streets with your hair blowing gently in the wind or tear across the cobblestones striking fear into the hearts of tourists? Almost everybody's got a scooter, so almost everybody's got an opinion.

3. **Italian Food vs. Any Other Country's Food**—Bad news: It's a very short conversation. Good news: It's usually followed by a great Italian meal.

4. **Skyscrapers vs. Florentine Architecture**—Rail against decorative ornamentation in favor of glass boxes and see if you can start a fight.

5. **Italian Soccer vs. American Football**—"Ah, foootbaall, but yew Americans do not like foootbaall. We Italians looove foootbaall. We live for foootbaall. Ah, but yew have foootbaall too, 'de American kind. So fast and strong. I don't understand. But it is not like our kind of foootbaall. Gracefuull and elegant. How do you say, beautiful."

are all filled with eye-catching shops including sandwich bars, pubs, and a high density of travelers attracted by several Internet cafes and laundromats. With the buzz of the modish cafe **La Dolce Vita** [see *bar scene,* below], Piazza del Carmine is the chosen site of the Florentine in-crowd, while the strobe lights gleaming from **Meccanò** and **Central Park** [see *club scene,* below, for both], the two summertime discos located at the easternmost edge of Viale degli Olmi *(10 minutes west of the station)*, are like laser sirens beckoning clubbers from miles away. Basically, Florence is a safe city for wandering, with a few rules: Guys, while the city center is fine for being out late into the night, don't go hanging around alone on the edges of town. Girls, don't walk anywhere at night by yourself—it's best to be with a guy or hang with a crowd. Gay guys, if you choose to dress in a majorly flamboyant way, be careful walking by yourself really late at night or in secluded areas.

bar scene

Despite having a cafe with a fully stocked bar on every corner, Italy has never traditionally had a very big drinking culture—outside of wine with dinner, of course. But with the relatively recent advent of the Irish/English/American pub and the pub-grub menu of foods like hamburgers and french fries, the landscape of Italy's drinking culture has changed somewhat. Simply by their nature, these pubs are not terribly original places, but they usually have chill atmospheres and a good selection of drinks and are popular with sightseers and Florentines alike. Despite their stock of liquor (which means you can have either espresso and/or vodka), most cafes close down around 10pm, although some do attract a late-night crowd. *Vinerie,* which specialize in wines and also other liquors, and the pub-like *osterie,* which offer beer, liquors, and a menu that generally consists of five to 10 meats and pastas, cater to late-night crowds. Outside the foreigner-heavy spots, Florentine-style drinking holes are relaxed; rowdiness and table-dancing are rarities. Still, as casual as the bar scene is,

dante meets beatrice

If they're breathing, foreign girls will have no problem getting picked up in any one of the major piazzas or clubs—Italian men have homing devices for women that are "more active" than their relationship-minded Italian counterparts. For traveling guys, the relationship thing *is* a major stumbling block in scoring a short-term tryst with an Italian lady. Once they come of age, Italian women are usually attached to a boyfriend or in the presence of family, which prevents them from straying too far off the traditional courtship path. The truth is that this "modesty" is an ironclad social pretense grown out of a culture where naked women are displayed just about everywhere—buses, stores, magazines, TV ads, public sculptures, museums. See, once the Florentine female gets to really *know you,* she is almost always wildly "forward" and willing to show you that she's in the know. Guys: Crack the ice by being funny and smart. Be sure to look them in the eye—they can sniff out an unworthy scoundrel from miles away (not you, of course!). Once you have their attention, you gotta shower them with gifts, praise, and kindness, and let them have their way. And remember, it's a small window before you have to meet papa and start planning the ceremony. Scared yet? The best places to make the approach are in cafes, Internet cafes [see *wired,* below], museums, and, yes, church (actually, *après* church).

Florentines like to dress up when they go out, so be prepared to feel out of place if you go grungy.

One of the quickest places to get crowded is **Dublin Pub** *(Via Faenza 27r; Tel 055/293-049; 5pm-2am daily; No credit cards)*, a cozy, centrally located Guinness-sipping drinking hole. Here it's not uncommon for expats and travelers to hit the pints right at opening time. The Irish photos and Guinness memorabilia on the walls and hardy wooden stools and tables make this the most authentic of Florence's Irish pubs. The small and cozy quarters help warm up the bones in December and January, and in summer, the open front door allows spillout into the streets.

A 5-minute walk south of Il Duomo, **Angie's Pub** *(Via de' Neri 35r; Tel 055/239-82-45; 2pm and on daily; No credit cards)* is a mellow, communal pub stop where you can nurse your drink and management won't seem to mind. Drinks are cheap (around L6,000), and the menu includes burgers, hot dogs, and bagels that are amazingly tasty by any standard. The picnic tables and the small, narrow seating area can make you feel like you're on a submarine, which actually adds to the overall fun and friendly atmosphere.

Equally as relaxed but somewhat more wacky is **Public House** *(Via Palazzuolo 27r; Tel 055/290-530; 8pm-2am daily; V, MC, AE, DC)*, with an assortment of not-so-usual mobiles—tennis racket, school desk and chair, ancient horn, iron kettle, and more—suspended from the ceiling. Cleverly placed light sources create cool shadows, and flickering film projectors run a perpetual feed of nonsense video. But there's more than interior design smarts at work here. The small, intimate bar, west of the city center, is an economical place to drink (medium beer L7,000, cocktails L6,000 to L8,000, wine L3,000) and packs in crowds of both young and more "mature" Florentines.

From the late afternoon to wee in the morning, **Cabiria Cafe** *(Piazza Santo Spirito; Tel 055/215-732; 8:30am-1am Mon, Wed, Thur, till 2am Fri, Sat, closed Tue; No credit cards)* is crowded with cheery, backpack-wearing students and student types from the nearby university district who'd rather be chatting than studying. In the summer, chic herds press into the covered outdoor seating area, while the tiny bar area gets packed in the winter. Cocktails during happy hour—everyday 6 to 9pm—are a mere L6,000. If you stay long enough, the yummy finger food could be a good substitute for dinner.

The crowds of beautiful locals at **La Dolce Vita** *(Piazza del Carmine; Tel 055/284-595; 11am-2am Mon-Sat, 5pm-2am Sun, restaurant open 12:30-2:30pm/7:30-11:30pm Mon-Sat; AE, DC)*, easily the trendiest place in Florence, conjure up images of Rome's sleekly dressed movie stars on the Via Veneto in the '60s. There may not be any Fellinis or Mastroiannis here, but the bar's all-too-hip vibe justifies the cinematic name. Olive-skinned women in Prada dresses and knickers, men in dark jackets and Dolce & Gabbana shirts, and everyone in Luxotica and Ray-Ban shades. Big after-work crowds gather at this slightly-off-the-beaten-path (south of the Arno and west of *centro storico*) spot around 6:30pm, but outdoor seating keeps it from feeling too packed. The shiny, curved bar and the mirrored walls give the patrons enough ways to check themselves and each other out shamelessly.

The relatively new **Sant'Ambrogio Caffè** *(Piazza Sant'Ambrogio 7; Tel 055/241-035; 10am-2am daily; V, MC)* is among a new generation of stylized bar/cafes with artsy, minimalist decor including high ceilings, a weird red twisty sculpture, Rothko- and Braque-style paintings, Pottery Barn-like wood and steel furniture, a long wine list, and a casual atmosphere. A few blocks west of the Duomo, it's the perfect place for an afternoon drink while discussing evening plans, catching up on reading, or whipping off a few postcards. Just remember to move in slow, tempered motions.

At **Kikuya** *(Via de' Benci 43r; Tel 055/234-48-79; 7pm-2am daily; V, MC),* in *centro storico,* the operative words are "happy hour." Every night from 7 to 10pm, pints are L5,000. Tuesdays and Thursdays, there's over-amplified live cover music: Cat Stevens, Foreigner, Rolling Stones, and maybe even an Italian tune or two. The good pub grub—hamburgers, burritos, and sandwiches named after stops on the London underground—is cheap and satisfying. Good place to mix with the locals.

Hailed as the oldest American bar in Florence (circa 1962), the **Red Garter** *(Via de Benci 33r; Tel 055/234-49-04; Open daily; V, MC),* a few doors down from Kikuya, is an indefatigable party place. Part small-time casino, part wood-paneled love den, the Garter pulls in American thrill-seekers in droves. Share your stories with other travelers, talk about the good ol' U.S. of A., and bitch about slow Internet connections. It's amazing how the patriotic sentiment wells up after a few Buds. Check out the mini-wall memorial to Hollywood's great femme fatales, and dance to live music (of various grades) under a disco ball. Happy hour, Friday and Saturday 9 to 9:30pm. Beer L8,000 and cocktails L10,000.

LIVE MUSIC SCENE

While Florence showcases endless artistic and architectural treasures, its modern musical tradition, though lacking in originality, can make for entertaining evenings. Be prepared to hear scores of badly sung English-language covers. Florentines who go out to hear live music tend to gravitate toward jazz, blues, and folk, and the best places for quality tunes of this variety are Chiodo Fisso and Caffè La Torre. Most rock, hip-hop, and alternative bands play at BeBop, which has a virtual monopoly on the beer-drinking grunge groupie crowd. For up-to-date information on the latest gigs in the ever-changing music and club scene, pick up a copy of the biweekly *Zero55* at local music stores like **Music Center** and **Pica-dilly Sound** off of Via Cavour [see *stuff,* below, for both].

Since 1979, locals and tourists have been cramming the picnic benches of the centrally located **Chiodo Fisso** *(Via D. Alighieri 16r, two blocks south of the Duomo; Tel 055/238-12-90; 11am-2pm/8pm till late; No credit cards)* to listen to traditional and original Italian folk ditties played and sung by local talent. The handwritten menu changes based on what's in

fIVE-O

While Italy's immaculately clad *caribinieri*—Italy's royal police force—are notorious for looking the other way, they are fairly strict about public drug consumption. It's not something anyone wants to be stopped for, 'cause it is definitely, no-question-about-it, illegal. Other than that, the cops are pretty laid-back in Florence.

the kitchen, but they always have a nice selection of cheap sandwiches and pastas that'll fill ya up. Most drinks are a steep L10,000, but there's no cover.

On Thursdays, local guitar and blues performers hit the small stage of **Eskimo** *(Via de' Canacci 12r, 3 minutes south of the train station; 8pm-3am daily; No credit cards)* to the delight of the twenty-to thirtysomething crowd. The establishment, which moonlights as a cultural association, also hosts live Italian pop music (Fri-Sun), ethnic and Italian folk music (Mon), and readings (Wed). In the words of the bar's promo flyer, the space is "at the disposition of everybody who would like to show their photography, paintings, sculpture—for free." If you're in Florence long enough and you're looking for a gig, give it a shot.

Come early (10pm) or come late (1am)—you'll still have fun at **Caffè La Torre** *(Lungarno Cellini 65r, 10-minute walk west of the Ponte Vecchio, 15 from the Duomo; Tel 055/680-643; 8:30pm-5am daily; No credit cards).* Jazz, pop, rock, blues, and soul are uncorked night after night by talented artists with no cover, all out under the stars. After a few drinks, you'll be feeling the vibe and convinced that you were born to get up in front of the crowd and shake your groove thang, but don't tire yourself out too

RULES Of THE game

The age for drinking here is practically nonexistent, and you can pretty much go to any Florentine piazza and uncork a bottle of wine or beer. In fact, it's almost a cultural norm, especially on hot summer nights. If you don't get rowdy, you shouldn't have any problems (except for running out of booze too quickly). But except for clubs and large concerts and sporting venues, you're probably not gonna smell pot/hash fumes in the open air. This doesn't mean it never happens. Piazza San Spirito is reputedly the place where people snoop out buying ops. Needless to say, with jail time lurking as a possibility, care should be taken to avoid that other trip so brilliantly evoked by Dante....

much—you have to walk home, you know. Nice place to bring a date, if you've got one.

While the main draw of the overtly cheesy "American-style" **Red Garter** [see *bar scene,* above], right near the Duomo, is the chance to mingle with a sweaty American crowd, the second-best attraction is watching tireless performers entertain the even more tireless college-age audience with mostly English and American pop and the occasional Broadway show tune. The full bar doesn't hurt, either.

The stuffy basement bar **BeBop** *(Via dei Servi 76r; Tel 055/239-65-44; Music starts 10-10:30pm, open 6pm-1am daily but erratic; No credit cards),* two blocks from the Duomo, is *the* place for the heady genius of the local metalheads, garage bands, and blues dudes. The brighter rooms in the back with picnic-table seating make it a little easier to carry on a conversation over the angst-ridden guitar progressions. There's no cover, which means steep drink prices—cocktails are 16,000L—but you can get around that by splitting a bottle of wine for 30,000L. The crowd is a mix of grungy locals and even grungier foreigners. The music ain't great, but it's a fun time.

Every Tuesday and Thursday, **Kikuya** [see *bar scene,* above] lets the best local cover bands wail away at their English song repertoire in its cramped and musty side room. The Americans in the audience love to sing along, especially after happy hour. The splintery-wood, fully stocked bar in the main room keeps the mix of American-European tourists and locals in good spirits. The mood here is more hardcore than at the nearby teeny-bopperish Red Garter.

club scene

Italians love to dance, so naturally there are quite a few discos in the center of town. Unfortunately, many of these close during the summer, as towns-folk seek refuge from the heat in the large, open venues outside the city congestion (this is a trend all over Italy). If you're traveling during this period, it can be a bummer, but there are a few large outdoor dance arenas within walking distance of the center. Florentine clubs, though possessed by a major pop preoccupation, have the same mix of music—house, techno, hip-hop, '80s—that clubs everywhere share these days. The full range of clubdom is here, from punky and pierced to light and pop-y to sleek and exclusive. Clubs usually open between 10 and 11pm, with fashionable people arriving fashionably after midnight. Though Florence isn't known for its happening late-late-night scene, there's plenty of action around.

Space Electronic *(Via Palazzuolo 37; Tel 055/293-082; 10pm-2am daily, closed Mon in winter; 25,000L cover; V, MC, AE),* west of *centro storico* near Via Palazzuolo, is a teenager's wet dream. You can drink, groove, drink, do karaoke, drink, hit on opposite sex, drink—just like you're a real, grown-up adult. Happily though, the club is large enough to accommodate a slightly older crowd as well, including many local men eager to practice their English (and more) with the female tourists. Playing a mix of American pop, disco, and alternative, this place, ultramodern and thoroughly hip, provides a lot of good, clean fun.

florence bars clubs and culture zoo

BARS/CLUBS ▲
Angies Pub **37**
BeBop **23**
Cabiria Café **6**
Caffe La Torre **36**
Central Park **11**
Chiodo Fisso **28**
C.S.A. RK Indiano **9**
Dublin Pub **16**
Eskimo **14**
Full Up **31**
Kikuya **40**
La Dolce Vita **8**
Maracana **34**
Meccano **10**
Public House **13**
The Red Garter **39**
Sant'Ambrogio Caffe **32**
Space Electronic **12**

CULTURE ZOO ●
Academy Gallery **21**
Baptistery of San Giovanni **26**
Bargello Museum **30**
Basilica di San Lorenzo **18**
Basilica di Santa Croce **35**
Basilica di Santa Maria Novella **15**
Boboli Gardens **1**
Gallery of Modern Art **3**
Giotto's Bell Tower **27**
Il Duomo **25**
La Sinagoga di Firenze **33**
Medici Chapels **17**
Museo Archeòlogico **22**
Museo Casa di Dante **29**
Museo San Marco **20**
Museum of the Duomo **24**
Old Bridge **44**
Orsanmichele **42**
Palatine Gallery/ Royal Aprtments **4**
Palazzo Medici-Riccardi **19**
Palazzo Vécchio **41**
Pitti Palace Silverware Museum **5**
San Miniato Monte **37**
Santo Spirito **25**
Uffizi Galleries **42**

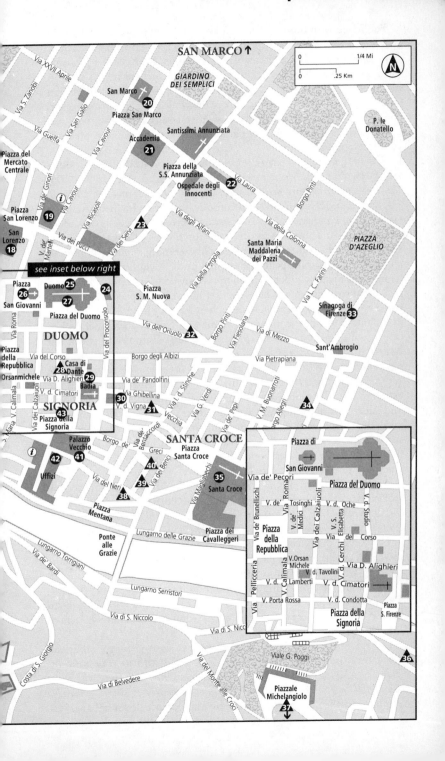

SAN MARCO ↑

Via XXVII Aprile

Via S. Zanobi

Via Guelfa

Via San Gallo

Via dei Ginori

Via Cavour

GIARDINO
DEI SEMPLICI

San Marco
20

Piazza San Marco

Accademia
21

Santissimi Annunziata

Piazza della
S.S. Annunziata

Ospedale degli
Innocenti
22

Via Laura

P. le
Donatello

Piazza del
Mercato
Centrale

Via Cavour

Via Ricasoli

Via de' Servi

Via degli Alfani

Via della Colonna

Borgo Pinti

Piazza
San Lorenzo
19

San
Lorenzo
18

V. de' Martelli

V. dei Pucci

23

Santa Maria
Maddalena
dei Pazzi

PIAZZA
D'AZEGLIO

Via della Fogola

see inset below right

Piazza
26
San Giovanni

Duomo **25**
27

24

Piazza del Duomo

Via Roma

DUOMO

Via del Proconsolo

Piazza
S. M. Nuova

Via dell'Oriuolo **32**

Borgo Pinti

Via Fiesolana

Via di Mezzo

Sinagoga di
Firenze **33**

Sant'Ambrogio

Piazza
della
Repubblica

Via del Corso

Orsanmichele

Casa di
28 Dante

Via D. Alighieri **29**
Badia

Borgo degli Albizi

Via Pietrapiana

Via de' Pandolfini

Via Ghibellina **30**
V. d. Vigna **31**

S. Maria – V. V. Calimala

Via dei Calzaiuoli

SIGNORIA

Piazza della
Signoria
43

Via de' Bentaccordi

Vecchia

Via I. d. Stinche

Via G. Verdi

Via de' Pepi

V. M. Buonarroti

Borgo Allegri

34

Palazzo
Vecchio
41
42

Borgo de'

Greci

SANTA CROCE

Piazza
Santa Croce

Via de' Benci

35
Santa Croce

Uffizi

Via del Neri

39
38

40

Via Magliabechi

Piazza
Mentana

Ponte
alle
Grazie

Lungarno delle Grazie

Piazza dei
Cavalleggeri

Lungarno Torrigiani

Via de' Bardi

Lungarno Serristori

Via di S. Niccolo

Via di S. Nicco

Costa di S. Giorgio

Via di Belvedere

Via del Monte alle Croc

Viale G. Poggi

Piazzale
Michelangiolo
37

36

Inset (below right):

Piazza di

San Giovanni

Via de' Pecori

Piazza del Duomo

Via de' Brunelleschi

V. de' Tosinghi

Via de' Medici

Via Roma

Via dei Calzaiuoli

V. d. Oche

V. S. Elisabetta

V. d. Studio

del Corso

Pelliceria

Piazza
della
Repubblica

V. Calimala

V.Orsan
Michele

V. d. Lamberti

V. d. Tavolini

V. d. Cerchi

Via D. Alighieri

V. d. Cimatori

V. Porta Rossa

V. d. Condotta

Piazza della
Signoria

Piazza
S. Firenze

Scale:
0 — 1/4 Mi
0 — .25 Km

Publicized with omnipresent handouts and wall flyers, **Full Up** *(Via della Vigna Vecchia 23-25r; Tel 055/293-006; 11pm-4am Mon-Sat, closed June-Sept; No cover before midnight, 15,000L after; V, MC, AE)* is probably the most popular disco in the city center among foreigners. Digs are a bit more formal, and the music is somewhat more diverse and soulful than Space Electronic, which means a more discriminating and mature clientele. The piano bar is another big draw. If you don't want to venture outside the city, and still want to get a taste of Italian discos, this is probably your best option.

About 10 minutes west of the city center, near Viale degli Olmi, **Central Park** *(Via Fosso Macinante 2 at Parco delle Cascine; Tel 055/253-505; Bus 1, 9, 26, 27 to Parco delle Cascine; Midnight-late Fri and Sat; 25,000L cover w/one drink)* is a slightly more upscale, slightly larger, just-as-popular version of its competitor, Meccanò, located across the street. Five outdoor dance floors and drinks stations keep the hordes of powdered twentysomething Florentines occupied till early morning. If you're important enough, then you can spend the evening in the exclusive, elevated V.I.P. section and literally "talk down" to the sweaty dancing serfs below. If you only want to dance, come late; the first hour or two, people like to just stand around in groups and check each other out.

Itching to dance the mambo? Wanna grind with a local? Get decked out in your cleanest, sexiest (preferably pressed) duds and check out **Maracana** *(Via Faenza 4r; Tel 055/210-298; Midnight-4am Tue-Sun, restaurant open 8:30-11:30pm, closed mid-June through Sept; 20,000L cover; MC, V)*, where you can funk to the Latin rhythms right in the center of town. The circular sunken dance floor invites shoulder-rubbing and table-dancing. When you get tired, there's ample seating, a huge bar, and a big video screen showing anything from Caribbean beach scenes to soccer matches to rock videos. On the way in or out, make sure to pay homage to the re-created Amazon jungle courtyard with an artificial creek and three very real, very loud peacocks.

If the dancing girls in high boots and low-cut dresses don't attract you to Florence's most renowned nightclub, **Meccanò** *(Viale degli Olmi 1; Tel 055/331-371; 11pm-6am Tue-Sat, restaurant 9:30pm-midnight; 20,000L cover w/one drink; AE, DC, EC, MC, V)*, about 10 minutes west of city center, then maybe the chance to sip martinis at the *Alice in Wonderland*-like table and chairs will. For those who aren't turned on by the dancing girls, there are also beefy dancing guys (sometimes dressed in chains) doing their best Chippendales renditions. Multiple dance floors—a couple indoors, a couple out—provide enough grooving options to keep even the headiest music snob happy, though Italians always seem to migrate toward mainstream pop.

If you're feeling adventurous and want to wear grungy clothes and slamdance to hardcore live music, **C.S.A. RK Indiano** *(Plaza dell'Indiano 1; Tel 055/307-210; Bus 17c to Piazzale J. Kennedy, then walk down Viale dell Indiano to the end; 10:30pm till whenever; 7,000L cover; No credit cards)*, the most active *centro sociale* in Florence, is your Shangri-La.

While these "social centers" are technically illegal, they're usually over-looked by the fuzz, so you probably won't end up being deported. (Can't say we didn't warn you.) At Indiano, punk and rock bands fill up the large squatter space nightly with brain-splitting original tunes. The low entrance fees and economical drink prices (remember, these guys are communists) attract tattoos, dyed hairdos, and piercings worthy of the Lower East Side, Haight-Ashbury, and Venice Beach.

ARTS SCENE

▶▶VISUAL ARTS

It's understandable why modern visual arts in Florence have not advanced very far. It's just too damned intimidating living in the shadow of the great masters, going up against Michelangelo and Botticelli. There are, however, several modern art refuges—all in the city center—trying to make a difference.

A good place to start is Florence's premier modern art gallery, **Galleria Pananti** *(Piazza Santa Croce; Tel 055/244-931; 10am-7pm, ticket office closes at 6:30pm Mon-Sat; 12,000L admission, 10,000L students),* east of the city center on Piazza Santa Croce. The museum-worthy exhibitions feature photography, paintings, prints, sculpture, and mixed media by Andy Warhol, Jackson Pollock, and other postmodern American masters.

A second stop is **Ken's Art Gallery** *(Via Lambertesca 15r-17r; Tel 055/239-65-87; 10am-8pm Mon-Sat; www.italink.com/kensgallery),* where exhibits include an ever-intriguing rotation of large abstract canvases and figurative sculpture created by local and national artists.

Visit the unusual tandem galleries **Art Point Black** *(Borgo Allegri 14; Tel 055/247-97-97; 3:30-7:30pm Mon-Sat),* showcasing abstract paintings, and **Art Point Red** *(Borgo Allegri 5),* which specializes in figurative etchings and sculpture. Just a few blocks east of Santa Croce.

You can watch the artists paint colorful, eye-pleasing abstract canvases at the mom-and-pop **Art Studio Karan** *(Via Borgo Albizi 9; Open late mornings & afternoons daily).*

Across Ponte alle Grazie, **Il Bisonte—International School of Specialization in Graphic Arts** *(Via San Niccolo 24r; Tel 055/234-25-85; www.ilbisonte.it)* often holds shows by the students; the large ceramics of **Akronos Gallery** *(Via dei Sapiti 18r; Tel 055/218-695; 11am-8pm Mon-Sat)* show a deep knowledge of art and fine craftsmanship.

▶▶PERFORMING ARTS

If you're looking for English-language film, theater, and classical music, you won't have trouble finding things that interest you here. Though Florence does not have as many city-sponsored events as Bologna or Rome, there's plenty to do, especially from June to September. The tourist offices [see *need to know,* below] have a ton of info on what's going on, as well as schedules for particular venues.

While most theaters feature American films, unless you know Italian, the dubbing makes it a little hard to *sapére.* To the relief of cineplex-aholics,

FESTIVALS AND EVENTS

The biggest festival in Florence is the **Maggio Musicale Fiorentino** *(May-June; Biglietteria Teatro Comunale; Corso Italia 16; Tel 055/211-158; 10am-4:30pm Tue-Fri, 9am-1pm Sat; www.maggiofiorentino.com),* now in its 62nd year. The festival presents an array of opera, dance, and classical music performances at the **Teatro Communale di Firenze, Teatro della Pergola,** and other venues in the city.

Dissolvenze *(June; Arena Estiva del Poggetto, Via M. Mercati 24b; Information at FLOG Centro Flog Tradizioni Popolari, Via Maestri del Lavoro 1; Tel 055/422-03-00; Tickets 8,000L per night)* is a cultural and ethnic festival featuring live music, dance, and film.

Mondo Culto! *(June-Sept; Information Tel 0339/726-37-32)* shows a series of "cult movies and incredible strange music."

On June 24, the city goes wild with **Festa di San Giovanni,** the celebration of Florence's patron saint. Parades and fireworks salute the angelic Saint John, and the crowds crunch onto the shores of the Arno. Another feature of the festival is the final match of the **Calcio Storico Fiorentino**—a competition exhibiting the medieval version of soccer played in a sandlot with small goals. Set in Piazza di Santa Croce, the spectator-filled bleachers become a rowdy foot-stomping exhibition of partisanship, chanting, and cheers. The intense action, with players diving in every direction in the sand pit, gives you a glimpse of how psychotically hard soccer was back in the day. Purchase tickets, usually around 15,000L, at the box office on Via Faenza 139r *(Tel 055/210-804).*

Odeon Cinehall *(Piazza Strozzi; Tel 055/214-068)* plays original-language films every Monday, and **Cinema Astro** *(Piazza San Simone, near Santa Croce; Closed Mon)* shows English-language films every other night.

The church of **Orsanmichele** *(Via Calzaiuoli; Info 055/477-805, box office Via Faenza 139r; Tel 055/210-804),* which plays host to the Florence Sinfonietta, is acoustically one of the best places to hear classical music—its Romanesque dome facilitates rich orchestral sounds.

Concerts of the Regional Tuscan Orchestra are often presented at **Santo Stefano al Ponte Vècchio.** Many other churches also have a regular schedule of free and low-cost concerts.

Teatro Communale di Firenze *(Corso Italia 16; Tel 055/211-158; Box office open 10am-4:30pm Tue-Fri, 9am-1pm Sat and one hour before curtain; Shows Oct-Apr; V, MC, AE, DC)* is Florence's main theater, with both opera and ballet seasons running from September to December and a concert season from January to April. Tickets cost 40,000L to 200,000L for the opera, 24,000L to 50,000L for the ballet, and 35,000L to 100,000L for concerts.

Teatro della Pergola *(Via della Pergola; Tel 055/247-96-51; Box office 9:30am-1pm/3:30-6:45pm Tue-Sat, 10am-noon Sun; Tickets 18,500-45,000L)* and **Teatro Verdi** *(Via Ghibellina 99; Tel 055/212-320; Box office 10am-7pm Tue-Fri, 10am-1pm Sat; Tickets 10,000-35,000L)* also hold many theatrical and operatic performances. If you're interested in catching a show, stop by the theaters to obtain a program of the current offerings. While the Pergola is slightly larger, both theaters are elegant spaces with gold-trimmed columns and walls, excellent acoustics, and balconies.

gay scene

The gay scene in Florence is not as out as in Milan or Rome, but, save for a few stares, there should be no major problems. Still, use common-sense caution [see *hanging out*, above]. Strangely, for a city built on the glory of such Renaissance artists as Leonardo da Vinci and Michelangelo Buonarroti—both now thought to have been less than straight—there aren't many gay-oriented stores and clubs in town. In fact, the entire country's gay scene lags behind that of other Western nations. The reason for this may lie in the fact that relatively few Italians have had extensive travel experience, and a fiercely religious, and somewhat suffocating, patriarchal family dynamic remains rooted in the Italian culture. Even so, most youth-oriented bars and clubs have an open, casual atmosphere that can be gay-friendly, even if they don't present themselves as gay establishments.

SMOKE IT UP

Anti-smoking stalwarts are going to have a tough time in Florence (and the rest of Italy). For many Italians, smoking is as much a reflex as taking a cup or two of espresso after dinner, and people do it in all the public places: train stations, trains, airports, planes, buses (occasionally), and hotel lobbies. The thing is, Italians seem to smoke (as they do basically everything else) to *enjoy*—not to stay calm or deal with stress. It's a social custom, and they make it so natural, it's like they were born with a cig poised on their lips.

If you speak Italian, the local branch of the national organization **ArciGay/Lesbian** *(Via San Zanobi 54r; Tel 055/476-557)* is a good source of information on the city, gay life, and gay-friendly eateries. For more info, check out a copy of **_Quir,_** Florence's bimonthly gay and lesbian magazine—available at ArciGay/Lesbian and newsstands, or **_www. dada.it/caffe/gay._**

The chic-est discopub in Florence, gay or otherwise, **Piccolo Café** *(Borgo Santa Croce 23r, right off Piazza Santa Croce; Tel 055/241-704; 5pm-late daily; No credit cards)* has neon and chrome accents and a stunning reflective, metallic ceiling, festooned with phallic light bulbs jutting out. Umm, what do you think? Though it opens at 5pm, the cute Italian boys (and girls) don't start showing up until 11pm. That's okay, 'cause they don't plan to go home early—and neither should you. Rotating art shows by gay and lesbian artists, live DJs. Drinks about 10,000L.

Owned by the same proprietors as Tabasco Bar, the slightly softer **Tabasco Disco** *(Via dei Pandolfini 26r, 5 minutes southeast of the Duomo; People arrive 11:30pm and stay till late, daily; 15,000-25,000L cover w/one drink; No credit cards)* has only one tiny dark room and lets in women (many others don't), but that doesn't mean you can't get raucous. Monday nights there's cabaret and karaoke in the Flamingo Pub on the top floor, where they also have theme nights and videos playing music, movies, and porn from all over the world. Thursday through Sunday, DJs spin house, hip-hop, and techno, while on other nights they succumb to their fetishes with Madonna, Gloria Estefan, Natalie Imbruglia, and other girl pop-drops.

Hey boys, you looking for daaark rooooms, for *molto* undergrowwwnd, for a place to be lascivious and naughty? Let your libido romp at seedy **Tabasco Bar** *(To find this secret spot, from Piazza della Signoría, with your back to Palazzo Vecchio, walk straight to Via Vacchereccia, then take a right on Vicolo Malespini, which heads into Piazza di Santa Cecilia; Tel 055/213-000; 10pm-6am Fri, Sat, till 4am other nights; 15,000L cover w/one drink; No credit cards),* reputedly the oldest gay discobar in Italy. No girls are allowed, so there's no fear of cross-gender cruising mistakes, and you can cut loose. The irony is, it's only steps from Piazza Signoría, yet straights, local or tourist, just don't know about it. Getting dressed up ain't that important, just gotta be gay and...oh, you know. Very hardcore.

The famous cruising skin bar **Crisco** *(Via San Egidio 43r; Tel 055/248-05-80; 9pm-3am Mon, Wed, Thur, Sun, till 5am Fri, Sat, closed Tue; No credit cards)* is the only match for Tabasco Bar, though it has a cleaner reputation and is slightly more upscale. Which may mean that you'll meet an Italian man with very deep pockets who will want to buy you and keep you for his very own. The clean dark rooms, tempting clientele, and gyrating tunes will keep your senses satiated.

La Vie en Rose *(Borgo Allegri 68r; Tel 055/245-860; Noon-3pm/7-11pm Mon-Sat; 10,000-22,000L per entree; No credit cards)* is a gay-friendly restaurant that is a great couples' place. Cozy, romantic, soft music, candles on the table—what could be better for a date? The nouveau-Italian dishes like risotto with fresh herbs (10,000L), asparagus and brie pie (10,000L), and fresh pasta with eggplant and cherry tomatoes (12,000L) are good on the stomach and the wallet. Rotating art exhibitions from local artists adorn the walls.

A number of hotels cater to the gay community, including the comfortable **Hotel Morandi alla Crocetta** *(Via Laura 50; Tel 055/234-47-47, Fax 055/248-09-54; 240,000L double; V, MC)* and the quiet, centrally located **Hotel Pensione Medici** *(Via de' Medici 6; Tel 055/284-818, Fax 055/216-202; 200,000L double; V, MC)*. Both are simply decorated with medium-size rooms (most with full bath, TV, phone, and drinks bar) and serve continental breakfast.

One of the best places to relax and look at hunks is in the **Florence Bathhouse** *(Via Guelfa 93r; Tel 055/216-050; 2pm-1am Sun-Fri, 2pm-2am Sat, summer hours: 3pm-1am Sun-Fri, 3pm-2am Sat)*, an exclusively gay sauna.

CULTURE ZOO

Towers and churches and frescoes and sculptures and about a billion Madonnas with Child: We've been salivating over the Renaissance-inspired masterpieces for centuries, and there's enough on every square block of Florence to keep you occupied for another century. There isn't much that hasn't been said except: Don't tire yourself out so much that you can't join in the late-night festivities. All of the following powerhouses are within walking distance of each other.

Galleria degli Uffizi (Uffizi Galleries) *(Loggiato degli Uffizi; Tel 055/238-865; Bus 23, 71 to the Duomo; 8:30am-9pm Tue-Fri, till midnight Sat, till 8pm Sun, holidays, Closed Mon; 12,000L admission):* The Uffizi, which was given to the city of Florence in the 18th century, is one of the world's greatest collections of Renaissance and Classical art—it's like an art history slide show brought to life. Most of the works in the collection are by Florentine masters who were commissioned by the immensely wealthy Medici family, who also donated this very museum to the city in the 18th century. To see everything in the Uffizi's 45 rooms would take months—luckily the place is organized into rooms by periods, schools, and artists, so you easily find what interests you. Rooms 2 to 6 are dedicated to Tuscan Gothic art. There are lots of works by Giotto and Cimabue, particularly noteworthy are Giotto's *Maesta* (room 2) and his *Pieta* (room 6). Rooms 7 to 10 are all about the Early Renaissance; in room 7, look for Piero della Francesca's double sided paintings with the Duke and Duchess of Urbino on one side, and representations of their virtues on the other. The highlight of room 8 is Fra Filippo Lippi's *Madonna and Child* and *Coronation of the Virgin*. Rooms 10 to 14 house some of the Uffizi's best stuff: the Botticelli collection. The crowds tend to gravitate towards the most famous ones like *The Birth of Venus* and *Allegory of Spring*. Room 15 holds works by a young Leonardo Da Vinci such as *The Annunciation* and the unfinished *Adoration of the Magi*. The

12 hours in florence

1. Climb up the Duomo or Giotto's tower (don't fall off) to see stunning views of the red tile on the ancient city.
2. Eat gelati at **Gelatería Carabe** or **Vivoli** [see *gelati wars*, below]—miss this and you might as well not come.
3. Chill on the steps at San Spirito and Piazza della Signoría (*con vino*)—you'll never want to leave.
4. Browse the tombs in Santa Croce—be careful to not walk on the buried guys.
5. See the *David* at the **Accademía**—The dude is truly spellbinding—don't let the crowds bother you! [see *culture zoo*, below].
6. Club at **Full Up, Meccanò,** or **Central Park** [see *club scene*, above, for all three]—do it all in one night and spin with delight.
7. Eat at **Sabatino, Contadina,** or **Mercato Centrale** for must-eat, cheap Italian soul food [see *eats*, below, for all three].
8. Take a hike up Piazzale Michelangelo—super views of the Duomo, Santa Croce, and Ponte Vècchio will take you out of time.
9. Visit the Botticelli room in the **Uffizi**—take a seat and salivate at how ahead of his time Botticelli was [see *culture zoo*, below].
10. Shop at San Lorenzo market and in the shops on Via Tournabuoni and near the Duomo and Palazzo Vècchio—Prada, Gucci, Versace: Just save some money for dinner, Miss Trump.

octogonally shaped tribune, with its mother-of pearl-domed ceiling, was designed to hold the Medici family's favorite works. Most notably, the room contains a reproduction of the *Venus of the Medici*. Look for the ancient Roman statues in the Arno Corridor; Michelangelo's bright Mannerist painting, The Holy Family, in room 25; Parmigiano's Madonna of the Long Neck *in room 29;* Raphael's Madona of the Goldfinch in room 26; and Titian's *Venus of Urbino* in room 28.

Galleria dell' Accademia (Academy Gallery) *(Via Ricasoli 60; Tel 055/238-86-09; Bus 1,6,7,11,33,67,68 to Via Alamanni; 8:30am-9pm Tue-Fri, till midnight Sat, till 8pm Sun, holidays, Closed Mon; 12,000L admission):* Admit it, you're like all the rest—you're just coming here to see *David*. The city of Florence commissioned the enormous marble statue from Michelangelo when he was just 29. Until 1873 it stood outdoors in front of Palazzo Vecchio, but was replaced by a copy when the original was moved to the domed room where it now stands for fear of wear and tear and vandals doing rude things to *David's* privates. But don't just see the naked guy and leave—the Museum also contains many other famous Michelangelo marble masterpieces (like *St. Matthew* and *The Four Prisoners,* which were intended for Pope Julius II's tomb) plus an important collection of paintings by 15th and 16th century Florentine bigshots like Botticelli, Pontormo, Fra Bartolomeo, Filippino Lippi, and Ghirlandaio. The Accademia was the first school in Europe to teach art techniques, founded in 1563. Many of the students' works from over the years are still displayed in the museum (just past the *David* room).

Pitti Palace and Boboli Gardens *(Palazzo Pitti; Tel 055/265-171; Bus D to Stazione galleria; 9am-6:30pm daily; 4,000L admission)* The enormous palace and the sprawling gardens, which are on the south side of the Arno, a few blocks from the river, make up a massive multi-museum palace which is one of Europe's greatest artistic treasure troves. The beautifully laid out and manicured garden is a great place to spend an afternoon wandering and recovering from sightseeing burnout. The gardens were begun in 1550, but not completed until a century later, and not open to the public until 1766. You'll find statues from the masters scattered among the greenery, plus an old amphitheater where, legend has it, the first ever opera performance was held. Bring a picnic lunch and wander from the perfectly clipped formal box hedges to the paths among the more wilder parts of the gardens.

The Palace houses three separate museums:

Galleria Palatina (Palatine Gallery) and Royal Apartments *(Palazzo Pitti; Tel 055/238-86-14; 8:30am-9pm Tues-Fri, till midnight Sat, till 8pm Sun, holidays, Closed Mon; 12,000L admission):* This is the most visited of the Pitti's museums. The paintings in the gallery are hung as they were during Baroque times—in no particular order, just piled on top of each other. Rooms 1 to 5 have gorgeous ceiling frescoes by Pietro da Cortona—remember to look up. The greatest works in the museum are by Raphael and Titian, but Botticelli, Perugino, Tintoretto, Caravaggio, Van Dyck, and Rubens also pop up. The Royal Apartments, which are included on the same ticket as the Galleria Palatina, is the former home of the Kings of Savoy. Built in the 17th century, these lavish Baroque rooms are frescoed by various Florentine artists and contain many Medici portraits, plus some works by Caravaggio and del Sarto. The rooms are ornately decorated, with lots of gold, flower prints, and rich colors—everything you'd expect from royal chambers.

Galleria D'Arte Moderna e Galleria del Costume (Modern Art Gallery and Costume Gallery) *(Palazzo Pitti; 8:30am-1:50pm daily; 12,000L admission):* If you're on a tight schedule, don't feel bad about skipping the Modern Art Gallery. The collection contains mostly Italian works from between 1784 and 1924, which was not exactly a high point in the history of Italian art. If there has to be a highlight, it's the 19th century collection of works from the *macchiaioli* school, which was Italy's

by foot

This walk, from **Piazzale Michelangelo** *(Bus 13 to Michelangelo)*—the Oltrarno square with picturesque views of the city—to the lovely **Piazza di Santo Spirito,** the nighttime outdoor hangout point for stylish university kids, is best from Thursday through Saturday, when all the locales are open for business.

Before you start, examine the beautiful vista. Santa Croce's right in front, the Duomo to the left, and the onion-domed Tempio Israeletico on the right. On a clear day, beyond the temple, in the camel hump formed by the rolling hills in the distance, you can make out Fiesole, a pretty town overlooking Florence. Go down the ramp, cross the road, and begin to make your way down through the terraced park. You should cross the road several times. At the bottom of the park, you will be at Piazza Giuseppe Poggi and in front of you will be the fine Poggi Tower. From there take a left on Via San Niccolo and head to **Mr. Jimmy's Bakery** [see *eats,* below], where you can fuel up on yummy American baked goods. Next, hang a right on Via dell'Olmo, then a left on Via dei Renai to the river, where you make a left toward the central city. Follow the river just past the Ponte Grazie and look across to the Florence Boating Club and mini-soccer field located on the grassy bank of the river. Dinner at the club is reputedly wonderful, but entrance is for members only. Continue to **Ponte Vècchio** [see *hanging out,* above], where you can inspect the jewelry stands, and then make a left on Via Guicciardini to Palazzo Pitti, a mega-museum with pretty **Boboli Gardens** [see *culture zoo,* above]. At Piazza San

answer to French Impressionism (notice, though, that you've never heard of the *macchiaioli* school before...). There are also a few Camille Pissarro paintings in the gallery. The Galleria del Costume (Costume Gallery), included in the same ticket, holds the Royal family's collection of costumes from the late 18th century to the early 20th century. The costume collection is actually more interesting than the modern art collection.

Museo degli Argenti (Silverware Museum) *(Palazzo Pitti; Tel 055/238-87-10; 8:30am-1:50pm Tues-Sat, Closed Mon; 4,000L admission):* Yeah, that's right, we said silverware museum. It's actually a really cool, quirky stop. This museum holds more than just silverware. The collection, which illustrates the enormous wealth the Medici family accumulated over the centuries, holds the family's collection of ancient glassware, rare and valuable silver, jewels, carpets, vases, furniture, and ivory. Come see how the other half lived in the 15th century.

Bargello Museum *(Via del Proconsola 4; Tel 055/238-86-06; Bus 14, 23 to Via Alamanni; 8:30am-1:50pm Tues-Sun, Closed Mon; 8,000L*

Felice take a left onto Via Mazzetta to the Piazza di Santo Spirito, where you can have a hard-earned drink at **Cabiria Cafe** [see *bar scene,* above].

This second tour brings you down one of the best shopping streets, Via del Corso, takes you to a series of bars, and leaves you off at Piazza della Signoría. Start at about 5pm at **Festival del Gelato** [see *gelati wars,* below]. Buy a cone and start strolling down Via del Corso. You'll pass a number of men's and women's clothing stores as well as **Fiori dei Tempo** [see *stuff,* below], a great antique jewelry shop. Continue straight on Borgo d'Albizi (which is what Corso is now called) to Volta di San Piero, where you can snack on a delicious sandwich at **Antico Noe** [see *eats,* below]. From this first stop, continue on Borgo d'Albizi and make a right on Via Verdi. The ugly fascist Post Office building should be on your left and you should pass an *Agencia Ippica* (off-track betting) on the right: Don't do it! Continue on Via Verdi for several blocks till it turns into Via de Benci and you come to **Kikuya** [see *bar scene,* above]. Go in and have a drink. Next stop in at the **Red Garter** [see *bar scene,* above] and say hi to the American sightseers. Now continue on and make a right on Via de' Neri where you'll find **Angie's Pub** [see *bar scene,* above], which serves some pretty good bagels. Drop in for a final beer. If you want, stay for another, or head up the road to Piazza della Signoría (it will be on your right) and rejoice in coming to the end of your journey.

Admission): The Bargello is housed in a fortress which was built in 1225 and was once a prison. The museum is dedicated to Florentine Renaissance sculpture and contains some of the world's greatest works by Michelangelo and Donatello. The Michelangelo room, on the first floor of the three floor gallery, holds his famous drunk *Bacchus,* and another different and smaller *David.* Among Donatello's best works in the museum are two of his *John the Baptist's,* his *St. George,* and his bronze *David.* You'll find it a few blocks east of Piazza della Signoria.

Museo San Marco *(Piazza San Marco 1; Tel 055/238-86-08 or 055/238-87-04; Bus 1, 6, 7, 10, 11, 17, 20; 8:30am-1:50pm daily, ticket office closes at 1:20pm, Closed 1st, 3rd, 5th Sun of month and 2nd and 4th Mon of the month; 8,000L admission):* The most amazing thing about this museum is the walls of the cells where the monks once lived—they're covered in allegorical frescoes and frescoes of scenes from the life of Christ by Fra Angelico, which are thought to be some of his greatest works. Seeing the building itself, with its courtyards and cloisters, is worth the price of admission. The library, which was designed by Michelozzo, is one of Europe's first public libraries.

Cathedral of Santa Maria del Fiore (Il Duomo) *(Piazza del Duomo; Tel 055/230-28-85; Bus B, 14, 23, 36, 37,71 to the Duomo; 10am-5pm Mon-Sat, 1pm-5pm Sun; free admission):* After the Vatican and St. Paul's in London, Florence's Duomo is the world's third largest church in Italy. It's Florence's most important monument, and tallest building, and the enormous dome dominates the city. Work was begun on the Cathedral in 1296, but the finishing touches weren't put on the building until 1887 when the existing facade was erected (the original had been demolished a few centuries before). From the 4th century the Church of Santa Reparata stood on the site, but was demolished to make way for the Duomo. Take a look in the **crypt** *(10am-5pm Mon-Sat, Closed for religious holidays)* of the Cathedral to see some of the remains and artifacts of the old church. The surrounding area is full of tourists bumping into each other straining to look up at the Cathedral. The inside is just as spectacular as the exterior, although it's decorated with a greater simplicity. The enormous dome of the Cathedral, the **Cupola del Brunelleschi** *(8:30am-7pm Mon-Sat, Closed Sun),* was designed by Filippo Brunelleschi and built between 1420 and 1434, and remains his greatest masterpiece. It was revolutionary at the time it was built, since he used no scaffolding or supports—instead, he devised a system of interlocking stones, so that the levels of the dome rose in progressively narrower concentric circles. Climb the 463 steps of the dome to get a closer look at Vasari's recently restored *Last Judgment* frescoes, and for fantastic views of the city.

Camponile (Giotto's Bell Tower) *(Piazza del Duomo; Tel 055/23-28-85; Bus B, 14, 23, 36, 37,71 to the Duomo; 8:30am-4:50pm daily Apr-Sept, 9am-5:20pm daily Oct, 9am-4:20pm daily Nov-Mar, Closed Jan 1, Easter, Sept, Christmas; 10,000L admission):* Adjacent to the cathedral is the Bell Tower, just six meters shorter than the Cathedral's Dome. The tower, which was built with the same white, green, and pink Tuscan marble as the Cathedral, was designed by Giotto in 1334. He worked on it until his death in 1337, but had only completed the first level, when Andrea Pisano took over the building and the carving of the reliefs along the bottom. There are fewer stairs to climb than in the Dome, and the view of Florence is just as beautiful from the Camponile.

Baptistery of San Giovanni *(Piazza del Duomo; Tel 055/23-28-85; Bus B, 14, 23, 36, 37,71 to the Duomo; 8:30am-7pm Mon-Sat, till 1:30pm Sun, holidays; 5,000L admission):* The Baptistery was built a few centuries earlier than the Duomo (making it the oldest building in Florence) and is named after the city's patron saint, John the Baptist. It's three sets of bronze doors, called *The Gates of Paradise,* are possibly the most famous in the world, and are definitely one of the most visited sights in Florence. The south door, sculpted by Andrea Pisano, is the oldest one and depicts scenes from the Life of St. John the Baptist. The north door represents scenes from the New Testament and was sculpted by Lorenzo Ghiberti with the help of his pupil, Donatello. The east door, which depicts scenes from the Old Testament, is considered to be Ghiberti's masterpiece and took him 27 years to finish. The doors you see now are good copies of the originals, which, after being restored, are on display in the Museum of the Duomo [see below]. Many people overlook the inside of the Baptistery after seeing the doors, but the Baptistery ceiling, with its golden and colorful 13th century mosaics of the *Last Judgment,* is also worth seeing.

Museum of the Duomo *(Piazza del Duomo; Tel 055/23-28-85; Bus B, 14, 23, 36, 37, 71 to the Duomo; 9am-6:50am Apr-Oct, 9am-6:20am Nov-Mar, Closed Sundays):* The Museum of the Duomo, located on the north side of the Cathedral, is full of sculptures and reliefs which have been removed for safekeeping from the Duomo, the Campanile, and the Baptistery over the years. The museum holds many masterpieces of Renaissance sculpture, including an unfinished Pietá by Michelangelo, which was carved near the end of his life. The main highlight of the museum is Ghiberti's original Gates of Paradise, which was removed from the Baptistery and recently restored. The courtyard of the museum is where Michelangelo is said to have carved David.

Basilica di San Lorenzo *(Piazza San Lorenzo; Tel 055/216-634; Bus 1, 6, 7, 11, 17, 33, 67, 68, to Piazza San Lorenzo; 7am-noon/3:30pm-6pm daily):* Since the Basilica di San Lorenzo was the Medici family's parish church, it has one of the most richest and ornately decorated interiors—don't let the simple unfinished facade fool you. The Renaissance Classical church was rebuilt by Brunelleschi in 1419 and contains several Michelangelo and Donatello masterpieces. Donatello's two bronze pulpits with reliefs depicting Christ's Passion and Resurrection, which he didn't begin work on until he was 74 years old, are in the center of the nave—they were completed by the artist's students after his death. Brunelleschi's Old Sacrsity, which is on the left side of the church, holds a few Medici tombs and doors designed by Donatello, which depict religious figures and martyrs. Exit the church, and to the left you will find the entrance to the **Biblioteca Medicea Laurenziana** *(Tel 055/210-760; 9am-1pm, Closed Sun)* and one of the world's most famous staircases, both designed by Michaelangelo.

Medici Chapels *(Piazza Madonna degli Aldobrandini 6; Tel 055/238-86-02; Bus 1, 6, 7, 11, 17, 33, 67, 68 to Piazza San Lorenzo; 8:30am-4:50pm Tues-Sat, till 1:50pm Sun, Closed Mon; 13,000L admission):* The entrance to San Lorenzo's most visited section, the Medici Chapels, is around the corner in the adjoining piazza. The Chapel, holds the New Sacristy and Michelangelo's Night and Day, and Dawn and Dusk funerary statues, which recline over the tombs of two of the Medici's. In an adjoining room, a series of 56 drawings, attributed to Michelangelo, were discovered on the walls and restored.

Orsanmichele *(Via dei Calzaiuolo at Via Arte della Lana; Tel 055/284-944; Bus 22, 36, 37; 9am-noon/4pm-6pm daily, Closed 1st and last Mon of each month; Free admission):* First this was a church, built to show the world how rich the city of Florence and its merchants were.

Then, in some bizarre twist, it was a food market, and then a church again. The exterior walls have 14 niches, which hold statues of each guild's patron saint. There was somewhat of a competition between the guilds to come up with the biggest and best statues, which were done by top artists of the time including Donatello, Giambologna, and Ghiberti. Most of the statues now standing in the niches are replicas—the originals have either been moved to the Bargello or the small **museum** *(9am-1:30pm daily; Free admission)* inside of the church.

Museo Archeologico (Archeological Museum) *(Via della Colonna 38; Tel 055/23-575; Bus 6, 31, 32 to Colonna; 9am-2pm Tues-Fri, 9pm-midnight Sat, till 8pm Sun, Closed Mon; 8,000L admission):* Florence has more than Renaissance art, you know. This excellent gallery of Egyptian, Etruscan, Greek, and Roman collections, like just about everything else in the city, started in the hands of the Medici's. Highlights include the Wounded Chimera, a 5th century B.C. Etruscan bronze lion with a goat sticking out of its back, and an Egyptian chariot made of bones and wood.

Museo Casa di Dante *(Via Santa Margherita 1; Tel 055/283-343; Bus B, C, 9; 10am-4pm Mon and Wed-Sat, 10am-2pm Sun; 5,000L admission):* It's not clear whether Dante actually lived in this house or if its just a typical period house turned museum. This place, which is four blocks north of Piazza della Signoria, probably won't be much of interest to anyone who's not a fan of the 13th-century Florentine poet. The house is mostly filled with photocopies of documents, Dante books, and other random and not-very-interesting souvenirs.

La Sinagoga di Firenze *(Via Farini 4; Tel 055/234-66-54; Bus 6, 31, 32; 10am-1pm/2pm-5pm Sun-Thur, 10am-1pm Fri Apr-Oct; 10am-1pm/2pm-4pm Sun-Thur, 10am-1pm Fri Nov-Mar; Closed Jewish holidays; 6,000L admission):* Though badly damaged in World War II, this 19th century synagogue, has since been restored to its Spanish/Moorish–style glory. You'll find it in the northeastern part of the city two blocks west of Borgo Pinti—look for the big green copper-covered dome. There's a small museum upstairs which tells of the history of Judaism in Florence and has many religious objects from as far back as the 17th century.

Ponte Vecchio (Old Bridge): What, you want me to go see some old bridge? Yes. This is the oldest, and most famous, bridge in Florence—the *only* one that survived the bombing in WWII. Located a few steps southwest of the Uffizi Gallery, it was built in 1345, but a bridge has existed on this site since the 10th century. The bridge used to be full of butchers and food shops, but gave way to goldsmiths and jewelers in the 16th century. The bust in the center of the bridge is of Benvenuto Cellini, a famous 16th century Florentine goldsmith. Beware of swarming tourists.

Palazzo Vécchio *(Piazza della Signoria; Tel 055/276-84-65; Bus 23, 71 to Piazza della Signoria; 9am-7pm Mon-Wed, Fri, Sat till 2pm Thur, 8am-1pm Sun, holidays; 10,000L admission):* Also known as the Palazzo della Signoria, this has been Florence's town hall since it was completed in 1332. The palazzo's 308 foot tall bell tower was originally used to warn Florentines of danger, or to call them to town meetings. When entering the Palazzo from Piazza della Signoria, you'll see a frescoed courtyard with a fountain designed by Vasari. Up the elegant staircase is the Salone dei Cinquecento (Hall of the 500), which is the highlight of the palazzo and is where government meetings used to be held. Most of the frescoes on the salone's walls are by Vasari, although the first ones were by Leonardo da Vinci, but were almost immediately destroyed because of the materials he used. Michelangelo's statue of Victory, which was originally intended for Pope Julius II's tomb, is nearby. The Sala dei Gigli (Hall of the Lilies), on the third floor, is one of the palazzo's most beautiful rooms and is full of golden tinted frescoes of Roman statesmen by Ghirlandaio.

Palazzo Medici-Riccardi *(Via Camillo Cavour 1; Tel 055/276-03-40; Bus 1, 6, 7, 11, 17, 33, 67, 68; 9am-1pm/3pm-6pm Mon-Tues and Thurs-Sat, 9am-noon Sun; 6,000L admission):* The Medici family lived in this old place before they made the move to the Palazzo Vecchio in 1540. The fairly simple brown stone palazzo was designed by Michelozzo in the mid-15th century after a design by Brunelleschi was rejected for being too extravagant. The entrance windows were a later addition designed by Michelangelo. There's a courtyard with walls made of Roman fragments, but the main attraction is the Medici Chapel, covered with mid-15th century frescoes by Benozzo Gozzoli.

Basilica di Santa Croce *(Piazza Santa Croce 16; Tel 055/244-619; Bus B, 13, 23, 71 to Santa Croce; 8am-12:30pm/3pm-5:45pm Oct-Easter; 8am-5:45pm Easter-Oct, till 1pm Sun, holidays; Free admission):* Come pay your respects—the Basilica di Santa Croce is filled with the elaborate tombs of many of the most famous dead Florentines. Michelangelo's tomb, the first one on the right side of the church, attracts the most visitors. He was first buried in Rome, and his body was later moved back to his hometown. Dante is not actually buried in his tomb, which is instead just a monument to the writer. Galileo was finally buried here (over in the left-hand aisle) more than a century after his death, when the Catholic Church finally decided to let him have a Christian burial.

Basilica di Santa Maria Novella *(Piazza Santa Maria Novella; The 055/215-918; Bus 6, 9, 11, 36, 37, 68 to the Piazza; 7am-12:15pm/3pm-6pm Mon-Fri, 7am-12:15pm/3pm-5pm Sat, 3:30pm-6pm Sun; Free admission):* This green and white marble church was built between 1279 and 1357 by the Dominicans, whose followers used to strip and whip themselves in front of the altar (now that's devotion!). It now contains many of Florence's most important works of art. The interior is spacious and elegant, yet a bit gloomy. The walls of the Tornabuoni Chapel, behind the high altar, are completely covered with Ghirlandaio's fresco cycle of The Life of John the Baptist. The Chapel of Filippo Strozzi contains Filippino Lippi's frescoes of the Life of St. Philip. The Spanish Chapel, located behind the Cloister, is decorated with scary frescoes of the success of the Dominicans and the themes of salvation and damnation.

Santo Spirito *(Piazza di Santo Spirito; Tel 055/210-030; 8am-noon/4pm-6pm Thur-Tues, 8:30am-noon Wed; Free admission):* Welcome to the most important church on the less visited southern side of the Arno. A church has sat on the site since the 12th century, but Brunelleschi redesigned it in 1444 and the simple flat facade, which remains unfinished, was added in the 18th century. The two aisles in the interior of the church are separated by two rows of elegant Corinthian columns designed by Brunelleschi. More interesting than the church of Santo Spirito is the Piazza di Santo Spirito [see *hanging out,* above], a great hangout spot.

San Miniato Al Monte *(Via Monte alla Croci; Tel 055/234-27-31; 8am-noon/2pm-7pm daily during Summer, 8am-noon/2:30pm-6pm daily during Winter):* Legend has it that after St. Miniato was executed on the bank of the Arno, he walked up the hill with his head and died on the spot where this pretty little church stands, far off the tourist path. To find it, head south a few blocks from Piazzale Michelangelo along Viale Galileo Galilei. The Romanesque church was began in the 11th century and took two centuries to finish. Much of the interior is decorated with marble—the floor is paved with marble symbols of the zodiac—and there are faded frescoes on the walls.

modification

Unlike Bologna and Rome, Florence is not home to hordes of grunge and punk kids, so there aren't a lot of places to get the Florentine spin on body art. At the centrally located **Alchimista** *(Via dei Ginori 49r; Tel 055/268-305; 1-7:30pm Mon-Sat, but call ahead; No credit cards),* the English-speaking tattoo artists will be more than willing to hip you up with original body designs.

great outdoors

In recent years, the Florentine footballers have become a feared and respected team capable of defeating perennial powerhouses Juventus of Turin and Inter of Milan. Florence's fans are equally as feared, commonly believed to be the rowdiest of Italian soccer hooligans. Tickets are available at the **Chiosco degli Sportivi** *(Via Anselmi, off Piazza della Repùbblica; Tel 055/292-363)* for as little at 30,000L.

The congested nature of Florence's layout does not leave much green pasture. For grassy lawn to spread out on, go to the gardens near Fortezzo da Basso or **Boboli Gardens** [see *culture zoo,* above]. A good jog can be had by running west along the Arno, and you'll definitely get a workout hiking up to Piazzale Michelangelo [see *by foot,* above].

stuff

If your baggage isn't too heavy already, you can do well shopping in Florence, best known for hand-tooled leather goods and decorative paper and stationery. With a host of good outdoor markets led by the profusely leathery-smelling **Mercato di San Lorenzo** *(Piazza di San Lorenzo;*

9am-7pm daily), which specializes in belts, wallets, jackets, bags, jewelry, and ties, you will be able to find lots of interesting gifts.

The bohemian **Mercato La Loggia** *(Via dei Neri; 8am-7pm Thur-Sun)* has clothing, foreign handcrafted jewelry, and drums, while the market at **Sant'Ambrogio** *(Piazza Ghiberti, open weekday mornings and some afternoons)* is a pack rat's dream: Old books, light fixtures, postcards, and assorted household goods are hawked by the stall keepers. Remember, always bargain for a lower price when shopping at the markets. Many vendors will knock off 10 to 20 percent when they see you're interested (but not *too* interested).

▶▶LEATHER

For years, the very clever Santa Crocians have been making and selling beautiful handcrafted leather goods to foreign visitors through the **Scuolo del Cuoio** *(Piazza Santa Croce 16; Tel 055/244-533; 10:30am-12:30pm/3-6pm Mon-Sat Apr-Oct, 9am-12:30pm/3-6pm Sun; closed Mon Nov-Mar; leatherschool@leatherschool.it; AE, V, MC)*. The bags and jackets are beautiful, but they are expensive, so you'll probably need to settle for crafty change purses or lipstick or cigar holders.

▶▶HOT COUTURE

If designer clothing is your thing, get your butt to Via Tournabuoni, home of the major boutiques such as Gucci and Ferragamo. There are also a lot of local shops you won't find elsewhere. For shoes galore, head to **Paoli** *(Via Calzaiuoli 21r; Tel 055/239-69-27; 10am-7:30pm, closed Sun; AE, V, MC)* or **Di Varese** *(Via Cerretani 49; No phone; 9am-1pm/4-7:30pm, closed Sun; AE, V, MC)*. There's also a bunch of shoe and clothing stores along Via Nazionale and Via del Corso.

Even if you don't love hats, you'll have a ball trying on local designer Antonio Bramini's handmade inventions at **La Nuova Modistera** *(Via Chiara 15r; Tel 055/282-02-94; 10am-1pm/2:30-7:30pm daily; V, MC)*.

▶▶THRIFT

For cheap, hip vintage boy and girl duds, **Used Clothing Store** *(Borgo Pinto 37r; No phone; 10am-6:30pm Tue-Sat; No credit cards)* is your answer.

▶▶GLAM

If you're looking for beauty aids, then makeup superstore **Profumeria Internazionale** *(Via Cavour 104r; Tel 055/239-69-61; 2:30-7:30pm Mon, 9:30am-7:30pm Tue-Sat, closed Sun; AE, V, MC)* will make you gape. Home to Christian Dior, Yves Saint-Laurent, Chanel, Clarins, and Helena Rubinstein products as well as lots of perfume and makeup samples. Look for the cellulite creams and tanning products not available in the U.S.

▶▶GIFTS

Since 1856, **Giulio Giannini e Figlio** *(Piazza Pitti 37r; Tel 055/212-621; 9:30am-7:30pm Mon-Sat, till 7pm low season Oct-Apr, closed Sun year-round; AE, V, MC)* have been handcrafting marbleized paper, greeting cards, and stationery.

The nifty notebooks, diaries, and other paper products at **La Tartaruga** *(Borgo Albizi 60r; Tel 055/234-08-45; 9am-7:30pm Tue-Sun,* *closed Mon morning, 10:30am-6pm last Sun of the month; No credit cards)* are made only from recycled paper.

You won't find just knickknacks at **Giraffa** *(Via de Ginori 20r; Tel 055/283-652; 9am-1pm/3:30-7:30pm Tue-Sat, closed Mon morning, Sun; V, MC)*, a unique store full of lava lamps, ceramics, scented candles, bags, key chains, planners, notebooks, bubble lamps, picture frames, soap, plastic inflatable furniture, and candle holders.

And finally, the mosaic-covered ceramics and lamps of **Frammenti** *(Via de' Pandolfini 11r; Tel 055/243-59-69; 10am-12:30pm/4-7:30pm, closed Sat in summer; No credit cards)* should not be missed.

▶▶BOUND

The Paperback Exchange *(Via Fiesolana 31r; Tel 055/247-81-54; 9am-7:30pm Mon-Fri, 10am-1pm/3:30-7:30pm Sat, closed Sun Apr-Oct, closed Mon Nov-Mar; papex@dada.it; V, MC, AE)* is absolutely the best English-language bookstore in Florence, boasting neatly arranged sections of books by Italian writers and books about Italy, as wells as mysteries, poetry, travel guides, romance novels, and philosophy. It also sells used books and is a good place to post notices and get information.

The English-owned **After Dark** *(Via del' Ginori 47r; Tel 055/294-203; 10am-2pm/3:30-7pm Mon-Sat, closed Sun; V, MC, AE)* also has some new and used English-language books, though it's better known for magazines.

The ubiquitous **Feltrinelli International** *(Via Cavour 12-20; Tel 055/219-524; www.vol.it/icone; V, MC, AE)* has a fair selection of both new releases and classics.

▶▶TUNES

Two of the best places to get used CDs and records are the **Music Center** *(Piazza Duomo 15a; Tel/Fax 055/211-538; 9am-7:30pm Mon-Sat, 11:30am-7:30pm Sun; AE, MC, V)* and the small, more relaxed **Picadilly Sound** *(Piazza San Marco 11; Tel 055/211-220; 9am-8pm Mon-Sat, closed Sun; V, MC, AE)*. Both stores carry the full range, from Coltrane to Britney Spears. But, sorry, no bootlegs.

€ats

Don't listen to anyone who says things like, "Florence has great museums, but the food isn't that great." If anybody says this, you have free license to knock them on the head. With an active university population, an endless flood of sightseers, and choosy locals who love fresh food, eating in Florence can be disappointing *only* if you settle for tourist dives. Otherwise, it should be top-notch. From bread to meats to pasta to fruits to vegetables, there's no reason here to settle for anything that isn't bursting with natural goodness.

Nightlife here begins with a late dinner, which winds its leisurely way through first and second courses, wine, dessert, espresso...add the casual service, and dinner can easily take an hour and a half, two hours, or more. Most spots are packed with large crowds around 8:30 or 9pm.

gelati wars

If you're human, you'll succumb to at least one gelato (ice cream) a day. Though it's very good, **Vivoli** *(Via Isola delle Stinche 7; Tel 055/292-334)*, the most famous *gelatería* in Florence, doesn't have the best stuff. For that, go to the real gurus at **Gelatería Carabe** *(Via Ricalosi 60r; Tel 055/289-476; Open daily; No credit cards)* who bring a slightly sweeter, more robust Sicilian flair to their scoops. With over 60 flavors, **Festival del Gelato** *(Via del Corso 75r; Tel 055/294-386; Open daily; No credit cards)* easily wins the prize for most varieties. They're particularly strong on fresh fruit flavors such as pineapple, lemon, strawberry, and blackberry.

▶▶**CHEAP**
Tight budgeters will melt on entering **Mercato Centrale** *(Piazza di Mercato Centrale, next to San Lorenzo; 9am-7pm daily)*, a huge two-story fresh food market a short walk north from the Piazza del Duomo.

For the best bread and focaccia and good slices of pizza, go to **Il Fornaio** *(Via Faenza 39r; Tel 055/215-314; 8am-8pm daily; No credit cards)*, near the train station. They also specialize in cannolis, eclairs, tarts, pies, and cakes, for a morning or afternoon snack.

Gran Caffè San Marco *(Via Cavour 122; Tel 055/215-883; No credit cards)* prepares pizza in slices with bundles of different toppings a few blocks northeast of the city center near Piazza San Marco and Accademía.

A quick take-out lunch of pasta or vegetables can be had at **Il Pirata** *(Via del' Ginori 56r; Tel 055/218-625; 9am-8pm Mon-Sat; 8,000L for a lunch's worth of pasta; No credit cards)* or **Chiaroscuro** *(Via del Corso 36r; Tel 055/214-247; No credit cards)*, both in the city center.

Since 1872, hordes of local workers have been coming up to Piazza del Mercato Centrale and crowding into **Nerbone** *(First floor of Mercato Centrale, make immediate left at Via S. Antonio entrance; 7am-7pm Mon-Sat; 6,000-12,000L per entree; No credit cards)* at lunchtime for sizzling, rich dishes of gnocchi, tagliatelle, sausage, or fried potatoes. Seating is across the way at communal booths. The food's so good you probably won't need to sit very long. One of Florence's secrets.

Imagine fresh rolls crammed with fresh meats, cheeses, and veggies. Think it'll taste good? *Duh.* A few steps from the Duomo, **Antico Noe** *(Volta di San Piero 6r; Tel 055/234-08-38; 8am-midnight, sandwiches till*

9pm daily; closed Sat for two weeks in August; 6,000-10,000L per entree; No credit cards), the best sandwich shop in Italy, has 17 panini on the menu to choose from, or you can get one custom-built just for you. The Vegetarian, with spinach, pepper, eggplant, mushrooms, and artichoke, is scrumptious, as is the turkey, brie, and sun-dried-tomato hero. Warning: Highly addictive.

The falafel sandwiches at **Il Nilo** *(Volta di San Piero 9r; No phone; Noon-midnight Mon-Sat; 6,000 Lper sandwich; No credit cards)* aren't award winning and neither are the gyros, but they are cheap, quick, and filling, and you can't find this sort of Middle Eastern takeout anywhere else in Florence. Across the vaultway from Antico Noe [see above].

Don't get **Trattoría Sabatino** *(Borgo San Frediano 39r; Tel 055/284-625; 18,000L full meal w/wine, dessert; No credit cards),* on the south side of the Arno over the Ponte alla Carraia, confused with the world-famous Sabatini's. Here, you'll sit next to strangers in a more traditional, communal setting decorated with mint-green walls and plastic tablecloths. The menu changes every day and offers some of the most delicious, economical grub in town. First courses are about 4,500L and seconds go between 5,000L and 8,000L. It's patronized by lots of hungry blue-collar worker types who look like they don't have a woman at home to cook for them.

With paper and pencil, Florence's health-conscious write their orders down from the chalkboard menu at **Il Vegetariano** *(Via delle Ruote 30r; Tel 055/475-030; Lunch and dinner Tue-Fri, dinner only Sat, Sun, closed Mon; 12,000L fixed menu; No credit cards)* and anxiously await the big portions of seitan, pasta, and tofu. The lack of meat doesn't mean the dishes aren't rich and filling as hell. The desserts are downright ambrosial. Kind of a hike (north of city center), but worth it: The garden in the back is as cool, green, and crunchy as the friendly, left-leaning crowd. One of Florence's best.

There are very few things better than knowing that you can get a first course, a second course, and wine, and pay less than 18,000L. With an awesome, prix-fixe menu, that's the case at **Trattoría Contadina** *(Via Palazzuolo 69/71r; Tel 055/238-2673; 8-11pm Mon-Sat; 15,000L fixed menu; No credit cards).* If you're staying in the center, it's well worth the 15-minute walk. If you're staying near the station, you'll probably become a regular.

With pastas at 7,000L, *ribollita* (a traditional Tuscan soup) at 5,000L, most meats at 9,000L, and lemon sorbet for 4,500L, it's a no-brainer that by 9pm you've got to fight for a table at **Trattoría La Casalingha** *(Via dei Michelozzi 9r; Tel 055/218-624; Noon-3pm/7-9:45pm Mon-Sat, closed Sun; V, MC, AE, DC),* probably the Oltrarno restaurant most popular with sightseers. There's another location at Borgo Tegolaio 5r.

The teddy bear of a baker who owns **Mr. Jimmy's** *(Via San Niccolo 47, Oltrarno; Tel 055/248-09-99; 10am-8pm Thur-Sun; No credit cards)* is a savior for all the yearning-for-bagels backpackers. He's also a clever businessman. Besides bagels, he offers Rice Krispies treats, apple pie (extraordinary), carrot cake (tremendous), cheesecake, chocolate cake, chocolate-chip cookies, and an assortment of muffins. Mr. Jimmy even delivers, so you can have some American-style goodies sent to your hotel.

▶▶**DO-ABLE**

Despite its name—**Osteria dei Pazzi** (pazzi means crazies) *(Via dei Lavatori 3r; Tel 055/234-48-80; Noon-3pm/7-11pm; 12,000-20,000L per entree; No credit cards)*—you won't go bonkers eating their x-tra yummy pastas and quaffing their fine wines. In fact, with its large outdoor seating area, you're crazy not to try it out. Just to the east of the city center.

A longtime crowd-pleaser near the central market, **Cellini** *(Piazza del Mercato Centrale 17r; Tel 055/291-541; Noon-3pm/7:30-11pm Thur-Tue, closed Wed; 12,000L; No credit cards)* has a fixed tourist menu with pasta/meat for 18,000L and brick-oven pizza from 8,000L to 14,000L, making it great for afternoon or evening hunger pangs. Half-liter of wine is 6,000L. The great piazza atmosphere is free.

▶▶**SPLURGE**

Locals and foreigners alike converge on **Il Barroccio** *(Via della Vigna Vecchia 31r; Tel 055/211-503; 7-11pm Thur-Tue, closed Wed; 24,000-35,000L per entree; AE, V, MC)*, a smallish, centrally located, elegant *trattoria*, to sample traditional dishes like asparagus *alla parmigna,* and *pollo alla cacciatora.* The artichoke salad is served over a bed of *rucola* (arugula), a favorite green of the Italians. Pastas are a smart light-dinner option at 8,000L to 12,000L. There's a good assortment of inexpensive wines, and the attentive wait staff is all smiles.

Weird name, weird water theme, weird little running fountain built into the translucent floor, and a weird-but-excellent mix of pastas, curries, grilled vegetables, and crêpes. The fun of the two-story **Hydra** *(Canto de' Nelli 38r; Tel 055/218-922; Noon-3pm/7:30-11pm; 20,000-40,000L per entree; AE, V, MC)*—besides the glowing blue ceilings—is that it doesn't fit into the common mold. The handiwork is the product of an imaginative local lady whose next idea is to move the restaurant upstairs and put a pizzeria downstairs. After dining here, a few blocks northeast of the Duomo, you can only wish her success.

crashing

With so much tourist fuss, Florence's hotel owners don't have to do much to attract visitors—usually an empty room that isn't astronomically priced will suffice. The result is that there are not many low-cost budget hotels (many *call* themselves budget), and it's almost impossible to get a single for under 54,000L or a double for under 145,000L. The good news is that there are a ton of clean hostels and a few campgrounds full of groovy people. But even with this bounty, there are still times—generally between May and September—when there aren't enough beds to go around. Make reservations if you can, and definitely *don't* waltz into town late on a Friday or Saturday without a room, 'cause it might end up costing you a bundle.

▶▶**CHEAP**

The benefits of the congested, dusty **Camping Italiani e Stranieri** *(Viale Michelangelo 80; Tel 055/681-19-77, Fax 055/689-348; Bus 13 to*

florence eats and crashing

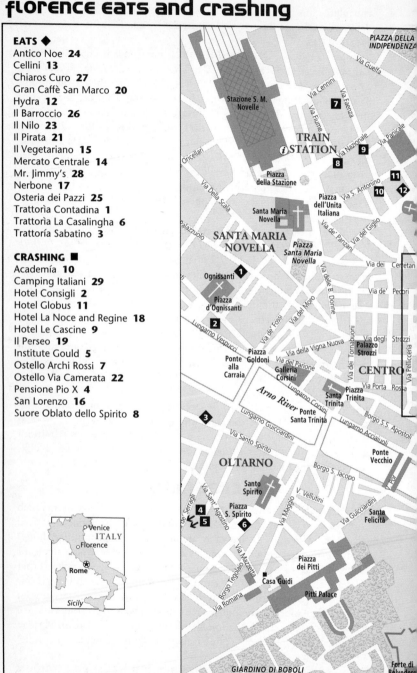

EATS ◆
Antico Noe **24**
Cellini **13**
Chiaros Curo **27**
Gran Caffè San Marco **20**
Hydra **12**
Il Barroccio **26**
Il Nilo **23**
Il Pirata **21**
Il Vegetariano **15**
Mercato Centrale **14**
Mr. Jimmy's **28**
Nerbone **17**
Osteria dei Pazzi **25**
Trattorìa Contadina **1**
Trattorìa La Casalinga **6**
Trattorìa Sabatino **3**

CRASHING ■
Academía **10**
Camping Italiani **29**
Hotel Consigli **2**
Hotel Globus **11**
Hotel La Noce and Regine **18**
Hotel Le Cascine **9**
Il Perseo **19**
Institute Gould **5**
Ostello Archi Rossi **7**
Ostello Via Camerata **22**
Pensione Pio X **4**
San Lorenzo **16**
Suore Oblato dello Spirito **8**

ITALY
Venice
Florence
Rome
Sicily

PIAZZA DELLA INDIPENDENZA
Via Guelfa
Via Cennini
Via Faenza
Stazione S. M. Novelle
Via Fiume
7
Via Nazionale
Via Panicale
TRAIN STATION
Oricellari
9
Via S. Antonino
11
8
Piazza della Stazione
10 **12**
Piazza dell'Unita Italiana
Via Della Scala
Santa Maria Novella
Via de' Panzani
Via del Giglio
Palazzuolo
SANTA MARIA NOVELLA
Piazza Santa Maria Novella
Via dei Cerretan
Via dei B. Donne
Via dei Pecori
Ognissanti **1**
Piazza d'Ognissanti
Lungarno Vespucci
Via de' Fossi
Via del Moro
2
Via della Vigna Nuova
Via dei Tornabuoni
Via degli Strozzi
Palazzo Strozzi
Via Pellicceria
Piazza Goldoni
Via del Parione
CENTRO
Ponte alla Carraia
Galleria Corsini
Lungarno Corsini
Via Porta Rossa
Piazza Trinita
Santa Trinita
Arno River
Ponte Santa Trinita
Borgo S.S. Apostoli
3
Lungarno Guicciardini
Lungarno Acciaiuoli
Via Santo Spirito
OLTARNO
Ponte Vecchio
Borgo S. Jacopo
Santo Spirito
V. Vellutini
de' Serragli
Via Sant'Agostino
4
Piazza S. Spirito
5
Via Maggio
Via Guicciardini
Santa Felicità
6
Via Mazzetta
Borgo Tegolaio
Piazza dei Pitti
Via Romana
Casa Guidi ■
Pitti Palace
GIARDINO DI BOBOLI
Forte di Belvedere
ⓘ Information

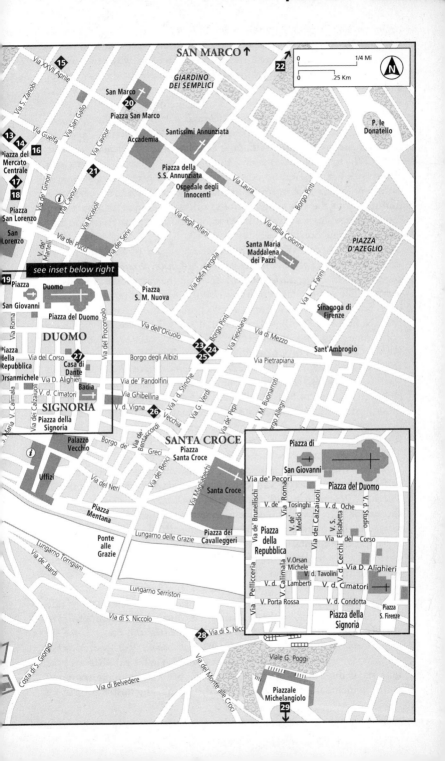

SAN MARCO ↑

GIARDINO
DEI SEMPLICI

22

0   1/4 Mi

0   .25 Km

N

Via XXVII Aprile

15

Via S. Zanobi

San Marco

20

Piazza San Marco

P. le
Donatello

Via Guelfa

Via San Gallo

Santissimi Annunziata

Accademia

13
14
16

Piazza del
Mercato
Centrale

21

Via dei Pucci

Via Cavour

Via Ricasoli

Piazza della
S.S. Annunziata

Ospedale degli
Innocenti

Via Laura

Borgo Pinti

17
18

Piazza
San Lorenzo

San
Lorenzo

V. de' Ginori

i

Via Cavour

Via dei Servi

Via degli Alfani

Via della Colonna

Santa Maria
Maddalena
dei Pazzi

PIAZZA
D'AZEGLIO

V. de'
Martelli

see inset below right

19

Piazza

San Giovanni

Duomo

Piazza del Duomo

Via de' Pergola

Piazza
S. M. Nuova

Via L. C. Farini

Sinagoga di
Firenze

Via Roma

DUOMO

Via del Proconsolo

Via dell'Oriuolo

Borgo Pinti

Via Fiesolana

Via di Mezzo

Sant'Ambrogio

Piazza
della
Repubblica

Via del Corso

27

Casa di
Dante

23
24
25

Orsanmichele

Via D. Alighieri

Borgo degli Albizi

Via Pietrapiana

V. d. Cimatori

Badia

Via de' Pandolfini

Via dei Calzaiuoli

V. Maria V. Calimala

SIGNORIA

Piazza della
Signoria

Via Ghibellina

V. d. Vigna

26

Vecchia

V. d. Stinche

Via G. Verdi

Via de' Pepi

V. M. Buonarroti

Borgo Allegri

Palazzo
Vecchio

i

Borgo de'

Via de' Benaccordi

Greci

SANTA CROCE

Piazza
Santa Croce

Piazza di

San Giovanni

Piazza del Duomo

Uffizi

Via del Neri

Via de' Benci

Santa Croce

Via Magliabechi

Via de' Pecori

Via de' Brunelleschi

V. d. Studio

Via de' Oche

Piazza
Mentana

Ponte
alle
Grazie

Lungarno delle Grazie

Piazza dei
Cavalleggeri

Via de'
Roma

Via de' Tosinghi

Via de'
Medici

Via dei Calzaiuoli

V. S.
Elisabetta

Via   del   Corso

Via D. Alighieri

Lungarno Torrigiani

Via de' Bardi

Lungarno Serristori

Via di S. Niccolo

Pellicceria

Via

V. Calimala

Piazza
della
Repubblica

V.Orsan
Michele

V. d. Tavolini

V. d. Lamberti

V. Porta Rossa

V. d. Cerchi

V. d. Cimatori

V. d. Condotta

Via D. Alighieri

Piazza della
Signoria

Piazza
S. Firenze

28

Via di S. Nicc

Costa di S. Giorgio

Viale G. Poggi

Via di Belvedere

Via del Monte alle Croci

Piazzale
Michelangiolo

29

Michelangelo; Check-in 7am-midnight; 13,000 L/person per night plus one-time 9,000L tent fee; No credit cards), a 10-minute walk southeast of the city center, are cheapness, great views, and camaraderie with other sweaty campers. The hot showers feel great, the toilets are kept admirably clean and de-scented, and it's only a short bus ride from the city center. Come early to grab a spot—there are always others itching to get in.

At **Institute Gould** *(Via dei Serragli 49; Tel 055/212-576, Fax 055/280-274; Office open 9am-1pm/3-7pm Mon-Fri, till 1pm Sat; 33,000L bed in quad, 48,000L single w/o bath, 72,000L double w/o bath, 105,000L triple; No credit cards),* there are private baths, towels, clean sheets, no lockout, and no curfew. Call early to get a room—there is simply no better deal in town. In the west end of Oltrarno (about 15 minutes from the city center), Gould offers small, quaint rooms with clean, springy single beds. The bathrooms and showers are clean, too, but could use airing out.

Ostello Archi Rossi *(Via Faenza 94r, Tel 055/290-804, Fax 055/230-26-01; Lockout 11am-2:30pm; 24,000L low season, 27,000L high season; No credit cards)* is clean, smack in the city center, and fills up quickly. The self-service laundry (10,000L), cafe/bar, fax machine, and patio are added bonuses. There are 96 beds in rooms with three, four, five, six, or nine beds. Breakfast 4,000L. Curfew 12:30am. Showers have good water pressure and stay hot.

Most rooms at **Pensione Pio X** *(Via dei Serragli 104-106r; Tel/Fax 055/225-044; 25,000L single, 22,000L double/triple, 2-day minimum stay; No credit cards)* are quads or quints and are clean. The generic, high-ceilinged rooms (54 beds total) don't fill up as quickly as some of the other hostels. Maybe it's because management keeps pretty good watch on things, maybe it's because of the midnight curfew, or maybe it's because it's slightly out of the way (a 15-minute walk west of center in Oltrarno). The bathrooms and showers are clean.

Depending on their mood, the sisters who preside over **Suore Oblato dello Spirito Santo** *(Via Nazionale 8; Tel/Fax 055/239-82-02; 30,000L single, 80,000L double, 90,000L triple; No credit cards),* a short walk from the train station, may pretend that they don't run a pension at all, but persistence will show that they have a nice little business, right near the train station, going from June to September. Though rooms are technically for women, guys can get in if they play married couple with a girlfriend/girl friend. (An inexpensive ring purchased from a street vendor helps.) Two-night minimum stay, 11pm curfew.

If you can deal with the midnight curfew and the 30-minute bus ride and walk from the central train station, **Ostello Villa Camerata** *(Via Augusto Righi 4; Tel 055/601-451, Fax 055/601-300; Bus 17, ask the driver to stop at the hostel; Check-in 1-10:30pm, lockout 9am-2pm; 25,000L per bed; No credit cards)* and its verdant grounds are for you. Rooms have four, six, eight, 10, or 14 beds. Continental breakfast with croissant and coffee is included. If you want to go dirt cheap, the hostel also runs a campground. One-time tent fees are 8,000L per site plus 19,000L per person per night. Bathrooms and hot showers are available.

▶▶DO-ABLE

Most of the 23 rooms in the charming, gingerbread-ish **Hotel Globus** *(Via San Antonino 24b; Tel 055/211-062, Fax 055/239-62-25; 80,000L single w/shared bath, 110,000L double w/shared bath; hotel.globus@firenzealbergo.it; AE, V, MC)* have views of the Medici Chapel; some even have small balconies. The young couple running the place are helpful, speak English well, and are constantly thinking of new ways to attract young travelers to their nice little spot just a few minutes' walk from the train station. Their latest idea: Internet hookups in each room. Breakfast consists of eggs, cereal, pastries, yogurt, and coffee. High-season (May-Sept) and low-season (Oct-Apr) prices vary greatly, so try to negotiate.

wired

As host to an endless flow of travelers from all corners of the globe needing to get in touch with friends and family and set up travel plans, Florence has caught the Internet bug—more than any other Italian city. The Internet cafes in Florence are great meeting places, and they hold a wealth of local information, and can be cruisy for both foreigner on foreigner and foreigner on locals. *Note to guys:* If you've lost your nerve, this may be the best bet to make a local girl yours. Just lean over to the damsel's computer and tell her you like to use another Internet company. (If she uses Yahoo, say Hotmail; if she uses Hotmail, then Yahoo.) Then ask her if you can show her why, and edge over into her computer space and do your thing. You know...your *thing*, Casanova.

The centrally located **Mondial Net Firenze** *(Via de' Ginori 59r; Tel 055/265-75-84; 10am-10pm Mon-Sat, noon-4pm Sun; mondialnet@rtd.it)* is one of the most popular places with American university students and has a good message board.

@CyberOffice *(Via San Gallo 4r; Tel 055/211-103; 10,000L one hour, 5,000L half-hour; gheri.fiers@dada.it; V, MC)* is also a hit with foreign travelers, as is the ubiquitous, somewhat generic **Internet Train** *(Via dell'Oriuolo 25r; Tel 055/263-89-68; Via Guelfa 24, Tel 055/214-794; Borgo San Jacopo 30, Tel 055/265-79-35; www.fionline.it; All locations open daily till late).*

The best deal in town is at the slightly out-of-the-way **Netik** *(Via dell'Angolo 65r, 10-15 minutes east of Duomo; Tel 055/242-645; 10am-8pm Mon-Sat; 6,000L/hour).* Coffee and soda are also served here.

One amiable man, Ivo, runs both **Hotel La Noce** and **Hotel Regine** *(Borgo La Noce 8; Tel 055/292-346, Fax 055/291-035; 110,000L single, 160,000L double; AE, V, MC),* two budget-traveler-friendly lodges a few blocks north of the Duomo. Though the 18 quiet and tidy rooms look like dorm rooms with their small beds and particle-board desks, they're cooled by central air, which makes a huge difference in the summer. Continental breakfast with coffee and croissants is included, and soda can be bought in the lobby. High- and low-season prices vary by as much as L40,000. Clean, somewhat stuffy bathroom/showers.

Open since 1993, the centrally located **Il Perseo** *(Via Cerretani 1; Tel 055/212-504, Fax 055/288-377; L85,000 single w/o bath, 125,000L double w/o bath; hotel.perseo@dada.it; AE, V, MC)* is one of the best budget hotels in Florence. Aussie expat owner Louise is dripping with niceness and full of info about Florence and Tuscany. While many of their large fourth-story rooms have great views of the Duomo, a fifth-floor double has a nearly unadulterated vista of Brunelleschi's masterwork. The cheerfully decorated breakfast/lounge room is full of mags and travel guides, and all 19 rooms have ceiling or floor fans and telephones. Continental breakfast with coffee, cereal, croissants, toast, and jellies included. The only drawback: 7am church bells.

San Lorenzo *(Via Rosina 4; Tel/Fax 055/284-925; 70,000L single, 170,000L double; V, MC)* is small and quaint and so close to the bustling San Lorenzo market you can practically smell the leather stands. All eight rooms have showers, hair dryers, TVs, and telephones. Management will gladly make restaurant and tour bookings.

▶▶**SPLURGE**

In addition to having 16 neat, air-conditioned rooms, the three-star jewel **Accademía** *(Via Faenza 7; Tel 055/293-451; 150,000L single, 220,000L double; AE, V, MC)* oozes character, as does its gregarious owner, Tea. She'll be quick to point out the painted wood ceilings, marble floors, crystal chandeliers, 14th-century fireplace, polished statues, and small outdoor seating area and garden. The only drawback is that the incredibly high ceilings create mini-echo chambers—ask for the large third-floor rooms where the effect is lessened. Continental breakfast with coffee, cereal/warm milk, croissants, toast, and jellies is included.

Hotel Le Cascine *(Largo F.lli Alinari 15; Tel 055/211-066; 220,000L double w/bath; V, MC, AE)* has spacious and elegant Victorian rooms that look out onto a tranquil courtyard. Stall showers have easy-to-use temperature modulator, and all bathrooms have a hair dryer. Air-conditioning and TV provide added comforts. The (included) continental breakfast is served in a nook beside the reception area, where you gleefully watch the two-person staff juggle phone calls and serving duties. One of the best on this hotel-laden street.

Hotel Consigli *(Lungarno A. Vespucci; Tel 055/214-172, Fax 055/219-367; 150,000L single, 260,000L double; hconsigli@tin.it; AE, V, MC)* is a former Renaissance palace situated along the Arno that will make you feel miles away from the madness of the frenzied center. The vaulted and frescoed 25-foot ceilings and the splendid second-story rooms that open onto the terrace are so amazing that Tchaikovsky spent a year of his life boarding here, as a guest of then-owner Prince Demidoff, the First General of Peter the Great. The present owner loves to practice his English and swears that he's installing air conditioning soon. Continental breakfast included, though you can order an American-style breakfast with eggs/bacon/sausage for around 13,000L. Sparkling-clean bathrooms have full tub. Free parking.

need to know

Currency Exchange Local currency is the **Italian lira (L).** Banks have best rates; most are open 8:30am-1:30pm/2:30-3:45pm Mon-Fri. You can also exchange money at **Central Post Office**'s foreign exchange office *(V. Pellicceria 3; 8:15am-7pm Mon-Fri)*, in the heart of the city, or for no commission at the **Stazione Santa Maria Novella (S.M.N.)** [see below] *(8:20am-6:30pm Mon-Sat).*

Tourist Information Azienda Promozione Turistica *(Via A. Manzoni 16; Tel 055/234-62-84, Fax 055/234-62-86; 8:30am-1:30pm Mon-Sat)*, near the train station; *(Via Cavour 1r, Tel 055/290-832, Fax 055/276-03-83; 8:15am-7:15pm Mon-Sat, till 1:45pm Sun)*, a few blocks northeast of the Duomo; or *(Borgo Santa Croce 29r; Tel 055/234-04-44; 8:30am-7:15pm Mon-Sat, till 1:45pm Sun, holidays)*, near the Piazza San Croce. The student travel organization **CTS** *(Via de' Ginori 25r; Tel 055/216-660; 9:30am-1:30pm/2:30-6pm Mon-Fri, till 12:30pm Sat)*, in the city center, helps out with reservations, tickets, maps, and advice.

Public Transportation Florence's orange buses are operated by **ATC.** Tickets *(1,500L, 24-hr pass 6,000L)* may be purchased at *tabacchi*; most buses run only until midnight or 1am. The bus station is located at **Piazza della Stazione** *(Tel 055/565-02-22)*, behind the train station. **ATC Information:** *055/56501.*

Bike/Car Rental Alinari *(Via Guelfa 85r; Tel 055/280-500; 9am-1pm/3-7:30pm Mon-Sat Nov-Apr, plus 10am-1pm/3-7:30pm Sun, Mar-Oct only)* rents both bikes and scooters. Must be over 18 with passport, driver's license, and valid credit card. **Avis** *(Borgo Ognissanti 128r; Tel 055/213-629)*, Budget *(Via Finiguerra 31r; Tel 055/287-161)*, and **Hertz** *(Amerigo Vespucci Airport; Tel 055/307-370)* will rent you cars.

American Express *(Via Dante Alighieri 20-22r; Tel 055/50981; 9am-5:30pm Mon-Fri, till 12:30pm Sat).*

Health and Emergency General Hospital of Santa Maria Nuova *(Piazza Santa Maria Nuova 1; Tel 055/275-81; Bus 6 to the Duomo and walk 3 blocks east)* is open 24-7, and you can always find *someone* who speaks English.

Pharmacies Farmacía Comunale *(Inside Stazione Santa Maria Novella; Tel 055/216-761)* or **Farmacía Molteni** *(Via Calzaiuoli 7r; Tel 055/215-472)*, open 24 hrs.

Telephone City code: *055*. See Milan chapter for general telephone information.

Airports Galileo Galilei Airport *(Tel 050/500-707)* is in Pisa, 58 miles west of Florence. No direct flights to United States. **Shuttle train** every hour or two (10 or 11am to 5 or 6pm) between airport and Stazione Santa Maria Novella, 8,000L one-way. **Amerigo Vespucci Airport** *(Tel 055/373-498)* is three miles northwest of the city. **Florence Bus 62** runs between airport and Santa Maria Novella station every 20 minutes, 1,500L.

Airlines Alitalia *(Lungarno degli Acciaiuoli 10-12; Tel 055/278-81)*, **Air France** *(Borgo SS. Apostoli 9; Tel 055/284-304)*, **TWA** *(Via dei Vecchietti 4; Tel 055/284-691)*.

Trains Stazione Santa Maria Novella (S.M.N.) *(Piazza della Stazione; Tel 01478/880-88)* offers fee-based hotel booking service (8:45am-8pm daily), **24-hr luggage storage** *(at Track 16, 5,000L/12 hrs.)*, and a **Eurail Aid Office** *(8am-noon/3-6pm)*.

Laundry You wanna dry or you wanna go? **Wash and Dry** has seven locations, including *Via dei Servi 105r, Via della Scala 52-54r*, and *Via Ghibellina 143r*. Hours for all are 8am-10pm daily, last wash at 9pm. There's also **Wash & Go** *(Via Faenza 26r; 8am-10pm; 6,000L wash, 6,000L dry)*.

everywhere else

cortona

Just because Cortona is small doesn't mean it's undiscovered—two very different factors at work here have brought tons of English-speakers to bitsy Cortona. First, and most importantly to you, the University of Georgia's independent campus in Cortona has been a hot spot for American students studying abroad for the past 30 years. There's no Italian university here, but plenty of locals in their 'teens and twenties hang out with these collegiate expats. All of this raging youth adds up to a much better bar scene than you'd expect in a town of just 20,000.

Then there's Frances Mayes. Of Tuscany's many walled towns, Cortona is the most picturesque, the best preserved, and the one most likely to make you say, "Hey, I could live here!" as you wander up the tiny, cobblestone streets into small dark *vicolos* (alleys) that open up to spectacular views of the dreamy lakes, knobby vineyards, and red-tiled rooftops surrounding the town. That's exactly what happened to Mayes, American-poet-turned-Cortona-resident, who wrote two best-sellers (*Under the Tuscan Sun* and *Bella Tuscany*) about her love affair with a house on a hill. She put this quirky little character-filled town on the map, and gave a big kick in the rear to the tourism industry. Now, during the day, the main streets and piazzas are packed with busloads of tourists on day trips. Luckily, rather than being royally p.o.'d that Mayes lured what sometimes feels like half of the U.S. here to *ooh* and *aah* and point and click, the locals love her. Maybe that's because even before the sun sets, the crowds thin, and the side streets and forgotten piazzas are returned to them—and to you, if you're one of the few smart ones who stick around. Whatever the reason, the locals—a generally refined, proud, and stylish bunch who love great wine and food—are very welcoming. The city retains its authentic charm; rather than herd its tourists through a manufactured experience, Cortona lets them make their own discoveries.

cortona

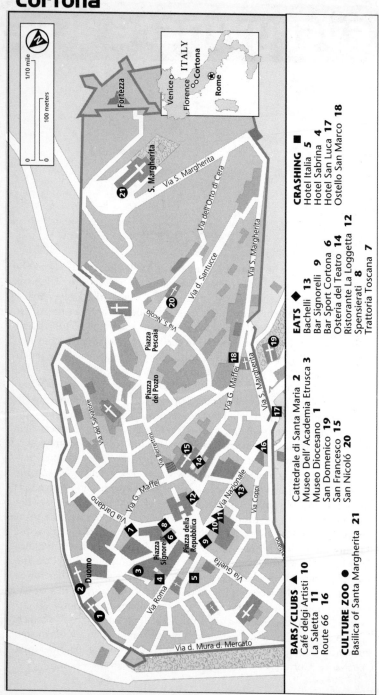

BARS/CLUBS ▲
Café delgi Artisti **10**
La Saletta **11**
Route 66 **16**

CULTURE ZOO ●
Basilica of Santa Margherita **21**

Cattedrale di Santa Maria **2**
Museo Dell' Academia Etrusca **3**
Museo Diocesano **19**
San Domenico **15**
San Francesco **20**
San Nicoló **20**

EATS ◆
Bachelli **13**
Bar Signorelli **9**
Bar Sport Cortona **6**
Osteria del Teatro **14**
Ristorante La Loggetta **12**
Spensierati **8**
Trattoria Toscana **7**

CRASHING ■
Hotel Italia **5**
Hotel Sabrina **4**
Hotel San Luca **17**
Ostello San Marco **18**

Cortonese legend has it that the town was founded by Dardanus, who later went on to build Troy. Of course, historians debate the truth in that—what's clear is that it was one of the most important Etruscan cities in Italy, and it still has the ancient city walls and archaeological treasures to prove it. The Romans had their time here, before being ousted by barbarians. Cortona was independently ruled by wealthy families during the medieval and Renaissance periods—these rulers were art patrons who graced the cities with the beautiful buildings Cortona is now known for—if they look familiar, it might be because they were used as a backdrop for the movie *Life is Beautiful.*

neighborhoods

Cortona sits on the side of a hill that rises high over the green **Val di Chiana.** Every sight within the city walls is just a few minutes' walk from the next, depending on how fast you can take the steep inclines. The city's main drag (and its only flat street), **Via Nazionale,** runs from east to west, with **Piazza Garibaldi** sitting on the western edge of the city wall. Whether you pull into town by bus or car (there's no train station here), Piazza Garibaldi will be your entrance. Fantastic views of the countryside and **Lake Trasimeno** can be had from here, and at night it's hopping with kids drinking beer and couples making out. The steep **Via Margherita** begins at Piazza Garibaldi and ends up at the **Basilica di Santa Margherita** [see *culture zoo,* below]. Via Nazionale cuts right through square at the social heart of the city, **Piazza della Repubblica.** The town hall is here, inside of the 13th-century **Palazzo Comunale.** At any time of the day or night, the steps of the palazzo are a favorite rendezvous point for Cortonese, American students, and anybody else who's feeling social. The town's other main streets also border Piazza della Repubblica: **Via Guelfa** on the western edge, and **Via Dardano** on the east. **Piazza Signorelli** is just north of Piazza della Repubblica, and houses the **Teatro Luca Signorelli** [see *arts scene,* below] and the **Museo Dell'Accademia Etrusca** [see *culture zoo,* below].

If you're wondering why everything in town seems to be named after the painter Luca Signorelli, it's because he was born in Cortona (1445-1523). Other names you should know are Pietro da Cortona (1596-1669), whom the town is named after, and Gino Severini (1883-1966).

The **Piazza del Duomo** holds the **Museo Diocesano** and the **Cattedrale di Santa Maria** [see *culture zoo,* below, for both].

The **Giardini Publici (Public Gardens),** located just east of the **Church of San Domenico,** down the hill, are the only green space in town. Bring a picnic lunch during the day or, better yet, come back around sunset with a bottle of wine. Either way, the gardens offer the best possible view of the countryside.

cafe scene

Cafe culture has really picked up since those tour buses started rolling in. Outdoor tables seem permanently packed with camera-clickers during the day, but at night, locals and students take their rightful places.

Tiny **Bachelli** *(Via Nazionale 68; No phone; 7am-midnight June-Aug; 7am-9pm Sept-May, closed Mon; No credit cards)*, on the eastern end of Via Nazionale, serves some of the best pastries in town. Its cultish following prefers to sit at the outdoor tables (rather than in the cramped interior) with a coffee and watch the world walk by.

Bar Signorelli *(Piazza della Repubblica; Tel 0575/603-075; 6am-1am daily; No credit cards)* has the foamiest cappuccino in town. Its outdoor tables are in a choice location, right on this busy piazza. Pay extra to sit here and enjoy your gelato—the fluorescent-lit interior is unspectacular and smoky.

Bar Sport Cortona *(Piazza Signorelli 16; Tel/Fax 0575/62-984; 7am-12am daily; No credit cards)* is exactly what it sounds like—Cortona's take on a sports bar. Local guys gather to watch soccer on TV, oblivious to the bustling cafe scene outside. The outdoor tables are quieter here than on Piazza della Repubblica, and are a perfect place to start your day with a cuppa' joe.

bar, club, and live music scene

During the dinner hours, Cortona's streets are eerily empty, but come 9pm, they fill up—particularly on Via Nazionale—with families, groups of teenagers, and kissing couples taking the typical Italian evening stroll. For most of the population, this leads to a little piazza- and barhopping. Most young Cortonese end up hanging out on the steps of the Palazzo Comunale at some point every night—its friendly atmosphere makes it an excellent place to meet some new friends. Then it's off to one of the bars, which are pretty cosmopolitan for a Tuscan country town. There are no clubs in Cortona, but during the summer, sporadic outdoor rave-like parties go on in several other small towns in the region—ask the guys at **Babilonia** [see *stuff*, below] about what's going down and how to get there.

Although every cafe has a fully stocked bar, **Route 66** *(Piazza Garibaldi 3; Tel 0575/62-727; 9pm-3am Tue-Sun, closed Mon; Route66@technet.it, www.route66cortona.com; No cover; V, MC, AE)* is the only *real* bar in town. It's also the only live music scene, offering everything from New Orleans blues to American covers to Italian rock bands. Located right on Piazza Garibaldi, it looks like every Italian's impression of an American bar—lots of license plates, old Coke signs, and beer-happy twentysomethings. There's even a computer for those emergency late-night e-mails (a 21st-century version of drunk dialing), and decent pub grub to take the edge off.

Local artists, as well as national artists who are in town showing their work, really do hang out at **Caffe degli Artisti** *(Via Nazionale 18; Tel 0575/ 601-237; 12:30pm-1am, closed Mon; V, MC, AE)*, on the north end of the main drag near Piazza della Repubblica. Well-heeled twenty- and thirtysomethings come to this trendy little bar to sip wine and cocktails at the outdoor tables, and to schmooze with friends in the pretty interior—show up by 10pm if you want a seat.

ot mail.com; Wines by the glass 3,000-12,000L; Cocktails 6,000-8,000L; V,
MC, AE, DIN). This cozy little mahogany-paneled bar, just a few steps
from the main sights on Via Nazionale, carries the best selection of wine
in Cortona, great cocktails, and 48 different types of grappa (we dare you
to find one you like). Sit at a table on the sidewalk out front, or head on
down to the comfy couches in the private tasting room down in the basement. Saletta is just as popular for its food [see *eats,* below].

ARTS SCENE

If it's more recent than the Renaissance, it's not Cortona's strong suit.
One room of the **Museo Dell' Accademia Etrusca,** [see *culture zoo,*
below] and a few galleries constitute Cortona's entire contemporary arts
scene. Cortona has a strong crafts tradition, and you'll find many stores
that sell ceramics and copperware. Performing arts is a different story—
Teatro Luca Signorelli hosts a great many different theater, dance,
and musical performances year-round, and the many festivals that swing
by in the summer [see *festivals and events,* below] mean free concerts in
the piazza.

▶▶VISUAL ARTS

Inside a drafty old building with a high, vaulted ceiling, right in the
center of Via Nazionale, is the **Commune di Cortona Ufficio Tech-
nico** *(Via Nazionale 45; No phone; Hours vary according to artist; Free
admission),* one of the coolest galleries in town. The works of mainly
Italian artists—paintings, photography, and sculpture—are on display in
the summer, spring, and fall. The **Galleria D'Arte Gino Severini**
(Piazza della Repubblica 3; 0575/630-666 or 0575/604-632; Hours vary

FESTIVALS and EVENTS

Although Cortona is technically in Tuscany, it's just a few
kilometers from the Umbrian border, so the renowned **Umbria
Jazz Festival** comes here for two days in late July, bringing world-
class musicians with it [see *festivals and events* in Perugia chapter].
On June 11th, hundreds of townsfolk take their medieval costumes
out of the closets and dress up for the **Archidado Games,** which
celebrate the 1307 marriage of a member of the Casali family (they
ruled Cortona from 1325 to 1409). The main event is the archery
competition in Piazza Signorelli, but religious ceremonies and processions go through the city on June 10th.

according to artist; Free admission) is a small space on the Piazza della Repubblica that hosts Italian and international artists and photographers year-round. The exhibits focus on one artist's work at a time, and are well worth a visit.

Many crafty artists make their home in Cortona, and **Galleria Umberto Rossi** *(Via Roma 2; Tel 0575/62-745; 10am-noon/4-8pm; Free admission),* just across from Piazza della Repubblica, showcases some of their work, along with namesake Umberto Rossi's specialty wooden carvings. The gallery displays a random mixture of Cortonese sculptures, drawings, photos, furniture, paintings, ceramics, and candleholders—all of which are for sale. A workshop around the corner at Via Guelfa 28 lets you watch Rossi in action.

▶▶PERFORMING ARTS

Simple but pretty **Teatro Luca Signorelli** *(Piazza Signorelli; Tel 0575/601-882; Movie tickets 12,000L, theater tickets 20,000L; V, MC, AE)* is the town's only theater, and it doubles as a cinema that shows the latest Hollywood tripe, and occasionally independent movies—all in English! The theater hosts performances of everything from ballet to opera, and during the summer, shows move outside, on Piazza Signorelli.

CULTURE ZOO

Cortona has many artistic treasures hiding in its dusty, scarcely visited museums and churches—all of which lie blocks away from the tourist-jammed Via Nazionale. Of the town's two museums, the Museo Dell'Accademia Etrusca is the highlight, although the Museo Diocesano contains works by several Renaissance masters.

Museo Diocesano *(Piazza del Duomo 1; Tel 0575/62-830; 9:30am-1pm/3:30-7pm Apr-Sept; 10am-1pm/3:30-6pm Oct; 10am-1pm/3-5pm Nov-Mar, closed Mon; 8,000L adults):* Located inside a former church (Chiesa del Gesú), this doesn't at first appear to be a first-class museum—it has bad lighting, dirty walls, and ancient curtains. But look around a bit: The first room is full of Luca Signorelli's works, most notably *The Deposition* and the *Communion of the Apostles.* There are several paintings by Fra Angelico, including an *Annunciation* that was painted in Cortona, and a *Crucifix* by Pietro Lorenzetti, who wasn't born in Cortona, but is considered a native son since he contributed so many paintings to the town. Rooms Seven and Eight, down the first set of stairs, aren't worth seeing unless you've got a thing for church vestments and chalices.

Cattedrale di Santa Maria *(Piazza del Duomo; 7am-12:30pm/3-8pm daily; Free admission):* Located directly across from the Museo Diocesano, this 16th-century church was built on the ruins of an 11th-century pagan-worship site. Many of the works of art inside come from other Cortonese churches that have been destroyed, but besides an *Adoration of the Shepherds* by Pietro da Cortona, there's nothing exceptional.

San Domenico *(Viale Giardino Pubblici, next to Piazza Garibaldi):* This church, which sits next to Piazza Garibaldi and right outside the city wall, is one of Cortona's most important medieval monuments. Fra Angelico once lived in the adjacent monastery, and painted the badly-faded fresco over the church's main door. The chapel to the right of the altar also holds an early 16th-century *Madonna and Child With Saints* by Luca Signorelli.

San Francesco *(Via Maffei):* Two blocks east of Via Nazionale and Piazza della Repubblica is this 13th-century church, which houses a few significant works. The third altar on the left displays the last unfinished work of Pietro da Cortona, *Annunciation* (1669). It is rumored that the crypt contains the tomb of Luca Signorelli, who died in 1523.

Basilica di Santa Margherita *(Via S. Margherita 1; Tel/Fax 0575/603-116):* Cortona's daily uphill walking will prepare you for what it takes to get up to the Basilica of Santa Margherita—a 25-minute-walk east of Piazza Garibaldi, along Via S. Margherita (there are no buses), that's lined with mosaics of the stations of the cross by Gino Severini. The preserved body of St. Margherita, a 13th-century saint who spent most of her life in Cortona, is on view in a 17th-century silver urn, designed by Pietro Berrettini, that's kept behind the altar. The original church was built in 1297, after St. Margherita's death, but was torn down in the 1800s to build this bigger and better one. The interior of the church is filled with Sienese frescoes, but the only artifacts surviving from the original church are the rose window in the facade, the 17th-century bell tower, and the external wall of the choir. Don't let the walk scare you off—this is definitely worth it. There's a snack bar next to the church, but the food looks like it dates from St. Margherita's time—bring your own picnic from back at sea level. After exiting the church, walk across the parking lot toward the sign that says *gabinetti* (restrooms), for yet another spectacular view.

San Nicoló *(Via San Nicolo):* If you head west from the parking lot of the Basilica of Santa Margherita and make your way down the trail that winds through a quiet residential area (complete with old ladies in black scarves knitting in the sun) until you hit Via S. Nicoló, you will come upon the shaded courtyard entrance to this 15th-century church. Notice the famous two-sided wooden painting by Luca Signorelli on the altar, which operates on an ancient pulley-system: The *Deposition* is painted on the front, and the Virgin Mary (noted for her expression) with Peter and Paul is on the back. The inside of the small church was modified in the 17th and 18th centuries.

modification

David and Francesco at **Nucio** *(Piazza della Repubblica 26 (for women) and Via Nazionale 5 (for men); Tel 0575/603-357; 8:30am-1pm/3:30-7:30pm Tue-Sat, closed Sun, Mon)* use American Tigi products, and can give you a wash, cut, and blow-dry for 60,000L. Expect a long wait on a Friday or Saturday (hey, this is a hip spot); stop by beforehand to make an appointment if you can.

stuff

Although the Cortonese love to flaunt their style, they obviously don't do their shopping here—the pickin's are slim. But it's kind of fun to stroll around and window-shop, though not on a Sunday or Monday, when most of the stores are closed.

▶▶DUDS

If you're in dire need of a new outfit, dig through the sales rack in the back of **Sixteen Abbigliamento** *(Via Nazionale 52; Tel 0575/631-079; V, MC, AE)*. As the name implies, clothes here are geared toward younger folks, with lots of funky, tight-fitting styles.

▶▶TUNES

The only music store in Cortona, **Babilonia** *(Via Nazionale 71; Tel 0575/604-201; 9:30am-1pm/4:30-8pm Tue-Sat, 10:30am-1pm/4:30-7:30pm Sun; babilo@freedomland.it; AE, V),* doesn't have much of a selection, but they do have a box office that sells tickets to concerts all over the region. The English-speaking staff can also tell you all about clubs and parties going on in the neighboring towns, and since this is a popular hangout, you just might meet someone to go with.

▶▶BOUND

Tiny **Nocentini** *(Via Nazionale 32; Tel/Fax 0575/603-692; 8:00am-1pm/4:00-8pm, closed Mon; giulnoc@inwind.it, www.toscumbria.com/nocentini; V, MC, AE)* is the only bookshop in town. Besides travel guides and a huge display of Frances Mayes's books, there isn't much of an English-language selection. If you're feeling inspired by Cortona's ancient walls and Etruscan art, you can also buy art supplies to paint your own masterpiece.

If you don't speak Italian and you're itching for some news in a language you can understand, **La Nazione** *(Via Nazionale 9; No phone; 8am-9pm daily; No credit cards)* sells the *International Herald Tribune*.

▶▶FOOT FETISH

Small towns like Cortona aren't usually the best places to shop for foot fashions, but they are always the best place to buy that great pair of classic Italian shoes that will last for years to come. **Lorenzi** *(Piazza Repubblica 18; Tel 0575/603-296; 9am-1pm/3:30-8pm; V, MC, AE)* is that kind of place. The soft, handmade shoes here are on the expensive side, starting at 170,000L and going way up from there, but they'll probably last you till *your* kids are doing this whole Europe thing.

EATS

Dining out in Cortona is something to look forward to. An abundance of cheap eateries cater to the college crowd, but even the home-style *trattorias* aren't that expensive, considering the fine food they serve. Though heartily Tuscan, there are some Umbrian influences of note on the menus—namely, fish and wine from Lake Trasimeno. It's a good idea to pop your head in and reserve a table if there's a specific place you want to try, since restaurants tend to fill up early. If you miss lunch, just about the only place open throughout the day is La Saletta—otherwise you'll be stuck with a slice of pizza from Spensierati (not that that's a bad thing).

▶▶CHEAP

East of Piazza Signorelli, **Spensierati** *(Via Dardano 1; Tel 0575/62-832; 8am-8pm daily; No credit cards)* is where the students come to buy

TO MARKET

What Cortona lacks in the way of clothes, shoes, and other stuff to buy, it makes up for in delicious local specialties like *pecorino* cheese (the older, the better ... and the more expensive), olives, and an enormous array of local wines. Most of the nicer food stores are located on Via Nazionale, like **Via Nazionale 81** *(No phone; 10:30am-1:30pm/4-8pm, closed Tue; V, MC, AE, minimum 50,000L)*, the first store on the street as you enter from Piazza Garibaldi. There are wooden tables in the back where you can have a sit-down snack. Although it lacks the gourmet feel of the other shops in town, **Enoteca Molesini** *(22-23 Piazza della Repubblica; No phone; 7am-1:30pm/4:30-8pm, closed Sun; V, MC, AE)* is the closest thing there is to a grocery store. **Fruttissiama** *(Via Nazionale 49; No phone; 7am-1:30pm/4:30-8pm, closed Sun; No credit cards)*, on the eastern end of Via Nazionale, is the best place in town to buy fresh fruit. If you want some fresh figs, but want to save a few lire, take a walk around the outside of the city walls and pick your own from the trees (it's okay, it's legal!). Every little food store sells wine, but the best selection can be found at **La' Cantinetta** *(Via Berrettini 15; No phone; 10am-7pm, closed Sun; V, MC, AE, DIN)*, two blocks northeast of Piazza della Repubblica.

their dinner. This bakery sells fantastic pizza by the slice, as well as other baked goods, like pastries, pies, and delicious Tuscan bread.

▶▶**DO-ABLE**

If you're prepared to wait for a table, **Trattoria Toscana** *(Via Dardano 12; Tel 0575/604-192; Closed Mon; Primi 6,000-16,000L, pastas 10,000-16,000L, secondi 14,000-20,000L; V, MC, AE)*, just north of Piazza Signorelli, is one of the best little family-run trattorias in town—complete with red-checkered tablecloths and arched ceilings—and is a favorite among the Cortonese. Everything at this fairly new restaurant is a good value. The *crostini* plate, a sampling of local antipasti (sautéed eggplant; various cured meats; crostini with olive spread, liver spread, and tomatoes), is a good introduction to Tuscan cuisine. The pastas and meat dishes are all even better with local Cortonese red wine. Try porcini or truffles, both regional specialties, if they're offered. Don't worry about having trouble with the menu here—the owner's helpful American wife is the waitress.

In the square next to Piazza della Repubblica, **Ristorante La Loggetta** *(Piazza Pescheria 3; Tel 0575/630-575; Noon-3pm/7-11pm,*

closed Mon; Secondi 5,000-24,000L; No credit cards) serves good, basic
Tuscan dishes at very reasonable prices. Students, families, and the occasional tourist pack into the no-frills dining rooms, order big carafes of
local wine, and pig out. The menu is small, but you can count on hearty
roasted meats and pastas.

Although the service is slow (even for Italy), **La Saletta** [see *bar, club,
and live music scene,* above] is worth a visit for the food alone. The cooks
put together a small but tasty menu of the day, and offer a huge selection
of appetizers, crepes, pasta, and pizza. The pizza with prosciutto and
arugula (10,000L) is life-changing, but save room for homemade gelato,
or a pastry from the glass cases along the bar.

▶▶**SPLURGE**
Even though it's not the most expensive, **Osteria del Teatro** *(Via
Maffei 5; Tel 0575/630-556; Noon-3pm/6-10pm daily; Secondi 12,000-
20,000L; V, MC, AE)* is probably the nicest restaurant in town. Around
the corner from the Teatro Luca Signorelli, this is *the* place to go for a
romantic dinner. Friendly service, candlelit dining room, soft opera
music, and black and white photos of old theater productions—oh yeah,
and excellent food—make this the most popular place around. The wine
list is stellar, as are the homemade desserts. The crowd is mixed, but
everyone is a little dressed up.

crashing

Cortona doesn't have many hotels, so if you plan to spend the night
during the high season, call ahead and make reservations. The tourist
information office will give you a list of all hotels, but they can't make
reservations for you. Prices tend to be reduced in the off-season
(November through March), when hotel operators are also more willing
to be bargained with (haggling is technically against the law). If all else
fails, stay at one of the *agriturismos* (literally, tourist farms), like
Cortereggio, out in the countryside.

▶▶**CHEAP**
Walk east on Via Margherita for about 10 minutes and turn left after the
Church of San Marco [see *culture zoo,* above] to get to the only youth
hostel in town, **Ostello San Marco** *(Via Maffei 57; Tel 0575/601-392,
Mobile 0335/315-987; Open Mar 15-October 15, midnight curfew; 10am-
3:30pm lockout; Bunk 18,000L, breakfast 1,000L, lunch and dinner 14,000L
each; 80 beds).* If your luggage is heavy, call before heading up the steep
hill—it's a real bummer to lug your stuff all the way up that incline just to
find there's no one there to answer the door. The hostel is housed in a
former monastery, with great views of the Tuscan valley that almost make
up for the insulting curfew. The rooms are spacious, with vaulted ceilings,
and the pretty dining room is always filled with backpackers swapping stories and playing cards. The hostel features several common rooms with
TVs, as well as laundry service, and bicycles for guests to borrow.

If just looking at the gorgeous countryside isn't enough for you, get
right into it at **Agriturismo Cortereggio** *(Loc. Terontola Alta 13;*

Tel/Fax: 0575/678-343; No credit cards), a five minute drive outside of Cortona. After a day or two on this farm, with its 2000 olive trees, wide swimming pool, and great views of the hills, you won't want to leave. The family-owned *agriturismo*, presided over by ever-helpful Bruno, has seven apartments, divided into several rooms each, most with kitchens and bathrooms. You're on your own here, but that's part of the fun—bring friends! You'll need a car to get here (unless you're a hard-core walker). If you don't have wheels, call and ask Bruno if he can give you a lift.

▶▶**DO-ABLE**

Smallish rooms at the friendly **Hotel Sabrina** *(Via Roma 37; Tel 0557/630-397, Fax 0575/604-627; www.emmeti.it/Welcome/Toscana/ Provarezzo/Valdichiana/ Cortona/Alberghi/sabrina.uk.html; 90,000-100,000L singles, 120,000L doubles, breakfast included; V, MC)* may be a little cramped, but they have a lot of character. Each room here is different, but all have old-fashioned furniture and a private bath, and most have TVs. The hotel is located on Via Roma, just north of Piazza della Repubblica.

Pleasant, family-run **Hotel Italia** *(Via Ghibellina 7; Tel 0575/630-254, Fax 0575/630-564; 100,000L singles with baths, 140,000L doubles with baths, 80,000L without baths, breakfast included; MC, V)*, on a little street that runs north of Piazza della Repubblica, is larger than the Hotel Sabrina. Rooms are simple and tasteful, with antique wooden furniture, timbered ceiling beams, comfortable beds, TVs, phones, and blow-dryers. The panoramic view of the countryside from its fourth-floor terrace is unforgettable.

The nicest thing about **Hotel San Luca** *(Piazza Garibaldi; Tel 0575/630-460, Fax 0575/630-105; L110,00 singles, L170,000 doubles; Breakfast included; V, MC, AE)* is the view of the Tuscan countryside and Lake Trasimeno from many of its rooms. The location, right next to the bus stop in Piazza Garibaldi, is a godsend if you're arriving with a heavy load. The rooms have TVs (but no English-language channels), nice firm mattresses, blow-dryers, and bizarre, half-sized bathtubs. The hotel is often overrun with tour groups and visiting students, so call way in advance.

need to know

Currency Exchange Banco Populare Etruria e Lazio *(Via S. Margherita 5; Tel 0575/604-609)*, at the intersection of Piazza Garibaldi and Via Nazionale, has an automatic money exchange machine. Several other banks with ATM machines can be found in Cortona, including **Banco Populare Di Cortona** *(Via Guelfa 4, near Piazza della Repubblica; Tel 0575/630-316)* and **Monte Dei Paschi di Siena** *(Via Nazionale 42; Tel 0575/630-284)*.

Tourist Info Inside a classical Tuscan building with high ceilings and Cortonese iron work, the **Cortona APT** *(Via Nazionale 42; Tel 0575/630-352 or 0575/630-353; 9am-1pm and 3-6pm Mon-Fri, 9am-1pm Sat Oct-Apr; 9am-1pm and 3-7pm Mon-Sat, 9am-1pm Sun May-*

Sept) has city maps and hotel lists, and lots of info on other nearby towns in the region, but can't make hotel reservations for you. There's also an ATM inside the same building.

Public Transportation The city is too small, and the streets too narrow, for **buses.** Walking is the only way to go in Cortona. If you need a **taxi,** call one of Cortona's **taxi drivers** *(Adreani Enzo Tel 0335/819-6313; Alberghini Tel 0338/700-59-59; Caleri Albino Tel 0368/738-6544).*

Health and Emergency Emergencies: *112;* Police emergency line: *113;* Cortona police station: *0575/603-006;* Ambulance services: *0575/630-707;* Medical emergencies: *0575/62-893.*

Pharmacies The most convenient pharmacy, **Farmacia Centrale** *(Via Nazionale 38; Tel 0575/603-206; 9am-1pm/4:30-8pm daily; V, MC, AE, DIN),* is located right in the center of the main drag. It posts a list of the rotating pharmacies in town that are open all night.

Telephone City code: *0575.* There's a **Telecom Italia** public phone center on Via Guelfa, right off of Piazza della Repubblica. There is also a pay phone at the entrance of the city, in Piazza Garibaldi.

Trains Cortona has no train station. The closest stations are **Terontola** (11 km) and **Camucia** (5 km), which lie on the Milan-Bologna-Florence-Rome line (a 90-minute ride from Florence), and are connected to Cortona's Piazza Garibaldi by a **shuttle bus** that runs about every half an hour, beginning at 6am and going 'til 9:15pm (both ways). The schedule is posted in Piazza Garibaldi, but if you need help figuring out which bus to get on, step inside Hotel San Luca and the concierge can help. **Tickets** can either be bought on the bus (2,800L) or at the *tabacchi* around the corner on Via Nazionale.

wired

Cortona isn't the most Internet-savvy city, but one place in town lets you check e-mail: **Neuromancer Internet Point** *(Vicolo Amandoli 18; No phone; 11am-11pm Mon-Sat, 3-8pm Sun; neuromancer—cortona@yahoo.it; 10,000L per hour; No credit cards).* Neuromancer, just half a block east off of Via Nazionale, doesn't have frills like food or drinks, but if you bring your own they won't mind. What they do have is fast connections, English-speaking staff, and English-language keyboards. If you need to send a fax, **Il Quaderno** *(Via Nazionale 4; Tel/Fax 0575/62-993; 9am-8pm, closed Mon; 5,000-6,000L a page)* can do it for you.

For information about Cortona on the web, check out ***www.toscumbria.com*** and ***www.cortona.net.***

Bus Lines Out of the City Buses run regularly from Piazza Garibaldi to Arezzo, the largest town in the area. The **bus stop** is near the Palazzo Comunale, on the southern side of the piazza. Buses also go to Castiglion Fiorentino, Foiano della Chiana, Mercatale, Terontola, Camucia, Pozzulo, Ossaia, Montecchio del Loto, S. Pietro a Dame, Chianciano, and Castiglion del Lago. For other destinations, take the bus to Terontola and then transfer to the **train. Tickets** can be bought on board the bus and the schedule is posted at the bus stop.

Bike/Moped Rental There's no bike rental store, but **Massimiliano Crivelli** *(Tel 0347/583-4419, Fax 0575/601-610)* rents mountain bikes and scooters and personally delivers them to your hotel. You can rent by the day or by the week.

Postal The most convenient way to send postcards home is to buy **stamps** from any *tabacchi* and then leave the postcards with the concierge at your hotel or stick them in one of the **red mailboxes.**

Internet See *wired,* above.

san gimignano

San Gimignano is called "the Manhattan of Tuscany" in honor of its distinctive skyline, dotted with medieval towers in place of skyscrapers. But any similarities to Manhattan end there. The jumble of picturesque palazzos, art-filled churches, and famous towers crammed inside its ancient city walls make San Gimignano a quintessential tiny Tuscan town. At times, particularly during the summer, it feels like a medieval stage set, built to attract tourists who step off the buses in the morning and back on promptly as the sun goes down. To experience the real San Gimignano, stay overnight and wander around after the day-trippers have left, when the town is peacefully romantic and silent. Plenty of hangouts will give you a lesson in Vernaccia, the town's prized *vino*—and the locals will welcome you with a heapin' helpin' of hospitality.

With its 13 surviving towers, this walled hill town dominates the Elsa Valley in central Tuscany. San Gimignano was once an Etruscan town, and was named in the 10th century when St. Gimignano was said to have saved it from invading barbarians. It's hard to imagine how magnificent—and intimidating—the town's 72 towers must have looked in the 13th and 14th centuries. They were built not only for protection, but as symbols of wealth, which was great back then because the town was located on a well-traveled trade and pilgrim route to Rome. San Gimignano was eventually torn into two by the dueling Ardinghelli family (known as the Guelphs) and the Salvucci family (known as the Ghibellines). When the Plague hit in 1348, and the population was drastically reduced, San Gimignano began its decline, which led to its takeover by Florence.

Today San Gimignano is a protected UNESCO World Heritage Site, and most residents work either in the tourism or wine industry. Compared

san gimignano

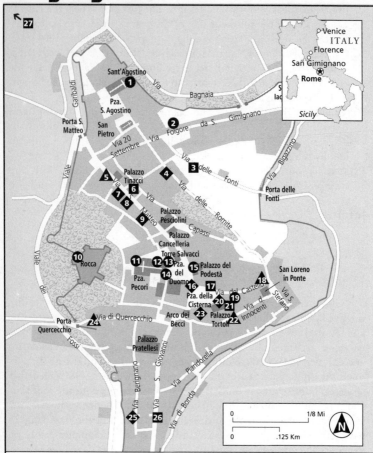

with other Tuscan cities, like Pisa, Siena, and Florence, San Gimignano has a vibe that's distinctly tilted toward the past, not the future. There's not much of a youth vibe here, and with a population of just 7,000, tourists grossly outnumber locals. The marketing here is geared toward wealthy Americans who want to feel like they've discovered the "true" Tuscany, and who will pay almost anything for the illusion. But if you reserve your room in advance, eat at the locals-only wine bars, and go for plenty o' picnics, San Gimignano doesn't have to cost a fortune.

neighborhoods and hanging out

San Gimignano's sights are all located within the city walls—you can easily trek from one end of town to the other in 10 minutes, which leaves plenty of time for exploring the less-visited back streets and surrounding countryside. The bus—the only way into town besides car—will drop you at **Porta San Matteo** on the northwestern edge of town, or **Porta Giovanni** on the southern end. Both are a five-minute walk from **Piazza Duomo,** the geographical and social center of town. From Porto San Matteo, **Via San Matteo** runs south through Piazza Duomo and **Piazza della Cisterna,** where it changes to **Via San Giovanni** and then ends up at **Porta San Giovanni.** Just south of Porta San Giovanni is the sprawling **Piazzale di Martiri di Montemaggio,** the southern tip of town. Almost all the shops are located on vias San Matteo and San Giovanni, and most of the sights, including the elaborately decorated **Duomo** and the **Great Tower** (the only one that can still be climbed), are right around the Piazza Duomo [see *culture zoo,* below, for both].

The best spots for hanging out and meeting your fellow travelers in San Gimignano are the Piazza Duomo and Piazza della Cisterna. If the scene at the local *enotecas* (wine bars) is too dull for you, bring a bottle of your own beverage of choice to one of the piazzas, like the young locals do. Tourists and locals of all ages gather on the steps of the Duomo to eat lunch during the day, and to chat with friends at night. The townsfolk are used to hordes of tourists descending on their city, but haven't gotten tired of meeting them, and seem more than happy to strike up a conversation. Most visitors don't stray off the well-worn tourist tracks, but you're not most visitors, right? The surrounding area is safe at night, so leave the city walls and go for a moonlit walk in the countryside—any directions you choose to go will provide you with gorgeous views.

cafe scene

With so many tourists milling around town, it's no surprise that caffeine and sugar (in the form of cappuccino, espresso, pastries, and gelato) are readily available at the town's many cafes and *gelaterías.* Take your jolt of choice to an outdoor table, or enjoy it on the Duomo's steps.

Jolly *(Piazza della Cisterna 34; Tel/Fax 0577/940-337; 9am-10pm daily; V, MC, AE, EC)* has some of the best ice cream in town, and their outdoor tables are perfect for people-watching. This brightly lit ice-cream parlor offers more than the typical cone—try a huge ice cream sundae in a pretty cocktail glass. The house specialties are *Zuppa Toscana* and *Terra di Siena,* but all flavors are homemade in the old tradition.

The competition, **Gelatería di Piazza** *(Piazza della Cisterna 4; Tel 0577/942-244; 9am-10pm daily; sedondo@tin.it; V, MC, AE, EC),* in the same piazza, also has very good ice cream, with loads of unique flavors. Even the local wine, Vernaccia, gets turned into ice cream.

Lucia & Maria *(Via San Matteo 55; Tel 0577/940-379; No credit cards),* a large, elegant shop with a few tables and chairs, has a nice selection of pastries, cakes, and ice cream. There's a pretty "tea room" where you can linger over an espresso or cup of tea and write a few postcards home. The crowd is a mix of locals and fellow travelers.

bar scene

Nightlife in San Gimignano is practically nonexistent, unless you're really into wine. You'll find no pubs or rowdy bars, but instead several *enotecas,* where you can sample the many varieties of San Gimignano's local white wine, Vernaccia. The wine is one of Italy's oldest, dating back to the 13th century, and it's deliciously refreshing and fruity. Many folks come here solely to visit the local wineries and stock up on Vernaccia.

Right on the main drag is the **Enoteca Bar da Gustavo** *(Via San Matteo; Tel 0557/940-057; Noon-11pm daily; V, MC, AE),* a small, family-run place that has one of the best selections in town. It's mostly a wine store, but there's a pretty little bar area where you can taste the local wines for as little as 3,000L a glass. Many of the customers in this tasting room take their wine very seriously—don't let them intimidate you!

Bar Enoteca il Castello *(Via di Castello 20; Tel 0577/941-845, Fax 0577/940-878; Noon-11pm daily, closed Jan 10-Feb 20; ricast@tin.it, www.tin.it/enocast; Wines by the glass start at 3,000L;V, MC, AE, DC),* just east of Piazza della Cisterna, is a little more lively. Also a wine store, it has tables where you can sit and drink your new purchases while ordering full meals [see *eats,* below]. This cozy, tranquil spot has more than 200 wines by the glass, and bread, cheese, salami, and olives that complement them.

From Via San Giovanni, take Via Quercechio west to reach **Enoteca Bruni** *(Via Quercechio 61; Tel 0577/940-442, Fax 0577/940-882; Noon-11pm daily; info@bruniluciano.com, www.bruniluciano.com; Wines by the glass start at 3,000L; V, MC, AE),* which has huge shelves stocked with local and national wines, and a small area for tasting, sitting, and unwinding. There's plenty of finger food for soaking up the wine, and the folks that hang here are friendly, down-to-earth sippers.

But probably the most enjoyable of all is **Enoteca Bar Il Vecchio Granaio** *(Via degli Innocenti 21; Tel/Fax 0577/941-919; Noon-11pm, closed Wed; No cover; V, MC),* two blocks east of Piazza della Cisterna. With pretty, terracotta-tiled floors and vaulted ceilings, the main room is host to a mix of tourists and locals, young and old. Try a few glasses of wine while listening to some live music—jazz, Celtic, and classical concerts are frequent and free, especially in the summer.

arts scene

A few galleries are scattered around town, really just specialty shops and artist's studios catering to the big wallets of tourists—it's all very conservative stuff. Several festivals go on, mostly during the summer, bringing full schedules of musical performances with them [see *festivals and events,* below], but for the rest of the year, the schedule is pretty sporadic.

▶▶VISUAL ARTS

A local artist, Alcon Falcone, exhibits his sculptures in his **Studio d'Arte la Rocca** *(Via della Rocca 1; Tel 0577/940-903; Hours vary; www.alcon-falcone.com).* The sculptures, he says, follow two principles of human existence: the tragedy of conflict and the redemption of the soul when it abandons itself to love. Heavy, man.

Atelier Novalis *(Via San Giovanni 1; Tel 0577/941-678, Fax 0577/906-063; Hours vary; cassandrawainhouse@yahoo.com),* right on the main street, is San Gimignano resident Cassandra Wainhouse's studio and gallery. Her contemporary art is Tuscan-inspired, with lots of brightly colored landscapes and collages.

▶▶PERFORMING ARTS

Teatro dei Leggieri *(Piazza del Duomo, Palazzo del Podestá; Tel 0577/940-742),* across from the Duomo, is the town's only theater. It hosts various theater, dance, music, and opera events, mostly during the town's festivals [see *festivals and events,* below]. The **tourist office** [see *need to know,* below] has up-to-date listings of performances, and sells tickets.

culture zoo

San Gimignano's sights are all within a few steps of each other, around Piazza Duomo. You can definitely cover them in a day or two. The highlights of this small town are the Duomo, which is also called the Basilica Santa Maria Assunta, and the Palazzo del Popolo and its Civic Museum (next to the Duomo), which contains the only tower in town that can still be climbed, the Torre Grossa. Of the town's many other small churches, Chiesa di Sant'Agostino is the nicest. From Via delle Fonti (a few blocks northeast of the Duomo), walk through Porta delle Fonti to see the Gothic medieval fountains, dating back to the 12th century. San Gimignano also has a few specialty museums, like the Museum of Religious Art, the Ornithological Museum, and the Museum of Torture—can you say "tourist trap"?

A combined ticket for practically all the museums costs 20,000L. Combined tickets for the Great Tower and the Civic Museum are just 12,000L. Both can be purchased at any one of these locations.

Basilica Santa Maria Assunta (Duomo) *(Piazza del Duomo; Tel 0577/940-316; 9:30am-7:30pm Mon-Fri, 9:30am-5pm Sat, 1-5pm Sun, Apr-Oct; 9:30am-5pm Mon-Sat, 1-5pm Sun, Nov-Jan 19 and March; Closed between Jan 20 and Feb 28; 6,000L Adults):* It's no longer technically a *Duomo* (cathedral), but the townsfolk still like to call it that. This

festivals and events

San Gimignano's biggest party and most interesting festival is **Carnival** (also called the Devilry Of The Witches Carnival) held on the last two Sundays in February, and the first Sunday in March. Ancient witchcraft practices, parades, masked races, parties, and lots of fireworks—the locals seem to enjoy it as much as the tourists. The **Harvest Festival,** which takes place in mid-June, is a reenactment of life in San Gimignano during medieval times. A parade runs through the city, and performances, games, and jousting competitions go on in the city's main streets and piazzas. The **International Mediterranean Festival of San Gimignano,** from mid-July to early August, brings a full schedule of open-air opera, symphony music, chamber music, cinema, theater, and dance to the piazzas. In September and October, the **San Gimignano Music Festival** brings classical concerts, by national and international performers. For more information on any of these events, contact the tourist office [see *need to know,* below].

12th-century Romanesque church is the artistic highlight of San Gimignano, and it's a lot more interesting inside than the unfinished facade indicates. Also known as *La Collegiata,* it's one of Italy's most elaborately frescoed churches—every corner of the museum-like interior is filled with high quality frescoes from the late 14th-century that are in surprisingly good condition. Highlights include the 26 *Episodes from the Old Testament* (in the left aisle) by Bartolo di Fredi, the *Episodes from the New Testament* (in the right aisle) by Barna da Siena, the *Scenes from the Life of Christ* by Lippo Memmi, and the *Last Judgment* by Taddeo di Bartolo. Be sure to check out the Cappella di Santa Fina (Chapel of St. Fina), which is decorated with frescoes depicting the life of local-girl-turned-saint Fina by Ghirlandaio.

Palazzo del Popolo and **Museo Civico (Civic Museum)** *(Palazzo del Popolo, Piazza del Duomo; Tel 0577/940-008; 9:30am-7:20pm, closed Fri, March-Oct; 10am-5:30pm, closed Fri, Nov-Feb; 7,000L Adults):* Enter the Palazzo Popolo, built in 1288 and now used as the town hall, through the courtyard next to the Duomo. In the courtyard, notice the faded coat-of-arms frescoes of ancient city mayors by Sodoma. Upstairs, in the museum, the first room is the *Sala di Dante* (Dante's room), in which the revered poet once spoke. It contains one of the city's artistic treasures—a *Maestá* by Lippo Memmi. The upper floors of the building house a small but important collection of Sienese and Florentine paintings from the 13th to the 15th century, including works by Pinturicchio (*Madonna With Saints Gregory and Benedict)* and Filippino Lippi *(Annunciation)*.

Torre Grossa (Great Tower) *(Palazzo del Popolo, Piazza del Duomo; Tel 0577/940-008; 9:30am-7:20pm, closed Fri, March-Oct; 10am-5:30pm, closed Fri, Nov-Feb; 8,000L Adults):* The 54m tower is the town's highest, and the only one that can still be climbed. A short exertion is worth it for the great views of the town and surrounding countryside.

Palazzo del Podestá *(Piazza del Duomo; Tel 0577/940-340; 9:30am-7pm daily, summer, 9:30am-5pm Tue-Sun, winter; Free admission):* Across from the Duomo, this palazzo contains one of the oldest towers in town, the Torre Rognosa (Clock Tower), which is 51m high. The building is the old mayor's palace, and in the 13th century a law was passed (which wasn't obeyed) making it illegal to build any tower taller than this one. Pop in and take a quick look around, but there's no need to stay. At the end of the 18th century, this place was converted into the **Teatro dei Leggieri** [see *arts scene,* above].

Museo della Tortura (Museum of Torture) *(Via del Castello 1-3; Tel 0577/942-243, Fax 0577/907-921; 10am-8pm daily Mar-July 18 and Sept 18-Oct; 9am-midnight daily July 19-Sept 17; 10am-7pm daily, Nov-Feb; torture/ats.it; 15,000L adults, 10,000L students):* This house of horrors has found its niche in the Torre del Diavolo (Tower of the Devil). The exhibits chronicle the history of torture, with more than 100 original instruments used for causing pain or death. Though overpriced, the museum is popular with the kiddies, and is a welcome diversion from churches and *Madonna con Bambino* paintings. You'll find it just east of Piazza della Cisterna.

Museo d'Arte Sacra (Museum of Religious Art) *(Piazza Pecori; Tel 0577/942-226; 9:30am-7:30pm daily Apr-Oct; 9:30am-5pm daily Nov-Mar; Closed Jan 21-Feb 28; 5,000L Adults):* Behind the western side of the Duomo, in a small piazza, this museum holds paintings, sculptures, and liturgical pieces from the Duomo and local monasteries. There is also a small collection of local Etruscan findings and tombstones. Unless religious art is your thing, skip it.

Chiesa di Sant'Agostino (Church of St. Agostino) *(Piazza S. Agostino; 7am-noon/3-6pm daily, Nov-Apr; 7am-noon/3-7pm daily, May-Oct; Free admission):* Sant' Agostino is a small, Romanesque/Gothic church on the northwestern edge of the city wall, built between 1280 and 1298, with a very simple facade. The most notable thing about the church is its magnificent Rococo interior and frescoes, particularly the ones around the altar, and *The Life of St. Augustine* on the choir walls.

Rocca di Montestaffoli *(Piazza Propositura; No phone; Free admission):* This 14th-century fortress occupies a good chunk of the city's western side. It also has a nice public garden with lots of fig and olive trees and sprawling views of the countryside—a great spot for a picnic lunch.

Museum Center *(Via Folgore da San Gimignano; 11am-6pm daily, June 1-Sept 30; 6,000L for all three museums):* This museum complex, housed in the former Convent of Santa Chiara, presents an odd mixture of permanent exhibitions, including Classical and medieval archaeological artifacts found around town, the Raffaele de Grada Gallery of Modern Art, and an herbarium displaying ancient pharmacy bottles, equipment, and techniques. Although there is some interesting stuff to be found in these exhibits, if you're only in town for a day or two you'll discover more by just wandering the streets.

CITY SPORTS

Awesome scenery makes San Gimignano a great place to get outside. The friendly staff at the Tourist Information office will help you plan your adventures, from hikes in the countryside to bike rides around town [see *need to know*, below].

Maneggio "C.E.M." *(Sant'Andrea 22, Uligno; Tel 0577/950-232)*, 5km out of town, offers horseback-riding lessons and equestrian tours. The local pool, **Piscina Comunale "Santa Lucia"** *(Loc. Santa Lucia; Tel 0577/940-350; 10am-7pm Mon-Fri, 9:30am-7pm Sat, Sun)*, 2km from the center, is where the locals go to cool off.

STUFF

Unless your goal is to stock up on wine to ship back home, forget about retail therapy in San Gimignano. Via San Matteo and Via San Giovanni are the main shopping streets, and have a few clothing and souvenir stores, but there's really nothing special here. Save your money for a major splurge elsewhere.

▶▶DUDS
Emporium *(Via San Matteo 21; Tel 0577/940-707; 9am-1:30pm/4-8pm daily; V, MC, AE)* sells their own handmade leather clothing and handbags along with a selection of designer labels like coccinelle, Fendi, Diesel, Moschino, and Francesco Biasia. They have a second location down the street at Via San Giovanni 29 *(Tel 0577/940-022; 9am-1:30pm/4-8pm daily; V, MC, AE)*, which is just as tempting, and just as expensive.

▶▶HOW BAZAAR
On Thursdays from about 8am till 1pm there are markets in Piazza Duomo, Piazza della Cisterna, and Piazza delle Erbe. Expect a random sampling of cheap clothes and housewares.

▶▶SOUVENIRS AND RANDOM STUFF
Leoncini *(Via San Giovanni 60-64; Tel 0577/942-086, Fax 0577/097-542; 9am-1:30pm/4-8pm daily; info@leoncini-italy.com, www.leoncini-italy.com; V, MC)* sells beautiful handmade Tuscan ceramics, at tourist prices. They have a few small items that would make great mementos—feel free to haggle.

EATS

During the day, especially in summer, most restaurants are packed with day-trippin' tourists. So if you're lucky enough to be staying overnight, save your mealtime energy for dinner, when the tourists are long gone and you can gobble up a great meal with locals at one of San Gimignano's

TO MARKET

Via San Matteo and Via San Giovanni are full of food shops—a great way to dodge the high restaurant prices without going hungry. **Fiaschetteria Antonella e Lorenzo** *(Via San Giovanni 94; Tel 0577/940-544)* has lots of locally made salami, meat, cheese, Vernaccia wine, grappa, and olive oil. **Mari dal 1920** *(Via San Giovanni 12; Tel 0577/940-673, Fax 0577/932-177; maridal1920@cyber.dada.it)* has a good selection of high quality, fresh, local foods and wines.

killer restaurants. Most of the food here is typically Tuscan, and made from fresh, local ingredients with an emphasis on hearty soups, wild mushrooms, and game—like *cinghiale* (wild boar) and *lepre* (hare). Several of the *enotecas* [see *bar scene,* above] double as casual restaurants serving homey, inexpensive meals—that's tip number one for saving money on your meal. Tip number two: tons of food stores [see *to market,* below] sell delicious, local ingredients for excellent picnic dinners.

▶▶CHEAP
La Mandragola *(Via Berignano 58; Tel 0577/942-110, Fax 0577/940-377; Closed Dec and Feb; Avg. meal 40,000-50,000L; V, MC, AE)* has the cheapest tourist menu in town, at 23,000L (if you order off the regular menu, prices shoot up dramatically). Homemade pasta dishes, particularly those with wild mushrooms, are fantastic. Located in the southern end of the city, one block west of Via San Giovanni.

▶▶DO-ABLE
The best thing about **Ristorante La Griglia** *(Via San Matteo 34; Tel 0577/940-005, Fax 0577/942-131; 12:30am-10pm, closed Thur, closed Jan-Feb; Avg. meal 40,000L; V, MC, AE)* is that it's open in those few hours between lunch and dinner, when it's nearly impossible to find anything to eat in small Italian towns. This pretty, two-tiered place, with red tablecloths and lots of knick-knacks, is popular with the locals, who linger over huge carafes of inexpensive Vernaccia. The menu is a study in extremes—simple dishes like lasagna next to hearty game specialties cooked with truffles. The tourist menu here is 32,000L, but ordering from the regular menu isn't much more expensive.

Bar Enoteca Il Castello [see *bar scene,* above] is a lively little wine bar known for its Tuscan home cooking. With more than 200 different types of wine by the glass, you're sure to find a few good matches with the house special—wild boar *alla San gimignanese* with *polenta.* With wine, a full meal in this rustic dining room will run you about 30,000L.

Few spots in town—or anywhere—are as charming as **Beppone** *(Via delle Romite 13; Tel 0577/943-135; beppone@cyber.dada.it; Noon-3pm/7-10pm, closed Sun; Avg. meal 40,000L)*, a casual trattoria one block west of Porta delle Fonti. Families, couples, and tourists eat Tuscan specialties and oversized pizzas under old brick arches. The red lanterns on every table cast a pretty glow over the room, which is lined with bottles of wine, ceramic plates, and tons of candles.

Although the dining room at **La Stella** *(Via San Matteo 77; Tel 0577/940-829, Fax 0577/940-444; Closed Wed, closed Nov, Jan-Feb; Avg. meal 40,000L; V, MC, AE)* is a little too brightly lit, you'll love the great family-run feel, from friendly waiters to super-fresh food. Try the *ribollita* (meat broth and vegetable soup) and the wild boar *cacciatore*. House wines are delicious and inexpensive, and the tourist menu is just 25,000L.

▶▶SPLURGE

Le Terrazze *(La Cisterna Hotel, Piazza della Cisterna 24; Tel 0577/940-328; 12:30-2:30pm/7:30-10pm Thur-Mon, 7-10pm Wed; Avg. meal with drinks 60,000L; V, MC, AE, DC)*, the restaurant of hotel **La Cisterna** [see *crashing*, below], is one of the city's finest. As its name implies, it features a terrace, which offers stunning views of the rolling Tuscan hills. The inside dining rooms are medieval-themed, with low ceilings, wooden beams, and lots of windows. There's a tourist menu for 35,000L, but you'll want to order a la carte here. The hearty *zuppa alla sangimignanese* is a perfect antipasto (and the house specialty), but don't miss out on the beautifully prepared game meats.

crashing

San Gimignano is small, but smart. The town has carefully planned its tourist industry to bring in as much money as possible. The idea, naturally, is to go for big bucks from those who can afford it (older, wealthier travelers) rather than for a continuous trickle of chump-change from tight-budgeted backpackers. The city isn't snobbish or pretentious, but they don't exactly roll out the red carpet for backpackers. So there are no cheap hotels in town, though there is a very popular hostel. Don't even think about showing up mid-summer without an advance reservation, because the hostel will be full and you could easily blow your entire budget on a room at one of the few hotels that does have space available. San Gimignano's saving grace is that you can rent a room in a private home (the tourist office will provide you with a list), and many restaurants and *enotecas* rent out their upstairs rooms to overnight guests.

▶▶CHEAP

The only cheap place in town is the non-HI **hostel** *(Via delle Fonti 1; Tel 0577/941-991; 7:30-9:00am/5-11:30pm reception Mar 1-Oct 31, 11:30pm curfew; 30,000L bed in a dorm room, 35,000L bed in a quad, 40,000L bed in a double, breakfast included; No credit cards)*, located inside the town walls near the Porta delle Fonti. With a total of 75 beds, most in dorm rooms, (there are four that serve as doubles or quads), this is one of Tuscany's most relaxing and comfortable hostels. The meals are tasty, and at 17,000L, a bargain compared to some of the local restaurants. Reserve well in advance. From Porta San Matteo take Via Cellolese east, then turn south on Via delle Romite; take an immediate right on Via delle Romite and then another immediate right on Via delle Fonti and you're there.

▶▶**DO-ABLE**

Located in a restored 15th-century palazzo at the northwestern end of Via San Matteo, **Hotel L'Antico Pozzo** *(Via San Matteo 87; Tel 0577/942-014, Fax 0577/942-117; 12:30am-6am reception closed; antpozzo//web.tin.it/antpozzo; 95,000-140,000L singles, 132,000-250,000L doubles, breakfast included; V, MC, AE, DC)* is one of the most pleasant hotels in town. At the end of the 18th century this place was a well-known house of ill repute, but now breakfast is served in the old ballroom. The concierge is extremely friendly and helpful; all rooms have phones, satellite TVs, private baths, and minibars. A computer by the bar in the basement is one of the only places in town to get online. If you need to work on your tan before heading home, there's even a solarium in the hotel.

Hotel Leon Bianco *(Piazza della Cisterna 13; Tel 0577/941-294, Fax 0577/942-123; leonbianco@see.it, www.see.it; 95,000-160,000L singles, 194,000-215,000L doubles; V, MC, AE, DC)* is in a restored 14th-century palazzo, with charming views of Piazza della Cisterna on one side and panoramic views of the countryside on the other. The theme here is very Pottery Barn-Tuscan Rustic; most of the 21 rooms are fairly spacious and come with private baths, phones, and TVs. There's no restaurant, but there is a bar and a few other common areas. Breakfast is included, and if the weather is nice, the best place to eat is up on the rooftop balcony.

Another renovated 14th-century palazzo, just across the main piazza from Hotel Leon Bianco, is home to **La Cisterna** *(Piazza della Cisterna 24; Tel 0577/940-328, Fax 0577/942-080; Closed Jan-Feb; lacisterna@iol.it; 95,000-160,000L singles, 155,000- 195,000L doubles, breakfast included; V, MC, AE, DC)*. The hotel was one of San Gimignano's first, and remains one of its best. Its 49 rooms are furnished in the classic Florentine style, and some have balconies with views of the countryside. The hotel offers a half-board option and the restaurant, **Le Terrazze** [see *eats,* above], is fantastic. All rooms have private baths, TVs, blow-dryers, and phones.

Villa Belvedere *(Via Dante 14; Tel 0577/940-539, Fax 0577/940-327; 95,000-160,000L singles, 132,000-270,000L doubles, breakfast included; V, MC, AE, DC)* is a 15-minute walk northwest of the city center, through Porta San Matteo. It has a garden with olive and cypress trees, and the hammock is heaven after a day of sight-seeing or traveling. All the rooms have private baths, TVs, phones, and minibars, and are super-lovely. If you don't mind the hike, this is a great place, and the pool is perfect for those quiet San Gimignano summer nights.

Bel Soggiorno *(Via San Giovanni 91; Tel 0577/940-375, Fax 0577/907-521; Closed Jan-Feb; 95,000L singles, 150,000-160,000L doubles, 15,000L breakfast; V, MC, AE, DC)* is at the southern end of Via San

Giovanni, a few steps from Porta San Giovanni. The hotel has been open since the late 19th century, and is tastefully decorated in the Tuscan style. About half the rooms have balconies, and all are comfortable, with private baths, TVs, and phones. There's even a bar—book this one ahead.

need to know

Currency Exchange The best place to change money is at the **tourist office. ATMs** are scattered throughout town.

Tourist Information The **Informazione Association Pro Loco** *(Piazza Duomo 1; Tel 0577/940-008, Fax 0577/940-903; 9am-1pm/2-6pm daily, Nov-Feb; 9am-1pm/3-7pm daily, Mar-Oct; prolocsg@tin.it, www.sangimignano.com)* is extremely helpful. They can place international calls for you (you pay the charges, of course), send faxes, change money, help out with bus, train, and ferry information for anywhere in the country, and give you more information than you could ever use on day trips from San Gimignano. The **Siena Hotels Promotion** *(Via San Giovanni 125; Tel/Fax 0577/940-809; 9:30am-12:30pm/3-6pm, closed Sun, winter; 9:30am-7:30pm, closed Sun, summer; hotsnagi@tin.it; www.hotelsiena.com)* office can make hotel reservations for you for a few thousand lira.

Public Transportation There is **no public transportation** in San Gimignano—not even taxis.

Health and Emergency Emergency: *113;* Police emergencies: *112;* Medical emergencies: *118;* Ambulance service: *0577/940-263.* There's a **police station** *(Piazzale Martiri di Montemaggio; Tel 0577/940-313)* on the southern side of town.

Pharmacies **Pharmacies** are in Piazza della Cisterna and Piazza delle Erbe—look for the green, neon crosses.

Telephone City code: *0577.* There are **pay phones** in Piazzale Martiri Montemaggio and Piazza delle Erbe.

Trains San Gimignano doesn't have a train station. To get here you must take either the **train** or the **bus** to Poggibonsi, step outside the station, and catch the next bus for San Gimignano. The train station in Poggibonsi, **Stazione F.S. di Poggibonsi,** *(Tel 0577/933-646 or*

wired

Wanna make a million dollars? Open a cyber-cafe in San Gimignano. Just about the only place in town with Internet access is **Hotel L'Antico Pozzo** [see *crashing*, above], which has one computer and charges high rates (10,000L per half-hour). For information on San Gimignano on the web try *www.sangimignano.com.*

0577/936-462), is about a 25-minute bus ride away and is connected by frequent trains from Florence and Siena.

Bus Lines Out of the City Frequent **TRA-IN** *(0577/204-111)* buses connect Poggibonsi and San Gimignano, from about 6am to 9pm. All buses arriving and departing from San Gimignano can drop you at either Porta San Matteo and Porta Giovanni on weekdays, but on weekends they only stop at Porta Giovanni. Tickets can be bought at the tourist office or at any bar or *tabacchi* (2,600L). Frequent buses also go from Poggibonsi to Florence (60-75 minutes) and to Siena (one hour). Day-trippers, take note: The last bus going in either direction leaves at 8:35pm.

Bike/Moped Rental Bellini Bruno *(Via Roma 41; Tel 0577/940-201 or 0348/412-54-88)* and **Pentacar** *(Viale Garibaldi 5; Tel 0577/940-575 or 0347/939-23-54)* rents, and can deliver, bikes and mopeds. Scooters generally cost 35,000L to 45,000L per half-day, and 50,000L to 65,000L for a whole day. For a half a day bikes are generally 15,000L to 28,000L, and 30,000L to 50,000L for full days. **Tourist Information** can help you organize your route, and will provide you with free maps of the province.

Postal There's a **post office** *(Piazza delle Erbe; 8:15am-7pm, closed Sun)* in the city center.

Internet See *wired,* above.

VOLTERRA

This little medieval village looks like a Gothic fortress rising up out of the hills, with a row of dark and craggy buildings forming a wall along a narrow ridge 1,800 feet above the valley below—it's all pretty dramatic. Behind the ridge, tiny curvy streets plunge down to meet the central piazza. The countryside around here is a bit wilder than in other parts of the region; a nice change from the sometimes overly manicured, post-card-ready Tuscan landscape. You could likely see all you need to see in Volterra in a day trip, but with less-than-regular bus schedule would make getting here and back out in day a real pain. So stay the night and soak in all that great "Tuscan hill town" atmosphere you've heard so much about.

Volterra crawls with tourists in the summer, a good number of whom show up in search of the famous white alabaster carvings that have been a part of the local culture for the past 3,000 years. Though you'll see low-quality chess sets and miniatures of Michaelangelo's David carved from alabaster hocked on the streets and in souvenir shops, don't get the wrong idea—alabaster carving is a serious art. Ancient Estrucean sarcophagi carved from alabaster fill the **Museo Etrusco Guarnacci** [see *culture zoo,* below], and you can major in alabaster carving at the local art school. If you want to see some of the good stuff, check out the

Società Coopertiva Artiere Alabastro *(Piazza die Priori 4-5; Tel 0588/87590),* an artists' cooperative that's been around since 1895.

It's easy to find your way around here. The bus will drop you at **Piazza Martiri della Libertà,** on the south side of town. Walk north for all of about two minutes to get to the **Piazza dei Priori,** the central part of the town.

CULTURE ZOO

There's only one ticket in town, which covers all three major museums (the churches and Palazzo are free). It's 10,000L for adults, 7,000L for students. The summer hours run from March 16 through October 15.

Palazzo dei Priori *(Piazza dei Priori; Tel 0588/86050; 10am-1pm/3-4pm Mon-Sat summer, 10am-1pm Mon-Sat winter; Free admission):* You can't miss this one—it dominates the Piazza dei Priori. It's worth at least a walk-by because it's the granddady of all Tuscan palazzos, and the one that Florence's Palazzo Vecchio, and most other palazzos in the region, were modeled on. The only thing of much interest inside is the town council chamber, which has looked pretty much the same for 740 years.

Duomo *(Piazza San Giovanni (also has entrance on Piazza dei Priori); No phone; Free admission):* You've got to stop in here for at least a few minutes to throw your head back and take a look at the amazing ceiling. It's carved and embossed with gold and azure, and filled with portraits od Volterran saints. There are a bunch of Baroque paintings scattered throughout the church as well, but no stand-outs. Go stare at the hills instead.

Museo Etrusco Guarnacci *(Via Don Minzoni 15; Tel 0588/86347; 9am-7pm daily summer, till 2pm winter, closed Jan 1 & Dec 25):* Okay, this is the real reason to buy that 3-for-1 museum pass deal. Who would have guessed that one of Italy's best archaeological museums was tucked away in tiny Volterra? The main event here are the funerary urns, many of which date from the 3rd century B.C., with some as early as the 9th century B.C. The earliest ones are in unadorned terra-cotta, but the majority are carved from the local alabaster or some other stone, with reliefs on the front and ornately sculpted lids depicting the deceased. There is room after room of these babies...maybe you don't need to see them all, but wander through at least a few—there's an incredible one in room XX of an elderly couple, holding on to each other till the bitter end. Oh and there's also the predictable collection of urns and busts and mosaics.

Museo Civico *(Palazzo Minucci Solaini; Tel 0588/87580; 9am-7pm daily summer, 9am-2pm winter, closed Jan 1 & Dec 25):* The best of what came out of Volterra, artistically, from the 12th to the 17th century has been rounded up and deposited here. Art students could spend hours, the rest of us may just want to take a quick stroll around. The only thing close to jaw-dropping is the *Deosition,* an early work by the young Rosso Fiorentini—his exaggerated use of light and color make this a real Renaissance original.

Museo d'Arte Sacra *(Palazzo Vescovile; Tel 0588/87580; 9:30am-1pm/3-6:30pm daily summer, no later afternoon hours in winter):* We'll give this place a half-hour, tops. The work here is older than at the Museo Civico, with some really neat medieval fragments. Check out the *Madonna of Ulignano,* by local boy Daniele da Volterra who struck out for the big city and became Michaelangelo's apprentice.

EATS

Haul yourself out of bed early if you're here on a Saturday morning for the **weekly market** held in the Piazza die Priori. Grab some provisions and go sit outside the city walls for the most picturesque picnic you may ever have.

The locals love the small and simple **Da Bago** *(Bgo. S. Lazzerro; Tel 0588/86477; Noon-2pm Thurs-Tues, closed July and Sept 1-10; 7-9,000L first courses, 9-14,500L second courses; No credit cards)* for it's commitment to traditional local dishes like the *zuppa alla Volterrano* (a thick stew with fresh veggies), *papparedelle alla lepre* (wide homemade egg noodles in a hare sauce), and the house specialty, *trippa alla Volterrano* (tripe stewed with tomatoes and herbs). You can honestly taste how fresh the ingredients are. It's outside the city walls, technically in the satellite village of San Lazzaro, but really only a 200-yard stroll away.

crashing

Yes, the buses are a little spotty, and you'll probably end up spending the night. But luckily there's a decent youth hostel in town. The non-HI **Ostella della Gioventù** *(Via Don Minzoni; Tel 0588/85577; Lock-out 9am-5pm, midnight curfew; 20,000L dorm bed, 50,000L double)* is standard in every way, but it's clean as can be and the staff is extra-friendly. You'll find it right down the street from the **Museo Etrusco Guarnacci** [see *culture zoo,* below].

If you've got a little more cash to blow, try the **Etruria** *(Via Matteoni 32; Tel/Fax 0588/87377; 60-80,000L double w/out bath, 80-100,000L double w/bath, breakfast 10,000L; MC, V),* right in the middle of town. It's housed in an 18th-century palazzo, but don't expect royal digs—the rooms are fairly simple, though immaculate, with vintage 1975 furnishings. The rooftop terrace, however, is worth the price of admission. It gives you a bird's eye view of all the rooftops in town, and, the coolest thing, has a gate the leads into Volterra's public gardens. Call ahead if you know what's good for you.

need to know

Tourist Information The helpful, well-stocked **information office** *(Via Turazza 2; Tel/Fax 0588/86150; 9am-1pm/2-7pm daily April-Oct, till 6:30pm daily Nov-March)* is just around the corner from the Piazza del Priori.

Bus Lines Out of the City There are 24 **SITA** buses a day from Pisa to Colle di Val d'Elsa, where you can transfer to one of the five buses a day that run to Volterra. It's even more of a pain in the butt from San Gimignano: You have to catch one of the four buses a day that run to

Poggibonsi and link up with buses to Colle di Val d'Elsa for the final transfer. It's easier from the big cities—SITA runs two mid-afternoon direct runs to Volerra, plus five daily buses to Colle di Val d'Elsa. Seven **APT** buses run here Monday to Saturday from Pisa, with only one transfer, in the town of Pontedera. There's no bus station in Volterra; you get tickets and information at the tourist office and catch the buses in Piazza Martiri della Libertà.

SIENA

Siena is often referred to as "Florence's little sister." It's got all the famous art museums, medieval architecture, shopping streets, fine restaurants, and tourist-filled piazzas that Florence does, but on a smaller, more intimate scale. Yet Siena feels more cosmopolitan and more modern than it actually is, probably because its narrow cobblestone streets are packed with boutiques, gourmet stores, Sienese residents dressed head-to-toe in the latest fashions, and grannies whizzing through the crowds on shiny Vespas. And tons of great bars, packed with students, Italian and otherwise.

It only takes a couple of days to check out the major sights, such as the famous fan-shaped, pink **Piazza del Campo** (one of the most romantic places in Europe to hang out after dark), but do yourself a favor and stick around for a little longer just to enjoy this really cool little city. Siena has a big-city feel, but it also has small-town friendliness, due to the size of its population (just 57,000). Hang out in most any bar and you'll bang into Italian students who will be happy to sit and yak, just to practice their English with you. Both the University of Siena and Università per Stranieri (for foreigners), are in session year-round, and together they fuel a vibrant nightlife. The scene is laid-back and welcoming—Italian girls wearing fierce high heels and grungy kids with pink hair and baggy jeans all hang out in the same piazzas, bars, and cafes.

But step away from the crowds, uphill into the residential areas, to see the other Siena: Residents hang pictures of their patron saints above their doors, old ladies dress in black aprons and kerchiefs (the mourning period in Italy is something like forever) and Italian housewives do their shopping once or twice a day just a few feet away from their front doors. The medieval spirit is alive and well in the ancient rites and traditions which remain a part of daily life, like the *contrade* (regions) into which the city and its citizens are divided [see *only here,* below], and the annual horserace between them, *Il Palio* [see *festivals and events,* below]. Il Palio is the city's ultimate party, and it's been going on since at least 1310, when the first written record of it was made.

Two legends tell the story of Siena's founding. The first says it was established by a tribe of Gauls. But the second, which says that it was founded by Senius, son of Remus, is the one the Sienese like to believe. A quick history lesson: According to legend, twins Romulus and Remus were raised by a she-wolf. Romulus killed Remus, and in 753 B.C. founded the village that eventually became Rome. You can spot statues of the she-wolf suckling her twins all over town.

Siena hit its cultural peak between the end of the 13th century and the beginning of the 14th, when the majority of the Gothic monuments, buildings, and artwork that still define Siena's image were created. Siena has a history of conflict with Florence, and in 1555, the Medicis took control of the town.

neighborhoods

Although the *contrade* define the city's social regions [see *only here,* below], Siena has no distinct geographic sectors—which doesn't matter all that much because it's so small that you don't need any further divisions to keep yourself oriented. The only major geographic landmark is the jagged ancient walls that enclose the historical center.

You'll likely start your time in Sienna at **Piazza Gramsci,** at the northern end of the city center. The buses from out of town will drop you here, as will the city bus that runs from the train station, which is located northwest of the city center on **Piazza Fratelli Rosselli,**. It's a fairly grueling half-hour uphill walk from the train station into the center, so the city bus (# 2,4,6, or 10) is really the way to go. Other than that, there's no need to take a city bus—most Sienese walk everywhere within the historic center, and only use the buses when they go outside the city walls. There's very limited bus service within the city since most streets are narrow and closed to traffic.

only here

There's a reason that people in Siena seem to know everyone who walks down their street: They do. Siena was once divided into 80 *contrade* (urban districts), but over the years the number has been reduced to the current 17. The *contrade* are bound to ancient rites—you're born into one, and not allowed to convert. Each *contrada* is named after an animal, and has its own mayor who takes care of everyday issues in the neighborhood. Signs of the importance and influence of the *contrade* are all over town: colorful animal flags, processions and celebrations on feast days, and weddings and other events in which most members of the *contrada* participate. If you want more info, each *contrada* has its own museum, visit-able by appointment only—the **tourist office** [see *need to know,* below] can give you phone numbers.

siena bars clubs and culture zoo

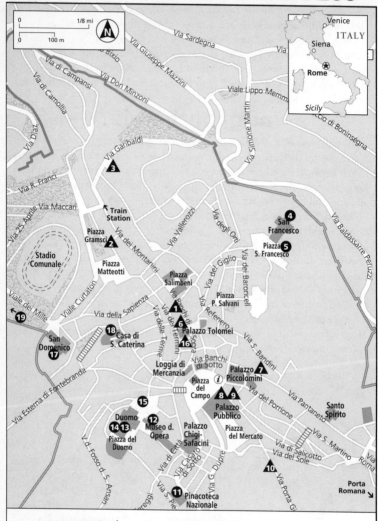

BARS/CLUBS ▲

Bar Le Logge 7
Barone Rosso 16
Caffé del Corso 1
The Dublin Post 2
Enoteca I Terzi 6
L'Officina Pub 3
Porta Giustizia 11
Tea Room 10

CULTURE ZOO ●

Basilica di San Domenico 17
Basilica di San Francesco 4
Battistero di San Giovanni 15
Duomo 13
Libreria Piccolomini 14
Museo Civico 8
Museo dell' Opera Metropolitana 12
National Picture Gallery 11
Oratoria di San Bernadino 5
Permanent Italian Wine Library 19
Sanctuary and House of St. Catherine 18
Torre del Mangia 9

The famous **Piazza del Campo,** about a 10-minute walk south of Piazza Gramsci, is the geographic, political, and social center of town. Most streets branch out from here. The **Duomo,** one of Italy's finest, sits a few blocks west from here.

hanging out

Piazza del Campo is the granddaddy of all Italian piazzas, and it's happening morning, noon, and night. Its seashell shape and pink hue make it unlike any other town square in Italy (you half expect a 150-ft Venus to pop up and scare the bejezzus out of all the tourists). If you want to blend in a little more with the locals, stay around the perimeter, instead of plopping down on the ground in the center like most tourists do. Bring a bottle of wine, a can of beer, or a picnic dinner, and you just might make some new friends. No other piazza can quite match Piazza del Campo— in size, beauty, or popularity—but **Piazza del Duomo, Piazza San Francesco,** and **Piazza Tolomei** attract those looking for quieter places to hang out. Siena's streets tend to be busiest during the evening *passeggiata* (stroll), when the entire population emerges onto the main streets in their finest duds for a bit of socializing. It's the beginning of the fun hours, and usually requires a few pit stops at local cafes and bars.

cafe scene

No matter how hard you try to resist the tourist-trap cafes in Piazza del Campo, sooner or later you'll probably cave. Those rows and rows of inviting little tables are just too tempting. Hey, it's vacation—lose your guilt. You pay for the setting on this grand piazza, and it's worth it once in a while—especially at sunset, when the *passeggiata* is in full swing. The three cafes we list here are all on the Pizza del Campo.

Drinks at most places on the piazza, like **Bar Il Palio** *(Piazza Il Campo 47; Tel 0577/282-055; V, MC, AE),* are twice what they are anywhere else—so have a coffee or a beer and plan on staying put for a while. (Don't you dare order food.)

One of Siena's favorite cafes is **Bar Pasticceria Conca d'Ora** *(Via Banchi di Sopra 24; Tel 0577/41-591; 7:30am-midnight Tue-Sun, 7:30am-8:30pm Mon; V, MC),* which is also a good place to try the Nannini family's famous Sienese sweets. The cafe is particularly proud of its rich and sticky *panforte* (fruit cake) and *nougat* (vanilla-infused, with nuts), which your sweet tooth will adore.

Any flavor of creamy, heavenly, homemade *gelato* you can imagine is available at **Gelateria Nannini** *(Banchi di Sopra 95-97; Tel 0577/44-225; 7:30am-8:30pm daily, 2,500L per cone; V, MC).* No trip to Siena is complete without a visit to this little take-away joint.

bar, club, and live music scene

Here's the thing about bars in Siena: There aren't very many. But don't let that scare you away. Forget the jaded local cabbies who tell you, "It's better to go to bed at night." They're just stuck in their Florence's-little-sister complex. Truth is, Siena's limited-but-quality nocturnal haunts are varied, inexpensive, and really fun. Locals, students, and tourists make their rounds between quiet *enotecas,* cafes with outdoor tables, and thumping live music venues. BYOB to Piazza del Campo and spend a few hours looking up at the stars (or across the piazza at everyone else doing the same thing).

During summer, and less often in spring and fall, outdoor rave-like parties rave on in the suburbs and small towns outside of Siena. Buses usually leave from Piazza Gramsci; pick up flyers from **Dischi Corsini** [see *stuff,* below] or call 0577/318-118 for information and schedules.

Your pierced waiter at **Caffé del Corso** *(Banchi di Sopra; Tel 0577/223-788; 8am-11pm daily; No credit cards)* serves espresso and croissants to old ladies in the morning, and then cocktails and beer to the young, tight-clothed Sienese after 8pm, when the music gets a little louder. The green marble bar isn't very big, but it's what the Italians call an "American bar," because highballs and other mixed drinks are the beverages of choice. Cool music—Italian pop mixed with reggae—and a hip crowd make this one of the focal points of Siena's scene.

L'Officina Pub *(Piazza del Sale 3; Tel 0577/286-301; 6pm-3am daily; No cover; V, MC),* two blocks northeast of La Lizza, is everything to everyone. Get here early to score one of the choice outdoor tables; otherwise, you'll have to elbow your way through the massive inside space. A huge screen shows cartoons, videos, and, on the rowdiest occasions, soccer games. The crowd is mixed—lots of students, tourists, and young professionals still in work clothes. Every now and then, the owners bring in local bands to entertain the masses.

Bar Le Logge *(Via Pantaneto 11; No phone; 6:30am-9pm daily; Avg. wine by the glass 4,000L; No credit cards)* is really just a cafe, but at night, it's one of the locals' preferred drinking establishments. The loft-like second floor, with its few tables, is much more comfortable than the packed-solid bar area. The music is your typical Top 40/Italian pop blend—show up around 8pm for a glass of local wine and the house specialty: small plates of cheese, olives, and salami.

Enoteca I Terzi *(Via de Termini 7; Tel/Fax 0577/4439; 12am-4:30pm/6:30pm-1am daily; Wine by the glass 5,000-15,000L, appetizers 12,000-20,000L; V, MC, DC, AE)* is definitely not for beer drinkers. Although it's a bit snobby, the long wine list and nice patio will make you forget all that. Located on a quiet street a few blocks north of Piazza Indipendenza, the bar has a patio surrounded by brick walls that's perfect for some juicy, wine-induced conversation. The inside area, with its brick walls, vaulted ceilings, and wooden tables, is just as intimate. Sample local and national wines from the long list, and try some delicious Tuscan snacks—*bruschetta* and *crostini* with various fresh toppings, cured meats and sausages, and cheese.

Barone Rosso *(Via de Termine 9; No phone; 9pm-2am or 3am daily; Beer 5,000-6,000L; No cover; V, MC)* is where the beer-drinkers go. Drinks are super-cheap, thus wall-to-wall students. There's often free live music;

it's typical Europop from the stereo otherwise. The place is so big that even during peak hours (which start around midnight), there's usually some space upstairs. Even if you don't find anyone interesting to talk to, checking out the random decorations on the wall should keep you entertained. If all else fails, eat a sandwich: all named after cartoon characters and all pretty tasty.

Every Italian town has to have at least one Irish pub. The **Dublin Post** *(Piazza Gramsci 20-21; Tel/Fax 0577/289-089; Noon-1am daily; Avg. beer 8,000L; V, MC),* just across from the bus terminal on Piazza Gramsci, is Siena's. It looks like any Irish bar in any corner of the world, with Guiness posters and pictures of Ireland on the walls, and Kilkenny on tap. The crowd, mainly tourists and students, is friendly, laid-back, and eager to meet new people.

The decor at **Porta Giustizia 11 Tea Room** *(Porta Giustizia 11; Tel 0577/222-753; 9pm-3am, closed Mon; No cover; No credit cards),* a few blocks southeast of Piazza del Mercato, includes a random mix of fantastic stuff that the owners probably took years accumulating at flea markets. If you're not into boisterous bar scenes, the Tea Room is a cool place to come for a late-night glass of wine, grappa, or tea. The crowd is down-to-earth at this tiny place—muscle your way over to the cozy fireplace and take a seat. Saturday night jazz bands pack 'em in, and, come summer, live music plays two nights during the week.

arts scene

Modern art takes a back seat to Siena's medieval and Renaissance masterpieces. The few contemporary spots feel more like shops than art galleries, but they're a welcome change when you've had enough of the past. Check in with the art crowd at **Tea Room** [see *bar, club, and live music scene,* above] to find out about openings and exhibitions. Performing arts abound, especially from June through September. The **tourist office** [see *need to know,* below] has detailed information.

▶▶VISUAL ARTS

Contemporary art exhibitions at the smallish **Alessandro Bagni** *(Via San Girolamo 13-17; Tel 0577/285-044, Fax 0577/270-673; 10:30am-1pm/4-7:30pm, closed Sun, Mon; alessandro.bagnai@si.nettuno.it; Free admission)* change frequently. The owner speaks English and will happily walk you through the gallery, explaining each piece.

Galleria d'Arte "Porto All' Arco" *(Via S. Agata 36; Tel/Fax 0577/247-586; 10:30am-1pm/4:30-7:45pm, closed Sun; Free admission)* holds more ambitious exhibitions of international (but mostly British and Italian) modern and contemporary art. The work on display in its six rooms, which ranges from installation pieces to straight sculpture, changes roughly once a month.

If ancient artifacts are your thing, go to **Fotoarte** *(Via C. Angiolieri 49; Tel/Fax 0577/226-080; 10am-7pm, closed Sun, Mon Oct-May; 10am-8pm Tue-Sat, 4-8pm Mon June-Sept; Free admission)* to admire black and white photos of ancient and medieval Tuscany.

fESTIVALS and EVENTS

Il Palio, held every July 2 and August 16, is one of Italy's longest-running and most dramatic annual events. Truckloads of sand transform Piazza del Campo into a racetrack for the big event—the Sienese spend all year planning for this. Other games, celebrations, parades, feasts, and religious ceremonies take place in the days before and after. The *Palio,* which is in honor of the Virgin Mary, has taken place practically every year since the 13th century, but now, only 10 of Siena's 17 *contrade* [see *only here,* below] can compete (straws are drawn). Even if you're lucky enough to be in town for the *Palio,* it takes some work and lots of cash to get a good view of it—tickets for seats around the edges of the piazza or for space in one of the balconies cost upwards of 400,000L. If you're on a budget, your money might be better spent on some sandwiches and beer to keep you occupied while you crowd into the center of the piazza with all the other young people in Siena (get there at least four or five hours early). If spending hours in hot, tight, dusty spaces isn't your thing, then do what the older Sienese do: watch it in a bar, on TV. If you're not in town for the race and want to know what this *Palio* thing is all about, do the touristy thing and watch *Il Palio*—the movie at the **Cinemo Moderno** *(Piazza Tolomei; Tel 0577/378-568, Fax 0577/378-698; 20-minute film shown from 9:30am-4pm Mon-Sat; 10,000L).*

Nothing beats the *Palio,* but a world-renowned international jazz festival also comes to town every July and August. Many concerts are held in the open air or at the Fortrezza Medici. For information about **Siena Jazz** call 0577/271-401.

▶▶PERFORMING ARTS

The **Accademia Musicale Chigiana** *(Via di Cittá 89; Tel 0577/46-152, Fax 0577/288-124)* holds concerts year-round and also hosts several popular annual events. Stop by **tourist information** [see *need to know,* below] to buy tickets.

The **Associazione Siena Jazz** *(Via Vallerozzi 77; Tel 0577/271-401, Fax 0577/281-404),* one of Europe's most prestigious music schools, can provide information about jazz concerts year-round in Siena.

Teatro dei Rinnovati *(Palazzo Pubblico; Tel 0577/292-265)* hosts a mixed bag of opera, theater, and ballet performances. Stop by **tourist information** [see *need to know,* below] to buy tickets.

Cinema Odeon *(Via Banchi di Sopra 31; Tel 0557/42-976)* and **Al Cinema Impero** *(Via Calzoleria 44; Tel 0577/48-260),* between Banchi di Sotto and Piazza Tolomei, both cater to an international crowd with films in the *lingua originale*.

gay scene

Unfortunately, there's no visible gay scene here, but **Arcigay Ganimede** *(Via Massettana Romana 18; Tel 0577/288-977; 4-8pm Mon-Tue, 9:30pm-midnight Wed, Thur)* is happy to share whatever inside scoop there may be.

culture zoo

Just wandering the streets checking out the Gothic architecture could keep you entertained for hours, but you should probably make time to check out at least a few of the amazing sights Sienna has to offer. The concave Palazzo Pubblico (Town Hall), which houses the Museo Civico, follows the curves of the Piazza del Campo; all of the other sights are just a short walk from

12 hours in siena

1. Visit the spectacular Romanesque-Gothic **Duomo,** one of Italy's finest. Dip into the **Battistero di San Giovanni (Baptistry of St. John)** while you're in the neighborhood, and admire the Renaissance baptismal font with its bronze reliefs by della Quercia, Ghiberti, and Donatello [see *culture zoo,* below].
2. Grab a gelato at **Gelateria Nannini** [see *eats,* below] a venerable institution in Siena, and then window-shop along Via Banchi di Sopra.
3. Head to Piazza del Campo and soak up some atmosphere in this huge, pink, seashell-shaped square.
4. Discover traditional Sienese cuisine at **Osteria la Chiacchera** [see *eats,* below].
5. Go to the **Pinacoteca Nazionale (National Picture Gallery)** to see Italy's greatest collections of 13th- to 16th-century Sienese art [see *culture zoo,* below].
6. Get off of the tourist track—explore Siena's side streets and stumble on some fantastic views of the Tuscan countryside.
7. Relax with a glass of local red wine at one of the outdoor tables at **Enoteca I Terzi** [see *bar, club, and live music scene,* below].
8. Check out the live music at the **Porta Giustizia 11 Tea Room** [see *bar, club, and live music scene,* below].

here. When visiting Siena's stunning Duomo, and other churches, remember to cover your knees, and any other flesh you wouldn't want Mother Superior to see (the caretakers are known to be pretty strict here.)

If you plan on seeing several sights, think about saving a few lira by buying a combination ticket. You have three options: 1) a combined ticket for the Libreria Piccolomini, Museo dell' Opera Metropolitana, and the Battistero is 9,500L; 2) all of that *plus* the Oratoria di San Bernardino and Chiesa di S. Agostino is 13,000L; and 3) the biggest money saver of all, a ticket that includes *all* the sights in town for 29,000L. Combo tickets are valid for seven days and can be bought at the ticket offices of any of these sights.

Museo Civico (Civic Museum) *(Palazzo Pubblico, Piazza del Campo; Tel 0577/292-230; 10am-6:30pm Nov-Mar 15; 10am-7pm Mar 16-June, Sept-Oct; 10am-11pm July-Aug; 10,000L Adults):* Enter through the courtyard of the Palazzo Pubblico to find a collection of important Sienese frescoes and paintings. Seek out the Sala del Mappamondo for the *Maestá* fresco by Simone Martini, painted in 1315—it's Siena's pride and joy. The well-known *Equestrian Portrait of Guiddoriccio da Fogliano* on the other side of the wall is sometimes attributed to Martini (and sometimes not). The frescoed vaults and marble portal sculpture in the Sala del Concistorio are worth a peek, and the chapel, with its frescoes by Taddeo di Bartolo, is stunning.

Torre del Mangia *(Palazzo Pubblico, Piazza del Campo; 10am-4pm Nov-Mar 15; 10am-7pm Mar 16th-June, Sept-Oct; 10am-11pm July-Aug; 8,000L Adults):* The hits just keep on comin' in the Palazzo Pubblico. Climb the 505 steps of the 335-foot 14th-century bell tower for an unrivaled view of the Siena skyline and Tuscan countryside.

Duomo *(Piazza del Duomo; Tel 0577/47-321; 7:30am-1pm/2:30-5pm Nov-Mar 15, 9am-7:30pm Mar 16-Oct, closed Sun mornings; Free admission):* Construction started on Siena's Duomo, which sits a few blocks southwest of Piazza del Campo, in 1229—200 years later, they were still building. The result is one of the most impressive churches in the country. Its long construction period allowed for many stylistic variations, and the Romanesque-Gothic one-two punch, right down to its zebra-striped black and white marble pillars, has enough intricate detail to occupy you for hours. Be sure to take a look in all the side chapels, particularly the Chapels of Madonna del Voto and St. John the Baptist, the latter of which contains a bronze statue of St. John by Donatello. Excavation work is being done on the left side, and you can look down and see the spot where the Torre del Mangia was recast in the 14th century. Highlights of the Duomo include: pulpit panels depicting the life of Christ, carved in 1265 by Nicola Pisano; the 56-panel, inlaid marble floor (one of the best panels depicts the *Massacre of the Innocents,* on the left side of the Cathedral); the Baptismal Font, created by Jacopo della Quercia with the help of Donatello; and sculptures of Saints Peter, Paul, Gregory, and Pius in the north aisle. You may also want to pop in to the **Libreria Piccolomini** *(Inside the Duomo; 10am-1pm/2:30-5pm Nov-Mar 15; 9am-*

7:30pm Mar 16-Oct, closed Sun mornings; 2,000L Adults), on the left side of the Cathedral. Built in 1495, it holds a collection of Pinturicchio's frescoes depicting the life of Pope Pius II.

Museo dell' Opera Metropolitana *(Piazza del Duomo 8; Tel 0577/283-048; 9am-1:30pm Nov-Mar 15; 9am-7:30pm Mar 16-Sept; 9am-6pm October; 6,000L Adults):* This museum is housed in the unfinished section of the Duomo, which was originally supposed to be the right aisle. Most of the museum's collection consists of stuff that was removed from the Duomo for safer-keeping. The ground floor hold architectural fragments that have been attributed to Giovanni Pisano, and the upper floor contains significant paintings, such as the *Maestá* by one of the greatest Sienese painters, Duccio di Buoninsegna, and the anonymous *Madonna of the Large Eyes,* which the Sienese used to pray to before going into battle.

Battistero di San Giovanni (Baptistry of St. John) *(Piazza San Giovanni; Tel 0577/282-992; 10am-1pm/2:30-5pm Nov-Mar 15; 9am-7:30pm Mar 16-Sept; 9am-6pm October; 3,000L Adults):* Take the steps to the right of the Duomo to get to the 14th-century Baptistry, which used to be the Parish Church of St. John. Its facade remains unfinished, but inside is what really matters—it's definitely worth the small admission price. The baptismal font is a Renaissance masterpiece, with incredibly detailed bronze reliefs of scenes from the Bible by della Quercia, Ghiberti, and Donatello. But don't overlook the gorgeous frescoes—grab a pew and use one of the magnifying mirrors lying around to get a closer look at the amazingly detailed ceilings.

Pinacoteca Nazionale (National Picture Gallery) *(Pallazzo Buonsignori, Via San Pietro 29; Tel 0577/281-161; 8:30am-1:30pm Mon, 9:30-7pm Tue-Sat, 8am-1pm Sun; 8,000L Adults):* From Piazza del Duomo, follow Via del Capitano east until it changes into Via San Pietro to find this museum. This is one of Italy's greatest collections of 13th- to 16th-century art from the Sienese school, and definitely has the highest concentration of different versions of *Madonna col Bambino* (Madonna and Child) in town. Rooms 3 and 4 are dedicated to Sienese master Duccio di Buoninsegno; *Madonna of the Franciscans* is said to be one of his masterpieces. Yet another important *Madonna and Child,* by Simone Martini, is in room 6. Scattered throughout rooms 5 through 8 are several works by the brothers Lorenzetti, leading Sienese artists of the 14th century. Ambrogio Lorenzetti's most outstanding painting is...you guessed it...*Madonna col Bambino.* Don't miss rooms 9 to 11, which hold amazing works by Bartolo di Fredi and Taddeo di Bartolo.

Basilica di San Francesco *(Piazza San Francesco; Tel 0577/289-081; 8am-noon/3-5pm daily; Free admission):* Most of the artwork from the original 14th-century Basilica was destroyed by a fire in the 17th century (Raphael was thought to have contributed to its frescoes). However, the interior of the eerily drafty and empty church still contains a few frescoes by the Lorenzetti brothers that are worth seeing if you're in the neighborhood—they're not really worth a special trip. The piazza out front, however, is a very cool spot, offering great views of the countryside and the city.

Basilica di San Domenico *(Piazza San Domenico; Tel 0577/280-893; 7am-1pm/3-6:30pm daily; Free admission, 5,000L to see head of St. Caterina):* St. Caterina, the patron saint of Siena, was the daughter of a tradesman who experienced visions from God, received the stigmata, and is best known for persuading Pope Gregory XI to return the seat of the Papacy to Rome in 1376. Now you can pay to check out her preserved, mummified head for 60 seconds. Like the Duomo, this Gothic Basilica took a while to complete—1225 to 1465, to be exact. The exterior of the church dominates Siena's skyline, but the interior, with its wooden rafters, is simple and bare. One of the most interesting things inside the Basilica is the portrait of St. Caterina by Andrea Vanni, located in the Chapel of the Vaults. It's said to be the only portrait ever made that was faithful to her, and you'll see it in countless different forms at every souvenir shop in town. From Piazza Matteotti, walk south on Via del Paradiso to get here.

Santuario e Casa di Santa Caterina (Sanctuary and House of St. Catherine) *(Vicolo del Tiratoio 15; No phone; 9am-12:30pm/3:30-6pm winter; 9am-12:30pm/2:30-6pm summer; Free admission):* From San Domenico, head east on Via della Sapienza, hang a right on Costa di San Antonio, and another right on Vicolo del Tiratoio to find St. Caterina's old house. Her childhood home is now a complex with a courtyard surrounded by chapels, cloisters, frescoed scenes from her life, and, of course, a souvenir shop.

Enoteca Italiana Permanente (Permanent Italian Wine Library) *(Fortrezza Medicea; Tel 0577/288-497, Fax 0577/270-717; Noon-1am Tue-Sat, noon-8pm Mon, closed Sunday; enoteca-italiana-siena/sienanet.it; Free admission):* This "museum" will cure the culture overload that can overcome you in jam-packed art cities like Siena. Take Viale dei Mille from Piazza San Domenico to get to the 16th-century Fortezza Medicea, whose museum claims to have a bottle of every type of wine produced in Italy. A bar area and a few outdoor patios with killer views invite you to taste wine by the glass or by the bottle. The prices are on the expensive side, so come here only if you're really interested in sampling a rare vintage—otherwise save your drinking for the *enotecas*.

modification

They're not particularly trendy, but the women at **Silvana** *(Via del Porrione 19-21; Tel 0577/40-235; 8:30am-noon/3:30-7:30pm; V, MC, DC)* have a great reputation among the locals. The salon is fairly big, and a wash, cut, and blow-dry will set you back about 60,000L. They don't speak English, so be prepared to gesture a lot—bring a picture to be totally safe....

city sports

Siena doesn't offer many opportunities for showing off your dance moves, but oddly enough, it probably has more dance studios and classes per capita than any other Italian town. At most places you can sign up for just one class if you want; it's a great way to catch some exercise (and meet new people) on the road. The **Dance School** *(Viale Cavour 188; 0577/593-519 or 0577/44-194)* has ballet, Latin, and tango classes. Francesca Selva, at the **Centro Danza Classica** *(Via Mentana 61; Tel 0577/223-267)* teaches classical, jazz, and "funky jazz" classes.

And when step-two-three-kick-two-three-keep-it-up-looking-good gets boring, go outside. The outdoor fanatics at centrally located **Club Alpino Italiano** *(Viale Mazzini 95; Tel/Fax 0577/270-666; 6am-7:30pm Mon-Wed, Fri)* will be more than happy to tell you about cool trails—they may even invite you to come along on one of their group trips if they have one in the works.

The **Centro Studi Arte e Movimento** *(Via Fiorentina 2; Tel 0577/288-199 or 0577/747-113)* offers yoga classes, and regularly welcomes travelers in need of a little downward dog.

Palestra Gold Gym *(Via Fiera Vecchia 9; Tel 0577/285-272; goldgym@tin.it, www.goldgym.it),* located a few blocks west of Porta Pispini at the southeastern edge of the city, has the typical gym set-up and a nice variety of dance classes, plus kung fu and kick-boxing. Hiii-ya!

STUFF

For a town of its size, Siena is a surprisingly great place to window-shop (or better yet, to shop-shop). The main shopping drags are Via di Città, Banchi di Sopra, and Banchi di Sotto, just west of Piazza del Campo. For one-stop shopping, try **UPIM** *(Piazza Matteotti 6; Tel 0577/41-390; 8:30am-7:30pm daily; V, MC, AE),* a department store selling everything from clothes and CDs to cosmetics and toiletries.

▶▶DUDS

You'll see **Sisley** *(Banchi Di Sopra 38; 9:30am-7:45pm; V, MC)* and **Stefanel** *(Piazza Matteotti 1; Tel 0577/281-086; 10am-8pm Mon-Sat, 3:30-7:30pm Sun; V, MC)* chains all over Italy. Although the clothes are a bit on the expensive side, you can't go wrong with the classic Italian styles.

Its headquarters are near Florence, but **Sasch** *(Via Banchi di Sopra 1; Tel 055/874-471, Fax 055/8744-7240; 10am-8pm Mon-Sat, 3:30-7:30pm Sun; sasch@sasch.it, www.sasch.it; V, MC)* also has a branch in Siena. It often has excellent sales (as low as 20,000L), but even when there's no sale on, the casual clothes and jeans here are a good value.

▶▶TUNES

Yeah, it's got a pretty good CD selection, but the real reason to go to **Dischi Corsini** *(Piazza Matteotti 5; Tel 0577/280-545; 9am-8pm, closed Sun; V, MC)* is its massive collection of flyers for parties, concerts, and bars in the area. The small store is located on Piazza Matteotti.

▶▶BOUND

Libreria Sienese *(Via di Città 62-66; Tel/Fax 0577/280-845; 9am-8pm, closed Sun; V, MC, AE)* has a decent selection of English-language books, newspapers, and magazines—everything from guidebooks to *Newsweek* to Danielle Steele novels.

Arte & Libri *(Via di Città; Tel 0577/221-325; 9:30am-8pm daily; V, MC, AE)* also carries many English-language books: classics, mystery novels, guidebooks, phrase books, and even cookbooks.

▶▶USED AND BRUISED

The garage sale-like **Secondamano** *(Via Milanesi 6; Tel/Fax 0577/588-148; 10am-1pm/4-8pm, closed Sun; No credit cards)*, located between Strada di Marciano and Strada del Patriccio e Belriguardo, has every type of used item, from CDs and musical instruments to clothes and shoes. Feel free to haggle.

You can paw through lots of '70s stuff like cool print dresses and pants at **Boutique dell' Usato** *(Via Pantaneto 63; Tel 0577/288-278; 9:30am-8pm Mon-Sat; No credit cards)*. They also have tons of great leather jackets.

▶▶HOW BAZAAR

Siena's sprawling weekly market takes place every Wednesday 8am-1pm (but be early to get the best stuff) in the area between La Lizza and the Fortrezza Medicea. They sell just about everything here, including surprisingly nice clothes.

▶▶FOOT FETISH

Romas Mori *(Banchi di Sopra 68-70; Tel 0577/280-528; 9:30am-1pm/3:30-7:30pm, closed Sat; V, MC, AE)* sells its own brand of Romas shoes for 140,000L to 200,000L. Make your friends at home jealous with these cool styles. The second branch *(Banchi di Sopra 30-32; Tel 0577/40-598; 9:30am-1pm/3:30-7:30pm, closed Sat; V, MC, AE)* is a bit more upscale and also sells leather jackets, skirts, belts, and pants.

If *stivale* are your thing, go to **Contrasti** *(Via Dupré 16; Tel 0577/286-109; 10am-7:45pm, closed Sun; V, MC)* for purple lizard-skin boots, red velvet boots, blue silk boots, red leather boots, pink-striped boots with flowers....

▶▶LEATHER

Florence is the best place to invest in leather, but if you must buy something in leather there are several good stores to hit—you'll just pay a lot more. **I Ponti** *(Via di Cittá 57; Tel 0577/41-638; 9:30am-7:30pm Mon-Sat, 10:30am-7:30pm Sun; V, MC)* has gorgeous leather bags, belts, and wallets. Down the street, **Furla** *(Via di Cittá 6-8; Tel 0577/281-287; 10am-8pm Mon-Sat; V, MC, AE)* also sells leather bags and wallets, along with pricey jewelry.

▶▶ARTSY STUFF

The smell of incense drifts down the street from **drago rosso** *(Via dei Pellegrini 13; Tel 0577/285-102; 10am-8pm Mon-Sat; V, MC, AE)*, right off of Piazza del Campo. This shop specializes in Asian art and has loads of cool jewelry and crafts. If you're interested in holistic healing or numerology Italian-style, this is the place to come for information.

Ruffini Dario *(Via delle Terme 44; Tel 0347/640-7437; 10am-8pm, closed Sun; V, MC)* sells his beautiful handmade glass objects at this little shop between Piazza Independenzia and Via di Città. For something small that won't break on the trip home, the glass rings are a good buy.

eats

Sienese cooking is characterized by its simplicity and heartiness, and its abundance of fresh herbs. Rich *ragùs* are on every menu—*pappardelle con la lepre* (pasta with rabbit) is a favorite. In the summer, nothing is more refreshing than *panzanella,* a salad of bread soaked in tomatoes, onions, and basil. *Cinghiale in umido* (braised wild boar), *ribollita* (vegetable soup), and *panforte* (a spicy, dense cake made with nuts, honey, and candied fruit) are other must-haves. The good news is, with all these students, there's lots of inexpensive options. The bad news is, with all these students, you may have to wait for a table. Show up early (before 8pm) to assure yourself a spot.

▶▶CHEAP

Outdoor tables at **Il Verrocchio** *(Logge del Papa 1; Tel 0577/284-062; Noon-3pm/6-10pm, closed Wed; Avg. meal 15,000L),* overlook a quiet, charming little square surrounded by pretty buildings just east of Piazza del Campo, between Via Banchi di Sotto and Via del Porrione. The clientele is touristy, and though the cheap menu contains the usual dishes, nothing too creative or unusual, it's all quality. The pizzas, on the other hand, are fantastic and cheap.

Crowds congregate at busy slice place **Il Cavallino Bianco** *(Via Città 20; Tel 0577/44-258; 11am-10pm, closed Tue; Avg. slice 4,000L; No credit cards),* where you can get thick-crusted pizza with several different kinds of toppings for next to nothing. The interior leaves a little to be desired, so grab a slice and a beer and head to the piazza.

A few steps east of the Battistero is the bakery **Panificio Il Magnifico** *(Via dei Pellegrini 27; No phone; No credit cards),* which sells fresh bread, pastries, and the best focaccia—with olive oil, Parmigiano cheese,

TO MARKET

The best (and biggest) place for food supplies is **Consorzio Agrario Provincale Siena** *(Via Pianigiani 5; Tel 0577/222-368; 8am-7:30pm daily; Visa, MC),* two blocks east of Piazza Matteotti. It sells lots of fresh Italian bread, cheese, meat, wine, and also tasty, ready-made meals. Behind the Piazza del Campo, **La Bottega** *(Via di Città 152; 8am-1pm/4-8pm, closed Sun; V, MC)* is a little place with a good selection of picnic fixings. **La Frutta Con Fantasia** *(Via Calzoleria 25; Tel 0577/282-433; 8am-1:30pm/4-8pm; No credit cards)* has the most delicious fresh fruit, along with drinks, meat, and cheese.

siena eats and crashing

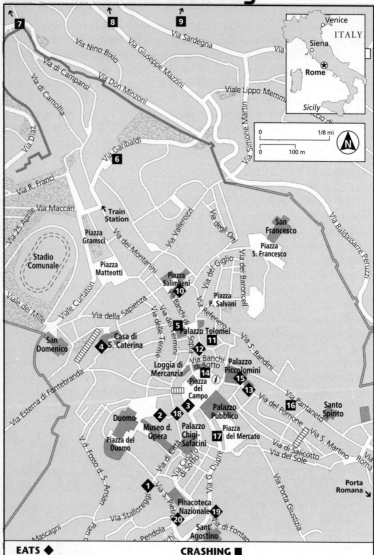

EATS ◆

Bar Il Palio **3**
Gelateria Nannini **10**
Il Cavallino Bianco **18**
La Taverna di San Giuseppe **19**
Nannini **12**
Osteria Da Cice **20**
Osteria Il Tamburino **1**
Osteria La Chiacchera **4**
Osteria Le Logge **13**
Panificio Il Magnifico **2**

CRASHING ■

Albergo Chiusarelli **5**
Guidoriccio **8**
Hotel Italia **7**
La Toscana **11**
Locanda Garibaldi **17**
Masianani **16**
Piccolo Hotel Etruria **14**
Piccolo Hotel Il Palio **6**
Siena Colleverde **9**

and rosemary—in town. It's the cheapest meal in Sienna, and one of the most delicious.

For a tasty, filling meal under 30,000L off the tourist track, check out **Osteria Il Tamburino** *(Via Stalloreggi 11; Tel 0557/280-306; 11am-3pm/7-11pm, closed Thur; V, MC, AE)*. To get to this popular, casual spot, walk south on Via di Città, which will turn into Via Stalloreggi. It's not the best place to come for a romantic meal (bright lights and cramped tables), but they serve good, typically Sienese food at great prices. If you're a vegetarian, stay away from the Sienese antipasto—it's just a big plate of meat. Try the *tagliatelle* (egg noodles in thin strips) with porcini mushrooms, fresh herbs, and olive oil—*delizioso*.

Osteria la Chiacchera *(Costa di S. Antonio 4; Tel 0577/280-631, closed Tue;Secondi 10,000L; V, MC)* translates to "the gossip," an apt name for this popular, locals-only haunt, one of the cutest little traditional restaurants in Siena. Right around the corner from the **Santuario e Casa di Santa Caterina** [see *culture zoo,* above], on a steep street, it has four wooden outdoor tables with longer legs on one side as an attempt to correct for the slope—beware the wobble. Friendly waiters speak English here, and the food is simple, delicious, and cheap. Order a bottle of house wine, and enjoy the cozy atmosphere.

▶▶DO-ABLE

If you go out for one nice dinner in Siena, **La Taverna di San Guiseppe** *(Via G. Dupré 132; Tel 0577/42-286, Fax 0577/219-620; Closed Sun; Secondi 20,000L; V, MC, AE, DIN)* is the place to do it. It serves typical Tuscan dishes in a historical building with exposed-brick walls, vaulted ceilings, candles on all the tables, a huge wine list, and waiters in tuxedos. No one will rush you—in fact, when it's all over, they'll expect you to linger all night over your wine, coffee, *digestivo,* and dessert. Try the *osso bucco* (veal shank marinated in red wine)—like most of the food here, it's a notch above the norm. Take Via G. Dupré south of the Piazza del Campo, and you'll find the restaurant just before the street changes to Via di Fontanella.

Osteria Da Cice *(Via S. Pietro 32; Tel 0577/288-026; Noon-3pm/7-11pm, closed Sun; Avg. secondi 20,000L; V, MC)* is a casual locals' favorite located near the **Pinacoteca Nazionale** [see *culture zoo,* above]. The unpretentious and traditional menu demonstrates the many ways you can prepare a wild boar, the specialty of Siena. The cozy dining room is conducive to long meals, especially with one of the great wine offerings.

▶▶SPLURGE

You have to look away from the tourist fare being pushed around Piazza del Campo to find a real gem like **Osteria Le Logge** *(Via del Porrione 33; Tel 0577/48-013; Noon-3/7:30-11pm, closed Sun; Avg. secondi 35,000L; V, MC, AE, DI)*. Perfectly set patio tables, waiters in long white aprons, old-fashioned decor, and the smell of *bistecca fiorentina* and freshly made pasta sauces make this place hard to resist. The food is a little on the expensive side, but worth it. It's the kind of place that never goes out of style, where grandparents celebrate anniversaries and young couples go out on first dates.

crashing

Siena has plenty of hotels—including lots of cheapies—but that doesn't make it easy to find a room (you're still in Tuscany). From March to November, especially during **Il Palio** or any other festival [see *festivals and events,* below], you've gotta book ahead for the hotels in the historical center. The ones outside of town aren't much cheaper, and they're a huge hassle as far as getting back and forth. The **tourist office** [see *need to know,* below] won't make reservations for you, but they will recommend places that "might" have rooms available. They can also give you a long list of *affittacameri* (family homes with rooms for rent), which sometimes are like mini-hotels with several rooms [see *Masianani,* below], and other times are just a spare room in somebody's apartment. The **Hotel Promotions** office [see *need to know,* below] will make reservations for you for a few thousand lira, and since proprietors reserve rooms especially for this office to fill, it's often worth it.

▶▶CHEAP

Siena Colleverde *(Strada di Scacciapensieri 47; Tel 0577/280-044, Fax 0577/333-298; Bus 3 or 8, tell driver to let you off near Campeggio; campingsiena@siena.turismo.toscana.it; 15,000L per person, per night),* north of the city center, is Siena's only campsite. Take bus 8 from Piazza del Sale or bus 3 from Piazza Gramsci. The site is open from March 21 to November 10, and at these prices, staying in a tent (or camper) has never been so much fun. All the amenities are yours to use, but admission to the swimming pool is 3,000L extra.

The non-HI youth hostel, **Guidoriccio** *(Via Fiorentina 89, Localitá Stellino; Tel 0577/52-212; Bus 4 or 10 from the train or bus station, 15 from the center, direction Lo Stellino; Front desk7:30-9am/3pm-1am Apr-Oct; 7:30-9am/3-11:30pm Nov-Feb; 25,000L beds, 7,000L breakfast; info@franchostel.it, www.franchostel.it/siost-uk.htm; No credit cards)* may be 4km away and a bit of a pain to get out to (20 min by bus), but with 120 beds, they almost always have room. Most rooms have just two or three beds, and there's a bar and common areas where backpackers hangout. And hey, no curfew!

Don't let the gloomy reception area at the family-run **Piccolo Hotel Etruria** *(Via delle Donzelle 3; Tel 0577/288-088, Fax 0577/288-461; 75,000L singles with bath, 65,000L singles without bath, 120,000L doubles with bath, 7,000L breakfast; V, MC, AE, DC)* scare you off—the 13 rooms are more pleasant, with tile floors and comfy beds. The hotel is located northeast of the Campo, between Banchi di Sotto and Via Cecco Angiolieri. Skip the breakfast.

The nice **Masianani** family *(Via Pantaneto 105; Tel 0577/287-342; 100,000L singles, 150,000L doubles; No credit cards)* runs a small pension with seven rooms in the same building as the University of Siena's library. The rooms are small and clean, simply decorated with antiques, botanical drawings, and flowery bedspreads, and all share one bathroom with a few showers at the end of the hall. A few of them offer an incredible view of the Basilica di San Francesco—waking up in the morning to that sight is so *Italy*. Unless your idea of breakfast is instant coffee and stale, plastic-wrapped cakes, grab your first meal of the day somewhere else.

If you really need to pinch pennies, try **Locanda Garibaldi** *(Via Giovanni Dupré 18; Tel 0577/284-204; 45,000L singles without baths, 85,000L doubles without baths; No credit cards)*, one of the cheapest hotels in town, located just south of Piazza del Campo. There are only seven rooms, so it's wise to call in advance. The place is simple and clean (although the shared bathrooms could use a thorough scrubbin'), and there are a few common sitting areas. No TVs or phones.

▶▶**DO-ABLE**

Hotel Italia *(Viale Cavour 67; Tel 0577/41-177, Fax 0577/44-554; 84,000L singles without baths, 130,000L singles with baths, 135,000L doubles without baths, 190,000L doubles with baths, breakfast included; V, MC, AE)* has 71 rooms, a small bar/restaurant, and a pretty patio. The rooms are clean and new-ish, with TVs, phones, and air conditioning (in some), but the decor is pretty uninspiring.

The best thing about the **Piccolo Hotel Il Palio** *(Piazza del Sale 19; Bus 3 to La Lizza; Tel 0577/281-131, Fax 0577/281-142; 130,00L singles with private baths, 160,000L doubles with private baths, 10,000L breakfast; V, MC, AE)* is its location—a 10-minute walk from the train station, and two blocks northeast of the La Lizza bus station. All of the rooms have minibars, TVs, and phones, and there's a bar near the lobby to ease late-night boredom. The place has just 26 rooms, so call ahead.

La Toscana *(Via Cecco Angiolieri 12; Tel 0577/46-097, Fax 0577/44-554; 100,000L singles with baths, 60,000L singles without baths, 140,000L doubles with baths, 100,000L doubles without baths, 15,000L breakfast; V, MC, AE)* is a conveniently located hotel—just east off Piazza Tolomei—with an unusually friendly receptionist. All rooms are clean, and have TVs and phones, but the decor is taaack-y. They'll happily lock up your bags in their storage room after check-out.

Housed in a recently restored 19th-century building between Piazza San Domenico and Piazza Matteotti, **Albergo Chiusarelli** *(Viale Curtatone 15; Tel 0577/280-562, Fax 0577/271-177; 125,000L singles with baths, 95,000L singles without baths, 185,000L doubles with baths, breakfast included; V, MC, AE)* gives you the impression that you're staying at a Tuscan villa. For this price range, it's one of the most authentically and tastefully decorated hotels in Siena. All 49 rooms have TVs, phones, bathrooms with blow-dryers, and air conditioning, plus there's a restaurant, bar, a few lounges, and a little garden.

need to know

Currency Exchange **Maccorp Italiana SPA** *(Via di Città 80-82)* offers student discounts (7.4 percent service charge instead of 10 percent), but it's still cheaper and easier to use the *bancomats* (Italian for ATM) for withdrawing money—you'll find a bunch of them along Via Banchi di Sopra. At the intersection of Piazza Tolomei and Via Banchi di Sopra is a **Banca Toscana,** with an automatic currency exchange machine.

wired

The **Internet Train** chain has two locations in Siena: *(Via di Pantaneto 54; Tel 0577/247-460; 10am-8pm Mon-Sat, noon-8pm Sun)*, one block east of the Logge del Papa, and *(Via di Città 121; Tel 0577/226-366; 10am-10pm Mon-Fri, 3-10pm Sun)*, one block east of the Duomo. They each have about 20 computers. The smaller **Internet Point** *(Via del Paradiso 10; Tel 0577/281-505, Fax 0577/247-747; internetpoint@sienaol.it)*, between San Domenico and Piazza Matteotti, isn't usually as crowded. **The Netgate** *(Via Dupré 12; Tel 0577/226-185; 10am-8pm Mon-Sat; siena.campo@thnetgate.it or info@thenetgate.it, www.thenetgate.it; V, MC, AE)* has student discounts and 18 superfast computers. And the **Internet Office Center** *(Via Cecco Angiolieri 51; Tel 0577/217-830, Fax 0577/226-811; 9am-8pm Mon-Sat; ioc@novamedia.it, www.novamedia.it/ioc; 150L/minute, 9,000L/hour; V, MC)* also provides copying, faxing, and many other services, just east of Piazza Tolomei. For info on Siena on the web, try: *www.comune.siena.it* or *www.sienaweb.it*.

Tourist Information Siena's very helpful **APT** *(Piazza del Campo 56; Tel 0577/280-551, Fax 0577/270-676; 8:30am-1pm/3-7pm Mon-Fri, 8:30am-1pm Sat, closed Sun Nov 11-Mar 21; 8:30am-7:30pm, closed Sun Mar 23-Nov 10; aptsiena@siena.turismo.toscana.it, www.siena.turismo.toscana.it)* has all the maps and info you need. They can give you a list of hotels and *affittacamere* (private rooms), but can't make the reservations for you—Siena's **Hotels Promotion** *(Piazza San Domenico; Tel 0577/288-084, Fax 0577/280-290; 9am-7pm winter; 9am-8pm summer, closed Sundays; promo@hotelsiena.com, www.hotelsiena.com)* office will, for a few lira.

Public Transportation Since the center of the city is closed to traffic (except taxis and hotel guests dropping luggage off), the only **buses** in town skirt the city walls. **TRA-IN** *(S.S. 73 Levante, 23 Due Ponti; Tel 0577/204-111)* buses stop at the train and bus station before heading out to the suburbs. If Siena's maze of streets gets too confusing—especially if you have heavy luggage—a taxi ride makes it all a breeze. The main **taxi stand** is at Piazza Matteotti *(Tel 0577/289-350, 0577/49-222)*, in front of the McDonald's. You can't hail cabs in Siena—if you're not near a stand, you have to call, and the operator will give you the number of the taxi that will come for you.

Health and Emergency Police emergencies: *112;* Ambulance service: *0577/222-199.* The **hospital** *(Vale Bracci, Tel 0577/586-466)* is just north of the train station, and the **police station** *(Via del Castoro; Tel 0577/201-111)* is between the Duomo and Via di Città.

Pharmacies Two conveniently located pharmacies, **Farmacia Antica Farmacia** *(Via Banchi di Sotto; Tel/Fax 0577/280-109; 9am-1pm/4-8pm; V, MC)* and **Farmacia Arbi Del Campo** *(Piazza del Campo 26; Tel 0577/280-234; 9am-1pm/4-8pm; V, MC)*, post a list of rotating 24-hour pharmacies.

Telephone City code: *0577*. **Telecom Italia** calling centers are at Via di Città 113 and Via Pantaneto 44.

Trains Siena's train station *(Tel 0577/888-088)* is located northwest of the city center at Piazza Fratelli Rosselli. Once you arrive in Siena, buy a **bus ticket** (1,400L) from the *tabacchi* inside the station, exit the station, and head to the bus stop directly across the road. There, you can take buses 1, 2, or 3 for a short ride to Piazza Gramsci. Or hoof it (uphill, about a half-hour) into town: From the train station walk southeast along Viale Giuseppe Mazzini. You'll enter the city walls at Barriera di S. Lorenzo. Regular trains depart for Florence (90 minutes), although many of them require a change at Empoli. Trains for Rome (180 minutes) are frequent. Left Luggage (10:30am-1:30pm/2:30-6:30pm, closed Sat, Sun) is 5,000L a piece.

Bus Lines Out of the City Most **buses** leave from **La Lizza** *(Piazza Gramsci; Tel 0577/204-246, 0577/247-934)* and then stop at **Piazza Domenico** *(Tel 0577/204-245)*. Siena is well-connected by bus, especially to other towns in the region. If you need to save time, check the bus schedule before you buy a train ticket, because the bus is often faster. Regular buses to and from Siena include such destinations as Rome, Milan, Florence, Pisa, Assisi, Perugia, and Bologna.

Bike/Moped Rental Several rental places service the town: **DF Bike** *(Via Massetana Romana 54; Tel 0577/271-905)*, **Automotocicli Perozzi** *(Via del Romitorio 5; Tel 0577/223-157)*, and **D.F. Motoricambi snc** *(Via dei Gazzani 16-18; Tel 0577/288-387)*. They all require deposits for bike rentals.

Laundry Located one block north of the Piazza del Campo is **onda blu** *(Via del Casato di Sotto 17; No phone; 8am-10pm daily)*, a self-service Laundromat where it's about 5,000L to wash a load, and another 5,000L to dry it. The prices and hours are the same at **Wash & Dry** *(Via di Pantaneto 38; No phone)*.

Postal There's a **post office** *(Piazza Matteotti 37; Tel 0577/41-482, Fax 0577/42-178; 8am-12:30pm/3:30-7:30pm Mon-Sat)* in the center, as well as many **red mail boxes** around town.

Internet See *wired*, above.

Lucca

Everything in Lucca is charmingly understated, from fantastic family-run Tuscan *trattorias* (restaurants) to spacious *piazzas,* to the wide ramparts that surround the city. Some other Tuscan cities can feel like

lucca bars clubs and culture zoo

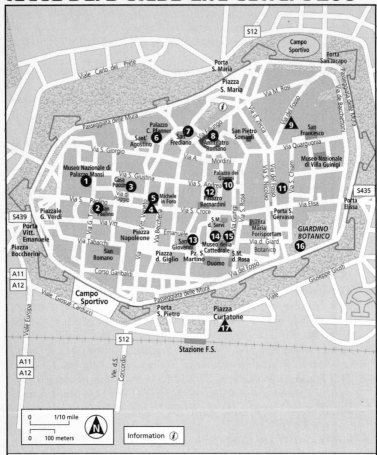

0   1/10 mile
0   100 meters

Information ⓘ

BARS/CLUBS ▲
L'Osteria del Neni **4**
McCullough's **17**
Miró **9**

Piazza del Mercato **8**
Pinacoteca Nazionale **1**
San Michele in Foro **5**
Torre Delle Ore (Clock Tower) **12**
Villa Bottini **11**

CULTURE ZOO ●
Botanic Gardens **16**
Casa Natale di Giacomo Puccini **3**
Chiesa di San Frediano **7**
Chiesa di San Giovanni e Reparata **15**
Chiesa di San Paolina **2**
Duomo di San Martino **14**
Museo della Cattedrale **15**
Museo Nazionale di Villa Guinigi/
  Torre Guinigi **10**
Palazzo Pfanner **6**

made-to-order tourist destinations, but Lucca isn't a prime spot on the Tuscan tourist trail. Day-trippers do stop in to check out the Romanesque churches, with their wedding-cake facades and fine art collections, but those folks head out by late afternoon, leaving the quiet streets and vibrant *enotecas* (wine bars) for you to explore.

Lucca welcomes tourists, but has not changed itself for them. The local population (100,000) is fairly conservative, and people jet around town on old-fashioned bikes, since most streets are closed off to traffic. Lucca's style is classic, simple, and elegant—but its youth culture plops a bit of creative disorder into that tidy image.

Though Lucca was settled by the Ligurians, and, later, the Etruscans, its Roman origins are the best-preserved, especially in the **Piazza Anfiteatro** and the beginnings of the **Ramparts** [see *culture zoo,* below]. Lucca went on to become a powerful, independent principality. The 12th and 13th centuries saw its greatest prosperity, and many of the buildings and churches from that period, like the Romanesque **San Michele in Foro** and the asymmetrical **Cathedral of San Martino** [see *culture zoo,* below], still define Lucca's image today. Its many lovely 15th and 16th century palazzos were modeled after Florence's great Renaissance examples. In 1805, Lucca lost its independence, and Napoleon gave the town to his sister, Elisa. The people loved her, and the city was prosperous, but just ten years later, Marie Louise de Bourbon took control—her statue now sits in the sprawling, tree-lined **Piazza Napoleone.**

neighborhoods and hanging out

Everything you'll want to see is neatly contained within *Le Mura,* or the city walls. The **train station** lies just outside the southern wall, five minutes from the center. Long-distance buses come and go from **Piazzale Verdi,** which sits next to the eastern corner of the wall. Everything within the town walls is walk-able; the Lucchese rarely drive anywhere themselves, opting to put their bikes to good use.

Lucca's Renaissance walls were built for protection, but today all 4km of tree-lined, elevated ramparts are used for jogging, roller-blading, romantic walks, and soaking up views of the country. Inside the walls, **Piazza Napoleone** is the town's main square for socializing; its benches are pleasant for a picnic lunch. One block north, **Piazza San Michele,** watched over by the beautiful **San Michele in Foro** church [see *culture zoo,* below], is one of Lucca's prettiest piazzas and busiest meeting spots. At night, the kids take over this piazza, and on warm summer evenings, the scene turns into a bit of party. The main shopping street, **Via Fillungo,** which leads to the shop-lined **Piazza Anfiteatro,** starts one block northwest of the San Michele. The **Duomo,** located a few blocks east of Piazza Napoleone through the adjacent **Piazza del Griglio** and **Piazza San Giovanni,** is on another pretty square, but it's not as popular for hanging out.

cafe sceNe

Laid-back Lucca is full of pleasant outdoor cafes. Skip your hotel's over-priced breakfast and start the day with a frothy cappuccino, or spend the afternoon people-watching while you suck up a frozen *granita,* Italy's equivalent of a slurpee.

Sitting right on the main piazza, **Bar San Michele** *(Piazza San Michele 1; Tel 0583/55-387; 7:30am-8pm Mon-Sat; No credit cards)* will give you a perfect view of the church—whether you sit indoors or out. Coffee, pastries, and cocktails are all good here, but the main reason to come is to be immersed in this crowd. On summer evenings, there's no choicer cafe.

Bar Casali *(Via Roma 1; Tel 0583/492-687; 7am-8:30pm, closed Wed; V, MC),* just off Piazza San Michele, has a little more hustle-bustle to it. Most people take their coffee standing at the traditional bar, but there are also a few outdoor tables if you don't mind a pricey cappuccino (5,000L).

Bar Gelateria Cubanatto *(Via Beccheria 16; Tel 0583/955-782; No credit cards),* one block south of Piazza San Michele, serves up some of the best gelato in town. This little take-away joint has tons of home-made flavors.

bar, club, and Live music sceNe

If you're a wino, you'll be in business in Lucca. Sipping the juice of the grape is the nocturnal activity of choice here, and the Lucchese prefer to do it in one of the town's cozy trattorias, many of which are open just as late as the bars. But if your teeth are starting to get those funky blue stains on them—or you're just craving a cool martini (stirred, not shaken)— check out **Mirò,** where the hip young crowd goes for real cocktails. Or join the party at McCulloughs, Lucca's only Irish pub. It attracts a lot of out-of-towners and gets very, very crowded.

L'Osteria del Neni *(Via Pescheria 3; Tel 0583/492-681; nicoladig@libero.it; Wines by the glass 30,000-10,000L; V, MC, AE),* on a small street just off Piazza San Michele, is a wine bar and simple restaurant with an old-fashioned Tuscan atmosphere that's perfect for quiet evenings. Sit outside at a table under the canopy, where wine lovers of all ages sip away the evening. The interior is pretty and homey, with rustic wooden tables and chairs, bottles of wine absolutely everywhere, and little knick-knacks hanging on the walls. Choose from a big selection of local wines, and lots of cheeses and salamis to sample as you drink.

Just outside the city walls, one block northeast of the train station, is **McCullough's** *(Piazza Curtatone 135; Tel 0583/469-067; 8pm-closing hours vary; V, MC, AE),* Lucca's beloved Irish pub. Its dark wooden tables, flowing Guiness, and friendly atmosphere attract both local kids and tourists. Try your luck at the dartboard in the corner before your vision starts to blur. True to the Irish soul of the place, the folks at McCullough's are known for their parties: St. Patrick's Day, Halloween, Carnivale, an "Irish pub birthday party" on October 18th, a summer festival on June

21st, and a twice-yearly beer-drinking competition are just a few of their select soirees.

Mirò *(Via del Fosso 215; Tel 0583/48-326; 8pm-closing hours vary, Closed Mon; Avg. drink 7,000L; V, MC)*, a few blocks east of Piazza Anfiteatro, is the city's coolest bar, attracting the city's coolest crowd. Decorated in homage to the surrealism of Spanish artist Joan Mirò, with reproductions of his work, lots of bright colors, and geometry-defying architecture, Mirò is much more cosmopolitan than the rest of provincial Lucca. It often features live music (jazz, blues, Latin beat), and occasionally art exhibitions. When the weather is nice, sit out in the garden with a Dadaist, Impressionist, Rococo, or Surrealist sandwich. To get here take Via del Portico to Piazza San Pietro Somaldi, then go east on Via della Fratta, which leads you to Via del Fosso.

Locanda Buatino [see *eats,* below], a popular locals' hangout that serves great food, is open until midnight and attracts a mixed crowd of the thirsty, from old men to college students. Live jazz concerts on Monday nights draw the masses to this casual nightspot, where folks are friendly and wine is cheap.

arts scene

To get the scoop on the local visual arts scene, head to **Mirò** [see *bar, club, and live music scene,* above] and talk to the local aspiring artists—who'll probably tell you to go to Florence. Locanda Buatino [see *eats,* below], which is popular with all kinds, holds exhibitions of its own every so often.

festivals and events

During August and September the **Musical Summer of Lucca** festival, in honor of Saint Paolino, patron saint of the city, brings lots of musical concerts and candlelit parades through the streets. The solemn **Luminara,** a traditional parade in honor of the *Volto Santo* [see *culture zoo,* above], takes place on September 13th and brings many native Lucchese back to their hometown. The whole center of town is lit by candles, while a huge parade of townsfolk dressed in medieval costumes makes its way through the city.

One of the most popular events is the **International Comics Fair,** which takes place one weekend in March each year. Comic book artists and collectors from all over the world descend on Lucca to indulge their passion. During the **Summer Festival** in July, the Piazza Napoleone turns into an open-air stage for musicians from all over Europe.

Music and performances are another story. There's a full schedule of concerts year-round, as well as many music-related festivals [see *festivals and events*, below]. During the summer, open-air concerts are also frequent (and often free)—you can get a schedule at the tourist office [see *need to know*, below]. Giacamo Puccini (the opera composer, dummy) was born in Lucca, and the Lucchese are very proud of him—expect to hear performances of his work.

▶▶PERFORMING ARTS

Teatro Comunale del Giglio *(Piazza del Giglio 13-15; Tel 0583/467-521 or 0583/46531, Fax 0583/490-317; 10:30am-12:30pm/4pm-6pm; teatro.giglio@comune.lucca.it, biglietteria.giglio@comune.lucca.it; Tickets 20,000-60,000L; V, MC)*, just off Piazza Napoleone, is the town's main venue. Predictably, a lot of Puccini is on tap here, and a good, varied schedule of theater, dance, and music. Tickets for everything from flamenco shows to *The Blue Room* can be bought for as little as 20,000L.

CULTURE ZOO

Other than Le Mura, there are no big-name tourist sights in Lucca, yet each church facade hides quiet masterpieces that are worth discovering.

San Michele in Foro *(Piazza di San Michele; Tel 0583/48-459; 7:40am-noon/3-6pm daily; Free Admission):* Although this pink-and-white marble, multi-tiered church right in the center of town looks grand

(12 hours in Lucca)

1. Start your day off Lucchese-style, with a foamy cappuccino and a *cornetto* (croissant) at **Bar San Michele** [see *eats*, below], and sit and admire the lovely pink-and-white marble, multi-tiered church of **San Michele in Foro** [see *culture zoo*, below].

2. Head to the **Duomo di San Martino** [see *culture zoo*, below] and look at Lucca's most sacred artifact—the *Volto Santo* [see *culture zoo*, below].

3. Have lunch at the family-style favorite **Osteria Baralla,** or try Italian comfort food at **Ristorante "Da Guido"** [see *eats*, below].

4. Work off all that pasta by walking the entire 4.2km of Lucca's tree-lined **Ramparts** [see *culture zoo*, below] or rent a bike and explore the town [see *need to know*, below].

5. Go window-shopping on **Via Fillungo** [see *stuff*, below].

enough to be Lucca's Duomo, it's not. As its name implies, this church stands on the site of an ancient Roman forum. Construction began in the second half of the 11th century and wasn't finished until the 14th century. The Pisan-Romanesque facade is incredibly ornate, with scenes depicting wild animals and hunters on horseback, swirling columns, and a big figure of St. Michael slaying a dragon with two angels standing on the pediment. Compared to the facade (which you could spend hours ogling), the interior is less interesting. Worth checking out are Andrea della Robbia's *Madonna and Child* and Filippino Lippi's *Saints Jerome, Sebastian, Roch, and Helena,* which was recently restored and is considered one of his finest paintings.

Casa Natale di Giacomo Puccini (Puccini's Birthplace) *(Corte S. Lorenzo 9; Tel 0583/584-028; 10am-1pm/3-6pm, closed Mon, March 14-May and Oct-Dec; 10am-6pm daily, June-Sept; Closed Jan-Mar 13; 5,000L Adults):* The 15th-century house where the great opera composer (and most famous resident of Lucca) was born is now a small museum full of mementos of his life, including costumes, paintings, his piano, sheets of music, and clothing. Even for those with no interest in opera, the museum is worth visiting for a glimpse at a gorgeous Renaissance building—it's half a block west of **San Michele in Foro,** on a small street just off Via di Poggio.

Duomo di San Martino *(Piazza San Martino; 7am-7pm daily summer; 7am-5pm daily winter; 3,000L entrance):* Lucca's Duomo, located two blocks east of Piazza Napoleone, has a long history of additions and renovations. The first church that sat on the site was a 6th-century monument to St. Martin. In 1070 it was rebuilt and enlarged, and between the second half of the 12th century and the end of the 15th century it was renovated in its current Gothic-Romanesque style. The church was built around the existing bell tower, which gives it a slightly lopsided look, and the facade is asymmetrical. But the interior is spectacular—highlights include Tintoretto's *Last Supper,* Jacopo della Quercia's statue of *St. John the Evangelist,* Ghirlandaio's altarpiece of *The Madonna Enthroned With Saints* in the sacristy, Giambologna's *Altar of Liberty* and statue of the *Risen Christ.* Check out the statue of St. Sebastian and the altar of St. Regalus, among the many outstanding works by Matteo Civitali, a little-known Renaissance painter from Lucca. Lucca's pride and joy, the *Volto Santo,* is a sacred wooden carving of Christ said to have been begun by Nicodemus and finished by an angel. The carving is paraded through town every year on September 13th at dusk. One of the Duomo's most prized possessions is the marble **Tomb of Ilaria del Carretto Guinigi** *(9:30am-4:45pm Mon-Fri, 9:30am-6:45 Sat, 9-10am/11:30am-noon/1pm-5pm Sun, Nov-Mar; 9:30am-5:45pm Mon-Fri, 9:30am-6:45pm Sat, 9-10am/11:30am-noon/1-5pm Sun, Apr-Oct; 3,000L Adults).* Carretto Guinigi was the wife of Paolo Guinigi, a 15th-century Lucchese lord—it's thought to be della Quercia's first work.

Museo della Cattedrale *(Via Arcivescovado; Tel/Fax 0583/490-530; 10am-6pm Apr-Oct, 10am-3pm Nov-Mar; 7,000L Adults):* This museum has been open for just a few years, and doesn't seem to be very organized yet. All the items on display in this 14th-century former Archbishop's palace were once in the Duomo—Jacopo della Quercia's figure of *John the Evangelist*, a 13th-century casket showing St. Thomas Beckett being attacked (which might have once contained a relic from him), an 11th-century stone carving of a king, and a bizarre medieval silverware collection.

Chiesa di San Frediano *(Piazza S. Frediano; Tel 0583/493-627; 8:30am-noon/3-5pm):* Located just north of Piazza Anfiteatro, near the middle of the city's northern wall, this church is said to have been erected by Bishop Frediano himself in the 6th century, in honor of St. Vincent. It was rebuilt and enlarged in the 12th century, and displays one of Lucca's most interesting works of art on its facade—a colorful 13th-century mosaic of *The Ascension*. The Romanesque baptismal font, on the right side as you enter, is carved with stories from the lives of Christ and Moses. Amico Aspertini's gorgeous frescoes, in the second chapel of the north aisle, show scenes of 16th-century Lucca.

Pinacoteca Nazionale (National Picture Gallery) *(Via Galli Tassi 43; Tel 0583/550-570, Fax 0583/312-221; 9am-7pm, closed Mon, 9am-2pm holidays; 8,000L Adults, 4,000L 19-25 years; Combined tickets for the Pinacoteca Nazionale and the Museo Nazionale di Villa Guinigi 12,000L Adults, 6,000L 18-25 years):* Three blocks west of Piazza San Michele, Palazzo Mansi is much more impressive than the collection it contains. The lavish, excessively decorated and furnished rooms of the 17th-century palazzo—especially the "nuptial room," flush with silk, mirrors, and a canopied bed decorated in ornate Baroque carved wood—are amazing. If you've got the energy, check out the interesting collection of Medici portraits, and the paintings by Sodoma, Pontormo, Andrea del Sarto, and Tintoretto.

Museo Nazionale di Villa Guinigi *(Via della Quarquonia; Tel/Fax 0583/496-003; 9am-7pm, closed Mon, 9am-2pm holidays; 8,000L Adults, 4,000L 19-25 years; Combined tickets for the Pinacoteca Nazionale and the Museo Nazionale di Villa Guinigi 12,000L Adults, 6,000L 18-25 years):* All the art in this red-brick former residence of the Guinigi family, who ruled Lucca in the 15th century—paintings, textiles, sculpture, architectural artifacts, and Etruscan findings—is from Lucca and the surrounding area. If time is limited, choose this varied collection over the Pinacoteca Nazionale.

Torre Guinigi (Guinigi Tower) *(Palazzo Guinigi, Via Sant' Andrea; Tel 0583/48-524; 10am-4:30pm daily Nov-Feb, 9am-7:30pm daily Mar-Sept, 10am-6pm Oct; 5,000L Adults):* Make sure to climb this tower, the city's most interesting landmark, while you're here. The views of Lucca are fantastic, and there's a tiny rooftop garden with a few trees whose roots have grown down to the room below. To get here, take Via del Portico to Piazza San Pietro Somaldi, then go east on Via della Fratta, which leads to Via della Quarquonia and the Museo.

Piazza Dell'Anfiteatro (Piazza del Mercato): The only trace of the Roman amphitheater that remains in the piazza, almost at the center of Via Fillungo, is its shape. In the 12th century, its stones were carted off to build the city's churches, and the medieval houses that sprouted up on its ruins were built around the amphitheater's perfectly preserved circular shape. Watch your head on those low archways.

Mura Rinascimentali (Ramparts): You can't miss 'em. The Ramparts, built between 1504 and 1645, have a 4.2km (2.5 mile) circumference that completely contains the *centro storico*. They're 12m high and 30m wide, with 11 bastions—you can't imagine their immensity until you're standing on top of them. The walls were built as fortifications to protect the city, and although they were never used militarily, they did save the city from floods in 1812. The walls were then declared a public park, chestnut trees were planted, and the Lucchese flocked there for their evening *passeggiata* (stroll).

Orto Botanico (Botanic Gardens) *(Via del Giardino Botanico 14; Tel 0583/442-160, Fax 0583/442-161; 9am-1pm Mon-Sat, 9am-1pm/3:30-6:30pm Sun, Apr-Oct; 9am-1pm Tues-Sat Nov-Mar; 5,000L Adults):* The gardens surround the southeast section of the ramparts. Come for a walk under shady trees and admire the wide variety of plants native to Tuscany.

Palazzo Pfanner *(Via degli Asili 33; Tel 0583/954-176; 10am-6pm daily Mar-Nov 15, Jan-Feb and Nov 16-Dec only group visits; 3,000L for gardens, 3,000L for palazzo, 5,000L combined):* With Baroque statues of the gods and goddesses of ancient Roman mythology surrounding the fountain, these manicured gardens are the prettiest in Lucca. The palazzo was built in the 17th century, but the gardens weren't laid out until the 18th. You can skip the eclectic lot of furniture and art inside, and admire the free view of the gardens from the middle of the northern ramparts.

Chiesa di San Giovanni e Reparata *(Via del Duomo; No phone; 10am-6pm Tue-Sun, June-Sept; 10am-1pm/3-6pm Tue-Sun Oct-May; 4,000L Adults):* This was Lucca's first cathedral, built, it's said, on an ancient pagan site. Extensive archaeological excavations on the interior have revealed a Roman house from the first century A.D. Excavators also found a 4th-century Christian church, 6th-century tombs, and a 9th-century crypt. It's worth going down into the darkness below the church to look at the excavations.

Torre Delle Ore (Clock Tower) *(Via Fillungo; 10am-4:30pm daily Nov-Feb; 9am-7:30pm daily March-Sept; 10am-6pm Oct; 5,000L Adults):* This tower has been in use since 1471, and though not as eccentric as the Torre Guinigi, the view from the top is awe-inspiring.

Chiesa di San Paolina *(Via San Paolina; No phone; 7:30am-12:30pm/3-6pm daily; Free admission):* San Paolina, three blocks west of Piazza San Michele, is dedicated to Lucca's patron saint, but it's most famous for the fact that Puccini played the organ here when he was a boy. The church is small and holds some interesting paintings and sculptures.

Villa Bottini *(Via Elisa; Tel 0583/494-136; 9am-1pm daily; Free admission):* The walled gardens of the 16th-century villa, the only gardens within the city walls, are a pretty place to stroll when the weather's nice, and make a good spot for a picnic lunch.

modification

Paradiso *(Via dei Marcelli; Tel 0583/491-666; 8:30am-12:30pm/3-7:30pm Tue-Thur, 8:30am-7:30pm Fri, 8am-12:30pm Sat, closed Sun, Mon; www.paradiso.it)* does state-of-the-art tattooing and piercing. The facility is huge, and includes a hair salon, just in case you want a total overhaul.

city sports

Most athletic activities here take place on the wide, welcoming ramparts. A brisk walk, jog, or bike-ride [see *need to know*, below] is an excellent way to start or end your day. If you want to get out of town and soak up some nature, seek out **Club Alpino Italiano** *(Palazzo Ducale, Cortile Carrara; Tel 0583/582-669; Meetings held 7pm-8pm Mon-Fri, 9:30pm-10:30pm Tue)*, which is located inside the Palazzo Ducale. They can help organize hiking trips in the surrounding areas.

stuff

Lucca's main shopping street, Via Fillungo, is lined with every kind of store for every kind of interest and budget. A lot of really cool little shops are tucked away on the small, quiet streets running off Piazza San Michele.

▶▶DUDS

The petite **Pesi e Vinci** *(Piazza Bernardini 39; Tel 0583/496-750; 9:30am-1pm/4-8pm Tue-Sat, closed Sun, Mon mornings; V, MC, AE)*, off Via Fillungo, is packed with shelves and racks of reasonably priced fine fashions for guys and girls. You might have to dig through many piles before you find something, but you will find something.

▶▶TUNES

Casa del Disco *(Via Vittorio Emmanuel 40; Tel 0583/53-496; 9:30am-1pm/4-8pm Tue-Sat, closed Sun, Mon mornings; V, MC, AE)*, located west of Piazza Napoleone; **Discomania** *(Via Fillungo 194; Tel 0583/496-287; 9:30am-1pm/4-8pm Tue-Sat, closed Sun, Mon mornings; V, MC, AE)*, on the main shopping street near Piazza Anfiteatro; and **Discoring** *(Via Vittorio Veneto 27; Tel 0583/467-353; 9:30am-1pm/4-8pm Tue-Sat, closed Sun, Mon mornings; V, MC, AE)* just north of Piazza Napoleone, have alright selections of CDs in every genre. None of them have used CDs or vinyl.

▶▶BOUND

Il Millenio *(Via Fillungo 211; Tel 0583/496-104; 9:30am-1pm/4-8pm Tue-Sat, closed Sun, Mon mornings; V, MC, AE)* has a small, random selection of pulp-fiction English-language books, with a few guidebooks and classics mixed in.

▶▶HOW BAZAAR

There's a market on **Piazza Anfiteatro** every Wednesday and Saturday 8am-1pm—it's your usual smattering of cheap clothes and housewares. On the third Saturday and Sunday of each month, check out the **antique market** on Piazza Antelminelli and Piazza San Giusto. An **arts and crafts market** occupies the same area on the last weekend of each month.

▶▶**FOOT FETISH**
You'll see **TT Bagatt** *(Via Calderis 16; Tel 0583/469-338; 9:30am-1pm/4-8pm Tue-Sat, closed Sun, Mon mornings; V, MC, AE)* in many Italian cities. It carries the coolest high heels, ladies—and a good selection of more sedate styles for both sexes.

Fillungo 89 *(Via Fillungo 89; Tel 0583/493-647; 9:30am-1pm/4-8pm Tue-Sat, closed Sun, Mon mornings; V, MC, AE)* is a bit more upscale, but for fine Italian shoes, the prices are reasonable.

▶▶**RANDOM STUFF**
Il Quetzal *(Via Cesami 8; Tel 0583/919-196; 9:30am-1pm/4-8pm Tue-Sat, closed Sun, Mon mornings; No credit cards)*, south of Piazza San Michele, is one of the funnest stores in town. It has a great selection of ethnic and tribal artsy stuff from India, Spain, Africa, and other countries. A huge pile of handmade Indian pillowcases can be found in the back, selling for 5,000L each.

EATS

Eating is one of the great pleasures of Lucca. Restaurants here fit every budget; choose from pizza joints like Sbragia and K2 Pizzeria and late-night *trattorias* where you can swill local wines and bliss out on simple, home-style food. You have to try *farro,* an ancient grain that locals still use in bread and in a delicious, thick, filling soup. Lamb with olives

TO MARKET

Lucca is packed with food stores that sell all the makings of your next picnic. **Ortofrutta Luccan Centro** *(Piazza San Salvatore; Tel 0583/491-203; 8am-1pm/4:30-8pm Mon, Tue, Thur-Sat, 8am-1pm Wed; No credit cards)*, one block north of Piazza San Michele, has a good selection of fresh fruit and drinks. **DelicoTezze di Isola Roberta** *(Via San Giorgio 5; Tel 0583/492-633; 8am-1pm/4:30-8pm Mon, Tue, Thur-Sat, 8am-1pm Wed; V, MC, AE, DC, EC)*, west off Via Fillungo, sells cured meats, salami, olive oils, and other tasty Tuscan products. **Cacioteca** *(Via Fillungo 242; Tel 0583/496-346; 8am-1pm/4:30-8pm Mon, Tue, Thur-Sat, 8am-1pm Wed; V, MC)* has Lucca's best selection of local, fresh cheese. Get your fresh-baked bread and warm *focaccia* at **Panificio Amadeo Giusti** *(Via San Lucia 18-20; Tel 0583/496-285; 8am-1pm/4:30-8pm Mon, Tue, Thur-Sat, 8am-1pm Wed; No credit cards)*, just north of Piazza San Michele.

Lucca eats and crashing

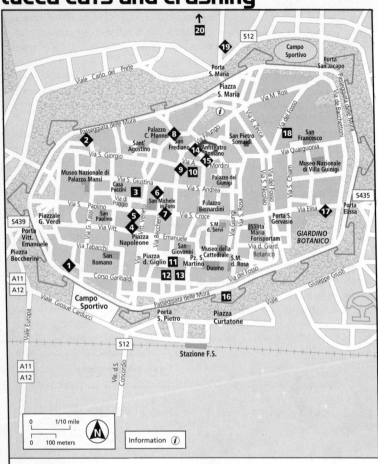

EATS ◆
Bar Casali **7**
Bar Gelateria Cubanatto **5**
Bar San Michele **6**
Da Giulio in Pelleria **2**
Gli Orti di Via Elsia **17**
K2 Pizzeria **15**
Locanda Buatino **19**
Osteria Baralla **14**
Puccini **1**
Ristorante "Da Guido" **8**
Sbragia **9**

CRASHING ■
Diana **13**
Hotel Rex **16**
Ilaria **18**
Il Serchio Youth Hostel **20**
La Luna **18**
Piccolo Hotel Puccini **3**
San Martino **12**
Universo **11**

(*agnello con olive*) is another local specialty, along with Lucchese olive oil, considered to be one of Tuscany's best.

▶▶**CHEAP**

Centrally located on the main shopping street is **Sbragia** (*Via Fillungo 144; Tel 0583/492-641; Noon-2pm/5pm-1am Tue-Sun; Pizza 4,000-10,000L; No credit cards*), a busy, inexpensive, self-service pizzeria that's popular with families, friends, and lunching tourists. You can pay a bit more to sit down at one of the little tables under the medieval arches (yes, that *is* an ancient pillar), or you can enjoy your meal out in one of the piazzas.

Ristorante **"Da Guido"** (*Via Cesare Battisti 28; Tel 0583/467-219; Noon-2:30pm/7:30-10pm, closed Sun; Primi 5,000-10,000L; Secondi 8,000-12,000L; AE*), one block northwest of Via Fillungo, is way off the tourist track and a favorite with locals. It looks like it hasn't changed a bit in years—waiters walk around the small, well-worn dining room with cigarettes in their mouths. The two brothers that preside over the kitchen cook up a small, daily-changing menu of comforting dishes for travelers tired after a day of sight-seeing—homemade tortellini and ravioli, roast rabbit, and various stews. There's a TV in the corner, which the old regulars watch while they eat. You can too.

The deliciously crispy pizza at **K2 Pizzeria** (*Via dell' Anfiteatro 107; Tel 0583/920-092; Noon-3pm/6-11pm, closed Wed; K2LU@onenet.it; Pizzas 10,000L; V, MC, AE*) is just one reason why it's so popular. Another is the extended, friendly family that runs it. Try the daily specials or the star dish—*polenta con funghi* (corn meal with mushrooms). The small, bustling dining room is brightly lit and has down-to-earth charm that's perfect for a relaxing dinner. Order a carafe of the inexpensive house wine.

Gli Orti di Via Elisa (*Via Elisa 17; Tel 0583/491-241, Fax 0583/491-241; Noon-3pm/7-11pm, closed Sun and Thur lunch; Pizzas and pastas 10,000L; V, MC, AE*), a few blocks east of Villa Bottini, cooks cheap and tasty meals that the locals pour in for. This cute, family-run restaurant serves stick-to-your-ribs Tuscan specialties like *risotto,* sage and rosemary ham, and rabbit *alla cacciatora.* The homemade desserts are fantastic, and the wine selection is huge. Remember salad bars? There's a great one here.

▶▶**DO-ABLE**

Da Giulio in Pelleria (*Via delle Conce 45-47; Tel 0583/55-948, Fax 0583/55-948; Noon-3pm/7:15pm-closing hours vary, closed Sun, Mon; Avg. meal 35,000L; V, MC, AE, DC, EC*), a few blocks north of the Palazzo Mansi, near the northwestern city gate, is always packed with locals and tourists who come here for the hearty, home-style dishes cooked with fresh ingredients. Try a stuffed pasta, like the ravioli, which are always filled with seasonal specialties. The restaurant itself is huge and a bit hectic, but a great value.

Don't leave Italy without experiencing a traditional *osteria* like **Osteria Baralla** (*Via Anfiteatro 5; Tel 0583/440-240; Noon-3pm/7:30-10:30pm daily; Avg. meal 30,000-35,000L; V, MC, AE*), located on Via

Anfiteatro, which curves around Piazza Anfiteatro. Come for wine, for a little snack of salami and olives, or for a huge, home-cooked meal. The decor is rustic and fun—you sit at long, communal wooden tables, and during the lunch rush, it's elbow to elbow. The small menu changes daily, and the *primi,* like polenta with wild boar and fresh pasta dishes, are big enough for a meal if you're not starving. The roasted meats are spectacular, the house wine is good, and the desserts are fantastic. Try the *tiramisu* if it's offered.

Just outside the town's northern gate, Porta San Maria, is **Locanda Buatino** *(Via Borgo Giannotti 508; Tel 0583/343-207; 8am-midnight Mon-Sat; Avg. meal 20,000-25,000L; No credit cards),* one of the coolest places in town. The food is simply prepared and delicious—try the delicate handmade pastas, the roasted meats, and whatever the server tells you is the special of the day. A full meal here costs around 20,000L, which explains the crowd. The kitchen stays open late, and on Monday nights, there's live jazz for your listening pleasure [see *bar, club, and live music scene,* above].

▶▶**SPLURGE**

One of the finest restaurants in town, **Puccini** *(Corte San Lorenzo 1-3; Tel 0583/316-116, Fax 0583/316-031; 12:30-4:30pm/7pm-1am, closed Tue, Wed lunch; pucciniLU@onenet.it; 60,000 to 70,000L Avg. meal; V, MC, AE, DC, EC),* off Piazzetta Cittadella near the western wall, specializes in seafood. The spacious dining room is tastefully decorated, with fresh flowers on the tables and warm, Mediterranean colors on the walls. The pastas are amazing—all the food is top notch. You pay for your fish by the gram, and it's completely acceptable to ask the price of your selected fish before the server gives it to the chef to grill, roast, or broil. When the weather's nice, sit outside and linger with a bottle of wine. You definitely want to break out your one nice traveling outfit for this meal.

crashing

Since Lucca isn't one of the most touristy towns in Tuscany, it doesn't have an abundance of hotels. But it's not difficult to find a room, even during the busy periods. There are hotels in Lucca to fit any budget, and even though the Tourist Information office won't make reservations for you, they can give you a list of hotels and of families who have private rooms for rent. The prices below reflect the high season (March through November), so expect some flexibility at other times of year.

▶▶**CHEAP**

The HI **"Il Serchio" Youth Hostel** *(Via del Brennero 673, Salicchi; Tel/Fax 0583/341-811 or 0586/861-517; Mar 10-June 4, Sept 1-Oct 10; Groups with reservations only Jan 1-Feb 29, June 5-July 31; Bed and breakfast 19,000L per person, full board 47,000L; No credit cards)* is north of the city, about a 20-minute walk outside the walls. To get here take Bus 1, 2, or 6 from Piazzale Verdi or the train station, and tell the driver to let you out at the *ostello.* The hostel is often booked solid with groups, so call ahead of time. It's typical dorm accommodation, with a kitchen and TV room where backpackers hang out and play cards late into the evening. The little garden is sometimes used for camping when space is tight.

Just behind the Duomo, **Diana** *(Via del Molinetto 11; Tel 0583/492-202, Fax 0583/467-795; aldiana@tin.it; 65,000L singles without baths, 115,000L doubles with private baths, 10,000L breakfast; V, MC, AE, EC)* is the best value for single travelers. Rooms are pleasant and tastefully decorated, and the staff is friendly and helpful. All rooms have TVs and phones—skip the overpriced breakfast.

Piccolo Hotel Puccini *(Via di Poggio 9; Tel 0583/55-421, Fax 0583/53-487; hotelpuccini@onenet.it; 95,000L singles with private baths, 130,000L doubles with private baths, 5,000L breakfast; V, MC, AE, DC, EC)*, one block west of Piazza San Michele, is one of the best values in town. It's run by a young local couple, who are constantly adding to and improving their hotel—they go out of their way to make sure you enjoy your stay. All of the 14 rooms are sparkling clean and comfortable, with phones, TVs, private baths, and cozy beds. The fresh croissants and coffee for breakfast are well worth the price.

▶▶DO-ABLE

If you plan on doing lots of shopping in Lucca, **La Luna** *(Corte Compagni 12; Tel 0583/493-634, Fax 0583/490-021; 150,000L singles with private baths, 170,000L doubles with private baths, 15,000L breakfast; V, MC, AE, DC, EC)*, just a block west of Via Fillungo, is the most convenient place to lay your head and rest your feet. The rooms are pleasant, spacious, and clean. Ask for one with a frescoed ceiling and antique furniture—all 30 rooms have TVs, phones, and minibars. Breakfast, however, will be more enjoyable and much cheaper at any cafe in town.

Just outside the southern city wall (a five-minute walk from the Duomo) and a stone's throw from the train station, **Hotel Rex** *(Piazza Ricasoli 19; Tel 0583/955-443 or 0583/955-444, Fax 0583/954-348; hotelrex@lunet.it; 130,000L singles with private baths, 170,000L doubles with private baths, 15,000L breakfast; V, MC, AE, DC, EC)*, is rather unremarkable and drab. The 25 rooms all have satellite TV, private baths, phones, and minibars.

San Martino *(Via della Dogana 7; Tel 0583/469-181, Fax 0583/991-940; albergosanmartino@albergosanmartino.it; 190,000L doubles with baths, 10,000L breakfast; V, MC, AE)*, on a small back street behind the Duomo, is a pretty, family-run place that's coveted by return-visitors for its friendly, cozy feel. All 10 rooms have TVs, phones, and minibars, and you can check your e-mail or surf the web on their one computer. Book in advance, if possible.

need to know

Currency Exchange Banca commerciale *(Piazza san Michele 4; Tel 0583/9720; 8:30am-1pm/2:30-4pm Mon-Fri)* and **Banca Toscana** *(Via Roma 6; Tel 0583/491-357; 8:30am-1pm/2:30-4pm Mon-Fri)* can exchange money and has **ATMs.** The exchange office at the train

wired

You'll find a computer with Internet access in the **tourism office** [see *need to know,* above], which costs 4,000L for 15 minutes. For info on Lucca, check out: ***www.comune.lucca.it*** or ***www.knowitall.com.***

station is open 5:30am-8:30pm daily. Money can be changed at the **post office** [see below] 8:15am-6pm.

Tourist Information Apt lucca *(Piazza S. Maria 35; Tel 0583/91-991, Fax 0583/469-964; 9:30am-6:30pm Apr-Oct; 9:30 am-3:30pm Nov-Mar; influcca@lucca.turismo.toscana.it, www.lucca.turismo.toscana.it)* also can change money. They'll give you a list of hotels, but won't make the reservations for you.

Public Transportation CLAP *(Tel 0583/587-897)* buses 3 and 6 connect the train station with Piazza Giglio (on the eastern corner of Piazza Napoleone), but it's just as easy to walk if your luggage isn't too heavy. Tickets are 1,500L and can be bought onboard or in *tabacchi* shops.

Health and Emergency Medical emergencies: *118*. Police: *113*. Ambulance services *(Tel 0583/49-233 or 0583/ 494-902)*. The Hospital **Campo di Marte** *(Tel 0583/9701)* is just beyond the northeast city walls on Via dell' Ospedale. The **police station** *(Tel 0583/4551)* is at Via Cavour 38.

Pharmacies Farmacia Comunale *(Piazza del Giglio 117; Tel 0583/491-398)* is open 24 hours a day.

Telephone City code: *0583*. There are **Telecom Italia** calling stations at Via Cenami 19 (between Piazza San Giusto and Via Fillungo) and Via Gonfalone 5. Both are open 7am-11pm daily.

Trains The **train station** is in Piazza Ricasoli *(Tel 0583/467-013, box office Tel 1478/88-088; box office 5:30am-8:30pm daily)*, a quarter-mile south of Lucca's center. Lucca is on the Florence-Viareggio-Pisa line. Trains connect Lucca and Florence nearly every hour.

Bus Lines Out of the City Lazzi *(Tel 0583/584-876 or 0583/584-877, Fax 0583/53-892)* has nearly hourly bus service to Florence (a 1 hour and 50-minute trip). Daily buses also go to Pisa and Rome. Buses leave from Piazzale Verdi and the train station. Buy tickets onboard.

Bike/Moped Rental Barbetti Cicli *(Via Anfiteatro 23; Tel 0583/954-444)*, **Cicli Bizzarri** *(Piazza S. Maria 32; Tel 0583/496-031),* and **Poli Antonio Biciclette** *(Piazza S. Maria 42; Tel/Fax 0583/493-787)* all rent bikes. Rentals start at 4,000L per hour and go up to 20,000L per day.

Laundry Lavanderia Niagra *(Via M. Rosi 26; Tel 0335/629-20-55 or 0368/257-064; 8am-10pm daily)* is self-service, just east of Tourist Information.

Postal The main **post office** *(Via Vallisneri 2; Tel 0583/43-351; 8:15am-7pm, closed Sun, 8:15am-12pm last day of each month)* is one block north of the Duomo.

Internet See *wired,* above.

pisa

You think of Pisa and you think of...the **Leaning Tower,** right? Yeah, that's here, and it's pretty cool, but it's not the best thing about Pisa, by far. Step away from the Tower—and the surrounding hordes of souvenir-hawkers and tourists—and you'll find the real Pisa: a vibrant city with some of Italy's finest architecture, fantastic shopping, and lots of nightlife. The **University of Pisa** brings a contemporary vibe and diversity to town that's totally different from its image. Pisa is actually quite cosmopolitan, and unlike other cities of its size (100,000), which seem stuck in glorifying their past, Pisa is content to revel in its present.

But what a past Pisa has. Its strong navy played a starring role in medieval history. Trade between Arabic and North African countries from the 11th to the 13th centuries made Pisa one of the region's richest maritime republics, and, before long, it had founded colonies throughout the Mediterranean. It was also during this time that many of Pisa's most beautiful buildings were constructed, and much of its best art created—particularly by the Pisano family, who were perhaps the greatest contributors to Pisa's artistic heritage. Pisa's good fortune began to reverse when the **Arno,** the river that runs through town toward the sea, started to silt up. Now there's nothing but marshland from Pisa to the coast.

neighborhoods

The jagged-shaped Pisa is surrounded by medieval walls, which are bisected by the Arno River. Everything you want to see is within these walls—the dreary suburbs aren't worth your time.

Pisa's most important sights are concentrated on the north bank of the river, on the **Campo dei Miracoli.** This sprawling square in the northernmost corner of town is where most of the tourists spend all their time, since it holds the **Leaning Tower,** the **Duomo,** the **Battistero,** the **Museo delle Sinopie, Museo dell' Opera del Duomo,** and the **Camposanto** [see *culture zoo,* below, for all]. **Tourist information** [see *need to know,* below] is just west of here, outside the city walls. **Piazza Cavalieri,** which is a few blocks south of the **Campo dei Miracoli,** is the city's most beautiful square, lined by palazzos with elaborately decorated facades. The city's main shopping street is **Corso Italia** (on the southern side of the Arno), which begins

pisa bars clubs and culture zoo

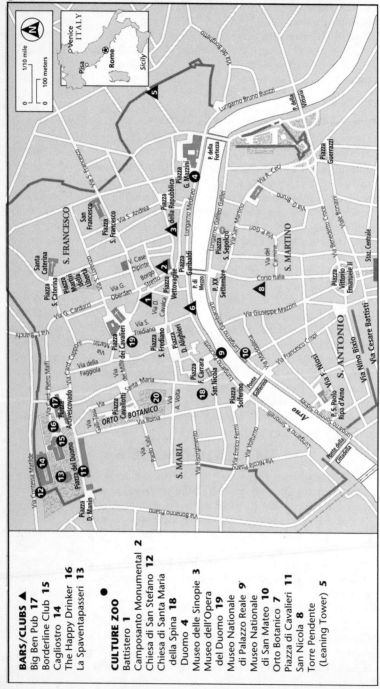

BARS/CLUBS ▲
Big Ben Pub **17**
Borderline Club **15**
Cagliostro **14**
The Happy Drinker **16**
La Spaventapasseri **13**

CULTURE ZOO ●
Battistero **1**
Camposanto Monumental **2**
Chiesa di San Stefano **12**
Chiesa di Santa Maria
della Spina **18**
Duomo **4**
Museo delle Sinopie **3**
Museo dell'Opera
del Duomo **19**
Museo Nazionale
di Palazzo Reale **9**
Museo Nazionale
di San Mateo **10**
Orto Botanico **7**
Piazza di Cavalieri **11**
San Nicola **8**
Torre Pendente
(Leaning Tower) **5**

at **Piazza Vittorio Emanuelle II,** near the main train station, and crosses **Ponte di Mezzo,** the most central bridge. On the northern side of the Arno, the street then changes into **Borgo Stretto,** and then to **Via Oberdan,** which is where many of the bars and clubs are located. From east to west, the bridges are **Ponte D. Cittadella, Ponte Solferino, Ponte di Mezzo,** and **Ponte D. Fortezza.** Shops, cafes, and bars cluster around all of them. **Piazza Garibaldi** and **Piazza Vettovaglie** are the happening hangouts on the north side of the Ponte di Mezzo, and **Piazza Settembre XX** is the social center to the south.

Unlike many other Tuscan towns, Pisa is relatively flat; its streets follow more of a grid-like pattern, and it's easy to find your way around. By train, you'll arrive at **Pisa Centrale** in **Piazza della Stazione,** about a 20-minute walk from the Duomo and the historical center at the southern end of Corso Italia. Pisa also has two bus stations, about a block apart, at Piazza Vittorio Emmanuele II and **Piazza Sant' Antonio**—both at the southern end of Corso Italia. Since everything in the center is so close and walk-able, there's no need to use the bus system, unless it's to lug those heavy bags to your hotel.

hanging out

When Pisans aren't hanging out in bars or restaurants, they take to the streets. Window-shopping seems to be the preferred leisure activity, with socializing in the piazza pulling in at a close second. The **Botanical Gardens** [see *culture zoo,* below] are full of picnickers and love-y couples, and offer a nice break from other tourists, who rarely make it up here. At night, the area around the Ponte di Mezzo, particularly Piazza Garibaldi and Piazza XX Settembre, fills up with Pisa's embittered youth. A block west of Borgo Stretto, on the northern side of the river, the green Piazza Vettovaglie, with its cafes, pizzerias, and park benches, is usually

wired

www.pisaonline.it/e-default.htm provides the lowdown on Pisa, in English.

Internet Planet *(Piazza Cavallotti 3-4; Tel 050/830-702, closed Sun; info@internetplanet.it; www.internetplanet.it; 6,000L per hour),* two blocks west of Piazza dei Cavalieri, has 45 computers, but on the off-chance that you have to wait, they also have a bar.

Internet Train *(Via S. Lorenzo 65; Tel: 050/970-596; 10am-1am Mon-Sat, 3pm-1am Sun; pisa.sanlorenzo@internettrain.it),* just east of Piazza dei Cavalieri, has about 20 computers, and offers many student discounts.

full of students. Pisans come here during the day to eat their lunch and again at night before heading off to a pub.

cafe scene

Pisans love their coffee, pastries, and gelato as much as the next Italian, but the student crowd here puts its own mark on the cafe culture. Step off the tourist track to these favorite spots for a little r&r.

La Bottega del Gelato *(Piazza Garibaldi 11; Tel 050/575-467; 8am-8pm daily; Avg. cone 3,000L; No credit cards)* has the best ice cream in town, with many home-made flavors to choose from. There are no tables—just a brightly lit, crowded, take-away shop—so grab your cone and hit the streets.

Caffeteria Dantesca *(Piazza Dante 8; No phone; Avg. dessert 5,000L, cappuccino 2,000L; No credit cards)* is the hangout of choice among Pisa's cool crowd. This stylish little place, with its hipper-than-thou waiters, is packed day and night with groups of friends catching up over delectable desserts. Cool acid jazz and reggae music play in the background, and the walls are painted with bright, colorful designs. You'd think this place would attract a bar crowd, but Pisans reserve it for chill moments. Try the heavenly *pannacotta,* a rich custard served with berry sauce.

bar, club, and live music scene

Pisa's nightlife feeds mostly on the student scene, but they seem to be a particularly studious lot—most of the bars tend to get going *and* wrap up relatively early. English-style pubs, like The Happy Drinker and Big Ben, are filled with Anglophile Italians just dying to practice their English. And since everything is within walking distance, plenty of pit stops are made in Pisa's piazzas, where young folks pass around beer and wine (and other curious intoxicants), play music, and chat the night away.

A few blocks east of the Borgo Stretto, one of Pisa's most beloved live music haunts, **Borderline Club** *(Via Vernaccini 7; Tel 050/580-577; 7pm-1am daily; Beer and cocktails 5,000L; Free admission; V, MC, AE)* bounces with activity. Expect an eclectic offering of free bands a few times a week, usually on weekends. Irish folk, blues, Greek folk, "surf rock," and jam sessions are frequent favorites on the large stage, surrounded by tables, Tex/Mex décor, and plenty of room for dancing. Every Saturday there's a '60s and '70s "funky soul and rock" night—just one of the many DJ parties these folks throw late-night. The crowd is young and fun—order a margarita and dive in.

The Happy Drinker *(Vicolo del Poschi 7; Tel 050/578-555; 7pm-1am daily; Beer pints 8,000L; No credit cards)* pub is hidden away in a dark alley, just off Borgo Stretto. Look for the sign advertising it as an "English speaking pub." The place has a good selection of beer, blasts cool Italian, American and British pop, serves light pub grub, and hosts a hip college crowd. British paraphernalia—paintings and old junk—lies scattered around the cozy room. It's one of the most popular bars in Pisa, and

festivals and events

Pisans aren't stuck in the past, but they do love reminding themselves of their former maritime might, every June during the **Regatta di San Ranieri.** On the night of June 16th, the street lights along the Arno in Central Pisa are shut off, and the city is lit by more than 50,000 candles and blazing torches. The next day, the Arno is full of boats representing competing Pisan neighborhoods. The whole town is filled with maritime exhibitions and events.

On the last Sunday in June, the ol' North-South battle is played out in the **Gioco del Ponte,** a huge tug-of-war on the Ponte di Mezzo, where locals from one side of the river battle locals from the other. The competition is a reenactment of an ancient medieval contest, and the members of the teams are decked out in medieval garb.

Held in mid-May, the **Palio della Balestra** is a traditional Pisan archery contest with teams from different quarters competing against one another. The **Maggio in Musica** festival, throughout the month of May, brings a full schedule of free open-air concerts to squares throughout the city.

During July, numerous musical concerts and theatrical events are organized for the **Stradafacendo** festival.

Strangely, Pisans also celebrate the New Year, or Capo d'anno, every March 25th. It's not the champagne and noise-maker kind of holiday that we all celebrate on December 31st; instead, it's a solemn, candlelit religious ceremony celebrating the **Feast of the Annunciation,** which also happens to fall on the zodiacal new year (when the sun passes Aries).

tourists often manage to find their way here. Finding their ways back to the hotel after all that Guinness may be a bit more difficult.

Easy to find just down the street from the **Teatro Verdi** [see *culture zoo,* below], **Big Ben** *(Via Palestro 11; Tel 050/581-158; 6pm-1am daily; Beer pints 8,000L; No credit cards)* pub is filled with loads of kitschy old English souvenirs—lanterns, stained glass windows with English drinking scenes, and miniature statues of London's Big Ben. Anglophile locals and tourists crowd the pretty mahogany bar, with its rows of Irish and Scottish whiskeys and beers on tap. There are a few rooms with tables where conversations roar over the rock music. If you happen to have a souvenir of your own hometown with you, give it to the bartender and you'll get a free pint.

Lo Spaventapasseri *(Via la Nunziatina 10; Tel 050/44-067; 11:30am-1am Tue-Fri, 4pm-1am Sat, Sun; Beer pints 6,000-7,000L; No credit cards),* just off Corso Italia, has a tavern-like atmosphere with wooden tables and arched doorways. The place is brightly lit and blares loud Europop, and is a favorite with the kids. The young crowd seems as content with ice cream and snacks as with their Italian beer.

Pub 2A *(Via Garibaldi 89; Tel 050/573-160; 11:30am-3pm/7:30pm-midnight, closed Tue; No credit cards)* has a huge pizza menu (over 50 types) [see *eats,* below], but its cheap wine and beer are just as popular with late-night diners. Since it's open later than most restaurants, it attracts more of a drinking crowd, and is a great spot to find out where the next party is going down.

The scene at **Cagliostro** *(Via del Castelletto 26-30; Tel 050/575-413, Fax 050/973-256; 12:45pm-2:30pm/7:45pm-1am daily; cagliostro@csinfo.it; V, MC, AE, DC, EC),* south of Piazza dei Cavalieri, is super-stylish—watch out for those air kisses and Prada pumps. Also a popular restaurant [see *eats,* below], the space is full of paintings, wrought-iron furniture, and funky decorations, and its cosmopolitan feel seeps over into the beverage of choice—the ever-cool cocktail. Drinks are discounted during happy hour every night, 7:45-9:30pm.

ARTS SCENE

Pisa's art scene is more medieval than contemporary—ask around at **Cagliostro** [see *bar, club, and live music scene,* above] to find out if any exhibitions are going on at alternative venues. Pisa's two theaters host a variety of dramatic, operatic, and musical performances throughout the year. The **tourism office** [see *need to know,* below] can give you an updated schedule.

▶▶PERFORMING ARTS

Teatro Verdi *(Via Palestro 40; Tel 050/941-104 or 050/941-154, Fax 050/941-158; Box office 9am-noon Tue, Thur, Sat, 5:30-7:30pm Mon, Wed, Fri; www.teatrodipisa.pi.it; V),* about two blocks east of Piazza Garibaldi, is the city's main theater, and hosts most cultural events in town. Sorry, guys—classical music concerts are the most frequent. Show your student ID for a discount.

A few blocks east of Ponte di Mezzo, and north of the river, **Teatro Sant' Andrea** *(Via del Cuore; Tel/Fax 050/542-364; santandrea@comune.pisa.it, www.archicoop.it/santandrea/; No credit cards)* is a smaller venue that hosts alternative and international theater performances. Housed inside an old church, it's a cool place for seeing a show, and tickets are usually less than 10,000L.

Pisa has a few cinemas, including **Cinema Splendor** *(Lungarno Pacinotti 25; Tel 050/580-969),* on the northern bank of the Arno between Ponte di Mezzo and Ponte Selferino, and **Cinema Teatro Nuovo** *(Piazza Stazione 1; Tel 050/41-332),* near the train station, both of which occasionally play English-language movies. Check in with **tourist information** [see *need to know,* below] for listings and show times.

CULTURE ZOO

You'll know you've hit Pisa's cultural epicenter, Campo dei Miracoli (aka Piazza del Duomo), by the throngs of unabashedly cheesy tourists, all lined up on the sprawling green lawn in front of the Leaning Tower, posing for that "Look, I'm holding it up!" shot. Many of Pisa's other attractions are right on this Campo—the Duomo, the Battistero, the Museo delle Sinopie, Museo dell' Opera del Duomo, and the Camposanto—all within a few feet of each other. Since this meadowy area in the northwest corner of the city was built on what was once marshland, all of the monuments are slightly off balance, but none more than the famous Leaning Tower. The square, with its incredible load of Romanesque architecture, is considered one of the most beautiful in Italy (posing tourists aside). All other sights in the city are just a short walk away. Most noteworthy are the Piazza dei Cavalieri (Pisa's second famous square), the Chiesa di Santa Maria della Spina, and the Museo Nazionale di San Matteo. Tickets for all of the sights in the Campo dei Miracoli are sold in the **ticket office** *(Tel 050/561-820 or 050/560-547)* inside of the Museo dell' Opera del Duomo. A full combination ticket is 18,000L; any three of the sights is 13,000L; any two of the sights is 10,000L; and entrance to just the Cathedral is 3,000L.

Torre Pendente (Leaning Tower) *(The tower wasn't open yet when we were there, but the tourist office will be more than happy to give you information):* It wasn't possible to climb the Leaning Tower from 1989 till June of 2001, but that didn't stop millions of visitors from coming to Pisa every year to see it. Now, after a $30 million restoration effort led by a 14-man team of international engineers—amid protests and political spats—the Tower is climbable once more. Granted, you can only go in on a guided tour of 25 or fewer people, so the lines are atrocious, but it's better than nothing. The engineers excavated 70 tons of earth from one side of the tower, wrapped metal cables around it as a harness, and placed big ugly metal girders at the bottom to anchor it (hence the protests and spats). It may not look great, but Pisa's treasure is safe from further lean for at least another 300 years. Construction on the tower began in 1173, in the Romanesque style of the Cathedral that it faces. Once the third level was built, construction was halted because the Tower had already begun to tilt (in the opposite direction that it does today). Nearly a century later, another architect thought that adding another four levels leaning in the other direction would straighten the building out. Obviously, it didn't. The Tower was finally completed in 1350, when seven bells were added. If you can remember back to your science classes, the Leaning Tower is what Galileo, who was born in Pisa, dropped objects from to disprove Aristotle's theory of falling bodies.

Duomo *(Campo dei Miracoli; Tel 050/560-921; 10am-5:40pm Mon-Sat, 1-5:40pm Sun Mar and Oct; 10am-12:45pm/3-4:45pm Mon-Sat, 3-4:45pm Sun, Jan-Feb and Nov-Dec; 10am-7:40pm Mon-Sat, 1pm-7:40pm Sun Apr-Sept; 3,000L):* Look closely at the Duomo (Cathedral) and you'll notice that it's also slightly leaning. If it weren't for the distraction of the Leaning Tower, the Duomo, which is one of the country's greatest examples of Romanesque architecture, would be a huge tourist attraction in itself. Work on the bright-white marble Cathedral began in the mid-11th century, but not until a century later was the building enlarged and completed. A fire in 1595 destroyed much of the Cathedral's interior, although many of the most important treasures survived, including Cimabue's mosaic of *Christ in Majesty* (1302). Giovanni Pisano's Gothic pulpit (1302-1311) is the Cathedral's most prized possession, even though it wasn't reassembled until the early 20th century. Pisan legend says that the large bronze lamp hanging outside the choir is called "Galileo's lamp" because the famous Pisan scientist came up with his principle of the pendulum by watching it swing. Notice also the bronze doors depicting scenes from the life of Christ by the Leaning Tower's original architect, Bonanno da Pisa, and the Islamic-influenced dome of the church.

Battistero (Baptistery) *(Campo dei Miracoli; 9am-5:40pm daily Mar and Oct; 9am-4:40pm daily, Jan-Feb and Nov-Dec; 8am-7:40pm daily Apr-Sept; Admission included in combination ticket):* To the west of the Cathedral, the Baptistery is yet another case of a building that took over a century to build. Work on the circular construction started in 1153; almost a century later, Nicola and Giovanni Pisano, who also contributed most of the sculptures that decorate the upper levels, took over. Most of the Baptistery's original decorations have also been moved to the **Museo dell' Opera del Duomo** [see below] for safekeeping, leaving the inside barer than the Cathedral. The highlight is Nicola Pisano's pulpit featuring scenes from the life of Christ.

Camposanto Monumentale (Monumental Cemetery) *(Campo dei Miracoli; 9am-5:40pm daily Mar and Oct; 9am-4:40pm daily, Jan-Feb and Nov-Dec; 8am-7:40pm daily Apr-Sept; Admission included in combination ticket):* A Pisan legend claims that the dirt this cemetery rests in was taken from the Holy Land by crusaders in the 13th century. Although the cemetery, which sits on the northern side of the Campo dei Miracoli, was damaged by bombs in World War II, it is still acknowledged as one of Italy's most beautiful sites. Marble walls surround the cemetery, and within its cloisters are several outstanding frescoes, particularly the anonymous *Triumph of Death and the Last Judgment.* At one time nearly all the cloisters were covered in frescoes, but the ones that survived were taken to the Museo delle Sinopie.

Museo delle Sinopie *(Campo dei Miracoli; 9am-5:40pm daily Mar and Oct; 9am-4:40pm daily Jan-Feb and Nov-Dec; 8am-7:40pm daily Apr-Sept; Admission with a combination ticket):* If the fresco fragments at the Camposanto pique your interest, cross the square to this museum. When the cemetery was bombed in 1944, the walls of some frescoes disintegrated, but the preparatory drawings for them—the *sinopie*—remained. The sketches—which the artists never intended the world to see—were removed from the walls, and brought to this museum for safekeeping. The building that houses the museum, constructed in 1241, is one of the nicest in Pisa.

Museo dell' Opera del Duomo (Cathedral Museum) *(Piazza Arcivescovado 8; 9am-5:20pm daily Mar and Oct; 9am-4:20pm daily Jan-Feb and Nov-Dec; 8am-7:20pm daily Apr-Sept; Admission included in com-*

bination ticket): The Cathedral Museum, in a 14th-century building on the eastern edge of the Campo dei Miracoli, contains works that were originally in the Camposanto, the Baptistery, and the Cathedral. There are good tourist-free views of the Leaning Tower from the second-floor portico of the cloisters and the quiet courtyard. One of the museum's most important pieces is a 10th-century Islamic bronze hippogrif (half horse, half gryphon, for those of you who haven't read Harry Potter), which was brought home by Pisan crusaders. The huge sculpture is one of the most important signs of Islamic influence on Pisan art—a result of the heavy trade and crusading. Several rooms are dedicated to Pisa's most important architects and sculptors: Nicola and Giovanni Pisano. There is also an archaeological section with important Roman and Etruscan antiquities found in the area around Pisa.

Torre di Santa Maria (Tower of Santa Maria) *(Campo dei Miracoli; 9am-6pm daily; 4,000L Adults):* If you don't want to leave Pisa without climbing *some* kind of tower, climb this one, which is along the city wall, next to the Campo dei Miracoli. The tower was used to protect the city, but when the Florentines attacked in 1499, it was almost completely destroyed, and wasn't rebuilt until the mid-19th century. The tower itself isn't worth seeing, but the view of the Campo dei Miracoli is fantastic.

Piazza dei Cavalieri: Just a few blocks south of the Campo sits Pisa's other grand square, which was built over a Roman forum. On the north side of the Piazza, the Palazzo dei Cavalieri now houses the *Scuola Normale Superiore* of Pisa University, which was founded by Napoleon in 1810 and is now one of the country's most prestigious schools. The palazzo (along with many other buildings on this square) was designed by the artist and writer Vasari, who decorated the facade by scratching designs into the wet plaster. Pisa's town hall originally stood on this site, but was destroyed by Cosimo I when the Florentines took over the city. The equestrian statue in the piazza depicts the man himself, and was constructed in 1596 by Pietro Francavilla. There are two churches in the piazza, the Chiesa di San Sisto on the western side and the Chiesa di Cavalieri di San Stefano on the eastern side. The latter was built by Vasari in 1572, and contains loot from the Turks, as well as an important bronze bust of San Rossore by Donatello. Also in the piazza is the Palazzo del Consiglio, which was designed as a home for the Knights of San Stefano. Palazzo dell' Orologio stands on the northern side of the piazza. Its tower was once used as a prison where a 13th-century Pisan military leader was imprisoned with his sons and grandsons until they all starved to death. He was falsely accused of treachery and was rumored to have eaten his sons, a grisly scene depicted by the poet Dante in his *Inferno*.

San Nicola *(Via Santa Maria; Tel 055/24-677; 8:30am-noon/3-7pm Mon-Sat, 5-7pm Sun; Free admission):* The church of San Nicola is also leaning into the sandy, unstable soil on which it was built. This small church, between the Campo dei Miracoli and the Arno, was built in 1150. With the exception of a painting showing the city's patron saint protecting Pisa from the Plague, the interior is unspectacular.

Museo Nazionale di Palazzo Reale (Royal Palace Museum)

(Lungarno Pacinotti 46; Tel 050/926-539; 9am-2pm daily; 6,000L Adults): An arcade connects San Nicola with the Royal Palace Museum, where paintings, sculptures, furniture, and other objects from royal families of Pisa's past are on display. The Medici, Lorena, and Savoia families' goods are on display, as well as other donations and special exhibits. A few works by major artists are here, but mostly it's a good collection of minor art and odds and ends from royal households.

Museo Nazionale di San Mateo *(Lungarno Mediceo; Tel 050/541-865; 9am-7pm daily, 9am-2pm holidays; 8,000L Adults):* Located on the northeastern bank of the Arno, this is one of Europe's foremost collections of paintings from the 12th to 15th centuries. The museum is housed in a 12th-century former convent, and contains many works by Pisan and Florentine masters Giunta Pisano, Simone Martini, Massaccio, Gentile da Fabriano, Beato Angelico, Ghirlandaio, Nicola and Giovanni Pisano, Donatello, Michelozzo, and della Robbia. There's also a significant collection of Pisan and Islamic ceramics. Although the place is poorly lit, labeled, and laid out, it's one of the city's artistic highlights.

Chiesa di Santa Maria della Spina *(Lungarno Gambacorti; Tel 050/910-365 or 055/321-54-46; 9am-1pm, closed Mon, winter; 11am-1pm/2:30-6:30pm, closed Mon, spring and fall; 11am-1pm/2:30-6:30pm Tue-Thur, 11am-1pm/2-8pm Sat, Sun, summer; 2,000L Adults):* This tiny Gothic church, with its ornately decorated facade, stands alone on the southwestern bank of the Arno, looking a bit out of place. The church, which was built in 1323, recently reopened after a long renovation, and is almost perfectly preserved. It gets its name from the fact that it was built to hold a *spina* (thorn) from the crown of Christ (although it's no longer there). Inside, the church is full of relics, statues, and paintings.

Orto Botanico (Botanic Gardens) *(Via Ghini 5; Tel 050/911-350 or 050/911-374; 9am-2pm Mon-Fri Museum; 8am-5:30pm Mon-Fri, 8am-1pm Sat Gardens; Free admission):* One block west of Piazza dei Cavalieri, the Botanic Gardens are a peaceful green spot away from crowds and pushy vendors. Founded in 1543 as part of the university, they're some of the oldest gardens in Europe, with plants that date back more than 200 years.

modification

Looking for a permanent souvenir from Pisa? **Tattoo Nik** *(Via di Gello 11; Tel 050/554-863)* and **Tattoo Pier** *(Via Napoli 3; Tel 050/555-181)* can tattoo or pierce you. Frequented by Pisa's alt kids, both shops have many designs to choose from and hyper-hypo-hygienic studios.

city sports

Pisa is the perfect place to get your blood pumping and burn off all those Tuscan treats. Signs are posted all over town for exercise courses, mostly geared toward Pisa's student population. Locals jog along the wide sidewalks on the banks of the Arno.

Pisa Centro Toning *(Via Viviani 12; Tel 050/577-811)* near Via Piagge, is a gym that offers diverse workout options, from weight-training to all kinds of classes. They also have massage and body-sculpting services, as well as a solarium. They're happy to let travelers pop in for a one-time visit.

Popular with student athletes, **Pisa Sport Club** *(Via Galli Tassi 12; Tel 050/560-353, Fax 050/834-442; geri@csinfo.it)*, on the north side of the **Botanic Gardens** [see *culture zoo,* above], has exercise rooms and courses in martial arts, judo, karate, jujitsu, Aikido, gymnastics, body building, aerobics, body sculpting, and ballet. They too welcome short-term users.

STUff

Pisa's cosmopolitan flair shines through when it comes to shopping—there's lots of good stuff to take your mind off the tacky tower souvenirs. The student crowd is a major alterna-cash cow, so there are lots of hip and funky boutiques. Pisa's main shopping street is Corso Italia, from Piazza Vittorio Emmanuele II, in the southern end of the city near the train station, to Ponte di Mezzo, several blocks north. Across the river, Borgo Stretto, and the small side streets that run off it, are packed with cool shops and the people who love them. But if it's clothes and shoes you're after, you'd do better to wait for Florence's cheaper prices.

▸▸BOUND
The Book Shop *(Via Rigattieri 39; Tel 050/598-687; 9:30am-1pm/3:30-7:30pm, closed Sun; No credit cards)* is one of the few foreign-language book stores in the area. This cool hangout for the international crowd has a huge selection of mostly English-language books, and smaller selections of tomes in other foreign languages.

▸▸USED AND BRUISED
Lula Hop *(Via Rigattieri 16; No phone; 9:30am-1pm/3:30-7:30pm; No credit cards)* is a tiny, cramped place full of racks of vintage clothing. The selection is mostly women's clothes, with some unisex offerings like tees and sweaters. Prices are a bit dear, but the unique vintage finds might be worth it.

▸▸HOW BAZAAR
The **Mercatino Antiquario** fills a huge area around the Ponte di Mezzo on the second weekend of every month (except for July and August). Here you'll find an enormous variety of antiques, old books, and furniture, as well as a lot of junk that looks like it spent lifetimes in the apartments of old Italian *signoras.*

▸▸FOOT FETISH
Malibu Shoes *(Via San Maria 58; Tel 050/554-815; 9:30am-1pm/3:30-7:30pm daily; V, MC, AE)* is a small, family-run store selling shoes and accessories. Prices here are reasonable—good quality shoes in funky Italian styles for around 120,000L.

▸▸OTHER STUFF
You can smell the sweet stuff of **Erborista** *(Corso Italia 25; Tel 050/24-*

590; 9:30am-1pm/3:30-7:30pm daily; No credit cards) from a few doors down. This all-natural store sells cosmetics, perfumes, oils, and soaps that make great gifts for your pals back home.

eats

Steer clear of the "menu touristicos" advertised around the Campo (translation: hidden charges, mediocre food) and you'll be fine. Pisa has a good range of restaurants, from charming trattorias to casual, inexpensive student hangouts. For good street food, head to the market area [see *to market,* below] around Borgo Stretto. Piazza Vettovaglie is another student haunt where you'll find take-away slices galore. The food here is typically Tuscan, although the Pisans do have a few unique specialties like *cecina,* a thin-crusted pizza made of crushed chickpeas and *trippa alla Pisana,* tripe with a pesto-like sauce. Menus in Pisa are also heavy on seafood, since it lies so close to the coast, and if you're brave, try another Pisan favorite—*cee all Pisana*—sautéed baby eels. Dinner in Pisa really gets going between 8pm and 9pm.

▶▶CHEAP

There's not much room to sit (or stand) with your pizza at **Pizza & Pizza** *(Via Curtatone Montanara 19; No phone; Avg. slice 3,000L; No credit cards),* the popular take-away joint north of the Arno near Piazza Garibaldi, so most people take their slices and sit on the benches in Piazza Dante. The pizza here, with its many choices of delicious toppings, is dirt-cheap—the line out the door attests to its quality.

The creative, Tuscan-inspired food—at super prices—at **Numeroundici** *(Via San Martino 47; 050/27-282; Noon-10pm, closed Sat and Sun morning; Avg. meal 8,000L; No credit cards),* a few blocks east of Corso Italia, is one of the best-kept secrets (from travelers, that is) in town. After you place your order (from the constantly changing menu) at the counter, head to the cupboard and grab your own silverware and napkin. Be sure to listen for your order to come up...they get a bit huffy when tourists don't understand the concept of self-service, Italian-style.

to market

The friendly owner of **Salumeria** *(Via San Martino 6; Tel 050/24-169; No credit cards)* doesn't speak English, but he'll express his enthusiasm when you pick out something good. Salumeria has a small selection of local wines, lots of meats and cheeses, and many other fresh local products.

Once you try this locals-only place, it's tempting to come here for all your meals while you're in town. Just because it's do-it-yourself, don't think you have to rush. This place sells great wines by the bottle and doesn't mind lingerers at its rustic, wooden tables. Try the lasagna, which gets experimented with (eggplant with bechamel sauce is a fave), or one of the many pastas, stews, or meat dishes.

Santa Maria *(Via S. Maria 104/106; Tel 050/561-881, Fax 050/551-204; 11:30am-3pm/7-10pm, closed Wed; No credit cards)* has a cheap self-service section, a pizzeria, and tourist menus that you can trust. This favorite student hangout, just a few blocks away from the Piazza dei Miracoli, is huge and a bit institutional-looking—head for one of the sunny tables outside. It's definitely not the place to come for a special dinner, but it will hit the spot if you've spent all morning sight-seeing and are starving.

Open till midnight, **Pub 2A** [see *bar, club, and live music scene,* above] is popular with the students for between-bar meals. But don't save it just for late-night snacks—this typical Italian pizzeria serves huge pies (10,000-15,000L) and traditional pastas and soups (8,000-12,000L) any time.

▶▶DO-ABLE

A few blocks east of the Piazza dei Miracoli, east of Via San Lorenzo, is **La Clessidra** *(Via S. Cecilia 3; Tel 050/540-160; 12:30-3pm/7:30-10pm daily; Tourist menus 18,000-45,000L; V, MC, AE),* serving traditional Tuscan dishes with some surprising, innovative twists. The pretty little homey dining room is filled with locals enjoying house specialties: gnocchi with pumpkin sauce, ravioli with shrimp and asparagus, and risotto. You'll probably want to order a la carte, but there are several set menus that you can choose from, all offering wine, and some, dessert. Try the excellent homemade gelato.

Il Vecchio Dado *(Lungarno Pacinotti 21-22; Tel 050/580-900; 12:30-3pm/7:30-11:30pm, closed Wed; Pizza 10,000-20,000L, avg. meal is 40,000L; MC, AE)* is a friendly little pizzeria with a nice view of the river—it's just west of the Ponte di Mezzo on the northern side. This place has a huge variety of pizzas—try something unusual, like gorgonzola and pancetta (Italian bacon). The pies are oversized here, which explains the heavy crowds. Come early to get a seat.

▶▶SPLURGE

The warm smells of good cooking hit you when you walk in the door at **Cagliostro** [see *bar, club, and live music scene,* above], south of Piazza dei Cavalieri, Pisa's favorite hipster hangout. Many folks come just for cocktails in this chichi scene, with its wrought-iron furniture and artsy walls, but stick around for the excellent food. The menu draws from the best of many Italian regions, and the food is artfully prepared. Seafood, roasted meats, homemade pastas, salads, and choice of cheeses put this offering a few notches above typical Tuscan fare. A full meal will cost about 50,000L, possibly more if you spring for one of its fine bottles of reserve wine. Make a reservation for a weekend meal, and break out something black and ironed to wear.

pisa eats and crashing

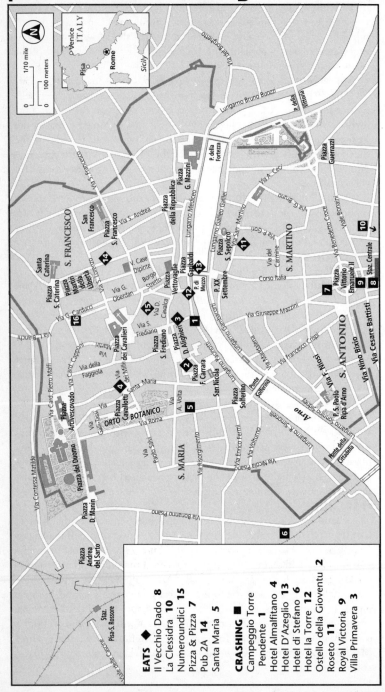

EATS ◆

Il Vecchio Dado **8**
La Clessidra **10**
Numeroundici **15**
Pizza & Pizza **7**
Pub 2A **14**
Santa Maria **5**

CRASHING ■

Campeggio Torre
Pendente **1**
Hotel Almalfitano **4**
Hotel D'Azeglio **13**
Hotel di Stefano **6**
Hotel la Torre **12**
Ostello della Gioventu **2**
Roseto **11**
Royal Victoria **9**
Villa Primavera **3**

crashing

Pisa has a good selection of hotels in all price ranges. The **Consorzio Turistico** [see *need to know,* below] can find you a room for a few thousand lire when you get to town, but during the high season (March through November), it's wise to book as far as possible in advance. All the hotels mentioned here are clustered within the city walls or just outside, and are easy walks from anywhere in town.

▶▶CHEAP

When was the last time you camped out? **Campeggio Torre Pendente** *(Viale delle Cascine 86; Tel 050/561-704, Fax 050/561-734; Bus 5 to campsite; Open mid-Mar-Sept; torrepen@campingtoscana.it, www.campingtoscana.it/torrependente; 9,500L per person, plus 8,500L for tent rental, 50,000-90,000L bungalow for up to five people, 40,000L camper for two people; Midnight curfew; No credit cards)* is just a 15-minute walk from the Duomo. If your backpack is too heavy, take bus 5 and tell the driver where you're going. This is not your good-old-fashioned campsite in the woods; it features a bar, a food shop, a pizzeria, coin laundry machines, Ping-Pong tables, and bikes to rent. Lots of backpackers stay here, so there's always something going on in the evening.

The non-HI **Ostello delle Gioventú** *(Via Pietrasanta 15; Tel 050/890-622; 22,000L single dorm bed, doubles, triples, and Quads available, sheets included; 6-11pm reception, strict 9am checkout and 11:30pm curfew; No credit cards)* is the only youth hostel around. From Stazione Pisa Centrale take bus 3 to the *ostello*—it's way too far to walk. Don't expect anything cozy—in fact, if you're not up in time to make the 9am checkout, the sisterly maids will rip the sheets right out from under you.

Just one block west of the station, **Roseto** *(Via Mascagni 24; Tel 050/42-596, Fax 050/42-596; 70,000L singles, 90,000L singles with private baths, 120,000L doubles with private baths, 10,000L breakfast)* has everything you need at low, low prices. Call ahead for one of the 25 simple and clean rooms, all with TVs and phones. There's also a small garden.

Hotel Di Stefano *(Via S. Apollonia 35; Tel 050/553-559, Fax 050/556038; 65,000L singles, 100,000L singles with private baths, 85,000L doubles, 125,000L doubles with private baths, 10,000L breakfast; V, MC, EC),* one block west of Piazza dei Cavalieri, is a pleasant and friendly hotel with 25 spacious, comfortable, and reassuringly simple *(almost* no tacky pictures on the walls) rooms. Sit back and enjoy satellite TV with British channels, a minibar, and blow-dryers in the bathroom.

Hotel La Torre *(Via C. Battisti 17; Tel 050/25-220, Fax 050/503-161; 60,000L singles, 85,000L singles with bathrooms, 95,000L doubles, 115,000L doubles with bathrooms, 12,000L extra for breakfast; V, MC, AE, DC, EC),* one block north of Stazione Centrale, is pretty tacky, with its turquoise furniture and bedspreads, but it's still a good value. The rooms have satellite TVs, phones, minibars, and blow-dryers in the bathrooms.

▶▶DO-ABLE

Villa Primavera *(Via Bonanno Pisano 43; Tel 050/23-537, Fax 050/27-020; 85,000L singles with bathrooms, 115,000L doubles with bathrooms, breakfast included; V, MC, AE, EC),* just outside the city walls, a few meters north of the Arno, exudes a Mediterranean feel. Palm trees sway in the small garden in front of the hotel, with benches for resting tired feet. The orange-and-pink hued rooms are simple, but spacious. All have private baths, TV's, phones, and minibars.

Hotel Almalfitano *(Via Roma 44; Tel 050/29-000, Fax 050/25-218; 90,000L singles, 110,000L doubles, 8,000L breakfast; V, MC, AE),* a block east of the **Botanical Gardens** [see *culture zoo,* above], is simple, comfortable, and tends to fill up quickly. Some rooms are quite spacious, and most have TVs. All rooms have private baths with blow-dryers, and phones.

▶▶SPLURGE

The elegant **Royal Victoria** *(Lungarno Pacinotti 12; Tel 050/940-111, Fax 050/940-180; 95,000L singles, 145,000L singles with private baths, 115,000L doubles, 175,000L doubles with private baths, breakfast included; V, MC, AE, EC),* on the northern bank of the Arno, just west of Ponte di Mezzo, isn't exactly luxurious, but its classic charm, though crumbling in places, is wonderful. Run by the same family since the early 19th century, the building has been painstakingly preserved. The walls and ceilings in most of the enormous rooms are completely frescoed, and about half have views overlooking the Arno. Be sure to wander through all the uniquely decorated sitting rooms, which are decked out in antiques. The hotel gives out complimentary collections of short stories and novel excerpts to all its guests, which come in handy on long train rides.

Hotel D'Azeglio *(Piazza V. Emanuele II 18b; Tel 050/500-310, Fax 050/28-017; 175,000L singles with bathrooms, 250,000L doubles with bathrooms, 15,000L breakfast; V, MC, AE, EC),* just north of Piazza della Stazione, looks modern and enormous from the outside, but the magnificent views make up for that. Rooms are comfortable and brand-new, with TVs, phones, and private baths, and there are lots of extras, like the rooftop garden that looks over Pisa's skyline.

need to know

Currency Exchange There is a **money exchange office** at the train station, and Corso Italia is lined with **banks** *(8:30am-1pm/2:30-4pm Mon-Fri).*

Tourist Information The main **apt** *(Via C. Cammeo 2; Tel 050/560-464, Fax 050/40-903; 9:30am-7pm daily Apr-Sept; 9am-5:30pm Oct-Mar; aptpisa@pisa.turismo.toscana.it, www.turismo.toscana.it)* office is just past the Campo dei Miracoli, outside the city walls. Another, smaller branch is outside Pisa Centrale *(Piazza della Stazione 11; Tel 050/42-291),* and keeps the same hours. Also inside of the main APT is the **Consorzio Turistico** *(Tel 050/830-253, Fax 050/830-243;*

9:30am-7pm daily Apr-Sept; 9am-5:30pm Oct-Mar; pisa.turismo@ traveleurope.it, www.traveleurope.it/pisa.htm, www.pisae.com), which can make hotel and restaurant reservations for a few thousand lire.

Public Transportation It's easier to walk than to take the **bus** in Pisa, since all major sights are within the city center. Tickets for the **CPT** *(Piazza Sant' Antonio; Tel 050/23-384; Tickets 1,500L)* city buses can be purchased at any *tabacchi.* From Pisa Centrale take bus 1 to Campo dei Miracoli. There are **taxi stands** in the Piazza Stazione *(Tel 050/41-252)* and the Piazza Duomo *(Tel 050/561-878).* Otherwise, call Tel 050/541-600 for a cab.

Health and Emergency Police emergencies: *112* and *113*; Ambulance: *118.* The hospital **Santa Chiara** *(Via Roma 67; Tel 050/992-111)* is south of the Duomo. The **police station** is at Via del Moro *(Tel 050/501-444 or 050/502-626),* on the southern side of the Arno, just east of Ponte di Mezzo.

Telephone City code: *050.* Pay phones are scattered throughout the city.

Airport Both international and domestic flights arrive at Pisa's **Galileo Galilei Airport** *(Tel 050-500-707),* which is 2km away and just a short bus or train ride from Central Pisa. **Trains** from the airport depart roughly every 30 to 60 minutes for Pisa *(2,000L, five-minute trip).* Bus 7 *(1,500L)* is just as quick and convenient, and arrives in Piazza della Stazione.

Trains Pisa Centrale *(Tel 1478/88-088 or 050/28-117; Box office open 7am-9pm daily),* in Piazza della Stazione, is about a 20-minute walk north of Campo dei Miracoli—it's a straight-shot south on Corso Italia. If you have heavy bags, take Bus 1. **San Rossore,** Pisa's second station, is a bit closer to the Duomo and Campo dei Miracoli. Just walk east on Via delle Cascine, which changes to Via Contessa Matilde, and then brings you to the Campo dei Miracoli, but it's harder to catch cabs and buses from this station. Pisa is connected by frequent trains to Rome, Florence, and Lucca.

Bus Lines Out of the City Pisa's **train connections** are more convenient and comprehensive than its bus connections. There are two **bus stations,** about a block apart. **Lazzi** *(Tel 050/46-288),* at Piazza Vittorio Emanuele II on the southern end of Corso Italia, has services to Florence, Lucca, Prato, Pistoria, Massa, and Carrara. **CPT** *(Tel 050/505-511),* at Piazza Sant' Antonio, has bus service to Lucca, Volterra, and Livorno.

Laundry Lavamatic Lavanderia *(Via Corridoni 66; Tel 050/49-558),* just east of Piazza della Stazione, and **Lavanderia Solferino** *(Via Roma 10; Tel 050/45-400),* just north of the Ponte Solferino, are both self-service. Loads cost around 10,000L.

Postal The main **post office** *(Piazza Vittorio Emmanuele ii 8; Tel 050/24-297; 8:15am-7pm Mon-Fri, 8:15am-noon Sat),* is just north of Piazza della Stazione.

Internet See *wired,* above.

abruzzo and le marche

abruzzo and Le Marche are regions of wild, natural beauty and small medieval towns that most visitors don't include on their itineraries—so hurry up and get there before it becomes the next Tuscany. Travelers who do make their way here carouse in the untamed terrain of the national parks, such as **Parco Nazionale D'Abruzzo,** and rest their tired bods in scenic towns like **Sulmona,** a village in Abruzzo surrounded by snow-capped mountains. They get their cultural fix in small, sophisticated cities like **Urbino,** in Le Marche, home to the world-renowned National Gallery of the Marches and great outdoor music festivals. And they don't expect any nightlife. With the exception of Urbino's college crowd, youth culture takes a back seat to small-town pleasures and the great outdoors in this region.

Le Marche and Abruzzo lie along the eastern coast of Italy, on the Adriatic Sea, and offer hundreds of kilometers of pristine coastlines. Much of Le Marche, which sits directly north of Abruzzo, consists of rural, hilly, and unspoiled countryside broken up by olive groves, poppy fields, and ancient towns. Its mostly rocky beaches are packed with Italian families escaping the city's summer heat—save your beach time up for another coast. Abruzzo is where you'll run into the mountains and the truly wild wilderness—it's dominated by the Appenine range. The sparse population of its many isolated villages and medieval walled towns, like Sulmona, is relatively poor. Since the economies of both regions depend heavily on agriculture, the food here is simple, rustic, and as fresh as it can get. Abbruzzo is most famous for its awesome sheep's milk cheeses. In Le Marche, truffles, rich cheeses, salamis and ham, stuffed olives, and fish soup are just a few regional treats you should try to sink your teeth into.

Many civilizations have touched down in Le Marche and Abruzzo over the centuries. Le Marche was colonized and heavily influenced by Greece in the 4th century; during the Middle Ages, the region marked the northern border of the Holy Roman Empire. In the 15th century, however, the Duke of Urbino turned his town into one of Europe's leading artistic and cultural centers, and his magnificent Palazzo Ducale is still standing (and is something you've just got to see). Abruzzo hasn't been so lucky—cursed with devastating earthquakes, it has spent as much time rebuilding as it has building. Settled by tribe after tribe during the Bronze Age, it became an important Roman outpost before being taken over by the Normans in the 12th century. After that, Abruzzo bounced around

abruzzo and le marche

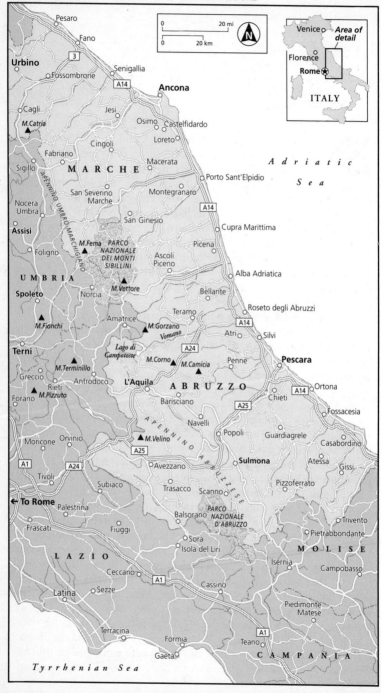

Much of Urbino's artistic heritage is dominated by its most famous resident, **Raphael,** who was one the great Renaissance masters. Visiting his childhood home in Urbino is a must. Urbino's **National Gallery of the Marches,** its **Museo Diocesano,** and its many oratories hold the regions best art. Abruzzo isn't one of Italy's foremost art regions, but its Medieval towns, like Sulmona, are worth visiting for their Medieval and Renaissance architecture—and its natural scenery was a muse to **Ovid,** the Latin poet who was born here.

between the Spanish, the French, and the Kingdom of Naples. It was hit hard in the World Wars, and the rebuilding process was slow.

Witchcraft, fertility rites, wizardry, and snake farmers have been a part of the Abbruzzian culture for centuries, and these things still play important roles in local culture today, though mainly in annual celebrations rather than in daily life. You'll often stumble on to rituals marking the changing seasons, for example, in the smaller towns.

getting around the region

Urbino and **Sulmona** both represent some of the best that their respective regions have to offer, and make pleasant places to base your stay: Urbino for its fantastic restaurants, bars, museums, and hotels, and Sulmona for its proximity to the national parks. The best way to travel in Le Marche and Abruzzo is, unfortunately, by car—many small towns and isolated villages aren't accessible by train, and are time consuming to reach by bus. If you're just passing through the regions and want to visit a few towns, traveling by bus or train, especially along the coast, can be slow, but will allow you to see much of the stunning, castle-speckled countryside. In Le Marche, **Pesaro** (not to be confused with nearby Pescara), is a transportation hub where trains and buses connect most towns in the region, as well as large cities in other regions. Ferries and ships leave for all over the world from the port of **Ancona** (65 km [40.4 miles] east of Urbino and 55 km [34.2 miles] south of Pesaro). For complete ferry information check out *www.informare.it/cgi win/imth.exe/_uk?HarbText= ANCONA&HFF= an1uk.htm.*

From Pesaro, Urbino can be reached by bus in under an hour. Sulmona can be reached easily from Rome by bus (2 hours) or train (45 minutes). There's not a train station in Urbino, so the easiest way to get there is to take the train to Pesaro, then take one of the 15 daily buses into town (a 55-minute ride, tickets are L3,700) from there. The trip between Sulmona and Urbino by way of Pesaro is about a 4-1/2 hour bus ride.

urbino

If it weren't for Urbino's college crowd, this little hilltop town would seem frozen in medieval times. The awe-inspiring **Palazzo Ducale** [see *culture zoo,* below], complete with its fairy tale turrets and imposing stone walls, towers over a jumble of Renaissance houses and wide piazzas. Native son Raphael is a tourist draw—people come to visit his home and the remarkable art treasures in the **National Gallery** [see *culture zoo,* below]. The pace here is pretty slow—old men leaning on their walking sticks stand around piazzas and street corners, and young folks hang out at cafe tables, admiring the stunningly green countryside. Even the presence of the University, which attracts lots of American students on year-abroad from September to June, doesn't liven things up too much—the general theme here is "laid back."

Despite the fact that there's little industry here, Urbino's 16,000 residents still retain a regal refinement cultivated when this town was the hot spot of the region. Women navigate the cobblestoned streets in high heels, and men look good in designer duds. The college students dress more casual—denim jackets are a uniform here—and they're really friendly. In fact, almost all the locals are nice to tourists, and proud to share the story of their town's history.

Founded by the Romans, then controlled by the Byzantines, Lombards, Franks, and various wealthy families, most notably the Montefeltros, Urbino put up a good fight before finally joining the Papal States. Most of the well-preserved brick buildings in the city were built during the 15th and 16th centuries. The Palazzo Ducale, former seat of the Montefeltro family, is the most important building in the region, and its twin towers, which can be seen from far into the countryside, are a symbol of the town.

neighborhoods

Since there's not a train station in Urbino, most people arrive at **Piazza Mercatale** by bus from the Pesaro train station, which is a 55-minute bus ride away [see *need to know,* below]. Piazza Mercatale is a 3-minute walk away from **Piazza della Repubblica** (take either **Via Mazzini** or **Corso Garibaldi** east), the very center of town. Don't even bother with the local buses—most of the city is closed to traffic, and all the sites, stores, restaurants, and bars are clustered within the city walls, in and around this piazza. The town's main streets branch off from here: **Via Raffaello** runs north and leads to a pleasant little green park with a monument to Raphael and great views. Via Mazzini and Corso Garibaldi both run west and end up a few blocks later at Piazza Mercatale, where the bus station is located. **Via Cesare Battisti,** with its many food stores, runs east from Republicca. **Via Vittorio Veneto** runs south and changes to **Via Puccinotti,** where the **Basilica,** the **Museo Albani** [see *culture zoo,* below], and the **tourist office** [see *need to know,* below] are located. The street then hits **Piazza del Rinascimento,** where the Palazzo Ducale is located.

The hill town is surrounded by ancient brick walls, and much of the northwestern section of town is occupied by the **Parco della Resistenza** (*Viale Bruno Buozzi; 9am-7pm daily; Free admission*), which holds the ancient **Fortezza Albornoz,** a 15th-century fortress with an excellent view of the Palazzo Ducale. The park that surrounds it isn't much of a park, but the uphill trek along Via Raffaello and then west on Viale Bruno Buozzi is worth it for a different perspective of the city. From the park, take **Viale B. Buozzi** west and walk around the outside of the city walls for a perfect photo op of the city. Check out the map that's posted at the entrance to the woods here—it outlines the areas hiking trails.

hanging out

The best places to watch and be watched are **Piazza della Repubblica** and its cafes [see *cafe scene,* below].

Throughout the day, and especially during the evening, folks hang out, chat, then gravitate toward drinks at one of the watering holes. For a quieter scene, head up the hill on Via Raffaello to the **Raphael Monument** and its quiet park, where few tourists venture. Couples sit on the park benches, college kids pass around beer or wine, and everyone enjoys the views. Another fave spot for the students are the steps of the Basilica, where they pass the quiet afternoons and evenings with a few bottles of beer, ducking across to **Cafe Cortegiano** [see *eats,* below] for sandwiches when they get hungry. The best streets for strolling—what locals call *la passagiata*—are the ones that lead straight across the town: Via Raffaello on the northern end, through Piazza della Repubblica, and along Via Vittorio Veneto to Piazza Rinascimento.

urbino

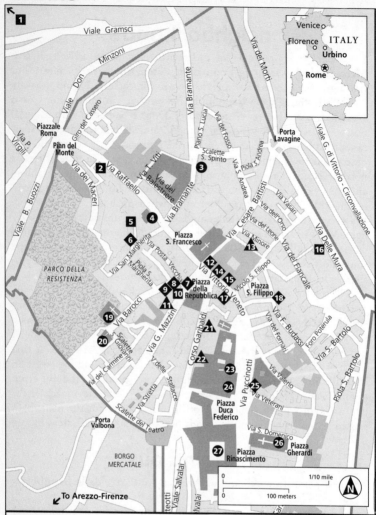

BARS/CLUBS ▲
Caffe del Sole **11**
Café Belpassi **21**
Gula **22**
Morgan's Pub **13**

CULTURE ZOO ●
Albani Diocesan
Museum **23**
Botanical Gardens **3**
Casa Natale di Raffaello **4**
Chiesa di San Domenico **26**
Metropolitana Basillica **24**

National Gallery
of the Marches **27**
Oratorio di San Giovani **20**
Oratorio di
San Giuseppe **19**

EATS ◆
Al Cantuccio **18**
Caffe Basili **12**
Cocktail and Drink **14**
Gelateria Via Veneto **17**
Il Coppiere **5**
Il Cortegiano **25**

Il Ghiottone **7**
La Vecchia
Fornarina **8**
Lo Sfizio **15**
Ristorante San
Giovanni **9**

CRASHING ■
Dei Duchi Hotel **1**
Fosca **2**
Hotel Raffaello **5**
Hotel Bonconte **16**
San Giovanni **10**

cafe scene

The cafe culture is intense here, with students, locals, and tourists constantly dipping inside for quick espressos, or lazily sipping cappuccinos outside.

Right in the center of all the action on Piazza della Repubblica is **Caffe Basili** *(Piazza della Repubblica 1; Tel 0722/2448; 7am-11pm daily; No credit cards)*, the social center of Urbino. The loud music blasting from the cafe's speakers isn't a problem at night, but it's pretty annoying when you're having breakfast. This traditional, pretty place is packed all day long, and when you've had enough caffeine, there are great sandwiches and pastries to fill you up.

Just next door sits **Cocktail and Drink** *(Piazza della Repubblica 2; Tel 0722/4415; 7am-11pm daily; No credit cards)*, which is much more typical than its funky name implies. There are a few game machines in the smoky room, which is crawling with old men reading newspapers, and locals catching up on the day's events. The outdoor tables are *the* place to sit—stick around and you'll probably meet some new friends. The sandwiches are decent, but the coffee, pastries, and drinks are the reason to come here.

Gelateria Via Veneto *(Via Veneto 8; Tel 0722/327-605; 2,000-5,000L a cone; No credit cards)*, just south of Piazza della Repubblica, has the creamiest, most delicious ice cream in Urbino. Try the rich *bacio*, made from the famous Perugian hazelnut chocolate.

bar scene

The activity in the piazzas, which starts early and ends very late, makes up for what Urbino lacks in clubs and live music. People hang at a choice bar for hours on end—Caffe del Sole is the coolest of the lot—and dip back into the piazza now and then to see what's going on. The rowdiest and loudest bars around are Gula and Morgan's Pub, which is where everyone ends up sooner or later.

Caffe del Sole *(Via Mazzini 34; Tel 0722/2619; 7am-2am Tue-Sat, 7:30am-1pm Sun, closed Mon; No credit cards)*, just west of Piazza della Repubblica, is a cool, dimly lit place with wicker tables and chairs, bamboo walls, and a copper bar. There are chess sets on the tables, which the students put to use when they're not studying massive philosophy tomes or spouting their latest theory. At night the place is a little livelier, with bouncier music—overall, a relaxing, unpretentious place to come sip a few drinks and meet some locals. There are sandwiches and snacks to take the edge off.

Cafe Belpassi *(Corso Garibaldi 3; 5am-2pm/4-8pm, closed Tue; No credit cards)*, also just west of Piazza della Repubblica, attracts an older beer-drinking crowd who seem to be fused to their bar stools. The scene is dark and thick with cigarette smoke—your typical Italian dive bar. But they have something no else has: a pool table. The kids love this place and they spend their afternoons shooting pool, drinking beer, and noshing on the inexpensive sandwiches.

Don't feel uncomfortable walking into the locals-only **Gula** *(Corso Garibaldi 23; V, MC, AE).* True, not many tourists find their way to this divey favorite, where the beer is cheap and the theme nights (everything from *Rock and Blues* to *Led Zeppelin*) are late-night free-for-alls. The crowd is collegiate, and they warm up after a while.

Morgan's Pub *(Via Nuova 3; Tel 0722/2528; 12:30-2:30pm/7:30-11:30pm; 6-8,000L; V, MC, AE)* is an English-style pub with a long, dark wooden bar, sturdy wooden tables, and the requisite beer posters hanging on the walls. College kids converse in little clusters across the big open space, and breathe deep in the non-smoking room—a rarity in Italy. The food—Italian basics and good pizza—takes a back seat to the Guinness, Harp, and Kilkenny on tap.

ARTS SCENE

Urbino's students aren't exactly an artistic bunch. From the looks of the non-existent visual art scene, academic pursuits take precedence. But there are plenty of performances that draw large crowds year-round. Pick up a copy of *Corriere Proposte* from the tourist office [see *need to know,* below], which lists (in Italian) all the exhibits, shows, and concerts. Or check it out on the Web at *www.corriereproposte.com.*

▶▶**PERFORMING ARTS**

Teatro Sanzio *(Scalette del Teatro),* a beautiful mid-19th-century building, is the center of the arts in Urbino. For information and tickets contact the **Assessorato alla cultura** *(Piazza della Repubblica 13; Tel 0722/309-601; Fax 0722/320-491; urbino.cultura@comune.urbino.ps.it, www.comune.urbino.ps.it).* Classical music, opera, dance, and shows—if it's coming to Urbino, it's coming here.

There are several cinemas in Urbino that occasionally show films in English, including **Supercinema** *(Via Viti 10; Tel 0722/2060),* located just west off Via Raffaello, and **Cinema Teatro Ducale** *(Via Budassi 13; Tel 0722/2413),* one block west of Via Vittorio Veneto.

CULTURE ZOO

The Palazzo Ducale, one of Italy's most beautiful Renaissance palaces, dominates Urbino's skyline as well as its history and artistic heritage. It holds the excellent National Gallery of the Marches, as well as the Archae-ological Museum and the Museum of Ceramics, which are included in the admission fee (but aren't really worth visiting for most of us). The Palazzo Ducale was built for Duke Federico da Montelfeltro, who ruled Urbino in the 15th century. The great Renaissance artist Raphael's child-hood home, Casa Natale di Raffaello, is a must see for everyone. Urbino also has several oratories, which are full of frescoes, paintings, and sculp-tures. The tourist office [see *need to know,* below] arranges tours of all the city's oratories on Saturday and Sunday afternoons (many are normally closed to the public) for just 6,000L. Stop by the office to sign up.

National Gallery of the Marches *(Palazzo Ducale, Piazza Rinascimento; Tel 0722/329-057; 8:30am-2pm Mon, 8:30am-7:15pm*

fESTIVALS and EVENTS

The **Urbino Jazz Festival** takes place every summer and features artists from around the world. Each day of the festival is dedicated to a different country, with music and cultural events held throughout the city, mostly in Piazza Rinascimento.

The **Festa del Duca,** at the end of August, is a medieval re-enactment of Urbino's glory days—residents dress up as nobility to play games, eat, and be merry.

The **Festa dell'Aquilone (Kite Festival)** has been held in Urbino for the past 50 years, in early September. This competition between the town's districts begins with a display of the best kites in the Albornaz Fortress [see *neighborhoods*, above], and ends with a sky-full of colors.

The **Frequenze Disturbate,** 4 days of totally free open-air Italian and international pop/rock concerts, is the most cutting-edge of Urbino's events. It usually takes place in the Fortrezza Albornoz in early August, and last year saw the likes of German industrial bands, as well as Scottish and Belgian groups.

The **Assessorato alla cultura** *(Piazza della Repubblica 13; Tel 0722/309-601; Fax 0722/320-491; urbino.cultura@comune. urbino.ps.it, www.comune.urbino.ps.it)* can provide more information on all of these events.

Tue-Sun, box office closes 1 hour before museum; 8,000L adults, 4,000L under 25ers, and price varies for special exhibitions): Located on the main strip a few blocks west of Piazza della Repubblica, this museum contains much of the best art from the entire region. Highlights include Raphael's *La Muta,* Piero della Francesca's *The Flagellation* and the *Madonna of Senigallia,* Pedro Berruguete's portrait of the Duke and his son, and Titian's *Last Supper* and the *Resurrection.* But by far the most famous, the most studied, and certainly the most interesting, is Piero della Francesca's *Ideal City,* a 15th-century depiction of an imaginary Renaissance town. The city, which is portrayed in perfectly measured perspective and is sur-really absent of any human activity, is thought by many to be Urbino back in the day.

Casa Natale di Raffaello (Raphael's House) *(Via Raffaello 57; Tel 0722/320-105, Fax 0722/329-695; 9am-1pm/3-7pm daily Mar 9-Oct 31; 9am-2pm Mon-Sat, 10am-1pm Sun Nov 1-Jan 31; Closed Feb 1-Mar 8; 5,000L adults, 2,000L students):* Even if you're not an art fan, Raphael's house is definitely worth visiting, if only to see what a Renaissance home looked like. The large residence occupies several floors and has a neat little courtyard where you can see the stone on which Raphael and his father mixed their paints. Raphael (1483-1520) was born and grew up in this house, but later spent much of his adult life in Perugia, Florence, and Rome. Not much of Raphael's own work is on display, but the beautiful *Madonna and Child* fresco, in the room where the artist was born, is thought to be one of his first works (although some historians say that it was painted by his father, Giovani Santi). The house contains many copies of Raphael's works, manuscripts, period furniture, and other household items which illustrate everyday Renaissance life—a nice change from the usual art museum format. It's located on Via Raffaello, two blocks north of Piazza della Repubblica.

Albani Diocesan Museum *(Piazza Pascoli 2; Tel 0722/2850; 9am-12pm/2:30-6pm daily; 3,000L adults):* There are a few treasures stashed away in this poorly-lit, gloomy museum next to the Basilica. The collection includes paintings dating from the early 14th century to the 18th, manuscripts from as far back as the 13th century, bronze sculptures and artifacts, ceramics and glass, and many religious items. Highlights include *Madonna col Bambino* by Scipione Pulzone, and the three grisly *Triumph of Death Over Adam and Eve* paintings by Giorgio Picchi, which are in the same room as the Pulzone.

Botanical Gardens *(Via Bramante 28; Tel 0722/2428, Fax 0722/4092; 8am-12:30pm/3-5:30pm Mon-Wed, 8am-12:30pm Thur-Sat; Free admission):* Urbino's pleasant and small botanical gardens, founded in 1806, contain thousands of species of rare plants, trees, and medicinal plants. Two blocks east from the southern end of Via Raffaello, this is a great spot for an afternoon picnic.

Metropolitana Basilica *(Piazza Federico; Closed at time of writing):* Urbino's Neoclassical Basilica, which sits right across from Palazzo Ducale, was rebuilt in 1789 after being badly damaged by an earthquake. The most outstanding part of the facade are the seven statues representing faith, hope, charity, and several saints. Inside, there are noteworthy paintings by Federico Barocci, including *The Last Supper* and *The Martyrdom of St. Sebastian.*

Oratorio di San Giovani (St. John's Oratory) *(Via Barocci; Tel 0347/671-11-81; 10am-12:30pm/3-5:30pm Mon-Fri, 10am-12:30pm Sat, Sun; 3,000L admission):* From Piazza della Repubblica, walk up the steep Via Barocci to reach Urbino's most famous oratorio, and an excellent view of the Palazzo Ducale. The only room that's open for visitors houses the finest frescoes of the Salimbeni brothers, Lorenzo and Jacopo. Painted in 1416, these Gothic depictions of St. John the Baptist's life are badly deteriorated, with the exception of the one behind the altar.

Oratorio di San Giuseppe *(Via Barocci; No phone; 10am-12:30pm/3-5:30pm Mon-Fri, 10am-12:30pm Sat, Sun; 3,000L admission):* A few doors downhill from the Oratorio di San Giovani, this 16th-century oratory is known for its life-sized Christmas Nativity scene, which was made in 1550 by a sculptor from Urbino named Federico Brandani. The figures are made from stucco, and the detail is amazing—there are even a few life-sized cows.

Chiesa di San Domenico *(Piazza Rinascimento):* The Gothic San Domenico, which dates back to the 14th century but was restored in the 18th, sits right across from the Basilica. Its walls and ceiling have been freshly covered in white paint, but there are several works of art worth stepping inside to admire, such as the glazed terra-cotta lunette by Lucca della Robbia.

STUff

Don't come to Urbino to shop, unless it's for postcards. Although the streets are fun to wander, there aren't many interesting thigns to buy. The streets that branch out from Piazza della Repubblica offer the best window-shopping.

▶▶DUDS

If you're looking for name brands, the only one in town is **Benetton** *(Via Vittorio Venetto 2; Tel 0722/320-404; 9am-1:30pm/4-8pm Mon-Sat; V, MC, AE, EC).*

Pierige *(Via Bramante 3; Tel 0722/320-015; 9am-1:30pm/4-8pm Mon-Sat; V, MC, EC),* just east of Via Raffaello, has cool leather pants and skirts. They also have lots of funky gold jewelry at good prices.

▶▶TUNES

Arte Musica *(Via Cesare Battisti 91; Tel 0722/2433; 9:30am-1pm/4-7:30pm Mon-Sat; V, MC),* just inside the city walls, is the only music store in town, but it's also a great one. A favorite of the locals and college kids, it's a great spot for picking up current concert and DJ-party flyers.

▶▶FOOT FETISH

Mazzini 81 *(Via Mazzini 81; Tel 0722/327-026; 9am-1:30pm/4-8pm Mon-Sat; V, MC, AE, EC),* west of Piazza della Repubblica, is a bit pricey, but the selection is the best in town. Boots, pumps, knock-arounds—this is a great place to pick up that pair of souvenir shoes.

▶▶OTHER STUFF

Koala *(Via Rafaello 79; Tel 0722/329-617; 9am-1:30pm/4-8pm Mon-Sat; V, MC, EC)* sells cool antique jewelry, hand-painted ceramics, and tapestries. This is a good place to buy unique souvenirs. Almost everything here is handmade by the proprietors, and prices are more than reasonable.

EATS

The student scene guarantees a lot of cheap places to grab a few slices of pizza, so you'll be able to save up for a really great meal at one of the elegant restaurants in town. Try the local specialties: *olive ripiene all'ascolane* (olives stuffed with chicken or veal, cheese, and herbs), *formaggio di fossa* (sheep's cheese aged in deep earth pits), *ciauscolo* (spreadable pork salami), and *vincisgrassi* (lasagna-like layers of baked pasta with chicken liver, truffles, cream, and sauce). It all goes better with a bottle of Verdicchio, the light local white wine.

▶▶CHEAP

Al Cantuccio *(Via Budassi 62; Tel 0722/2521; Pizza 10,000-18,000L; 2-course meal 30,000L; No credit cards),* one block southeast of Via Veneto,

TO MARKET

Via Rafaello and Via Cessare Battisti, which both run from Piazza della Repubblica, are full of little food stores and fresh fruit markets. **Margherita Conad** *(Via Rafaello 37; Tel 0722/329-771; 7:30am-1:55pm/4:30-8pm daily; V, MC)* is the biggest grocery store in town (notice the Virgin Mary encased in glass over the door). **La Bottega del Duca** *(Via Vittorio Veneto 46; No phone; 7:30am-1pm/4:30-7:30pm, Closed Sun; No credit cards)* is a small store with a good selection of fine foods and wines. The best place to buy wine and other Italian liquor specialties is the **Enoteca** *(Via Raffaello 54; Tel 0722/328-438; 9:30am-1pm/4:30-7:30pm, closed Sun; V, MC, AE)*, at the top of Via Rafaello. A few steps south, **Enoteca Caffé Raffaello** *(Via Raffaello 41; Tel 0722/329-534; 9:30am-1pm/4:30-7:30pm, closed Sun; No credit cards)* also sells wine and snacks. **Conad Macelleria** *(Via Raffaello 11; Tel 0722/320-061; 7:30am-1:30pm/4:30-8pm daily; No credit cards)* is the place to stock up on basic food supplies.

is a small restaurant/pizzeria that's popular with the college crowd. The decor borders on bland, but they play cool music—a mix of Italian, American, reggae, and jazz—and the scene is congenial and comfortable. Stick with the pizza—it's better than anything else on the menu.

If you want to spend as little as possible, check out **Lo Sfizio** *(Via Vittorio Veneto 19; Tel 0722/2824; 9am-8pm, closed Sat; 1,500-3,000L; No credit cards)*, the great slice place just south of Piazza della Repubblica. This tiny student haunt full of Italian football banners has a few stools, but most people take their slices to go.

Il Ghiottone *(Via Mazzini 10; No phone; 11:30am-3:30pm, 7-10pm, Closed Sun; Slices and sandwiches 2,000-4,500L; No credit cards)*, just off Piazze della Repubblica, elevates Urbino's slice obsession to an art form. Pizza, sandwiches, and calzones of every type are available here. Try the *paposcia con crudo e mozzarella,* a long, thin sandwich made from pizza dough, prosciutto, and mozzarella. The walls are hung with plastic trophies and pictures of beaches, and the counter and stools are always packed.

The quietly charming **Ristorante San Giovanni** *(Via Barocci 13; Tel 0722/2286; Tourist menu 20,000L; Pizza 10,000L; No credit cards)* is right below Hotel San Giovanni [see *crashing,* below], and is a favorite with both visitors and locals. Soft Italian music plays in the background and the walls are decorated with old black and white prints of Urbino and different versions of the *Ideal City*. The tourist menu is a good deal, but so is everything else on the traditional menu. If you haven't already been pizza-ed to death, these wood-fired ones are fantastic.

▶▶**DO-ABLE**

The cool crowd hangs out at **Il Cortegiano** *(Via Puccinotti 13; Tel 0722/320-307; Avg meal 35,000L; V, MC, AE)*, whose outside tables face the Basilica. Inside, the cafe/bar has a fun, artsy feel—the bright orange walls are filled with funky paintings, and the long bar offers free cookies and snacks. The dining room, which is in the back, leads out to a romantic candle-lit garden, where you can dine on their great homemade pasta with *porcini* and zucchini sauce, *gnocchi* with wild mushrooms, and truffles galore.

The locals all know about the fantastic food at **Il Coppiere** *(Via S. Margherita 1; Tel 0722/322-326; Closed Sun evening, Mon; Avg meal with wine 35,000L; V, MC, AE, EC)*. From the southern end of Via Raffaelo, take Via S. Margherita west to reach this pleasant little home-style restaurant. Specialties of the house include *insalatina*, potato *gnocchi* with wild boar, and marinated beef stew in red wine sauce.

▶▶**SPLURGE**

La Vecchia Fornarina *(Via Mazzini 14; Tel 0722/320-007; Noon-3pm/6-10pm Mon-Sat; Avg meal with wine 40,000L; V, MC, AE, DC, EC)*, centrally located on Via Mazzini, serves all the classics—with a twist. Try *tagliata* (ribbon-shaped pasta) with porcini mushrooms, and rabbit stuffed with bacon, fennel, and garlic, then baked with red wine. The fixed price menu for 35,000L, which comes with two courses and a good house wine, is a great deal. Come alone or bring a date—the brick walls, vaulted ceilings, pink and white tablecloths, and dim lights make this one of the prettiest spots in town.

crashing

Le Marche is one of the least-visited regions in Italy, so it's usually not a problem to find a room for the night in Urbino (unless it happens to be parents' weekend on campus.) There are no youth hostels or campsites here, but there are a few budget options in the city center. The tourist office can't help you make reservations, but they can make suggestions. If you decide you want to stay in Urbino a little longer, the bulletin boards by the bus stop in Borgo Mercatale and in some of the pizzerias always have ads from students in search of roommates.

▶▶**CHEAP**

Not all the 33 rooms in **San Giovanni** *(Via Barocci 13; Tel 0722/2827; Fax 0722/329-055; 40,000-58,000L single, 60,000-90,000L double; No credit cards)* have bathrooms, but most have at least a sink and all have phones and TVs. There's a good restaurant [see *eats*, above] and bar down below, and it couldn't be more centrally located—one block west of Piazza della Repubblica on Via Barocci.

You should book ahead for a room at **Fosca** *(Via Raffaello 67; Tel 0722/2542 or 0722/329-622; 35,000-40,000L single; 55,000-60,000L* *double; No credit cards)*. If you're saving pennies, this centrally located hotel is the best choice. Don't expect any frills for these low prices: the seven rooms (three with private baths) are simple—no phones, TVs, or other diversions—but they're clean. There's a small campsite in the back, if you're really desperate (or love the outdoor life...).

▶▶**DO-ABLE**

If you'd rather see trees from your window than old buildings, haul your bags to the **Dei Duchi Hotel** *(Via Dini 12; Tel 0722/328-226; Fax 0722/328-009; Bus G. Dini to Via G. Dini; 50,000-110,000L single with private bath; 90,000-160,000L double with private bath; info@viphotels.it, www.viphotels.it; V, MC, AE, EC)*. The hotel, which has its own pretty garden, is in a private residential area 10 minutes from the center of town by bus. Some of the rooms are absolutely huge, others are tiny, but all have TVs, phones, and private baths. The staff is friendly and there's a lobby with lots of magazines and a little bar. Breakfast is a few thousand lira extra, but it's just coffee and croissants.

The nice family who runs **Hotel Raffaello** *(Via Santa Margherita 38-40; Tel 0722/4784 or 0722/4896; Fax 0722/328-540; 100,000-150,000L single, 150,000-200,000L double; www.poliedrosnc.com/hotel-raffaellourbino; V, MC, AE)* will pick you up from the station when you get to town. This was Urbino's first seminary, and the views of Palazzo Ducale and the surrounding countryside from some of the rooms are reason enough to stay here. Everything is modern and comfortable, and all rooms have TVs, phones, radios, and mini bars. From the southern end of Via Raffaello, take Via Margherita west for a few blocks to get here.

▶▶**SPLURGE**

Two blocks south of Piazza della Repubblica is **Hotel Bonconte** *(Via della Mura 28; Tel 0722/2463; Fax 0722/4782; 100,000-140,000L single with bath; 150,000-260,000L double with bath; 25,000L breakfast; info@viphotels.it; www.viphotels.it; V, MC, AE, EC)*, one of Urbino's most elegant hotels, housed in an old villa with a panoramic view of the city. The hotel has a charming little garden where you should take your breakfast if the weather is nice. The recently renovated rooms have lots of antique furniture, TVs, and phones.

need to know

Currency Exchange There's a **Banca Nazionale del Lavaro** *(Via Vittorio Veneto 58)* and a **Banca della Marche** across the street *(Via Vittorio Veneto 47)*. Both have ATMs, and can change money during bank hours *(8:30am-1pm/3-7pm)*. At **Casa di Risparmi** *(Via Puccinotti 1)*, there is a 24-hour automatic change machine.

Tourist Information The very helpful **I.A.T.** *(Via Puccinotti 35; Tel 0722/2613, Fax 0722/2441; 9am-1pm/3-6pm daily; urbino.turismo@comune.urbino.pr.it or iat.urbino@regione.marche.it, www.comune.urbino.pr.it)* is directly across from the Basilica. They can't make hotel reservations for you, but they'll give you a list of places to try.

wired

HSA Service *(Via della Campane 4; Tel 0722/327-958; 9:15am-1pm/3:15-7:30pm Mon-Fri, 9:15am-12:30pm Sat; V, MC)* has cheap Internet access for 2,500L per hour—but it's really more of a copy shop, and is always full of students. Though a bit more expensive, **Agenzia & Copisteria Studenti** *(Two locations: Via Mazzini 51; Tel 0722/322-520; 9am-1pm/3:30-7pm, closed Sun; and Via Saffi 27; Tel 0722/350-808; 9am-1pm/ 3:30-7pm, closed Sun)* is the most popular place for Urbino's students to surf the web. If you're running out of lira, tourist information [see *need to know*, above] has a computer with Internet access that you can use once a day for no more than 15 minutes.

Public Transportation Urbino's **buses** skirt around the city walls, so there's no need to use them. There are **taxi stations** at Piazza della Repubblica *(Tel 0722/2550)* and Borgo Mercatale *(Tel 0722/327-949)*. You can call **RadioTaxi** *(Tel 0360/753-121)* 24/7.

Health and Emergency Ambulance and police: *118;* fire brigade: *115.* **Ospedale Civile** *(Via B. Da Montefeltro-Centralino; Tel 0722/3011, Emergencies Tel 0722/328-089)* is east of the town. The **police station** *(Piazza della Repubblica 1; Tel 0722/309-300)* is right on the main square.

Pharmacies There is a pharmacy with a **big red sign** *(Piazza della Repubblica 9; Tel 0722/329-829)* on the main square, and another, just off of it *(Corso Garibaldi 12; Tel 0722/2787)*.

Telephone City code: *0722.* There are **Telecom Italia** calling centers at Piazza Rinascimento 4, next to San Domenico, and Via Mazzini 3. There are also pay phones at Piazza Mercatale.

Bus Lines Out of the City Fifteen **SOGET** *(Tel 0721/371-318)* buses a day connect Urbino's Piazza Mercatale to the nearest train station, in the town of Pesaro. The first one leaves both locations at 6:45am, and the final one leaves at 7:45pm. Tickets are 3,700L and can be bought onboard. Train and bus schedules are posted in Urbino's Piazze della Repubblica. From Pesaro, buses (and trains) connect most big cities in the region.

Laundry At the self-service **Eccezionale a Urbino** *(Via Battisti 35)* it costs about 14,000L to wash and dry one load.

Postal There's a **main post office** *(Via Bramante 28; Tel 0722/377-917; Fax 0722/377-907; 8am-7pm Mon-Sat)* in the center.

Internet See *wired,* above.

suLmona

For nature lovers and adrenaline seekers, it doesn't get better than this. Tiny Sulmona, nestled down in the Gizio River valley in central Abruzzo, is surrounded on all sides by national parks. The town's quiet piazzas and narrow medieval streets are dwarfed by the highest snow-capped peaks in the Apennine range—just being here would be awesome even without the hiking, climbing, and hang-gliding. There's no better home base for an exploration of Abruzzo's untamed charms. The bar scene is quiet—people spend more time in the cafes.

It's no surprise that Ovid, the classical poet of *Metamorphosis* fame, made Sulmona his home. The great Latin poet was born here in 43 B.C. and is still the town's most famous son. Sulmona has always encouraged the arts, especially gold and copper smithing. But these days, Sulmona's most famous artists are in the kitchen. The town is known for its confectionery almonds called *confetti* [see *only here,* below], which supposedly bring good luck. They definitely seem to bring good spirits: The people of Sulmona (pop. 25,000) are regarded across the region as a kind and helpful lot. They welcome tourists, who are a bit of a curiosity here, with open arms—and *confetti,* if you're lucky.

neighborhoods

Parts of Sulmona are still surrounded by ancient walls and town gates. Everything you'll want to see is inside, except for the train station, which is about 2 kilometers (1.24 miles) away in the boring, suburban outskirts. It's an easy (though uphill) walk from the station to the center of town, but you can also take Bus A, which runs every half-hour between the station and the **Corso Ovido,** the town's main drag. If you arrive at the bus station, which is just south of town on **Via Iapasseri** just off **Via di Circonvallazione,** a shuttle bus can bring you to **Piazza Tresca,** across from the **Cathedral of San Panfilo** [see *culture zoo,* below].

There's no other need for buses. You can walk from one end of Sulmona to the other in less than 10 minutes. Nearly all of the shops lie on the main street, Corso Ovido, which runs from **Porta Napoli** on the west to Piazza Tresca and a big park on the east. Just about everything worth seeing lies between Piazza Tresca and **Piazza Garibaldi.** Garibaldi is a few blocks west of the **Palazzo della Santissima Annunziata,** and is where all of the town's special events, festivals, and markets are always held. The large piazza holds a few churches, several cafes and shops, but the most striking sights are the **Aquedotto medievale (medieval Aqueduct)** and the view of the mountains to the south. The Renaissance **Fontana del Vecchio,** built by local artisans in the 15th century, sits in the center of the piazza. **Piazza XX Settembre,** between the Palazzo and Piazza Garibaldi, contains a statue of Ovid, one of the few reminders of Sulmona's most famous resident.

hanging out

Maybe it's those big mountains in the distance that draw the residents of this town outside—Corso Ovido and the town's piazzas are constantly buzzing with activity. The steps of the Palazzo della Santissima Annunziata are a favorite meeting place, but the busiest square is Piazza XX Settembre. There's a small park full of rose bushes and palm trees at the end of Via Mazara, next to Porta San Antonio, the city gate. The park is surrounded by apartment buildings, with old ladies hanging laundry out on their balconies. Day or night, the benches here are a great spot for a picnic or a bottle of wine.

cafe scene

With such great views, it's no surprise that Sulmona's outdoor cafes are always jam-packed. **Attilio** (*Piazza Garibaldi 28-29; Tel 0864/34-271; 7am-8pm daily; 1,500L cappuccino; No credit cards*) is the busiest of them all, and once you taste their gelato, you'll know why. The downside to this place is the bad disco music that's constantly blaring—but hey, location is everything. Once you get used to it, it's pleasant to sit here and sip a coffee: to your left, enormous mountains; to your right, the aqueduct; straight ahead, the Renaissance fountain. Bellissimo.For the best pastries in town, try **Bar Schiazza** (*Corso Ovido 280; Tel 0864/ 34-033; 7am-8pm daily; 1,500L cappuccino; No credit cards*). Near the Palazzo Santissima Annunziata, and right on the main drag, it's crammed with caffeine guzzlers and cone-licking kids.

bar scene

Most people around here would rather hang out in outdoor cafes than inside bars, but there are a few spots to get good cheap beer and hook up with young locals.

sulmona

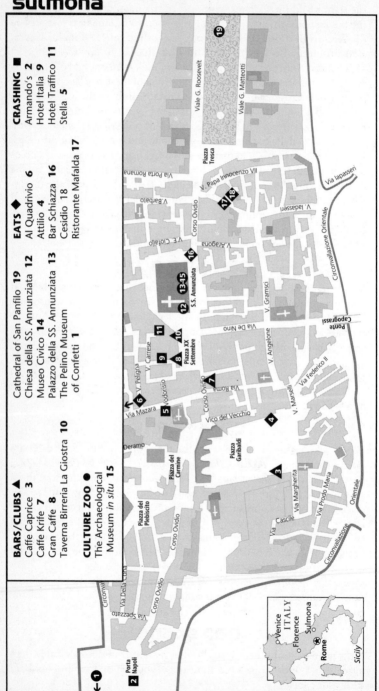

BARS/CLUBS ▲
Caffe Caprice **3**
Caffe Krife **7**
Gran Caffe **8**
Taverna Birreria La Giostra **10**

CULTURE ZOO ●
The Archaeological
Museum *in situ* **15**

Cathedral of San Panfilo **19**
Chiesa della SS. Annunziata **12**
Museo Civico **14**
Palazzo della SS. Annunziata **13**
The Pelino Museum
of Confetti **1**

EATS ◆
Al Quadrivio **6**
Attilio **4**
Bar Schiazza **16**
Cesidio **18**
Ristorante Mafalda **17**

CRASHING ■
Armando's **2**
Hotel Italia **9**
Hotel Traffico **11**
Stella **5**

Sulmona isn't a very wired town. The only place to check e-mail is **Elmer Technology** *(Via Barbato 9; Tel 0864/207-306; 9:30am-1:15pm/4-8:15pm, closed Sun)*. Internet use is 5,000L for the first hour and 4,000L for the second hour. They also sell international phone cards.

The English-style pub **Taverna Birreria La Giostra** *(Piazza XX Settembre 11; No phone; 8pm-1am daily; Avg drink 3,500L; No credit cards)*, situated back in a small alleyway behind Piazza XX Settembre, pours cheap beer to the town's young citizens and blasts your typical selection of American Top 40 and Italian pop. This is a cool hangout to meet some locals, but beware: it gets a little rowdy during the soccer games. Otherwise, this small, dark room is a great place to tie one on.

Gran Caffe *(Piazza Settembre XX 14; 8am-midnight daily; Avg drinks 4,000L; V, MC, EC, AE)* is by far the busiest bar in Sulmona, day or night. Teenagers, old men, twentysomethings—everyone hangs out in this enormous place, and on busy summer nights, the crowd spills out into the Piazza. There are couches upstairs, tables in the bar area, and an arcade/game room in the back with foosball, air hockey, and video games. The music is commercial, the decor is non-descript—ignore it and focus on the cool crowd and great drinks.

Caffe Caprice *(Piazza Garibaldi 41; No phone; 8am-midnight daily; Wine 3,000L; No credit cards)* is an elegant yet laid back place for sipping a glass of wine or an *apertivo*. Small and quaint, with just a few tables inside and a few more outside, it's a nice spot for journal writing and people watching. Italian arias play softly on the stereo, and they bring little plates of chips and cookies when you order a drink. This is *not* the place to visit when you're in the mood to get a little crazy—it tends to attract romantic couples and serious conversationalists.

Getting homesick for your friendly neighborhood dive bar? **Caffe Krife** *(Corso Ovido 202; Tel 0864/33-860; 8am-10pm daily; drinks 4,000L; No credit cards)*, located almost directly across from Gran Caffe, has a slightly seedy feel to it, complete with a strong odor of stale tobacco. There's a pool table in the back room that's popular with the kids, and a bunch of old men sit around smoking cigarettes and pipes in the front room.

arts scene

For a small town, Sulmona has a pretty big schedule of cultural events, especially classical music and opera. For tickets contact the **Associazione Musicale** *(Vico dei Sardi 9; Tel 0864/212-207; 10am-1pm/5-7pm daily)*, which is east of Corso Ovido, across from Piazza XX Settembre.

festivals and events

The **concert season** runs from October to April—contact the tourist office [see *need to know,* above] for details. The **Annual International Singing Competition,** which means free opera all over town, is held in mid-October, and attracts young opera singers from all over the world. For information contact the **Associazione Musicale Maria Caniglia** *(Vico del Sardi 9; Tel 0864/212-207; Fax 0964/208-668).*

During the **Festa della Madonna che Scappa in Piazza** on Easter Sunday, the whole town partakes in a reenactment of the Risen Christ meeting Mary.

In September, the **International Exhibition of Contemporary Art** brings artists and photographers from around the world to Sulmona to showcase their work.

▶▶**PERFORMING ARTS**

Teatro Comunale *(Via Guiseppe Andrea Angelari; Tickets 80-160,000L, but reduced fares available),* two blocks south of Corso Ovido and the Palazzo della Santissima Annunziata, features all types of performances— opera, modern dance, and concerts with international performers like jazz pianist Mulgrew Miller. **Cinema Pacifico** *(Via Roma 27; Tel 0864/210-953),* one block from Corso Ovido, occasionally shows films in English.

CULTURE ZOO

Sulmona doesn't have any first-class museums or well-known masterpieces, but that just means you can see all the sights fairly quickly and have plenty of time left to check out the cool buildings around town. The narrow streets off Corso Ovido are packed with venerable buildings— overwhelmingly medieval, but also Renaissance, Baroque, and Gothic. The gem is the gorgeous Palazzo della Santissima Annunziata, which houses the Museo Civico.

Palazzo della Santissima Annunziata *(Corso Ovido 208; Tel 0864/210-216; 9am-1pm/3:30-7pm Tue-Fri, 10am-1pm/4-7pm Sat, Sun; 1,000L admission):* Construction on this Gothic/Renaissance palazzo started in 1415, and was not completed until the end of the 16th century. Both the palazzo and the adjacent church combine elements of Gothic, Renaissance, and Baroque Sulmonese architecture. Originally built as a hospital, today it houses the town's museums.

Chiesa della Santissima Annunziata *(Corso Ovido 208; Tel 0864/210-216; 9am-1pm/3:30-7pm Tue-Fri, 10am-1pm/4-7pm Sat, Sun; Free admission):* This spacious former church has been cleared of its pews and is now mainly used for concerts. Rebuilt in the 18th century after a devastating earthquake, the facade is ornately Baroque. The marble altars are beautiful, and if you take a closer look at some of the statues, you'll see that some of the saints are holding *confetti* in their hands.

Museo Civico (Town Museum) *(Palazzo della Santissima Annunziata, Corso Ovido; Tel 0864/210-216; 9am-1pm/3:30-7pm Tue-Fri, 10am-1pm/4-7pm Sat, Sun; Free admission):* The town's museum is divided into two sections: the medieval and the archaeological. The medieval section holds sculptures, paintings, old documents and manuscripts, gold religious artifacts, jewelry, local coins, and baroque chalices. The pride of the museum is a land register document from 1376, which is one of the oldest of its kind in Italy. The archaeological section holds prehistoric ceramics, Roman bronze statues, and fragments of sculptures and mosaics found nearby. Skippable except for history buffs or urban planning majors.

The Archaeological Museum "in situ" *(Palazzo della Santissima Annunziata; Tel 0864/50-970 or 0864/33-222; 10am-1pm, closed Mon; Free admission):* This small museum, on the ground floor of the Palazzo, shows off artifacts found in the west wing of this very building during repairs and subsequent digs shedding light on the 1st century B.C. Roman city. Check out the remains of a Roman house and a drawing of the wedding of Dionysus and Ariadne.

Cathedral of San Panfilo *(Viale Matteotti; Tel 0864.34065; Only open upon request; Free admission):* Sulmona's cathedral was built over a Roman temple in the 14th century, and had later additions added that encompass many styles. The church, on the eastern end of the Piazza Tresca park, was heavily damaged in an earthquake in 1706, and the inte-

only here

The multi-colored, sugared almonds known as *confetti* will most likely be the first thing that grabs you about Sulmona. Practically every other store on Corso Ovido is dedicated to selling hundreds of different types of this sweet stuff, which is delicately shaped into faux floral arrangements. In traditional weddings in Abruzzo, the couple is pelted with them for good luck (Ouch!). Want to know more about the tradition? Visit the one and only Italian *confetti* museum [see *culture zoo,* above].

rior remains fairly empty. The crypt is Romanesque and displays the sarcophagus of a bishop who died in 1422.

The "Pelino" Museum of Confetti *(Via Staz. Introdaqua 55; Tel
0864/210-047; 9:30am-noon/3:30-6:30pm Mon-Fri; 2,000L admission):*
If you find yourself liking the Sulmonese *confetti,* or you're just into food,
take a stroll around this little museum that traces the history of the tradition and illustrates how the candy is made.

great outdoors

Sulmona sits on the outskirts of the sprawling **Parco Nazional de
Maiella,** home of the Maiella mountain range. It's more rugged and
wild than many of the national parks in Italy, with ragged cliffs and steep
inclines covered in gnarly old trees that are home to a number of endan-
gered species. If you have camping gear, you should commit a couple of
days to a visit here—the buses run to the small towns inside the park, but
they don't run too frequently. To do it all in one day, you'll have to get up
and out before the crack of dawn and pack it in while there's still plenty
of good hiking time left. There's certainly opportunity for blister-inducing
hard-core hikes here, but there's also plenty of flat ground for strolling,
admiring the wildflowers, and enjoying the shade of the trees. The park
stretches out to the coast of the Adriatic Sea, ending up at long stretches
of untouched beach and grassy, gentle cliffs.

Pescocostanzo is a decent place to start out, reachable by an ARPA
bus from Sulmona [see *need to know,* below]. It's a well-preserved little village that has been slightly overrun with the resort crowd, but is just fine
as a home base, as it puts you right on the doorstep of the park. The
tourist office in Pescocostanzo *(On the main square (you can't miss it, trust
us); Tel 0864/641-440; 9am-1pm/4-6pm Mon-Sat, no later afternoon hours
Sun)* can give you detailed trail maps and weather conditions, and info on
the nameless camping sites scattered around the park.

stuff

Via Ovido is the central nervous system of Sulmona, and that applies to
shopping as much as everything else. There are some decent clothing
stores in Sulmona, but if you can, wait for Florence or Rome, where
prices are lower and selections are better. But by all means, do stock up
on *confetti* [see *only here,* below]. Practically all stores in Sulmona, except
for a few *confetti* shops, are closed on Sundays. Stores here generally open
from 9am to 1pm and again from 4 to 8pm.

▶▶**DUDS**
Benetton *(Corso Ovido 197; Tel 0864/51-708; 9am-1pm/4-8pm, closed
Sun; V, MC, AE, EC),* an Italian staple that never disappoints, is right on
the main drag.

For all kinds of cool clothes and accessories at reasonable prices, try
Max Street Corner *(Corso Ovido 145; Tel 0864/51-115; 9am-1pm/4-
8pm, closed Sun; V, MC, AE, EC).* Pick up a pair of Diesel jeans at a fraction of their cost in the States.

▶▶CLUB GEAR

Girls, need something strappy? Guys, some tight-fitting T-shirts to show off those pectorals? **Phard** *(Corso Ovido 151; Tel 0864/52-657; 9am-1pm/4-8pm, closed Thur morning; V, MC, AE, EC)* sells cool club gear at even cooler prices.

▶▶TUNES

Dimensione Musica *(Vico dei Sardi 7; Tel 0864/50-269; 9am-1pm/4-8pm, closed Sun; V, MC, AE, EC)* may not be the hippest music store, but at least it knows what it's good at—classical CDs galore.

Kaos *(Corso Ovidio 213; Tel 0864/51-972; 9am-1pm/4-8pm, closed Sun; V, MC, AE, EC)* sells a wide variety of CDs and is the preferred music store for Sulmona's pierced and pout-y population. The karaoke machine in the back is a greatly under-utilized cure for a boring afternoon.

▶▶HOW BAZAAR

There's a **flea market** in Piazza Garibaldi in the morning hours every Wednesday and Saturday. Tables are piled high with used clothes, various types of junk, and lots of cheap new duds. If you dig, you can find some useful stuff. As always with markets like these, haggling is the norm.

▶▶OTHER STUFF

Orient *(Corso Ovido 83; Tel 0864/56-378; 10am-1:30pm/4-8pm, closed Sun; No credit cards)* sells cool beaded jewelry and tribal Asian, African, and Indian arts, crafts, and jewelry. Prices are reasonable for such a great selection.

La Bottega del Rome *(Piazza Garibaldi 18; Tel 0964; 210-053; 10am-1:30pm/4-7pm daily; No credit cards)* is a neat little store overflowing with glittering copper pots, a specialty of Sulmona. Remember Mom!

EATS

There are few restaurants in Sulmona, and they're often full of families, young couples, and whatever tourists happen to be in town. Show up early (no later than 8pm) to make sure you get to try some of the local specialties. Much of Abruzzo still depends on agriculture for its livelihood, so the produce here is out of this world. Don't miss the *maccheroni alla chitarra,* a handmade egg pasta cut into squares with a tool that looks vaguely like a guitar—hence the name. The *brodetto* (fish soup), which usually comes to the table in a huge covered tureen, is usually enough for two. You'll see *zaffereno* (saffron) on many menus—the pricey and unforgettably flavorful spice is grown locally, and is used in many dishes. Top it all off with a bottle of Montepulciano d'Abbruzzo, a local, hearty red, or Trebbiano, a crispy white wine.

▶▶CHEAP

The meals at **Ristorante Mafalda** *(Via Solimo 20; Tel 0864/34-538; Noon-3pm/7-11pm, closed Sun; Avg. meal 30,000L; No credit cards),* just east of the Palazzo Santissima Annunziata, are hearty and soul-satisfying. The popular family-run place is decorated with hundreds of wine bottles, and it has a real unpretentious, neighborhood feel. The dining room is brightly lit, and there's a TV in the corner that shows all

TO MARKET

Almost everything is closed on Sundays, including food shops, so plan ahead. **Enoteca di Loreto Vinattieri** *(Via Aragona 39 and Via Gramsci 39-41; Tel 0864/51-919; 9am-1:30pm/4-8pm, closed Sun)* has a big selection of local, national, and international wine. Don't miss **Soldo di Cacio** *(Piazza Plebiscita 7; Tel 0864/54-026; 9am-1:30pm/4-8pm, closed Sun)*, Sulmona's best food market. You can smell the salami down the street, and once you're inside, homemade pastas and cheeses, and fresh breads are all yours.

the soccer games. Try the *cotoletta alla Milanese* (breaded veal), or *spaghetti alla carbonara*.

The very busy, family-run **Cesidio** *(Piazza Solimo; Tel 0864/52-724 or 0864/34-940; Noon-3pm/7-11pm, closed Thur; Avg. 3-course meal 30,000L; No credit cards)*, right off Corso Ovido, may not have the best food, but it's definitely the restaurant of choice for many locals. Huge extended families come in for huge extended meals—it's all traditional dishes here.

▶▶**DO-ABLE**

Al Quadrivio *(Via Mazara 38; Tel 0864/55-533; Noon-3pm/7-11pm, closed Sun and Mon evenings; Avg. meal with wine 50,000L; V, MC)* is one of the town's best restaurants, and it barely qualifies as a "do-able," it's so reasonable. Tables are candle lit, the lights are dim, the music is soft, and the food is excellent. Try the handmade pasta dishes, or dig in to one of the roasted meats. Reservations are recommended.

crashing

Sulmona, like much of the region, is almost unknown to tourists. There are just four hotels in town, but even during the town's big events [see *festivals and events,* below], it's usually not difficult to find a room. If you do have trouble, there are several hotels 2 kilometers (1.24 miles) west of town and along Bus A's route—but this should be a last resort.

▶▶**CHEAP**

There are reasons why **Hotel Traffico** *(Via Degli Agghiacciati 17; Tel 0864/54-080; 35,000-40,000L single with private bath; 30,000-35,000L single without; 70,000-80,000L double with private bath; 50,000-70,000L double without; No credit cards)* is so cheap. The reception area is musty, you may not have hot water, and the blankets are ancient. But the elderly couple that runs it couldn't be nicer, and neither could the location—it's right in the middle of things, just around the corner from the Palazzo della Santissima Annunziata. The rooms don't have TVs or phones, but you don't need those modern distractions, right?

Hotel Italia *(Piazza S. Tommasi; Tel 0864/52-308; 90,000L double with private bath; 70,000L double without private bath; No credit cards)* has tons of character, with stained-glass windows, vaulted ceilings in some of the rooms, antique furniture, and huge windows with great views. Each floor in this old-fashioned hotel has its own little sitting room. Even though technically there aren't singles, they'll usually give solo travelers a discount on a double.

The smallest hotel in town is **Stella** *(Via Mazara; Tel 0864/52-653; 50,000-65,000L single; 90,000-100,000L double; No credit cards)*, with just nine rooms, all with private baths. The rooms are clean and pleasant, if a bit Spartan, and there's a dining room where you can sign on for full or half board. It's located one block west of Piazza XX Settembre, just off Corso Ovidio.

Armando's *(Via Montenero 15; Tel 0864/210-783; Fax 0864/210-787; 70,000L single with private bath; 120,000L double with private bath; No credit cards)* also has a restaurant attached that serves hotel guests a la carte meals. If the other hotels are booked, you'll have a better chance of finding a room here since it's just outside Porta Napoli on the western edge of town, the farthest from the train station of all the hotels. The 18 rooms are clean and relatively new.

Need to know

Currency Exchange The best places to change money are the banks, several of them along Corso Ovido. There is also a **Banca di Napoli** *(Piazza XX Settembre 3),* and several ATMs in the center of town.

Tourist Information Sulmona's tourist office, **Informazione Accoglienza Turistica** *(Corso Ovido 208; Tel 0864/53-267; 9am-1pm/3:30-6:30pm Mon-Sat, open Sun mornings during the summer),* is inside the Palazzo Santissima Annunziata. They can help you arrange tours or itineraries of the surrounding national parks, but can't make hotel reservations for you.

Public Transportation The only bus you'll need is **Bus A.** It starts from the train station and runs straight along Corso Ovido and to the hotels. You can buy tickets onboard. There are **taxi stands** in **Piazzale Stazione** *(Tel 0864/31-746),* **Piazza XX Settembre** *(Tel 0864/31-747),* and **Piazza Carmine** *(Tel 0864/317-48).*

Health and Emergency Emergency: *113;* Police emergency: *112;* Medical emergency: *118.*

Pharmacies There are many pharmacies in town that rotate hours so that at least one is open at night and during lunch—Corso Ovido 214 *(Tel 0864/210-830),* Corso Ovido 179 *(Tel 0864/52-645),* and Piazza del Carmine 9 *(Tel 0864/51-260).*

Telephone City code: *0864.* There are pay phones on Piazza XX Settembre.

Trains The train station, **Sulmona Stazione Centrale** is located in Piazzale Stazione Centrale, 2 kilometers (1.24 miles) from the historic center of town. Bus A goes back and forth between the station and the center every half hour. Trains regularly connect Sulmona with Rome and Pescara.

Bus Lines Out of the City ARPA buses connect Sulmona with several of the region's small towns. There are nine daily buses to L'Aquila, five to Pescara, and two to Naples. Take note that there are none to Urbino—you have to transfer in Pesaro. Buses leave from both Piazza Tresca and the bus station (which is more like a parking lot where the buses hang out) on **Via Iapasseri.** The station is south of Piazza Tresca, on Via Iapasseri, just off of Via di Circonvallazione.

Postal The **main post office** is in Piazza Brigita Mariella *(Tel 0864/2471; 8am-7pm Mon-Sat),* but there are **red postal boxes** throughout the town.

Internet See *wired,* above.

milan &
lombardia

milan & lombardi

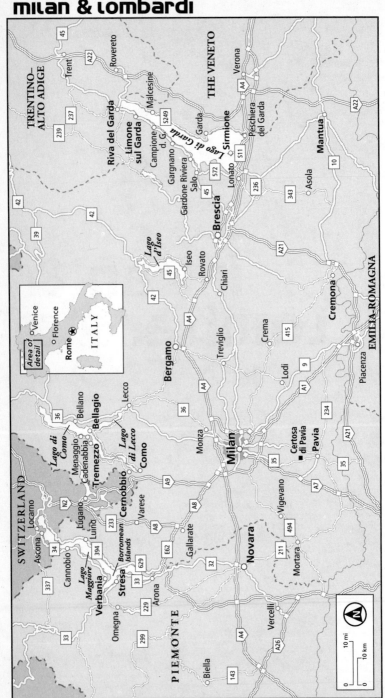

nowhere on earth are people more chic than in Milan, the heart of Lombardia. People here ooze style from their pores, and they know it. They distinguish themselves as Lombards first, Italians second (which doesn't make them exceptionally popular outside of their own territory in Northern Italy). Everything they do, they do with style. Even outside the city, the resort towns of the northern lake regions aren't just outdoorsy, they're "fashionably rustic." **Milan** is like a gorgeous supermodel who looks unbelievably great no matter what she's wearing. So don't waste time on envy; just pick up a few fashion tips and be prepared to max out your VISA card.

And if the whole too-cool-for-school thing is getting to you, you can always take consolation in the fact that Milan's party scene is totally mediocre. Happy hour has caught on in a big way, and you can catch decent music almost any night of the week, a rarity in Italy, but the club scene is disappointing. As you might expect, especially in the clubs, the Milan scene is all about seeing and being seen.

Once you've seen it all, leave Milan to the Milanese, and check out the northern lake region, home to **Lago Maggiore, Lago di Como, Lago d'Orta,** and **Lago di Garda.** Rustic chic aside, all of these little lakeside towns are a refreshing break from Milan's urban ego-trip. For centuries, renowned authors and intellectuals from Kafka to Nietzsche and Hemingway found inspiration along the lakeshores. Today the lakes offer tourist pleasures from the tacky (Sirmione, a tourist trap in the best sense of the word) to the sublime (grandiose Isola Bella). You can indulge in every form of outdoor adventure from intense windsurfing to alpine rock climbing or a 255-meter bungee jump off a dam.

The lure of this region is not new. Lombardia bears the footprints of northern barbarians, Roman Centurions, and Napoleon's armies—all of whom coveted its agricultural wealth and strategic position south of the Alps. And soldiers haven't been the only invaders; after Milan's post-WWII industrial boom, hordes of southerners trekked north in search of higher wages and better opportunities. Today, immigrants from all over the world still crowd the major cities, peddling imitation Gucci bags and cheap sunglasses, much to the distaste of native citizens. Lombards have tried several times to secede from the country, claiming that the poorer southern regions are undermining their economic strength (not to mention their acute fashion sense), but it looks like the hoi polloi will be sticking around, at least for the foreseeable future.

One thing that hasn't been diluted is Lombardia's rep for amazing food. The regional cuisine is based around entrees featuring fresh water fish, risotto, and meat galore. In the Lake region, dishes such as *alborelle fritte e salvia impanata* (little breaded fried fish covered in sage) and *filetto di pesce persico alle erbe aromatiche* (a lake perch fillet pickled in herbs) are

TraveL Times

All times by train except:
* bus
** ferry/water steamer
***hydrofoil

	Milan	Pavia	Como	Lecco
Milan	-	:30	1:00	1:00
Pavia	:30	-	2:00	1:45
Como	1:00	2:00	-	1:30
Lecco	1:00	1:45	1:30	-
Domaso	3:00*	4:00*	2:00	3:30*
Riva del Garda	3:30*	4:30*	5:00*	5:00*
Sirmione	1:45*	2:30*	3:00*	3:00*
Stresa	1:00*	1:45	3:00	3:00
Isola Borromee	1:30**	2:00**	3:00**	3:30**

a culinary staple. Meat dishes like *scalamino allo spiedoe fagioli* (beans and grilled sausages) and *lombo di coniglio marinato in agretto di limone e mist-icanze* (rabbit loin pickled in lemon sauce and vegetables) go nicely with a tall bottle of local wine, such as *Vespolina*. In Milan, risotto rules the day, often prepared in melted provincial cheeses, appropriately named *risotto alla Milanese.*

Milan's duomo is by far the most recognized and impressive example

Domaso	Riva del Gorda	Sirmione	Stresa	Isola Borromee	Lago di Orta
3:00*	3:30*	1:45*	1:00	1:30**	2:00
4:00*	4:30*	2:30*	1:45	2:00**	3:00
2:00	5:00*	3:00*	3:00	3:30**	4:00
3:30*	5:00*	3:00*	3:00	3:30**	4:00
-	7:00**	5:00**	5:00*	5:30* **	6:00*
7:00*	-	4:00**	5:00*	5:30* **	6:00*
5:00**	4:00**	-	3:00*	3:30* **	5:00*
5:00**	5:00*	3:00*	-	:30	2:00
5:30***	5:30***	3:30***	:30	-	2:30**

of Lombardia's architecture. However, the duomo and da Vinci-designed Carthusian Monastery outside of Pavia are only the tip of the iceberg in a region which boasts architectural contributions from both the ancient Romans and royal families of the Renaissance, who left the lake region strewn with their gilded-lily villas and palazzos.

geттıng around тнe regıon

High-speed trains and swarms of buses cover Lombardia in every direction, making it one of the most accessible and convenient destinations in Italy. **Milan** is the most logical starting point for touring the region, as just about all trains and buses run through it. From Milan, heading north to the lakes is easy and quick. A train line runs from Milan to **Lago D'Orta** (30 minutes) and continues up to **Lago Maggiore** (one hour). From there, you can travel north as far as Switzerland. Heading east to Lago Di Como by train requires a trip back down to Milan; the only slightly quicker trip by bus is very expensive (L80,000). Two train lines connect Milan to Lago Di Como, one leaving from Stazione Centrale and the other from Stazione Nord. The trip takes about an hour. The trains that run from Stazione Nord are privately owned and do not recognize Eurorail passes. Cities east of Milan, including Bergamo (one hour), Brescia (two hours), and Mantova (three-and-a-half hours), are serviced by inter-city and Eurostar high-speed trains almost every hour. To reach Lago Di Garda from Milan, you must take a train or bus to Brescia, and then take a local bus around the lake.

milan

Milan is its own entity: confident, brash, sometimes a little too cool for school. It's a city that doesn't rely on the curiosity of foreigners to dictate its rhythms. You're welcome to join in, but remember, they don't really need you. Milan is big and diverse, a sprawling architectural grandiosity. It's more like London than Rome. Though it has some of the best museums around, you don't come to Milan to be a passive sightseer; you come to wander around its distinctly different neighborhoods, lose yourself in the urban funk, *shop* (exchange rates be damned!), and groove on Italy's most genuinely modern culture. Still, if you look closely at Italy's "Second City," you'll get a glimpse of old Italy tucked inside its hardcore urban veneer.

Southern Italians would have you think the secession-happy, fiercely protectionist Milanese are uptight aliens. While the people you'll meet are basically friendly and congenial, they, unlike their southern countrymen, don't communicate as much with their hands. And kids from Milan have a greater sense of purpose than those coming from other, poorer Italian towns. You won't see hordes of moped-riding students with brightly colored Invicta backpacks lounging or chatting for hours in the streets or in the neighborhood bars. Here, twentysomething culture is shaped by university classes and steady jobs. At night, kids hang out in the Ticinese, Navigli, or Garibaldi districts with friends. While Milan is one of the best cities in which to pull out your fancy clothes and play dress-up—and the few established clubs here do deliver the goods—a lovely evening can be had pursuing less-frenzied activities: seeing a flick at one of many local theaters, sipping martinis by the canal, or eating a

milan bars clubs and culture zoo

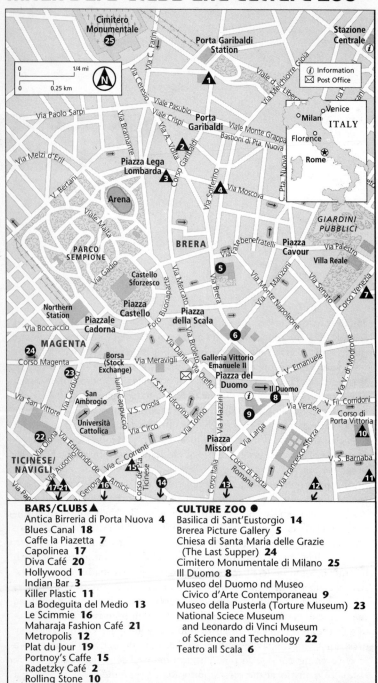

BARS/CLUBS ▲
Antica Birreria di Porta Nuova **4**
Blues Canal **18**
Caffe la Piazetta **7**
Capolinea **17**
Diva Café **20**
Hollywood **1**
Indian Bar **3**
Killer Plastic **11**
La Bodeguita del Medio **13**
Le Scimmie **16**
Maharaja Fashion Café **21**
Metropolis **12**
Plat du Jour **19**
Portnoy's Caffe **15**
Radetzky Café **2**
Rolling Stone **10**

CULTURE ZOO ●
Basilica di Sant'Eustorgio **14**
Brerea Picture Gallery **5**
Chiesa di Santa Maria delle Grazie
  (The Last Supper) **24**
Cimitero Monumentale di Milano **25**
Ill Duomo **8**
Museo del Duomo nd Museo
  Civico d'Arte Contemporaneau **9**
Museo della Pusterla (Torture Museum) **23**
National Sciece Museum
  and Leonardo di Vinci Museum
  of Science and Technology **22**
Teatro all Scala **6**

pizza on Via Dante and then taking a long, slow, gelati-filled *passegiata* along the porticos of Corso Vittorio Emanuele.

The few slackers around mostly set up camp in the Parco Sempione, but outside the park grounds, you won't see many tie-dyed, dreadlocked street kids banging on drums or spinning a Chinese top. Other than in the Piazza del Duomo, where a sparse few trade their talents for lira, Milan isn't kind to spare-changers—the layout of the city doesn't really permit it. Unlike Rome, the city of a thousand squares, Milan is a town of grumbling boulevards-less about stopping and sitting and more about getting from here to there. But once you land wherever *there* might be, the city and its inhabitants warm up after a couple glasses of wine, inviting you to join them in their weird mix of metropolitan grit and sophisticated splendor.

The best period to visit Milan is from late April to July, when the skies are usually blue, and the sun hasn't reached its hottest. This is also the time when most outdoor events take place. In August, the city practically shuts down as residents escape to the sea and Lake Como. Whatever time of year you decide to visit, pick up a copy of ***Hello Milano*** at the tourist information office [see *need to know,* below] for indispensable information on what's current and happening culturally around town.

neighborhoods

One of the great things about Milan is its completely distinct neighborhoods, characterized as much by the stores and buildings as by the folks who live and/or hang out there. Milanese youth tend to bypass the bureaucratic and regal **Centro** and snobby **Brera,** heading instead to the artsy **Porta Ticinese** area or the canals of the **Navigli** district to see and be seen. Two Amsterdam-ish canals let Navigli rival Rome's Trastevere for the most happening 'hood in Italy. Late into the summer nights, the scene is like some sort of hipster boardwalk, with the streets on either side of the narrow strips of water teeming with crowded outdoor bars, restaurants, loud live music, and an unending stream of dressed-up kids. Farther down along **Corso di Porta Ticinese** and **Via Gorizia,** the snappier artsy set sits, smokes, and talks at cafes and bars like **Soup du Jour** [see *bar scene,* below]. For a slightly lower-octane experience, the Garibaldi section—especially along **Corso Como** and around **Piazza Moscova**— has a mess of scattered bars and pizzerias. Here, the lay of the land is more upscale and the prices are higher, but the mood is still casual. At about 11pm, the decked-out club kids begin to line up outside **Hollywood,** one of the hippest nightclubs in town [see *club scene,* below].

One element Milan *does* share with other Italian cities is its ability to get you lost. The centuries-old street layout has no clear pattern, and the streets themselves often change names from one block to the next. The city center is a confounding mess of Vias, Viales, and Vicolos, built around the **Piazza del Duomo.** Running from this central point are roughly 30 streets of varying size, the largest being the store-laden **Corso Vittorio Emanuelle** (eastward), **Via Mazzini** (southward), **Via Manzoni**

fɪve thɪngs to talk to a local about

1. **Milan vs. the rest of Italy**—the Milanese think the rest of Italy is a siphon that sucks their commerce and stringent work ethic dry. They're basically right, so play it however you want.

2. **Milan vs. the rest of Italy, part deux**—same thing, except play the other side and commiserate on how the Milanese are treated like second-class citizens. You'll make a lifelong friend.

3. **Milan vs. Rome and Paris**—the Milanese are a haughty bunch and really think their city is the capital of Europe and much more beautiful than Paris or Rome. As far as fashion goes, they're right, but they take it too far.

4. **Inter vs. AC Milan**—Just say one thing about this football rivalry, and you'll be sucked into an hour-long discussion pretty much every time. Choose your words carefully—this is a division on a par with Mets vs. Yankees.

5. **The best shopping street**—Sure, Via Montenapoleone is the summit of splurge, but there's a bunch of other places to spend a buck or a hundred that only the locals know about.

(northward), **Via Torino** (southwestward), and **Via Dante** (northwestward), which runs out to **Parco Sempione.** In this inner quadrangle of squares of streets you'll find most of the cultural sites, including the impressive, glass-covered mall known as the **Galleria,** the **Ambrosiana Library and Picture Gallery,** and the **Museo Civico d'Arte Contemporaneau** [see *culture zoo,* below], plus the tourist office [see *need to know,* below], which is adjacent to the Piazza del Duomo. The other major geographic hub is the **Piazza della Scala,** due north of the Duomo. From this piazza, you can walk north on **Via Verde** to the fashion district around the upscale **Via Brera** and continue on to the happenin' **Garibaldi** area. The Navigli/Porta Ticinese neighborhood is a little farther out, southwest of the Duomo by roughly 1.5 miles.

The city is connected by three efficient **Metro lines** (red: M1, green: M2, yellow: M3) and a confusing hodgepodge of orange **ATC bus** and **tram routes.** Everything you'll want to see in the city center can be walked between, but it's quicker and easier to use the Metro to get to Brera/Garibaldi (M2 to Garibaldi or Moscow), Navigli/Porta Ticinese (M2 to Stazione Genova), and off-central sites like **Chiesa di Santa Maria delle Grazie** (which houses Leonardo's *The Last Supper*) and **Cimitero Monumentale** [see *culture zoo,* below, for both].

hanging out

Milan lacks the active street life of the other big Italian cities—there really aren't any quaint piazzas made for hanging out under the stars. Your best bet at any time of day or night is **Piazza del Duomo,** where all types and ages congregate in the shadow of the great cathedral. Listen to dressed-up minstrels, watch kids chase pigeons, and browse the makeshift stands of cheap jewelry and other knickknacks. If you have a thing for riff-raff, take a seat in front of the huge and strangely appealing **Central Train Station** [see *need to know,* below], where freeloaders do their loitering thing. When the droning traffic gets to be too much for you, make for the tree-lined public gardens, or **Giardini Pubblici** *(in the northeast of the city center between Via Daniele Manin and Corso Porta Venezia).*

bar scene

Several years ago, to help the hip young poor afford the steep drink prices that this cosmopolitan city commands—or maybe just to get them to buy more—the happy-hour phenomenon was introduced. Now almost every Milanese cafe/pub has one. Even better for the impoverished traveler are the happy-hour snacks, or *stuzzichini.* This finger food, commonly consisting of focaccia, pastas, salads, and vegetables, is better than most meals back home and goes far to calm hunger pangs.

The cool tunes on the beat-up stereo system at **Portnoy's Caffè** *(Via de Amicis 1 at Corso di Porta Ticinese; Tel 02/58-11-34-29; 8am-2pm daily; V, MC)* sound even better when you realize how cheap the drinks are here—pints are 4,000L, and fresh-squeezed orange juice is just 3,000L. The breezy atmosphere—plus the occasional poetry readings and art exhibits—make this *the* place to feel Euro-chic. In the morning, you'll often find coffee and beer drinkers sharing a table. A 10-minute walk south of the Duomo.

Beginning at 6:30pm, Milan's twenty- and thirtysomething crowds descend on the congenial **Diva Café** *(Via Vigevano 3; Tel 02/89-40-30-53; M2 to Porta Genova; Happy hour 6-9pm Mon-Sat; No credit cards)* in the Navigli for its delicious happy-hour buffet. There's always-packed outdoor seating, plus an open and airy inside with light-toned walls. If it's too hot, the owners may even turn on the air conditioning, a godsend in July and August. A good early-evening place.

You'll feel at home at **Antica Birreria di Porta Nuova** *(Via Solferino 56; Tel 02/659-77-58; M2 to Moscova or Garibaldi; 6pm-2am; No credit cards),* a classic microbrewery dating from 1877, up in the Garibaldi district. The tables on the first floor are restored sewing-machine stands minus the machines, and the windows are fitted with neat English-language displays on the art of beer barrel knots and tap devices. The tapas-rich happy hour that runs from 6 till 9pm makes the very good Porretti microbrew taste even better. An ambient basement-level restaurant serves a small menu of pastas and seconds.

You can spend hours drinking coffee or beer in the flower-filled **Caffè la Piazzetta** *(Piazza Lima at Via Ozanam; Tel 02/29-52-92-25; M1 to*

Lima; 7:30am-11pm; No credit cards), feeling oh-so-calm amid the frenetic activity of Corso Buenos Aires, to the west of the city center. Covered outdoor seating provides the shade; you do the rest.

If you want to be a part of the cocktail-toting fashion elite, just put on some fresh duds, motor over to **Radetzky Café** *(Corso Garibaldi 105; Tel 02/657-26-45; M2 to Moscova; Noon-3pm/8pm-midnight daily, closed Mon afternoon; No credit cards)* and order up a 10,000L drink. The large, open windows let you chat with your cool, cocktail-holding comrades mingling on the streets of the Garibaldi.

Word is that Indian food and slinky pumps are a great match. You'll have to go to **Maharaja Fashion Café** *(Viale Gorizia 8; Tel 02/89-42-03-19; M2 to Porta Genova; 2pm-midnight, closed Monday; No credit cards)* in the Navigli district to find out for yourself. The food's more pricey than back home, but who comes to eat? Come late, when all the other pretty boys and girls do—as the night goes on, the focus shifts more to the bar and away from the restaurant.

Loud American music streams out from **Indian Bar** *(Corso Garibaldi at Via Moscova; Tel 02/29-00-03-90; 5pm and on; No credit cards),* a dark, two-story bar with indoor/outdoor seating just down the road from the Radetzky Café. The crowd is kind of young and definitely friendly—it's a good place to ask locals about their views on life, soccer, music, and anything else that comes to mind. Just don't fall for a 16-year-old (and if they *look* 16, they're probably 13). Strippers perform on and in the bar on Sunday nights—be sure to bring plenty of cash to cover the 10,000L entrance fee, and for tips for the ladies....

Plat du Jour 1999 *(Viale Gorizia 28; M2 to Porta Genova; 7pm-2:30am Tue-Sun, closed Mon; No credit cards)* serves yummy fruit drinks and gives overstimulated kids something different than what's offered by the more standard bars on the Navigli canals a block over. The Keith Haring-esque wall murals, tropical theme, and the dirty floor combine to create an alluringly edgy atmosphere. The slick bottle-spinning bartenders like to play loud continuous cuts of rap/rock/reggae. Wine 3,000L, beer 7,000L, and long drinks 9,000L.

Castro would be proud of the Mojitos they mix up at **La Bodeguita Del Medio** *(Viale Col di Lana 3; Tel 028/940-05-60; Noon-2am, closed Sun; V, MC, AE),* sister bar to a local hangout in Havana. This bar serves up everything from genuine Cubano cigars to live Cuban music and those Mojitos (10,000L), which will clean your throat as well as your head. The walls are plastered with Cuban baseball relics and autographed photos of Cuban musicians, and there's a small shrine dedicated to Hemingway. The crowd is super hip and when the bands are jamming it can get down right nasty.

LIVE MUSIC SCENE

Most folks don't come to Milan expecting to catch a good gig, but even in a nation as music-poor as Italy (except for opera, of course), the city offers some pretty happening venues. As with many other aspects of

ragazzo meets ragazza

Girl travelers in Milan will have no trouble getting hit on—this is still Italy, after all. Traveling in all-female packs is one solution. While doing so will directly increase the number of catcalls received, it can also provide some protection against come-oning local goons. Guys, on the other hand, may experience problems getting chummy with local chicks. The Milanese are way more conservative than their southern brethren, which means that there is less interaction between strangers, both in the streets and in the bars. A good tactic for guys: Try frequenting the same bar for a couple days and get chummy with the *male* bartender. Tell him that you're trying to meet a local *bella donna* (not the poison kind), and he can and almost always will willingly act as matchmaker. Granted, this approach takes some time and finesse, but save for rare drunken exceptions, it's really the best way.

Milan, the live music scene revolves around the Garibaldi and Navigli areas. Many bars on the major canal streets of Alzaia Naviglio Grande and Alzaia Naviglio Pavese have nightly lineups of local bands. Of these, the smaller **Charlie's** (*Via Argelati 1; Tel 02/89-40-35-60; 7am-3am Mon-Sat, closed Sun; No credit cards*) and the enormous **Naviglio Blues** (*Via Ascanio Sforza 11; Tel 02/58-10-39-29; 1pm-late daily; No credit cards*) are two of the more popular, pumping out blues, rock, and English/American covers to a young, beer-guzzling crowd. The CD shop **Supporti Fonografici** and megastore **Messagerie Musicali** [see *stuff,* below, for both] are good sources of information on what's up around town.

Milan's most established music venue, **Capolinea** (*Via Ludovico Il Moro 119; Tel 02/89-12-20-24; M2 to Porta Genova; Music 10:30-1am, doors open at 8pm daily; No credit cards*), offers nightly jazz/blues/rock from accomplished local and international artists. It's slightly south of the city center, the crowd is subdued and somewhat older, and, though there's no cover, the obligatory drinks are expensive. Still, after so many tired cover bands, the high-quality licks you'll hear are worth it. The adjoining restaurant opens at 8pm for dinner, and the shows start at 10:30pm.

Bands tend to play longer sets at the more lively **Le Scimmie** (*Viale Card. A. Sforza 49; Tel 02/840-22-00; M2 to Porta Genova; Music 10:30pm-4am, doors open 8pm daily; Cover 12,000L; No credit cards*), where a mix of conservative button-ups, blue-collar folk, and punky kids, local and tourist alike, come together. Unfortunately, the sound system stinks, but a couple of stage spots flicker periodically in the large-ish room to create a rock 'n' roll effect. Scimmie (which, by the way, means monkey) is a common stop for bands doing the traditional trek through

milan eats and crashing

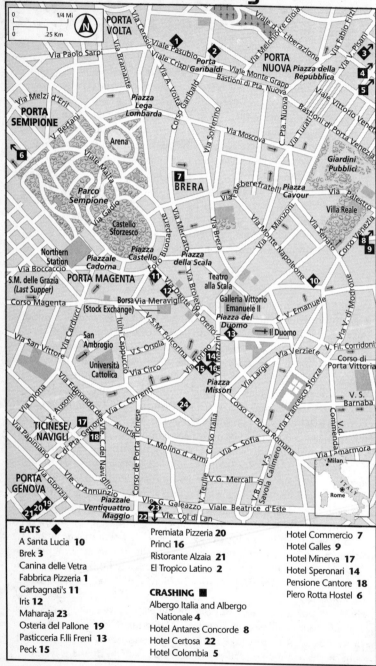

EATS ◆

A Santa Lucia **10**
Brek **3**
Canina delle Vetra
Fabbrica Pizzeria **1**
Garbagnati's **11**
Iris **12**
Maharaja **23**
Osteria del Pallone **19**
Pasticceria F.lli Freni **13**
Peck **15**

Premiata Pizzeria **20**
Princi **16**
Ristorante Alzaia **21**
El Tropico Latino **2**

CRASHING ■

Albergo Italia and Albergo
  Nationale **4**
Hotel Antares Concorde **8**
Hotel Certosa **22**
Hotel Colombia **5**

Hotel Commercio **7**
Hotel Galles **9**
Hotel Minerva **17**
Hotel Speronari **14**
Pensione Cantore **18**
Piero Rotta Hostel **6**

fIVE-O

Because of the high level of commerce and great amount of wealth flaunted on every corner in the center of Milan, the police have a more austere, watchful presence than in other major Italian cities. Some actually walk a beat!

Europe. On some nights a one-drink minimum replaces the cover. With dark wood paneling and music memorabilia—like photos and concert posters on the walls, this is also a good, homey place, south of the city center, to just stop in for a drink.

The spacious "Irish" pub **Blues Canal** *(Via Casale 7; Tel 02/836-07-99; M2 to Porta Genova; 6pm-3am, music starts around 9pm daily; No credit cards),* down in the Navigli, has a bizarre aquamarine interior and a nightly billing of jazz ensembles and cover bands playing English pop/rock. It's kind of a cheesy take on the House of Blues, but the hip, enthusiastic crowd is intoxicating, and you can have a blast trying to figure out the garbled words of your favorite hits from the '80s and '90s. Large wraparound sofas in the back are great for tired legs.

Rolling Stone *(Corso XXII Marzo 32; Tel 02/733-172; Tram 12 or 27; 10:30pm-4am daily, closed July, Aug; Cover 12,000-25,000L depending on the night; No credit cards),* a youth-culture breeding ground since the '60s, has rock 'n' roll oozing out of its pores. Aggressive heavy-metal and hardcore bands take the stage and pepper the crowd with incomprehensible lyrics and mind-numbing riffs. There are about 75 seats and some cramped standing room in the black-walled space, to the east of the city center.

In addition to being a favorite local watering hole, **Indian Bar** [see *bar scene,* above], has a dirty gig pit hosting live bands and ska, funk, hip-hop, and reggae DJ nights, which the young slackerish crowd just eats right up. There are few other outlets in Milan where you can listen to such a variety of music. Call or stop by ahead of time; there's no set schedule.

cLub SCEnE

For a city as classy as Milan, one of the big disappointments is the total lack of good clubs in the city center. This can be explained partly by the dirty habit locals have of keeping the best things for themselves and away from tourists, partly by the magnetic draw of the canals out in Navigli, and partly by the harsh difficulty the clubs have paying their bills and keeping their doors open in this finicky and faddish fashion scene. Fortunately, the ones that have survived do kick some ass. It's in clubs, more than in any other scene, that you'll probably smell hash wafting. A fairly snobbish vibe hangs around most clubs, but for the most part it's just a

rules of the game

There's no legal age limit for purchase or consumption of alcohol here—instead you're completely at the mercy
of the shopkeeper and the barkeep. As long as you're not acting like
a drunken fool, you shouldn't have any problem securing some
hooch. Drinking and carousing in Milan is usually concentrated in
ubiquitous *locali* (bars, cafes, and other going-out places), not on
the streets. While you *can* bring a bottle of wine outside around the
Piazza del Duomo, it's not a common thing—the general anti-inti-
macy of Milan's traffic-heavy streets kinda takes the allure out of it.
Milan does have a local pot-smoking street scene in Parco Sempione
(though marijuana is technically illegal here), where scores of bongo-
playing hippie anarchists hang out.

facade put on by the club owners—the clubbers themselves are cool.
They're also dressed to the teeth, as you should be if you want to get in:
Girls, go with the sexiest thing you can throw together. Guys, stay away
from tees and shorts, and maybe gel your hair up to fit in with the local
boys. The doormen are strict, but not beyond anything you would find
in any other big urban place. Locals don't go out till 11 or midnight and
don't pack it in till sunrise.

You'd have to be comatose to not have fun at **Hollywood** *(Corso
Como 15; Doors open around 10pm Thur-Sun; Cover 20,000-25,000L; No
credit cards),* up in Girabaldi. The small dance floor encourages a lot of
flirty nuzzling among the extremely done-up, bouncy girls and boys. The
music varies from commercial to techno, and to do it right, you should
stay till at least 2 or 3am. If you get drowsy, you can always grab a drink,
plop down on a sofa or chair, and people-watch one of the most elite
crowds in Milan's nighttime scene.

The slightly out-of-the-way location (far southeast of the city center)
of Milan's hippest club, **Killer Plastic** *(Viale Umbria 120; Tel 02/733-
996; M3 to Lodi TBB, then catch Bus 92 at Viale Isozno and take it north on
Viale Umbria, or take the 30-minute walk up Viale Umbria from the Metro
stop; Thur-Sun, gay/lesbian Thur; No credit cards),* isn't keeping away the
style-setting youth. Wear your party best and groove with the other exhi-
bitionist trendoids in the sprawling, tropical-themed outdoor space.
Music-wise, it alternates between eardrum-popping drum 'n' bass samples
and more mainstream discs. No matter what the DJs have in store, you'll
have a great time, especially if you're looking for pickup action. Call
ahead—sometimes the schedule changes unexpectedly.

Metropolis *(Via Broni 10; Tel 02/56-81-55-70; 11pm and on nightly,
gay Tue, Fri, Sat; No credit cards)* is a haven for choreographed multiple-
DJ theme nights of punk, funk, drum 'n' bass, bebop, and pop. The col-

lege-age crowd likes to shake it out hard. Video and space-age doodads should keep you occupied during rest periods. Entrance is reduced for ArciGay members [see *gay scene,* below], but usually costs 15,000L to 25,000L. Also slightly out of the way, south of the city center.

ARTS SCENE

▶▶VISUAL ARTS

Via Brera is quickly becoming the center of Milan's exciting gallery scene. You can cover everything from neo-post-Impressionism to post-neo-Modernism in just a few blocks.

At **Galleria Ponte Rosso** *(Via Brera 2; Tel 02/86-46-10-53; 10am-7pm Tue-Sat),* you'll see a collection of Impressionistic canvases from local artists, as well as sculpture.

Zammarchi *(Via Brera 29; Tel 02/86-46-04-88; 9:30am-8pm Tue-Sat)* is a cozy little space featuring local and national minimalist painting and sculpture.

The bars around Corso Garibaldi are where you should go to discuss all the metaphysical values of the modernistic, anti-directional brush strokes responding to the primal need to violently re-create our ontic placement in the universe, etc. etc. etc.....

▶▶PERFORMING ARTS

Led by the world-renowned Teatro alla Scala [see *culture zoo,* below], the performing arts are alive and well in Milan. Scores of theaters and concert halls present music, dance, opera, and drama. The theaters in Milan

---

FESTIVALS and EVENTS

National and International Dance Festival *(Mid-June to mid-July; For info and reservations, call Comune di Trezzo sull'Adda—Ufficio Cultura 02/90-98-70-52 9am-noon, or visit www.commune.trezzo-sulladda.mi.it).*

Festival del Teatro D'Europa *(June; Held at Teatro Strehler, Largo Greppi, M2 to Lanza; Teatro Grassi, Via Rovello 2, M1 to Cordusio; and Teatro Studio, Via Rivoli 6, M2 to Lanza; For information, call the Tourist Office).*

Festival Cinematografico Gay/Lesbico *(Early June; Held in various theaters throughout town, call the Tourist Office for details. Via Sturzo 51)* held in June, is now in its 13th year.

International Cinema Competition and Festival of Milan *(Early June; Via Milazzo 9; Tel 02/659-77-32; M2 to Garibaldi or Moscova)* is hosted by Anteo Spazio Cinema [see *art scene,* below].

are not cheap, but if you can muster up a few bucks to catch a show, it'll be worth it.

Despite what the modern and, therefore, ugly reinforced concrete frame of **Teatro Smeraldo** *(Piazza XXXV Aprile 10; Tel 02/29-00-67-67; M2 to Garibaldi or Moscova)* might lead you to think, this theater shows one of the most progressive lineups of national and international music and theater troupes. It's best to go to the theater, north of the city center, to pick up a season brochure and to purchase tickets.

Great classical and operatic programs can be heard at **Centro Culturale Rosetum** *(Via Pisanello 1; Tel 02/48-70-72-03; www.rosetum.it).* Established in 1956, this small and quaint venue has plush seating, chandeliers, and a marble-decorated interior that offers a welcome change from the packed bars along the Brera and Navigli sections of Milan.

English-language movies are screened on various nights at: **Anteo Spazio Cinema** *(Via Milazzo 9; Tel 02/659-77-32; M2 to Garibaldi or Moscova)* Mondays, **Arcobaleno** *(Via Tunisia 11; Tel 02/29-40-60-54; M1 to Porta Venezia)* Tuesdays, and **Mexico** *(Via Savona 57; Tel 02/48-95-18-02; M2 to Porta Genova)* Thursdays. All of these are just your basic nondescript movie theaters, and all seat about 300.

gay scene

As one local put it, "Milan is the out-est Italy gets." Don't expect Chelsea or the Castro, but there's plenty to do here. In Via Sammartini (adjacent to the train station), Milan even has a so-called "Gay Street." With Groove Caffè, Libreria Babele, Afterline, and a few other stores, Via Sammartini is the place to be for gays and lesbians. The scene is also kickin' around Nuova Idea International (in the Garibaldi district) and Zip (near Parco Sempione). **ArciGay** *(Via Torricelli 19; Tel 02/58-10-03-99)* is the leading gay organization, and sponsors events, conferences, and social outings. Its gay/lesbian/trans information and help line *(02/89-40-17-49; 9am-11pm Mon, 8am-midnight Tue, Thur, Fri, 8am-11pm Wed)* is in Italian only.

To get funky with the boys of Milan, go to **Nuova Idea International** *(Via de Castillia 30; Tel 02/69-00-78-59, 02/689-27-53; M2 to Garibaldi; 10pm-4am Thur-Sun; 15,000L cover w/one drink, 25,000L Sat; No credit cards).* This well-known dance pad north of the city center is the softcore club for gay men of all ages and types. Its two big rooms hold a lot of sweaty, muscular bodies, and you're bound to bump into one.

Even though it's a *club privato*, the raunchy, cross-dressing crowd at **Zip** *(Corso Sempione 76 at Via Salvioni; Tel 02/331-49-04; 1pm-late Thur-Sun; No credit cards)* will gladly accept you. To enter, blow a kiss to the beefy bouncer, wave your passport (make sure to bring this) and some lira in front of his face, and wiggle your butt on in there, baby. The club's in a seedy 'hood, so be alert.

In one of its ads, the gay nights at **Metropolis** [see *club scene,* above] are described in the following words: "Hi-tec, modern, megavideo, jolly self massages, and sex box." Hmm, wonder which ones caught your eye?

You'll have to go to satisfy your curiosity on gay Tuesdays, Fridays, and Saturdays.

On Thursday nights, queens take over **Killer Plastic** [see *club scene*, above] for *Man2Man* night (girls are also welcome).

Next Groove *(Via Sammartini 23, Tel 02/66-98-04-52; 10am-2am daily, till 9:30pm Tue; No credit cards)*, located on "Gay Street," is advertised as the only gay bar open all day.

The name of the popular leather bar **Cocksucker** *(Via Derna 15; No phone; 10pm-whenever Wed, Fri, Sun; No credit cards)* is pretty self-explanatory.

The slightly grungy **Recycle** *(Via Calabria 5; Tel 02/376-15-31; 9pm-2am or 5am Wed-Sun, gay men allowed Wed, Thur; No credit cards)* is the oldest and perhaps the most well-known lesbian bar among locals, expats, and foreigners. The decor is pretty standard—light-brown wood and marble—and the crowd mixes between butch-grunge pierced trendoids and a variety of more sophisticated ladies. It's a good place both for coffee and for stiffer drinks. You may want to call ahead, as hours sometimes vary.

Girls can also have fun at **Cicip e Ciciap** *(Via Gorani 9; Tel 02/867-202; 8:30pm-late, closed Mon, Tue; No credit cards)*—a bar with restaurant—and **Sottomarino Giallo (Yellow Submarine)** *(Via Donatella 2; Tel 02/29-40-10-47; 10pm-2 or 3am daily, but call ahead, gay males allowed Wed-Fri; No credit cards)*, the only lesbian disco in town.

CULTURE ZOO

The strong modern-art presence in Milan is a welcome relief in this Old Master-centric country—emphasizing once again that, despite a huge stockpile of Medieval and Renaissance treasures, the city and its residents are not living on past glories. The single most important work in Milan is, obviously, Leonardo's *The Last Supper*, but in a different vein, the Museum of Torture [see below] provides a creepy antidote to your average museum excursion.

Il Duomo *(Piazza del Duomo; Tel 02/86-46-34-56; M1, M3 to Duomo; 7:15am-6:45pm daily; Free admission to cathedral floor; Roof open 9am-4:30pm daily, 6,000L stairs, 8,000L elevator; Crypt open 9am-noon/2:30-6pm daily, 2,000L; Baptistery open 10am-noon/3-5pm Tue-Sun, 3,000L):* With its delicately spired facade straight from a fairy tale, Milan's famous Renaissance Duomo is unlike any other in Italy. Look up to the highest pinnacle and see the superb *Madonnina*—covered in 3,900 sheets of gold leaf—watching over the piazza below.

Museo del Duomo and **Museo Civico d'Arte Contemporaneau** *(Palazzo Reale, Piazza del Duomo 12 and 14; Tel 02/860-358; M1, M3 to Duomo; 9:30am-5:30pm, closed Mon; Free admission):* The Museo del Duomo is your typical church museum, chronicling six centuries of the illustrious landmark's history. The permanent collection at the Museo Civico includes some works by Picasso and Modigliani—a welcome break from the typical Italian museum.

Chiesa di Santa Maria delle Grazie (The Last Supper) *(Piazza Santa Maria delle Grazie 2; Tel 02/498-75-88, must call 199-199-*

walking tour

At first it's just a few: Young professionals return from a hard day's work and check in to the pubs for the happy-hour haven of cheap drinks and finger food. Slowly more and more trickle in, until the place is so crowded you can hardly hear yourself think! On this walk, you get an inside look at this oh-so-Milanese post-work phenom.

Jump on the M2 line to **Porta Genova,** and as you exit the station (at 6:30pm precisely), remember that here workers get their first whiff of freedom. Take a whiff of your own and make a right on **Via Gorizia.** On your way to stop number one, **Bar Diva,** you'll pass **Maharaja Fashion Café** [see *bar scene,* above]—keep it in mind for later; it's a hot late-night spot. At **Bar Diva,** get a glass of wine, eat some munchies, and make your way across to **Porta Ticinese.** Yes, this is taking you away from the perfect pub-crawlin' of the **Navigli canals,** but don't worry, we'll get back there in a minute. Along **Corso Porta di Ticinese** you can window-shop at the clothes boutiques. Hang a right at **Via Vetere.** Here, take your choice between **Coquetel, Open Space,** or **Up To You,** all American-style bars. Now, back-track and make a left on P. Ticinese, and window-shop till you get to **Portnoy's Caffè** [see *bar scene,* above], where the drinks are dirt cheap. Take two cocktails. Afterward, if you want to peep around a bit, check out the incongruous Parthenon-like columned piazza, reached by walking under the **Ticinese Arch.** Now, as a finale, find a bar of your very own, and top it off with one quick shot. There, you've made it. Now high-five your friends and take the night from here....

100 in advance for reservations; M1 to Cadorna, Tram 24; 8am-1pm Tue-Sun; 12,000L admission): Making reservations in advance can be a drag, but seeing this late-15th-century da Vinci is worth the trouble. And given the painting's state of near-decay, who knows how much longer you'll have the opportunity?

Brera Picture Gallery *(Via Brera 28; Tel 02/867-518; M2 to Lanza, M1 to Cairoli or M3 to Montenapoleone; 9am-9pm Tue-Fri, till 11:40pm Sat, till 8pm Sun, holidays, closed Mon; 12,000L admission):* If you've got a one-museum limit, this has to be your choice. Relatively small, but jam-packed with masterpieces by the likes of Piero della Francesca, Raphael, Mantegna, Bellini, and Caravaggio. One of Italy's best.

Teatro alla Scala *(Piazza della Scala; Tel 02/72-00-37-44 for ticket info; Tickets 10,000-160,000L; www.lascala.milan.it; No credit cards):* Even if you can't imagine a bigger snorefest than a night at the opera, the overwhelming beauty of the interior of this truly grand ol' opry will blow your mind. The 200 standing-room-only tickets are sold till 30 minutes before curtain. If you're really into it, drop by the on-site La Scala museum, **Museo Teatrale alla Scala** *(9am-noon/2-5:30pm daily, closed Sun Oct-Apr; 6,000L admission)*, too.

12 hours in milan

1. **Get lost in the Duomo:** The most impressive church in Italy—maybe in the world. When you finish gawking at the interior, steal a pair of binoculars and salivate over the hundreds of dazzling spires [see *culture zoo,* above].

2. **Check out the Torture Museum:** Hands-down, the best museum in Milan— a great break from the traditional Renaissance masterpieces [see *culture zoo,* above].

3. **See *The Last Supper*:** We are not worthy, and as long as it lasts, it will remain one of the world's greatest artistic treasures [see *culture zoo,* above].

4. **Barhop on the Navigli Canals:** So many happy-hour deals, so little time. Start early, end late, stumble home [see *bar scene,* above].

5. **Splurge on Something Designer:** In this fashion mecca, with Gucci, Prada, Versace, Armani, Krizia, Dolce & Gabbana, and others at your fingertips, you can't pass this up [see *stuff,* below].

6. **Chill out in Le Scimmie:** See both local and touring acts and, if you're halfway decent, maybe land a gig yourself [see *live music scene,* above].

7. **Go to a soccer game:** There's nothing better than watching the best in the world at their sport in the middle of 60,000 chanting lunatics. A change-your-life experience [see *great outdoors,* above].

8. **Opera at Teatro alla Scala:** You are completely thrust into a time warp. Standing-room-only tickets are available for some shows [see *culture zoo,* above].

9. **Party at Hollywood:** This accessible, only-somewhat-pretentious spot will get you in the groove. Wear the designer something that you bought earlier [see *club scene,* above].

10. **Eat a gelato at Rinomata Gelateria:** Nothing else in Milan compares for price, taste, and variety. You'll probably end up having two or three [see *gelati wars,* below].

At the **Museo della Pusterla (Torture Museum)** *(Via Carducci 14; Tel 02/805-35-05; 10am-7:30pm Mon-Sat; 10,000L admission)*, discover exactly how twisted human beings can be. The torture devices in this bizarrely kitsch museum range from a chastity belt to an elaborate pulley system used to tear victims limb from limb. The English-language descriptions are a laff riot.

National Science Museum and Leonardo da Vinci Museum of Science and Technology *(Via San Vittore 21; Tel 02/48-01-00-40; M2 to Sant'Ambrogio; 9:30am-5pm Tue-Fri, till 6:30pm Sat, Sun, closed Mon; 10,000L admission):* Housed in a former Benedictine monastery, this tribute to all things Leonardo will truly knock your mind on its proverbial butt.

Basilica di Sant'Eustorgio *(Piazza Sant'Eustorgio 1; Tel 02/58-10-15-83; M2 to Porta Genova; 7:30am-noon/3-6:30pm daily; Free admission to basilica, 5,000L admission to chapel):* Near the charming Navigli area, this simple church is notable for its 13th-century bell tower and for having the first tower clock in the world, made in 1305. Good pre-barhopping spot.

Even if you know nothing about Milanese history or the rich and famous Milanese buried here, a stroll through **Cimitero Monumentale di Milano** (Monumental Cemetery) *(Piazzale Cimitero Monumentale; Tel 02/659-99-38; M2 to Garibaldi or Tram 3, 4, 29, 30, 33; 8:30am-4:30pm Tue-Fri, till 5pm Sat, Sun, closed Mon)*, a veritable hall of fame, is a nice rest from the city streets.

modification

If you want to get a big spider on your back or etch the name of your love on your bicep, call the very competent **Tatuggi di Rottino Mauro** *(Via Vigevano 9; Tel 02/58-10-21-95; M2 to Porta Genova; 3-7pm Mon-Fri)* in advance, since appointments are required.

Tattoo Pittan *(Corso di Porta Romana 6; Tel 028/323-072; 10:30am-7:30pm Wed-Sat, 3-7:30pm Mon; V, MC)* is a hip, professional joint to put a hole through your nose or a Celtic War band around your arm. Most days you can walk in and get serviced, but weekends tend to get a little backed up as there are only two artists and one piercer in house.

great outdoors

The best city places for outdoor relaxation on a spot of green are the **Giardini Pubblici** [see *hanging out*, above] and **Parco Sempione.** The sprawling Sempione is not what you would call well-maintained, and has quite a few shady characters—women shouldn't go there alone past evening—but it's a good spot for a daytime jog. The better option is the public gardens, a peaceful manicured refuge with running creeks, flowers, mule rides, and playing children. The crosscutting gravel paths make for a good run or walk.

Milan's two hometown soccer teams—Milan A.C. and Inter F.C.— have a history of fierce rivalry, with each spending billions and billions of liras each year to attract the latest international star. For Milan A.C. tickets, head to **Bank Cariplo** *(Via Verdi 8; Tel 02/886-61)* or the **Milan Point Shop** *(Via Verri 8; Tel 02/796-481)*. For Inter tickets, stop by **Banca Populare di Milano** *(Piazza Meda 4; Tel 02/770-01)*. **Milano Ticket** *(Corso Vittorio Emanuele Pavillion)* shows no favoritism—it sells tickets for both teams. The **Meazza Stadium** *(San Siro; Via Piccolomini 5; Tel 4870-71-23; M1 to Lotto)* is where all the action goes down.

STUFF

Milan definitely lives up to its reputation as a shopping megalopolis. Yeah, most goods are pricey, but there are also places to find bargains. The best window-shopping is on the famed Via Montenapoleone and Via della Spiga—with a crush of designer boutiques like Gucci, Ferragamo, Prada, Armani, Krizia, and Sisley—Porta di Ticinese and Corso Garibaldi running a close second.

do they really look better in their armani

Fashion is to Milan as canals are to Venice, prosciutto is to Parma, and the Coliseum is to Rome: an inseparable component of its identity and the personality of its people. But on a more basic level, fashion plays out in a more complex way. Don't go to Milan looking for fashion models. Unless you're an insider or have the dough to hang at the most expensive restaurants and bars, you almost certainly won't find them. They're pretty much shielded from the rest of the city's society. So what does fashion mean to the average Milanese? In Milan, dress is a public statement, and for the most part, that translates to costly, conservative, efficient lines. The locals wear much more expensive clothing, shoes, jewelry, and accessories than do other Italians. On men, you'll see lots of smartly cut suits and Dolce & Gabbana shirts, while the women, especially in the Brera area, go for expensive suits and lots of gold. In the summer, *la moda* turns to high-cut knicker pants, tank tops, and heels or raised sandals. And just about everyone has a rich, brown tan, à la Donatella Versace. But look a little closer, and another fact becomes clear: Despite spending more, Milanese don't look any better than their more easygoing Roman or Florentine counterparts. Why? Good old-fashioned stress. What some might even call *uptightness*. Of course, covering up that stuff is what keeps the Guccis, Armanis, and Versaces in business....

▶▶MARKET

Line up with locals at **Mercato Communale** *(Next to Piazza XXIV Maggio; 8am-7pm Mon-Sat)* for fresh fruits, vegetables, and fish. For all this, plus books, housewares, and used clothes, check out the **outdoor market along Via Marcello** *(M1 to Lima, walk west toward Stazione Centrale)*.

▶▶BOUND

Messagerie Musicali *(Galleria del Corso 2 near Vittorio Emmanuele; Tel 02/760-551; M1 or M3 to Duomo; 9am-8pm, closed Mon; V, MC, AE)* is Milan's version of a Barnes & Noble or Tower Records superstore (there's actually a Virgin megastore near the Duomo), with a huge selection of English-language books, newspapers, magazines, and music. You can also pick up concert tickets for large events.

For all kinds of English-language reads, check the tight shelves of the **American Bookstore** *(Via Camperio 16; Tel 02/878-920; M1 to Cairoli; 9:30am-7pm Tue-Sat; No credit cards)*.

▶▶TUNES

The collection of new and used CDs and records at **Supporti Fonografici** *(Corso di Porta Ticinese 100; Tel 02/89-40-04-20; 9am-7:30pm Tue-Sat, 3-7:30pm Mon; supporti@sti2.starlink.it; AE, V, MC)* will service less-mainstream music addicts.

▶▶THRIFT

You only wish grandma had a trunkful of clothes as hip as the ones in **Il Baule (The Trunk)** *(Ripa di Porta Ticinese 21; Tel 02/837-39-37; M2 to Porta Genova; 3:30-7:30pm Mon, 11:30am-7:30pm Tue-Thur, till 11:30pm Fri-Sun, closed two weeks in Aug; No credit cards)*. This adorable shop in the Navigli sells lovely affordable vintage women's clothing.

For the best men's and women's used clothing go to **Lo Specchio di Alice** *(Corso di Porta Ticinese 84; Tel 02/58-10-34-81; 3-8pm Mon, 10am-1pm/38pm Tue-Sat, 10am-8pm Sun; V, MC)*, the biggest store of its kind in Milan.

▶▶HOT COUTURE

Cut *(Corso di Porta Ticinese 58; Tel 02/83-94-13-5; 9:30am-7pm Tue-Sat; No credit cards)* has the most funky and original leather clothing and bags you'll see anywhere. Sexy pants, skirts, and cropped tops set the style quotient sky-high. Everything's handmade and originally designed in an amazing array of animal skins.

If that's not your thing, try **Anna Fabiano** *(Corso di Porta Ticinese 40; 10am-7pm, closed Mon; AE, V, MC)*, a boutique with fun and colorful handmade women's clothing, like see-through shirts and funky floral pants.

▶▶MULTI-TASKING

One of the chic-est stores in Milan, multilevel **High-Tech** *(Piazza XXV Aprile 12; Tel 02/624-11-01; M2 to Garibaldi or Moscova; 10:30am-7:30pm Tue-Sun, closed Mon; AE, V, MC)* sells an assortment of housewares and neat products that showcase the multifaceted talents of Milan's artisans and designers. Everything from clocks to shoes, candles to sofas, cards to soaps, and much, much more. Walking around with a High-Tech bag shows you're an insider.

Follow the crowds veering off busy Corso Como, in the Garibaldi district, and into **10 Corso Como's** *(Corso Como 10; Tel 02/29-00-25-74; M2 to Garibaldi; AE, V, MC),* through the verdant palazzo garden with its charming cafe to the main floor where you can browse through the gorgeous designer clothing, shoes, and jewelry, as well as their unique housewares. Upstairs there's also a bookstore that hosts readings (unfortunately not in English) and other events occasionally.

▶▶BEAUTY

Profumo *(Via Brera 6; Tel 02/7202-33-34; 9:30am-7:30pm Tue-Sat; AE, V, MC)* sells Kiehl's products, shaving materials, Listerine, and other bathroom/beauty stuff you may not be able to find elsewhere in Italy's pharmacies, so stock up.

The fantastic, fresh, and all-natural handmade soaps, shampoos, bath and beauty products carried at **Lush** *(Via Fiori Chiari 6; 9am-7pm daily; No credit cards)* are probably similar to what the Body Shop carried before it went corporate. Beat the rush and say you knew Lush when.

EATS

Like its bars, Milan's restaurants are pretty pricey—and there's no happy hour to help out here. Both pizzas and pastas usually run between 10,000L and 20,000L, with meats often higher. Most restaurants serve good salads (around 10,000L) that are usually big enough to be shared. Both the Navigli and Garibaldi sections have a ton of good choices and enough bars with happy hours (read: free appetizers) nearby that you'll be able to get by with only one dish at dinner. Most restaurants have per-person covers *(copertos)* ranging from 1,000L to 6,000L. If this is the case, don't pay a tip; otherwise 7 to 10 percent will do. Another way to save some lira is to make sure you specify water from the tap *(aqua al rubinetto)*; otherwise you'll be paying for bottled.

▶▶CHEAP

Pasticceria F.lli Freni *(Corso Vittorio Emanuele 4; Tel 02/804-871; and Piazza Duomo, corner of Via Torino; Tel 02/877-072; M1, M3 to Duomo; Both 9:30am-7pm daily; Both no credit cards)* has been making marzipan, *ciambelle,* and other Sicilian-style goodies since 1914. The glittery display window and glitzy interior may look cheesy, but trust us—this is the real deal. Both locations are just steps from the Duomo.

Princi *(Via Speronari 6; Tel 02/874-79 and Piazale Istria 1; Tel 02/606-854; Both 8am-8pm; Both no credit cards)* has so cornered the market on fresh, fast-ish food that this bright, upscale chain deserves to be on every street corner. Pizzas by the slice, focaccia, pastas, salad, fruit, vegetables, cakes, pies, tarts—try 'em all. The large central location on Via Speronari has a few stools and opens to a bakery in the back, so you can watch the workers expertly fashion new treats. A slice of mushroom pizza costs 3,500L.

The self-service fresh-food chain **Brek** *(Via Lepetit 20; Tel 02/670-51-49; M2, M3 to Centrale F.S.; 9am-8pm daily; 3,500-12,000L lunch or*

gelati wars

As soon as you walk into **Rinomata Gelateria** *(Ripa Porta Ticinese, corner of Viale Gorizia; Tel 02/58-11-38-77; M2 to Porta Genova; No credit cards)*, you know you've discovered something special: The cabinet-lined walls hold hundreds of cones and the gelati is protected by brass coverlets. Tell them to whip off those coverlets and give you a chocolate with mint or strawberry with Nutella. A few flavors are even made from soy milk for you vegans. Two close seconds to Rinomata are **Cremeria San Marco** *(Via San Marco 14; Tel 02/65-90-08-67; No credit cards)*, where the cones feature the largest scoops in all Milan, and **Venezia Gelateria** *(Corner of Buenos Aires and Piazza Gugliemo Oberdan; Tel 02/29-51-39-44)* which, at 2,500L per cone, may be the most economical place to get Straciatella, Bacio, or Fragola.

dinner; No credit cards), up by the train station, is a favorite of Milan's business crowd. Ignore the suits and enjoy the mouth-watering pastas, meats, fish, and salads that are prepared right in front of your greedy face. A plate of pasta with bread and drink is around L8,000. All this, plus air conditioning.

The centrally located **Iris** *(Via Dante 7; Tel 02/877-498; M1 to Cordusio; 11am-10pm, closed Mon; 10,000-25,000L per entree; AE, V, MC)* has pretty standard fare, but the brick-oven pizza stands out, with its scrumptious crispy crust and slightly sweet sauce. The magnanimous crew of waiters loves to chat it up with the patrons, a good percentage of whom are tourists. Outdoor seating lets you keep an eye on the finely dressed locals, and, if you're lucky, you may be serenaded by a local busker.

Anywhere lots of young people roam, you'll find great options for quick, cheap meals. **Maharaja** *(Via Vetere 12; Tel 02/58-11-34-36; Noon-3pm/6pm-midnight Tue-Sun, closed Mon; 6,000-12,000L per entree; No credit cards)*, down in the Navigli, is one of them. Don't get this confused with the other **Maharaja** [see *bar scene,* above]. Including an order of the soft fresh bread *nan* (2,000L), most takeout dishes will set you back a mere 10,000L—the chicken curry is especially nice. The only takeout *indiano* in Milano.

With outdoor seating on wire chairs, a tidy menu of panini and salads, cheap beer (including Guinness on tap), and an old-world feel, **Osteria del Pallone** *(Viale Gorizia 30; Tel 02/58-10-56-41; M2 to Porta Genova; 11am-2am Tue-Sun, closed Mon morning; 8,000-18,000L per entree; No* *credit cards)* is the perfect place to chow and drink around the Navigli. The "Brillante" sandwich, with *speck* (Italian ham), cheese, and olive pulp, lives up to its name, and the vegetarian "principe," with mushrooms, lettuce, tomatoes, and mustard dashed with olive oil and salt, is tasty too. "Insalata Primavera" is a mongo salad of tuna, fresh mozzarella, tomatoes, and dressing.

Garbagnati's *(Via Dante 14; Tel 02/86-46-06-72; M1 to Cordusio; 7am-7:30pm; 8,000-20,000L per entree; AE, V, MC)* covered outdoor seating area is a great place to sit down, take a break, have a sandwich and a beer or soda, and bask in the glow of being in Europe. When you're done basking, make sure you try the gelati—made on the premises, of course. Just steps away from Iris.

▶▶DO-ABLE

The pizza and pasta are so good at **Fabbrica Pizzeria** *(Viale Pasubio 2; Tel 02/655-27-71; M2 to Garibaldi; 12:30-3pm/7:30pm-1am Tue-Sat, 7:30pm-1am Sun, closed Mon; 11,000-30,000L per entree; V, MC)* that locals sometimes wait an hour to get a table at this spot just off Porta Garibaldi. The prep area and oven are out in the middle of the dining room, so you can really check out the pizza maker's skills. There's another location at Alzaia Naviglio Grande 70 *(Tel 02/835-82-97)*. Sit back, have a carafe or two of wine, and stuff your face.

Don't blink—the huge, sizzling pizzas at the Navigli's **Premiata Pizzeria** *(Via Alzaia Naviglio Grande 2; Tel 02/8940-06-48; 7:30-11:30pm; 10,000-25,000L per pizza; AE, MC, V)* will be ready in 5 minutes, which fits right in with busy Milanese schedules. Starting at 8pm, hordes of casual young people crash through the doors, sometimes making dining hard on the ears. Great place for big groups, especially out on the second-story patio. Two pizzas, one salad, and a half-carafe of wine for less than 50,000L.

Though the centrally located self-service **Peck** *(Via Victor Hugo 4; Tel 02/861-040; M1, M3 to Duomo; 7:30am-9pm; 10,000-20,000L per entree; AE, V, MC)*—a sibling of the famous full-service restaurant down the street—is a bit more expensive than most *tavola calda*-type places, the rich soups, risottos, and fish dishes will satiate the traveler's appetite. With a piece of bread, the *minestrone di riso* is particularly hearty and filling. The red, twirling, butt-molded seats and modern lamps make eating here fun and relaxing. At around 5,000L, panini are the best bet to not break the bank.

Cantina della Vetra *(Via Papa Pio IV 3, in Piazza Vetra; Tel 028/940-38-43; Noon-3pm/7pm-1am, closed Mon; V, MC, AE)* is a sexy little wine bar bistro located just off Via Ceasare Correnti two blocks south of the Duomo. It offers a new menu every day, filled with lush vegetarian pasta dishes and a killer wine list. The candle-lit tables make for a romantic place to begin the evening.

▶▶SPLURGE

Guys put on the jackets, girls slip on the heels, and all head for **Ristorante Alzaia** *(Alzaia Naviglio Grande 26; Tel 02/832-35-26; M2 to*

Porta Genova; 8pm-midnight daily; 40,000L and up per person per meal; AE, V, MC), one of the finest restaurants in the Navigli. The decor is basic white walls with wood paneling on the bottom half and some exposed brick—and the nouveau-Italian menu centers around smaller, fancier, well-thought-out gourmet dishes. The eggplant parmesan, gnocchi, ravioli, and lamb dishes are excellent. The wine list contains scores of local, Tuscan, and foreign varieties.

At first, the framed photos of Hollywood stars and others crammed onto the walls at **A Santa Lucia** *(Via San Pietro all'Orto 3; Tel 02/76-02-31-55; M1 to San Babila; Lunch noon-3pm, dinner 7:30pm-midnight daily; 45,000L and up per person for a meal; AE, V, MC)* seem tacky. But hang on. The kitchen here is bad-ass—anyone who knows anything about food does not leave Milan without a stop here. The fish and meats are worth every last lira, and even the simple *spaghetti al pomodoro* will leave you obsessively sopping up the sauce. If you want to fill up for less cash, the calzones are a good deal. The service, of course, is expert. A meal like this makes staying in hostels, taking night trains, and eating bread, cheese, and jam every stinkin' day—except today—worth it. No shorts, no sneakers, no kids, and reservations are a must. Just a few blocks east of the Piazza del Duomo.

Tired of Italian? Take a break in the cool, dark, candlelit underground cantina of **El Tropico Latino** *(Corso Como 2; Tel 02/659-04-44; M2 to Garibaldi; 8pm-midnight; 15,000-35,000L; AE, V, MC)*, a very un-chain-like chain. While the menu ain't traditional Tex-Mex, the entrees are well-seasoned and well-portioned, and taste even better after a couple of margaritas. Young, casual locals hang in this Garibaldi spot, both chowing in the restaurant and downing tropical drinks in the downstairs bar.

crashing

Milan will never be known for its hotels, at least not the kind your average traveler can afford. While there are tons of medium-priced and business-class choices, budget varieties are scarce and usually pretty drab. When you call a hotel, make sure to ask for the current rates—they can fluctuate greatly, especially during the high season and/or whenever there is a large convention. Because Milan is so freakin' big and spread out, it's more important here than in other cities to get a hotel close to where you're going to be hanging. Because as quick and efficient as they are—with electronic signs telling you how long you'll have to wait for the next train—subways are subways are subways, no matter what.

▶▶CHEAP

The long hike from the center out to the well-managed **Milan City Camping** *(M2 to Gambara, then walk to Via Triluzio and take Bus 72 to Quinto Romano, which leaves you 500 meters from campground; Check-in 8am-10pm; 12,000L/person per day plus 10,000L tent fee; V, MC)* is worth it if you're budgeting—it's the cheapest option in Milan, especially if you're staying more than a few days. Sites have electricity hookups and hot showers.

giovanni, phone home

Italians are tireless consumers, always on the go, and lovers of convenience, so it's no big shocker that over 30 percent of the population owns *celluari*: cell phones. Mobile phones go off in classes, in the middle of church services, during funerals, during concerts, at the movies, on scooters, and on and on. Italians, in comparison with other cultures, do not shirk from having conversations, no matter where they are or how intrusive it may be to others. Of course, this increasing phenomenon has not gone without the classic Italian debate. Part of the population detests the little plastic nuisances and wants to pass etiquette rules dictating their use. Until this happens—and most likely it never will—Italians will continue to listen to their mamas chew them out on one end of the line while their neighbors shush them till they disconnect.

With an 11:30pm curfew and location away from the bustle of the city to the northwest of the city center, **Piero Rotta Hostel (HI)** *(Via Martino Bassi 2; Tel/Fax 02/39-26-70-95; M1 to Q.T.8, then walk down Via Pogatschnig to Martino Bassi; Lockout 9am-5pm; 23,000L/bed; No credit cards)* probably isn't the place you want to stay the whole time you're in Milan, but it's a good place to hole up for a couple of nights if you need to budget, or if everywhere else is full—with 388 beds, the hostel almost always has a vacancy. An HI card is required, but you can buy one there for 30,000L, giving you access to other HI hostels as well.

Fancy ain't the word you'd use to describe **Pensione Cantore** *(Corso Porta Genova 25; Tel 02/835-75-65; M2 to Porta Genova; Desk open 8:30am-2am; 40,000L single, 65,000L double, breakfast 5,000L; No credit cards),* but it's so close to the Metro and the bar-laden Navigli/Porta Ticinese neighborhood, who cares! Plus, fairly spacious doubles start around 65,000L. The bathrooms could use more spic-and-spanning, and if you want to party all night long, this may not be the best option—the Cantore closes at 2am every night. There are only 11 rooms, so in the high season it sometimes fills up quickly. Usually closed in August.

Close to the Brera-Garibaldi section of town, **Hotel Commercio** *(Via Mercato 1; Tel 02/86-46-38-80; M2 to Moscova; 90,000L double w/shower; No credit cards)* has got more grit than shine but, like the Cantore [see above], its location makes up for its shortcomings. Plus, the 12 rooms all come with a private bathroom—a rarity in this price range. Definitely book ahead.

Hotel Certosa *(Corso San Gottardo 7; Tel 02/89-40-21-05; M2 to Porta Genova; 65,000-85,000L doubles w/o bath; No credit cards)* is close to both Porta Ticinese and the Navigli, and there's no curfew. If that doesn't win you over immediately, here are a few more positives: Though the 26 rooms are nothing to gush about, the beds are made every day, and the friendly staff won't get too mad if you decide to—or end up having to—sleep in. Watch for price swings.

The bright rooms in the **Albergo Italia and Albergo Nazionale** *(Via Vitruvio 44/46; Tel 02/670-59-11; M2, M3 to Centrale F.S.; 55,000L single, 85,000L double; No credit cards)*, complete with sink, mirror, and green shutters, have surprisingly more character than the hotel's hole-in-the-wall exterior would betray. Between the two side-by-side establishments, owned by the same congenial proprietor, there are 42 rooms. Its proximity to the train station makes it a good late-night arrival option, but there is a catch: The curfew's at 1am and the desk doesn't reopen till 6:30am.

▶▶DO-ABLE

For the price and *centralissimo* location, the clean rooms at **Hotel Speronari** *(Via Speronari 4; Tel 02/86-46-11-25, Fax 02/72-00-31-78; M1, M3 to Duomo; 70,000L single w/o bath, 100,000L double w/o bath; V, MC)* are among the best bargains in Milan. Rooms that look into the courtyard are drab and muggy, but the ones overlooking the busy street below are airy and bright—choose your lesser of two evils. Staff is friendly and used to backpacker and student guests. Some shared bathrooms are not great, but the fully stocked bar next to the lobby desk is. Ask for rooms on the third and higher floors—the views from up there are lovely.

The charmless-yet-clean rooms at **Hotel Minerva** *(Corso C. Colombo 15; Tel 02/837-57-45, Fax 02/835-82-29; M2 to Porta Genova; 115,000L single, 125,000L double; V, MC)* are slightly overpriced, but all have TV and private bathrooms. About half of its 38 rooms look out onto a quiet, treeless courtyard; the others look onto side streets. Some doubles have two single beds that can be pushed together if you're traveling with a sweetie. Close to the Navigli and curfew-less, this is a good option if the cheaper pensions are booked.

The management at **Hotel Colombia** *(Via R. Lepetit 15; Tel 02/669-21-60, Fax 02/670-58-29; M2, M3 to Centrale F.S.; Closed in Aug; 100,000L single, 140,000L double; AE, V, MC)* is a bit solemn, as are the rooms, but all in all, it's not a bad choice. A private bath comes with every room, and the ground-floor sitting room, bar, and backyard garden area are nice homey touches. Northeast of the city center toward the train station.

▶▶SPLURGE

Hotel Antares Concorde *(Viale Monza 132; Tel 02/403-02, Fax 02/48-19-31-14; M1 to Turro; 320,000L single, 450,000L double; antares.hotel.rubens@traveleurope.it; AE, V, MC)* is part of a trio of Best Western "Antares" hotels catering to the omnipresent Milanese business crowd. The spacious, air-conditioned rooms have soundproof windows—so that businessmen can get their sleep, you know—and the bathrooms have full bathtubs. A basic continental breakfast of cereal, croissants, and coffee is included. The modern design of the gray-tone hotel falls within the Italian post-World War II guidelines—that is, must be butt-ugly—but if you want to relax and catch some CNN, this is a pretty good choice. Out to the east of the city center.

Our old friend Best Western does it right again with **Hotel Galles** *(Piazza Lima; Tel 02/204-841, Fax 02/204-84-22; M1 to Lima; 230,000L single, up to 400,000L double; galles-mi@mbox.it.net; AE, V, MC),* a renovated turn-of-the-century palazzo-esque offering. The large, air-conditioned rooms are charming but not overly charming, decorated with quasi-Victorian touches. The glistening bathrooms invite you to take long baths, the downstairs bar pours pricey-but-fun late-evening cocktails, and the rooftop garden features a solarium and Jacuzzi. The sunny terrace restaurant serves up a great American-style all-you-can-eat breakfast for 25,000L that will hold you till late afternoon; a less elaborate continental breakfast is gratis. The helpful staff speaks English better than most Americans and knows how to make you feel welcome and forget the steep prices. Keep an eye out for off-season rates which go down to 85,000L for a single. If you want to indulge, do it right—do it here. In the same area as its brother [see above].

need to know

Currency Exchange The currency of Italy is the **Italian Lira (L).** Exchange currency and traveler's checks at **Stazione Centrale** or either airport for a 1-2 percent fee. ATMs or exchange machines (charging a 1 percent fee) are all over the city.

Tourist Information The great **Azienda di Promozione Turistica del Milanese** *(Piazza del Duomo at Via Marconi 1; Tel 02/725-241; 8:30am-8pm Mon-Fri, 9am-1pm/2-5pm Sat, 9am-1pm/3-5pm Sun)* or *(Stazione Centrale; Tel 02/669-05-32; 8am-7pm Mon-Sat, 9am-12:30pm/1:30-6pm Sun)* provides priceless info as well as a place to pick up the monthly English-language *APT Events Guide* and the English/Japanese newspaper *Hello Milano*. **CTS** *(Corso Ticinese 100; Tel 02/58-47-52-23; sale Reps speak English)* is the student information center.

Public Transportation Buses run every 10-20 minutes 5am-1am; the **Metro** runs 6am-midnight. A bus/metro ticket costs 1,500L, or get a one-day (5,000L) or two-day (9,000L) travel pass at the tourist office. The **ATM Information Offices at Stazione Centrale** *(Tel 02/800-001-68-57; 8am-8pm Mon-Sat)* or the **Metro station Duomo** *(Tel 02/480-311; 7:45am-7:15pm Mon-Sat)* both provide free bus/metro maps. Free information: *167/016-857.*

American Express *(Via Brera 3; Tel 02/72-00-36-93, 02/86-46-09-30; 9am-5pm Mon-Fri).*

Health and Emergency Police: *115;* Fire, medical emergency, ambulance: *118* or *113.* The hospital **Ospedale Maggiore Policlinico** *(Via Francesco Sforza 35; Tel 02/550-31)* has English-speaking doctors.

Pharmacies There is a 24-hour pharmacy at **Stazione Centrale** *(Tel 02/669-07-35).*

wired

The websites *www.rcs.it/inmilano/english/ benven.html* and *www.traveleurope.it/milano.htm* have good general info on the city and its venues.

The site *www.CityLightsNews.com/ztmimp2.htm* has great maps.

The Milanese are ahead of the rest of Italy in terms of Internet usage, but that's not saying much. There are only a handful of public places to check your Internet account. The best option is **Terzo Millenio** *(Off Via Veneto; Tel 02/205-21-21; 8:30am-7:30pm Mon-Sat; 10,000L/hour, 5,000L/half-hour; Call ahead for times, as info changes regularly)*, which has about a dozen computers and is best set up for Internet access. The friendly employees will help you with any glitches that might arise. Two other options are the centrally located **Gallery Games** *(Via S. Sisto 5; Tel 02/72-00-46-02; 10am-7:30pm/9pm-midnight daily; 18,000L/hour, 11,000L/half-hour; No credit cards)* and the bohemian **Netkiosk** *(Via Solari 56; Tel 02/230-003; www.netkiosk.it)*, in the southwest end of the city, managed by the owners of **Sherwood Café** *(Via Solari 52; Tel 02/472-470; 7am-1pm/3-6pm)*. Of these two, the computers at Gallery Games—which is really an arcade—offer better performance than the computers at Netkiosk. But if you're all for helping the little guy....

Telephone Country code: *39;* city code: *02;* information: *12;* English-speaking operator: *170.* Local calls cost 200L. **Phone cards** are available in denominations of 5,000L, 10,000L, and 15,000L (a 10,000L phone card should give you about 4 minutes of talk time to the U.S.), and are sold at cafes and *tabacchi*. Deposit a refundable 200L to use your credit card. **AT&T:** *06/172-10-11;* **MCI:** *06/172-10-22;* **Sprint:** *06/172-18-77*. You can also make credit card calls at the Telecom offices in **Galleria Vittorio Emanuele** *(between Piazza del Duomo and Piazza della Scala; Open 24 hours daily)* or **Stazione Centrale** *(8am-9:30pm daily)*.

Airports General flight and airport information: *02/74-85-22-00; 7am-11pm.* **Aeroporto di Linate** is about 4 miles southeast of the city. ATM buses leave Piazza San Babila *(Corner of Corso Europa; Tickets 1,500L)* for Linate every 10 minutes 5:30am-12:20am. STAM buses *(02/66-98-45-09, 02/40-09-92-80; Tickets 4,500L)* run between Piazza Luigi di Savoia *(Right side of Stazione Centrale)* and Linate every 30 minutes 5:40am-9:05pm. **Aeroporto della Malpensa** is 31 miles northwest. Air Pullman buses *(02/40-09-92-60)* leave Piazza Luigi di Savoia *(on the right side of Stazione Centrale)* every 20 minutes 5:20am-

10pm for 13,000L one-way; STAM buses depart every half-hour for Stazione Centrale 6:30am-11pm. Tickets for both are 13,000L.

Trains Stazione Centrale *(Piazza Duca d'Aosta; Tel 1478/880-88, is toll-free in Italy only for bilingual information about all trains and stations; Information office 7am-11pm daily; M2, M3 to Centrale F.S.; No credit cards),* to the northeast of the city center, is the main station. You can catch the M3 and M2 lines from Centrale. Luggage storage open daily 4am-1:30am *(5,000L/12 hrs).* The other two are **Stazione Garibaldi** *(Information office 6am-10pm),* to the north of the center, and **Stazione Nord** *(Piazza Cadorna 14; Tel 02/48-06-67-71; Information office 6:30am-8:30pm daily),* to the west of the city center.

Laundry Vicolo Lavanderia *(Via degli Zuccaro 2; 8am-10pm; 9am-7pm daily; 6,000L wash, 6,000L dry)* will help you look your spiffiest.

Internet See *wired,* above.

everywhere else

pavia

For a break from urban traffic jams—and a chance to check out some amazing old-world architecture, plus a casual collegiate party scene—take a day trip from Milan to the lively little town of Pavia, about 20 miles to the south. Leonardo da Vinci visited the town way back in 1515, and he left behind some monuments that put the city on the map. There's no high fashion or frenetic football scene here, and the nightlife is pretty much impromptu, but it's a surprisingly fun place to spend a day—or a night if you luck into a cool party.

The **Università degli studi di Pavia,** founded in 1361, serves as a link to Pavia's history but also keeps it from stagnating—the students it brings in year-round, from all over Italy and the world, help Pavia stay young. Romanesque towers rise above the university's neoclassical **Piazza Leonardo da Vinci,** in the heart of town, where many of its 28,000 students attend classes. Distinguished alumni and past faculty include Christopher Columbus and Alessandro Volta (apparently they couldn't get da Vinci to give a senior seminar).

The best places to hang out and soak up the local culture are the piazzas of the old town: **Piazza della Vittoria,** the main piazza in the center of town just southwest of Piazza Leonardo da Vinci, and **Piazza del Duomo,** just a few steps to the south of that. A few blocks farther south is the **Ponte Coperto,** which bridges the old town with the area surrounding **Piazzale Ghingaglia** [see *culture zoo,* below], where you can dine *al fresca* and gaze across the Ticino at the sandstone architecture of the *centro storico.* Corso Strada Nuova is the main north-south avenue that connects all of these piazzas and ends up at Ponte Coperto.

bar, club, and live music scene

You'll find the kids from the university hanging out and drinking in the piazzas till late (weather-permitting, of course). If you make friends, they'll probably show you where that night's local parties are. Anyone really cool, of course, will probably be heading for Milan's hipper-than-thou scene (well, at least it's hipper-than-Pavia).

Any time during the summer, bars like the central **Il Broletto** *(Piazza della Vittoria 14; Tel 0382/67-541; 9am-3pm/8pm-2am daily; No credit cards)* are swarming with Pavia's baddest and brightest. You'll find a lot of the same crowd just down the street, to the west of the Piazza, at a little dive called **Lo Stagno** *(Corso Cavour 66; 9am-10pm Thu-Tue; No credit cards)*. "The Pond," as the name translates, serves, among other things, the greasiest local specialty, *gambe di rane* (frog's legs). In addition to giving you nightmares of hundreds of frogs on tiny little crutches, they're likely to increase your need for liquid refreshment by at least a few notches.

CULTURE ZOO

Culture in Pavia is all about architecture. In addition to the buildings designed by Leonardo the Great, there are structures dating back to the 9th century. To see the mothership of the da Vinci sites in this area, you'll have to take the train about six miles west to the nearby Certosa de Pavia monastery.

Certosa di Pavia *(On the road between Pavia and Milan; 9am-11:30am/2:30-5pm Tues-Sun; Take the train 6 mi. west of Pavia on the Pavia-Milan line):* One of the most lavish buildings of the Renaissance, this 15th-century da Vinci-designed monastery is an absolute must-see. The canals that he placed here were so far ahead of their time that to this day they're studied by architects and historians alike. Among the eclectic art displayed in the vestries of the monastery are numerous *tromp l'oeil* murals and an amazing statue made entirely from hippopotamus teeth (obviously those wild-and-crazy monks could've taught Damien Hirst a thing or two). You can also pick up a bottle of liquor distilled on the premises by the monks who still live here.

Basilica Di San Michele *(Via San Michele; 8am-noon/3-8pm daily):* This Romanesque basilica, the most striking structure in the city, was built in 1090 on the site of a 7th-century church. Long a favorite spot for coronations, this is where Charlemagne was crowned in 774, and where Frederick Barbarossa was crowned Holy Roman Emperor in 1155. The intricate carvings on the sandstone exterior have faded over the years, but if you squint, you can imagine how they looked in their prime.

Cattedrale Monumentale di Santo Stefano Martiro *(Piazza del Duomo):* Pavia's other major architectural gem is a work-in-progress. Da Vinci was among the architects who began work on the building in the 15th century. But the cupola—the third largest in Italy—wasn't completed until 1885, the impressive interior wasn't finished until Mussolini was in power, and the brick exterior is still waiting for the marble facade that was part of the original design. Hey, this is Italy—nobody really expects an ornate cathedral to be finished on schedule in a country that can't get its trains to run on time. The Torre Civica, the tower once adjoining the duomo, collapsed in 1989, killing four people and destroying much of the left chapel. Not a trace of it is left.

Castello Viconteo *(Strada Nuova; Tel 0382/338-53 castle, Tel 0382/30-48-16 museum; 9am-1:30pm Tues-Sat, 9am-1pm Sun; 5,000L admission, 2,500L under 18; No credit cards):* Set in a gorgeous landscaped park that once extended to Certosa di Pavia, this castle has beautiful stained-glass windows and terracotta decorations on three sides of its vast court-yard. The fourth wall was destroyed in 1527 during the Franco-Spanish Wars. The building now houses Pavia's Museo Civico, which exhibits an extensive sculpture collection and paintings by Bellini and Correggio. A walk around the park is just as breathtaking as the castle itself.

eats

Set in the town's central square, **Ristorante-Pizzeria Marechiaro** *(Piazza della Vittoria 9; Tel 0382/237-39; 6,000-18,000L pizzas; V, MC, AE, DC)* serves the standard assortment of pasta and pizzas at reasonable prices, especially considering its prime location. For a hearty meal in a more idyllic setting, walk across the Ponte Coperto and enjoy local cuisine from one of the places along the picturesque Via Milazzo. Try **Osteria della Malora** *(Via Milazzo 65; Tel 0382/343-02; 10,000-20,000L first courses; V, MC).*

crashing

There's a distinct shortage of good places to stay here, so you should probably make it a daytrip from Milan. Get in, see the da Vinci sights, and get out. But if you get stuck—or have such a good time at one of the local parties that you just don't feel like staggering back to Milan—there are a couple of passable places to crash.

The most convenient, **Hotel Stazione** *(Via Bernardino de Rossi 8; Tel 0382/35477; 60,000L singles, 90,000L doubles; No credit cards),* is right off the train station. It isn't most people's idea of either comfort or charm, but if the sound of passing trains has a soporific effect on you, you just might have the best night's sleep ever.

Located between the train station and the *centro storico,* **Hotel Aurora** *(Viale V. Emmanuele 25; Tel 0382/236-64, Fax 0382/212-48; 80,000L singles, 125,000L doubles; V, MC)* is clean and convenient, with modern art hanging from pristine white walls. All rooms come equipped with phone, TV, and AC.

need to know

Currency Exchange Try **Banca Commerciale Italiana** *(Corso Cavour 12)* or **Banco Ambrosiano Veneto** *(Corso Cavour 7),* both of which have ATMs. You can also exchange money on the second floor of the **post office.**

Tourist Information The **tourist office** *(Via Filzi 2; Tel 0382/27-23-81; 8:30am-12:30pm/2-6pm Mon-Sat)* is just north of the bus and train stations, off Piazza Dante.

Public Transportation The town is small enough that you can walk everywhere. The only time you might need a ride is from the train station to the center of town. Bus 3 or 6 will save you a 10-minute walk.

Health and Emergency Emergency: *113*. Ambulance: *118, 0382/52-76-00* nights and holidays. The local hospital is **Ospedale San Matteo** *(Piazza Golgi 2; Tel 0382/50-11)*.

Pharmacies Vippani *(Via Bossolaro 31; Tel 0382/223-15; 8:30am-12:30pm/3:30-7:30pm Mon-Fri)*, at the corner of Piazza del Duomo, posts a list of pharmacies offering night service.

Trains The **train station** *(Viale Vittorio Emmanuele, Tel 1478/880-88)* is at the western end of town. Train service is available to Milan every hour, 6:08am-11:40pm. Trains also arrive from Genoa every hour, 6:33am-10:45pm.

Bus Lines Out of the City Bus service to Milan and Certosa di Pavia is provided by **SGEA** *(Tel 0382/37-54-05)*. To get to the bus station, turn left as you exit the train station.

Postal The **post office** *(Piazza della Posta 2, Tel 0382/297-65; 8:05am-5:30pm Mon-Fri, 8:05am-noon Sat)* is off Via Mentana, a block from Corso Mazzini.

COMO

Some 30 miles north of Milan, crystal-clear Lago di Como was an idyllic weekend getaway for Italy's elite as long ago as the 12th century. Their elegant villas are still scattered throughout the surrounding countryside, used now as vacation homes for wealthy Milanese business people. But Como's romantic allure has definitely decreased as the water has gotten more and more polluted. It looks clear enough, but it's actually not fit for nighttime skinny-dipping or even afternoon wading. It does still attract a small contingent of windsurfers, though, and they jam the bars on a nightly basis, along with the too-hip-for-words students from the small local design school. There's also a handful of wealthy Milanese *fashionistas,* local entrepreneurs, and tourists taking advantage of easy rail access from Milan. Put all this together and what you end up with is a small but diverse social scene, noted for its live music and jamming DJs. For more laid-back times on Lago di Como, try **Lecco** or **Domaso** [see below for both].

Como sits at the foot of the Alps, a stone's throw from the Swiss border. The surrounding mountains create a cool temperature year round, while snow-capped peaks remain visible to the north. Unlike the more touristy lake towns, Como isn't littered with insta-condos, inflatable rubber-ducky stands, or double-decker tour boats. This mini-Milan is known as the center of the silk industry and offers some of that high culture Italy's known for, including an eponymous cathedral and worthwhile art museum. But the real attraction of Como lies in the cafes, bars, and boutiques in the city center, on and off the main drag, **Piazza Cavour.**

Trains arrive from Milan at **Stazione San Giovanni,** on the southern end of town. To reach the city center, follow the stairs down from the

como

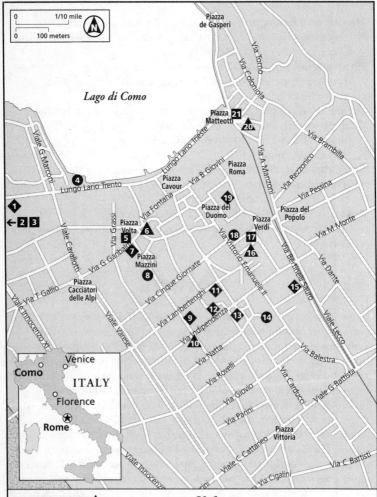

BARS/CLUBS▲
Bac **16**
Greenwich Pub **10**
The Hemingway Pub **6**
O'Sullivan's Irish Pub **20**

CULTURE ZOO ●
Basilica di San Fidele **14**
Duomo di Como **18**
Pinacoteca Palazzo Volpi **8**
Tempio Volitiano **4**

EATS ◆
A Brasileira **19**
Café Dea **15**

GS **1**
Guerci **11**
Osteria del Gallo **12**
Pizzaria Messicano **13**
Taverna Spagnola **7**
Trattoria Scaldasole **9**

CRASHING ■
The International Camp Grounds **2**
Ostello Villa Olmo **3**
Albergo Sociale **17**
In Riva al Lago **21**
Albergo Posta **5**

main doors of the station to **Piazzale S. Rocchetto** and continue north on **Via Gallio,** through **Piazza Cacciatori delle Alpi,** straight down **Via Garibaldi,** and through **Piazza A. Volta.** From there, Via Fontana will lead you into Piazza Cavour. From Piazza Cavour, the cobblestoned, carless **Via Vittorio Emanuele II** takes you past the towering Duomo, a kind of Mini-Me of the cathedral in Milan.

bar, club and live music scene

Como isn't as cosmopolitan as it wants to be—as far as nightlife goes, it's no Milan. But along the traffic-free roads in Como's center you'll find some laid-back, loungey watering holes and enough interesting conversation to make for a memorable evening.

During the years after WWII, Ernest Hemingway supposedly frequented **The Hemingway Pub** *(Via Filipo Juavara; Tel 031/261-088; Noon-4pm/7pm-2am Tue-Sun; No cover; V, MC, AE),* just past the arches off Piazza A. Volta. If he didn't, he might wish he had—today, shrines throughout the bar are dedicated to earnest Ernest and his many, many accomplishments as spokesmodel for his Lost Generation. But it's the deep red velvet curtains, stained glass windows, and bottomless couches that make it an inspiring place to guzzle down a pint of beer (8,000L). Live music, mostly acoustic duets of old and new Italian folk songs, entertains the older, after-dinner crowd (the latest lost generation?) every night of the week.

Outside the Hemingway, follow the red carpet east down Via Luini, hang a right on Via Independenza, and you'll come to the **Greenwich Pub** *(Piazzolo Giuseppe Terragni 7/8; Tel 031/267-872; Noon-4pm/8pm-3am Tue-Sun; No cover; V, MC),* the hippest hangout for today's wasted youth. Inside the three separate rooms of this giant bar, young'uns slug back whiskey and cokes (10,000L) and chain-smoke their lives away. They also munch on sandwiches, play chess, and watch Milan's soccer teams go at it on the big-screen TV. The beer selection is very bitter

wired

The city's website is *www.lakecomo.com.*
Several places in town offer Internet access. To get the most bang for your buck, pull up a computer in the back room at **Click Zone** *(Via Alessandro Volta 29; 9am-1pm/5-10pm Mon-Sat; 3,000L for 30 min., 5,000L per hour; No credit cards),* a local computer store. Don't mind the pit bull running around, he's really friendly. Slower and more expensive is **Lauritel** *(Via Vittorio Emanuele II 93; 9am-6pm Tue-Sat, 2-6:30pm Mon; 10,000L per hour; No credit cards).*

(8,000L pints), and shots are three finger pours in a well glass (12,000L). The manager, Jonnie, cranks out semi-alternative fare like Red Hot Chili Peppers and Air from the stereo day and night, but he'll gladly shut down the music for any acoustic musicians willing to play a set of Eagles covers (at which point you might want to make your exit).

More of today's youth, both wasted and unwasted, come from near and far to double-fist some of the finest Guinness and Boddingtons pints around at **O'Sullivan's Irish Pub** *(NE corner of Piazza Amendola; Tel 031/304-465; Noon-4pm/7:30pm Fri-Wed; No cover; No credit cards)*, right across the street from Stazione Como Nord. Since thick pints of Guinness (8,000L) and late night bar food go hand in hand, they also serve up little pizza-bread things (10,000L) that provide a nice base for towering shots of Jagermeister on the rocks (12,000L). The place is packed any night of the week, and even though the bar's spread out over four rooms, it still gets really stuffy and smoky as the night wears on—just like the pubs in Ireland! Prime real estate is on the couches left of the entrance, where you can strike up a good word with the friendly waitresses, and also get a breath of fresh air now and again.

All-in-black vino aficionados sit in candlelight communing with the crushed grapes at **Bac** *(Via V. Emanuele 27/A; Tel 013/270-996; 6pm-1am, closed Mon; No cover; V, MC, AE)*, a chill little wine bar at the northeast corner of the Duomo. This grapevine cult will inspire you to moisten your own palate with a glass of wine (5,000L), which also buys you a couple of hours far from the frenzied crowds shopping along Via Vittorio Emanuele II. The stone walls are stacked 10 rows high with an amazing collection of local and French wines; ask one of the fresh-faced, in-the-know waiters for his personal recommendations.

CULTURE ZOO

Como offers more high culture than you'd expect from a town its size. But hey, this is Italy—you can't swing a dead cat without hitting an architectural mini-masterpiece. Pretty much all the sights worth seeing are in the city center.

Cattedrale di Como *(Piazza del Duomo; 7am-noon/3-6pm daily; Free)*: Walking through Piazza del Duomo for the first time may make you do a Duomo double-take. You might think you're back in Milan, but as your retinas focus in, you'll realize it's just a mini-Milan Duomo. Como's cathedral was constructed over the 14th-17th centuries with the Lombard Gothic style in mind. Things got a little Romanesque along the way, with decorations by the Rogari brothers clinging to the facade, including statues of all Rome's beautiful people (gee, there had to be more than two...). The interior is less impressive, with hanging tapestries and massive pillars, and frescoes by Luini and Morazzone.

Attached at the Duomo's hip is its little black and white striped brother, the Broletto. Begun in 1215, this town hall was pushed back in 1415 so that big brother could get more space. Its tri-colored marble scheme is worth a peek.

only here

Como has been making silk since Marco Polo returned with silkworms from the Orient. Today, it's still the silk capital of the world, with bigwig designers like Armani, Versace, and Bill Blass still meeting here to plot domination of the fashion industry with Como's silk honchos. The city is also home to a silk museum, **Museo Didactico delle Sete** *(Via Vallegio 3; Tel 031/303-180; 9am-noon/3-6pm Tue-Fri; 15,000L; No credit cards)*.

Basilica di San Fedele *(Piazza di San Fedele; 8am-noon/3-6pm daily; Free):* Grab a fork, because this five-sided church, built in the 6th century on one-time pagan worshipping grounds, is a feast for the eyes. Go ahead, gobble up its stunning external apses, medieval figures, and long rolling windows. It's a couple blocks east of the Duomo.

Pinacoteca Palazzo Volpi *(Via Diaz 84, inside Palazzo Volpi; Tel 031/269-896; 9:30am-12:30pm/2-5pm Mon-Sat, 10am-1pm Sun; Admission 4,000L, 2,500L students; No credit cards):* Also in Como's center, this small gallery offers a collection of medieval and Renaissance paintings. The anonymous Youth & Death and St. Sebastian (looking quite serene, despite being pierced with multiple arrows) will stay with you long after you leave.

Tempio Volitiano *(Viale Marconi; 031/574-705; 10am-noon/3-6pm daily Apr-Sept, 10am-noon/2-4pm Tue-Sun Oct-Mar; 4,000L admission; No credit cards):* This temple is dedicated to local hero Alessandro Volta, inventor of the battery and noteworthy man of electricity! It houses instruments and relics from Al's life and work that will give all you fanatical Volties a charge. It's right on the water, in the town gardens.

modification

If checking out the arrow-riddled St. Sebastian at the Pinacoteca gallery inspires you to do some decorative piercing of your own, you won't have far to go. Head for **Studio Di Tatuaggi e Piercing** *(Via Diaz 39; Tel 031/260-602; 10am-2pm/5-10pm Mon-Sat; 60,000L and up; V, MC)* down the street, where the tattoo artists and piecers can make that picture in your mind's eye a reality. Heading north down Via Giovio until Via Contrada will bring you to the other tattoo parlor in town, **Jigen Tattoo** *(Via Contrada 38; No phone; 3-10pm, closed Sun; 60,000L and up; V, MC)*. It's a little smaller, but very professional, with at least two artists in house offering some fancy penmanship.

great outdoors

The big attraction here is, of course, Lago di Como itself. Because of the nearby factories, many Italians have written it off as a lost cause, but in fact, most of the heavy industry in the region is far from the lake and the towns that border it. Although the waters at the southern end, near Como, look clear, swimming here is still better left to the fish. Wind-surfing is better accomplished in nearby **Domaso** [see below], but from Como it's easy to take a lake cruise. Head for Lungo Lario, just off Piazza Cavour, and buy your ticket at the window of the **Societa Navigazione Lago di Como** *(Lungo Lario; Tel 031/304-060; Hours vary, Easter-Sept only; Tickets 13-20,000L; No credit cards).* You'll feel just like a 15th-century bigwig. Really.

Or take a spin on the **funiculare** *(7,200L roundtrip)* for great views of the lake. It runs every 30 minutes from Piazza dei Gasperi, on the northern shore of town, up to the end of Lungo Lario Trieste, in the town of Brunate. If you want to get in a little physical activity, hop off the funiculare in Brunate and make your way back to Como on one of the well-marked trails that run along the lake. Ask for trail maps at the tourist info booth in Piazza Grimoldi [see *need to know,* below].

EaTS

Even though Como isn't known for its cuisine, eating out here can get a bit pricey. But if you know where to look, there are still cheap eats to be had (don't worry, we're about to tell you where to look).

▶▶**CHEAP**

If you're in the picnic mood, grab some fried eggplant in marinara sauce, pecorino cheese, and salami to go at **Guerci** *(Via Francesco Muralto 33; 9am-1pm/4-8pm daily; No credit cards).* The old men running the place are super-friendly and will let you sample anything you're unsure of.

For a quick afternoon bite, **Café Dea** *(Via Vitini 46; No phone; 9am-8pm daily; Sandwiches 8,000L; No credit cards),* two blocks south of the Duomo, serves up basic Italian panini: mozzarella, bread, tomatoes. It's a chill spot to meet some local students.

TO MARKET

The biggest supermarket in town is **GS** *(At Viale Fratelli-Rosselli and Via F.lli Recchi; 9am-1:30pm/3-9pm Mon-Sat),* across from Tempio Volitiano. Don't even think of shoplifting here—the security guard is about 6-foot-5 and carries one hell of a six-shooter.

Craving some greasy Tex-Mex cuisine, Italian-style? You won't have to fight for a stool at **Pizzaria Messicana** *(Piazza San Fedele 2/B; Tel 031/348-811; Noon-3pm/6-11:30pm, closed Wed; Avg. entree 15-18,000L; V, MC)*, nestled in the northern corner of the piazza. The locals haven't really caught on to the whole sloppy-joe concept quite yet. Maybe they need to lighten up a little—this place is fun, with authentic 1950's Coca-Cola ads and faded movie posters. There's a big bar with a couple of TVs (very American), where you can enjoy a Tex Burger with steak fries (18,000L) and a milkshake (8,000L) made from ice cream, not gelato. Even though they have quite an extensive collection of 50's and 60's music, the pretty-cool staff just plays the radio instead.

Or try your luck with some Spanish grub at **Taverna Spagnola** *(Via Grassi 10; Tel 031/272-460; Noon-3pm/7:30-midnight, closed Wed; Avg. entree 12-15,000L; V, MC, AE)*. With techno music blasting away, the atmosphere's not exactly what you'd expect from a Spanish restaurant, but the paella (50,000L), available with meat or seafood, is yummy, and enough for two. Call ahead to order; it takes an hour to prepare. The service and seafood antipasto aren't anything to write home about, but the huge bowls of spaghetti Bolognese and lake trout aren't half bad. To get there, head south from Piazza Cavour, on Via Fontana, toward Piazza A. Volta.

Grab a table outside **Trattoria Scaldasole** *(Via Armando Diaz 39; Tel 031/677-0222; Noon-3:30pm/6-11:30pm; Avg. entree 13,000L; V, MC, AE)* and indulge in a bottle of crisp white wine as you suck the pits from local spiced olives. The dining area inside is equally charming, with high oval ceilings, wooden wine racks covering the walls, and opera arias (not live, thankfully). For main courses, try the delicious *penne zucchine e mente* (pasta with zucchini and mint sauce) or *orata con funghi e patate* (meat with mushrooms and potatoes). To get there, head east out of Piazza A. Volta down Via Armando Diaz.

One of the oldest eateries in town, **Osteria del Gallo** *(Via Vitani 16; Tel 031/272-591; Noon-3pm/6pm-midnight; Avg. entree 20,000L; V, MC, AE)*, seats only 20, so reservations are a must. The house specialty is *linguini di verdure* (linguine with red vegetable sauce), and the fish entrées are equally delectable. The staff is friendly, but the wine list is a little skimpy. It's just two blocks north of Piazza Volta.

Samba beats blare all night long at **A Brasileira** *(Piazza Grimoldi 8; Tel 031/337-00-08; 7pm-2am, closed Mon; Entrees 10-20,000L, 5-course menu 45,000L; V, MC, AE)*, one block south of Piazza Duomo. Tropically dressed waiters and waitresses serve a five-course a la carte menu with a Brazilian flare. It includes the drink of your choice, antipasto, a selection from a variety of Brazilian meat dishes, a fish entrée, and some bananas and cheese for dessert. After dinner settles, dip into the tropical drink specials (12,000L) and take to the dance floor with some of the Brazilian dancers.

crashing

Como offers some good options for such a small town; the tourist office will even help you make reservations.

If you feel like roughing it, take a 15-minute walk up the west shore of the lake to **The International Camp Grounds** *(Via Cecilio; Tel 031/521-435; Bus 1, 14; Open Mar-Oct; L8,000 per person; V, MC)*. Call ahead to reserve a plot down by the water.

During the summer months, backpackers use the boisterous **Ostello Villa Olmo** *(Via Bellinzona 2; Tel/Fax 031/573-800; Bus 1, 6, 11, 14; Open Mar-Nov, curfew 10pm; 20,000L bed and breakfast; Shared baths; HI cards, no credit cards)* as a home base for day trips around the lake. Located about a kilometer west of town, this crowded hostel features the usual dorm rooms, a restaurant with hefty dinners (16,000L), and a very friendly couple at the helm. The place is designed for the backpacker on the go: you can rent mountain bikes (20,000L a day), get discounts on various activities around town (like the funiculare ride), or do a load of laundry (5,000L). One major bummer is the curfew: 10pm is a crying shame. Hey, you can always stay out till 7am when the doors open again in the morning.

Centrally located, right next to the Duomo, is **Albergo Sociale** *(Via Maestri Comacini 8; Tel 031/264-042; 35,000L singles, 65,000L doubles, 90,000L triples; Shared baths; No credit cards)*. The place has an actor's guild motif, with autographed photos of local thespians covering the walls. The rooms are basic and the bathrooms are a little skanky, but there's no curfew—if you come stumbling in late at night, all you'll get is a good laugh from the cops who are usually sucking down coffee at the bar downstairs.

Another frugal alternative with a central locale, **In Riva al Lago** *(Piazza Matteotti 4; Tel 031/302-333, www.inrivaallago.com; 45,000L singles, 75,000L w/ bath, 90,000L doubles, 110,000L w/ bath; V, MC, AE)* sits right behind the bus station. Every room is clean and comes with a phone, and rooms with baths have TV's. Hearty breakfasts are just 5,000L.

The northern-facing rooms at **Albergo Posta** *(Via Garibaldi 2; Tel 031/266-012, www.hotelposta.net; 70,000L single; 120,000L double, private baths; V, MC, AE)* have great views of the lake, and *all* the tidy rooms come with TVs, phones, and little radios. The managers are a little uptight, and make it clear that there will be no late night sneak-ins. The restaurant downstairs is way overpriced, but the bar's a decent place to grab an afternoon coffee with a shot of grappa.

If you're planning on staying in Como for the week, ask the tourist office for a listing of apartments for rent. This list of about 25 agencies can find you an apartment in town or further up the lake. One of the bigger agencies is **Appartamenti Como Sole** *(Salita Cappucini 18; Tel 031/296-6611)*.

need to know

Currency Exchange There are a slew of banks in and around **Piazza Cavour;** all exchange money and have ATMs.

Tourist Information The **main tourist office** *(Piazza Cavour 16; Tel 031/269-712; 9am-1pm/3-6pm Mon-Sat)*, on the southern side of the main drag, is helpful when it comes to ferry schedules and room reservations. Another **tourist info booth** set up in the middle of Piazza Grimoldi *(9am-1pm/3-6pm Mon-Sat)* offers maps and extensive info on hiking and other outdoor activities.

Public Transportation It's easy getting around town on foot, but there's also a very reliable bus system that runs until midnight. Most buses leave from the train stations; tickets are 1,500L.

Health and Emergency Emergency: *113.* Two blocks north of Piazza Cavour, **Ospedale Valduce** *(Via Dante 11; Tel 031/324-111)* has a 24-hour emergency room.

Pharmacies Fill your prescriptions at **farmacia centrale** *(Via Plinio 1; Tel 031/42-04; 8:30am-12:30pm/3:30-8pm, Tue-Sun).*

Trains There are two train stations in town. **Stazione San Giovanni** *(Piazzale San Gottardo; Tel 1478/880-88)* is in the southern end of town, a 15-minute walk from the center. Trains run into Switzerland and Milan. **Stazione Nord** *(Tel 147/888-088)* is located one block north of Piazza Cavour. The trains leaving this station are owned by a private company and *do not,* we repeat *NOT,* accept Eurail passes.

Bus Lines Out of the City Buses leave from **Stazione Nord,** one block from Piazza Cavour. **SPT** *(Piazza Matteotti; Tel 031/304-744)* provides service to other towns around the lake.

Boats **Navigazione Lago Di Como** *(Tel 800/551-801)* runs ferries and hydrofoils that service most of the towns on the lake; they leave from the port opposite Piazza Cavour. Schedules are distributed from the tourist info booths and at the booth on the port.

Bike Rental Guests of the **hostel** [see *crashing,* above] can rent bikes from them; everybody else is SOL.

Laundry There's a self-service **laundromat** *(Via Vittorio Emanuele; No phone; 9am-8:30pm daily; 1,600L per load; No credit cards)* with 20 machines two blocks north of Piazza Duomo.

Postal Mail stuff home from the **post office** *(Via T. Gallio 4; Tel 031/277-30-20; 8:15am-6pm Mon-Sat).*

Internet See *wired,* above.

LECCO

The little industrial city of Lecco, perched at the end of the eastern leg of Lago di Como about 20 miles east of the city of Como, offers some of the most challenging rock climbing in the area. The 2,000 or so locals get a kick out of all the adrenaline-seeking backpackers en route to conquer their rock faces—they'll tell you you'll never catch *them* risking their lives that way. Climbing and hiking are the only game in town—risk your life during the daylight hours and take the bus back to Como after the sun sets for accommodations and libations.

The climbing here ranges from novice to expert and is mostly lead climbing, although some of the smaller faces can be top-roped (if that's all Greek—or Italian—to you, you probably shouldn't be climbing these rocks). There are no rental or guide shops in town, but **La Dama Café** *(Via Principale 12/r; No phone; 8am-9pm daily; 2-3,000L; No credit cards)*, right on Lecco's only Piazza, usually has some climbers hanging around who know about the faces and can offer some assistance in tackling them. The café also serves small sandwiches and drinks. For other provisions, try **GS supermarket** *(Via N. Sauro; No phone; 8:30am-2pm/4-9pm Mon-Sat; No credit cards)*, just off the western side of the piazza—just don't expect to find any PowerBars.

If you're more interested in dramatic scenery than death-defying feats, lace up your boots and head for the hiking trails. Walk out toward the rock faces that border the town to the east, and you'll find them easily. The hikes, that take only 90 minutes to 2 hours round trip, wind through amazing spire-shaped rock formations known as **Le Grigne,** and offer inspiring views of the lake far below. They begin steeply, but level out after the first 15 minutes or so. Like the rock faces, the trails are made of hearty granite. During wet or dry conditions, you can end up flat on your behind if your footing isn't steady. The scattered pines and indigenous shrubbery are thin enough that you can do some trailblazing.

need to know

Tourist Information **Azienda promozione turistica del lecchese** *(Via N. Sauro 6; Tel 034/136-23-60; 9:30am-noon/2:30-6pm Mon-Sat),* located on the northern side of Lecco's Piazza, has information on climbing and hiking in the area.

Directions and Transportation Buses from Como make the ride to Lecco every 60-90 minutes, leaving from **Stazione Nord,** one block north of Piazza Cavour. It's 4,200L one way. You can also reach Lecco from Como by **hydrofoil,** but the ride is long (three hours), as you have to go almost to the top of the lake and then down the eastern leg to reach Lecco, but it sure is a purty ride if you've got the time. Buy tickets through **Societa Navigazione Lago di Como** *(Lungo Lario, Como; Tel 031/304-060; Hours vary, Easter-Sept only; No credit cards).* It's L6,500 one way.

domaso

During the summer and fall, VW vans stacked with boards, sails, and young dreadlocked windsurfers questing for the perfect thermal winds *(breva)* pour into this tiny town, infesting it's beaches with fly-by-night bonfire bonanzas. The winds howl through Domaso, Lago di Como's northernmost town, all year long, making it a mecca for windsurfing and sailing. With its slate-roofed houses and rustic winding streets, the town maintains an old-time Northern Italian feel, with only a few nightspots. The 2,000 or so locals are very friendly as long as you don't come off as one of those windsurfer-types with nothing better to do than surf, get drunk, and keep the town awake all night (so try and pretend you're not, okay?).

On a clear day, the view from the waterfront is spectacular, expanding across the eastern edge of the Alps to the north. The water is soft and blue, and ice-cold year round. The center of town is **Piazza Cavour,** which is intersected by the two main drags, **Via Case Sparse** and **Via Regina.** Following Via Regina four blocks east from the piazza will bring you to the waterfront. From the bus station, follow Via Case Sparse south to get to Piazza Cavour. If you arrive by boat—which you likely will, as Domaso is connected with virtually every big town on the lake via boat—just follow Via Regina west for four blocks and you'll be in the center of town.

If you want to get in on the scene here (and why wouldn't you?), some of the cheapest rentals of windsurfers and equipment are available through **Ostello della Gioventu** [see *eats,* below]. Other possibilities include **Windsurfcenter Domaso** *(Via Case Sparse 14, near Camping Paradiso; Tel 393/449-74-90, Fax 393/449-75-19; No credit cards)* and **Surfin Progress** *(Via Case Sparse 54, Tel/Fax 393/449-62-08; masta@mclink.it; No credit cards).* Both offer boards, canoe, bike, and catamaran rental, plus repair service.

eats

Everybody flocks to **Pub Crazy Games** *(Via Case Sparse, 42; Tel 034/496-095; 1pm-2am daily; No credit cards),* the wild bar in the center of town, before and after their daily poundings on the lake. Nine out of ten surfers agree that the beers (8,000L) alleviate some of the pain of their injuries, while the greasy food brings them back down to earth (that tenth guy's just a pain). As the night goes on, the hard liquor tends to flow a lot more freely and the surfing tales get a lot taller. If you haven't had enough sport for the day, there are two pool tables in back.

The hearty, mouth-watering pizzas at **Ristorante Pizzeria Bar Madonnina** *(Via Garibaldi 34; Tel 034/495-200; Noon-11pm Tue-Sun; 10-15,000L pizzas; V, MC, AE)* are ready before you can say *"pronto."* At this swanky pizza parlor, bustling with backpackers all day and night, you can rest your surf-weary bones at one of the tables inside or out, and add to your dining pleasure by checking out the funky old school photos of Domaso on the walls.

If you want to pick up some daily brown baggin' rations there's a **GS Supermarket** *(Via Case Sparse 11/r; 9am-2pm/4-9:30pm, closed Sun)* with all the essentials three blocks north of the Piazza, at Via Regina.

crashing

Ostello della Gioventu *(Via Case Sparse 12; Tel 034/497-449; Open Mar-Oct; 20,000L dorm bed, breakfast included, shared baths; HI cards accepted, no credit cards)* is very modern, very clean, located right on the water, four blocks west of Piazza Cavour. It offers the cheapest board and equipment rentals in town, as well as Internet access (12,000L per hour). During the summer months, reservations are required. There's also a strict midnight curfew, but things are usually dying down by midnight around here anyway.

Two blocks east of the hostel, toward the center of town, is **Modonnina** *(Via Case Sparse 44/3; Tel 034/496-294; 30,000L singles, 40,000L w/bath, 55,000L doubles, 65,000L w/ bath; No curfew; No credit cards)*. From the outside, it looks like a dump, but the inside is all recently renovated. The simple bedrooms and baths are clean—more than adequate for a good night's sleep. Pretty much anyone staying here is a backpacker passing through to check out the windsurfing scene.

need to know

Tourist Information The **tourist office** *(Via Garibaldi 12; Tel 034/496-322; 9am-1:30pm/3-7pm daily)* has the skinny on Domaso. You could also log on to the fairly comprehensive ***www.domaso.it/english/***.

Directions and Transportation Domaso is easily accessed by boat from any of the major lake towns like Como or Lecco. **Navigazione Lago Di Como** *(Tel 800/551-801)* runs ferries and hydrofoils from Como that service most of the towns on the lake; they leave from the port opposite Piazza Cavour. All boats arrive and depart Domaso from the docks down by the water. The ticket office, to the right of the docks, is open 7am-8pm daily. The bus ride from Como to Domaso is a two-hour ordeal that doesn't offer the views that the boat does.

riva del garda

Rock climbing, wind surfing, slamming late-night pubs, and hold-onto-the-rail party cruises separate Riva, on the northern shore, from the rest of the towns on the Lago di Garda, the largest lake in Italy (370sq km). Surrounded by mountains that seemingly dip right into the aqua-velvet waters, it's overrun in the summer by crowds of fresh-out-of-school urban sherpas on a quest for adrenaline and bacchanalia. On a sunny day, you can lose yourself to the warm rays at the same pebble beaches where Kafka and Nietzsche once perfected their doggy paddles.

Riva suffered through a long custody battle between Austria and Italy, which the end of WWI settled for good by handing the tiny town over to the Italians. Of course, the Austrians (and Germans) still get visitation rights in the summer. A barefoot stroll through Riva's sweeping cobblestone streets and *piazze* is the best way to get oriented. The older center of town is the massive **Piazza III Novembre,** which branches out to the main thoroughfare of **Via Roma.**

bar and live music scene

Despite Riva's teeming international thrill-seekers, the most popular evening entertainment consists of a couple of cheap 40-ounce beers, an agreeable drinking partner, and a comfortable seat on the edge of the lake after sunset. The clear skies and blaring stars make for a quintessential Italian moment—hope you remember it the next day.

There are, of course, more organized options. The largest, most crowded one is **Discoteca Tiffany** *(Giardini di Porta Oriental, Tel 046/455-25-12; 7pm-3am Thur-Sun; No cover),* not far from the tourist office. It's your standard small-town disco, but it's pretty fly.

The newest additions to Riva's nightlife are the booze-boats that rage with eurodisco and samba beats till the breaka breaka dawn. The bluntly named **Party Boat** *(Tel 046/49-14-95-11;Boats leave the docks at Giardini di Porta Orientale at 8pm, Jul-Aug; 22,000L cover includes first drink; No credit cards)* offers debauchery Julie McCoy couldn't imagine in her wildest dreams on a liquor-soaked tour around the lake. We're not talking shuffleboard on the Lido deck here—good thing you have a designated driver.

For beer-swilling landlubbers, **Pub al Gallo** *(Via San Rocca 11; Tel 046/455-11-77; 6pm-1am daily; No credit cards)* serves up pints of German beer (8,000L) to a mostly German crowd, which has an insane kind of logic to it. You may find a few international backpackers here as well. It's just north of Piazza III Novembre.

CULTURE ZOO

Riva's not big on culture, but that doesn't mean there isn't any really old stuff around to gape at—just follow the German tourists.

Torre d'Apponale: The town's most evident human-made landmark is this 13th-century watchtower, standing high above the port on Piazza Novembre III, which was probably intended to ward off invasions. It's not open to visitors, but be sure to stop by and take a look—and don't forget to wave to the angelic trumpeter on top.

La Rocca *(Piazza Battisti 3; Tel 046/457-38-69; 9am-noon/4-10pm Jul-Aug; 9am-noon Tue-Sun, Jan-Jun, Sep-Dec; 8,000L admission; No credit cards):* This ghostly 12th-century castle, once owned by the Viennese Hapsburgs and the Veronese Scaligeri princes, was also used as a prison. Today, it imprisons bored tourists who venture inside to explore exhibits of local art and traditions in the Museo Civico La Rocca. Not really worth missing out on beach time for.

great outdoors

All year long, the winds from the Dolomite mountains swoop down and provide a constant source of natural energy which makes Riva the fastest spot in the country for windsurfing. **Nautic Club Riva** *(Viale Rovereto 132; Tel 046/455-24-53; Closed Nov-Easter; 60,000L per half-day rental plus deposit; No credit cards)* and **Bouwmeester Windsurfing Centre** *(On the water by Hotel Pier; Tel 046/455-17-30; 55,000L per half-day; No credit cards)* both rent out boards, wet suits, and life jackets. They also offer hourly lessons.

The solid, jagged faces of Riva's mountains, some of them hanging right over the lake's edge and ascending over 100 meters, definitely aren't for tennis-shoe climbers. For solo or lead climb info, partners, and guides, head to **Ufficio Guide Alpine** *(Via Segantini 64; Tel 046/451-98-05; 9am-12:30/3-6pm daily; 110-680,000L excursions; No credit cards)* or **Orizzonti Trentini** *(Via Segantini 41; Tel 046/451-02-02; 9am-noon/3-6pm daily)*. Both shops have gear and lists of locals and tourists to pair up with, as well as maps and guides.

Another option for exploring the trails around Riva is to two-wheel it. Bikes are available for rent at **Centro Cicli Pederzolli** *(Via Canella 12; Tel 046/455-18-30; 9am-12:30/3:30-7pm daily; 25,000L per day; No credit cards)* and **Superbike Girelli** *(Via Damiano Chiesa 15/17; Tel 046/455-66-02; 22,000L per day; No credit cards)*, both in the old part of town south of Piazza Novembre III.

If you only trust your own two feet, take advantage of the local trails leading to **Cascato Varone,** a waterfall chiseling its way through the granite. It's an easy hike up into the base of the mountains, about three kilometers outside of town. Trail maps are available at the tourist office [see *need to know,* below].

EATS

Pizza and seafood are the choices in this town. For a cheap, quick bite to go, grab a slice at one of the booths along Via Roma.

On a sunny day or moonlit evening, the tables outside **Le 4 Stagioni** *(Via Maffei; Tel 046/455-27-77; Noon-3pm/7-11:30pm daily; 8-15,000L pizzas; V, MC)* make for authentic pizza eating as well as authentic people watching. The service is quick and friendly, the pizzas covered in marinara with loads of mozzarella. Families pack in during the dinner hour, so eat late unless you like the soothing sounds of young, high-pitched voices.

The photos of local fishermen on the walls of **Osteria al Pescatore** *(Via Castello 19, just south off Piazza Carducci; 046/443-03-63; Noon-3pm/5:30-11pm, closed Mon; Avg. entree 15,000L; No credit cards)* spell out Riva's fishy history. You know that if the local fishermen recommend the fresh fish entrees, this place has to be good. You can't go wrong with a steaming bowl of *zuppa di pesce* (fish soup) and a bottle of local white wine. The long pine tables are packed during lunch and dinner.

The Neapolitan spirit, along with some fresh mozzarella and marinara sauce, makes **Bella Napoli** *(Via dei Fabbri 34; Tel 046/455-73-45;*

TO MARKET

Stock up at the **open-air market** in Piazza della Erbe, weekday mornings from 8am-noon. Local venders sell all sorts of veggies, meats, and cheeses at great prices.

Noon-3:30pm/5:30-10pm daily; 12,000L pizzas; V, MC) the liveliest restaurant in town. It's no coincidence that Neopolitans are the best pizza makers in Italy. The brick oven here will cook your *pizza con salmerino* (pizza with fish) faster than you can guzzle down your glass of *Schiava* (local red wine). This place also makes a great antipasto (13,000L) with loads of seasoned *prosciutto* and *mozzarella di bufalo.*

Set back from the lake on one of Riva's main shopping streets is **Ristorante San Marco** *(Viale Roma 2; Tel 046/455-44-77; Noon-2:30pm/7-10pm Tue-Sun, closed Feb; 20-35,000L entrees; AE, DC, MC, V),* housed in an old 19th-century hotel. The classic Italian menu includes such possibilities as spaghetti with clams or tortellini with prosciutto. There's also plenty of seafood on hand, from sole to grilled scampi. You can eat outside in the garden in the summer months.

crashing

Like most Italian lake resorts, Riva is full of high-priced digs. Finding something within your budget takes a bit of doing, but it is possible—just keep an open mind about where you sleep. A lot of the windsurfers visiting Riva skip the hotel scene altogether and camp out instead. For a complete listing of campgrounds in the area, call Campeggio Riva *(Tel 046/191-44-44).*

▶▶CHEAP

Somewhere along the line, someone designated **Campgrounds Bavaria** *(Via Rovereto 100; Tel 046/455-25-24; 10,000L per person, 16,000L per site, showers 1,500L; V, MC, AE)* the official windsurfer hangout, which makes perfect sense—you can roll out of your sleeping bag and into the lake. (Maybe try some coffee first, though.) It's on the way to the neighboring village of Torbole, the first stop on any bus headed down the west side of the lake. Call ahead to reserve a plot—you'll have a blast.

One look at some of the other prices in town will send most budget backpackers scurrying on over to **Ostello Benacus** *(Piazza Cavour 9; Tel 046/455-49-11; Open Mar-Oct; 22,000L dorm, breakfast included; Shared bath; HI cards accepted, no credit cards).* To find it, take a left turn off Via Roma and proceed under the arch. It's basic hostel chic (which means there is no chic). There are two dorms (one for boys and one for girls), a small cafeteria, clean bathrooms, and a lounge with battered books and a TV. And no curfew!

▶▶DO-ABLE

The best feature of **Albergo Portici** *(Piazza Novembre III; Tel 046/455-54-00; 80,000L singles, 130,000L doubles; Private baths; V, MC, AE)* is the rooms on the piazza side, which all have little balconies perfect for scanning the buzzing square before setting out on the party scene. The super-cool owners don't really care if you get a single or double and let someone crash on the floor—just offer them a little bit more money to show your gratitude. There are only 20 rooms (some of them with old-fashioned porcelain tubs), so it's difficult to get a reservation; be sure to call ahead.

need to know

Currency Exchange There are **ATMs** and **banks** all along Via Roma.

Tourist Information The **main tourist office** *(Giardini di Porta Oriental 8; Tel 046/455-44-44; 9am-noon/3-6pm Mon-Sat)* is down by the water, behind the park off Via della Liberazione. They have maps of all the trails surrounding the town, and tons of info on festivals and tours around the lake. They can't book rooms for you, but they're happy to share hotel vacancy listings. Log on to *http://gardaworld.com* for info about the whole Lago di Garda area.

Public Transportation Local buses and taxis can be found at the bus station, but the town is small enough to be covered easily on foot.

Health and Emergency Emergency: *118*. There's always a doctor on call at Farmacia Dante.

Pharmacies You can re-stock your meds at **Farmacia Dante** *(Via Dante Aligieri 12/c; Tel 046/455-25-08 8:30am-12:30pm/3-7:30pm Mon-Sat, 9am-12:30pm/4:30-7pm Sun).*

Trains There's no rail access to Riva del Garda. The nearest train station is at Roverto, where you can connect with frequent buses making the trip to Riva.

Bus Lines Out of the City Eight buses a day make the trip from Trento to Riva—it's 6,000L one way. For info on schedules and fares, call the **Autostazione on Viale Trento** *(Tel 1478/880-88).* Buses also run from Verona and Rovereto, which has rail access [see above]. Call *Tel 046/455-23-23* for info.

Boats **Navigazione Lago di Garda** *(Piazza Matteotti; Tel 030/914-95-11)* runs daily ferries and hydrofoils to Sirmione (13,900L) [see below]. Covering the entire lake via boat is a four-hour trip (14,500L).

Bike/Moped Rental Bikes are available at **Centro Cicli Pederzolli** and **Superbike Girelli** [see *great outdoors,* above, for both]. If you like your two wheels motorized, speed over to **3-S Bike Scott Rental Tour** *(Viale Rovereto 47; 046/455-20-91).*

Riding a moped around the lake's winding roads will definitely test your skills and raise your pulse.

Postal The local **post office** *(Largo Bensheim; Tel 046/455-23-46; 8am-6:30pm Mon-Sat)* gets those letters out to the world.

SIRMIONE

For most of the year, Lago Di Garda's tiny peninsula town Sirmione is dead to the world. But from May to September, it becomes the buzzin'-est beehive on the lake. Tourists from points north (most notably Germany) drag their surly pubescent teenagers into town for a fun-filled summer vacation of wind surfing, sun bathing, and neurosis-inducing sit-down dinners. If you can distance yourself from the family trauma and keep a bemused, ironic distance, Sirmione is good for a lively daytrip or evening bar-hop from Milan or one of the bigger resort towns. There are a couple of decent beaches on either shore of the town, and the summer heat is continually refreshed by breezes off the water. Sirmoine evidently quite impressed the Roman poet Catullus, who hung here whenever he got the chance. Hoping to lure in even more tourists, some local pseudo-historians also claim that Roman emperor Julius Caesar and infernal poet Dante also did some fishing here from time to time (no, not together, duh).

You've just got to accept that you're in a tourist trap here. A wooden sign reading "Welcome" (in German first and Italian second) leads out onto the main drag, Viale Marconi, which stretches the five-kilometer length of the town. Here you'll be confronted with a stretch of brightly painted wooden shanties, beachball carcasses, and anything else but what you would expect from a medieval Italian lake town. Things get a little better in the next half-mile, beyond the old entrance to the town at **Scagligero Castle** [see *culture zoo,* below], where you'll find somewhat charming cobblestone streets and panoramic lake views—a kind of medieval Disneyland. Just don't look too closely: the neon-filled streets offer overpriced, over-rated dinners, a plethora of hotels, and some decent teen/adult nightlife, all orbiting the overcrowded tourist epicenter, **Piazza Marconi.**

bar and live music scene

Nightlife is about the best thing this town has to offer. Everything's clumped into the streets beyond the castle, which start to feel a bit like that island where Pinocchio turned into a donkey-boy.

Retro music blares all night long under a canopy of deep day-glo blue neon and disco lights at **Kursaal** *(Via San Martino d/B, one block north of the castle; Tel 030/91-91-63; 6pm-1am daily; No cover; No credit cards),* one of the bigger discos in town. The stiff drinks, like everything in Sirmione, are overpriced (12,000L), but if you're looking for alcohol content, you may get your money's worth. The crowd of teenyboppers sneaking puffs of cigarettes usually filters out after 9pm, when older (but not too much older), more energetic fun-seekers fill the two dance floors, getting good and sweaty as the night rages on.

Even though **Break's Beer** *(Via Mazzarona; Tel 030/990-69-99; Noon-1am daily; No cover; No credit cards)* bills itself as a disco, you won't find anyone practicing their Travolta imitations here. Break's is a simple little watering hole, with musty wooden tables and one long bar where you can slug back cold pints of German draught (8,000L) and vodka tonics (10,000L). Day and night, it's filled with beer-swilling couples tappin' their toes to the latest Madonna remixes on the radio.

Heavy disco blares through the night at **Mean River** *(Via Verona; Tel 030/91-94-01; 6pm-1am, closed Tue; No cover; No credit cards),* one of the only discos in town that brings in DJs from other cities. Ultraviolet lamps keep the atmosphere cool and mysterious, and most of the crowd on the small dance floor has finished going through puberty, which is always a plus. Drinks run about 8,000L.

If you're in that Billy Joel kind of mood, put some cash in the jar at **Piano Bar Divinia** *(Via Verona; Tel 033/880-88-55; 1pm-midnight Tue-Sun; No cover; V, AE).* If you don't want the guy behind the ivories to sing you a song 'cuz he's the piano man, this crowded piano bar is a bit of a bore, with a much older crowd and the requisite overpriced drinks (12,000L).

CULTUrE ZOO

Note how everyone bursts out laughing when you ask them about culture in Sirmione. Okay, okay—but this *was* a medieval town, so there's got to be something to check out....

Scagligero Castle *(Piazza Castello; 9am-6pm daily, Apr-Sep; 9am-1pm Tue-Sun, Oct-Mar; 8,000L; No credit cards):* Constructed in 1250 by the all-powerful Scaglieri princes of Verona, this moated castle isn't all that spectacular as castles go (my, aren't we jaded?), but it most likely gave the locals the idea to turn their town into a wannabe Disneyland. On a clear day, you get an amazing view of the points east and north of the lake from its towers.

Grotte di Catullo *(Via Catullo, at the northern most end of the town; Tel 030/91-61-57; 9am-4pm Tue-Sun; 12,000L admission, under 17 free):* This Roman Villa, at the northern end of town, has deep black baths once frequented by pleasure-loving Roman poet Catullus, which were in operation until 11th century. The baths are no longer open to soak your bones in, but the ruins, along with the lake view, are worth a look-see.

grEAT OUTdoors

The cleanest and most pleasant beach to grab some lakeside tanning is **Lido delle Bione,** off Via Dante just east of the castle. Vendors will rent you a chaise lounge and umbrella for 15,000L. Smaller strips of beaches can be found on both sides of **Viale Marconi.**

If the wind is howling, try your luck at some wind surfing. **C. Surf Martini** *(Porto Gajeazzi; Tel 033/076-76-72-36)* and **C. Surf Sirmione** *(Lido Brema; Tel 033/862-24-36-50),* on the docks outside the castle, offer classes and wind surf rentals from April to September. If you're looking for a bit more speed, **Bisoli** *(Via XXV Aprile; Tel 030/91-60-88)* and **Minozzi** *(Porto Gajeazzi; Tel 033/754-99-82-75)* provide water-skiing excursions and lessons by the hour.

The crystal clear waters of Lago Di Garda are ideal for scuba diving. **Asso Sub Il Pellicano** *(Viale Marconi 32; Tel 030/990-49-12; 8am-4pm, closed Mon)* is a diving school located on the main road, just before the castle walls, that offers lessons and group dives around the lake.

EATS

Just about every restaurant in Sirmione is overpriced and as authentically Italian as a chalupa. The cheapest way to grab a decent meal in town is

TO MARKET

There's an **open-air market** *(Piazza Montebaldo; 8am-1pm Fri)* one block north of the castle with veggies, cheese, meats and other backpack reserves.

from one of the pizza stands in the city center along Pizza Carducci or Via Vittorio Emanuele.

For some good Mexican/Spanish food, head for **Chica Loca** *(Via G. Piana 8; Tel 033/990-57-87; 11am-3pm/5-10pm Tue-Sun; 15,000L entrees; V, MC)*. Ponchos and Mexican rugs hang from the walls, and speedy waiters throw large portions of rice, beans, and tortillas at you faster than you can eat them. The margaritas (10,000L) are weak, but that's nothing a couple shots of tequila (10,000L) can't handle.

One of the best home cooking eateries in town is **Grifone** *(Via Vittorio Emanuele; Tel 033/91-60-97; Noon-3pm/5pm-11:30pm Thu-Tue; V, MC, AE)*. The views from the terrace will prepare you for your meal: fish pulled right from the lake, served over hefty pasta platters (20,000L). Other options include *gnochetti dragoncella* (potato dumplings) and *costello di Manzo* (beef cutlets). This old stone house is separated from the castle by a moat.

The best eating in Sirmione isn't in Sirmione—it's just outside of town (a 10-minute walk north), at the base of the peninsula, at **Vecchia Lugana** *(Piazzale Vecchia Lugana 1; Tel 030/91-90-12; 12:30-2pm/7:30-10:30pm Wed-Sun, closed Jan to mid-Feb; 18-30,000L entrees; AE, DC, MC, V)*. Chef Pierantonio Ambrosi serves up inventive dishes made with fresh ingredients in a kick-back setting. The fresh fish is grilled to perfection, and any of the fresh pasta dishes (*tagliatelle, orecchiette,* etc.) will make the trip to Sirmione worthwhile.

crashing

If you don't have to sleep in Sirmione, don't. Even though there are over 100 hotels crammed into the 5-kilometer stretch of town, they're usually booked through the summer and not worth the pocket change.

If you've gotta stay and don't want to spend a bunch, head over to **Albergo Progresso** *(Via Vittorio Emanuele 18; Tel 030/91-61-08; 55,000L singles, 65,000L doubles, 70,000L w/bath; Private baths available; V, MC)*, two blocks north of the castle. The rooms are simple, the bathrooms clean, and there's a nondescript cafe and restaurant downstairs.

Outside the castle gates, just two minutes on foot, you'll find **Venezia** *(Via XXV Aprile 36; Tel 030/91-60-92; 49,000L singles, 54,000L w/bath; 60,000L doubles, 67,000L w/bath; Private baths available; V, MC, AE)*.

This little piece of the Veneto has a beach out back looking east over the lake, and a bar for sipping pina coladas in the sun—squint your eyes funny and for a second you may actually believe you're in Venice. The rooms are small and practical, with fresh linens and towels, a sink, and a bidet (fancy!).

need to know

Currency Exchange There are **ATMs** and **exchanges** all along Via Vittorio Emanuele.

Tourist Information In a circular building just outside the castle gates, the **main tourist office** *(Via Guglielmo Marconi 2; Tel 030/91-61-14; 9am-9pm daily Apr-Oct, 9am-12:30pm/3pm-6pm Mon-Fri, 9am-12:30pm Sat, Nov-Mar)* offers little more than a listing of local outdoor concerts.

Public Transportation There are buses that run the full length of Sirmione. They leave from in front of the castle; tickets are 5,000L.

Health and Emergency Emergency: 113. The nearest hopital, **Ospedale Di Desenzano** *(Tel 030/914-51)* is 10 kilometers south of town, toward Brescia.

Pharmacies If walking Sirmione's day-glo streets gives you a headache, head for **Farmacia** *(Via Vittorio Emanuele 73; Tel 030/91-60-04; 9am-8pm daily; No credit cards)*. For nightly service dial *Tel 800/20-87-55*.

Trains and Buses Getting to Sirmione is something of a pain in the butt. Trains from Milan or Venice stop in either Verona or Brescia; from there, buses run every hour to Sirmione. Tickets are 4,600L from Verona and 5,400L from Brescia. You can take a hydrofoil or boat to the other towns on the lake (contact the tourist office for info).

Bike/Moped Rental **Adventure Sprint** *(Via Brescia 9; Tel 030/91-90-00)* can hook you up with a set of wheels, motorized or people-powered.

Postal The **post office** *(Lago Fasele Bitinico; Tel. 030/91-61-95; 8am-1pm Mon-Fri/8-11am Sat)* is one block south of the tourist office, just outside the castle walls.

stresa

Once a quiet fishing village on the western shore of Lago Maggiore, Stresa has evolved into an international resort where tourist from all walks of life come for lakeside views, alpine adventure, and high culture at the town's most popular attractions, the **Borromean Islands** [see below]. In the 17th-century, all the beautiful people used to come here to enjoy the views of the sublime landscape, and they covered the islands with their grandiose villas and lush gardens. Today, we ignore the landscape and instead *ooh* and *ahh* at the sublime wealth expressed by these one-time playgrounds of the extremely rich and famous, which would leave even Robin Leach speechless.

Even before the Borromeo family had left Stresa behind, it became a stop on mere mortals' itineraries, around the beginning of the 19th century. It's been a vacation magnet for everyone from Dickens, Lord Byron, and Hemingway to mountain-bike adrenaline slaves and famous musicians from all over the world, who convene for Settimane Musicali and Jazz Fest [see *festivals and events,* below].

The town of Stresa begins at the base of Monte Mattorone, to the west, and stretches downhill to Lago Maggiore, to the east. The main road, **Via Principe Tommaso,** runs from the mountains down toward the docks at the lake. It first passes through the smaller squares **Piazza Posi** and **Piazza L. Cadorna,** and ends up at the spacious **Piazza Marconi,** right on the water, which is the social center of town. Lined with wrought-iron lampposts and massive palm trees that sway in the subtle breezes off the lake, Marconi is always teeming with barhoppers, hungry families, and boat owners trying to cut you the best deal for a ride out to the islands. The train station is on **Via Principe di Piemonte,** at the northern end of town. To reach Piazza Marconi from there, take a right out of the station, and turn right going down the hill at **Viale Duchessa di Genova** until you come to the water. Then continue right down **Corso Umberto** until you reach the piazza—it's about a five-minute walk total. From there, you can easily access the entire town on foot by heading inland on Via Principe Tommaso or **Via Roma,** which run parallel.

bar and live music scene

The minor nightlife scene here focuses more on music than liquor, as you you should be able to pick up from the excitement around the annual festivals: Settimane Musicali and the Jazz Fest [see *festivals and events,* below]. But of course, there's plenty of liquor to go around, too.

Live rock and the bluest of the blues set the tone at **L'Idrovolante Café** *(Piazza Lido 6; Tel 032/33-13-84; 8-2am daily; No credit cards),* where steel guitars, slammin' waitresses, and three-finger shots make for the hippest spot in town. It's all the way at the northern end of Corso Umberto, which runs along the lake starting at Piazza Marconi. On Blues nights, the mostly younger crowd lolls about the wooden stage in back, looking to soak up some soul from the band. Oldsters generally stick to the Budweiser-strewn bar ("We have more than enough soul already, thank you."). Everyone gets good and liquored up on pints of beer (7,500L) and shots of whiskey (10,000L), 'til closing time leads the hedonists down to the water's edge to indulge in a cool dip and howl at the moon. Weekends generally have the best bands; music kicks off at about 9pm.

Take the short hike one block up the hill from Piazza Marconi to find the creatively named **Irish Bar** *(Via Principe Margherita 9; Tel 032/33-10-54; Noon-3pm/7pm-2am daily; No cover; No credit cards).* Young backpackers guzzle down pints of Guinness and other Irish pours (8,000L) and throw darts, while family men come in to escape the wife and kids and indulge in a little male bonding. The radio blares hip hop and funk, just like in Ireland.

stresa

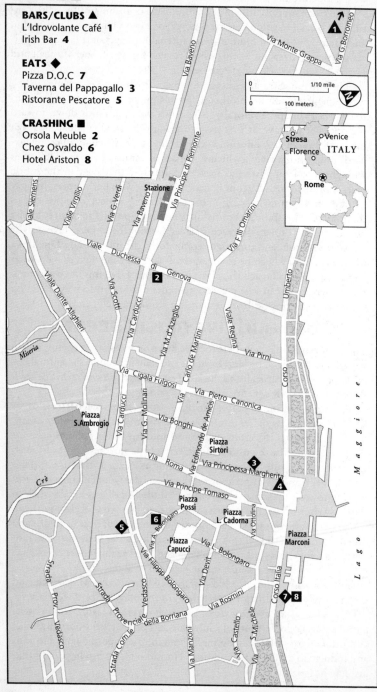

BARS/CLUBS ▲
L'Idrovolante Café **1**
Irish Bar **4**

EATS ◆
Pizza D.O.C **7**
Taverna del Pappagallo **3**
Ristorante Pescatore **5**

CRASHING ■
Orsola Meuble **2**
Chez Osvaldo **6**
Hotel Ariston **8**

CITY SPORTS

For outdoor adventure, get advice and equipment from **Bicico** *(Piazzale della funivia; Tel 032/33-03-99, jurio@tin.it; 9am-5pm daily; V, MC, AE).* This extreme outfitter offers the usual mountain bike rentals (20,000L per day, 50,000L deposit) and guided excursions on Mount Mattarone (15-20,000L for three hours) for the average thrill-seeker. Adrenaline junkies who need a stronger hit (you know who you are) can hire a helicopter to drop them off at the top of a glacier for the cycling adventure of a lifetime. Then there's always the "007 Bungee Jump" off the Verzasca Dam, in the nearby Swiss town of Locarno. Dropping 255 meters, it's the longest in the free world. The whole package, including travel over the border, runs about 200,000L.

Another local company, **Bici Company** *(Piazza Funivia 2/B; Tel 032/33-03-99; 9am-6pm daily; V, MC, AE)* offers helicopter excursions and downhill bike rides daily and nightly (200-250,000L). Trips begin with a ride up the cable car in Piazza Lido.

If you're into the outdoors but happy enough with your life to resist death-defying feats, pick up a copy of *Lago Maggiore Trekking* at the tourist office [see *need to know*, below]. This multilingual trail guide covers 18 organized and detailed hikes, including the Val Grande National Park, Lagoni Park, and Switzerland's Mount Zeda.

And the truly anti-sweat can take the cable car (10,000L roundtrip) from Piazza Lido up Mount Mattarone to the pretty **Giardini Alpinia** *(Via Canonica 8; Tel 032/33-13-08; 9am-6pm Tue-Sun, Apr 1-Oct 15).* This garden, first opened in the 1930s, has over 700 different species of predominantly Alpine and medicinal flowers and herbs—beautiful *and* good for you!

You can also cruise the waters of Lago Maggiore by motorboat or hydrofoil—contact the **Navagazione Sul Lago Maggiore** *(Tel 0322/46-651)* in the nearby little town of Arona for schedules and details.

EATS

Eating in Stresa is intimate and elegant across the board—even the pizza places have class.

Enjoy pizza with a view at **Pizza D.O.C.** *(Corso Italia 60; Tel 032/33-00-00; Noon-2:30pm/7pm-midnight daily; 8-20,000L; V, MC, AE),* a pizza joint so classy it makes you reconsider calling it a "joint." The dining room is on the balcony of Hotel Artison [see *crashing*, below], which offers panoramic views of the mountains and the lake, and a mind-boggling 75 different kinds of pies. During dinner hours, the place gets a bit crowded, but a table with a view is worth the wait.

For some down-to-earth Stresa hospitality in an elaborate garden setting, head to **Taverna del Pappagallo** *(Via Principe Margherita 46; Tel 032/33-04-11; Noon-3:30pm/6-11:30pm, closed Mon; 18,000L; V, MC, AE),* just two blocks up the hill from Piazza Marconi. Enjoy the specialty of the house, *scalamino allo spiedoe fagioli* (beans and grilled

TO MARKET

Fill your picnic basket at the **GS super-market** *(Stresa Via Rome 11; 8:30am-12:30pm/3:30-7:30pm Mon-Sat, 8:30am-12:30pm Sun)*, between Via Principe Tomaso and Via Roma. Aside from the usual supermarket staples, it has brick-oven pizzas and freshly made sandwiches to go.

sausages) with a cold mug of beer. Other possibilities include *saltimbocca alla romana* (veal and prosciutto), and the tourist's favorite, pizza Regina (with ham and mushrooms).

For an intimate dinner, call to reserve one of the three garden tables at the tiny **Ristorante Pescatore** *(Vicolo del Poncivo 1; Tel 032/33-19-86; Noon-3pm/6-11pm;15-18,000L entrees; V, MC, AE)*. The menu includes Galician influences from Spain, as well as Lago Maggiore specialties like *filetto di pesce persico alle erbe aromatiche* (lake perch fillet pickled in herbs). Ask your attentive waiter to recommend one of the local white wines, such as *Colline Novarsi*. For dessert, try *torta di carote*—it may not look as exotic as it sounds, but carrot cake's delicious in any language. Add a shot of *grappa* with that *caffè* and you're a real Italian.

crashing

It's almost impossible to find a place to stay in Stresa from May to September without calling ahead to make a reservation. It's even more of a feat to find someplace cheap (what'd you expect—this is the playground of the stars, 17th-century and otherwise). If you're down and out, you can always ask for a detailed listing of all the campsites up and down the lake at the tourist office [see *need to know*, below]. And there's always the train back to Milan....

The rooms at **Orsola Meuble** *(Via Duchessa di Genova 45; Tel 032/33-10-87; 50,000L singles, 60,000L w/bath, 80,000L doubles, 100,000L w/bath; V, MC, AE)* are clean and simple, but nothing to write home about. So why's it so hard to book a reservation? Location, location, location—this place is just a couple blocks from the water in the center of town. From the train station, hang a right and head down F.lli Omarini until you come to the intersection at the bottom.

It's more difficult to get a room at **Chez Osvaldo** *(Via A.M. Bolongaro 57; Tel 032/33-19-48; 50,000L singles, 75,000L doubles; Private baths in doubles; V, MC, AE)*, which is even closer to the center of town. Hemingway would have liked any of its nine rooms—each is a clean, well-lit space. The restaurant downstairs serves breakfast for 5,000L.

The frugal but respectable **Hotel Artison** (*Corso Italia 60; Tel 032/33-11-95; 75,000L singles, 130,000L doubles; Private baths; Breakfast included; V, MC, AE*) offers the best value in Stresa, as well as much-sought-after rooms with a view. On warm summer nights, you can eat dinner on the terrace [see *eats*, above] and bask in the subtle breezes off the lake. There's a 1am curfew, but you can ask for a key if you're going to be out all night.

need to know

Currency Exchange The best exchange rates in town are in a little store called **Borroni Travel** (*Piazza Marconi; Tel 032/33-02-51; 9am-8pm daily, Apr-Oct*), on the north side of the piazza. Look for the big yellow letters that say "CHANGE." They also offer limousine and taxi service.

Tourist Information Signs on almost every corner direct you to the tourist offices. There's the **main tourist office** (*Via Canonica 8; Tel 032/33-13-08; 10am-noon/3-6:30pm daily*), north of Palzzo dei Congressi, which offers information on musical events as well as the trail guide, *Trekking Lago Maggiore*. The **regional tourist office** (*Via Principe Tomaso 70/72; Tel 032/33-04-16; 8:30am-12:30pm/3-6pm Mon-Sat*) is on the right at the lake-side end of Via Principe Tomaso. It offers info on activities and cultural sights around the lake. Don't bother asking—neither office can help you find a room.

Public Transportation You can cover Stresa on foot in about 30 minutes. For the most part, the town relies on the ferries running out to the islands and other lake towns. The **public ferry** leaves the dock about every half-hour; the cost is 2,000L. Smaller, private boats also run from the docks; they run 50-90,000L, depending upon how well you can bargain in Italian. Local buses leaving from Piazza Marconi

festivals and events

July 20-29, Stresa hosts its annual **Jazz Fest** (*Tel 032/304-16*). The smooth grooves get going at 9:30pm down by the water, and last well into the night. All performances are free and open to the public.

From the last week in August till the third week in September, the towns holds **Settimane Musicali** (*Tel 032/33-10-95; www.stresa.net/settimanemusicali; 30-100,000L adults, 10,000L students*). Begun in 1961, this "Festival of Weeks" features some of the world's greatest orchestras and classical musicians, drawing crowds from all over Europe.

run to the smaller towns along the lake, both to the north and south. They leave every hour, 8am-7pm; tickets are 3-10,000L.

Health and Emergency Emergency: *112;* Ambulance: *Tel 032/33-18-44.*

Pharmacies Fill'er up at **farmacia capucci** *(Piazza Capucci; Tel 032/35-01-62; 8:30am-noon/2:30-8pm Mon-Sat).* For pharmaceutical emergencies, a local doctor, **Dottore Polisseni** *(Tel 032/393-38-33)* is on call 24 hours.

Trains Trains *(Tel 032/393-38-33)* run from Milan to Stresa (22,000L) and continue north to Domodossola. Trains pass through Stresa pretty much every hour during the summer; in winter, they're less frequent. The **train station** in town is on Via Principe di Piemonte. The **Lago Maggiore Express** *(Tel 800/55-18-01)* is a private train that runs from Stresa to Domodossola (41,000L) and than on to Locarno, Switzerland (49,000L), winding through old mountain towns and offering incredible views of the lake. The return trip is by old-school ferry.

Bus Lines Out of the City Buses for Milan and other cities leave from Piazza Marconi, on the waterfront. The trip to Milan costs 30,000L.

Boats **Navigazione Lago Maggiore** *(Tel 032/223-32-00; 7am-7pm daily)* runs ferries to the islands and just about all the lake towns, including Pallanza, Baveno, and Locarno. Detailed timetables are distributed at the dock and the tourist office [see above]; one-way tickets to Locarno are 35,000L. Ferries leave from Piazza Marconi, where you can also hire private boats to take you to the islands or other towns.

Bike/Moped Rental Most of the outdoor outfitters in town offer bike rentals [see *city sports,* above]. **Affito, al Lido** *(Piazzle Lido 8; Tel 032/33-03-99; 10,000L per half-day, credit card deposit required; MC, V, AE),* located at the base of the cable car, can also hook you up with a set of wheels.

Postal The **main post office** *(Via A. Bolongaro 44; Tel 032/33-00-65; 8:15am-6:30pm Mon-Fri, 8:15-11:40am Sat)* is just off Piazza Rossi.

borromean islands

Lago Maggiore comes with Fantasy Islands all its own. Once the playground of the all-powerful (and now dead and gone) Borromeo family, **Isola Bella, Isola Madre,** and **Isola dei Pescatori** were filled with exquisite villas and lavish gardens—those Borromeos knew how to live in style.

Could it be named anything else? The *bella bella* Isola Bella is home to the stunning **Palazzo e Giardini Borromeo** *(Tel 032/330-556; 9am-noon/1:30-5:30pm daily, Mar 27-Oct 24; 15,000L admission; No credit cards).* The original design of the garden called for it to be built like a ship in honor of everyone's favorite noble family, but instead it came out looking like a triple-decker birthday cake. White peacocks wander the botanical labyrinths wrapping around the palace, which are dotted with glistening pools and fountains, orange and pomegranate trees, and harmonious flower arrangements of orchids and jasmine. The Baroque palace, built in 1607 by Count Borromeo himself, showcases ornate architecture as amazing as the views of the lake and the towering Alps that surround it. Guided tours offer background on the grotto rooms, which were built piece-by-piece like mosaics, and the ghastly tapestries that look like something from Hannibal Lechter's rumpus room.

A couple of ripples north is the largest of the islands, Isola Madre, where Chinese pheasant hens and white peacocks run wild (refugees from Isola Bella, maybe?) The terraced gardens in the **Orto Botanico** *(Tel 032/331-261; 9am-noon/1:30-5:30pm; 15,000L admission; No credit cards)* boast some of the tallest and oldest palm trees in all of Italy, as well as such rarities as a cypress tree imported from the Himalayas. The 17th-century palace on the grounds can't match the splendor of Isola Bella, but it does have Countess Borromeo's collection of 19th-century French and German dolls, and a 19th-century marionette theater complete with light, sound, and other special effects that would have Kermit and the other muppets green with envy.

Isola dei Pescatori doesn't have any flashy palaces or manicured gardens, but it's a worthy place to throw down the beach towel and soak up some rays. The old cottages that dot the island, still inhabited by fishermen and their families, are slowly giving rise to souvenir shops and other tourist "necessities."

need to know

Directions and Transportation The islands are easily reached by **public ferry** from Stresa's Piazza Marconi. Boats leave the dock about every half-hour; the trip out takes about three hours. Tickets are available at **Navigazione Lago Maggiore** *(Tel 032/223-32-00; 7am-7pm daily)*. It's 2,000L each way, but the excursion fare of 18,000L is a better deal—it allows you to go back and forth between all three islands all day. Smaller, private boats also run from the docks. They generally run 50-90,000L, although rates are negotiable.

orta san giulio

Only one hour south of massive Lago Maggiore is the smaller Lago Di Orta. The towns on this forested lake offer little as far as nightlife goes—actually, they offer little as far as *towns* go, although little rustic farms and cottages periodically reveal themselves up and down the 15-kilometer (9.3 miles) shoreline. With great hiking and fishing, it makes for a relaxing day trip from Milan or one of the Lago Maggiore towns, a chance to get even farther away from it all.

The train lets you off at the Orta Miasino stop, where you can connect with almost all of the trails that wind around the lake. It's a little more than a mile west uphill to charming, rustic Orta San Giulio, the main village. The only notable landmark in town is the **Crespi Tower,** which is two blocks inland from the lake's edge, on the main square, **Piazza Ragazzoni.** The primary thoroughfare, **Via Panoramica,** runs east-west from the lake out to the edge of town.

Just off shore is the little island of Isola di San Giulio, with its Romanesque 12th-century **Basilica San Giulio** *(Boats head to Isola di San Guilio from the docks in Orta every 15 minutes or so, roundtrip ticket 5,000L; 9:30am-12:15pm/2-6:45pm Tue-Sat, 8:30-10:45am/2-6:45pm Sun, 2-6:45pm Mon; Free admission).* You didn't actually think you could find a town in Italy without a church, did you? The story of this one goes way back to the 12th-century, when the superstitious townsfolk of Orta banished San Giulio to the island, believing that if they let this stranger build his church in their town, they'd all be damned (go figure). Not to be deterred, the plucky future-saint built the church on the island all by himself. After he died, the villagers came around and decided they liked the poor guy after all. They liked him *so* much, evidently, that not only did they name their town after him, they dressed his skeleton up in some pimpin' duds and enclosed him in a glass case for all eternity. (No lie— you can see it for yourself downstairs). Aside from the basilica, the island offers beautiful views of the lake, and some chill little beaches for sunning. Be warned that some villagers still live out here—don't go ripping it up late at night. The locals have proven themselves a feisty bunch.

But legendary churches aside, the reason to come to this lake is to get outside. One good hike begins on the northwestern edge of town and heads up the eastern shore of the lake, where you'll get some amazing views of the Alps to the north. The trek takes about four hours round trip (depending on how energetic or sober you're feeling), and the terrain's relatively easy, except for a few tricky parts. Be sure to wear sturdy shoes.

More challenging hikes run through the woods parallel to the road that goes north to Lago Maggiore. Detailed trail maps can be found at the tourist office [see *need to know,* below].

A fishing store called **Il Pescatore Fresca** in Orta San Giulio's center, one block east of Piazza Ragazzoni will rent you poles and basic tackle for 20,000L for the day; no deposit is required. You can fish just about anywhere on the lake, but the further from the boat activity in Orta San Giulio, the better. Ask the old guys at the store for their advice—hope you've brushed up on your Italian.

eats

One of the more popular and festive places to grab a bite is **Pizzeria La Campana** *(Via Giovanetti 41; Tel 032/290-211; 11am-9pm, closed Tues; 9-12,000L pizzas; No credit cards).* As you wait the full five minutes for your piping hot pizza, suck down a mug of frosty beer and grab a handful of fresh marinated olives. Upstairs from the pizzeria is the more sedate **Taverna Antico Agnello** *(Via Olina 40/r; Tel 032/290-56-56; Noon-*

3pm/5:30-11pm Tue-Sun; 18-27,000L entrees; V, MC), which has a lot going for it: high wooden ceilings, folky Italian music, and a friendly staff. Go for the daily specials, which are always some sort of fresh fish creation. As the night goes on, some younger folks usually drop in for drinks at the bar.

crashing

There are only a few places to stay in Orta, and all are on the expensive side—you're better off staying in Stresa and making it a day trip down here. Otherwise, your best bet is **Piccolo Hotel Olina** *(Via Olina 40, Tel 032/290-56-56; 110,000L singles w/bath, 150,000L doubles w/bath; V, MC, AE)*. The hotel, like the town, is small and charming. With great views of the lake, the rooms hardly need decoration at all, but Mama's proven herself an overachiever with old-school lace curtains and ceramic bedpans.

If you came prepared to rough it, you can enjoy some peace and quiet on the lake's shores at **Camping Orta** *(Via Domodossola 28; Tel 032/290-267; Open Mar 15-Oct 31; 8,000L per person, 14,000L per plot, 17,000L lakeside site; V, MC, AE)*. From Piazza Ragazzoni, follow the main drag Via Panoramica down to the water's edge and look for the campsite's big wooden sign.

need to know

Tourist Information The **tourist office** *(Via Panoramica 2; Tel 032/290-56-14; 9:30am-1pm/2:30-7pm daily, Mar 1-Nov 1)* is across the street from the Crespi Tower in Orta San Giulia's center. They can provide you with detailed hiking maps around both Lago di Orta and Lago Maggiore, as well as information on nearby campsites, but can't help you out with hotels.

Directions and Transportation Orta lies on the **Domodossola-Novara trainline,** which connects to Milan and passes along the western shore of Lago Maggiore (4,200L). Tickets for Orta can be bought on board the train from the conductor, or from the tickets offices in any of the major towns on Lago Maggiore. You can also catch a bus to Orta from Stresa (5,500L).

genoa &
the italian
riviera

So, you've been burning it at both ends for awhile, and you've taken in more than you can possibly process. It's time for a little vacation from your way-too-active vacation. Liguria, essentially the Italian version of the Riviera, is the place to head. It's all about simple pleasures: kicking back, leisurely dividing your time between sunning, hiking, tasting the local wines, and marveling at awesome beach and mountain views. It's all about relaxing. A typical day might be dragging yourself out of bed for a frothy cappuccino, heading to the beach or a rock in the sun to work on the tan, hiking some portion of the spectacular trails that run through this area, tasting some of the local wine at a laid-back *enoteca* (wine bar), then maybe—if you've got the energy—getting down at a beachfront disco. The international social scene—on and off the beach—makes for a hoppin' time from May to September, when the party rages all along the Ligurian coast. There's a mixed crowd of travelers here: hard-core backpackers in for a day and zooming out at night, lazy beach bums crashing for a week, wine connoisseurs tingling their palates, and honeymooners fresh from the altar. (But beware: the closer you get to France, the older and more Griswold-*Vacation* the scene gets.)

Backpackers and other tourists swarm the beautiful coastal villages of **Cinque Terra, La Spezia,** and **Finale Ligure** in search of "authentic Italy," but as is typically the irony in places like this, it's their own damn fault that they won't find it. As the tourists have descended, locals have wasted no time turning their small villages into a maze of hotels, restaurants, and shops—the mom-and-pop fishing and olive industries have given way to tourism, and most of the towns have lost their simple Italian charm. Yes, Ligurians welcome tourists. They have to. Tourism is now the region's largest—and sometimes only—source of income. But the novelty of visitors from all over the world seems to be wearing off.

The region's biggest claim to historical fame is Christopher Columbus—or so they say. Several towns and cities (not just in Italy) claim Senore Columbus as their native son, but most historians (not just in Italy) argue that **Genoa** was indeed his birthplace. Today, Genoa is still a buzzing port, a scrappy industrial city, and an increasingly cosmopolitan urban center that's worth at least a day of your time even if you don't think Columbus is quite as cool as your elementary school textbooks made him out to be.

genoa & the Italian riviera

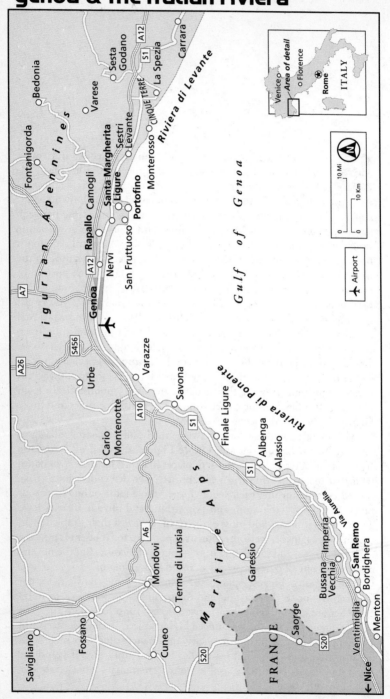

You should use La Spezia as your transportation hub for trips up the eastern section of Liguria—it's a nice little port town, but really, better things await you up the coast. It's the starting point not only for the local trains, but also for a number of Ligurian hiking trials. Finale Ligure, over on the western end of the coast, is where to head if your idea of relaxation includes packed bars and discos. Educated rock-jocks should recognize the name of this town—it serves up some of the best climbing spots in all of Italy.

Cinque Terra is a collection of five tiny fishing villages: **Monterosso, Vernazza, Corniglia, Manarola,** and **Riomaggiore.** Multicolored buildings like washed-out children's blocks manage to snuggle improbably into the steep, rocky cliffs, giving the towns a storybook look. The beaches are a big draw, of course, but don't expect calm little waves lapping at a smooth, sandy shore—it's rocky here, and jumping off the rocks will put you in deep water that can be dangerous if seas are rough. The ideal amount of time in Cinque is probably two to three nights—just enough time to recharge with a calming break from the travel frenzy, and not enough time to get bored.

But no matter how tempting it may be, you can't come to this beautiful region and only check out the notorious beach scene—you've got to shake the sand out of your clothes and spend at least a little time on solid ground. The towns of Liguria are full of angelic churches and grandiose palazzos that can compete with the grandiosity and antiquity of the big boys down in Tuscany and Umbria.

getting around the region

Getting around Liguria is a piece of cake. The train and bus companies haven't failed to notice the amazing amounts of visitors this area gets every summer, and they have planned their routes to keep up with the hoards.

Trains are, as usual, your best bet. Dozens of trains coming and going from France pass through every day. It's easiest to make **Genoa** your first stop, as trains to just about everywhere else in the region branch out from there. Warning: When you get out to the coast, it can be tricky finding which trains are local and which are intercity—it's best to ask at the station to make sure. You'll need to get on local trains to get to the smaller villages. The trains to reach **Finale Ligure** and points further west are sometimes infrequent and indirect. Your best bet if coming from the north is to take the intercity from France headed to Genoa, which makes stops along the coast and will put you smack dab in the middle of the action. Coming from the east, head for either **Pisa, La Spezia,** or Genoa and transfer to local trains from there.

The ticket to moving through—or to—**Cinque Terra** is the "milk run" train (it doesn't actually carry the moo juice anymore) that runs constantly from 5am till 1am. The name is a lot cuter than the train itself, which is a slow, double-decker deal. Jump on the milk run in Genoa if you're coming from northern parts, or in La Spezia from the south. Schedules are posted at the station and at many local businesses—just make sure that the train you're taking stops in all five villages. Tickets are cheap, 1,800L, so there's no point in wasting a punch on the Eurail Pass. Train stations in **Vernazza, Corniglia,** and **Manarola** are hardly ever staffed, so buy your ticket at the nearest newsstand or tobacco shop. It's rare that you'll even see a conductor on the trains, so tickets are essentially on the honor system. There is boat service between the towns, but it's probably not worth the price, unless you're just dying to get on a non-descript yacht-like boat. One-way fares are from 8,000L to 15,000L, and the boats only run from 10am to 5pm. Schedules can be picked up at the harbor of each town.

If you're heading south after your stay in Liguria, take note: There are no direct trains to **Florence** once you pass Genoa headed south or east. You have to stop and change trains in Pisa or La Spezia—preferably Pisa, where the trains are quicker and more frequent.

TRAVEL TIMES

(Cinque Terre includes five towns w/in five-mile radius—travel times here are to Monterosso)	La Spezia	Genoa	Finale Ligure	Cinque Terre
La Spezia	-	1:30	2:30	:30
Genoa	1:30	-	1:00	1:30
Finale Ligure	2:30	1:00	-	3:00

genoa

From a distance, Genoa looks like nothing but one big, ugly jumble of skyscrapers and ocean liners—and it sort of is, at least on the surface. It's got a rep as sort of a sleazy, gritty port town, and Italians from other cities will swear that it's a scrappy, dangerous city. (Kind of like out-of-towners who think New York is a cesspool full of whores and pickpockets.) Don't pay too much attention to them. Look closer and you'll find colorful mansions, medieval castles, and massive, vivacious piazzas hidden away within the cityscape. From the moment you leave the train station and head down Via XX Settembre, Genoa's main avenue, you'll see that this humming port city has potential. Cafes, bars, expansive parks and gardens, and chic little eateries line just about every main avenue in the city center—there's even a small university here. And the *Porto Antico* (the old port) is kind of like downtown Seattle: There are shopping malls, movie theaters, and a panoramic lift that raises you above the city for a killer view—surrounded by mountains on three sides and facing the sea, Genoa's got some of the best views around. But hang on before you take that comparison too far—Genoa is decidedly *not* Seattle, so don't hold your breath waiting for the hip young crowd to appear or the nightlife to rock. But do take in the daytime stuff—there's enough charm to last till around midnight.

Genoa has been an important port since the days of Christopher Columbus. Old Chris is still a major local hero, even though he practically ruined the local economy by blazing a trail to the New World and shifting the balance of trade over to the new ports in the Atlantic. But nobody here seems to care much about that. He's Christopher Columbus.

genoa bars clubs and culture zoo

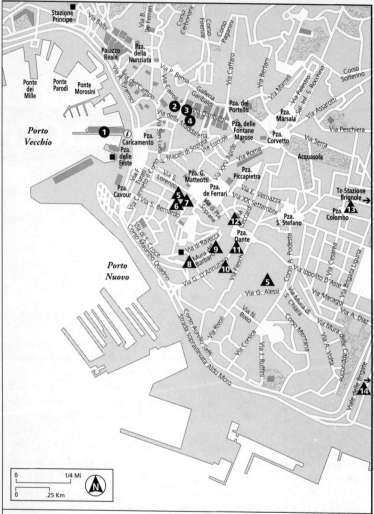

BARS/CLUBS ▲
Barbarossa **9**
Borderline **12**
Café Degli Specci **6**
Hot Wires **7**
Koala Pub **11**
La Mura Café **8**
Le Café des Artistes **13**
Le Corbusier **5**
Mako **10**
Vanilla **14**

CULTURE ZOO ●
Acquaria di Genoa **1**
Galleria di Palazzo Bianco **3**
Galleria di Palazzo Rosso **4**
Galleria Nazionale
 di Palazzo Spinola **2**

He da man. In fact, Italians all over the world seem to think of Columbus as some sort of relative who made it big and therefore is not to be blamed for whatever grief he left in his wake. So keep negative opinions and pesky little historical facts to yourself—especially in his hometown. Nobody's remotely interested in being reminded that Columbus was relieved of his maritime duties and sent back to Europe because of the numerous atrocities he committed on the job. Fuhgeddaboutit.

12 hours in genoa

1. **Be a kid.** If the baby seals and penguins in Europe's largest aquarium, **Acquario di Genova,** don't make you feel like a young pup, then grow up and get serious with the 3-D underwater show [see *culture zoo,* below].

2. **Get high.** Take a ride up the panoramic thingamabob in the middle of the port to get the a gull's eye view of the city and the massive ships docking in the harbor [see *only here,* below].

3. **Mansion hop.** The Genovese built some larger than life shacks in their heyday—take a stroll down Via Garibaldi and take them in [see *culture zoo,* below].

4. **Get down (under).** Practice your boomerang tosses with a pint of Aussie beer at **Koala Pub** [see *bar scene,* below].

5. **Rev-up the Ferrari.** Piazza de Ferrari is one of the biggest and baddest squares you'll come across in northern Italy, and that's really saying something.

6. **Faniculi, Fanicula.** Take a ride on the cable car that heads off into the hills that surround the city [see *need to know,* below]

7. **Culturize.** With a little something for everyone, **Galleria Nazionale di Palazzo Spinola** is Genoa's premier art museum [see *culture zoo,* below].

8. **Coffee, tea, or beer?** **Barbarossa** has tea and beer for all occasions, as well as sandwiches hot off the grill [see *bar scene,* below].

9. **Get Lost!** Put away your compass and check out all the old market shops in Genoa's oldest part of town, around Via San Bernardo [see *to market,* below].

10. **Ship off.** Throw some confetti to the thousands of tourists coming in and out of the port on cruiseliners that look like cities on the sea.

festivals and events

Regata *(April 20-23)* is Genoa's Tall Ship Expo, when hundreds of antique cruisers come into port. Contact the local tourist office [see *need to know,* below] for more information.

neighborhoods

Trains arrive at **Stazione Principe,** in the northwestern part of town; it's at least a half-hour walk from here to the city center, through a neighborhood you don't want to be in after dark (or ever, if you can avoid it). It's easier and safer to catch a local train directly to **Stazione Brignole** in the old city center (they leave every 5 minutes), or to catch one of the 10 buses that goes from Principe to **Piazza de Ferrari,** Genoa's largest square, which sits to the east of the old city center, halfway to the port.

Stazione Brignole is in the northeast corner of the old section of town. When you exit the main doors of the station you'll step right into **Piazza G. Verdi.** Heading south down **Via Fiume,** bordering the piazza on your right-hand side, will bring you to the biggest street in town, **Via XX Settembre.** Lit up with more neon than *Miami Vice,* this massive boulevard runs east-west through the center of town and can be covered on foot in about 10 minutes. Heading west on Via XX Settembre will take you through Piazza de Ferrari. This place—and the newly renovated mansions that surround it—has been undergoing major construction for quite some time, according to the locals, and completion isn't expected any time soon. From Piazza Ferrari, you can get down to **Porto Antico** (the old port) by walking further west on **Via San Lorenzo,** (which is also under perpetual construction). You don't have to be in town very long to discover that the city functions around Porto Antico, which forms a new moon-like curve along the rounded edge of the **Gulf of Genoa.** It's where the city began, and it's where you'll find the most cultural treats like the aquarium and dozens of old sailing vessels—and, of course, the mall. You really can't say you've been to Genoa unless you've taken a walk along the port.

For nightlife—what there is of it—stick to the old section of town between Stazione Brignole and the port. Day or night, it's teeming with shoppers, business people, and small markets selling everything from produce to beat-up used books. Just about all the clubs, bars, and cafes worth checking out are here and around Piazza de Ferrari and the smaller streets to its west. As you get closer to the water, you'll notice that the streets start to shrink in size: Large thoroughfares like Via XX Settembre give way to the city's original narrow side streets like **Via San Bernardo** and **Via Sottoipa.** Here you can wander aimlessly, at least during the day, and see some of the oldest mom-and-pop shops in the city.

   With over 800,000 residents, Genoa is a traffic-worn city. From the crack of dawn until sunset, the streets are packed with commuters and buses. The most efficient way to get around the old city is on foot—you'll see a lot more without wasting your time trying to figure out the complicated bus system. The main public bus terminals are in front of both the major train stations, but figuring out where they go requires a bit of asking around. If you do get on a bus, be sure to ask one of the locals to let you know when you reach your destination. There's a metro line you can pick up at Stazione Principale, but it only heads away from the city center out into the suburbs, not toward port where you want to be.

hanging out

During the day the city literally hums with activity. All the suit-and-tie types clutching their briefcases as they stampede toward the skyscrapers surrounding Piazza Dante will remind you how sweet vacation is. If you want to sit back and take in Genoa's industrial buzz, pull up a seat at one of the 50 or so sidewalk cafes along **Via XX Settembre. Porto Antico** is a more laid-back daytime scene. The massive mall complex, constructed on the waterfront for the World Expo in 1992, will open your eyes to how westernized Italy is becoming. Looking toward the west, you can watch the cruise lines shipping off hordes of Italians toward the Greek Islands and points east. The small student population congregates up on the hill south of Piazza de Ferrari toward **Mura del Barbarossa**—look for the old castle entranceway called Porta Saprana and start climbing.

bar scene

A big city? Yes. A big bar scene? No. Like any Italian city, Genoa has what they *call* bars, but are in reality little cafes where old men fuel up on espresso or maybe a shot of grappa—the real bar scene is kind of lacking. The daytime city is occupied by a working crowd that comes in, goes to work, and then gets the hell out of Dodge. Happy hours are nonexistent, and the place looks like a ghost town after midnight.

down and out

For about 5,000L you can take a ride up the **Funic-ulare Zecca Righi.** This cable car connects the city with its high-elevation residents, and offers some great views of the sea and city. To find it, take bus 34 from either train station to Piazza Largo Zecca.

fIVE-0

Genoa's rep as a scrappy city isn't reflected by its police force. The non-threatening cops swarm the new mall constructed down by the old port; the city's invested a lot of money here and will be damned if out-of-work immigrants will screw it up. Unfortunately, you won't see any cops on the waterfront at night, creating a sort of "Where are they when you need 'em?" attitude among tourists and locals alike.

The streets around Via Calata, just west of Stazione Brignole, are roped off from car traffic during the evening hours. Because most of the cheaper places to crash are right around here, it's overrun with the back-packing crowd. Kick your night off with a glass of vino in this area at **Le Café des Artistes** *(Viale Sauli 1; No phone; 2pm-1am daily; No credit cards)*. The name of the bar doesn't really have much to do with the crowd that hangs here, but it's a chill spot if you can grab a seat outside. There are usually street performers just across the way, spitting balls of fire and trying to juggle devil sticks to the rhythms of heavy, heavy German grunge. A pint of beer will only set you back 5,000L and on weekday nights you can get devastating pitchers of margaritas that make the rainbow-colored walls inside look a lot more colorful.

The old section of town near Piazza delle Erbe is your best shot for doing a shot. Work your way through the tiny winding streets, but leave a trail of bread crumbs because getting in is a lot easier than getting out. Along the little street Via Strada San Agostino, you have your choice of mellow lounges and rough riding, whiskey-chugging watering holes. Earlier on in the evening all the bars are a bit dull, but as the night goes on and the smoke builds, things usually pick up. Lit up like a jack-o-lantern, **Hot Wires** *(Sal. Pollaioli 24/Via San Donato; Tel 010/589-355; 5pm-2am daily; No credit cards),* 2 blocks south of Piazza Matteotti, offers up some of Genoa's hippest bohemians. The walls are tiled in a Sunkist shade that complements the intense local oil pastels on the walls, donated by the starving artist community-at-large. Sipping one of the exotic cocktail specials (10,000L) while slumping back into the orange polyester couches is almost guaranteed to make you feel a little more cool, and the women working the bar provide some incentive for guys to practice a little loose-lipped Italian. The DJ positioned way in the back has a mind-blowing collection of Bob Marley vinyls that completes the free and easy atmosphere.

Just up the street from Hot Wires, heading west, you'll find **Le Corbusier** *(Via San Donato 38; Tel 010/246-86-52; 10am-2am Mon-Fri, 6pm-2am Sat-Sun; V, MC)*—look for the bar with the black and white photos of beautiful nude women. Don't get too alarmed (or excited, whichever the case may be) by the pics on the wall, this place is actually pretty reserved. The older, better-dressed crowd puffs on cigarettes and sucks down martinis (12,000L) on one side of the bar; the other side is for sitting down and having a less grown-up drink and maybe a bite to eat.

Along the same strip is **Café Degli Specchi** *(Via Pollaili 43; Tel 010/556-23-22; 11am-2am daily; V, MC)*. Don't be intimidated by the pseudo fogged-up windows; it's all a ploy to scare off the less than hip. Specchi, as the regulars call it, is a trendy little hangout, a bit like a New York City lounge. Drinks are a bit pricey (10,000L-12,000L), and the bartenders can give some serious attitude if you ask for something too pedestrian like a jack and coke or a vodka tonic, so throw them a curveball and order something snazzy. After 10pm the upper-class professionals head out and the place is filled up by a younger, student crowd.

If you're looking for a more international scene, walk up the hill from Piazza Dante toward Porto Soprana onto Mura del Barbarossa, a street shadowed by fragments of the old wall that once surrounded the city. Keep your eyes open for the life-sized statue of Elvis—once you've spotted The King, you've found **Barbarossa** *(Via del Barbarossa 21; Tel 010/298-21-82; Noon-1am daily; V, MC, AE)*, the liveliest student bar in town. Fuel up on the edible goodies displayed in the glass window behind the bar [see *eats,* below] and then dive into the extensive menu of exotic elixirs, which features spiked tropical smoothies and international teas, as well as plain old beer and coffee. Your best bet is to take a seat upstairs and order from the waitress; things get a bit chaotic downstairs. Despite Elvis's presence outside, this old Italian brick building funks to the sounds of Otis Redding.

If you'd prefer a little more open space, try **La Mura Café** *(Via del Barbarossa 27; No phone; 11am-1am Tue-Sun; No credit cards)*, just one block west of Barbarossa. On a sunny day, you can pull up a chair outside and catch a view of the mountains surrounding the city or the port down below. Staple beers on tap are 8,000L, and mixed drinks will run you about 10,000L. There's typically a service charge for sitting outside; ask how much it is before you decide to order. The crowd's a bit older-touristy, with the occasional backpacker mixed in.

Feeling a bit *down under* the weather? **Koala Pub** *(Piazza Palmetta; Tel 010/469553; 11am-2am daily; V, MC)* has the cure. This haven for Aussie expats and wannabes, 1 block south of Piazza Dante, is decked out like a kangaroo on Christmas, with boomerangs hanging from every spare inch of wall space. The bar is proud of its Castlemaine XXXX Lager, and serves some damn good fries and little pizzas (8,000L-15,000L) as well. You might even run into a couple of real Australian backpackers while you're here.

LIVE MUSIC SCENE

There's not much to Genoa's live music scene, but you can try **Vanilla** *(Via B. Salerno 4r; No phone; Bus 12, 22 from Stazione Brignole; 8pm-2am, Tue-Sun; No cover; No credit cards)*, a club that alternates between DJ music and live performances. The headliner's usually unannounced unless there's a big band playing. It's more of a disco than live music set-up, and the bands that do play are pretty much local Italian rock bands, with more of a reggae-type scene floating in for the summer. The crowd tends to reflect the band, and DJ nights draw teeny-boppers and those who love them.

You might also get lucky at **Borderline** [see *club scene,* below] or, for acts you might have actually heard of before, the **Teatro Carlo Felice** [see *arts scene,* below].

club scene

Clubbing is not Genoa's favorite pastime. But a couple of decent clubs have surfaced over the past 10 years or so, as there's been more demand for them. Most of the bigger clubs are way outside the city—figuring out how to get there and back could give you a hangover before you even take a drink. During the summer months, some of the open-air cafes down by the port hire DJs on the weekends to draw in the warm weather tourists.

In the center of the city near Piazza de Ferrari is **Borderline** *(Via Cercardi 24, between Via XX Settembre and Piazza Dante; Tel 010/880-069; 8pm-4am Thur-Tue; Sat drinks 5,000L, other days 8,000L; No cover; No credit cards),* a multi-themed club with plenty of room to dance and breathe. Housed in the basement of one of the larger banks in Genoa, the club has three different lounges with squishy couches, three bars, and two dance floors. A trippy alien motif complements the deep black walls and barrage of strobe and disco lights. During the week there's a younger crowd until after midnight, when all the stragglers from the bars come in to dance off their booze-inflated bellies. Eurodisco is the primary focus, but the music changes as often as the DJs. Friday retro nights draw older, better-dressed crowds, while on Saturday the records are put away in favor of live funk and indie music. If even the Baccardi Limon drink specials (5,000L) can't get you out on the dance floor, go stand in the corner and look mysterious.

rules of the game

Don't be misled by the hash pushers down by Salita Pollaivoli—hash and any other drugs are not tolerated or taken lightly by the Genovese public-at-large. People sell everything from drugs to their bodies down by the port and in the older part of the town. Don't mess with 'em. A lot of these people have nothing better to do than follow you down one of the side streets to take your valuables by force. Watch yourself, and don't walk alone, especially down by the water at night.

four things to talk to a local about

1. **Genoa, and why no one comes here.** The Genovese are pretty pissed that the rest of Italy, if not all of Europe, gives it such a bad rap as a tourist city.
2. **Construction.** The center of Genoa is constantly under construction, so like the weather, it comes up often in conversation.
3. **Christopher Columbus.** There are a lot of places that try to claim Mr. Columbus' fame, but Genoa will be argued as his rightful birthplace till the sun goes down.
4. **Soccer.** Hey, they've got a team—but really, who needs a reason to talk to an Italian about soccer?

Another club to check out is the slightly smaller **Mako** *(Corso Italia 28; Tel 010/505-936; 9pm-3am Tue-Sun; Drinks 8,000L; No cover; No credit cards)*, located 2 blocks south of Piazza Dante. Mako is pure Eurotrash, but that's the whole idea, right? The crowd is all international twentysomethings, so it's a great place to get your flirtation groove on— if you can manage to hold a conversation over the blasting disco.

arts scene

There's no gallery scene to speak of here, but you'll do alright if you're looking for ballet, operas, and straight-up theater. We wouldn't call the scene here avant-garde, but there's a fair representation of the alternative, eclectic, and underground.

▶▶PERFORMING ARTS

After some major destruction during WWII, Genoa's opera house, **Teatro Carlo Felice** *(Piazza de Ferrari; Tel 010/589-329; 10am-1pm/3:30-7pm Mon-Fri, 2 hours before shows; 20,000-200,000L for tickets; V, MC, AE)*, sagged until its full-blown renovation in 1991. They wasted no time in lining up acts for both young and old—frequent performances range between jazz, classical, and alternative music. Even if you don't go to a show, you should check out Felice's neoclassical facade when you pass through Piazza de Ferrari.

Theater companies from around the world can be seen at **Teatro della Tosse** *(Piazza Renato Negri 4; Tel 010/247-07-93; 9:30am-2pm Mon-Sat; Ticket prices vary; No credit cards)* throughout the summer months. They tend to book more experimental theater during the off season. Performances are in Italian (what'd you expect?). A monthly listing of shows can be obtained at the tourist office [see *need to know,* below]. Il Tosse, as the Genovese thespians call it, is located 5 blocks south of Piazza Matteotti.

gay scene

Genoa's gay scene is still somewhat unpublicized. **ArciGay** *(Viale Salita Salvator 15r; Tel 010/545-02-24; 10am-2:15pm/5-8pm daily)* offers information for gay events throughout the city. The office is right next to the Arches that lead to Piazza Dante, up the hill from Piazza dei Ferrari.

The festive spirits and stiff drinks at **La Cage** *(Via Sampierdarena 167r; Tel 010/645-45-55; 9pm-3am Tue-Sat; No cover; No credit cards)* make it a great place to kick off an evening. It's generally packed with a twenty- to fifty-something male crowd who chat up the bartender at the small bar or lounge on the comfortable couches. They're not unfriendly to breeders, they may just be surprised to see you there.

culture zoo

Following a major cultural depression that lasted for several decades after World War II, Genoa chose to commemorate the 1992 quincentennial of Columbus' voyage in a big way, by hosting the World Expo. In no time, the city's rundown mansions and antiquated port were transformed into modern-day treasures. Today, with over 20 museums, Europe's largest aquarium, and exquisite 500-year-old villas, Genoa is a more than just a great place to kill time on a rainy day. The Genovese mansions grouped together along Via Garibaldi, known as "museum row," are worth at least a walk-by. Most of these gems are due to the patronage of Genovese families like Giustiani, Doria, and Grimaldi, who built and commissioned some of the most grandiose homes in the region. From Piazza de Ferrari, head due north on Via XX Aprile, which will bring you to the west side of Piazza delle Fontane Marose—Via Garibaldi stretches west toward the port from here.

Galleria Nazionale di Palazzo Spinola *(Piazza Superiore di Pelicceria 1; Tel 010/247-70-61; 9am-8pm Tue-Sat, 1-8pm Sun and*

only here

If you're down at the old port and have 5,000L to blow, take a ride up to the top of the panoramic **Il Brigo** tower *(Porto Antico; 11am-1pm/3-6pm Tue-Sat, 11am-1pm/2:30-6:30pm Sun, Mar-Aug; 11am-1pm/2:30-4:30pm Tue-Fri, 11am-1pm/2:30-5pm Sun, Sep-Feb; 5,000L; No credit cards),* built in 1992 for Columbus' quincentennial. This lift goes straight up 500 feet, offering a great photo op of Genoa on high, or a momentary head-rush if you're already high on too much vino.

holidays; 8,000L admission, 4,000L 18-25; No credit cards): This mansion, built for the Grimaldi family in the 16th century, now boasts the largest collections of Flemish and Italian art in the city, including Van Dyck's elaborate paintings of the four evangelists. From the aquarium, head due east across Piazza Del Caricamento; the museum is 1 block east of the piazza.

Galleria di Palazzo Bianco *(Via Garibaldi 11; Tel 010/247-63-77; 9am-1pm Tue, Thur, Fri; 9am-7pm Wed, Sat; 10am-6pm Sun; 6,000L admission; No credit cards):* Although it primarily features paintings by 14th- and 17th-century local greats such as Murillo, Strozzi, and Magnasco, this museum's main attractions come from northern artists. Crowds stand slack-jawed in front of Memling's *Jesus Blessing the Faithful,* Van Dyck's *Christ and the Coin,* and Sir Peter Paul Rubens' depiction of *Venus and Mars.* Regardless of your artistic interests, it's worth a look—just about every hall is filled with old statues and relics.

Galleria di Palazzo Rosso *(Via Garibaldi 18; Tel 010/247-63-51; 9am-1pm Tue, Thur, Fri; 9am-7pm Wed, Sat; 10am-6pm Sun; 6,000L admission; No credit cards):* This massive palace must have hosted some raging house parties back in the 17th century. Opened to the public in 1874, it now hosts paintings by Veronese, Reni, Preti, Castiglione, and Rubens. The walls were frescoed by Genoa's own De Ferrari, Guidobono, and Piola.

Acquario di Genova *(Porto Anitco, Ponte Spinola, down by the water; Tel 010/248-12-05; 9am-7pm Mon-Fri, 9:30am-8pm Sat-Sun and holidays; Closed Mon Nov 1-Feb 28; 22,000L; www.acquario.ge.it; MC, V):* But enough about art and palazzos—housed in the ship that never sinks, this aquarium, the largest in Europe, is Genoa's real pride and joy. Even if you're not a fish buff, it's a must see. Just try not to step on any of the hundreds of Italian school kids that run around the place on any given day, gaping at the 50-plus tanks filled with dolphins, sharks, penguins, and seals. Every tank creates its own environment, from the Caribbean Sea with its nurse sharks and parrot fish to the Amazonian rain forest and its chomping piranha. There's also a 3-D show every hour on the hour that's not lame.

great outdoors

Like any well-rounded industrial city, Genoa has its fair share of sanctuaries. One of the best is **L'Orto Botanico** *(Corso Dogali; Tel 010/252820; 9am-4pm daily; Free admission),* whose gardens spread to the north of Piazza de Ferrari along via Roma. A guided tour gives insight into the city's evolution and explains how industrialization has slowly robbed it of its once expansive parks and gardens, but you could also just come and smell the pretty flowers and leave the thinking for another day.

If you really want to get away from it all and see the city from afar, take a 3-hour ride on the **private train** *(Via alla Stazione per Casella 15, bus 33 from Brignole station; Tel 010/839-32-85; 17,000-31,000L each way; fgc@ferroviagenovacasella.it; No credit cards)* that lifts off into the outlying mountains and valleys. The ride begins at the city walls on Piazza Manin and slowly begins its ascent past the ruins of the city's old aqueducts. Shortly, you'll pass by **Cemetary Staglieno** *(Piazzle Resasco; Tel 010/870-184; Buses 12, 13, 14, 34, 48 from Brignole station; 7:30am-5pm daily; Free admission),* which has inspired the likes of Nietzsche, Mark Twain, and Guy de Maupassant. A true city for the dead, the cemetery includes Hebrew, English, and Protestant burial grounds, as well as a chiseled church built almost entirely of marble. The views of the ocean and the city from here are some of the best the mountains offer.

STUff

If you've got money to spend and have the urge to do some shopping, you might consider waiting till you get out of Genoa—it's not really known for great finds.

▶▶DUDS

Well-known Italian stores like **Coin** *(Via XX Settembre 16; Tel 010/335-23-44; 9am-2pm/4:30-9pm daily; V, MC, AE)* and **Berti** *(Via XII Ottobre 4; Tel 010/543126; 9am-2pm/4:30-9pm Mon Sat; V, MC, AE),* the local equivalent of Gap or Urban Outfitters, line the sidewalks along Via XX Settembre.

Two young supermodel-esque women started **Feng Shui** *(Via XX Settembre 233, northeast corner off Piazza Ferrari; 10am-1:30pm/4-10pm Mon Sat; V, MC)* about 5 years ago, and they've been setting styles in Genoa ever since. This is the place for fresh ethno-Italian clothes for boys and girls alike: day-glo shirts and pants run about 80,000L, but the ladies will be more than happy to cut you a deal if you fill up your shopping basket.

If you're looking to spice up the romance in your life, check out **L'ultima Volta che Violi Parigi** *(Via Settembre 139; 10am-1pm/3:30-9:30pm daily; V, MC, AE)* for some of the most lavish lingerie you'll ever lay eyes on. Silk undies run anywhere from 30,000L to 150,000L, but hey, at least they're Italian. It's just 3 blocks east of Piazza de Ferrari.

▶▶BOUND

Two blocks east of Piazza de Ferrari, **Feltrinellis** *(Via XX Settembre 233; 9am-2pm/4-9:30pm Mon-Sat; No credit cards)* stocks a decent selection of English, French, and Spanish books.

▶▶TUNES

Wade through the loads of American, British, and Italian vinyls at **Temptations** *(Via Galata 76; No phone; 10am-2pm/5-10pm Tue-Sat; No credit cards).* The guys that work here speak pretty good English and are more than psyched to give their opinion on what's good and what's not. You can also get flyers for local live concerts and hip-hop parties.

▶▶USED AND BRUISED

There are a couple of student-run secondhand stores up on the hill near Teatro delle Tosse. **Grigio Vecchio** *(Stradone San Agostino 3; 9:30am-3pm Mon-Sat; No credit cards)* is a great place to buy your next retro dance party outfit or add to your Cavaricci jean collection.

▶▶FOOT FETISH

Just about every other store on Via XX Settembre and Via E. Vernazza is a shoe store. **Il Tacco** *(Via E. Vernazza 22; 10am-2:30pm/5-8:30pm Tue-Sat; V, MC, AE)* offers the cutting edge for the Italian foot, with sneakers, boots, high heels, fancy shoes, walking shoes, working shoes...Italians can never get enough to satisfy their shoe obsessions.

EATS

Typical Genovese cuisine revolves around fish, pesto sauce, and salami. Some of the more delectable local treats include *farinata* (fried pancakes made with chick pea flour) and *pansotti* (stuffed ravioli, usually filled with spinach and ricotta served with a creamy walnut sauce). But the best eating isn't in the restaurants at all, but at the open-air markets along Via San Bernardo [see *to market*, below].

▶▶CHEAP

If you're just getting into town and need a quick, quality bite to eat, you have a couple of choices near the train station. **Pizzaria Policino** *(Galleria degli Artigiani 116; 11am-10pm daily; Pizzas 8,000-15,000L; No credit cards)* has three menu's worth of pizzas, including vegetarian, sardine, and fruit-of-the-sea pies. Walking out of Stazione Brignole, go north up Via Amicis; its 2 blocks up on the right. Grab a plastic table in the back or get pizza to go. The fun little **Pizza Point** *(Via Montevideo 11/r; Tel 010/362-05-05; Noon-11pm daily; Pizzas 10,000-15,000L; No credit cards)* offers quick service and a mean pizza pie. It's just two blocks east of Stazione Brignole, and always packed with people coming and going from the trains.

TO MARKET

The greatest culinary treats in Genoa aren't in the restaurants, but in the little authentic *carnerceria* (butcheries) and *mercati* (grocery stores) along **Via San Bernardo.** Everything from hazelnuts roasted beneath a medieval warehouse to candied fruit dipped in chocolate can be found along one of the oldest streets in the city. The area along Sottoripa, 1 block north of the port by the mall, is the closest you're going to get to being in an old time Genovese bazaar, where you can buy shark fins from the Orient (yes, they're illegal here, too), kalamata olives, lentils from Egypt, and ouzo from Greece. It's a pretty chaotic scene in the morning—be sure not to come when you're hungover.

genoa eats and crashings

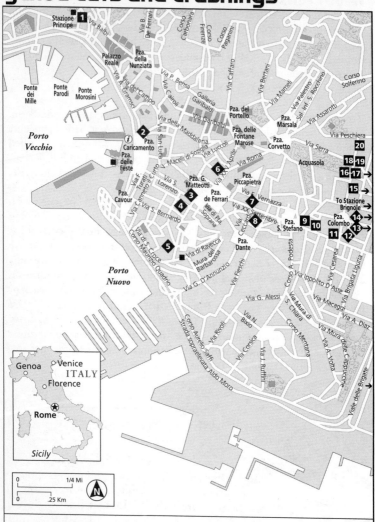

EATS ◆

Caffe degli Specchi **4**
I Tre Merli **2**
La Cantine di Colombo **7**
Le Cantine di Squarifico **3**
Osteria del Teatro **5**
Osteria dell'Antico Campanile **8**
Pizza Point **13**
Pizzeria Policino **14**
Sola **12**
Trattoria da Maria **6**

CRASHING ■

Albergo Argentina **19**
Albergo Astro **9**
Albergo Carola **18**
Albergo della Posta Nuova **16**
Albergo Moderno Verdi **17**
Albergo Parigi **1**
Albergo Rita **20**
Hostel Genova **15**
Pensione Barone **11**
Soana Dip **10**

Barbarossa [see *bar scene,* above] has great salads, panini, nachos, and every other bar food you can think of, all under one roof. The portions are huge and they load you up with bread if you grab a salad.

▶▶**DO-ABLE**

Located between Via XX Settembre and Via Dante, **Osteria dell'Antico Campanile** *(Via Novembre 20; Tel 010/592-541; 11am-4pm/8pm-midnight; Entrees 12,000-15,000L; MC, V)* serves up huge portions for poco dinero. It's a big, noisy place, but it's Italian noisy—the waiters and cooks are pretty much all related and never stop talking to each other. You can get a menu in English if need be, but it's safe to go with any of the Genovese fish specials. Try the *spaghetti vongole* (pasta with clams in red or white sauce) or *torte di verdura* (vegetable medley).

On a little street that branches off Via XXV Aprile to the west, **Trattoria da Maria** *(Vico Testa d'Oro 14; Noon-4pm/6-11pm Tue-Sun; Pasta dishes 8,000-10,000L; No credit cards)* serves up thick pasta dishes like *linguine alla Genovese* (linguine with pesto sauce) accompanied by good house wine. The service gets a little slow around dinnertime, when the place is usually packed with friends and families.

La Cantina di Colombo *(Via XX Settembre 57; Tel 010/399-34-98; 11am-4pm/7-11pm Tue-Sun; Entrees 15,000L; MC, V),* located 2 blocks east of Piazza de Ferrari, specializes in traditional Genovese grub, primarily seafood. The dining room complements the home cooking, with its worn oak tables, dusty wine racks, and family pictures on the walls. For a little of everything, try *la zuppa di pesce.* Despite the dozens of sea creatures featured in this soup, it doesn't taste overly fishy—it's spicy, and comes with loads of thick, whole-grain breads.

During lunch, **Caffe Degli Specchi** *(Via Fieschi 12; 8:30am-10pm daily; Entrees 10,000-22,000L; No credit cards)* is always packed with locals devouring hearty sandwiches and pizzas. But what's really special in this cool little sit-down cafe are the pastries, all made in the bakery across the street—it's well worth an early rise in the morning to get them hot from the oven. You'll find this place 2 blocks south of Piazza Dante.

Le Cantine di Squarifico *(Via Invrea 3r; Tel 010/247-08-23; 5pm-midnight; Entrees 15,000L; MC, V)* is an intimate little restaurant tucked away on a side street 1 block west of Piazza de Ferrari. The ever-changing menu has a little bit of everything. Pasta dishes like *pansotti* (ravioli stuffed with spinach and ricotta) come in generous portions, and the house wine will loosen you up for a night out on the town. Late in the evening, the nine-to-fivers head home, making way for a hipper, more artsy crowd.

Feel like a thespian at **Osteria del Teatro** *(Via Vernazza 8; Tel 010/570-23-27; Hours vary, open for lunch and dinner; Entrees 15,000L; MC, V),* which is all decked out with photos and memorabilia from Teatro Carlo Felice, across the street. Follow the lead of the dramatically inclined locals, who chow down on amazing pesto pastas and succulent marinated calf livers.

▶▶SPLURGE

A fancy little wine bar in the cool part of town between the port and Piazza de Ferrari, **Sola** *(Via C. Barabino 120r; Tel 010/594-513; 7pm-1am daily; Entrees 25,000L; MC, V, AE)* offers a wide variety of fine wines and meat dishes. The wood-paneled ceilings and floors, rustic dinner plates, and Italian folk music whistling from the radio make for a genuine Italian meal. Start with the cheese platter—it may smell like feet, but it tastes like heaven—or the traditional Genovese *cotelette di acciughe* (stuffed fried anchovies). Hundreds of bottles of Ligurian wines like Arcola line the walls, and the waiters are more than happy to let you taste a few, assuming you'll buy one with dinner.

Festive and romantic, **I Tre Merli** *(Palazzina Millo, near the aquarium; Tel 010/246-44-16; Hours vary, open for lunch and dinner daily; MC, V)* offers up great views of the waterfront. The menu is primarily seafood, appropriate for a joint so close to the aquarium. Dishes like *risotto alla pescatore* (rice with catch of the day) and *insalata di pulpi* (octopus salad) are served on tables covered in Belgian lace and small black candles. Waiters are attentive and polite, diners are well dressed but boisterous, and a good time is had by all (except the fish).

crashing

Compared with what you'll find in some of Italy's other big cities, sleeping in Genoa is a bargain. Fortunately, the cheaper places tend to be close to Stazione Brignole, where it's safe to walk home late at night.

▶▶CHEAP

A 5-minute walk west from Stazione Brignole on Via Amicis will bring you to two charming *albergos* in the same building, run by the same person: Carola, a lovely lady who's more than familiar with the backpacker's circuit. On the third floor of the building is **Albergo Carola** *(Via Gropallo 4; Tel 010/839-13-40; Reception 9am-midnight daily; 50,000L single, 80,000L double, 110,000L triple, 120,000L quad, private bath available in triples and quads; No credit cards).* All rooms come with sinks and clean towels, and the giant bathtub in the sparkling common bathroom is a welcome sight after a long day of trekking through the city. Carola's quite the hostess: she's set up a little library in the front hall, and if you're desperate to check your e-mail, she'll even let you use her fancy computer for free. The first-floor **Albergo Argentina** *(Via Gropallo 4; Tel 010/839-13-40; Reception 9am-midnight daily; 45,000L single, 75,000L double, 100,000L triple, 110,000L quad, private bath available in doubles, triples, and quads; No credit cards)* is slightly smaller, slightly cheaper, and newly renovated. Because of their proximity to the train station and bargain rates, both hotels are almost always full, so call ahead, even during the off season.

One block north of Carola's place you'll find **Albergo Rita** *(Via Gropallo 8c; Tel/Fax 010/870-207; 40,000L single, 65,000L w/bath, 65,000L double, 85,000L w/bath; No credit cards).* Rita runs this clean, quiet little family place like it's her own home. There's a fish tank in the

wired

The city's primary website, ***www.genova.it,*** offers links to all sorts of events and venues throughout the city.

To check your e-mail or surf the web, go to **Internet Village** *(at the corner of Via Brigata Bisagno and Corso Buenos Aires; Tel 010/570-48-78; 9am-1pm/3-7pm daily; 15,000L per hour; No credit cards)*, near Piazza Vittoria.

lobby that's in really bad shape—if you know anything about fish and their tanks, Rita could use your advice.

Hostel Genova *(Via Costanzi 120; Tel 010/242-24-57; Bus 40 from Bignole and Principe; 23,000L dorm, breakfast included; HI card required; No credit cards)* is situated a bit outside the city's center: from Stazione Principe, walk east on Via Balbi to catch bus 40, which will take you up the hill to the hostel. It's too far—and arguably too dangerous—to walk from the center of town, so you really should take the bus. The hostel is relatively clean, with free lockers, a cafeteria, and a TV room. The crowd usually consists of immigrant workers and backpackers. The distance from town makes trying to get home to meet the midnight curfew an adventure every night....

If you want to stay near Stazione Principe for an early departure, **Albergo Parigi** *(Via Pre 72/1; Tel 010/252172; 40,000L single, 60,000L double, shared baths; No credit cards)*, 1 block north of Via XX Settembre on the corner of Via Brera, is your best bet. Just don't expect gay Paris—it's in a pretty shady part of town and offers just the barest essentials. Bedrooms and bathrooms are relatively clean, and so are the towels. If the place isn't booked, you can bargain for a room—try to knock 10,000L off the price, but be prepared with a back-up plan.

▶▶**DO-ABLE**

Right on the main drag, **Soana Dip** *(Via XX Settembre 23/7 A; Tel 010/562-814; 50,000L single, 80,000L double, shared baths; V, MC)* is a respectable, family-run hotel that puts you in the center of Genoa's action. Each room has a sink, clean towels, and fluffy pillows, and there's a little bar where you can get an early morning coffee or evening cocktail. Just don't expect to sleep in—it's close to the street, and the morning rush hour traffic gets pretty loud.

A little further down toward the water, **Albergo Astro** *(Via XX Settembre 3/21; Tel 010/587-86; 50,000L single, 80,000L double, 110,000L triple, private baths; V, MC)* offers well-lit rooms and a little more peace and quiet. There's a bar and restaurant downstairs, and once you walk out the door, you can head in any direction and find something cool to do, day or night.

Along the strip of Via Balbi, you'll find over a dozen places to crash. One of the bigger ones is **Albergo della Posta Nuova** *(Via Balbi 24; Tel 010/246-20-05; 75,000L single, 90,000L double, private baths; V, MC, AE).* The rooms are large and the beds are super-soft. All the rooms have phones and there's a bar downstairs. Some rooms have balconies that look out on the boulevard, perfect for throwing catcalls to the Italian hard bodies.

Pensione Barone *(Via XX Settembre 2/23; Tel 010/587-578; 50,000L single, 70,000L w/bath, 70,000L double, 80,000L w/bath, 110,000L triple w/bath; V, MC)* is a small, homey place to crash close to Stazione Brignole. The owners aren't super friendly, but the beds are, and the bathrooms are always clean. You can grab some stiff coffee at the cafe downstairs. Definitely call ahead for reservations—only about 15 people can sleep here. From the station, walk west down Via Fiume to Via XX Settembre for 3 blocks.

▶▶**SPLURGE**

It may be worth splurging at the four-star **Albergo Moderno Verdi** *(Piazza G. Verdi 5; 010/553-21-04; 150,000L single w/bath, 220,000L double w/bath; V, MC, AE)* to get a room right on the piazza. All the usual four-star amenities are here, including televisions, phones, and mini-bars in every room. Beware the allure of the mini-bars—the happy little bottles they're stocked with aren't included in the price of your room. The deep bathtubs are a great place to waste away the better part of the evening with some trashy Italian tabloids. There's a great bar downstairs, but the so-so food in the restaurant isn't worth the high prices.

need to know

Currency Exchange ATMs are available at both train stations and all over the city. The best places to exchange money are in and around **Piazza Colombo.**

Tourist Information The main tourist offices are down by **Porto Antico** *(Palazzina Santa Maria; Tel 010/24-87-11; 9am-6:30pm daily)* and off **Piazza Corvetto** *(Via Roma; Tel 010/576-791; 9am-5pm daily).* Both offices have maps and listings for shows and concerts in and around the city, but they won't make hotel reservations for you.

Public Transportation City buses run from both train stations from 5am to 1am. Tickets (1,500L, no free transfers) can be purchased at just about any tobacco stand or train station. If you need to get from one station to the other, you're better off catching one of the trains that pass through on their way to points north and south. The **Funiculare** *(3,000L),* which goes to the towns up on the hill north of Genoa, runs every 15 minutes. Maps and schedules can be obtained at the tourist offices.

Health and Emergency Emergency: *113.* **Ospedale San Martino** *(Via Benedetto XV 10; Tel 010/55-51)* is the city's biggest hospital.

Pharmacies Two blocks north of Stazione Principe is the 24-hour **Farmacia Ghersi** *(Corso BuenasAires 18; Tel 010/54-16-61).*

Airports Aeroporto Internazionale de Genova Cristoforo Colombo *(Tel 010/601-51 for flight info)* is about 2 miles outside the city. It's easiest to get into town from the airport by train, but a taxi to the city center will run you about 40,000L.

Trains The primary local train stations are **Stazione Principe** *(Piazza Acquaverde)* and **Stazione Brignole** *(Piazza Verdi)*. Both are connected by trains running almost every 5 minutes, as well as by buses 18, 33, and 37. If you find yourself arriving at Stazione Principe, grab one of the local trains or buses to Stazione Brignole, which will put you closer to the center of town.

Bus Lines Out of the City Buses that leave the city for domestic and international destinations can be caught from **Piazza della Vittoria.** Tickets can be purchased at the **bus station** *(Via D'Annunzio; Tel 010/558-114).*

Boats This port city is very accessible by boat. If you're headed to international points such as Barcelona (100,000L) or Corsica (70,000L), your best bet is **Grandi Navi Veloci** *(Via Freschi 17; Tel 010/58-93-31).* They offer high-speed hydrofoils that also go down to Sicily (130,000L). From Stazione Principe, take bus 20; from Stazione Brignole, take bus 11.

Bike Rental Get some wheels at **Nuovo Centro Sportivo 2000** *(Piazza dei Garibaldi 18r; Tel 010/254-12-43; 9am-5pm Mon-Sat; 10,000L per day; No credit cards).*

Laundry Centrale wash *(Via Di Amicis 32; No phone, 9:30am-8pm daily; 8,000L per load; No credit cards)* is 1 block west of Stazione Brignole, on the left along Via Amicis.

Postal The **post office** *(Piazza Dante 4/6r; Tel 010/259-46-87; 8am-7pm Mon-Sat)* is 2 blocks southeast of Piazza de Ferrari.

Internet See *wired,* above.

everywhere else

la spezia

Ever since nearby Cinque Terra began booming in the '70s, La Spezia has been a little bitter about its lowly position on the tourist food chain. This little port town, situated smack dab on the southern tip of the "Italian Riviera," is mostly used as a layover spot where people come to catch the local trains up the coast and maybe crash when the beach towns are all booked up (which will likely be your MO as well). The local yokels are friendly enough—just don't tell them where you're headed if you're only here as a jumping-off point for somewhere up the coast. La Spezia doesn't have the wild scene you can find further north, but it does have its good points, especially if hiking's your thing—this is the place to hop on the trails that take you up along the coastline.

The city is surrounded by mountains in every direction except to the south, where it opens up to the Mediterranean. This keeps the climate warm and humid all year long. Almost two thousand years ago, poet Ennio invited many of his fellow citizens to Spezia, and so it became known as "the poet's gulf." Today, you're more likely to run into sailors on the prowl than any potential Kerouacs (ladies beware!). During the day, the streets are pretty much dead, except for locals running their chores and stray backpackers making the trek down from Cinque Terra for some provisions. The main streets, **Via del Prione** and **Corso Cavour,** both running north-south from the port, are filled with little boutiques, rustic cafes, and strolling couples. Corso Cavour runs into and through **Piazza Cavour,** the main square, about a 5-minute walk from the port. The town is easily covered on foot, but walking up the stairs connecting to the bigger villas on the mountainside makes for a sweaty brow. As evening sets in, the gardens and parks down by the port make for a chill spot to drink some local vino and watch the sun set over the Riviera.

bar and live music scene

There aren't many people who really let loose in La Spezia, but if you feel like getting rowdy with some Italian sailors, there's no better place. On any given night you'll find a mob of nautical types down by the port on Viale Italia. The other options lie on the main drag, Via del Prione.

La Spezia's hippest and best dressed hangout is **Oficine Nuvoletti** (*Via Prione 235; No phone; 9am-2pm/4pm-2am daily; No credit cards*), where the beautiful and the soulful come to slurp back martinis (10,000L) and smoke loads of tobacco. This place is your best chance to find one of the poets that supposedly live in the poet's gulf. From the outside it looks like a fashion boutique, with giant glass windows looking out onto the street. Upstairs, local musicians do the unplugged thing Monday through Friday, accompanied by an all-you-can-drink wine special (10,000L), which is not a bad deal considering the quality of the local wines served.

The crowd at **Tavernetta** (*Via del Prione 16; Tel 018/7544590; 10am-2pm/5pm-2am Tue-Sun; No cover; V, MC*) ranges from young people doing the beer-pizza thing (they offer just about every Italian beer on tap [8,000L for a pint]), to families stuffing mountains of pasta into their bambini's mouths. Copper plates hang from the raw wooden beams that hold the place up, and the kitchen's open to the dining room. Like every good-spirited Italian, the cooks toss their pizza dough high into the air before throwing it into the brick oven in the back. If you're hungry, they'll serve you up a cheesy calzone called a *braccio di ferro,* stuffed with spinach, parmesan, and ricotta cheese (10,000L-14,0000L). Should you run into Antonio, the owner, mention soccer to get an earful on the teams from La Spezia and Genova.

The biggest international hangout in La Spezia is **Mad Max** (*Via M. Vinzoni 24; Tel 018/7807127; 9:30pm-4am daily; V, MC*). They don't call it Mad Max for nothing; any bar opening this late is going to draw more than its share of drunken olive-trawlers. The stereo blares out classic rock and the likes of Pearl Jam, and the crowd is pretty hip—a pleasant mix of locals and backpackers. Beers run about 7,000L, mixed drinks about the same. The bartenders are super cool—when the owner isn't around, it's buy-backs galore.

No one seems to know what the KKK in **The KKK Bar** (*Via Paleocapa 5; No phone; 10am-2pm/5pm-2am Wed-Mon; No credit cards*) stands for, but rumors say the bar is changing its name. I wonder why? This little place 1 block off Piazza Garibaldi, toward the train station, and a bit dingy, but the bottled beers are only 5,000L. It's a good place to fuel up if you've got a long train ride ahead of you.

culture zoo

Much of the culture in this port town revolves around ships and the men who love them.

Naval Museum (*Piazza Chiodo; Tel 018/770750; 9am-noon/2-6pm Mon, Wed, Thur, Sat; 2-6pm Fri; 8:30am-1:15pm Sun; 2,000L; No credit*

LA SPEZIA

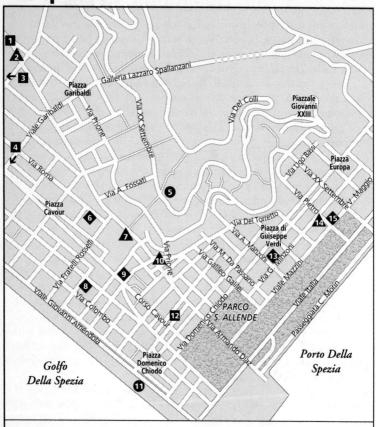

BARS/CLUBS ▲
Tavernetta 7
Oficine Nuvoletti 10
The KKK Bar 2
Mad Max 14

CULTURE ZOO ●
Naval Museum 11
Pinacoteca Civica Amedeo Lia 5

EATS ◆
Ristorante della Mama 13
All Inferno Vino 8
Vegio Caroggio 6
Dino 15
Il Caffe 9

CRASHING ■
Terminus 1
Giglio Rossi 12
Astra 4
Il Birillo 3

cards): Housed in the dockyard across from the canal, this museum has some amazing models of old Italian sailing ships, as well as beautiful carved busts of women that rode the helms and reminded the sailors what they were missing all those nights at sea (like they needed reminding). The naval base across the way opens its doors to visitors each year on March 19.

Pinacoteca Civica Amedeo Lia *(Via del Vecchio Ospedale 234; Tel 018/731100; 10am-6pm Tue-Sun; 12,000L, 8,000L with student ID; No credit cards):* This museum manages to cram over 2,000 works of art into a small space just off Via Prione. You'll find medieval, Renaissance, and modern paintings by Italian stalwarts like Bellini, Sansovino, and Tintoretto.

CITY SPORTS

Ditch your gear and take a hike. You can take the local mountain trails all the way up the coast, and a number of local hiking clubs are dedicated to doing just that.

Detailed maps and expert advice for hiking and mountain biking can be found at **Natura Trekking** *(Via Bragarina 56/9; Tel 018/7504264; 9am-1pm/4-8pm Mon-Sat; All day bike rentals 12,000L, credit card deposit required; V, MC)* or **Club Alpino Italiano** *(Viale Amendole 196; Tel 018/228-73; 8:30am-1pm/3-7:30pm Wed-Mon).*

If you're more of the aquatic type, don't worry—they've got some of that, too. The islands and lava rock coastline off La Spezia and Cinque Terra are ideal for scuba diving. For info on gear rental and hired boats, head to **La Federazione Italiana Pesca Sportiva** *(Via V. Veneto; Tel 018/7511222; 8am-3pm daily).*

EATS

Hope you like fish, because that's what you're going to be eating here. There are a couple of nice sit-down restaurants on the harbor that drag the sea life right out of the water and onto your plate.

TO MARKET

The supermarket trend sweeping the rest of Italy hasn't quite caught up to La Spezia. So if you're packing a lunch for a boat ride up the coast or a train trek to Genova, the daily market along Corso Cavour known as **La Piazza** *(7am-1pm Mon-Sat)* has everything from salted pork meat to local homemade cheeses.

▶▶CHEAP

Ristorante Della Mama *(Viale Mazzini; Tel 018/7778312; 4pm-midnight Tue-Sun; Entrees 15,000L; V, MC)* is a schwank little joint with a nice view of the water—if you can get a seat outside. Inside, things get a bit more romantic with candle-lit tables and soothing Italian opera as the backdrop. Try the *insalata frutti di mare,* which includes just about all the local shellfish they can get their hands on, or the stuffed *calamari.* Chances are they've gone from net to kitchen to plate in a matter of hours.

If you're heading up into the center of town from the waterfront, look for **All Inferno Vino** *(Via Lorenzo Costa; Tel 018/729-458; Noon-4pm/7pm-midnight daily; Entrees 15,000L; MC, V),* a home-style restaurant tucked into an old wine cellar. It's just 1 block off Piazza Cavour. The setting is intimate—both the stone ceilings and the lighting are low. There are no menus; the youthful waiters will tell you what your dinner choices are. If your Italian isn't what it should be, keep an eye out for what other people are eating, and don't be afraid to point. Try the *spaghetti cicale* (spaghetti with all sorts of clams and octopus), and wash it down with a half-liter of the house white, which is served from giant oak barrels.

If you're looking for a good old pizza pie, check out **Vegio Caroggio** *(Via S. Lorenzo 41; Tel 010/2541390; Noon-5pm/8pm-midnight Tue-Sun; Entrees 15,000L; MC, V),* 1 block east of Piazza Cavour. You can pretty much get any plate your palate desires, but you can't beat the *pizza ai funghi* (mushrooms) or *pizza 4 formaggio* (four cheeses). If you can't stand the heat from the brick oven, get your pizza to go and munch it on the piazza.

If your sweet tooth is acting up, **Il Caffe** *(Piazza Ramiro Ginochio 2; No phone; 8am-10pm daily; No credit cards)* has a wild assortment of pastries and a cup of coffee that will put some zip in your steps. It's between Via Prione and Corso Cavour.

▶▶DO-ABLE

In the mood for some thick Tuscan cuisine? **Dino** *(Via Cadorna 18; Tel 018/7736157; Noon-4pm/8pm-midnight, closed Sun evening; Entrees 20,000L; MC, V)* can serve it up. The *tagliolini al tartufo bianco* (pasta with a white truffle cream sauce) is one of kind, and goes nicely with some of the local red wine. The dining room's a bit on the fancy side, decked out with old copper plates and cups hanging from the walls, and the friendly staff is at your beck and call. It's 2 blocks off Via Prione, at Via F. Cavalloti.

crashing

La Spezia can come in handy if you can't find a room in Cinque Terre or if you miss the last train headed up the coast. The best places to stay are down by Giardini Pubblici, near the harbor.

Terminus *(Via Paleocapa 21; Tel 018/703436; 40,000L single, 60,000L double, shared bath; No credit cards)* is one of the cleaner places to crash out. The rooms are a bit small, but the park and harbor are just across the street.

Only a block away is **Giglio Rossi** (*Via Carpenino 31; Tel 018/ 731374; 40,000L single, 60,000L double, shared baths; No credit cards*). It isn't as warm as some of the other joints in town, but it's a place to leave your gear and get a quiet night's sleep.

▶▶**DO-ABLE**
If you're looking to be a little closer to the center of the action, grab a bed at **Astra** (*Via Costantini 48; Tel 018/511105; 60,000L single, 90,000L double, private baths; MC, V*), which is a couple blocks north of Piazza Covour. You get a free breakfast, clean towels, and a color television.

Conveniently located for a clean getaway, **Il Birillo** (*Via dei Mille 15; Tel 018/732-666; 60,000L single, 90,000L double, private baths; No credit cards*) sits right across the street from the train station. The rooms are very simple and relatively clean. Don't plan on sleeping in—it gets pretty noisy when the trains start running in the morning.

need to know

Currency Exchange There's a handy **ATM** at the train station.
Tourist Information The **main tourist office** (*Viale Mazzini 45; Tel 018/770-900; 9:30am-12:30pm/2:30-5:30pm Mon-Sat*) is about a 15-minute walk from the train station. Follow Via Prione all the way down to Via G. Mazzini, almost at the port, and take a left; the office is 3 blocks down on your left. Another, smaller **tourist office** (*Tel 018/771-89-97; 9am-12:30pm/4-7pm Tue-Sat*) in the train station is also very helpful.
Public Transportation There isn't really any need for public transportation in La Spezia—it's that small. You can usually find a **taxi** right outside the train station if you need one to help you get your bags to your hotel.
Health and Emergency Emergency: *118*. **Ospedale S. Andrea** (*Via M. Asso 118*) offers medical attention.
Pharmacies Try **Farmacia dell'Aquila** (*Via Chiodo 97; Tel 018/732-162; 9am-12:30pm/4-8pm Tue-Sat*) for all your pill-popping needs.
Trains La Spezia is on the Genova-Roma line, as well as the line that runs from Pisa to Turino. All trains terminate in La Spezia, where you can switch to the local "milk run" train that runs up the coast to get to Cinque Terre.
Bus Lines Out of the City The **bus station** is on Piazza D. Chiodo, down by the naval museum. Buses are your only way of getting to the tiny surrounding towns, but to get to Cinque Terre, or anywhere else, take the train.
Boats Soc. Navigazione Golfo dei Poeti (*Viale Mazzini 21; Tel 018/732-987*) runs the local ferries up and down the coast, from La Spezia to all the coastal towns and Genova, April through October. Ferries run about every hour at about 10,000L to 25,000L. If you're trying to get to Corsica, try **Happy Lines** (*Tel 018/7651273; 6:30am-noon/3:30-6:30pm daily; Tickets 125,000L in summer, 90,000L in the low season*).

Postal Get connected at **Phone Center** *(Via Fume 1, Piazza S. Bon; Tel 018/7777805; 9am-10pm Mon-Sat, 10am-9pm Sun; Internet 12,000L per hour),* which offers Internet, UPS, and fax facilities. It's 2 blocks toward the port from the train station.

finale ligure

With its breezy palms, wide beaches, surrounding mountains that keep temperatures warm and climbers happy, and late night bar-hopping scene, the little tropical town of Finale Ligure is an ideal spot to kick off the sandals for some r&r. It may not be the place for a week-long beach fiesta, but it's worth a day or two of tanning, partying, and rock climbing. You could easily make it a day-trip from Genoa.

The entire town is only about a mile long and 10 blocks deep. From the train station, it's only a 5-minute walk due south to the beach. The town is broken into two primary parts, **Finale Marina** (down by the beach, south of the train tracks) and **Finale Borgo** (the older part of town, north of the tracks). Both neighborhoods are very small and can be walked on foot in about 10 minutes.

Almost all the noteworthy bars and more lively piazzas and spots to chill are in Finale Marina. The sunset strip of Finale is **Via della Concezione,** running parallel to the beach. It's a great place to eat or find a place to stay. **Via S. Pietro** also runs east to west, parallel to the beach, 1 block inland from Concezione. Sitting between these two main drags is **Piazza V. Emanuele,** the biggest, most festive piazza in town, where you can kick off the night and hook up with the rest of the international crowd. From the piazza you can pretty much amble down any street and come across a decent (usually better than decent) bar or restaurant. Finale Borgo is only worth a visit if you're interested in finding mom-and-pop restaurants, cheaper accommodations, rock-climbing partners, or pigeons. The locals, at least the ones who aren't running the bars and restaurants, hang out with the aforementioned pigeons in Finale Borgo near **Piazza del Tribunale** and **Piazza San Biagio.**

From May to September, Finale literally explodes with tourists, mostly northern Europeans—the population surges from 16,000 to 60,000. During this time, Finale locals are almost nonexistent. Most flee the swarms of tourists, packing up for less crowded digs and living off the exorbitant rents they charge those same tourists to stay in their houses for the summer. The ones that do stick around are a happy-go-lucky bunch who run their businesses and milk the tourist season for all it's worth.

bar, club, and live music scene

As in any hopping beach town, most of the action in Finale can be found down around the water.

Kick the night off with some Latin beats at **Cuba Libre** *(Via Torino 12; Tel 019/695-56-84; Noon-2am daily; No credit cards)*. With Finale's best selection of liquor in their arsenal, the bartenders are very generous with their pours, and the all-day mojito specials (10,000L) draw in tanned travelers rip-roaring for a night of bar hopping and skinny dipping. Don't feel bad if you begin *and* end your night here—you won't be the first.

Louie Armstrong is the unofficial mascot of **Birreria** *(Via Giusseppe Garibaldi 72; No phone; Noon-2am daily; No credit cards)*, (check out his statue out front) but don't expect any sort of jazz inside. The music is toe-tappin' Italian rock and assorted European radio disco, the scene is laid-back and international, and the dimly lit bar is decked out in photos of days past. Beers are about 8,000L and the bartenders might actually buy you one if you stay long enough, which almost never happens in Italian pubs. With its relatively chill atmosphere, this is a good spot to either kick off the night or kill it.

If you're in the mood for a cocktail, **The Scotch Club** *(Via Colombo; Tel 019/681-60-94; 4pm-2am Tue-Sun; No credit cards)* offers some of Ireland's finest malts. Chat it up with other vacationers at the long bar, or plop down with friends at one of the tables or booths. From time to time, travelers juiced up on shots of whiskey (5,000L) and beer (5,000L-8,000L) go a little wild with the six strings, drawing in passersby late into the night.

Watch the sunset with a glass of local vino at **Acrobaleno, Pub 59** *(Piazza del Vittore Emanuele; No phone; 11am-1am daily; No credit cards)*. Sit a few yards from the water, take in the salty air, and get mellow watching the seagulls annoy the fishermen unloading their daily catch. The bar is close enough to the beach to draw in everybody and their Aunt Irma searching for a cold drink, but as the sun goes down and the younger kids get put to bed, a livelier crowd packs in.

arts scene

Finale has a good number of local artists and galleries for a small beach town. If you're looking for an air-conditioned break from the beach, check out some local contemporary art at **Sala Gallesio** *(Via Pertica 24; No phone; 9:30am-2pm/4:30-8:30pm Mon-Sat; No credit cards)*, 2 blocks east of Piazza V. Emanuele. Further down the street is **Galleria Arte Bersani** *(Via De Raymondi 27; Tel 019/693-513; 9:30am-2pm/4:30-8:30pm Mon-Sat; No credit cards)*. Most of the works are tripped-out oil paintings of fishermen pulling in their loads at some absurd time of morning. They're all for sale, of course, and artists are somewhat lenient with their prices if you bargain a little.

city sports

Compared with most others on the coast, the beach in Finale is huge. Tossing the Frisbee or kicking the soccer ball is no problem, but you should probably practice your sincere apology in Italian for the occasional stray projectile. The entire beach is open to the public and there are spots where you can rent a chair and umbrella for about 8,000L a day. The water itself is very pleasant in the warmer months: crystal clear and not too hot or too cold.

Climbers from all over Europe head to Finale to assault the wicked rock faces. The two hot spots are **Rocca di Perti** and **Rocca di Feglino,** both well outside town (about 10 kilometers [5 miles]); buses from the train station will drop you at the trailheads that lead to them. Unless you're really prepared and experienced, it's advisable to tackle the faces with somebody who is. In Finale Borgo, **Free Climbing c/o Rock Store** *(Piazza Garibaldi; Tel 019/690-208; 8am-2pm/3:30-7:30pm daily in summer; Deposit of 100,000L or credit card on climbing gear; V, MC, AE)* provides gear rental and daily guided expeditions. Renting gear and a guide, preferably with a group, will run you about 60,000L per person, but you can stay up at the rocks the whole day. Pack a lunch and lots of sunscreen. If you've got the experience and the gear and just need a climbing partner, there's a message board used to connect with people just like you. There's a similar board at **Caffé Centrale** *(Piazza Garibaldi 28; Tel 019/691-778; 7:30 am-2am Tue-Sun; No credit cards),* a climber's hangout.

If you're not the death-defying type, head to **Race Ware** *(Via Brunenghi 124; Tel 019/680-639; 8:30am-2pm/3:30-8pm daily in summer; Rental and maps 40,000L, plus deposit; V, MC, AE)* or **R.C. Bike** *(Via Brunenghi 65; Tel 019/681-058; 8:30am-2pm/3:30-8pm Tue-Sun; Rental and maps 40,000L, plus deposit; V, MC, AE)* to rent out mountain bikes and pick up trail maps for the novice trail grunter. Both bike rental shops are along Via Brunenghi, about halfway between Finale Marina and Finale Borgo.

There are at least five places along the beach that rent gear for fun in the surf. **Wind-Surf c/o Bagni Mariella Varigotti** *(On the beach; Tel 019/698-760)* offers lessons and daily windsurfer rentals. They're open as long as there's sunlight—no deposit, no credit cards, 'nuff said.

EATS

Finale offers the usual beach town options. If you're looking to pack a lunch of fresh mozzarella and proscuitto for the beach, **Chiesa** *(Via Pertica 13; No phone; 8:30am-2pm/4-8:30pm, closed Sun; No credit cards),* 1 block west of Piazza V. Emanuele, has everything except bread. Luckily, you can get that across the street at the local **Paneria** *(No phone; 8am-3pm, closed Sun; No credit cards).*

▶▶CHEAP

For a quick slice, your best bet is **Pizzeria Le Petit** *(Via San Pietro 3; No phone; 10am-midnight daily in summer; pies 10,000L; V, MC).* They've got just about every kind of pizza you can imagine. But be warned that the sauce is a little funky and they don't like giving change for 50,000L bills.

La Betulla *(Via Concezione 12; Tel 019/692-326; 9am-11pm daily in summer; Avg. entree 10,000L; V, MC)* is a comfortable sit-down restaurant

TO MARKET

Finale is nirvana for market freaks. All year
long, there's some sort of open-air market
going on just about every day of the week.
Mondays, there's a food market with hung
chickens, fresh cheeses, and all sorts of nuts (the
edible kind) along Via S. Pietro in Finale Borgo.
On Thursdays from 8am till noon there's a giant market
along the beach with fresh vegetables, used clothes, and more stupid
beach toys than you can shake a shovel at. In the summer, there's
also a seafood market along the beach from 8am to noon on Mondays, Wednesdays, and Saturdays.

right on the beach that offers great salads filled with fresh seafood and all
the bread you can eat. Girls, don't worry about coming in for lunch
wearing just your bathing suit, but guys—you should put on a shirt
(funny how that works, isn't it?).

▶▶DO-ABLE

If you really want to dive into some rich Finalese home cooking, grab a
table at **Ristorante Campara** *(Via Garibaldi 38; Tel 019/600-44-29;
11:30am-3:30pm/5pm-midnight Tue-Sun, 5pm-midnight Mon; Entrees
15,000-20,000L; MC, V)*. They serve up a wild flattened polenta bread
called *panissa fiarinata* that's worth a taste. This busy restaurant feels like
a big homey kitchen, and the waiters are friendly and patient. It's just off
Piazza Garibaldi in Finale Borgo.

The rustic **U Quarte** *(Via Fiume 33; Tel 019/692-28-84; 5pm-mid-
night Tue-Sun; Entrees 18,000-20,000L; MC, V)*, also located up in Finale
Borgo, offers seafood entrees like linguini with red clam sauce that will
make you think twice about saving room for dessert.

Finale is also a good place to indulge your sweet tooth. Just off the
west side of Piazza V. Emanuele, **I Frutti del Grano** *(Via Pertica 32; Tel
019/337-68-34; Noon-3pm/5:30-11:30pm; Entrees 16,000-24,000L; V,
MC, AE)* has homemade candy and pastries that you can smell a block
away. Further down the street, you'll find thick coffee and bowls of
complimentary chocolates at **Caffetteria Garibaldi** *(Piazza Garibaldi
45; No phone; 9am-10pm Wed-Mon; No credit cards)*, for the ultimate
caffeine buzz.

crashing

Finding a place to stay in Finale gets tricky during the summer; if you
don't call ahead, sleeping on the beach might have to suffice. About 6
kilometers (3.73 miles) north of town, there are two campsites for those

of you traveling with gear: **San Martino** *(Localita' Manie; Tel 019/698-250; Bus ACTS from the train station; Sites 10,000L; No credit cards)* and **La Foresta** *(Localita' Manie; Tel 019/698-103; Bus ACTS; Sites 10,000L; No credit cards).*

▶▶**CHEAP**

Youth Hostel Wuillermin *(Via Caviglia 46; Tel 019/690-515; Curfew 11:30pm; 20,000L for dorm bed and breakfast, shared baths; HI cards accepted, no credit cards)* is housed in an amazing red stone castle atop the town, looking over the ocean. The hostel was renovated only a couple of years ago, so everything from the bathroom to the garden is neat, tidy, and beautiful. The food in the cafeteria is pretty decent; you can grab a veggie dinner for 15,000L from 5 to 10pm. There are also laundry facilities to get all the sand and seasalt out of your swimsuit; a load of wash is 8,000L. It's about a 15-minute walk to get here from the train station: go left onto Via Mazzini, continuing onto Via Torino. Make another left on the little, almost unmarked, street of Via degli Ulivi, which heads up way too many stairs. The walk is worth it when you finally see the castle.

You can manage some good deals across the tracks in Finale Borgo. Along Via S. Francesco are hotels **Il Faro** *(Via Francesco 5; Tel 019/692-369; 40,000L single, 70,000L double, private baths; No credit cards)* and **Santa Maria** *(Via Brunenghi 71; Tel 019/692880; 35,000L single, 70,000L double, 90,000L triple, private baths available in doubles and triples; MC, V).* Both are within walking distance of the beach, and are comfortably situated between the old and new towns. The rooms are a bit on the stale-smelling side, but you can open the big windows to let in the ocean breeze. The beds are soft, clean, and comfy.

▶▶**DO-ABLE**

Hotel San Marco *(Via Concezione 22; Tel 019/692-533; 60,000L single, 100,000L double, 130,000L triple, private baths; V, MC)* has rooms looking right over the main drag onto the water. Rooms with a view are difficult to score; call ahead to reserve one. They may try to charge you more for a seaside room, but you may be able to talk them out of it.

Further down the strip on the other side of the piazza is **Albergo Marina** *(Via Barilli 22; Tel 019/692-561; 45,000L single, 80,000L double, private baths; V, MC, AE)*, just a block off the beach. Rooms are spacious and clean, and there's a little cafe downstairs.

If you're planning on staying in Finale for a week or more, you could rent out one of the local's pads. **Residenza Adelaide** *(Via Brunenghi 87; Tel 019/681-11; 9am-5pm daily)* rents outs apartments with all the amenities by the week and the month.

need To Know

Currency Exchange Money can be exchanged along **Via de Ray-mondi.** There are ATMs all throughout town.

Tourist Information The main **IAT office** *(Via San Pietro 14; Tel 019/681-019; 9am-1pm/4-8pm daily; iatfinale@infocomm.it)* offers maps of the town and hiking trails. Unfortunately, they can't make room reservations for you.

Public Transportation Finale is walkable, but local **buses** do run from the train station, linking up Finale Borgo and Finale Marina. Tickets are 2,000L.

Health and Emergency Emergency: *113;* Ambulance: *118.*

Pharmacies Farmacie assirelli *(Via Fiume 2; Tel 019/690-623; 9:30am-1:30pm/3-8pm Mon-Sat; V, MC)* in Finale Borgo and **Faramacie Communale** *(Via Ghiglieri 6; Tel 019/692-670; 9:30am-1:30pm/3-8pm Mon-Sat; V, MC)* in Finale Marina rotate 24-hour shifts.

Trains The **train station** is on the northern edge of Finale Marina, on Piazza Vittorio Veneto, offering local connections to Genoa, where you can transfer for a train to points beyond. It's walking distance from just about anywhere in town.

Bus Lines Out of the City Buses to other cities leave across the street from the train station.

Boats Locals give tours of the coast in small fishing boats from the pier on the beachfront. Rates vary, and are sometimes negotiable.

Bike/Moped Rental R.C. Bike [see *city sports,* above] rents out mountain bikes and mopeds.

Laundry Pura Acqua *(Via Aurelia 73; No phone; 9am-8pm daily; 6,000L per load; No credit cards)* is a good spot to wash the sand out of your jeans.

Postal Mail stuff at the **main post office** *(Via Concezione 28; Tel 019/692-838; 8am-6pm Mon-Fri, 8am-1:30pm Sat).*

cinque terra

monterosso

When you step off the train at Monterosso, you'll be standing on a strip of road with hotels, restaurants, and cafes that face the water. Immediately to your right is a pharmacy, and immediately to your left are an ATM and a wall with hotel and temporary residential listings. This is not the town center, however: Walking east, you'll see a tunnel with rail tracks on top. Don't bother craning your neck to see the tracks—you can't see them. Just pass through the tunnel to enter the heart of town—10 minutes or so from the train station. The largest of the five towns, Monterosso has the most amenities: sandy umbrella-ed beaches, boat rentals, real hotels rather than rooms for rent, and more than one nightspot to choose from. It tends to attract a mix of people, from vacationing Italians to American college kids. Locals are really friendly, and it's sort of a town custom to help out hard-up travelers with nowhere to crash. If you find yourself homeless, head to **Il Casello** [see *bar scene,* below] and appeal to Signore Bacco. He'll hook you up and probably offer you a drink. Gianluigi's **Cantina de di Sassarini** [see *bar scene,* below] is one of the best wine bars in Cinque Terra—the guy's motto is "to taste is free," and he sticks to his word. Just be careful not to "taste" too much if you're going hiking later on. Your next stop should be the multipurpose **Fast** [see *eats,* below]. Monterosso gets a bad rap for being touristy and not quaint enough, but don't count it out. It definitely has the best beaches, and it's not so far gone that a McDonald's or anything of that ilk has turned up on a street corner.

bar scene

Each of the Cinque Terre towns has a multi-purpose bar that is also your link to the town. In Monterosso, **Il Casello** (*On the hill just past Piazza Garibaldi; Tel 0187/818-330; Noon-2am daily July, Aug, closed Tue rest of the year; No credit cards*) is the place to go whether you're desperate for a room or dreaming about a mug of creamy, rich "killer" draught (4,000L). Signore Bacco is the Sam Malone of Casello. As the Paul Simon tunes play, he immediately lets you know that drinks are 500L cheaper if you sit in the century-old bar interior rather than at the tables outside (although the outside ones overlook the ocean). Bacco has been known to help out room-less travelers by magically producing lodging from his myriad contacts. He tells every traveler the same thing: Make friends with the locals and go out with them! And he's right—you'll get cheaper meals and have more fun. (It's par for the course that the person who lets you a room becomes your local buddy while you're here.) Casello is the home of the *bazara,* a 6,000L adventure of liqueur and fruit juices that is Bacco's secret weapon. Casello is not about dancing on the tables singing "I Will Survive"—the atmosphere is laid-back and casual, with a generally under-35 crowd at night. Il Casello also offers cheap and fast Internet access (*3,000L for 15 min*).

cinque terra

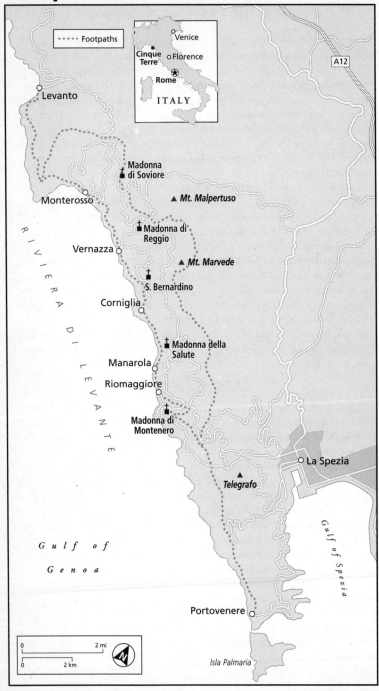

Footpaths

Venice

Cinque Terre

Florence

Rome

ITALY

A12

Levanto

Madonna di Soviore

▲ *Mt. Malpertuso*

Monterosso

R I V I E R A

Madonna di Reggio

Vernazza

▲ *Mt. Marvede*

✝ S. Bernardino

D I

Corniglia

L E V A N T E

✝ Madonna della Salute

Manarola

Riomaggiore

Madonna di Montenero

La Spezia

▲ *Telegrafo*

Gulf of

Genoa

G u l f   o f   S p e z i a

Portovenere

0   2 mi

0   2 km

Isla Palmaria

Down the hill from Il Casello, in the center of town, is the much less chill **Il Paradiso** *(13 Via Roma; Tel 0187/817-164; 8am-2am daily; V, MC).* The walls are plastered with posters of everyone from Fishbone to the Ramones, and Cake is playing on the stereo. Paradiso has a younger crowd at night, lots of college kids doing the European adventure. The bar is filled with tables and chairs, making it a communal party. Try one of the musical sandwiches (6,500-8,000L) like: Red Hot Chili Peppers (Parma ham and Brie cheese), Limp Bizkit (pickled veggies and cheese), Beastie Boys (raw ham and veggies), and wash it down with a cold one. This is definitely a draught beer joint: Moretti, Baffo d'oro, Labatts Extra, and La Rosa are on tap at 4,000L for a small, 12,000L for a large. If the beer and sandwiches leave you in need of a refill for your wallet, there is an ATM (or *bancomat,* in common parlance) 2 minutes up the street from the Paradiso.

Enotecas are everywhere in Cinque, but there's only one that has "To Taste Is Free" written on the door: **Cantina di Sassarini** *(7 Via Roma; Tel 0187/817-828; 10am-midnight daily; V, MC, AE),* run by the wonderful Gianluigi. Try to hit this place during the day when he's not too busy, and he'll taste you through the wines and grappas of the area, throwing in a smattering of history about Cinque Terre's grapes and a shot of *limoncina* [see *wine,* above] to finish you off. You'll learn that the reason the local Sciacchetra is 18 percent alcohol is a result of its 10 kilos of grapes per bottle ratio instead of the usual 1 kilo per bottle. And did you know that red wine should breathe one hour for every year that has passed since its birth? These and many other tips come courtesy of Gianluigi himself.

The oldest wine shop in town, **Enoteca Internazionale** *(A block north of Piazza Garibaldi; Tel 0187/715-512; 9am-1pm/5-8pm, closed Mon; V, MC, AE)* is stacked with reds and whites from all over the region. The women who run the store will let you have a taste from one of the open bottles, but if you don't buy anything, they'll definitely give you the evil eye on your way out.

beaches

Monterosso's main public beach, located right below the train station, is packed with young inebriated American travelers checking each other out (picture spring break in Fort Lauderdale). If that's not your scene, walk north for about 5 minutes until you come upon a parking lot on your left. Just past the lot, you'll see the "Il Gigante" statue carved into a rock ledge. In front of that is a small public beach with clear water for snorkeling and less of a crowd. Families tend to migrate here, but the swimming is good, and you won't have to listen to drunken tales of glory for hours on end.

There are also private beaches with changing rooms in front of the train station and on the other side of the harbor. This is the same sand as the public beach, but it's sectioned off for the special people. Plots of sand are rented for 5,000L per person, which includes use of the shower and

hiking

Cinque Terre is famous for the hiking trail that connects all five towns. It's a narrow dirt trail and nothing more, so wear good shoes and don't plan to hold hands while you walk.

The annoyance about hiking in Cinque is the families and groups who insist upon walking in a little line like ducks. They walk together, they stop together, and there's never room to pass. Meditation might be a good idea in these cases: Picture yourself on a deserted backwoods trail and try to block out the explanations of local flora and fauna.

For hardcore hiking, buy a trail map at any of the newsstands for 7,000L. It includes long hikes to Levanto and La Spezia, as well as the higher and more difficult hikes around Cinque Terre. Even if hiking is not your thing, the views from atop Cinque Terre's hills are worth the sweat. It's a humbling site to see monstrous waves crash against a town's breakwater while the sun sets behind the adjacent hills.

This is a breakdown of the main Cinque Terre trail, which runs roughly north-ish. All the hikes are do-able for someone who exercises regularly. Many people hike the whole damn thing, which takes about four and a half hours. There are signs along the paths so you won't get lost. Don't hike this in the rain—these trails are literally dirt on cliffs. Also, it's not good form to camp at the picnic sites along the way. Above all, bring food and water!

toilet facilities. Throw in an umbrella and two chaises, and the price is 18,000L. The private beaches also rent boats; a paddleboat goes for 15,000L an hour. If the water isn't rough, you can paddle out and find a cove to hide in.

eats

▶▶CHEAP

Even if you're not hungry, your first stop in Monterosso should be a pair of cafes on Via Roma where you can hang out, surf the web, get the inside scoop on the local scene, and, of course, fill up on good, cheap eats. First you'll hit **Fast** (*Via Roma 13; Tel 0187/817-164; fastpub@tin.it; 8am-2am daily; Sandwiches and burgers 6,500-8,000L, salads 6,000L, bruschetta 7,000L, 15 types of beer, wine and cocktails, breakfast all day*), then **Fishnet** (*Via Roma 17, in the dark alleyway just off the street; Tel/Fax 0187/817-373; fishnet@inwind.it; 10am-1pm, 4-8pm, 9:30pm-12:30am daily; Four high-speed computers, access 12,000L per hour*). Locals call Fast (named for

Monterosso to Vernazza: This one takes you about one and a half hours to conquer. It's the hardest of the four hikes, but it's still not *that* hard. There are really narrow places along the way, so it's not a good idea to walk with a big pack. Glimpses of the ocean can be had and are spectacular from these heights, but much of your time is spent in the trees.

Vernazza to Corniglia: You'll still walk for about one and a half hours, but the trail is not as steep or as narrow as the first. Lots of people like to grab a pre-hike drink at **The Blue Marlin** [see *bar scene* in *Vernazza,* below]. This hike affords more ocean views, but at a slightly lower vantage point than the first.

Corniglia to Manarola: This 45-minute journey is more of a walk than a hike, and the path is actually wide enough to let you walk beside someone and chat. It's pretty level, so you won't be stopping to catch your breath, and there isn't much jungle-like tree and shrub growth, so you get to gaze at the rock cliffs and ocean spray.

Manarola to Riomaggiore: Hike? Please. This thing will take you 20 minutes. The **Via dell Amore** (lovers' lane) is the name for this stretch of the trail, as the smooching couples who come here illustrate. There are benches and gardens along the way, and even a little snack bar. The tunnel leading into Manarola is pleasantly grafittied with underwater scenes and ocean views.

owners FAbio and STefano) a "snack bar," but it's a far cry from the tacky cotton-candy-and-hot-dog snack bars you'd find on the boardwalks along America's New Jersey shore. Fast is actually a tiny cafe-bar that serves really tasty, fresh food for little money. You can get absolutely yummy bruschetta (four) with tomatoes and garlic for about 7,000L. At night it's packed with kids who appreciate the good, cheap dinner and a fun place to hang out. Get your food there, then go next door—right around the corner, actually, in a little alleyway—to Fishnet, the best place in town to check your e-mail, download and burn disks of your digital photos, and get the line on the coolest spots in Cinque Terra and the rest of Italy from the super-friendly owner, expat Texan Kate Little (Fabio's wife). She'll help you book air, rail, and ferry tickets or track down a place for you to stay—not just locally, but almost anywhere in Europe. Or you can just kick back on her soft, comfy blue couch (goes great with the lime-green walls), listen to the great tracks Kate plays over her sound system, check out books from her travel library, browse through her English-language

WINE

Not *all* of Italy swears by red wine; in Cinque Terre they don't even make it. *Enotecas* do carry reds from other regions of Italy—including the rather disturbing Sieg Heil, with its picture of Hitler on the front—but if you want authentic local wine, stick to whites. Vermentina is an unusual spicy white, and sweet Sciacchetra is the dessert wine with a whopping 18 percent alcohol content. Yet another wine unique to the region is Chachetrá, a smooth sweet dessert wine locally made all along the coast. Cinque also produces lots of grappa and *limoncina*. Grappa is made from the skin of grapes that have been fermented beyond your wildest dreams. Olive- and lemon-flavored grappas are a bit smoother than the straight version, which leaves you in a sweat after a few shots. *Limoncina,* a lemon liqueur that is a result of Cinque's booming lemon-tree industry, is also shot-able, but mixing it into drinks and soda works well too. It ranges in taste from sickly candy-like lemon to the fresh stuff, so ask for a taste before you commit to a bottle. Most of the *enotecas* let you taste any of their products before you buy.

In Monterosso, pass by **Cantina di Sassarini** [see *bar scene,* below], run by Gianluigi, who is as well-versed in the English language as he is in wine. In Manarola, check out **Bramante** *(186 Via Disclovolo; Tel 0187/920-442; 9am-midnight daily, closed Thur; V, MC),* where twentysomething Gabriel gives wine virgins tastes of his elixir.

newspapers and magazines, or take advantage of her book exchange, where you can trade the books you've already read for different titles (1,000L) or just buy one you haven't read yet (10,000L). There were more than 150 books there at last count. Between Kate's high-tech/down-home hospitality and Fabio's great Italian food, this pair of cafes is bound to become your second home in Cinque Terra. During the hours that Fishnet is closed (Kate has to go home to feed her baby), you're welcome to use the Internet connection on her "old, crappy computer" at Fast for free (15 minutes max). Oh, and one more thing, Kate says you don't need to be afraid of the family dog, Chili, a Doberman/German shepherd mix who's a constant presence at both Fast and Fishnet. He's really a sweetie.

It's difficult to sit down in a restaurant and eat cheap in any part of Cinque Terre. One exception to this rule is **Midi Bar** *(Across Bar Centrale at Piazza Garibaldi; Tel 0187/817-003; 7am-midnight; No credit* *cards)*. This backpackers' hangout has outdoor tables where you can grab a quick snack or sit for hours and read a book. Pizza is 2,000L, focaccia is 1,000L, and gelato ranges from 2,000L to 6,000L, depending on size.

Il Casello and **Il Paradiso** [see *bar scene,* above, for both] also have reasonably priced food. Castello's focaccia sandwiches are really good and cheap (5,000L). Paradiso has coffee and snacks for breakfast from 1,000L. If you want groceries for a beach picnic, **Super Market-Europio** *(Just up the street from Il Paradiso; Via Roma 61)* has a nifty selection of cheap food-stuffs.

▶▶SPLURGE

Expensive does not necessarily mean good. The **Ristorante Belvedere** *(38 Piazza Garibaldi; Tel 0187/817-033; Noon-2pm/7-10pm; 7,000-26,000L per entree; V, MC, AE)* is a favorite of locals (Bacco from Casello recommends it), but the food is just okay, not spectacular. It's the seafood that is worth coming for—their specialty is the *Amphora,* filled with steamed seafood for two for 75,000L. Santina is the chef and owner, and her English-speaking son Frederico greets guests. The interior is kinda boring, so sit outdoors if possible. Try the house wine at 6,000L a liter and grab dessert somewhere else.

crashing

Monterosso is the place to stay if you want a real hotel room rather than a room-for-rent (read: no staff catering to your whims) or apartment. Of course, you'd better be prepared to pay real hotel prices; rooms here are way more expensive than in the other towns.

▶▶DO-ABLE

Just to the south of the train station is the one-star **Pension Agavi** *(30 Lungomare Fegina; Tel 0187/817-171, Fax 0187/818-264; Desk open 9am-8pm and phone after; 80,000L single, 130,000L double; No credit cards)*. Situated right on the beach promenade, it's convenient and much cheaper than the other waterfront hotels. Four people can probably pack into one of the doubles without notice—play it by ear. Rooms are plain, and there's no air-conditioning, but each has its own private bath, fridge, and phone.

Rooms at the **Albergo Marina** *(Via Buranco 40; Tel 0187/817-242; 50,000L single, 95,000L double),* are simple, hyper-clean, and inexpensive, but the place is not on the waterfront, so forget the beach views. The atmosphere is also a bit on the uptight side, so don't go there if you're looking for a laid-back, party-friendly hotel scene.

▶▶SPLURGE

Hotel Villa Steno *(109 Via Roma; Tel 0187/817-028, Fax 0187/817-056; Desk open 7am-9pm; www.pasini.com, steno@pasini.com; 130,000L single, 200,000L double, 240,000L triple, 260,000L quad; V, MC, AE)* is a family-run affair, with English-speaking Matteo at the helm. There is an incredibly fragrant lotus-like smell to the hotel. Fourteen rooms have balconies with ocean view, and a real breakfast of more than just bread and jam is included: You'll get hard-boiled eggs, croissants, muesli, and fruit.

All rooms have AC and TVs, and the service is super-friendly, making Steno's only drawback the 10-minute uphill hike from the station.

Midway down the hill from Steno is the partially hidden **La Colonnina** *(6 Via Zuecca; Tel 0187/817-439, Fax 0187/817-778; Desk open 8am-10:30pm; 140,000L double, 190,000L triple, 225,000L quad; No credit cards)*. Its shaded outdoor garden and rooftop sundeck are always nice, as are the small terraces on each floor. The room decor is a bit cheesy (vinyl surfaces, comforters, brass-edged nightstands), but chances are, you won't be in the room much, so who really cares? Each room has a satellite TV and a fridge but, alas, no AC. The breakfast buffet isn't worth the 15,000L per person unless you're really pressed for time.

need to know

Currency Exchange The best places around town to get money are **ATMs** *(bancomats)*. There's an ATM immediately adjacent to the train station, and another one 2 minutes up the street from the Paradiso [see *bar scene,* above]. Note: This is the only of the five Cinqua Terra towns where you can exchange money!

Tourist Information You can get information at the **tourist office** *(To the right as you exit the tunnel from the train station to the town center; Tel 0187/817-506; Open daily 9:30am-12:30pm/3:30-5:30pm, closed Sun 3:30-5:30pm).*

Public Transportation The "milk-run" train services all five towns daily from 6am until 1 or 2am [see *regional intro,* above]. You can easily walk anywhere you want to go in Monterosso, but there's a **taxi** service that runs from the train station *(Tel 0335/616-58-42).*

Emergency Medical emergencies: *118;* Police: *112.* Medical Corps on call to go to hospital in La Spezia: *800-973, 817-687, 730-500.*

Pharmacies There is no 24-hour pharmacy, so call the Medical Corps if an emergency pops up while you're in the region. Otherwise, regular pharmacy hours are 8am-1pm/4pm-7pm, closed Sat afternoon, Sun. There's a pharmacy in Monterosso *(42 Via Fegina; Tel 817-148).*

Telephone Local dialing code: *0187.*

Trains La Spezia *(Tel 714-735)* is the nearest major station. From La Spezia, you can reach Monterosso on the milk train.

vernazza

Vernazza cannot support the numbers of tourists it gets. Because other guidebooks have touted it as their favorite, it is filled with Americans—you hardly feel like you're in Italy. Unlike Monterosso or Riomaggiore, Vernazza draws more middle-aged and older folks than wild youth. The Rick Steves tour groups, the kings of the package-deal trips, descend upon Vernazza all summer long, and you're sure to notice the clusters of 20 to 30 West Coasters who take over local establishments upon arrival.

It's obnoxious, really—a group that large just dominates a town this small. If you see them at a restaurant, don't bother going in; service is sure to take forever. In terms of daylight activities, the beach at the breakwater is tiny, so you might just want to hike or train it to Monterosso for swimming. Most people sun themselves on the rocks near Vernazza's harbor; swimming is not allowed off the docks. Vernazza by night revolves around the only nightspot worth going to, **The Blue Marlin.**

bar and live music scene

In this town, **The Blue Marlin** *(43 Via Roma; Tel 0187/821-149; 6:30am-midnight, daily July, Aug, closed Thur rest of the year; bmarlin@tin.it; No credit cards)* is where it's at. Run by the boisterous Massimo and his partner Franco, this place has everything you'll need during a stay in Vernazza. Everyone shows up here at some point, and people come dressed casually, some in bathing suits. There's even Internet access (300L per minute), but be prepared to wait a bit for the lone computer. There's live music playing nightly and plenty of drinking going on. Draught beers are 3,000L to 6,000L and cocktails are 7,000L. Massimo helps people find rooms, so if you're in need, go straight to the Marlin. They also own the self-service laundry, **Lavsciüga** *(8am-10pm, 5,000L/load)*, next door.

eats

▶▶CHEAP

Once again, welcome to **The Blue Marlin** [see *bar and live music scene,* above]. Breakfast tarts and brioche go for 6,000L, cappuccinos for 2,500L. Massimo did an impromptu poll, and everyone agreed that the cappuccinos were cheaper and better here than at other places. For lunch try the tasty Caprese salad with tomatoes and mozzarella (3,000L) or any of the sandwiches (5,000L).

▶▶SPLURGE

All of the harbor restaurants in Vernazza are gonna set you back. The best is **Gambero Rosso** *(7 Piazza Marconi; Tel 0187/812-265; Noon-3pm/7-9:30pm daily, closed Mon; 12,000-38,000L per entree; V, MC, AE),* which has an outdoor seating area right on the square, with white linen tablecloths, napkin rings, the whole shebang. There are five-course prix-fixe menus for 55,000L and 80,000L. The *pansotti,* a tube-shaped pasta made with cocoa (don't worry, it doesn't taste like chocolate) and filled with ricotta and pesto, is a house specialty. Reservations are a good idea in summer; walking in wearing your bathing suit ain't.

crashing

▶▶CHEAP

If the idea of sharing a bathroom doesn't faze you, **Albergo Barbara** *(30 Piazza Marconi, 4th floor; Tel/Fax 0187/812-398; Office open 9am-9pm; 70,000-90,000L doubles; No credit cards),* on the main square, has nine decent rooms with three bathrooms between them. The rooms range in price depending on size and view, and none have AC. If you have the means, request one of the big doubles with an ocean view. Giuseppe and Patricia both speak English and like to make reservations by phone.

▶▶**DO-ABLE**

A more traditional atmosphere can be had at **Pension Sorriso** *(4 Via Gavino; Tel 0187/812-224; Desk open 8am-11pm; 90,000L single, 150,000-180,000L double; V, MC).* Sorriso is a "real" pension, which means that the price includes breakfast and dinner. The food was described as "okay" by a visitor; still, it *is* homemade Italian fare. Try to arrive before 6pm, otherwise you're paying for a dinner you don't eat. The rooms (some with private bathroom, some with shared) are simple and spotless; none have AC, but four have balconies. A bar downstairs with drinks and ice cream is open until 11pm.

need to know

Tourist Information Vernazza's information office is in the train station, but it is rarely open.

Public Transportation The "milk-run" train services all five towns daily from 6am until 1 or 2am [see *regional intro,* above]. You can easily walk most everywhere in Vernazza.

Emergency Medical emergencies: *118;* Police: *112.* Medical Corps on call to go to hospital in La Spezia: *800-973, 817-687, 730-500.*

Pharmacies There is no 24-hour pharmacy in the region, so call the Medical Corps if an emergency pops up. Otherwise, regular pharmacy hours are 8am-1pm/4pm-7pm, closed Sat afternoon, Sun. There's a pharmacy in Vernazza *(2 Via Roma; Tel 812-396).*

Telephone Local dialing code: *0187.*

Trains La Spezia *(Tel 714-735)* is the nearest major station. From La Spezia, Genoa, or any of Cinque Terra towns, you can Vernazza on the milk train.

corniglia

Corniglia is the least visited of the five towns, probably because it sits on a hill rather than on the water. It's quiet except at the nudie beach, **Guvano** [see *beaches,* below], and has few restaurants, but exceptional wine. The walk to town from the train station is all uphill, and most people call Corniglia the "mountain village." You also don't see anyone hanging out on the streets here—it's a fairly reclusive place. Artsy types like the solitude here. Rounding the corners of buildings, you're bound to run into someone with watercolor paints and sketchbook having a go at re-creating the hilltops.

bar scene

Corniglia isn't the liveliest town in Cinque Terre, but there are still a few revelers about. The homey **Bar Nunzio** *(154 Via Fieschi; Tel 0187/812-138; 7am-midnight daily; No credit cards)* is *the* nightspot in town. There's a nice boar's head on the wall and trophies over the doorway, they play jazz and pop, and the bartenders are quite friendly to the young ladies. Try the strange orange cocktail *Aurora*...but don't expect to find out exactly what's in it. **Bar Matteo** [see *eats*, below] is right across the street.

beaches

To get to the nude beach, **Guvano** *(5,000L admission)*, start at the Corniglia train station. Follow signs pointing to a tunnel, pass through it, and you'll come to the entrance. This beach has suited bathers as well, so you won't feel like an idiot if you don't strip. But there are plenty of naked, pierced (nipples and elsewhere) Europeans to stare at. The beach is far from white and sandy, so you'll want to search out the flattest rock to lie upon. If you're pressed for time and need some George Hamilton to go, the public beach directly below the train station may or may not be there, depending on the tide. It's a narrow strip of sand, but usually not crowded, and at least there's a snack bar.

eats

▶▶CHEAP

For snacks and a cheap lunch, check out **Bar Matteo** *(151 Via Fieschi; No phone; 7:30am-12:30am daily; 4,000-5,000L sandwiches; No credit cards)*. The *panzerotto (4,000L)*, basically a pita pocket filled with tomato and cheese, is good, and the *café fredo* (iced coffee) *(2,500L)* is exceptionally good. There's outdoor table service, but indoors is self-service. At night, this turns into a bar with shots for 3,000L to 4,000L.

▶▶SPLURGE

The **Restaurant Cecio,** part of **Pensione Cecio** [see *crashing*, below], is by far the best restaurant in town. Entrees run 15,000L to 25,000L, and dinner is served from 7pm (closed Wed). An outdoor garden has

(ragazzo meets ragazza)

Cinque is an easy place to meet people. When everyone is on the same beach by day and in the same bar by night, you're bound to get familiar. Riomaggiore's **Bar Centrale** [see *bar scene* in *Riomaggiore*, above] is the perfect pickup spot. You don't even have to be obvious about it—conversations overlap on the wooden deck outside, and there's always room for one more at a game of cards. Nabbing an Italian love thang in these parts is not likely to happen, as there just aren't a whole lot of local young people around. If you get desperate for some lovin', hang out at the entrance to Via dell Amore [see *hiking*, above] and wait for someone to ask you to pose with them for a smooching picture.

tables that overlook the ocean, but the restaurant interior, with exposed rock walls and log furniture, is equally impressive. The house wine is 9,000L for a half liter, and the *risotto al Cecio,* cooked in a terra cotta pot with seafood and local herbs, is the house specialty.

crashing

At almost every doorway there's a sign for *camere*-Italian for "rooms"— but if you're the kind who prefers to make reservations in advance, try **Pensione Cecio** *(Via Serra; Tel/Fax 0187/812-138; Ask about rooms in the restaurant 9am-11pm; 90,000L double; No credit cards).* The family-run Cecio is a cut above most places in Cinque Terre. Just off the town's main square, Cecio has a pension upstairs from its very solid restaurant. Rooms are whitewashed and have simple, classy furnishings and views of the water, each with its own bathroom. Included in the price is breakfast in the **Restaurant Cecio,** with a nice selection of pastries, breads, and yogurt.

need to know

Tourist Information Corniglia's information office is in the train station, but it is rarely open.

Public Transportation The "milk-run" train services all five towns daily from 6am until 1 or 2am [see *regional intro,* above]. You can easily walk most everywhere you need to go in Corniglia.

Emergency Medical emergencies: *118;* Police: *112.* Medical Corps on call to go to hospital in La Spezia: *800-973, 817-687, 730-500.*

Pharmacies There is no 24-hour pharmacy, so call the Medical Corps if an emergency pops up. Otherwise, regular pharmacy hours are 8am-1pm/4pm-7pm, closed Sat afternoon, Sun. Corniglia is so small it doesn't have a pharmacy, but all the other Cinque Terra towns do. Just jump the milk train [see above] to an adjacent town, if you need some medicine.

Telephone Local dialing code: *0187.*

Trains La Spezia *(Tel 714-735)* is the nearest major station. From La Spezia, Genoa, or any of Cinque Terra towns, you can get to Vernazza on the milk train.

manarola

Manarola is the most spread-out of the Cinque Terre villages—it has no real "center." The town is essentially an uphill road dotted with businesses and plenty of restaurants that cater to the German and Scandinavian families who make it their vacation base. The vibe can be semi-snotty in Manarola; if one of the towns were to be called "upscale," this would be the one. Dinners are expensive, and you won't find too many young people here. Keeping with the family vibe, every year at Christmas the town constructs a manger on the western slope of a hill in a vineyard adjacent to the town. The best parts of Manarola are its youth hostel and **Cantina da Zio Bramante** [see *bar scene,* below]. The nightlife is so-so—more lively than Corniglia, less lively than Monterosso and Vernazza. Finally, there's no beach at Manarola's port, so walk to Riomaggiore [see below] or train it to Monterosso [see above] if you crave sand.

bar scene

If hanging out and listening to young locals sing the "Manarola Blues" sounds like a jammin' night out, make a beeline for **Cantina da Zio Bramante** *(186 Via Disclovolo; Tel 0187/920-442; 9am-midnight daily, closed Thur; V, MC).* Twenty-something Gabriel—not the guy from **Toretta** [see *crashing,* below]—always has a guitar on hand and loves to make up impromptu tunes to entertain his customers. "Manarola Blues" is one of his many creative efforts, and only a true curmudgeon would find his home-grown lyrics less than charming. Also charming is his willingness to let you sample his wine. In fact, if you supply the bottle, he'll fill it up with his own white for 5,000L. This is the oldest cantina in Cinque Terre, so there is tradition to be had along with good music and fine wine. And Gabriel's prices are lower than the norm for bottles to go.

Across the street, the generic-as-it-sounds **Bar Gelateria** *(181 Via Disclovolo; No phone; 8am-midnight daily, closed Sun Sept-June; No credit cards)* serves up big draughts for 5,000L and a shot of whisky for 3,000L. There's also an outdoor deck where locals and travelers hang out at night with picnic tables where you can plop down and make new friends.

eats

▶▶CHEAP

Hankering for a hot dog? **Bar Gelateria** [see *bar scene,* above] serves up those greasy little tastes of home *(5,000L),* along with grilled panini sandwiches filled with veggies or meat *(4,000L to 7,000L)* and splendid home-made gelato (try the coconut).

▶▶SPLURGE

Ristorante Aristide *(290 Via Disclovolo; Tel 0187/920-000; Restaurant open noon-2pm/7-10pm, snack bar open 8am-8pm; 15,000-35,000L per entree; V, MC)* is not the friendliest place, but locals love it. It has outdoor dining overlooking the water as well as an indoor restaurant with a snack bar downstairs. It's the "best restaurant in town," so to speak, so it's packed most nights in the summer. The food is gourmet-ish and expensive, and the seafood dishes—their specialty—are especially excellent.

crashing

▶▶CHEAP

Manarola has a bona fide youth hostel atop town across from the church, **Ostello Cinque Terre** *(21 Via B. Riccobaldi; Tel 0187/920-215, Fax 0187/920-218; Desk open 7am-1pm/5pm-1am; ostello@cdh.it, www.cinqueterre.net/ostello; 25,000L/bed, 100,000L private quad; V, MC, AE).*

There's no hanky-panky in the single-sex rooms, which hold four to six people with shared bath. The private rooms can sleep up to four and are 100,000L flat, no matter how many people. Conveniences abound: a bread, jam, and coffee breakfast for 5,000L, Internet access for 4,000L per 15 minutes, and laundry for 11,000L per load. The rooms are your typical bunk-bed hostel types, but the roof terrace has a great view. The maximum reservation is three nights, and there's a 1am curfew.

▶▶DO-ABLE

Across from the youth hostel is a family-run bed-and-breakfast that is definitely worth checking out. **La Toretta** *(14 Vico Volto; Tel/Fax 0187/920-327; Desk open 8am-11pm; 70,000L double, 90,000L apartment, 150,000L large apartment for 4; toretta@cdh.it; No credit cards)* is managed by the young architect Gabriel Baldini, who designed many of the rooms. He also personally picks up guests from the train station or a nearby airport if you arrange it in advance. Toretta's rooms have ocean views, TVs, terraces, and antique-looking furniture. The apartments are a good deal, since they have a kitchen and a sitting room with a fold-out. Breakfast is 8,000L per person. There are only seven rooms, so be sure to reserve in advance.

need to know

Tourist Information Manarola's information office is the train station, but it is rarely open.

Public Transportation The "milk-run" train services all five towns daily from 6am until 1 or 2am [see *regional intro,* above]. You can easily able to walk most everywhere you need to go in Manarola.

Emergency Medical Emergencies: *118;* Police: *112.* Medical Corps on call to go to hospital in La Spezia: *800-973, 817-687, 730-500.*

Pharmacies There is no 24-hour pharmacy, so call the Medical Corps if an emergency pops up. Otherwise, regular pharmacy hours are 8am-1pm/4pm-7pm, closed Sat afternoon, Sun. Manarola has a pharmacy *(Via Disclovolo; 949-209-30).*

Telephone Local dialing code: *0187.*

Trains La Spezia *(Tel 714-735)* is the nearest major station. From La Spezia, Genoa, or any of Cinque Terra towns, you can Vernazza on the milk train.

riomaggiore

Bar Centrale [see *bar scene,* below] is an ongoing party from morning to night, the pebble beach is big enough so that you're not inhaling the suntan lotion from the sunbather next to you, *and* this is the home of Cinque Terre's scuba club. The mayor took it upon himself to cable the town to a hilltop satellite, providing residents with cable TV and views from the bizarre "spy cam" that sporadically zooms in on various parts of the town! Smaller than Monterosso, but with much more character, Rio is happy to let students take over. The buildings along the town road stay in families for generations, so any of the rooms that you stay in here are lovingly cared for and individually decorated.

bar scene

There is but one bar in town, the infamous **Bar Centrale** *(144 Via Colombo; Tel 0187/920-208; 7:30am-1am daily; barcentr@tin.it; No credit cards)*. Ivo and Alberto run this place with an iron fist. The cafe interior is where you'll place your order, but all drinking and hanging out is done on the wooden deck outside. One of the duo is always around to joke with strangers and serve up the 20,000L pitchers of beer that are guzzled down at night. On the patio outside there's drinking, late-night card games, and easy fun. They have been known, however, to blast the *Pulp Fiction* CD all night long. Internet access costs 350L per minute, and be gentle—Ivo is very protective of his PC.

beach

It's not sandy, but the sun, rocks, and pebbles grow on you. Wear shoes and walk down Via Colombo until the staircase takes you into a tunnel that goes to the harbor. The beach is around the rock to the left. In that tunnel you'll pass the **Cinque Terre Diving Center** *(Tel 0339/543-17-00; By appointment; info@acquario.ge.it; No credit cards)*, which will most likely be closed. To arrange a dive or snorkel trip, call the center's English hot line. Dives are 80,000L for students and 100,000L if school is a memory. The price includes all equipment, and you have to be scuba-certified. They may allow a shallow introductory dive without certification if it's not a full trip. Snorkeling gear is 20,000L per day. Area diving is actually good, because all of Cinque Terre's waters are protected marine land. You'll see colorful fishies and gorgeous reefs with anemones and sea sponges.

eats

Unless absolute laziness has set in, there's no reason to eat out in Riomaggiore. It's easy to pick up food from any of the five street markets and whip up an Italian feast in the kitchen. If you must have your food made

rules of the game

Cinque Terre is so small that no one hassles you about drinking on the beach or on the street, and even if you throw up on the street they're likely to laugh it off (still, it's always preferable *not* to have to throw up on the street). Drug use seems nonexistent; what goes on behind closed doors doesn't seem to draw much attention.

for you, sandwiches are the best and cheapest option from these markets, at 2,000L for focaccia with prosciutto and cheese.

▶▶**DO-ABLE**

Dau Cila *(84 Via Colombo; Tel 0187/760-032; 8am-12:30am; 5,000L breakfast; V, MC, AE)* is a cutesy ground-level cafe with tooled iron chairs and Formica tables. This little place can help you fend off the urge for a real breakfast with its killer buffet—complete with muesli, yogurt, croissants, and the infamous Nutella (1,500L per item). Fresh-squeezed OJ pressed right before your eyes is only 3,000L, and at night they serve wine for only 3,000L a glass.

▶▶**SPLURGE**

Locals describe this waterfront eatery as chichi, but **La Lanterna** *(Marina; Tel 0187/920-589; 11am-3:30pm/7:30-11pm daily, closed Thur night; 7,000-25,000L per entree; V, MC, AE)* won't necessarily empty out your wallet. Lanterna's small outdoor terrace overlooks the harbor, so it's no surprise that fresh seafood is the house specialty. A blackboard outside lists the day's specials, which might include spaghetti cooked in cuttlefish ink or scampi roasted on a spit. The food is fine to good, but the real draw here is the atmosphere.

crashing

There are no hotels in Riomaggiore, and that's not a bad thing. Instead, locals rent out private "rooms," which are usually apartments with kitchens and living rooms. Try to get here early for a room, but if you come in on the 11pm train, go straight to **Bar Centrale** [see *bar scene, above*], and Ivo will hook you up with a place if it is at all humanly possible. More than a few sleep-deprived travelers have slumped in desperately late at night.

▶▶**DO-ABLE**

For a more traditional approach, e-mail Anna Michielini and stay in one of her flats at **Anna Michielini Rooms** *(143 Via Colombo; Tel/Fax 0187/920-411; No office, call between 8am-10pm; 80,000L double apartment, 160,000L apartment for up to six people; camichie@tin.it; No credit cards)*. Anna's daughter Daniella went to school in London and speaks perfect English, and her husband, Camillo, hooks guests up to the Net for free. The apartments vary in sizes—one is an enormous two-bedroom and another is a studio—but all have homey and simple decorations and come complete with kitchens and cookware (eating out does, in fact, get old).

   Edi Apartments *(111 Via Colombo; Tel/Fax 0187/920-325; Office open 9am-8pm; 80,000L double; edi-vesigna@iol.it; No credit cards)* are run by Edi himself, who presents guests upon arrival with bottles of his homemade *limoncina*. Don't drink it all in one sitting—this ain't lemonade. The apartments vary in size, but all have kitchens and bathrooms.

   Run by a great guy who has caught on to the backpacker craze in town, **La Dolce Vita** *(Via Colombo 122; Tel 018/770-56-24; 40,000L/person summer, 25,000L/person winter; V, MC)* has three apartments that sleep two people, six apartments that sleep four, and a giant one for 12. As long as you pay the basic amount, you can have more friends sleep over at no extra charge—the owner doesn't care. Every apartment is totally hooked up with full kitchen and utensils, living room, clean bathrooms, fridge, and washers and dryers. During the summer reservations should be made a week in advance; ask for apartments with balconies.

Vivaldi, Ugolino, Grazie *(Via S. Antonio 113; Tel 018/792-0192; 40,000L single, 80,000L double; No credit cards)* is a small, three-room pensione run by an old man and his wife who have lived in town their entire lives (with exception of a brief stint in Long Island). Apartments have full facilities (kitchen, bathroom, etc.), and an amazing view of the sea. The old man brews his own Chachetrá, a sweet dessert wine, in his basement and is always happy to get sauced with one of his renters.

need to know

Tourist Information Rio Maggiore has an information office at the train station, but it's rarely open.

Public Transportation The "milk-run" train services all five towns daily from 6am until 1 or 2am [see *intro, above*]. You can walk (or climb) anywhere you need to go in Rio Maggiore.

Health and Emergency Medical emergencies: *118*; Police: *112*. Medical Corps on call to go to hospital in La Spezia: *800-973, 817-687, 730-500.*

Pharmacies There is no 24-hour pharmacy, so call the Medical Corps if an emergency pops up after hours, but during daylight hours you can get help for what ails you at the local pharmacy on Via Columbo *(Tel 122/920-160).*

Telephone Local dialing code: *0187.*

Trains La Spezia *(714-735)* is the nearest major station. From **La Spezia,** you can reach Rio Maggiore on the **milk train.**

piedmont &
the valle
d'aosta

Laid out at the foot of the mighty Alps, the Piedmont region is known for its tall mountains, culinary genius, and cultural wealth. It's a granola-head's paradise, with 11 national parks and an urban capital, **Turin,** that's greened up by a bunch of botanical gardens and parks. The region also has some of Italy's best climbing, whitewater rafting, parasailing, hiking, and (last but most definitely not least) skiing. With its gigantic mountains to the north and its rolling farmland to the south, Piedmont is a great place to chill, whether that means exploring a small cobblestone village like **Asti** for a day, or planning a week of skiing in the **Valle di Susa.** The winter season up in these parts runs from October through June, with the first snowfall usually coming in early November.

With all the mountains around, it's easy to forget that Piedmont was among Italy's industrial big shots not so long ago. Southern Italians moved here by the thousands in the 1920s to get work in the car and engine factories (including the fabulous Fiat). It was only after World War II, when Turin was bombed to smithereens, that the boom fizzled out.

As you tour the area you'll see remnants of a much earlier boom. Thanks to the wealthy royal Savoy family, which first landed here in the 11th century and stayed for about 800 years, the countryside around Turin is sprinkled with cool old castles, mansions, and Baroque art. Today, Turin locals continuously fund multibillion-lira restorations of these monuments, while still keeping admission costs unbelievably low so slackers like us can enjoy the fruits of their labor (21,000L covers all the museums you can see in 48 hours). Culture vultures will most definitely want to linger in Turin to fully enjoy its promenades of Baroque architecture, halls of celebrated Flemish and Piedmontese works, and an excellent Egyptian museum.

One of the region's most cherished and controversial artifacts, the holy shroud of Christ, won't be available for viewing until the year 2006. After making a brief public appearance in 2000, it's been whisked away from public view until the 2006 Winter Olympics, which Turin is hosting. Allegedly the very cloth that Jesus was wrapped in after the crucifixion, the shroud was almost reduced to ashes after a fire in 1997 in Cappella della Santa Sindone (which is also off limits until 2006).

But what you can definitely enjoy without any restrictions is the region's bounteous food. Locals pride themselves on cultivating some of Italy's heartiest wines, moldiest mushrooms, and highest-calorie meals—

pιedmonτ & τhe vaλλe d'aosτa

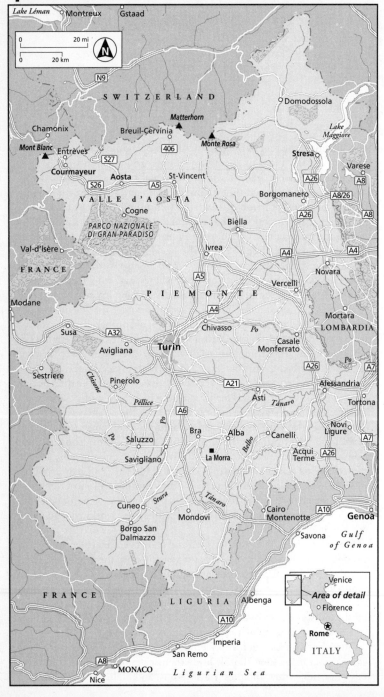

Lake Léman   ○ Montreux   ○ Gstaad

0 ——— 20 mi
0 ——— 20 km
N
N9

S W I T Z E R L A N D   ○ Domodossola

Matterhorn ▲
○ Chamonix   ○ Breuil-Cervinia   Monte Rosa ▲   Lake Maggiore
▲ Mont Blanc   Entrèves ○   406   **Stresa**
                S27   A26   ○ Varese
Courmayeur   **Aosta** ○ St-Vincent   A8
                S26   A5   ○ Borgomanero   A8/26
V A L L E d' A O S T A   A8
    ○ Cogne   A26
PARCO NAZIONALE   ○ Biella
DI GRAN PARADISO
                        ○ Ivrea
Val-d'Isère ○   A4   ○ Novara   A4
                        A5   ○ Vercelli
F R A N C E
                   P I E M O N T E   ○ Mortara
○ Modane   A4   **LOMBARDIA**
                                    Po
○ Susa   A32   ○ Chivasso   ○ Casale   Po   A7
    ○ Avigliana   **Turin**   Monferrato
                                              A26   ○ Alessandria
○ Sestriere   ○ Pinerolo   A21   ○ Tortona
         Chisone   ○ Asti   Tánaro   A7
                   Péllice   A6   ○ Novi
                   Po   ○ Bra ○ Alba ○ Canelli   Ligure   A7
         ○ Saluzzo   ■ La Morra   ○ Acqui   A26
         ○ Savigliano   Terme
                   Po   Belbo
                        Stura   Tánaro
         ○ Cuneo   ○ Cairo   A10
    ○ Borgo San   ○ Mondovi   Montenotte   **Genoa**
      Dalmazzo
                                        ○ Savona   Gulf
                                                  of Genoa

F R A N C E   L I G U R I A   ○ Albenga   Venice ○
                              A10   *Area of detail*
                                                      ○ Florence
                        ○ Imperia
         A8   ○ San Remo   ★ **Rome**
      MONACO   L i g u r i a n   S e a   **ITALY**
○ Nice

this is *not* a good place to be on a diet. And culinary staples vary from town to town, so you'll never get a chance to get sick of any new-found favorite dish. In laid-back southern Piedmont, for example, folks seem to be obsessed with finding the biggest, stinkiest *tartufos* (truffles) in the world, especially in the fall, when they're in season. Southern Italians will go to hell and back to uncover this subterranean delicacy, which they serve over pasta with butter, or in various meat dishes.

Because Piedmont is close to France, the food here is a little different from what you'll find elsewhere in Italy. The winner by a mile is the region's most famous recipe, *bagna caoda.* This meal-in-itself is a huge pile of vegetables (primarily potatoes, beet root, Jerusalem artichokes, cabbage, and butter onions) covered in a garlic, anchovy, and olive oil sauce. Another well-known dish is *tajarin,* a handmade pasta mixed with eggs, covered in a meat or chicken liver sauce, and smothered in Parmesan cheese. The amazing list of cheeses (like *castelmagno, gorgonzola, and toma*), wines (*Barolo, Cortese,* and *Caluso Passito*), hearty bread sticks, and mouthwatering deserts (*krumiri, panna cotta,* and *gianduiotti*) are reason enough to explore the restaurants and cafes here.

valle d'aosta

Pocketed up in Piedmont's northwestern corner is the mountainous **Valle d'Aosta.** Join the rest of the snow-happy tourists who flock to the wealthy mountain towns of **Courmayeur** and **Aosta** for awesome winter sports. And if you're more of a cocoa-in-the-lounge than adventure-on-the-slopes type being dragged along by an outdoorsy friend, don't worry—these pretty little villages have plenty of cozy bars and cool boutique shops, and Aosta even has some great old ruins you can wander about while your buddies are out risking frostbite.

People first settled in the Valle d'Aosta in 3000 B.C., and Augustus and his Roman centurions contributed to local culture early in the first millennium. Today the folks here speak an interesting mix of Italian, French, and German—or so they like to think. From time to time you'll hear them say things like *voilá* instead of *ecco,* but the real French influence comes in the culinary form. If cheese doesn't settle well on your palate, get a new tongue, because every kitchen in Aosta goes crazy with blends of mountain cheeses. The most popular French-Italian dish is *fonita,* a fondue-like blend of Gouda and Brie cheese that's served over a flame with meats and bread. Borrowing more from the Italian bag of kitchen tricks is *carbonada con polenta,* a thick steamy soup with hunks of *polenta* (cornmeal mush) and meat.

Due to heavy snowfalls and some downright nasty weather, almost all the older homes up in the northern end of this region are covered in shale stone tiles that can measure three or four square feet in size. From Aosta up to France, you'll also see dozens of Romanesque and Gothic castles that, on a foggy day, look like something in Transylvania. The castles form a chain up the center of the valley, and visits cost anywhere from 4,000 to 10,000L. You can get to the castles by car or via the bus from

Aosta to Switzerland. (The tourist office in Aosta has a complete map, with visiting hours and other info.)

The walled city of Aosta is the best place to check out some Roman ruins, including a Roman amphitheater, the 11th-century cathedral Chiesa di Sant'Orso, and Augustus's personal monument, Arco d'Augusto. If you're more interested in the mountains outside of town, Courmayeur has the most direct access to the nearby lifts. For outdoor fun at a slower speed, Parco Nazionale di Gran Paradiso has lots of great hiking and cross-country trails.

getting around the region

Turin is Piedmont's transportation hub. Trains run from the city's Stazione Porta Nuova in just about every direction, including Milan to the north, Genova to the south, and France to the west. Trains are the cheapest and most efficient way to get around, although if you're headed to a ski resort you may want to take the bus instead: Many have direct connections from Turin, whereas taking the train involves switching at various stations.

Although Piedmont is the second-largest region in Italy (over 24,000 square km), you'll likely find yourself not straying far from the middle, where most points of interest run in a vertical line (except, of course, the western ski resorts). To explore the region from bottom to top, you can catch a train from Savona in Liguria, head north through Turin and up to Lago Maggiore, and eventually continue on to Switzerland. Coming from the north via Switzerland will bring you through the Italian Alps along Italy's biggest lake, Lago Maggiore. From here you can pretty much shoot through the northern expanse of the region until you reach Turin. From Turin you can catch a bus up to the region's most beautiful park, **Parco Nazionale del Gran Paradiso.** Busing it from the park, you can either head back down to Turin or into the smaller mountains in **Valle di Susa.** From Valle di Susa you can train it west to France, or hop a bus or train back to Turin.

Since fall 2000, train service into the Valle d'Aosta from the rest of Italy was suspended, after heavy flooding completely demolished the tracks. Unless officials fix the tracks by the time you visit—and we've been told it "could take years" for things to get back to normal—the best way to take in this region is by bus. The train line that once ran to Valle d'Aosta now stops in **Chivasso** and **Ivrea,** two towns down in Piedmont, and from there a connecting network of buses will take you where you need to go.

The main route through the Valle d'Aosta, A5, goes pretty much down the middle of the region, passing through St. Vincent, Aosta, and Courmayeur. All buses from towns and cities to the south travel on this route. Aosta also has a little 5km train line that winds through the mountains on its way to **Pre Saint Didier** (you'll get some great views of the valley's castles). From Pre Saint Didier, you can catch a bus to Courmayeur.

With your starting point at **Aosta,** you can take a day trip north through the Valle del Gran San Bernardo, check out some Roman ruins, see the authentic stuffed Saint Bernard (the dog, not the monk) at the Swiss border, and amble through one of the oldest mountain passes in the region, Route 27. Heading south from Aosta, you could catch a bus through the Valle di Cogne and explore some amazing hiking trails in **Parco Gran Paradiso.** Heading west from Aosta, strap on your snowboard for some of Italy's best ski resorts—or your lifejacket for wild whitewater rafting—in and around **Courmayeur.**

TRAVEL TIMES

All times by train unless otherwise marked:
* by bus

	Turin	Asti	Valle di Susa	Aosta	Courmayeur	Parco Nationale
Turin	-	1:00	1:00	2:00	3:30*	3:00*
Asti	1:00	-	3:00 via Turin	3:00	4:30*	4:00*
Valle di Susa	1:00	3:00 via Turin	-	3:00 via Turin	4:30* via Turin	4:00* via Turin/ Aosta
Aosta	2:00	3:00	3:00 via Turin	-	1:00*	1:00*
Courmayeur	3:30*	4:30*	4:30* via Turin	1:00*	-	2:00* via Turin

TURIN

If the phrase "intellectual party town" sounds like an oxymoron to you, you've obviously never been to Turin. You'll find plenty of discos, bars, cafes, clubs, and plazas to occupy your time here—new bars are springing up every day, and the streets are literally packed with students from the huge local university all year long. Although they're a little more reserved than their southern peers, the students here know how to rip it up on the party scene. But this teenage riot is balanced out by rare and prestigious Baroque art and architecture to check out when you're not scoping the scene from a park bench or barstool.

Turin's history rivals the best of Italy's cities: The royal Savoy family settled here in the 11th century, and during their 800-year rule they united the Italy we know today. They made Turin Italy's capital city for a short-lived four years. Today the city's two largest piazzas are named after the prominent Savoy family members who put Turin on the map for good: Vittorio Emanuele and Camillo Cavour.

In more recent history, Turin is known for its manufacturing role during both world wars, during which it was severely bombed, and as the home of the first **Fiat factory** [see *culture zoo,* below], where workers turned out Italy's famous car until the factory was shut down in 1982. The city is close to a million strong these days due primarily to the migration of southern Italians during the factory's peak production.

But it's easy to forget about all those smokestacks on the outskirts of the city when you're downtown: On a clear day, you can see the Alps, and the city's public sanitation crews seem to always be keeping the streets and parks of Turin so clean it could be mistaken for an outdoor museum.

From the banks of the Po River and the streets surrounding Piazza Vittorio Veneto, Turin's bars, discos, and cafes come alive when the sun falls. The university students are well aware that their city doesn't get as many tourists as, say, Milan, and maybe that's why their attitude toward international crashers is so innocent and inviting.

For big city dwellers, Turin locals are a chill bunch. They love their city, their food, and their province. You'll feel like you're hanging in one big friendly neighborhood instead of a big city. Just about every cafe has its regulars who spend countless hours talking about their families, politics, and, of course, soccer. *Enotecas* (wine bars) like **Il Bottigliere** [see *bar scene,* below] are always popular places to get an earful of local gab.

12 hours in turin

1. Swing by **Caffe Flora** [see *bar scene,* below] for a glass of white wine with Pellegrino and watch the boats go by on the river Po.
2. Grab a slice of some thick-crusted pizza while you do some shopping for a new cowboy hat on Via Po [see *stuff,* below].
3. Practice your Frisbee toss or take a bike ride along the river in **Parco Del Valentino** [see *city sports,* below].
4. Walk like an Egyptian down Turin's fanciest boulevard, Via Roma, and straight into the world's third-largest Egyptian museum, **Museo delle Antichita** [see *culture zoo,* below].
5. Suck down a pint of Ireland's finest brew at **The Shamrock Inn** [see *bar scene,* below] and mingle with Turin's wild university crowd.
6. Brown bag a lunch from a student sandwich booth on Via Giovanni Giolitti and take a boat ride up the river to check out the old Fiat factory and the Savoy fortress [see *city sports,* below].
7. Get in tune with Italy's oldest and most cutting edge technology from the silver screen in the cinema museum, or catch an amazing view of the city, in Turin's largest building, **Mole Antonelliana** [see *culture zoo,* below].
8. Catch some rays with the university students in Piazza Cavour.
9. Fire off some cannons at the royal armory museum [see *culture zoo,* below].
10. Rub elbows to the reggae rhythms at **Hiroshima Mon Amour** till the early hours [see *club scene,* below].

turin bars clubs and culture zoo

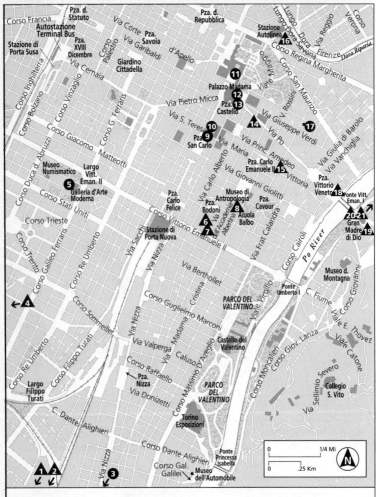

BARS/CLUBS ▲

Birreria **15**
Caffé Flora **18**
Club Varadero **2**
Coors Colorado **8**
Fratelli Marx **16**
Hiroshima Mon Amor **1**
Il Bottigliere **6**
Magazzini Reddocks **19**
Naxos **21**
Road Roars **14**
The Shamrock Inn **7**
The Supermarket **4**
Zoo Bar **20**

CULTURE ZOO ●

Duomo di San Giovanni
 (Capella della
 Santa Sindone) **11**
Galleria Civica D'Arte Moderna
 e Contemporanea **5**
Galleria Sabauda **9**
Mole Antonelliana **17**
Museo dell'Automobile **1**
Museo delle Antichita **10**
Palazzo Madama **13**
Royal Armory in
 Armeria Reale **12**

Jolly and usually drunken, these age-old watering holes appear on practically every other block.

The best place to get the lowdown on local goings-on is in the weekly Italian-language edition of *La Stampa,* printed every weekend. The entertainment section, *Torino Sette,* has listings of summer concerts in the parks, theatrical performances, and club parties. The lobbies in the university buildings [see *hanging out,* below] also have copies of student newspapers and flyers with info on DJs, live concerts, and festivals.

neighborhoods

Unlike in other European cities we could mention, you don't have to be a brain surgeon to find your way around here. Except for the area east of the river, the streets in Turin's city center pretty much run north-south and east-west, thanks to the genius of hometown architects Filippo Juvarra, Guarino Guarini, and Carlo di Castellamonte. The center of the city is **Palazzo Madama** [see *culture zoo,* below], the mother of all the city's palaces. The Palazzo is connected to the cultural epicenter of the city by **Via Po,** which runs east to the **Po River**—most of the action goes down here on the west bank of the river, and in the upper-class residential areas that lie east of the river up in the hills.

Within the city's center, there are a number of colossal piazzas. **Stazione Porta Nuova,** where you're likely to arrive, is about a dozen blocks south of **Palazzo Madama.** One of Turin's main streets, **Corso Vittorio Emanuele II,** runs east-west in front of the station. Right across that street is **Piazza Carlo Felice,** a grand circular piazza built around a garden. **Via Roma,** one of the city's oldest and most decorative avenues,

when you gotta go

For some reason, conventional toilets are practically nonexistent in Turin and throughout much of Piedmont. Instead of Mr. Toilet Bowl, you will become quite close to his distant cousin, Mr. Stand 'N' Drop (you know, the kind with the kung-fu-grip feet plates and the bulls-eye hole to nowhere?). These intimidating contraptions are quite common in cafes and smaller bars in and out of the city. It has something to do with cold weather and poor septic systems, or so the locals say. So if you're in your nice hotel room or some fancy restaurant, take advantage of the "normal" toilet, because your next option may require much more coordination.

runs north from Carlo Felice and connects Piazza Carlo Felice to **Piazza San Carlo** and then to Palazzo Madama. At the northern edge of the city center is the huge **Piazza della Repubblica,** which becomes an antiques free-for-all every Sunday [see *to market,* below].

Clearly the most active part of town—day or night—is the area of town east of Via Roma over to the river, between Corso Vittorio Emanuele II at the south and Via Po to the north—especially *on* Via Po. This is the university district, and it's teeming with posh little *enotecas,* three-story bars and pubs, and laid-back students' parks. Students and young out-of-towners tend to flock in and around **Piazza Cavour** to trade philosophy notes, tune their guitars, and get a buzz on. The more cultural and commercial pulse of Turin is centered along the section of Via Roma that runs between Palazzo Madama and Piazza delle Rupubblica.

The farther north you go in Italy, the more efficient the public transportation becomes. Turin has a major network of trams and buses that are—for the most part—organized and on time during the day. At most stops an electronic board tells you when the next bus or tram is arriving, give or take a minute. During the night, however, arrivals tend to be a little less punctual. Public transportation shuts down at about 1am and kicks off at 5am. But if you're just hanging out in the city center, it's always more interesting to walk.

hanging out

For all its history and grandeur, Turin is a giant college town in a lot of ways. The more than 30,000 students from all over the region and Italy who flock here year-round to be close to the mountains, to party, and hopefully to attain *some* scholastic enlightenment can be seen sprawled all over the city at any

four things to talk to a local about

1. **Music.** Turin being the cultural city that it is, with over a dozen festivals for music alone, you're sure to strike up a tune with this subject.
2. **Fiats.** Since Turin was once the car capital of Italy, older Turin locals have lots of stories to tell about what the city was like when just about everyone in town was working for the factory.
3. **Vino.** With more than 200 different kinds of wine made in the region and some 50 or 60 wine bars in the city, there's plenty to talk about while you drink it.
4. **Festivals.** The city has always got some sort of festival going on that they can give you the inside scoop on.

hour. If you want to find the motherlode, head to the campus—it spreads out between Via Po, the river, and Corso Vittorio Emanuele II.

Chewing the fat in some piazza or on a park bench is an age-old Turin pastime. **Piazza Cavour,** and **Piazzas Valdo Fusi** and **Carlo Emanuele II,** all located around the university, are always teeming with Turin scholars. Or you can grab a seat at one of the 30 or so outdoor cafes on **Via Po** and bump into other travelers. As in most major Italian cities, cafes here generally open at 8am and close around 11pm. An old Turin cafe specialty is *bicerin,* an espresso coffee with chocolate and cream. **Cafe delle Scienze** *(N.E. corner of Piazza Castello 2; No credit cards)* is a cheap place on the main drag to suck down a coffee (3,000L), write a postcard, and take in the city's peaks and freaks. You can do some more people watching across the street at **Caffé Gallery** *(Via Po N. 58/A; Tel 011/817-01-07; 9am-10pm daily; No credit cards).* Fill your belly with a big frothy cup of *caffè* with *nutella* (5,000L) while you people-watch from the tables outside. To hang with the everyday Turin folk, have a pistachio gelato in **Master Club Coffee** *(Via Roma 121; Tel 011/562-16-82; 8am-8pm Mon-Sat; No credit cards)*—or get it in a cone and walk out onto fancy Via Roma for some window-shopping.

To meet some of Turin's cutting-edge hipsters, club kids, and punks, try wandering past the row of *bizzarro* boutiques along Via Po toward the river [see *stuff,* below]. The chain-smoking crew hanging here is usually listening to some deep bass groove, and they eagerly invite all foreign beings to hang.

Public displays of affection are always welcome in **Giardini Real** [see *city sports,* below], the gardens behind the city palace. As evening falls, the riverbanks down by Ponte Vittorio Emanuele I, the bridge at the end of Via Po, are swarming with strolling locals, pub-hopping students, and wine-swilling backpackers.

bar scene

Plain and simple, Turin rocks when the sun goes down. There's a high concentration of massive pubs along Corso Vittorio Emanuele II that seem to bear the brunt of the university crowd seven days a week, from dusk till dawn.

The Shamrock Inn *(Corso Vittorio Emanuele II 34; Tel 011/817-49-50; 7pm-4am daily; No credit cards)* has two floors jam-packed with eclectic Turin youth. Upon entering, you'll find yourself shoulder to shoulder with the local long-beards and hippy chicks crowded around the tap-filled bar. If listening to Peter Gabriel and feeling like a sardine in a smoke-filled tin can is your fetish, this is as far as you need to go. If not, follow the oriental carpets up the stairs past the philosophical squatters on the landing to the second floor. Upstairs you can share an oak bench with the lounge crowd and tap your toes to the likes of Men at Work. There's a bar in the back with a huge selection of English and Irish beers (a pint of Beamish will cost you 8,000L). You can easily make a night of it here: Grab a seat at any table, buy a round, and strike up a conversation about whatever floats your boat.

rules of the game

Turin is filled with lax people who love to party.
On any given night you'll see locals young and old stumbling through the streets, singing to their heart's content. Unlike many other Italian cities, Turin stays up way past its bedtime and into the early morning, especially on weekends. Students and elders alike party late into the night. Unlike their elders, though, the students tend to fill the parks and piazzas with the scent of Moroccan "incense," very rarely drawing the attention of anyone.

If you're in the bar mood but want more of an international scene, your best bet is **Road Roars** *(Via Carlo Alberto 3; Tel 011/812-01-71; 11pm-4am daily; V, MC)*, a bar/restaurant tucked amid the dimly lit streets between Piazza Castello and Via Po. Choose from a main avenue of tables and stools or a labyrinth of private wooden stalls where you can talk about top-secret travel plans or whisper sweet nothings. The speakers pump R&B when there isn't a soccer game on the telly, and they have a huge grub menu that's about 15,000L for a filling platter. The bartenders specialize in daiquiris (10,000L) and it's got sweet red ales (8,000L) and whiskey shots (4,000L) during happy hour. The younger evening crowd generally rolls in at about 11:30pm.

"Life Is Too Short to Drink Bad Wine" is slogan on the bumper sticker/business card for **Il Bottigliere** *(Via San Francesco Da Paolo 43; Tel 011/836-050; 5pm-2am daily; V)*. This chill little wine bar in the university district loves its wine—and wants its customers to drink only the best. It has just about every regional wine imaginable stacked along the walls in the lounge and behind the bar; order by the bottle or the glass (4-8,000L). A house favorite is the Nebbiolo D'Alba, a thick, tangy red wine with 14 percent alcohol. The crowd at the bar is very welcoming and the bartender will be more than happy to hook you up with a complimentary corkscrew.

For a glimpse at the local riff-raff, grab a beer just down the street from Bottigliere at **Birreria** *(Via S. Massimo 7; Tel 011/839-52-54; 7pm-4am daily; MC, V)*. As in many establishments in Turin, you have to buzz to get in because of the unpredictable crazies (that we never got a glimpse of) who apparently roam the streets after dark. In addition to stale air and funky stained-glass lamps, the bar has a great German beer called Kapuziner Weisse that is served with a slice of lemon (8,000L). The coal-oven pizzas (10,000L) are thin crusted, loaded with cheese, and over-baked.

Caffe Flora *(Piazza Vittorio Veneto 24; Tel 817/15-30; 10am-2am daily; No credit cards)* is a perfect place to start the night if you're down by the river near Via Po. Dim lights, blue velvet upholstery, chill Italian music, and equally chill bartenders will help you pace yourself for a long night ahead. The bar is stacked with booze and the *bellisima* bartenders can mix up just about any request. There's a bulletin board near the entrance with au pair and other English-speaking job opportunities in the city.

If you're looking for a Rocky Mountain high, hike on over to **Coors Colorado** *(Via dei Mille 24; Tel 011/837-547; Noon-3:30am daily, closed Wed; No credit cards)*, just a couple blocks toward the river from the train station—it's Turin's tribute to American bars. Cheesy, loaded with televisions, and surprisingly packed, the Colorado serves up America's most watered-down draft (8,000L). The crowd here tends to be a little bit older, but can get a little crazy as the night progresses.

If sipping a cocktail, picking at tapas, and watching a movie (in Italian, duh) on a giant screen with 50 other people gets your goat, snuggle in at **Fratelli Marx** *(Corso Regina Margherita 97, behind Giardini Reali; Tel 011/814-11-34; 7pm-3am daily; No credit cards)*. Subtle music by the DJ for Radio Flash plays in the background, and the drinks run from 4,000L for beers to 10,000L for most cocktails. If you want to check some soccer action from that same giant screen on Sundays, the entrance fee is 3,000L.

club and live music scene

Over the past decade, the club scene in Turin has exploded with more than a hundred venues. Some clubs might hassle you about a membership disco card; just tell them you're a tourist and wave some moolah at them and you'll get in. Or you can buy a temporary card at the door of most clubs if you're going to be in town for a little while. The staff at **Beat** [see *stuff*, below] always knows the best parties and has the scoop on the latest underground raves.

One of the most popular discos with the university crowd is **Hiroshima Mon Amour** *(Via C. Bossoli 63, Bus 34, 1 to Lingotto Centro Fiere; Tel 011/317-66-36; 11pm-Dawn daily; 15,000-20,000L cover; No credit cards)* in the university district. The cutting-edge crowd rocks everything from colorful handmade dresses to Diesel jeans. The music is generally reggae and rock. Things start to pick up around 1am

five-o

Big brother doesn't have to be on the streets of Turin because he's watching you from hundreds of cameras strategically placed around the city. The police and God knows who else can keep an eye on you from these surveillance cameras, which are nestled on top of lamp posts, under cafe awnings, and in what you thought was just an innocent stone goblin carved on a church.

on weekends and go strong until the house lights go up in the wee hours. The women are slammin' beauties and unlike what we've seen at many other Italian discos, and the guys actually dance rather than drool over the women from the bar. There is live ska, reggae, and rock music sometimes on the weekends.

One of the biggest and baddest clubs in the city is **Zoo Bar** *(Corso Casale 127; Tel 011/819-43-47; 8pm-4am, closed Mon, Tues; Weekdays no cover; Weekends 15,000-20,000L; No credit cards),* which sits nicely along the Po River near **Parco Michelotti.** Inside, it's separated into two floors with two lounges, two bars, and two dance floor rooms. The crowd is very diverse but young to the core, very trendy, and expensive in attire. Admission comes with a free drink (otherwise 10,000L). Thursdays is usually live music—very, very loud live music—ranging from reggae to rock. Fridays usually feature DJ Ale and DJ Gino Latino, who spin a nasty mix of deep bass beats, hip-hop, and ska. Saturday nights seem to draw an older crowd, the spins are usually a little more laid-back, and the music leans more toward retro and R&B. There's a pizza place in the club where you can grab a beer and a slice or two until 3am.

A little bit more on the techno side of things, **Naxos** *(Piazza Guala 147; Tel 011/616-169; 9pm-4am, closed Mon; Cover 15,000L Fri-Sat with free drink; No credit cards)* is definitely a sweet place to get good and psychedelic. It features some of the best DJs in Turin on the weekends—the club's premier DJ, Ricky Martini, spins a decent mix of techno, progressive, and hard house along with other local DJs. There is a main stage/DJ booth in the center of the club with a 25-foot-tall replica of the Statue of Liberty under dozens of steel rafters covered in hundreds of lights and strobes. Admission during the week is almost free when local rock and punk bands are playing. The live music crowd is a little young, but it's very hip and way into the music. When punk bands jam, the place gets very moshy. Getting in on a weekend night might require a bit of a wait. It's just down the street from the Zoo Bar.

A bit outside of the city center to the west is **The Supermarket** *(Via Madonna di Campagna 1; No phone; Bus 64 from Stazione Porta Nuova; 9pm-4am, shows start around 10pm; 20,000L cover; No credit cards).* Bands jam out every weekend to grunge, rock, and poppy Italian stuff. During the week DJs spin hip-hop and reggae.

After being closed for several years for renovation and God knows what else, local club favorite **Magazzini Reddocks** *(Via Valprato 68, Tram 10 or Bus 75; No phone; 10pm-5pm Thur-Sat, closed in August; Cover 20,000L including free drink Fri-Sun; No credit cards)* is back by popular demand. This classic Turin club/art exhibition hall/theater/concert venue near the river on the south side has spread its wings and begun to get hip to the onslaught of techno and house music. Drinks run from 8,000 to 15,000L and the DJs are some of the city's best.

For more of an ethnic spin on things, check out **Club Varadero** *(Strada delle Cacce 20; Tel 011/344-534; Opening times vary; No cover weekdays; 10,000-15,000L weekends; MC, V).* This place is always jamming and packed with a somewhat older crowd. During the week there's no entrance fee, and the music is pumped through an endless line of speakers lining the walls. On Fridays, when live Brazilian music plays (15,000L cover), the place is jamming, so you could wait up to an hour to get in (and don't even *try* tipping the bouncers). But by far the craziest night of the week is Saturday, when the salsa bands get the crowds good and steamy (10,000L cover). If the 6-foot-tall Latina dancers in bikinis don't get your salsa groove on, drink another margarita (10,000L).

ARTS SCENE

Turin's filled to the brim with culture. Today the old Savoy villas are home to many of the city's prestigious art galleries and museums, which frequently feature university exhibitions.

▶▶VISUAL ARTS

For a smaller gallery scene, take a peek in **Artlab** *(Viale Risorgimento 31; Fax 011/397-20-08; MC, V)*, which is always looking to make a sale and

festivals and events

The Music Fest: Every September, Turin hosts jazz, rock, reggae, and classical musicians from around the world. All over the city—in concert halls, palace courtyards, and churches—you can join thousands of Italians and international music buffs day and night. See the tourist office for concert listings.

The International Photography Fest: Held twice a year, in the Spring and Fall (see tourist office for exact dates), this exhibition is the only one of its kind in Italy. The festival presents an international perspective through displays of provincial photographers and artists.

The International Festival of Young Filmmakers: This fast-growing fest is held every summer in cinemas all over the city.

The Turin International Gay/Lesbian Film Fest *(Piazza San Carlo 161; Tel 011/534-888; www.assioma.com/glfilmfest):* This small and friendly festival comes to town every April, and showcases feature films, shorts, and documentaries from around the world. It also dedicates part of the festival to the history of gay film, screening old classics and honoring early gay film folks.

The Turin Marathon: While Americans are busy playing jokes on each other, the Italians are racing each other in this April 1 marathon, a renowned European tradition that first kicked off in 1897. Runners follow some of the most beautiful roads in the province, from the town of Susa to the piazza in front of Palazzo Madama.

has reproductions of old classics and limited original editions of cityscapes and landscapes by local artists.

▶▶PERFORMING ARTS

The epicenter of performing arts in Turin is **Teatro Regio Torino** (*Piazza Castello 215; Tel 011/881-52-41; Tickets start at 20,000L; MC, V*). From its choice spot in one of the most impressive piazzas in Turin, the city's theater hosts a number of operas, ballets, and symphonies throughout the year, but primarily in the fall and winter. Unless you've bought tickets well in advance, tickets go on sale about an hour before performances at the main ticket window; depending on the show, the line can wrap around the building.

gay scene

Turin is the birthplace of the gay movement in Italy—the first Italian gay and lesbian organization, FUORI, was created here in 1970. The scene here is still politically active, and all the bars are cozy and welcoming. The strongest organizations today are **Fondazione Sandro Penna** (*Via Santa Chiara 1; Tel 011/521-20-33, Fax 011/540-370; www.geocities.com/WestHollywood/6263/*), **InformaGay** (*Via Santa Chiara 1; Tel 011/436-50-00, Fax 011/436-86-38; www.arpnet.it/~infgay*), and **Arcigay/Arcilesbica "Maurice"** (*Via della Basilica 3; Tel 011/521-11-16, Fax 011/521-11-32; www.arpnet.it/~maurice*). InformaGay publishes a monthly magazine, the eponymous *InFormaGay,* full of reviews and articles. Every Saturday afternoon from 5 to 8pm the InformaGay HQ turns into a laid-back cafe serving up coffee, tea, and drinks. ArciGay organizes social events and cultural gatherings for the gay and lesbian community, and runs a hotline. The most renowned gay event in Turin is the **Turin International Gay/Lesbian Film Fest** [see *festivals and events,* below].

The friendly **Il Male** (*Via Lombardore; No phone; 9pm-1am, closed Mon*) is the perfect place to lounge about with a group of friends, either at the comfy tables or sprawled right out on the carpet.

Come feel the history at **Matisse** (*Via Garibaldi 13; No phone; 9pm-1am, closed Mon*), where that first gay organization came together way back at the beginning of the 70s. Today it's still the pretty, spacious cafe it's always been—come on in and have a latte, play checkers, and watch the crowds go by.

culture zoo

Like so many other Italian cities, Turin's cultural scene is steeped in religion and royalty, and the city has made visiting the sites easy with the Torino Card. For 21,000L, you get free access to most museums and transportation for 48 hours. The card also offers discounts on some concerts, theater performances, car and bike rentals, parking, and tours within the city. To purchase a card or get more information, go to any of the tourist information offices [see *need to know,* below].

Palazzo Madama (*Piazza Castello; Tel 011/521-5960; 9am-5pm Tues-Sun; 8,000L admission*): It would be tough to miss this majestic palace, which is surrounded in the rear by the city's largest garden, **Giardini**

Reali [see *city sports*, below]. The palace was closed for restorations for over a year and just recently reopened.

Duomo di San Giovanni and **Cappella della Santa Sindone** *(Piazza San Giovanni; Tel 011/521-59-60; 9am-noon/3-5pm daily; Free admission):* Located just off Via XX Septembre, this cathedral house what is perhaps Italy's most controversial religious relic, Christ's Holy Shroud (the cloth that supposedly wrapped Christ's body after crucifixion), aka the Shroud of Turin. Although many authorities (mostly from Turin) have argued that the shroud is the real deal, carbon dating and DNA tests have scientifically challenged its validity. Much speculation and argument has persisted since. Unfortunately, the shroud will not be unveiled to the public again until Turin hosts the winter Olympics in 2006.

Museo delle Antichita *(Via Accademia delle Scienze 6, in Palazzo dell'Accademia delle Scienze; Tel 011/561-7776; 9am-7pm Tue-Sat, 9am-*

by foot

The best walking tour of Turin starts in Piazza Carlo Felice, in front of Stazione Porta Nuova. Fuel up on a quick caffè at **Ristorante Brek** [see *eats,* above], then walk north through the park. From here you'll be able to see one of the oldest streets in Turin, Via Roma.

Walking north up Via Roma, you'll pass by two large cathedrals into Piazza San Carlo. From Piazza San Carlo, continue down Via Roma and take a quick peek into the Egyptian museum, **Museo delle Antichita** [see *culture zoo,* above]. A couple of blocks further down, you'll find yourself in front of the majesty of **Palazzo Madama** [see *culture zoo,* above]. After admiring the royal digs, stop and smell the flowers in the public gardens behind the palace [see *city sports,* below]. Walking back through the gardens and the palace, head east toward the river on Turin's chaotic commercial street, Via Po. Buy yourself that funky Ecuadorian hat you always fancied from one of the street vendors. About halfway down Via Po, make a quick left on Via San Montebello. Look up at what was once Europe's tallest building, **Mole Antonelliana** [see *culture zoo,* above]. Then head back to Via Po, and continue on toward the river Po. Cross the Ponte Vittorio Emanuele I, walk through Piazza Gran Madre di Dio, and follow Via Vittozzi, which will turn into Via Gidanetti. From here, walk up the hill and take in the amazing view of the city until you reach the Museo Nazionale della Montagna. Here you can study the cultural and economic importance of the Piedmont mountains and check out some amazing photos.

*2pm Sun and Holidays; 12,000L entrance fee):*If you're into all things Egyptian, this is a must. It's the third-largest Egyptian museum in the world. Above the vast collection of Pharaoh statues on the first floor, the second floor has an intact 14th century tomb of Egyptian architect Kha and his better half. There's also an amazing documented exhibit on Egyptian burials. It's a couple of blocks south of the Palazzo Madama.

Galleria Sabauda *(9am-2pm Tue-Sat, 10am-7pm Thur, 8,000L admission):* Housed in the same building as the Museo delle Antichita on the third and fourth floors, this prominent art museum has what is perhaps the region's wealthiest art collection. While it focuses primarily on provincial favorites, it also has an amazing array of Flemish works. Famous paintings include Botticelli's *Venus,* Rembrant's *Sleeping Old Man,* Duccio's *Virgin and Child,* and the local favorite, *Views of Turin* by Bellotto.

Galleria Civica d'Arte Moderna e Contemporanea *(Via Magenta 31; Tel 011/562-99-11; 9am-4pm closed Monday; 8,000L admission; No credit cards):* Had enough of those old masters? There's also excellent contemporary art in Turin. This massive modern warehouse has collections of Chagall, Picasso, Renoir, and Courbet, just to name a few. The styles of work range from Dadaism to Pop Art (like Warhol's *Orange Car Crash*) to an eclectic array of Divisionist works.

The Royal Armory in Armeria Reale *(On the right next the gates in front of the Palazzo Reale; Tel 011/426-14-55; 9am-7pm Mon, Wed, Sat/ 2:30pm-7:30pm Tue-Sat, closed Mon; 8,000L admission):* If you're in the museum mood but want a bit of a blast, check out the local armory. Guns, cannons, and other tools of destruction have been collecting dust here since the royal Savoy family decided that the pen was mightier than the rifle. All in all, this museum is a one-of-a-kinder. If you believe the guards that there's a firing range in the back, I've got a small bridge in Brooklyn you can invest in....

Mole Antonelliana *(Via Montebello 20; Tel 011/815-42-30; 10,000L museum entrance, 8,000L students)* Above and beyond the rest of the city, literally, the Mole towers almost 500 feet above the city; the glass elevator ride to the top is the best way to check out the city. The tower was once a synagogue during some religious and political instability in Turin eons ago. Scared of heights? Check out the new Museo del Cinema, dedicated to Turin's role in Italian cinema, at the base of the monument. The Mole and museum are two blocks east of Palazzo Madama, on the right-hand side off Via Giussepe Verdi.

Galleria Civica D'Arte Moderna *(Via Magenta 31, corner of Corso G. Ferraris; Tel 011/562-99-11; 9am-7pm Tues-Sun; 10,000L general admission, under 26 5,000L):* Turin's hippest collection of 19th and 20th century art includes works by Chagal, Renoir, Picasso, and Warhol, to name just a few. It's also one of the few museums in town where you might actually meet some people who don't look like they belong in one. It's west of the train station.

Museo Dell' Automobile *(Corso Unita d'Italia 40; Go South along Via Nizza from Stazione Porta Nuova for about 15 minutes, it will be on the* *right; Tel 011/677-666; 10am-6:30pm, closed Mon; 4,000L admission; No credit cards):* Once famous for turning out fabulous shiny new Fiats, the factory-turned-museum now showcases almost 200 cars, from Mercedes to BMWs. While the Fiat is definitely the star of the show, you'll also find displays exploring the evolution of the automobile and the automotive industry.

modification

Turin's premiere tattoo parlor is **Kaifa's Studio** *(Via Mercanti 1/L; Tel 011/546-407; 10am-10pm, closed Sun; MC, V).* With more than 15 books of customized designs, tattoo artists Kaifa and Iva are often booked at least a day in advance, so call ahead or stop by to set up an appointment. The parlor is four blocks west of Piazza Giovanni down Via Giuseppe Garibaldi.

One of the most renowned and expensive salons in Turin, **Carrucchiere** *(Via Po 5; 9:30am-2pm/4-10pm, closed Mon; AE, MC, V)* is where you will find beautiful people trying to become a little more beautiful. The old barber chairs the staff sit you in will set you at ease for the cut of a lifetime, which will run you anywhere from 50,000L for guys and 70,000L for the ladies. It's located a block from the river.

city sports

Considering that Turin will host the 2006 Winter Olympics, sports are sure to get star billing here in the next several years. And while most events will be held in the mountains to the west and north of the city, many of the ceremonies and after parties will surely take place here in town.

If you're more interested in an out-of-city adventure, **C/o ES.PA Sport** *(Corso Matteotti 10; Tel/Fax 011/463-159; 9am-2pm/3:30-7pm, closed Sun; AE, MC, V)* organizes canoeing, kayaking, and rafting trips throughout the region. But they can set you up with cool activities within city bounds as well, including canoeing down the Po River and bicycling through the many parks in the city.

More than 22 percent of Turin is covered by parks and gardens along the river and around various monuments. The most prestigious of all the city gardens is **Giardini Reale** *(Behind Palazzo Reale; Same hours as the palace).* It has some beautiful strolling paths where you catch some shade under a 500-year-old tree or pick a rose for your loved one.

You can take a cruise up and down the river with **Pro Sailing** *(Via Murazzi 65; Tel 011/888-010; Open from April to October),* which offers three different rides. The shortest one (4,000L) will take you from Ponte Vittorio Emanuele I up to Borgo Medioevale (a medieval village and castle) and back. The second ride (8,000L) will take you to the medieval castle and then further up by the automobile museum [see *culture zoo,* above]. The third and longest ride (10,000L) will take you all the way to Savoy's largest fortresses, Moncalieri. This enormous castle was built more than 800 years ago and is definitely worth the ride.

If you've rented a bike [see *need to know*, below] and want to get some fresh air, pedal your way through **Parco Del Valentino** *(along the Po River between Corso Massimo D'Azeglio and Corso Vittorio Emanuele II)*. You can take a break and check out the medieval castle or watch the university rowing teams sweating it out on the river.

If you'd like to something a little more bold, try your luck at some more extreme sports like parasailing with **VDS AEC Torino** *(Via Salbertrand 48; Tel 011/752-073; 9am-4pm daily; No credit cards)* or **Federazione Italiana di Volo Libero** *(Via Salbertrand 48; Tel 011/744-991; 9am-1:30pm/4-7:30pm, closed Wed-Sun)*. Both places organize parasailing and hang gliding trips in the mountains east of the city. If you've never done it before, you have to take a mandatory intro class (offered in English) and fly tandem.

STUff

Turin isn't exactly the fashion capital of Italy, but some of the stuff you'll find here is original and usually a bargain. The side streets around Via Garibaldi sell some of the coolest and most down-to-earth fashions in the city. The area around the university is also a good place to dig up some bargains on footwear, secondhand garb, and accessories. For more chic, trendy Italian fashions, take a window-shopping gander down Via Roma.

▶▶DUDS

For some crazy outfits and T-shirts, check out the row of shops along the western side of Via Po. One in particular is **Equoe Solidad** *(Via Po 13; 10am-9pm, closed Mon; No credit cards)*. This little ethnic boutique features clothes from South and Central America, along with a dash of Italian fashion.

More ethno-Italian fashion can be found at **Kassida** *(Via Carlo Alberto 7; 9am-1pm/4-10pm, closed Sun; No credit cards)*, right next to **Road Roars** [see *bar scene*, above]. All clothes are made by hand in a little shop behind the store, and if you have the time and the money, the designers can tailor one of their simpler dresses or shirts to fit your *stilo*, or mend your lack thereof.

On the main shopping drag, **Pimpkie** *(Via Roma 12; 10am-3pm/6-11pm; MC, V)* has got some of the sleekest women's fashions Turin has to offer. Minidresses and sleeveless tees set the tone, and although the clothes don't cover much of the body, they will surely uncover the money in your pocket.

▶▶CLUB GEAR

Watch out for the hip-hop and jungle music blaring from the monster sound system at **Beat** *(Via Po 3; 10am-11pm daily; MC, V)*—it just might get you in the mood to buy some shiny pleather leggings and 12-inch-high platform shoes. The crowd here is Turin's hardest of hardcore clubbers. The staff always has the scoop on current raves, although usually they're well outside the city.

▶▶TUNES

Millennium *(Corso Regina Margherita 111/b; 10am-10pm; No credit cards)* is a two-story CD and vinyl wonderland. Although the new CDs are a bit pricey, the vinyls and used CDs are quite a bargain. The young guys who run the joint could care less if you spend hours flipping through their collection.

▶▶BOUND

Turin's hippest bookstore is **Libreria Luxemburg** *(Via Cesare Battisti 7; Tel 561/38-96; 9am-2pm/5-11pm; MC, V)*. The store is wall-to-wall books; follow the cast iron stairs winding up to the international section. There's also some great Ginsberg poetry (in Italian) and interviews plastered on the walls throughout.

Situated right off Turin's major piazza, **Feltrinelli** *(N.E. corner of Piazza Castello; 9am-2pm/5-11pm, closed Sun; MC, V)* has a decent selection of travel guides and paperbacks in all languages.

▶▶USED AND BRUISED

On the corner of Corso Regina Margherita is **Jako** *(Via Delle Orfane; 10am-2pm/5-10pm, closed Sun; No credit cards)*, a small secondhand clothes store with mostly old World War II Italian army garb, which is really hard to find in other cities.

▶▶FOOT FETISH

One of the most eclectic shoe stores in all of Turin, if not the province, **Corrado** *(Via Po 1; 9am-2pm/5-11pm; V, MC, AE)* is where you'll find the latest fashions in leather, the most outlandish European sneaker designs, and simple leather sandals for decent prices. Things tend to get a little crazy on the weekends when new styles come in.

▶▶SADDLE UP

John Wayne meets Pavorotti at **Riders Shop** *(Piazza Vittorio Veneto 21; 10am-2pm/5-11pm; AE, MC, V)*. This Italian Western shop has got 10-gallon hats (or would that be in liters?), Italian leather stirrups, and everything else you would expect to find in Wyoming, except with an Italian twist.

▶▶HEMP SPAGHETTI

For a look at how the Italians market their hemp, check out **Biosfera** *(Via San Dalmazzo 7, off Via Garibaldi; No credit cards)*. Okay, it don't actually sell hemp spaghetti, but it does have one-of-a-kind hemp tees with pro-hemp slogans in Italian.

EATS

Cheese, butter, and mushrooms are the three ingredients that are the basis of Turin's (and Piedmont's) cuisine unique. While the city is loaded with little *Mamma e Pappa* produce stands that sell your basic olive oil, tomatoes, and fresh basil, it's the mountains of multicolored mushrooms and seriously odiferous cheese that will catch your attention.

▶▶CHEAP

Right next to the train station is a simple but quality self-serve joint called **Ristorante Brek** *(Piazza Carlo Felice 22; 8am-midnight daily; No credit cards). They have slices of pizza to go (4,000L) and a huge salad bar with pasta, fruit, and sandwiches.*

All along Via Po are some great sandwich and pizza places if you're not in the mood to cop a squat. **La Piramide** *(Via Po 34; 11am-11pm*

TO MARKET

Every other Sunday, the chaotic **Gran Balon Mercato** takes over the immense Piazza della Repubblica. This secondhand antique bazaar is a great place not only to practice your bargaining skills in Italian, but also to enhance your sense of claustrophobia. Immigrants and Italians alike are trying to push everything from broken lampshades to bronzed baby shoes.

daily) has amazing homemade calzones with loads of ricotta for only 3,000L.

A few doors down, **Bricolage** *(Via Po 41; 10am-11pm daily)* is basically a booth in the side of a wall that sells long baguette sandwiches with cheese and prosciutto for 4,000L.

Bar Tavola Calda *(Via XX Septembre 36; Tel 011/530-141; Closed Sun-Mon for dinner; No credit cards)* is a sit-down restaurant with simple regional grub, lightning quick service, and large portions.

For some simple, cheap Indian cuisine, grab a seat at **Kashmir** *(Via Gioberti 4; 11am-11pm daily; V, MC)*. Even though the place is laid out like an Italian restaurant (with some pictures of India hanging from the wall), the food is quite authentic and the portions are huge.

▶▶**DO-ABLE**

If you're tired of seeing menus stacked with seafood, poultry, and meats, Turin's only vegetarian restaurant, **Il Punto Verde** *(Via S. Massimo 17; Tel 011/885-543; Noon-2:30pm/7-10:30pm Mon-Fri, 7-10:30pm Sat, closed Sun; Avg. entree 20,000L; MC, V)* has a huge menu of creative and tasty vegetarian dishes. Had enough pasta? You're in luck: Many of the entrees come with whole-grain rice potatoes instead. Italians on the whole eat pretty healthily, but there's something about the crowd that eats here that makes you think they've betrayed their country and the food it prides itself on.

For some downright proper pizza pie with some lively pizza pie tossers, fill up at **Punto A Capo** *(Via Principe Amedeo 11/N; Tel 011/817-12-10; Noon-3pm/7pm-midnight, closed Tues; MC, V)*. You'll feel like one of the family here as you munch on homemade brick oven-baked pizzas (12-15,000L) and liters of light Italian lagers (12,000L).

Arcate *(Via dei Mercanti 3; Tel 011/517-10-83; 5pm-when the last person wants to leave; Avg. entree 12,000L; AE, MC, V)* offers a more intimate meal. Just head through the brick arches. Housed in what looks like an old brick warehouse, Arcate is all about candlelit meals. The dozens of shelves of provincial wine (8-15,000L a bottle) are sure to spark romance, or at least honest conversation, and the oak tables and lovely waitresses will hopefully distract you from the tasty but unfortunately skimpy entrées.

Popular with the university crowd, **Nuove Salette** *(Via Gioti 7; Tel 011/650-28-98; 6pm-1am, closed Mon; Entrées 12,000-14,000L; MC, V)* is a trendy little wine bar and restaurant that serves up giant plates of pasta (12,000L) and an amazing meat and potatoes dish (14,000L). The waiters are a bit slow, but that's only because they're mostly students chatting it up with their friends.

For a beer swilling, fried-food sort of meal, pull up a stool at **Brasserie** *(Piazza Carlo Emanuele II 21; Tel 011/887-644; Noon-midnight daily; MC, V)*. It's set up more like a bar, but the burgers and fries (15,000L) are so far Mad Cow-free, and the beer (7,000L) is smooth and frosty.

▶▶**SPLURGE**

With jazz in the background and a warm selection of red wines, **Locanda Del Litro** *(Via Principe Amedeo 21/C; Tel 011/812-94-89; 7pm-1am, closed Mon; AE, MC, V)* is a hip but mellow place to spend the evening. As you wait for a table, preferably by the window, check out the local artists' oil paintings and sip a glass of *Malvasia di Casorzo*, a sweet but snazzy local red wine (4,000L). For an appetizer, try the Piedmontese cheese platter (*Grasso d'Alpe* and *robiola*) with some spicy olives. For dessert we recommend the local favorite, *sambajon* (a creamy pudding covered in chocolate hazelnut sauce). The women who run the restaurant are very friendly and very, very *bellisima*. The crowd borders on the younger side and you can easily spend two or three hours over dinner.

Antica Vineria Bianco *(Via San Massimo 11; Tel 011/835-565; 7pm-midnight daily; Avg. entree 25,000L; AE, MC, V)* offers a soothing meal in a laid-back, jazzy atmosphere. The owners and chefs, like many others in the city, pride themselves on their wine selection, which is packed into the shelves behind the bar. The waiter will be more than happy to let you try a couple of different wines, and the bartender will let you flip through his music collection and pick something out. The crowd is very laid-back and almost all the food is prepared with wine. They offer a two-person bowl of *panissa* (salami sautéed with hearty beans and garlic) that's served over fresh spinach pasta or rice and will surely help the *Monferrato* (local red wine) settle nicely.

crashing

While there's dozens of party places to play social butterfly here, Turin does not have a huge amount of places to crash if you're on a tight budget.

▶▶**CHEAP**

The cheapest place to crash (besides on the banks of the river) is the youth hostel, **Ostello Torino** *(Via Alby 1; Tel 011/660-44-45; Bus 52 from Stazione di Porta Nuova, second stop after crossing the bridge; 19,000L for a bed and breakfast; HI cards accepted)*, east of the Po River. The best thing going for this place is its view of the city and the mountains. You'd be wise to call ahead for reservations, though, since the hostel houses lots of long-term guests who are working in and around the city. Rooms are

Turin eats and crashing

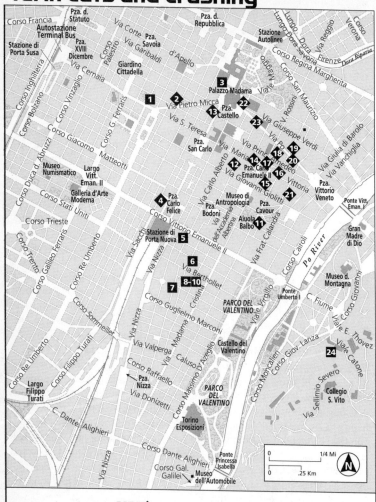

EATS ◆

Antica Vineria Bianco **16**
Arcate **21**
Bar Tavola Calda **2**
Brasserie **14**
Bricolage **20**
Café delle Scienze **22**
Caffé Gallery **23**
Il Punto Verde **11**
Kashmir **12**
La Piramide **19**
Locanda del Litro **17**
Master Club Coffee **13**
Nuove Salette **15**

Punto A Capo **18**
Ristorante Brek **4**

CRASHING ■

Canelli **7**
Don Chisciotte **1**
Hotel Centro **8**
Hotel Genio **5**
Hotel Sori **9**
Lux **6**
Ostello Torino **24**
Principe Tommaso **10**
Venezia **3**

clean, and the place is always busy. There's a common room downstairs, a cafeteria (dinner 15,000L), and a computer with a slow Internet connection in the lobby. The rooms sleep four people and the curfew is 11:30pm sharp, but if you leave your passport they'll give you a key so you can come in later.

Closer to the main train station is **Lux** *(Via B. Galliari 9; Tel 011/657-257; 40,000L single w/out bath, 50,000L w/bath, 50,000L double w/out bath, 100,000L w/bath; No credit cards)*. Given the cheap price and the fact that this place only has 12 rooms, reservations are the way to go. The bathrooms are clean, they give you clean towels and clean beds, and you can sleep soundly, since there's virtually no outside traffic noise.

Hotel Centro *(Via Principe Tommaso 12; Tel 011/650-95-11; 40,000L single w/out bath; 70,000L double w/out bath, 95,000L triple w/bath; No credit cards)* offers even cheaper, if slightly dingy, accommodations. The lobby reeks of tobacco, but fortunately the rooms don't. The rooms are small and relatively clean, but the bathrooms leave something to be desired (like Ajax).

Big and always busy, **Canelli** *(Via S. Dalmazzo 7; Tel 011/537-166; 25,000L single w/out bath, 40,000L w/ bath, 35,000L double w/out bath, 55,000L w/ bath; No credit cards)* is a hotspot for immigrant workers doing some temp work in the city. The hotel is surprising clean and so are the rooms, which are very difficult to get if you just show up. There's a little bar and pay phone downstairs in the lobby.

Principe Tommaso *(Via Principe Tommaso 8; Tel 011/669-86-12; 30,000L single w/out bath-40,000L, w/ bath, 50,000L double w/out bath-80,000L w/ bath)* is a place to sleep, and that's about it. While the rooms and bathrooms aren't exactly Ritz status, it's fairly big and not usually packed.

▶▶DO-ABLE

Hotel Bellavista *(Via B. Gallari 15, 6th floor; Tel 011/669-81-39; 55,000L single w/out bath, w/bath 70,000L, 110,000L w/ bath, 120,000L w/out bath, w/bath 140,000L; breakfast 8,000L; MC, V)* is a bright hotel

wired

Turin's main websites are: ***www.comune.torino.it www.unito.it;*** and ***www.torino2006.it***

There aren't many cyber cafes in Turin. On the second floor of **Alice** *(Piazza Statuto 9; Tel 011/562-88-90; 9am-midnight; No credit cards)* there are about 10 computers with slow Internet access (7,000L an hour). If you hit this cafe on a weekend night they've got free food downstairs at the bar.

You can also check your e-mail at the more spartan MailBoxes Etc [see *need to know,* below].

that's constantly filled with backpackers opting out of the hostel routine. The 19 rooms are clean and relatively spacious (you could throw a party for you and 30 of your closest friends in the triple rooms) and most have TVs and phones.

Right off Piazza Cristina near Parco Velentino is **Hotel Sori** *(Via Principe Tommaso 12; Tel 011/650-95-11; 70,000L single w/bath, 12,000L double w/bath; AE, MC, V)*. Every room has a television, phone, big bed, and clean marble bathroom, and there's a little bar near the desk. The owner is very hard of hearing, so speak to his wife.

Don Chisciotte *(Corso Giulio Cesare 132; Tel 011/281-311; 80,000L single, 120,000L double, 130,000L triple, all with private bath; AE, MC, V)* is one of the newer and nicer hotels in Turin. There's a cool little cafe/restaurant downstairs, and the big, bright rooms have little fridges and televisions—but there are only seven of them, so call ahead. The owner is from Spain and loves yapping it up with his guests—you can usually find him in the cafe when he's not running around keeping the place immaculate.

▶▶SPLURGE

If you want to wake up to an amazing view of the palace, it's got to be **Venezia** *(Via XX Septembre 70; Tel 011/562-37-26; 180,000L single, 230,000L double, 260,000L triple; V, MC, AE)*. You can smell the roses in the gardens behind the palace when you open your window. Most of the guests in this 67-room hotel are older business professionals, but that won't matter when you lay your pack down in what would pass for a royal suite in most places. The rooms, of course, come with all the amenities. This is the kind of place where you could meet a bunch of people and have an after-party (hey, at these prices, you might as well get your money's worth!).

Hotel Genio *(Corso Vittorio Emanuele II 47; Tel 011/650-57-7; hotel.genio@torino.alpcom.it; 170,000L double w/ bath; Breakfast included; AE, MC, V)* is a 200-year-old castle of a hotel that's just a couple of blocks from the river and the train station. Each room is fully loaded with antique Piedmontese furniture, TV, stocked minibar, and AC for those hot summer nights. Don't expect to have any backpackers as your neighbors down the hall—and if you show up at breakfast smelling like a day-old 40 ouncer, don't expect a warm reception, either.

need to know

Currency Exchange There are **ATMs** at both train stations and some exchanges on Via Roma and around Palazzo Madama.

Tourist Information The main office is in **Piazza Castello** *(W. side of the piazza; Tel 011/535-181 or 011/535-901; 9am-7pm Mon-Fri, 9am-noon/1-6pm Sat, closed Sun)* and another is in **Stazione Porta Nuova** *(Tel 011/561-70-95; Same hours)*. Both offer monthly listings of shows, markets, festivals, and outdoor concerts. They do not make hotel reservations.

Public Transportation Turin is an easy city to walk around in, but the **buses** and **trams** *(Tel 800/019-152 for both)* are very prompt. A single ticket costs 1,800L, but you can also buy multi-day unlimited passes starting at 4,500L. You can pick up a tram/bus map at the train station or tourist office. Unfortunately for night owls, Turin's public trains shut down at 1am and resumes service after 5am, so if you're trying to get back to your hotel in the wee hours, your feet or a cab are your only alternatives.

Health and Emergency Emergency: *118*; Police: *113*. The main hospital is **Ospedale Mauriziano Umberto** *(Largo Turati 62; Tel 011/508-01).*

Pharmacies **Farmacie Boniscontro** *(Corso Vittorio Emanuele II 66; Tel 011/538-271)* is open 24 hours.

Airports The main airport servicing Turin and Valle di Susa is **Aeroporto Caselle** *(Tel 011/567-63-61 for flight information).* For 17,000L, you can hop the connecting train into Turin; they leave about every 30 minutes for the half-hour trip.

Trains The other smaller train station in the western part of the city is **Stazione Porta Susa,** but usually it only services local trains. The main train station in Turin, **Porta Nuova** *(Tel 011/531-327)* is closer to the center of the city, and it services trains to Milan, Florence, Genova, and Rome. As of press time, all trains leading into this region were suspended due to terrible floods to the north in Aosta. To get to Aosta [see below] from Turin you must take a train to Ivrea and then a bus serviced by the train company into the mountains. Just to be safe, ask at the APT office in the station.

Bus Lines out of the City The main national and international bus station *(Tel 011/332-525)* is on Corso Inghilterra 1. Buses go wherever the trains do.

Bike and Moped Rental Ciclopark *(Near baggage storage in Stazione Porta Nuova; No phone; 6am-midnight; MC, V)* has cruisers and mountain bikes that you can rent for 5,000L for 5 hours, 7,000L for 12 hours, or 12,000L for 24 hours (plus a cash or credit card deposit).

Laundry **Lava E Asciuga** *(N.W. corner of Piazza della Repubblica 5/g; 8am-10pm daily)* has more than 25 washers and dryers and charges 7,000L a load.

Postal The **main post office** *(Tel 011/546-800; 8am-7pm Mon-Sat)* is on Via Alfieri 10. There is a **MailBoxes Etc.** *(Via San Francesco Da Paola 10d; 9am-8pm Mon-Sat)* that has UPS, Federal Express, and Western Union.

Internet See *wired,* above.

everywhere else

SESTRIERE

Taking a winter jaunt to Italy? Grab your skis, your board, or your snow-shoes and make a beeline to the way north, way cool Valle di Susa. From December to May, it's filled to the gills with weekenders in search of snow. And it is on these very slopes that the best skiers in the world will duke it out in the 2006 Winter Olympics. With more than 20 ski resorts stretching from Turin to the French border, the Valle di Susa has some-thing for the glamorous ski bunny *and* the shaggy, small-town snow-boarder. And though every town in the valley has its merits, we recommend Sestriere for its hordes of cool young skiers and snowboarders, and direct ski-lift access to no less than 400 kilometers of runs and 2,000 meters (6,000 feet) of vertical drop. Just a stone's throw from the French border, and a perfect day trip from Turin, Sestriere is the Valle di Susa's biggest and most developed resort town.

Spend any time at all here and you won't fail to notice what looks like Italy's version of the Great Wall. Slinking its way up the side of the nearby Via Lattea mountain, it includes a 15-part castle that was used in its heyday for protection against invaders.

The town's resort boasts 118 runs, accessible by an extensive system of 66 lifts. You can find skis or snowboards at any one of the many rental shops in the area, including **Centro Sci Sestriere, Fonara Gimmy, Yaya Sport,** and **Ski Man,** all on or right off the main drag. Ski and boot rental will typically run you about 22,000L a day, while snowboards are slightly pricier at 30,000L a day.

You'll have a bunch of options to choose from when purchasing a lift ticket, but don't worry—even the most expensive pale in comparison to the astronomical prices in resorts in the States like Aspen or Vail. Sestriere is part of the "Milky Way," a connected ski area with easy access links between **Sestriere, Sauze d'Oulx, Sansicario, Cesana, Claviere,** and **Montegenevre.** If you plan to ski on any of the other slopes in the area, it's worth it to buy a one-day pass to the entire Milky Way for 49,000L, or the discounted six-day pass for 215,000L. A one-day pass for Sestriere alone is 44,000L, or 205,000L for six days. There are also lift passes available for half-days, and up to 15 days, but remember to bring a photo if you are skiing for more than six days.

For 80,000 to 120,000L a trip, **Elisusa** *(Tel 034/822-01-88)* arranges heli-skiing trips.

But don't think you'll have nothing to do if you end up here in the summer—there's plenty going on. You can try your luck at hang gliding over the valley with **Velum Volitans** *(Via Cavour 36; Tel 011/953-15-48; www.velumvolitans.org; 8:30am-5pm daily; AE, MC, V)* . It's based in Turin, but makes pickups throughout the valley and does most of its flying in the mountains closer to Sestriere. Guides and gear for climbing and hiking can be found at **GA Favro Giancarlo** *(Fraz. Constance 2; Tel 012/296-874)* located in Oulx, a 15-minute walk from Sestriere. There are all kinds of trails around here, from easy-strollin' walking paths to rugged trails that require clamp-ons. Or how about horseback riding? Contact **Circolo Ippico Sestriere** *(Via Sauze di Cesana; Tel 012/270-109 or 012/277-466)* for trips through the valley and in Sestriere.

eats

There's a string of interchangeable fast food joints and restaurants along the main drag and at the ski resorts—they'll all fill you up good, and none is worth recommending above the others. But if you're dying to indulge your monster skier's appetite someplace special, try **Al Braciere** *(Via Agnelli 2; Tel 012/276-129; Noon-3:30pm/5-11:30pm, closed Tues; Entrées 20-30,000L; DC, V)*, which is always packed with hungry downhillers. Like so many restaurants in Sestriere, it's great when it comes to food, not so great when it comes time for the bill. You might be able to catch a glimpse of the photos of Sestriere's own Alberto Tomba (Italy's most famous downhill skier) on the wall through the waves of waiters running to and from the kitchen. On weekends you can load up on the prix fix meal (60,000L), which includes a glass of regional wine, appetizers, and a hefty entrée.

crashing

The only campground in Sestriere is **Chisonetto** *(Via al Colle 5; Tel 012/277-546, Fax 012/277-546; Open May-Nov; 7,500L per person, 11,000L for a plot, includes bathroom use)*.

If you're here in the winter—or would just rather have a solid roof over your head—you could head for the youth hostel up the road in **Fenestrelle,** 10 minutes away by public bus. Called **Centro Soggiorno** *(Pra' Catinat 2, Fenestrelle; Tel 012/176-555; Open year-round; 50,000L bed and breakfast, 70,000L single w/bath; V)*, it's a simple hostel with 58 private rooms and 200 beds. Some rooms come with private baths. During the winter it's packed with snowboarders and ski bums mountain-hopping through the valley. There are four communal bathrooms on every floor that are kept fresh and clean. The cafeteria offers a meager dinner for 15,000L.

The cheapest place to crash in Sestriere is **Centro** *(Strada Nazionale 17; Tel 77/138; 80,000L single w/ bath; 120,000L double w/ bath; 110,000L triple w/ bath; MC, V)*, a basic hotel with semi-spacious rooms and a bar and restaurant downstairs. It's almost impossible to get a room without reservations during ski season.

A bit more pricey, but also less crowded, is **Sciatori** *(Via San Filippo 5; Tel 70/323; 120,000L single w/ bath, 150,000L double w/ bath, 165,000L triple w/ bath; AE, MC, V)*, billed as a three-star hotel. The rooms are cozy and some have great views of the mountains.

need to know

Travel Info The **tourist information office** *(Piazza Agnelli 11; Tel 012/275-54-44; 9am-1pm/3-8pm Mon-Sat)* is just across the street from the bus station; hotel reservations can be made through the hotel board outside the office free of charge or by dialing Tel 012/230-76-06.

Health and Emergency The **mountain rescue emergency** number is 118. Dial the same number to reach the **ski patrol.**

Directions/Transportation To reach Sestriere from Turin, you can take the direct **bus** (15,000L), or catch the **train** (12,600L) to **Oulx,** where you can transfer to another line going into Sestriere. You're looking at a two-hour trip either way. If you're driving, beware of a Friday trip—the traffic leaving Turin for the mountains is horrendous.

aosta

Surrounded by the magnificent Alps, Aosta is where ski-junkies and hard-core hikers land at night after they come down from the mountains in **Courmayeur** or the **Parco Nazionale di Gran Paradiso** [see below for both]. The party scene isn't exactly hopping by big-city standards, but it's the best you'll find up here in the mountains. Aosta is by far the biggest town around (population 36,000), and it's right in the center of the out-door action, whether it be hiking in the summer or skiing in the winter (although diehard skiers should know that the best skiing is really 20 miles north in the smaller Alpine town of Courmayeur).

Situated between the Dora Baltea and Buthier rivers and at the feet of Mount Emilius (3559m), Becca di Viou (2856m), and Becca di Nona (3142m), Aosta is a charming mountain village where locals milk tourists for everything they're worth. Winding streets stemming out from the central Piazza Chanoux are lined with small cafes, candy shops, restaurants, and wine bars like **Le Gran Paradis** [see *bar scene,* below]; buildings are roofed with giant slabs of stone to ward off the unbelievable amounts of winter snow. But you can easily pay a too-high price for all this charm, so check out the menu in advance or you may be unpleasantly surprised when you get your dinner tab.

Action-central status is nothing new in this neck o' the woods. As far back as 2900 B.C., Aosta was the military center for citizens of Salassi, who were later romped by Augustus and his troops (25 B.C.). Back then, Aosta was known as the Rome of the Alps and was a prime site because of its relatively easy access to France and Switzerland. Eventually, after everybody and their brother had tried to pry Aosta from Roman control, the Piedmontese royal Savoy family succeeded in taking over, and placed the city under the rule of the new Italian State. Today, Aosta has a diverse array of churches, monuments, and mostly Roman ruins like **Arco d'Augusto** and **Teatro Romano** [see *culture zoo,* below, for both].

neighborhoods

The whole town can be covered on foot, starting with **Piazza Chanoux,** the social hub of Aosta. Like most kids from small towns, the youth of Aosta jump at the opportunity to leave home and study at universities in bigger cities. But thanks to a constant flow of tourists, mountaineers, and ski-resort employees, there's always a decent contingent of young people hanging around inside the Romans' crumbling city walls. Day and night, human activity hums in and around the cobblestone streets leading to the piazza. Most cafes, restaurants, and bars that are worth going to line the pedestrian streets **Via P. Pretoriane,** which runs east from Chanoux and eventually turns into **Via S. Anselmo,** and **Via de Tillier,** which runs west from Chanoux and turns into **Via E. Aubert.** The best place to learn about any festivals or markets going on is at the **tourist information office** [see *need to know,* below], on the north side of Piazza Chanoux.

bar, live music, and club scene

Nightlife starts early in Aosta, mostly because the sun sets so early behind those huge mountains surrounding the town. But don't expect too much sizzle; the scene doesn't exactly heat up—it warms a bit and then simmers.

A cool, authentic *enoteca* that's a great place to start your night is **Le Grand Paradis** *(Via Sant'Anelmo 121; Tel 016/544-047; 9:30am-1pm/4-11pm, closed Sun; MC, V for bottles only, not drinks),* nestled on the ground floor of an old weathered house one block east of the **Torre dei Signori di Quart** [see *culture zoo,* below]. Rummage through baskets of mini wine bottles outside to find your poison, or head inside for the full effect. Purchase bottles of regional wine for a picnic at the counter up front, or head into the back room with the locals and pull up a seat at one of the musty, oak wine barrels. If you're not familiar with the regional wines, as most of us aren't, owner Isero will be more than happy to give you a few samples. Although the music could use some help, the local wines, like Gros Jean, Eleve en Fut Chene (both Pinot Noir), Torrete, and Chanteletre (a lethal Muscat), sold by the bottle or glass (3,000-4,000L), could not. The back room technically only holds about a dozen people, but that doesn't seem to discourage hordes of locals from trouping in to

aosta

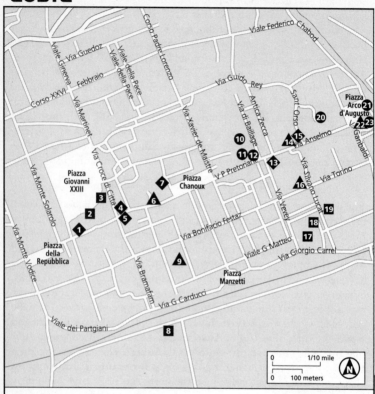

BARS/CLUBS ▲
Le Grand Paradis **14**
Old Distillery Pub **16**
Victoria Pub **6**
CD **9**
La Compagnia dei Motori **22**

CULTURE ZOO ●
Ponte de Pierre **23**
Porta Pretoria **12**
Torre dei Signori di Quart **11**
Anfiteatro Romano **10**
Collegiata di Sant' Orso **9**
Arco d' August **21**

EATS ◆
Pizza Antonio **7**
Hostaria del Calvino **4**
Vecchia Aosta **13**
Trattoria Praetoria **15**
Trattoria/Creperie Carillon **1**
Break House **5**

CRASHING ■
Milleluci **17**
Ville D' Aosta **18**
La Belle Epoque **2**
Albergo Pila **8**
Monte Emilius **19**
Albergo Bus **3**

——— Railway

munch on super-stinky platters of Swiss and chevre (12,000L), crack a bottle, and chat about what they're going to have for dinner.

Just up the block from Grand Paradis, heading through the archway onto Via Pres. Fosses, you'll find the **Old Distillery Pub** *(Via Pres. Fosses 7; Tel 016/523-95-11; 6pm-2am daily; No credit cards),* where you can slug down a pint. With its tap-fitted English bar and old drinking relics strewn about, this English-speaking pub is a fine tribute to drinking British-style. Locals and tourists flock to this watering hole for a frothy pint (8,000L). Things usually warm up after 8pm, and from time to time you can catch some mellow live music.

For a more local pub scene, check out **Victory Pub** *(Via De Tillier 60; Tel 016/540-324; 6pm-2am, closed Wed; No credit cards),* just west of Piazza Chanoux. It's totally packed during lunch, when they serve up some pricey dishes of *fonduta* (Italian fondue served with meat and vegetables) and pasta. But at other times you can sit for hours at one of the oak tables and yap with the bartenders over a pint of German lager (8,000L) and a complimentary bowl of nuts. During the weekend, grab a table in front of the giant glass windows and watch the tourists spend their lunch money in the little boutiques along Via Tillier. The crowd here is usually pretty boisterous and loud, hence the lack of music from the stereo that doesn't exist.

Chic and relatively trendy, considering where you are, **CD** *(Via Bramafam 22; Tel 016/526/24-74; 6pm-2am, closed Mon; No credit cards)* is a swank little place for an after-dinner martini (10,000L). The generally twentysomething crowd is open-minded enough to be into the wild oil paintings on the walls, such as that fuzzy rendition of the Statue of Liberty. This place is huge, and serves up every mixed drink under the sun (10,000L), plus a giant selection of French and regional wines. After 6pm on weekends, there's a little free buffet in the table section with cheeses, meats, and pickled onions. An old analogue recorder behind the bar sets the mood for the smooth R&B and jazz wafting from its speakers. This place is about three blocks south of Piazza Chanoux, just before you reach the main road and the train tracks.

La Compagnia dei Motori *(South side of Piazza Archo D'Augusta; Tel 016/536-34-84, 8pm-3am, closed Mon; No cover)* is right outside the city walls, near the river Buthier. It's your best bet for gettin' down with your bad self in Aosta. Although the metallic interior design is a bit retro, the Eurodisco mixes and numerous dance floors make things lively. Grab a stiff cocktail (12,000L) at one of the three bars, where you can brush elbows with some older local beauties. On weekends the crowd tends to be more touristy and younger, and the music more diverse, with hints of hip-hop, light house, and R&B. A couple of lounge-like rooms with rock-hard couches offer plenty of mirrors to check your hair in.

CULTURE ZOO

Thanks to Augustus and his merry band of Roman marauders, Aosta is jam-packed with cool old weathered churches, towers, and ruins. If you come into town from the east, you'll pass over Ponte de Pierre (stone bridge), where you may ask yourself, "But why is there no water under this bridge?" It's because hundreds of years after the bridge was built (1 B.C.), the Buthier River decided to change its course. The bridge is still intact today and its endless layers of ancient stone still serve as the thoroughfare for entering the city.

Arco d'Augusto *(On the eastern edge of Via Anselmo in Piazza Arco d'Augusto):* One of the most important Roman artifacts in Aosta is Arco d'Augusta, just down the street from the Pont de Pierre. Built in 25 B.C., the arch's axis is perfectly aligned between the Ponte de Pierre and the Pretorian Gate (Porta Pretoria). These three monuments used to serve as the official eastern entrance to the city. The arch was built to commemorate the

on the road again

Heading north from Aosta via bus or car on Route 27, you'll travel through one of the oldest mountain passes connecting Italy and Switzerland, so bring your passport. First stop on this scenic route is the little mountain town of **Gignod,** where the French/Italian festival of **Fete du Teteun** is held every summer in the town square. This gastronomic festival ensures that everybody gets good and fat munching on slices of the local specialty, (salted and spiced cow udders). It's an acquired taste.

A few more mountain peaks to the north is **Etroubles.** Named after what the Romans used to call the entire mountain pass leading to Switzerland, this quiet mountain village is famous all over the region for its *jambon de Bosse* (dry-cured ham). After passing by Saint Oyen, the pass will zig-zag a bit before reaching the ancient Roman village of **Saint-Rhemy-En-Bosse.** Much more touristy than most of the other mountain pass villages, this community is regarded as one of the best producers of fontina cheese. From here you can set out for **Colle del Gran San Bernardo** (The Great St. Bernard Pass), the same road Napoleon marched his destined-to-die soldiers down in the beginning of the 19th century. The wooded gorge road heads into Switzerland and passes right by a stuffed St. Bernard, patron dog of all mountaineers. Take in the awesome mountain views at the **Hospice of St. Bernard,** built in 1050 by the archdeacon of Aosta Cathedral. Today, brandy-drinking monks continue to raise those famous lifesaving dogs.

defeat of the Salassi tribe, and had a vault containing a 15th-century wooden crucifix that was later placed in the treasure museum in the cathedral.

Porta Pretoria *(Via Sant' Anselme and Antica Zecca):* The third part of the eastern passage, this former entryway to the city is by far the largest and most intact Roman monument in town. The gate comprises three slab archways, two of which were for pedestrians, with the center one used for chariots on the go.

Torre dei Signori di Quart *(Via P. Pretriane; 9:30am-noon/2-6:30pm daily winter; 8am-7pm daily summer; Free admission):* Located on the northern side of the gates, this 100-foot tower was built in the 12th century and used as a sort of toll booth for incoming goods to keep the Bishop of Aosta's deep pockets nice and lined. Today the tower's ground floor is used for photo exhibitions.

Anfiteatro Romano *(Via Baillage; 9:30am-noon/2:30-6:30pm summer; 9:30am-noon/2-4:30pm winter; Free admission):* This 2,000-year-old amphitheater was Augustus's tribute to the arts and is similar to the one in Pompeii. Once upon a time, it had a roof that covered the public seating area. Today, small theatrical productions are staged here in the summer; check the tourist office or posters on the lampposts on Piazza Chanoux for a schedule of upcoming performances. It's just up the road from the Porta Pretoria.

Collegiata di Sant'Orso *(Via and piazzetta Sant'Orso; Tel 016/526-20-26; 9:30am-noon/2-5:30pm winter; 9am-7pm summer; Free admission):* Recognizable by its gothic bell tower and fortress-like stone facade, this former church is the best place to experience medieval works of art and architecture in Aosta. It was built in the 12th century in a Romanesque style and later altered by a more Gothic facade. Check out the Romanesque frescoes decorating the Gothic-cross vaults throughout the church. A fascinating fresco worth a look-see is *'il miracolo',* as one local called it, which depicts a crippled boy and hangs above the altar on the left side of the church. The church also houses crypts that date back to the 11th century.

Town Hall: Just off Aosta's central Piazza Chanoux, this was built at the beginning of the 19th century. Two statues on the columns of the building represent the two rivers that flow through the city; two bronze plaques under the portico pay tribute to the Aostan Valley soldiers who have died in battle.

great outdoors

We've told you once and we'll tell you again: Use Aosta as a jumping-off point, and do your skiing and outdoor trekking elsewhere in the region. If you're the stubborn type and don't want to heed our advice (or if you only have time to come through Aosta and can't make the journey to the back of beyond), you should head out to the nearby village of **Pila,** where you will get some decent skiing in. There is a **cable car** that takes you from Aosta up to this little mountain village; the tourist office will give the current schedule [see *need to know,* below]. Pila is really just a ski area masquerading as a town—there's not much else here besides the 13 runs that wind down the mountain. You are herded directly to the lifts when the cable car deposits you in town. You'll find a good variety of runs here, from little bunny slopes to a competition slalom course. There's also 10km of cross-country skiing for those of you who like to glide rather than *woosh*. In the precious few warmer months (July-September), a few of the lifts remain open to haul you up in the mountain so you can hike your way down.

eaTS

Every little winding street and cobblestoned corner offers a culinary surprise in Aosta, and you can actually get by fairly cheaply on cheap but delicious pizza or a bowl of yummy minestrone.

▶▶CHEAP

For a quick meal that won't drain your lira supply, the great little pizza joint **Pizza Antonio** *(On the northwest corner of Piazza Chanoux; 11am-3:30pm/5-8pm, closed Sun; No credit cards)* is your best choice. Try the pizza (4,000L a slice), or an unbelievable spinach calzone (3,000L). Owner Antonio loves to play 20 questions with anyone who even remotely looks like a tourist.

▶▶DO-ABLE

You can have a great sit-down lunch or dinner at **Hostaria Del Calvino** *(Via Croce di Citta 12; No phone; 11am-3pm/5-11pm daily; pizza 11,000-14,000L; AE, MC, V)*. For a more fancy-restaurant atmosphere try one of the tables upstairs, but if you want pizza, head down into the crypt-like basement. Surrounded by cold stone and frescoed brick walls, you'll find plenty of warmth watching the pizzas go in and out of the brick oven faster than you can say *parmesano*. The menu offers more than 30 kinds of pizza, like *diavola* (spicy salami), *mare monti* (salmon and mozzarella cheese), and *mais* (corn). Families and young people alike spend hours on end sipping the house wines and losing themselves in the ROYGBIV ceiling lights. It's two blocks west of Piazza Chanoux.

For a pizza pie in more of an international setting, head over to **Break House** *(Via Lostan 3/5; Tel 016/536-15-34; Noon-3pm/5-11pm, closed Sunday; No credit cards)*, two blocks west of Piazza Chanoux, across the street from Hostaria Del Calvino. The vibe is a little cheesy (no pun intended), but the pies (12,000-15,000L) are piping hot and the beers (7,000L) ice cold.

Conveniently situated between the inner and outer walls of Porta Pretoria, the two-story **Vecchia Aosta** *(Piazza Porta Pretoria 4, south side; Tel 016/536-11-86; Noon-3pm/7:30-11pm, closed Wed; Avg. entree 40,000L; AE, MC, V)* is like something out of *Gladiator*. Fill up on the a la carte menu at one of the private oak tables. There's a huge list of local and regional wines, any of which will serve as a nice palate cleanser after a hearty meal of homemade ravioli stuffed with minced mushrooms and basil. If you happen to catch sight of what you think is a local eating dinner, pay close attention—sometimes they have the inside scoop on dishes that aren't on the menu. Don't be afraid to ask for "what she's having".

Just down the street is a great little family-style restaurant called **Trattoria Praetoria** *(Via Sant'Anselmo 9; Tel 016/544-356; Noon-2:30pm/7-10pm, closed Mon in winter; AE, MC, V)*, which is always packed with hoards of hungry locals, hikers, and ski bums. The menu is huge and the waiters will gladly let you know what's tasty. They dole out delicious bowls of creamy linguini with bits of ham and vegetables (12,000L), and a huge antipasto with regional cheeses, meats, and veggies (15,000L) that can easily fill up two people.

If you find yourself wandering the streets with a bit of an appetite and a sweet tooth, indulge yourself at **Trattoria/Creperie Carillon** *(Via E. Aubert; Tel 016/540-106; Noon-3pm/5-10pm, closed Thur; Avg. entree 20,000L, crepes 8,000L, AE, MC, V)*. The French/Italian cuisine features pasta dishes with very thick cream sauces and meats heavily marinated in red and white wines. The entrées are good, but the specialty of the house, the crêpes, will most definitely take you back to gay Par-ee; they're wafer-thin and very sweet, and you can fill them with anything from fresh strawberries and Nutella to homemade coffee ice cream.

crashing

Aosta is a relatively cheap place to crash compared to the towns stretching west toward the mountains, plus it has two campgrounds located just outside the city. Inside the city walls, the prices tend to inflate during the summer and the heart of the ski season.

▶▶CHEAP

The campground called **Milleluci** *(Via Porossan 15, localita Roppoz, Tel 016/5235278; Bus 11; Open year round; 9,000L per person, 16,000-19,000L for a plot, bathrooms 1,000L, laundry 8,000L)* is just across the river on the eastern edge of town. A little further to the north (another 5 minutes of walking) is another tent haven, **Ville D'Aosta** *(Via de Seigneurs de Quart; Tel 016/536-13-60; Open June 1-Sept 30; 8,000L per person, 16,000L per plot)*. Take the bus headed to Courmayeur and ask them to drop you off en route. Neither of these places rents out tents; you have to come equipped.

wired

Bar Snooker *(Via Lucat 3; 8am-5pm daily)* offers Internet access for 10,000L an hour. It also offers video games and a pool hall, but you'll notice we didn't write it up in bar scene....

▶▶DO-ABLE

One relatively frugal option is **La Belle Epoque** *(Via D'Avise 18; Tel 016/526-22-76; 45,000L single w/out bath, 50,000L single w/bath, 90,000L double w/bath, 120,000L triple w/bath; AE, MC, V)*. For what you're paying, you might expect more—don't. And always make reservations if you're coming during the ski season. The rooms are pretty small, with limited views, but the bathrooms are clean and there's no curfew. Walls are paper-thin, which might disrupt your afternoon siesta but won't your nightly snooze—the place falls silent by 11pm. The restaurant downstairs is always loaded with friends of the owners' and other locals. One of their home-style entrées will run you about 20,000L, but don't expect special treatment just because you're staying there. Head three blocks west of Piazza Chanoux, and follow the sign down a little side alley on the right-hand side.

Just outside the city walls, across the train tracks, is **Albergo Pila** *(Via Pavavera 12/B; Tel 016/543-398; 45,000L single w/out bath, 55,000L single w/ bath, 80,000L double w/ bath, 115,000L triple w/ bath; MC, V)*. It's not exactly in the middle of town, and it's a bit too close to the tracks, but the rooms are spacious and clean. The owners are friendly but their rooms are often booked through the ski season, so call ahead.

Monte Emilius *(Via G. Carrel 9, upstairs from restaurant Le Ramoneur; Tel 016/535-692; 50,000L single w/bath, 100,000L double w/ bath; No credit cards)* is just outside the city walls, in the southeastern part of town near the soccer fields. With only 20 beds, reservations are a must all year long. The hotel is close to the highway, so things can get a bit noisy at night, but the owners are friendly, the beds comfy, and the bathrooms clean.

A little pricier but in the center of the city is **Albergo Bus** *(Via Malherbes 18; Tel 016/543-645; 90,000L single w/ bath, 170,000L double w/ bath; AE, MC, V)*. The rooms in this typical Aostan house make you feel like you're in a real home, with handmade drapes on the windows and embroidered down comforters on the beds. The bathrooms are equipped with deep bathtubs that are perfect after a long day of skiing or hiking.

need to know

Currency Exchange **ATMS** and **banks** *(9am-1:30pm/3:30-6pm Mon-Fri)* are all along Via dei Tillier.

Tourist Information The main **tourist information booth** *(Northwest corner of Piazza Chanoux 8; Tel 016/523-66-27; 9am-1pm/3-8pm Mon-Sat, 9am-1pm Sun)* offers a detailed map of the region and prices for the ski centers in the valley. They will not make hotel reservations for you.

Public Transportation The city is small enough to cover on foot. **Buses** *(2,500L)* get you to the outskirts of the city and leave from in front of the train station. To get to the ski lifts you have to take the bus to Courmayeur *(8-11,000L)*.

Health and Emergency Emergencies: *113;* mountain emergencies: *118.* The **hospital** *(Tel 016/53-041)* is on Via Ginerva 3, just north of the city walls.

Pharmacies Farmacie chenal *(Tel 016/526-21-33; 9am-12:30pm/3-7:30pm, closed Wed)* is on Via Croix de Ville 1.

Trains and Buses As we said you in the regional introduction: Train service to Aosta has been suspended since the fall of 2000 due to heavy flooding that almost destroyed the tracks that run through here. Buses now run at similar times to the same places. The **train station** and **bus station** are across from each other in Piazza Manzetti.

Postal The main **post office** *(8:15am-7:30pm Mon-Fri, 8:15am-1pm Sat)* is on Piazza Narbonne.

Internet See *wired,* above.

courmayeur

Italy's oldest skiing mecca, and still home to the best skiing in the country, Courmayeur sits under the towering shadow of the highest peak in Europe, Monte Bianco (Elev. 4,810m). Surrounded by snowcapped mountains, sliding glaciers, and steep hillside vineyards, the town itself is tiny and oozes wealthy, après-ski charm. The only permanent residents you'll encounter here will most likely be working in one of the restaurants, town offices, or tobacco shops; this is a year-round tourist spot. No matter when you visit, it's difficult finding a place to crash, since Courmayeur's close proximity to the mountains makes it a prime year-round destination for outdoor-sport junkies. The steep slopes and huge powder bowls dotted with pine trees and filled to the gills with freshies will motivate even the most sluggish skier or snowboarder, and the gorgeous woods and rivers are perfect for checking out in the warmer months (July-September).

Balanced on a steep incline, Courmayeur revolves around the church **Chiesa Parracchiale,** the largest building in town. The two main drags

wired

There are no true cybercafes in Courmayeur, but if you're dying to check your e-mail, try asking the bartender at **The American Bar** [see *bar scene,* above] if it's okay to use the computer behind the bar. *www.courmayeur.net/>http://www.courmayeur.net* and *www.emmeti. it/Welcome/Valdaosta/Valdigne/Courmayeur/index.uk.html* are good local info sources.

courmayeur

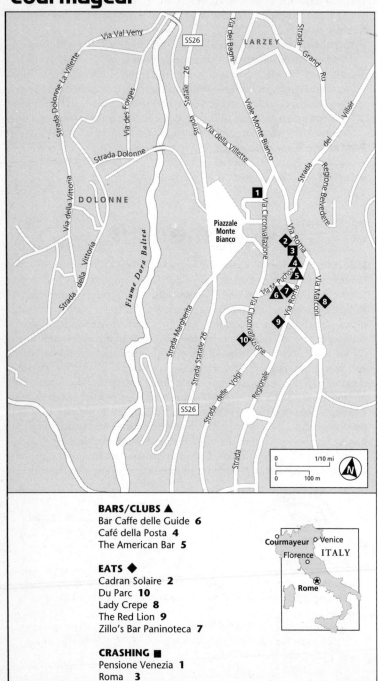

BARS/CLUBS ▲
Bar Caffe delle Guide **6**
Café della Posta **4**
The American Bar **5**

EATS ◆
Cadran Solaire **2**
Du Parc **10**
Lady Crepe **8**
The Red Lion **9**
Zillo's Bar Paninoteca **7**

CRASHING ■
Pensione Venezia **1**
Roma **3**

are **Via Roma,** a pedestrian street where you'll find a few bars and some good places for a hearty meal, and **Viale M. Bianco.** To the north of these streets are the mountains; to the south is the main highway and the **Dora River.** The bus station and the tourist office are near the **Piazzale Monte Bianco.**

During the day, women in furs (or luxe twinsets in the warmer months) can be seen shopping in the itsy-bitsy boutiques and outdoor stores along Via Roma, while everybody else is off in the mountains skiing, hiking (when the weather allows), or attempting some other extreme sport—be it white-water rafting, hang gliding, rock climbing, or some steep, steep snowboarding. You can pick up information on ski-lift prices and local events from the tourist information office [see *need to know,* below].

The heart of the social scene is in and around the bars and cafes along Via Roma. The crowd tends to be diverse in age, since Courmayeur lures young and old alike.

bar scene

The most hopping hangout in Courmayeur by far is **The American Bar** *(Via Roma 43; Tel 016/584-67-07; 10am-1am daily; No credit cards),* always packed with downhillers in winter, rock jocks in the summer, and anybody looking for a decent party scene all year round. The back room has cool little stools around equally small tables, couches, and a fireplace to warm your toes when the weather is biting. The likes of Lauren Hill and spacy background Arabic music fill the bar while you slurp down an Irish coffee (12,000L) or one of the eight beers on tap (8,000L). On a clear day, you can see the ski slopes and mountains to the south from a table in the back. The bartender (Stefano) might let you use the computer behind the bar if you need to check your e-mail—smile pretty and ask nice.

Next door is the more reserved and decorative **Café della Posta** *(Via Roma 51; Tel 016/584-22-72; 8:30am-1am daily; MC, V),* serving a somewhat older crowd. The bar is technically a cafe during most of the

fur's the word

Should you find yourself traveling though Aosta in the winter, prepare yourself for dead-animal central. Wealthy women from Milan, Turin, and local communities love their mink, raccoon, and fox furs. Wearing furs in Italy is a cultural norm, always has been, and unfortunately probably always will be, despite protests and demonstrations.

day, but that doesn't stop people from getting good and lit. Sip a mixed drink (10,000L) at the bar, or doze off in the couches around the fireplace.

Bar Caffe Delle Guide *(Viale M. Bianco 2; Tel 016/584-24-35; 10am-1am daily; AE, MC, V),* just down the road from Caffe della Posta, off Via Roma, is another cozy joint to relax those muscles. Grab a liter of German beer (20,000L) and head for the deep couches in the back room, where the vibe is young and friendly. This place offers small sandwiches (5,000L) and other bar food to munch on, and on weekends has DJs who mix hip-hop, reggae, and Italian rap. As at the other two bars in town, when the mountaineers return from their daily adventures, the place fills up with young and old.

great outdoors

In winter, from October through June, tourists and downhillers by the thousands flock to Courmayeur for a good reason: snow. And lots of it. Two ski resorts are within the immediate area: **Checrouit-Val Veny** *(Tel 016/584-20-60; 100,000L for five-day equipment rental, one-day pass 40,000L)* and massive **Monte Bianco** *(Tel 016/584-20-60; 100,000L for five-day equipment rental, one-day pass 40,000L).* Ski passes are valid for these and any one of the other 24 resorts throughout the valley, and cross-country ski passes are free. From the **bus station** [see *need to know,* below], buses (2,000L) run every 15 minutes to both resorts. Checrouit-Val Veny's four cable cars, two cableways, and 20 ski lifts shuttle more than 23,000 people up the mountain (elevation 2,746m) every hour. Monte Bianco covers a little less terrain, but has steeps and cliffs for the adrenaline seekers in all of us. You can find up-to-date ski pass and rental prices in *White Weeks,* an English-language weekly that's distributed at the resorts and tourist offices. Generally, it costs 144,000L for a consecutive three-day pass, 255,000L for a five-day, and 338,000L for a seven-day. Non-consecutive multiple-day passes go for 215,000L for four days, 319,000L for six days, and 420,000L for eight days.

The resorts in Courmayeur also offer hourly guided skiing and snowboard lessons for 50,000L. If you've already taken more than enough ski lessons, or have been skiing for about as long as you've been walking, try the longest and most challenging run in the valley: the Monte Bianco trail from Courmayeur to Chamonix. This amazing trail crosses over high granite peaks, crevasses, and some of the most virgin snow around. From December to May you can hire a guide to make the run with you for 120,000L.

A little more extreme, and altogether thrilling is heli-skiing the peaks in Vel Veny. The resorts offer heli-skiing with vertical drops between 1,000m and 2,700m from January to May. Every adventure is led by an expert guide, and specific peak drops can be requested. For a group of three people it's 290,000L for one flight; for a seven-person group it's 205,000L. For more information, call the **tourist office** [see *need to know,* below].

Snowshoeing the back woods is a little less adventurous but much more stimulating for the cardiovascular system. A mountain guide, equipment, and pass for a group of seven costs 120,000L a day. If interested, contact the tourist office for more info.

If your journeys don't happen to coincide with the snowy season, you shouldn't cross Courmayeur off your itinerary completely—there is gorgeous hiking to be done here in those precious few summer months. The **Società Guide di Courmayeur (Mountain Guide Society)** *(Piazza Henry 2; Tel 0165/84-20-64)* organizes treks around the area, from one-day jaunts to seven-day journeys. They also do rock climbing trips, if solid ground starts getting a little too boring for you. For information on guides and trips for kayaking, and rafting (and ice climbing in the winter), head to **Rafting** *(Piazza Monte Bianco, above the tourist information office; Tel 888/809-977; 9am-4pm daily; AE, MC, V)*. They can help you with just about anything, or at least point you in the right direction if they don't have what you need.

To check out the mountains from a heavenly height without all the physical exertion any time of year, hop on the **Funive Monte Bianco** *(8am-1pm/2-5pm daily, departs every 20 minutes; 45,000L)*. Cable cars leave from La Palud, a 10-minute bus ride from Courmayeur (3,000L), and make two stops along the way as they pass over the French border (no passports needed). The first stop is at Pointe Helbronner (Elev. 3,459m); the second is at Aiguille Du Midi, at a whopping elevation of 3,843m. On a clear day you can see just about everything, including the Matterhorn in Switzerland, the peaks in the Parco Nazionale di Gran Paradiso, and the sleek ice sheets off Monte Bianco.

EATS

The restaurants along Via Roma and its small side streets are the best—and only—places to fill yer belly, unless you've got a car and can drive to other nearby towns. Like most Italian mountain cuisine, Courmayeur fare is thick, cheesy, and meaty, and it's almost always served hot. Even though small pizza-to-go places have sprung up over the past five years, there are still plenty of traditional *Mamma e Papa* eateries in town.

▶▶CHEAP

Zillo's Bar Paninoteca *(Viale Monte Bianco 23; Tel 016/584-66-73; 10am-10pm daily; MC, V)* is a cool little cafe/restaurant where you can slurp down a *caffé* (3,000L) or get your fill of grease with a hefty cheeseburger and fries (15,000L). It's just north of where Via Roma and Viale Monte Bianco intersect.

For more of a festive sit-down lunch or dinner, try **Du Parc** *(Via Circonvallazione 88; Tel 016/584-25-90; 11am-3pm/5-10pm daily; Pizzas 10,000-17,000L; V, MC)*, just off Via Roma. With seating for over 150 people, don't expect an intimate dinner over a bottle of local wine—be ready for a boisterous pizza adventure. The service is great and the old oak beams, stone walls, and real brick oven offer the most authentic Italian pizza experience in town.

The Red Lion *(Via Roma 54; Tel 016/584-37-04; 10am-11pm daily; Avg. entree 12,000-18,000L; MC, V)* dishes out giant plates of pasta, served with all the free bread you can fill your pockets with. Lunch lines are long, but they tend to shuffle everyone through pretty quickly.

With France just across the mountains, it's safe to indulge in some delicious crêpes. Just off Via Roma, **Lady Crêpe** *(Via Marconi 7; Tel 016/584-41-44; 9am-1pm/3:30-7:30pm Tue-Thur; Crêpes 5,000-10,000L; No credit cards)* serves, yes, fresh crêpes and all sorts of breads and pastries.

▶▶**SPLURGE**

Cadran Solaire *(Via Roma 122 H/3; Tel 016/584-46-09; 12:30-2pm/7:30-midnight Wed-Sun; Avg. dish 15,000-22,000L; AE, MC, V)* is one of the most renowned and hard-to-get-into restaurants in the entire valley. If you do manage to score a seat (easier during lunch), you'll experience a typical Aostan meal of spinach casserole, dried mountain hams, and piping bowls of minestrone in a room filled with weathered floorboards and long pine ceiling beams. The bar is enclosed with giant slabs of mountain stone; even if you have to wait an hour for your table, you'll enjoy sipping a glass of white wine and talking to other travelers.

crashing

All year long, Courmayeur is packed with Italians from Turin and Milan and foreigners from France and afar, so it's almost always tough to find a cheap (or any) place to stay. The absolute busiest times of the year are during the Christmas and Easter holidays. In Piazzale Monte Bianco, where the bus station and tourist office are, a switchboard is connected to all the hotels in towns. Consult the map for your hotel of choice, then use the free phone to call and see if there's a vacancy.

▶▶**CHEAP**

Campgrounds **Grandes Jorasses** *(Tel 016/586-97-08; Open from July 1-Sept 30; 10,000L per person, 7,000L for a plot)* and **Tronchey** *(Tel 016/586-97-07; Same open time and prices)* are just outside of town and are easily accessible by the local bus headed for Val Ferret. Both places have public showers. If you don't have your own tent you can rent one for 10,000L.

▶▶**DO-ABLE**

One of the best bargains in town, just up the street from Piazzale Monte Bianco, is **Pensione Venezia** *(Via delle Villette 2; Tel 016/584-24-61; 45,000L singles w/out bath, 59,000L double w/out bath; MC, V)*. There are only 15 rooms in the entire place, so you should make reservations at least two weeks in advance. The rooms are well-lit and comfy, and breakfast will cost you 8,000L. The people who work the desk can get super grumpy because of all the tourists who ask for rooms that are *never* vacant, so beware.

Another place worth a shot is **Roma** *(Via Roma 101; Tel 016/584-67-65; 48,000L single w/out bath, 68,000L double w/bath; No credit cards)*. It's right on the main drag, and almost always impossible to get a room in. People book months in advance to get one of the tiny but quaint rooms. Some bathrooms are shared.

need to know

Currency Exchange There is an **ATM** in Piazzale Monte Bianco and **banks** *(8:30am-1:15pm/3-6pm, closed Sat, Sun)* and **ATMs** all along Via Roma.

Tourist Info The main **tourist office** *(Tel 016/584-20-60; 9am-12:30pm/3-6:30pm Mon-Sat, 9:30am-12:30pm/3-6pm Sun)* is on Piazzale Monte Bianco. It has listings of ski lift prices and maps for hiking. While they don't make hotel reservations for you, a board right outside, listing all of the hotels in town, is connected to a free phone.

Public Transportation The town is easily covered on foot. **Taxis** are always waiting outside the bus station in Piazzale Monte Bianco. When you're ready to hit the slopes, there's a **gondola** that connects Courmayeur with Checrouit-Val Veny. To get to the gondola from Piazzale Monte Bianco, take Via Proda up the hill for about five minutes; the gondola will be on your right-hand side. There are also **buses** that leave from Piazzale Monte Bianco for both resorts every 15 minutes.

Health and Emergency Emergencies and mountain rescue: *118.* **Ospedale Regionale d'Aosta** *(Tel 016/530-42-56)* is an ambulance network servicing the valley based in Aosta. The biggest nearby **hospital** is in Aosta [see *need to know,* Aosta].

Pharmacies Farmecie Roma *(No phone; 9am-12:30pm/3-8pm Mon-Sat)* is on Via Roma 112.

Bus Lines out of the City You can get into Courmayeur by car or bus. The **bus station** *(Tel 016/584-13-05)* is on Piazzale Bianco. Buses run up the only highway that goes through the valley, the Auto Strada Regionale.

Bike/Moped Rental Neleggio Ulisse *(Via Proda, across the street from the chair lift; Tel 016/589-570; 9am-2pm/4-7:30pm daily in spring/summer)* rents bikes.

Postal The main **post office** *(8:30am-1pm/2:30-5:30pm Mon-Fri, 8:15am-noon Sat)* is on Via Roma 22.

Internet See *wired,* above.

parco nazionale gran paradiso

The Grand Paradise National Park is just what it claims to be: a paradise, especially for hiking, horseback riding, and cross-country skiing. But it wasn't always a park. Way back when, it was a hunting ground for royal types; it became Italy's first national park in 1922, thanks to King Vittorio Emanuele III. King Vitto's dad had actually started the process in

1856 when he made it a royal hunting reserve, nearly wiping out the already diminished population of ibex (mountain goats). But the younger Vitto saved the land, and the goats, by making the area a public park where, of course, hunting is strictly forbidden. If you're lucky, you may spot one of the few remaining ibexes—now that they're protected, the goats have made a significant comeback. You can identify the male ibex by its white shaggy fur and the towering black horns that curve behind its head.

Park territory is split between the Piedmont and Aosta regions, and covers more than 7 million acres of alpine terrain, from glacial lakes and colossal mountains like Gran Paradiso (4,000m/12,000ft) to the three major valleys of **Valle Di Campiglia, Vallone di Lavina,** and **Testata della Valle Di Rhemes.** If it's ruins you're after, take a hike through Vallone di Lavina, along the breathtaking routes people from the valley once traveled to get to the commercial centers in **Valle Di Cogne.** Winding green trails deep in the valley lead to ancient villages, abandoned decades ago. Or visit **Testata della Valle Di Rhemes,** where you'll get a glimpse of the glaciers from the high open valleys that slope down from **Granta Parei.** Most of the hiking trails in the park are pretty easy, but never set out alone or without telling someone where you're headed, since the weather can change at the drop of a hat.

Information on guided hikes, rock-climbing guides, and gear rental in the park can be obtained through **Guide Alpine Valli Orco-Soana, c/o Capo Guide Valerio Nazareno** (*Piazza Chanoux 11, Cogne; Tel 012/428-515; 9:30am-2pm/4:30-7pm, closed Sun; No credit cards*). Their outfit provides detailed maps of the parks as well as guided tours through some of the more desolate areas. Guide costs vary.

Guide Alpine Aosta (*Via Monte Emilius 13/A, Aosta; Tel 016/544-448; 9am-1:30pm/3:30-7pm, closed Mon; AE, MC, V*) rents everything from ice-climbing gear to snowshoes and cross-country skis. If you're planning on buying gear, it's best to look elsewhere, since they're a bit pricey.

From the Piedmont side in Ivrea, contact **GA Giolitti Alberto** (*Via Monte Navale 8/E; Tel 012/544-158; 9am-1pm/3-6pm, closed Sun; MC, V*), a small outdoor store just south of the park that has little to offer beside maps of the park, friendly advice on hiking, and basic camping accessories. You can also try **GA Mantoan Silvio** (*Vicolo dell'Arco 14; Tel 012/548-753*).

For horseback riding, contact **Centro Turismo Equestre Val Di Rhemes** (*Loc. La Fabrique 7, Rhemes-St.Georges; Tel 016/590-76-67 or 016/590-76-1, info@casegranparadiso.com; 8am-5pm daily, Easter-Nov 1; Horse rental for half-day 150,000L; MC, L*).

need to know

Hours/Days Open The park is open all year long. Generally the best time to go hiking, horseback riding, or camping is from April to October.

Directions/Transportation The quickest and most scenic way to get to the park is from Aosta. Several **buses** leave daily from Aosta's bus station for the town of Cogne, about an hour away (4,000L). Once you reach Cogne, you can catch a **local bus** to the park entrance. You can also catch a bus to Cogne From Turin.

Eats The only place to eat in the park is at the **visitor's center,** and it's closed in the winter, so grab some supplies from one of the markets in Cogne before you head in to the wild.

Crashing For camping in Cogne, choose from the **Vallee de Cogne** *(Fabrique, Cogne; Tel 016/574-079 or 016/574-92-04; 8,000L per person, 10,000L site, bathrooms included)* or **Gran Paradiso** *(Valnontey, Cogne; Tel 016/574-105; 8,500L per person, 7,000L for a site)*. To get to both campgrounds, take one of the **buses** (2,500L one way) that leave hourly from Piazza Chanoux in Cogne. Both campgrounds are tidy and spacious and situated in a nice peaceful corner in the park, close to many of the main hiking trails. The grounds do not provide sleeping bags, but you can rent a tent.

If you'd rather have a roof over your head, try the **Youth Hostel Centro Di Soggiorno** *(Frazione di Noasca, in the park; Tel 012/490-11-07; 25,000L bed and breakfast; Curfew midnight; No credit cards)*. It's also in a peaceful corner of the park and offers your basic sleeping accommodations. The dorm rooms and communal bathrooms are relatively clean, and the staff is pretty cool. During the summer (May-August), reservations are mandatory.

bologna &
emilia-
romagna

Eat the incredibly delicious food in **Parma** and **Modena,** then burn it off dancing until morning in the hot nightclubs and underground music spots in **Bologna.** Check out the glittering gold mosaics in **Ravenna,** catch some rays at **Marina di Ravenna's** sun-drenched beaches, and indulge in the glitzy nightlife in **Rimini.** The entire area has literally fueled musical and artistic geniuses since the middle ages: Corregio, Verdi, Toscanini, Pavarotti, and Fellini all claim Emilia-Romagna as their home. Ferrari, Ducati, Lamborghini, and Maserati—those mythical machines that make grown men drool—are all designed and made here. In six words: You'll get ridiculously spoiled, amazingly quickly. It's tough to pace yourself when there's so much hedonistic pleasure within reach, but you can redeem yourself for your sins of excess by making your last stop **San Marino**—one of the smallest independent republics in the world—where a hike up awesome Mount Titano will be a veritable religious experience (and much more fun than going to confession). Emilia-Romagna can keep you busy for weeks—just do it all.

Until 1948, it was two separate regions (with distinctly different personalities): Emilia and Romagna. To this day, the two regions function as individual entities, each with its own culture, character, and tastes. And the towns within the now-combined Emilia-Romagna still cling to the unique identities they developed during centuries of independent rule. The only real trait that's shared by both regions is the liberal mentality, which has been the fundamental mindset of the entire area since the early 1900s—this is one of the most open-minded regions in all of Italy. Political and intellectual conversations flow as freely as wine and beer in every corner bar, and the active pursuit of free speech rubs off on tourists. As the original home base of the Italian Communist Party, which became the Italian Democratic Left Party, Emilia-Romagna is proud of its leading position in the Resistance movement against the Nazis during World War II. The University of Bologna is one of Europe's oldest, and since the 11th century it has cultivated many of Italy's most influential free-thinkers.

Emilia—the western part of the region—is often regarded as more refined and sophisticated than Romagna. A diverse and prosperous area nestled between the Appenine mountains and the Adriatic, it's one of the wealthiest and most culturally stimulating places on the Italian peninsula. Every night locals get all dressed up before they pour out into the piazzas for their nightly fix of socializing. Cities that popped up along Via

bologna & emilia-romagna

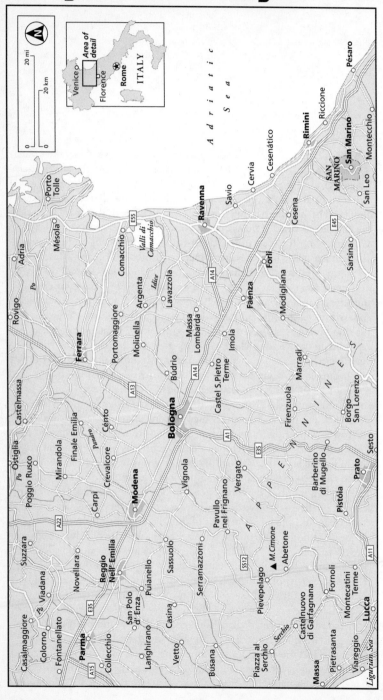

N

20 mi
20 km

Area of detail

Venice
Florence
Rome
ITALY

Adriatic Sea

Pésaro
Riccione
Rimini
San Marino
SAN MARINO
Montecchio
San Leo
Cervia
Cesenático
Savio
Ravenna
Cesena
E45
Sarsina
Forlì
Faenza
Modigliana
Comacchio
Valli di Comacchio
E55
Argenta
Lavazzola
Idice
Massa Lombarda
Marradi
Portomaggiore
Molinella
Imola
Mésola
Adria
Po
Rovigo
Ferrara
Búdrio
Castel S.Pietro Terme
Firenzuola
Borgo San Lorenzo
Porto Tolle
A14
A13
Bologna
A14
Cento
A1
E35
Barberino di Mugello
Sesto
Prato
Castelmassa
Finale Emilia
Crevalcore
Mirandola
Panaro
Vignola
Vergato
Pistóia
Ostiglia
Poggio Rusco
Carpi
Modena
Pavullo nel Frignano
A11
Po
Suzzara
Novellara
Sassuolo
M.Cimone
Abetone
Fornoli
Viadana
Reggio Nell'Emilia
Puianello
Serramazzoni
SS12
Pievepelago
Montecatini Terme
Casalmaggiore
Colorno
Po
San Polo d'Enza
Casina
Busana
Castelnuovo di Garfagnana
Lucca
Fontanellato
E35
Langhirano
Vetto
Piazza al Serchio
Pietrasanta
Viareggio
Parma
Collecchio
A15
Serchio
Massa
Ligurian Sea

APPENNINES

Emilia—the Roman road that connects the port in Rimini to Piacenza in the west—came to flourish during the Renaissance rule of art-patron royal families like the Estes, Borgias, and Farnese. To this day, Via Emilia still functions as the main drag in Ferrara, Parma, and Modena, and their cultural legacy has seeped into the contemporary in every regard. The appreciation for the arts that began with the residents of the Este Castle in Ferrara resonates today down the winding, medieval back streets of town. Bars share space with galleries, live music erupts from every other club, and the whole town is on the edge of a renaissance of its own. Today Parma's tourists, who typically come to see operas at Marie-Louisa Borgia's Teatro Regio, dig the food as much as the music. And Modena, the second home of the Estes after they were banished from Ferrara, gets its kicks with tons of wine bars, restaurants, and live music venues. And compared to those places, Bologna seems like Sin City. Here's where you'll find Emilia's most exciting—and tolerant—nightlife, from early evening cabaret shows to late-night dance clubs and a vibrant (out) gay scene.

All of Romagna, on the other hand, has a much more rowdy rep than Emilia. Hedonistic Rimini is a perfect example. Long ignored by American tourists, it has become one of Southern Europe's most hopping resort towns. People come from all over the continent just to go wild on vacation (think spring break, Italian-style). It's famous for unabashed fun-in-the-sun and unashamed larks-after-dark. On the surface, Ravenna seems more like an Americans' image of Romagna, with its celebrated Byzantine

art + architecture

The Romans, the wealthy duchies, and the Renaissance all played major parts in the development of Italy's most artistic region. Charting the Via Aemilia, the major Roman road that goes through most of the towns in the region, you'll stumble across ornate marble arches and sturdy stone bridges. Verona remains the best example of classical architecture, with its coliseum being one of the best examples of the form in Italy, but Rimini and Ravenna both have many lasting vestiges. The tradition of mosaics in Ravenna dates back to when the Holy Roman Empire was based here, and its glittering gold is a nod to the eastern tiles of Constantinople. When the gloomy dark ages gave way to the Renaissance, the prominent families of the region were there to patronize the arts. Ferrara's Estes, Parma's Farnese, and the Malatestas all across Romagna, acquired massive collections of local painters like Correggio and Parmigiano, so each town boasts impressive *musei civici*.

mosaics. But locals pretty much ignore the art and stick to the more important business of eating, drinking, and being merry. So eat a big meal and get on over to a locals-only bar; you'll forget about the whole tourist thing in a New York minute.

And as long as you're doing the local thing, get ready to chow down, because some of the best food in Italy is right here in Emilia-Romagna. It's been called the belly of Italy, which is meant as a compliment—everything from pasta and cheese to vinegar has been elevated to an art form. The verdant Po valley is its garden for fresh produce, grains, and wheat, the Adriatic produces its seafood, and some of the most skilled chefs in the world labor away in the kitchen. Eating here ranks up there with sex and art—and locals talk about it accordingly. What you ate, where you ate it, who made it, and what you hope to eat later are all topics of intrigue.

You can sample a lot of this great food for free by taking a little grazing tour during the Italian version of happy hour. A few hours before dinner, many bars lure you in for just one more *aperitivo* with a generous buffet of finger foods, hams, cheeses, and breads. For locals, it's a nibble. For you, it can be free dinner. Try the *mortadella* (the stuff we turned into baloney) and the *culatello,* which is even more delicate—and expensive— than prosciutto. And whatever you do, don't miss the unbelievably delicious *gnocco* (fried bread).

Emilia is most famous for its pasta. You've never seen such a dizzying array—from *tagliatelle* to *pappardelle, cappellacci* (tortellini filled with winter squash and cheese) and *capelletti* (what we think of as tortellini), to *passatelli* (hand-hewn strips), *Garganelli* (twists), and of course, lasagna. Pasta is still made by hand here in even the humblest of restaurants—you can often see the result of the morning's work drying in the dining room before lunch. (When you see a *Tris* on the menu, order it—they'll bring you a plate with three of the chef's best pastas.)

Romagnan fare, on the other hand, is peasant food—hearty bean soups, chewy flatbreads, and the catch of the day. You'll see *piadina*—a buckwheat flat bread rolled by hand and cooked on large griddles— everywhere, from the nicest restaurants to streetside snack shops. They're often filled with meats and cheeses. The abundance of seafood means you'll find it prepared hundreds of ways—either simply *grigliata* (grilled), deliciously *fritti* (fried), or *arrosto* (roasted). Rimini's fish stews *(brodetto)* are as popular as the *fritti misti,* which can include anything from shrimp to sardines.

getting around the region

Traveling by train in this region couldn't be easier. None of the major cities and towns of interest are more than two hours from the next big stop. Efficiency in public transportation (as well as most other government agencies affecting tourists) far exceeds the unfair Italian stereotype.

The cities profiled here are arranged in a relatively V-shaped wedge. The V starts (like where you would start if you were writing a V) in **Parma,** to the northeast. One train line runs from there and follows the old Via Emilia route southeast through **Modena** and **Bologna** to **Rimini,** which is at the fulcrum of our V. From Rimini, you can jump off the V to the **Republic of San Marino,** just to the southwest, a daytrip by bus. Once safely back in Italy (remember: San Marino is it's own country), you turn from Rimini north to **Ravenna** and close neighbor **Marina di Ravenna.** After you've seen those towns, follow the same train line north to **Ferrara,** which sits near the border of the Veneto region, and is the end-point of the V. If coming from the northeast, take the whole trip backwards (duh). If you get to Rimini first, or arrive by international train in Bologna, you'll have to cross the same ground more than once in order to see everything, but since it's all close together, you won't waste too much time doubling back. (Remember, the V is imaginary, so don't go asking conductors about it.)

TRAVEL TIMES

All times by train unless otherwise marked:
* By bus
† By bus and train combined

	Bologna	Ferrara	Parma	Modena	Ravenna	Rimini
Bologna	-	:45	1:00	:30	1:30	1:30
Ferrara	:45	-	1:45	1:30	1:00	2:15
Parma	1:00	1:45	-	:40	2:30	2:30
Modena	:30	1:30	:40	-	2:00	2:00
Ravenna	1:30	1:00	2:30	2:00	-	1:00
Rimini	1:30	2:15	2:30	2:00	1:00	-
San Marino	2:15†	3:00†	3:15†	3:00†	2:00†	:45*

bologna

If you're looking for Partyville, Italia, you've found it. But not many others have—compared to Florence, Milan, and Rome, Bologna's a virtual secret, which, of course, makes it all that much cooler. On summer nights, it's almost impossible to escape the series of free, groovy outdoor concerts and festivals held in Piazza Maggiore and its surrounding streets. The large student population brings an edgy, carefree energy to the streets, and there's no better place to experience this than along Via Zamboni, the heavily postered main drag of the university district. Here students mingle at all hours of the day and night, talking shop, making plans, or checking out the betty on the other side of the street. With a healthy mix of slackers, skaters, straight-edgers, punks, preppies, and nerds, Bologna has a wide variety of discos, clubs, and discopubs [see *live music and club scene,* below]. Many of these, unfortunately, close for the summer when classes let out (which, combined with the humidity and heat that descend in the summer months, make July and August the worst times to visit Bologna). But it's not *all* about the students—the compact metropolis has a mood and swagger of its own. The headquarters of Italy's communist party, the city government here is one of the most forward-thinking, embracing the arts like few others in Western Europe.

While there's no big attraction like the Uffizi or Saint Peter's—which is probably why the tour groups don't swarm here. But they should— Bologna has one of the best-preserved city centers in Italy. Their on gorgeous porticoes [see *singin' in the rain,* below] and towers that crumble and lean. Europe's oldest university, **Alma Matter Studitorium,** was founded here, and to this day it fills the city with intellectual intensity and a liberal attitude. Pretty much all of the attractions you'll want are in the *centro* (city center) and easily reached by walking. The efficient-yet-somewhat-confusing ATC bus system will take you beyond the ring road that borders the central city. Few people here, even the students, are fluent in English. Still, overall proficiency is higher than in most towns—there are quite a few English schools—but less than in a tourist haven like Florence. And, the attitude is very, very welcoming to young travelers. All that said, Bologna does have more than its fair share of street punks, so watch your back.

Talk aBOut, the monthly English language glossy that includes bar, restaurant, and event listings, is by far the best way to get a grip on the expat scene here. You may be able to score some free copies at Tourist info, but if not, call Tel 051/251784 or check out www.talkabout.it to find out where it's being sold (or just to speak English with the all-knowing editors). Another great source of info is **The British Council** *(Strada Maggiore 19; Tel 051/ 225142; Bus 25, 27, 30, 37, or 50 to Due Torre; 3-7:30pm Mon-Wed, 10-1pm Thurs, Fri),* a language school that has an English library open to English-speaking travelers. Their newsletter, which you can pick up at the library, lists current events of an English-speaking nature. They also have a few internet-connected computers that they're happy to let you use for browsing, but not to check e-mail. For info on *la vita della notte,* pick up *Uscita di Sicurezza,* the free monthly guide to bars, live music, and clubbing. Any respectable venue will have a few sitting out on the bar.

neighborhoods

The historic center of Bologna is laid out like an egg-shaped wheel, with **Piazza Maggiore** in the quasi-exact center and about a dozen streets shooting off from it. The central artery is **Ugo Bassi,** which to the west turns into **Via San Felice** and to the east turns into **Via Rizzoli** and then **Via Strada Maggiore.** The **university district** is anchored by **Via Zamboni,** which runs to the northeast. The big park, **Giardini Margherita,** is situated on the northeast side of the *centro* outside the road (which changes names several times) that forms the outer circle of the egg shape. The **Stazione Centrale** is located north of Piazza Maggiore, several streets off from **Via Indipendenza,** the major north-south thoroughfare. At its largest, the *centro* is 2.5 miles (east-west) by 1.5 miles (north-south), which makes basically everything in the tightly compacted center easily walkable. Modern Bologna, with its dull yellow and tan stucco buildings, lies outside of the central oval and stretches on for several miles in all directions. There's not much to see out there except for the **Stadio Communale** [see *great outdoors,* below], **Made in Bo** [see *club scene,* below], and the **city cemetery,** but if you do decide to venture, it's easy to do, thanks to the remarkably efficient ATC buses [see *need to know,* below].

five things to talk to a local about

1. **Why tourists don't come to Bologna in droves:** Just about every Bolognese has a theory why their city hasn't become a tourist hotbed on the scale of Florence or Siena.
2. **The difference between Bologna's region, Emilia Romagna, and the rest of Italy:** While a little more complex, this topic will also get the locals' vocal cords limbered.
3. How far **Bologna's soccer team** will go in Premier Division: The Bolognese are not as crazy as the Florentines, but they are loyal and, as their team has been improving, finally have something to cheer about.
4. **The role of the communist party in Bologna's history:** This will get any resident talking, red or not.
5. **Bolognese chow:** Bologna is famous for its food—tortellini, tagliatelle, lasagna verde, zampone, sausage, bolognese sauce—and hitting locals up for their fave will make ordering at a restaurant even better.

hanging out

The grandiose **Piazza Maggiore** is the perfect place to plop down and uncork a chilled bottle of wine with some friends. People of all ages pass through here throughout the day and night—walkers, bikers, and scooters using the square as a shortcut, flirty teenagers hanging around the Neptune fountain in the adjoining **Piazza del Nettuno,** jamming guitar players with their cases open for tips, and travelers like you lounging on the cathedral steps. **Via del Pratello** gets rolling around 8pm, when hordes of hipsters hit the streets in search of food and fun. The bar-filled Via Zamboni and restaurant-happy **Via delle Belle Arti** get crowded a bit earlier, once classes let out. One of the coolest spots to chill out around here is the **Giardini del Guasto,** a big, poured concrete public space full of scrap metal art, wind chimes, grafitti, and picnic tables. To get there, hang a right on Via del Guasto from Belle Arti, and take a right up the stairs to what appears to be Bologna's answer to Mount Trashmore. Kids sit around on the ground playing guitar while skate punks navigate the slopes on their boards.

For a greener refuge, head to **Giardini Margherita,** the most popular destination for runners, rollerbladers, and sunbathers. South of the **Duomo** [see *culture zoo,* below], **Piazza Cavour** is a small, clean patch good for taking a break and eating a sandwich.

bar scene

With so many students hanging out in abject procrastination (you'll meet some who are pushing 30 and have 10 exams left till graduation), you'd better believe there is a bonanza of cafes and pubs. The most crowded street, with a variety of large English/Irish-style pubs, is Via Zamboni, where literally thousands of students swarm like busy little beer-guzzling bees. Via del Pratello and Via Mascarella are also prime streets for scoping out the leaders of slackerville.

With a great outdoor patio, the trendy **Golem Caffè D'Arte** *(Piazza San Martino 3b; Tel 051/262-620; 7pm-2:30am daily; No credit cards)* provides the perfect place to sip specialty coffees or drinks and wax intellectual with your mates (and pretty much *only* your mates—the artsy crowd here isn't really outgoing). There's abstract art and projections on the walls by local artists, dishes named after the likes of Gauguin and others, a range of talks and theme evenings, and sometimes even music. Mellow, if a little snooty, it's a good pre-clubbing stop, over to the east of Piazza Maggiore; cocktails L10,000.

Except for Via Zamboni, where every place is an "Irish Pub," there are few in other parts of town. One of the best is the **Celtic Druid** *(Via Caduti di Celefonia 5c; Tel 051/224-212; 6:30pm-2:30am daily; No credit cards),* over by Piazza del Nettuno. Done up in dark wood paneling hung with Irish memorabilia, with an almost all-Irish staff, it's a favorite port of drink for English speakers, expats, students, and locals alike. Happy hour is from 6:30pm to 8:30pm—pints are only L6,000 (as compared to the normal 8,000L). The authenticity ends with the bar snacks, which are mostly (really good) bruschetta and pizzas.

The chic **Far Magia-Moro Moro** *(Via Isaia 4b/c; Tel 051/644-95-61; Noon-3:30pm/7pm-2am, closed Mon; V, MC),* east of the *centro,* has it all, including the most imaginative decor in town. Fantastic abstract murals cover the back walls, and suspended from the ceiling is a stunning Chinese dragon kite. There's even an upright piano, which offers inebriated partiers a place to practice their "skills." A restaurant in the back serves up savory lunches, dinner, and some of the fanciest happy-hour munchies in town. With Friday night DJs, the speed picks up, the

fIVE-O

Bologna's major police congregation is usually found in the area around Piazza Maggiore, the site of large, city-sponsored, open-air concerts and the occasional demonstration. Though Bologna's police are relatively unassuming and leave you alone, with so many students, they also like to make sure things stay in order.

bologna bars clubs and culture zoo

BARS/CLUBS ▲

Birraria del Pratello **3**
Celtic Druid **15**
Chalet Margherita **26**
Circolo Grada **6**
Cohiba **19**
Corto Maltese **18**
Far Magia-Moro Moro **1**
Golem Caffe D'Arte **16**
Kinky **23**
Link **7**
Naked Urban Café **17**
Pavese **4**
Riff-Raff Sud Wine Bar **5**
Soda Pop **24**
Sushi Bar **2**

CULTURE ZOO ●

Basillica di San Domenico **26**
Basillica di San Pietro (Il Duomo) **13**
Chiesa di San Giacomo Maggiore **22**
Collezione Communali d'Arte Bologna **10**
Fountain of Neptune **11**
Museo Civico Archeologico **14**
Museo of Giorgio Morandi and
 Palazzo Communale **8**
Museo Morandi **9**
National Picture Gallery **21**
Teatro Anatomico **12**
Tower of Asinelli and Garisenda **20**

bar turns dance floor at around 10:30pm, and happy souls spill out onto the street.

The no-cover **Corto Maltese** *(Via del Borgo di San Pietro 9/2a; Tel 051/229-746; 7:00pm till whenever; No credit cards)* is smack in the center of things. As with most Bologna locales, the dancing doesn't get started till past midnight, after the clean-cut regulars have downed at least a couple of drinks. Weekends can get crazy here, so if you want a more civilized crowd, show up early or during the week. Good pub grub, including sandwiches and hot dogs. Two very basic, square, fairly brightly lit rooms with live DJs playing hip-hop, commercial, and house for the one dance floor.

Primarily a disco bar, **Chalet Margherita** *(Via Meliconi 1; Tel 051/307-593; 8am-2am daily, closed May-Sept; No credit cards)* heats up in the summer with decent live music and highly entertaining karaoke and cabaret. On the northern side of **Giardini Margherita,** the whole deal is outdoors, except for the tent-like structures with seating that are scattered about. Get busy with the giddy locals on the dance floor, and order up some snacks from the gigantic menu selection to share between sets. Very laid-back, a little cheesy, and a lot of fun.

No longer the makeshift disco-pub that it used to be, Riff-Raff has gone uptown. Now called **Riff-Raff Sud Wine Bar** *(Via Pratello 3/c; Tel 051/222888; Any bus to the end of Ugo Bassi; 11am-2:30am Tues-Sat; Wines by the glass 5-10,000L; No credit cards),* this cozy, newly renovated space appeals to the Bolognese elite—those cell phone-toting, slick-dressed twenty and thirty somethings who sip wines out of ridiculously oversized glasses. The small wooden tables and front bar are packed nightly, and since it's right in the midst of Via Pratello's madness, it's a great spot to meet other bar-hoppers. The wines here all come from the southern part of the world...the south of France and Italy, South Africa, southeast Australia. Even if you're not imbibing, it's a worthwhile spot for the innovative salads and snacks [see *eats, below*].

If you've had your fill of the carbon-copy Italianate Irish pubs, but still love a cold one every now and then, then **Birraria del Pratello** *(Via del Pratello 24A; Tel 051/238 249; Any bus to the end of Ugo Bassi; 7:30am-2:30am Mon-Sat; Beer 5-14.000, Panini 7,000L; No cards)* will hit the spot. This old-style German bierhaus is serious about its brews—each beer's temperature is separately controlled, and is poured out of ceramic taps into a glass specifically designed to make *that* beer taste better. Pierre Alberto and his family started importing Franziskaner, Spaten, Brigand, and Deutchland's Guinness alternative, Diebels, almost thirty years ago—in fact, that's his collection of beer glasses and taps that's wrapped around each room, rattling against the walls as the bass kicks in the juke box. With long, wood tables and spacious booths, this is a favorite with the college kids, who tend to get a bit rowdy after a liter or two of beer. The crowds peak around 10 or 11, before they start dancing away their beer bellies away at **Soda pop** or **Circolo della Grado** [see *live music and club scene, below*].

The coolest new kid on the block is **Sushi Bar** *(Piazza Malpighi 14; Tel 051/221773, for reservations 051/221773; Bus 20, 17, 16, or 30 to Piazza Malpighi; 8pm-10:30pm kitchen, 11pm-2am club; Closed Mon; V, MC, DI),* a tiny, blue-lit space that looks more like an Arctic art gallery than a restaurant [see *eats, below*] or a nightclub. The stark white room at the bottom of the stairs, with its faux ice and waterfalls, fake fur, and psychedelic projections, plays host to 8 low-level cube tables and a long bar. After the dinner crowd dissipates around 11, the DJs come in and the party begins. Every night draws a different crowd—each of them heavily arty: Tuesday is gay night, Wednesday is international music, Thursday is open mike, Friday and Saturday are techno, and Sun is all about the lounge. You don't have to pay to get in, but you're expected to order at least one of their chi-chi cocktails (this place is so small, the bartenders can keep their eye on you). Angelo blues, Capirinhas, and mojitos all cost 10,000.

Techno and house spun by a live DJ shake the PacMan-esque painted walls of **Naked Urban Café** *(Via Mascarella 26b; Tel 051/264-738; 10pm to late; No credit cards)*, a dark, underground bar in the city center. The funky metallic bar stools are more comfortable than they look. Chic and goth student types mix here, but make sure you go late, 'cause the scene often doesn't pick up till after midnight. Cocktails go for L8,000, beer L7,000, and wine L3,000.

LIVE MUSIC and CLUB SCENE

Bologna's nightlife is as funky as it gets in Italy. Dark industrial discos, sprawling outdoor party plazas, and screaming young instrument-bashing bands are all at the disposal of the curious sightseer. To find out what's going on in the ever-changing scene, pick up the monthly 'zine *Uscita ai Sicurezza* at local CD and music stores like **Joker** or **Casa del Disco** [see *stuff,* below, for both] and many area clubs listed below. Bologna is definitely late-night-oriented: Things usually get going *no* earlier than 10 or 10:30pm and last way into the night, till 3 or 4am on weekdays, later on weekends. The look is very casual—some girls do it up in heels, skirts, capri pants, and skimpy shirts, and some boys go for pants and button-down shirts; but for the most part, it's jeans and T-shirts across the board. In places like **Naked Urban Café,** things get even punkier and more casual. And it really doesn't matter what you're wearing; the scene is totally snob-free, completely open, and inviting. There may be a bouncer at the door of some clubs, but he's there to keep the peace, not to turn people away.

When heading into many of Bologna's most popular clubs, you *may* be stopped at the door and asked for your *tessera* (card), or whether or not you're a *membro* (member) of the soci (pronounced like the preppies in *The Outsiders*) or club. ARCI and FITeL are both national groups of members-only clubs and bars. A lot of cool places in this region of Italy function as a part of one of these collectives, that is, by law, they have to charge a nominal yearly membership to let you in. The good news is, if you tell them that you're just passing though town for the night, they'll usually usher you in with a warm welcome. If not, though, just consider the 5-10,000L as a cover charge, and you get yourself a cool souvenir that might come in handy in other Northern Italian towns.

The granddaddy of music clubs in Northern Italy **Link** *(Via Fiora-vanti 14; Tel 051/530-971; www.linkproject.org; Bus 10 or 27 to Sacre Cuore; 9pm-late daily, closed Jun-Sept; 6,000L drinks, 5,000L beer pints, 3,000L bottled beer; No credit cards)*, is a bit off the map, a 10-minute walk northeast of the train station. This huge ex-pharmaceutical warehouse started out, like many such cool spots, as an illegal squat, but now operates above ground as a member of the leftist ARCI association. The graffiti-ed exterior gives a shady feel to the place, but the atmosphere inside is

rules of the game

As is the Italian norm, the liquor laws here are lax, which means that kids start drinking at about 16, and nobody'll bat an eyelash at a group of people passing around a bottle on the street. While plenty of hash smoking is done on Via Zamboni, it *is* illegal—though if all you have on you is what you're smoking at the moment, you'll only face "administrative sanctions" (read: fines and community service and "social reintegration" programs), not hard jail time. Many seem to stick to secluded spots, like discos, clubs, or the Giardini Margherita, which has plenty of nice, hidden nooks. As with almost anyplace in the world, a considerable amount of drugs can be found in most clubs.

friendly enough. Once inside, join the crowd in the do-it-yourself vibe of the downstairs Sala Blu ("the blue room"). Drinks are served in paper cups from the ramshackle bar while folks listen to national and international acts on the grubby stage. You can catch anyone from a local acid-jazz group to Kim Gordon here. There's also a bookstore with political ëzines, and art books and a small but eclectic collection of used and new CD's from 16-30,000L. Upstairs in the Sala Bianca ("White Room"), bare walls, professional lighting, and a large stage give a slicker feel to this international electronica and hip-hop venue. *Zen,* the Wednesday night dance party, features cutting-edge local DJs. The cover charges for the two areas are usually separate, so if you're coming for a specific show, make sure you know which floor you want. If you're trying pot-luck, the Sala Blu offers more diversions, in case you don't like the band. The covers (8-12,000L most nights, 20,000L on Saturdays, free on band-less Thursdays and Sundays) and the hours vary—this isn't a rules kind of place. The one hard and fast rule: you have to buy an ARCI membership card (tessera) for 5,000L [see *intro*, above].

Circolo della Grada *(Via della Grada 10; Tel 051/554322; Bus 32 or 33 to Porta San Felice; 9pm-late daily, shows start at 11pm; No cover; No credit cards)* is well worth the 15-minute walk west of the center. It's just one street north of Via Pratello, a few feet before the ring road Viale G. Vicini—look for the signs on a metal chain-link fence to the left...you'll see a driveway packed with kids sitting on cars, drinking beer, shooting the shit. Make your way through the pack to the industrial looking building, and step inside to the cozy, candle-lit bar. Don't lose that drink card they handed you—the first drink will cost 11,000, but they get con-siderably cheaper the more you have. By the end of the night, you can be tossing back margaritas for a mere 2,000L. The front room is a chill bar, but head to the open area around back where, depending on the night, folks could be rocking out to live bands, taking Tango lessons, breaking into a jazz jam session, or busting a move to the DJ-beat. There's no cover for this entertainment once you pay your annual membership fees (6,000L a year—part of the FITeL-E TSI associato)—well worth it. There's also weekly changing photography, painting, and sculpture exhibits, a library, and cheap snacks (5,000L panini).

Bologna has jumped on the Latin-crazed bandwagon with the commercial and cheery **Cohiba** *(Via Borgo san Pietro 54 a/b; Tel 051/6390527, infoline/reservations 051/6390527, Fax 051/4213924l; From the station, bus 50 to Zamboni; www.cohiba.bo.it; 8pm-late daily; No cover; V, MC),* located just north of the student center (From Zamboni, hang a left (north) on Via Marsala, then a right on Via Mentana, which becomes San Pietro after it crosses Moline Castagnoli.) The closest thing to the Tropicana in Italy—complete with waitresses in ruffly, revealing costumes, fake palm trees, and a bar fashioned to look like a straw hut—this Cuban club is packed every night with an all-ages crowd of folks who are willing to really shake a leg—a rarity in these parts. Yeah, it may be a cheese-fest, but it's also a lot of fun. Though blender drinks (10-20,000L) keep the bartenders busy, the caipirinas (12,000L) are super potent, and the beer (9,000L) goes down quickly. Ladies, the men can be pretty persistent in their search for dancing partners, so if you're alone and not in the mood for company, you may want to avoid this scene.

Is it a bar? A club? A theater? A gallery? The extremely well-rounded and welcoming **Pavese** *(Via de Pratello 53; Tel 051/550221; Bus 20, 17,*

ragazzo meets ragazza

As with any Italian town, foreign girls have the major upper hand in the cruising scene here. Italian men are hornier than cats in heat, and American women are considered "easy." But for brave, insistent backpacker boys, Bologna is the place where you may strike gold. Younger Bologna women are more urbane and independent than the traditional Italian damsel—though they still like a guy who will be attentive to their need to be coddled. The crowded bars on Via Zamboni, which are crawling with tipsy co-eds, are the best places to make your move. Start a conversation with a Bolognese babe interested in practicing English, which shouldn't be too difficult—English is quickly becoming an important commodity for Italians. And be sure to buy her a drink. Girls, your strategy has more to do with how to keep Bolognese guys *away*. Try holding hands with or kissing your friends—male or female— or saying *"lasciami in pace"* (leave me in peace) while giving them the frowning of a lifetime.

16, or 30 to Piazza Malpighi; www.pavese.bo.it, 9pm-3am Mon-Sat; Beers 8,000L; popcorn 5,000L, No cover for members; No credit cards) defies classification, but guarantees an all around good time whatever night you stumble in. Everything about this space, located down a long alleyway off Via Pratello, is big and fun—imagine a junior high school that's been taken over by anarchist artists and performers. A huge, oblong bar has been put in the center of the cafeteria, with busy bartenders passing out pints of Heineken and scooping up popcorn from the big, state fair–sized popcorn popper. All the chairs have been pulled out of the auditorium and replaced with little round tables in front of the stage, which can be removed to make room for the dance floor. Modern art hangs in the long hallway that leads to the garden and the theater—exhibitions change on a monthly basis. Every night begins with a live act—cabaret, Flamenco, or world music—and ends with a DJ. Check out the listings at Tourist info or on their website. This "soci" group usually requires ARCI membership (9,000L per year, intro) for entry, but they may make an exception for visitors.

The pierced punk kids (and their requisite dogs) make their home at the **Naked Urban Café** *(Via Mascarelli 26 b; Bus 11,27, 37, or 30 to Due Torre; Tel 051/264-738; 10:30pm-2:30am Mon-Tues; 6;30pm-2:30am Wed-Sun; No cover, different DJ every night)*, a dark and dingy disco-bar in the smack-dab center of town. There isn't a shred of pretension here—bang your head to the reckless, DJ-created techno, drum 'n' bass, and hardcore beats in your rattiest pair of jeans and sneakers. The dècor is similarly lax—that is to say, non-existent. Aluminum bar stools around wood tables around a small dance floor, and a non-descript wood bar, and that's about it. The drinking is cheaper than most spots—7,000L for a pint, 3,000L for wine, 9,000L for cocktails.

The popular disco/discobar **Soda Pop** *(Via Castel Tialto 6; Tel 051/272-079; 11pm-late; One-drink minimum; No credit cards)* has one of the most diverse selections of DJ-inspired theme nights from rock and funk to Brit pop to ska and reggae to hip-hop. A favorite with expats, it's also in the center of the city, which means you won't have to figure out late-night bus schedules or take a taxi. Of course, it also means that you'll have to put up with the meat-market mentality. The decor is nothing special—basic wood bar and a couple of nondescript things on the wall—and it's not a big place, but they sure pack 'em in.

ARTS SCENE

In between stuffing your face, dancing, and guzzling huge quantities of wine, you can explore Bologna's other virtues, namely its very active arts culture. In the summer, on most nights, you can find a free city-sponsored outdoor theater, music, or dance event, like a Puccini opera, an outdoor art exhibit, or a fife-and-drum exhibition. Most of the festivities fall under the auspices of the well-known Bologna Sogno series, which runs from July to September. Giardini Margherita is also a site for many free outdoor concerts.

▶▶VISUAL ARTS

Bologna's not exactly known for its modern art prowess, but it does have a few worthwhile galleries in the city center. **Galleria d'Arte Maggiore** *(Via D'Azeglio 15; Tel 051/235-843; 10:30am-12:30pm/4:30-7:30pm),* **Galleria d'Arte del Caminetto** *(Via Marescalchi 2; Tel 051/233-313; 4-8pm, closed Mon),* and **Galleria Falcone-Borsellino** *(Piazza Galileo 4d; Tel 051/235-292; 10am-12:30pm/4-8pm)* show a mix of works by local and regional artists. Maggiore is the largest and has the most eclectic collection, both of abstract painting and sculpture, while the others concentrate solely on 2-D art.

▶▶PERFORMING ARTS

Teatro Comunale *(Via Largo Respighi; Tel 051/529-999),* southwest of the *centro,* is the best known venue for opera, ballet, modern dance and orchestral music, with the occasional free performance.

If you happen across Bologna in the summer months, **Made in Bo** [see *festivals and events,* below] offers a nightly fix of free live musical entertainment.

gay scene

Though understandably small given the size of the city, gay life here is fairly active. **Arci Gay** *(Porta San Sarrogozza 2; Tel 051/644-69-02),* the main gay organization in Bologna, organizes conferences and events concerning gay and lesbian issues, HIV/AIDS, and safe-sex awareness. In addition to the office, the historic 17th-century building, well southwest of the city center, also houses **Il Cassero** *(7pm-late daily)* a happening discobar, whose adjoining open-air terrace is open in the summer. Like the Arci Gay office, Il Cassero is a central meeting point for both the gay and lesbian communities and one of the few places in Bologna that is open year-round. June and July, when other centrally located clubs close, are its most popular months. Drinks run between L4,000 and L8,000, and there are regular theme nights and live DJs. It's a good place to either start or end an evening.

One of the local favorites is **Paquito** *(Via Polese 46c; Tel 051/243-998; 9:30pm-late Wed-Sat, 10pm-late Sun; L15,000-20,000 cover; V, MC)* a hardcore all-boys club (though brave girls sometimes go) with heavy groping, heavy gasping, and very dark near the Giardini Margherita. No one gets here before 11:30pm, so if you go, you may not be getting up before noon. It's said that they are particularly welcoming to boys from abroad. Just remember to behave yourself.

Gay Thursdays bring out an almost religious following of guys and gals to **Kinky** *(Via Zamboni 1; Tel 051/268-935 10pm-late Wed-Sun; Cover varies from L15,000-25,000; No credit cards),* as do gay-heavy Saturdays. The gregarious crowd doesn't usually go much beyond T-shirts and jeans.

Right on the Via San Felice (same thing as the Via Ugo Bassi running through the heart of the city), the **New Vigor Club** gym *(Via San Felice 6b; Tel 051/232-507; 5-minute walk from Piazza Maggiore; 2pm-2am;*

fESTIVALS and EVENTS

With rides and games on one side of the hill, and vendors, bars, restaurants, discos, and live performance areas on the other, the sprawling outdoor entertainment hub **Made in Bo** *(Parco Nord-Via Stalingrado; Tel 051/264-738; Bus 25 to Parco Nord; 10pm-late July, Aug; No credit cards)* resembles a patchwork theme park. There is something for everyone here, which means attendees range from parents with crying kids to hyper teens to lovey-dovey couples to single guys and girls cruising each other. The outdoor dance floors don't get revved up till 11pm (and rage on till 4am and sometimes later), so while you wait for someone to take the plunge, try your hand at the carnival games. All types of music, live bands, and comedy.

The large classical music festival, **Bologna Festival** *(Information: Via delle Lame 58; Tel 051/649-33-97, 051/649-32-45; bofest@tin.it)*, is held each year from April to June and features national and international talent. Venues are scattered about Bologna in various churches and theaters.

L18,000 cover; No credit cards) is a great place to: a) make sure your buff build doesn't go to pot by burning off the seemingly endless mounds of carbohydrates you've been ingesting, and b) get a date! When you're done working out, you can towel off and do some more sweating in the sauna. Mostly guys, but women aren't unwelcome.

Another good relaxation venue is **Cosmos Sauna** *(Via Boldini 22, interno 16; Tel 051/255-890; 5-minute walk from train station; 2pm-late; 22,000L Mon-Thur, 25,000L Sun, Sat; No credit cards)*. Larger and more modern than the New Vigor Club, the facility is for men only, which creates an unabashed cruising atmosphere.

CULTURE ZOO

For the museum- and church-weary traveler, Bologna is the place to be. There are fewer "must-see" stops, more charming nooks and crannies. Because of the almost anemic number of visitors, sightseeing is much less stressful, and, except in the high season, you might actually find yourself looking at a painting *by yourself* for a few minutes. One thing you really shouldn't miss is the climb up La Torre Asinelli. For about a buck fifty, get a great workout and an awesome skyscape view. The most obvious place to start your Bologna cultural tour is Piazza Maggiore, the social, spiritual and political heart of the city. The old and the new fuse together beautifully in this sprawling, cafe-lined square. Some of the city's best preserved medieval and Renaissance buildings now house facilities of a more modern

singin' in the rain

So what if it's raining? With more than 20 miles of arcaded galleries (more than any other city in the world), you can get almost anywhere you need to go without getting wet. Bologna's main architectural feature, the beautiful stone porticos that wrap around buildings in the historic center, make Bologna one of the most pedestrian-friendly cities in the world. The designs vary widely—from baroque flourishes to gothic simplicity to ultra-modern interpretations of a traditional design.

nature (like the tourist office in Palazzo Comunale, to the right of the Duomo), and huge, colorful banners advertise the current exhibits inside.

Basilica di San Petronio (Il Duomo) *(Piazza Maggiore; Tel 051/225-442; Buses 25 and 30 from the train station to Piazza Maggiore; 7am-1:30pm/2:30-6:30pm daily Apr-Sept, 7:25am-1pm/2-6pm daily Oct-Mar; Museum open 9:30am-12:30pm Mon-Sat; Free admission):* Construction stopped on Bologna's biggest church once the papacy found out it was intended to be larger than St. Pete's in Rome (blasphemy!), which explains why the facade only goes abut a quarter of the way up before it gives way to brick and mortar. Don't believe anyone who tells you the ladders were too short. Started in the last decade of the 14th century, it didn't have a roof until the 1700s—apparently the building was so big, they couldn't figure out how to construct one. The enormous, dark interior is host to many important works of art (most housed in the small museum), but one of the most interesting is Cassini's sundial. Follow the brass line, which runs along the floor, diagonally, from the center of the aisle in the back to the hole in the wall that lets the sunlight in. Four hundred years later, it's still right on time.

Fountain of Neptune *(Piazza Nettuno, just east of Piazza Maggiore):* It's fitting that such a shocking bronze sculpture should become the pride and joy of Bologna, a town that has always been known for its liberal philosophies. Completed in 1566 by the French artist who was nicknamed by the locals "Giambologna," the muscular water god caused quite a controversy when the world found out just how manly this man was. Legend has it that though the citizens were fine with his washboard chest, and his posse of naked dolphin-abusing kids and heavy-bosomed sirens, the artist was forced to rework his masterpiece's masterpiece toward more human proportions. Giambologna got the last laugh—take a look from about 30 feet behind the statue, about ten feet from the steps on your right, and just try not to blush.

Teatro Anatomico at Palazzo e Biblioteca di Archiginnasio

(Piazza Galvani 1, behind San Petronio; Tel 051/236488 or 051/276811; 9am-6:30pm Mon-Fri (closed in afternoon occasionally), 9am-1pm Sat; www.comune.bologna.it/archiginnasio; Free entrance): Today, Palazzo Archiginnasio houses Italy's most important and comprehensive library— a not-so surprising feat considering that the Bologna's University is one of Europe's oldest. This beautifully decorated building was built to be its epicenter of learning in 1563. Wind your way through the porticos, which are frescoed with professor's visages and prominent student's coats of arms, up to the Anatomy Theater, which will make even the most solid-stomached med student a bit queasy. Designed in 1637 by Antonio Levanti, this hall contains beautiful wood sculptures of famous physicians, and two skinless representations of the human form. Yes, those would be muscles. The marble table in the center of the room that once set the stage for human dissections is watched over by Apollo and his heavenly consorts. Climb up into one of the wooden benches that surrounds the room, and thank God for modern medicine. Ask the friendly security guard who let you in for information in English—the free pamphlet describes how the Teatro was rebuilt after an allied bombing on Jan 29, 1944.

Collezioni Comunali d' Arte Bologna

(Piazza Maggiore 6 in Palazzo d'Accursio; Tel 051203629 04 203111; Fax 051/232312; museicivici@comune.bologna.it; 10am-6pm Tues-Sun; closed Mon, Christmas, and New Year's Day; 6,000L admission) houses local painters from the 15th century onward. Wander through beautiful frescoed rooms filled with sculptures and paintings. For a more modern take on Bologna's artistic output, there's the **Museo Morandi** *(Piazza Maggiore 6 at Palazzo d'Acccursio; Tel 051/203646 or 203386, Fax 051/203332; mmorandi@commune.bologna.it; 10am-6pm Tues-Sun; Admission 8,000L; students 4,000L)* houses the most complete collection of the local modernist painter's work. Pastel abstracts, sculptures, and even a rendering of the artist's studio are on display. Travelling exhibits for more well-known modernists, like Paul Klee, are featured here as well. You can purchase a joint ticket for both museums for 12,000L, and guided tours are given on Wed and Sat in English (25,000).

Palazzo Communale and Museum of Giorgio Morandi

(Piazza Maggiore 6; Tel 051/203-526; 10am-6pm Tue-Sat; Each museum separate admission, L8,000 adults, L4,000 ages 14-18, combined tickets L12,000 adults, L6,000 ages 14-18): Restored for the year 2000 Jubilee, the 14th-century Bologna town hall houses two small museums of artwork donated from several private collections, as well as the tourist information office.

Basilica di San Domenico

(Piazza San Domenico 13; Tel 051/640-04-11; 7am-1pm/2:15-7pm daily; Free admission): Regardless of whether you've seen Michaelangelo's *David* in person, you'll be spellbound by his *San Procolo,* said to be the artist's "rehearsal" for his later masterpiece.

(12 hours in boLogna)

1. **Catch a free outdoor play:** In the summer, many of the piazzas in the city center become sites of free local musical and theatrical productions. Even if you can't speak Italian, it's fun to check out the scene.
2. **Climb the Tower of Asinelli:** You might get dizzy climbing the winding wood staircase, but gazing down on the red tile cityscape and confusion of Ugo Bassi are worth it [see *culture zoo,* above].
3. **Cruise the steps of Piazza Maggiore:** This is *the* place to hang out and strike up a conversation with a potential love interest. Offer to buy a coffee or gelato, and your odds increase a thousandfold [see *hanging out,* above].
4. **Party on Via Zamboni:** You'll probably be told that the student area is seedy—and it is! That, and the crush of undergrads, make it great [see *neighborhoods,* above].
5. **Dine on Via del Pratello:** One of the best, cheapest streets for restaurants, pubs, and cafes is also a student favorite [see *hanging out,* above].
6. **Go to Made in Bo:** This sprawling, outdoor nighttime carnival-disco-mall keeps the masses entertained on those hot summer evenings when most other bars and discos in the city are closed [see *festivals and events,* above].

Tower of the Asinelli and Tower of the Garisenda *(Piazza di Porta Ravegnanna; 9am-6pm daily May-Sept, till 5pm Oct-Apr; L5,000):* Need a bit of exercise? After a satisfying climb up the Asinelli's wooden staircases (about 500 steps in all), you'll be rewarded with the best view in central Bologna. Looking like it may topple any day, Garisenda is closed. (Don't be afraid to get close: It's been leaning since Dante wrote the *Inferno.*)

Chiesa di San Giacomo Maggiore *(Piazza Rossini or Via Zamboni 15; Tel 051/225-970; 8am-noon/3:30-6pm daily; Free admission):* The Bentivoglio Chapel in this 13th-century structure is best known for its stunning (though somewhat dirty-looking) frescoes by Francesco Francia.

Pinacoteca Nazionale (National Picture Gallery) *(Via delle Belle Arti 56; Tel 051/243-222; 5-minute walk from Piazza Maggiore; 9am-1:50pm Tue-Fri, 9am-12:50pm Sun, closed Mon; L8,000 adults, under 18 free):* A one-stop tour of Bologna's greatest art offerings from the Byzantine to the Baroque. The Giotto altarpiece is a must-see, as is Raphael's "Ecstasy of Santa Cecilia."

7. **Chill out in Giardini Margherita:** Big open fields, shaded woodsy areas, and a couple of kiddy amusement rides, and in the summer, free concerts filled with the university's soccer-playing, frisbee-chucking, rollerblading, suntanning student body [see *great outdoors,* above].

8. **Take a photo by the Neptune fountain:** Designed in 1566, the fountain depicts a buff Neptune with his foot on the head of a dolphin, surrounded by four very sensual sirens. Great place to take a seat and cool off [see *hanging out,* above].

9. **Get lost at Link:** Revel in the kind of freewheeling fun only a night at an abandoned pharmaceuticals company can offer. The coppers are closing down anything that used to be a casa occupata, one-by-one, but the folks behind link joined up with the ARCI association and saved their souls. Not that it cramped their style any—they're still moshing and head banging with the rest of them. [see *live music and club scene,* above].

10. **Eat a Pizza:** Nicola's Pizzeria, a local favorite with students and non-students alike, is smack in the middle of town [see *eats,* below].

Museo Civico Archeologico *(Via dell'Archiginnasio 2; Tel 051/233-849; 9am-6:30pm Tue-Sat, 10am-6:30pm Sun, closed Mon; L8,000, L4,000 students):* All you archeology buffs will love this "Civic Archeological Museum," with its excellent Egyptian collection and a good showing of Greek, Etruscan, and Roman treasures.

great outdoors

Located just outside the southern rim of the city center, **Giardini Margherita** is one of Italy's most pleasant urban parks. Basketball and volleyball courts, large fields for sunbathing and frisbee, and smoothly paved pathways make this the perfect escape from the loud, scooter-filled streets. Another park option, though much less impressive, is **Giardino della Montagnola,** located in the northern half of the city. The most notable feature is a large, fish-filled fountain.

If you're visiting Bologna during the sweltering summer months, hike over to **Stadio** *(Via A. Costa 174; Tel 051/615-25-20; Bus 14, 21 from Porta San Isaia to Via A. Costa)* or **Sterlino** *(Via Murri 113; Tel 051/623-70-34; Bus 13, 96 from Porta San Stefano to Via Murri),* two public swimming pools open every day from mid-June to Sept, 10:30am till 7pm. Entrance costs about L10,000.

STUff

Bologna is not among Italy's best shopping cities: Clothes and shoes are wicked expensive. The stylish Via d'Azeglio and Via Farini have an array of designer boutiques like Gucci and Armani as well as some nifty jewelry stores, but you won't find many bargains. With a bunch of clothing and specialty shops, and a McDonald's, Via Ugo Bassi and Via Indipendenza are great window-shopping and walking streets. At the outdoor market in Piazza Aldrovandi, vendors hawk fresh fruits and vegetables, breads, Italian books, housewares, and some clothing at fair prices. Generally though, in Bologna, money is better spent on food and drink than pretty much anything else.

▶▶BOUND

Feltrinelli International *(Via Zamboni 7B; Tel 051/268-070; 5-minute walk from Piazza Maggiore; 9am-7pm Mon-Sat; AE, V, MC)* has an assortment of good English books, as well as magazines, travel guides, and newspapers.

▶▶TUNES

For relatively cheap CDs, tapes, and vinyl ("relatively" is the operative word) of basic international pop, alternative, hip-hop, rock, and the latest Italian versions of all of the above, go to **Casa del Disco** *(Via Indipendenza 30c; Tel 051/234-224; 9am-12:30pm/2:30-7:30pm, closed Thur afternoon, Sun; AE, V, MC)* or **Joker** *(Via Ugo Bassi 14e; Tel 051/265-016; 2-minute walk from Piazza di Maggiore; 9:30am-1pm/4-8pm, closed Sun; V, MC).*

▶▶DUDS

For the hippest styles from Stussy, Pickwick, and Carhartt, head over to **Scout** *(Piazza VIII Agosto 28e; Tel 051/249-825; Bus 12, 9:30am-7:30pm; AE, V, MC).* They also carry a wide selection of hats, Jansport

moda

The large student population here has cornered the style market on punk and grunge. Sneakers, ripped or baggy jeans, T-shirts, tank tops (for girls), and colorful Invicta backpacks are the look of choice. Blue, green, white, or purple hair is not uncommon, nor are tattoos. All of which makes fitting in easy for scrubby travelers. The best place to check out the current styles is in the university district near Via delle Belle Arte and Via Zamboni.

and Eastpak bags, and sneakers, though some stuff like the shoes and bags are more expensive.

▶▶GIFTS

You can knock off some of your obligatory gift-shopping at **Images** *(Via delle Moline 8; Tel 051/227-630; 9am-12:30pm/3:45-7:30pm, closed Thur afternoon),* a store full of posters, postcards, T-shirts, murals, and various souvenir knickknacks.

EaTS

Don't worry about emptying your travel wallet on good food here. The westward Via Pratello, and eastern Via Zamboni, bookend Bologna's centro storico with bargain eateries and self-service restaurants that are packed with locals day and night. The food at these pizzerias and buffets are very good, however, you are in the gastronomic heart of Italy, and if there's any place where you should splurge, it's here.

Being the largest city in Emiglia Romagna, all the best products from around the region can be found in abundance—*Prosciutto di Parma* (cured ham); *Balsamico* (balsamic vinegar); *Parmigiano Reggiano* (aged parmesan cheese) are the best-known. Some of the best loved are the slightly sweeter *Prosciutto di Langhirano; Cotechino,* an enormous, spiced pork sausage that is boiled and served hot; and *Mortadella,* the finely minced pork sausage that was the inspiration for b-o-l-o-g-n-a! Pastas are an art form here, and most of cooks at the trattorias here spend their mornings rolling out the egg, flour, and water dough by hand. Simple as can be, the ubiquitous *tortellini in brodo* is one of the most soul-nourishing dishes imaginable. Heartier appetites defer to the equally popular *Tagliatelle Bolognese,* which is made with a *rag*— (sauce) of tomatoes, pork, and veal and topped with a sprinkling of Parmigiano.

▶▶CHEAP

You'll walk away from **Osteria Alle Due Porte** *(Via del Pratello 62a; Tel 051/523-565; Noon-3pm/7pm-2am, closed Tue; L10,000-25,000 per entree; V, MC)* licking your lips with gusto. If you're on a very low budget, you can make a meal of the perfectly spiced *pennette all'arrabiata* (L6,000) and a carafe of wine, but if you have a bit more dough, go for one of the scrumptious beef, veal, or fish dishes. For vegetarians, the eggplant parmagiana and caprese are heavenly. The decor is nothing special—basic white walls, wood paneling, marble floors—but the waitstaff is friendly and speaks just enough English to help you get by. Arrive early to beat the student crowd for an outside table.

Also right in the heart of studentville, the Greek hole-in-the-wall **To Oteki** *(Largo Respighi 4E; Tel 051/268-012; 11am-11pm, closed Sun; L6,000-15,000 per entree; No credit cards)* is a university favorite. The kitchen serves up drippy gyros, healthy moussaka, and stuffed pitas seconds after you order. There is outside seating, but you'll be hard-pressed to upend the "studious" academics.

The difficulty in finding an empty table at the vegetarian **Clorofilla** *(Strada Maggiore 64c; Tel 051/235-343; 12:15-3pm for lunch, 7:30pm-*

boLogna eats and crashing

EATS ◆
Clorofilla **15**
Due Torri **9**
Mercato delle Erbe **4**
Nicola's Pizzeria **8**
Osteria alle due Porte **1**
Riff Raff Sud Wine Bar **3**
Sushi Bar **18**
Tamburini **17**
To Oteki **10**
Trattoria Belle Arti **12**

CRASHING ■
Albergo Accademia **12**
Albergo Centrale **6**
Albergo Minerva **7**
Albergo Panorama **5**
Garisenda **16**
Ostello per La Gioventu San Sisto **13**
Pensione Marconi **2**
San Vitale **14**

midnight for dinner; 9,500-14,000L per entree; AE, V, MC) is proof that in the land of spaghetti, there *is* life after pasta. The cheerful yellow-and-green interior matches the colorful plates of rice, couscous, seitan, and tofu. At 6,500L, the veggie burger makes a nutritious and light lunch or dinner. Largely full of travelers—Italians generally like their meat. Right on the Piazza di Porta Ravegnanna.

The mod dècor of the inexpensive self-serve **Due Torre** *(Via de' Giudei 6/f; Bus 11,27, 37, or 30 to Due Torre; Tel 051/237718; Noon-3pm/7-9pm Mon-Sat, open for dinner Sept-June only; 4-6,000L pastas, 6-9,000L main dishes; No cards)* features aomeba-shaped swivel stools, and yellow and teal tables that are all occupied come lunchtime, when the line for food extends all the way out the front door. But don't let all the slickness fool you—this homestyle Italian cafeteria serves up rustic, no-frills classics at rock-bottom prices. *Tortollini in brodo, gnocchi Bolognese,* a salad, a hunk of bread, and a quarto of wine, all for less than 12,000L. Get in line.

Since 1932, the beautiful, tile-floored **Tamburini** *(Via Caprarie 1; Tel 051/234726; Fax 051/232226; www.tamburini.com; tambinfo@tin.it; Any Bus to Rizzoli; 8-14,000L main dishes; V, MC, DC)* has sold fresh pastas, meats, cheeses, and breads. The buffet that winds its way through the back of the store is one of the most popular lunch options in town. Line up, grab a tray, and point to whatever looks good. Bolognese specialties like homemade *gnocchi al ragù,* tagliolini with asparagus and ham, warm *Tomo* cheese with walnuts, and *bollito misto* cost much less than you'd pay at a sit-down meal. The atmosphere in the dining room, where you sit at long tables with other diners, is convivial and cheery. If you buy a roll (500L), the great olive oil and cheese on every table makes a meal in itself.

▶▶**DO-ABLE**

In the summer, you can't find a more sought-after outdoor table than at **Nicola's Pizzeria** *(Piazza San Martino 9a; No phone; Noon-3pm/7:30pm-midnight; L15,000-35,000 per entree; V, MC)* on the Piazza di Porta Ravegnanna. Couples, students, and families come here for the same thing: cheap and delicious food served in a great, lively atmosphere. Starting at L5,000, the brick-oven pizzas have a 100 percent satisfaction rating. The pastas (L9,000-11,000)—try the traditional bolognese or ragú sauce—won't disappoint. Everything's better with a jug of local red wine.

TO MARKET

Why go to a supermarket when you can get everything you need at the **Mercato delle Erbe** *(Via Ugo Bassi 27; No phone; 7am-1pm/4-7pm Mon-Sat; Closed Sun all day and Thurs and Sat afternoons; No cards),* the enormous covered food market on the western end of Ugo Bassi. All the makings of your picnic—bread, cheese, salami and sausages, vegetables, fruits, and wines—are sold in this maze of busy stalls. Other grocery basics, like sodas and cereals, are for sale here too. On the other end of Ugo Bassi, just two blocks east of Piazza Maggiore, Via Drapperie functions as the other food market in town. Old, established food stores like **Drogeria Gilberto** [see *stuff,* above], fishmongers, and produce purveyors create dizzying displays of their goods, and bargain abound around 7pm, just before the stores close for the day.

down and out

Considering it's a student town, Bologna is not as cheap as you might expect. Still, there are a lot of things to do for the monetarily challenged. Sit in Piazza Maggiore or lounge in Giardini Margherita—the continual influx of all kinds of humans make these spots legendary for people-watching. Cheap eats are best found on Via delle Belle Arte and Via del Pratello. Even cheaper eats can be had by getting made-to-order sandwiches from local *alimentari*. Italians usually don't order sandwiches, so you'll have to tell the shop help exactly what you want—i.e., two slices of prosciutto (*due figlietti del proscuitto*), one slice of cheese (*una pezza del formaggio*), etc. Since everything is weighed separately, this will cost as much as buying bread, cheese, and meats separately and putting it together yourself, so the choice is yours....Finally, buy a couple of bottles of vino and find a stoop. It's totally legal and part of everyone's Italy experience. If it's the malt you're after, **Birre + Bevande** *(Via Petroni 15A; Tel 051/034-787; Bus 11,27, 37, or 30 to Due Torre; 11am-8:30pm Mon-Sat; No credit cards)* is a great alternative to the Bologna Bar Tax. Donati Gianfranco has transformed his family's old *latteria* (milk store) into a beer store that rivals any in the states. With more than 150 beers from around the globe, this little, fluorescent lit storefront offers Peroni and Moretti for a mere 2,500L, and specialties like Leffe and Orval for a 5,000L.

Not to be confused with the non-descript place of the same name down the street, the hip and hectic **Restaurant Belle Arti** *(Via Belle Arti 14; Tel 051/225581; Bus 11,27, 37, or 30 to Due Torre; 11am-3pm/6-11pm daily, closed Wed; Entrees 12-20,000L; V, MC)* is one of the most popular trattorias in this part of town. The décor, with Victorian looking floral wallpaper under high, brick arches, and blue and yellow plaid tablecloths, doesn't look like it would attract the hordes of actors and performers from the nearby theater, students, and decked out young professionals. No, they all flock here for the food, even if it means being served by some of the snootiest, hipster waiters in town. *Gnocco,* or fried pizza dough, is brought to the table warm and sprinkled with Parmigiano cheese and olive oil. The tortolloni with hazelnuts and four cheeses is dessert-like in its decadence. Fish is the thing here—try *Pasta Scoglio,* with mussels, clams, shrimp, served with an al dente pasta, or the *rombo humido,* an entire Turbot cooked in tin foil with tons of fresh vegetables. Make sure you know the price of the wine before you order—though the wine list is incredible, they're known for pushing the more expensive bottles.

Though you're in the culinary capital of Italy, sometimes too much of a good thing breeds boredom. The palate-shifting **Riff Raff Sud Wine Bar** [see *bar scene, above*] will hit the spot with it's inspired menu items from southerly places around the world. Have a plate of cheese, salami, and sliced hams from Calabria or Sicily. Try an oversized Sardinian salad (12,000L). And since this little wood and copper trimmed spot is primarily a wine bar, there's a glass (5-10,000L) to go with everything. Come by on the weekends for a leisurely brunch (15,000L).

Swathed in intentionally antiseptic, white minimalist décor, **Sushi Bar** [see *club and live music scene, above*] is the last place you'd expect to see hungry hordes chowing down on colorful little cubes of raw fish. 6 pieces of sushi, 6 pieces of roll, miso soup, salad, and fruit is a little bit pricey at 30,000L, but that's the price you pay for the coveted table here. Hot or cold sakis are just 5,000L a glass. Reserve your table for dinner, which runs from 8 to 10:30pm, and you're guaranteed a spot when the party starts around 11.

▶▶**SPLURGE**

A huge wine list, goofy wait staff, and a menu of hearty Bolognese and Lucan dishes are the major draws to **Trattoria Belle Arti** *(Via Belle Arte 6f; Tel 051-267-648; Lunch 11am-3pm, dinner 5-11pm; L20,000-40,000 per entree; No credit cards)*. All pastas are fresh, and meats, epecially the roast lamb, are slow-cooked and tender. Also try the *zucchine trifolate alla crema di yoghurt*—a yummy zucchini cream concoction. The one catch is that the waiters don't write down your order, so you may get something unexpected, but it's usually still delicious. The inside and outdoor tables are covered in real linen and decorated with fresh flowers. Conveniently located at the northeast corner of the *centro*.

gelati wars

Scoops from **Gelateria Moline** *(Via Moline 13)* are perennial favorites for students here, though the comparatively little-known **Gelateria Gianni** *(Via Montegrappa 11; Noon-1am daily, 11am-1pm Sun, closed every other Wed)*, hidden away one street north of Ugo Bassi, exceeds it in scoop size, taste, and number of flavors. Gianni also has a full bar and seating in the back and an assortment of *granita* (Italian-style slurpees) for anyone looking for a refreshing alternative to gelati. **Occhi di Venere** *(Via San Vitale 37a; 5-minute walk from Piazza Maggiore; Closed Mon)* is another good choice for big cones.

crashing

Even in the height of summer, Bologna's center will never be crawling with disoriented map readers. You'd think this would make cheap hotel rooms and beds relatively easy to snag, but unfortunately there just isn't a big pool of low-cost options. There are a few budget hotels in the center, but virtually none by the train station, and the youth hostel is located well outside the center. Call ahead to the cheaper hotels and make a reservation, especially during the summer. Once you reach a hotel, speak up, because there is also some chance that you'll be able to negotiate a better price, as hotel owners customarily have off-season and high-season prices. Many visitors come here for the well-established business-fair circuit that runs mostly in the spring and fall, so make sure you have reservations if you're in town then.

wired

There are so many free places to check email and surf the web in Bologna, there's hardly any reason to pay. Here's a list of the most convenient spots: **Iperbole** *(Piazza Maggiore 6, in the tourist info office; Tel 051/203184; 9:30-6:30 Mon-Sat; 9:30-1:30 Sat; Closed Sunday; Free):* toward the back of Bologna's well-equipped tourist info office in Piazza Maggiore, the city government has six computers that they lend out to the internet-starved masses daily. Though you're supposed to reserve at least a day in advance, there's always empty space if you're willing to wait for someone not to show up. The only downsides are that you can't print, use word processing, or download files to disk. Sorry guys, but **ServerDonne Internet Tea Room** *(Palazzo Notai on Via De'Pignattari 1, just off piazza Maggiore; Tel 051/203401 or 051/233863; http://Orlando.women.it; 9-1 Mon, Wed, Sat; 3-7 Tues, Thurs, Sat; Free)* is strictly for the ladies. This women's organization houses the second floor of an old palazzo, and besides organizing lecture groups, discussions, and meetings regarding women in technology, they provide the female public with seven computers equipped with Microsoft Office in a narrow computer room at the back of their lecture hall. It's first come, first serve, and you're allowed to print if you bring your own paper. Though you may have to fill out a short questionnaire, **Informagiovani** *(Via Pier De Crescenzi 14; Tel 051/525842; 10-1/3-6 Mon, Tues, Fri; 3-6 Wed; 10-6 Thursday)* has a few computers that they lend out for browsing. No download, no discs, no printing, but this is a great place to meet folks and get the 411 on the scene.

▶▶CHEAP

Ostello per La Gioventu San Sisto (HI) *(Via Viadagola 5; Tel 051/501-810, Fax 051/391-003; Bus 93, 21B to Localita San Sisto; Desk open 7-10am/3:30-10pm, closed Dec 20-Jan 20; L21,000 per bed, L26,000 w/o HI card; V, MC)* is by far the cheapest choice in town, but you pay in other ways: There's a midnight curfew, a 10am to 3:30pm lockout, and it's a 30- to 40-minute bus ride east of the city center. Most of the rooms in the converted villa contain five beds and sinks, with (very clean) bathrooms and showers in the hallway. The young staff is eager to help. Continental breakfast included.

Due Torri *(Via Viadagola 14; Tel 051/519-202)* is run by the same folks and has all the same vitals.

Though its rooms are plain and let in a load of street noise, **Pensione Marconi** *(Via Marconi 22; Tel 051/262-832; L68,000 single w/bath; L110,000 double w/bath; No credit cards)* is a great cheap crash pad near the train station. The staff likes to point out that most rooms have ceiling fans, an absolute must in summer.

You can't get more central than **Garisenda** *(Galliera del Leone 1; Tel 051/224369, Fax 052/221007; Bus 37 to Due Torre; 70,000L singles, 100,000L doubles; V, MC)*, so if bar-hopping in the student district is on your agenda (hello!), this should be one of your first choices. With only seven standard rooms, this place feels more like a bed & breakfast, only there's no breakfast (or TVs and phones, for that matter).

Just a three-minute walk from the student center and the two towers, **San Vitale** *(Via San Vitale 94; Tel 051/225966, Fax 051/239396; Bus 37 to Due Torre; 60,000-100,000L singles with bath, 95,000-135,000L doubles with bath, price depends on season)* is a fave with budget travelers, students, and young families. There's a pretty garden where you can feel free to hang out, and all of the 17 rooms have phones and TVs, comfy beds, and cozy décor.

▶▶DO-ABLE

Sure, the rooms are antiseptic, but **Albergo Minerva** *(Via de Monari 3; Tel 051/239-652; 100,000-130,000L double; V, MC)* is only a 5-minute walk from the university quarter-which makes it slightly easier to make the 2:30am curfew—and not a bad price if you share the room. The tongue-in-cheek Sicilian-born owner mans the desk for psychotically long shifts (18 hours) and likes to chat with guests. The shared bathrooms are somewhat muggy, and you may literally bump into fellow travelers in the narrow hallways.

The name says it all: every room in **Albergo Panorama** *(Via Livraghi 1; Tel 051/221-802, 051/227-205, Fax 051/266-360; L95,000 double w/shared bath; AE, V, MC)* has a pretty view, some looking down on the hectic Via Ugo Bassi; some onto the cute and tranquil courtyard and terracotta roofs of its neighbors. The 13 rooms are large and provide ample space to stretch your legs. The women who run the hotel are friendly, and operate the establishment like proud aunts. Bathrooms are clean and location can't be better. By far the best reasonably priced hotel in Bologna.

▶▶SPLURGE

The pleasant, three-star **Albergo Centrale** (*Via della Zecca 2; Tel 051/225-114, Fax 051/235-162; L100,000 single w/bath; L140,000 double; AE, V, MC*) puts you about a 2-minute walk from Piazza Maggiore. Ask for a top-story room—most have nice rooftop vistas. Phones and TVs found in all rooms provide good diversions, and the efficient staff keeps the lounge stocked with coffees and liquor. twenty-two rooms.

Albergo Accademia (*Via delle Belle Arte 6; Tel 051/232-318, Fax 051/263-590; www.hotelaccademia.com; L150,000 single, L210,000 double; V, MC, DC*) is pricier than some others in the area, but it's within earshot of the student activity and has big, yet cozy, rooms. The complimentary breakfast of croissants and coffee does the belly well. Twenty-eight rooms, all with private bath.

need to know

Currency Exchange There are banks with **ATMs** along Via Rizzoli and Via Marconi, or at the train station, which are probably your best bet.

Tourist Information The main office of the **tourist bureau** (*Piazza Maggiore 6; Tel 051/239-660; Buses 25 and 30 from the train station to Piazza Maggiore; 8:30am-7pm Mon-Sat, 8:30am-2pm Sun, 9am-1pm holidays, closed Jan 1, Easter, Christmas, San Stefano*) provides free Internet access by reservation only, as well as the standard info, maps, and pamphlets. There's also a small tourist office at the train station (*8:30am-7:30pm Mon-Sat*). Or try the **Student Travel Agency (CTS)** (*Largo Respighi 2f; Tel 051/237-501; Buses 32-33 from Piazza Maggiore to Via San Vitale, or any other bus that makes a University stop*). ***www.hotelreservation.com*** can book a room for you before you arrive.

Public Transportation Bologna runs on the great **ATC bus system.** Every bus stops at the centrally located Piazza Maggiore. Night buses (87-99) have limited stops. Tickets (*2,000L for one ticket; 10-ticket packs for slightly reduced rate*) may be purchased at *tabacchi* (tobacco shops), and bus maps found at the ATC information office at the train station or at *atc.bo.it.* Buses run 5:30am-12:30am.

Health and Emergency Emergency number: *113*; Fire: *115*; Medical Emergency: *118*; Police: *112*. Hospitals in and near the city are **Ospedale Santa Orsola** (*Via Massarenti 9; Tel 051/636-3111*) and **Ospedale Maggiore** (*Via 1 Nigrisoli 2; Tel 051/647-8111*).

Pharmacies Farmacia **Comunale Centrale** (*Piazza di Maggiore 6; Tel 051/238-509; Buses 25 and 30 from train station to Piazza di Maggiore*) is always open.

Telephone City code: *51*. The red telephone booths scattered around on the squares and street corners take coins as well as phone cards, which you can buy at *tabacchi* (tobacco shops).

Airports Aeroporto Guglielmo Marconi (*Borgo Panigale; Tel 051/647-96-15; Aerobus (L6,000) from the train station; 6am-midnight*) is 4 miles north of city center. The **Aerobus** *(6:30am-11pm; L6,000)* runs from airport to train station every half hour.

Train There's only one **train station** *(Piazza delle Medaglie d'Oro; Tel 055/630-21-11, 1478/88-088)* here. 24-hour luggage storage, L5,000 for 12 hours. Info desk open daily 8am-8pm. Buses 25 and 30 run between the station and Piazza Maggiore; Buses 11, 17, 25, 37 go to the center.

Bike/Car Rental Bikes can be rented at the **train station** *(Piazza delle Medaglie d'Oro; Tel 051/630-20-15; Buses 10, 21, 25, 30, 31, 32, 33, 35, 36, 37, 38, 39, 50, 81, 90, 91 to Piazza delle Medaglie d'Oro; 6:30am-10pm Mon-Fri; 7am-3pm Sat; L3,000/hour, L15,000/day; No credit cards).*

Laundry Wash & Dry *(Via Petroni 38; Tel 051/237-174; 9am-9pm daily; L6,000 wash, L6,000 dry)* will let you do just that. Just don't try putting coins in the washing machine—you have to get a *gettone* (token) from the machine against the wall.

Internet See *wired*, above.

everywhere else

ferrara

For some reason Ferrara's not on the basic Rome-Florence-Venice tourist circuit, but it should be. It's right on the way to Venice from Florence, it looks even better than the postcards, and it's got a great art scene and hopping nightlife. The infamous Este family, who ruled during the Renaissance, spent a lot of time and money keeping up Ferrara's good looks. But apparently 19th-century steamer trunk crowd on the Grand Tour of Europe didn't feel it was chic enough, so they wrote it off—and old reps die hard in Europe.

No matter. What Ferrara lacks in fame, it makes up for in elbow-room and a sincerely welcoming attitude. Unlike most other beautiful Italian cities with a rich history, Ferrara isn't totally stuck in its past. Over the past few years, artists, chefs, DJs, bartenders, and college students have made modern Ferrara a very cool destination in its own right. Bars and clubs of every form have been popping up left and right. For a town of just 150,000, it's got an edgy, urban sophistication that merits at least a night or two.

neighborhoods and hanging out

Ferrara is a very walkable city, with all it's cultural sights neatly packed into the *centro storico.* If you arrive at the train station, just outside the city walls on the northwestern part of town, you're a 15-minute walk from where you'll want to be. If you arrive at the bus station, just inside the city walls along the river on the southern side of the city, you're just five minutes away from the action.

The main east-west street that divides the town is called **Viale Cavour.** It turns into **Corso Giovecca** when it passes **Castello Estense (Este Castle)** [see *culture zoo,* below] to the east. The southern part of town, where you'll find **Il Duomo** [see *culture zoo,* below], is still a medieval maze. Most of the cool bars and restaurants are south of the Corso

Giovecca and east of the cathedral, but the main sights are spread out across town. Lucky for you, that means there's no one street or piazzas clogged with map-holding tourists, but barhopping is easy. Unless you're lugging all your gear from the train station to your hotel, don't waste your time with buses.

Most of the stately Renaissance palaces were built in the northern half of the town, and the sprawling gardens hidden behind them are a good bet for free relaxation.

Walk from the castle east on Corso Giovecca, and hang a left (north) on **Via Palestro,** which heads north to **Piazza Ariostea**—the whole walk will take you about 10 minutes total. This enormous green piazza is home to the annual *Il Palio* horse race, but on any nice day, it's filled with picnickers and folks just hanging out, enjoying the weather.

Piazza Cattedrale, the lively square in front of the Duomo, is a prime spot for early-evening people watching. **Piazza Trento Trieste,** to the east of the Duomo, is lined with market stalls and cafes. **Via San Romano** and **Via Mazzini** form an angle that contains the coolest, liveliest part of town. Wander around the winding streets, and you're bound to bump into bar after bar and many *studenti* in pursuit of beer.

To the west of the church is the arcaded **Piazza Municipio,** the starting point of **Via Garibaldi,** which is the main street of the old town, where people sip their morning coffee, do their food shopping, and stop to talk with neighbors.

festivals and events

Since the 1200s, Ferrara has celebrated **il Palio,** the horse race, with an enthusiasm rivaled only by Siena. But things are done a bit differently here. The festivities kick off with everyone in town leaving their homes dressed in one of many stock Renaissance characters. The dames, the lords, the banner carriers, the warriors, musicians, and color guards all strut their stuff before the races begin. To find out more about il Palio, contact **Ente Palio della Citta di Ferrara** *(Via Mortara 98; Tel 0532/751-263, Fax 0532/52207).*

The summer music festival **Ferrara Sotto Le Stelle,** which runs in July and August, offers outdoor concerts from all over the world almost every night of the week. Many of the concerts—from reggae to Siberian throat-singing—are free, and those that aren't cost less than 45,000L. For more information call **ARCI Ferrara** *(Via Cortevecchia 57; Tel 532/202-135, Fax 0532/248-207; www.4net.com/stelle).*

ferrara

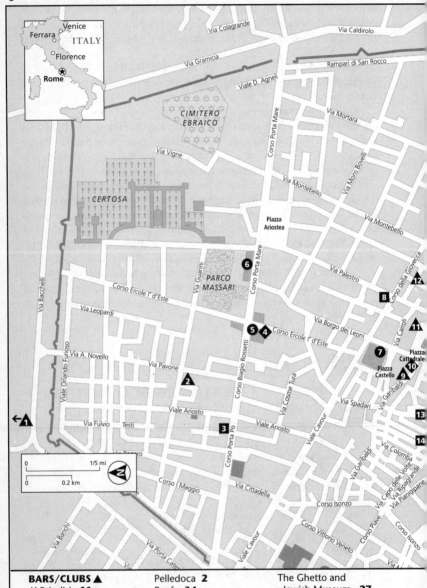

BARS/CLUBS ▲
Al Brindisi **11**
Anima Latina **22**
Birdland **1**
Club Nichola House **19**
Il Mago e La Strega **9**
La Corte **30**
Messisbugo **23**
Non Sul Collo **32**

Pelledoca **2**
Renfe **34**
Reset **12**
Zuni Arte
  Contemporanea **20**

CULTURE ZOO ●
Casa Romei **31**
The Este Castle **7**

The Ghetto and
  Jewish Museum **27**
Il Duomo &
  the Duomo Museum **16**
Palazzo Bevilacqua Massari **6**
Palazzo Diamanti **5**
Palazzo Schifanoia **33**

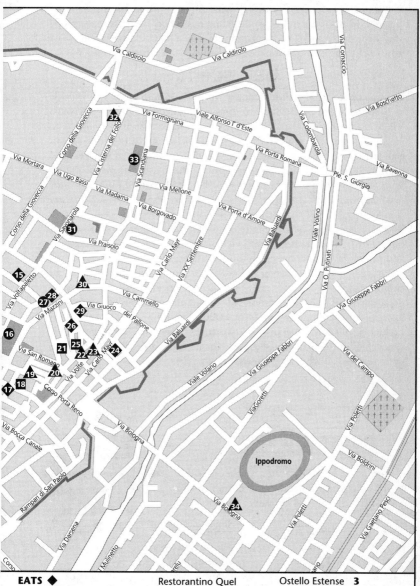

EATS ◆

China Expresso **10**
Este Bar **29**
Gelateria Mazzini **28**
Guido Ristorante **26**
L'Osteria **15**
Pizzaria Cris **4**

Restorantino Quel
Fantastico Giovedí **24**
Ristorante Centrale **17**

CRASHING ■

Albergo Lupa **25**
Hotel Centro Storico **14**
Hotel Europa **8**
Hotel Santo Stefano **13**

Ostello Estense **3**
Pensione Artisti **21**
Nazionale **18**

If you really want to fit in, bike around town [see *city sports* and *need to know,* below, for rental outfits]. Most streets within the city walls are blocked off from car traffic, so bicycling has become the preferred mode of transport. No sight—or bar—is more than a bike ride away, and at any time of the day or night you'll have plenty of two-wheeled company.

bar scene

Ferrara's bar scene is without a doubt the liveliest in the province, outside of Bologna. Most of the bars are compacted into the old town, between Via Mazzini and Via Porta Romano, where everyone seems to migrate to around 7pm for the venerable ritual of *aperitivo* hour. All the bars set out elaborate spreads of free finger-foods (similar to *tapas*) that are meant to be munchies but can easily become dinner—the free food flows till around 9pm. The *aperitivo* at Italy's oldest wine bar, **Al Brindisi** *(Via degli Adelardi 11; Bus 2 to Castello or Mac Donald's; Tel 0532/209-142; 10-1am Tue-Sun; V, MC, AE)* is legendary—no trip to Ferrara should go without it. The free spread here is made up of regional finger foods like salty olives, little foccacia bread sandwiches with cured meats and sausages, and strong raw milk cheeses. Almost 600 years after it first opened, the place is still hopping—young and old alike cram into its candlelit interior or hover over the sidewalk tables and drink glass after glass after glass of great vino. Get your mitts on one of the menus and choose from forty or so wines by the glass, ranging from 4,000L for local wines to 15,000L for fancier *Recito* or *Barolo,* or just try a suggestion from the friendly bartenders. This place is also celebrated for its reasonably priced meals and great selection of cheeses [see *eats,* below].

buskers unite!

For more than a decade, buskers (street musicians) from every street corner in the world have come to Ferrara in August to do their thing and rub shoulders with the competition. Not your typical trade convention, this festival brought over 700 buskers last year, and 800,000 people showed up to hear them play everything from steel drums to washboards. For three days straight, the town smells like a patchouli factory and sounds like a giant music school—there's dancing and drinking in the streets, and music lovers are generous with spare change. To find out more, contact festival headquarters for more info *(Via De' Romei 3; Tel 0532/249-751; www.ferrarabuskers.com).*

Il Mago e La Strega *(Via Garibaldi 16/18; Bus 2 to Castello or Mac Donald's; No phone; 9-1am, closed Thur; 2100L cappuccino; No credit cards)* looks like the rec room you would have grown up in if your dad rode a Harley and your mom took her D & D character a little too seriously. At first glance, this place, located just west of Piazza Cattedrale on the main drag, might strike you as your typical Italian bar: Old men wave salutations as they toss back an espresso, and women drink their wine spritzers standing up. But take a look closer, and you'll notice that most of the wall hangings are airbrushed fantasy scenes and motorcycle paraphernalia, and heavy lead troll statuettes fight beer glasses for space on the bar. Weird. But there's a foosball table in the front room, lots of board games in the back room, and cheaper drink prices than in most of the scene-y bars around town. At night it's crowded with beer-drinking high school and college students, but the daytime scene, with room to sit and read or play "Stratego," is a fun world unto its own.

The crowd at **Messisbugo** *(Via Carlo Mayr 95; Tel 0532/764-060; Bus 2 to Piazza Verdi; 6pm-2am Sun-Friday, closed Sat; 10,000L cocktail, 8,000L pint, 4-8,000L wine; V, MC)* is very Young Professional. Prada bag-toting women sip glasses of wine and cigar-smoking gents sample from a long list of whiskies from around the world while the jazz plays. But don't get the wrong idea—it's more laid back and less cliquey than it appears. Occupying the bottom floor of a 14th century Palazzo just inside the southern city wall, Messisbugo has been renovated beautifully. Look up above the bar—the chalkboards list the wines by the glass, which change weekly. The best time to come is the after-work *aperativo* hour, a tradition that Messisbugo holds up very well with slices of salami and prosciutto, and toothpicked slivers of great cheese. Messisbugo is experimenting with a no-smoking night once a week—very California.

Ferrara is the last place you'd expect to stumble across a place like **Reset** *(Via Dei Romei 36/A; Tel 0532/241-777; Bus 5, 9 to Via Dei Romei; Noon-1am daily, 'til 2am on the weekends, closed Mon; 12-20,000L main entree, 10,000L cocktail, 6,000L beer; V, MC, AX, DC)*. This restaurant/bar looks straight out of the pages of "Wallpaper" magazine: the orange plastic goldfish hanging from the ceiling, blue walls, and a glowing white frosted glass bar make for an eerie aquarium vibe [see *eats,* below, for info on the restaurant half]. Wine is poured from industrial-sized stainless steel drums, and smartly dressed trendsetters sip alcohol-infused power drinks from test tubes. This place, in fact, is used as a location for fashion mag photoshoots, which are on display alongside the trendy English and Italian reading material. Right on Via Romei, a block south the main drag of Corso Giovecca, it's a slice of postmodern life in medieval Ferrara.

La Corte *(Via Saraceno 36; Tel 0532/206-379; Bus 2 to Mac Donald's; 5:30pm-1:30am Tue-Sun; 7,000L beer pint; No credit cards)*, right in the old town, is Ferrara's equivalent of a neighborhood dive bar. Owner Gilberto Buzzoni worked in this popular after-work hangout for 8 years before buying it out, and has transformed it into a unlikely fave destination. During the week, the back rooms are filled with college kids hanging out, drinking beer, and playing video poker. But come Thursday, and all through the weekend, it turns into a popular disco-pub. The music is commercial, the crowd is laid back in their tank tops and jeans, and the vibe is fun and welcoming.

There's nothing very Latin about **Anima Latina** *(Via Ragno 35/37; No phone; Bus 2 to S. Romano; 9pm-2am Mon-Sat; 3-4,000L glass of wine, 7,000L beer pint; No credit cards; ARCI membership required)*, unless you consider the faux fresco a nod to the Roman era of indulgence. And this place is all about indulgences. Arty collegiate types spend hours nurturing glass after glass of wine, or Guinness on tap, while reading the existential heavyweights, holding whispered conversations and smoking hand-rolled cigarettes. (Those *are* cigarettes, aren't they?) The beaten-up wood tables, high-backed chairs lining the brick walls, and newspapers and board games on low tables give this place a rustic, country cabin sort of feel. But far from being bloodless intellectuals, the warm staff here will go out of its way to make you feel at home. Like **Zuni** [see *arts scene,* below], which is right across the street, this is an ARCI, so they'll ask you for your card when you enter. If you haven't already shelled out the 8 bucks for national ARCI membership, you can always buy it here [see **regional introduction,** above, for more info on ARCI].

LIVE MUSIC and CLUB SCENE

As in most Italian cities, the mega-clubs are way out in the countryside, and impossible to reach by public transport. A **discobus** ferries the fab from the train station to clubs outside of town on late-summer Saturday nights, but the itinerary and hours vary wildly. Check with the bus ticket booth outside the train station. But if you miss the bus, don't sweat it. There are enough music and dancing options in town to blow out your eardrums.

Birdland *(Via Massarenti 3 in Gualdo; Superstrada to Gualdo or Uscita; Tel 0532/328-038; Open Tue-Sun; Cover varies)* is the best nightspot around, but you can only get there if the bus is going your way, or better yet, you meet a new friend with a car. It's not your typical Italian Club. The DJs here are famous all over the province for their parties, which writhe with energy in this oversized space. House, electronica, trip hop— every night's a different theme. The crowd runs the gamut as well, from students to thirty-somethings. Like many of the hotspots in town, Bird-land is part of the very cool ARCI association [see regional introduction, above].

The scantily clad pre-club crowd congregates at **Club Nichola House** *(Via Gobette 16/18; No phone yet; Bus 2 to Castello or Mac Donald's; 9-2am everyday; 6,000L for Panini and Piadine, 5000L for revolving hot-dogs, 6,000L beer, 6,000-25,000L cocktail, No credit cards)*, a new excuse to start the night early. This new-ish local hot spot is run by Antimo, a gregarious DJ who worked the big-league club scene around Rimini (he still spins at Birdland), and seems to know all his patrons by name. The upsides to this pal-sy ownership are the cheap drinks and plenty of good house, pop, and funk. The downside is that the buddy-buddy crowd tends to take over the turntable at whim. Keep your ears open for the siren that periodically blares over the sound system—drinks are a few thousand lira cheaper for the next few minutes. And eat beforehand: Antimo is proud to offer perpetually rolling hot dogs á là 7-11, but they look like they've been on display for one too many nights. It's just two blocks south of Piazza Cattedrale, on the wide pedestrian walk, where the party migrates to on summer evenings.

Been a while since you went stage-diving, or are you missing the kind of fun that cheesy Italian cover bands just can't offer? Put on some comfortable shoes and take the 25-minute hike south on Via Bologna to **Renfe** *(Via Bologna 217; Tel for ARCI headquarters and info on shows 0339/415-02-08; 9:30pm-4am Thur-Sat & weekdays when bands are scheduled, Happy Hour from 10-11pm; 10-20,000L for most shows; ARCI card required; No credit cards).* Industrial-looking and boxy from the outside, this place resembles every college-town music venue in the States once you walk in. A huge, dark expanse stretches from the stage to the bar in back, which is presided over by a monosyllabic metalhead. A cloud of smoke hangs over the shows, where everyone from mods, rockabilly kids, and 15-year-old Goth girls come out to hear local and international alternative acts. Hoegarten and pale ales come in little plastic cups at big prices, but from the aroma in the air, that's not what a lot of folks are indulging in anyway. The telephone infoline is not in English, but the band names on posters around town should give you a pretty good idea (Italian for punk is *lo Punk*).

Non Sul Collo *(Via Cisterna del Follo 39; Tel 0532/40748; Bus 1 to P.le Medaglie d'Oro; 9pm-1 or 2am Mon-Fri, open at 8pm Sat-Sun; 7,000L beer, 9,000L cocktail; ARCI card required)* is definitely more chill. It's hard to find Via Cisterna del Follo on a map, because it's called Via Adelardi when it's by the cathedral, then Via Voltapaletto, Via Savonarola, and finally Cisterna del Follo just before it runs into the eastern city wall, but that's where you'll find this jazz club. It features local musicians on Thursdays 'til late, and the rest of the week plays American jazz discs. The owners call this very laid-back spot a "relax club"—you'll find young people playing board games and sipping wine or cocktails at the tubular metal tables underneath the neatly framed jazz posters. The crowd is friendly, and yes, relaxed—except on weekends when they pile big TV's on the small stage and show the *calcio* (soccer) matches. Once again, this is an ARCI club (have you read that sidebar in the regional introduction yet?)

Club kids without cars head to **Pelledoca** *(Via Arianuova 91/93; Tel 0532/248-952; Bus 3C to Via Ariosto; Reservation line 0338/250-41-37; 10pm-4am Fri-Sun; www.pelledoca.it; No set dress code),* the flashy, three-level nightclub on the northeastern edge of the town center. This place runs like a well-oiled machine: Droves of decked-out college kids and twenty-somethings are ushered through the lobby, issued drink cards, and poured into the never-never-land that is Pelledoca. The central space rises up three stories from a serpentine bar and raised dance floor combo, and it's crowded with bobbing heads and flailing arms all the way up. The scene here is non-pretentious and inoffensive—a welcome change from the imported meat-markets in more touristed towns. When lethargy sets in, or you get an opportunity to chat with a new friend, you can retreat to the booths and tables on the upper levels, which overlook the chaos below. There's no cover, per se, but your first drink will cost you 20,000L. The price goes down with every drink, and the bartenders keep track with the card that guests are issued on the way in. Don't lose it, or you'll have to start over. If you can manage to work your way down the card, a night of overindulgence here won't cost much more than getting hammered at the corner bar. But nursing that first drink ain't cheap. The music varies, with house and techno one night, early eighties the next. Occasional guest DJs spin more interesting fare—posters in the town center publicize these nights well in advance. Things get going around midnight.

arts scene

There are a surprising number of cutting-edge art scenes in Ferrara, and they all converge at **Zuni Arte Contemporanea** (*Via Ragno 15; Tel 0532/760-776; Bus 2 to S. Romano; 11am-1am Mon, Wed-Sat, 6pm-1am Sun, closed Tue, Kitchen open from noon-2:30pm; 8-11pm, closed Tue; 10,000-15,000L main entree, 10,000L cocktail, 4,000L wine, 7,000L beer; V, MC*). Hidden behind frosted glass on a quiet street off Via S. Romano in the southeastern part of town, this is one of the coolest art or drinking spaces in Italy—the brainchild of a group of local artists who were sick of going to Bologna to get their cultural fix. Gallery meets bar meets performance space meets fusion restaurant in this overlit, loft-like space that's crowded day and night with art-minded and multiple-pierced twenty- and thirty-somethings. The long, narrow room packs in multidisciplinary Italian exhibits, making it hard to tell where the art ends and the party begins. That container overflowing with scrap metal in the middle of the floor, for example, isn't a sign of negligent management, it's the work of Ferrara's finest young sculptor. And there's no one yelling at you every time you near the bathroom—it's a motion-detecting sound installation. Word to the wise: call ahead to reserve a table for the performances and readings, so you can eat while you watch. Even the food is artfully prepared: the artist/chef has a penchant for exotic fare like aspics and curries [see *eats*, below]. Check for flyers on upcoming events, performances, and opening parties at tourist info. Like many of the region's coolest spots, this is an ARCI Circolo [see **regional introduction,** above]. Keep in mind that aside from the initial charge, most performances are free, or close to free.

The gorgeous neoclassical 18th-century **Teatro Comunale** (*Theater and offices at Corso Martiri della Liberta 5; Ticket booth at Corso Giovecca 12; Tel 05332/218-311, Fax 0532/247-353; Bus 2 to Castello or Mac Donald's; Tel 0532/202-675; 10am-12:30pm/4-7:30pm Mon, Fri,*

Sat; 4-7:30pm Tue, Wed, Thur, closed Sun; www.teatrocomunaleferrara.it; V, MC, AE) is Ferrara's main venue for concerts, opera, orchestra, and dance. Just sitting in a box seat in one of the theater's five balconies and watching the other patrons is a performance unto itself. People under 27 get a whopping 50 percent discount with the "Carte Verde," which is given out at the ticket booth. Located at the main intersection of town, where Corso Martiri della Liberta meets Viale Cavour.

If you're wondering what "Over the Rainbow" would sound like in Italian, check out some of the shows at **Teatro Nuovo** *(Piazza Trento Trieste 52; Tel 0532/207-197; Bus 2 to Castello or Mac Donald's; Ticket prices vary),* which sits right on the popular piazza Trento Trieste, across from the Duomo. This place is popular and pedestrian—don't expect the avant-garde.

L'Embassy Theater *(117 Porta Po; Tel 0532/203-424; Show dates and times vary; No credit cards),* near the station just inside the city walls, shows Hollywood box office hit movies in *lingua originale* (that's usually English, bub) once a week. Check in at the tourist office for current show times and listings.

CULTUrE ZOO

Between the 13th and late-16th centuries, the Estes made Ferrara one of the most beautiful cities in Italy. Though it waned in power after it fell to the Papacy, it's cultural and artistic legacy lived on. The university, founded in 1391, has taught many Italian luminaries, including Tasso and Ariosto, two of the Renaissance's most prized poets. Start your tour at the Este Castle. All the sights are within walking distance of each other. Though many visitors try to cram it into one day, you'd be much better off spreading it out over a leisurely two days.

The Este Castle *(Largo Castello; Tel 0532/299-233; Bus 2 to Castello; 9:30am-5:00pm Tue-Sun; 8,000L adults, 6,000L w/student ID; No credit cards):* This imposing fortress and palace has been the focal point of Ferrara since construction began in 1385. You can hardly go about your merry way without catching a glimpse of its archetypal brick towers, especially at night when they're brilliantly illuminated. Any stroll along the surrounding moat is easily accompanied by visions of mounted warriors charging over the drawbridges. There's a reason for this: The beautifully preserved structure was commissioned by Duke Nicolo II to both intimidate rebellious citizens and protect the Estes from outside armies. Once the hostilities passed and the Renaissance kicked into high gear, the castle was renovated to keep up with the Joneses (actually the Medicis, up in Florence.) Marble balconies, lush courtyards, and royal apartments were added as grandiose flourishes.

Though its interior is now used for municipal offices, there are still plenty of gems inside that give a sense of the luxurious, lascivious, and brutal history of the Estes.

Anyone who has read Robert Browning's poem "My Last Duchess"— that would be, anyone who's ever gone to high school—may want to check out the prison cells of Ugo and Parisina. Browning based his grisly verses on the story of Nicolo III's cradle-robbing wife, who took young Ugolino, his son from a previous marriage, for her lover. When the Duke discovered her wandering ways in 1425, he locked them in these dungeons until he got around to beheading them.

The Ducal apartments lend an idea of the over-the-top lifestyle the Estes enjoyed. The Bacchanalian Room, complete with 16th century paintings devoted to the god of wine and other fun things, show their seedier side. On a more wholesome tip, sports fans will want to take a stroll past the frescoes in the Hall of the Games. Here, every activity—from "A Game with Leather Bags" to "Throwing of a Discus"—was artfully depicted in a time when athletes were actually wholesome.

If you need to climb a few more stairs after all this, a visit to the top of the castle—the Lion's Tower—will cost you 2,000L *(10am-4pm, Sat and Sun only)*.

Il Duomo & the Duomo Museum *(Piazza Cattedrale; Tel 0532/207-449; Bus 2 to Castello or Mac Donald's; 10am-noon/3-5pm Tue-Fri, 10am-noon/4-6pm Sat, Sun, and holidays; Free admission, but donations encouraged):* The facade of Ferrara's Duomo bears witness to the town's endurance through the ages: practically every period of Italian architecture is evident in this 12th-century church, which towers over a wide piazza around the corner from the castle. It's lower half is buzzing with Romanesque arches, griffins and grimacing sinners holding up columns. The top was rebuilt in the more uplifting Gothic style. The Renaissance bell tower was designed by Leon Battista Alberti, who ushered in some of Florence's finest architecture. The flowery, neo-classical interior was an unfortunate renovation in the 18th century, and unless you're into hymnbooks and religious art, the museum can be skipped.

Palazzo Bevilacqua Massari *(Corso Porta Mare 9; Tel 0532/206-914; Bus 3C to Piazza Ariostea; 9am-1pm/3-6pm daily; 8,000L for Boldini, 4,000L for Pisis, 10,000L combined ticket, student discounts; No credit cards):* You'll find a little of the old and a little bit of new in this pretty palace. The **Giovanni Boldini Museum** is devoted to Ferrara's famous portrait painter from the early 1900s. Boldini's depictions of his subjects are far from boring, and a trip to this museum lends insight into the inner lives of Ferrara's finest. Also located in this palace is the **Filippo De Pisis Museum of Modern and Contemporary Art.** This collection isn't exactly a one-man show of this modern painter: other 20th-century Italian luminaries, such as Previati, Mentesse, and Sironi, are also on display.

Casa Romei *(Via Savonarola 30; Tel 0532/240-341; Bus 5 to Casa dello Studente; 8:30am-7:30pm Tue-Sun, closed Mon; 4,000L adults, 2,000L under 25 and student; No credit cards):* This Renaissance house, found just south of Corso Giovecca, east of the castle, belonged to the Duke Borso D'este, and was frequented by the notoriously lascivious Lucretia Borgia. With the exception of some stunning frescos of sibyls in two rooms, and one excellent inlaid ceiling in the Duke's study, there isn't much left of the original decor. Other works of art and sculpture have been brought in to add more bang for your tourist buck, but some poisoned chalices or secret rooms would add some much-needed spice to the sparse exhibits....

Palazzo Diamanti *(Corso Ercole I d'Este 21; Tel 0532/205-844; Bus 3C to Palazzo Diamanti; 9am-2pm Mon-Wed, 9am-7pm Thur-Friday, 9am-1pm Sat, Sun; 14,000L admission, 12,000L under 25 and student, free under 18):* You'll spot the pride of the Este's palaces blocks before you get to it—a five minute walk north from Viale Cavour. Built in 1493 and named for the 8,500 diamond-shaped stones that completely cover this building, it truly is the coolest palazzo in town. Step inside to discover the Ferrarese masters: Tura, Roberti, Garofalo, and del Cossa are all represented here. There's also a great modern art museum, which hangs a collection of local and national artists, and draws some pretty cutting-edge exhibits and big collections traveling from international museums.

Palazzo Schifanoia *(Via Scandiana 23; Tel 0532/64178; Bus 1 to P.le Medaglie d'Oro; 9am-7pm Tue-Sun; 8,000L admission, 4,000L students; No credit cards):* The Este Castle was great for protection and intimidation, but a drag to live in. The Palazzo Schifanoia, on the other hand, was where the Estes threw all the A-list parties. It's a little bit out of the center, a five-minute walk east of town near Piazza Medaglie d'Oro. *Schifanoia* is Italian for "disgusted by boredom" and the easily-bored dukes spent much effort decorating the pad. You can easily spend all afternoon staring up at the *Salone dei Mesi (Salon of the Months),* the intricate astrological fresco cycle featuring Ferraran celebrities and dignitaries that adorns this 14th century palace. They are the collective work of Cosme Tura, Ercole de Roberti, and Francesco del Cossa, who are attributed with the founding of the Ferrarese School of Renaissance Art. These frescos overlooked a lot of ducal shindigs and mark an important stage in the city's artistic spirit.

The Ghetto and Jewish Museum *(Via Mazzini 95; Tel 0532/210-228; Bus 2 to Castello or Mac Donald's; 10am-12pm Sun-Thur, closed Jewish holidays; 7,000L admission, 3,000L students):* Aside from all the oppression and beheading, the Estes were known for being pretty open-minded, at least culturally. They welcomed artists and poets, like Ariosto, who were on the run from the long arm of the law elsewhere, as well as a large community of Sephardic and Askenazi refugees from Spain. It wasn't until 1626, when the Estes died out and the Pope took over the town, that the first ghetto was formed (it took up the length of Via Mazzini). The keys used to lock the ghetto gate are on display in the Jewish Museum along with many other interesting relics of religious significance—documents, holy books, and art. The Jewish cemetery is just north of Corso Porta Mare. The Jewish community is still one of the largest in Italy, and their history is well preserved and documented.

CITY SPORTS

Ferrarans love bikes like Texans love big hats, and there's a really cool bike path running along the top of the city. The 8.5km ride is hardly strenuous, even after a night of barhopping, and the views are incredible. Start your bike ride in **Piazza Travaglio,** which is a short walk south from the castle and leads into Via Bologna, one of the main streets south from the city walls. When you see the things that look like watchtowers attached by tall walls, you're there. Get on the path to your right and follow it west. You'll pass the old horse market, the old gates called the **Porta Romana,** and the soccer stadium, up and over to the north of the city center. You're almost halfway home when you get to the Jewish cemetery. Go through **Piazzale Medaglia d'Oro** and around the southeastern part of the city, where you'll be riding along the Po river.

Signore Trevisan at **Estense Bici** *(Via Voltapaletto 11/A; Tel 0340/236-69-34; Bus 5, 9 to Via dei Romei; 9am-1pm/2:30-6pm Mon-Sat 9am-1pm Sun; 20,000L for 8 hours, 35,000L for 2 days; No credit cards, deposit required),* a tiny little shop right in the center of town, is the Italian grandpa you wished you had. He lets you rent great bikes for as few as 2 hours, which will cost you only 8,000L. You can also rent bikes at the train station [see *need to know,* below].

Because Ferrara is a university town, there's a bunch of sports clubs that organize events and distribute info about your sport of choice. Some of the more popular ones are the **Canoe Club** *(Via Darsena 62; Tel 0532/764-340),* the **Mountain Biking Club** *(Via Porta Catena 73, Tel 0532/54394),* and the **Tennis Club** *(Via Gramicia 41; 0532/750-396).*

The community pools are a great place to cool off or to burn off all those pasta carbs. The **Piscina Comunale** *(Via Beethoven; Tel 0532/900-886; 12:30-4pm Mon-Fri, 1-8pm Sun; 10,000L entrance, 6,000L student ID; No credit cards),* which is covered from October to May, is the one nearest to the *centro storico.* It's outside the city walls, to the southeast and right along the railroad tracks—you're better off taking the bus from the station. Look for the one with the "Piscina" stop.

STUFF

Ferrara has tons of cool stores, from collegiate bookstores to comic book boutiques. And since Ferrara isn't exactly tourist central, you don't have to pay the visitor tax!

▶▶TUNES

Despite the huge numbers of hipsters in Ferrara, there's not a lot of cool record and CD shops. **Music Hall 18** *(Via San Romano 18; Tel 0532/761-626; Bus 2 to S. Romano; 9am-12:30pm/3:30-7:30pm daily, closed Sun in summer; No credit cards)* is pretty much the best there is, with a large selection of pop, Italian, and commercial CDs from 18,500 to 36,000L.

▶▶BOUND

Though it's the Italian equivalent of Barnes and Noble, **Libreria Feltrinelli** *(Via Garibaldi 30; Tel 0532/240-570; Bus 2 to Castello or Mac Donald's; 7am-7:30pm Mon-Sat, 10am-1pm/3:30-7:30pm; V, MC, AE)* is also the only place in town with a large collection of English titles that you would actually *want* to read. Prices hover around 15,000L for classics, and go up to 30,000L for best sellers. Look for it just west of the Duomo.

If you have even the slightest interest in comic books *(fumetti)* or old magazines, you have to check out **Mercatino Del Libro e Del Fumetto** *(Via Mazzini 66/68, on the corner of Vigatagliata; Mobile phone 0335/662-61-90; bus 5,9 to Via dei Romei; 9:30-9pm daily; No credit cards).* This gem of a used bookstore is unlike any other in Italy. Pull open the creaky doors of what appears to be an abandoned warehouse, and you'll find yourself tearing through piles and piles of books for hours. The collection here is amazing—boxes of old postcards dating back to the turn of the century for 1000L a pop, Fascist propaganda posters and fashion magazines from the forties for 5,000L, and early Spiderman comics in Italian are just a few of the highlights. It's on Via Mazzini, near the university district.

▶▶**HOW BAZAAR**
Ferrara's piazzas bustle with activity during the first Saturday and Sunday of every month when the markets come to town. You can score anything from an antique doorknob to old military patches at the antique market in **Piazza Municipale** *(8am-6pm, closed in Aug and during holidays).* Pottery and woodworks, along with other artisanal crafts from the region, are on display at **Piazza Savonarola** *(8am-6pm, also closed in Aug and during holidays).*

EATS

For a town of its size, Ferrara has a happening food scene. People start strolling the streets around seven or eight, poking into one bar for a glass of wine and another to check out the happy-hour *aperitivo* spread [see *bar scene,* above]. Dinner-for-real starts between 8 and 10:30pm; it's not unusual to see people still sitting at the dinner table well after midnight.

Meanwhile you're probably wondering what the hell those huge, bell-shaped moldy things are hanging from restaurant windows. They're *Salama da Sugo,* spicy, hearty sausage that's steeped in wine and aged for a year before it's brought to the table. They cook it for hours and serve it over a huge mound of mashed potatoes—it's Italian comfort food. And when you're trying to figure out the menu, look for *capelletti* (literally, little hats), the Ferraran version of tortellini. They're filled with a blend of meats and are usually served in chicken broth. When you're ready to go deep into food bliss, try *cappellacci,* the same as cappelletti only bigger and usually filled with *zucca* (pumpkin), tossed with butter and sage, and served piping hot. (Yes, sometimes size does matter.) *Bigoli,* a handmade buckwheat pasta that's served with a rich duck sauce, is a stick-to-your-ribs kind of meal. Though you won't see it on many menus, stop by a bakery and try *Pampepato,* Ferrara's cross between a fruitcake and a brownie. But the pride of Ferrara is, *La Coppia* bread, an ornate holdover from court kitchens. The recipe is attributed to the Estes' most famous chef, Cristoforo da Messisbugo. It's beautiful when brought to the table, all twisted and golden brown, but unfortunately there's much less there than meets the eye: It's usually dry and flavorless. Try adding a little olive oil.

TO MARKET

Conad Supermercato *(Via Garibaldi 51; Bus 2 to Castello or Mac Donald's; 8:30am-8pm Mon, Tue, Fri-Sat, 8:30am-1:30pm Thur, closed Sun)* is conveniently located on the main drag in the southern part of town, and has a good take-out section where you can get roasted chicken, risottos, and salads for just a few thousand lire. There's also a specialty **food market** *(7am-1:30pm/4:30-7pm Mon-Sat, closed Thur and Sat afternoons, Fri mornings, and all day Sun)* in the huge industrial space on the corner of Via Vegri and Via del Mercato, where you'll find all the makings of your picnic lunch, as well as a lesson in local foodstuffs. Tip: *un etto* (100 grams), is the unit of measurement at most Italian markets. *Un mezz'etto* of prosciutto or salami is more than enough for a sandwich, but you may want to spring for a whole *l'etto* of gorgonzola.

▶▶**CHEAP**

Pizzaria Cris *(Via Palestro 113; Tel 240-781; Bus 3C to Piazza Ariostea; 8am-1:30pm/4-10pm Tue-Sun; 2,000L per slice; No credit cards)* couldn't be in a better location. This take-out slice place serves one function—to feed the hungry hordes that descend upon Piazza Ariostea every afternoon, and remain there 'til the wee hours of the morning. They must pump the good food smells out into the street, because by ten o'clock, when the crowd seems to collectively realize that they skipped dinner and have a huge case of the munchies, the line is out the door. Mushrooms, peppers, sausages—the toppings are standard and delicious. Someone should convince them to stay open later.

You may not even be aware that you're missing wontons, spring rolls and MSG until you walk past **China Expresso** *(Via Garibaldi 12; Tel. 0532/212-238; Bus 2 to Castello or Mac Donald's; 10:30-2:30pm/5-11pm daily; No credit cards),* on the main drag in the southern half of the town center. This crowded storefront has a little counter where you can slurp up some cheap *zuppa agro-piccante* (sweet and sour soup, 3,000L) and munch on multiple *involotini primavera* (spring rolls, 1,500L). None of the fifty or so Chinese classics, from roast duck to chicken with bamboo and mushrooms, cost more than 9,000L, but the *Menu Fisso,* which includes fried rice, a spring roll, and any main dish, is a real steal at 8,500L.

Al Brindisi [see *bar scene*, above], next to the Duomo, may be known for its long tradition of excellent wines, but their food—traditional, osteria-style favorites—are delicious and inexpensive *(Kitchen open noon-3pm/6-11am Tue-Sun; 6-15,000L main entree)*. A small menu of simple pasta dishes, large green-leaf salads, and an interesting selection of cheeses is available all day and evening. And though the food is memorable, perhaps the best part about eating here is that it's roomier than the bar area. You can sit either in the wine room, surrounded by vintage bottles and old wine tools, or up in a spacious loft, where your table looks out over the crowd.

The sweet, grandmotherly Anna Maria Rosati, who runs **Gelateria Mazzini** *(Via Mazzini 91/A; Bus 2 to Castello or Piazza Verdi; No phone; 7:30am-11:30pm daily; closed Sun in the winter; No credit cards)* makes a mean gelato. You'll pay 2,500L for a cone with three *gusti* (flavors), a bargain when you consider that each scoop was handmade. Roasted *Pignoli* (pine nuts) should not be missed, but the cheesy, bubble gum Italian music that's piped into the shop might make you want to take your cone outside to enjoy.

▶▶DO-ABLE

Cool as the decor and bar scene is at **Reset** [see *bar scene,* above] it's the food that shouldn't be missed *(12-20,000L main dish)*. While other places close for siesta, the hip London-trained chef at Reset cooks all day, serving up inventive dishes like *Shabu Shabu, Spaghetti alla chitarra,* and haricot verts with pancetta. If you're planning on coming in the evening call and reserve a table, since the bar crowd starts coming around 11pm.

Everyone seems to agree that **Este Bar** *(Via Scienze 13/15; Tel 0532/240-323; Bus 2 to Castello or Mac Donald's; 12-3pm/6pm-1am, closed Mon; 8-13,000L pizza, 9-12,000L primi piatti, 10-22,000L secondi; V, MC, AE)* serves the best pizza in town. This nondescript fluorescent-lit bar, with a dining room off to the side, has a wood-burning oven that turns out over 40 kinds of pizzas. Whether it's a conventional Quattro Stagione, or a more inventive Speck, Gorgonzola, and Arugula (beef, blue cheese and greens), these pies all hang off the plate, they're so huge. Other house specialties are Sicilian in nature—fiery sausages, satisfying *scallopinis* (cutlets in sauce), and crunchy *fritto misto* (mixed fried seafood).

Zuni Arte Contemporanea [see *arts scene,* above] gives "dinner theater" new meaning *(Kitchen open noon-2:30pm/8-11pm, closed Tue)*. This alternative art space serves meals throughout performances, but the food itself is art. Prepare for a lot of fresh vegetables and Asian seasonings, like curry, coconut milk, and lemongrass. The menu changes often, but there are usually a few innovative salads, with great local cheeses, and soups (10,000-15,000L for main dishes). If you stumble in off-hours, you won't even see the bistro tables where folks take their meals—when it's not mealtime, they're whisked away to make room for more gallery guests.

If you want to catch a meal at **L'Osteria** *(Via dei Romei 51; Tel 0532/207-673; Bus 5, 9 to Via dei Romei; 7:30pm-1am Tue-Sun, closed Mon; 12-20,000L primi, 20,000L secondi; V, MC)*, make a reservation. Otherwise, you'll end up drinking a bellyful of wine while you wait for a table at the bar of this subterranean restaurant located a few blocks south of Corse Giovecca (which isn't necessarily a bad thing). There's a reason why this casual, traditional osteria is so popular—the food is damn good, and this cavernous cellar of a Renaissance palazzo is as welcoming as Grandma's house. Room after little room, this place is a maze of brick and wood that opens up to the kitchen, where you can watch the cooks at work. The menu changes with each season, and features local specialties with the chef's inventive twists. Pumpkin flan, *Bigoli al Torcio,* and ravioli are all cooked to order and fantastic. The four-course set menu is a steal at 40,000L, and the enormous wine list has plenty of bargains.

Guido Ristorante *(Via Vignatagliata 61; Tel 0532/761-052; Bus 2 to Castello or S. Romano; 12-3pm/6pm-1am daily; 4,000L service charge per person; Closed Thur; V, MC, DC)* offers a welcome break from the traditional dishes that are available at most restaurants. *Gnocchi al curry* with zucchini and black olives, duck breast with raddichio rosso, and liver paté with pepe verde are a few of the specialties prepared by Guido himself, a friendly restaurateur who seems to be more popular with adventurous, foreign diners than with the locals. The restaurant is funky and cozy— tables draped in linen line the exposed brick walls, under a canopy of antique musical instruments that hang from the old wood beams. You'll find it south of the Duomo, on the road that connects Via Mazzini and Via San Romano.

On the other hand, if you *do* want a lesson in how the locals eat, head to the completely unpretentious and friendly **Ristorante Centrale** *(Via Boccaleone 8; Tel 0532/206-735; Bus 2 to Castello or Mac Donald's; 12:30-3:30pm/7-10:30pm Mon-Sat; Closed all day Sun and Wed eve; 10-18,000L primi, 15-30,000L secondi, 6,000L dolci, 15-30,000L wine; 3,000L per person service charge; V, MC, AE),* a bustling, family-run restaurant just around the corner from Piazza Municipio. The modern stained-glass hangings and wood paneling aren't an attempt at retro—they're leftovers from when the Masseti's first opened the restaurant 50 years ago. Young and old come here for traditional Ferrarese dishes at very reasonable prices. Try the *Tortelli Misti,* a plate of three different local specialties of *capellacci—zucca al Bolognese* (pumpkin in a meat sauce), *taleggio* (the creamy local cheese), and *speck al nocciolo* (smoked ham in a nutty cream sauce). The *capellatti in brood* is a cure all for over-indulgent travelers— an Italian chicken-soup-for-the-soul. The wines are local and cheap—try the *Morellino di Scansano,* Signore Massetti's recommendation.

▶▶**SPLURGE**
Restorantino Quel Fantastico Giovedí *(Via Castelnuovo 9; Tel 0532/760-570; Bus 2 to Piazza Verdi; 11am-4pm/6pm-1am Thur-Tue, closed Mon; 14-30,000L primi and secondi, 50,000L seasonal tasting menu; V, MC, AE, DC),* in the southeastern edge of the *centro storico* close to Piazza Travaglio, is the hottest table in town. This tiny (8-10 tables) low-lit restaurant is a favorite with the twenty- and thirty-something crowd, who make reservations weeks in advance to feast on dishes like fish soup

with wild fennel, or roasted calamari with eggplant. Everything here is a notch above—from the kind of rice in the risotto (canoroli rather than Arborio) to the great mix of music. The ambiance is as whimsical as the name (which means "that fantastic Thursday"—go figure). Oversized Chagall prints next to elegant, candle-lit table settings make this place a great first date option.

crashing

Ferrara's a wealthy town, so most tourists and business travelers expect to spend 200,000L for a night's sleep. Even the one-star hotels are slightly more expensive than in other northern Italian towns, but at least there are plenty of them and they're all right in the center of town.

▶▶**CHEAP**

Your first choice should be **Pensione Artisti** (*Via Vittoria 66; Tel 0532/761-038; Bus 2 to S. Romano; 36,000L single w/out shower, 65,000L double w/out shower, 90,000L double w/shower, 100,000L triple; V, MC, AE*), a comfortable, clean, and centrally-located hotel run by a cool, friendly couple. It's on a quiet little street that runs south from Via Mazzini. By far the best bargain in town, the 21 rooms are spacious and cozy, which means they book very early. Many have bathrooms, but there are newly restored facilities and showers in the hallway. Another bonus: there are two tiny kitchens upstairs that the proprietors let guests use, and a coin-operated coffee machine to get things going in the morning. Not that you should have too much trouble—this place enforces a pretty strict 12:30am curfew.

wired

Ferrara isn't the easiest place to get online. **Off Limits Internet Point** (*Via Contrari, 31; Tel/Fax 0532/247-699; Bus 2 to Mac Donald's or 5, 9 to Via dei Romei; 11am-7pm Mon-Fri, 4-7pm Sat; www.olworld.it; info@olworld.it; Closed Sun*) is the very best for high speed access, though there's only three machines, and the environment is less than cozy. This media shop also does international faxing, and has headphones if you want to make free phone calls home with dialpad (www.dialpad.com). Access is 10,000L per hour (*6,000L half-hour, 3,600L 15 min*). It's just a short north walk from Viale Cavour, on the corner of Via Palestra and Via Psis. Other than that, **informagiovane** [see *need to know*, below] has a few old, slow machines you can use.

www.fromitaly.net/english/region/emilia/tourism/ferrara/ferrara/index.htm will give you inside info on the town.

Ostello Estense *(Corso Biago Rosetti 24; Tel 0532/204-227; Bus 3C from the station to Via Ariosto or Corso Biago Rosetti, but only a 10 min walk; Open 7am-10am/5pm-11:30pm, open all year; hostelferrara@hotmail.com; 25,000L for a bed in a room of up to five people, 28,000L in a private family room; 84 beds total; V, MC)* just opened last year, and is one of the better hostels in the region. Just off the main drag Corso Ercole I d'Este, it's a short walk to most of the Palazzi, and a bike ride to most of the bars and clubs. Sure, it's dripping with institutional cheeriness, with a bright IKEA-looking TV room and plaid-covered bunks, but the price is right. Expect the normal hostel routine—lock out after 10am, lock in by 11:30pm.

The tiny **Albergo Lupa** *(Via della Lupa 15; Tel 0532/760-070; Bus 2 to Piazza Verdi; 60,000L single w/bath, 70-90,000L double w/out bath, wheelchair accessible; V, MC, AE)* is located on a quiet street right in the middle of things between Via Mazzini and Via Porta Romano. The ruffled awning and potted plants out front are just an indication of the kind of care the owners take to make sure you enjoy your stay.

Hotel Centro Storico *(Via Vegri 15; Tel 203-374, Fax 20948; Bus 1, 9 to Posta (Post Office); 50,000L single w/out bath, 70,000L double w/out bath)* used to be called *Tre Stelle* (three stars), and it's easy to tell why they recently changed names. None of the 15 grim rooms have baths, and all are badly in need of a renovation—but at least the mattresses are new and each room has a sink. There's apparently no maid service here, though clean towels, which are nothing more than extra-large napkins, are handed to you upon entry. The two bathrooms per floor are huge and new, and it is, just as the name suggests, centrally located, just steps from the market and Via Garibaldi.

Backpackers love the **Nazionale** *(Corso Porto Reno 32; Tel 209-604; Bus 2 to Castello or Mac Donald's; 80-120,000L single w/bath, 70,000L w/out bath, 120,000L double w/shower, 110,000L w/out shower)*. It's the cheapest central hotel, it's just around the corner from the cathedral, and it's reasonably clean. The management is exceedingly warm and helpful, and willing to turn almost any room into a dorm. This place hasn't been renovated since the early eighties—the "Hang in There" kitty-cat posters are curling around the edges, but hey, it's the thought that counts.

▶▶DO-ABLE

One of the more popular mid-range hotels in town is **Hotel Santo Stefano** *(Via Bocca Canale di S. Stephano 21; Tel 0532/206-924; Fax 0532/210-261; Bus 1, 9 to Posta (Post Office); 35,000-52,000L single w/out shower, 80,000-120,000L double w/shower, 60,000-95,000L double w/out shower; V, MC, AE)*, a cozy pensione a few blocks southwest of the Duomo near the market, with a little bar/TV room that caters to the Italian families and business travelers who stay here. The price is right for the comfortable if a little out-dated rooms. There are TVs in some rooms, but unless you're dying to see "Knight Rider" in Italian, don't get too excited.

▶▶SPLURGE

Hotel Europa *(Corso Giovecca 49; Tel 0532/205-456, Fax 0532/212-120; Bus 2 to Boldoni; www.hoteleuropaferrara; info@hoteleuropaferrara.com;*

90-135,000L single w/bath; 130-195,000L; double w/bath; Breakfast included; V, MC, AE) is well worth the splurge, especially if it's been a while since you treated yourself. Located just down the block from the castle, this renovated Renaissance palazzo has been *the* place to stay in Ferrara since 1880, when it opened for business. Giuseppe Verdi lived here back in the day, and over the years it's hosted everyone from Mussolini to Prince Charles. All the creature comforts are here: TVs and bathrooms in all rooms, hair dryers, and more antiques than most museums. Their prices go down considerably in low season, so go ahead, ask for one of the rooms with original frescoes. There's a pretty garden for hotel guests, as well as a bar and sitting rooms that cater to your every need.

need to know

Currency Exchange Though there's exchange kiosks at the station, there's plenty of **ATMS** all over town—at the station, in Piazza Cattedrale, and in Piazza Castello. You'll get the most current rates at the ATM, and the only fee you'll be charged is the normal ATM fee *(between $1.75-3US)*.

Tourist Info There's a super helpful tourist info office at the **Este Castle** *(In the castle; Bus 2 to Castello; Tel 0532/209-370; Fax 0532/212-266; 9am-1pm/2-6pm; daily/www.commune.fe.it; infotur@provinci.fe.it)*, where the English speaking staff will unabashedly shell out advice on everything from nightclubs to budget hotels. **Informagiovane** *(Via de Pisis 43/49; Tel 0532/210-408; Bus 2 to Boldoni; 11am-1pm/5-9pm Mon, Tue, Thur, Sat, 5-9pm Fri; informagiovane@commune.fe.it;)* isn't as young-centric as it sounds, and can lead you to cool events and locales. They also have a few old computers in the back that you can use, once you fill out a brief questionnaire. Ask them about the *carta sconti*, which will give you discounts at stores around Ferrara. Neither one of these places will make hotel reservations for you.

Public Transportation It's much easier to walk or ride a bike than it is to take a bus or a car in Ferrara, since so many of the venues in town are in pedestrian zone. Unless you're really loaded down with bags, walking can usually save you 30 minutes in the heart of the city center. But if you must, buy a ticket for the **bus** *(1,600L)* at any *tabachi* or from the automated machines out in front of the train station. You're supposed to validate the ticket once you get onto the bus. If you'd rather be driven about town, call for a **taxi** *(Tel 0532/900-900)*. The taxis are metered, safe, and available 24/7.

Health and Emergency Ambulance: *118;* Police: *113.* The hospital, **Ospedale Sant'Anna** *(Corso Giovecca 203; Tel 052/236-111, open 24 hours)*, is just east of town.

Pharmacies Pharmacies are marked by the green illuminated crosses you'll notice all over town. Each pharmacy is required to post the night-time rotating schedule, and will provide an address for the one that's on duty that particular night. The only one that's open 24/7 is **Communale No.1** *(Corso Porto Mare 114; Tel: 0532/753-284)*.

Telephone You can use either coins or cards **carte telefonici** (cards) that you buy at the tabacchis.

Trains The **Ferrovia del Stato** *(Tel 147/888-088 for schedules)* train station is located on the western edge of the city, just outside the city walls. Ferrara is on the main Bologna-to-Venice line, and trains to and from come twice an hour. If you're day-tripping from Ferrara, you can leave your bags at the station *(5,000L)*. To get to the center from the station (1km walk), take Bus 2 to the Castello stop (when you see the big castle, press the "fermata" request on the bus). You could walk it (15 min) by hanging a left out the front doors of the station and then taking Viale Consituzione until it turns into Viale Cavour.

Bus Lines Out of the City the **Acft bus station** *(Via Rampari S. Paolo; Tel 0532/599-492; 6:15am-8pm Mon-Sat)* is on the southwestern edge of town, along the river and the city walls, though most buses destined for out of town locations leave from the train station. You can buy tickets at the **Biglietterua Centrale** *(Piazza Municipale 11, Tel 0532/599-491; 9am-12pm Mon-Fri),* directly across from the Duomo.

Bike Rental There's a huge **bicycle garage** just to the right of the station *(Piazzale Stazione; Tel 0532/772-190).* You can also rent bikes from **Bici Estense** [see *city sports,* above].

Laundry Lavanderia Self Service Ad Acqua *(105 Via Palestra; No phone; Bus 3C to Piazza Ariosto; 8am-10pm daily, 7,000L per wash, 500L per 4 minutes dryer time)* is conveniently located across from the Piazza Ariostea, in the northern part of town, next to **Pizzaria Cris** [see *eats,* above].

Postal The **main post office** is located at Viale Cavour 29 *(Tel 0532/297-206; 8am-7pm Mon-Sat),* but you can buy stamps (francoboli) to the states at most Tabacchi.

Internet See *wired,* above.

modena

The Italians who tell you that Modena's 175,000 inhabitants all have their noses up in the air aren't entirely mistaken. Emiglia's largest town, just 40km west of Bologna, has come to represent the finer things in life; sports cars, opera, and fine foods are just a few of its modern accomplishments. Ferrari, Maserati, and Lamborghini are based outside of the city center, drawing hordes of designer-clad business types here to talk shop. Luciano Pavoratti hails from here, but for tax reasons, we're told, he only leaves his Monaco home to live here for a month or two each year. And then there's Balsamic vinegar, the sweet-sour concoction that started making Modena millions when it was first imported to the States back in the eighties. (Salads have never been the same since.)

All this means that Modena has money to burn, and budget travelers will find their wallets crunched at every turn. But just like the cool kid in school you always had a crush on, Modena isn't really as surfacy as it seems. International travelers don't particularly impress locals—they're as accustomed to business people who fly in for meetings as they are to camera-toting tourists—but they do welcome visitors. As in any conservative place, the alterno spirit thrives underground—and from the used clothes stores to the punk pilgrimage **More** [see *bars, clubs, and live music scene,* below], there are plenty of diversions for the open-minded travelers.

As the second home of the Este empire back in the late Renaissance, Modena has always been a friend to free expression. After being banished from Ferrara when the papacy took over, the Estes continued the same beautification policy they upheld in their old 'hood, commissioning

WILL THE REAL BALSAMICO PLEASE STAND UP

Balsamic vinegar put Modena on the international culinary map. Hordes of hungry Americans come to Modena every year in search of that magical stuff that saved their salads back in the eighties, but they don't find it. That's because traditional balsamic vinegar is a rare condiment that takes at least 12 years to produce, and fetches upwards of $100 for a 3.5 ounce bottle, depending on its age. Its history is long, and inextricably linked to that of Modena, its climate, its grapes, and its families. The aging process requires the transfer of the vinegar into successively smaller barrels (as evaporation takes place) made of different woods (to impart different flavors). Finally, concentrated sweet/sour syrup remains, and this is the stuff that's drizzled over Parmigiano, and sipped as a cordial at the end of special meals. Many stores will try to hawk lesser products at the same high prices, but beware: Unless it comes with a gold or red wax stamp, in the long necked, bulbous-bottomed bottles, and unless it reads *Aceto Balsamico Tradizionale,* then it's not the real thing. The Modenese are so serious about this stuff that they set up an official *Consortium of Balsamic Vinegar Experts* to taste every batch of vinegar that's bottled before it can be sold as *Tradizionale. Balsamico* counterfeiters are caught and fined every year, but all they do is mix their lesser product with red wine vinegar, boil it down 'til it acquires that certain sweetness, and sell it to Americans as a *condimento* they call Balsamic Vinegar.

modena bars clubs and culture zoo

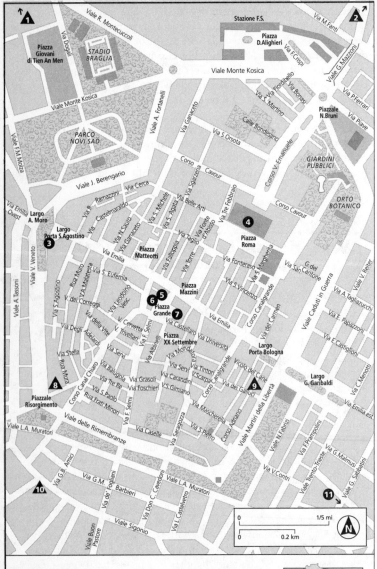

BARS/CLUBS ▲
Griffin's Irish Pub **9**
More **2**
Red Lion Pub **10**
Snoopy's Countdown **1**
Stallo del Pomodoro Enoteca **8**

CULTURE ZOO ●
Il Duomo **5**
Palazzo Communale **7**
Palazzo dei Musei **3**
Palazzo Ducale **4**
Galleria Ferrari **11**
Ghirlandina Tower **6**

palaces, municipal buildings, and funding artists for public works. From the Ghirlandina tower that hovers over the cobblestone Piazza del Duomo, to the fine Galleria Estense, which houses paintings by Correggio, Veronese, and Tintoretto, Modena's Renaissance spirit looms large. But its history goes even deeper. A Roman colony founded in 183 B.C., Modena was the stage for the battle between Mark Anthony and Brutus in 43 B.C. (we all now how that story ends). The Roman road upon which so many towns flourished is still thc lifeblood of the region. Now called Via Emilia, it runs right through the center of town, and even though you're more likely to spot a Max Mara than Circus Maximus here, or a temple dedicated to Gucci than to Jupiter, the feel is still exclusively upscale.

Thanks to Modena's deep pockets, the city underwent a facelift since it was half-destroyed by heavy bombing during World War II, making this a great place to stroll, snap pictures, and admire the beautifully renovated Renaissance buildings. Public gardens, sprawling piazzas, and plenty of palazzo steps are popular places for kicking back and enjoying the scenery.

MusicPlus.net, the glossy, hyper-designed, music monthly lists live music and DJ events in and around Modena. *News Spettacolo Modena* is more comprehensive, including not just bars and clubs, but theater, dance, and performance art.

neighborhoods

Although Modena has considerable urban sprawl, most of where you'll want to be spending your time, in the *centro storico,* is pretty compact and walk-able. Don't bother with the efficient urban bus system unless you're schlepping your bags from the train station to your place of rest or vice versa [see *need to know,* below]. **Via Emilia,** the elegant shopping

wired

The super-swank **tourist office** has twelve computers for your browsing, downloading, and printing pleasure, and you don't have to sign-up in advance. You pay first at the front desk, and the more hours you buy, the cheaper it will cost you. The two-hour minimum will cost you only 2,500L. **Bibliotecha Delfini** [see *performing arts,* above] also has a few computers that they loan out for free use. Check out *www.emmeti.it/Welcome/Emilia/Modena/index.uk.html .http:// www.emmeti.it/Welcome/Emilia/Modena/index.uk.html* for good basic town info.

street, bisects the *centro storico* into north and south. The grandiose **Piazza Mazzini,** on the north side of Via Emilia, in the very center of town, is home to a beautiful synagogue, and to hordes of hanger-outers who catch a slice at **Pizza Alt** [see *eats,* below] before their nightly *passegiata*. **Via Taglio** (otherwise known as tourist central) forms the northern side of Piazza Mazzini. The restaurants here cater to the busloads, but the shops are very cool—exploring is encouraged. A block north of Taglio is **Piazza Roma,** home to the **Palazzo Ducale,** Italy's main military academy. Just off to the east of the Palazzo are the **botanical gardens** [see *hanging out,* below]. Picnickers, roller bladers, and all-around slackers spend their days navigating this wide green expanse.

On the southern side of Via Emilia, almost directly across from Piazza Mazzini, sits **Piazza Grande,** one of the true masterpieces of medieval Italy. The cobblestones are the size of your fist, so it's almost painful to walk here in flip-flops or other flimsy footwear. The **Duomo** and its attached **Ghirlandina tower** sit on Piazza Grande, across from the **Palazzo Communale** (where the tourist office and other city offices are housed). To the southeast of Grande you'll find the busy **Piazza XX Settembre,** whose daily market functions more as a social center than a place of commerce.

Bars and restaurants are spread all throughout the *centro storico,* though the area south of Via Emilia is certainly the most hopping as far as neighborhoods go.

hanging out

The Modenese seem to have better things to do than spend their afternoons drinking wine in public places, but after lunch—and then again right before dinner—they do take to the streets for a daily stroll, walking arm and arm with their better half (or just with their buddies) down **Via Emilia, Canal Chiaro** (to the southwest), or **Corso Canal Grande.**

After stopping for a gelato at **Gelateria Ducale** (see *eats,* below), many wanderers end up at the **Giardini Publici,** just north of Piazza Mazzini. Fish ponds with ducks, duck ponds with fish, shaded walking paths, benches and fountains make this the perfect place to chill for a few hours, catch up with your reading, or take a nap. All the rare breeds of trees, foliage, and flowers are in the **Orto Botanico (Botanical Gardens)** *(Viale Caduti in Guerra 127; Tel 059/439-07-11; 9am-1pm Mon-Fri and by appointment; Free),* off to the right of the public gardens.

bar, club, and live music scene

There are plenty of places to wet yer whistle here in Modena, but most are civilized joints you'd take your parents to for a *caffe coretto,* and nothing more. The real night scene hinges around a group of popular bars and clubs that skirt (if not pass into) the outskirts of town.

There's nothing really very Irish about **Griffin's Irish Pub** *(Largo Hannover 65/67; Tel 059/223-606; 6pm-1am Tue-Thur, Sun; 6pm-2am Fri, Sat; griffins@Ireland.com; No credit cards),* but that said, it's much more comfortable and fun than most Italian attempts at Gaelic gaiety. It's located just to the right of the popular **Osteria Pomodoro** [see *eats,* below] in a building that they share, so folks wander between the two and hang out in the spacious gardens out in front. Inside you'll find high ceilings, stained glass and wood details, typical medieval arches, and folks crowded around big booths, drinking Guinness (8,000L) or sipping cocktails (9-10,000L). The Wednesday-night live shows are usually Celtic music, but Italian pop and rock cover bands do show up every once in a while. You'll never have to pay a cover to hear them butchering "Bad to the Bone" and other American, uh, favorites. The oversized sandwiches (8,000L) are popular with the regulars. Try the Mr. Green (Speck, mozzarella, and grilled zucchini) or the Shannon (Gorgonzola or Arugula).

Twenty- and thirty-something scenesters make the 15-minute trek south, out of the center for the happy hour at the **Red Lion Pub** *(Via Carlo Signonio 160; Tel 059/30-27-45; 6pm-1am Mon-Sat; 6-8:30pm, happy hour daily; No credit cards).* Half-price beers (full price is 8,000L) in this smoky, nondescript bar would be reason alone, but the cool, laid-back bunch that comes here is a nice change from the typical, conservative Modena crowd. Rockabilly kids rule the jukebox as art students smoke clove cigarettes and talk politics at the bar. There's not a lot of seating, so if you score one, hold onto it. The Tuesday beer festival means 5,000L for all beers, including Guinness.

The fashionistas and their fans spend the evenings swilling wine at the styly **Stallo del Pomodoro Enoteca** *(Via Calle di Luca 9; Tel 059/21-72-10; 6pm-2Aam Tue-Sun; V, MC).* Don't let the crowd frighten you off—this place has an incredible wines-by-the-glass list at reasonable prices (4-8,000L), and is spacious enough to house you and your whole crew. From *aglianico* to *primitivo,* Italy's most obscure wines are here for the tasting. Most folks crowd around the beautiful wood bar out front, but the two rooms off to the left and to the back have comfy tables and

moda

The fashion sense in Modena is diametrically opposed to nearby Bologna. Conservative and costly are the two operative words here—most of the twenty and thirty-somethings who stroll down Via Emilia on the nightly *passagiata* are decked out in expensive designer duds. Though none of the bars here have an actual dress code, the unwritten rule is clean, pressed, and smartly dressed, like young business students in America.

chairs where you can spread out, write in your journal, or just stare into the abstract art that hangs from the wall [see *art scene,* below]. It's just a five-minute walk from Piaza del Duomo, on the southwestern edge of the city walls.

So where do all the punks, Goths, gays, and grrrls in Modena hang out? Bologna. The restrictive scene here has driven most folks out of town, to party at more welcoming venues in the big city. But there is one place that keeps 'em in town: **More** *(Via dei Lancillotto 10B; Tel 059/45-05-03; 8-4am Tue-Sun, bands start around 11pm; Giordano@incretech.it; Cover ranges from free up to 20,000L; No credit cards)* is the place in Modena for live music, DJs, and all-around hell-raising. You'll find it just north of the train station (6,000L taxi ride or a 30-minute walk from the center of town). This industrial-looking building seems abandoned from the outside (don't they always?), but walk inside and you'll be overwhelmed by art, sculpture, and big open spaces. Everything's black, from the big, sunken dance floor to the long bar that wraps around it. On the other end of the room, nine computers have been connected to the Internet for your browsing or game-playing pleasure (free! freeee!!), so you can watch the band on the small stage down below while you check your email. The crowd here is a totally mixed bag of Modena's fringe folks, and the diversity makes for an overwhelmingly welcome attitude. Wednesday, Friday, and Saturday nights bring national and international alternative acts, and a DJ spins a mix of electronica, hip-hop and R&B afterward. The party doesn't break up 'til the wee hours of the morning.

Think of the cheesiest disco in the smallest town you've ever been to, and that's **Snoopy's Countdown** *(Piazza Della Cittadina 2, at the corner of Via del Corso; No phone; 10pm-2am Mon-Sat; Cover varies; No credit cards).* If you *really* want to dance, take the 10-minute walk north east of the stoplight at the west end of Via Emilia. You'll know it by the two stone lions under the awning, and the red indoor/outdoor carpet that ushers you in. The music is commercial Italian with some American Top 40, but it's popular with the college kids and divorced moms on the prowl. Good luck!

arts scene

With culturally stimulating Bologna and Parma so close by, Modena doesn't manage a very vibrant arts scene. There are a few locales worth checking out, though.

▶▶VISUAL ARTS

The painting and sculpture at **Circolo Degli Artisti** *(Via Castel Maraldo 19; Tel 059/214-161; 1-6pm Mon-Sat; No credit cards)* is sometimes the work of under-talented members, but there is often good stuff from the locals, as well as shows by artists from elsewhere in Italy. This "Artist's Club" also publishes a monthly newsletter listing art happenings around town.

▶▶PERFORMING ARTS

Biblioteca Delfini *(Corso Canalgrande 103; Tel 059/20-69-40; 1-8pm Mon, 9am-8pm Tue-Sat, closed Sun; No credit cards),* a Baroque town library just south of Piazza Roma, hosts a series of plays, poetry readings, and lectures. It also has a few computers that it lends out for Internet use [see *wired,* below].

Everything from classical ballet or a violin concerto to an homage to Jimi Hendrix plays in **Teatro Comunale** *(Via del Teatro 8; Tel 059/200-020, Fax 059/200-021, For information and reservations 059/223-244 between 9am and 1pm; www.commune.modena.it/teatro comunale; 20,000L-50,000L per ticket; V, MC),* a beautiful mid-nineteenth century theater house with crystal chandeliers, gold and white balconies, and a painted ceiling and blackout curtain. Matinees and evening shows are available throughout the year. Check their website, or stop by the tourist office for their current listings of performances. The theater is just south of Piazza Roma.

If you're starved for entertainment in English, you're in luck. **Cinema Embassy D'Essai** *(Vicolo dell' Albergo 8; Tel 059/22-51-87; Box office hours 1-9pm; Voice over movies every Wednesday; 10,000L admission, 8,000L reduced price; No credit cards),* on the east side of the town center, shows movies in English once a week—call ahead or stop by the tourist office to find out which ones are playing. They're all pretty current.

Culture zoo

The cobblestone Piazza Grande is the natural place to start a tour of Modena. One of the most pristinely preserved in all of Italy, this square sits in the shadow of the Ghirlandina tower, the Duomo, and the Palazzo Comunale. The other sights—the Palazzo Ducale and Palazzo dei Musei—are just a short walk from here.

Il Duomo *(Corso Duomo; Tel 059/21608; Bus 7, 12, 14; 6:30am-12:30pm/3:30pm-7pm daily; No admission):* One of the finest examples of Romanesque architecture in all of Italy, this cathedral is seriously worthy of a few hours of exploration. Don't forget to peek in at the slightly disturbing remnants of San Gimignano, the patron saint of Modena, housed in the chapel back behind the alter, but be ready to wait in line—they're

festivals and events

The Modenese celebrate their favorite condiment every year during the **Balsamic Vinegar Fair** *(Tel 059/220-022, Fax 059/206-688; www.comune.modena.it/balsamica/calendario.html).* Downtown transforms into a vinegar lovefest, with tastings, exhibits, and samples galore. The festival takes place in May or June each summer, and attracts foodies from around the world, so make sure you book your room ahead.

one of the Duomo's main attractions. Started in 1099 by architect Lanfranco, it wasn't finished until the 14th century, and architectural influences that span the centuries are evident inside and out. The 14th-century rose window designed by Campione hovers over Wiligelmo's 12th-century sculptures from the Book of Genesis. His detailed carvings adorn most of the church doors. Inside, the high vaulted space is overwhelming.

The Ghirlandina Tower *(Piazza della Torre; 10am-1pm/3-7pm daily; 2,000L entrance; No credit cards):* This ever-so-slowly sinking tower beside the Duomo is a symbol of the city, as it once housed, of all things, the "stolen bucket of Bologna." Legend has it that during the Battle of Zappolino in 1325, the Modenese snatched this bucket from the Bolognese, and since then, it's been a symbol of local pride and courage (whatever floats your boat, guys). Started in 1169, this 87 meter-tall tower (95 if you count the anachronistic Gothic spire they stuck on top) used to be the base for the city guards, who would signal for the town's gates to open or close.

Palazzo dei Musei *(Piazza Sant'Agostino 48, off Via Emilia Est; Tel 059/222-145; Bus 7, 12, 14 to Palazzo dei Musei; Gallery hours: 9am-7:30pm Tue, Fri-Sat; 9am-2pm Wed, Thur, 9am-1pm Sun; Library hours: 9am-7pm Mon-Sat; 8,000L for the gallery, free for the library):* What are El Greco and Velasquez doing here? This collection was acquired by the art-loving Estes, during their reign first in Ferrara, and then here. They amassed a great collection of Emilian art too, but most come to see Spanish artists' works, such as El Greco's triptych, and a Velasquez portrait of Francesco I. Coreggio. Bernini, Tintoretto, Guercino, and Veronese make an appearance as well. In the same building sits one of Europe's most renowned libraries, with more than 500,000 tomes and 13,000 manuscripts (many of which are decoratively painted). The Bible of Borso d'Este sits under glass for your inspection, and it's a shame you can't flip through all 1,200 stunningly bordered pages. The *De Sphaera,* from the 1400s, is regarded as one of the most beautiful astrological books from the period, and the *Cantina Map of the World,* from the turn of the 16th century, offers an interesting glance into the early age of exploration.

Palazzo Communale *(Piazza Grande; Tel 059/206-669; 7am-7pm Mon-Sat, 10am-1pm/3-7pm Sun; 2,000L admission; No credit cards):* The L-shaped medieval building that flanks the northeast side of Piazza Grande, with the beautiful clock tower, is still the heart of the city. Old men play cards under the shade of its porticos, tourists run in and out of the city's tourist office, but few wander up the stairs to learn about Modena's political history (and we're not really recommending you do either, unless you're really into Italian antiquity). It now houses the original bucket that brought Ghirlandina Tower it's glory, as well as many frescoed rooms that shed light on the Modena of times past. The Sala del Furoco, painted by Noccoló dell'Abate in 1547, is perfectly preserved, and depicts the war of Modena back in 46 B.C.

Palazzo Ducale *(Accademia Militare; Piazza Roma; Tel 059/206-600; Tours given on Sundays by appointment only; 10,000L):* This ominous and ornately decorated building is significant not only as the Este's home in Modena from 1635 until 1859, but also as the headquarters of Italy's main military academy since 1947—this is where army officers are trained for permanent positions within the government. The *Appartemento di Stato* contains an impressive collection of Renaissance portraits of the royal family, but it's enough to just stroll outside and admire the facade.

Galleria Ferrari *(Via Dino Ferrari 43; Tel 0536/943-204; Fax 0536/949-714; Bus 2 from the bus station toward Sassulo, ask the driver for the right stop; 9:30-12:30pm/2:30-6pm Tue-Sat; gallerie@ferrari.it; 15,000l admission; 10,000l student; No credit cards):* This official Ferrari museum will make you see red—the prominent color of the archetypal sports cars. Located southeast of Modena in Maranello, it's only worth the trip and trouble if you're a die-hard gear-head. A good bit of history, manufacturing the cult of the Enzo Ferrari legacy, is on display, as well as some of the early prototypes. Just make sure that you call first to assure that there will be someone there to give you a tour.

If you're interested in touring the Lamborghini, Maserati, or De Tomaso plants you should contact the tourist office [see *need to know,* below] to arrange a visit.

CITY SPORTS

When the going gets tough, the Modenese go swimming. Dive in with the locals at the covered and uncovered pools around Modena. These are great places to meet and mingle—after working off lasts night's beer binge with a few laps, you can start off all over again at the convivial pool bar. Both are open all year. The large public **Piscina Pergolesi** *(Via Divisione Acqui 152; Tel 059/373-337; 7am-4pm Mon-Fri, 8:45am-11pm Friday, Sat, 9am-1am Sun; 9,000L)* is east of the center, and kind of a long haul (a 20-30 minute walk). **Piscina Dogali** *(Via Dogali 12; Bus 2, 7,9-12, 19 to Piscina; Tel 059/217-525; 7am-4pm Mon-Fri, 7am-1am Sat; 8am-11pm Tue, Wed, Thur; 9am-1am Sun; 9,000L)* is closer to the middle of town, just north of Parco Novi Sad, on the northwest corner of the center of town.

The huge **Palazzo dello Sport** *(Viale dello Sport 25; Tel 059/375-121)* has everything from basketball to workout rooms, if swimming isn't your thing.

For all you rock jocks, there's a climbing wall at **Modena Sporting Club,** *(Via Padovani 45; Tel 059/346-456; 7am-11pm daily; No credit cards).* For more information about climbing in the area, contact **Associazione Equilibrium c/o Polivalente Unione 81** *(Via Tincani Martelli 32; Tel 059/253-452).*

STUFF

Modena's shops are pricier than their equivalents in Bologna, but the alternative undercurrent means that you'll find some cool vintage shops that double as hangouts during the day.

▶▶DUDS

Not only is this the only place in town to pick up a used snakeskin jacket or a replacement pair of Levis, but **Seta Cotta** *(Corso Canal Chiaro 34; Tel 059/244-660; Noon-7:30 daily; No credit cards)*, southwest of Piazza Grande, is a hangout for hipsters with their pulse on the nightlife. Pick up some flyers from the counter, or ask the regulars who hang out in the back room where the party is. This place has better bargains than its American equivalents—old Izod sweaters for 70,000L, vintage dresses, and handbags by the bushel.

For slinkier fashions to sport on the dance floor, ladies should check out **Anna Ruggenti** *(Via Rismondo 12; 9:45am-1pm/4-8pm Mon-Sat; V, MC)*, in the town center north of Via Emilia. Faux snakeskin pants (60,000L) with a rhinestone-studded tank-top (25,000L) should do it.

▶▶BOUND

There's a **Feltrinelli** *(13 Cesare Battisti; Tel 059/222-868; 9am-7:30pm Mon-Sat; V, MC)* right in the heart of town that has a fairly large English book selection. Most new titles hover around 20,000L.

▶▶TUNES

The widest (though mostly commercial) selection of CDs at the best prices can be found at **Ricordi Media Store** (10 Via Cesare Battisti; Tel 059/226-566; 9am-7:30pm Mon-Sat; V, MC), right on the corner of Via Emilia. With two well-stocked floors, and headphone for listening to the latest Italian hits, it's worth a browse.

▶▶HOW BAZAAR

Bargains abound at the **Piazza XX Settembre Market** *(Piazza XX Settembre; No phone; 7am-7pm, closed Sun and Mon)*. The offering at these small kiosks lined up in the narrow piazza is slightly more interesting and diverse than usual market far. You can find everything from used clothing to disposable razors at rock-bottom prices.

EATS

It's surprisingly easy to eat on the cheap here. Just beware of the traps around Via Taglio, where hungry travelers are lured in with wholly unsatisfying *Menu Turistiches* (set priced multi-course meals with limited choices). A heavily stickered door is usually a bad sign.

Local specialties include the delicious chewy fried bread called *Gnocco*, and *Maltagliata*, roughly cut strips of pasta cooked in a bean soup. More adventurous eaters will relish in *Zampone*, a spicy sausage that's put into the skin of a pig trotter (lower leg), and served with beans or lentils. *Cotechino* is the less-scary local pork sausage. In Modena, many meats and fowl are swathed in the inimitable flavor of Balsamic Vinegar—don't pass up the chance to try some drizzled on chips of Parmigiano Reggiano. For dessert, keep an eye out for *tortelli fritti*, or fried tortelli, which is usually stuffed with sweet cheese and marmalade. And the meal isn't over until you've downed a glass of *Nocino*, the surprisingly good *digestivo* made out of walnut hulls. The local wine is *Lambrusco;* watch out, though, it's light and fruity and it goes down dangerously easy.

▶▶CHEAP

The cheery **Gelateria Ducale** *(Piazza Roma 4; Tel 059/23-51-24; 8:30am-midnight, closed Mon; 3,000-6,000L for a cup or cone)*, on Piazza Roma across from the Palazzo Ducale, is packed year round with kids, couples, and entire families who come here for the best artisan-made gelato in town. With 32 flavors, there's something for everyone. If you happen in during winter, order up their bittersweet *ciocolate con panna* (4,000L), an intensely thick and dangerously decadent version of hot chocolate that's topped with homemade whipped cream.

Conveniently located just across the street from Modena's most popular happy hour at the **Red Lion Pub** [see *bar, club, and live music scene,* above], **Bella Rosa Rosticceria Cinese** *(Via le C. Signonio 45; Tel 059/21-68-07; 10:30am-3pm/5:30pm-10:30pm daily; No credit cards)* is packed for lunch and dinner. This tiny takeout joint does awesome rotisserie chickens (5,000L) as well as some typical Chinese food faves. The 8,500L menu fisso is Modena's best meal deal—fried rice, a spring roll, and your choice of main dishes will fill you up without breaking the bank.

If you've had your fill of the trattoria staples, and just want a damn good pie, head to La Mamma *(Via Taglio 38; Tel 059/216-427; 10am-2:30pm/6-11pm daily, closed Thur; 6-12,000L pizza; 10-20,000L entree; No credit cards)*, the no-frills pizzeria in the center of town. There's nothing fancy about this place (thank gawd), but the oversized pizzas and other Italian grandma food really hit the spot. It's loud and crowded constantly, with students, soldiers, families, and couples who down the house wine by the literful.

Euro Kebab *(Via Voltone 1 and Castel Marald 57; Tel 059/23-43-64, Fax 059/439-36-66; Restaurant 11:30am-3pm/6pm-midnight daily Paninoteca 11:30am-midnight daily; 15,000L main entree; 6,500L pita;*

TO MARKET

Housed in a beautiful gated building, the **Albielli food market** *(Via Alninelli, just south of Piazza Settembre; 7am-2pm/4-6pm Mon-Sat)* buzzes with activity every day. This is *the* place to try the best of Modenese food. Don't miss the local Nostrano ham, which is similar to Prosciutto di Parma and is awesome with some gorgonzola between a couple slices of bread. All the making of a yummy picnic can be bought here, cheap.

modena eats and crashing

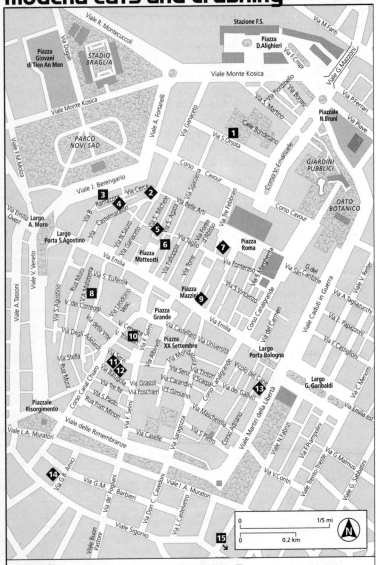

EATS ◆

Bella Rosa Rosticceria Cinese **14**
Euro Kebab **4**
Gelateria Ducale **7**
Hermes **2**
La Casa della Strega Bionda **12**
La Mamma **5**
Pizza Alt **9**
Stallo del Pomodoro Trattoria **13**
Taverna dei Servi/Club 37 **11**

CRASHING ■

Albergo Bonci **3**
Hotel Centrale **6**
Hotel La Torre **10**
Hotel San Marino **15**
Locanda Sole **8**
Ostello San Filippo
  Neri **1**

No credit cards), in the area between Via Emilia and the east side of Parco Novi Sad, just may well be the first pan-Middle Eastern restaurant in Italy. What looks like your typical kebab shop, with bean salads and skewered meats sitting in illuminated deli-cases and crowds of students and couples sipping chai at the standing-room-only bar, hides a pretty dining room off to the right. You can always order Gyros, hummus, babaganoug, or kofte to go, or sit down for a real Middle Eastern feast, complete with the sticky-sweet baklava for dessert. The homemade pitas are light, airy, and unforgettable.

It's virtually impossible to eat between the hours of 3 and 6pm in a town as efficiently run as Modena. But let's say you find yourself sleeping in for some reason, and are in dire need of nourishment—drag yourself on over to **Pizza Alt** *(Piazza Mazzini 46; Tel 059/223-506; 9am-9pm Mon-Sat, 3-9pm Sun; No credit cards).* This by-the-slice place on Piazza Mazzini is just a little fancier than most (hey, this is Modena, whaddaya expect?), with such varied toppings as *funghi* (mushrooms) and *carciofi* (artichoke hearts) for 1,900-2,300L per slice. But perhaps the real reason to come here is for the super-size fountain Cokes with *ice* for 4,500L.

▶▶**DO-ABLE**

If you really want to eat like the Modenese, book yourself a table at **Stallo del Pomodoro Trattoria** *(Largo Hannover 63; Tel 059-21-46 64, Fax 059/439-22-73; Noon-2:45pm/8-11:30pm Mon-Sat, closed Sun all day and Sat lunch; 15-25,000L per entree; V, MC, AE).* The beautiful, two-tiered restaurant south of Via Emilia on the east side of the town center has a more down-to-earth feel than its uptown branch, the wine bar of the same name [see *bar, club, and live music scene,* above], with heavy wood tables, dark wood, and candle light everywhere. The small bar that sits under the dining room loft is usually crowded with folks who just stopped in for a small cheese or salami plate (around 10,000L). The wines by the glass are listed on the blackboard, and none cost more than 8,000L. Busy waiters whisk seasonal dishes from the open kitchen out into the dining room-baby lamb in *balsamico, tortolloni* with four cheeses, *rucola* and *balsamico* salad. Don't risk it—book ahead.

If you get the sense that you're being stared at, don't take it personally. It's just that locals would rather not let word of **Taverna dei Servi/Club 37** *(Via dei Servi 37; Tel 059/21-7-134; 8pm-2:30am, closed Monday; 10-12,000L first course, 12-30,000L per entree; Cover 3,000L; No credit cards)* out of the bag. It doesn't look like the kind of place where life-changing meals take place, with it's long wood tables, big screen TVs constantly showing soccer games, and loud crowd of sports fans—oh, but it is. The talented young chef, Lorenzo Migliorini, has cooked all over Italy, and recently returned home to Modena to work with the ingredients he knows best. The pastas are his specialties—light and ethereal dough holds a mixture of four cheeses, tossed in butter and sage (12,000L). Homemade sausages are sweet with fennel, grilled, and served with potatoes (20,000L). Chips of Parmigiano Reggiano are drizzled with syrupy 25-year old *balsamico,* and brought out before the dessert carts rolls past. All the wines are local and chosen to match the food—there's no bottle over 25,000L. Ask for a taste of the chef's *Nocino digestivo,* and you just might leave there a local. You'll find this place southeast of Piazza Grande, just off Corso Canal Chiaro.

Hermes *(Via Giancetto 89; No phone; Noon-2:30 Mon-Sat, lunch-only; 30,000L prix fixe; No credit cards)* will transport you back to your grandmother's dining room, with frilly *tchotchkes* on the wall and great food smells knocking you down as soon as you walk in the door. This is a peculiar place—Hermes, the husband, runs the front of the house with great flair, bossing his son around to bus tables while his wife toils away in the kitchen. They only do a fixed price lunch, so come hungry: 30,000L gets you the whole Modenese meal, including antipasti, a first course, second course, vegetable, dessert and coffee. People make a point of eating here when they come to town, and you should to. It's right down the street from the market, north of Via Emilia on the west side of the center.

▶▶**SPLURGE**

Just wait until you meet the "blonde witch" who runs **La Casa della Strega Bionda** *(Vicolo Frassone 10; Tel 059/238-080; 6pm-midnight Mon-Sat; 15-20,000L first course, 22-30,000L entree; V, MC).* This former model left the fashion industry to focus on good food—you can tell she has her heart in it. This elegant restaurant located on a dead-end street off Corso Canal Chiaro is beautifully decorated with abstract paintings, fine crystal and linen, yet the prices don't approach the fine dining quota you'd expect. Modenese specialties, like *tortolloni* and *tagliatelle,* are all prepared with the freshest ingredients. The main courses are slightly more innovative, mixing non-traditional flavorings with Modenese fare. The wine list is comprehensive, and has some good local bottles—ask for a recommendation.

crashing

Budget sleeps aren't hard to find in Modena, but you should call ahead if it's important to you to stay in the *centro storico.* If you're willing to walk, you can often get much nicer rooms for the same or less money at hotels outside the city walls.

▶▶**CHEAP**

Yeah, there's a midnight curfew. Yeah, it's bright and overly cheery. And yeah the cleaning ladies will rip the sheets off your bed if you're not out by 10am. But really, **Ostello San Filippo Neri** *(Via San Orsola 48-52; Tel 059/23-45-98; 10am-2pm lock-out; 28,000L dorm bed, 30,000L for a bed in a family room w/ private bath, 85 beds total; IYH card required or else pay 6,000L for a stamp (six stamps and you're a member!); No credit cards)* is a great bargain if you're just spending a night in town. This hostel opened in 1999, and it couldn't be more central. Located almost exactly between the train station and the Piazza Grande, it's a popular spot with visiting families and students who stay here during the semester.

Locanda Sole *(Via Malatesta 45; Tel 059/214-245; Bus 7 to Via Emilia Centro; Reception desk open from 9am-midnight, closed August,*

Xmas, and Easter; 45-60,000L single, 80-100,000L double, no private baths; No credit cards) is centrally located, well-maintained, and clean. The 70's refugee decor may be off-putting to some, but the small tile-floored rooms are cool in summer and warm in winter. The rooms are basic enough, but have TVs, sinks, and those inscrutable bidets.

▶▶DO-ABLE

Albergo Bonci *(Via Ramazzini 59; Tel 059/223-634; Bus 7 to Via Emilia Centro; 35-75,000L single, 60-120,000L double, none w/bath, 15 rooms; No credit cards),* north of Via Emilia, has huge, comfortable rooms that are spic and span. There's a tiny mezzanine level lounge that fits a few vending machines, a couch, and a TV. The grouchy guy who runs this place grows on you—he's incredibly helpful with directions and traveler advice. Take caution when walking around alone at night—there's a rowdy bar next door that's just on the other side of seedy.

Hotel San Marino *(26 Via Vignolese; Tel 059/306-158; Bus 3 from the station to Medagli d'Oro; 78,000L single, 114,000L double, 144,000L triple, all w/private bath; No credit cards)* is a little bit out of the way (a five-minute walk southeast of the city walls), but you get so much more for your money here. The directions are pretty simple: From Largo Garibaldi, hang a right on Viale Trento-Trieste, a quick left on Viale L.A. Muratori, and a fast right on via Vignolese. This modern, boxy building has 18 new-ish, well-equipped rooms, with TVs, phones, and a nice tile bath in each. The super-friendly owners like to play tourist guides, and will give you advice over a coffee in the bar downstairs.

You couldn't find a better location than the centrally located two-star **Hotel La Torre** *(Via Cervetta 5; Tel 059/222-615, Fax 059/216-316; Bus 7 to Via Emilia Centro; 75,000L single w/bath low season, 90,000L high season, 45,000L single w/out bath low season, 60,000L high season, 110,000L doubles w/ bath low season, 140,000L high season, 145,000L triple low season, 185,000L high season; 15,000L breakfast; 15,000L garage; V, MC).* They make an effort to act like a two-star here—nice towels, carpeting, and televisions and phones in most room.

▶▶SPLURGE

Why not spoil yourself with a little MTV? **Hotel Centrale** *(Via Rismondo 55; Tel 059/218-808, Fax 059/238-201; Bus 7 to Via Emilia Centro; 95,000L single, 50,000L singles w/ shared bath, 150,000L double, 195,000L triple; V, MC)* is central—just off Via Emilia and down the block from Piazza Grande—and cush. This hotel has all the creature comforts. If you've been suffering from floral print overload, you'll appreciate the tasteful decor of these squeaky clean, recently renovated rooms (40 in all). Call in advance, as this is a favorite with business travelers and families.

need to know

Currency Exchange There are plenty of **ATMs** scattered around town, but for changing money, **Credito Italiano** on Via Emilia, is a good bet.

Tourist Information the brand new **tourist office** *(Piazza Grande 17; Tel 059/206-660, Fax 059/206-659; 8:30am-1pm/3-7pm Mon-Sat (closed Wed afternoon), 9:30am-12:30pm Sun; www.comune.modena. it/infoturismo/)* is north of Via Emilia on the west side of the center and is extremely helpful, though they won't make hotel reservations for you. They also have a dozen computers that they rent out [see *wired*, above], and next door, a few that you can use for free if you promise to be surfing the tourist office site.

Public Transportation You'll really only need to use the **city bus system** to get to and from the train station *(Bus 7 to Via Emilio Centro)*, as Modena is an easily walk-able city once you get into the *centro storico*. Tickets for the ACTM buses cost 1,600L and can be purchased at any tabaccherie or newsstand. For information, call 059/222-220. And of course taxis *(Tel 059/374-24-42)* run 24/7.

Health and Emergency Emergencies: *112;* Ambulance: *113;* Fire: *115.* The **main police station** is located on Viale Amendola 152; *Tel 059/200-700;* The main hospital is the **Ospedale Civile Sant'Agostino** *(Largo Porta Sant'Agostino 228; Tel 059/435-111),* northeast of the town center.

Pharmacy S. Filomena *(Corso Duomo 4; Tel 059/223-916; 9am-12:30pm/2:30-7pm Mon-Sat; No credit cards),* between Via Emilia and the back of the Duomo, is your best choice.

Trains The **train station** *(Tel 059/218-226)* is located in Piazza Dante, a 20-minute walk to the northeast of town. Take buses 7 or 11 to Piazza Grande, which is right in the center of town. Trains leave every 30 minutes to Bologna and Parma.

Bus Lines Out of the City For schedules and information for regional buses, call 059/222-220. The **bus station** is location at Via Bacchini, and open from 7:30am-6:30pm.

Bike Rental You can rent bikes in Parci Novi Sad *(Tribuni Novi Sad; Viale Monte Kosica; Summer only),* in the beautiful park just north of the bus station.

Postal the **main post office** is on Via Emilia 86 *(Tel 059/243-509; 8am-7pm Mon-Sat).*

Internet See *wired,* above.

parma

The Parmagiani (the people, not the cheese) have a rep for being super-refined, if not downright snooty. They wear uptight clothing that makes them look like they just came from Brooks Brothers; and they talk with a slight French accent that sets them apart from most other Italians. But they've kind of earned the right to be snobs: Their food is world-renowned, and people still come from all over the world to hear the works of native-son Guiseppe Verdi in Parma's beautiful Teatro Regio. But beneath that stuffy surface—way beneath—this town's got a serious wild streak. Once you hook up with some local college students from the **Università degli Studi di Parma,** you'll find plenty of places to party, as well as a raw-edged contemporary arts scene that's a good antidote to the Renaissance overdose. School's in session year-round, and there's a huge student population, so stick around at least long enough to check the place out.

For a town of just 170,000 people, Parma is extremely cultured and cosmopolitan. Even the superficially uptight Parmigiani are closet hedonists—they love the finer things in life, often to excess. So do as they do. Eat some great food, dig some classical music, gape at Renaissance architecture, and get into some spirited, late-night conversations in fashionable bars. (Remember: A wine buzz is as good—or as bad— as a beer buzz.)

Though the town itself dates back to 183 B.C., when it was established along Via Emilia as a Roman colony, it wasn't until the Middle Ages that it really matured into the cultural capital it is today. In the 16th century, it was declared an autonomous state under the Farnese family (which also happened to be Pope Paul III's family), who governed the city for about 200 years. The French Bourbons inherited the duchy when the Farnese failed to produce a male heir. They sent Maria Luigia, Napoleon's consort, to rule at the start of the 19th century. She had an affinity for the arts, and Parma further blossomed during her reign. When she died in 1847, it went back to the Bourbons, but the city never stopped being infatuated with her. She's responsible for the city's good looks—many of the standout buildings, like the Teatro Regio, were her ideas to begin with. The yellow facade set the stage for a trend that lasts even today— this color is washed over the city, and you can hardly go a block without seeing a patch of it.

neighborhoods and hanging out

Parma was built around the intersection of **Via Emilia** and the River Parma, so most of its sights crowd around this junction. The train station is about 1km north from here, just to the east of the river. To get to the center of town from the station, just stroll down **Via Verdi,** to **Piazza della Pilotta,** the Renaissance home of the Farnese family. Heavily bombed in the WWII, it's been rebuilt, and now is home to some of Parma's finest museums and most avant-garde contemporary art exhibits. From this piazza, head due east down **Strada da Pisacane.** When it crosses **Cavour,** it turns into **Strada da Duomo.** Here in one of Italy's finest Romanesque squares, the Duomo, the baptistery, and, just behind the two, the Abbey of John the Baptist, converge. For a striking juxtaposition of the old and the new, turn right and head south down **Via XX Marzo,** the fashion center of Parma. Boutiques and restaurants line this street, and smart-suited couples window shop on their way back to work in the afternoon. At its north end, this street intersects with **Strada della**

parma

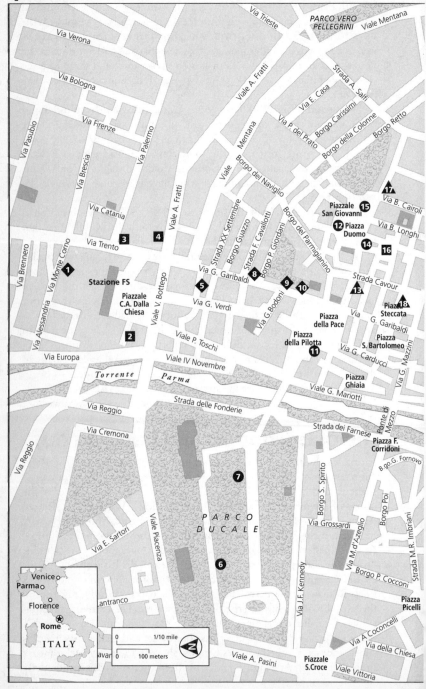

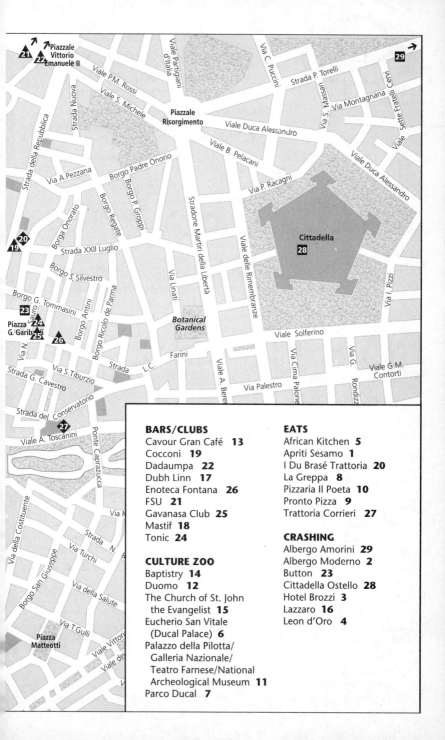

BARS/CLUBS
Cavour Gran Café **13**
Cocconi **19**
Dadaumpa **22**
Dubh Linn **17**
Enoteca Fontana **26**
FSU **21**
Gavanasa Club **25**
Mastif **18**
Tonic **24**

CULTURE ZOO
Baptistry **14**
Duomo **12**
The Church of St. John
  the Evangelist **15**
Eucherio San Vitale
  (Ducal Palace) **6**
Palazzo della Pilotta/
  Galleria Nazionale/
  Teatro Farnese/National
  Archeological Museum **11**
Parco Ducal **7**

EATS
African Kitchen **5**
Apriti Sesamo **1**
I Du Brasé Trattoria **20**
La Greppa **8**
Pizzaria Il Poeta **10**
Pronto Pizza **9**
Trattoria Corrieri **27**

CRASHING
Albergo Amorini **29**
Albergo Moderno **2**
Button **23**
Cittadella Ostello **28**
Hotel Brozzi **3**
Lazzaro **16**
Leon d'Oro **4**

five things to talk to a local about

1. **Those Miserable Modenese:** People from Parma never tire of striking comparisons between their hometown and Modena.

2. **The river:** What is usually a trickle has turned into a torrent over the past few years. The main bridge that leads from Via Mazzini to Via M. d'Azeglio has closed several times in recent years, stranding hundreds of bar goers on the other side of town. What to do? Is the situation getting worse?

3. **Compare and contrast Alexi Lalas/Lucy Lawless:** The former used to play for the AC Parma soccer team before moving to the States, and is almost as popular as the latter.

4. Boy's night: Sounds like gay night, but no, no, no. What it is, actually, is a testosterone-infested room packed with hootin' and hollerin' fans of AC Parma, known affectionately to locals as "the boys." You may find a closet queen in there somewhere, but don't count on it.

5. **The real thing:** People really do talk about Parmigiano-Reggiano cheese with a sense of collective pride and accomplishment. Ask them what they think about the knock-offs by Kraft and others.

Republicca, which is called **Via Mazzini** when you take a right. This is the main drag in town, which follows the old Via Emilia route. Take it toward the river, and you'll pass **Piazza Garibaldi,** which is crowded day and night with folks chatting with grocery bags in their hands, kids skateboarding, couples taking a break in the sun. If you continue over the **Ponte di Messo,** you head into what is now the university district, with its old crumbling classroom buildings. The students don't really hang out here, since the bar and restaurant scene is all around Piazza Garibaldi, but if you're staying at one of the cheap hotels across the river, you'll be caught up in the mass exodus that occurs around 3am when everyone is emptying out of the bars.

Off Piazza Garibadi, to the south, is **Via Farini,** the central nervous system of Parma's nightlife. Restaurants, pubs, and wine bars line the main street, and are hidden in the maze of windy alleys that run off to the side. If you walk all the way south down Farini, it will lead you straight into **Cittadella** *(Viale delle Rimembranze 5; Tel 051/961-434; Bus 9; Via Martiri della Liberta; 6:30am-8pm April-Sept, 7am-7pm Oct-March, 7:30am-7pm Nov, Feb, closed Dec, Jan; Free),* a sprawling public park that's housed in a pentagon-shaped military fortress that was constructed in 1546 by the almighty Farnese. As you stroll around the preserved ramparts, just imagine that all 2.5 acres were once surrounded by a man-made moat. Then take a nap in the grass. You can also get your lazing about done in the Ducal Gardens [see *culture zoo*, below].

bar and live music scene

This is a college town, so for every funky cool bar, there are five cookie-cutter college pubs. Before you drop 10,000L on a fruity cocktail, consider your options. The best places make a nod to Parma's rich culinary, cultural, and artistic history. Pick up *Parmagenda*, the free weekly guide to clubs, bars, and shows. Any self-respecting bar will have a few on the counter.

Just a few steps from the tourist info office sits the very un-touristy **Cavour Gran Café** *(Via Cavour 30/B; Tel 0521/206-223; Bus 1 to Garibaldi; 10,000L cocktail; 1,600L cappuccino; 8-2am daily; No credit cards).* With its classic crystal chandelier and flowery Baroque paintings, this wouldn't strike you as the preferred coffee shop of Parma's hip-n-trendy set. We're not sure what brings them in—maybe it's the old-school waiters who bring you the most elegant silver sugar bowl you've ever seen. Maybe it's the spritzers, which the busy bartenders seem to find the time to adorn with a long spiral of orange peel, even if they're slammed. But most likely, it's the history—this place has been around so long, many of the cool kids hanging out here have grandparents who drank here (and still do).

The nomination for the Prettiest Bar Award (and we don't mean pretty in some sissified bad way) goes out to the half-century-old **Cocconi** *(Via Reppublica 22; Bus 1 or 14 to Piazza Garibaldi or Mazzini; Tel 230-351; 7:30am-8:30pm daily; 10-12,000L cocktails; V,MC),* which is probably looks just as lovely as it did when it first swung open its doors. Walk past the wooden tables and deli cases packed with pastries and head straight to the beautifully detailed wood and marble bar. This is *the* place to go for happy hour—everyone from the twenty-something suit just off work to the jokester grandpa on his fifth Campari and soda is here. From 7:30 to 8:30pm, there are no drink specials, but the free *aperitivo* spread is generous, with bite-sized foccacia sandwiches, olives, chips, nuts and bruscetta, all yours to nosh on when you order a drink. This place is known for its cocktails...they make all their fruit syrups and mixers from scratch. The *Belle Epoque* is an intense infusion of fresh mandarin orange syrup, with gin, Cointreau, and sweet vermouth (10,000L), so think twice before you order a beer. It's also known for its chocolates, particularly the famous Duchessa cake [see *eats*, below]. The local AC Parma soccer players come here a lot, and are treated like rock stars.

To see it during the day, you'd never guess that **Gavanasa Club** *(Via Farini 22/A; Tel 0521/231-036, for reservation 0328/596-82-84; Bus 1 or 8 to Piazza Garibaldi, or 15 to Farini; 7:30am-4pm Mon, Tue, Thur; 7:30am-4pm/9pm-1am Wed, Fri, Sat, closed Sun; No cover; No credit cards)* turns into one of Parma's most rocking disco-pubs come nightfall. This little Italian cafe, on the eastern side of Strada Farini just south of Piazza Garibaldi, is bright and lively around lunch, but when it re-opens at 9pm, the DJs start spinning commercial dance music from Ibizia, the lights dim, and the crowds come out in hordes (get here this early and score a seat; otherwise, it's shoulder to shoulder). This place is laid back...ladies in tank tops and gents in jeans. Some 40 types of wine by the bottle go for 3-7,000L, big beers go for just 5,000L, and good news—there's never a cover. The narrow front room is reserved for drinking and noshing on a wide selection of panini (6,000L)—the party breaks loose in the back.

Parma's coolest hangout by far is the arty, loud, and rambunctious **Tonic** (*Via N. Sauro 5; Tel 052/239-174; Bus 1 or 8 to Piazza Garibaldi, or 15 to Farini; 9:30pm-3:30am Mon-Sat; No credit cards*). The front room is covered with sculpted forms made from molds of some of their regular customers—that's right, head to toe. Walk past the bar and into the back two rooms, past the abstract paintings and montages, and try to score yourself a table. If you come after 11, you'll have to dodge the dancers, who by this time are often on top of the tables, doing their thing. There's no formal DJ, but Luca Ferraglia, the owner, has one of the best CD and vinyl collections in town, and he and his wife seem to encourage the crowd to get down. There are beers on tap, but try one or four of their awesome fresh mint mojitos (10,000L). If you like the stuff on the walls, ask Luca to take you back to the small gallery that shows his work in the courtyard. This guy is no minor talent. His oversized works are a combination of found objects, fish bones, and raw emotion. You'll find it one block south of Piazza Garibaldi.

The whimsical furniture and loud, lively scene make **Dubh Linn** (*Borgo del Coreggio 1/A/B/C; Tel 052/284-038; Bus 1 or 8 to Piazza Garibaldi; 8pm-2am Thur-Sat, 6:30pm-2am Wed-Mon; No credit cards*), located a few blocks northeast from Piazza Garibaldi, more fun than the other Irish pubs in town. It looks tiny when you first walk in, but two rooms off to either side of the bar hide plenty of space for you and your newfound friends. The dark wood tables and chairs, church pews, stained glass, and curtained confessionals may start to make you feel a little guilty about all that Guinness you've guzzled—get over it. The music is mostly English & Irish rock—U2, Sex Pistols, and the Stones. Folks start pouring in around 8pm, and it's crazy busy until around midnight.

Parma's most popular wine bar looks like the inside of someone's garage, if that someone happened to be a wine connoisseur. **Enoteca Fontana** (*Strada Farini 24/A; Tel 0521/286-037; Bus 1 or 8 to Piazza Garibaldi, or 15 to Farini; 9am-3pm/4:30pm-9pm Tue-Sat; 3,500-8,000L sandwich; 8,500-9,000L pasta; No credit cards*), right on the main drag, doesn't have the sleek appeal that characterizes so many establishments in Parma. To get to the bar and restaurant, you have to walk through a tiny room that's crowded floor-to-ceiling with cardboard cartons of wine. The main room, with its long wood bar and barrels for tables, has seen better days, but with this laid back, all ages crowd, and 45 or so wines by the glass, who cares? And the back room, which is crowded with heavy, square tables, smells of the best home cooking you can imagine. Hearty pasta dishes, plates of cheese, sliced hams and meats, and homemade desserts are there for the devouring at super reasonable prices. The friendly folks that work here can help steer you toward a few great wines. The best time to arrive is right before dinner, during *aperitivo* hour.

With its neon signs and loud jukebox music, **Mastif** *(Via Mamelin 9/A; Tel 0521/200-665; Bus 1 or 8 to Piazza Garibaldi; 8pm-2am daily; No credit cards)*, just north of Piazza Garibaldi, looks like every college bar in the States. The clientele, with their appetite for copious amounts of beer and their preference for skimpy, flashy clothes, are hauntingly reminiscent of college life circa 1985. Rock out with the rest of them to heavy metal's softest hits—Gun's and Roses and Bon Jovi are on heavy (no pun intended) rotation here. This big open room has lots of cozy nooks to settle into in the big booths. The crowds pile in around 11pm. The beers are yours for 7,000L a pint, and cocktails are 8-10,000L.

club scene

The choice of clubs isn't large here, but what there is has style. Prepare to look good to fit in.

The latest greatest place to hit Parma's nightlife is **FSU** *(Via Emilia Est 142; Tel 0339/581-840; Bus 3 to San Lazarro; 6pm-2am daily; V, MC)*, *which stands for* Falana Sushi Underground. Just a short cab ride east on Via Emilia (or a 30-minute walk), this ultra-modern spot sports all the trappings of a scenester hangout—cool decor, fancy cocktails, and pretty people. The popular happy hour from 6 to 8pm attracts students and young professionals alike, all of whom mingle over free *aperitivo* and relief from the normally high drink prices (10-15,000L for cocktails). With a kitchen/dining room, a "living room" or bar space, and a dance space, each playing different music, there's something for everyone. Music tends to be more alternative or DJ-crafted.

The fashion crowd still flocks to **Dadaumpa** *(Via Emilia Est 48; Tel 0521/483-802; Bus 3 to San Lazarro; 10pm-late; Cover 20,000L; No credit cards)*, which is just a few minutes closer to town. An elegant, slightly formal feel surrounds the small dance floor. Everything about Dadaumpa is exclusive and elegant, from the styly, sleek decor to the conversation clusters. You get the sense that no one wants to mess up their Prada slingbacks by having tipsy businessmen stepping all over them, but they're more than happy to make conversation and sway back and forth a bit.

Gavanasa Club [see *bar and live music scene,* above] is another, slightly more chill, DJ-fueled option.

arts scene

It doesn't come as a surprise that an artsy town like Parma would have more than its fair share of galleries, theaters, and public art spaces. Even some of the bars, like **Tonic** [see *bar scene,* above], have turned into makeshift exhibition spaces.

VISUAL ARTS

The tiny, brightly-lit **Kalos Arte Contemporaneo** *(Via F. Petrarca 1/C; Tel 0521/503-454; 9:30am-12:30pm/4-8pm Mon-Sat; V, MC)* exhibits some of the most cutting edge paintings and sculptures in Italy. The two-storied gallery is worth a visit—and maybe you'll be lucky enough to stumble into one of their famous opening parties. Just around the corner from the Duomo.

Gallery Spaces at Palazzo Pilotta [see *culture zoo*, below] have exhibited international shows from big names like Richard Serra and Peter Greenway—much more avant-garde than you'd expect for a municipal space. Painting, sculpture, multi-media exhibits are common.

Galleria S. Ludovico *(corner of Via Cavour and Borgo del Parmigiano; Tel 0521/218-041; 10am-1pm/4pm-7pm Tue-Sun, Closed Mon)* attracts intriguing modern shows that you can explore for free. Architecture and design is the main focus.

▶▶PERFORMING ARTS

Teatro Teatro Cinghio *(Largo 8 Marzo; Tel 0521/967-088; 10:30am-1:30pm/3:30pm-showtime; Cover varies; V, MC, DC)* is a popular venue for music, from classical piano or blues to symphonies. This tiny theater, with no more than 150 seats, is also the seat of Parma's Music Academy, which explains their diverse, and often excellent, lineup.

With its 1-ton chandelier and accompanying neo-classical decorations, **Teatro Regio** is the pride of Parma. *(Via Garibaldi 16; Tel 0521/218-685; 10am-1pm/4-6pm Mon-Fri, 10am-noon Sat, closed Sun; 5,000L entrance, 1-3,000L student; V, MC, AE)*. Built to the lavish standards of its patron, one very wealthy Mary-Louise, it opened for opera performances in 1829. Opera lovers come from all over to pay this house a visit—you should at least duck inside and steal a glance. It's the main venue for the annual Verdi Opera Festival, but you can also catch jazz and orchestral concerts here.

There are performances year-round in affiliation with the **Serata al Parco** *(Il Teatro al Parco; Tel 0521/992-004 or Tel 0521/993-818; Shows begin between 8-9:30pm; 20,000L tickets; 16,000L students; V, MC)* music series. Stop by tourist info for a list of upcoming outside concerts. You'll find international world music acts, from opera singers to Italian gypsy music, as well as visiting theater groups. Good news—there's a bar.

CULTURE ZOO

Every Italian city has a favorite square, and Parma's is Piazza Garibaldi, as good a spot as any to start your cultural tour. The facade of the Palazzo Comunale (1673) is a stunning example of Parma's architecture, though there really isn't anything inside to drag you in. Since most visitors are here for music and food, the churches are often empty and the museums quiet.

Duomo *(Piazza Duomo; Tel 0521/235-886; Bus 1 to Via Garibaldi; head toward Duomo down Via Melloni; 9am-1pm/3-7pm daily; Free* *entrance):* Construction started on this, one of Italy's best examples of a Romanesque cathedral, back in 1059. When an earthquake seriously damaged it in 1117, pious old Parma had a chance to re-decorate. Three levels of colonnades, or loggias, adorn the facade, and the 13th-century bell tower that rises off to one side is all that remains of the twin towers that used to bookend the church. Inside, Coreggio's masterpiece, *The Assumption of the Virgin* (1522-1534), draws a heavenly glance upwards. As you gaze at Mary rising into a billow of pink and yellow light, you can understand why Correggio is heralded as ushering in the Baroque period.

Baptistry *(Piazza Duomo; Tel 0521/235-886; 9am-12:30pm/3-7pm daily; 5,000L admission; 1,000L students; No credit cards):* Resist the temptation to strike comparisons between Parma's famed Romanesque Baptistery and a big, pink, birthday cake. Completed in 1307, this octagonal building is a stunning architectural feat. Home to Antelami's beautiful sculpture cycle of the 12 months, the seasons, and their corresponding astrological signs.

The Church of St. John the Evangelist *(Piazzale San Giovanni; Tel 0521/235-592; Bus 1 to Via Garibaldi; Head toward Duomo down Via Melloni; 9am-noon/3-6pm daily; Free entrance; The Pharmacy is open from 9am-1:30pm Tue-Sun; Tel 0521/233-309; 4,000L admission; No credit cards):* Parma's quirkiest collections of sights are housed in this complex, off behind the Duomo. The church and Abbey next door date back to the 10th century, even though they've been souped-up with a Baroque facade. Correggio again steals the show here, this time with his *Vision of San Giovanni,* one of the artist's finest works. The abbey, just outside the church, consists of three curious rooms that make up the *Historical Pharmacy,* where monks mixed up some witchy potions to cure everything from the common cold to a case of the evil spirits. The "Hall of the Mortars" is decorated with frescos of ancient medical luminaries, such as Hippocrates, Avicenna, and Eusculapius, and the "Hall of the Mermaid" displays old medical books and documents.

Palazzo della Pilotta *(Piazza della Pace; Bus 1 to Via Garibaldi, get out when you see the palace on your right; See numbers for respective museums below):* You can't miss this imposing fortress of a building on Via Garibaldi. It was once the homestead of the influential Farnese family that ruled during Parma's flourish during the Renaissance. The lawns are a great spot for an afternoon picnic, where you can soak up what's left of this Renaissance timepiece and admire the juxtaposition of the old with the modern additions. Heavily bombed during WWII, it's been restored into a public arts and museum space.

Galleria Nazionale *(Pilotta Palace; Tel 0521/233-309; 9am-1:30pm Tue-Sun; 12,000L admission; No credit cards):* Parma's most comprehensive collection of artwork from the 13th to the 19th centuries owes its success to the good taste of Marie-Louise. Important pieces from many genres are housed in room after grandiose room. Some stars of the show are Leonardo da Vinci's *Head of a Woman,* local talent Parmigianino's *St. Catherine's Marriage,* and many, many paintings by Correggio.

Teatro Farnese *(Pilotta Palace; Tel 0521/233-309; 9am-:30pm Tue-Sat; 4,000L; No credit cards):* Giovanni Battista (Argenta) Aleotti was the creative force behind this 17th-century theater carved from wood. Officially opened in 1628 for the marriage of Margherita de' Medici to Duke Odoardo Farnese, it came to house the kind of over-the-top theatrical performances the Renaissance actors were known for. A machine for moving actors above the stage, for changing scenes, and most impressively, for flooding the auditorium for the celebrated mock water battles are just a few of the innovations you can study here. It all came to an end in 1944, when the theater was badly bombed. Reconstruction began almost immediately, and today the place is completely restored.

National Archeological Museum *(Palazzo della Pilotta; Tel 0521/233-718; 9-6am Tue-Sun; 4,000L admission; No credit cards):* The best known artifact on display here is the *Tabula Alimentaria* (no, it's not a grocery list), an etched tablet found near Piacenza, dating back to around 100 B.C. Though the collection may not be the most stunning you've seen (a mixed bag of Etruscan, Roman, and Greek art, sculpture, and pottery), it is pretty cool that this museum dates back to 1760, when it was built to display the findings from excavations.

Parco Ducal (Ducal Gardens) *(Entrance just over Ponte Verdi, from Pilotta Palace; Tel 0521/230-023; Bus 11 to Via Piacenza; 7am-5:30pm Dec, Jan, 7am-6pm Nov, Feb, 6:30am-7pm Oct, Mar, Apr, 6am-12pm May, Sept):* Spotted with sculptures, centuries-old trees and foliage, and a few palaces thrown in for good measure, this is one of the city's most relaxing spots for soaking up some culture. The Ducal Gardens occupy a large chunk of the city on the western bank of the river, across from Piazza Pilotta. If you haven't had your fill of Parmigianino frescos, there are a few more in the palace **Eucherio San Vitale** *(9am-12pm Mon-Sat; 5,000L; No credit cards),* which was built by Giorgio da Erba in 1520. The awesome Ducal Palace, with it's ornate facade, is a marvel to walk around and observe. Now used for municipal purposes, the inside offers little to visitors.

modification

Tattoo Daniele *(Borgo G. Tommasini 12/A; Tel 0521/231-455; 11am-8pm daily; No credit cards),* affiliated with the Academia Beauty Workshop, is not your average tattoo parlor. It looks more like a salon, which may be a good thing, if you're getting ready to change your look forever. There are books of designs that you can flip through, but these guys are also happy to help you bring your own original idea to life.

city sports

In the summer, folks flock to **Parma Piscina Comunale** *(Via Moletolo c/o Centro Polisportivo Moletolo; Tel 0521/853-646; Bus 5 to Piscina; 9am-7pm daily from June to Sept; 9,000L weekday, 11,000L weekend)* for a little exercise. Located north of town, about 8 blocks north of the station, the pool is just a short bus trip on the number 5. If you're visiting in the winter, the covered **Giacomo Ferrari Piscina** *(Via Zarotto 41; Tel 0521/486-856; 1-3pm/7-11:30pm Tue; 8:30am-11:30pm Thur, 1-3pm Fri; 9:30am-12:30pm/2:30-5:30 Sat, 3-7pm Sun; Closed summer; 11,000L)*, on the eastern edge of the Parco Ferrari, is a popular place to warm up.

There's a climbing wall at **Sprint** *(Strada Martinella 88; Tel 0521/648-802; Bus 2 to Alberi di Vigatto)*, a fitness center a 15-minute bus ride south of town. Call ahead to reserve a climb time. For the real thing, contact **CAI (Club Alpino Italiano)** *(Viale Piacenza 40; Tel 0521/984-901; 6-7:30pm Wed, 6-7:30pm/9-10:30pm Thur)*, a group of locals who plan two or three outdoor events weekly. It's appropriately positioned just north of the Parco Ducale, where the town's athletes congregate all day, every day. Give a call to tag along.

STUFF

Parma's personality is a mix of collegiate liberalism and cultural sophistication, so the shopping's varied and interesting. Borgo XX Marzo, between Strada della Reppublica and the Duomo, is jam-packed with small family-run businesses and funky boutiques. Go to Via Mazzini for big-name, commercial stores.

▶▶**BOUND**

Fiaccadori *(Via al Duomo 8; Tel 0521/282-445; 10am-1:15pm/4pm-7:30pm Mon-Sat; V, MC)*, on the main drag between Strada della Reppublica and the Duomo, is the kind of family-owned bookstore that's sadly disappearing rapidly across Italy (and in almost every other country). Since 1829, this small but comprehensive store has sold fiction, art books, textbooks, and an enormous collection of cultural guides to the city for its English-speaking visitors. Their selection of fiction in English is more robust than other places.

▶▶**DUDS**

Going to the theater with nothing to wear? Stop by **Gazzabuglio** *(Via 20 Marzo 13b; Tel 051/283-379; 10:30am-12:30pm/5-8pm; V, MC)* and pick up something as theatrical as the stage sets. Since 1975, this tiny store has specialized in great vintage clothing from the turn of the century to the sixties, with jewelry, hats, gloves, and other accoutrements to match. Don't expect thrift store prices—do expect to spend some time here, drooling over these fashion timepieces.

If your fashion sense is more Kate Moss than Holly Golightly, check out **Central Park 3** *(Strada Reppublica 21/E; Tel 0521/208-070; 10am-2pm/3:30-7:30pm Mon-Sat, noon-3pm Sun; V, MC)*, a big, brightly lit, music-booming kind of place that sells all the brands that are fit to sell—Replay, CK, Guess, the works.

▶▶**TUNES**

Indie, dance, jazz, heavy metal, and rock classics are squeezed into the tiny **La Nuova Crispoli** *(Via Farini 5; Tel 0521/289-508; 9am-7:30pm Mon-Wed, Fri, 9am-1pm Thur, 9am-1pm/3:30-7:30pm; No credit cards)*, which is presided over by one of the sweetest punks in town. The owner here has the 411 on the local live music scene (uh, Bologna), and is happy to chat with you for a while. There's always a sale bin, and a listening station for the album of the week. Located in the heart of town, on the road that Via Mazzini turns into as it heads east.

eats

If Bologna is the belly of Italy, Parma is the pantry where all the best ingredients came from. People make pilgrimages here to taste Parmigiano-Reggiano and Prosciutto di Parma straight from the source [see *ham and cheese, parma style,* below]. That huge rep—and all those out-of-towners—make it easy to stiff tourists, so try to stick to where the locals hang. A handwritten menu is always a good sign, and there are a lot of them here in Parma. Don't pass up the opportunity to try ingredients you won't find anywhere else in Italy, including *Culatello di Zibello, Salame* from the little town of Felino, and wild mushrooms from Valtaro. The pastas are of unsurpassed quality and variety—all of the places listed below make theirs by hand.

▶▶CHEAP

It is possible to overdose on tortellini and pizza, you know. Should that time come, check out **M. African Kitchen** *(Via Albertelli 4/A; Tel 0521/289-527; Bus 1 to Garibaldi; 10:30am-2:30pm/5:30-10:30pm Tue-Sun; No credit cards),* a little take-away joint between the station and downtown. Coconut rice with shrimp (10,000L), curry stew (10,000L), fried plantains (7,000L), and okra soup (3,000L) are a nice change from red sauce, and the bright, busy storefront, filled with immigrants and other curious eaters, is fun and welcoming. There's not a lot of atmosphere, but with food like this, who cares?

What **Pizzaria Il Poeta** *(Via Garibaldi 21/A; Tel 0521/207-588; Bus 1 to Garibaldi; 10:30am-2:30pm/5-10pm Tue-Sun; No credit cards)* lacks in ambiance, it makes up for in taste. This popular little take-away pizza-by-the-slice joint across from Palazzo Pilotta answers every traveler-on-a-budget's dining dilemma. Entire round pizzas will cost you only 6-7,000L, so grab one and a bottle of wine and head for Piazza Garibaldi. There's a whole range of *piandina* (flat bread sandwiches) stuffed with ham, artichokes, red peppers, and other tasty treats for no more than 3,500L. The large square slices and calzones cost 3,000L.

Il Poeta's rival, **Pronto Pizza** *(Strada Garibaldi 55; Tel 0521/38-69-27; Bus 1 to Garibaldi; 12:30-2:30pm, 6-11pm daily; No credit cards)* is just as cheap and just as good, but offers a little more elbow room and a few stools if you'd rather eat inside. This family-run place serves up innovatively prepared pies and slices for 2,000-4,000L. Try the *gorgonzola,* with huge chunks of melted blue cheese, or the four seasons with ham, artichokes, and mushrooms. A slice and a drink for 3,000L is one of the best deals in town.

▶▶DO-ABLE

Parma's most celebrated restaurant is relatively new to the scene. **I Du Brasè Trattoria** *(Piazze le Cervi, 5; Tel 0521/286-098; Bus 1, 8, or 15* *to Via Mazzini; 12-3:30pm/7:30-10:30pm Mon-Sat, Closed Sun; 10,000L first course; 12-18,000L second course; Cover 3,000L; V,MC),* hidden in a quiet courtyard just off Via Reppublica, serves rustic Parmigiano food at great prices. The decor is formal—antique prints hang on pale yellow walls, spacious tables are set with fine silver and linen. Vittorio Trappase, a retired train engineer, and his amazing cook of a wife, Louisa, run this place with their hearts and souls. Start with one of her soft and hearty pasta dishes, like fettuccine ai funghi porcini or tortelli d'erbetta (fresh herbs and cheese ravioli), are awesome. You can smell the tartufi neri

ham and cheese, parma style

They're two of the world's most famous foods, and even a small serving costs an arm and a leg. So you can understand why local groups that promote their sales are interested in your knowing everything that goes into the cultivation of Parmigiano Reggiano cheese and Prosciutto d' Parma ham. A little history and hard work, and an understanding of why they tastes the way they do, helps sales.

Prosciutto d' Parma owes its soft texture and intense flavor to patience, skill, and good air. The hind legs of pigs are cured in sea salt for a month, washed, and then hung to dry for anywhere from 8 months to 2 years. Though the process varies very little from producer to producer, every ham tastes different. The **Consorzio del Prosciutto di Parma** will happily let you sample the goods when you take a free publicity tour. Contact Signore Lepoati, Schianchi, or Rossetti at 0521/243-987, or stop by Via M. Dell'Arpa 8/B to arrange an outing.

The salty, almost spicy, Parmaggiano Reggiano is about as different from the powdered stuff that Kraft sells in those green cardboard shakers as it is from Swiss cheese. Reggiano can trace its culinary roots back to the 13th century, when its cows were first raised on the plain between Parma and Reggio Emilia for their milk to be made into cheese. Though the cheeses made in Parma were always considered a different thing entirely from those made in Reggio, in the fifties the towns came together to strengthen forces and take over the world. Today, the **Conzorzio Del Parmigiano Reggiano** *(Via Gramsci 26/C; Tel 521/292-700)* will show you how it's done during a two-hour tasting tour, and teach you a few shopper's tricks to help you spot the real thing.

risotto (which has to be ordered for two people and is a bargain at 16,000L) as soon as it leaves the kitchen, but nothing prepares you for the intense taste. The main courses are mostly grilled meats with sauces— chicken with black truffles, rabbit with red wine, etc. The wine list is reasonable, with many local choices hovering around 20,000L. Try the torta di ricotta (5,000L), a sweet cheesecake covered with melted bittersweet chocolate, for dessert.

Trattoria Corrieri *(Via Conservatorio 1; Tel 0521/234-426; Bus 8 or 15 to Piazza Garibaldi; 12-2:30pm/7:30-10:30pm, Closed Sun; V, MC, AE),* just a block to the east of the Ponte di Mezzo off Via Oberdan, is packed with English-speaking tourists sent over by their hotels for a real "local" meal, but this isn't just some tourist trap—take a look in the kitchen and you'll see the tortellini being rolled by hand and the soup being stirred in big steaming crocks. The dining room feels more touristy, loud and fun—you'll hardly notice that your waiter hasn't been by in an hour or so. Start with one of their great *affettati piatti,* plates of slice local salamis and prosciuttos (12,000L) and *Gnocco,* delicious fried bread with cheese (5,000L). The pastas and gnocchi are all super-fresh and filling, and much better than the meat dishes.

Vegetarians and flava hounds should pilgrimage up near the train station to eat at **Apriti Sesamo** *(Via Montecorno 4; Tel 0521/270-274; 12:30-3pm Mon-Thur, 12:30-3pm/8-11pm Fri-Sat, closed Sun; www.studiopag.it/apritisesamo; apritisesamo96@hotmail.com; 20,000L lunch fixed price, 30,000L dinner fixed price; V, MC),* a *ristorante biologico* (macrobiotic restaurant). This sunny dining room has yellow walls with murals of green plants and smiling suns, colorful tablecloths, and shiny, happy people to serve you. Everything on the organic menu is Italian-inspired, from the vegetarian lasagna to the carrot cake. The menu is a multi-course set meal, so bring your appetite. Pay close attention to directions: On the right hand side of the station (to the east, stage left), there's a large street called Via Trento. Hang a left onto it, heading away from the center of town, and then take your first left, onto Via Monte Corno. The restaurant is just to the left.

▶▶**SPLURGE**

If you have one good meal in Parma, save up your lire for **La Greppa** *(Via Garibaldi 39/A; Tel 0521/233-686; Bus 1 to Via Garibaldi; 12:30-2pm/7:30-10:30pm Wed-Sun, closed July; 22-32,000L main entree; V, MC, AE, DC),* located across from Pilotta Palace. Another talented husband-and-wife team runs this cozy restaurant. The specialties of the house will send you back in time—most of the recipes are culled from a vintage collection that dates back to the 1500s. *Quadracci* (cabbage and ham pasta) and the eponymous *Pappardelle alla Greppia* (with mushrooms and cream) are just a few of the dishes that'll knock your socks off.

crashing

There is no shortage of beds in Parma, but only a few of them are in the center of town, so make sure you call ahead.

▶▶CHEAP

For being in such a cool location inside the ramparts of the Cittadella Fortress, **Cittadella Ostello** *(Parco Citadella 5; Tel 0521/961-434; Bus 9 from the station, or walk down Strada Farini until you reach Viale delle Rimembranze, and hang a right on Via Passo Buole. Walk through the gates, and you'll see the hostel; 17,000L per bed; Non-members pay an extra 6,000L for a stamp, and after six stamps at any IYH hostel, you're a member; No credit cards)* is pretty inconvenient. With its 11:30 curfew, and lockout during the day, it's almost better to cough up the few extra thousand lira to come and go as you please without having to deal with a 20-minute walk. But just in case you're looking forward to a night of R & R, this is a cozy spot, situated within the medieval walls of an old fortress.

You're almost better off camping at **Cittadella** *(Via Parco Cittadella 5; Tel 0521/961-434; Open April September 1; 15,000L per night)*, the adjacent campground, if you have all the equipment.

▶▶DO-ABLE

Without a doubt, your first hotel choice should be **Lazzaro** *(Via XX Marzo 4; Tel 052/127-27-17; Bus 1 to Via Garibaldi, head east down Strada da Pisacane, and after you pass the baptistery, hang a right on XX Marzo; 58,000L single w/out bath, 70,000L single w/bath, 95,000L double w/bath; V, MC)*. It couldn't get more central than this—your windows will overlook the busy, pedestrian-packed street that leads from the Duomo to Via Mazzini/Strada Reppubblica. The restaurant downstairs is a little touristy and overpriced, but the rooms are the best bargain in town. The seven cozy and clean rooms fill up quickly, so calling ahead is essential.

You're totally on your own at **Hotel Brozzi** *(Via Trento 11; Tel 052/127-27-17; 55,000L single, 78,000L double w/out bath, 90,000L double w/ bath, 12,000L breakfast; No credit cards)*. Totally. In fact, to check in, you have to lug your stuff next door to the three-star Astoria (stop yer drooling), where you'll get the key for your much more modest digs and be sent on your merry way. Although it's rough around the edges, and looks a little dormy, it is safe. The brand-new showers in the hallway are spacious, though the furniture in the rooms could be in better shape.

Albergo Moderno *(Piazza la Stazione via Cecchi 4; Tel 0521/772-647 and 772-648; Bus 9; 60,000L single w/out bath, 80,000L single w/bath, 90,000L double w/out bath, 110,000L double w/bath, 7,500L breakfast; V, MC)* is within a stone's throw of the station—you'll see the sign to the right as soon as you exit. This simple, institutional hotel has 46 rooms, all equipped with phone.

The Albergo Amorini *(Via Gramsci 37; Tel 0521/983-239; Bus 1 to Via Mazzini; Change to Bus 3 at Piazza Garibaldi to Ospedale Maggiore stop; 55,000L single w/out bath, 80,000L double w/out bath, 110,000L doubles w/bath; V, MC)* is about a 20-minute walk out of town, down through Via M. D'Azeglio, which turns into Via Gramsci after it crosses Piazza Santa Croce. It's an easy, 10-minute bus ride, and all 18 rooms are clean and equipped with phones. There's a huge Co-op market just across the street.

The favorite choice for staying close to the station is **Leon d'Oro** *(Via Le Fraggi 4; Tel 052/177-31-82; 50,000L single w/out bath; 80,000L double w/out bath),* a cozy *albergo* above a busy restaurant that looks like it was decorated by your grandmother. There are only 16 rooms, and the price is right, so call ahead.

▸▸**SPLURGE**

If you're looking for a splurge, check into **Button** *(Strada San Vitale; Tel 0521/20809; Bus 1 or 8 to Via Mazzini; Fax 0521/238-783; 175,000L double, all with private bath, breakfast included; V, MC, AE, DC).* Right off Piazza Garibaldi, this place has all the fine features...in addition to TV, phones, and nice tile baths, there's comfy linen and a 24-hour bar (yep, you heard right).

need to know

Currency Exchange There are numerous **ATM's** on and around **Via Mazzini.**

Tourist Information The kids who work at **(I.A.T)** *(Via Melloni 1/B; Tel 0521/218-889; Tel/Fax 0521/234-735; turismo@commune.parma.it)*

wired

Parma is pretty well connected. The cheapest, fastest, and most comfortable places to get online are:

Informagiovani *(Via Melloni 1/B; Tel 0521/218-749; 9am-1pm/3pm-7pm Mon-Sat; Free),* located in the same office as tourist info, has two computers that they lend out to the internet-starved masses. You're supposed to reserve ahead, but just ask nicely, and if no one's working on them at the moment, you'll usually be able to hop on and check email.

Libreria Fiaccadori [see *stuff,* above] has a pretty slow computer that it rents out by the hour (10,000L) and half hour (6,000L) from 9am-7:30pm, Mon-Fri and 10am-1pm/3:30-7:30pm Sun. If you're in a pinch, go ahead, but Informagiovani's just down the block.

Definitely the best-equipped and most comfortable spot to get online is **PC Help Cyber Point** *(Via D'Azeglio 72/D; Tel 0521/504-148; 9:30am-8pm Mon-Thur, Sat; 10,000L/hour; No credit cards).* Six super-fast computers are hooked up to DSL, each with printer access. Located right in the heart of the student district, it's also not a bad place to meet up with other cyberites.

know their town inside and out, and are happy to unload their knowledge on you. You're on your own as far as making hotel reservations, though. The office is located on the small street that runs from Via Garibaldi, across from Pilotta Palace, to the Duomo. There's a 24-hour automated info service in Italian: *Tel 0521/218-218.*

Health and Emergency Emergency: *113;* Ambulance: *118.* The main police station *(Tel 0521/2194)* is located at Borgo della posta 14. The **Opsedale Maggiore** *(Tel 0521/991-111, Bus 3)* is located down Via Gramsci, the small street that runs from Via Garibaldi, across from Pilotta Palace, to the Duomo.

Pharmacy Guareschi Farmacia *(Strada Farini 5; Tel 0521/282-240; 8am-1:30pm/4-7:30pm Mon-Fri; V, MC)* is smack in the middle of town.

Trains The **station** *(Tel 147/88088 for info, 0521/771-118 to reserve tickets)* is located at Piazza Carolo Alerto della Chiesa. Parma is right on the main Bologna-Milano line, and trains leave regularly for both.

Bus Lines out of the City The **TEP Bus line** *(Tel 0521/2141)* service both city stops and out of town destinations. The bus station is located just in front of Pilotta Palace, on Via P. Tosci. Tickets are 1,500L if you buy them before you get on the bus, but there are only automatic ticket machines, so bring change. Most stops are covered by the night buses 1N, 2N, 3N, and 4N that run after 8:30pm. For a taxi *(Tel 0521/206-929)* call any time.

Bike Rental City Bike *(Viale Mentana 8/A; Tel 0521/235-639; Summer only)* is just south of the train station on the main road.

Postal Just east from Pilotta Palace, across Via Garibaldi, is the **main post office** *(Via Pisacane 1; Tel 0521/233-623, Fax 0521/208-279; 8:30am-5:30pm Mon-Fri; 8:30am-1pm Sun).*

Internet See *wired,* above.

ravenna

When most of Italy was stuck in the dark ages, Ravenna was its one bright spot. Nowadays, busloads of fanny-packed tourists pour into the domed churches to gaze at Ravenna's star feature, the shimmering Roman and Byzantine mosaics—and to buy cheesy plaster reproductions of them at every other corner store. The good news is that most of these visitors wearing nylon walking suits are day-trippers, so when they hop back on the bus around five or six in the evening, the city is yours.

Ravenna isn't very large, and though you can easily check it out in a day or two, it's worth a long weekend. You'll see a lot more than just mosaics: there are great galleries, bars, and restaurants, and a beautifully preserved city center for strolling. There are more galleries, more alternative art spaces, and more theaters here than most Italian cities of its size (pop. 136,000). Don't expect a huge youth vibe here, but the piazzas and

ravenna bars clubs and culture zoo

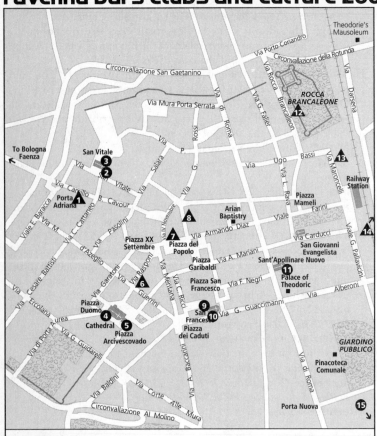

BARS/CLUBS ▲
Bar Rocca Brancaleone **12**
Bierhaus **13**
Buddy's Pub **14**
Horny Gap **6**
La Cantina del Capello **8**
Tazza D'Oro **7**
Verderame Café **1**

CULTURE ZOO ●
Basilica di Saint Apollinaire Nuovo **11**
Basilica di San Francesco **10**
Basilica di San Vitale **2**
Basilica di Sant'Apollinare in Classe **15**
Dante's Tomb **9**
Mauseleo di Galla Placidia **3**
Museo Arcivescovile **4**
Neoniano Baptisry **5**

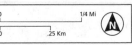

parks are popular hangouts every evening. There's no major university, but there are lots of art students; the University of Bologna's art history and preservation program draws international students year-round.

Ravenna feels more like a small town than a city, probably because most people live in the sprawling suburbs. But the city center bustles with friendly activity, and locals welcome tourists with open arms. People here are super-polite, from the way they courteously maneuver their bicycles around hordes of clueless tourists to the way they cordially tip their hats to one another when they pass on the street.

Ravenna is the oldest city in the region of Romagna, and has some of the best-preserved buildings from every architectural period. In fact, eight buildings are on the UNESCO world heritage list [see *culture zoo,* below]. It's not just the dazzle and glitter, nor the craftsmanship, but also the way in which religious and political themes were depicted that make the mosaics on these buildings so important. In order to understand the stories told by these *tesserea* (mosaics), you have to brush up on your history: Honorious, the emperor of a struggling Roman Empire, moved the capital from Rome to Ravenna in 402 A.D. The surrounding marshland was perceived as impenetrable, but as history would have it, the Visigoth-Barbarian armies took over in 473 anyway. Honorius's daughter, Galla Palacido, married the last of the Barbarian kings, Aleutia. In 540, Ravenna was re-conquered by Justinian, who established the city as the eastern capital of the Eastern Roman, or Byzantine, Empire. He and his wife, Theodora, were huge patrons of the arts, and commissioned some of Ravenna's most sparkling mosaics. The Byzantines ruled until the Lombards took over in 752. Don't search for external clues to the Byzantine influence, since most of the churches and buildings have been revamped and renovated to fit changing fashions over the years. Ravenna's medieval and Renaissance buildings are very well preserved, making it a joy to just stroll through the streets, snapping pictures. But all you need to do is step inside to be reminded of earlier influence of the East.

neighborhoods

The view isn't exactly dazzling when you walk out of the train station, east of the city center on **Piazza Farini.** Cheap hotels line the street in front of the station, to the north and the south, and there's a congested line of buses right out front—don't be tempted! To use buses when everything is within a 10-minute walk defeats the whole purpose of visiting Ravenna. One of the best things about coming here is strolling from church to church, through the beautifully preserved city center. To get to the center of town, walk straight down **Viale Farini,** which becomes **Via Diaz.** You'll pass a bunch of cafes and street-side candy vendors before you reach **Piazza del Popolo,** the heart of the city, where people meet and mingle all day long. **Tazza d'Oro,** the piazza's most popular cafe, should be your first stop in town. Everyone comes here at least once—maybe twice—a day, and it's a great place to get a sense of what's going on around town.

Via IV Novembre, is a pretty, pedestrian street that leads right into **Piazza Andrea Costa,** where the busy food market buzzes with activity. This Piazza marks the beginning of Ravenna's swankiest shopping district, **Via Cavour.** You can hang a right on **Via Salara** to get to tourist info, or follow your wallet down Cavour, dipping into boutiques, shoe stores, and other fashion-inclined establishments. **San Vitale and the museum complex** [see *culture zoo,* below] is just one block north, at the end of **Via Argentario.**

Ravenna's other sights are scattered around town. There's no grid pattern to the streets—they change names as you go, unexpectedly turn into dead-ends, and inevitably confound the crowds of map-holding tourists. And the map that the tourist office hands out doesn't help at all, unless your goal is to get lost. It shows the train station at the top of the map, as if it were north of the city center, but the station's actually east, so you'll be disoriented from the jump. Either rely on your own sense of direction or blindly follow the map, but don't try to combine the two. Actually, Ravenna is so small that you can see all the sights in one long day of trekking around and still leave plenty of time for getting lost, so don't worry about it.

hanging out

There are plenty of outdoor areas and cozy indoor cafes where you can just chill or kick off your night on the town. One of the most popular spots is **Rocca Brancaleone,** the remains of a 15th-century castle in the northern part of town. It's been restored into a public park; during summer there are free concerts and movies at the small outside amphitheater, where you can bring picnic baskets and blankets and plenty o' wine. The little **Café Brancaleaone** [see *bar, clubs, and live music scene,* below] is bustling morning, noon, and night with hanger-outers on the patio, reading the paper, writing in journals, making friends. Other popular spots for mid-day conversation and relaxation include **Verderame Café,** which looks like it was decorated by pre-Raphaelite drag queens [see *eats* below], and the central **Tazza d'Oro** [see *bars, clubs, and live music scene,* below].

Piazza del Popolo is be the epicenter of Ravenna's social life, but the covered galleria that links Via Ricci with **Dante's Tomb on Via Polenta** [see *culture zoo,* below] is the hangout of choice for Ravenna's rowdy youth. Groups of friends and amorous couples drink wine straight from the bottle, and cavort on the grass next to the poet's tomb. Very Goth.

bars, clubs, and live music scene

Ravenna's small, but it has a big rep as a tourist destination. But there aren't many bars and clubs, so most of the locals hop over to Marina di Ravenna, just a few kilometers to the east, to party [see **marina di ravenna,** below]—that's where to find a hell-raisin' good time.

Ravenna's most popular Italian bar—you know, the kind with the bow-tied waiters, where everyone from the cute couple with matching pierced eyebrows to the geezer drinking his morning grappa crowds the bar—is **Tazza d'Oro** (*Piazza del Popolo 11; Tel 0544/212-331; 11am-2pm/5:30-8:30pm daily, aperitivo hour 7-9pm, closed Sun in the winter, stays open until 2am in summer; 5-7,000L wine by the glass, 5,500L beer; No credit cards*). Located right on the corner of Ravenna's main piazza and Via IV Novembre, Tazza d'Oro is packed inside and out, morning, noon, and early evening. Without a doubt, their *aperativo* spread is the best in town—maybe even in all of Romagna. You won't just find your requisite bruschetta and olives with your drink, but cheese plates, assorted salamis, stuffed mushrooms, and other tasty treats are spread out on the long marble bar. Order a spritzer, or a glass of wine, and the bartender will fix you a plate and bring you a fork and knife. Once a week, they feature the wines and foods from a particular region in Italy, which means more free stuff for you.

The crowds of locals spill out of **La Cantina del Capello** (*Via IV Novembre 41; Tel 0544/219-876; 11-2am Mon-Sat, closed Mon afternoon; No credit cards*), just north of Piazza del Popolo, and into the street every night. If it's between 6:30 and 8:30pm, pass through and head straight for the bar, where an awesome spread of free finger food awaits you. The wines are what all these people come here for—there's a black board behind the bar that lists all the wines by the glass (3,000-10,000L). The tables in the amber-lit front room are for patrons of the wine bar, and if you snag one, hold on to it—this place gets packed with a young after-work crowd. If you're ready to move on to a whole meal, take a seat in the back dining rooms [see *eats,* below], where rustic Romagnan dishes are served.

Hidden away in Ravenna's prettiest park is **Bar Rocca Brancaleone** (*Via Ronca Broccaleone; Tel 0544/36094; 8am-7pm Mon-Sat, 9am-7pm Sun Oct-Mar, 8am-8pm Mon-Sat, 9am-8pm Sun Apr-Sept; 3-5,000L beer pint, 3,500-5,000L panini; No credit cards*), the narrow, wood-paneled

festivals and events

The annual **Ravenna Festival** (*Via Dante Alighieri 1; Tel 0544/249-211; Fax 0544/36303; www.operabuse.com/ mkhouse.cgi?house = wiraf*) is a week-long music event held in June and July that, since 1990, has attracted some of the finest musicians and conductors from around the world. Not to mention the crowds. The music is a mix of classical and contemporary. The entire town transforms itself into one big walking concert, and the bands and orchestras playing against the backdrop of Ravenna's churches are an unforgettable sight.

bar that's the perfect spot to unwind from your long day of church-hopping. The gregarious owners go out of their way to welcome guests to their little refuge, and are full of advice on where to go and what to see (they know the coolest clubs). In the summer, you can sit outside and eat one of the best bargain meals in town: 12,000L gets you a *piandina* (Romagnan flatbread sandwich), wine, gelato, and a coffee.

A cross between Chuck E. Cheese and a sports bar/disco, **Buddy's Pub** *(Via Magazzini Anteriori 18; Tel 0544/591-059; 7am-1pm/7:30pm-2:30am daily, 'til 3:30 on weekends; No cover; No credit cards),* back behind the train station, is a surreally fun experience. Buddy's pub looks just like your average Italian cafe from the front. But walk through the bar, past the bathrooms and the four computer terminals where backpackers browse the web (9,000L per hour), and you're in the world of flashing lights, neon bar signs, and overly enthusiastic DJs. The crowd here is young and lively, running between the tables to chat while they're chowing down on a late dinner, and then bouncing out to the mezzanine dance floor. There's no consistent vibe to this place—the themes change nightly, bringing a mixed crowd of locals, backpackers, and students, all looking for fun. Each Monday night brings music and food from a different country each week—Greece, France, and Germany have all had their turn. Tuesday night is blackjack night, when there are some pitchers of beer to be won. Wednesday is Tattoo and Astrology night (huh?), Thursday is Mexican food with Latin dancing, and Friday is "Roulette", with whatever music they feel like playing. Saturday and Sunday are DJ nights, with free pizza on Sundays. Main dishes cost between 8,000 and 18,000L, but there's always free popcorn.

On the flier for **Horny Gap** *(Piazza Kennedy, off Via Guerino; Tel 0544/215-572; Bus 1, 2, or 3 to Piazza Caduti; 8:30pm-2am; www.localionline.com; No cover; No credit cards),* it says that you're not allowed to call it "ex-Kennedy", Kennedy being the name of the bar that used to occupy this dark and sprawling subterranean space southwest of Piazza del Popolo. Someone should tell these guys that their name just does *not* translate well in English, because it's really a very cool place, with reasonably priced drinks. Punks, preps, club kids—they're all here, rubbing shoulders and getting along famously. Like Buddy's, Horny Gap throws on a different theme each night: Monday nights they air a radio show, Tuesday is always live music, Wednesdays they play house, Thursdays they play soft rock, and Friday through Sunday they bring in DJs from Rimini and Riccione. The occasional and ever-so-popular strip night, when local lovelies strip down to their bikini and make good use of the slicked-up pole, is a sight to behold, and it's all in good fun—if you miss it, be sure to check out the photos on the wall.

The dark, dank, and smoky **Bierhaus** *(Via Maroncelli 5; Tel 0544/30098; 8pm-3am Mon-Sat, closed for a few weeks in July or August depending on the owners' vacation schedule; No credit cards)* is where all the local punks and Goths get their fix of cheap beer and loud music. This narrow bar, located right down the block from the station across from

Hotel Ravenna, is filled with unfinished wood booths (watch for splinters in yer keister). There's a great selection of German beers on tap (6-8,000L pint), and a menu of bar snacks, like panini and fries, is available till closing time. Perhaps the best juke box in town, with a huge collection of early punk and pop classics from the Sex Pistols to the Smiths.

arts scene

Ravenna's contemporary art scene is hopping, from photography to abstract painting, sculpture to modern mosaics. Churches have been born again as makeshift galleries and public buildings with a spare room or two constantly exhibiting the latest-greatest talents. A few conventional gallery spaces attract international modern exhibits, and admission is almost always free.

▶▶VISUAL ARTS

Art M Studio *(Via G. Mazzini 62; Tel 0544/407-070; 10-noon Tue, Wed, Thur, 5:30-7:30pm every afternoon except Thursday, closed Sun; V, MC)* is a small white space that is the canvas for local and international contemporary artists. A mix of media is on display. To get there, walk south from Piazza dei Caduti, in the southern part of town along Via Mazzini.

Imagine an enormous Renaissance church stripped of all the religious art, all the pews, and the alter. The effect is expansive and perfect for the kinds of exhibitions being shown at **Chiesa di San Domenico** *(Via Cavour; Tel 0544/219-938 or 800/303-999; 10am-6pm Tue-Sun; www.Ravennaservice.net; 5,000L admission)* a former church now being used as an exhibit space displaying well-researched, beautifully-curated shows that change every few months. Marc Chagall's *Bible sketches* were last seen here. Located right on Via Cavour, close to Via IV Novembre.

Palazzo del Tribunale *(Via D'Azeglio 2; Tel 0544/482-515; 9am-6pm Mon-Fri, 10am-1pm Sat, Sun; www.commune.ra.it/eventi; Suggested donations)* is another public art space, located in the west end of town, that focuses on photography and documentary studies exhibits.

More modern than contemporary, the two-story **Galleria Patrizia Poggi** *(Via Argentario 21; Tel 0544/219-898; 4-7:30pm Tue-Fri, 10:30am-12:30pm/4-7:30pm Sat, closed Sun; www.galleriapoggi.com; Free)* hosts the kind of exhibits that people come from out of town to see, like a recent collection of Man Ray photographs. They have great materials in English, so you can understand what you're looking at. Just one block south of San Vitale, on a small road that runs perpendicular between Via San Vitale and Via Cavour.

▶▶PERFORMING ARTS

Music and art go hand and hand here, and from the operas at the newly renovated **Teatro Aliglieri** to the street concerts during the **Ravenna Festival** [see *festival and events,* below], the music of this city is as much a reason for the city's popularity as its mosaics.

You can't miss the **Teatro Rossini** *(Piazza Cavour 17; Tel 0545/38542, Fax 0545/38482; Performances start at 8:30pm; www.teatro*

rossini.it; teatro@provincia.ra.it; 9-37,000L tickets, depending on your seat); it sits on Piazza Cavour, just northwest of Piazza del Popolo. Drop by tourist info [see *need to know,* below] for the current offerings that run the gamut from opera and dance to Shakespeare. Built in 1757, it was recently restored to its original elaborate, formal, and plush Baroque design.

Teatro di Tradizione Dante Alighieri *(Via Mariani 2; Tel 0544/32577, Fax 0544/215-840; 10am-2pm daily, 4-6pm Tue and Thur; www.teatroalighieri.org; 15-60,000L (under 25ers get a 30 percent discount); V, MC, AE, DC),* built in 1838, has been renovated back to its earlier age of splendor. The opera sets here are known to be quite a spectacle, and locals and tourists alike get all gussied up for them. Much of Ravenna's music festival [see *festivals and events,* below] take place here, as do ballet and other dance performances. Located just east of Piazza Garibaldi, on the main road to the station.

CULTURE ZOO

The first thing you should do is plunk down 12,000L for a **Ravenna Visit Card** *(www.ravennavisitcard.com),* available at any of the sights it gives access to. The one-time fee gets you into the Basilica di San Apolinaire Nuovo, the Basilica dello S. Santo, the Archepiscopal Museum of San Andrea, the Basilica of San Vitale, the Mausoleum of Galla Placidia, the Adrian Baptistery and the Battistero della Neoniano.

Museum and Basilica of San Vitale (Museo e Basilica di San Vitale) *(Via San Vitale 17; Tel 0544/219-938; Bus 1 to Via Marche; 9am-6:30pm daily; 6,000L admission; No credit cards):* The mosaics in this 6th-century domed church are some of the most brilliantly dazzling in all of Ravenna. The ring of green marble columns and huge arches seems impressive until you situate yourself under the beardless Christ, the focal point of this mosaic cycle—it blows those columns and arches right out of the water.

Mauseleo di Galla Placidia *(Via San Vitale, behind the church and through the gardens; Tel 0544/219-938; 9am-6:30pm daily; 4,000L):* Although it looks like nothing more than the ancient equivalent of a tool shed from the outside, this small mausoleum is home to both the remains of Galla, the sister of Honorius and wife of Visigoth king Ataulf, and some of Ravenna's most stunning mosaics. The arch above the crypt is covered in a 3-D labyrinthine design.

Basilica di San Francesco *(Piazza San Francesco; Tel 0544/33256; 7:30-noon/3-9pm daily; Free admission, donations encouraged):* As you stand looking at the underwater mosaics, you'll find yourself wondering where all the tourists are. This church was the site of Dante's funeral on Sept 15th, 1321, but he's laid to rest next door (where all the tourists are). This gargantuan church has always had an unlucky history—the original structure started sinking in the 1100s, and the Roman mosaics that once adorned the floor behind the alter are now submerged in about 3 feet of water. Despite the fact that these beautiful black and white mosaics are a little soggy, they're beautifully preserved. Check out the lucky goldfish who make this their home. A visit here is a must.

Dante's Tomb *(Via Dante Aliglieri; 8am-7pm daily; No admission):* The poet's final resting-place is here in this little ornamental mausoleum. He died in Ravenna while under the patronage and protection of the Di Polenta family. So where are the guards? Nowhere in sight. Anyone can wander in and pay their respects, at any hour. You gotta wonder if it's really him in there. He wasn't always so unprotected—the locals had him buried in a concrete bunker to escape WWII bombing raids.

Neoniano Baptistery *(Via Battistero, off Piazza del Duomo; Tel 0544/219-938; 9:30-4:30 daily; 5,000L including admission to the Museum):* Pagan meets Christian in this octagonal baptistery that was built over the site of Roman baths, off Piazza Duomo. The frescos were commissioned by Bishop Neonei, and were completed in 458 A.D. Their style reflects the earlier, more classical mosaic motifs. The faithful would get dunked in the octagonal font in the center, looking up at the mosaic of John baptizing Jesus. Notice how each of the apostles surrounding Jesus is made to look like an individual through different facial features and hairstyles. The old man off to the side is the personification of the river Jordan, an artistic trope that's more pagan than Christian.

Museo Arcivescovile *(Piazza Arcivescovado; Tel 0544/219-938; 9:30am-4:30pm daily; 5,000L including admission to the baptistery):* Your ticket to the Baptistery includes a visit to this little museum, which includes Archbishop Maximian's carved ivory throne and some impressive mosaics in the Capello di St. Andrea. The mosaics depict a heavily ornamented warrior Christ, but other than that, there's not much to see.

Basilica of Sant'Apollinare in Classe *(Via Romea Sud; Tel 0544/473-643; Bus 4 or 44 to Piazza Caduti; 8:30am-7:30pm daily; 4,000L):* Located 5 miles southeast of town (don't even try walking—bus 44 leaves from the station every hour), this dedication to Ravenna's influential bishop, St. Apollinare, contains an apse with some of Ravenna's most dazzling mosaics, dating back to the sixth century. The birds, the blue and gold hues, and the twelve apostles—represented by sheep that stand attendant to the saint—are the reasons to come here. The church is awe-inspiring and the mosaics may be the best ones this side of Istanbul.

Basilica of Saint Apollinare Nuovo *(Via di Roma; Tel 0544/219-930; 9:30-4:30 daily; 5,000L):* To many, this is the grand-daddy of mosaic cycles—or should we say, grand-mommy. The depiction of women saints on the long, uninterrupted panel on one wall of the church is an early nod to women's studies. And on the opposite side, the individual attributes of the male saints are just as impressive. This famous mosaic cycle had many imitators in Northern Italy—make sure you don't miss these so you can sniff at the knockoffs dismissively.

great outdoors

You'll see pesky yellow bikes all over the place. They're everywhere because they're free. In one of the coolest moves made by a city government anywhere, Ravenna filled its racks with bikes that anyone can use. (We hope the highly successful *Centro in Bici* initiative rubs off on other cities.) All you have to do is swing by tourist info, drop off your license or passport as collateral, and pick up the key. Don't get the wrong idea, though. These bikes are for use in the city center only...if you even attempt to take them outside of the city walls, a huge alarm goes off and *carabinieri* will be called to the scene. Just kidding—but seriously, don't be the bad kid who gets all the other kids' toys taken away.

On the other hand, if you've *rented* a bike and want to do a little exploring outside Ravenna, there is a lot to see [see *need to know,* below, for places to rent]. In fact, this area is known for its cycling. The "Cycling in Romagna" booklet (in English!) given out at tourist info states that there are more bicycles in Romagna than anywhere else in Italy, and outlines some of the best routes for both road and mountain bikes around the province. These are serious trips, in the 30-200km range, and shouldn't be attempted with the map they give you alone. Ask for the Provincia di Ravenna (1:18,000) map. For starters, you can head east, on a straight-shot to the beach—it's 13km (8 miles) away, and is a nice, flat, easy ride. From Piazza Caduti, head east on Via Guaccimanni, which turns into Alberoni, and then, once it crosses the railroad tracks, Candiano. After 2km, this road becomes Via Trieste, and then Viale dei Navigatori, and then at the water, Piazza a Saffi, where you can hang a left, and continue down Lungomare Cristoforo Columbo 1.5km, until you hit Marina di Ravenna. You'll see a big climbing wall on your right, and what appears to be small-town USA. This is the Ravenna's beach-side, and what it's lacking in mosaics, it makes up for in serious outdoor fun [see **marina di ravenna,** below]. If you'd rather trek around in the nature reserve of **Parco Regionale del Delta del Po,** than don't turn left at the end of Via Navigatori. About .75km before it ends, take a right on Via Alessandro Manzoni (if you hit Via della Fiocina, you've gone too far—it's the street before that). This will take you past the small Lido Adriano, over the Ponte Bailey. Hang a left on Via Marabina, which will take you to Lido Dante, the beach that butts up against the natural preserve. There are some paths that lead into the park, but they're not well sign-posted. Just follow the families of birdwatchers and nature lovers. The variety of wildflowers, foliage, and trees is exhaustive. Try to borrow some binocular from your hotel so you can spy on all the different kinds of wildlife that live here—from white cranes to wild deer.

STUFF

▶▶BOUND

Located just north of Piazza del Popolo, **Feltrinelli** *(Via IV Novembre 5/7; Tel 0544/34535; 9am-7pm Mon-Sat, 10am-1pm/3:30-7:30pm Sun; V, MC)* has a great selection of English books, at the usual, slightly inflated prices for the novelty of reading them in Italy. 12-22,000L for classics and best-sellers.

▶▶DUDS

Don't you need some gold lame? Some leather pants? They, and many other funky finds, can be yours for just 140,000L at **Selz** *(Via S. Alberto 29; Tel 0544/454-600; 9:15a,-12:30pm/3:30-7:30pm daily, closed Fri evenings; V, MC)*. The shop has all the makings of a club-kid outfit extraordinaire. And if you left home without that little black dress, there are many to choose from here. Just one block south of San Vitale, on the northwestern part of town.

EATS

Don't let Ravenna's refined attitude fool you: The food here is definitely down-home in a sort of gourmet Italian way. Flavors are strong, preparations are rustic, portions are hearty, and every meal is a reason to linger late, drink another *limoncello,* and enjoy. You won't find as many tourist menus here as you will in other cities. Places like Ca' de Ven still roll out their *piadina* (buckwheat flat bread) by hand and cook it on hot griddles, and tiny surprises like Cupido attest to the staggering number of ways you can stuff a *tortelli* (ravioli). Ravenna isn't exactly a smorgasbord of cheap eats, but there are a few inexpensive gems if you know where to look.

TO MARKET

Don't miss the market where Via Cavour runs into the tiny Piazza Andrea Costa *(7:30am-2pm Mon-Thur; 7:30am-7:30pm Friday, closed Sun)*. The classical-looking building has a gorgeous facade, and the inside looks like it was built to serve as a market. There's one area devoted solely to fish, where high-booted men hose down the catch of the day. The fruits and vegetables are in the center, surrounded by specialty retailers. Chat with these guys—you'll learn a thing or two about the local cheese, salami, and pasta.

Your mom would die for this place. **Salumeria Alpine** *(43 Via Cavour; 8am-12:45pm/4:45-7:15pm daily, closed Thur afternoon; V, MC)* is conveniently situated right next to **Cupido** [see *eats,* above]. Great cheeses, hams hanging over the counter, breads, wines, pastas, all displayed with just the perfect eye for detail.

Bargain hunters should check out the **Mostra Mercato Antiquariato,** held in Piazza San Francesco on the third Saturday and Sunday of every month. This is one of those mixed-bag bazaars, where you can pick up almost anything old.

ravenna eats and crashing

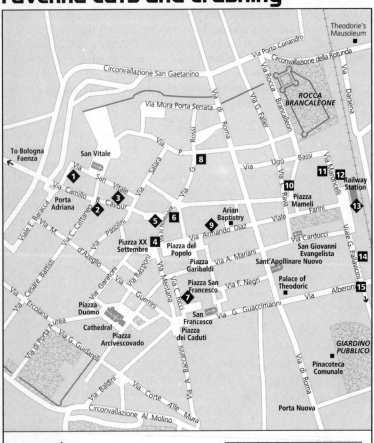

EATS ◆
Bizantino **5**
Ca'de Ven **7**
Cupido **3**
Da Rose Pizzeria **9**
Ristoromagna Mensa **13**
Spasso Bistrot **1**
Verderame Café **2**

CRASHING ■
Albergo Cappello **6**
Hotel Al Giaciglio **10**
Hotel Centrale Byron **4**
Hotel Diana **8**
Hotel Italia **14**
Hotel Minerva **12**
Hotel Ravenna **11**
Ostello Dante **15**

▶▶CHEAP

One of the best bargains in town is actually in the train station. The totally non-descript **Ristoromagna Mensa** (*Piazzale Farini 18; No phone; 11am-3pm/6-9:30pm; No credit cards*) is the railway worker's cafeteria, but it's open to the public and the food is pretty great for the price. Fill up a tumbler of red wine for 2,000L, feast on *penne al broccoli* for 5,500L, and know your mother would be glad that you're getting your meat (*tacchino* breast) and two veggies (spinach and squash) for less than 10,000L.

The intellectual, black-clad art crowd hangs out at **Verderame Café** (*Via Cavour 82; Tel 0544/32248; 8:30am-8pm Mon-Wed, Fri, Sat; 8:30am-2pm Thur; 3-8pm Sun; No credit cards*), the beautiful and exclusive coffee shop on Via Cavour. This place looks like something out of a pre-Raphaelite painting—the orangy/pink walls are dotted with gold and brightly colored broken-plate mosaics, there's lots of flowing, velvety fabric, and the furniture is ornate and plush. The glass case in the back is home to decadent pastries, and the oversized cappuccinos are Ravenna's answer to the wants of the visiting Starbucks crowd. No booze here (too bad, a drink might loosen these folks up...), but still a great place.

Ravenna's most popular "ristorantino free-flow," is **Bizantino** (*Piazza A. Costa 2-6; Tel. 0544/32073; 11:45am-2:45pm Mon-Fri; 5-6,500L pasta, 6-10,000L main dish; Cover 1,000L; No credit cards*). Though these self-service places are usually drab and utilitarian, feeding the masses with rustic but hearty foods, this one, located in the covered market, is actually kind of hip and fun. The funky dining area looks like an Ikea show room, with lots of brightly colored chairs around Formica tables. And the food is great—walk through the buffet line and get a bowl of spicy bean soup, a vegetarian lasagna, some focaccia, and a beer. Business people, students, workmen, and families are all eating a meal while they can—this place, unfortunately, isn't open for dinner. Walk in from Piazza Andrea Costa, off Via IV Novembre, and look for the door to the restaurant to your right.

▶▶DO-ABLE

The brightly lit **Da Rose Pizzeria** (*Via Diaz 46; Tel 0544/34771; 6:30am-12:30am daily; 4,500L pizza by the slice; No credit cards*) gets a lot of tourists, as it's right between the station and the downtown, but its pizza by the slice is among the best around. To answer the needs of backpackers, who plop their rucksacks down for an hour or two as they write away in their journals under the frescoed-ceiling, the owners have installed two internet-enabled computers on a little mezzanine in the back (10,000L/hour).

You'd never know this little gem of a bargain eatery was here if you weren't looking for it. Hidden in a little vine-covered courtyard, down an alleyway off Ravenna's main drag, Via Cavour, is the delightful **Cupido** (*Via Cavour 43/A; Tel 0544/37529; 8:30m-8:30pm Tue-Sun; 5-8,000L pasta; No credit cards*). This takeout shop serves up homemade pastas in an array of sauces, *piandina, bruschetta,* pizza by the slice, and delicious desserts. The hordes of folks that line up at the register to shout out their order to the busy husband and wife team usually don't wait until they get home to eat their meal. There are five or six tables, and a few benches, out in the courtyard, where you can pop open a bottle of wine and dive into your heavenly *tortelli al zucca* (pumpkin ravioli), or *gnocchi al gorgonzola* (blue cheese gnocchi).

A trip to Ravenna isn't complete without at least one meal at **Ca'de Ven** *(Via Corrado Ricci 24; Tel 0544/30163; Bus 1, 2, or 3 to Piazza Caduti; 11am-2:45pm/5:30-10:15pm Tue-Sun; 1,500-15,000L first course or sandwich, 16-25,000L main entree, 3-5,000L wine by the glass; No cover; V, MC),* and the owners know it. Located right on the corner of Via Ricci and the ever popular hangout, Via Polenta, the huge, convivial spot couldn't be in a more convenient position. Though even the locals, who flock here at their lunch break, all agree that the food here is fantastic, you won't be able to fight the feeling that you're on the tourist track. The cheeky waiters speak perfect English, and there's promo pamphlets touting this place's long history (as if 1975 is *that* old). That said, the building dates back to 1542, and this place is a local institution, serving up classic Romagnan fare that's made in a traditional, hand-crafted manner. Their wheaty *paindina,* the dense flatbread made of buckwheat flour, are the basis of incredible sandwiches. Try the *prosciutto, formaggio,* and *rugula* (7,500L). The menu of pastas and meat dishes changes daily, and is completely seasonal. But don't leave without trying the cheese plate, which contains five or six local cheeses served with a spicy/sweet *mostardo* (fruit and mustard preserves) for just 10,000L. A meal here is more of an experience than just nourishment—you eat at long communal tables under brick arches and frescos. Wine casks and other paraphernalia decorate the room.

Not to be confused with the fine-dining restaurant owned by the same people, right next door and to the left, **La Cantina del Capello** *(Via IV Novembre 41; Tel 0544/219-876; 11-2am Mon-Sat, closed Mon afternoon; 10-14,000L first course, 13-20,000L main course; V, MC),* is the casual eatery wedged into the little room off to the back of the chi-chi wine bar that goes by the same name [see *bars,* above]. The room is lined with bottles of wine, and filled with good food smells—which explains why many of the square, wood tables are reserved days in advance. Try not to fill up on the free food during *aperativo* hour at the bar. The dishes here are generally Romagnan, some with innovative twists, such as blue cheese gnocchi with peas and walnuts. This place is big on slow-roasted meats, so angry vegans beware. The prices shouldn't break the bank at all.

▶▶**SPLURGE**

Looking more like a chic LA restaurant than an Italian trattoria with great food, **Spasso Bistrot** *(Via Mura di San Vitale 10; Tel 0544/218-100; Bus 1 to Via Marche; 12-2:30pm/7:30-11pm Tue-Sun; 10-12,000L first course, 20-25,000L main course; Cover 3,000L),* is Ravenna's latest hotspot. It's just south of San Vitale, on the eastern-most edge of the city's walls. Leather banquettes with zebra-striped pillows and ultra modern suspension lighting drive the impression home. The menu breaks the mold of pasta dishes—game birds with wild rice, a duck prosciutto with olive paste, a curried cous-cous, and *radicchio garganelle* are all inventive and beautifully presented. Though this place is decidedly showy, it delivers a great meal. The wine list is long, and there are some good values to be found in the 20-30,000L range.

crashing

It's essential to book ahead in Ravenna. People fly in just to see the mosaics—don't let them get your room. Most of the budget accommodations are around the train station.

▶▶CHEAP

Your first choice in town should be **Hotel Ravenna** *(Via Maroncelli 12; Tel 0544/212-204; Reception open 7am-midnight; 50-70,000L single w/out bath, 60-80,000L single w/bath, 70-90,000L double w/out bath, 80-110,000L double w/bath, V, MC)*, the two-star that acts like a three-star, but has one-star prices. Just a stone's throw north of (and on the same street as) the station, and a five-minute walk from the major sights, this three-story hotel provides a pleasant refuge from the crowds and cultural overload of Ravenna. Elevators, telephones, TVs, matching furniture (praise be) and comfortable duvets make this one stand out above the rest. There's a cozy bar and TV room with leather couches downstairs. The front door closes at midnight, but the sweet Signore will give you a key if you ask nicely.

wired

Get the latest scoop on Ravenna at *http://www.adriacoast.com/en/localita/prora/index.htm.*
   Multimediateca *(Via da Polenta 4; 2;30-6pm Mon-Fri, 8:30am-noon Sat, closed Sunday; 2,000L per 30 min; No credit cards)* Right upstairs from informagiovane. The two large rooms are decorated with old movie prints—the front is for computers, the back, for satellite TV. These are the fastest connections in town. **Rock Caffe** *(Via Castel San Pietro 9; Tel 0544/213-523; 7am-1am Tue-Sun; 5,000L beer pint, 10,000L per hour Internet access; No credit cards)* has six computers on a huge, rectangular table, surrounded by old men smoking cigars and playing cards. Both **Buddy's Pub** [see *bars scene,* above] and **De Rose's Pizzaria** [see *eats,* above]are profiting on the information highway with a few machines that they rent out at 10,000L an hour.

Located 1km east of the station and the center in Ravenna's neighborly suburban outskirts is **Ostello Dante** *(Via Aurelio Nicolodi 12; Tel 0544/421-164; Bus 1 or 11, ask the driver when to get off; Open April 1-Dec 31; Reception open 7-9am/3:30-11:30pm, curfew 11:30pm, lockout 9:30am-5pm; 25,000L per person in dorm, 27,000L in private family room, breakfast included; No credit cards).* Even if hostels aren't usually your thing, consider this one. First of all, there's so much to do and see during the day in Ravenna, so the bright and early kick-in-the-butt isn't such a bad thing. This hostel is less institutional-feeling than most. Housed in a modern building right across from a super Co-op, it has a huge TV where backpackers scan the satellite dish while drinking beer, a large dining room where they play cards late into evening, and a management crew made up of Ravenna's alterno-youth. They no longer have the internet-enabled computers, but the guy at the desk may let you check your email on his.

The best budget deal in town is **Hotel Al Giaciglio** *(Via Rocca Brancaleone 24; Tel/Fax 0544/39403; Closed for two weeks in November; 40-45,000L single w/out bath, 50-55,000L single w/bath, 50-65,000L double w/out bath, 70-80,0000L double w/bath, 7,000L breakfast; V, MC),* located right across and down the block from the Rocca Brancaleone Park. The owners have been renovating this place for the past few years, slowing but surely building a brand-new hotel. The rooms all have new furniture, the tile bathrooms are spacious and clean, and there are even TVs in a few rooms. Call ahead as far as you can.

▶▶DO-ABLE

Hotel Minerva *(Viale Maroncelli 1; Tel 0544/213-711; 100,000L Single,; 150,000L double, 35,000L extra for a triple, private baths; V, MC)* is right across the street from Hotel Al Giaciglio, and though it's more expensive for about the same level of accommodation, the triples are a good deal. Nice furniture, TVs and phones in every room, and lots of space. Just remember, breakfast is extra.

It doesn't get more central than **Hotel Centrale Byron** *(Via IV Novembre 14; Tel 0544/33479, Fax 0544/34114; 75-95,000L single w/bath, 86,000L double w/out bath, 103-146,000L double w/bath, 7,000L breakfast; V, MC, AE, DC),* located just a few steps north of Piazza del Popolo. The English-speaking signora who runs it makes sure you get the most out of your visit to Ravenna, as the maps, travelers' tips, and personal anecdotes start coming as soon as you check in. This is a lovely hotel, a favorite with Italian families here on vacation. The rooms are spacious and simply decorated, with TV, phones, and frigobars. The downstairs lobby is elegant, and a nice cool place to chill out before venturing back out into the mosaic madness.

Hotel Diana *(Via G. Rossi 47; Tel 0544/39164, Fax 0544/30001; Single w/out bath 97,000L, 115,000L w/bath, 134,000L double w/out bath, 160,000L w/bath; V, MC, AE)* is actually a very nice hotel, but it reserves about a third of its 33 rooms for budget travelers. The budget rooms might be a little less cushy, but some of the amenities remain the same: you get reasonable bike rental, sweet service from an English-speaking staff, and breakfast out on the patio regardless of the caliber of your room. It's just north of Piazza del Popolo.

▶▶SPLURGE

Hotel Italia *(Viale Pallavioni; Tel 212-362, Fax 217-004; 75-150,000L single w/ bath, 100-200,000L double w/bath, depending on the season; V, MC, AE),* just south of the station, is you're typical "fancy Italian" hotel. The rooms are institutionally clean, but well-equipped with all the requisite features like satellite TV, frigobars, and phones, and the bar is always busy and open late.

If you only treat yourself once on your trip, there's no question that it should be here, at Ravenna's most magical **Albergo Cappello** *(Via IV Novembre 41; Tel 0544/219-813, Fax 0544/219-814, for reservations call 0544/219-889; 145,000L-180,000L single, 200-240,000L double and suite, all with private bath; V, MC).* Located in an old palazzo that has recently been renovated, it's upstairs from a fine dining restaurant, art gallery, and *enoteca/cucina,* all of the same name, and all cultivating the same romantic attention to detail. The seven rooms are each given names that are as imaginative as their decor—the *Sogno Amaranto,* or lover's dream, for example, sits under a timbered ceiling, with remnants of frescos still clinging to parts of the walls. Each room is indescribably different from the next, with a different color scheme, different linens (all luxurious), and different antique wood furniture, but all have gorgeous tiled baths, TVs, frigobars, flowing curtains, phones, and hairdryers. Modern design magazines and English newspapers are set out in the comfortable common rooms.

need to know

Currency Exchange There's a **Bancomat (ATM)** at the station, and at **Cassa di Risparmio di Ravenna** *(Piazza del Popolo 3, 5; Tel 0544/480-511).*

Tourist Information The well-equipped and super-helpful **tourist office** is located at Via Salara 8 *(Tel 0544/482-077, Fax 0544/35094; 8:30am-6:30pm daily).* There's a 24-hour infoline in Italian *(Tel 0544/482-444).* Also, **Informagiovane** *(Via Guido da Polenta 4; Tel 0544/482-456; 9am-1pm Tue-Sat, 3pm-7pm Tue-Thur; www.racine.ra.it/informagiovani/ravenna),* the youth-oriented service center where volunteers often speak English and are happy to point fun-seeking youth in the right direction, is a huge source of information on not just the sights, but clubs, bars, and other hangouts. Neither of these offices will book rooms for you.

Public Transportation The **ATM Buses** *(Azienda Transporti Municipale; Via delle Industrie 118; Tel 0544/689-961; atm.ra.it)* are a reliable way to get you out to the hostel, but Ravenna is very walk-able. There's a kiosk right in front of the train station where you can pick up schedules and request information. Local buses will also get you out to the beach *(lido)* from the station, and back: Bus 70 runs year round from the station, and 60 is added in the summer for Marina di Ravenna; Bus 1 and 70 go to Marina Terme, Bus 44 goes out to Lido Dante (and Basilica Apollinare in Classes.) Tickets cost 1,700L. For a **taxi,** call 24/7 *(Tel 0544/36592* or *0544/338-888).*

Health and Emergency Emergency: *113;* Ambuance: *118.* The **police station** is located in **Piazza Mameli** *(Tel 0544/482-999).*

Pharmacy Farmacia Dradi *(Via IV Novembre 35; tel 0544/35449; 8}30am-7:30pm Mon-Sat; No credit cards).* The 24-hour pharmacy is **Comunale N. 8** *(Via Fiume 124; Tel 0544/402-514).*

Telephone There are public telephones on Via G. Rasponi 22.

Trains The **train station** is located just east of town, a five-minute walk from Piazza del Popolo, in Piazzale Farini *(Tel 0544/217-884; 8:30am-12:30pm/2:30-5pm daily).* There's a *deposito babagli* (Luggage room) which is open from 9am-1pm/1:30-5:45pm daily.

Bus Lines Out of the City The bus station is located at Piazzale Aldo Moro, right behind the railway station. For information, call **ATRI** *(Tel 0543/27821)* or **ACFT** *(0532/771-302),* the two local lines.

Bike/Moped Rental In Piazza Farini, just to the right of the station, is a huge warehouse that rents out bicycles *(Tel 0544/37037; 6:45am-8pm Mon-Sat; 20,000L a day, deposit required; No credit cards).* But unless you want to go out into the countryside, why rent, when the city gives them out for free? [see *great outdoors,* above]

Laundry There's a coin-operated **laundromat** on Via Candiano, just a around the corner from the station and Hotel Italia *(7am-10pm daily; 6 washers, 6,000L, 3 dryers, 6,000L are all coin operated.)*

Postal the **main post office** *(Tel 0544/31348)* is located at Piazza Garibaldi 1.

Internet See *wired,* above.

marina di ravenna

This is the beach town you always wished your parents would take you to when you were a kid. People walk around in their bathing suits and flip-flops from morning 'til night, towels wrapped around their waists and syrupy popsicles dripping down their wrists. There are no high rises. No massive water parks. Just a main drag that's short enough for you and your newfound friends to walk from one end to the other ten times over the course of the evening. This is the kind of town that still has local-locals, and has attracted a serious contingent of surf bums and dropouts who live here year-round. It's not pretentious or classy. People come here to stick their toes in the sand, get a tan, and catch a wave. And if you're not convinced yet, it's the best seaside deal around.

You'd be hard-pressed to bump into those American art-students you met under the mosaics back "in town." The only people who even know about the beach just 6 miles away from Ravenna (connected by a canal) are the Italians and a handful of Germans, Russians, and Slavs. With the flashy and boisterous twin towns of Rimini and Riccione just a 10km walk south down the beach, Ravenna di Marina has been pegged the quiet cousin, which is a good thing for you. It's your big chance to soak up some of the best bargains and outdoor activities on the Adriatic—and get into a very cool small-scale beach party while you're at it.

Just a bit of background: Augustus built the port of Classis right around here in the 1st century A.D., and it grew to be the largest Roman Naval center on the Adriatic. King Theodoric of Ravenna kept his boat here. Ravenna di Marina is still a working port, and the new **Marina** *(Tel 0544/218-931; www.marinara.it)* located right at the canal in the northern part of town, is a sight to be seen. Boats from all over the Adriatic and the Middle East dock here, and come nightfall, the wooden boardwalks are full with vacationers from all over the world.

Via Delle Nazioni, the main drag, runs north-south through town. Marina di Ravenna proper is only about 5 blocks long and 10 blocks wide—getting oriented is not a problem. **Lungomare** is the street that runs along the water, and gives you access to most of the beaches. If you're not used to sunbathing the Italian way, be prepared. Most of these beaches are private, and though you can likely catch a wave of two for free, you have to pay a nominal hourly or day rate for your chair. The good news is, all of these beach resorts have bathrooms, snack bars, music, and cabanas for rent, and some have restaurants. Most also have volleyball and badminton nets, shuffleboard, and of course, bocce ball. You may want to plan your day at the beach around where you want to eat—seaside restaurants like **La Maree** [see *eats*, below] for example, have a beach reserved for restaurant guests. 10,000L gets you a chaise lounge for the day, and the volleyball, beaches, and restaurant are yours to enjoy.

bar, club, and live music scene

It says a lot that many of Marina's most popular spots are named after modern literary and jazz greats...the scene here is lower-key than down the road at Rimini, but it's also a little smarter, less cruisy, and more laid-back.

Taverna Bukowski *(Viale delle Nazioni 176; Tel 0339/582-75-03 or 0544/530-845; Noon-late daily; No credit cards)* is more of a complex than just a bar. The little ramshackle building is set back from Via Nazioni, surrounded by all the stuff you want to play with: a brand new skate park to the left, a 50 meter climbing wall to the right, and tons of picnic tables and chairs spread out across the lawn and under the shade of the trees. But don't think you can just wander in—all these attractions are reserved for paying customers. Taverna Bukowski is an ARCI Sportivo [see book intro for info on ARCI], so they may ask you to pay a nominal fee to join in the fun. Whatever the cost (it varies), it's well worth it. Inside looks like an old harbor bar, with lots of wood and sawdust on the floor, but you and everyone else will spend most of your time outdoors. In the afternoons, people hang out at the picnic tables, drinking beer and walking the climbers. At night, the music is turned up a few notches and the lawn party goes into full swing. The owners host lots of special theme parties over the summer, and do regular poetry readings as well.

The place to see and be seen come nightfall is **Cafè Hemingway** *(Viale T. de Revel 62; Tel 0544/530-681; 7-3am Tue-Sun; 10,000L cocktails, 60,000L full meal; Wed is ladies night, Tues is gay night; Cover 10-25,000L if you're not dining; V, MC),* the seaside bar, restaurant, and club that attract all the cool kids in town. Located right next to the Marina, on the northern end of Nazioni, this newly renovated space is home to one of the summer's most hopping parties, and it's absolutely essential to reserve a spot ahead if you want to join in on the fun. This place is pretty without being pretentious—it feels like a party at the rich kid's parents' beach house, with everyone dancing under cathedral ceilings and out on the deck. People spill over onto the sand, bumping and grinding to the commercial blend of house, hip-hop, and disco. Despite its beachy allure, this is a wine and beer, more than fruity cocktail, kind of club. If you're willing to drop the 60,000L on a full meal, you can forgo the cover, and assure yourself a table for the night. The food is great—owner Marco Bonamico comes from a cooking family, and serves up traditional Italian food with innovative twists. The multi-course meal offers vegetarian choices as well.

BB KING Dinner Club *(Viale C. Colombo 171, Punta Marina Terme; Infoline 0338/650-98-00, table reservation 0333/310-13-93; 7am-late Wed-Sat; info@bbking.it; 10-30,000L; V,MC)* is something else entirely. Located about 1-1/2 km south of Marina di Ravenna (an easy walk), where Via Nazioni turns into C. Colombo, this club/restaurant complex is a nod to Rimini's excess and exploits—and it's also a whole lot of fun. With a beach-front dance floor that rocks 'til dawn, a stylish bar and great food inside, it's no wonder that this place is a destination in its own right. The dining room teeters somewhere between elegance and theatricality, with accents in wood, velvet, concrete, and glass, plus metal spirals twisting their way to the ceiling. Cozy banquettes provide a bit of respite from the undulating crowds. The bar looks like something out of an "X-files" episode—smokey and underlit with blue light—and serves up cocktails in whimsically shaped glasses. The crowd is hip and flirty, the girls are prone to sport bikinis, and both sexes like to get a little crazy on the dance floor.

CULTURE ZOO

You've seen the mosaics. You've visited the churches. You need a break, and Marina di Ravenna is the perfect place for it. Unlike larger coastal cities that share space with museums, galleries and churches, there's nothing here to make you feel guilty for wanting to do nothing but lie on the beach.

The Historical Diving Society Museum *(Viale IV Novembre 86/A; Tel 0544/531-013; Fax 0544/531-013; 9-11am Wed, Thur from June-Sept, 3-6pm Sat, Sun Oct-May; www.racine.ra.it/perglialtri/*

hdsitalia; Cover 5,000L; No credit cards); This quirky homage to underwater exploration is the one attraction that might get you up off that chaise lounge. This is actually a very cool collection outlining the history of diving, and their exhibits tour cities around the globe. Dive into the tradition of hard hat diving, with paraphernalia that dates back to the turn of the century.

great outdoors

Beach bumming is definitely a priority here, but there also are tons of adrenaline-pumping activities available for people who just can't stand the idea of doing "nothing." From surfing to bike riding [see *need to know,* below, for bike rentals], this place is all about fun in the sun.

There's a brand new **skate park** on the corner of Via Nazioni and Via IV Novembre, with awesome quarter pipes and lots of crowds—all for you, totally free of charge. You might be able to jump into a basketball game right next door—and unlike most courts in Italy, these have real nets.

If you can get some folks together for a day at sea, check out **Easy Sea Boat Hire** *(Tel 0333/331-166, call anytime; V, MC).* For 50,000L an hour, you and up to 7 friends can rent a 15-foot motor boat. You don't need a boating license...hell, you don't even need a drivers license. You can call for info, but to actually book, you have to go to tourist info [see *need to know,* below].

To go scuba-diving, or to find out about a day of instruction, contact **GS Sub Delphinus** *(P.le Adriatico, 5; Tel. 0544-530-500).* This local club does everything from booking dives to hooking up interested parties with classes. You'll find them on the northernmost part of the Marina, right on the water.

You can't miss the climbing wall that's right out in front of Taverna Bukowski. Since 1994, **Istrice Climbing Wall** *(Tel 463-044; No regular hours—usually open daily during daylight hours, closed in winter)* has been the site of international competitions, but on most days it's open to the public.

eats

Via Nazioni is packed with low-priced eateries that cater to crowds. Though most of the food is Romagnan in spirit (pastas, tortelli, and *piadina*), you shouldn't skip the super fresh and cheaper-than-usual seafood options. Fish is often sold by the gram, so before you pick your catch, ask them to weigh it for you. Otherwise, the ubiquitous beach fare—fried calamari—is a delicious and reliable choice.

If you're picnicking, or just eating on a budget, there's a **Mini Co-op** *(Viale Nazioni 138; No phone; Mon-Sat 8am-1pm/4-7pm, closed Thur afternoon; No credit cards)* right in the heart of town.

Don't expect goat curry or jerk chicken at **Bar Jamaica** *(Viale delle Nazioni 179; Tel 0544/530-853; 7am-4am summer, 7am-midnight winter; 3,5000L pizza, 6,000L panini, 6,000L beer; No credit cards),* the tiny terrazzo of a restaurant on Via Nazioni. Its name probably stems from the fact that it's the most laid back joint in town, really more of a bar than a restaurant. Take away a pizza or stuffed *piadine* (a pizza-like disk with cheese or vegetable toppings) to eat on their porch, or sit down and order at a table. There's no atmosphere to speak of, but at these prices, who's complaining?

The pies at **Chez Nous** *(Viale delle Nazioni 48; Tel 0544/530-111; Noon-3pm/7pm-1am Thur-Tue; 12-15,000L first course, 13-25,000L main entree; V, MC)* are internationally renowned—seriously. Daniela and Walter Botrogno have brought their secret recipe to the International Pizza Expo in the States, and won top awards. Located under **Albergo Adriatico** [see, *crashing,* below], which the Botrognos also run, Chez Nous is a happening spot come early afternoon and evening. Try the *funghi e salsiccie,* or even more decadent, the *funghi tartufati,* redolent with truffles, mozzarella, and red sauce. The specialty pizzas listed on the back of the menu are a bit more expensive, but twice the meal. The truffle oil, arugula, and parmagiano is just 13,000L, and is the kind of pie you'll pine for when you return home. These folks also specialize in fish (surprise, surprise). The paella-esque *Pescatrice in padella con frutti di mare,* or the *zuppa di frutti di mare e crostacei,* both loaded with crabs and shellfish, are to die for. Order a bottle of wine from the area—none is more than 25,000L.

After a few days at the beach, the urge to wash the salt off and get dressed for a nice meal is natural. In that case, head to **Restaurant Maree** *(Viale delle Nazioni/Arenile Demaniale 10; Tel 0544/530-652; 6:30pm-midnight Mon-Thur, 6:30pm-2:30am Fri, noon-2:30am/6:30pm-2:30am Sat, 12:30pm-2:30pm/6:30pm-midnight Sun, closed Sun in winter; 16-30,000L first course, 18-30,000L main course and seafood, 6,500L beer, 3,000L cover; V/MC, AE).* This place looks like it would be more at home in Los Angeles than here in little old Marina di Ravenna, so it's no surprise that the motto on the menu is "enjoy design food." The huge, circular room is decked out in festive blues and yellows, with all the trappings of an Italian fine-dining experience. Oversized wine glasses, lengthy fresh breadsticks, and plush linen napkins are waiting at the table when you sit down. The seafood here is spectacular—try the grilled swordfish, or the whole flounder. There are pasta dishes *(gnocchi al gorgonzola,* is awesome) and the wood-burning oven turns out some great, if small, pizzas. The tiki huts out front might tip you off to the fact that this isn't just a restaurant. On Wed, Fri, and Sat nights, they bring the DJs in, and the place transforms into a commercial Italian disco inside and out (the Djs begin around 11:30). The theme is reminiscent of a Hawaiian luau, with citronella torches and drunken dancers trying not to spill their Mai-tais.

crashing

Like any good beach town. Marina di Ravenna has a fair number of places to lay your sunburned head, most of which are reasonably priced. There's also a fun camping area.

▶▶CHEAP

The huge **Piomboni Camping** *(V.le Lungomare, 421; Tel 0544/530-230 May-Sept, Tel 0545/27559 in the off-season, Fax 0544/538-618; info@camp ingpiomboni.it; Open from May-Sept 30; 7,500-11,000L per person with own tent, 15-20,000L camper rental; V, MC),* located north of Via Nazioni on the coast, is a community of campers, mobile homes, and tents, all of which can be rented. Expect to fight for beach space with tons of toddlers and teens (the sites are just 50 meters from the water), to get that stupid feeling when invited to partake in group activities, and to enjoy yourself more than you expected to at their little disco. There's also a small grocery store on site.

Run by the sweet, cherubic Daniela Botrongno, **Albergo Adriatico** *(Viale delle Nazioni 48; Tel 0544/53011; 70-80,000L double w/out bath, 80-90,000L double w/bath, only a few w/TVs, 10,000L per extra person; Closed Nov 15-Dec 15; V, MC, AE)* right on the main drag, is the best deal in town. Rooms are cozy and grandmotherly—and who needs TV and phones when you're at the beach? **Chez Nous,** the restaurant downstairs [see *eats,* above] serves up great, inexpensive food, and is hopping 'til the wee hours. For a room in August, you'll have to book by June.

Hotel Maddalena *(Viale delle Nazionale 345; Tel/Fax 0544/530-431; 45-70,000L single w/out bath, 55-80,000L single w/bath, 60-90,000L double w/out bath, 80-110,000L double w/ bath; V, MC)* is a five-minute walk along the main drag out from the center or town, but at this price, it's worth it. The 21 rooms are homey and cozy, the proprietors have some bikes that they'll let you use, and there's a pretty little garden where you can chill out with your journal or meet some new friends. Breakfast is an additional 10,000L—skip it and grab a pastry in the attached bar.

▶▶DO-ABLE

The water views from the terraces off the rooms at **Albergo Oasis** *(Via Bernardini 53; Tel 0544/530-404, Fax 0544/531-637; Closed Dec 20-Jan 7; 115-120,000L double, 30,000L for an extra bed, private bath, breakfast included; V, MC, AE)* are unforgettable. These super-clean, newish rooms are comfortable and beachy, with lots of seashell art, TVs, phones, and creature comforts. There are 38 rooms, but you should still call in advance.

Hotel Internazionale *(Viale delle Nazioni 163; Tel 0544/530-486, Fax 0544/530-310; Open year-round; 70,000L single, 90,000L double, 120,000L triple, private baths; V, MC, DC)* is on the western side of Nazioni, and priced accordingly. This three-star hotel is run by the sweetest couple you'll ever meet—don't you dare tell them that shag carpet and wood paneling is no longer the epitome of cool. All the rooms are perfectly clean and comfortable, and have TVs and bathrooms.

need to know

Currency Exchange Get yourself some lira at **Corso del Risparmio di Ravenna** *(Viale delle Nazioni 86; Tel 0544/530-129; 9:30am-12:30pm/4-7pm June 21-Aug 17, 9:30am-12:30pm/3-6pm April 14-June 20 and July 9-Sept 22, Closed Sept 23-April 13).* You can also change money at the **post office.**

Tourist Information The **tourist info office** at Marina di Ravenna *(Viale delle Nazioni 159; Tel 0544/530-117; Hours vary depending on season)* holds irregular hours. Just to be sure, you can pick up all the same materials at Ravenna's super efficient tourist office [see **Ravenna,** above] Log on to ***www.emmeti.it/Welcome/Emilia/Romagna/MarinaRavenna/index.uk.html*** for even more info.

Public Transportation You can call a **taxi** at 0544/464-648 or 0544/33888

Bus Lines Out of the City Ravenna's **public bus 70** goes out here (in the summer you can catch bus 60 as well), but there's no station *(Tickets 1,700L),* There are stops all along Nazioni.

Health & Emergency Police: *113;* Fire: *115;* Ambulance: *118;* Water emergency: *1530.* There's a hospital, **San Maria delle Croce** *(Viale Randi 5; Tel 0544/285-11-10),* just east of the southern end of Via Nazioni.

Pharmacy Farmacia Communale n.8 *(Via Fiume Abbandonato 124; Tel 0544/402-514)* is open 24/7. It's at the end of Viale Lungomare, east of Viale della Nazioni.

Bike Rental You can rent bikes at **Sporting Shop** *(27 Viale dei Mille; Tel 0544/538-482).*

Trains The nearest train station is in **Ravenna,** at Piazza Farini [see **Ravenna,** above]. To get there, take **bus 1** to the station.

Postal *(Viale delle nazioni 76; Tel 0544/530-221; 8:30am-12:45pm/3:15-7pm Mon-Fri).*

rimini

Rimini is the Daytona Beach of Italy, and possibly the Myrtle Beach, too. The Amalfi Coast may get more tourists, the Ligurian coast might be quainter, but the Adriatic coast parties like a rock star. For much of central and northern Europe, this is the beach, warm weather, summer break, and mating grounds rolled up into one sleazy, flashy, friendly, fun town. Lodging here is dirt-cheap, but book way-ahead for August, when all of Europe has two-weeks off, and much of it comes here. The clubs are some of the biggest and trendiest in Europe—this of course makes a few of them amazingly cool, and the rest of them amazingly lame imitators. Outside of peak season's dancing and sunburn, the locals look forward to the off-season private party, and you should, too. Many chic clubs and bars open only after the summer crowds have gone home. There is a vibrant and growing art scene, and some of the restaurants away from the beach are first-class.

For a town founded in Roman times (where the Via Emilia met Via Flaminia) and dominated by a great arts patron during the Renaissance, there's not that much sightseeing and museum-hopping. (Of course, that's not why you come to Rimini in the first place.) But if you must see "sights," Rimini's *centro storico* is full of architectural masterpieces from the medieval and Renaissance periods; most locals take their afternoon strolls here.

The beach and the town are two separate entities, even though they're just a 15-minute walk from one another. In the winter, the town is hopping and the beach is dead. In the summer, the opposite is true. Spring and fall are delicate balancing acts, as local hipsters try to determine the right moment to appear on the beach in a bikini, or when to appear in one of the town's sidewalk cafes wearing a suit.

neighborhoods

First off, most tourist info maps will probably just confuse you. They show the beach at the bottom, below the center of town, which makes you think the beach is to the south, right? Wrong. The beach is actually to the northeast—the top of the map points southwest. Once you get used to this, you'll be fine. Hey, this is Italy.

The **town center** *(centro storico)* is the historical part of town, inside the city walls. It has most of the good restaurants and bars, and all the cultural sites. The **train station** separates the center from the beach area on the northeast side of the walls. There are no bus lines in most of the town center, so get used to walking.

Centro Marina is the main beach area. The numbered beaches (real sand!) start here, and get higher as you head southeast toward **Riccione,** the suburb where tons of clubs writhe with action every night. The **beach road** *(Lungomare)* goes under many different names, starting with **Lungomare Tintori** at the northeast and becoming **Lungomare Murri** and then **Lungomare Giusepe di Vittorio** as you move down the beach. One street in from the water, parallel to the Lungomare, is the main road for traffic, called, in turn, **Viale Vespucci, Viale Regina Elena,** and **Viale Regina Margerita.** The two roads pass through several piazzas, **Piazza Kennedy** and **Piazza Tripoli** being the most important. Most of the bars and restaurants near the beach are clustered along this main road, and the most important services, like pharmacies and laundries, are on or around the piazzas. The bus that goes down this road *(Bus 11)* has convenient, numbered stops (no, they don't correspond with the beach numbers), which get higher as you head toward Riccione.

North of Centro Marina and the town center is the **Porto,** a canal running inland where most of the town's pleasure boats are moored. There are several restaurants and great places for strolling in this area, which is crossed by the ancient **Ponte di Tibero** [see *culture zoo,* below] and the more modern **Ponte dei Mille.** Across the bridges is **Borgo San Giuliano,** an old medieval neighborhood that is home to both old folks and a new influx of local artists. There are several terrific restaurants here, and the quiet streets are worth exploring to see the **murals** that residents have painted over the years—there must be 20 of them.

rimini bars clubs and culture zoo

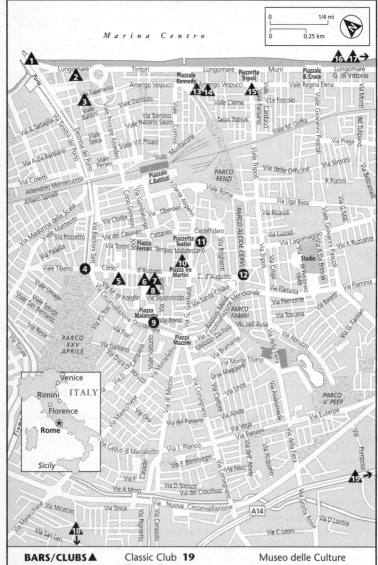

BARS/CLUBS ▲

3Sei5 **5**
Antica Cafeteria **10**
Antica Drogeria **6**
The Barge Guinness
  Pub **2**
Betty Page **3**
The Black Cock **7**
Bio Bar **13**
Carnaby Club **17**

Classic Club **19**
CoCoRiCo **16**
IO Street Club **14**
Rock Island **1**
The Rose and Crown **15**
Vecchia Pescheria **8**
Velvet **18**

CULTURE ZOO ●
Arco D'Augusto **12**

Museo delle Culture
  Extraeuropee
  "Dinz Rialto/
  Castello Malatestiano **9**
Ponte Tiberio **4**
Tempio Malatestiano **11**

hanging out

Piazza Tre Martiri in the *centro storica* is the center of activity when it's not beach season. The weird mish-mash of styles—lightsaber-esque modern lights stick out from the ground, and Armani stores occupy neo-classical buildings that face off against a Renaissance clock tower. This square is the place to see and be seen as you duck in and out of cafes and bars in the early evening. The locals take their *passagiata,* or evening walk, in the little streets radiating out from here, over to the **Tempio Malatestiano** [see *culture zoo*, below] and **Piazza Ferrari.**

Vecchia Pescheria, the beautiful old covered fish market on **Via Piscane** with its Renaissance marble slabs and whimsical fountains for cleaning the day's catch, marks the entryway to the most hopping bar scene in the city center. In the summer, the five bars along this street and down **Piazzetta Gregano da Rimini** put out cafe tables, making this one big, rowdy night-spot. People pack themselves like sardines in the Piazzetta, with music pouring out of all the bars and conversation bouncing up and over the rooftops. The vibe is let-loose, fun, and easy—this is where most of the locals head before they take to the clubs, so it's a great place for finding out where the action is going to be later on.

The **beach,** referred to as *centro marina,* and sometimes just *il lido,* is a different hang-out scene entirely. Most of the strips of beachfront are private, but you can sit on the sand closer to the surf for free, and if you rent a chair for a half day or longer, you can use the other facilities of the beach area [see *city sports,* below]. There's tons of foot traffic between the bars and video game parlors on the Lungomare and the Viale, as this is where most of the restaurants and clubs are clustered. Keep your eyes out

wired

Play Zone *(Corso Giovanni XXXIII; 2pm-1am daily; 6,000L per 30 min; No credit cards)* has 4 PCs, some with US-style keyboards, in a back room that looks like something out of "Mystery Science Theater 3000." The drawback: it's a video arcade, filled with obnoxious Italian pre-teens. The advantages: It's a video arcade, filled with video games, it's in the center east of Piazza Ferrari, and they sell beer. Tokens are 800L. Try "Radikal Bikers," the most Italian video game you've ever seen: you ride around Rome on scooters (it's a handlebar game), delivering pizzas. You may forget all about emailing Mom.

http://www.adriacoast.com/en/localita/prorn/index.htm will give you good local info.

for **Bio Bar** on Viale Vespucci between piazzas Kennedy and Tripoli [see, *bar scene,* below], which is open 24-hours on the weekends. Morning, noon, or night, this cheery spot is full of folks just bumming around, drinking beer, eating lunch, and trying to muster up enough energy to hit the beach again.

bar scene

The bar scene is more meaningful off-season, when people hang out in them longer—maybe all night—instead of rushing off to the club of the moment. The drinking scene here is more diverse than in most Italian towns—you can actually avoid getting sloshed in an "Irish pub."

The street sign out front of **3Sei5** *(Vicolo Beccari 3; Tel 0541/50117; Bus 1 to Circonvallazione Occidentale; 8,000L cocktail, 6,000L beer pint; No credit cards)* doesn't scream "bar," but it is the only Japanese lettering on the block—maybe even the whole town. This long, mirrored, industrial-hip space, in the town center east of Piazza Cavour, is where the cool locals hang out, drink beer, smoke dubious cigarettes, and listen to local DJ's—but not in summer. 3Sei5 is closed from March 15th to Sept 15th, when all the action moves to the beach, anyway. You have to be a member of ARCINova [see **regional intro**, above] to get in—15,000L for a membership card here, but you may be able to talk them out of it, since you're just passing though and all. But if they don't, cut them some slack—the local cops are just waiting to pounce on the place for admitting non-members.

Bio Bar *(Viale Vespucci 77; Tel 0541/391-334; Bus 11, stop 13; 8am-8pm Sun-Thur; 24 hours Fri-Sat; 7,000L beer; 3,000L wine; No credit cards)* is next-door to IO Street Club, has the same owner, and was also designed by Roberto from RM12. The cool pastel '60s furniture, red tile bar, and bright yellow walls will remind you of a juice joint, but the fare here is classic Italian bar. Espresso, cappuccino, and pastries are available all day, as well. The real beauty of this place is that it's open round the clock on weekends. The outside tables are always a choice spot, whether it's breakfast, beer on a beach break, before dinner warm-up,

ruLes of the game

Being a party town, Rimini has a pretty tolerant reputation. However, that does not always bear out, as **Echos** found out [see *gay scene,* above]. Certainly the various *circoli* care more that only members are allowed in then what they smoke once they're inside. The mammoth clubs, like **CoCoRiCo** [see *club scene,* above] are too chaotic for people to know what's going on, or who's doing what. That being said, watch yourself and what you inhale in public. You're not fooling anybody in this town—they've seen it all before.

between clubs, or breakfast again. The off-season crowd is young and hip, but in the summer it's more of a grab-bag, since the beach location draws everybody in.

Antica Cafeteria (*Piazza Tre Martiri 47; Tel 0541/27946; Bus 1 or 2 to Arco d'Augusto; 5:30am-9:30pm winter, 5:30pm-3am summer; 2,500L cappuccino, 4,000L campari cocktail; No credit cards*) anchors the Piazza's social scene like a big department store anchors a mall. The outside tables that line the south side of Piazza Tre Martiri (compete with heaters when required) are always packed in the evening, and people line up three-deep at the marble bar inside for cocktails, wine, espresso with grappa, or hot chocolate as thick as crude oil (in season). This is a seriously old-school Italian cafe, with all the staff in dapper vests. There's a tea-room upstairs, with views over the piazza, which may offer some respite from the shoulder-to-shoulder upscale all-age crowd. Come between 7 and 9pm for the free spread of *aperitivo* snacks. Nothing fancy, but a handful of chips, peanuts, and bruschetta provide needed protein after a day of sun and suds.

From the look of the tiny, ancient **Vecchia Pescheria** (*Via Pisacane 10; Tel 0541/27337; Bus 1 to Giovanni XXIII; 12-3pm/5pm-late; No credit cards*), you'd assume that this was a vineyard workers' hangout, not a hotspot for artists, coders, cooks, DJs, and other interesting twenty- and thirty-somethings with cool jobs. The owner, Roberto, is not only a big, loud, friendly, bear of a guy, but one of the hottest club impresarios in Rimini—though you may not be able to guess it from watching him stomp around on the peanut shells that litter the floor, slice big hunks of cheese at the bar, and slap down plates of fried calamari on the rough-hewn table that dominates the center of this rustic watering hole. But this guy knows the skinny on the coolest nightspots, and you'd be smart to get on his good side. When weather's nice, the crowd spills out the door and sips wine or guzzles beer under the roof of the real *vecchia pescheria* (the Old Fish Market). Outside you'll find a huge open-air bar, which begins here and continues down Piazzetta Gregano da Rimini and towards the Black Cock, where the crowds from several bars come together.

Antica Drogeria (*Piazza Cavour 5; Tel 0541/23439; Bus 1 to Giovanni XXIII; 10:30am-9pm Mon-Tue, closed Sun; 5,000L glass of wine; No credit cards*) is in a 19th-century drugstore on the west side of Piazza Cavour. The long main room is expertly lit for maximum cool, and the glass jars and dried herbs and antique wooden tables make everything seem fancy-schmancy. It's all very "Wallpaper" magazine. They have 680 kinds of wine in the bottle, and offer a rotating selection by the glass. The crowd consists of laid-back twenty- and thirty-somethings with a bit of cash to spend.

Don't say a word about the name of this pub. Don't even think it. **The Black Cock** (*Piazzetta Gregano da Rimini 3; Tel 0541/785-307; Bus 1 to Giovanni XXIII; 8pm-5am daily in summer, 8am-late Wed-Mon, 8am-3pm Tue winter; No credit cards*) has a pub atmosphere, but doesn't commit the sin of trying too hard. It gets really lively at night, but in the afternoons it's an intellectual hangout. The piano is usually covered with flyers for local clubs, but it gets played occasionally, and there are chess sets and board games on shelves. During the day, the shadowy interior has a grad-student feel that might be perfect for escaping the beach when your tender skin gets too burned. Wednesday, in fact, features poetry and prose readings. You can also buy a piece of cake or pastry here for 4,000L to go with an espresso at any time of day. But make no mistake, this is a bar. Cocktails are 8,000L, and they have a nice selection of English, German and Belgian ales for 6,000L a pint. The pub is just south of the *vecchia pescheria,* and the crowds from the two places spill out into the streets and merge when the weather is good.

     The Rose and Crown *(Viale Regina Elena 2/A; Tel 0541/391-398; Bus 11, stop 15; 11am-late daily in summer; 8,000L Guinness; V, MC)* is one notch faker than most Italian "Irish pubs." This place is more like an Italian version of a Daytona Beach version of an Irish pub. Still, it's near the beach and Piazzale Tripoli, a good place to let your sun-bleached hair down and meet some other weary travelers. It's been here since 1964, and as one of the first "English pubs" in Italy, something of a local institution. Rather nasty pub grub is served till late (eggs on toast for 7,500L or burgers for 7,500L). But if it's very late, how much will you care?

LIVE MUSIC SCENE

Rimini has one big venue that would be considered a real music club in the States. The others are bars that have bands in order to draw more of the beach-blanket-bingo crowd. Go on, enjoy it—there's a time and place for stumbling in off the sand, drinking a yard of ale from a plastic glass, and deciding that the "Fabulous Thunderbirds" cover band is pretty good after all, and this is it.

     Velvet *(Via S. Aquilina 21; Tel 0541/756-111; 10:30pm-4 or 5am Fri, Sat; www.velvet.it; slego@iper.net; Cover 20-30,000L; No credit cards),* in the hills southwest of the city center, bills itself as "the House of Rock" and is a mega-dance/rock club. This big converted warehouse has bare black walls, a big stage, a huge dance floor and long bar, and a glass wall that overlooks a lake and pretty lights. The crowd here is totally mixed and casual—the only thing they seem to have in common is their mutual appreciation for head-banging. There's a little store, *Shopop,* that sells T-shirts and clubby gadgets. Big international names swing through every once-in-a-while: Paul Weller, Stephen Malkmus of Pavement, and Michelle Shocked played here in 2001, and the house DJs are always big names in club circuit. A "Rockbus" runs on Saturday nights from the station in Rimini to the club from 11:15 on (every 45 min, the last buses back leave at 4-4:45am). Since the bands tend to start at 11pm, on concert nights the buses start at 9pm and run every 30 minutes, and then start running back after the show. Tickets are from 20-30,000L.

     The behemoth of a bar and music venue, **The Barge Guinness Pub** *(Lungomare Tintori 13; Tel 0541/22685, Fax 0541/708-204; Bus 7 Est to Porto; 7pm-4am daily in Summer, closed Mon in winter; 8,000L pint,*

10,000L cocktail; No cover; No credit cards), is on the beach, just across the street from the Grand Hotel. They have rock and blues cover bands and the occasional little-known American performers almost every day from 10pm to midnight, and you never have to pay a cover. Little-known or not, the bands really pack people in, especially in summer. The crowd is young, and seems to think it's always Mardi Gras, except on Thursday afternoons, when the Emilia-Romagna Harley Club meets here. And the barge name isn't for nothin'—this place actually *looks* and *feels* like a boat. There are two sprawling levels inside, and a big terrace, plus the "Celtic Room," with tree-trunk tables sprouting Celtic crosses at the corners— it's kind of like a Disney version of an Irish pub. A good time is always had by all—if you're too snobby for this place, you probably shouldn't be in Rimini. Did we mention the free popcorn?

They call themselves the only club in the middle of the ocean, which isn't far from the truth. **Rock Island** *(Porto Canale; Tel 0541/50178; Bus 7 to Largo Boscavich; 7:30pm-4am Tue-Sun; www.rockislandrimini.com; Cover varies; No credit cards)* is all the way out on the causeway at the eastern end of the beach. The 5-minute walk out on the concrete causeway is pretty cool, if a little harrowing, with waves crashing on either side. And when you get to the bar, which is built on stilts (stilts!) out over the Adriatic, you wonder if this will be the night that it sinks. Apparently, the threat of being reclaimed by the sea adds to the sense of wild abandon inside, where Rimini's most trashed thrash about to the electronica spun by DJ Master Freeze and Sabbia. Bands also play just about every night in summer, usually indie-rock, reggae, or ska. The inside looks pretty good for a ramshackle fort. Even though it's been out there for 10 years, we wouldn't recommend attending during a storm.

The **Rose and Crown** [see *bar scene,* above] has bands in the summer, mostly of the local cover variety, but you don't pay to see them.

club scene

The most easily accessible—and some of the coolest—bars stretch out along the beach from Rimini to Riccione. Since many of the clubs are not really within walking distance of Marina Centro (at least not in those shoes, dahling), and since the city buses stop running at midnight, there's a night bus for your partying pleasure. The Blue Line runs all night from Rimini to Riccone, stopping at most clubs along the way. You can catch it at the train station if you're in the *centro storico,* but otherwise, it'll stop along the Viale. It starts at 2:20am and runs every 30-40 minutes until 6am. Tickets can be bought on board for 5,000L.

IO Street Club *(Via Vespucci 77; 0541/391-334; Bus 11, stop 13; 11pm-5am Fri, Sat, Oct-May; www.ioclub.com; Cover 10-20,000L; No credit cards)* is great eye candy for design lovers. It was laid out by Roberto from RM12 [see *arts scene,* below], and cool is ingrained in every chair, in all three of the red bars, in the huge dance floor, and in the fur walls. DJ Willie Sintucci presides most nights, and spins drum 'n' bass, new wave, trip-hop and '70s grooves. IO also has live music, usually high-end Italian pop bands. Plus, as a non-summer bar, the crowd is local and non-touristy. Theme nights can be anything from a glitzy MTV Europe-sponsored event, to Mod night, where you ain't getting in without a shiny suit. Usually there's a bit of a dress code, but nothing's set in stone. Look sharp and you'll be fine. Cover varies according to the night and whether or not there's a band. Try to find a flyer that mentions a *ridotto* (discount). The cheapest you'll ever find (except for sponsored events) is 10,000L, including first drink.

It's everything you'd expect from a place called **Betty Page** *(Via Esperanto 1; Tel 0541/294-837; Bus 7 Est to Porto; 7:30pm-2am daily in the summer, 7:30pm-2am Thur-Sun winter; No cover; V, MC):* An ultra-modern homage to Betty in her "jungle" days, this swank club/restaurant caters to Rimini's cultured crowd of jet-setter wannabes. Beautiful people lounge on curvaceous red leather banquettes, sipping from a long list of brightly colored martinis. The fake-fur throw pillows, zebra-striped wallpaper, and black velvet curtains are all over-the-top decadent. The wall behind the half-moon bar is lined with not just liquor bottles, but black, white, and red patent leather platform heels—very drag queen. The party starts early here—between 5pm and 9pm, Chef Ilde Vadini hauls out the most impressive *aperativo* (pre-dinner free food) spread you've ever seen. A whole ham *(porchetta)* stuffed with good stuff and sliced for you, little turkey and chutney sandwiches, chicken with Mediterranean vegetables, and the list goes on and on. The DJs start around nine, and before long, the doors swing open and the dancing extends out onto the patio. Their theme nights are awesome—they give away free CDs of their dance party on the first Saturday of every month, there's live music on Sunday, and the Thursday night cabaret is a burlesque tribute to the woman herself. If you're still hungry, the restaurant off to the other side serves up some of the most innovative food in town [see *eats,* below].

ragazzo meets ragazza

C'mon, that's what this town is designed for— go to a club, relax, start dancing. Women, as usual, will have plenty of guys to choose from, it's getting rid of the unchosen that's difficult. Men will find that Italian women let their hair and their guard down when they're in Rimini—almost like it's a vacation from playing the fun-but-good Italian girl stereotype. (But that happens to tourists, too...) Look for them at **Barnaby** and **the Barge.** For a slightly higher class of quarry, men and women alike should look to **CoCoRiCo** and **IO Street Club.** Try the line, "I'm lost, which way to the Grand Hotel?"

CoCoRiCo *(Via Chieti, Riccione, Blue Line to Cocorico; Tel 0541/605-183; 12-4am Fri, Sat Sept-Jul, 12-5am daily Aug; Cover 50,000L; No credit cards)* is the Colossus of Rimini/Riccione nightlife. From the outside, it looks like the pyramid from the Louvre, from the inside, it looks like your brain on drugs. There are 10-foot swooping bird sculptures hanging from the ceiling, giant pink fur tree trunks, walls made of vertical rows of chains. CoCoRiCo has three main halls, each spinning its own blend, and hosting its own devotees. The DJ's are among the best in the Rimini scene, which also make them the most sought-after in Italy. Everyone can get in the main dance floor (house, underground, drum 'n' bass), but you have to endure a 30-minute wait (at least) and pass the discerning eye of the selectors to get in the two side rooms. The VIP room *(prive)* is one of the best in Italy, and snob appeal is the sole measurement for entry. **Titilia,** is the gay club within CoCoRiCo, and entry depends on both snob appeal, degree of fabulosity, and the selector's finely-tuned gaydar.

There's something for everyone on the three floors at **Carnaby Club** *(Viale Brindisi 20; Tel 0541/373-204, Fax 0541/370-984; Bus 11, stop 26; 10pm-late; carnaby@infotel.it; Cover 15,000L; No credit cards)*, especially if you're a 19-year old Scandinavian, or the people who love them. The crowd is *molto* young and Northern European, and the dress code is loose—shorts and jeans are OK. In fact, dressing too cool might get you looked at funny. The "Cave" in the basement plays hip-hop, indie-rock, and dub. There are some lit dance-floor areas here, but there's as much standing and drinking at the full bar as there is moving on the floor. The second floor, the main dance level, has cool day-glo painted columns, and plays house, progressive and commercial dance hits. The top floor is just a loud bar (discopub, in Italian), but fun and cool nonetheless. You're as likely to hear disco as R&B or Moby's "Play" here. Beware of the tequila body shots. The cover hovers around 15,000L, and it includes your first drink—a good deal for Rimini.

ARTS SCENE

There's definitely a contemporary arts scene to see and people to meet here in Rimini—certainly more than the town's beach image would lead you to believe. What's here is choice, or at least working damn hard trying to be choice.

▶▶VISUAL ARTS
RM12 Arte Design *(Via Giovanni XXIII 12; Tel 0541/57372; Bus 1 to Giovanni XXIII; 10am-1pm/4-8pm, closed Mon; V, MC, AE)*, in the town center, is both a working industrial design studio and an exhibition space. Roberto, who designs sexy couches and whimsical cabinets, among other things, is all about putting Rimini on the contemporary art map. He designed the interiors of some of the coolest nightspots [see *bar scene,* above], and exhibits all kinds of cutting edge art, making sure that cool music is playing while you take it all in. So hip. While you probably won't be buying a set of chairs or a 12-foot canvas to take home, Robert knows

fellini, esq.

Federico Fellini (1920-1993), native son of Rimini, was one of the most important moviemakers after World War II and before Jar-Jar Binks. He was, above all, an autobiographical filmmaker who used his family as models for his *La Dolce Vita* and *8 1/2*. Though not set in Rimini, these films still resonate locally. In 1974, he finally set a movie in Rimini, *Amarcord,* which won him his fourth foreign film Oscar. People here already knew him as *il Maestro,* but this sealed the deal for his local immortality. Fellini's movies and the effect that have on people gave the world the words paparazzi, Fellinesque (duh), and introduced another film maestro, actor Marcello Mastroianni. If all of this is news to you, you gotta do some serious boning up if you want to go home all worldly and pretentious.

The **Fellini Association** *(Via Anghera 22; Tel 0541/50085, Fax 0541/24885; 10am-12:30pm/2:30-6pm Mon-Fri)* has archives with drawings, films, journals, and essays by and about the director. It's in the center, west of the train station. You can also visit his grave, if you're a serious fan or a nut, in the city cemetery *(Via dei Cipressi, bus 9 to Cimitero),* north of the center. His is the one with the sail on top. The **Borgo San Giuliano** neighborhood [see *neighborhoods,* above,] still gives the quaint yet oddball feeling of a Fellini movie, and the residents have painted murals of him and scenes from his work on exterior walls.

the latest crazy-cool art hangouts and is happy to give advice. Try a few words in Italian, and he'll probably break out his slightly rusty English.

Galleria Fabjbasaglia *(Via Soardi 19; Tel 0541/785-646, Fax 0541/785-646; Bus 1 or 2 to Corso Augusto; 9:30am-12:30pm/2:30-7:30pm, closed Sun; No credit cards),* or "Fabbi," as most people call it, is dedicated, for the most part, to established current Italian and international painters. There is always a healthy amount of contempo sculpture and non-figurative paintings. It's a 2-minute walk north of Piazza Tre Martiri.

▶▶PERFORMING ARTS

Teatro Ermete Novelli *(Via Cappellini 32; Tel 0541/24152, Fax 0541/21700; Bus 7 to Porto (L.go Boscovich); Box office: 11am-7pm Tue, 11am-1pm/4-7pm Wed-Sat; novelli@commune.rimini.it; 25-30,000L tickets; V, MC)* has boring modern architecture, but nice acoustics. The space puts on a good variety of Italian theater, modern dance, classical concerts, operettas and the occasional pop concert.

There are poetry and prose readings, mainly in Italian, on Wednesday nights at **The Black Cock** [see *bar scene,* above].

gay scene

Finally, an Italian town where there is an above-ground gay scene. You'll find the atmosphere runs anywhere from slightly cruisey to full-on meat marketing in many Rimini gay clubs. There are also a lot of cool drag nights, theme parties, and other weekly gay events all over town. The **Arcigay-Arcilesbica Alan Turing** *(Viale D'Annunzio 164, Riccione; Tel 0541/648-658; 9-11pm Wed, Fri),* in Riccione, is the local gay and lesbian association. They are a wealth of knowledge about the ever-shifting scene. They also organize movie nights and bus trips to Gay Pride festivals in Italy and Europe.

Classic Club *(Via Feleto 11; Tel 0541/731-113 or 0335/585-46-40, Fax 0541/731-234; 11pm-late daily; www.clubclassic.net; info@club classic.net; Cover varies; No credit cards)* has been around since 1987 and is a landmark in the local gay movement, having been the site of the first heavily-publicized gay wedding in Italy in 1988. The club features two dance floors, three DJ's playing electronica and disco, four cocktail bars, a swimming pool, a video room, and a "relax" room where very little relaxing actually takes place. Classic Club is a circolo of the ARCIGay network [see **regional introduction,** above], so you need a membership to enter. The crowd, mostly in the late 20s and 30s, is friendly and welcoming to both gay and straight travelers.

While **Titilia,** inside **CoCoRiCo** [see *club scene,* above], is not a freestanding locale, it is one of the best gay clubs in Italy. **Echoes,** one of the better gay clubs, was busted in the winter of 2000 for letting people use drugs on premises—watch for it to reopen.

culture zoo

Say it over and over like a mantra: "I don't have to visit the cultural sites, I don't have to visit the cultural sites." Don't feel guilty for ignoring Rimini's cultural side, but do know that it does exist. Rimini dates back to Roman times, and the *centro storico* is overflowing with remnants from every period in its long history.

Tempio Malatestiano *(Via IV November/ Tel 0541/51130; Bus 1 or 2 Tempio Malatestiano; 8am-1pm/3:30-6pm Mon-Sat, 9am-1pm/3:30-7pm Sun; Free):* The is only cultural thing you *have* to see before you leave Rimini. The official cathedral of Rimini, it's about as extravagant and carnal as a Riccione nightclub—at least considering that it's a Renaissance church. Sigismondo Malatesta (literally, "Headache"), was a conquering soldier and the mid-15th century ruler of Rimini. In addition to being a great patron of the Renaissance, he was a huge enemy of Pope Pius II. He had many of the leading lights of the day rebuild this Franciscan church into what is essentially a monument to Sigimondo and his lover, Isotta. The Florentine architect, Leon Battista Alberti, designed the exterior that, though unfinished, shows a near-perfect balance and classical line that kicks the butt of anything he did in Florence. The interior is decorated with naughty cupids, Greek gods, astrological symbols, marble elephants, the life of St. Sigismund of Burgundy (get it?), and the Malatesta family crypt. Renaissance superstars like George Vasari, Agostino di Duccio, and Piero della Francesca all had a hand in the interior. The intertwined initials "SI", for Sigismondo and Isotta, are everywhere. If the church was a little less over-the-top, it would be recognized as one of the high points of Renaissance Humanism. There's a whole lot of Man (especially named Malatesta) and not so much God here. The Pope, who Malatesta once sent armies against, never really got over this "pagan temple." It was one of the reasons he gave for making Malatesta the only person ever to be canonized to hell after his death.

Museo delle Culture Extraeuropee "Dinz Rialto" *(Piazza Malatesta; Tel 0547/665-850; Bus 1 or 2 to Piazza Malatesta; 8am-1:30pm/3:30-6pm Tue, Thur; 5,000L; No credit cards):* This dull ethnographic museum is housed in Castello Malatestiano, the castle along the Western wall that was Sigismondo's stronghold. Skip the museum unless you're really into Italian history, and just go to check out the cool building. It's about as imposing and pretty as the Death Star, but unfortunately has a busy parking lot and traffic circle out front that ruins the ambiance and makes photography dangerous. It's a brawny-looking castle, the kind that would make you feel really safe if you lived there and the Pope hated you. The structure used to be 3,000 square meters, but when the Pope defeated Malatesta and took over Rimini, he had most of it knocked down.

Ponte Tiberio *(Over the Porto, where corso D'Augusto meets Viale Tiberio):* This Roman bridge connects the center with the Borgo San Giuliano to the north. It is one of the longest-lasting Roman bridges in Italy, surviving bombings and summer beach traffic since it was commissioned by Emperor Augustus in 14 AD, and finished by Tiberius seven years later. Via Emilia, from which the region takes its name, starts right here. This one-lane bridge is one of two bridges that lead into the Borgo, and it's worth a long look for the inscriptions, remaining detail, and beautiful views.

Arco D'Augusto: A white marble triumphal arch built by Augustus early in his career (27 B.C.), it marked the start of Via Flaminia, another major Roman road. Now it is just a fitting bookend to Rimini, at the city walls on the southern end of Corso D'Augusto. It features busts of the Roman Fab Four: Jove, Neptune, Apollo, and Minerva.

modification

Who says sun and salt are bad for new tattoos? The guys at **Central Tattoo** *(Viale Derma 1/B; Tel 0541/381-515; Bus 11, stop 13; 6pm-8pm Fri-Sat; eyepop3@blu.it; No credit cards)* do, umpteen times a day. That probably doesn't stop anyone from getting inked up, boozed up, and burned up, though. If you are going to spend 50,000L for a small, simple tattoo or 60,000L for a non-naughty bit piercing (there is a "handling fee" for some piercings), stay out of the salt water, for God's sake. This split-level shop has plenty of books of photos for you to peruse, as well as black-and-white tattoo pictures and piercing videos, to help you get an idea of how exactly you'd like to improve yourself. This very arty place will gladly go beyond the tribal, geometric, and dragonz 'n' skullz flash for some original designs. And you gotta love their motto "101 percent in *dolore*" (pain). Via Derna runs away from the beach off Viale Vespucci, about halfway between piazzas Tripoli and Kennedy.

CITY SPORTS

So, you're an expert in Shaolin fighting techniques, but it's been a while since you sparred with anyone wielding wicked-looking halberds or spears? Show 'em what you got at the Thai kick-boxing school at **Fitness Club** *(Via Oberdan 34; Tel 0541/21262; Bus 1 or 2 to Via Oberdan; 11am-10pm daily; Fees vary; V, MC)*. The rest of us can stick with hitting the weight room, sauna, or tanning beds before showing our pale and sickly bodies on the beach. The tanning beds are 15,000L for 20 minutes, and the sauna and hydro-massage is 25,000L a sitting. For the weight room there's a 30,000L membership fee and 70,000L a month charge, but if you explain that you're just visiting and really need to work out, they may work something out. Especially if you fling some throwing stars at their throats and wrap a pair of nunchuks around their heads.

great outdoors

From water-skiing to jogging, basketball to sailing, Rimini has it all and has it cheaper, simply because of good old capitalistic competition. Carry a Frisbee with you and you're bound to meet some new friends (or at least some friendly dogs, if you like dogs).

You can rent a boat at **Noleggio Barche** *(Destra di Porto, 0347/279-78-13; Bus 7 to Porto (L.go Boscovich); Sunrise-sundown daily in summer; 180,000-300,000L; V, MC, DC)*, right where the harbor meets the sea-side, 50 meters southwest (away from the beach) of the intersection of Destra di Porto and Columba. A 20-foot center console powerboat (fits 6 people) with a 40 horsepower engine is just 180,000L for a half or 250,000L for a full day. There is a limit on going more than 6 miles out to sea. For a boat with two 40 horsepower engines, the price goes up to 200,000L half day and 300,000L for a full day.

You can get a game of tennis, round of putt-putt, or find a place for a jog in the **Public Park** between Via Cristoforo Colombo and Lungo-mare Tintori. It's across the street from the end of the beach near Rock Island. You can rent clubs for the mini-golf, but will have to find some-body with an extra racket if you want to hit the courts. Take the 7 Est bus to get there and get out at Largo Boscovich.

And, of course, there's the **beach.** The entire beach is blocked off into numbered lots—most of these are private. Many hotels have deals with beach operators, but the cheaper ones don't. Running around in the surf is free, but you'll have to rent a beach chair for the day. Before you decide to do this, walk around a bit—lots of the beach areas have volleyball and basketball, changing rooms, and other amenities that are free if you just rent the chair. Find a place you like, and suddenly the concept of paying to sit doesn't seem like such robbery (Well, not as much, anyway). Other services, like jet-skiing *(75-85,000L per half hour)* or sailing a catamaran *(100,000L per half day)* rental, or water skiing *(75,000L for half hour)*, are available as well. Just so you don't think you're being scammed: the prices for such outdoor activities are fixed by the city, and should be the same, by law, at every locale.

With low winds and waves, the Adriatic is perfect for sailing. **Riminisail** *(Via Flaminia 82/A; Tel0541/392-422, Fax 0541/392-744; No credit cards)* is a sailing school for first timers. By the end of the course, you'll know all the sailing basics, from rigging a boat to navigating winds. And at only 65,000L for 2 hours, with no more than 4 students, this is a great bargain.

So you came all the way out here—why not learn to scuba dive? There are tons of places along the Rimini/Riccione stretch, but **Dive Planet** *(Via Ortigara 59; Tel 0541/21506; Bus 2 to Via Ortigara; www.guest.net/home/dive; 350,000L for a full course, with all equipment; V, MC)* is one of the old standbys, and is regarded as the place to get your license (or at least take a few classes).

STUFF

Rimini is a fun, crass town, with fun, crass things to buy. If it's a book, it's Robin Cook, if it's a bathing suit, it's butt-floss. There's also some decent music in the center, as well as an array of weird specialty stores.

▶▶NOW, PAY ATTENTION, 007

In a conspiracy-theorist's prime location, just off Piazza Kennedy, the **Spy Store** *(Viale Vespucci 69b; Tel 0541/53156 or 0541/59455; Bus 11, stop 12; 2:30-7:30pm, closed Sat, Sun; spystore@spystore.it; V, MC, AE)* seems pretty damn legit. At these prices, the clientele is much more Russian businessman on holiday than backpacker looking for novelty items. Once they buzz you in through the barricaded door, you can have some fun browsing the night-vision goggles, metal detectors, phone tracer, mace pen (115,000L), or mini-spy kit (complete with earphone and listening device—270,000L). They also have a franchising plan, in case you want a career in counter-espionage.

▶▶BOUND

Libreria Gulliver *(Via Vespucci 10; Tel 0541/53390, 2nd location at Via Regina Elena 23, Tel 0541/391-058; Bus 11 to Stop 13 or 15; 9:30am-1pm/3-7pm Tue-Sun Oct-Jun, 9am-12am Jul-Sept, closed Mon; V, MC, AE),* east of Piazza Kennedy, carries a good selection of beach reads in English from 9,000 to 12,000L during the summer. Between September and April, they don't bother restocking, however.

▶▶TUNES

The kinda-ramshackle **Dimar** *(Corso D'Agosto 49; Tel 0541/786-292; Bus 1 or 2 to Arco d'Augusto; 8:30am-12:30pm, 3:30-7:30pm; V, MC, AE),* in the center of town, feels like record stores used to, before everything became part of a chain—except that it's something of a chain with 3 stores locally. Still, you can get used 45s for 1,000-3,000L, and tapes (remember them) for 29,000L—the perfect way to brings some Italian pop home without investing 41,000L in a CD that you might listen to a few times before you realize that Italian pop is much worse when you are back home. For non-novelty purchases, Dimar has a full collection of international rock, folk, jazz and hip-hop CDs.

EATS

You'd think you'd have to pay a premium for your meals during high season, but the competition keeps the prices low. In another strange twist of tourist fate, the restaurants all seem to give a damn, which means your beach food favorites like **calamari fritti** are usually crisp and delicious, rather than soggy and rubbery. And when you get all gussied up for a nice meal, that's exactly what you're going to get. Seafood here is out of this world, and the variety is staggering. And since you're in one of the most ancient strongholds of Romagna, the trattoria food is rustic, unrefined, and gutsy. *Piadina* (buckwheat flatbread sandwiches that look like quesadillas) is Rimini's favorite snack, which is a good thing for beach-bums on the move.

▶▶**CHEAP**
Piada e Cassoni da Jonni *(Via Giovani XXIII 101; 0541/29675; Bus 1 to Giovanni XXIII; 4:15-9:15pm Sun-Tue, closed Monday; 1,000L piadina, 3,500-5,000L cassono; No credit cards)*, in the town center, serves local variations on *piadina,* which is to Romagna what tortillas are to Mexico. The walk-up counter feels a little like a Southern BBQ stand: You can watch the ladies roll out the flat bread and cook it on the crack-

TO MARKET

One street from the water, **Standa** *(Via Regina Elena 133; Bus 11, stop 14; 8:30am-7:30pm Mon-Sat, 9:30am-7:30pm Sun; V, MC, AE)* supermarket has all the cheap grub you can fit in a bag.

If the urge to plan a picnic strikes when you're in the *centro storico,* Rimini's most impressive food market is on the corner of Via Tempio Malatestano and M. Rosa, on Largo Gramsci *(7am-1pm/3-7:30pm Mon, Wed, Fri, Sat, 7am-1pm Tue, Thur)*. Cheese, salami, fruit, veggie, and wine stalls are all housed in this huge, covered space. Surprisingly enough, the market butts up against a huge supermarket.

rimini eats and crashing

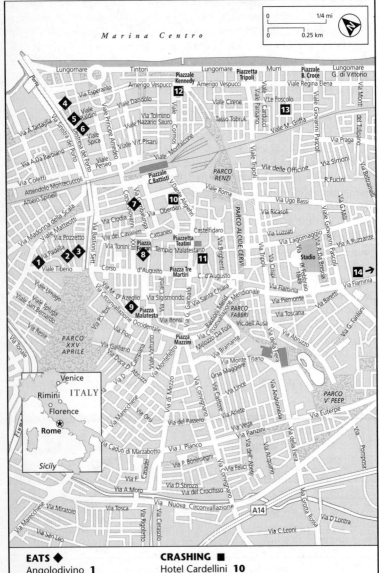

EATS ◆
Angolodivino **1**
da Pilado **5**
Gelateria Romana **8**
Grand Cina **6**
Il Lurido **3**
Osteria di Borg **2**
Osteria Santa Columba **9**
Piada e Cassoni da Jonni **7**
Ristorante Cavalieri Mare **4**

CRASHING ■
Hotel Cardellini **10**
Hotel Gasparini **13**
Hotel Sorriso **12**
Julio Cesare **11**
Ostello per la Gioventu "Urland" **14**

ling griddles as you wait for your to-go order. You can get a piece of the fried bread as is, or get some Nutella smeared on top. *Cassoni* are piadina stuffed with a sausage and cheese (think calzone), and they make more of a meal. A word to the timid—the decidedly non-Kosher *piadina* are made with pork lard. *Mmmm,* lard. *Sfogliata* are made with olive oil instead.

In the summertime, the coolest place to eat breakfast is **da Pilado** *(Via dei Ragazzi dei '99 2b, just by the harbor; No phone; Bus 7 Est to Porto; 6am-7pm summer; No credit cards)* just by the harbor. This may or may not be the actual name; not even the owner (Pilado) seemed to know what to call it. The after-club and Richie-Rich boating crowds alike eat a light breakfast indistinguishable from any other in Italy (coffee and roll) in these two big sunrooms. The view of the boats in the harbor is nice, the breeze is refreshing, and it's in a little grassy park.

What's a beach town without ice cream—or in this case, gelato? **Gelateria Romana** *(Piazza Ferrari; Tel 0541/55297; Bus 1 to Giovanni XXIII; 10:30am-12:00pm; No credit cards),* on the big piazza near the Tempio Malatesta, has tons of handmade flavors, but you have to dodge all of Rimini's yard apes if you go in the evenings, when mamma takes them out for a cone *(3-5,000L).*

▶▶DO-ABLE

One of the Borgo's most happening dinner spots is also one of its prettiest. **Angolodivino** *(Via San Giuliano 43; Tel 0541/50641; Bus 9 or 9A to Piazza Vannoni; 7:30pm-late, closed Tue; 10,000L Affettati della Romagna, 9,000L formaggio misto (mixed cheese plate), 10,000L crostini, 7-8,000L salad 5-6,000L dolci, 18-25,000L wine; No credit cards),* which can translate to either "divine corner" or "corner of wine," is actually both. The two rooms have long wooden tables under low brick arches and are packed nightly with couples and large groups of friends who come to sip wines, nosh on plates of salami and prosciutto, or have a huge, all-out meal. Stefano and Yvette make some of the best over-sized salads in town, and the assortment of bruschetta, with anything from cod to smoked mozzarella on top, is impressive. Pick a spot with a view of what's going on in the open kitchen.

You have to call ahead if you want to eat at **Il Lurido** *(Piazza Ortaggi 7; 0541/24834; Bus 9 or 9A to Piazza Vannoni; 12-2:30pm/7:15-10:30pm; Wed-Mon; Cover 2,000L; 12,000L first course, 20-35,000L main dish; V, MC, DC).* This bright yellow building tucked into a back street in the old Borgo serves great, down-home local food at great prices. To find it, cross the Ponte di Tiberio from the center of town, and take the second right, via Ortaggi. It's not all that impressive when you walk into the bar up front, which doubles as a hostess stand. But the two back rooms are filled with families, friends, and nuzzling couples out for a great meal, and in the summer, there are a few outdoor tables set up out front. The risottos, which start at 12,000L, are some of the best in town. Other pasta first courses are a good start, but the fish soup, a heaping tureen of shellfish and crustaceans, is the real reason to come here. Otherwise, pick your fish and have them grill it, or go for the *grigliati misti,* or mixed grilled fish platter. The wine is cheap, and comes to the table in big glass pitchers.

Grand Cina *(Destra del Porto 119; Tel 0541/56336; Bus 7 Est to Porto; 11-17,000L main dish; Cover 2,000L; V, MC)* is the Chinese restaurant you first went to as a little kid with your parents on a Sunday afternoon. It was jammed with after-Church folks trying "exotic" foods like egg rolls and gamely attempting to use the chopsticks. The decor was all red, gold, and mirrored, and the hostess wore a silk gown with a slit up the side. Maybe there was an aquarium with giant carp and some shiny wooden laughing Buddha. Well, it's moved to Rimini, just across from the port. If your tired of the best Italian food in the world, come try Chinese food designed for Italian palates. Located right on the canal, in the town, this is a great place to wash the hangover blues away with a cheap set menu (12,000L for soup, rice, rolls, and a main dish).

Osteria Santa Columba *(Via Agostino du Ducco 2; Tel 0541/780-048; Bus 1 or 2 to Piazza Malatesta; 7:30pm-12am Mon-Sat, closed Sun; 11,000L first course, 12,000L main dish; V, MC)* is a gorgeous spot in the lower brick vault of a medieval bell tower that serves traditional dishes prepared by someone who really cares about the traditions. The owner, Maurizio, is from Tuscany, and mixes the food from his region with the tastes of Romagna. The prices hover around 11-16,000L for such delightful dishes as the homemade *strozzapreti al salsicce,* simple and satisfying *pasta e ceci* (chick peas), or *polpetti* (squid) in *umido con formaggio.* The grandmotherly homemade desserts, like *torta della Nonna* or *Zuppa Inglese,* are not to be missed. The menu changes according to the season and is scribbled on notebook paper every week. There are only 10 tables in this intimate and romantic little space, so book way ahead, and take care trying to find it. It actually is in that bell tower (entrance to the side), a few hundred feet from Castello Malatestiano, east of the Piazza.

▶▶**SPLURGE**

Osteria di Borg *(Via Forzieri 12; Tel 0541/56074; Fax 0541/56071; Bus 9 or 9A to Piazza Vannoni; 7:30-11pm weekdays, 12:30-2pm/7:30-11pm weekends; 12-15,000L primi piatti, 15-24,000L secondi piatti; No credit cards)* is a great rendition of the typical Italian osteria. The pastas are homemade and fresh, the bread is a meal in itself, and the wines are a study in the local viticulture. The decor is simple—Fellini posters on sponged, amber walls, wooden tables and shelves filled with rows of wine bottles. Everyone from families to young lovahs will wait for hours for a table here, so try to book ahead.

The eating is as flashy as the crowds, but that's a good thing. The dining room at **Betty Page** [see *club scene,* above], is all dressed up for fine dining in leopard prints and leather. The modern lighting, fine stemware, and oversized plates give this an LA celebrity-chef sort of feel. That chef, Ilde Vadini, gives you the option of ordering from the fish menu, the meat menu, or both. You've got shrimp linguini with a Thai sauce, duck ragout over *pappardelle,* a generous cheese plate with the spicy *mostarda di frutta* sauce to look forward to *(15-20,000L first course;*

20-30,000L main course). Every dish comes with a wine by the glass suggestion, but you should give a glance to the enormous bottle list—look for the good, local bargains.

Ristorante Cavalieri Mare *(Via F. Gioia 7; Tel 0451/22777; Fax 0338/274-61-63; Bus 7 to Porto (L.go Boscovich); 7:30-11pm Tue-Sun; 15-20,000L; V, MC)* is the kind of seafood place that older folks will swear is the best in town—not inventive, just fresh fish prepared correctly. The two big bright rooms are always packed after 8pm every night with families who choose their local catches from the ornate octagonal ice table in the center of the main dining room. Except for the slightly overwhelming brightness, this place is good-looking, with vivid yellow walls, fairy lights embedded in the ceiling, and big cut-out swoops and round columns. *Primi piatti* are either your basic pastas or wonderful *frutti del mare* such as shrimp *(gamberetti),* squid *(calamari),* and little sardiney fish. All the main courses are fresh fish, and priced by the kilogram. In case your memory needs refreshing, a kilogram is equal to seven US miles. Just kidding, it's 2.2 pounds.

crashing

Sleeps are cheap here and hotels cater to the market that most *pensiones* distrust the most—rowdy youth. Curfews are few and far between, maids expect people to sleep late, and breakfasts are served later than elsewhere in Europe.

Over the past couple of decades, every house or apartment within 3 blocks of the water has transformed itself into a hotel, driving the competition wild and the prices down. Though hotels are supposed to print their seasonal rate ranges, they're actually flexible. The fact that the annual scooter rally is coming to town when you happen to arrive could cause a sweet little old signora to double her prices. Prices here are usually figured per person—Rimini is no stranger to large parties crashing in one room, so you probably won't get away with any freebies that way.

▶▶CHEAP

Ostello per la Gioventu "Urland" *(Via Flaminia 300, Rimini Miramare; Tel 0541/373-216; Bus 9 or 11 to Miramare; 7-10am/2:30pm-12am; 14,000L shared bath, 12,000L meal; No credit cards):* This HI youth hostel is 500 meters from the station in Miramare, a little suburb. It has 41 beds, a curfew of midnight and lockout from 10am to 2:30pm. The price is right, but ask yourself if the curfew defeats your purpose in coming to Rimini. If not, you're golden. HI Members only.

Hotel Gasparini *(Via Boiardo 3; Tel and Fax 0541/381-277; Bus 11, stop 15; Open all year; 30-50,000L single, 60-80,000L doubles w/ bath, 7-8,000L breakfast; V, MC April-Sept only),* just a few blocks from the main seaside road, has mini-bathrooms in every double room and some singles, and TVs in 11 of the 22 rooms. A big buffet breakfast is available in a glassed-in sunroom. If the owner deems you trustworthy, you get your own key for late-night entry. Services (and prices) go down in the winter, when lots of temporary workers fill local hotels. Credit cards are not taken off-season, and breakfast isn't served.

▶▶DO-ABLE

Hotel Sorriso *(Via Trento 7; Tel 0541/25921; Bus 11, stop 12; 40-60,000L single, 80-120,000L, double, 120-180,000L triple, all with private bath; 20,000L lunch and dinner; V, MC)* near Piazza Kennedy, is a great choice in the beach area—especially because there's no curfew. It has modern, light-filled rooms, renovated back in 1997, all with TV and private bath. Lunch and dinner in the attached restaurant are not gourmet meals, but filling and reasonable. The elevator ride up is a welcome break from lugging your pack in the hot sun.

Hotel Cardellini *(Via Dante 50; Tel 0541/26412; Fax 0541/54374; Any bus to Station; Open all year; card@adhoc.net; 45-100,000L single, 70-100,000L doubles, some w/bath, 90-140,000L triples, some w/ bath; V, MC, AE)*, is a good choice if you need to be near the station for a quick morning getaway, or you hate the beach. About 100 meters from the station down Via Dante, Hotel Card (as it's known) has 24-hour desk reception for late entry, 63 rooms with mini-bars, phones and satellite TV rooms. The lobby has seen better days, but the Spartan rooms are spacious. It's more of a business hotel in the spring/summer and more of a workers' place in the winter. Breakfast is 3,500L and they supply you with microwave dinners if you want to eat in bed.

Julio Cesare *(Via Batarra 3; Tel 0541/51303; Bus 1 or 2 to Tempio Malatestiano; Open all year; 40-68,000L single, 70-90,000L double, some with private baths; No credit cards)* is also in the town center, in a prime location for off-season travel, right off the Piazza Tre Martiri. It's a reasonable option, but looks like the only renovation done since the sixties has been to hang soccer jerseys and paraphernalia on every available surface in the lobby. The rooms are OK, and the bathrooms in some are an added bonus that you don't pay too much of a premium for. There are phones in every room. The hotel has more of a quaint Italian old-lady-run feel to it than most in town. The particular lady who runs this one seems like she's on speed, and hands out flyers for the place that must have been printed up in 1968. They make good souvenirs, but sadly, you can see how much nicer the place was then. Some years they work out an arrangement with a private beach, and some years they don't. Make sure to ask.

need to know

Currency Exchange You'll trip over the **ATMs** on Viale. Rolo Banca, on Viale Amerigo Vespucci 75, near Piazza Kennedy, changes traveler's checks.

Tourist Information There's a helpful office just outside of the station *(Via Dante 86; Tel 0541/51331; Fax 0541/27927; 10am-4pm Mon-Sat)*. The office at the beach, the location *(Piazza Fellini 3; Tel 0541/56902, Fax 0541/56598; 9:30am-12:30pm/3:30-6:30pm; info-marinacentro@riminiturismo.it)* is larger and a little more tanned. They'll both give you enough maps and pamphlets to weigh you down good, but they can't (or maybe just won't) make hotel reservations for you.

Public Transportation Bus tickets are 1,700L and can be bought in any *Tabachi* (tobacco shop) or newsstand. Line 11 runs along the beach road, but don't bother taking the bus within the town center, as your destination is probably closer than the stop. The Blue Line runs to all the clubs down the coast road from 2 to 6am and costs 5,000L. Most buses stop in front of the train station. Taxis cost 7,000L for the first 5 minutes, then 1,850 per km; add 1,000L for each suitcase.

Health and Emergency Ambulance *118*; Police *113*. The local hospital, **Ospedale Infermi** *(Via Settembrini 2; Tel 0541/705-111)* is south of the city center, inland from where Viale Regina Elena turns into Viale Regina Margherita.

Pharmacy Like all Italian pharmacies, **Farmacia al Lide** *(Piazza Tripoli 7; Tel 0541/390-640; 8:30am-12:30pm/3:30-7:30pm; Closed Thur)* has the rotating weekly schedule for the 24-hour pharmacy posted on the window.

Telephone **Phone cards** *(carte telefoniche)* come in 5,000 and 10,000L denominations and are available at newsstands.

Airport **Aeroport Civile** *(Via Flamia, Miramare di Rimini; Tel 0541/715-711)* has direct flights to Berlin, Brussels, Cologne, Dusseldorf, Hamburg, Helsinki, London Gatwick, Luxembourg, Manchester, Moscow, and Rome. The airport is 3km south of the town center; Bus #9 goes from the airport to the train station.

Trains The **train station** is in Piazzale Battisti; *Tel 1478/88088* for railway information.

Bus Lines Out of the City **Bonelli** *(Tel 054/137-24-32)* leaves from the train station to San Marino on the hour. For anywhere else, you're better off on the trains.

Bike Rental You can rent a bike at almost any of the beaches; there are a ton of little stands.

Laundry *Onde Blu Lavandrie Self-Service (Pizzale Tripoli; 137e behind pharmacy; 8am-10pm daily winter, 7am-11pm daily summer; 7,000L wash, 7,000L dry; No credit cards)* has plenty of machines and comparatively long hours.

Postal The **main post office** is beside the Arco d'Augusto, on the south of the town center *(Largo Giulio Cesare, 1; Tel 0541/784-839; 8:10am-5:30pm Mon-Sat; No credit cards)*.

Internet See *wired*, above.

San Marino

You've gotta see San Marino for the cobbled streets and the killer scenery, but don't say we didn't warn you. Surrounded by Italy on all sides, this tiny country of 22,000 people is cooler in concept than it is in reality. Europe's smallest republic (only 23.5 square miles), and the only one to be founded by a saint, celebrates a long history of autonomy and pride—it's a perfect example of how the little guy came out ahead in the end.

san marino

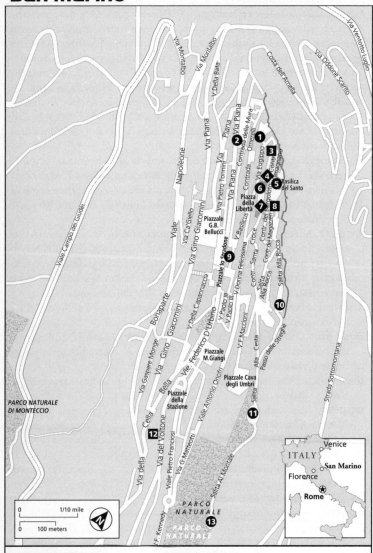

CULTURE ZOO ●
Basilica of San Marino **5**
Montale **13**
Museo delle Curiosita **2**
Museo Storico della Tortura **9**
Museum of Emigration **1**
Palazzo Pubblio **6**
Rocca Cesta **11**
Rocca Guaita **10**

EATS ◆
Righi La Taverna **7**
Trattoria La Balestra **4**

CRASHING ■
Bellavista **3**
Diamond **8**
Hotel Montana **12**

Since the 1400s, the *Sammarinesi* have governed themselves from their village atop Mt. Titano, minted their own coins, and trained their own army. Somewhere along the line, they figured out how to make a buck or two out of their small numbers and big views. The result is an interesting study in what tourism can do to a place, and is worth a day trip.

You can't resist the worn-out Disney World comparison as you pass the caravan of buses braving the hair-raising switchbacks up the mountain. The buildings are stunning, in that glittery, unreal way—all the stone has been whitewashed, and the new buildings are fashioned to look neo-gothic, nuevo-Roman, whatever. The street signs lead the crowds through the uphill maze from sight to sight, clearly indicating when you've reached a Kodak moment. But you won't see a real butcher, baker, or candlestick maker anywhere (alright, there *is* a woman making those ornamental ribbon candles). Most of the stores are selling not just your typical San Marino souvenirs, but everything from beanie babies and discount liquor to frighteningly real-looking plastic handguns—the three together are a terrifying combination. Forget about food—everything here is super-expensive and geared toward palates that wouldn't know any better. Bars? No way.

So where's the costumed character actor dressed up as San Marino, the town mascot? As the story goes, this Dalmatian stone cutter was brought to work on the port in Ravenna, but made his mark by spreading the gospel. When a woman claimed to be his abandoned wife, he skipped town, finding refuge on the slopes of Mt. Titano. After inflicting paralysis on, and then curing, the owner of the mountain's son, he converted them both and was given the mountain as his own. Local legend has it that this happened around 301 A.D., and San Marino has been a free city ever since. It's governed by the *Arengo,* a political body which was originally an assembly of family representatives, but today is made up of 60 elected officials. The locals are supposedly hardy independent souls, who have kept their tiny nation free for all this time—but mainly the ones you will meet sell plastic trinkets and seem a little tired of all the tourism.

neighborhoods

Leave your flip-flops at the hostel. A visit to San Marino means a lot of walking up uneven, cobblestone streets, so hiking boots are a better option. The bus lets you off in front of **Porto San Francesco** in front of the big 15th-century gate that used to be the entrance to town. (Make a mental note that the bus that goes back to Rimini will leave from about 100 meters down the shore, to the right, in **Piazzale della Stazione.**) Walk through the gate and start the twisty, turny ascent that will take you past **Piazza Garibaldi** and then to **Piazza Liberta** where you'll find the **Palazzo Pubblico.** Just a block northeast of here is the **Basilica of San Marino** [see *culture zoo,* below]. The cable car station is just behind the basilica. Take note that at this point, you've seen 50 percent of the town's historical sights. From Piazza Liberta, continue heading up, up, up, on

Via Salita alla Rocca, which will bring you to San Marino's three famous fortresses, all in a row: **Rocca Guaita, Rocca Cesta,** and **Montale** [see *culture zoo*, below]. From up here, you can see straight out over the farmland to the ocean.

When you've seen all three, we've got a little surprise for you—a little nature hike. There are a few seemingly unexplored rock paths that leads down from the **Montale** fortress through the Parco Naturale. The paths aren't clearly marked, but they all end up on **Viale Kennedy** or Via **Giacomo Mateotti,** which take you right back into the center of town.

Culture zoo

Don't bother leaving Rimini if the weather's crappy. The only way to enjoy San Marino is to laugh at the touristy cheese, seriously appreciate the views, which are some of the most awesome in Italy (have you heard that a thousand times yet?), and check out the big fortresses and the facade of the Basillica. The sight of the sun breaking through the heavy coastal clouds and illuminating the farmland below could well make you forget about the tacky trinket stands and make you wonder what it was like to be a Saint in 300 A.D.. In foggy weather, you'll just be damp and pissed off. Most of San Marino's museums are private, touristy, and utterly skipable.

Museo delle Curiosita *(Salita alla Rocca 26; Tel 0549/99105; 10am-5pm Nov-Feb, 9am-6:30pm Mar-June, Sept 16-Oct, 9am-midnight July-Sept 15; 10,000L admission; No credit cards):* It's easy to find this one—just look for all the tourists lined up outside, waiting to get in. Home to lots of little "treasures" like the sandals of a Grecian prostitute or the preserved fingernails of a hermit. It's missable.

Museo Storico della Tortura *(Porta San Francesca; Tel 0549/991-215; 9am-7pm daily; 10,000L admission; 6,000L reduced fee):* Medieval implements of torture more up your alley? The Iron Maiden, the Guillotine, and even the Chastity Belt are all here. But more interesting are the lesser-known devices, like the Skinning Cat and the Heretic's Fork. There seems to be one of these places in every touristy town....

Palazzo Pubblico *(Piazza della Liberta; Tel 0549/885-370; 9:30am-5pm daily, unless the Arengo is in session; 4,000L admission; No credit cards):* Rebuilt in 1894, this government building in the center of town is the pride and joy of San Marino. Fashioned to look like a neo-gothic palace, it's home to the *Arengo* (the Congress, remember?) who meet here every six months. There's not much to see inside, just a collection of political portraits and historical documents. The pointed arches and ornate balcony on the facade, however, are quite beautiful.

Rocca Guaita *(Salita di Rocca; Tel 0549/991-369; 9am-5pm daily Oct-Mar, 8am-8pm daily Apr-Sept; 4,000L admission, 6,000L combined ticket with the other fortresses; No credit cards):* To arrive at this lookout point, take Via Salita di Rocca from Via Contrada dei Magazzeni, just north of Piazza Liberta. It was built in the 11th century, but restored many times. The most impressive aspect of this fortress is the cobblestone path that winds up here along the slope of Mt. Titano. Just left of the entrance sits a small chapel that was built in the 1960s, and down below are some prison cells that were used as late as 1970. The pentagonal turret is one of Italy's oldest.

Rocca Cesta *(Salita alla Cesta; Tel 0549/991-295, 9am-5pm daily Oct-Mar, 8am-8pm daily Apr-Sept; 4,000L; No credit cards):* The "second fortress," which looms over town from Mt. Titano's highest peak, dates back to the 13th century. This is your Kodak moment. Gape at the exterior, skip the collection of medieval weaponry inside, and hike down the trail that leads off behind the fortress to Montale.

Montale *(Salita al Montale):* The third and last fortress is closed to visitors, but the views are awesome from here, and there is a picnic table right off to the side where you can chill from the crowds. Look for the stone path that leads through the woods and back into town—this is the one part of San Marino that's least likely to be congested with tourists.

Basilica of San Marino *(Piazza Domus Plebis; Tel 0549/882-380; 8am-12:30pm/2:30-6pm daily; Free):* This church was rebuilt in 1838, though it's thought to date back to Roman times. The inscription on the face translates to "The government and the people of San Marino are authors to their freedom." Inside is a Corinthian flourish of columns, with paintings and sculptures that date back to the 1600s. The main draw here is San Marino himself, whose final remains are contained in the urn over the altar.

EATS

San Marino was made for picnickers, with all those great views. There's a supermarket on **Contra del Coleggio 13** *(7am-2pm/3:30-8pm daily; No credit cards)* and a food market on Thursday mornings (until noon) in Borgo Maggiore, at the southern base of the cable car. Beware of the tourist traps that line the streets, offering *menu touristiche* and air-conditioning.

Though it's the kind of place you'd run from anywhere else—with cheesy tablecloths, fluorescent lights, and blaring TV sets—just the thought of a meal under 20,000L in this town will lure you in to **Trattoria La Balestra** *(Contrada del Pianello 10; Tel 0549/991-928; 8am-midnight daily; Pizzaz 8-14,000L; V, MC).* Located near the Palazzo, it serves up decent wood-fired pizzas. Stick with the classics, like *Quatro Stagione* and *Diavolo.* Other than that, there's good standard trattoria fare: *Gnocchi, tortellini,* and heavily sauced pasta dishes.

Righi La Taverna *(Piazza della Liberta 72; Tel 0549/991-196; 11am-3pm/6-11pm daily, closed Wed in winter; 15-20,000L first course, 20-30,000L main entree, 4-7,000L apertivo; V, MC)* is a favorite with the locals, even though it's right smack-dab in the center of tourist central. The food is as traditional and rustic as the decor. Under the brick arches, folks chow down on simple, hearty pasta dishes, grilled meats, and fish. There's a *tavola calda,* or hot table, at the bar, where you can nosh on some *bruschette* or a panini with a glass of wine.

crashing

We'd definitely recommend making this just a day trip (most travelers do), but if you find yourself stuck, you can choose from the few budget one-stars right in the center.

Bellavista *(Ontrada del Pianello 42-44; Tel 0549/991-212; 65-70,000L single; 90-95,000 double, some with private bath; Breakfast included; V, MC)* has a great location (perpendicular to the top of the cable car station), spacious, clean rooms, and a convivial restaurant down below. It only has six rooms, so call ahead.

Just a few steps from the Basilica and the Palazzo del Governo sits the comfortable and reasonably priced **Diamond** *(Contrada del Collegio 50; Tel 0549/991-003; 65-70,000L single, 90-95,000L double, all with showers; Open Mar-Nov only; Breakfast included; V, MC)*. With five large, comfortable rooms over a popular (and totally overpriced) pizzeria, it's as good as it gets in this price range.

The more modern **Hotel Montana** *(Via del Voltone 20-21; Tel 0549/992-709; 70,000L single, 56,000L double; V, MC)* is close to the bus stop. All rooms have bathrooms, TVs, phone lines—all the basic amenities. Rooms are clean, and nondescript.

need to know

Currency Exchange San Marino uses the **lire,** but they print their own coins, which have become collector's items in Italy. The **post office** will cash travelers checks for you.

Tourist Information The **main office** is located at Contrada Omagnano 20 *(Tel 0549/882-400; statotourismo@omniway.sm; Hours vary widely by season)*. There's another office on Contrada del Collegio *(Tel 0549/882914)*. Both are jam packed with hundreds of fliers, brochures, pamphlets on the area, but won't make hotel reservations for you. You can look on line at *http://inthenet.sm/rsm/intro.htm.*

Public Transportation There aren't any city buses, but there's a fun **cable car** that runs between the bottom of the mountain, at Borgo Maggiore, and San Marino's city center *(Tel 0549/885-590; 8am-9pm summer, 8am-6:30pm winter; 4,000L one way, 6,000L round trip; No credit cards)*. You can get a **Taxi** *(Tel 0549/991-441; 1,500L per km)* if you really need to be carried.

Telephone To call San Marino from the states, replace Italy's *039* with *038*. You don't have to worry about using the prefix from within Italy, though.

Health and Emergency Emergency: *112;* Ambulance: *118;* Police: *0549/887-777*. There is a local **Ospedale** *(Via Scialoja; Tel 0549/994-111)*.

Pharmacy There's a 24-hour pharmacy on Via Scialoja, near the hospital *(Tel 0549/994-222)*.

Bus Lines Out of the City Rimini is the only place you can come from and go to by public transportation, which must explain why the

Bonelli *(Via Calzecchi 18 in Miramare di Rimini; Tel 0541/372-432)* and **Fratelli Benedettini** *(Via Ovella 13 in Miramare di Rimini; Tel 0549/903-850)* buses are so cush—they're running a monopoly here. You buy your tickets on the bus, which you catch in front of Porto San Francesco.

Postal The **main post office** is on Viale Onofrio *(Tel 0549/882-905; 8:30am-6pm Mon-Thur, 8:30am-2pm Tue, Wed, Fri; 9am-1pm/2-6pm Sat, Sun).*

VENICE & VENETO

news flash: Venice isn't the only city in Italy that's full of romantic canals. The allure of this legendary city draws backpackers to Venice like rows of ants marching to a picnic, but don't get stuck in this one city. **Reviso, Verona, Vicenza,** and **Padua** all have those cool winding canals, architectural gems, and artistic monuments without the shoulder-to-shoulder hordes of summer tourists. And each has its own unique kind of fun, from Vicenza's raucous live music venues to Padua's college hangouts.

Locals in the Veneto region are well-dressed (Benetton and Diesel are based here) and well-read (Padua and Vicenza are university towns), but not necessarily well-rested (there's tons of nightlife here). It doesn't matter if you're on a tight budget or traveling with a platinum gold card—there are cool places here that cater to all sorts. And since the main towns are just short train rides (30 minutes to 2 hours) away from one another, people hop all over the region for the most exciting clubs, the best bars, and the most cutting-edge art scenes this side of Milan.

Venice is obviously the crown jewel of the Veneto, even though it's showing signs of wear after almost a thousand years. But the fading beauty is part of Venice's perennial charm; every sagging palazzo and proud cam-panile is a reminder that the city was once much more than just a pretty face. At the height of the Venetian Republic five centuries ago, the city was the center of European and Middle Eastern commerce, and a pivotal point of the early trade routes. The finest spices, fabrics, jewelry, and art-work from many cultures around the world were sold in Venice's markets, which gave Venetians a permanent sense of multicultural sophistication—and a taste for living large.

Today, millions of tourists descend each year to gobble up Venice's past, but few venture far from the souvenir-lined streets to discover how the locals live—not that there are an enormous number of locals to discover. Most Venetians have taken note of the rapidly sinking state of the city center and moved out to more solid ground—very few actually *live* on the 118 swampy lagoons anymore. So there's not the big, glitzy nightlife that you might expect, since there's just not enough of a local crowd to support it. But don't give up and settle in to the tourist bars quite yet. There is a local scene to be found, it's just quiet. There are the *bacaro,* where Venetians stop in for a quick *ombre* of wine and a few *cicheti,* plus garden restaurants and smoky jazz dens that stay open until the wee hours of the morning.

VENICE & VENETO

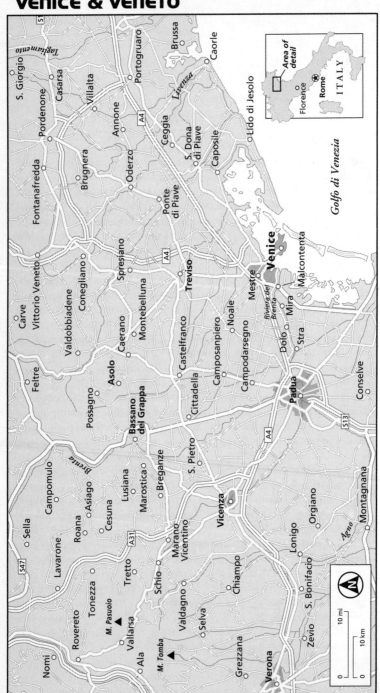

Meanwhile, over in Treviso, canals carve through the beautifully pre-served and renovated Renaissance streets, creating a fairy-tale setting in which to take a stroll. This is a wealthy little city with a quiet nightlife that revolves around the wine bars in the *centro storico*. Since there isn't a budget option within the old walls, most folks make it a day-trip from Venice, or stop on the way out of town.

Padua, another canal-curvy city, should not be skipped. Its university is one of the most legendary in the country, and attracts a large and lib-eral bunch. Discos open up onto river views, old-fashioned cafes are packed with budding intellectuals, and pubs abound. And the Scrovegni chapel, filled with Renaissance painter Giotto's vibrantly preserved fresco cycle, is reason enough to come here.

Verona also gets its fair share of visitors, most of whom come in the name of star-crossed lovers Romeo and Juliet. Those fictional victims of teen angst aside, Verona does have some very real history, packed with remains of Rome's ancient glory. Everywhere you look, there's a crum-bling arch, a stubborn bridge, or a fragment of a city wall. Its first-century arena, the third largest in the country, is absolutely overwhelming. Verona also fared well during the Renaissance; today the city's piazzas and streets are lined with ducal palaces, castles, and wide piazzas that trans-form into makeshift hangouts in the cool of the evening.

Vicenza's claim to fame is Renaissance architect Palladio, whose palaces and villas speckle the Veneto's landscapes, and have influenced the course of building over the past 500 years. But behind Vicenza's conservative facade, a nightlife like none other in the region stirs. Great live music, alternative dives, and chi-chi wine bars make this a great town to unwind from cultural overload.

Food from the Veneto is as unique as the region itself. Polenta and risotto are the starches of choice, and everything from slow-cooked game birds to fried local asiago cheese is served on top. People from this region are big-time carnivores—beef, pork, and *horse meat* feature prominently on every menu. And of course, Venice is home to a dizzying selection of seafood. For dessert, Treviso's famous tiramisú is legendary. The wines from the Veneto are also awesome, from the weighty Bardolino and fruity *valpolicella* reds, to the crisp white soave.

getting around the region

Since **Venice** is a major national and international train hub, getting around in the Veneto is fast and efficient by train. Most of the cities and towns are in a nice straightish path, evenly spaced about a half-hour to an hour away from each other. **Verona** is on the western end, then there's **Vicenza, Padua,** and we're back at Venice. **Treviso** is not in line—it's slightly north of Venice and is best taken as a day-trip from there.

If you're coming up from Emiglia-Romagna, start in Verona and work your way west. If you're coming from the north, start in Venice and head east. If you only have a short time to spend, Venice and Padua are close to each other and the highlights of the region.

TRAVEL TIMES

All times by train.

	Padua	Verona	Vicenza
Venice	:30	1:30	1:00
Padua	-	1:00	:20
Verona	1:00	-	:30

mardi gras, VENICE STYLE

Back in the 18th century, Europe's upper crust flocked to Venice every April for **Carnivale,** a week-long debauchery-fest where everybody could get all the sinning out of their systems before Lent, the period of abstinence and penitence that leads up to Easter. Napoleon stomped out the whole tradition when he swooped into town in 1797, .but it was resuscitated in the name of flagging tourism in 1980. In the first years of its return, what seemed like the entire student population of Europe showed up and took the town over, blanketing the train station and the piazzas with sleeping bags and clogging the streets day and night. The tourism board wasn't so pleased—a backpacker's free-for-all wasn't what they had in mind when they brought Carnivale back. So they retooled things a bit, and now there's a better balance between young folks stumbling through the streets and wealthier tourists attending elegant balls and parties.

You can easily do Carnivale on a budget. The streets are full of free music—from reggae to classical—and free people. The only thing you should spend a little money on is a costume: everybody's got one on. At the very least, get a mask, so you too can be one of the nameless, faceless revelers. As you might expect, Carnivale crowds are killer. You've just got to give in to the crunch .

Contact the tourist office [see *need to know* in **venice,** below] for this year's exact dates.

VENICE

It *is* possible to come to Venice and hate it. No one likes a hot, sticky August, being pushed around by the flocks of tourists and pigeons in and around Piazza San Marco or getting ripped off by the wolf-like predators in the bad restaurants and trinket shops. But it's also possible to come to Venice and never want to leave. For every bad restaurant, there's a terrific *osteria* just off the beaten path serving dishes worth writing home about. For every tacky snow globe or postcard stand there's a deserted alley ending in a canal that will burn its image into your mind forever. For every cheesy piano bar and cookie-cutter Irish pub, there's an *enoteca* where locals invite travelers out into the cobblestone piazza to dance and blow off some steam. And somewhere in Venice, right now, there's a Renaissance church that's empty except for one awestruck traveler, one old lady with her head bowed in prayer, and one of the most important paintings in the world.

Yes, there's plenty of nightlife in Venice (mostly for tourists), but from the moment you arrive, you get the odd sense that the real party's over. It's true. Venice's glory ended more than a couple centuries ago. But it was a helluva party—its remnants are more amazing and inspiring than most civilizations' treasures are at their peak. The people on these 118 swampy little islands shook the world and did it in style. In 810, Italian fishermen were gradually forced deeper and deeper into the lagoon by successive waves of attackers—the Huns, the Lombards, and finally Charlemagne's son Pepin, and moved their government to this soggy area. They figured the sheer insanity of trying to build on such inhospitable land would keep them safe—who'd want to take it from them?

venice bars clubs and culture zoo

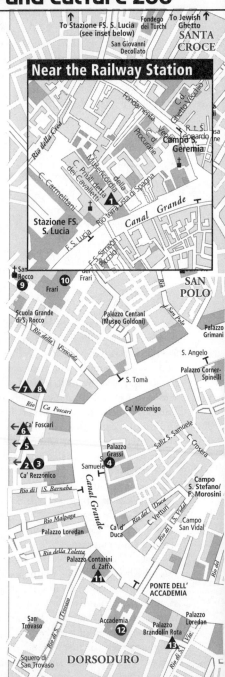

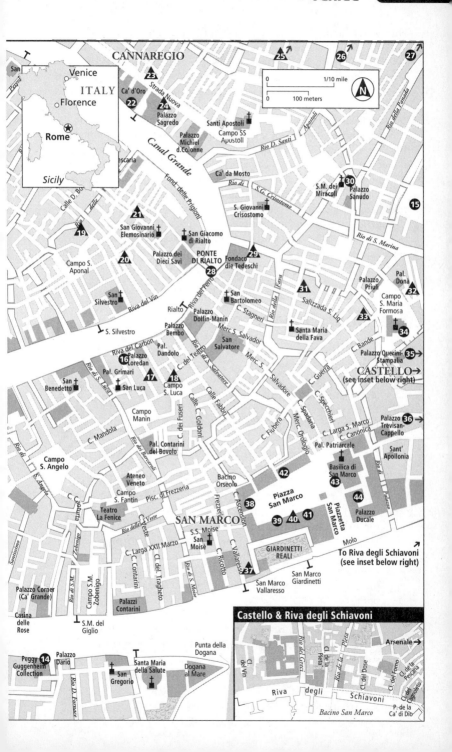

They manufactured dry land with landfill techniques, and within 20 years had stolen a patron saint from powerful Alexandria and started construction on St. Mark's Basilica, with the goal of making it the most dazzling church in the world. Within 200 years, Venice was the hub of an empire, soon to become the dominant economic, naval, military, and cultural power on the Mediterranean—at one point it was considered the wealthiest and most beautiful city of the Renaissance.

Venice's art and architecture are a visual montage of the many influences that shaped the city. Byzantine-style onion domes, bright blue tile, and gold mosaics are reminders of the city as gateway to the East. The Renaissance brought elegant Gothic arches to the façades of many of the town's most grandiose buildings. Palladio, the influential Renaissance architect, left his mark here as well, kicking off the mannerist trend in the 16th century.

Venetian painters and architects were like rock stars, with their volatile semi-religious passion, youthful indiscretions, wealthy sponsors wanting to bask in their glory, and even fanatical groupies. But they lived and

12 hours in Venice

1. Put on your walking shoes
2. Hop on Vaporetto 82 and enjoy the views along the **Grand Canal**—jump off at Piazza San Marco.
3. Get a cup of coffee at **Caffe Florian** [see *bar scene,* below].
4. Revel in the splendor of the **Basilica di San Marco** [see *culture zoo,* below].
5. Wander north to Santa Maria Formosa for an afternoon *chiceti* at **Al Mascaron** [see *eats,* below].
6. Go to Dorsoduro and get lost in the Venetian painting craze at the **Accademica** [see *culture zoo,* below].
7. Stop at Campo Santa Margherita's **Bar Duchamp** [see *bar scene,* below] for a little well-earned downtime.
8. Continue north to San Polo, and stop for a typical Venetian meal at **La Patinanta** or **Antica Dolo** [see *eats,* below, for both].
9. Take a traghetto to the other side of the Grand Canal and wander up and around the **Rialto Bridge** [see *culture zoo,* below].
10. Head north through Cannaregio, following the Strada Nova, stopping in at **Vecchina Carbonera** [see *live music scene,* below] for a little jazz and wine.
11. Wave goodbye from the steps of the train station.

breathed to create beauty, and that's reflected in their work. You know the names: Bellini, Titian, Tintoretto, Veronese, El Greco, Canaletto, Tiepolo...they were Elvis, the Beatles, and the Rolling Stones. You can see their genius by dipping into the Academia [see *culture zoo,* below], or simply by strolling through the streets and gazing up at the lofty church spires and domes.

With the invasion of Napoleon in 1797, the Venetian trading empire, the fleets, the territories, everything but the city itself seemed to sink back into the sea. Venice surrendered its sovereignty, ending 1,000 years as *La Repubblica Serenissima* ("the Most Serene Republic"). Now Venice survives only as a tourist destination. The permanent population is half of what it was in 1945. Venetians have moved onto the mainland to make room for paying visitors (and for the benefits of more solid ground); the few locals who do still live on the lagoon mostly work in the tourist trade. So there's a lot more English spoken in Venice than in the rest of Italy, though it's usually being used to sell you something. Skip the standard tourist routine of taking the mandatory gondola ride, snapping a few photos that can never even hope to capture the grandeur of the Basilica, and complaining about the high prices. Forget the souvenirs. Forget about seeing the things people have told you that you just have to see. Just hang out, wander around, get lost. Then you'll have the real fun of stumbling across the treasures—even the tiny ones—that make this city so amazing.

But let's be practical for a minute: One of the first things you should do is slap down 5,000L for the ***Rolling Venice*** card, available to people age 14-29, that gets discounts and freebies at museums, plus 10-30 percent off at restaurants and hotels. To get one, bring two passport photos of yourself (you can get them at the photo booths at the train station) to the Rolling Venice Box *(Tel 041/524-28-52; 8am-8pm daily Jul 1-Sep 30)* at the Santa Lucia train station. During low season, you have to go to the tourist office. There are also two free must-have tourist guides for listings of cool events: *Un'Ospiti a Venezia* and *Venice Pocket* list everything from concerts to plays to gallery exhibits. The catch is, they're hard to find. The tourist offices and most hotels have a stack of them behind the desk, but they go fast. When you grab hold of one, don't let go. An online edition is also available at ***www.meetingvenice.it.***

neighborhoods

Your first impression of Venice will be overwhelming in many ways. The sight of the misty Grand Canal that greets you outside the train station will blow you over, if the chaotic crowds don't. First of all, good luck. Second, don't panic. You will get lost, but everyone does, so enjoy it. Just remember a few essentials:

1. Venice's train station is **Santa Lucia Venezia,** not Venezia Mestre (this is the mainland suburb where many of the locals live).

2. *Vaporetti* are like buses for the canals. # 82 is the fast way down the Grand Canal, stopping only at the main stops, while # 1 stops at every single one.

3. Gondolas are for chumps, and the occasional hopeless romantics. Go for *Traghetti,* which cost 1/100th of the price.

4. There are only three bridges where you can cross the Grand Canal by foot. From the train station, moving southeast, they are Ponte Scalzi, Ponte Rialto, and Ponte Accademia.

5. Don't attempt to do Venice without a map with a complete street index. And remember: *rios* are canals too. There is, believe it or not, a method to the madness of finding an address in this topsy-turvy city. Buildings in Venice have both a street address and a mailing address, the latter lacking a street name. In this book, we list the name of the street, the number, and then the neighborhood (*sestiere*).

The city is divided into six sestiere: **San Marco,** to the southeast, where most of the attractions are; **Cannaregio,** to the northwest; **Castello,** east of San Marco; **Dorsoduro,** west across the Accademia bridge; **San Polo,** and **Santa Croce,** both north of Dorsoduro.

Most guidebooks say Venice looks like a big fish. It doesn't. In fact, the shape of Venice defies description. The most important things for you to

oh solo mio!

A flirty Fabio, in his red and white striped shirt and broad-brimmed straw hat enthusiastically serenades a pair of tourists as he navigates the narrow canal from the edge of his gondola. Depending upon how you look at it, a gondola ride can be either the height of romance, the epitome of cheese, or yet another ploy to shake down the dopey tourist.

If you can appreciate the gondola's history, you just might be tempted to dig deep into your pockets and take a ride yourself—especially if your significant other gives you that look you can't refuse.

Gondolas are a later interpretation of the flat-bottomed lagoon boats that early Venetians used when the islands were first settled. They're about 33 feet long and 4 feet wide. 10,000 gondoliers once sliced through the serene waters of Venice 400 years ago; only 450 remain today. They may lose a little bit of their nobility hawking rides on the edges of Piazza San Marco, but the job of a gondolier has always been much-respected, often passed down from father to son. They know the Venetian waterways like the backs of their hands—whether you're just along for the ride, or have romance on your mind, they'll get you where you want to go.

know are that the train station is at the far northwest corner of the city, connected to the mainland by the **Ponte della Libertá.** From here, the **Grand Canal** weaves through the city in a backwards "S" shape and opens up into the **Canal of San Marco** right in front of Venice's legendary **Piazza San Marco.**

The **Cannaregio** neighborhood spreads from the train station all the way down and around to meet the neighborhood of San Marco. The train station opens its doors on the **Fondamenta Santa Lucia,** a gorgeous hustle-bustle avenue that overlooks the water, where *vaporetti* depart for all areas around town, and everyone from hotel owners to peddlers of Prada knock-off bags will try to tempt you. If you follow the masses from here as they hang a left onto the **Lista di Spagna,** Cannaregio's main drag, you'll find cheap sleeps, souvenir shops, and neon galore. Lista di Spagna ends at the grandiose **Ponte Giulie,** which crosses the **Canale di Cannaregio** and officially marks the end to tourist trapdom. On the other side of the canal, it becomes **Rio Terra San Leonardo,** which wraps around north to **Fondamenta dell Misericordia,** the long strip of sidewalk that runs along **Rio della Misericordia,** a wide canal. During the day it's one of the more picturesque and tranquil areas in town, but at night it turns into a festive block party. Southeast of Lista di Spagna is **Ca' d'oro,** a jumble of quiet alleys hiding countless buzzing *bacari* and osterie. The winding **Strada Nova** is this area's central nervous system and shopping central. In the evenings, it's crawling with Venice's embittered youth.

San Marco, the mythic heart of Venice, is cradled by the twisting Grand Canal to the north, west, and south. Perhaps the most recognizable open square in the world, **Piazza San Marco** sits on the southeast corner of the sestiero, and despite the camera-toters tripping all over each other, it's still a magical place (try to go early in the morning). The piazza's sprawling space is dominated by the illuminated golden facade of the **Basilica San Marco** and flanked on three sides by the **Procuratie Vecchio and Nuovo,** whose porticos are blanketed with cafe tables and roaming musicians [see *culture zoo,* below for all]. The Grand Canal empties into the bay here, right in front of the piazza, and you get a killer view.

The best **tourist information office** [see *need to know,* below] is here also, on the southwest side of the piazza. Everything immediately around San Marco has *"sucker"* written all over it, but if you head east, past the Rodeo Drive-y **Salizzada Moise,** you'll come to some quieter areas. **San Samuele,** in the eastern part of the sestiero toward the Grand Canal, is the gallery district, and also where you'll find the sestiero's only real nightlife scene, around **Campo San Luca.**

One block east of Piazza San Marco begins **Castello,** perhaps Venice's most diverse sestiero. **Riva degli Schiavoni** is a waterfront promenade whose antiquated beauty hints at the era when this was Venice's social core. Today, Castello's scene has shifted to **Campo Santa Maria Formosa,** the enormous piazza around where you'll come across cheap sleeps, great eats, and tons of bars. **Corsa Lunga Santa Maria Formosa** stretches out to the east, a narrow little street that's full of popular oste-rias and enotecas. To the west, **Mondo Nova** is filled with bars and gro-cery stores that cater to the locals who do their shopping on the wide **Salizzada San Lio.**

Dorsoduro, right across the **Ponte Accademia** from San Marco, is Venice's answer to a hipster neighborhood. The tour groups come here to visit the **Peggy Guggenheim** collection and the **Gallerie dell'Ac-cademia** [see *culture zoo,* below, for both], and some stick around for great gelato, cafes and people-watching on the **Zattere,** the piers on the Grand Canal, but very fewer venture west over the **Rio San Trovaso,** where the real youth scene begins. Just a little further north from here is the huge expanse of **Campo Santa Margherita** (aka Il Campo), the meeting ground of Venice's hip-n-trendies. Crowds from a handful or two of bars that rim the square spill out onto the benches here. The streets that stretch just north of here are packed with a sleeker set of bars that are virtually tourist-free.

Back at the height of Venice's power, **San Polo,** just west over the Rialto Bridge, was the center of the Republic's famous markets, the final destination for all the spices, gold, fabrics, and other luxurious curiosities on the trade route from the east. Today, the only things being hawked here are cheap beads and other plastic souvenir junk—the real fruit, veggie, and fish markets still take place on the water just north of here. The streets that shoot off San Polo's main drag, **Ruga Vecchi San Giovanni,** are speckled with some of the town's most ancient osterie, a whole bunch of art that never gets seen by most tourists, plus, surpris-ingly for this sleepy area, a more modern art scene. Just north is the even quieter **Santa Croce** sestiero, with plenty of shady, narrow alleys and one of the best jazz clubs in town, **Non Risorto** [see *live music scene,* below].

hanging OUT

In mid-afternoon, all the bars, osterie, and cafes are full of folks ready to put their feet up and sip a cool beverage. There aren't any green, open spaces where you can just stretch out and breathe for a while (there's the Ex Reali Gardini off St. Mark's, but it's tiny). There's *nothing* relaxing about Piazza San Marco, though a seat at **Café Florian** [see *bar scene,* below] affords an unforgettable view, and try as they might to rush you out after you finish that cappuccino, you can stay as long as you like.

Most of the locals do their sunning and shading in the smaller, out of the way squares, like **Campo Bartolomeo,** by the Rialto Bridge, and **Campo Sant'Angelo,** in the middle of San Marco sestiero. Each of the other sestieros have their equivalent—in Castello, it's **Campo Santa Maria Formosa,** in Dorsoduro, it's **Campo Santa Margherita,** in San Polo, **Campo San Polo,** and in Canareggio, the wide **Strada Nova.** Another favorite hangout, for tourists and locals alike, it seems, are the vaporetti. There's hardly a better way to blow an hour or two than sitting in the misty bow of a boat....

bar scene

The people who say Venice is not the city for nightlife either don't try hard enough, or aren't very flexible in their definition of nightlife. There's plenty to do after dark, you just gotta poke around a little to find it. Campo San Margherita in the heart of Dorsoduro, and Fondamenta di Misericordia, in northern Cannaregio, are homes to the biggest scenes. Other pockets of fun can be had in surprising places across the city—Santa Croce hosts a few jazz clubs, Castello is full of pubs, and San Marco's Campo San Luca hides a few local haunts.

One of the coolest things in town is the *bacari* bars. A *bacaro* is a wine bar that serves up *ombre,* or tiny glasses of wine, for just a thousand lire or so, and has a long bar lined with platters of food, known as *cicheti.* You can order a bit of anything you see, be it *polpetti* (meatballs) or *sarde in saor* (sardines with onions), for a few thousand lire each.

Many tourists don't see anything more of Venice's bar scene than **Caffe Florian** *(Piazza San Marco, 56 San Marco; Tel 041/528-53-38; Vaporetto San Marco; 9:30am-midnight daily; V, MC, DC, AE).* This Baroque masterpiece of a cafe, which dates back to 1720, sits under the shade of the Procuratie Nouve's Portico. In spring, summer, and fall, their outside tables offer a memorable, if ridiculously expensive, Venetian experience. All the Italian literati used to hang here, as well as a few British heavyweights like Lord Byron. Now, the worn, red velvet cushions are packed solid with tourists everyday—Japanese hipster kids and Grandmas from the Midwest alike rest their weary souls while munching on 5,000L pastries and ogling the 18th-century painting hanging on the wall.

Harry's Bar *(Calle Vallaresso, 1323 San Marco; Tel 041/528-57-77, Fax 041/520-88-22; Vaporetto San Marco; 10:30am-11:30pm Tue-Sun; 19,000L Bellini; No cover; V, MC, AE, DC)* just a few steps west of San Marco, made the Bellini famous. Opened up in 1931 in an abandoned rope store, this place became the haunt of literary heroes like Hemingway, who undoubtedly enjoyed quite a few of the peach juice and *prosecco aperativo*s in his day. It's worth stepping inside this jet-set Disneyland to see the crowd of air kissers—a mixed bag of flashy Europeans and American dotcommers. Poor fools must not know where the cool kids hang

fIVE-O

Since Venice lives on tourism, the police here exist to make sure your pockets don't get picked. Though general carousing is tolerated, throwing things (or people) into the canals is not. Just because the twisty-turvy streets limit sightlines, don't think you can get away with anything.

out. The upstairs restaurant serves up expensive classics in a lovely, brightly lit room, but the smaller, darker, and more low-key downstairs is where the action is. Order anything off the menu while you nurse a glass of wine or three. It's always crowded, especially in the early evenings, so if you score a seat at the bar, hold on to it.

It's a fact: **Bar Torino** *(Campo San Luca, 4591 San Marco; Tel 04/520-76-34; Vaporetto Rialto; 7am-7:30pm/10pm-2am Tue-Sat, 7am-7:30pm Mon; No cover; No credit cards)* is one of the consistently happening spots in San Marco. It looks like a typical Italian bar, but acts like a typical American one. Other than the tile floor and bizarre fashion-plate wall hangings, there's no decor to speak of. The big V-shaped bar hosts both a hipster local crowd and a handful of tourists, who down long cocktails (4-7,000L) and beers (7,000L) from early evening to late night. There's some room between the bar and the bistro tables that line the wall for half-hearted, drunken dancers; the music is a good, loud mix of American pop, jazz, reggae, and commercial Italian. You'll find it a few blocks north of Piazza San Marco.

By Venice's standards, **Vitae** *(Calle S. Antonio, 4118 San Marco; Tel 041/520-52-05; 9am-1am Mon-Sat, closed Sat morning; No cover; No credit cards)* is urban hip. This little local hangout off Campo Santa Luca, north of Piazza San Marco, gets crowded around 8pm for the famous *aperitivo* hour, when free finger foods are laid out and spritzers (7-8,000L) are the drink of choice, and stays that way until the wee hours of the morning. Later in the evening, around 10pm, the lights dim, the rock and pop music gets louder, and the normally civilized crowd turns ugly (but in a good way). The narrow interior is too small to house the hordes of twentysomethings who pile in, so they hang out at the picnic tables out front, lean up against the walls of the alleyway, and seep out into the piazza in front.

It's touristy, yes, but your stay in Venice won't be complete without a visit to **Bácaro Jazz** *(Salizada del Fontego dei Tedeschi, 5546 San Marco; Tel 041/528-52-49; Vaporetto Rialto; 10:30am-3pm/5:30pm-2am Thu-Tue; No cover; V, MC, AE, DC),* located at the San Marco end of the Ponte Rialto. Alfredo, the paternal, pot-bellied owner, works the bar like a PR agent, introducing you to these folks from Florida and those from Illinois, and will drop down an armful of journals where travelers have scribbled their thanks and impressions of the bar. The back bar is a mural of jazz moments, and the deli cases are filled with inventive *cicheti*—big scallops on the half-shell with carrots and fresh herbs, *sarde in saor,* and *bacala bruschette.* Happy hour runs from 2-7:30pm everyday, with half-price Raffo d'oro Italian beer. Jazz plays second fiddle to conversation here, making a chill backdrop for the evening.

Located on Castello's main drag, just west of Campo Santa Maria Formosa is **Inishark Irish Pub** *(Mondo Novo, 5787 Castello; Tel 041/523-53-00; Vaporetto Rialto; 6pm-1:30am Tue-Sun; No cover; No credit cards).* It looks laid-back and local during the day, but at night it's packed with everyone under 30 in the neighborhood, from the waiter who served you dinner to the kid you met at the hotel. This is the craziest Irish pub you've ever seen, crowded with antique fishing equipment and presided over by an enormous stuffed shark. The free live music on Thursday nights usually starts around 10pm, and can be traditional Irish, blues, or jazz. Folks down Kilkenny (7-8,000L), nurse Irish whiskeys (6-20,000L), and when the hunger pangs strike, order one of the little *prosciutto e formaggio* sandwiches (2-3,500L). There's also a coin-operated computer where you can surf the web (15,000L/hour).

Enoteca Mascaretta (*Calle Lunga S. Maria Formosa, 5183 Castello; Tel 041/523-07-44; 6pm-1am daily; Vaporetto Rialto; No cover; No credit cards*) is the sister wine bar of the Ostaria Mascaron [see *eats,* below], and is just down the block from its sis, through the sprawling Campo Santa Maria Formosa. Young couples, waiters unwinding after work, and middle-aged tourists sip wine and nosh on little plates of salami, prosciutto, and cheese from the bar at intricately carved antique tables. They offer over 30 wines by the glass (3-6,000L), and the cheese selection here is one of the best in town for the price. Come before dinner for a glass of wine, or later, when Mascaretta offers a relaxing escape from more touristy venues.

Right off Piazza San Lio sits a busy little pub called **Taverna L'Olandese Volante** (*San Lio, 5658 Castello; Tel 041/528-93-49; Vaporetto Rialto; 10am-midnight daily, later in high season; V, MC*), known in English-speaking circles as "the Flying Dutchman." With windows that look out over a little piazza, this big, open room is the hangout of choice of hostellers and young locals, who sprawl out in the wooden booths for hours nursing a Murphy's Irish Stout or a Double Diamond (7-8,000L). In the afternoon, you can relax with a pot of tea or a whiskey—whatever gets your juices flowing—but at night, the music gets turned up and the crowds pour in.

Touted as the oldest Irish pub in Italy, **The Fiddler's Elbow** (*3487 Canneregio; Tel 041/523-99-30; Vaporetto Ca' d'Oro; 5pm-1am daily; No cover; No credit cards*) is frequented by crusty old men with tobacco-stained facial hair who are nodding off into their drinks (6,5000L), rockabilly hipsters who hang out at the booths for hours, and young rowdy local boys who flirt with the bartenders until beer gets thrown in their faces. This is the epitome of a dive bar, and for that alone, it's worth a visit. The heavy, guitar-solo music's loud, the beer's cold, and it's all right in the heart of Cannaregio, off Strada Nova.

Iguana Bar (*Fondamenta della Misericordia, 2515 Cannaregio; Tel 041/71-35-61; Vaporetto Madonna dell'Orta; 6-3am Tue-Sun; No cover; V, MC, AE*) is a tiny Mexican-themed hangout on northern Canareggio's main drag, where the margaritas come cheap (6-8,000L) and South American folk art and carpets decorate the walls—very Mexican fiesta. There's generally live music rock, pop, and jazz on Tuesday nights around 9pm, but on other nights the wooden booths are packed with an international crowd, which doesn't really pile in till 'round midnight. You may want to come a little earlier: happy hour's from 6-7:30pm, and until 11pm, you can order from their Tex-Mex menu—carne asada (16,000L), tostadas (12,000L), and tacos (8,000L) hit the spot after all that seafood.

The doors open up on either side of the long, corridor-shaped **Cantina do Mori** *(Calle dei Do Mori, 429 San Polo; Tel 041/522-54-01; Vaporetto San Silvestro; 8:30am-8:30pm Mon-Sat; No cover; No credit cards)*, on the San Polo side of the Rialto bridge, letting in a nice cool breeze. Big copper pots hang from every inch of the ceiling, and a few well-worn stools line the walls. This enoteca has been here almost as long as Venice itself, playing an important role in the city's economy by getting the Rialto shoppers drunk and happy. They serve every kind of wine imaginable by the glass (3-5,000L), as well as bruschette, cheeses, and other finger food (2-5,000L).

Although it looks like the kind of harbor-side joint frequented by crusty old fisherman, **Senso Uncio/The Corner Bar** *(Corso Nuova Piscina Forner 684, Dorsoduro; No phone; Vaporetto Accademia; 11am-1am Tue-Sun; No cover; No credit cards)* actually attracts one of the most artistically bent crowds in town. The decor's certainly not artistic, just three rooms with a bar and a jumble of mismatched tables and chairs. If you want a drink on the go, the bartenders will happily serve you a beer through the window that opens up onto the street so you can keep on strolling. There are also ten wines by the glass (2-5,000L) and great sandwiches (5,000L) on. It's located right around the corner from the **Peggy Guggenheim Museum** [see *culture zoo,* below].

With wood beams, stylish bistro tables, mirrors, and a curvaceous bar, the sleek **Duchamp** *(Campo Santa Margarita, 3019/a Dorsoduro; Tel 041/528-62-55; Vaporetto Ca' Rezzonico; 9am-2am Mon-Sat, daily in summer; No cover; No credit cards)* is *the* hangout of choice on the Campo, popular both for late nights and weekend brunches. The crowd is professional and ultra-stylish. Backpackers in ratty old clothes will get the sub-zero stare-down the second they walk in the door. Like the rest of the haunts on the Campo, it's a good mix of locals and tourists, the tie that binds being a love of the brightly colored chi-chi cocktails that come in martini glasses (10-13,000L). They play commercial electronica, but everyone's a little too cool to dance.

You can spend hours at the classic **Il Caffe** *(Campo Santa Margarita, 2963 Dorsoduro; Tel 041/528-79-98; Vaporetto Ca' Rezzonico; 8-1am daily; No cover; No credit cards)* and never actually step inside—this place thrives on its cluster of 30 or so outdoor tables. The crowd here is just as civilized (and the drinks just as pricey) as at Duchamp, but not as concerned with appearances. The tiny, brightly lit, narrow interior is typically so packed that just walking around can be a challenge.

North of Santa Margherita off Campo San Pantalon, **Cafe Blue** *(Salizada San Pantalon, 3778 Dorsoduro; Tel 041/710-227; Vaporetto San Tomà; 3:30pm-2am Mon-Sat; No cover; No credit cards)* caters to a laid-back crowd of twenty- to thirtysomething tourists and locals, who chill for hours playing board games and drinking beer. The music is bluesy, and the pretty exposed brick walls and arches give this winding, L-shaped space a more grown-up and romantic look. The 8:30 to 9:30pm happy hour packs 'em in for half-price Guinness and Bulldog (down to 3,500L from 7,000L), and the Friday night live music draws even bigger crowds. Expect American-inspired rock and jazz bands, starting around 10pm. An added bonus: there's a PC off to the side where paying customers can check their email for *niente*.

LIVE MUSIC SCENE

We should really just call this section "jazz scene." The city's music venues are all about "the jazz," though you may be lucky to stumble across a good rock band playing in a bar [see *bar scene,* above], or a classical concert at Teatro Goldoni [see *performing arts,* below].

You'll see crowds lining up at the door of Paradiso Perduto [see *eats,* below], which is as well-known for its jazz as it is for its food. Every evening in the summer (and just on the weekends during the off-season) this big fish shack of a trattoria serves up live jazz. With wine just 1,500L and beers for 7,000L, everyone from salt-weathered fishermen to fresh-faced college kids get a little rowdy come late night. Make sure to try the seafood before the kitchen closes at midnight.

A flickering candle marks **Cantina Vecia Carbonera** *(Strada Nova, 329 Canneregio; Tel 041/710-376; Vaporetto Ca' d'Oro; 4pm-midnight Tue-Thur; 4pm-1am Fri-Sun; No cover; No credit cards),* just over the Calle Anconetta Bridge. There's also a boat laden with wine barrels roped to the open side door—it's all very Venetian. This place, parked on the corner of Ponte Sant' Anotonio, is on its way to becoming Cannaregio's fave hangout. Maybe it's the whole revitalization of the *bacaro* that's swept through the city over the past few years, or the free jazz shows on Sunday night, or maybe it's just that it's just so damn quaint. Antique musical instruments hang from the walls, heavy, dark wood paneling wraps around clusters of farmhouse tables, and a long, beat-up looking bar welcomes guests upon entrance. There's a perfect balance between civility and chaos, with young hipsters wandering through the three little rooms, sipping *ombre* after *ombre* of wine (1,500-3,500L) and yelling at each other over the hot jazz. The bands start between 9-10pm; come early to score a table.

It looks like your typical wine bar, but **Antico Ostaria Ruga Rialto** *(Calle del Sturion, 692 San Polo; Tel 041/521-12-43; Vaporetto San Silvestro; 11am-3pm/6pm-midnight daily; No cover; V, MC, AE, DC),* located just north of the Rialto bridge, hides one of the most eclectic art spaces in Venice. A warm, friendly crowd of locals and international students crowds around the bar here or one of the big tables, drinking beer (6-10,000L) and listening to a jazz trio or a poetry reading, whatever the night might bring. Tuesdays and Sundays tend to be jazz, starting around 10pm. The walls double as an art gallery for local contemporary artists and photographers.

You never have to pay to listen to the Thursday night jam sessions in the garden at Al Nono Risorto [see *eats,* below], deep in the heart of San

Polo. Jazz bands usually start around 8-9pm. The beers are cheap, the crowd is cool and mixed, and if you're hungry, you just so happen to be in one of the better restaurants in the 'hood.

The only thing hip about **Pizzaria Jazz** *(Campiello del Sansoni, 900 San Polo; Tel 041/522-65-65; Noon-3pm/7:30pm-12:30am; No cover; No credit cards)* is the music. People take jazz seriously here—a mix of middle-aged music maestros and young devotees of new jazz, both locals and travelers, listens with reverence. Otherwise the place (and the pizza) is pretty nondescript—it's just a jumble of tables in a low-lit, big open room stretching out behind the front bar. But with a groove this smooth, who needs anything else? Wednesday is its most popular night.

club scene

The coolest place in town has the cheesiest name: **Round Midnight** *(Fondamenta dello Squero, 3102 Dorsoduro; Tel 041/523-20-56; 7pm-4am; 5-12,000L cocktails; No cover; V, MC, AE)*. Maybe it sounds hip if you're Italian. This tiny, modern place in Dorsoduro hardly sees any tourists, but it's the destination of choice for the cool-kid crowd that works in the city's bars and restaurants, who come here for the late-night parties to blow off steam. The low-lit and loungy space gets so crowded that people hold their drinks up over their heads. There's at least one night each week devoted to trip-hop and trance, another to lounge, another to jungle. The theme nights are varied and tremendous, usually involving costumes—*Barbarella* and Starsky and Hutch are a couple of the favorites. There's also a gay night at least once a week (which night varies). Drink prices also vary: beers that are 4,000L before 11pm will cost you 5,000L after 11pm, and 7,000L after midnight.

Just a year old, **Casanova Disco Music Café** *(Lista di Spagna, 158/a Cannaregio; Tel 041/275-01-99; Vaporetto Ferrovia; 7pm-4am daily; 15-20,000L cocktails, one drink minimum; V, MC)*, the only club on the Lista di Spagna is big and commercial, bordering on cheesy, but really popular and a lot of fun—it's also the best place to meet an international crowd. With a different DJ every night, the music runs the gamut: hip-hop, funk and house on Tuesday, rock on Thursday, Latin on Friday, and

boy meets girl

All traditional Italian rules of dating are off here in Venice, where the local guys and girls have grown up with international friends and tend to be a little more liberal. Realistically, unless you've got your eye on a waiter or bartender, you're more likely to hook up with another traveler, which wouldn't be such a bad thing, would it?

all-out disco on Saturday. There's no dress code—women take to the huge dance floor in tanks and skirts, guys in jeans and tees. The front room is just a big open bar with red leather booths and candelabras, but walk through the red velvet curtains in the back and the place opens up onto a huge, high-ceilinged dance floor. Mainly because it's the only club in the area, folks start piling in through the doors early. Gear up with the happy hour that runs from opening till 10pm every night—by 11pm, the place is packed.

Mick Jagger used to hang at **Piccolo Mondo** (*Corfu Gambara, 1056 Dorsoduro; Vaporetto Accademia; Tel 041/520-03-71; 10pm-4am daily; 15,000L cocktails; 12,000L cover; V, MC, DC*) when he was in town, but today, the only stars who come here are the ones who don't buy the right guide books. To find it, cross the Accademiainto Dorsodoro, hang a right, pass the vaporetto stop, and walk down the narrow street ahead, looking for a tiny brass sign hanging from a black door. It's very discreet and insidery outside, but inside's a different story. The patterned upholstery, pocked with cigarette burns, smacks of every chain-hotel bar in the States, and the DJ plays the same old, tired dance tracks over and over. The median age is around 45, and the vibe is very cruisy. It's not worth the cover charge, but if you decide you want to haggle your way in, take a gander at the wall that's posted with photographs of faded stars who make this their home away from home. We were wondering what Brigitte Nielson was up to these days....

arts scene

The Renaissance may be long over, but the artistic soul still resides in Venice. Many of the more alternative arts take second stage to the traditional stuff that appeals to tourists, but there's a little pocket of contempo galleries around San Samuele in San Marco, and another around the **Peggy Guggenheim Museum** [see *culture zoo*, below] in Dorsoduro. The slightly seedy **Corner Bar** [see *bar scene*, above] is a fave of the international art crowd, and a great place to start looking for fresh art.

▶▶**VISUAL ARTS**

A favorite of the gallery-hopping San Samuele crowd, **Gallery Holly Snapp** (*Calle delle Botteghe, 3127/3133 San Marco; Tel 041/521-00-30; Vaporetto San Samuele; 10am-3pm/5-8pm daily; Free; No credit cards*), goes from ancient to modern. The pretty commercial space has wide windows and a diverse collection of hangings. Expect anything from a tribute to Tiepolo to an installation by a young Venetian talent.

Just north of the Piazza San Marco, **Bugno Art Gallery** (*Campo San Fantin, 1996A San Marco; Tel 041/523-13-05, Fax 041/523-03-60; Vaporetto San Marco; 10:30am-12:30pm/4-7:30pm Tue-Sat, 4-7:30pm Sun-Mon; Free; No credit cards*) opened in 1991 under the name Bugno & Samueli. Though its name has recently changed, it's still one of the most well-known galleries in town for international contemporary artists. Oversized abstract canvases from a mixed bag of artists tend to dominate, but don't expect anything too conceptual or avant-garde.

Bac Art Studio *(San Vio, 862 Dorsoduro; Tel 041/522-81-71, Fax 041/241-92-01; Vaporetto Accademia; 10am-1pm/3-7pm Mon-Sat; Free; No credit cards)* offers one of the most vibrant art scenes in town. The gallery looks more like a few stalls from a local art fair—a mish-mash of sculpture, paintings, photography, and crafts are for sale, and though many of them are astronomically priced, there are also plenty of small, framed lithographs that make nice souvenirs. It's right on the Dorsoduro's main drag—when you step off the Accademia bridge, continue straight, then hang your first left.

▶▶PERFORMING ARTS

500-year-old musical traditions echo around the beautiful, Rennaisance walls of **Scuola Grande di San Rocco** [see *culture zoo*, below], situated right across from Santa Maria Frari. The house opens for classical musical performances every Tuesday and Saturday, and you can stroll upstairs to look at the Tintorettos during intermission.

Venice's famous opera house burned down in 1996, but you can still hear the city's world-class orchestra, which operates now on the island of Trochetta, at **PalaFenice** *(PalaFenice, Tronchetta; Tel 041/520-40-10; Vaporetto Fenice; Box office open two hours before performance, tickets at the door; www/teatrolafenice.com; 30-60,000L, 15,000L under 26; V, MC, AE)*, a make-shift auditorium. A vaporetto marked "Fenice" stops at San Marco to pick up concert-goers 45 minutes before the show; performances usually start around 8pm. Tickets are also available at **Cassa di Risparmio di Venezia** *(Campo San Luca, 4216 San Marco; Tel 041/521-01-61; 8:30am-1:30pm Mon-Fri; V, MC, AE)*.

On the seaside street looking north to the Canale delle Fondamenta Nuova, **Teatro Fondamenta Nuova** *(Fondamenta Nuova, 5013 Cannaregio; Tel 041/522-44-98; Hours and ticket prices vary; No credit cards)*, is the city's main venue for avant-garde theater and conceptual art. It also stages modern dance performances on a regular basis.

Take a short walk southeast from the Rialto bridge to find the **Teatro Goldoni** *(Calle Goldoni, 4650B San Marco; Tel 041/520-54-22 or 041/520-52-41; Vaporetto Rialto; Box office 9am-1pm/3-7pm Mon-Sat; Ticket prices vary widely; V, MC, AE, DC)*, home to the local theater company, as well as visiting performers and huge concerts.

A movie-house with a past, **Giorgione Movie D'Essai** *(Rio Tera de Franceschi, 4612 Cannaregio; Tel 041/522-62-98; Vaporetto CA' d'Oro; Noon to last showing, usually between 9-10:30pm; 12,000L tickets)* was formerly a porn theater. Today it's one of the most modern cinemas in Venice, with comfy seats and big screens. The two-screen miniplex holds over 300 seats and shows films in *lingua originale* (which usually means English) every Thursday.

gay scene

At the height of its fashionable stage in the early 20th century, Venice was an open-minded playground for people of every form, fashion, and fancy. Sadly, as the tour groups have poured in, the gay-centered businesses have moved out to the 'burbs, with most of the local population. While there's not one exclusively gay bar in town, many, like Duchamp, are extremely gay-friendly [see *bar scene,* above]. For information on the queer community, as well as gay-friendly establishments and events, contact one of the local community groups: **Arcigay Archilesbica Nove** *(San Polo 1507 Santa Croce; Tel 041/721-197; Vaporetto Riva San Biasio; 6pm-late daily),* directly over the Rialto Bridge in San Polo, or **Arcigay** *(V. A. Costa 38/a Mestre; Tel 041/753-84-15; 7pm-9pm Mon, 9-11pm Thu).*

Out in the suburb of Mestre, **Metrò Venezia** *(Via Capuccina 82/b, Mestre; Tel 041/538-42-99; 8pm-3am Mon-Sun; 25,000L Mon-Sat, 30,000L Sun, discounts for under 26; No credit cards)* is Venice's only gay sauna, and as you would expect, it's strictly men only. There's a bar, a big, open room with two saunas, and a huge Turkish bath with showers. When you're all nice and clean, go check out the video bar, and the relax room, where much more flirting than relaxing is going on. You can easily reach it from Venice in 10 minutes by bus or train. It's a few steps from Mestre Station, at the beginning of Via Cappuccina, 100 meters on the left.

CULTURE ZOO

The entire city of Venice is a work of art; you could spend forever here and never run out of beautiful things to see. First and foremost, there are the gilded wonders of Piazza San Marco, the eye of the tourist hurricane. But there are also the works of the Venetian school painters, and the city's many lovely churches and galleries. It's all worth seeking out, if only for the opportunity to travel the canals and get lost in the *calle* of Venice. If you plan on seeing more than a couple of churches, consider the Chorus pass, available at any of the participating sites, which allows entrance to 15 Venetian churches for 15,000L. All of this culture frenzy can be overwhelming—the sights that shouldn't be missed are St. Mark's and the Accademia. Don't get so caught up in the art that you forget to take a trip up and down the length of the Grand Canal—Vaporetto 1 or 82, toward San Marco, gets you the best views.

Ponte Rialto: One of the most famous bridges in the world, the Rialto crosses the narrowest part of the Grand Canal between San Marco and San Polo, in the absolute center of Venice. In 1587, Antonio da Ponte won the right to replace the wooden drawbridge that served as the only Grand Canal crossing. His 6,000 wooden pilings continue to hold steady hundreds of years later; the way the blocks in the base are stacked diagonally is still imitated in concrete bridges today.

Piazza San Marco: This huge square is the only one in Venice called a piazza, not a campo. It was enlarged to its present size in the 9th century by filling in a canal and flattening a vegetable garden in order to provide a grander setting for St. Mark's Basilica and by extension, the Republic. Between the Piazza and the Grand Canal is the Piazzetta San Marco, where the winged lions of the city's patrons, St. Mark and St. Theodore, welcome vessels to La Repubblica Serenissima from atop their

FESTIVALS and EVENTS

Millions of masked madpeople descend upon the city each year for **Consorzio Carnevale di Venezia** *(Campo S.Maurizio, S. Marco 2668, 30100 Venezia; Tel 041/277-78-14, Fax 041/277-78-11)*, during the two weeks in February leading up to Lent, the wildest time to be in Venice. You'll pay double for everything during Carnivale, but if you can handle the crowds and the prices, you'll have a blast. People put on their costumes in the early morning, and don't take them off until the day's through. The city organizes a series of street concerts, indoor recitals, and outdoor parties. Most of the activities are centered around the campos in San Marco, but the crowds spill out into all the sestiere. Don't expect the kind of seedy debauch you'll see in Rio or New Orleans—for the most part, the only falling-down-drunk people are Americans stupid enough to request hurricanes from the bartenders.

In a city where art is life, **The Venice Biennial** *(June-Nov, San Marco 1364/a Ca' Giustinian for main office; Giardini di Castello for exhibition spaces; Tel 041/521-871, Fax 041/521-00-38; Vaporetto Giardini; dae@labiennale.com, www.labiennaledivenezia.net/gb/index.html; tickets: www.ticket.it/labienale; 10am-8pm daily; 25,000L entrance, 20,000L reduced; V, MC, AE)* is the most prestigious art exhibit. Each year emerging artists from around the world come to showcase their work for a few months in the permanent palazzo space. Artworks are arranged outside, stretching from the Italian Pavilion in Castello Gardens through to the Arsenale. Tickets are available at the garden entrance on the far eastern edge of Castello; they can also be ordered by phone or online.

Lido's slightly run-down streets are packed with outlandish fashion, bursting flashbulbs, and air kissing in the late summer for the **Venice Film Festival** *(Lungomare Marconi, Palazzo del Cinema, Lido; Tel 041/272-65-01, Fax 041/272-65-20; www.labiennaledivenezia.net/gb/cinema.html)*. Screenings are open to the public (10,000L for normal showings, 30,000L for special tributes), but it's harder to score a seat at any of the speeches or award ceremonies.

columns. During summer evenings, the cafes under the loggias that line the Piazza all have free classical music outside.

Basilica di San Marco *(Piazza San Marco; Tel 041/522-56-97; Vaporetto 1, 52, or 82 to San Marco; Main church 9:30am-5pm Mon-Sat, 2-5pm Sun, Oct-Mar, open till 5:30pm Apr-Sep; Treasury and presbytery 9:45am-5pm Mon-Sat, 2:30-4:30pm Sun; Main church free, treasury*

4,000L, presbytery 3,000L, gallery 3,000L; No credit cards): More than just prime snowglobe filler, this huge domed church is at the heart of Venice's identity. Begun in the 1100's on the ashes of the 9th-century original, the Basilica was intended as the most glorious church in the world. It was adorned with the most beautiful art in the world, which the Venetians got any way they could, whether as the spoils of war, loot from outright thievery, extravagant purchases, or six centuries of labor from the city's artisans and artists. These artistic treasures make St. Mark's a truly multicultural structure, connecting Venice to ancient Rome, Byzantium, the Ottomans, Egypt, Greece, and, through its entombed saint, the man who put the Christ in Christianity, St. Mark (Even the saint's body was "borrowed" from the city of Alexandria). The Greek cross structure of the building, with the five onion domes, is a direct descendant of Byzantine architecture. The famous four horses perched atop the church are Byzantine as well, taken from Constantinople during the Crusades. The gold mosaics that line the domes are the highlight of the free portion of the church and show the progression from Byzantine to Renaissance styles.

The Treasury, with its 4,000L entrance fee, is full of what remains of gold chalices and saints' relics, and the Presbytery, hidden behind an Islamic-style screen, contains the tomb of St. Mark, backed by the *Pala d'Oro,* a jewel-studded golden altarpiece from Constantinople. You have to call ahead to reserve a viewing of the Baptistry, with its stunning mosaic of Salome dancing with St. John the Baptist's head. The Gallery, behind the loggia of the facade on the second floor, offers the original copies of the *Quadringi,* the four horses, Paolo Veneziano's painted wooden "everyday" cover for the Pala d'Oro, and an expansive view of the piazza. Entry is 3,000L. Although huge throngs of tourists crowd through here every day, remember that the Basilica is not a theme park—Venetians take the Basilica very seriously. Services are still held here, and there are always people praying in the areas reserved for worship. No matter how long you've waited in line, you will *not* be allowed to enter in shorts, spaghetti straps, tank tops, etc. Talking and photography are also strictly forbidden.

Campanile di San Marco *(Piazza San Marco; Vaporetto 1, 52, 82 to San Marco; 9am-7pm daily; 8,000L; No credit cards):* This 100-meter tower is a 1912 reconstruction of the 16th-century original, which collapsed at the beginning of the last century. The elevator ride is a nice change from the usual grueling climb you endure for a rooftop view, but you pay a premium for it (8,000L). The five bells at the top each had a special purpose and name, back in the day. It's located right across from the Basilica, closer to the Grand Canal—the two structures gaze across the piazza at one another.

Palazzo Ducale *(Piazzetta San Marco; Tel 041/522-49-51; Vaporetto 1, 52, 82 to San Marco; 9am-5pm daily, Nov-Mar; open till 7pm Apr-Oct; Last admission 2 hours before closing; 18,000L; No credit cards):* The Venetian Doge and Senate ruled over the Republic from this palace, which still rules over the Piazzetta San Marco. It's a stony primer on Venetian architecture, high Renaissance paintings, and tough law enforcement. The Giant's Stairway, named after the mammoth Sansovino figures on either side, leads to the upper floors, where you'll find artwork by Veronese and Tintoretto. The *Sala del Consiglio dei Dieci* is where the 10 infamous judges met to condemn criminals to torture and death. Downstairs, these poor guilty bastards crossed the famous "Bridge of Sighs," usually for the last time, to meet their fates in prison. **Biblioteca Nazionale Marciana/Marciana Library** *(Piazzetta San Marco, 7 San Marco; Tel 401/520-87-88, Fax 041/523-88-03; Vaporetto 1, 52, 82; Monuments Hall 9am-7pm daily, Apr-Oct; Open till 5pm Nov-Mar; Last admission 2 hours before closing, reading rooms 8:10am-7pm Mon-Fri, 8:10am-3:30pm Sun-Fri, Sat; Monuments Hall included in Palazzo Ducale ticket, reading rooms free; No credit cards):* The "Monuments Hall" section of Venice's Library was designed in 1537 by the Florentine architect Sansovino, but after the roof caved in on the collection of ancient texts, he was put in prison. Today you'll find ancient statuary, as well as works by Veronese and Titian. There's also a pre-Columbus, post-Marco Polo map of the world—things looked a lot different back then....It's worth a look if you already have the ticket from the Doge's Palace, but don't spring for 18,000L just for this.

Procuratie Vecchie and **Procuratie Nuove:** The two long buildings on either side of Piazza San Marco date back to the 1500s, when they were apartments for procurators, high officials of the Republic. The Clock Tower at the east end of the Procuratie Vecchie is home to two clockwork Moors who not only ring the bells every hour, but also tell the tide, the zodiac sign, and the lunar phase. You can't go inside these buildings—they house private apartments or offices—but looking up at their ornate facades gives you a good sense of Venice way back when. The loggias on the outside of the Procuratie were the site of Venice's first coffeeshop in 1638—it was overpriced then and it's overpriced now.

Ala Napoleonica/Museo Correr and **Museo Archeologico Nazionale** *(Piazza San Marco; Correr Tel 041/522-56-25, Archeologico Tel 041/522-59-78; Vaporetto 1, 52, 82 San Marco; 9am-7pm daily Apr-Oct; Open till 5pm Nov-Mar; Last admission 2 hours before closing; Same ticket as Palazzo Ducale; No credit cards):* In 1807 the conquering Napoleon knocked down the Church of San Geminiano to build a palace for himself and his puppet government. Today it's put to better use as the Correr Museum, which holds paintings by Venetian masters from the 14th through the 16th centuries, as well as a copy of Marco Polo's published travelogue. The Archaeology Museum has an extensive collection of Egyptian, Greek, Roman, and Assyrian statuary, but nothing that can't be found in many other cities.

Palazzo Grassi *(San Samuele, 3231 San Marco; Tel 041/523-51-33; Vaporetto San Samuele; 10am-7pm daily; www.palazzograssi.it; Cover varies; No credit cards):* The late 18th-century palace, designed by Massari, that holds this museum is one of the most gorgeous buildings on the Grand

Canal, and certainly one of the largest. Its facade features ornately detailed windows overlooking a sprawling square. And the exhibitions inside are usually a hit—expect extremely thorough and well-researched main events, with a number of smaller shows that tend to be a little more cutting-edge. Shows have been diverse over the years, including archaeological and anthropological studies as well as retrospectives of major art movements. When art is the main focus, it's usually not contemporary, but the Palazzo does provide space for small, contemporary exhibits as well.

Chiesa di San Zaccaria *(Campo di San Zaccaria, Castello; Tel 041/522-12-57; Vaporetto 1 or 82 to San Zaccaria; 10am-noon/4-6pm Mon-Sat, 4-6pm Sun; 2,000L museum, church free; No credit cards):* This 9th-century church, just east behind the Piazza San Marco in Castello, was largely renovated in 1458. The beautifully decorated facade, with Gothic arches and columns, is by Mario Codussi. Inside you'll find the usual breathtaking paintings and frescoes (usual for Venice, anyway), by masters like Andrea del Castagno, Tintoretto, Titian, Bassano, and Antonio van Dyck.

Chiesa di Santissimi Giovanni e Paolo *(Campo SS. Giovanni e Paolo; Tel 041/523-59-13; Vaporetto 1 to Fondamenta Nuove; 8am-1:30pm/3-6pm Mon-Sat, 3-5:30pm Sun; Free):* Many of Venice's Doges called this 1430 Gothic brick church *"Zanipolo"* for short. It's located right at the area where Canareggio and Castello meet. The ceiling of the Chapel of the Sacrament, by Giovanni Battista Piazzetta, is considered a minor masterpiece of 18th-century painting. Verrochio's equestrian statue of the fierce Venetian soldier, Bartolomeo Colleoni, which stands in front of the church, is one of the most famous of its kind.

Chiesa di Santa Maria dei Miracoli *(Campiello dei Miracoli, Castello; Tel 041/275-04-62, Fax 041/275-04-94; Vaporetto 1, 3, 4, 52, and 82 to Rialto; 10am-5pm Mon-Sat, 1-5pm Sun; www.chorus-ve.org, chorus:tim.it; 3,000L or 15,000L for chorus pass):* Right on the main piazza in central Castello is this colorful church with the carved marble facade. It was one of the first Renaissance buildings in Venice, and was designed by Pietro Lombardo to house the painting above the altar, *Madonna with Child* by Nicolò di Pietro, which is said to work miracles.

Chiesa di Santa Maria Formosa *(Campo Santa Maria Formosa, Castello; Tel 401/275-04-62, Fax 041/275-04-94; Vaporetto 1, 52, 82 to Rialto; 10am-5pm Mon-Sat, 1-5pm Sun; 3,000L or 15,000L for Chorus Pass; No credit cards):* Formosa means, uh, busty. Legend has it that St. Magno saw a vision of Mary as a "buxom matron of the people" who told him to follow a certain white cloud and build a church (with a big steeple, perhaps?) where it landed. In the chapel there's an altarpiece of Santa Barbara by Jacopo Palma the Elder. Santa Barbara is the patron saint of artillery soldiers *(bombardieri),* because a bolt of lightning from the sky avenged her murder at her father's hands.

Scuola di San Giorgio di Schiavoni *(Calle dei Furiani, Castello; Tel 401/275-04-62, Fax 041/522-88-28; Vaporetto 1 to San Zaccaria; 9:30am-12:30pm/3:30-6:30pm Tue-Sat Apr-Oct, 10am-12:30pm/3-6pm Tue-Sat, 10am-12:30pm Sun Nov-Mar; 5,000L; No credit cards):* This *scuola,* or religious fraternity, in eastern Castello was for Venice's Croatian or *Schiavoni* minority. Inside, Carpaccio's 1508 painting cycle portrays the three patron saints of the Croatian coast: George, Jerome, and Tryphon. His placid, scholarly painting of Jerome's death is upstaged by the fire-breathing, blood-n-guts *St. George and the Dragon.*

Basilica di Santa Maria Gloriosa dei Frari *(Campo dei Frari, San Polo; Tel 401/275-04-62, Fax 041/275-04-94; Vaporetto 1, 52, 82 to San Tomá; 9am-6pm Mon-Sat, 1-6pm Sun; 3,000L or 15,000L for Chorus Pass; No credit cards):* Most cities would find this treasure trove of Renaissance art quite enough to build their image around, but in Venice it loses out to the Basilica, which has a better marketing campaign. It's hard to get to—a 15-minute walk south of the Rialto, or north of the Accademia, in the deep heart of San Polo. Your best bet is the San Toma *traghetto* stop. It's worth the trip to see Titian's *Assumption of the Virgin,* which made his reputation, and the wooden John the Baptist, Donatello's only work in Venice. The Sacristy holds Titian's *Ca' Pesaro* altarpiece and Giovanni Bellini's triptych, *Madonna with Saints.*

Scuola Grande di San Rocco *(Salizada San Rocco, 3052 San Polo; Tel 041/523-48-64, Fax 041/525-64-85; Vaporetto 1, 52, 82 to San Tomá; 9am-5:30pm daily; 6,000L; No credit cards):* Behind Santa Maria Gloriosa sits one of the wealthiest guild fraternities in Venice. As the protector from the Plague, San Rocco had a large following in what was at the time a disease-ridden city. Frat brother Tintoretto's *The Flight into Eygpt,* on the first floor, and *The Crucifixion,* on the top floor, are considered some of the finest paintings in Europe.

Gallerie dell'Accademia *(Campo dell Caritá, 1050 Dorsoduro; Tel 041/522-22-47; Vaporetto 1, 82 to Accademia; 9am-2pm Mon, 9am-9pm Tue-Fri, 9am-11pm Sat, 9am-8pm Sun; 12,000L; No credit cards):* The masterpieces housed here make up something of a laundry list of definitive Venetian painting: *The Coronation of the Virgin,* by Paolo Veneziano, a whole room of Madonnas with their bambini by Giovanni Bellini, *The Tempest,* by Giorgione, and Paolo Veronese's *Banquet in the House of Levi.* This last one was meant to be a representation of the Last Supper, but the party was way too hopping for Church authorities at the time, who asked that it be renamed (hey, we all know the apostles could par-tay). Take advantage of the long hours and pace yourself. As you might have already guessed from the name, this place is right near the Ponte Accademia, on the Dorsoduro side.

Peggy Guggenheim Collection *(Palazzo Venier dei Leoni, 701 Dorsoduro; Tel 041/240-54-11, Fax 041/520-68-85; Vaporetto Accademia; 11am-6pm daily; 12,000L adults, 8,000L students; No credit cards):* This is as much an homage to art diva Peggy Guggenheim as it is one of Europe's most interesting collections of modern art. Peg hung with a fast crowd—Samuel Beckett and Marcel Duchamp were two of her buds, and Jackson Pollock was one of her discoveries. She opened galleries in New York and London before moving into this palazzo on the Grand Canal in 1948 (it's just over the Accademia in Dorsoduro). Today you can see her collection of modernist, realist, surrealist, and cubist art. We're talking Modern Art 101: Picasso, Chagall, Magritte, Picabia, Duchamp, Kandinsky, Klee, Mondrian, de Kooning, Rothko, Pollock, and of course, her husband, Max Ernst, are all here. The sculpture garden is a great place to chill for an hour or two.

Chiesa di San Sebastiano *(Fondamento di San Sebastiano, Dorso-duro; Tel 041/275-04-94; Vaporetto 61, 62, or 82 to San Basilio; 10am-5pm Mon-Sat, 3-5pm Sun; www.chorus-ve.org, chorus@tim.it; 3,000L or 15,000L for chorus pass):* After Veronese greatly exceeded all expectations with his commissioned Old Testament paintings in the sacristy of this church, the church officials gave him the keys to the place and said, "Have fun." And he did. The paintings of the story of Esther that adorn the ceiling, the frescoes of political and religious figures on the upper por-tion of the nave walls, the Madonna altarpiece, the many depictions of pin-cushioned martyr Saint Sebastian—all are splendid. There are also works by Tintoretto, Palma, Titian, and Sansovino here, but the spotlight is placed upon Veronese.

Ghetto Nuove and **Jewish Community Museum** *(Campo di Ghetto Nuovo, 2902B Cannaregio; Tel 041/715-359; Vaporetto 1 or 82 to San Marcuola; Museum 10am-5:30pm Sun-Fri, closed Sat and Jewish hol-idays, guided tour in English 3:30pm, 4:30pm Sun-Thurs; 5,000L museum, 12,000L tour; No credit cards):* In 1516, the less-than enlightened Doge decreed that the city's Jews had to live in this once-walled area of Cannaregio. Not only was this Europe's first ghetto, but also the first high-rise neighborhood—the overcrowding of this small space forced building upward as high as seven stories. There's a synagogue for each of Venice's Jewish communities: German, Spanish, Italian, Swiss, and Turkish. The Spanish synagogue is the oldest functioning synagogue in Europe. Walking tours last about an hour.

Chiesa della Madonna dell'Orto *(Campo della Madonna del-l'Orto, Cannaregio; Tel 041/275-04-62, Fax 041/275-04-94; Vaporetto 57 to Madonna dell'Orto; 10am-5pm Mon-Sat, 1-5pm Sun; www.chorus-ve.org, chorus@tim.it; 3,000L or 15,000L for chorus pass):* This Gothic church on the extreme north of Cannaregio, with its unusual brick facade and onion-domed campanile, was Tintoretto's parish church, and is filled with his artwork. The artist's 19th-century tomb is in the Tintoretto Chapel, while the miracle-working Madonna statue, which gives the church its name, is in the Chapel of San Mauro. (Just how many of these miracle-working things were floating around back in the day?)

Ca d'Oro Galleria Giorgio Franchetti *(Campo Santa Sofia, 3932 Cannaregio; Tel 041/523-87-90; Vaporetto 1 to Ca' d'Oro; 9am-2pm daily; 6,000L; No credit cards):* True to its billing, this "House of Gold" was originally covered in precious metal on the canal side when it was built in the early 15th century. The gold and the bright red and blue paint have worn away, but the facade remains one of the best on the Grand Canal. For the best views, take the vaporetto here. Baron Franchetti donated this palace and his impressive collection of art to the nation during WWI.

CITY SPORTS

Walking all over town's not enough? There's a **"Fitness Point"** *(Calle del Pestrin, Santa Maria Formosa, 6141 Castello; Tel 041/520-92-46; Vaporetto Rialto; 9am-10pm Mon-Fri; 9-5 Sun; Free)* with modern equipment. This spacious gym is open to the public, offering mainly weights and a few classes (everything from aerobics to weight-training). It's also a great place to meet some local hardbodies. Resist the urge to dive into the canal (really, you don't even want to *think* about what's in that water) and swim with the locals at **Piscina Sant' Alvise** *(Sant'Alvise, 3161 Cannaregio; Tel 041/713-567; 1pm-2:30pm/8:45-10:15pn Mon, Wed, Fri; 3-4:15pm Tue, Thu, 3-4:15pm/6:30-8pm Sat, 10am-noon Sun; 7-11,000L, No credit cards)* instead. It's located in Northern Cannaregio, close to the Canale delle Fondamenta Nuova.

STUFF

You really don't want to shop in Venice. It's more expensive than Rome or Florence. But do pick up a piece of Venetian glass—just be sure to shop as far away from San Marco as possible. You can literally watch the same glass ornaments decrease in price as you walk away from the Piazza toward Castello.

▶▶BOUND

Located at the end of Lista di Spagna, **Libreria Demetra** *(Campo San Geremia, 282/283/284 Cannaregio; Tel 041/275-01-52; 9am-midnight daily; V, MC),* is in a prime location—it'll cost you an arm and a leg for its English paperbacks and guides to the town because it knows it can. A few blocks north of the Accademica, off the square given the same name, **Toletta** *(Calle della Toletta, 1214 Dorsoduro; Tel 041/523-20-34; Vaporetto Accademia 9am-12:45pm/3:30-7:30pm Mon-Sat; V, MC, AE)* also has a small selection of English titles.

▶▶GIFTS

A Murano factory outlet, **Top One** *(Calle Saoneri, 2718 San Polo; Tel 041/523-86-80; Vaporetto San Tomà; 10am-1:30pm/2:30pm-7:30pm daily; V, MC, DC, AE)* is run by the girlfriend of the glassmaker's son. There are tiny *millefiore* globes, hanging lamps the size of light bulbs, cordial glasses—everything in the store is small enough to fit in your backpack. The quality is higher and the prices are better. Not only can you afford to buy Mom a candy dish, but you can also get her some glass candies to put in it.

▶▶DUDS

Calle Vallaresso is packed solid with designer duds. **Dolce e Gabbana** *(Calle Vallaresso,1314 San Marco; Tel 041/520-57-33; V, MC)* and **Gucci** *(Calle Vallaresso 1317; Tel 041/520-74-84; V, MC)* are likely neighbors in San Marco, but you probably can't even afford to look at their merchandise. But you can score the same duds at discount prices at a tiny sample store on San Lio, between Piscina Vernier and Fondamenta Vernier. Armani, D&G, Replay—this place is the real deal. We can't say when it's open, or even what its name is. The woman who sells designer men's and women's samples for no more than 50,000L a pop will only let us say that she's open most weekend evenings in the summer. Look for the storefront window where mannequins wear high fashion, and women walk out loaded down with shopping bags. If by some travesty it's closed, there's always the well-stocked **Coin** *(Salizzada San Giovanni Grisostomo, 5785 Cannaregio; Tel 041/520-35-81; 10am-1pm/3:30-8pm daily; V, MC),* your typical Italian department store, where everything from soccer shirts to little black dresses can be had for less. It's just off Campo Bartolomeo in northern San Marco.

▶▶**TUNES**

Not only is **Parole e Musica** *(San Lio 5673, Castello; Tel 041/523-50-10; 7:30am-7:30pm Mon-Sat, 3:30-7:30pm Sun; V, MC, AE, DC)* a well-stocked music store, with a great selection of rock, jazz, and indie cuts, but it also functions as an info-point for the scene, where you can pick up flyers for live music shows, and even buy tickets for big concerts at Teatro Goldoni [see *arts scene,* above]. It's one block east of Campo Santa Maria Formosa.

EaTS

Travelers are often so conditioned to think that there's no such thing as a good meal in tourist-drenched Venice that they willingly submit themselves to mediocre, overpriced food. That's a shame, because Venice does have a cuisine all its own as well as many reasonably priced restaurants (as well as *osterie, trattorie, bacari, enoteche...*) where you'll eat like a king. You've just got to know the basic rules.

Rule 1: Don't ever order fish on Monday. The market isn't until Tuesday morning, so anything you order will be a carryover from last week.

Rule 2: Beware of *menu turistiche,* which serve three course meals that will still leave you hungry. Stick to the a la carte.

Rule 3: Eat like the Venetians do—standing up—at least once a day. Many restaurants have a colorful and diverse spread of cicheti up at the bar, and though you can order it and eat it there, it's perfectly acceptable to sit down and tell the waiter what you'd like. *Cicheti misti,* a mixed plate of all the restaurant's bar offerings, usually runs between 15-25,000L; it's the best way to sample everything from stuffed scampi to marinated mozzarella.

The seafood dishes in Venice are stunning, from grilled fish sold by the pound, to fish soup *(zuppa di pesce),* to pasta and risottos with every kind of sea creature imaginable. Look for *bacala mantecato,* salted cod re-hydrated with cream and mashed with herbs; *sarde in saor,* small, fried sardines marinated in vinegar; and *seppia in nero,* cuttlefish served in its own ink. Venice's wine bars and restaurants are stocked with some of the best bottles from all over the region—cabernet, merlot, refosco, soave, and malvasia.

▶▶**CHEAP**

Okay, so it's not food, but we thought you should know about **Nave de Oro** *(Calle del Mondo Novo, 5786/B Castello; Tel 041/523-30-56;*

VENICE EATS and CRASHING

EATS
Ai Promessi Sposi **23**
Barbanera **34**
Chat Qui Rit Self Service Restaurant **39**
CIP CIAP **31**
Da Sandro Pizzaria **16**
La Colombina Enoteca **20**
La Zucca Osteria con cucina **10**
Ostaria Antica Dolo **17**
Osteria Al Marscaron **43**
Osteria Al Ponte "La Patatina" **9**
Osteria N.1 **37**
Paradiso Perduto **18**
Pizza e Poi **19**
Ristorante ai Barbicani **30**
Ristorante Cantina Canaletto **28**
Taverna San Trovaso **11**
Tokyo Sushi Restaurant **33**
Trattoria Ai Cugnai **14**
Trattoria Ca' d'Oro Vedova **22**
Trattoria da Remigio **45**
Tre Spiede **25**

CRASHING
Albergo Doni **42**
Albergo San Samuele **15**
Antica Locanda al Gambero **38**
Archie's House **21**
Casa Gerotto **6**
Foresteria Valdese **44**
Hotel Adua **5**
Hotel Agli Alboretti **12**
Hotel ai Do Mori **36**
Hotel Barnardi-Semenzato **24**
Hotel Bruno **27**
Hotel Canada **26**
Hotel Canaletto **29**
Hotel Caprera **4**
Hotel Casa Linger **46**
Hotel Galleria **13**
Hotel Iris **8**
Hotel Messner **40**
Hotel Minerva e Nettuno **3**
Hotel Moderno **1**
Hotel Rossi **2**
Locanda Canal **35**
Ostello di Venezia **41**

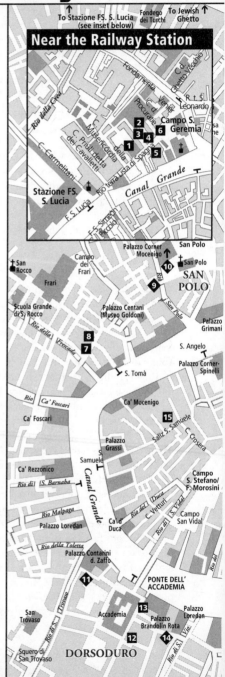

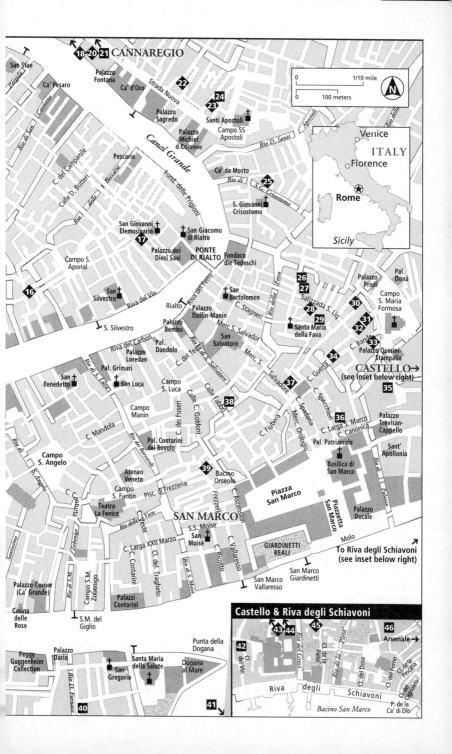

Vaporetto Rialto; 9am-1pm/5-7pm Thu-Tue, closed Sun and Wed; No credit cards). This tiny wine shop, filled top to bottom with barrels, is an essential stop on the way home for most Venetians. You bring the empty container (the humble plastic water bottle will do), and for 2,800-3,800L, they fill it up with a liter of pinot Nero, rabuso, or whatever strikes your fancy. Don't picnic in Venice without it.

Just west of Piazza San Marco, **Chat Qui Rit Self Service Restaurant** *(Angolo Frezzeria, 1131 San Marco; Tel 041/522-90-86; 11am-9:30pm daily, high season, closed Sat and Mon low season; 11-16,000L entrees; 1,000L cover; No credit cards)* is in the business of nourishing thousands of tourists a day. With crazy floral wallpaper and fake trees in the *"sala giardino,"* this bright, cheery place looks like it was decorated by a grandma on acid. But the food is pretty good, super-fast, and very cheap. Try the grilled sardines, or the lasagna.

This is what you think of when you think of Venice: old men drinking *ombres* of wine, and after a while, breaking out into song. Happens all the time at **Ai Promessi Sposi** *(Calle dell Oca 4367 Cannaregio; Tel 041/522-86-09; 9:30am-3/6-10pm daily; 1-3,000L cicheti; No credit cards)*, a long, narrow bar where people stop in for a few quick cicheti. There's no decor to speak of—just a few things that were taped up to the wall years ago, and now are yellowed and curling at the edges. But you can't argue with the quality of the buffet—try the heavily seasoned *polpetti*. Wine costs between 1,000L and 3,000L per ombre, just a few gulpfuls each. It's just a five-minute walk east from the train station.

A popular pizza by the slice place, **Pizza e Poi** *(Via V. Emanuele/Strada Nova, 2222 Cannaregio; Tel 041/522-86-71; 11:30am-3pm/5-9:30pm daily, later in summer; 3,500L slice of pizza; No credit cards)* caters to the crowds of Cannaregio bar-hoppers. Students and tipsy tourists hang outside the little fluorescent-lit takeaway joint, drinking wine out of paper cups that they buy for 1,000L. It may be the cheapest way to get a buzz on, and the best way to find out where all these cool kids are headed. Oh, there's also pizza—the oversized slices are topped with everything from sausage to mushrooms.

Locals come from all over town for the innovatively topped slices at **CIP CIAP** *(Calle del Mondo Novo, 5799 Castello; Tel 041/523-66-21; Vaporetto Rialto; 9am-9pm Wed-Mon; 3,000L slice of pizza; No credit cards)*, a tiny, brightly lit take-out joint on Castello's popular main drag, Mondo Novo. It intersects with San Lio to the west and Campo Santa Maria Formosa to the east.

▶▶DO-ABLE

Seaside fish shack **Paradiso Perduto** *(Fondamenta della Misericordia, 2540 Cannaregio; Tel 041/720-581; Vaporetto San Marcuola; 7am-2am daily; 1,5000L wine; 7,000L beer; 13-20,000L entrees; No credit cards)* serves up the freshest catch-of-the-day in a dining room that look like the inside of your dad's garage. It's the most happening spot in northern Cannaregio. Busy waiters drop off big platters to strangers who've become fast friends sitting at the long communal tables. Try the *fritto misto* (fried calamari, shrimp, sardines—big enough for three), or *spaghetti al cozze e vongole* (mussels and clams). In the summer, live jazz moves in [see *live music scene,* above]. The neighborhood artists have also started their own Perduto beautification campaign—thus the arty ceiling, with post-modern murals and found object sculpture hovering overhead.

The two cozy-but-cramped rooms of old-style trattoria **Tre Spiede** (*Salizzada San Canciano, 5906 Cannaregio; Tel 041/520-80-35; Vaporetto: Rialto; Noon-3pm/7-10pm Tue-Sun, closed Sun afternoon; 15 30,000L entrees; No reservations; V, MC)* are filled every night with locals and in-the-know tourists chowing down on great, no-frills seafood and downing white wine by the carafe. You get to pick your fish from the catch of the day on ice—it's priced by weight. It's all just one block from the Grand Canal, equidistant from the Ca d'Oro and Rialto vaporetto stop.

Wine drinkers crowd around the alley outside **Trattoria Ca' d'Oro Vedova** (*Ramo Ca' d'Oro, 3912 Cannaregio; Tel 041/528-53-24; 11:30-3pm/6:30-11pm Fri-Tue, closed Sat morning; Closes down Jul-Aug; 13-18,000L entrees; No credit cards),* waiting for a table at one of the most famous osterie in town. Run by the Doni family for most of its 130 years, this place is known for its seafood pastas. The spicy scampi with spaghetti is simple and sublime, and the sweet crab sauce has everyone diving into the bowls with their fingers. Homemade bilberry grappa, or limoncello, is the perfect end to a meal. Although the two big rooms look casual, with candles and fresh flowers on the tables, there's definitely a hipper-than-thou vibe here. This is the best food that will ever be served to you by Goth girls with attitude.

If **Barbanera** (*Corso de la Guerra Cassellaria, 5356 Castello; Tel 041/521-07-17; 10am-midnight daily; 9-14,000L pizza, 7,000L beer pints; V, MC, AX)* looks all too familiar, it's probably because you spent your college years in a joint a lot like it. With graffiti covering the oversized wooden booths, big-screen satellite TVs, loud alterna music, and lotsa, lotsa beer, you may start having flashbacks. A young, diverse crowd drops in day and night for the huge, dripping pizzas, cheap drinks, and quality chill-time. The refreshingly un-Italian salads—try the Mexican salad with salsa verde—and sandwiches of all kinds (6-12,000L) are a nice change from the typical panini. If the food didn't steal the show, the beer would—five types on tap (6-7,000L per pint), and more than 30 by the bottle. It's just a few blocks north of San Marco square, near the beginning of San Lio.

Just around the corner from San Lio, the ultra-modern **Tokyo Sushi Restaurant** (*Calle delle Bande, 5281-2-3 Castello; Tel 041/277-04-20; Noon-4pm/6pm-midnight daily; V, MC)* looks as out of place here as a gondola would in Tokyo. The pretty abstract art and streamlined furniture say modern Japan, but you're still in Venice—with all the fresh seafood available, you'd better believe you're going to get wonderful sushi. It's also surprisingly cheap: miso soup for 5,000L, tempura for 10,000L, and a six-piece sushi combo with salad and soup for 20,000L. Big ceramic mugs keep filling up with all-you-can-drink green tea, and there's also Asahi beer (5,000L). Expect a 12% service charge on top of the bill.

As soon as you see the old tile floor and beat-up tables crammed with locals at **Osteria Al Marscaron** *(Calle Lunga Santa Maria Formosa, 5525 Castello, Tel 041/522-59-95; Vaporetto Rialto; 11:30am-3pm/7:30-11:30pm Mon-Sat; 18-32,000L entrees; No credit cards)*, you know you've stumbled onto something good. Located just north of Santa Maria Formosa, this is one of Venice's famed osterie. Morning, noon, or night, it's the site of a cicheti frenzy, packed solid with people pointing their requests for a little of this, a little more of that. Join in, or take a seat and order something even more sensational like *pasta vongole* (spaghetti with clams) or grilled fish. Wash it all down with a liter of the house red (12,000L).

Old-school trattoria all the way, **Trattoria Ai Cugnai** *(Corso NouvoPiscina Forner, 857 Dorsoduro; Tel 041/528-92-38; Vaporetto Accademia; 11am-2:30pm/6-9:30pm Tue-Sat; 14-20,000L entrees; No credit cards)* comes complete with wood paneling, fake flowers in the porcelain vases, cheesy sad clown prints, and front windows boasting the catch of the day on ice. Ignore the rest and focus on that last part. The elderly waitresses mean business—by the time they come to the table, you'd better know whether you're ordering the daily special of boiled crabs or the pasta vongole. It's right down the block and around the corner from the Guggenheim museum, and always stocked with a good mix of tourists and locals.

The newest osterie in the 'hood, **Osteria Ai 4 Feri** *(Calle Lunga San Barnaba, 2754/a Dorsoduro; Tel 041/520-69-78; Vaporetto Ca' Rezzonico; 11:30am-2:30pm/6:30-10:30pm Mon-Sat; Avg. entree 20,000L; No credit cards)* is also the most popular with the locals. It's just a five-minute walk north from the Accademia Bridge in Dorsoduro, and south of Campo Santa Margarita. Copper pots and old photos of Venice decorate the walls, but the centerpiece is a phenomenal *cicheti* bar. Order a *cicheti misti* sampler plate (20,000L) to try one of everything—stuffed peppers, grilled shrimp, fried oysters, the works. Otherwise, you can order a fish entree and pay by the kilogram—tell them how much you want to pay (20,000L is about normal), and they'll throw one on the grill for you.

Vegetarian and fusion foodies should experience the charm of **La Zucca Osteria con Cucina** *(San Giacomo dell Oria, 1762 Santa Croce; Tel 041/524-15-70; 12:30-2:30pm/7-10:30pm Mon-Sat; 10-32,000L entrees; V, MC, AE, DC)*. This little, winding restaurant looks over a quiet canal in un-touristy northern Santa Croce, many of its rooms perching perilously over the water. The modern design mirrors the menu—prepare for innovative dishes heavy on the vegetables and eastern spices, but rooted in Italian tradition. Pumpkin soup is served with a fragrant Indian poori bread, the penne is tossed with broccoli and smoked ricotta, and the roast turkey breast is drizzled with a curry yogurt sauce.

With the flirtiest waitresses in town, the traditional **Osteria Al Ponte "La Patatina"** *(Calle Saoneri, 2741/a San Polo; Tel 041/523-72-38; 9:30am-2:30pm/4:30-9pm Mon-Sat; 13-18,000L entrees; V, MC, AE)* is the kind of place where workmen come for lunch day in and day out. The waitresses probably have something to do with its enduring appeal, but there's also the food: hearty, traditional fare like homemade *pappardelle* with everything from *musetto* sausage to slow-cooked rabbit. The cicheti stacked on the bar make a great lunch if you muster up the strength to push your way through the crowd. The 20 or so wines by the glass are 2,500L or less. It's just south of the Rio di San Polo.

A popular spot during the off hours, when all the other restaurants are closed, is **Da Sandro Pizzaria** *(Campiello Meloni, 1473/1411/1412 San Polo; Tel 045/523-48-94; 11:30am-11:30pm Fri-Wed; 8-13,000L pizza, 12-20,000L entrees; V, MC)* serving some of the best pizzas in San Polo. This is the kind of place where wine is poured straight out of the barrels, and the *tagliatelle* is homemade, delicious and light, with just enough bite. The three-course meals are a great deal—spring for the fresh fish. Folks hang out under the canopies outside, or take a breather from the busy streets in the pretty dining room, which is covered with a mishmash of cheesy paintings. It's just east of Campo San Polo.

▶▶**SPLURGE**

Stepping into **La Colombina Enoteca** *(Campiello Anconetta, 1828 Cannaregio; Tel 041/275-06-22; Fax 041/275-67-94; Vaporetto San Marcuola; 12:30-2:30pm/8:30pm-12:30am Mon-Sat, closed Mon morning; 12-16,000L first courses, 14-26,000L main dishes; No credit cards)* feels more like visiting family friends than dining at Venice's latest greatest. Owners Biba Candiani, the director of a TV food program, and Alberto Metope, a former taxi driver, have retired to serving up creative, decidedly non-Venetian food. There's no menu, so listen carefully: Biba cooks up a few appetizers, like radicchio with tome goat cheese and potatoes, or sea scallops over wilted greens, and a few fresh pastas and main dishes, like tortelli filled with pumpkin or roast cod over wilted greens. Whenever Alberto takes a break from waiting tables to talk to some pals, Biba shoots him angry looks from the small kitchen and yells, *"Pronti!"* The stucco walls are embedded with mosaics and tiles, and adorned with photos of family and friends. Make a reservation—this place is booked long in advance. Since they stay open late, you can usually score a table after 11pm. It's a five-minute walk east from the station, just where Rio Terra curves around and runs into Campiello Anconetta.

The warm, friendly vibe at **Al Nono Risorto** *(Sotoportego de Siora Bettina, 2338 Sante Croce; Tel 041/524-11-69; Noon-2:30pm/7-11pm Wed-Mon, later in summer; 9-13,000L first courses, 15-20,000L main dishes; No credit cards),* deep in the heart of Santa Croce, just northwest of Campo San Polo, makes up for the lack of atmosphere. If all the seafood in Venice has left you with an appetite for something else...*anything* else...the menu will leave you satisfied. Go for homemade gnocchi in rich ragu, or gigantic, irregularly shaped pizzas with gorgonzola and radicchio (13,000L). In the summer, bands take the stage a few nights a week in the garden out back, while an appreciative crowd lingers late under the trees. Even in the off-season, there's jazz every Thursday [See *live music scene,* above].

Hip American and Italian pop plays in the background at **Ostaria Antica Dolo** *(Ruga Rialto, 778 San Polo; Tel 041/522-65-46; 9:30am-*

3pm/5:30-10:30pm daily; 14-20,000L first courses, 14-25,000L main dishes; V, MC, AE), which is both the most traditional and the funkiest restaurant in town. The floors are black and white tile mosaics, and the dark red walls are covered top to bottom with everything from fin-de-siecle porn to abstract art to copper pots and pans—it's all very post-modern. But you should also notice that they spell *ostaria* the traditional way, with an "a" rather than an "e," and take the preparation of traditional dishes like *spaghetti al nero di sepia* and *sardi in soar* just as seriously. Cool thirtysomething owner Matteo pours shots of grappa for the regulars at the tiny wood bar, and offers *crostini* and cheeses from the deli case. It's right on Ruga Rialto, the main thoroughfare that runs from the Rialto area in San Polo, toward Campo San Polo.

crashing

Sweet dreams in Venice don't come cheap, but because of the competition, they're not astronomical either. Decide where to stay based on your agenda. Want loud, rowdy nightlife? Stay in Dorsoduro. Prefer laid-back wine bars? Stay in Cannaregio. Of course, the vaporetti run all night long, so if you're willing to wait for your ship to come in, it really doesn't matter where you stay.

wired

The cheapest—and most fun—way to check your email is with a beer in one hand and your mouse in the other. **Café Blue, Café Noir,** and **Innishark** [see *bar scene,* above, for all] all have a few computers with net access.

Venetian Navigator Internet Point *(Calle delle Bande, 5269 Castello; Tel 041/522-60-84; 10am-10pm daily; 12,000L; No credit cards),* right off San Lio, is also a great little place to check your email and call home with *dialpad.com.* There are just a few computers, but since it's not really on the tourist track, you rarely have to wait. As institutional as it gets, **Net House** *(Campo Santo Stefano, 2967-2958 San Marco; Tel 041/277-11-90; 10am-8pm daily; 15,000L per hour; V, MC, AE)* is crammed with over 30 computers. To call it a cybercafe would be a stretch—it's just a big room filled with money-sucking machines that have DSL access. The **Net Gate** *(Crosera S. Pantalon, 3812/a Dorsoduro; Tel 041/244-02-13; 12,000L per hour; No credit cards),* just north of Campo Santa Margherita, is geared toward all the students who hang out in "The Campo." It's more a computer store than anything else, but offers a good rate, for Venice anyway.

High season runs from March to November, and from the end of December to mid-January, and throughout Carnivale (the two weeks before Lent). Expect all published prices to get thrown out the window during this time—call ahead and haggle. Try to make reservations as far in advance as possible. If you show up without reservations, and don't want to stay at the hostels, you can try to book a room through the AVA board [see *need to know,* below].

▶▶**CHEAP**

Though **Foresteria Valdese** *(Palazzo Cavagnis, 5170 Castello; Tel 041/528-67-97, Fax 041/241-62-38; 36,000L dorm, 1,000L discount for multiple nights, 100,000L double with TV, 130,000L double with TV and bath, 180,000L quad, 190,000L apartment; Reception open 9am-1pm/6-8pm daily; No credit cards)* is affiliated with the Waldensian Methodist church, you don't need religious reasons to stay in this beautiful guest house. The location is choice, right at the end of Castello's main drag, down the block from Santa Maria Formosa. The huge common space is decorated with heavy wood furniture, a baby grand piano, and Venetian chandeliers, and there's a TV room covered with remnants of old frescoes still clinging to the wall. The dorm rooms really pack 'em in, so if you want some space, spring for a double. Sheets are provided, and breakfast is included.

Located on the island of Giudecca, **Ostello di Venezia** *(Fondamenta delle Zitelle, 86 Giudecca; Tel 041/523-82-11, Fax 041/523-56-89; Vaporetto 82 or 52 to Zitelle; Closed Jan 16-Jan 31; Reception 7am-midnight; Lockout 9:30am-2pm; 30,000L dorm, breakfast inlcuded; No private rooms or baths; No credit cards)* isn't as inconvenient as it sounds—it's actually just a quick vaporetti ride across from San Marco. The 260 beds, as well as the guests sleeping in them, are just what you'd expect in a big hostel. The pretty main room functions as hangout central, where folks play cards, make a meal out of bread and cheese, and annoy one another. Bring your own wine—after the 11:30 curfew, the nights can seem pretty long.

Literally steps away from Piazza San Marco is **Hotel ai Do Mori** *(Calle Larga San Marco, 658 San Marco; Tel 041/520-48-17 or 041/528-92-93, Fax 041/520-53-28; reception@hotelaidomori, www.hotelaidomori. com; 80-100,000L single without bath; 120-160,00L double without bath; 160-230,000L double with bath; 160-215,000L triple without bath; 180-280,000L triple with bath; V, MC),* one of the best deals in town. Each room is painted in a different color scheme, with tasteful furniture and comfy beds. The painter's room is one of the prettiest in Venice, with a private terrace that looks out over the city. All of the recently restored rooms feature TVs, phones, and air conditioning.

Your mother would kill you if she knew you were staying at **Archie's House** *(San Leonardo, 1814/b Cannaregio; Tel 041/720-884; 25-30,000L dorm, 2,000L extra per shower; No credit cards).* You'll think you're entering an abandoned building when you walk through the door of this 19th-century palazzo; old bikes, piles of clothes, and a strange stench welcome you. Luckily, things are a bit cleaner upstairs. The rooms are relatively small, and lined with beds, but you're not really cramped for space. Run by the docile Archie, a doctor of philosophy who's conversant in 12 languages, and his friendly, smelly dog, this place is popular with hardcore budget travelers and Aussies. The vibe is very friendly, the location, right at the end of the Lista di Spagna, east of the Campo Giuglie, oh so convenient.

Also known as Hotel Calderon, **Casa Gerotto** *(Campo S. Geremia, 283 Cannaregio; Tel/Fax 041/715-361 or 041/715-562; 31,000L dorm, 100-120,000L double without bath, 140-150,000L double with bath; 1am curfew; No reservations; No credit cards)* is the hostel half of this part-hostel/part-budget hotel. But the dorm rooms buzz with international energy, and the private rooms are spacious, clean, and utilitarian. Four computers offer web browsing by the hour (12,000L), and there's a microwave where you can heat up dinner. You'll have to abide by the 1am curfew, but it's super-close to the Cannaregio nightlife around Misericordia and Lista di Spagna.

▶▶DO-ABLE

Your first choice in the entire city should be **Hotel Barnardi-Semenzato** *(Calle d'Oca, 4366 Cannaregio; Tel 041/522-72-57, Fax 041/522-24-24; mtpepoli@tin.it; Vaporetto Ca d'Oro; 60,000L single without bath, 100,000L double without bath, 150,000L double with bath, student discounts available; V, MC, AE)*, located just a few steps away from Strada Nova. Since 1981, this charming hotel has been run by Maria Theresa, who's a language teacher, and her husband, and both go out of their way to make sure you feel at home. The rooms are spacious and cozy, with phones and some with TV. There's a rooftop terrace where you're welcome to chill and take in the views, and a breakfast room that doubles as a sitting room late into the evening. They also have an annex around the corner in an old palazzo. These rooms are the height of elegance, with antique furniture and lovely linens, inlaid wood floors, tile bathrooms, and more space than you know what to do with. Some of them even have canal views. Call *way* in advance; you'll be glad you did.

Lucky for you, **Albergo San Samuele** *(Salizzada San Samuele, 38 San Marco; Tel/Fax 041/522-80-45; 70-80,000L single, 120-130,000L double without bath, 160-170,000L double with bath; V, MC)* is right in the heart of the gallery district. It's also one of the nicest budget hotels in town. Each of the rooms has a personality all its own, with funky art and furniture. The young, hip owners really put their all into this place—there's even a lending library in the sitting room well stocked with English titles.

Sweet and family run, **Hotel Caprera** *(Calle Gioacchina, 219 Cannaregio; Tel 041/715-271, Fax 041/715-927; 90,000L single without bath, 120,000L double without bath, 200,000 double with bath, 150,000L triple without bath, 250,000L triple with bath, 12,000L breakfast; 21 rooms; V, MC, AE)* is on a quiet side street off Lista di Spagna, and strangely enough, doesn't get the tourists that the noisy Lista hotels do. Comfortable and clean, it's a great bargain. Go for a room without a bath—the bathrooms in the hallway have been recently renovated and will do just fine.

Housed in a 17th-century palazzo, **Hotel Galleria** *(Rio Terra Antonio Foscarini, 878/a Dorsoduro; Tel 041/523-24-89; Fax 041/520-41-72; Vaporetto Accademia; 180-220,000L double with bath; 150-160,000L double without bath; 100,000L single without bath; V, MC)* is one of the best stays in town. It's a one-minute walk from the Ponte Accademia in Dorsoduro, and the views of the bridge are stunning. The rooms are *so* Venetian, with glass-blown chandeliers and lace curtains, antiques and old paintings. This is what *Le Serenissima* is all about.

Just across the street from the train station, over Ponte Scalzi, is **Hotel Marin** *(Campiello delle Muneghe, 670B Santa Croce; Tel 041/718-022, Fax 041/721-485; 130,000L double without bath; 160,000L double with bath, 205,000L triple with bath, 240,000L quad with bath; V, MC).* The sitting rooms and breakfast area are lovely, with old marble columns and tile floors, but the 19 rooms are a bit cramped. All have modern furniture, TVs, phones, and AC. The doors lock at 1am; if you're going to be out and about, ask if you can get a key.

▶▶SPLURGE

The look and feel of **Hotel Canaletto** *(San Lio, 5487 Castello; Tel 041/522-05-18, Fax 041/522-90-23; 90-350,000L single, 110-380,000L double, breakfast included; All rooms have showers; V, MC)* is much fancy-schmancier than others in the neighborhood, with its nice furnishings and classy wall art. All rooms have satellite TV, showers, phones, safes, and AC. Remember to **Just Say No** to the ever-tempting minibars. The rates fluctuate wildly over the course of the year—call ahead to see exactly how *much* splurging you'll be doing before you book a room. It's right on Castello's main north-south thoroughfare.

In a pretty Renaissance building just a few minutes south of Santa Maria d'Salute, **Hotel Messner** *(Fondamenta Ca' Balà, 216 Dorsoduro; Tel 041/522-74-43, Fax 041/522-72-66; Vaporetto Salute; 110-140,000L single, 175-220,000L doubles; Private baths; V, MC)* offers a great location and lots of personal service. The friendly, English-speaking owners will change money for you, and give you advice on restaurants and bars in the neighborhood. The recently renovated lobby, awash in wood details and fresh flowers, is as charming as the cozy courtyard where guests take their breakfast. The modern rooms are all satellite-TV-enhanced.

need to know

Currency Exchange There's a **Banco d'Italia** *(San Marco 4799; Tel 041/270-91-11)* right off the main Piazza. The **American Express office** provides all the usual financial services, as well as some tourist assistance. Beware of the hundreds of "cambios" around town that charge exorbitant fees for changing foreign currency into lire.

Tourist Information There are plenty of great tourist offices that offers everything from advice in English to free maps to tours and personal guides. The **San Marco office** *(Piazza San Marco, 71F San Marco; Tel 041/520-89-64; 9:30am-5:30pm daily http://www.comune.venezia. it/index.asp)* is helpful, but the real prize is the new **Venice Pavillion** *(Tel 041/522-51-50; 9:30am-5:30pm daily),* located right on the Grand Canal, next to the Ex Reali Gardens. The folks equipped to answer your every tourist need are available on one side, and there's an interesting bookstore/souvenir shop on the other. There's another small tourist office at the train station, right in front of the exit. If you're looking for help in booking a room, the local hotel association, **AVA (Associazione Veneziana Albergatori)** *(Tel 041/522-86-40, 1-800-843006 toll-free; 9am-9pm daily; Deposit required)* has one location to the left of this tourist office and another near the bus station in Piazzale Roma. Be aware that you'll end up paying a slightly higher rate.

Public Transportation The **bus station** *(Piazzale Roma; Tel 041/528-78-86),* in Santa Croce, is the only area where buses come in and out. It's open 24/7, with buses running to Mestre and other surrounding neighborhoods on a regular basis; tickets can be purchased from *tabacchi* and newsstands. The rest of the city, with the exception of Lido, is closed off to auto traffic.

The most efficient way to get around Venice, all day and all night, is by **vaporetti,** the ferries that whiz around the Grand Canal and the islands. Tickets cost 6,000L one-way, 10,000L roundtrip; discounts are available for groups (15,000L for three, 20,000L for four, and 25,000L for five). A 24-hour ticket costs 18,000L; a three-day pass is only 25,000L with a Rolling Venice Card. The city center routes that you'll use most are Vaporetti 82, which stops at the major stops along the Grand Canal, and Vaporetti 1, which stops at *all* stops on the Grand Canal and Lido. Both vaporetti and bus service are provided by **Actv** *(Azienda Consorzio Transporti Veneziano; 3935 Cannaregio; Tel 041/27-22-11-11, lost and found Tel 041/27-22-17-91; www.actv.com).*

Traghetti are the gondolas that cross the Grand Canal, often dodging vaporetti and motorboats in the process. At 900L per crossing, they're the cheapest way to ride a gondola, though you'll have to share it with as many people as can fit standing up (a lot). They're marked on most maps—keep your eye out for the yellow signs around town that point to the nearest launch. Each traghetti is operated independently, and hours fluctuate widely. There used to be more than 20; today, there are only 8.

Gondolas are more for atmosphere than transportation. Gondoliers are supposed to follow the set prices per hour trip established by the tourism board. For up to 6 people, the first 50 minutes is 120,000L, and every additional 25 minutes is 60,000L. Between 8pm-8am, when it's most romantic, that price goes up 300,000L for the first 50 minutes. Call the **Gondola Association** *(Tel 041/528-50-75) for more info.*

Water taxis *(Tel 041/522-203)* cost an arm and a leg, and should only be used in the direst circumstances. Getting to or from the airport will cost somewhere around 150,000L.

American Express: *(Salizzada San Moise 1471-2 San Marco; Tel 041/520-08-44; 9am-5:30pm Mon-Fri; 9am-12:30pm Sat).*

Health and Emergency Ambulance *118;* Medical emergency: *041/260-71-11;* Police emergency: *113.* The **main police station** *(Piazzale Roma, 500 Santa Croce; Tel 041/271-55-11)* is in Santa Croce. The hospital, Ospedale Civile *(SS. Giovanni e Paolo 6777 Castello; Tel 041/529-41-11)* is in northern Castello, facing the Canale di Fondamenta Nuove.

Pharmacies **Farmacia al lupo coronato** *(Campo SS Filippo e Giacomo 4513; Tel 041/522-06-75; 9am-12:30pm/3:45-7:30pm Mon-Fri, 9am-12:45pm Sat; V, MC)* is just a few steps northeast of Piazza San Marco. **Farmacia Santa Lucia** *(Cannaregio 122E, Lista di Spagna; Tel 041/716-332; 9am-12:30pm/3:45-7:30pm Mon-Fri, 9am-12:45pm Sat)* is right on the Lista di Spagna.

Telephones City code: *041.* There are clusters of pay phones in most main squares. Though many are coin-operated, they all take phone cards, which you can pick up in 5,000L increments at any newsstand or tabacchi.

Airports The **Marco Polo International Airport** *(Tel 041/260-92-60 for flight info)* is 12 kilometers away by land, and 10 by sea. To get to and from the airport, you have a few options. You can take the **Alilaguna line boat** *(Office San Marco 4267/a; Tel 041/523-57-75; www.alilaguna.com; 17,000L),* or the Bus 5 from Piazzale Roma (every half-hour, 30-40 minutes, 1,500L).

Trains Venice's main station is **Venezia Santa Lucia** *(Tel 041/147888088; Info office 8:30am-1:30pm/3:30-5:30pm),* just west of Canareggio, in the northwest corner of the city. Many of the trains headed to Venice will first stop at Mestre, Venice's suburb—although the signs will say Venice, hold your horses for the next stop. Trains fill up *fast,* so if you're planning on leaving town on a weekend, reserve your seat well in advance. Reservations can be made at the station, or by calling 1-478-88088. Don't forget to validate your ticket yourself before hopping on—if you don't, you'll be fined.

Bus Lines Out of the City ATVO *(Tel 041/520-55-30)* operates most out-of-town bus trips. The main hub is the huge concrete sprawl on Piazzale Roma, across from the train station. Buses leave for Mestre (1,500L), Chioggia (1,400L), and out of town destinations on a regular basis. There are buses to and from Padua (6,000L one way, 10,000L round trip) every 20 minutes between 4:55am and 7:15am, and every hour until midnight.

Postal The **main post office** *(San Marco 5554, Salizada del Fontego dei Tedeschi; Tel 041/271-71-11; Vaporetto Rialto; 8am-7pm Mon-Sat)* is right between Canareggio and San Marco, on the block leading north out of San Bartolomeo Square.

Internet See *wired,* above.

everywhere else

padua

There are three reasons to come to Padua: the amazing art, the cool party scene, and the anything-goes atmosphere. Padua rivals Siena or Assisi in terms of art, with works by Giotto and other Renaissance stars so gorgeous they'll make you a groupie for life. One of the coolest alternative scenes in Italy is here, fueled by students at Italy's second-oldest university and hidden away amid the beautiful Renaissance piazzas in the old medieval city center. And best of all, the city has a wild spirit, which has overcome everyone from Austrian conquerors to modern-day fascists.

Local legend says Trojan elder Antenor founded Padua after the fall of Troy in 1185 B.C. It became an official Roman city in 45 B.C., got sacked by Lombards six centuries later, and became an independent *comune* in 1163, joining in the political struggle against the Roman Emperor.

The University was founded in 1222, and attracted Renaissance whiz kids like Giotto, Galileo, Dante, and Petrarch. When Venetians conquered the city in 1405, they built walls around the city and erected the usual winged-lion statues. During that period, in 1592, Shakespeare used Padua as the setting for *Taming of the Shrew,* that tale of a fierce woman named Katharina who refused to be dominated by her husband.

In 1797 Napoleon came, saw, conquered, then went away the next year, handing Padua over to the Austrians. But angry students led the resistance forces that threw the Austrians out, and Padua joined the Kingdom of Italy in 1866. The city's shrewish spirit (and a tough university Chancellor) gave the fascists no end of problems during World War II—locals liberated their city on their own 10 days before the Allies showed up in 1945.

Today, fiery student activism has faded into mere intellectualism, which peacefully co-exists with major industry and business. The town is always filled with college students, even during the summer. Half of them speak English, as does at least one person working in any restaurant or bar. Students and locals alike are friendly and informal; they're fine with tourists.

neighborhoods

Directly across from the train station, which is perched at the north end of town, is **Corso del Populo,** the beginning of Padua's main north-south drag. As you follow it south toward the center of town (about a 20-minute walk), the Corso crosses a canal that completely encloses the center of town. Once you're inside the canal, the street becomes **Corso Garibaldi,** passing by the Roman Amphitheater and Giotto's masterpiece, the Scrovegni Chapel [see *culture zoo,* below], which is located on the grounds of the **Giardini dell'Arena** gardens. A few blocks past the gardens, the Corso passes through **Piazza Garibaldi, Piazzetta Pedrocchi,** and then **Piazza Cavour,** getting a bit narrower as it goes. From here it becomes, in turn, **Via VIII Febbraio, Via Roma,** and **Via Umberto I** before it hits the mammoth **Prato della Valle,** one of the largest squares in Europe, drawing big crowds to its monthly market.

Just west of **Piazza Cavour** is the true heart of the city, known simply as **Le Piazze** ("the squares"): **Piazza dei Frutta** and, just to the south, **Piazza delle Erbe.** Here you'll find some of the city's finest Renaissance buildings, as well as a bustling food market. South of the Piazza delle Erbe are the narrow, twisty streets of the 17th-century **Ghetto,** full of good restaurants and bars. To the east side of **Corso Garibaldi,** the streets are wider and arc gracefully south toward **Piazza del Santo,** about a two-minute walk from Prato della Valle, where you'll find a few budget hotels and the Basilica di Sant'Antonio, aka "Il Santo."

ı2 hours ın padua

1. Grab a table at **Caffe Pedrocchi** [see *cafe scene,* below].
2. Run, don't walk, to the **Scrovegni Chapel** [see *culture zoo,* below].
3. Join the crowds on **Via Soncin** [see *hanging out,* below].
4. Eat at **Per Bacco** [see *eats,* below], just like the locals do.
5. Catch **Cantina Cabaret** [see *arts scene,* below] to learn some choice local lingo.
6. Get an anatomy lesson at **Palazzo del Bo** [see *culture zoo,* below].
7. Chill in the **Orto Botanico** [see *culture zoo,* above]

padua bars clubs and culture zoo

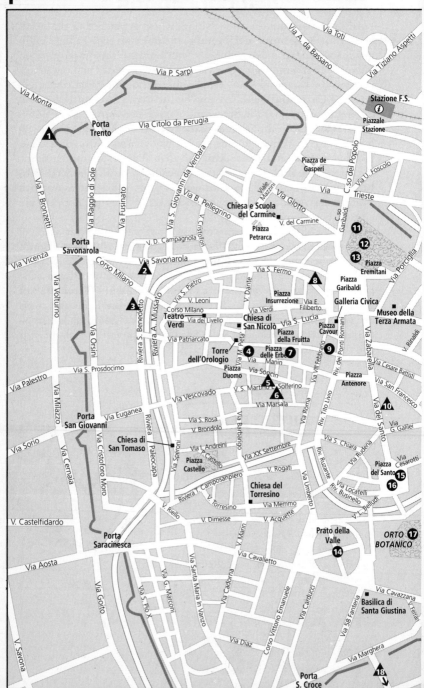

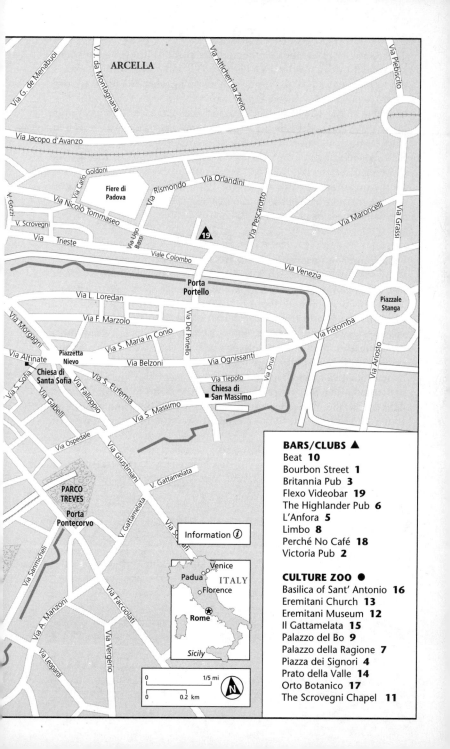

BARS/CLUBS ▲
Beat **10**
Bourbon Street **1**
Britannia Pub **3**
Flexo Videobar **19**
The Highlander Pub **6**
L'Anfora **5**
Limbo **8**
Perché No Café **18**
Victoria Pub **2**

CULTURE ZOO ●
Basilica of Sant' Antonio **16**
Eremitani Church **13**
Eremitani Museum **12**
Il Gattamelata **15**
Palazzo del Bo **9**
Palazzo della Ragione **7**
Piazza dei Signori **4**
Prato della Valle **14**
Orto Botanico **17**
The Scrovegni Chapel **11**

Information ⓘ

Venice
Padua   ITALY
Florence
Rome
Sicily

0   1/5 mi
0   0.2 km

hanging out

There's no central campus, so the students in Padua just hang out where everyone else does, mainly in Le Piazze. You'll find people rushing around or just kicking back all day, from early morning when the markets open to late at night when the bar crowd takes to the streets. You can still buy fruit here in Piazza della Frutta("piazza of fruit"), but don't get any funny ideas about Piazza del Erbe ("piazza of grass")—marijuana is illegal and will get you into major trouble. The weekend crowds are so large on the main east-west drag of the Ghetto, Via Soncin, that you can hardly walk through. Even during the day, people chill in Piazza Duomo. At the southern end of the town center, the Prato del Valle's grassy expanses, gravel paths, marble benches and outer ring of statues are still a hotspot after a hundreds of years.

café scene

Padua's most historic hangout, **Caffé Pedrocchi** *(Piazzetta Pedrocchi 15; Tel 049/876-25-76; Bus 3, 8, 12, or 18 to Corso Garibaldi or MP to Piazza della Frutta; 9:30am-12:30pm/3:30-8pm Tue-Sun; 3,000L espresso; V, MC)* has been around since 1775. When it re-opened in 1831, with a neo-classicist facade and concert hall interior, it became a Nationalist meeting-point for the anti-Austrian resistance. Nowadays, it seems more like a museum than it does a place to grab a cuppa joe and plot revolution. With its echoing marble rooms in the colors of the Italian flag, crystal chandeliers, and huge murals of world maps, this could be a movie version of a dictator's office. All the furniture seems to be rubbed with gold leaf, wrapped in red velvet, or sprouting lion's feet, and the waiters teeter around in tuxes. Order a cappuccino (4,000L), super-thick hot

wired

The 16 internet-connected PCs at **In Collegio** *(Via Petrarca 9; Tel 049/658-484; 10,000L per hour; No credit cards)* are usually full of kids playing online games. It's just off Piazza Pertraca, across the canal, north of the city center. Gay- and lesbian-friendly **Arcibe Walchiria** *(Via Savonarola 167; Tel 049/87-14-31-2l; 10am-8pm Mon-Sat; 15,000L Arci membership required; No credit cards)* is across the canal, northwest of the town center. It has a pool table and a video room, in addition to PCs where you can get online.

You can get up-to-the minute info on Padua at *www.emmeti.it/ Welcome/Veneto/Padova/index.uk.html.*

chocolate (*ciocolato in tasca,* 5,000L) or *aperativo* (10,000L) and hang out for a while. Tip: the espresso that costs 1,900L while standing at the bar will set you back 3,000L if you sit down. Drink slowly and take in the decor.

Can't afford the coffee and drinks at Padrocchio? Head a couple blocks east on Via Cesare Battista to the sprawling **Milk Bar Pasticcheria Gelateria** *(Via Cesare Battista 17; Tel 049/826-10-33; 7am-9pm Mon-Sat winter; 7am-11pm Mon-Sat summer; No credit cards).* A winding staircase takes you up to a packed mezzanine of tiny round tables, one of Padua's fave hangouts. Everyone from kids who are too cool for school to couples who are too old for it orders coffee and drinks from the long bar. Of course there's cappuccinos (3,200L) and gelato (5,000L), but the huge case of oranges on display is a reminder that the fresh fruit juices rule here.

With a tea shop upstairs and a wine bar below street level, **Sottosopra** *(Via XX Settembre 77; Tel 049/664-898; Bus 3, 8, 13 to Riviera Tito Livio; 11-1am Tue-Sun winter, 11am-3pm/7pm-1am summer, closed Mon; web.tiscalinet.it/sottosopra; V, MC)* is aptly named (*sottosopra* means "under-over"). The comfy booths lining the walls, Moby on the stereo, backgammon sets lying around, and semi-pretentious books on the stairwell make this a relaxing place to waste a rainy day. The friendly owners, Diego and Giorgio, specialize in a wide selection of exotic teas—50 kinds from all over the world—but the well-stocked bar also offers Italian *aperitivi* like campari, and Irish, Scotch, and American whiskeys (3-10,000L). A stylish, laid-back crowd enjoys large salads, *bruschette* and desserts until the kitchen closes at 1:30am.

Situated just northeast of Piazza del Santo, **Pasticceria Forin** *(Via Cesare Battista 17; Tel 049/826-10-33; 9am-12:30pm/3:30-6pm; 2-5,000L pastries; No credit cards),* takes *Santantonio* cake seriously. Every day, this little bakery is packed with locals stopping in for this chocolate and powdered sugar indulgence, which is shaped to look like a crown and traditionally eaten on St. Anthony's feast day. Feast day or not, go ahead and indulge—the patron saint of lost things will help you gain back some weight.

bar, club, and live music scene

The student-filled nightlife here is dominated by bars. The Ghetto and the area between Corso Garibaldi and Piazza del Santo are the best places to grab a few good beers and meet some students. Hip clubs are harder to find: Limbo is the only dance club in the city center, and it's not very good. But Bourbon Street manages to succeed as a bar, club, and performance space, depending on the night.

Just northwest of the city walls, **Bourbon Street** *(Via P. Bronzetti 8; Tel 049/871-97-11; Bus 11 to Porta Trento; 6-8,000L beer; 15,000L Arci membership; No credit cards)* is an authentically divey, New Orleans-themed bar and club. Iron columns, ceiling fans, and murals of riverboats go for that "Nawlins" look, but the crowd is cooler then the decor, full of

fIVE-O

Looks can be deceiving. Though there's a lot of hanging out going on in Padua—mostly around Via Soncin, and Piazza delle Erbe—the cops have their eyes out for any illegal behavior, as is usually the case when they're surrounded by students. Be on your best behavior.

Italian and foreign students who are friendly and eager to strike up a conversation, especially about left-wing politics (remember: globalization is bad). The alternative crowd makes for the best dancing in Padua, with a different theme every night. Wednesday is English-speaking night, when Italians will practice their Robert De Nero impressions on you. Thursdays and Saturdays (Red Night and Blue Night) bring electronica-spinning DJs, and Friday is Country Night, with line dancing lessons from 9-10pm. Sunday is 60s Night, which often features live music from local bands. You have to be a member of ARCI [see **book intro**] to get in, but it's well worth it—consider the 15,000L membership a cover charge. To get there, go though the Porta Trenta and take a left on Bronzetti.

Smack dab in the middle of the Ghetto, **The Highlander Pub** *(Via San Martino Solferino 69; Tel 049/659-977; Bus 3, 8, 13 to Riviera Tito Livio or minibus MP to Piazza Erbe; Noon-3pm/5pm-2am Mon-Sat, closed Sun; No cover; V, MC, AE)* is too big and rowdy to pull off its quaint little Scottish pub act. But it's a great place to meet English-speaking exchange students, as well as all those locals talking in Italian. Choose from seven beers, including real ale (6,000 to 8,000L) and chow down on pub grub like mushroom pie (15,000L) and burgers (7,000L) until 1:30am. The music is pretty standard U.S. and U.K. Top 40 rock, with some Italian pop hits thrown in. Things get hopping after 11pm.

With fake marble columns hung with red Roman banners, the entrance to **Limbo** *(Via San Fermo 44; 049/656-882; Bus 6, 9, 15 or MP to Via Dante; 7:30pm-4am Fri-Sat, 11pm-12:30am Sun, Wed-Thu, closed Mon-Tue; Cover 15,000L Wed-Fri, 20,000L Sat, 10,000 Sun, one drink included; No credit cards)* is pretty impressive. But once inside, you'll feel like you're in an 80s comedy club. Exposed brick, chrome, and neon pop out all over this two-level dance hall, located in an open-air mall north of Piazza della Frutta—there's a balcony on the second level for ogling the dancers. The music is cheesy and commercial, like the club, and tribute and swing bands come through every few weeks, usually on Wednesdays or Thursdays. Despite its drawbacks, it *is* popular, with a mixed crowd that ranges from 17-year-old pop tarts to middle-aged suburban coffee cake—pretty much anyone who just wants to dance.

Walk northeast from Piazza della Frutta and cross the canal at Corso Milano to find the **Britannia Pub** *(Riviera San Benedetto 22; Tel 049/871-98-01; Bus 6, 5, or 10 to Corso Milano; 7pm-4am Mon-Sat,* *closed Sun; No cover; No credit cards)*. It's quite a dive, but that seems to be the point. The local hoodie-wearing wallet-chain-swinging lads squeeze into the narrow room while alterna-lasses loiter around the covered patio out back—occasionally the two groups mix and mingle. The small bar has McEwan's lager and Bulldog ale on tap (6-8,000L a pint).

In March of 2000, **Beat** *(Via del Santo 9/11; No phone; Bus 8, 12, 18, or 22 to Riviera Businello or MB to Via del Santo; 10am-3pm/7pm-3am; 15,000L CSEN membership required; No credit cards)* opened with a very simple philosophy: everyone should be happy. The free food at midday and free buffet in the evening (7:30-9:15pm) help do the trick. Then there's happy hour, with two-for-one drink specials from 6:15-7:30pm (beers are typically 7,000L a pint; cocktails are 7,000L). The constantly cheery music from the likes of Stevie Wonder and the Village People makes people even happier; ditto for the yellow walls and plastic sunflower motif. Then there are the theme nights: Monday is Erasmus Night, when college students meet and greet. Thursday brings live music, Friday and Saturday there are DJs and dancing, and Sunday offers theater or spoken word performances. All this cheer draws a hipster crowd of twentysomething fashion plates that's friendly, open-minded, and...happy. Beat is on the east side of Via Del Santo, just south of Via San Francesco.

On the south side of Via Soncin, **L'Anfora** *(Via Dei Soncin 13; Tel 049/656-629; Bus 3, 8, 13 to Riviera Tito Livio or minibus MP to Piazza Erbe; 10am-10pm Mon-Sat; Cover 3,000L for food, no cover for music; V, MC, AE)*, takes both its jazz and and its wine seriously. This is no small feat, considering that the wine is from small, offbeat producers (3-6,000L by the glass), and the jazz is almost all recorded, because there just aren't that many jazz bands around Padua. Even so, the rickety old tables are packed with arty intellectual types who pile in for the great, rustic meals, whatever the chef decided to cook that day—hot dishes like risotto, sausage and peppers, and lasagna served up buffet-style (10-15,000L). And if you really want some live jazz, you're welcome to tickle the ivories on the beat-up old piano in the corner.

arts scene

The University's presence creates a demand for contemporary arts of all kinds. Theater and the performing arts are predominant, but are generally in Italian only. There are a few galleries popping up all the time—unfortunately they go out of business just as quickly. Artists who can afford it hang out at Sottosopra and Beat [see *bar, club, and live music scene*, above]; the latter has cool shows of paintings and photography that rotate monthly.

▶▶VISUAL ARTS

The first-class **PerugiArtecontemporanea** *(Via Altinate 66; Tel 049/663-996; Minibus MB to Via Altinate; 5:30-8:30pm Mon-Sat; www.artist-info.com/gallery/Perugi-Artecontemporanea; V, MC)*, located east of Piazza Garibaldi, showcases Italian and international artists. Photography, painting, sculptures, and conceptual art all find a temporary

home here. The gallery prides itself on hosting foreign artists' first Italian
show. They're also happy to point you toward any of the newly opened
galleries in town.

▶▶PERFORMING ARTS

A small theater with murals of old Padua on the walls, **Cantina Cabaret**
*(Via Savonarola 84; Tel 049/872-00-74; Bus 6, 5, or 10 to Corso Milano;
9pm-2am daily; cancab@cantinacabaret.com, www.cantinacabaret.com;
Ticket prices vary; No credit cards)* doubles as a serious wine bar. Shows are
traditional cabaret (satire, parodies, sketch comedy, songs and dancing),
all in Italian. Of course after a little wine (3-8,000L a glass) even impro-
visational political satire in another language starts to sound kinda funny.
Shows start at 10:30pm and last about an hour. The theater is just north
of the city center, across the canal at Via San Cristofori.

gay scene

Padua has more to offer gay travelers than many other Italian cities—again,
you can thank the college. The most popular bars, including Beat and Sottosopra [see *bar, club, and live music scene,* above for both] are gay-friendly,
and Bourbon Street [see *bar, club, and live music scene,* above] and ArciBé
Walchiria [see *wired,* below] are both part of the Arci gay network. For local
gay info, try the **ArchiGay-Archilesbica Centro Nuovo** *(Via Santa
Sofia 5; Tel 0498/762-458; Bus 3, 8, 13 to Riviera Tito Livio or minibus MP
to Piazza Erbe; 9am-1pm/2:30-5pm Mon-Fri),* which operates out of the
student center off Riva Tito Livio, the street between Via Roma and Via
Del Santo. The helpful folks at the desk in the back will be happy to tell you
the news of the day, events of the week, and flavors of the month.

Just outside the city walls east of Prato della Valle is **Perché No Café**
*(Via Alessandro Manzoni 4; Tel 049/687-775; Bus 24 to Via Cavazzana;
7pm-1am daily; No cover; No credit cards),* a gay and lesbian club with a
mixed-age crowd, but mainly young folks. Most kids visit here to hook
up before heading off to other clubs, but the creative theme nights sometimes inspire them to stick around. Beers are 8,000L, while a glass of wine
is 3-7,000L.

Offering high-tech cruising, with lots of porn playing around the bar
and something called a "Dark Labyrinth," **Flexo Videobar** *(Via Tommaseo 96/a; Tel 049/807-47-07; Bus 5 to Tommaseo or 8 to Fiera; 9:30pm-
late Wed-Sun; 12,000L Wed-Thu, Sun; 15,000L Fri, 20,000L Sat; V, MC)*
is exactly what it sounds like. The second and fourth Sunday of every
month is Leather Night. It's not a lesbian sort of place, really...lotsa men,
though. It's a five-minute cab ride east on Via Tommaseo from the train
station, between Via Ugo Bassi and Via Venzia.

culture zoo

Because of Padua's long, mixed history, you'll find tangible evidence of
the course of Italian civilization everywhere you turn.

The Scrovegni Chapel/Eremitani Museum *(Piazza Eremitani; Tel 049/820-45-50; Bus 3, 8, 12, or 18 to Corso Garibaldi; 9am-*

7pm daily, Feb-Oct; 7am-6pm daily, Nov-Jan; 10,000L; No credit cards): Situatued on the grounds of the old Roman Arena, just inside the city walls off Corso Garibaldi, this chapel is as good as Italian art gets—and that's pretty good. Scrovegni was a merchant who needed to redeem himself for the sin of usury (charging interest), so he commissioned Giotto for some artistic money-laundering. The resulting 38-panel "Life of Mary and Jesus" fresco cycle is pretty much the high point of 14th-century painting. Sadly, the frescoes are being destroyed by dirty, dirty visitors, who bring in dust and pollution from outside. Nowadays, you have to wait at a new side entrance while contaminants are removed from the air. Groups of 25 are let in for 15 minutes at a time; call for reservations. While you're waiting, browse through the nearby Eremitani Museum, which includes an amazing Giotto crucifix and miniature armed angels by Guariento.

Eremitani Church *(Piazza Eremitani 9; 049/875-64-10; Bus 3, 8, 12, or 18 to Corso Garibaldi; 8:15am-noon/4-6:30pm Mon-Sat, 9:30am-noon/4-6pm Sun, Apr-Sep; 8:15am-noon/4-5:30pm Mon-Sat, 9:30am-noon/4-5:30 Sun, May-Aug; Free):* In 1944, this church was bombed, destroying priceless frescos completed in 1457 by 17-year-old prodigy Andrea Mategna. Killed in a street brawl before he reached 20, this James Dean of Italian art didn't leave many works behind; his "Martyrdom of St. Christopher," on display here, is the best preserved. The murder-through-the-window motif in the painting is pure Hitchcock.

Basilica of Sant'Antonio *(Piazzo del Santo 11; Tel 049/878-97-22; Bus 8, 12, 18, 22, M or T to Riviere; 6:30am-7:45pm daily Apr-Sep; 6:30am-7pm daily Oct- Mar; Free):* The extravagant final resting-place for Padua's favorite adopted son was built in the Romanesque and Gothic styles, with a bronze altarpiece by Donatello and Byzantine domes and towers topping things off. Pilgrims from all over the Catholic world come to touch the tomb of Saint Anthony, the patron saint of lost things. Now's your chance to find all those things you've lost over the years: phone numbers, car keys, your youthful idealism....

Il Gattamelata: Dominating the square outside the basilica is the work that brought Donatello to Padua. Depicting Erasmo da Narni, a mercenary employed by the Pope and Venetian republic, it was controversial in its day because, until then, only kings were portrayed mounted in statuary. (These days, any old shmoe can be mounted in statuary.)

Palazzo della Ragione *(Via VII Febbraio; Tel 049/82-06-50-06; Bus MP to Piazza della Frutta; 9am-7pm Tue-Sun; 12,000L; No credit cards):* This 13th-century palazzo separates Piazzas della Frutta and della Erbe. It features a roof shaped like a ship's hull, and a giant wooden horse from which no Greeks have leapt (not so far, anyway—you never know). The interior includes frescos of astrological symbols by Giotto and his school, which were destroyed by fire in 1420 and restored five years later.

Piazza dei Signori: The Venetians placed a winged lion atop a column in this Piazza to remind everyone who was boss (never a good idea in Padua), but the real sight to see here is one of the oldest clock towers in Italy, dating to 1344, which also tracks the positions of the planets and constellations.

Palazzo del Bo *(Via VIII Febbraio 2; Tel 049/820-97-11, Fax 049/820-97-26; Bus 3, 8, 12, or 18 to Corso Garibaldi or MP to Piazza della Frutta; Guided tours hourly, 9-11am/3-5pm; 5,000L; No credit cards):* The main building of Padua's University, located just east of Piazza Della Frutta, includes a 1594 anatomy theater that's the oldest permanent structure of its kind. The Sala dei Quaranta has 20th-century paintings of the university's forty most famous teachers and students, and the so-called "Chair of Galileo." Galileo, everyone's favorite prof, had to lecture in the Great Hall next door to accommodate his hordes of eager groupies.

Orto Botanico: *(Via Orto Botanico; Tel 049/827-21-19, Fax 049/827-21-20; Bus 3, 8, 12, 18, 22, 24 to Prato della Valle; 9am-1pm Mon-Sat Nov-Mar; 9am-1pm/3-6pm daily Apr-Oct; 5,000L; No credit cards):* If you're weary of all the cold stone of Italian cities, a quiet afternoon in the gardens may cure what ails you. This botanical garden was founded in 1545 to cultivate herbs and medicinal plants, some of which are hundreds of years old.

Prato della Valle: Another open area, just east of the Orto Botanico, this Enlightenment-era piazza was built on a swamp in 1775. The 87 statues that ring the oblong space, all famous Paduani, resemble the white pieces in a giant chess set. It makes for a slightly surreal picnic.

modification

If Giotto's work is inspiring you to consider some full-body frescoes of your own, take a look at **Little London Tattoo & Piercing** *(Via Giotto 20; Tel 049/652-792; Bus 11 or 13 to Via Giotto; 10:30am-12:30pm/3:30pm-7:30pm Mon-Fri, 1-7:30pm Sat, closed Sun; No credit cards),* across the canal from Corso Del Popolo. The artists at this brother shop of Helter Skelter [see *stuff,* below], have books of inked flesh available, and also do original inkwork.

city sports

Across from the Prato Del Valle, **Tre Pini** *(Prato del Valle 56; Tel 049/875-54-58; Bus 8, 12, or 18 to Prato del Valle; 10,000L; No credit cards)* is the most centrally located of Padua's handful of public swimming pools. It's also a popular hangout for University students on hot summer days. That doesn't necessarily mean *your* student card will get you a discount, but it's worth a shot.

stuff

You won't find many super-stylish clothes or cool gifts, but there are great selections of books, music, and a London-style punk shop—a rare find in Italy. For those with more mainstream tastes (at least, mainstream Italian), the chain shops clustered in the area north of Le Piazze and west of Via Garibaldi make a virtual open-air shopping mall. You'll find your Sisleys, Pradas, and Benettons there.

▶▶TUNES

Look past the new releases at **Il Ventitre Dischi** *(Via Barbarigo 2; Tel 049/875-06-89, Fax 049/875-43-57; Minibus MD to Duomo; 8:45am-1pm/3-7:45pm Tue-Sat, 3-7pm Mon, closed Sun; shop@23cdstore.it, www.23cdstore.it; V, MC),* and you'll find a wide selection of CDs, tapes, a little vinyl, some concert DVD's and even cult videos. CDs are 13-39,000L; K-Tel-style "Super Buy" stuff is only 9,900L. Ventitre also has an excellent selection of jazz, classical, electronica, and world music. It's just south of Piazza Duomo.

▶▶DUDS

The store for anyone with a serious London fetish, **Helter Skelter** *(Galleria Storione 4; Tel/Fax 049/656-322; Bus 3, 8, 13 to Riviera Tito Livio; 10am-12:30pm/1:30-7:30pm; V, MC)* has everything for the punk, SHARP, or mod on your Christmas list, including Ben Sherman shirts, 3- to 20-eye Doc Martens, Lonsdale hoodies, spike bracelets, bomber jackets, tongue studs, Sta-press trousers, and bondage pants. You'll find it under a pedestrian walkway just south of Via San Francesco, between Via VII Febbraio and Riviera Tito Livio.

▶▶BOUND

Near the corner of Riviera Tito Livio, **Feltrinelli International** *(Via San Francesco 14; Tel 049/875-07-92, Fax 049/875-42-53; Bus 3, 8, 13 to Riviera Tito Livio; 9am-7pm Mon-Fri, 9am-1:30pm/3:30-7:30 Sat; V, MC)* has a great selection of the classics and modern fiction in English. It's a student bookstore, so the prices aren't bad, either.

EATS

Padua is a budget eater's dream, overflowing with great grub on the go. The self-service cafeteria has taken off here, thanks to the student population, who refer to places like this as "free-flow" (go figure). All these bargains have done a good job of driving the price of all-out, traditional meals way down, too. Keep your eye out for polenta and risotto, prepared in every way imaginable. Padua also has great local wine, produced in the neighboring hills. Try a crisp white soave, a hearty bardolino, or a fruity valpolicella.

▶▶CHEAP

The students have moved into **Bar Target** *(Via Zabarella 27; Tel 049/651-867; 7am-8pm, closed Sat and Sun; 1,500-4,000L beer pints, panini and fruit drink 6,000L; No credit cards),* and they refuse to leave. Upbeat, loud, and bright, this little cafe east of Le Piazze has great food at awesome prices—and it's a super place for mixing with the locals. Panini, like the grilled vegetables with prosciutto crudo and mozzarella, come on hearty breads, and the lasagne radicchio is delicious and healthy. The sandwich and drink special is the best deal in town. Finish it off with an Italian fruit smoothie called a *frullati,* made with fresh fruit like strawberries, mango, and kiwi.

Literally hundreds of people—mainly students—pack the totally non-descript, florescent-lit pizza-by-the-slice joint a few doors down from

TO MARKET

You've never seen a **food market** *(8am-1:30pm/3:30-7:30pm   Mon-Fri;   8am-1:30pm/3-7:30pm Sat, closed Sun)* like this one, spanning the gap between Piazza della Frutta and Piazza delle Erbe. This picnicker's dream offers every kind of *comestible* imaginable—cheeses, meats, cured hams and salamis, breads, wines, nuts, beans, rice, coffee, and even gelato. There's also a horse butcher (bad! *very bad!*) who caters to traditional tastes for this highly seasoned meat. We could do without the hanging body parts.

L'Amphora, **Soncin Aurora** *(Via Soncin 7; Tel 049/876-06-84; 10am-11pm Tue-Sun; 2,000L slice; No credit cards).* What's in that pizza anyway? Order a beer (4,000L by the bottle; 8,000L by the pint) and a few slices to find out for yourself before heading out onto the street with all the others.

The dowdy **Al Ricordo** *(Via San Francesco 175; Tel 049/663-908; 8, 12, 18, 22 to Riva Businello or MB to Via del Santo; Noon-2:20pm/7-9:30pm Mon-Fri, noon-2:20pm Sat and Sun; No credit cards),* just north of Piazza Del Santo, is packed with local workmen everyday for lunch. Why? Because it serves the kind of food Mama would fix up at home. The 19,000L three-course meal includes pasta with a simple sauce, a grilled meat or fish main course, and a tossed salad. The crusty yet flirty waitresses are like Italian versions of Flo from Mel's Diner. Daily offerings are scrawled with neon marker out front—you better know what you want *before* you sit down.

▶▶DO-ABLE

One block south and two blocks east from Piazza Cavour, **Ristorante Vecchia Padua** *(Via Zabarella 41; Tel 049/857-96-80; Bus 16, 22, 8; Noon-2:30pm/5:30-10:30pm Tue-Sun, closed Mon; 6-12,000L lunch entrees, 10-20,000L dinner entrees; V, MC, DC)* serves great, inexpensive, self-service food by day, and great, almost fancy trattoria fare at night. Decor consists of old radios and typewriters from the 1940s, vases of fresh flowers, and heavy wood detail. There's a steady hum of conversation coming from the comfy, upholstered booths, which are packed solid day and night. Expect traditional dishes from the Veneto, like rabbit with tagliatelle, *risi e bisi* (rice and pea soup), and grilled radicchio. The wood-burning stove turns out great, oversized pizzas (9-14,000L).

It may look a little touristy, but **Pizzeria/Trattoria Marrechiaro** *(Via D. Manin 37; Tel 049/875-84-89; Noon-2:30pm/5-10:30pm Tue-Sun, closed Mon; 7,000 and 11,000L pizzas; No credit cards)* sure knows how to make great pies. This cheery, modern pizza place is great for refueling after a day of sightseeing. Try the *frutti di mare,* with calamari, shrimp, and tomatoes with a liter of house wine (only 9,000L). It's right in tourist central, just off Piazza delle Erbe, so you'll hear lots of English being spoken here. The waiters like to strike up conversations with the scores of American year-abroad students who make the comfy booths their second home.

▶▶SPLURGE

The best restaurant in a town filled with great restaurants is **Per Bacco** *(Piazzale Ponte Corvo 10; Tel 049/875-46-64, Fax 049/876-28-10; Bus 13 or 16 to Via Faccolati, 7:30pm-midnight daily; 22-32,000L entrees; perbacco@libero.it; No credit cards).* The chefs use only the freshest ingredients in seasonal, classic dishes from the Veneto and Tuscany. The San Daniele prosiutto is cut by hand, and the *cingale* (wild boar) is cooked till it's falling off the bone. The formal dining room in back caters to businessmen sealing deals and young would-be lovers trying to do the same. The front room is much more informal—you'll often find the staff of the local bars and restaurants having wine and dessert here around closing time. You'll find it behind the Basilica di Sant'Antonio, across the canal.

Treat yourself to **La Vecchia Enoteca** *(Via San Martino e Soleferino 32; Tel 049/875-28-56; 12:45-2pm/7:45-10pm Tue-Sat; 30-40,000L entrees; V, MC)* if you can afford it. This cozy, amber-lit restaurant in Padua's old Ghetto has been a destination for gourmets for the past six years. Everything about this place says class, from the bookshelves stocked with wine bottles, books, and other knickknacks to the plush banquettes, shiny silver service, and white linen tablecloths. Start with tiny gnocchi tossed with olive oil, thyme, and scallops; move on to grilled swordfish with a piquant caper sauce; and finish it all off with the most amazing chocolate torte ever. Be sure to break out your good clothes for this one. Ignore the snotty waiters—they look at everyone like that.

crashing

College towns mean cheap, plentiful accommodations, and Padua is no exception. Most of the hotels are either near Piazza del Santo or west of Piazza dei Signori.

▶▶CHEAP

The youth hostel **Ostello Cittá di Padua** *(Via Aleardi 30; Tel 049/875-22-19, Fax 049/654-210; Bus 3, 8, 12, 18, 22, 24 to Prato della Valle; Reception 7-10am/2:30-11pm; 24,000L per person; No private baths; No credit cards),* is right in the center of town, just a 10-minute walk south of Le Piazze—a nice break for hostellers used to catching the last bus to a dark and faraway castle. Features include luggage storage (after 2:30pm Mon-Fri, 4pm Sat), laundry room, and a common room with Dalí-inspired murals, and the usual annoying hostel rules (lockout 9:30am-4pm, curfew at 11pm sharp).

Situated just on the northeastern side of Piazza Del Santo, **Locanda La Perla** *(Via Cesarotti 67; Tel 049/875-89-39; Bus 8, 12, 18, 22 to Riva Businello or MB to Via del Santo; 45,000L single, 68,000L double, 5,000L extra person; No private baths; No credit cards)* couldn't be more convenient

padua eats and crashing

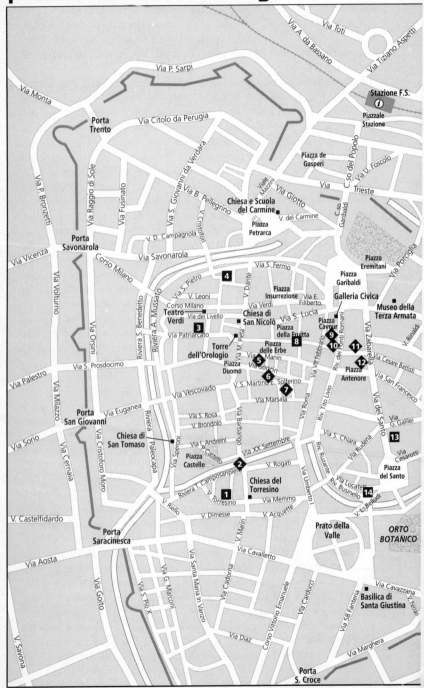

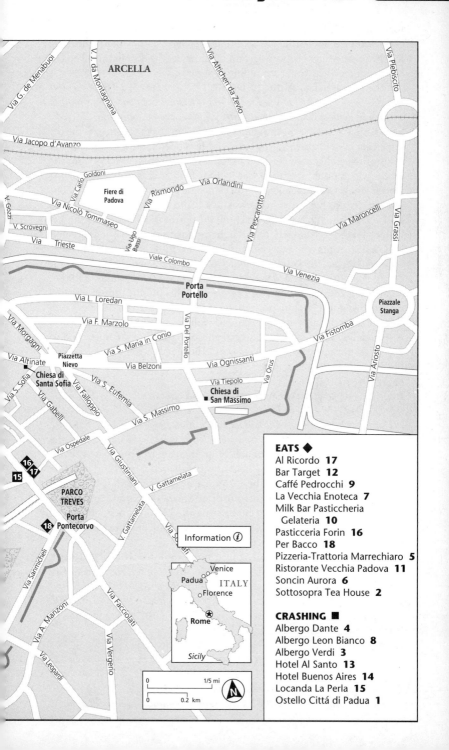

EATS ◆
Al Ricordo **17**
Bar Target **12**
Caffé Pedrocchi **9**
La Vecchia Enoteca **7**
Milk Bar Pasticcheria
  Gelateria **10**
Pasticceria Forin **16**
Per Bacco **18**
Pizzeria-Trattoria Marrechiaro **5**
Ristorante Vecchia Padova **11**
Soncin Aurora **6**
Sottosopra Tea House **2**

CRASHING ■
Albergo Dante **4**
Albergo Leon Bianco **8**
Albergo Verdi **3**
Hotel Al Santo **13**
Hotel Buenos Aires **14**
Locanda La Perla **15**
Ostello Cittá di Padua **1**

for visiting the Basilica. The owners are friendly and helpful, the rooms clean, with tile floors and phones. Some even have TVs, which is shocking for the price. Many people with family in the nearby hospital stay here, so be very quiet when you're stumbling in at night.

The typical Italian **Albergo Dante** *(Via San Polo 5; Tel 049/876-04-08; Bus 6, 9, 15 or MP to Via Dante; 50,000L single without bath, 68,000L single with bath or double without bath, 75,000L double with bath; No credit cards)* is run, of course, by la Signora (is it just our imagination, or is she the same lady in every town?). The basic, old-fashioned rooms, decorated with Jesus prints and watercolor landscapes, are up the marble stairs from the lobby, which doubles as the front hall for La Signora's apartment. Don't worry; you get your own key so you can come and go at all hours without waking her up. Every two rooms share a bathroom—not a bad ratio. To find it, leave the Piazza dei Signori from the northeast corner, following Via Dante. Take your third left, then a right on quiet side street Via San Polo.

Local students who can't sneak their friends into their dorms put them up at **Albergo Verdi** *(Via Dondi Dell'Orologio 7; Tel 049/875-57-44; Bus 6, 5, or 10 to Corso Milano; 40,000L single, 64,000L double, 85,000L triple; No private baths; No credit cards).* Call this the anti-hostel—there's no curfew, and the staff can tell you where the current hotspots are. Rooms are acceptably clean and usually full, so call ahead. Albergo Verdi is remodeling in Spring 2001, so call ahead to see if they're open, and to check the prices (remodeling brings out the greed in some people). It's a block north of the Duomo.

▶▶DO-ABLE

A terrific one-star, **Hotel Al Santo** *(Via del Santo 147; Tel 049/875-21-31, Fax 049/878-80-76; Bus 8, 12, 18, 22 to Riva Businello or MB to Via del Santo; 50,000L single without bath, 65,000L single with bath, 85,000L double with bath, 115,000L triple with bath; V, MC),* is a cut above the cheaper places without that much of an increase in price. The ground floor holds a restaurant run by a saintly, gray-haired *signora* and her even saintlier and grayer mother. The 17 rooms are kept spic and span, and all have phones. The location, just north of Piazza del Santo, couldn't be better. If you come back after hours, ring the bell and the night porter will let you in. There are plans to renovate, and add another star or two, so make sure to check the prices before unpacking.

It's a big step up to the air-conditioned rooms at **Hotel Buenos Aires** *(Via Luca Belludi 37; Tel 049/665-633 or 049/651-844, Fax 049/658-685; Bus 8, 12, 18, 22 to Riva Businello or MB to Via del Santo; 100,000L single, 140,000L double, 160,000L triple all with bath, 80,000L extra person; V, AE, DC),* all with private bathrooms, TVs, and phones. Book ahead. It's just off Piazza del Santo.

▶▶SPLURGE

Built in the late 1800s, **Albergo Leon Bianco** *(Piazzetta Pedrocchi 12; Tel 049/657-225, Fax 049/875-08-14; Bus 3, 8, 12, or 18 to Corso Garibaldi or MB to Piazza della Frutta; 143,000L single; 175-185,000L double, all with bath; 16,000L breakfast; leonbianco@toscanelli.com; V,*

MC, DC, AE), is still going, and has a great perk-per-lira ratio. The friendly, English-speaking management are at the front desk 24/7, and the 22 tastefully designed, comfortable rooms all have air conditioning, phones, and TVs. There are even free bikes at your disposal! The breakfast buffet isn't worth the 15,000L price, but it's served on the rooftop terrace, which offers sweeping views. It's easy to find, just around the corner from Café Pedrocchi [see *cafe scene,* above].

need to know

Currency Exchange There are banks with **ATMs** along Corso Garibaldi/Via VIII Febbraio. You can also change money in the **train station** (the rates aren't as good), or at the **post office.**

Tourist Information The **main tourist office** *(Vicolo Pedrocchi; Tel 049/875-20-77; 9am-7pm Mon-Sat, 9am-noon Sun Apr-Oct; 9:15am-5:45pm Mon-Fri, 9am-noon Sun Nov-Mar)* is near Cafe Pedrocchi, offering plenty of information and an online info kiosk with a printer. A smaller office in the train station and a kiosk in Piazza del Santo *(Tel 049/875-30-87)* hold the same hours. None of them can help you book a room.

Public Transportation Most buses stop at the train station, and run until 11pm. Tickets can be purchased at the newsstand in the train station, and at *tabacchi* which you can find on almost any street (look for the blue sign with a white "T"). After 11pm, try **Radiotaxi** *(Tel 049/651-33-33; 8,300L first 2km, 1,450L per km thereafter).*

Health and Emergency Emergency: *118;* Police: *113.* The local hospital, **Complesso Clinico Ospedale** *(Via San Giustiniani 1; Tel 049/821-11-11)* is west of Piazza Al Santo.

Pharmaces Al Duomo *(Via Manin 67; Tel 049/875-83-63; 9am-12:30pm/3:30-6pm Mon-Fri; No credit cards)* is pretty central, and has the weekly schedule of which pharmacy is open after hours posted in the window.

Telephone City code: *049.* Phone cards come in 5,000L or 10,000L and are available from any newsstand.

Trains The **train station** *(Piazzale dell Stazione; Tel 049/875-20-77)* is north of the city center. There are good connections to Venice (every half-hour; 4,000L one-way) and Milan (every hour; 20,000L one-way), as well as to most of the other smaller towns in the Veneto.

Bus Lines Out of the City The **bus station** is at Piazzale Boshetti, just across the canal northeast of the Roman Arena. Buses to Venice and Vicenza leave every half hour and cost 5,100L.

Laundry Spiff yourself up at **Lavandaria Ad Aqua** *(Via Ognissanti 6; Tel 049/775-759; 6,000L wash, 6,000L dry; No credit cards)* is a bit of a hike east of the town center. Follow Via Altinate east for just under 2 km until it becomes Via Ognissanti.

Postal Direct your postcards to the **main post office** *(Corso Garibaldi 33; Tel 049/820-85-11; 8:10am-6pm Mon-Fri)* It also changes money.

Internet See *wired,* above.

verona

Verona was a first-century outpost of ancient Rome, and the spirit of Bacchus still runs wild here today. The local students chug barrel after barrel at swanky wine bars, swing to the groove in late-night music dives, and shake their money-makers in the riverside disco. When morning comes (if it hasn't already), you won't want to miss the Roman arena and amphitheater or the Renaissance art in the city's gorgeous piazzas.

There are more ancient artifacts here than anywhere outside of Rome, from the remnants of the old city gates to the enormous gladiatorial arena to the Ponte Pietra. The elegance of the Renaissance is also alive and kicking; Verona was the home turf of the Scaglieri family from 1263 to 1398, and they blessed it with dazzling *palazzi* and *castelli* as well as beautiful old churches, all still standing. Verona has its own orchestra, an annual opera festival, and a ton of contemporary art galleries.

And then there are the Capulets and the Montagues. Throngs of tourists make quick stopovers here, rushing off the bus to stand below the balcony where Juliet ostensibly gave her famous speech. Don't buy it. As if Verona didn't have enough going for it, they had to turn Shakespeare's setting into a theme park. Save your romantic urges for nighttime, when the blush of first love can be witnessed for real in any of the city's hopping college bars.

Despite Verona's many tourist attractions, the city of 50,000 people manages to retain its individual spirit. The locals are very style-conscious—and a little more uptight than in many Italian cities. But all are accommodating to tourists, who are, after all, the city's lifeblood. English is widely spoken, thanks to all those tourists, plus the presence of the Universitá degli Studi di Verona. Students from all over Italy get the Veronese population to lighten up considerably, and spur on the city's nightlife. Ignore the tourist traps and keep your eyes fixed on the sublime beauties that are only available in fair Verona—a few sleepless nights will leave you with memories to last a lifetime.

neighborhoods

The **Adige river** weaves through Verona, forming what looks like a giant "S" that fell over on its left side. The bulk of the sights are tucked into the bottom part of the "S," on the eastern side of town, though you shouldn't ignore what's on the other side of the three main bridges that cross the Adige—there's some good stuff over there too. The train station is a good 20-minute walk southeast of the center of town. As you exit the main doors of the station, turn to your right and walk until you reach **Porta Nuova,** then head northeast on the busy main street, **Corso Porta Nuova.** This will lead you to Verona's largest piazza, the sprawling asphalt **Piazza Bra,** where you'll find the first-century **Amphitheater Arena** [see *culture zoo,* below]. Welcome to tourist central—you'll be bombarded with street-side souvenir cards and touristy cafe hawkers entreating you to sit down for an overpriced cappuccino. Resist!

Instead, hang a left onto **Via Oberdan,** heading north, where you'll begin to see how the real Verona lives. This street is speckled with stores, restaurants, and cafes, and when you get to its end, you can hang a left and backtrack southwest a bit down **Corso Cavour.** This stylish street is studded with bookshops, designer boutiques, and other local stores. You'll pass through the stunning first-century **Arco dei Gavi,** a gate into the old Roman town, and see the grandiose **Castelvecchio** on your right. Once home of the Scaglieri family, today it's Verona's most prestigious museum [see *culture zoo,* below].

But let's go back to Piazza Bra: You can stroll north from here on the ritzy pedestrian street, **Via Mazzini,** until you hit **Piazza delle Erbe,** which has been the heart of the city since it was a buzzing Roman forum (you can still see some of the artifacts in an exposed excavation below the piazza). People hang out in the piazza's market and dip into the surrounding bars for an *aperitivo* before settling down to dinner. Just a block northeast of here, under the arches, sits **Piazza Signori.** The oldest of Verona's famous bridges, **Ponte Pietra,** is a five-minute walk due north of here; crossing over it will bring you just a few steps northwest of **Teatro Romano.** The youth hostel sits on the hill just above this first-century amphitheater.

The other bridge you'll find yourself crossing, over and over again, is **Ponte Navi,** five blocks east of Piazza Bra. This bridge leads into **Via San Polo,** which becomes **Via XX Settembre,** the center of the student scene. Verona's bus system is efficient, and will whisk you anywhere you want to go in no time. Though regular bus service stops around 8pm, night buses run until midnight, and hit all the hotspots.

hanging out

Piazza delle Erbe is the best plaza for creative time-wasting. The small daily market takes up valuable meandering space, but the cafes that line the area are great for people watching. It's also the center of activity of the nightly *passegiata,* or stroll, where almost all Veronese put on their Sunday best and wear out some expensive shoe leather along the trendy Via Mazzini, Piazza del Signori, and Via Stella. There are other little pockets of activity on Via Leoncino and around Piazza delle Erbe. If you're looking for Verona's students, you'll find them along **Via XX Settembre,** west of the Ponte Navi. Bars, clubs, and restaurants line this street—on weekends, it's an all-out block party.

bar scene

Verona's university keeps the city's powerful nocturnal drive alive. The only problem is there's no real epicenter of fun, so a night out on the town usually requires a lot of walking. Things get going early on and around Piazza delle Erbe—the Via Mazzini strollers stop in for a drink at Caffé delle Erbe before deciding where the night will take them. For students, that usually means heading west to the more manic scene along Via XX

verona bars clubs and culture zoo

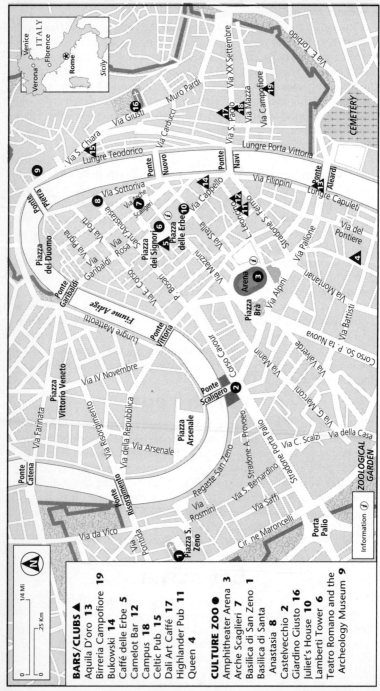

BARS/CLUBS ▲
Aquila D'oro **13**
Birreria Campofiore **19**
Bukowski **14**
Caffé delle Erbe **5**
Camelot Bar **12**
Campus **18**
Celtic Pub **15**
Dali Art Caffé **17**
Highlander Pub **11**
Queen **4**

CULTURE ZOO ●
Amphitheater Arena **3**
Arche Scaglieri **7**
Basilica di San Zeno **1**
Basilica di Santa
Anastasia **8**
Castelvecchio **2**
Giardino Giusto **16**
Juliet's House **10**
Lamberti Tower **6**
Teatro Romano and the
Archeology Museum **9**

Settembre. Though most college kids are gone in the summer, their hang-outs don't close up completely—they're just not as packed.

Verona's fashionistas get all gussied up and head out to **Caffé delle Erbe** *(Piazza delle Erbe 32; Tel 045/591-403; Bus 70, 71 to Piazza Duomo; 7:30am-2am Tue-Sun; 5-8,000L cover for bands; No credit cards)*, the happening spot on the main piazza in town. The twenty- to thirtysomething crowd here acts much older than they look, with pinkies extended as they sip from their wine glasses. The traditional Italian bar transforms into a happening club late every night, serving up beer (8,000L), wines by the glass (3-8,000L), and a wide range of cocktails (10-13,000L). The lights dim around 9:30pm, the candles come out, and the tables out in the piazza fill up faster than you can down a glass of *moscato*. Folks spill out into the piazza with drink in hand and a sway in their steps. There's usually live music on weekends—expect Italian pop.

On any given night, the **Highlander Pub** *(Via Leoncino 11; Bus 70, 71, 72 or 73 to Piazza Bra; Tel 045/800-22-61; 11am-3pm/5pm-2am*

wired

E-mail junkies, rejoice! **Cyber Club Internet Café** *(Via San Antonio 13; Tel 045/801-55-50; 9am-midnight Tue-Sun; 4,000L per hour, free with a drink from 9-9:30pm; No credit cards)* southwest of Piazza Bra, just may be the best Internet bar in Italy. This gigantic space lacks all the cold, calculating, and technical aspects of the hi-tech age. With its flickering candlelight and red, gold, and orange fabric-draped walls, it looks more like an opium den than a cybercafe. The front bar is full of tea-drinkers and wine-sippers, while the Internet-inclined gather around the 20 super-fast computers that line the room, each positioned on their own, long, wood tables, with plenty of room for spreading out. While you're checking the scores on all the ball games you've missed, you can click on a desktop icon and order a drink. Beautiful.

Between the hostel and the Teatro Romano, the creatively named **Internet bar** *(Via Redentore 9; No phone yet; 7am-midnight daily in the winter; 8:30am-2:30am daily in the winter; 8,000L per hour; No credit cards)* is cheery enough, offering beer and panini to the hostellers that check their e-mail on the six fast machines.

Chain outfit **Internet Train** *(Via Roma 19; Tel 045/801-33-94; 8am-8pm Mon-Sat; 10,000L per hour; No credit cards)* has a small shop just west of the Arena with 15 computers. During happy hour, you can stay online for half-price.

Verona is on the web at ***www.emmeti.it/Welcome/Veneto/Verona/index.uk.html.***

five things to Talk to a Local about

1. **Romeo and Juliet.** Or Leonardo di Caprio and Clare Danes, if you must.
2. **Tourists.** Love 'em or hate 'em? Can't live with 'em or without 'em?
3. **Graduation.** Once diplomas are handed out, Verona becomes a massive bacchanalia. Find out about last year's exploits.
4. **Subtitles in movies.** Even the most erudite Italian will argue their case for dubbing American movies into Italian.
5. **Roman ancestry.** Who at the table can trace their family tree back to the dear, departed Roman Empire?

daily; no cover; V, MC, DC, AE) west of Piazza Bra, is the most packed bar in town. This place is massive—the huge front room is flanked by a long, wooden bar, and decorated with the kind of oil paintings only a grandmother could love. The wood tables and booths carry on around back to the side rooms, where college kids, couples, and young professionals down Newcastle and Beamish Ale by the pint (7,000L). The wooden ledge that lines the entrance is covered with flyers for clubs and bars around town. Chances are most of the cool kids have late-night plans, and guess what? They're friendly, and more than likely will invite you along if you make the first move. Catch a bite to eat before it gets too late—the food here is a nice break from the Italian fare you've been living on for the last few weeks. Try the fish and chips (13,000L).

The ads promise "Knights and Dragons!" and **Camelot Bar** *(Via Leoncino 7; Tel 045/800-10-96; Bus 70, 71, 72 or 73 to Piazza Bra; 5pm-2am Tue-Sun; 8,000L pints; No credit cards)* delivers. Yes, that would be a guillotine by the door, and there are more coats-of-arms on the walls than you can count. This tiny, two-tiered medieval theme bar is as cheesy as they come, but it's so crowded with students and charged with loud rock music that you can't help but enjoy yourself, if that's the type of thing you enjoy. It's proximity to the ever-popular Highlander Pub, two doors down, means that folks go back and forth between the two, stopping to hang out in the street for a de facto block party. The American servicemen who make this place their home away from home can get a little rowdy, but the fiery wenches behind the bar keep them in line.

Somewhere between swank and alterno, **Bukowski** *(Vicolo Amanti 6; Tel 045/801-14-17; Bus 70, 71 to Piazza Duomo; 7pm-3am Wed-Mon; Gay nights Thu, Sun; No cover; V, MC, AE)* is all about "the scene," but the vibe is always low-key—whether you're gay, straight, punk, or prep, you'll feel welcome. Located on a tiny side street west of Piazza Bra, this big, beautiful bar attracts everyone from fashionistas to not-so-starving artists.

The regulars sip brightly colored cocktails (12,000L) and boutique beers (8,000L), make conversation over the mosaic bar, and play pool in the back. Ambient sounds escalate into a DJ-driven house party around 10pm on the weekends, but there's never any cover.

The bright, cheery **Dalí Art Caffé** *(Via XX Settembre 17; Tel 0333/294-93-68; Bus 11, 12, 51, 91, 90, 98 to Via XX Settembre's first stop; 7am-2am Mon-Thu; 7am-4am Fri-Sat; No cover; No credit cards)* is currently the latest greatest with Verona's college crowd, packing 'em in from early evening to late, late night—with beer at 5,000L a pint, you can understand why. The decor is modern and Ikea-inspired, although there are Dalí prints on the walls, as the name promises. Music—a combo of European and American pop, rock, and commercial faves—plays at a level that makes conversation impossible, but there's not enough room for dancing. Come around midnight, when the crowd's at its best.

Catering to college kids with its board games, live music, and lots of beer, **Campus** *(Via XX Settembre 18; Tel 045/801-47-87; Bus 11, 12, 51, 91, 90, 98 to Via XX Settembre's first stop; 7pm-2am Tue-Thu; 7pm-3am Fri-Sat; 2:30pm-2am Sun; No cover; No credit cards)* couldn't be more appropriately named. This place, across from Dalí Art Caffé, has a great selection of beers on tap—you can get Leffe, Hoegarden, Becks, or Murphy's by the liter for just 12,000L. American Top-40 blares from the speakers, and come late night, the music kicks up a few notches and dancing on the tables begins. Snacks from the full kitchen are pretty darned good and absolutely cheap. The snack of choice seems to be the nachos with salsa and cheese (6,000L), but the panini (5,000L) are something else, each one named after another college major—there's the *giurisprudenza* (law school), with speck and mozzarella on rustic bread, or the *matematica* with fontina and pancetta on focaccia.

If you're staying at the hostel, you'll be glad to know about **Celtic Pub** *(Via Santa Chiara 1; Tel 045/590-704; Bus 73 or 90 to Piazza Isolo; 7pm-2am Tue-Thu, Sun, 7pm-3am Fri-Sat; No cover; No credit cards),* the walk-in closet-sized Irish pub right on the corner before you start your ascent up the hill, the perfect place to stop in for one more drink (8,000L beer pints; 7-8,000L whiskey) before curfew. The owner is a sharp-tongued, take-charge woman who loves to talk to foreigners. The wall behind the bar is covered with bills that she's collected from around the world over the past 15 years—if you give her one she doesn't already have, she'll probably offer you a beer on the house. This is a chill space (there's not much more room for anything else), with Italian and American rock at a conversation-friendly level. In the early evenings, you can sprawl out in one of the round wooden booths and order from a small menu of beer-related food—beef cooked in stout (15,000L) and a Guinness chocolate cake (5,000L) are some of the better options.

LIVE MUSIC SCENE

Verona is surprisingly short on live music options. A restaurant first and foremost, Al Carro Armato [see *eats,* below], found on Vicolo Gatto, a tiny street east of Piazza Dei Signori, is single-handedly filling Verona's live music void. Wishing there was some place in town to hear live music themselves, the owners started booking bands right in their dining room—mainly indie rock, jazz, and folky stuff. The crowd ranges from high school kids to middle-aged couples, all sitting at the same long wooden tables where diners slurped pasta just hours ago. A small bar offers wine by the glass (2-6,000L) and a space to talk away from the main event.

club scene

Verona offers a laid-back scene, free from the restraints of dress codes and VIP rooms. (That's the nice way of saying "there aren't really any clubs".) Aquila d'Oro would be the lamest club in town in most places, but here, it's second best. Luckily, the crowd makes its own fun.

The wildest parties are at Verona's best and brightest, **Queen** *(Via Bertoni 1; Tel 045/800-02-03; Bus 70 to Pallone; 11pm-late; Cover varies from free-20,000L; No credit cards)*. It's recently been renovated, with super slick decor and drinks to match—tall, funny-colored cocktails (12-15,000L) are the accessory of choice, perfectly suited to the high-fashion and hipster crowd that hangs here. The music is just the other side of commercial, with a little bit of everything—house, disco, and electronica. Keep an eye out in bars around town for discount entry fliers, which can bring the cover down from 20,000L to 10,000L. It's a bit out of the way, about four blocks south of Via Pallone, which runs between Piazza Bra and the Ponte Aleardi.

For most Veronese, a night on the town ends at **Aquila D'oro** *(Via Macello 5; Tel 045/592-630 or 045/592-776; Bus 70 to Via Pallone; 10,000L cover includes first drink; No credit cards)*, the cheesy but popular dance club right on the water near the Ponte Alerdi, the next bridge south of Ponte Navi. Also known as Gold Station, it's located in an enormous old public pool building and packed with patio furniture and swinging chairs. A glass wall offers views of the pool itself. People wander around inside and out, drinks in hand, stopping to get a glance at the river, or to sit on the white rattan furniture out on the porch. A small space is reserved for dancing up by the stage, where the mc/keyboard player belts out com-

romeo meets juliet

Not only is Verona the quintessential college town, but it's also the home of history's most famed star-crossed lovers. Love always seems to be in the air, even when it isn't. Don't be surprised to find very generous doses of flirtatious behavior in the bars, the piazzas, even in the streets. If all this attention is unwelcome, *"Lasciami in pace, Romeo"* should get you a little solitude.

mercial Italian and butchers classic American pop songs—it can feel like the longest school-sponsored post-prom party ever. If you can turn off your cheese detector, you can have a good time, but get here late, after midnight at least, when it's packed. This place would be way too depressing empty.

arts scene

Modern galleries, the latest movies in *(gasp!)* English, local music, and avant-garde theater are just a few of the cultural advantages Verona has over most Italian cities of its size. Some of the country's most influential galleries are based here, and new, raw spaces are opening up every day.

▶▶VISUAL ARTS

Housed in a renovated Renaissance palace northeast of Piazza Dei Signori is **Galleria d'Arte Moderna "Pallazzo Forti"** *(Vicolo Volto due Mori 4; Tel 045/800-19-03; 9am-7pm Tue-Sun; Admission fee depends on the exhibit, reduced rate for students; V, MC),* one of Verona's largest modern and contemporary art spaces. With a few exhibits going on at any given time, you can stumble across conceptual multimedia presentations, photography, or an early modern collection of paintings (Kandinsky, Malevich, and Chagall are a few recent shows). All the exhibits are accompanied by well-written info in English; it also distributes information for other galleries around town.

Cutting-edge exhibits and presentations of new talent make **Galleria Dello Scudo** *(Vicolo Scudo di Francia 2; Tel 045/590-144; Hours vary with exhibit; Free; No credit cards),* right on Piazza delle Erbe, a must-see. It's been at the forefront of Italy's international art scene since 1967. Many of the artists it has featured have moved on to important modern art museums around the world.

East of Piazza Bra, **Studio la Città** *(Via Dietro Filippini 2; Tel 045/597-549, Fax 045/597-028; 9am-1pm/3-7:30pm Tue-Sat; www.artnet.com/citta; Free; No credit cards)* has been drawing gallery-hoppers for 32 years. Specializing in the Italian art movements after WWII, it recently expanded its interests to include photography, multimedia, and other genres. Recent shows include the first-ever exhibit of Gianni Versace's fashion.

East of Ponte Nuovo, you'll find **Galleria La Giarina** *(Via Interrato dell'Acqua Morta 82; Tel 045/803-23-16; 3:30-7:30pm Tue-Sat; Free; V, MC),* the little gallery with a heart of gold. Single-artist exhibits showcase paintings, installations, video, and photography by some of the freshest talent in the country.

▶▶PERFORMING ARTS

Whether it's serious drama or musical theater, **Teatro Nuovo** *(Piazza Vivani 10; Tel 045/800-61-00 or 045/803-08-15; 15-45,000L tickets; V, MC, AE)* is Verona's main venue. Most performances are in Italian, of course, but tickets are so much more reasonable than they are in other Italian cities, you might consider checking it out.

With its lovely 17th-century red and gold draped tiered interior and wonderful acoustics, **Teatro Filarmonico** *(Via dei Mutilati 4/k; Tel*

045/800-28-80; Box office 9am-noon/3:15-5:45pm Mon-Fri, 9am-noon Sat; 13-25,000L tickets; V, MC), is perfect for a night of Mozart or Mahler. Seeing the locals all dressed up for a night at the symphony is a performance in itself.

Check out Verona's great jazz tradition in the weekly concerts at the **Sala Maffeiana** (Via Roma 3; Tel 045/800-74-33 information; 045/801-11-54 box office; 10,000L; No credit cards), a room in the Verona Philarmonic's original theater, west of Piazza Bra. Shows start at 9pm; stop by the tourist office [see need to know, below] for a listing of current performances. You can usually score discount tickets on the night of the show.

Lucky for you that **Cinema Teatro Stimate** (Piazza Cittadella; Tel 045/800-08-78; 6-9pm Tue; 10,000L tickets; No credit cards), south of Piazza Bra, is anti-dubbing. They bill Tuesday night's mainstream Hollywood movies in lingua originale as "impara l'ingleses al cinema" ("learn English at the movies"). You're welcome to come along even if English is your mother tongue.

gay scene

Though there are very few gay-only bars, Verona has a vibrant gay community. Places like Bukowski [see bar scene, above] and Queen [see club scene, above] feature specifically gay nights, but pretty much any night of the week is gay-friendly, if not gay-all-the-way. To hear the buzz on the best places, stop by **Arcigay/Arcilesbica** (Via Santa Chiara 7; Tel 045/801-28-54; 9-11pm Mon, Wed, 6-9pm Sun), the local gay and lesbian group.

The unassuming **Birreria Campofiore** (Via Campofiore 35; Tel 045/803-25-34; 9am-midnight daily; 6,000L beer; 8,000L cocktails; No credit cards) doesn't look like much, but it's considered one of the few cool gay bars in town, attracting men and women of all ages. Picnic benches are the only attempt at decor in this little space, although there's video poker in the corner, and a deli case filled with big, bountiful bruschette and panini (3-7,000L). It's worth the walk over the Ponte Navi to the student neighborhood to meet some friendly folks. In the daytime this place is neither gay, nor a bar, but a cafe mobbed by the annoying little beasties from the high school across the street. The night crowd arrives around dinnertime.

culture zoo

The problem with sightseeing in Verona is figuring out where to start, and when you're finished. No matter where you are, there's always something else worth seeing. The Verona Card, available at tourist info for 22,000L [see need to know, below], is a really good deal, getting you entrance into all the sights and free bus travel to boot.

Amphitheater Arena (Piazza Bra; Tel 045/800-32-04; Bus 11, 12, 13, 14, 51 to Piazza Bra or 70, 71, 72, 73 to Piazza Municipio; 9am-7pm Tue-Sun, last entry 6:30pm, 3:30pm performance nights; 6,000L adults, 4,000L students; No credit cards): You're standing on the stylish Corso Cavour, contemplating whether you should buy the latest Radiohead album, or that cute pair of capri pants. You turn around, and bam! There

festivals and events

The Verona Opera Festival *(Ente Lirico Arena di Verona, Piazza Bra 28; Tel 045/800-51-51; July-August; www.arena.it)* is a sight to behold. In the summer months, folks flock to Verona to see classical Italian and European opera in the most classical of settings— the ancient Roman Arena. Though reserved seats are astronomically expensive, you can buy yourself a general seating ticket for 25-40,000L. Wait for the first aria—when the high note hits you all the way up in the nosebleed seats, it'll give you chills.

it is: a very loud reminder of Verona's early days, one of the most complete Roman arenas in Italy, with its inner wall intact, and four taller arches of the outer wall remaining. It used to woo the masses with gladiator combat, but today it's used for much more civilized cultural events. During the summer, you can book a seat with 20,000 others to hear the great operas [see *festivals and events,* below]. After nearly 2,000 years, the acoustics still rock—no microphones necessary.

Piazza dei Signori: Everywhere you look in this elegant piazza, you're confronted with Verona's Renaissance splendor. The daunting Palazzo Governo sits behind the even more daunting statue of *Inferno* poet Dante. The Loggia del Consiglio, with its Venetian detail and towering statues, was built on the other end of the piazza in 1493. The Arco della Costa medieval gate leads into Piazza delle Erbe, and the 274-foot 12th-century **Lamberti Tower** *(Cortile Mercato Vecchio; Tel 045/803-27-26; 9am-7pm daily; 4,000L; No credit cards)* presides over it all. An elevator trip to the top will get you the best views of the city.

Piazza delle Erbe: While Piazza dei Signoria was home to regal pageantry and political ceremonies, Piazza delle Erbe was the main center of commerce back in the day—*way* back in the day, actually, since it was originally built over a Roman Forum. Unfortunately, the markets that remain are more about sending the tourists home with snow globes and other cheesy junk. But look past all that to one of the most beautiful Renaissance piazzas in Italy. A reminder of Verona's loyalty to the Venetian republic, the winged lion, sits on a column that looms large over the square, surrounded by beautiful 14th-century palazzos.

Arche Scaglieri: If only we could all rest in peace with such style. Right around the corner from the piazzas, you'll come across these ornate, gothic tombs of the noble family. The equestrian statue that sits on top of the tomb is a copy—to see the real thing, venture over to Castelvecchio. But really, once is enough.

Juliet's House *(Via Capello 23; Tel 045/803-43-03; Bus 11, 12, 13, 14, 51 to S. Fermo; 9am-7pm Tue-Sun; 6,000L adults, 4,000L students; No* *credit cards):* It's cheesy. It's fake. But c'mon, where's your romantic side? Everyone knows that this house between Piazza Erbe and Ponte Navi doesn't *really* contain the balcony where Juliet made her big speech. The building was bought in 1905 by the city of Verona, which propped up a statue of Ms. Capulet for an instant tourist attraction. People come from all over the world to suspend their disbelief for a few hours, and scrawl their lover's name on the outside gate—*R+J= Tru luv 4eva.*

Teatro Romano and the Archeology Museum *(Rigaste Redentore 2; Tel 045/800-03-60; 9am-7pm Tue-Sun; 5,000L adults, 3,000L students; No credit cards):* To think that first-century poet Catullus, a Verona native, used to come to this stone ampitheater across Ponte Pirtra for an evening of theater really puts things in perspective. Though it's not in as good a shape as the Arena, it's one of the best-preserved ancient theaters in the world; performances were held here until about 10 years ago. The archeological museum, housed in the little church above, contains more remnants of Verona's ancient past.

Castelvecchio *(Corso Castelvecchio 2; Tel 045/94734; Bus 31, 32, 33 to Via S. Stefano; 9am-7pm Tue-Sun; 6,000L adults, 4,000L students; No credit cards):* This archetypal castle on the Adige River west of Piazza Bra was the home of the Scaglieri, lucky stiff. Completed in 1355, it's now used as Verona's main art museum, but just strolling around the ramparts and brick passages is exciting enough—cross the Ponte de Castelvecchio for one of the most beautiful views of the city on the river. Inside, there's lots of art to behold, from Roman sculpture to endless examples of paintings from the Veronese school. Tintoretto's *Madonna Nursing the Child* and *Nativity* are two of the more famous works. If you have a post-modern bent, you'll want to pay the additional fee to revel in the contemporary exhibitions housed in the gallery space (admission varies depending on the show).

Basilica of Santa Anastasia *(Piazza Sant'Anastasia; Tel 045/592-813; Bus 70, 71 to S. Anastasia; 9:30am-6pm Mon-Sat; 9:30am-1pm Sun; Free):* Built between 1290 and 1481, Verona's biggest church dominates the northwestern end of Via Sant'Anastasia. The facade remains unfinished, and the Gothic portico is stunning in comparison to the striated brick that rises up to the top. Inside, take a moment amid the enormous columns, Gothic arches, and tall windows to see Pisanello's fresco of St. George and the Princess.

Basilico di San Zeno *(Piazza San Zeno; Tel 045/592-813; Bus 32, 33 to Piazza Pozzo; 9:30am-6pm Mon-Sat, 1-6pm Sun; Free):* One of Verona's oldest churches, dating back to the 4th century, San Zeno's been restored, rebuilt, and revisioned many times since, most significantly in the 12th and 13th centuries. The front bronze doors detail the life of San Zeno, who is laid to rest in the crypt below the altar. Mantegna created the altarpiece in the apse, and there are some 13th- and 14th-century frescoes on either side. But the real beauty inside the church is the ceiling, which was designed to look like the keel of ship.

Giardino Giusto *(Via Giardino Giusto 2; Tel 045/803-40-29; Bus 73 to Piazza Isolo; 9am-8pm daily; 8,000L adults, 3,000L students; No* *credit cards):* If you've had enough of Roman ruins and Renaissance architecture and art, and cultural overload has set in, walk east from Ponte Navi to chill out in some of the most beautiful gardens in Italy. Pay no attention to the Renaissance details, like the fountains, the mythology-themed statues, and the hedged labyrinth, which are attributed to Agostino Giustini's 16th-century design. Okay, so there's culture here, too, but at least you can enjoy it on the grass with your shoes off.

CITY SPORTS

Verona's all about the art, the ruins, the music. But if you insist on getting more exercise than trampling around first-century ruins provides, go to the city's public pool, **Piscine Comunale Santini** *(Via Santini 15; Tel 045/835-04-70; Bus 23, 24 to Piscina; 10am-2:30pm/6:15-8:30pm Mon-Fri, 10am-8:30pm Sat, 10am-1:30pm Sun; 6,500L adults, 5,500L students; No credit cards).* It's just over a kilometer northeast of the center, easily accessible by bus.

STUFF

A fixture on tour-bus routes, Verona has its fair share of tacky souvenir shops. But there are student-oriented shops as well, with everything from cool art to comic books to vintage clothing, all hard to find in other Italian cities. Many of the coolest shops are along Via Fama, just west of Piazza Erbe.

▶▶BOUND

North of Piazza Bra, where Via Oberdan meets Corso Bosari, **Giubbe Rosse Bookstore** *(Corso Porta Borsari 49; Tel 045/803-34-63; 9am-8pm Mon-Thu; 9am-noon Fri-Sat; 10am-8pm Sun; V, MC)* specializes in art and design books, with an outstanding collection of titles, although few of them are printed in English. Ask them what they have on your fave artist. There are some English-language titles as well.

Just five blocks northeast of Piazza Bra, **Passwords** *(Via Stella 17/a; Tel 045/801-54-56; 9am-1pm/3-7pm Mon-Sat; V, MC)* specializes in foreign titles, with an enormous collection of academic and contemporary best-sellers. This is the place to run into fellow English-speakers.

The best way to learn a language is with a comic book in hand—everything is written at a fifth-grade reading level, with accompanying drawings, and punctuated with slang and vernacular phrases—it's the quickest road to fluency. **Fan City** *(Via Fama 4/a; Tel 045/592-456; 10am-12:30pm/3:30-6:30pm; No credit cards)* has a large collection of Italian comics, called *fumetti,* including the fave of Italian preteens (and certain American guidebook writers), *Dylan Dog.* This shop, on the corner of Corso Portoni Borsani, also stocks other distractions, like models of classic Vespas and old retro toys, that make great gifts for the friends back home.

▶▶TUNES

Sandwiched among all the other cool stores on this block, **I Dischi Volante** *(Via Fama 7; Tel 045/801-25-31; 9:30-2:30pm/3-7:30pm Tue-Sun, 3-7:30pm Mon; V, MC)* is a great little record shop, with an enormous collection of indie artists from all over—there are even some Italian alternative bands worth checking out. CDs run 25-40,000L.

▶▶**DUDS**

Offering all the cool clothes you've been seeing in shop windows all over town for less, **Happy Moda** *(Via Roma 12; Tel 045/803-18-73; 10am-12:30pm/4-8pm daily; No credit cards)* will make you a happy shopper. Located west of Piazza Bra, near the intersection of Via Manin, it's a great place to pick up a skinny tank or tee before hitting the town. Skirts are 15-25,000L, jeans 30,000L. There are dressing rooms in the back, but the line of bargain shoppers is usually pretty long.

EATS

There are tons of tourist traps to avoid—you can recognize these places by the laminated menus outside their front doors—but there are also plenty of perfectly good restaurants where you can score hearty, cheap meals. Verona also has lots of local *osterias* and *trattorias* that serve unfussy, regional specialties at reasonable prices—try the polenta. *Pasta e fagioli* is different here—soupier and richer—with fresh pasta tossed in. And don't miss out on anything made with *radicchio,* the best of the local veggies. The wines here are amazing—from light, fruity red Valpolicella to crisp, white Soave. Pony alert: Horse meat is another local specialty, so avoid anything with *cavallo* in the name unless you want to take a bite of Trigger.

▶▶**CHEAP**

When you're through touristing around the Arena, desperate for some instant gratification, **Brek** *(Piazza Bra 20; Tel 045/800-45-61; 11:30am-3pm/6:30-10pm Sun-Fri; 9-13,000L entrees; No credit cards)* is your answer. Conveniently located on the west side of Piazza Bra, this spacious self-service restaurant has it all. The pretty upstairs marble-floored dining room is filled with everyone from business folks to students to tourists, all devouring heaping plates of lasagna and oversized salads. The pasta bar serves up innovative dishes like spaghetti with ricotta and saffron, and there's a whole table full of pastries for dessert. Score a table outside on the piazza for a view of the Arena.

Always first in line for great cheap food, the college kids have moved into the bright and cheerful **Pizza e Café Nogara** *(Via Scala 2; Tel 045/803-47-17; 7:30am-midnight Tue-Thu, Sun; 7:30am-1:30am Fri, Sat; 8,000L first courses; 10-13,000L pizzas; No credit cards).* There's nothing funky about this two-story place four blocks northeast of Piazza Bra—in fact, it's pretty sterile—but the crowds keep lining up anyway. The tagliatelle with pesto and shrimp is tasty and filling, as is the *tortellini al ragu,* but pizza is the specialty of the house. It's open "non-stop," which means they don't close down after lunch.

The lines go out the door at **Pizza Doge** *(Via Roma 21/b; Tel 045/596-853; 10am-8:30pm Tue-Sun; No credit cards)*—everyone comes to this tiny, fluorescent-lit storefront on the western end of Via Roma for Italy's best slice to go. The ingredients are organic; the breads, home-made; the cheeses, sublime. The owner/chef rolls her dough out by hand,

and offers inventive concoctions like walnuts with smoked provolone, feta with spinach and tomatoes, and brie with arugula and smoky speck. Her *panzerotti* are like calzones in shape only: each dough is seasoned individually, and filled with complementary stuffings—try the pumpkin panzerotti filled with prosciutto and smoked mozzarella. Everything is priced per kilogram—tell how much you want to spend, and a slice'll be cut accordingly.

▶▶**DO-ABLE**

For the past 12 years, Annalisa Morandini has been the creative force behind **Al Carro Armato** *(Vicolo Gatto 2/a; Tel 045/803-01-75; 11am-3pm/6pm-2am daily, kitchen closes at 12:30pm Thu-Tue; 11-18,000L entrees; No credit cards),* located in a former carriage house on a tiny street east of Piazza Dei Signori. She's a dominant force on the floor as well, greeting everyone as they come into the dining room, finding them a seat at one of the long communal wooden tables, and bringing them a glass of wine to start the evening. Though the food here is great—classic Veneto chow with an emphasis on grilled meats—people really show up for the atmosphere. The high carriage-house ceilings, with enormous wooden beams, set the tone for the decor, the waiters are the friendliest guys in town, and on weekends rock and jazz bands come in to play for the crowd [see *live music scene,* above]. There's a little wine bar off to the back that serves up more than 40 regional choices by the glass (2-6,000L). The food is rustic and hearty—try lamb *spedinini* (13,000L) or the pasta e fagioli soup with lots of *parmegiano* cheese. For dessert, nothing beats some aged goat cheese, drizzled with chestnut honey and served with a glass of moscato sweet wine.

If you need a break from pasta and polenta, check out **Sushi Itto** *(Via Stelle 13/a; Tel 045/803-00-66; Noon-3pm/7pm-11pm Tue-Sat, 7pm-11pm Sun; 3-5,000L sushi; 14-28,000L combo plates; V, MC).* This beautiful new place, northeast of Piazza Bra, hasn't been embraced by the locals yet—something about raw fish doesn't appeal to the Veronese. But the food's great, from the chicken and vegetable tempura (14,000L) to the six-piece sushi platter with rolls, soup and salad (28,000L). The chef, who comes from Mexico by way of Tokyo, has integrated some local ingredients into his menu—try the radicchio roll, stuffed with rice, nuts, carrots and fresh ricotta. Minimalist and white, the decor is as soothing and refreshing as the food, with a modern, bleached-wood bar and an underlit sushi bar in the back.

Nestled in a tiny litle street between Piazza Delle Erbe and the Ponte Nuovo, **Trattoria alla Trota** *(Via Trota 3; Tel 045/800-47-57; Noon-3pm/7-10:30pm Mon-Sat; 10-18,000L entrees; No credit cards)* may look like nothing more than a rec room, but it serves up some of the best (and cheapest) mama food in town. Check out the daily specials, scribbled in bad handwriting on the blackboard outside the front door: spaghetti with sardines, *spezzatino al manzo con polenta* (beef steak), *tacchino arrosto con funghi* (roast turkey with mushrooms), and best of all, *faraona al forno* (oven-roasted game birds), which you pick up and eat with your hands.

verona eats and crashing

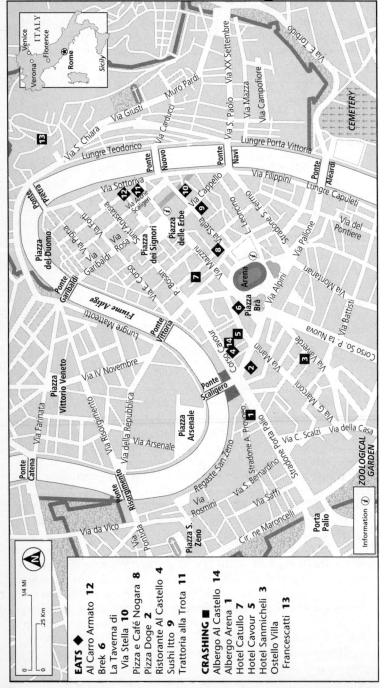

EATS ◆
Al Carro Armato **12**
Brek **6**
La Taverna di
  Via Stella **10**
Pizza e Café Nogara **8**
Pizza Doge **2**
Ristorante Al Castello **4**
Sushi Itto **9**
Trattoria alla Trota **11**

CRASHING ■
Albergo Al Castello **14**
Albergo Arena **1**
Hotel Catullo **7**
Hotel Cavour **5**
Hotel Sanmicheli **3**
Ostello Villa
  Francescatti **13**

This is a very popular place with the locals—the little yellow room is packed with families and friends enjoying a great meal loudly and enthusiastically. A liter of great house wine is just 8,000L, so drink up.

Don't miss out on a meal at **La Taverna di Via Stella** *(Via Stella 5C; Tel 045/800-80-08; 10:30am-2:30pm/6:30-11:30pm Tue-Sun; 13-20,000L entrees; No credit cards)*—it'll be one of your best in Verona. Everything about this big, crowded osteria southeast of Piazza Bra is delicious. The bar looks like something from a different era, with old-fashioned butcher weights and a deli case filled with every kind of sausage, cured ham, salami, and cheese available. The dining room is down in the cellar, under the arches and old metal hooks that were once used for hanging cured meat. Start off with one of their many polenta dishes or a homemade pasta. For dessert, try the tiramisu, a specialty of nearby Treviso that these folks have perfected.

▶▶**SPLURGE**

The beauteous **Ristorante Al Castello** *(Corso Cavour 43; Tel 045/800-44-03; 12:30-3pm/7:30-10pm Mon-Sat; 16-25,000L entrees; V, MC, DC)* is right in front of the Roman arch, on Corso Cavour. If you come too early for dinner, you may interrupt the owners' entire family sitting down to eat together before the crowds rush in. With yellow walls, amber light, and homey details everywhere you look, this is a comfortable spot to enjoy some great, regional cooking. Start with the *rape rosse* (beetroot ravioli with smoked ricotta cheese), and move on to the duck breast in *balsamico,* the roasted rabbit, or the white fish simmered in Vernaccia wine. The house wine (12,000L per liter) goes down easy, so watch out.

crashing

Tourist-friendly Verona is full of centrally located accommodations, but booking ahead is essential, especially in the summer season.

▶▶**CHEAP**

If you stay in one hostel on your whole trip to Italy, make it **Ostello Villa Francescatti** *(Salita Fontana del Ferro 15; Tel 045/590-360, Fax 045/800-91-27; Bus 73, 90 to Piazza Isolo; Reception open 7am-11:30pm, 11:30 curfew, 9am-5pm lockout; 23,000L dorm, 26,000L private family room with bath; Breakfast included; No credit cards),* a 16th-century villa surrounded by gorgeous landscaped gardens and sweeping views. It's located up on the hill near Teatro Romano, a beautiful 15-minute walk northeast from the city center—follow the Ostello signs up, up, up. The main house has a big communal room where hostellers hang out under the frescoes and in front of the fireplace, drinking wine and playing cards. This is also where dinner is served—14,000L for three courses isn't a bad deal. There's also a washer and dryer, and a PC for email (8,000L/hour). The grounds are so lush and lovely, you almost won't want to leave.

▶▶**DO-ABLE**

A cozy little hotel with just 16 rooms in a central location, **Albergo Arena** *(Stradone Porta Palio 2; Tel 045/803-24-40; 65-80,000L single, 100-120,000L double, 146,000L triple; Private baths available; V, MC,*

AE) fills up fast, so book ahead. From Piazza Bra, head down Via Roma and hang a left on Porto Palio; the hotel will be on your right. Ask for a room with a bath—not only are they bigger, but the owners have taken more care in decorating them. There's also a little TV room near the front desk, where you can chat it up with the English-speaking management.

Located down a quiet, little alley right off Via Catullo, and up two flights of stairs, **Hotel Catullo** *(Via Valerio Catullo 1; Tel 045/800-27-86; 40-60,000L single without bath, 60-90,000L double without bath, 70-110,000L double with bath; V, MC)* is Verona's best deal. An elderly husband and wife team go out of their way to make you feel at home—the lack of TVs and phones is more than made up for in homey hospitality. The rooms are spacious, and many have little terraces overlooking the main street.

Right on the corner of Via Valverde and Via Sciesa, **Hotel Sanmicheli** *(Via Valverde 2; Tel 045/800-37-49, Fax 045/800-45-08; 80-120,000L single, 105-150,000L double, all with bath; No credit cards)* makes a great central base for seeing all there is to see in Verona. All the rooms have phones, TVs, and cozy, grandmotherly furniture, and the downstairs sitting room and bar is a good place to retreat and collect yourself after Roman ruin overload.

Don't let scary Grandma at the front desk scare you off—**Albergo Al Castello** *(Corso Cavour 43; Tel 045/800-44-03; 75-85,000L singles without bath, 100,000L singles with bath, 110-120,000L doubles without bath, 130-150,000L doubles with baths; V, MC),* right across the street from Castelvecchio, is a great little find filled with homey touches like the floral carpets on the winding staircase. The nine rooms are basic, but comfy.

▶▶**SPLURGE**

A little pricier than most hotels in town, **Hotel Cavour** *(Vicolo Chiodo 4; Tel 045/590-508; 92-124,000L single, 124-180,000L double, all with private bath; Breakfast included; No credit cards)* is worth the extra lire for a lot more comfort. For the past 27 years, this family-run hotel, just north of Via Roma, on a quiet side street, has catered to vacationing visitors with a personal touch. All the rooms are decorated differently, and each has a TV and phone. In warm weather, breakfast is served in the pretty gardens.

need to know

Currency Exchange You'll have no problem finding **ATM** machines anywhere in town. There's also a **Cassa di Risparmio** on Piazza Bra, as well as a booth at the train station.

Tourist Informaton Lodged into a storefront on the southeast end of the Arena, the **tourist office** *(Via Degli Alpini 9; Tel 045/806-86-80; 1-7pm Mon, 9am-7pm Tue-Sat, 9am-3pm Sun)* is a little hard to find. There's a small, helpful office at the train station as well *(Tel 045/8000861; 8am-7:30pm Mon-Sat)*. Both have tons of booklets and pamphlets, but neither books rooms.

Public Transportation Buses run from 6am-8pm daily; most stop in front of the train station. For information, contact the **AMT office** *(Via F. Torbido 1; Tel 045/887-11-11)*. Tickets are 1,6000L and are valid for one hour.

Health and Emergency Emergency: *113;* Ambulance: *118;* Fire: *115.* The hospital, **Ospedale di Verona Borgo Trento** *(Piazzale Aristide Stefani 1; Tel 045/807-111, Fax 049/918-75)* is northeast of the town center, across the Adige River.

Pharmacies Agli Angeli *(Corso Porta Nuova 28; Tel 045/800-66-70; Hours vary; V, MC, AE)* is in the northern part of town, near the arch. For other pharmacies, look for the **green flashing crosses** all over town. 24-hour service is available on a rotating basis—check the notice that's posted on all pharmacy doors to find out which one is open for emergencies.

Trains Verona is a major transportation hub for the region. Trains run from here to Milan, Venice (by way of Padua and Vincenza), and Florence (by way of Bologna). The train station, **Verona Porta Nuova** *(Via XXV Aprile; Tel 1478/88088 for fares and schedules)* is located southwest of the city center, accessible by Buses 72, 73, 11, 12, 13, 14, 51. By foot, it's a 20-minute walk.

Bus Lines Out of the City The **APT bus station** *(Piazzale XXV Aprile; Tel 045/800-41-29)* is just across from the rail station. Buses leave for smaller cities in the province, as well as biggies like Venice.

Laundry Euro Lavandaria Fa Da Te *(10 b/c Via XX Settembre; 7:30am-10:30pm daily; 4,000L wash, 2,500L dry; No credit cards)* has loads of machines. You'll notice lots of college kids in this area, west of Ponte Navi, all dreaming of some day having clean clothes again.

Postal There's a **Mailboxes, Etc.** *(Via Cattaneao 24; Tel 045/901-30-38; 9am-1pm/3-7pm Mon-Fri)* north of Via Roma.

Internet See *wired,* above.

VICENZA

Work hard, play hard—that's Vicenza's motto. Thanks to a centuries-old gold trade and a more recent computer industry boom, this is one of Italy's wealthiest towns. And, lucky for you, the good life rubs off on visitors. Vicenza's compact *centro storico* is jam-packed with winding streets full of architectural flourishes and Renaissance reliefs, and losing yourself in their maze is great fun. The town's nightlife, while small, is one of the most diverse in the region, spanning the spectrum from punk clubs to chi-chi cocktail bars that most tourists don't stick around long enough to discover. Don't make the same mistake they make! Stay the night here and scope the scene.

Most tourists come here for the Palladian architecture, and with good reason. In 1994, the town was added to the UNESCO World Heritage

VICENZA

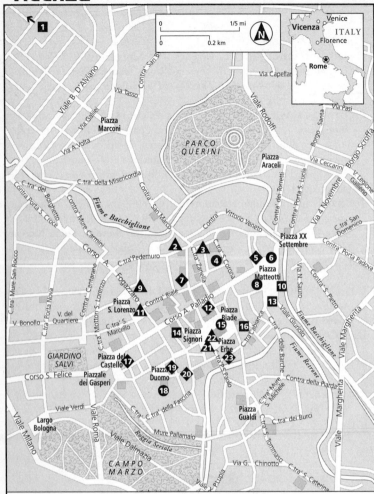

only here

If you don't know Palladio's work already, you will when you see it. Considered the most influential architect in the western world, he's responsible for every two-story colonial in your neighborhood that's held up with egregiously enormous columns. From 1540 to 1580, Vicenza was the famous architect's workshop, and the outskirts of town are speckled with villas he built for wealthy Venetian families. The most famous example is Monticello, upon which Thomas Jefferson based his home.

Palladio set the standard that architecture would follow for the next 400 years. His book, *I Quattro Libri Dell'Architettura* ("The Four Books of Architecture," 1570), become the most widely used architectural reference in the world.

list for the abundance of buildings designed by architectural genius Andrea di Pietro della Gondola—aka Palladio (1508-1580). Palladio is considered the most influential architect in the world—you'll recognize the columns and terraces typical of his work in everything from the White House to suburban homes with delusions of grandeur. Way prior to Palladio, Vicenza was the seat of a Lombard Dukedom, but in 899, it was sacked by other, more barbaric barbarians. In 1404, it joined the Venetian Republic, and remained a loyal outpost until Napoleon brought down the state in 1797.

Nowadays, Vicenza is a working city of 110,000 people, who go about their more-or-less normal lives amid the splendor of Palladian monuments. Travelers typically pass through town just long enough to check out a few examples of Palladio's work—you'll automatically get points just for sticking around. The friendly locals are almost all eager to point you toward your next meal, drink, or late-night party. Be warned, however, that there's a U.S. Army base nearby—Yanks, you might have some cultural ambassador work to do, since servicemen aren't always on their best behavior.

neighborhoods

This is a small town—everything you'll want to see is jammed into the **centro storico,** a small jumble of streets that revolve around **Corso Palladio,** the main street, which runs southeast from **Piazza Matteotti,** home to Palladio's last work, the **Teatro Olimpico.** Amidst the camera-toting crowds, here's where you'll find the tourist office and hostel [see *crashing,* below]. The train and bus stations are within the city walls, a 10-minute walk southeast down **Viale Roma.** As you walk from the station, the sprawling **Campo Marzo** will be on your right. Unfortunately, this park is more asphalt than greenery, and since the tour buses park right around here, it's always full of picnicking tourists. Where Viale Roma hits Corso Palladio is **Piazzale de Gasperi,** with the entrance into the **Gardino Salvi** straight ahead. Hang a right through the arch onto **Corso Palladio**—almost everything is on this street or within a few blocks north or south of it. To the north is the university district, with a bunch of cool bars and restaurants. Even farther north sits **Parco Quernini** with its rushing streams, green lawns, and paths for walking and bike riding. South of Corso Palladio lies the pride, the joy, and the lifeblood of town, the **Basilica Palladiana** [see *culture zoo,* below]. **Piazza Signori, Piazza Biade,** and **Piazza delle Erbe** surround this massive structure; any afternoon stroll requires a good amount of time in all three.

The neighborhoods just outside the city walls leave something to be desired. In fact, they can be downright sketchy. Though you don't need to use the efficient city buses to get to most spots in the main town, do use them if you're venturing out a bit.

hanging out

Corso Palladio is the big hot spot. This pedestrian zone is full of fancy shops and cafes, and during lunch and early evening it transforms into a massive cruising zone. Everyone chooses this path on their way to or from work, lingering to talk with neighbors or do a little window-shopping. As in every Italian town, folks kill time in the main piazza as well. The Basilica Palladiana breaks Vincenza's main piazza into three little piazzas, but the concept is the same. The cafes that line the squares are super-expensive—you'll find better ones on the street that spindle out from this area.

Teenagers hang out at the southwestern end of the Corso, near the Brek and the pretty **Gardino Salvi.** These gardens are a great place to sneak away from the crowds for a while—most of the people lounging around on the grass are students and other travelers who had the same idea.

bar, club, and live music scene

As you're walking into town, bumping into all the Palladio-pointing tour groups, you may start wondering where the hell you're going to have any fun around here. But behind its squeaky-clean, conservative exterior, Vicenza hides an impressive little nightlife. There's no shortage of stylie cocktail bars, which attract everyone from international jetsetters to gussied-up couples, but the real deal is the underground music scene.

How Vicenza ended up with so many cool live music venues is a mystery. It's totally possible to start your night with a little jazz, move on to some rockabilly, and wrap it all up with heavy metal head-banging. The only things missing are discos—you can only shake a leg at Osteria Grottino, and only a few nights a week. Pick up the monthly magazine, *Press Music,* your all-around guide to what's going on, at the tourist office [see *need to know,* below].

Vicenzo's beautiful people start (and often come back to end) their evenings at **Belle Epoque American Bar** *(Piazza Badia; Tel 0444/321-862; 7-3am Wed-Mon; No cover, V, MC)*, the tiny, stylish bar on the edge of Piazza Badia. This place evokes a Paris-in-the-twenties kind of indulgence. Sip long cocktails and sway to the sounds of early jazz, as bow-tied waiters sweep by and women dressed to the nines wave to their friends. The upstairs is a nice little breather from the thunderous conversation and the air kisses—good luck scoring one of the ten bistro tables, though. The drink of choice is the spritz, a Veneto classic cocktail made with campari, seltzer, and white wine, garnished with a slice of orange. If that doesn't float your boat, pick from the over 90 cocktails listed on the menu (10-15,000L), or let Frederico, the gregarious English-speaking owner, surprise you.

Just out the door and down the steps is another local fave, **Osteria Grottino** *(Piazza delle Erbe 2; No phone; 10am-3pm/5:30pm-3am Tue-Sun; No cover; No credit cards)*. The atmosphere isn't as high-class as what you'll find at Belle Epoque, but that's fine, because come 2am, after the American Bar's lights are out, this place is still rocking. Starting off as a restaurant and wine bar, somewhere along the line Grottino became Vicenza's rowdiest late-night discopub. The front room has barrel tables and a small bar serving up wines by the glass (3-8,000L); people order food in the big back room [see *eats,* below]. But come 10pm, the ambient music explodes into DJ-ed house, pop, and indie rock, and the same people you met at Belle Epoque really let loose, pouring out into the piazza, drinks in hand, for one of the hippest block parties you've ever seen. Currently this only happens on Tuesday and Thursday nights, but more frequent parties are planned in the future.

Don't be mistaken: **Sir William Wallace** *(Contrà Zanella 8; Tel 0444/325-095; 5pm-2am Wed-Mon; No cover; No credit cards)* isn't your typical Irish Pub wannabe. No, this place is *Scottish*—a little corner of the highlands just north of Corso Palladio, filled with college kids who chat the night away at the dark, wood tables. Not only does the owner really know how to pour a scotch (5-15,000L), he also carries some great brews (4-8,000L a pint), like the hand-drawn cask ale made by McEwan's. If you skipped dinner, go for one of their filling baked potatoes (4-7,000L), packed with anything from mozzarella to prosciutto.

Covered top to bottom with comic strips from the sixties and seventies, with a few classic 45 records, and vintage movie posters, **Art Café** *(Corso Fogazzaro 52; Tel 0444/321-047; Noon-2am Wed-Sun, music starts 10pm; 8,000L beer; No cover; No credit cards)*, is hipper than hip. Scenesters line up at the long bar to order beer (8,000L) and cocktails (6-9,000L) from the busy bartender, but all the action happens in the back room, where a small stage hosts rock, blues, and jazz bands every night. The flavor of the crowd changes with the style of the band—typically they're the kind of hipsters who haunt used record stores, but there are also rockabilly kids, skinheads, and even punks from time to time. If you stumble across this spot northeast of Piazza Dei Signori during the day, you'll notice the same crowd, solemn in the daylight, downing copious amounts of coffee.

Unless they have a penchant for Judas Priest, Primus, or the Dead Kennedys, locals avoid **La Cantinota** *(Stradella del Garofolino, behind the theater Corso; Tel 0444/323-722; 7pm-2am, music starts at 10pm Wed-Mon; 7,000L beer pints, 13,000L liters; No cover; No credit cards)* like the plague. They just don't know what to make of this big, dark, subterranean space, perhaps the only punk and hardcore club in the Veneto, where *everything's* painted black. But the cast of characters that come out to listen to the nightly selection of aspiring speed metal and punk bands are a warm and refreshing change from the same old scene. There are some mild-mannered beer-bellied long-hairs, a few American military types from the local US Army base, and a collection of Goth girls. Run by a sweet, thirtysomething punk couple (her name is Psicho), this place feels like a surreal clubhouse. Off to the side, there's a comfy little nook with a web-computer where you can surf for 10,000L an hour. All in all, this place looks a lot scarier than it actually is. This is the best fun in town. If you're walking north on Corso Fogazzaro from Corso Palladio, Stradella del Garofolino is the first street on your left.

With Cruzcampo on tap (6,500L), and a loud, Latin vibe streaming out of the speakers, Vicenza's only tapas bar, **Pub Spagnolo** *(Contrà San Biagio 92; Tel 0444/321-142; Noon-3pm/6pm-2am Tue-Sun; No cover; No credit cards)* doesn't look or act like an Italian haunt. Everyone comes here to order the small, savory tapas (5-10,000L per plate), drink wine (3-7,000L), and linger long into the evening. The crowd's a little older and more "young professional," but you get the sense that if they'd just loosen up a little, they'd be salsa dancing on the tables. To find it, walk north on Contrà Proti from Corso Palladio and take a left on Contrà San Biagio.

ARTS SCENE

There aren't any private galleries to speak of in Vicenza, but a few public places host contemporary art shows every once in a while. Performing arts are also a little light—but there are movies in English!

▶▶VISUAL ARTS

Palladio designed the grandiose **Palazzo Barbaran da Porto** *(Contrà Porti 11; Tel 0444/323-014; 10am-6pm Tue-Sun; Admission varies depending on exhibit; No credit cards)* in 1570. Today, this palace north of Corso Palladio is the main office of C.I.S.A (The *Centro Internazionale di Studi di Architettura di Palladio*), which invites international modern art talents to exhibit their work. It's also worth checking out just for the building: it's one of the best examples of the architect's residential works. Some Palladio nuts say it's very different from his other works because the front door isn't set in the exact center of the building and the facade is over-decorated. Other Palladio nuts say that the first Palladio nuts need to get out more.

Among other things, **Basilica Palladiana** [see *culture zoo*, below] is home to international and local modern art and architecture exhibits.

There are usually a few going on at once—check in with the tourist office [see *need to know,* below] for the latest offerings.

Connected to the University of Vicenza, **Biblioteca Civica Bertoliana** *(Contrà Riale 5; Tel 0444/323-832; 8am-7pm Mon-Fri, 8am-12:30pm Sat; Free)* is a library that holds occasional contemporary art exhibits and lectures. It's a popular place with students, worth a visit just catch the vibe of the local scene.

▶▶PERFORMING ARTS

Going to the movies has never been so exciting: **Odeon Cinema** *(Corso Palladio 176; Tel 0444/546-078; Box office 3:30-10pm daily; 10,000L admission; No credit cards)* on the south side of Corso Palladio, shows subtitled current films every Monday night. The old theater is at just the right stage of decay to make it look cool—the paint is chipping off the baroque columns, and the mezzanine's velvet chairs have lost all semblance of comfort. This theater also routinely hosts film festivals, so check at the tourist office [see *need to know,* below] for the current listings.

CULTURE ZOO

Culture in Vicenza is all about über-architect Palladio, the man who inspired public buildings all over Italy, and later the rest of the world. The Vicenza Card, available at the tourist office [see *need to know,* below] or any of the locations that accept it, offers various itineraries—from palaces, to museums, to villas. If you're staying in town, the Biglietto Unico (12,000L) is your best bet; if you'd like to venture out of town to see some of Palladio's country villas, reachable by bus, you should get the Vicenza e Ville (40,000L).

Your cultural tour will begin right around Palladio's earliest designs, Basilica di Palladiana. Just across Piazza delle Erbe from the Basilica sits the flourish of architectural swoops and swirls called the Loggia del Capitaniato. One of Palladio's later works, it consists of four gigantic half-columns, with smaller columns within. Piazza Biade, on the northern

FESTIVALS AND EVENTS

Each December, the Vicentini celebrate the **Radicchio Festival** *(Tel 0444/872-167)* with a week's worth of culinary events, from tastings in the piazza to a market and lecture in Campo Marzo. The bitter, maroon-colored green from the chicory family flavors everything from risotto to gnocchi to salads. Although there are many varieties (radicchio di Treviso is longer and darker, radicchio di Verona is more loose-leafed with firm white ribs), all are welcome here, on Vicenza's neutral ground.

side of the Basilica, contains two tall columns, the one on the right nodding to Vicenza's history as a member of the Venetian Republic with a winged lion. To the south, you'll pass the Torrione del Girone, also known as the tower of torment because it used to be a prison.

Basilica Palladiana *(Piazza dei Signori; Tel 0444/323-681; 9am-5pm Tue-Sun, winter; 10am-7pm Tue-Sun, summer; Free):* When Palladio was handed that task of renovating Vicenza's Gothic Palazzo della Ragione in 1548, no one expected him to succeed. The city had rejected renovation plans from some of the area's leading architects. When Palladio came along and mounted an extension of double loggias to encase the old facade, the critics went nuts. This was his first big success as an architect, and many think it is still his finest work. Step inside to see the gorgeous copper ceiling, and check out some of the contemporary art exhibits [see *arts scene,* above].

Teatro Olimpico *(Piazza Matteoti; Tel 0444/323-781; 9am-5pm Tue-Sun Jan 2-Jul 2; 10am-7pm daily Jul 4-Aug 31; 9am-5pm daily Sep 1-Jan 31; 12-14,000L adults, 6,000L students; No credit cards):* Palladio died before his final plans for this theater were completed, so the master never got to see his masterwork. Built between 1580 and 1585, it was mainly executed by his star pupil, Vincenzo Scamozzi. The Teatro was commissioned so that Vicenza would have a place to perform the classical tragedies, and to this day the tradition is carried on every summer, when traveling and local theater troupes perform here.

Museo Civico Pinacoteca *(Piazza Matteoti; Tel 0444/323-781; 9am-5pm Tue-Sun Jan 2-Jul 2; 10am-7pm daily Jul 4-Aug 31; 9am-5pm daily Sep 1-Jan 31; 12-14,000L adults; 6,000L students; No credit cards):* Housed across the square from the Teatro, in one of Palladio's masterpieces, the outstanding Palazzo Chiericati, this museum features an impressive collection of Italian paintings from the 18th and 19th centuries. The exterior is stunning enough, with a huge double portico and mannerist sculptures lining the top of the building.

Museo Naturalistico e Archeologico *(Contrà Santa Corona; Tel 0444/320-440; 9am-5pm Tue-Sun Jan 2-Jul 2; 10am-7pm daily Jul 4-Aug 31; 9am-5pm daily Sep 1-Jan 31; 12-14,000L adults; 6,000L students; No credit cards):* This museum is more interesting than your typical small-town archaeological collection, including history and artifacts from the surrounding Iberici hills. There's also an impressive collection of Roman statues from the city's ancient theater, as well as Lombard artifacts and other precious metalwork. It's housed in an old convent, north of Corso Palladio.

Cripto Portico Romano *(Piazza Duomo 6; Tel 0444/321-716; 10am-11:30am Wed, Sat; Free):* Evidence of the Roman era here in Vicenza rings out loud and clear under the Proti palace in Piazza Duomo. This chilly, stone burial place offers the usual cryptic sights—some Roman mosaics, arched walls, and remnants of columns. It's worth a quick visit for the atmosphere if you're already in the piazza and have an active imagination.

EATS

The Vicentini know how to eat. The food here combines Venice's rich seafood tradition with the vegetables, grains, and meats from the surrounding Veneto hills. It's not difficult to eat on a budget here, either. Check out some of the super-cheap self-service restaurants, but don't pass up an opportunity to eat at one of the osterias, which serve up traditional fare. Vicenza's most famous dish is the creamy *baccalà alla Vicentina,* dried cod that's been rehydrated in milk, heavily seasoned, and served over polenta.

▶▶CHEAP

It's the sort of cheery, chain spot you want to hate, but with prices like this, you can't help but adore **Brek** *(Corso Palladio 10/12; Tel 0444/327-829; 11:30am-3pm/6:30-9:30pm Tue-Sun; Entrees 9-13,000L; No credit cards).* Situated right on Vicenza's main drag, this self-service restaurant is one of the busiest spots in town. Students, families, and tourists line up, trays in hand, at the pasta counter, where fresh ingredients are tossed into their tagliatelle or penne. This isn't your typical cafeteria—the dining room is decorated with wood and brass detail, and the service island is a work of art in itself, from the meat station to the salad bar, where fresh baby greens and every vegetable imaginable are yours for the taking.

There's a method to the madness at **Righetti** *(Piazza Duomo 3; Tel 0444/543-135; Noon-3pm/7-9:30p daily; No credit cards),* Vicenza's most popular self-service restaurant, just south of Corso Palladio: You walk in and grab yourself a table or a booth, throw down your stuff, and then make a beeline for the front room, stopping to pick up a tray and some silverware. Business folks, students, retired couples—everyone's here, pushing and shoving and not waiting their turn like good Italians. It's helpful to know that the left-hand side is reserved for the *primis,* the middle for the *secondis,* and the right side is for vegetables, cheese plates, bread, and dessert. When the cook looks at you, you have to tell him

TO MARKET

The **Thursday morning market** in Piazza delle Erbe brings all of the food artisans and producers from throughout the province to sell their goods. You can also do your picnic shopping at the **Big Pam** *(Viale Roma; 8:30am-7pm daily; No credit cards)* supermarket, right on the corner of Piazzale de Gasperi.

which of the many things written on the blackboard you want—or point. Then go back to your seat, scarf it down, then go to the register and tell the sweet check-out man what you ate. This place works on the honor system, so if you had a long list of things, you may want to write down the Italian names—unless you want to hold up the line while saying "Turkey? You know, *tur-key!*" really loud.

▶▶DO-ABLE

If you ask anyone in town what their favorite Vicentini restaurant is, **Antica Casa Delle Malvasia** *(Contrà delle Morette 5; Tel 0444/543-704; Noon-3:30pm/6pm-midnight Tue-Sat, noon-3:30pm Sun; 12-18,000L entrees; 2000L cover; V, MC, AE)* is usually at the top of their list. Not only is the food fantastic, but this traditional osteria, found between Piazza Dei Signori and Corso Palladio, has such a following that the owners decided to stay open as a bar on Thursday and Friday nights, when they bring in local rock, pop, and jazz bands—call ahead and book yourself a table. Heavy wood tables are packed into the two quiet dining rooms like puzzle pieces. Dishes are classic, with fresh ingredients, and inventive twists. The bright pink gnocchi di rapa, tossed in a rich sauce of bacon and pumpkin, is life-altering, and the baccalà alla Vicentina is the best in town. Stop by in the afternoon for a bargain: a 10,000L cheese and wine tasting plate.

The best pies in town slide from the wood-fired ovens at **Pizzaria Zí Teresa** *(Contrà San Antonio 1; Tel 0444/321-411; 11:30am-3:30pm/ 6:30pm-midnight Thu-Tue; 7-12,000L pizzas; 18-23,000L entrees; V, MC, AE, DC).* This big, traditional Italian trattoria/pizzaria east of Piazza Duomo is nothing special to look at, but the fantastic pizzas are so large they come to the table dropping off the plate. Try the spinach and ricotta pie. The rest of the menu is a little pricey for what it offers, so stick to the 'zas.

Your first clue that something healthy's in the air at **Nirvana Caffe degli Artisti** *(Piazza Matteotti 8; Tel 0444/543-11-11; 7:30-midnight daily; 3-4,500 teas, 2,500L-6,000L sandwiches, 7-10,000L main dishes; www.nirvanacaffe.3000.it; No credit cards)* is that you can't smoke—a first for Italy. The second is all the Buddhas mixed in with the typical Italian decor. Third is the inventive and healthy food issuing from the kitchen. Lunch brings sandwiches like the Panda (tofu with mozzarella, tomato, soy mayo and oregano), or the Bear (asiago, mustard, and wheat bread). Stick with the aptly named Nirvana salad, which is loaded with vegan ingredients. In the evenings, everyone orders their three-course all-vegetarian dinner (15,000L), and sips from the enormous selection of teas and tisanes. More or less once a week, the owners invite a different world music band to play for the crowd, with a corresponding ethnic menu—call ahead for the current schedule.

People come to **Osteria Grottino** [see *bar, club, and live music scene,* above] looking for a little wine, conversation, and eventually, dancing on tables. The great, local dishes at super-cheap prices are an added bonus. The menu isn't extensive—in fact, there isn't even a menu anywhere to be found, but dishes typically run between 7 and 10,000L. Try a little hand-sliced prosciutto from the bar, a plate of baccalà alla Vincentina, or some asiago cheese.

▶▶**SPLURGE**

The newest osteria on the scene, the hip, slightly formal **Antica Osteria al Bersagliere** *(Contrà Ponte San Paola 11; Tel 0444/540-400; 10am-4:30pm/6-11pm Mon-Sat; V, MC, AE),* is already being embraced by the locals. Run by a mother and son team, this tiny, two-tiered space just south of Piazza Erbe turns out rich Vicentina cuisine with favorites like pumpkin gnocchi sprinkled with smoked ricotta (13,000L), radicchio risotto (14,000L), and baccalà alla Vicentina (18,000L). Ask for a table upstairs in the small loft space looking over the long bar and wooden tables below. The wine list features many local bottles, some of them pricey—ask for the *vino della casa* if you don't want to over-splurge.

crashing

Fortunately, most of Vicenza's accomodation options are right in the center of town. You should book reservations as far in advance as possible to beat out the crowds of Palladio groupies.

▶▶**CHEAP**

If you're going to stay at a hostel, **Ostello per la Gioventu "Olimpico"** *(Viale Giuriolo 7/9; Tel 0444/540-222, Fax 0444/547-762; Bus 1, 2, 4, 5, 7 to Ostello; Reception open 7-9:30am/3:30-11:30pm; 25,000L dorm, 27,000L family room; No private baths; No credit cards),* in a Palladio look-alike around the corner from Teatro Olimpico, is a pretty good one. It's run by a bunch of cool English-speaking kids who can clue you in to what's happening around town. Cool as they may be, don't expect them to budge on the 11:30pm curfew. The inside of the building is institutional and pretty drab, but you get added amenities like Internet access (1,500L/hour) and bike rentals (8,000L/day).

▶▶**DO-ABLE**

It doesn't get more central than **Palladio** *(Via Oratorio dei Servi 25; Tel/Fax 0444/547-328; 60-70,000L single without bath, 100-110,000L single with bath; 100,000L double without bath; 110-120,000L double with bath; No credit cards),* the old-fashioned hotel right around the corner from Piazza Matteoti. Each of the 24 rooms is basic and sort of comfortable, with bad art on the wall, mismatched comforters and furniture, and TVs hanging hospital-style from the ceiling. But everything's very clean, the owners are sweet and helpful, and the bar downstairs is a cozy place to chill for a while. Ask for one of the rooms with a terrace.

It's a little more expensive than the others, but once you see **Due Mori** *(Contrà Do Rodi 26; Tel 0444/321-886, Fax 0444/326-127; 65-70,000L single with bath; 60-95,000L double without bath; 80-135,000L double with bath; V, MC, AE),* you'll understand why. Situated just around the corner from Piazza Signori, this is by far the most comfortable, lovely, and dare we say it, romantic hotel in town. You enter into a cold stone lobby with modern red velvet chairs and architectural draft prints on the wall, but walk upstairs and you'll enter a dream world. The narrow, winding stairway leads to plenty of little nooks where the owners have lovingly placed antique furniture and modern art, breakfast is served in a big ballroom. Each of the 26 rooms has its own unique character. Some have wooden beams or irregular shapes, others have terraces, but all of them have the nicest linens, antique furniture, and the most comfortable beds in town. Need we say it? Call ahead.

Hotel Vicenza *(Stradella Dei Nodari 5/7; Tel 0444/321-512; 80-10,000L single, 110-120,000L double; Private baths available; V, MC)* looks like the kind of place where your grandparents stayed on their honeymoon, and seems like it hasn't been renovated since. Located in the dead center of town, this place charges the same prices as Due Mori, but offers a fraction of the ambiance and service—but that's okay, it's still a good bargain. Although the mattresses have seen better days, the rooms are spacious, many have oversized bathtubs, and everything is kept super-clean. The elderly couple that runs this place hang out in the cozy TV room all day, and are happy to lend you some travel advice.

▶▶SPLURGE

If you were coming to Vicenza on business, you'd stay at the recently renovated **Hotel Giardini** *(Via Giuriolo 10; Tel/Fax 0444/326-458; 50-200,000L single, 80-250,000L double; Private baths; V, MC)*. Located just across from Teatro Olimpico, this hotel is modern and stylish, with minimalist furniture, modern art poster prints, and big tile baths in every room. But despite all the extra amenities (frigobar, satellite TV, air conditioning), all the professionalism and anonymity leave you a bit cold. But doesn't that AC feel good?

need To know

Currency Exchange There's an **ATM** at the train station, and plenty more in the town center.

Tourist Information The **main tourist office** *(Piazza Matteoti 12; Tel 0444/320-854, Fax 0444/027-072; 9am-1pm/2:30-6pm Mon-Sat, 9am-1pm Sun; www.ascom.vi.it/aptvicenza)* is tiny, but extremely helpful, with reams of printed information. They can't book rooms for you, but they'll do just about everything else, offering advice and walking directions, and circling every point of interest on your map, even if it's already labeled. The folks at the smaller office *(Piazza Duomo; Tel 0444/544-122; 8:30am-1pm/2:30-6pm Mon-Fri)* are just as eager.

Public Transportation The super-efficient bus system, **AIM** *(Via Fusinieri 85; Tel 0444/394-909)*, is great, though you'll really only need it to get from the train station to the town center, and vice versa. You can buy tickets for local and suburban destinations for 1,700L at the kiosk in front of the train station, 6:30am-11:10pm. If the bus doesn't suit your needs, try **RadioTaxi** *(Tel 0444/920-600)*, which is available 24/7.

Health and Emergency Emergency: *116;* Ambulance: *118;* Fire: *115.* The **police** *(Tel 0444/250-811)* are at Via Muggia 3. The local hospital, **Ospedale Civile** *(Via Ferdinando Rodolfi 37; Tel 444/993-111)* is north of the center, above the big Parco Querni.

Pharmacies Farmacia Doria *(Piazza Dei Signori 49; Tel 444/321-241; 8:45am-12:30pm/4-7:30pm; No credit cards)* is right in the center of town. Look for **flashing green crosses** to find others. All pharmacies will have the 24-hour rotating schedule posted in the window in case of emergencies.

Trains The **Ferrovia Dello Stato train station** *(Viale Venezia and Viale Roma; Tel 0444/147888088 or 0444/326-707)* is just southeast of the city center, about a five-minute walk. Trains run regularly to Venice (7,000L), Treviso (6,200L), Padua (4,500L), Verona (9,800L), and Milano (17-27,000L).

Bus Lines Out of the City The **FTV Ferrovie e Tramvie** *(Viale Milano 138; Tel 0444/223-115)* is based just to the left of the train station. Buses come from and go to all the surrounding towns.

Bike Rental You can rent bikes from the **Deposito Bagaglio** office at the train station *(Tel 0444/392-528)* for 1,500L an hour or 15,000L a day. You have to leave a passport or other valuable document as a deposit. Credit cards might work, but you can't pay with them. The hostel [see *crashing,* above] also has a bunch of bikes that they lend out to only their guests.

Laundry Across the bridge to the east of Piazza Matteoti, **Euro Lavanderia Fai da Te** *(XX Settembre 27; 7:30am-10:30pm daily; 5,000L wash, 5,000L dry; No credit cards)* has dozens of machines for your wash 'n' dry pleasure.

Postal The **central post office** *(Contrà Garibaldi 1; Tel 0444/332-077; 8:10am-6pm Mon-Sat; No credit cards)* is between Piazza Dei Signori and Piazza Duomo.

Internet The only place around to get online seems to be **La Cantinotta** [see *bar, club, and live music scene,* above]. You can get online info about Vincenza at ***www.emmeti.it/Welcome/Veneto/Vicenza/index.uk.html.***

TRENTINO-
ALTO ADIGE

Three things you should know before arriving in Trentino-Alto Adige: 1) The natural beauty will knock your socks off, 2) you'll definitely get your adrenaline pumping on the slopes, and 3) technically, you're not in Italy anymore.

At the tippy-top of the country, Trentino-Alto Adige flanks the Eastern Alps, known as the Dolomites, where the mountain peaks are incredible, the rivers are all rushing, and rolling valleys are so lush (in the summer, that is) you'll think the color green was invented here. It's just two hours from Milan and Venice, but most American tourists skip it entirely—bad for them, good for you.

These mountains aren't just eye candy. Depending on the season, you could be skiing. Or snowboarding. Or hiking. Or engaging in some other sport that'll get your heart pumping. And you won't stress over what to wear on the slopes; except for bordering-on-pretentious **Cortina,** the ski scene here is pretty easygoing. And speaking of seasons, the snow falls from roughly November to April, and July-September are considered "summer."

So what's the deal on not being in Italy? Well, Trentino-Alto Adige is actually an autonomous state, which basically means it can make its own laws and govern itself any way it wants. They get some financial aid from Rome, but really, that's about the extent of their relationship with the Italian government. The area is composed of two distinct regions—the northern, heavily Austrian **Alto Adige** and the southern, predominantly Italian **Trentino**—which were fused together only after WWII, and granted autonomy in 1948. The two regions couldn't be more different (who ever heard of an Austrian train that was late or an Italian one that was on time?) but they share an understated tolerance born of centuries of cultural and political flip-flops. In the Middle Ages, Goths, Franks, Lombards, and Bavarians struggled to keep power here, but it was the Holy Roman Empire that won out, allowing Roman Catholic Bishops friendly to the emperors to reign. Both Trentino and Alto Adige were outposts of the Austrian Hapsburgs in the latter part of the 18th century, before the World Wars brought them into dispute yet again. Today, though, people get along great and are relieved to have it all settled. Ask anyone—autonomy feels damn good. Locals speak both German and Italian fluently, and because of the diversity of language you'll meet more local English speakers here than anywhere else in Italy. One other very interesting feature of autonomy: In general, any spot in the region calling

TRENTINO-ALTO ADIGE

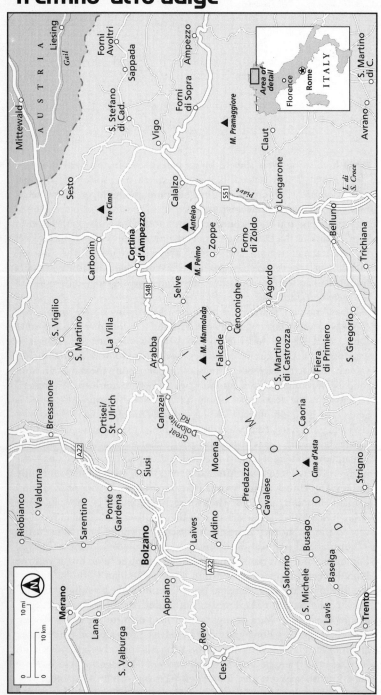

itself a "night club" instead of a "club" is a pay-to-play place—specifically, it's the kind of place where men go looking to pay for dates. Guess what's legal here and not in the rest of Italy?

The northern part, Alto Adige, called *Südtirol* in German, looks like something out of a fairy tale, à la Hansel and Gretel. White limestone and rose-colored granite peaks poke through the clouds, which hover over sprawling meadows dotted with small villages, castles, and farmhouses. (Or was that Snow White and the Seven Dwarfs?) Depending on the time of day, the dramatic mountain peaks can look blue-gray, deep amber, or golden. **Bolzano** (*Bozen* in German) is its cultural capital, and a hopping university town. **Merano,** the small town just north of Bolzano along the Adige river, came to affluence in the mid-19th century as a spa resort. You can still sit in the thermal spas and get a deep-tissue massage, but the real reason to come here is to hike around the town's perimeter. The weather is almost always sunny, the air is fresh and crisp, and though it's at a high altitude, the climate is sheltered from extreme cold. The people here have stuck steadfastly to their Germanic culture and language—they're cheerful, hardworking, agrarian types who love life, beer, and a good pair of *lederhosen.* You should fit in just fine.

Trentino, on the other hand, has always been more Italian. You can see it in the elaborate porticos and frescoed facades of its elegant palazzos—an influence of the nearby Venetian Republic. The Trentini cling to their Italian characteristics—fashion is a serious preoccupation, as is chatting enthusiastically (yes, they really do talk with their hands), eating passionately, and living indulgently. **Trento,** the region's capital, has for centuries fostered an intellectual and artistic spirit that continues to thrive today, with its university and spectacular Modern art museum. The city sits in the shadow of **Mount Boldone,** which transforms from hiker's delight in the summer to shredder's paradise in the winter.

Cortina d'Ampezzo and the **Ampezzo Valley** are technically part of the Veneto region, but we dropped 'em in here because they're mountain towns at heart, and are really more tied to their Trentino-Alto Adige neighbors than to the rest of the Veneto. This Alpine playground comes with all the requisite entertainment: mulled wine and hot chocolate in cozy mountain lodges, and rowdy bars filled with *simpatico* ski bums. Though Cortina is known to cater to upper-crusties, the slopes can be done on a budget, and over the past few years this resort has taken on a slightly more youthful vibe.

Food here is different from what you've been sampling throughout Italy. Pork rules—smoked, roasted, grilled, aged, and made into sausages of all kinds. German classics like goulash and strudel abound, but there are also a fair share of culinary curiosities worth exploring, including *canederli* (*knodel* in German), hearty bread and flour dumplings often seasoned with herbs and smoked, and cured ham known as "speck." This area is also famous for its fruit, nuts, and cheeses. You'll see *zuppa di castagne* (chestnut soup) on many menus, and *mele* (apples) integrated into many dishes. Trentino is known for wild mushrooms, and *asiago* cheese. The wines of Trentino-Alto Adige are world-renowned: Gewürztraminers,

Rieslings, and Sylvaners are the star whites, while Pinot Nero, Cabernet, Merlot, and the hearty Terolego Rotaliano are the great reds.

GETTING AROUND THE REGION

The major towns of Trentino-Alto Adige are very close together, and can be easily reached by bus or train, though trains are faster, easier, and more direct. To get from **Trento** to **Merano** by train, you must change in **Bolzano** to the slow train, which is not part of the Italian Ferrovia del Stato—don't even try to use your Eurail pass. But don't worry—it's very inexpensive, and more efficient than most Italian transport. Bolzano is on the Verona-Bolzano-Innsbruck line, as is Trento, so it's just as easy to come from east or west. **Cortina** and the **Ampezzo Valley** can be reached via bus from Bolzano via a transfer in Dobbiaco; if you're coming from the south, you can train it from Venice to Calalzo, where you transfer to bus service.

Cortina and the Valley are worth at least a couple of days of your time, for skiing, hiking, and other sports. Many people do Merano as a day trip, since it's such an easy jaunt from Bolzano, but if you're interested in hiking or skiing around the dramatic Alto Adige landscape, Merano is actually a better base. Of course, Bolzano's nightlife puts all others to shame, so if you've come to party, stay there. Trento is often the city that's skipped in the region, but it's also the most cosmopolitan; any Renaissance art and architecture lover would be sorry to miss it. Reserve at least an afternoon for wandering its winding streets.

TRAVEL TIMES

All times by train unless otherwise marked: * By bus	Merano	Trento	Cortina
Bolzano	1:00	1:00	4:00*
Merano	-	:45	5:00* via Bolzano
Trento	:45	-	5:00* via Bolzano

***Monte Bondone: day trip from Trento, cable car every 30min.
***Ampezzo Valley: in and around Cortina

TRENTO

While most American tourists on the train coming from Bolzano blink and miss Trento, Italians come here to explore beautiful **Monte Bondone,** just 15km east of town [see below]. Endorphin-junkies hike the mountainside by day and wander the streets at night; touring snowboarders, hikers, skiers, and other outdoor buffs keep the bars from getting boring.

Trento's a lot more fun than you might think a town whose heyday came during a religious convention (the Council of Trent) more than 500 years ago would be. This medieval city has aged remarkably well. Original frescoed Renaissance buildings still stand, but there's a solid contemporary arts scene—many of the old palazzos are now makeshift galleries—and the college population helps keep things fresh. The Universita degli Studi di Trento is in full force all year long, attracting lots of international students, many from the States, so the ancient piazzas are filled with scenester kids in baggy pants every night.

Trento is the capital city of Trentino, a region that has been treated like a political checkerboard over its long history. It all started when the Romans came through on their northern treks, and named the town Tridentum. Later, power shifted to the Goths and Lombards, and, in 1027, to the Bishops of Trento, who were supported by the Holy Roman Empire. The most famous bishop came along during the Renaissance: While Florence had its Medicis, and Ferrara its Estes, Trento found an art patron in Prince Bishop Bernardo Cles, a humanist who ruled between 1514 and 1539. Deciding it was high time Trento caught up with the Joneses, he initiated an urban renewal program that started with a little

TRENTO BARS CLUBS AND CULTURE ZOO

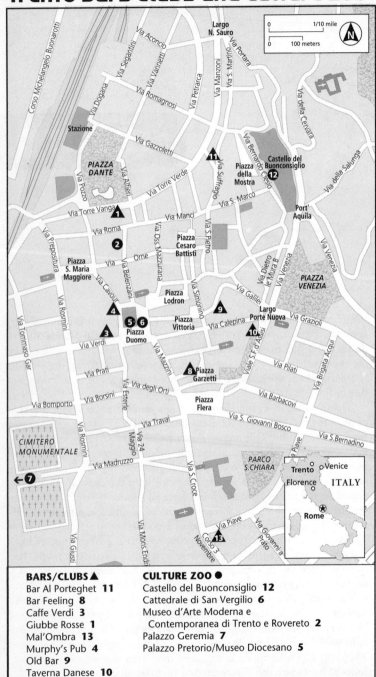

BARS/CLUBS ▲

Bar Al Porteghet **11**

Bar Feeling **8**

Caffe Verdi **3**

Giubbe Rosse **1**

Mal'Ombra **13**

Murphy's Pub **4**

Old Bar **9**

Taverna Danese **10**

CULTURE ZOO ●

Castello del Buonconsiglio **12**

Cattedrale di San Vergilio **6**

Museo d'Arte Moderna e
  Contemporanea di Trento e Rovereto **2**

Palazzo Geremia **7**

Palazzo Pretorio/Museo Diocesano **5**

paint and ended with a city full of frescoed murals and grand palazzos. Not long after, Trento became the home base of the European Counter-Reformation with the establishment of the Council of Trent. During the Napoleonic Wars, the French took over and gave the region to Austria in 1814—which the Italian townsfolk didn't much like. After WWI, Trento became part of Italy, but remained in dispute until 1948 when it was paired up with Alto Adige and named an independent state.

Despite Trento's autonomous standing, a visit here still feels like a visit to Italy: The people are much more Italian than their Austrian-leaning neighbors to the north. Old men walk arm and arm in the early evening, young women tote designer bags, everyone's constantly chatting on their cell phones, and people eat *gnocchi,* not *spatzle.* Spend a day or two in Trento, surrounded by the beauty of the past and the energy of today. You won't be disappointed.

neighborhoods

Trento is easy to figure out. It's not a very big town—just a 10-minute walk from one side to the other—and the places you'll want to see are all within a few blocks of one another. A word of warning, though: The map given out by the tourist office has north on the left instead of the top, which can cause all kinds of confusion if you're not aware.

Okay, here are your major landmarks: **Monte Bondone** hovers over the town, just west of the **Adige River,** which is crossed by **Ponte San Lorenzo.** The train station sits between the river and the city center. **Castello Del Buonconsiglio** [see *culture zoo,* below], once home to the bishop princes, looms over the eastern edge of town.

From the train station, you're a five-minute walk to the city center; just take a right turn down **Via Pozzo** as you exit the station. The big, green **Piazza Dante,** a comfortable, grassy park complete with duck pond and lots of benches, will be on your left. Via Pozzo changes names a few times as it runs south into town, eventually becoming **Via Cavour** and leading right into the sprawling **Piazza del Duomo,** at the heart of the city. **Cattedrale di San Vergilio** [see *culture zoo,* below] dominates this space. The streets spindling out from this piazza are some of the main strolling and shopping venues—**Via Belenzani,** running north from the Piazza, is the site of several municipal buildings, including the tourist office. **Via Mazzurana,** heading northeast out of the piazza, is restaurant-land.

Via Verdi heads west from the piazza down to **Via Roberto da Sanseverino,** which runs along the river. Around the back of the Duomo is **Via Mazzini,** which heads southeast, crossing the beautiful remains of an old Roman wall, and into **Piazza Fiera,** a popular hangout and strolling square in the early evenings. Continuing down the same street, which changes its name to **Via Santa Croce,** you'll pass the beautiful **Santa Chiara** church, with its gorgeous gardens [see *culture zoo,* below]. The area southeast of here is student central, where you'll find everything from high-rise student housing to the Laundromat.

wired

Callme *(Via Belenzani 58; Tel 0461/983-302; 9am-noon/2-10:15pm daily; 10,000L per hour; V, MC),* right down the block from Palazzo Geremia, is actually one of those foreign call centers, where people go just to make international calls. The individual Internet access cubbyholes get claustrophobic, but hey, they do the trick.

Biblioteca Comunale *(Via Madruzzo 26; Tel 0461/884-572; 10am-6:30pm Mon-Sat),* the general library just north of the Duomo, is your only shot at free browsing. The main lobby has six computers, loaned out by the hour. Though they're typically booked weeks in advance, if someone doesn't show up, which happens often, you're welcome to hop on. The library also has a great reading room, with English-language magazines such as *Time* and *Vogue.*

You can find Trento on the web at ***www.apt.trento.it/inglese/rent.htm.***

The northeastern side of town, over by the castle, is another pretty spot for strolling. **Via Suffragio,** its main drag, is packed with students making their nightly bar-crawl—to find it, head up **Via Mazzurana** from Piazza del Duomo for a few blocks till you hit **Via Manci.** Take a right here (it turns into **Via San Marco** as you head east); Via Suffragio will be three blocks up on your left.

hanging out

Trento's high student-to-normal-person ratio makes it a great hang-scene, whether it's for reading a book over cappuccino, chatting with friends, or grabbing a quick glass of wine before heading back to class. The piazzas are hopping morning, noon, and night—Piazza Fiera, near Santa Chiara, always draws a good crowd. Piazza del Duomo is also usually fairly packed (in a good way) with people meeting friends, dropping in on a bar or two, or just hanging out around the Baroque Fountain of Neptune.

bar, club, and live music scene

For a college scene, Trento's nightlife isn't as diverse as it probably should be. There's no live music venue, no disco, no full-fledged club in the town center. But there are tons and tons of bars, and they cater to just about any personality you could invent.

Day and night, **Old Bar** *(Via Roggia Grande; Tel 0461/231-145; 7:30pm-2:30am Mon-Sat; No cover; No credit cards),* east of Piazza del Duomo, is packed with college kids sipping wine, shooting the breeze, and catching up on their reading—in that order. This tiny, wood-paneled room is a casual place to chill for an hour or two, meet some locals, and find out what's going on about town. The loud background music is upbeat American pop and rock—whatever the flirty bartenders feel like hearing. These women pour generous glasses of wine (2,200-4,000L) and pints of beer (6,000L), and make kick-ass sandwiches (4,000-8,000L) on the best bread ever. Scotch is the thing here (4,000-8,000L)—the 27 bottles mounted on the wall make the intellectual, chain-smoking crowd feel more grown-up.

If your Irish grandpa opened a bar in Italy, it would look like **Murphy's Pub** *(Piazza del Duomo 31; Tel 0461/235-353; 9am-1am daily; Till 2am in summer; No cover; No credit cards),* which sits on the western side of Piazza del Duomo. It's decorated with what looks like the contents of someone's garage, with old musical instruments, tools, and fishing equipment sprawled about, and a few bookshelves full of vintage Irish titles. The front room's got a long wooden bar, cushy upholstered banquettes, and some wooden tables. Irish folk music plays on the stereo, along with some U2 and Cranberries, of course. Order a stiff drink (7,000-8,000L) or fine Irish ale (8,000L) and stick around for a while—this place gets crowded when the locals stop in after work for a pint. There's pretty good grub as well—Irish breakfasts, all named for Gaelic celebs (like Molly Bloom of *Ulysses* fame, or Van Morrison of "Brown-eyed Girl" fame) come with a pint of beer, and more sausage than you would usually eat in a week. Beer and sausage—now *that's* breakfast!

Caffe Verdi *(Via Verdi 31/33; Tel 0461/232-562; 7:30am-1am Mon-Fri, 7:30am-2am Sat; No cover; No credit cards)* sits a block east of the Piazza del Duomo on Via Verdi. It's a big, open, brightly lit space with kitschy oil paintings of landscapes and sad clowns, and modern chrome chairs where Trento's cool kids sit and drink cheep beer by the pint (3,000-6,000L) and try to talk over the trance-y music. Two big TVs become the center of attention on game nights—good luck getting a seat.

Mal'Ombra *(Corso Novembre 43; Tel 0461/390-696; 9am-1am Mon-Sat; No cover; V, MC, DC)* is the kind of cozy, local place where old men mix with hipsters over a glass of good wine and some smooth jazz. The narrow wooden bar up front is crowded with bottles of wine and grappa, and a small deli-case serving up bruschetta and other snacks (2,000-4,000L); most folks grab their food and drink and head to the back of the room where they can have a seat and maybe even play checkers. With more than 30 wines by the glass (3,000-6,000L), this is a great place to familiarize yourself with local offerings. Owner Andrea Massarelli gladly offers his expertise when you give him that "Uh, I don't know...a red, I guess" look. The feel is civilized and down-to-earth. It's about a five-minute walk south of Piazza del Duomo, just past Parco Santa Chiara.

If you're wondering where Trento's pierced and tattooed populace hangs out, look no further: Rockabilly kids, skins, punks, and Goths share space at **Bar Al Porteghet** *(Under Portico Dorigoni at Sottoportico di Via Suffragio; No phone; 2pm-2am Wed-Mon; No cover; No credit cards),* scuffing the black-and-white tile with their combat boots and slouching into the red leather booths of this fifties-diner-gone-bad. It's actually pretty welcoming to all types; you're just as likely to hear Lou Reed as you are an Italian Oi band. The tiny bar snakes up into a crowded mezzanine covered with old license plates from the States. Beers are 5,000L a pint, 2,000L during happy hour *(10:30-11:30pm Thu and Fri)*. At those prices, there's no excuse for drinking anywhere else.

Only a small chalkboard outside hints at the carousing that goes on downstairs at **Giubbe Rosse** *(Galleria Torre Vanga 14, enter off Via Roma after 8pm; Tel 0461/234-715; 7:30pm-1am Mon-Sat; 10,000L cover when there's live music, includes first drink, entrees 20,000-32,000L; V, MC, AE, DC)*. Housed in what looks like a shopping mall, off Via Torre Vanga, across from Piazza Dante, this hip Cuban bar serves up refreshing mojitos, Mexican beer (4,000-7000L), and more beat than your boogie can handle. Tiny, candlelit wooden tables crowd the bar in the front room, but there's more sitting space in the two back rooms, as well as a small stage where international live music-acts play on Thursday, Friday, and Saturday nights. Band or no, music gets going at 10:30pm, and the entire space transforms into a heated dance party. Caribbean one night, Brazilian the next—the only constant is that it's let-loose and wild. The owner is a diehard Cuban patriot, so Cuban radio-shows air here once a week, and TV broadcasts of *Buena Vista Social Club* play ad infinitum. The food [see *eats,* below] is a nice break from all that pasta.

The award for Cheesiest Bar Name in Trento goes to **Bar Feeling** *(Via Prima Androna 20; Tel 0461/230-868; 8pm-3am Mon-Sat; No cover; V, MC),* just west off Piazza Garzetti. Sure, it looks like a '70s ad for Riu-nite on Ice—all heavily upholstered and candlelit, with brass detailing, and back-lighted cognac glasses on display. But because the place *thinks* it's classy, it actually works. After a few Manhattans in tall, chilled glasses (9,000L), you too will be swaying to easy-listenin' hits by Barry Manilow and friends, and dipping into martini glasses filled with corn nuts. Trentino's suave twenty- to thirtysomethings all seem to be in on the ironic joke, making this a pretty cool destination. You're bound to meet a sexy Sagittarius or an airy Aries; *"Che cos'e il tuo segno?"* ("What's your sign?") is the line of choice.

Ignore the sports-bar look of **Taverna Danese** *(Via San Franceso 8; Tel 0461/238-069; 8am-1am Mon-Sat; No cover; No credit cards)*. Sure, it's packed with rowdy college kids, the beer selection is mostly *chiara* (lighter beer, 7,000L pint), there are TVs playing sports everywhere, and the staff wears golf shirts with the company logo. But move straight through the bar and its commercial music blasting at an unbearable decibel level, and head down the stairs, and you'll find the rec room of your dreams. Pool tables, air hockey, and every video game, bar game, and board game you can imagine. You think you got game?

arts scene

Trento has a happening art scene, thanks to a little help from the city gov-ernment. A lot of old palazzos are now gallery spaces, showing off the town's young artists. Pick up a copy of the free monthly art journal, *Le Muse,* at the **tourist office** [see *need to know,* below] to find out what's going on.

▶▶**VISUAL ARTS**

Studio d'Arte Raffaelli *(Via Travei 22; Tel 0461/989-595; 11am-12:30pm/5-7:30pm Tue-Sat; Free admission; V, MC),* off Via Santa Croce near Santa Chiara, is one of the most respected galleries in town. The owner seeks out cutting-edge Italian talent, showcasing work in this small, white-box space. Look for postcards around town touting the next opening party.

Housed in an old palazzo a few streets west of the Castello, **Galleria Civica di Arte Contemporaneo** *(Via del Suffragio 35/Piazza della Mostra 19; Tel 0461/985-511; 10am-6pm Tue-Sun; Free admission; V, MC)* displays traveling shows as well as local Modern art. Events range from lectures to films to opening parties; get a list at the **tourist office** [see *need to know,* below].

▶▶**PERFORMING ARTS**

With a diverse program of performances, the beautiful opera house **Teatro Sociale** *(Via Oss Mazzurana; Tel 0461/986-488; Box office 9am-6pm Mon-Sat, tickets also available by phone and at the door; 30,000-70,000L; V, MC, AE),* just north of Piazza del Duomo, is a destination in its own right. Performances are in Italian, but modern and traditional dance, opera, and music comes from all over the world.

Teatro Auditorium *(Via Santa Croce 67; Tel 0461/239-917; Box office hours and ticket prices vary with each performance, tickets available by phone; V, MC)* hosts musical performances of all kinds, all year long. The shows are in Italian, but with modern dance and music, who cares? Tickets are usually less expensive than at Teatro Sociale, and it's a great place to catch a show before heading out for a drink. You'll find it in the Parco Santa Croce complex.

CULTURE ZOO

History, art, and culture are all combined in Trento's wonderful old buildings. Piazza del Duomo should be your starting point in Trento's cultural history lesson. This sprawling piazza is beautifully preserved, with the imposing cathedral straight ahead, and the grand medieval clock tower to the left. The Fountain of Neptune, which dates back to the mid-18th century, provides a perfect vantage for admiring the frescoed Cazuffi houses that run along the northern edge.

Cattedrale di San Vergilio *(Piazza del Duomo; No phone; 6:30am-noon/2:30-7:30pm daily; Free admission):* Looming large over Piazza del Duomo is this Romanesque church, named after the region's first bishop, who converted much of Alto Adige and Trentino to Christianity in the 4th and 5th centuries. The facade is a stunning mix of Romanesque and Gothic detail. Inside, there's a large collection of religious art and sculpture, as well as some fading 13th- to 15th-century frescoes still hanging on for dear life.

COUNCIL OF WHA?

C'mon, dig deep into the recesses of your brain, where the remnants of European History 101 are lodged. Martin Luther? The Reformation? Is *any* of this ringing a bell? Okay, refresher time: Trento played a significant role in the religious politics of the last, oh, 500 years or so. After Martin Luther posted his "95 Theses" on the door of his church, calling for reform *now*, all the big Catholic heavyweights, including the Pope, were shaking in their boots, too afraid to do anything. When Pope Paul III came to power a few years later, he called for the Council of Trent to strengthen the church by outlining Catholic dogma and at the same time refuting Luther's points. Discussions began on December 13, 1545, and continued until 1564. The Council actually succeeded in unifying Catholics across Europe, but it never healed the wounds that led to the Reformation, or the creation of the Protestant denominations, which are obviously here to stay.

Palazzo Pretorio/Museo Diocesano *(Piazza del Duomo; Tel 0461/234-419; 9:30am-12:30pm/2:30-6pm daily; 9,000L admission, 5,000L students; No credit cards):* Once the home of Trento's bishops, today this elegant palace, just to the left of the cathedral, houses Trento's most interesting artifacts. The seven Flemish tapestries representing the Passion of Christ are also some of the most famous. Woven in Brussels between 1511 and 1520 by Pieter van Aelst, they decorated the walls of the rooms where the Council of Trent was held. Other Council items, as well as a large collection of religious art, are also on display.

Castello Del Buonconsiglio *(Via Bernardo Clesio 5; Tel 0461/233-770; Bus 2, 6, or 7 to the castle; 9am-noon/2-5:30pm Tue-Sun, Apr 1-Sep 30; 9am-noon/2-5pm Tue-Sun, Oct 1-Mar 31; 9,000L Adults, 6,000L students and under 18; No credit cards):* With its turreted tower and stone ramparts, this former home of the Bishops of Trento looks like your archetypal medieval castle. And it is. The Venetian influence is evident in its beautiful Gothic arches, which date back to 1475. The *Torre dell'Aquila* (eagle tower) includes an impressive collection of Gothic frescoes depicting the cycle of the months. Bernardo Cles's Renaissance addition, Palazzo Magno, is next door. Today both buildings have been restored and house two museums: The Provincial Art museum includes everything from Medieval mosaics to fresco fragments, while the Historical Museum contains documents from Trento's past. They loom over the town from atop the hill to the east of the center.

Museo d'Arte Moderna e Contemporanea di Trento e Rovereto *(Via R. da Sanseverino 45; Tel 0461/234-860; 10am-6pm Tue-Sat; www.mart.trento.it; No credit cards):* Also known as MART, this is the region's most important Modern art museum. Gorgeous Palazzo del Albere houses more than 3,000 works from the 19th and 20th centuries, with an impressive collection of paintings, drawings, and sculptures from the early Primitive and Italian Futurist movements. Rarely seen outside of Italy, works by Bonazza, Boldoni, and Garbari arc just a few of the obscure surprises here. Traveling exhibits from Modern art museums around the world often stop in.

Palazzo Geremia *(Via Belenzani):* You start to take all the frescoed Renaissance buildings in Trento for granted after awhile. But when you look up at the finely detailed forms painted on the outside of this 15th-century palazzo, you remember how amazing it is that they've endured the centuries. Just north of Piazza del Duomo, these are some of the most outstanding frescoes in the area. The inside of this building is impressive as well, but it's mainly used by the city for official events, and is not generally open to the public.

CITY SPORTS

Trento locals like nothing more than a super endorphin rush. The town's great sports facilities are advertised heavily to tourists, though most prefer hiking (climbing?) Monte Boldone [see below] for getting the blood pumping. Just south of town, the **ASIS** *(Via IV Novembre; Tel 0461/992-990; 1-11pm Mon-Sat, 7am-11pm Sun)* sporting center organizes classes (rock climbing, etc.) and offers information on outdoor options. You can pay a visit to the **Piscine Comunali** *(Via Fogazzaro; Tel 046/924-248; 9am-9pm Mon-Fri, 9am-7pm Sat, 9am-1pm Sun; Admission varies)* at any time of year—they've got both indoor and outdoor lap pools. There's also **Stadio del Ghiaccio** *(Loc Ghiaccio; Tel 0461/922-055; 10am-noon/2-6:30pm Mon-Fri, 9pm-11pm Wed and Fri, 2-6:30pm/9-11pm Sat; Admission varies),* an ice-skating rink south of town, right along the water, for the cooler months. Skate rental is available.

STUFF

Trento doesn't cater to hordes of tourists, so the shopping scene here is the real deal. The region's fine foods, chocolates, and pastries make great authentic souvenirs, so stock up on that stuff here and save your clothing budget for Bologna or Padova.

▶▶GIFTS

Press your nose up against the long, sweet-filled cases at **Casa Del Cioccolate** *(Via Belenzani 21; Tel 0461/4352; 8:30am-12:15pm/3-7:15pm Mon-Sat, 9am-12:30pm Sun, closed Mon mornings; No credit cards)*—you won't be alone. It seems like everyone in town stops off at this spot just north of Piazza del Duomo to pick up a bag of homemade candy, and nibble a few on the way home.

▶▶HOW BAZAAR

On the second Saturday of every month, Piazza Garzetti turns into a bustling **flea market** *(For information, Tel 0461/235-062; 7:30am-about 6pm)*. Folks from all over the province lay out their housewares, books, old jewelry, and clothes on fold-out tables for curious shoppers to poke, pick through, and haggle over.

EATS

There's a local saying: *"Si mangia molto bene a Trento"* ("One eats very well in Trento"). This is a kick-ass food town, with a menu that borrows slightly from Austrian and German influences, and heavily from Italian. And though accommodation is costly here, the food's a bahgin', dahlin'. There are lots of uptown-chic places where local recipes have gotten the modern treatment, but also a heaping helping of traditional trattorias where you can order local specialties like *formaggio fuso* (fried cheese served over polenta), and *ravioli alla Trentino* (filled with pork, beef, chicken, and herbs). This area is known for its fruit, nuts, and mushrooms, so you'll see them all over just about every menu. Originating in a town by the same name just south of here, *asiago* is the cheese of choice.

▶▶CHEAP

The bakers in this region are famous, and any trip to **Pasticceria Bertelli** *(Via Oriola 29; Tel 0461/984-765; 8am-12:30pm/3-7:30pm Tue-Sat, 8:30am-1:30pm/3:30-7:30pm Sun; pastries 1,500-3,000L, cappuccino 1,600L; No credit cards)* shows why. These lovely little works of art are the bane of any dieter's existence, from homemade chocolate truffles to fresh figs filled with almond paste. Mid-afternoon, people are packed into this pretty little shop shoulder-to-shoulder.

TO MARKET

Filled top to bottom with regional treats, **La Gastronomia** *(Via Mantova 28; Tel 0461/235-217; 8:40am-1pm/4-7:30pm daily, closed Sat afternoon; No credit cards)* is reason enough to plan a picnic. There's an enormous deli-case full of cured hams and salamis, great cheeses, and rotisserie chicken and game birds, as well as breads, vegetables, and fresh herbs—who needs a supermarket? Don't worry, you can still pick up a bottle of Coke—or go native and give San Pellegrino a try. It's a few blocks east of Piazza del Duomo, intersecting with Via Calepina.

Bright and cheery, the eat-on-the-run self-service restaurant **Due Gigante** (*Via San Simonino 14; Tel 0431/237-515; 11:30am-3pm/6-10:30pm; Entrees 9,000-15,000L; V, MC*), a few blocks east of Piazza del Duomo, offers the most bang for your buck in Trentino. Wind your way through three splendiferous food bars, with a pasta station serving up favorites like tagliatelle with wild mushrooms and gnocchi gorgonzola, a salad bar where you can create your own heap o' greens, and a deli counter with roasted meats, chicken, and fish entrees, vegetables, cheeses, and even desserts. There's nowhere more popular for lunch, so come either early or late to avoid the rush.

For almost 80 years, the massive **Pedavena** (*Piazza Fiera 13; Tel 0461/986-255; Restaurant 8am-midnight Wed-Mon, pizzeria noon-2:15pm/4pm-midnight; Entrees 8,000-16,000L; V, MC, AE*) has been Trento's trattoria of choice. The dining rooms are always packed, and the front bar is crowded with locals stopping in for a beer (at 9,000L per liter, one of the cheapest in town), but it's well worth braving the crowds. The traditional food is cheap, the servings generous. Try the *piatto Pedavena* for a taste of all the local specialties, or the *canederli al sugo* if you want to pad your stomach before a night of heavy drinking. The goulash is spicy and meaty, and the wood-fired pizzas are an oversized force to be reckoned with. A cheesy piano player entertains the hungry masses on Wednesdays and Thursdays, making these the most popular nights of the week.

Located between Piazza del Duomo and the old walls on the north side of Piazza Fiera, **Trattoria Tre Garofani** (*Via Mazzini 33; Tel 0461/237-543; Noon-2:30pm/7-11pm Mon-Sat; Entrees 14,000-22,000L, three-course meal 32,000L; V, MC, AE*) is the kind of family place that makes you want to go into the business. The Linardi family has managed this cozy restaurant since 1947—Mom cooks away in the kitchen while her son handles the dining room, and Dad talks to his pals at the front bar. The food is a notch above traditional trattoria fare: Try the *canederli in brodo* or homemade tortellini. And vegetarians won't feel cheated—the *polenta con asiago fuso,* a big slab of local cheese, deep-fried and served over a plate of polenta, is amazing. The three-course meal is a good deal—start off with canederli, move on to slow-cooked rabbit, and finish up with a homemade torte. A liter of local wine costs 15,000L.

▶▶DO-ABLE

Everyone from the cool, blue-haired punk-rocker to the cool, blue-haired auntie heads northeast of Piazza del Duomo to **Först Birreria Pizzeria** (*Via Oss Mazzurana 38; Tel 0431/235-590; 10am-11pm Tue-Sun; Entrees 7,000-18,000L, three-course meal 22,500L; No credit cards),* for great food at great prices. Old men drink at the front bar while diners devour heavily sauced pasta dishes and meaty entrees under painted arches and murals of family crests. The food's cheap and unfussy, and everyone orders the three-course deal. Shy away from the pizzas, which are a bit small. Wine comes in oversized ceramic pitchers—a bargain at 12,000L per liter.

Been awhile since your last burrito? Head for **Giubbe Rosse** [see *bar, club, and live music scene,* above], the happening Cuban bar located

TRENTO EATS and crashing

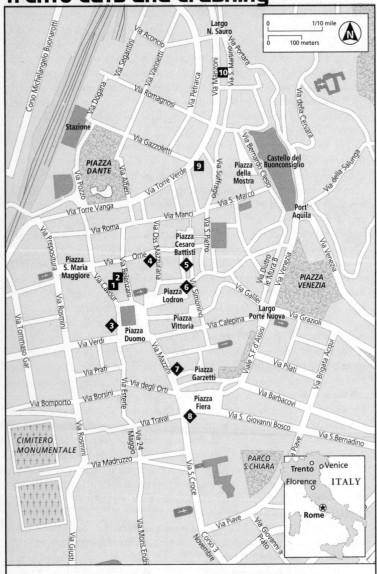

EATS ◆
Due Gigante **5**
Först Birreria Pizzaria **4**
Pasticceria Bertelli **6**
Pedavena **8**
Scrigno del Duomo **3**
Trattoria Tre Garofani **7**

CRASHING ■
Al Cavallino Bianco **1**
Hotel America **9**
Ostello Giovane Europa **10**
Venezia **2**

inside a shopping mall off Via Torre Vanga—they don't get any better than the ones here. A plate of chicken, beef, and/or bean burritos (13,000L) hits the spot, and the sizzling fajitas (20,000L) are more than you can eat. For something out of the ordinary, try *langostine en salsa con Paella* (lobster in salsa with paella). Three levels of spiciness are offered, but none are for the uninitiated. Wash it all down with some Corona or Dos Equis in the bottle (7,000-9,000L).

▶▶**SPLURGE**

The coolest kid in town is also the newest. With its elegant garden out front, and Billie Holiday tellin' it like it is in the background, the super-sleek **Scrigno del Duome** *(Piazza del Duomo 29; Tel 0461/220-030; 9am-2:30pm/5pm-1am; www.scrignodelduomo.com; Entrees 22,000-30,000L, 65,000L tasting menu with more courses than you can count, 85,000L with matching wines; V, MC, AE)* is the epitome of *scene*. The upstairs wine bar puts all others to shame, with *stuzzichini* (snack plates) of salami, cheese, and stuffed olives, each of which comes with a paired glass of wine (8,000-15,000L). You can perch at the marble bar or grab a seat at one of the wooden tables in the room next door, but the real treat is the downstairs, which has been renovated to modern standards, with a Picasso-esque relief mural on the wall mixing it up with Medieval columns and detail. Look up through glass tiles into the piazza above, or down into the ancient Roman foundation below. Third-generation restaura-teurs, the Bettucchi family offers gourmet interpretations of traditional local foods, from candederli in gorgonzola to the surprisingly simple spinach and potato soup. If you save up for one meal in Trento, this should be it. It's easy to find, on the western side of Piazza del Duomo.

crashing

Trento is not a budget-friendly spot, especially for overnighters. There are only a few central options, so call as far ahead as you can. If you're plan-ning on skiing or hiking, it's actually cheaper to sleep on Monte Bondone than to base yourself here.

▶▶**CHEAP**

Don't get too excited about **Ostello Giovane Europa** *(Via Manzoni 17; Tel 0461/234-567, Fax 0461/268-434; Reception open 7am-midnight; closed Jan 6-31; 23,000L dorm, 32,000L single, 26,000L per person double, no private baths; No credit cards)*—it's a typical, institutional youth hostel catering to busloads of visiting student groups. But given Trento's hotel situation, you might consider cramping your style for a night or two. All the usual amenities—bunk beds with sheets included, standard breakfast, TV room, curfew—are here. It's an easy 10-minute walk northeast of the station: Hang a right on Via Pozzo, then make the first left on Via Vanga. This street curves to the left, and changes its name to Torre Verde, before it becomes Via Manzoni. The hostel is on the right.

▶▶**DO-ABLE**

If you're doing Trento on a budget, but don't want to bother with a curfew, **Al Cavallino Bianco** *(Via Cavour 29; Tel 0461/231-559, Fax*

0461/234-114; 67,000L single, 94,000L double, all with private showers and shared toilets; No credit cards) should be your first choice. Its best feature is its location: right in the heart of town, just down the block from the hostel on the main road. It *is* a little weird—a cross between a hostel, a one-star hotel, and Romper Room—but you know what they say about beggars and choosers. Many of the rooms open out onto a shadowy sunroom with a mural of trees and flowers that looks like something from a nursery school. The rooms are spic-and-span, but tiny, and the furniture's a little worn down. This is a popular spot, and it gets crowded, which means noise. At all hours.

Two hotels have recently merged to become **Venezia** *(Via Belezani 70; Tel 0461/234-559, Fax 0461/234-114; 72,000L single, 120,000L double, all with private baths, breakfast included; V, MC).* The resulting hotel has an elderly feel, both in terms of its decor and clientele, but the simple rooms are spacious. The main entrance is on a side street that runs into Piazza del Duomo, but another entrance is right on the piazza, and some of the rooms have spectacular views.

▶▶**SPLURGE**

Named **Hotel America** *(Via Torre Verde 50; Tel 0461/983-010, Fax 0461/230-603; 100,000L single, 160,000L double, private baths, breakfast included; V, MC)* because it was opened by Grandpa Giovannini when he came home from a stay in Wyoming in 1923, this hotel is still run by the same family. Considering the limited options in town and the service, amenities, and all-around good time you get here, it's well worth the price if you can swing it. This is a hotel with style—a nice break from the mismatched floral prints and scratchy towels you get all over the rest of Italy. Each of the 67 rooms, some of them mini-apartments, has personal touches—a vase of sunflowers here, a skylight there—as well as spacious tile bathrooms with hairdryers, and cable TV.

need to know

Currency Exchange There's a **bancomat** at the train station, and the streets leading to the center of town are lined with **banks** where you can change money and cash travelers checks.

Tourist Information Located on the corner of Via Manci and Belezani, halfway between the station and the Duomo, the super-helpful **tourist office** *(Via Manci 2; Tel 046/983-880; www.apt.trento.it; 9am-7pm daily)* functions as a home base for both the city and Monte Bondone. Helpful staffers will assist you with anything from ski passes to equipment rental. They cannot, however, book rooms for you.

Public Transportation Walking's the way to go in Trento, but if you need a ride you can always call a **24-hour taxi** *(Tel 0461/930-002).*

Health and Emergency Ambulance: *118;* Police: *113;* Fire: *115.* The nearest hospital, **Ospedale Santa Chiara** *(Tel 0461/903-111),* is a 20-minute walk south from town.

Pharmacies All your pharmaceutical needs can be met at **Farmacia Giallo** *(Piazza delle Erbe; Tel 0461/234-387; 8am-1:30pm/3-7:30pm*

Mon-Sat; V, MC), just east of the Duomo, off Via Simonino. Look on the door for a posting of which pharmacy in town is on the 24-hour rotating schedule.

Trains Trento is well-connected by train. Multiple trains run every hour to Bolzano (4,500-6,000L) and other nearby towns. Trains for Venice, Verona, and Bologna leave several times a day. The **train station** *(Tel 0461/891-411)* is right on the water, a five-minute walk west of the city center, on Piazza Dante.

Bus Lines Out of the City Buses connect Trento to its suburbs. **Atesina bus lines** *(Tel 0461/983-627)* are based at the bus station on Via Pozzo.

Bike Rental Just east of the Duomo, **Sportler** *(Via Mantova 12; Tel 0461/981-290; 9am-noon/3-7pm daily; 30,000L per day, deposit required; No credit cards)* rents wheels, as well as ski equipment in the winter months.

Laundry This brightly lit, coin-operated, self-service **Laundromat** *(Via Travai 23; 8am-10pm daily; wash 5,000L, dry 5,000L)* in the student quarter is a little more expensive than most. Bring lots of change—the machines don't give it back.

Postal The **post office** *(Piazza Vittoria 20; Tel 0461/987-270; 8am-6:30pm Mon-Fri, 8am-1pm Sat)* is just east of Piazza del Duomo. The postal code is 38100, in case you were wondering.

Internet See *wired,* above.

bolzano

Whether you come here to trip around the Dolomite Mountains or to pig out on sausage and beer, Bolzano is a place you won't forget. "You are now leaving Italy, *willkommen* to Austria" isn't on any of the road signs, but it might as well be. This small, sleepy town—called *Bozen* in German—is the German-speaking capital of Italy. With more nightlife and cultural sites than the even-smaller towns in the rest of Alto Adige, Bolzano is a perfect place to check out Austrian culture without ever leaving Italy.

Bolzano began its life as a part of the Roman Empire around 15 B.C., and after Rome fell, the Goths, Franks, Lombards, and Bavarians all held the reins here for short times. But it wasn't until the 11th century, when the Holy Roman Emperor gave the Bishop of Trento this land, that there was any real stability. In 1366, Austria's Hapsburgs took over, and held onto the alpine town tightly until after WWI. The Italian Fascists paid a lot of attention to Bolzano when they seized power in 1924, enforcing Italian-only codes, renaming everything they could find, and building monuments designed to rub defeat in the faces of the Austrians. Most of these monuments to intolerance still stand (check out Piazza Vittoria, or the train station), even after a 1970s terrorist bombing campaign tried to get rid of them once and for all.

Today the conflict between German and Italian speakers in this town has been resolved. The truce probably went something like this: "Let's speak *both* Italian and German, learn English too, and make lots of money." The tourist trade has made this a wealthy place. Austrians come here for the sun, Italians come for the snow, and schoolchildren come to see the remains of an ice-age mummy found nearby [see *culture zoo,* below]. Bolzano is also home to the Free University of Bolzano, founded in 1997, Italy's newest university and the only one in Europe where students are *required* to speak three languages: German, Italian, and English. And where there are students, there are bars. Most of the watering holes in the city center are less than three years old, and they're basically empty when students go home for the summer.

The locals are reasonably friendly, but don't expect to feel like the adopted son or daughter of the people you meet. They've got that Austrian reserve thing going on, unlike their gregarious counterparts in Italian Italy. You came here to get a little taste of Austria, *capiche?*

neighborhoods

Be aware that both Italian and German names are used for just about everything in this town. We give Italian names first for the sake of clarity, followed by German names in parentheses. Most things to see and do in Bolzano are compacted into the small **city center,** which can be crossed in less than 15 minutes. The center is basically shaped like a triangle with the long side (or *hypotenuse,* as they say in geometry class) made up by the **Talvera (Talfer) River** and its riverside park, **Passeggiata Lungo Talvera (Wassermauerpromenade)** on the west. The triangle's northern angle is at the **Castel Mareccio (Schlott Maretsch)**—a castle and, of all things, convention center. From here, **Via San Osvaldo** slants southeast to the **Funivia del Renon (Rittner Seilbahn),** a cable car station and the easternmost point of the city center. **Via Renon** runs southwest from here, past the train station to **Piazza Verdi,** where it becomes **Via Marconi** and runs along the small **Isarco (Eisack) River** until they meet the Talvera River at the southern angle of our happy little triangle. **Piazza Walther (Waltherplatz)** is Bolzano's main square, situated more or less in the center of the old town [see *culture zoo,* below]. The **Duomo** backs onto the west side of Piazza Walther, and opens onto **Piazza Duomo** on the west. Piazza Duomo and **Piazza Erbe,** to the northwest, are both central meeting points. East of Erbe is **Piazza Grano,** where you'll find a bunch of hotels. The main drag, **Via Museo,** runs west from Piazza Erbe, and crosses the river as the **Ponte Talvera** bridge.

wired

The only public place to get online is **Bar Vecchia Bolzano,** [see *bar and club scene,* below]. But competitors will doubtless start hooking up computers in their bars any day now. *www.sudtirol.com/bolzano/1e.htm* is Bolzano's home on the web.

bolzano bars clubs and culture zoo

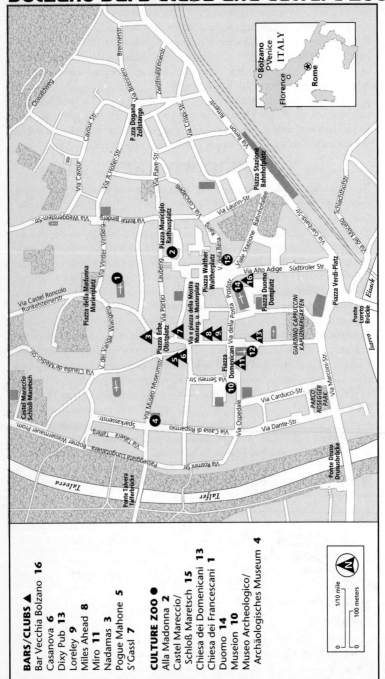

BARS/CLUBS ▲
Bar Vecchia Bolzano **16**
Casanova **6**
Dixy Pub **13**
Loreley **9**
Miles Ahead **8**
Miro **11**
Nadamas **3**
Pogue Mahone **5**
S'Gassl **7**

CULTURE ZOO ●
Alla Madonna **2**
Castel Mareccio/
Schloß Maretsch **15**
Chiesa dei Domenicani **13**
Chiesa dei Francescani **1**
Duomo **14**
Museion **10**
Museo Archeologico/
Archäologisches Museum **4**

If you're not an outdoorsperson, there's really no need to venture beyond the city walls—you'll find all your cultcha, accommodations, and after-dark fun within. But if you're here to see the mountains, try a hike up the **Passeggiata San Osvaldo,** or take the **Funivia del Renon cable car** up into the Dolomites [see *great outdoors,* below, for both].

hanging out

The bulk of Bolzano's quality slacking goes on in the center of town, mostly in the main square, **Piazza Walther (Waltherplatz),** which always seems to be powered by manic shoppers and other assorted time-wasters. **Via Goethe,** which runs north into Piazza Erbe (Obstplatz), two blocks west of Walther, is the axis of the bar scene, as well as a major thoroughfare for the townspeoples' obligatory evening stroll. The stretch of **Via Portici** between Piazza Erbe and Piazza Municipo (Rathausplatz) is prime window-shopping grounds. The shore of the Talvera River, north of the Ponte Talvera bridge, has the **Passeggiata Lungo Talvera** (Wassermauerpromenade), a terrific city park with lots of benches and shady knolls for lazing around.

cafe scene

Exil Lounge Café *(Piazza Grano 2A; Tel 0471/971-814; 10am-midnight Mon-Wed, 10am-1am Thu-Sat; Coffees 1,800-3,000L, wines by the glass 3,000-7,000L, large Italian panini from 2,000-10,000L, huge salads with bread 8,000L; No credit cards),* on the east side of Piazza Grano, is as close as it gets to a San Francisco-type coffeehouse in Bolzano. The space is huge and uncluttered, with plenty of options for sitting and watching the day go by. There are newspapers in library-style racks, but everyone seems more interested in checking everyone else out than current events. With 450 Italian and Tyrolean wines by the glass, beer specials (3,000-6,000L), and lots of strong Italian coffee, you may never want to leave.

You can sip your morning cappuccino with ladies in Chanel suits and your evening *caffe corretto* (espresso with grappa) alongside sophisticated young businessmen at **Monika Pasticceria Cafe** *(Via Goethe 13; 0471/977-744; 7:30am-7:30pm; 1,800 cappuccino; No credit cards),* a stylish Viennese cafe. You'd fit right into this Baroque atmosphere if you hadn't been wearing the same jeans for three weeks! They also serve the city's best pastries (1,500-4,000L), for that quick snack to tide you over till the next meal.

bar, club, and live music scene

Over the last three years, more and more bars have opened their doors in the city center to serve those hard-rocking, trilingual econ students from the new Universitá di Bolzano. Bolzano's noise ordinance, however, says that they've gotta close by 1am. So the scene doesn't get as wild as it could—but when they *are* open, the bars are pretty cool. While some places (Pogue Mahone, Dixy Pub) fudge a bit on closing time, Miro is the only real exception, being legally open until 4am. Almost everyone speaks German, Italian and English, in that order.

Late-night in Bolzano means **Miro** *(Piazza Domenicani 3/b; Tel 0471/976-464; 11pm-4am Thu-Sat; www.miro-club.com; Cover from 12,000L with drink; No credit cards),* a small club in an arched, stone-walled Renaissance cellar on Piazza Domenicani, just west of the Duomo. The groove is the main attraction here—Thursday nights bring house from DJ Corrado, and Friday is a fun '70s night (embrace the cheese). Miro also hosts infrequent bands of all types and indifferent quality (there's not much to choose from in Alto Adige). The cover varies according to who's spinning, the theme, and whether there's live music. The extremely friendly crowd is a little older than you'll find in most Italian clubs (mid-thirties), which may explain how they can afford the overpriced cocktails (from 12,000L) at the fully stocked tiki bar. Most locals come here around midnight, as other bars are winding down.

Bolzano's currently having a love affair with **Casanova** *(Vicolo Erbe 8; No phone; 10am-1am winter; 5pm-1am summer; No cover; No credit cards),* just west of Piazza Erbe. It's an appropriate name for a bar devoted to the cult of the diva. Brightly painted walls are swathed in a Modern art homage to fifties femme fatales—everywhere you look, there's another picture of Elizabeth Taylor in her prime. With two large front rooms and a cavernous back room where folks sip wine and play cards by candle-light, this place can really pack 'em in. There's fabulous '70s camp playing in the background, and talk of live music in the near future. Frozen drinks, such as the Very Berry Margarita, cost 10,000L, and there's always a student beer special for 4,000L. The vibe and crowd are young, relaxed and—a first for Bolzano—gay-friendly.

Right next door is **Pogue Mahone** *(Vicolo Erbe 20; 5pm-1:30am; No cover; V, MC, AE),* a pretty good stab at an authentic (upscale) Dublin pub. Pictures of Joyce, Beckett, Shaw, Wilde, and Yeats hang on the green-sponged walls, and classic rock plays in the background (with a few Irish bands thrown in for good measure). Lots of nooks and crannies invite a quiet word or two and a shot of Irish whiskey (4,000-12,000L) with your mates. Things get pretty hot by midnight or so on Friday and Saturday nights, when students pack the place for imperial pints of Guinness (8,000L). Cold panini (5,500L) can keep you going till last call—one of the few in town later than 1am.

On the west side of Piazza Erbe, **Nadamas** *(Piazza Erbe 43/44; Tel 0471/980-684; 12:30pm-1am bar, 12:30-2:30pm/7-10:30pm for food, closed Sun; Entrees 12,000-13,000L, main courses 20,000L; No cover; No credit cards)* is the old standby of Bolzano's newborn scene—everyone passes through here eventually, some drawn by the restaurant [see *eats,* below], others by the pleasantly shady location. Decor is part traditional Tyrolean—heavy beams with red and green woodwork details—and part arty, college-town bar, with paintings from local artists and candles that look like they've been dripping for years. Indie rock plays on the stereo and posters up front tell what's going on in the region this month. The cool slacker crowd enjoying Guinness (8,000L) and cocktails (7,000-10,000L) at the long, well-stocked bar may be the first class of students-turned-townies, since the university just opened in 1997. Drop in anytime—folks are here all day, and they don't seem to be going anywhere anytime soon.

On the local Italian-to-Austrian bar scale, **S'Gassl** *(Via Argentieri 30; Tel 0348/882-0128; 8:30am-1am daily; No cover; ATM cards)* weighs in at the extreme Austrian end. This homey bar is just below street level, filled with blond wood furnishings and fixtures and an enthusiastic German-speaking crowd. They're open mornings for coffee (1,800L) and pastries (3-6,000L), but from Thursday to Saturday after 10pm, the place is sardine-can full of students, who often end up dancing on the tables and bar to techno and indie rock on the stereo. Ten wines by the glass are 3,000-7,000L, and concoctions such as the Green Cuba Libre—rum and green tea—are 9,000-10,000L. Three brothers own and run this place, as well as Dixy Bar and Miles Ahead.

Opened as a jazz club in 1999, the airy and open **Miles Ahead** *(Via Goethe 20; Tel 0338/405-3173; 7pm-1am daily; No cover; No credit cards)* has settled into a happy groove with house and alternative DJs on Friday and Saturday, and recorded jazz Monday through Wednesday. Twinkly blue lights above the bar and large color-field canvases on the brick walls brighten the place up. Thursday's Student Night draws the young and rowdy, who shake it to old soul and belly up for ever-changing drink specials. Beers typically run 4,000-10,000L; cocktails are 9,000-12,000L.

The long-established **Dixy Pub** *(Via Cappuccini 6; Tel 0471/970-511; 7pm-1:30am daily; No cover; No credit cards),* at the southern end of Via Goethe, where it turns into Via Cappucini, looks like a rustic cabin, with big wooden beams, plaster walls, and wrought-iron fixtures. Christoph, the oldest of the three brothers who own this bar (as well as Miles Ahead and S'Gassl), holds court here till late (1:30am), cheating just a little on the town's official closing time. With German and English beers on tap for 6,000L, and classic rock on the sound system, the Dixy is huge with the student crowd, especially on the weekends, when things get warmed up around 11pm. They also serve ham and cheese "toast," a Wonder Bread-looking sandwich that only a college student could love.

If you've downed enough beer and seen enough lederhosen, head to **Bar Vecchia Bolzano** *(Piazza Parrocchia; Tel 0461/981-919; 7pm-1am Mon-Sat, closed Sun; No cover; No credit cards),* across from the Duomo. During the day, this Italian-style bar is a chill place to hang out and check e-mail over a beer (5,000L), but around 10pm, it starts to fill up with a very Italian crowd—younger, more animated, and more inquisitive than you'll find in many of the more Austrian places. The place looks like it was decorated by Spring Break backpackers: U.S., Aussie, and Italian flags hang from the ceiling, and a mishmash of "kangaroo crossing" signs and old Coke calendars decks the walls, all by the light of blue and red lightbulbs and five TVs playing Italian music videos and football matches.

Your average Italian bar hawking beer (6,000L) and wine (4,000) by day, **Loreley** *(Via Goethe 28; Tel 0471/976-230; 11-1:30am daily; No cover; No credit cards)* transforms into one of the town's rockin'-est disco pubs after 11pm. Girls show up in maximum glitz, while guys sport their coolest leather jackets and jeans. The evening bartender, Max, turns DJ on Thursdays, Fridays, and Saturdays, spinning a good mix of house, disco, and early-80s dance hits—there's not much space to dance, but the booths in the back serve as impromptu mini-stages. It's all very styling, in a collegiate kind of way. You'll never get any elbowroom, but you'll also never have to pay a cover.

arts scene

Not much of an independent art scene here—the kids who come for school are on the economic and poli sci track—but some great community-funded galleries and an awesome Modern art museum [see *culture zoo*, below] keep the artistic community alive.

▶▶VISUAL ARTS

Galleria Les Chances de l'Art *(Via Visitazione 16/a; Tel 0471/272-408; 10am-12:30pm/3:30-7:30pm Mon-Fri, 10am-12:30pm Sat; Free admission; No credit cards)* is what happens when art students open galleries—you get an edgy, arty scene that borders on pretentious. Ask a stupid question, you'll get a dissertation. Ignore theoretical blathering and focus on the exhibits—they're international and excellent, spanning from conceptual installations to abstract paintings and sculpture. Of course it's located outside the conventional environs of the city center, just west of the river, down Viale Druso.

Can you believe the coolest art space—with exciting exhibits from all media and contemporary styles and great literary readings in both German and Italian—is run by the city? **Galleria Civica** *(Piazza Domenicani 18; Tel 0471/500-483; 10am-1pm/3-8pm daily; Free admission; No credit cards)* is comprised of two large rooms, incorporating architectural remnants of the original medieval building. Two or three artists, some regional, some from afar, exhibit at a time.

gay scene

Bolzano's lively gay and lesbian activist and social club, **Centaurus** *(Via Talvera 1; Tel 0471/976-342; 9pm-midnight Wed, 9pm-midnight Sat; Arci NA or ArchiGay membership card required, available for 25,000L; No cover; No credit cards)*, operates from its location near the riverside park as the central nervous system of the entire region's queer scene. Phone lines are open Tuesdays 8-10pm for local gay info in Italian, German, and occasionally English. Weekly meetings, called *Treffpunkt,* are Wednesdays 9pm-midnight. On Saturdays, a makeshift disco pub springs up in their HQ, with dancing 9pm-midnight. On other nights, you can find the gay crowd mixing in at **Casanova** [see *bar scene,* above] or **Hopfen & Co** [see *eats,* below].

CULTUre ZOO

While Bolzano's art and museum collections may not be as mind-blowing or extensive as what you'll find in Tuscany or Rome, they provide a cool glimpse into the inner life of this one-of-a-kind region. And don't forget the famous mummy!

Museo Archeologico/Archäologisches Museum *(Via Museo 3; Tel 0471/982-098, Fax 0471/980-648; 10am-6pm Tue, Wed, Fri Sun, 10am-8pm Thu, May 1-Sep 30; 9am-5pm Tue, Wed, Fri-Sun, 10am-8pm Thu, Oct 1-Apr 30; 13,000L adults, 7,000L students under 27 with card; museo.archeologico@provincia.bz.it; No credit cards):* Remember the Iceman? No, not the Iceman who cometh, or the 1984 sci-fi flick. The *real* Iceman. In 1991, a hiker found an Ice-Age mummy sticking out of a glacier near the Austrian border, so well-preserved that you could make out his tattoos and the pattern of his coat. After much international bickering, Bolzano—specifically the second floor of this museum, halfway between the river and Piazza Erbe—was chosen as the Popsicle's final resting place. The first-floor exhibits outline the prehistoric history of the region, with artifacts and models, English-language audio guides (3,000L extra), plenty of multilingual plaques, and other top-of-the-line visual aids (learning is fun!). Soak up as much Neolithic background as you can stand before heading up to the second floor to see the star mummy. Ötzi, as the locals nicknamed him, looks like an alien made of beef jerky—not too bad for 5,300 years old. Upper floors follow the region's history through the Roman period and early Middle Ages.

Duomo *(Piazza Duomo 1; Tel 0471/306-208; 9:45am-noon/2-5pm Mon-Fri, 9:45am-noon Sat; Free admission):* Begun by the Lombards in 1295, and completed by the Swabians after 1340, this Gothic church towers over the southwest side of Piazza Walther, but its Romanesque facade actually looks out on Piazza Duomo. The high bell tower was a Renaissance addition, while the multicolored roof is reminiscent of Vienna's cathedral. Inside, you get a taste of the differences between Germanic and Italianate religious art. Carved wooden sculptures are more common than marble or canvas and, for the most part, the frescoes don't hold a candle to the artistry of the Italian Renaissance. Germans also seem to be more interested in the pain and suffering of religion than in its abject beauty—just ask the souls writhing in flames at the base of the 14th-century wooden crucifix as you enter.

Museion *(Via Sernesi 1; Tel 0471/977-116, Fax 0471/980-001; 10am-noon/3-7pm Tue-Sun; info@museion.it; 5,000L; No credit cards):* Bolzano's Modern art museum splits its space between traveling shows of international and local artists and a large permanent collection. Works by Modern heavy hitters like Duchamp, Klee, and Picasso roll through every so often, but the main focus is exploring the dynamics of local cultures through exhibits of Austrian, Italian, and German art. Other exhibits explore the borders of aesthetics "between art and sound, art and writing." Guided tours (of the museum, not the areas between art and sound) are on Thursdays at 6pm. They're officially in Italian and German, but it's a safe bet that there will be someone around who can help you out in English.

Chiesa dei Dominicani *(Piazza dei Dominicani 1; Tel 0471/280-694; 9:30am-5:30pm Mon-Sat; Free admission):* The interior of this 13th-century church is stark and German Gothic, except for the very Italian frescoes added by Giotto's school from Padua. Check out the wicked depiction of St. George battling the dragon on the right wall. Walk through the arch that leads to the altar and hang a right to view the heavily frescoed side chapel. Piazza dei Dominicani is connected to Piazza del Duomo by Via Posta.

Chiesa dei Francescani *(Via dei Francescani 1; Tel 0471/978-625; 10am-noon/2:30-6pm; Free admission):* This 14th-century church contains some of the best examples of Gothic woodcarving in the region. Altar doors, carved by master-of-the-genre Hans Klocker in 1500, are worth the trip up Via Francescani, which runs north from Piazza Erbe. The covered walkways of the cloisters outside have more fresco cycles, by students of imported Paduan Giotto, from 1330. Local legend says that Francis of Assisi visited this site with his father during his pre-sainthood wonder years.

Via dei Portici: Running east from Piazza Erbe right through the center of town, this street, the first laid out by the Bishop of Trento in the 11th century, is lined with brightly colored porticos, dormers, and balconies. Most of its structures date to the 16th and 17th centuries. This thoroughfare has been shared by two cultures for a long time: Ancient records show the city's plan to increase foot traffic by placing the Italian merchants on the north side of the street, where the Germans lived, and the Germans on the south, where the Italians were. This medieval marketing scheme must have done the trick: The locals still do all of their shopping here today, though there's not much to interest travelers.

Alla Madonna *(Via Portici 17; Tel 0471/976-749; 8:30am-noon/3-7pm Mon-Fri, 8:30am-noon Sat; Free admission; No credit cards):* Looking for some ancient herbal remedies, or just a refill on your Ritalin prescription? Alla Madonna, in the heart of the town center, on Via Portici, is both a historic apothecary shop dating back to the Middle Ages and a working, modern-day pharmacy. One wall is lined with little wooden drawers containing hundreds of dried herbs, oils, poultices, dyes, and teas, all for sale. (Nothing beats a good poultice for a pulled hamstring.) The usual OTC and prescription drugs are also available.

Castel Mareccio/Schlott Maretsch *(Via Castel Mareccio; Tel 0471/976-615, Fax 0471/300-746; 8:30am-12:30pm/3-7pm; Free admission when there is no convention; No credit cards):* This 13th-century castle has the usual turrets and towers, but it's built at the bottom of one of Bolzano's valleys (perhaps not the most strategic location for fending off Barbarian invaders...). The castle itself, set in a vineyard, has some well-preserved frescoes of Tristan and Isolde. It also doubles as Bolzano's convention center, so if there's a dentists' convention in town, you might have to fake your way in.

CITY SPORTS

Meet the alpine experience head-on with a visit to either of Bolzano's terrific urban parks. **Parco Petrarca,** located on both banks of the Talvera River, just west of the city center, has two soccer fields, putt-putt golf, a baseball diamond, bike paths, and jogging and walking trails. In the winter, there's an ice skating rink where all the local kids make like Michelle Kwan.

Campo Sportivo Druso *(Viale Trieste; Tel 0471/911-000; 7-8am/12:15-2:30pm/4-9:30pm Mon-Fri, 2-9:30pm Sat, 9am-12:30pm/2-9:30pm; 8,000L, 4,000L students under 26 discount; No credit cards),* the more sports-oriented park, is located just over the river southwest of town, where the Isarco and Talvera Rivers meet. The covered swimming pool is a choice spot for both aquatic exercise and scantily-clad socializing. The new **Fitness Center,** in the same complex, offers a sauna, steam room, solarium, and massages. On Wednesdays, only men can use the sauna, but the rest of the week it's unisex, so wear something you don't mind being seen in. Admission fees vary according to peak times of the day (10,000L 10-11:30am, 15,000L noon-2:30pm, and 20,000L 4-11pm). The soccer field nearby offers pick-up games daily, while the basketball court has no nets and no tall guys.

If the feeling of mud under your tires gets your blood pumping, you're in the right place—some of the best mountain biking in the world is right here. The **Centro Nazionale Mountain Bike (aka Alp Bike)** bike club *(Via C. Flavon 101; Tel 0471/952-266; Hours vary; www.alpbike.it; No set rates; No credit cards)* is run by Andrea Trivellato and Giancarlo Bolognese, instructors at the world-renowned *Scuola Nazionale Maestri di Mountainbike.* They plan weekly mud-happy excursions up into the hills, at varying prices. It's a pretty informal place, so check the website or call for latest news. If you'd rather make a go of it on your own, you can rent a sturdy mountain bike at **Sportler** *(Via Grappoli 56; Tel 0471/977-19, Fax 0471/309-710; 9:30am-12:30pm/2:30-7pm Mon-Sat; Bikes 30,000L per day, 45,000L per weekend; V, MC).* The city also provides bike rental at **Campo Sportivo Druso** *(Viale Stazione 5; No phone; 9am-sundown, summer only; Bikes 20,000L a day; No credit cards),* located outdoors between the station and Piazza Walther.

GREAT OUTDOORS

Although you can take in the gorgeous Alpine peaks without ever leaving town, it's more rewarding to break a sweat and get a look up close. For sweeping views and crisp mountain air, a trek up to the mountain village of San Osvaldo is a must. From Piazza Erbe, take via Museo east to the Ponte Talvera, the bridge over the river. Turn right before you cross the river and take the Passeggiata Lungotalvera into the riverside park. After about 400m, you'll come to the Castel Mareccio (you're about a third of the way through the park). Keep on for 20 minutes or so until the Passeggiata ends (after about 1,200m) and take a right when you see the Ponte St.

Antonio bridge on the left. Here Via Beato Arrigo curves to the right, just where the Passeggiata San Osvaldo starts. The well-maintained walking path winds uphill past benches and scenic overlook after scenic overlook. After an easy, 20-minute stroll, you'll reach a junction. The path to your left keeps going uphill and leads to an unimpressive restaurant; the path to your right leads back down to the town center (another 20-minute walk) and comes out on Via San Osvaldo. Straight ahead is a slightly long, level walk to the wine-growing, hilltop village of **Santa Maddalena,** which is worth wandering around for a half-hour, and is a nice spot to eat your packed picnic lunch (you did bring a lunch, didn't you?). From here, you can walk back down to town, coming out near the Gatto Nero hotel in about 20 minutes.

If you'd rather ride than walk, take the **Funivia del Renon cable car** *(Via Renon; No phone; 7:10am-7:30pm daily Jul-Aug; 7,200L round trip; No credit cards)* for a sky-high view of the Dolomites, whose jagged peaks change colors as day moves into night. It's east of the city center, just a quick walk from the train station,

STUFF

While no one comes to Bolzano for the shopping (take your platinum card over to Florence or Milan), the town has lots of cool markets, both the food and flea market types. For info, call the police—who issue licenses to the vendors at the markets and therefore know where they're all taking place—at 0471/997-669 (really, we're not kidding).

▶▶HOW BAZAAR
Expect the usual mishmash of cheeses, vegetables, and socks at Bolzano's permanent **outdoor market** *(Piazza Erbe; 8am-7pm Mon-Sat).* Bolzano's **flea market** *(Passeggiata Lungotalvera; Tel 0471/981-011; 8am-4pm, first Sat of every month)* offers the usually useless yet irresistible crap that someone else is throwing out.

▶▶WHEELS
Buy your own Vespa at the **used car and motorcycle market** *(Piazza Vittoria; Tel 0471/981-011; 8:30am-1pm, second Sat of every month; zotass@supereva.it).* Be warned that if you really do want to buy an old bike, you'll need residence papers to own it legally, unless it's a scooter with an engine of less than 200cc.

EATS

Eat up while you still can. As soon as you leave Alto Adige, you'll be hard-pressed to find tasty *candederli (knodel)* dumplings, not to mention any Germanic sausage and pork dishes done up a hundred different ways, anywhere else in Italy.

▶▶CHEAP
Unlike the rest of Alto Adige, Bolzano has tons of cheap eats—maybe the restaurant owners have taken pity on the student population.

Imbliss Talvera *(Parco Stazione; No phone; 10am-10pm, closed Sun; Hot dog 4,000-5,000L; No credit cards),* a fast-food stand in the park

TO MARKET

Check out the well-stocked **Supermarket A&O** *(Via Museo; No phone; 8:30am-7:15pm Mon-Sat, 8am-6pm Sun; V, MC)* for the absolute cheapest way to stay nourished and eat local. Grab some cheese and bread and cater your own low-budget dining experience. At least you won't have to tip.

For flowers, fruits, and veggies, try the **general market** which rotates piazzas, depending on the day *(8am-2pm; Piazza Vittoria, across Ponte Talvera from the center, Saturdays; Piazza Don Bosco, Mondays; Piazza Bersaglio, Tuesdays; Piazza Matteotti, Thursdays)*. There's also a **farmer's market** *(Vicolo Gumer, 7:30am-noon Fri)* in the center south of via Portici, between Piazza Grano and Piazza Municipo, and the **permanent outdoor market** [see *stuff*, above].

across from the train station, sells a concoction called *currywurst* for 7,300L. A popular fast food in Germany and Austria, it's finding fans here as well. If you love both curry and hot dogs, give it a shot, but the spicy sauce they pour over it is definitely an acquired taste—*wurstel* (plain hot dogs) are available for non-curry heads. Follow the locals' lead and eat your wurstel with mustard, *not* ketchup. The ketchup *(salsa pomodoro)*, available by request, is a little runny and tangy—but hey, maybe you're into that.

You'll find anything from eggplant parmesan to Hungarian goulash at **Don Pedro** *(Via Goethe 34; Tel 0471/975-195; 10am-7pm Mon-Fri, 9am-2pm Sat; Entrees 7,000-10,000L; No credit cards)* a *tavola calda*, or steam table, on the west side of Via Goethe. You can rest your foil container of pasta on the narrow counter if you don't want to eat outside, but unless it's raining, you can probably find a better place to eat your take-out chow. The choice food is the attraction here, drawing crowds of local business folks during the day and students in the evening.

The professional lunch crowd flocks to **Arma-Self Service Ristorante** *(Via Renna 1-3; Noon-2pm Mon-Fri; Entrees 8,000L; No credit cards)*, right across from the train station. It offers hearty and filling lunches in an American-style cafeteria setting. The place is surprisingly hip for what it is, with blue, lemon-yellow, and chrome paint everywhere, and two-toned blue tile walls. The carrot soup (4,000L) is a winner, and while the pastas aren't up to Emiglia or Veneto levels, they're good enough for the price. Fish-lovers, take note: Like any good Catholic eatery, it serves fish on Fridays.

bolzano eats and crashing

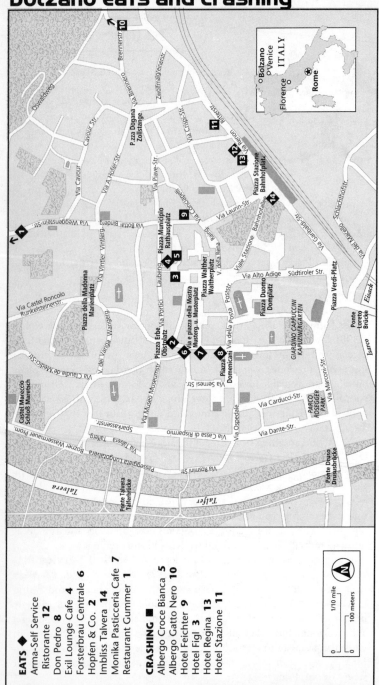

EATS ◆
Arma-Self Service
Ristorante 12
Don Pedro 8
Exil Lounge Cafe 4
Forsterbrau Centrale 6
Hopfen & Co. 2
Imbliss Talvera 14
Monika Pasticceria Cafe 7
Restaurant Gummer 1

CRASHING ■
Albergo Croce Bianca 5
Albergo Gatto Nero 10
Hotel Feichter 9
Hotel Figl 3
Hotel Regina 13
Hotel Stazione 11

▶▶DO-ABLE

Diners from all over make the long trek to **Restaurant Gummer** *(Via Waggenstein 36; Tel 0471/970-280; Noon-2pm/6-9:30pm Mon-Fri, noon-2pm Sat; Three-course meal 26,000L; No credit cards),* a 10-minute walk north of the city center. Take a bite of one of the hearty and honest Italian dishes and you'll understand why. The food is some of the best in town—try a risotto with radicchio and arugula, or one of the perfectly roasted meats, all made with the best regional ingredients. Local wines are on tap, and pannacotta and other homemade desserts finish things off. Cheesy decor, with paper napkins stuffed in the wineglasses and plastic flowers on the wood paneling, just adds to the place's hokey charm. Make sure to get a card, which has cutouts of flowers laminated on the surface—it looks like the handiwork of a little girl or sweet old lady. It looks like an old-man bar when you first walk inside—just turn right to find the dining room.

Hopfen & Co. *(Piazza Erbe 17; Tel 0471/300-788, Fax 0471/303-387; 2:30pm-midnight daily; Entrees 12,000-22,000L; V, MC, DC),* situated on the east side of Piazza Erbe, may be the first Tyrolean brewpub. Pass through the small bar into a large dining room filled with dark, exposed beams in the low ceiling, rustic, locally made furniture, and—my God, look at that plate of ribs! It's not part of the decor, but it might as well be. The *stinco di miale* is slow-cooked until it's falling off the bone, but the real winner has to be the *costate di miale,* or beef short ribs, served with two sauces (tangy or hot) and lots of napkins. Dark beer, brewed downstairs in huge copper drums you can watch through a glass wall, is smooth and hoppy. At 7,000L for a huge one-liter mug, the price can't be beat. The menu, logically, is a long list of things that taste great with beer, including sausages, beer-and-bread soups, and more pork than you can shake a stick at. Two more floors upstairs are arranged in quiet, cozy nooks, some with views over the Piazza.

Walk through the bar and under the stone arch at **Nadamas** [see *bar and club scene,* above] to find the roomy *Sala Trattoria,* or dining room. Candles light cozy, mismatched tables, and chill classic jazz plays in the background. The adventurous menu includes couscous plates (up to 20,000L), as well as Italian classics like gnocchi (13,000L), cheese plates (12,000L), and oversized salads (12,000L).

▶▶SPLURGE

Owned by the Forst brewery, local-favorite Austrian-style suds-makers, **Forsterbrau Centrale** *(Via Goethe 6; Tel 0471/977-243, Fax 0471/326-966; 11:30am-2:30pm/7-9:30pm, 11:30am-2:30pm/7-11pm Thu-Sat, bar open till 1am Mon-Sat; Entrees 25,000L; V, MC, AE),* on the corner of Via Goethe and Via da Vinci, is surprisingly upscale. The decor is traditional Tyrolean—light wood and some rustic bric-a-brac—but with a hip, minimalist twist. Forst's product (5,400L for a pint) is as superior to mass-marketed American and Italian beers as this restaurant is to Mickey-D's. Dishes include smoked salmon for 16,000L, seven kinds of quiche (3,000-15,000L), and regional specialties like *Canederli di fegate in brodo* (soup with dumplings flavored with liver—better than they sound, wimp!). Italian dishes, like ravioli, are 12,000L.

crashing

Despite the new university, Bolzano's still basically a village, so there are only a few places to stay, but a few of the few are cheap—a rarity in pricey Alto Adige. The tourist office is too small to help with accommodations, so you're on your own (lucky you've got us, huh?).

▶▶CHEAP

Guest rooms at **Albergo Gatto Nero** *(Via St. Magdalena 2; Tel 0471/975-417, Fax 0471/325-028; 80,000L doubles, No private baths; Closed Dec 22-Jan 16; V, MC)* are above the local-est of Bolzano's local bars, also called Gatto Nero, which doubles as the hotel's reception area. Expect to see lots of old men smoking and playing cards, as well as some families. The staff look like St. Pauli girls, and you get the feeling that the customers' lederhosen are in the wash, or they'd be wearing them too. The slightly noisy downstairs might bug you if you're a very-early-to-bed type, but the Palladium it ain't. The rooms all have an outside entrance, with a key for the guests, so you don't have to go through the initial stare-fest in the bar if you don't want to. Every room has two single beds and a sink, but not much more. To get there, walk to the eastern end of Via Brenner, bear to the left, and walk uphill toward the cable car entrance.

Albergo Croce Bianca *(Piazza del Grano 3; Tel 0471/977-552, Fax 0471/972-273; 52,000L singles without bath, 88,000L with bath, 104,000L doubles with bath; 132,000L triples with bath; No credit cards)*, on the east side of Piazza Grano, is family-run, but the family seems to pay a little more attention to the unremarkable restaurant by the same name downstairs. The place is perfectly comfortable; it's just that the furniture, beds, and decorations have gotten a little old, especially compared to most places in Bolzano. But that's why it's so cheap. Watch your head coming up the stairs.

▶▶DO-ABLE

Hotel Statzione *(Via Renon 23; Tel 0471/973-291, Fax 0471/974-910; Reception 8-midnight, ring bell after hours; 50,000L singles without bath, 60,000L with bath, 120,000L doubles with private bath, breakfast 5,000L; V, MC)* is, as advertised, near the station. The 20 rooms, spread out over three walk-up floors, are clean and spartan, with TVs and coffee bars. It's not a bad place, but anywhere else in Italy it would be cheaper, especially considering the noise from the trains pulling into the station across the street.

Right down the block is **Hotel Regina** *(Via Renon 1; Tel 0471/972-195, Fax 0471/978-944; 90,000-110,000L singles, 130,000-150,000L doubles with private bath; reginahotel.regina@pns.it, www.gattei.it; V, MC, AE, DC)*, which looks like an American Holiday Inn, minus the cheesy art. The carpeted rooms are big by Italian standards; all have TVs and phones, and bathrooms are spacious and new, though who can tell why anyone would choose that ugly brown tile. Nonsmoking rooms are also available, a rarity in nicotine-happy Italy.

The older couple that runs the homey, comfortable **Hotel Feichter** *(Via Grappoli 15; Tel 0471/978-768, Fax 0471/974-803; 90,000L singles, 140,000L doubles; 170,000L triples, all with private bath, breakfast included; No credit cards),* just south of Piazza Municipo, are justly proud of their sweet, clean little place. Most rooms are accessible through a mezzanine above the garden, which also offers a nice view of a small piazza. Each room has a phone and TV.

▶▶**SPLURGE**

If you're into oh so-trendy Scandinavian design, you'll catch your breath when you walk into **Hotel Figl** *(Piazza del Grano 9; Tel 0471/978-412; 130,000-140,000L singles, 150,000-180,000L doubles, 210,000-300,000L apartments, all with private bath; info@figl.net, www.figl.net; V, MC),* an ultra-modern fashion plate. Lots of the furniture is either ultra-suede or mustard-colored leather, which goes well with all the aluminum and frosted glass. The only furnishings having anything to do with the region are the rustic booths and chairs in the otherwise industrial-hip breakfast room. Rooms are as contemporary and stylish as public areas, with deep carpets, magnetic keys that turn on the lights, and big, fully-stocked bathrooms (hello, towel warmers!). Apartments sleep up to four people, and if you catch it in low season (not summer or pre-Christmas) and skip the 20,000L breakfast buffet, you and three friends may just be able to afford the place.

need to know

Currency Exchange Several **ATMs** and **banks** can be found along Piazza Walther. Try **Unicredito.**

Tourist Information The **tourist office** *(Piazza Walther 8; Tel 0471/307-000, Fax 0471/980-128; 8:30am-12:30pm/2:30-5pm Mon-Sat; info@bolzano-bozen.it)* answers questions and offers maps and flyers. The staff is too small to help with booking rooms.

Public Transportation Everything in town is walk-able, but if you feel the need to be carried, you can catch a ride at the **A.C.T. Bus station** *(Via Perathoner; Tel 800/846-047).* Tickets (1,700L) are available at the orange machines.

Health and Emergency Emergency: *118;* Police: *113.* The local hospital, **Ospedale Generale di Bolzano** *(Via Lorenz Boehler 5; Tel 0471/908-111),* is west of the town center.

Pharmacies Alla Madonna, [see *culture zoo,* above] on Via Portici, is both medieval landmark and working pharmacy. Pharmacies in town participate in a rotating schedule for 24-hour service. To see which one is open after hours, check the schedule on the door.

Telephone Phone cards, with either 5,000 or 10,000L worth of calling time, are available from any newsstand. **Public telephones** are available in Piazza Walther and Piazza Municipo.

Trains The main **train station** is **Bolzano Bozen** *(Piazza Stazione; Tel 1478/88-088).* Bolzano is on the main line from Verona (1 hour 35 minutes) to Innsbruck (1 hour 15 minutes).

Bus Lines out of the City **Buses** depart for Merano (one hour, 5,500L) four to five times daily from the **S.A.D station** *(Via Conciapelli 60; Tel 0471/450-111)*, near the train station.

Bike Rental You can get a set of wheels at **Campo Sportivo** [see *city sports,* above], south of the bridge on the last street on the west before the river. The bikes themselves are on a rack outside the building.

Laundry Suds your duds at **Lava e Asciuga** *(Via Rosmini 81; No phone; 7:30am-10:30pm daily; 5,000L wash, 5,000L dry; No credit cards)*.

Postal Send those clever ice-age mummy postcards at the **main post office** *(Via Poste 1; No phone; 8:05am-6:30pm Mon-Fri, 8:05am-1pm Sat)*, across from the Duomo.

Internet See *wired,* above.

everywhere else

merano

Remember *The Sound of Music*, that famous World-War-II-meets-the-Partridge-Family musical? Well, this could be it, folks. In Merano, edelweiss grows all over the meadows, with craggy white-granite Alpine peaks in the background. And not only does the place look like a movie set, but some of the townspeople could definitely make a few bucks as extras: Old men walk around in lederhosen like they're rehearsing for *Heidi*. Yodel-ay-ee-hoo! (You're not going crazy. Merano actually used to be part of Austria, hence the whole Tyrolean motif.)

Don't worry, you're still in Italy and it's still the 21st century. Merano's just a harmless little time warp, which is precisely what makes it such a great place to visit: It's completely unspoiled. And the hills are alive with more than show tunes here. Bars and clubs stay open way late—those lederhosers can really put away the brew. This place is a party that won't quit, and in summer the main street buzzes with activity through the wee hours of the morning.

Merano is situated about 30km northwest of Bolzano, upstream on the **Adige river**—you'll know you're getting close when you see a sprawling carpet of green rolling down the valley, interrupted only by castles, church steeples, and bright-blue mountain streams. The landscape makes you want to jump right in—and you should. Merano attracts tons of outdoor enthusiasts, who come to soak up the views on mountain hikes, bike rides, and ski at the nearby **Merano 2000** resort [see *great outdoors,* below]. And when you're beat, you can relax in the **Terme di Merano** [see *modification,* below], the natural spa that made Merano famous.

Despite the northerly location, the temperature rarely falls below freezing here. Surrounding mountains temper the weather, which mainly consists of crisp air and lots of sunshine. Though just walking around the small town is invigorating enough for most tourists, you really should hike some of the beautiful paths that lead out of town into

merano bars clubs and culture zoo

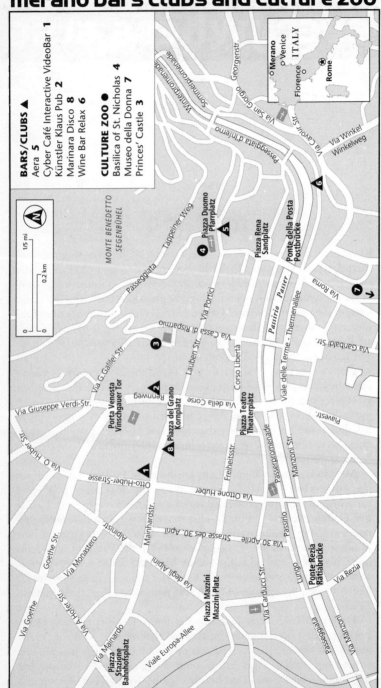

BARS/CLUBS ▲
Aera **5**
Cyber Café Interactive VideoBar **1**
Künstler Klaus Pub **2**
Marinara Disco **8**
Wine Bar Relax **6**

CULTURE ZOO ●
Basilica of St. Nicholas **4**
Museo della Donna **7**
Princes' Castle **3**

the hillsides. The most famous is the **Tappeiner Way** [see *great outdoors,* below], which takes you up to the tiny hilltop village of **Dorf Tyrol,** with its well-preserved medieval castle.

Just a little over 80 years ago, this was all Austria. In fact, the town of Merano, with a population of just 33,000, was the capital of Tyrol back in the 13th century. When the Counts of Tyrol moved to Innsbruck 200 years later, Merano remained a chic playground for Hapsburg hotshots, who built some castles and laid out mountain paths for their leisurely strolls. Tourists arrived in the 19th century, when some town doctors, who must've taken a course in marketing, started advertising the cool mountain air and thermal springs as the next fountain of youth.

By the turn of the century, Merano was one of Europe's most famous spa towns, catering to intellectual heavyweights like Freud and Kafka, who came to try the mysterious grape cure and let their minds wander where their feet led them. Both world wars had heavy consequences for Merano: The town was handed over to the Italians after World War I, causing tension between local German- and Italian-speakers that still lingers today.

As you might have guessed, German is more prevalent than Italian here, but more young people speak English here than in the rest of Italy. Tourism has been an integral part of Merano's economy for what seems like forever, so the friendly locals welcome visitors with open arms. Young or old, Italian or German, sporty or artsy, they're all here—diversity is definitely one of the town's strong suits.

neighborhoods

The train station on **Piazza Stazione** is just a five-minute walk northwest from the center of town. To get into the middle of things, head down **Viale Europe Allee** and through **Piazza Mazzini.** From this piazza, continue straight down **Via Freiheit** to **Piazza Teatro,** a major intersection. **Via Renweg,** to the north, is full of restaurants and bars; it runs in to **Piazza del Grano,** which seems to be the stomping ground of local hipsters. **Via Mainardo,** leading west out of Piazza Mazzini, also buzzes with crowds day and night.

Merano's main drag, **Corso Libertà,** runs due east from Piazzo Teatro. Sprinkled with cafes, restaurants, and bars, this pedestrian street passes the town hall and tourist office, ending up at the modern **Piazza Rena.** Heading south from Piazza Teatro, you'll run into the **Passirio** river and most popular bridge in town, **Ponte Poste,** dating back to 1903, which was recently restored to its original grandeur. Another bridge, a few blocks to the east, leads south down **Via Piave** to Merano's famous spa (on the left), and the **Merano Arena** sports complex (on your right). Heading due north from the center, you'll reach **Via Portici,** the city's most charming street. Covered porticos lining this street provide relief from the intense summer sun—they were laid out in the 13th century at the request of Mainhard II, Count of Tyrol, and today are home to some of the city's best shopping. Breathe deep and enjoy the smokey smell a of curing *speck,* the regional cured ham (think prosciutto, but drier and smokier). Vegetarians, stay away. Here you'll also come across the **Basilica of St Nicolaus,** with its imposing bell tower [see *culture zoo,* below]. Follow Via Portici to the end, and you're back to Piazza del Grano.

café scene

Groovy, baby, yeeeah! You may feel like you've wandered back into the shagalicious sixties at **Café Imperial** *(Corso Libertà 110; Tel 0473/237-172; 8am-8pm Mon-Sat, till midnight in the summer; Coffees 2,000L, teas and tisanes 2,000-5,000L, cocktails 5,000-8,000L; No credit cards),* but it's not retro, it's for real. It's looked like this since it was renovated—in 1963. Original fiberglass swivel chairs with pink-velvet seat cushions slink around matching pedestal tables. The back room is similarly covered in pink and red, from shag carpeting to velvet walls. Even the ceiling is a geometric-paneled work of art, and the menu's font is like something out of *Wallpaper* magazine. The waitresses are all holdovers from the swingin' era as well, and they tend to be a little grumpy about it. Though this looks like it should be a bar, it's really an old-fashioned *pasticeria* (pastry shop)(though you can get a drink here). The menu goes on for pages: Homemade cakes and muffins are to die for, and teas, coffee drinks and hot chocolates are the real deal. It's hands down the most popular hangout on Merano's main drag.

bar, club, and live music scene

For a town this small, Merano has a serious nightlife. Revelers walk Corso Liberta till the wee hours of the morn, disappearing again and again into dark, cavernous haunts that thump with live music. You'll find a few great

wired

If you're looking for atmosphere while you e-mail, check out the shiny, happy **Cyber Café Interactive VideoBar** *(Via Mainardo 116; Tel 0473/221-644; 8am-8pm daily; 10,000L per hour, 5,000L beer pint; No credit cards),* between Piazza del Grano and Via degli Alpini; a great place to get online, drink a beer, and meet some other cyberians. **Tangram** *(Via Portici 204; Tel 0473/210-430; 8am-noon/3-7pm Mon-Fri; www.tangram.it; 5,000L per hour; No credit cards)* offers the next best solution for the wayward web traveler. With 12 new computers hooked up to an ISDN line, this little computer-learning shop is doing the community a good deed.

Check out ***www.emmeti.it/Welcome/Trentino/AltoAdige/ Merano/index.uk.html*** before you travel for the latest Merano info.

places to dance, from the styling Aera to the down-to-earth disco Marinara. Pick up a copy of the cool fold-out publication *MeMO* at the **tourist office** [see *need to know,* below], or stop by their editorial offices *(Corso Libertà 45; Tel 0471/977-100; 9-12:30pm/2:30-6:30pm Mon-Fri, 9:30-12:30pm Sat),* for a listing of the month's coolest events.

Just across Ponte delle Poste, on the southern side of the river, **Wine Bar Relax** *(Via Cavour 31; Tel 0473/236-735; 7:30pm-1:30am daily; No cover; V, MC)* puts on all the airs of a latest-greatest, but it's really an old standby, ranking as one of the world's largest South Tyrolean cellars for the past 15 years. Beautiful people sip wine from oversized glasses around the curvaceous bar, while sophisticates populate the mezzanine, chewing on olives, cheese, and other snacks from the bar menu. Try a spicy Gewurtztraminer, or a Reisling dessert wine (3,000-10,000L by the glass). And if you get hungry, all you have to do is return downstairs to catch some of Merano's best pizza [see *eats,* below]. Come early—by 10pm, this place is packed solid, and the roar of conversation overpowers soothing jazz and blues music.

Discopub? Mexican restaurant? Sports bar? It's hard to put your finger on **Pub 1** *(Via Roma 96; Tel 0473/210-505; 8pm-1:30am daily; No cover; No credit cards),* located down Via Piave, a ten-minute walk south from Ponte Teatro. But one thing's for sure: It's hopping. Adobe is the operative word here, driving the Mexican theme home, and the music is reminiscent of college bars everywhere—loud, commercial, and dance-inducing. The upstairs isn't anything spectacular, but most of the grooving goes on in the downstairs bar, with its leather banquettes and huge chandelier. Arrive around midnight to join the college crowd as they munch on nachos and sip tropical cocktails, pints of beer, and Corona in bottles. Avoid the laminated menu's offerings—they're strictly Old El Paso.

Unless lots of smoke, loud music, and rowdy behavior in cramped quarters get on your nerves, **Künstler Klaus Pub** *(Via d. Corso Rennweg 2/b; Tel 0473/212-522; 7pm-2am Mon-Sat; No cover; No credit cards)* is a great time. This tiny subterranean space, on Corso Rennweg across from Piazza del Grano, is covered from top to bottom in years' worth of graffiti, and old beams holding up sagging walls gives it a real bunker feel. The girls behind the bar pour beers (6,000L) and choose the music, which is usually Sex Pistols, The Smiths, etc. Everyone here is too filled with teen angst to dance, but there's definitely some subtle head-banging going on. It's packed the minute the doors open in the early evening, so get there by 8pm to snag a table.

All right, so there aren't many clubs in Merano, but when you've got **Aera** *(Pfarrplatz 232; Tel 0473/232-825; 9:30pm-3am Thu-Sat, 9:30pm-2am Wed summer only; No cover; No credit cards),* what else do you need? This is one of the coolest clubs you'll ever dance the night away in, and you'll know it by the line of folks waiting to get in—it wraps all the way around to nearby Piazza Duomo. Dating back to 1563, this sprawling, many-roomed wine cellar recently underwent a renovation accentuating all its old stone arches and walls, narrow paths, and chilly, wide open spaces. Modern touches include three gorgeous wood bars, lots of comfy nooks for conversation, and best of all, elevated loft spaces like tree houses. Climb up with your pals, sip your drinks (5,000L beers, 10,000L cocktails), and observe the gyrating crowds below. Thursdays bring live music—even the usual Italian cover bands draw impressive crowds. On Friday nights, the DJs spin pop; on Saturdays, it's rock and reggae. Things start relatively early—get here by 11pm to find a spot.

Okay, so it's not the best-looking club you've ever seen: The small but adequate dance floor suffers from light-show overload, and that NYC skyline mural is totally cheesy. But **Marinara Disco** *(Mainardo 9; Tel 0473/230-671; 10pm-3am Mon-Sat; 12,000L cover includes first drink; No credit cards),* not far from Piazza del Grano, is laid-back, loose, and totally fun. The scene here isn't cruise-y at all—everyone's in jeans, tank tops, and tees, dancing like crazy to commercial dance hits, with a lot of disco and early-eighties stuff thrown into the mix. Come after midnight to blow off some steam.

ARTS SCENE

With Bolzano nearby, Merano's art community suffers from shy-little-sister syndrome. You won't find many galleries or cutting-edge theaters, but what there is is seriously worth checking out.

▶▶VISUAL ARTS

Listen to the heartbeat of Merano's art world at **ArtFORUM Gallery** *(Piazza Duomo 27/a; Tel 0473/212-643; 9:30am-12:30pm/3:30-6:30pm Mon-Fri, 9:30am-12:30pm Sat; Free admission; No credit cards).* This foundation exhibits visual arts, literature, music, and design from regional and international artists. By the time you read this, the space across from the Duomo will have given way to "The Art House," a huge new building on Via Portici.

The owner of **Galleria Art Dependent** *(Via Portici 108; No phone; Hours vary; Free admission)* lends out this beautiful old space to aspiring young artists to show their work. The artists schmooze with visitors over refreshments in the main room, while two rooms upstairs are devoted to the artwork itself. Hours are irregular, and there's no phone, so drop by or stop in at the tourist office [see *need to know,* below] to find out what's on exhibit.

Close to the Duomo, **Ateigen Gallery Masten** *(Via Portici 169; Tel 0473/236-189; 8:30am-12:30pm/3-7pm Mon-Fri, 8:30am-12:30pm Sat; Free admission; No credit cards)* is a small, minimalist space displaying modern works from international artists. Exhibits typically include paintings and sculptures—-nothing too abstract.

▶▶PERFORMING ARTS

Stadtetheater *(Corso Libertà 27; Tel 0473/211-623, Fax 0473/275-140; 9am-12:30pm/3:30-showtime, performances 8:30pm; Prices vary depending on show and seat; No credit cards)* is an avant-garde German theater that performs plays...in German. The subterranean theater space, close to the tourist office on the main drag, offers a very cool spectacle, with a sunken stage surrounded by elevated seats.

The turn-of-the-century **Puccini Theatre** *(Piazza Teatro 2; Tel 0473/233-422; Hours vary; Prices vary depending on show and seat; V, MC, AE)* is a beautiful example of Austrian Art Nouveau architecture (or "Liberta," as it's called here). Designed in 1900 by Martin Düfler, it's still used today as one of the town's preeminent venues, with a mix of plays in Italian and German, some modern dance, classical music, and opera.

CULTURE ZOO

Few come to Merano for their shot of culture. Your best chance for mind-expansion is taking in the beautiful Art Nouveau buildings that line the streets. You can get into any of the little museums in town with the Museumcard Merano, which is only 12,000L for adults and 9,000L for students at either the **tourist office** [see *need to know,* below], or any participating venue.

Basillica of St. Nicholas *(Piazza Duomo, Tel 0473/230-174; 7:30am-9pm Mon-Fri, 7:30am-6:30pm Sat and Sun; Free admission):* This tribute to the patron saint of Merano was begun in 1320 and completed at the end of the 15th century. Its beautiful bell tower is one of the tallest in the region, at 83m. There's not much to see inside, besides some modern frescoes. This is a working church, and people come here more for worship than for photo-ops.

Museo della Donna *(Via Portici 68; Tel 0473/231-216; 9:20am-12:30pm/2:30-6:30pm Mon-Fri, 9:30am-1pm Sat; Admission 7,000L; No credit cards):* Merano is the unlikely site of a museum dedicated to the contributions of women—here it is, hear it roar. This small exhibit examines the roles of Merano women through local crafts, costumes, and cultural contributions. It's worth a stroll-through.

Princes' Castle *(Via Galilei; Tel 0473/230-102; 10am-5pm Tue-Sat, 10am-1pm Sun; Admission 4,000L; No credit cards):* The Archiduke Sigmund once made his home in this castle, one of the best-preserved in the region and the pride of Merano. Now visitors pile inside to see its collection of antique furniture, musical instruments, and weapons. It's located just behind the town hall.

MODIFICATION

Don't even think about leaving Merano without checking yourself into **Terme di Merano** *(Via Piave; Tel 0473/237-724; Bus 11 or 12 to Terme; 7am-8pm Mon-Sat; V, MC),* the spa that put Merano on the map. It's just south of town, a five-minute walk down Via Piave. The outdoor thermal pools are a slice of heaven. Try a 25-minute therapeutic massage (50,000L), a less intense hydromassage (25,000L), or a mud bath *(fango con doccia,* 43,000L*),* or just splash around in the thermal swimming pools (15,000L) and saunas (24,000L). Or go for the works with the *Pacchetto Relax* package: one trip to the sauna, a 25-minute massage, a dip in the pool, and a visit to the solarium, all for 85,000L. Week-long curative and beautifying packages are also available, from 100,000L to 760,000L.

CITY SPORTS

International competitions are held here, but you don't have to be a bronze medallist to visit the Olympic stadium at **Merano Arena** *(Via delle Palade 74; Tel 0473/236-982; 9-11am/2:30-4:30pm/9-11pm Tue, 9-11am/2:30-4:30pm/9-10pm Wed, Fri, 9-11am/2:30-4:30pm Thu, Sat, 10am-noon/2:30-4:30pm Sun; No credit cards)*—just cross the Ponte Teatro and follow Via Piave for about 10 minutes. You'll pass the horse track at Via Pertrarca; about five minutes later, hang a right on Via delle Palade. Facilities include an indoor ice-skating rink (5,500L), where you can rent skates and practice your triple Lutz, and an Olympic-size covered swimming pool (8,000L), where you can swim laps or dive. Right behind the pool and the rink is the big attraction—**RockArena** *(Merano Arena; 4-10pm Tue, Thu, 6-10pm Wed, Fri, 2-7pm Sat, 4-6pm Sun, Oct-Easter; 6-10pm Mon-Thur, 2-7pm Sat, closed Sun, Easter-May 30; 8,000L Adults, 6,000L under 18; No credit cards),* one of the best climbing walls in Italy. There's a 32-foot tower, not to mention various boulders, nooks, crannies, and challenging slants for you to scramble over, under, and around. Ropes, shoes, and all other necessary equipment are available for rental, and instructors are always on hand to help. For more information, visit RockArena's offices in town *(Via Galilei 45; Tel 0773/234-619; 9am-11:45am Mon-Fri).*

GREAT OUTDOORS

▶▶ON FOOT

For the past 150 years, the great and nearly great have come to soak up Merano's sunshine and breathe its cool mountain air. Follow in their footsteps on the *passeggio d'estate* (summer promenade), on the southern bank of the river Passirio. The promenade begins right over the Ponte Poste, at the statue of Empress Sissi, an Austrian socialite who spent many a day here. This walk is shaded some of the way, and it passes gorgeous rose beds and trees. On the northern side of the river is the *passeggio d'inverno* (winter promenade), known for its cool breezes, bright sun, and gorgeous mountain views.

If you think strolls along the river are for sissies, don't worry—there's serious hiking around here, too. The **tourist information office** [see *need to know,* below] schedules day-hikes with expert guides, free of charge, July through September. They also print an English-language guide called "Mountain Walks on the Sunny Side of the Alps," which includes more than 60 diverse hikes for every type—nature lovers, thrill-seekers, and even birdwatchers. Another resource is the **Italian Mountaineering Club, CAI** *(Corso Libertà 188; Tel 0473/448-944; Hours vary).* Be warned: The office holds extremely irregular hours.

One of the best walks is also a historic one—up the Tappeiner Way from Merano to Dorf Tirol, then down the mountain, back to your starting place. This circular walk shows off the best of the region's scenery, and passes some historic highlights, like St. Peter's Cathedral in the little village of Gratsch, and the famous home of the Counts of Tirol, Schloss Tirol (*Castello Tirolo,* in Italian). The Tappeiner Way was established by Dr. Franz Tappeiner (1816-1902). The city cares for its preservation and maintenance, thus it's in extremely good shape, and lined with trees and foliage collected from all over the world. The views on this easy three- to four-hour walk are stunning, and there are just a few steep inclines. (If you're feeling wimpy, you can do the walk in reverse and miss the steepest climb, between the castle and the town of Dorf Tirol, but it's a little anti-climactic that way.) The trail is never officially closed, but use your judgment—it can get tricky when there's snow, ice, or mud.

Start on Via Portici, looking on the sides of the road for signs to the *Tappeinerweg,* which begins just behind the Duomo. The path is well marked, and heads up and under the cable car that leads up the Tiroler road into Dorf Tirol. Continue straight and you'll pass a small castle, which is a private residence, to your right—keep following the path until it ends in the village of Gratsch. You'll see a signpost for the steep "pilgrim's path," which leads up to **St. Peters Cathedral.** This church dates back to the 11th century, and houses some impressive frescoes from the period; admission is free.

From the church, it's just a short walk up Via Vecchia Roman to **Schloss Tirol** *(Tel 0473/220-221, Fax 0473/221-132; 9:30am-noon/2-5pm Tue-Sun; Free admission).* Built in the 12th century, this castle was the ancestral home of the Counts of Tirol. It also lent the region its name—that's right, this is where it all began. It's been restored many times over the centuries, and the hodge-podge of towers and keeps, jutting out from the mountain, is truly magnificent. Inside, the castle houses a small archaeological museum, as well as some historical documents charting this independent province's history.

From here, it's a short walk on an easy trail known as the Falkner promenade to **Dorf Tirol.** At 1,600 feet, you can't help but feel like king or queen of the world. Dorf Tirol is a quaint little town of no more than 2,000 inhabitants, all of whom seem happy to play the part of adorable Alpine townsfolk. It doesn't have many reliable food options, and the hours are so variable that you shouldn't plan your day around getting a meal here—bring a snack. There's one main street, which begins at the town's highest point near the church and the cemetery, called the **Tiroler Path.** It's served by buses heading back to Merano every 20 minutes, if you decide to poop out here. Tickets are 3,300L and can be bought on the bus, which leaves from the traffic circle in the center of the village. Otherwise, you can take the path down yourself, and get back on the Tappeiner Way at the bottom of the Tiroler Path. The path will take you right back to your starting point, at the Duomo.

▶▶SKIING

If you want to swoosh down the slopes, and can't wait till you get to Cortina, **Merano 2000** *(23,000L half-day; 39,000L full day of skiing; No credit cards)* is your answer. From December to the end of March, the 36km *pistes* at this tiny resort just above town are packed with skiers and snowboarders.

Cross-country tracks, toboggan runs, and equipment rental are available as well. All information and arrangements should be made through the **tourist information office** [see *need to know,* below]. The resort is accessible by the cable car just east of town, **Funivia di Ivigna/Ifinger Seilbahn** *(Via Val di Nova 37; Tel 0473/234-821; Bus 1 to lift; 9am-noon/1:15-5pm daily; 14,000L single ticket; No credit cards).* From the center of town, cross the Ponte delle Poste, hang a left on Via Cavour, and follow it to Piazza Fontana Brunnen. From there, continue straight through on Via del Ruscello, which merges with Via Scena Schenna. This road curves to the left at almost 45 degrees; the cable car will be just a few minutes ahead on your right.

EATS

Though Merano is ethnically more Italian than the smaller villages in the mountains nearby, you'll find that when it comes to dinner, it's Austrian all the way. Expect heavily smoked sausages, dumplings, and other belly-bombs. But don't get the wrong idea; food here is amazing, and you should take every opportunity to sit down and enjoy a meal. The predominant flavors are so *not* Italian: Herbs and seasonings of choice include cinnamon, cloves, caraway, anise, and dill, as well as poppy seeds and horseradish. Try *canederli,* heavy bread and flour dumplings seasoned with anything from liver to speck. Ah, speck—the cured and smoked aged ham is at it's best here. Mountain *trota* (trout), served roasted or boiled, is on many traditional menus, as is *carre di miale affumcato,* or smoked pork loin. There's goulash, often made with *cervo* (venison) or *capriolo* (baby goat—awwww), and *gröstl,* a potato-and-meat hash that hits the spot after a night on the town.

only here

Known for their mysterious healing powers, the grapes of Merano are meant to cure everything from gastrointestinal problems to weakness caused by disease—hey, it's worth a shot. People from all over come to drink grape juice during harvest-time (September-November), but doctors recommend eating the grapes one at a time, and chewing on the skin to extract all of its vitamins. The Grape Cure has been a popular Merano tradition for the last 120 years—Dr. Freud himself came here to try it out. Every year, locals celebrate the harvest in mid-September. Brass bands play in the streets, and wine is sold by the glass on every corner. Exact dates change each year, but the tourist office [see *need to know,* below] can give you all the details.

▶▶CHEAP

The region's cheapest eats are at **Cappricci** *(Corso Libertà 68; Tel 0473/233-882; 10am-midnight daily, later in the summer; 2,000-4,500L; No credit cards)*, a bright snack shop, right on the main drag, where local kids down the ever-popular currywurst (4,500L) by twos and threes. Pizza by the slice (2,000L) may be your only bet in the later hours—this is the only place in town that stays open after midnight.

Just downstairs from the similarly relaxed wine bar, **Relax Pizzeria** *(Via Cavour 31; Tel 0473/236-735; Noon-3pm/5:30-midnight; Pizzas 9,000-14,000L; No credit cards)* is a world away in look and feel. A cheery mural on the back wall sets a festive scene, but busy waiters funneling in and out of the open kitchen make it clear that it's all about the oversized pies, dripping with mozzarella and tangy sauce. Hordes of families pile into the massive wooden booths to devour classic pizzas like *quatro stagione* (artichokes, mushrooms, ham, and olives). While the upstairs wine bar specializes in bottles, you can order carafes down here.

Don't let the waitresses in Tyrolean garb turn you off; **Birra Först** *(Corso Libertà 90; Tel 0473/260-111; 10am-11pm Fri-Wed; Entrees 11,000-20,000L; V, MC, AE)* is the most popular spot in town for good reason: They not only serve cheap, terrific traditional food, but also the best beer in Merano (anywhere from 2,600-13,500L a pint). Try the Först Sixtus, or if you think you can hold your liquor, the super-strong Dopplebock. Ask for the menu in English, if you must, but you won't go wrong ordering the longest name on the list: *Tyroler speckknodelsuppe/canederli in brodo* (bread dumplings with speck and herbs, in a light broth). Choose between two huge modern rooms, plus the prettiest beer garden you've ever seen.

▶▶DO-ABLE

La Veneta Trattoria *(Via Monestero 2; Tel 0473/449-310, Fax 0473/220-257; Noon-3pm/6:30-10:30pm Mon-Sat; info@laveneta.it, www.laveneta.it; Entrees 20,000-30,000L; No credit cards)*, located right under the budget hotel of the same name [see *crashing*, below], isn't the tourist trap you might expect. This is the kind of restaurant where local hockey teams have their pre-game dinners, extended families get together for leisurely Saturday dinners out in the garden, and folks stop in for a *limoncello* on their way home. Rustic and hearty Italian specialties change on a weekly basis: First courses could be *tortellini in brodo* (tortellini soup), tagliatelle with wild mushrooms, or a big salad; entrees are often hearty meat dishes like roast chicken or pork. The wine-by-the-jug is local, cheap, and great.

To find out what Tyrolean food is all about, get a table at **Haisrainer** *(Lauben Portici 100; Tel 0473/237-944; 8:30am-2:30pm/5-11pm Mon-Sat; Entrees 15,000-30,000L; V, MC)*. Make absolutely sure, though, that you're in the right place. This old standby is located down an unmarked alley off Lauben Portici, and there's another "typical" restaurant nearby that opens up onto the street. Don't be fooled. When you spot number 100, go down the alley, past an aquarium filled with trout (dinner?), and

merano eats and crashing

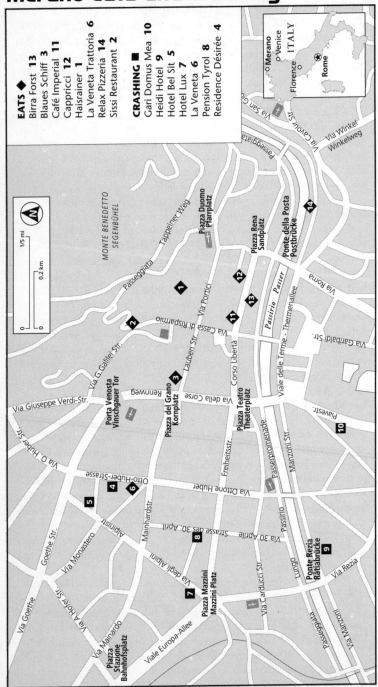

EATS ◆
Birra Forst **13**
Blaues Schiff **3**
Café Imperial **11**
Cappricci **12**
Haisrainer **1**
La Veneta Trattoria **6**
Relax Pizzeria **14**
Sissi Restaurant **2**

CRASHING ■
Gari Domus Mea **10**
Heidi Hotel **9**
Hotel Bel Sit **5**
Hotel Lux **7**
La Veneta **6**
Pension Tyrol **8**
Residence Désirée **4**

enter the door on your right with wrought-iron windowframes. An enormous, carved chandelier hovers over the small, square dining room. The wood detail on the walls is ornate, and the medieval-looking chairs are gorgeous, if a little uncomfortable. Elderly waiters offer a wealth of information about local cuisine—and they speak English, so ask questions. Start with a smoked *wurtzel* (11,000L), served with sauerkraut and mustard, but leave room for canederli, and the main courses, which span the spectrum from roasted pork to pan-fried trout.

▶▶**SPLURGE**

Chef Andrea Fenoglio recruits the brightest culinary talents from the States to work in his kitchen at **Sissi Restaurant** *(Via Galilei 44; Tel 0473/231-062; Noon-2:30pm/7:30-10pm daily; Lunch 16,000-22,000L, entrees 32,000-38,000L, four-course dinner, 75,000-90,000L, dessert included; V, MC),* easily the nicest place in town. The large downstairs dining room is elegant, yet comfortable; you won't feel totally overwhelmed. The menu changes seasonally—you might find cured salmon with fennel, chickpea cream with shrimp and olive oil, foie gras *involitini* with grapes, or baby lamb with a spicy pear sauce.

crashing

Merano has no shortage of hotels, but budget accommodations get booked up really fast all year long, and the tourist office can't book rooms for you. *Call Ahead.* Be aware that rooms are often quoted at a per-person rate—make sure you know the total cost before you commit.

▶▶**CHEAP**

Your best bet for budget accommodation is the homey **La Veneta** *(Via Monestero 2; Tel 0473/449-310, Fax 0473/220-257; 50,000-90,000L per person, private baths; info@laveneta.it, www.laveneta.it; No credit cards).* Each of the cheerful 10 rooms can accommodate up to five people, and has a private bath, a TV, creature comforts like downy comforters. One of the best things about staying here is that you're just upstairs from the hopping restaurant of the same name [see *eats,* above]. If you're a light sleeper, don't worry—the sound doesn't travel.

▶▶**DO-ABLE**

You'll feel right at home at **Residence Désirée** *(Via Otto Huber Strasse 17; Tel 0473/449-564, Fax 0473/230-644; 85,000L-100,000L for a two-person apartment, 115,000-130,000L for 2-3 people, 150,000-175,000L for 3-5 people, all with private baths; www.desireemeran.com/english/apparte ment.htm; V, MC).* This turn-of-the-century building has been completely renovated into a hotel with apartment suites, and really has it all: a pool, a workout room, and even a laundry room at your disposal. Apartments range from a studio with a fold-out couch and a kitchenette hidden in an armoire to a two-bedroom with a dining nook. Everything's newish—nice, solid furniture, satellite TVs, tile baths, and even hairdryers.

Just a short walk southeast from the train station, three-star **Hotel Bel Sit** *(Via Penddelstrasse 2; Tel 0473/446-484; 55,000-89,000L doubles, private baths, breakfast included; No credit cards)* is an older, family-run villa that's been completely renovated. The spacious rooms, elevator, TV room, and sixties-looking dining room are all homey and welcoming. A lovely garden and great views justify the rates.

Don't let the elevator-ride to the second floor of this professional office building make you think that **Gari Domus Mea** *(Via Piave 8, 2nd floor; Tel 0473/23-677; 48,000-52,000L per person, private baths, breakfast included; No credit cards)* will be sterile—Senora Lee runs this very charming, 12-room guesthouse with a careful, personal touch. It's only a 10-minute walk across the Passe river to the main part of town.

Just two blocks east of the train station, on a quiet side street, is **Pension Tyrol** *(Via Aprile 30, No. 8; Tel 0473/449-719; 40,000L per person, private baths; No credit cards)*, run by a sweet, little old signora...who rules with an iron fist. Still, it's worth staying in any of this alpine-style hotel's eight rooms. There's a comfortable sitting and dining room downstairs, and a big shared garden space. And after awhile, she does warm up...kinda.

Located down a long, unlit driveway, **Heidi Hotel** *(Via Ugo Foscoli 50; Tel 0473/449-594, Fax 0473/449-594; 48,000-60,000L per person with breakfast, private baths; No credit cards)* isn't the best choice for women traveling alone. But this cheery, three-story hotel is central and cheap, with all the basic amenities. The cozy downstairs sitting room/bar and backyard garden are always crowded with fellow travelers. It's located a few blocks south of the train station, and over the river, near the tracks.

Some basic rooms are for rent above **Café Imperial** *(Corso Libertà 110; Tel 0473/237-172, Fax 0473/237-172; 50,000-60,000L per person, private baths; No credit cards)*—it's your typical *zimmer* (room for rent) experience—small, friendly, and high on the comfy factor. A simple room with nothing more than a telephone is yours, right in the heart of Merano, above one of its most popular hangouts [see *cafe scene,* above]. Not such a bad deal, is it?

Hotel Lux *(Piazza Stazione; Tel 0473/447-451; Open all year; 70,000L singles, 140,000L doubles with breakfast, private baths; No credit cards)* has a lot of personality. Run by a friendly German-Italian man who's more than happy to tell you how he would spend *his* vacation in Merano, this is a great place to pick up local tips. Some rooms have balconies with views of the snow-capped mountains, and all of them have a small fridge, a TV, and a big bathroom. The decor is seventies all the way—real seventies, not hip-retro. You'll run into it across the street from the train station.

need to know

Currency Exchange There's no bancomat or place to change money at the train station, but **Corso Liberta,** a five-minute walk away, is packed with **banks,** and the entire town is spotted with **ATMs.**

Tourist Information Right on the main drag, the **Merano Tourist Authority Office** *(Corso Libertà 35; Tel 0473/235-223, Fax 0473/235-524; 9am-12:30pm/2:30-6:30pm Mon-Fri, 9:30am-12:30pm/2:30-6pm Sat, 10am-12:30pm Sun; winter, 9:30am-12:30pm Sat, closed*

Sun; www.meranoinfo.it) gives out more information than you can shake a stick at—ask for hiking maps, and it will provide. It can also arrange a trip to the local Merano 2000 ski resort [see *great outdoors,* above], and even arrange for experienced hiking guides free of charge, July-September. The one thing it *can't* do is book rooms for you, though the staff will happily hand you a list of all accommodations, from four-star hotels to humble zimmers.

Public Transportation Most of Merano is walk-able, so there's no transportation to the outskirts of town. A **cable car** connects the city with the Merano 2000 ski resort [see *great outdoors,* above]. For **24-hour RadioTaxi,** call 0473/212013.

Health and Emergency Emergency: *113;* Alpine Rescue: *0473/211-111;* Police: *(22/a Via Petrarca, Tel 0473/447-445).* The **general hospital** *(F. Tappeiner 5, Via Rossini; Tel 0473/263-333)* is a two-minute walk northeast from the train station.

Pharmacies Druso farmacia *(Via delle Corse 58; Tel 0473/236-357; 8:30am-1:30pm/3:30-6pm daily; No credit cards)* is south of the river, off Via Pave.

Telephone Phone cards are available from the **Merano Tourist Authority Offices** [see above] and tobacconist's shops for 5,000L, 10,000L, and 15,000L. **Phone kiosks** are all over town, with central offices on Via Roma near the main post office

Trains The **train station** *(Piazza Stazione; Tel 0473/147-888-088)* is a 10-minute walk northwest of town. Trains leave on the hour for Bolzano, where you can make connections.

Bus Lines Out of the City The **ACT bus line** *(Tel 800/846-047 for schedules and ticket info)* operates out of Merano's train station, and connects to local and nearby town destinations. A Merano/Tyrolo bus leaves every 40 minutes, 7am-8:20pm daily; buses leave on the hour for Bolzano as well.

Bike Rental You can rent a bike for free at the **train station** from the end of May to the end of September. A small deposit is required. Call 0473/147-888-088 for information.

Laundry There's no Laundromat in Merano, although some of the **hotels** provide laundry service.

Postal The main **post office** *(Via Roma 2, Tel 0473/237-713; 8am-7pm Mon-Sat, open Sun mornings)* is just south of the Ponte della Posta bridge.

Internet See *wired,* above.

monte bondone

Whether you're a full-on shredder or just someone who loves to be out in nature, you're going to love Monte Bondone. This mountain looms large over the Trentino landscape, like a billboard for itself. In winter (October through April, with the first snow usually falling in November), it's heaven for downhill speed-skiing and snowboarding, cross-country treks, and even dog-sledding. When spring arrives in May and the ski runs close down, the slopes morph into green Alpine meadows—a hiker's paradise for cool walks and sweeping views. Most travelers spend a whole day in Monte Bondone, but you can also easily lock up your bags at the train station in Trento (15km away) and spend just one afternoon tripping around the mountain. There are a few places to stay overnight [see *need to know*, below].

To clear up any confusion: This isn't just one lonely mountain. Monte Bondone actually refers to the *group* of mountains just west of Trento, and includes a park called **Riserva Naturale Integrale delle Tre Cime del Bondone.** You'll catch a great view of those three *cime,* or peaks— **Cornetto** (2188m), **Dosso d'Abrama** (2133m) and **Cima Verde** (2102m)—on your way up to **Monte Palon,** the main downhill ski run.

Monte Bondone is covered with little clusters of mountain chalets and lodges—to call them villages, or even hamlets, would be overstating the matter. The first one you'll pass is **Candriai;** then comes **Vaneze, Norge,** and finally, **Vason,** epicenter of activity here. The bus from Trento stops off at each of them.

Since 1934, the mountain has been home to Italy's most laid-back ski scene. You won't see any uppity ski-bunnies in fur coats, and snow-boarding, cross-country skiing, and even carving are welcomed—if not encouraged. A new snow-park with quarter- and half-pipes is getting a good rep in Italy's snowboarding community. Vason is Ski Central, with 15km of *pistes* (slopes), and 10 lifts across the mountain [see *need to know,* below, for ski pass costs]. The ski school here, **Scuola Italiana Monte Bondone Vason** *(Tel/Fax 0461/948-211; Hours and prices vary; V, MC, AE)* boasts 15 instructors, four of which teach nothing but snowboarding, so you can rip it up even if you've never been on a board before. There are a number of classes daily, and you can rent all the equipment you need. At the school you can get on or off any of the lifts—the most impressive is the harrowing ride up to Monte Palon, which gives you an amazing 360-degree panoramic view. Cross-country skiing in the **Viote Valley,** a high plateau between two of the peaks, goes on for 26 square km, through a natural preserve and snowed-over botanical gardens.

When snow disappears and flowers start to bud, check out Monte Bondone's botanical garden, **Giardino Botanico Alpini** *(Via Calepina 14; Tel 0461/270-311; 9am-noon/2-6pm daily June-Sept; 3,000L adults, 2,000L students; No credit cards).* It has more than 2,000 types of trees, plants, and flowers. It's a 10-minute walk east from Vason, along a well-marked route. The 1,000-meter hike through the gardens is signposted, and you'll learn more about foliage than you ever thought you wanted to know.

Other excursions can be arranged by contacting any of the clubs in the area. Trento's **Mountain Biking Club** *(Via Verdi 13; Tel 0461/236-420; Hours vary)* regularly schedules free trips up Monte Bondone. The

Collegio delle Guide Alpine della Provincia di Trento *(Via Manci 57, Trento; Tel/Fax 0461/981-207)* can't hook you up with a guide, but can provide some suggestions based on your interests. There are hikes for all skill (or energy) levels on Monte Bondone. But the Big Daddy group here is the **Consorzio Pro Loco Tre Cime Monte Bondone** *(Tel 0461/842-586, Fax 0461/843-098)*. Whether you're into rock-climbing or hang-gliding, they'll put you in touch with the right folks.

need to know

Tourist Information You can purchase your ski pass, and collect all the hiking maps you'll need, at the **Trento tourist office** *(Via Manci 2; Tel 046/983-880; 9am-7pm daily; www.apt.trento.it; Passes 36,000L adults, 29,000L under 18)*, or at the cable car office at the base of the mountain. One day's pass includes all 10 lifts. The tourist office also arranges hotel, ski instruction, and packages. Inquire about their holiday-offers publication. You can also find Monte Bondone on the web at *www.apt.trento.it/inglese/bondon.htm.*

Directions and Transportation If you just want to get up to the top and start skiing or hiking, you can take the **bus** from the Trento station [see **Trento,** above]. It follows the main road up, stopping at all the little towns, and drops you off in Vason. But the scenic route would be to start your ascent with the cable car, **Funivia Monte Bondone** *(Tel 0461/910-332 or 948-187; 1,500L one way, 4000L all day, free with ski pass)*, which leaves every 30 minutes from Ponte di San Lorenzo, just behind Trento's train station, and runs year-round. After a steep and beautiful incline, you'll be let off at **Saardagna** (571m), the first of Monte Bondone's little chalets. Wind your way up north, along the only road, and before long, you'll find yourself in **Candriai** (984m). From here, the views only get better. Continue crawling upward to Vason, where you can hop on a lift and hit the slopes.

Rental In winter, you can rent everything you need at Vason's **Monte Bondone Ski School** *(Tel 0461/948-211; Hours and rates vary; V, MC)*. If you want to get your gear in Trento, check with **Sportler** *(Via Mantova 12; Tel 0461/981-290; 9am-noon/3-7pm daily; Rates vary; No credit cards)*.

Eats Unfortunately, it's all bad hamburgers and hot dogs at the snack shops in the lodges. You're better off bringing some provisions and waiting until you're back in Trento for hot food, unless you get *really* hungry.

Crashing To be in the middle of all the action, base yourself in Vason. But the bus does run up and down the main road nonstop, so staying in Candriai is another option. There's nothing to do come nightfall in either of these little spots, and a slim-to-none chance for a good meal, so unless you're going for the total-immersion experience, staying in Trento is always your best bet. The tourist office in Trento keeps an up-to-date list of *rifugi* and hotels, and which seasons they're open.

Hotel Montana *(Localita Vason; Tel 0461/948-200, Fax 0461/948-177; 55,000-85,000L per person, private baths; www.hotelmontana.it/webcam.htm; V, MC)*, with its incredible views and cozy, mountain lodge-y decor, is a great pick for an overnight ski or hiking trip. Each of the rooms has a TV, comfy furniture, and a big bath you can soak in after a day on the slopes. You're just a few feet from the lifts here, and the owners are super-knowledgeable about all the trails and *pistes*.

Alla Posta *(Localita Candriai; Tel 0461/947-207, Fax 0461/947-207; 50,000L single, 85,000L double, prices go up 10,000L in high season, private baths available; No credit cards)* is a comfortable, small hotel located in Candriai. You can't beat it for the price—it has a pretty little winter terrace, a TV room, and a bar. The 19 rooms are basic as can be, but it's cheaper than anything you're going to find in Trento.

cortina d'ampezzo

Both James Bond *and* Hitchcock movies have been set here—what more do we have to say? Cortina D'Ampezzo, known simply as Cortina, is Italy's most fashionable ski resort, the playground of the rich and European. Its winter population definitely projects that 007 image, without the blood or the chase scenes. Lodging is expensive in winter (November-April), coats are mink, and there are plenty of professionally thin young trophy women on the arms of graying Viagrites. But the skiing in the surrounding Ampezzo Valley is spectacular, and there's a cheerful camaraderie in town that insulates you from the worst of the snobs—maybe it's because everyone is worn out from skiing all day. When cocktail time comes around, you and all the tourists, resort workers, and mink-clad ski bunnies bond like army buddies or winning teammates. In the summertime, prices go down, the chichi crowd is on the Riviera, and Cortina becomes a hiking destination. Any time, though, it's a great town to come and play, with sweeping views, fun bars, and a nightlife that teeters on till dawn.

The crowd that flocks here is mainly Italian and German, though more and more package tours are dumbing down the place every year. The only crowded times of the year are when Italians have their bank holidays (Christmas, and the last two weeks in February).

neighborhoods

The town has only a few streets. Four of them make a box around the center of town. Along the north edge and uphill from everything is **Via Marconi,** home to the bus station and the Faloria cable car. The shorter **Via Grohman** marks the west side of the box. Downhill and to the south is **Via Battisti,** which turns into **Via Mercato;** the tourist information office is here. **Via Franchetti** is on the east.

wired

You can get online at **Dolomiti Multimedia** *(Largo Poste 59; Tel 0436/868-090, Fax 0436/866-704; 8:30am-12:30pm/3-7:30pm; dailycortina@sunrise.it, www.sunrise.it; 15,000L per hour; No credit cards)*, in a strip mall on Largo Poste. They have seven PCs, with only dial-up connections for the time being. Printing is 200L a page, and you can use disks or word-processing. But cheaper, and much more relaxing, would be the one little computer in the side room of **Hotel Victoria's bar** [see *bar, club, and live music scene,* below]. Get info on Cortina on the net at *www.dolomiti. org/dengl/Cortina/index.html.*

Inside the town center are the pedestrian-only **Corso Italia,** and **Largo Poste;** most of the bars are along the latter, across from the post office. **Via Roma,** which is lined with hotels and restaurants, leaves town to the east, then curves south.

In winter the piazzas aren't too inviting (most people spend their days on the slopes anyway), but in summer they're great spots for lounging. Corso Italia is always popular for strolling in the late afternoon, when the sun has had a chance to warm things up.

bar, club, and live music scene

Three things most important to skiers are: a big downward slope, snow, and lots of bars. Cortina has a plethora of bars for what is basically a three-street town—unless otherwise noted, they're all around Largo Poste. Whether you choose the rarified atmosphere of a cocktail lounge, or the democratic rowdiness of the Clipper, remember this: No ski boots inside. In France the *aprés-ski* drinking begins as soon as the bottom of the run is in sight, but not so here—people go home, shower, change clothes, and have a bite to eat, then go out around 10pm.

There's really only one place to throw down in Cortina, and that's **Bar Cristallino (aka The Clipper)** *(Via Stazione 4; Tel 0436/867-999; 12:30pm-3am daily; No cover; No credit cards).* Everybody, from heiresses to dishwashers to ski instructors, comes to this sprawling, nautical-themed bar that's *so* cheesy, you can't help but throw away those pretenses and have fun. This is the kind of place where foreign women dance on tables while men serenade them, singing along with Italian pop hits. You can go in alone and leave with friends from every part of town. Six kinds of beer flow from the taps (6,000-8,000L), but most folks get sloppy with the strong cocktails (10,000L). Passable panini (8,000-11,000L) can also help take the edge off.

A mild alterna-crowd packs into the dank, subterranean **Orange** *(Largo Poste 9/a; No phone; 6pm-3am Mon-Sat; No cover; No credit cards).*

The decor is a weird mish-mash—a straight-faced attempt at Goth that falls somewhere between Liberace and Anne Rice. But there's Leffe and Hoegarden on tap (6,000-8000L), video poker, and the promise of Internet access to come. Unscheduled live bands sometimes play in the back room, free of charge.

Barato *(Largo Poste; No phone; 6pm-3am Tue-Sun; No cover; No credit cards)* is more downtown-NYC edgy than Alpine-chic. The wood-paneled nook of a bar has one wall entirely lined with Sambuca bottles, the repetition more a tally of the drink of choice than any attempt at style. If you buy the last drink out of a bottle, you get to sign the white label, and it goes on the shelf. Beer (6,000-8,000L) and wine (2,000-4,000L) are also available. The crowd hovers just under thirty, though they act much younger when they move downstairs to the game room for foosball, pinball, and retro arcade games.

More intellectual and off-season crowds converge at **Osteria "Pane Vino e San Daniele"** *(Corso Italia 137; Tel 0436/870-067; 11:30am-2pm/5:30pm-3am Tue-Sun; www.losteriacortina.com; No cover; V, MC)*, a funky little candlelit space hidden off an alley behind Corso Italia. Couples catch a glass of wine (4,000L) and a plate of cheese and San Daniele prosciutto (16,000L) before dinner, club kids sip *aperitivi* before hitting the dance floor, and far into the small hours, groups of friends linger in the back room, sharing bottles of wine and talking on and on. The spray-painted graffiti that covers the walls has been covered with art posters and farm tools, but the spirit is still fringe-y. The music is laid-back, but not drippy—to get a sense of the owner's inclinations, head to the bathrooms, where somewhat-modern heroes like Janis, Bowie, Cobain, and Morrison have been lovingly painted on the tile for your WC enjoyment.

A window seat at **Febar's** *(Corso Italia 17; Tel 0436/867-580; No cover; No credit cards)* is the best people-watching spot in town. Cozy leather banquettes are perfectly situated for staring out into the crowd of folks on their *passeggiatta* (evening stroll) down Corso Italia. The grape comes relatively cheap here, so stick around for a while and taste a few of the more than 20 wines by the glass (2,000-4,500L) offered over the pretty marble bar—cocktails cost a little more (9,000-16,000L). Although it's popular with local ski bums and upscale tourists alike, this place never loses its *tranquilo* vibe, even in the late hours, when folks move out back to the tiny *terrazzo* to watch the moon shining over the mountains.

Happy hour at the **Victoria Hotel** *(Corso Italia 1; Tel 0436/3246; 11am-1pm daily; No cover; V, MC, DC, AE)*, the plushest digs in town, is a little-known secret you'll be glad to know. Though most of the hotel clientele is cut from the mink-coat-and-platinum-dye-job mold, the bar and restaurant are open to all. Few public spaces are as welcoming as the enormous "great room," which offers everything half-price from 6 to 7pm each night. More sofas than you can count are arranged in little nooks under timber arches—head straight for the leather ones in front of the glowing fireplace. There's a pool table in the back corner, and little rooms off to the side for hushed games of poker or a quick log-on to check e-mail (12,000L per hour). And if that's not convincing enough, the Victoria has the largest bottled-beer selection in town.

Down a dark corridor in Cortina's only shopping center, on the hillside between the Clipper and the station, is the **Blu Room** (*Largo Poste in the Centro Nuovo; Tel 0436/4366; Midnight-4am Tue-Sun; info@blunotte.it, www.bluenotte.it; 20,000L cover on weekends, 15,000L drink minimum on weekdays; V, MC, AE, DC*). This decidedly stylish bar attracts a mixed crowd of Italian and foreign partyers who are happy to take the dress code seriously (no jeans, sneakers, or ski clothes—look as sharp as possible and you *might* get in). This place is as commercial as it gets, with candles perched on wrought-iron candelabras around the tiny dance floor, bottle-blonde ski bunnies bopping away to bubble-gum Italian dance hits, and more yards of velvet than should be allowed. But this *is* a ski resort for most of the year; no one's expecting much. Go and have fun.

If you're hankering for a bit of single-malt scotch, check out Cortina's only whisketeria, **Bar Arnika** (*Galleria Croce Bianca 102; No phone; 7:30pm-12:30am Mon-Sat, 8:30am-8pm Sun; No cover, No credit cards*). More than 250 bottles line the walls, all behind lock and key; shots are 5,000-12,000L. Cocktails and beers are also available for those who just came for the cozy atmosphere—the decor is strictly plaid. Hidden in a little shopping center just off Corso Italia, this place is packed all week long.

culture zoo

If you hadn't already guessed, no one really comes here for culture. Artists and writers come to Cortina once they've already made it, but all they leave behind are their bar bills.

Parochial Church of Saints Filippo and Giacomo (*Corsa Italia; No phone; 9am-12:30pm/2:30-6:30pm daily; Free admission*): This church, which towers over the middle of town, dates back to 1775. The bell tower was built between 1851 and 1858, and today is the town's main symbol. Its bells chime the same tune as Westminster Abbey's. The interior of the church is sweet, but it's really more useful as a landmark than anything else.

great outdoors

▶▶**WINTER**

Um, skiing, skiing, and more skiing? All of the slopes are easily reachable, either by bus or by one of the two **cable cars** [see *need to know*, below]. All you need now is to rent equipment and maybe arrange a lesson. Both of these things can be done on the slopes, but why not plan ahead? [We only list the local suppliers and outfitters here; for more info on the slopes themselves, see **Ampezzo Valley Skiing**, below].

What? You didn't stuff a ski jacket and pants into your backpack? The guys at **Snow Service** (*Via 29 Maggio 11; Tel/Fax 0436/866-635; 8:30am-7:30pm daily; snowservice@sunrise.it; skis 25,000L per day, boots 9,000L per day; V, MC, DC*) want to see you on the slopes; they'll do whatever they can to help you out. They're skiers and boarders themselves, and have tips and opinions on every facet of the sport. They aren't always right, but the prices are great and there's a keg down in the rental room.

No Limits *(Via del Stadio 18; Tel 0436/860-808; www.sunrise.it/cortina/link/nolimits.html, nolimits@sunrise.it; 8:30am-7:30pm daily; V, MC)* is a snowboard, sports equipment and clothing store. The kids who work here are pretty much just bored employees, not the aficionados you'll find at Snow Service, but they'll hook you up. But though the store part of No Limits is just mediocre, the activities they run out of their "adrenaline center" kick butt. **Taxi-Bob,** a guided bobsled run down the old Olympic bobsled track, and **Snow Rafting,** a rubber-raft ride down the nearby Olympic ski jump, are both awesome alternatives to another day of skiing—don't worry, they're safety nuts, and won't let you near the mountain without a helmet. Rumors have it that Taxi-Bob is not going to be around much longer, so ask for details. They also run a bunch of great warm-weather excursions [see *summer,* below].

SkiPass *(Via del Castello 33; Tel 0436/862-171; 8:30am-12:30pm/3:30-7:30pm Mon-Sat, 8:30am-12:30pm/5-7:30pm Sun; info@dolomitisuperski.com, www.dolomitisuperski.com; V, MC)* is the only place in town that sells—you guessed it—ski passes. Located behind the bus station, this is HQ for the association of Ampezzo Valley slopes and cable car operators, who've agreed to let you in for the price of 51,000-58,000L per day, depending on peak season. For 56,000-63,000L a day, you can ski any slope or ride any cable car almost anywhere in the Italian Dolomites (460 lifts, 1,200km of ski runs), but that would be silly. For that much territory, the weekly pass for 292,000-332,000L makes more sense. Both passes are sold in one- to 21-day increments.

On the south side of Corso Italia, **Guide Alpina Cortina** and **Scuola Sci Cortina** *(Corso Italia 69/a; Tel/Fax 0436/868-505; 8am-7:30pm daily; info@guidecortina.com, www.guidecortina.com; V, MC)* is a consortium of 25 accredited Alpine guides, who will arrange to meet you at any of the local slopes for lessons *(125,000L per person, three people minimum; 55,000L for each additional person).* More extreme options include heli-skiing, where you fly to mountaintops no one else can get to and ski down them *(390,000L per person; six people minimum).* In between are night-skiing trips, off-run skiing, snowboard lessons, and other packages.

▶▶SUMMER

When all that snow melts, there's still plenty to keep your adrenaline pumping in and around Cortina. The cable cars still run up and down the mountains, so you can explore away.

No Limits [see *winter,* above] is your ticket to all things extreme. They'll get you wet, hurl you down the mountains, and generally tire you out. Example: they've taken one of the bobsleds from their Taxi-Bob attraction [see *winter,* above], ripped off the runners, tricked it out with wheels and brakes (thankfully), and set it up on a concrete track so that you can have the bobsled experience even without snow. They call it the

Taxi-Bob Wheel, and, as it says on their website, it "perform[s] like a Formula 1 racing car" and gets up to 70mph. Don't worry, one of their staff members drives the thing while you hold on—they don't give you the reins. If you'd rather be on the water, they can take you **rafting, kayaking, canyoning** (hiking, climbing, and generally sliding about in waterfall-filled gorges) or what they call **"Hydro-Speeding,"** which is careening through the rapids on individual rafts that are kind of like very high-tech, highly padded wave runners.

There are 90+ numbered trails around Cortina at every level of difficulty from totally flat to steeper than steep. The tourist office [see *need to know,* below] will provide you with detailed maps so you can strike out into the woods. **Guide Alpina Cortina** [see *winter,* above] organizes day-long to week-long group hikes and canyoning trips, and runs climbing courses. You're in good hands with these guys.

The excellent website ***www.dolomiti.org/dengl/Cortina/ce/mtb/ index.htm*** outlines 15 mountain biking itineraries, complete with detailed maps, organized into 4 levels of difficulty. You can rent a bike at **No Limit** or any of the other outdoor outfitters around town, and can take them on the cable cars with you.

If that all sounds like a bit more than you're looking for, you can relax on the links at **Circolo Golf Miramonti** *(PezIè, 104/a; Tel 0436/867-176; May-end of October; golfmiramonti@sunrise.it)* or do the backstroke at the local **Swimming Pool** *(Loc Guargné; Tel 0436/4380; May-September).* You equestrian types can find a nice piece of horseflesh to carry you around the base of the mountains at **Fattoria Meneguto** *(Tel 0436/860-441).*

EATS

Cortina is not really a foodie's paradise. Many choose to pay the surcharge for full- or half-board at their hotels—never really a money-saving option. The expensive restaurants tend to be expensive and not really good, and even the cheap places are expensive. Bright spots are where the locals eat, places like Pizzaria Perla and Vienna.

▶▶CHEAP

With its knotty pine walls and aqua tablecloths, **Pizzaria Perla** *(Piazzatta San Francesco 3; Tel 0436/4681; 11:30am-3pm/5:30pm-midnight Tue-Sat; Pizza 8,000-13,000L, entrees 11,000-20,000L; No credit cards)* isn't exactly the chic-est place in town, but that's half the appeal. This place, located right beside the tourist office, is where ski instructors and locals (yes, there are a few) go for delicious, reasonably priced meals and the best pizzas in town. Luckily it keeps a few menus in English, just in case. The local specialty, *pappardelle de capriolo* (flat noodles in a red sauce with goat kid meat, 13,000L), makes a great stick-to-your ribs meal after a day of riding the slopes.

Cortina's answer to the ubiquitous "free-flow" restaurants that are popping up all over Italy, **Cortina Bar-Ristorante Self Service** *(Autostazione, Via G. Marconi 9; Tel 0436/2529; 11am-2:30pm/5:30-*

9pm daily, May 1-Dec 15 only; Entrees 12,000L; No credit cards), isn't bad for a cafeteria, and the food is cheaper than most. It's attached to the bus station—just head through the glass doors from the station bar and you're there. The dining room is a sweet attempt at Cortina chic—the result is just Italian fancy, with lots of dark wood and green plants.

Vienna Pizzaria Ristorante *(Via Roma 66/68; Tel 0436/866-944; Noon-4:30pm/7-10:30pm daily; Pizzas 8,000-13,000L, entrees 15,000L; Cover 1,800L; V, MC, AE, DC)* is just a far enough walk from the center of town (about five minutes) to make you think that it won't be tourist-ville. And it's not. This homey trattoria is a real find, and though there's no English spoken or on the menu, the staff is super-friendly—you can get by with pointing. Try the smoked *scamorza* cheese and *pancetta* (thick bacon) pizza (13,000L) cooked in the wood-burning oven, or the region's specialty, *casunziei,* beet ravioli filled with nuts and cheese (10,000L). Homemade bilberry grappa, or the vodka-spiked lemon *sorbetto* with *prosecco* are usually offered at the end of the meal, and the beer is a real bargain—go for the *stivalo,* more than a pint in a boot-shaped glass. The decor is suburban rec room—knick-knacks and souvenirs from around the world share space with three-foot trophies and sports paraphernalia.

▶▶**DO-ABLE**

A welcome surprise in this suave town, **Restaurant Birreria Hacker** *(Via Stazione 7; Tel 0436/867-625; 8-2am Tue-Sun; No credit cards)* is a smoky old-man bar/restaurant, tended by some of the sweetest waitresses in town and packed with beer-swilling locals. This place is rustic—unpainted Alpine wood tables and chairs sit under a chandelier made of deer antlers. The tall *heffeweizen* (6,500L) is the cheapest glass o' suds in town, and the *wurstel* (hot dog, no bun, 7,000L) with a plate of greasy fries (3,000L), is a heaven-sent hangover cure. It's right across the street from the Clipper.

crashing

Cortina's population swells from 3,000 to 30,000 in high season (winter), which means two things. One, there are plenty of hotels; two, it's a vicious seller's market. Be warned: Rates are typically per person, not per room. Watch out for the often hidden breakfast charge, especially if you have no intention of eating breakfast. You can get a copy of the legally allowable rates at the **tourist office** [see *need to know,* below], but good luck scaring the management into abiding by it. They'll charge whatever they want during ski season.

The way to save is to stay in a hostel-like *rifugio,* or mountain lodge [see *Ampezzo Valley,* below], open year-round. The drawback in the winter is that you're stuck up there after the last lift runs at 6pm, so you miss out on the nightlife in town. The good part is you're the first one on the slopes in the morning.

▶▶**DO-ABLE**

Meublé Montana *(Corso Italia 94; Tel 0436/862-126, Fax 0436/868-211; 52,000-90,000L single without bath, 68,000-112,000 single with* *bath, 10,0008-136,000L double without bath, 120,000-216,000L double with bath; hmontana@cortinanet.it, www.cortina-hotel.com; V, MC)* is every student's first choice, so calling ahead is essential. This 30-room family-run inn right across from the church is the best value of the three-stars in town. Beautiful knotty-pine rooms are spacious and well-equipped with TVs, phones, and tiled-tub bathrooms (some with crazy colored-light hydromassage). The cozy breakfast room serves up all the carbs you need for a day on the slopes (breakfast is included). In winter, the sweet owner, Adriano, is more than happy to help you arrange for a ski pass and rentals.

On the western end of Corso Italia, **Hotel Cavallino** *(Corso Italia 142; Tel 0436/2614; 60,000-70,000L per person low season, 120,000-125,000L per person high season, no private baths; V, ATM cards)* is the only typical little-old-lady-run hotel in town. The ever-present Recafina brothers and sisters keep the seven small rooms, all with TV, clean and homey. Breakfast is included, and a larger coffee-bar/common room should be ready by the time we go to print. The combination of good price and in-town location makes this a preferred spot for travelers on a budget. Be prepared, though, for the confusing pricing scheme.

The **Hotel Panda Meublé** *(Via Roma 64; Tel 0436/860-344, Fax 0436/860-345; 65,000-130,000L single, 130,000-250,000L double with bath and breakfast; hpanda@sunrise.it; V, MC)* is a short walk east of town center, but the bus stops right in front. Rooms are cozy and Alpine, and a few have mountain views. There's a comfy sitting room where kids hang out and watch TV.

Further out on Via Roma, **Hotel Dolomiti** *(Via Roma 118; Tel 0436/862-140; 80,000-170,000L single, 11,0000-210,000L double, private baths; V, MC, AE, DC)* is unattractively located beside a service station—all the beauty is out the back windows, with their unbroken view of the mountains. The hotel itself hasn't been renovated since the '60s, when it was built, but it's been well-maintained. There's no elevator, but hallways and rooms are spacious. A buffet breakfast is included and served in the downstairs restaurant, which also offers popular home-style lunches and dinners (60,000L).

▶▶SPLURGE

The small **Hotel Meublé Oasi** *(Via Cantore 2; Tel 0436/862-019, Fax 0436/879-476; 60,000-150,000L per person with minimum stay of seven days year-round, private baths; info@hoteloasi.it, www.hoteloasi.it; V, MC)*, sitting just beside the bus station, couldn't be better-looking. The owners, Giovanni and his wife, completely remodeled their family home from top to bottom in 1998. The new furniture is made of light-colored wood, the carpet is springy, and the breakfast room has a panoramic view. Two of the 10 rooms have balconies, and all have satellite TV and an external line. Prices and minimum-stays vary wildly according to the week in the snow season.

The **Parc Hotel Victoria** *(Corso Italia 1; Tel 0436/3246, Fax 0436/4734; 80,000-210,000L single, 125,000-380,000L double,; private baths; victoria@dolomiti.it, www.victoria.dolomiti.it; V, MC, AE, DC)* has been reigning over Cortina since 1892. Yes, there are some new super-luxury places hidden in the hills, but tradition counts in these things, dahling. The same family has run this hotel since the beginning, surviving the Austro-Hungarian Empire, two World Wars, and several occupations. The rooms aren't huge, but the antique furniture, warm reddish walls, thick comforters, TVs, phones, and high level of service more than make up for it. Yes, they can have those pants pressed by tomorrow.

NEED TO KNOW

Currency Exchange There's an **ATM** at the **Banca Populare dell'Alto Adige** on Largo Poste, near the **post office** [see below], which also changes money and cashes traveler's checks.

Tourist Information The **tourist office** *(Piazzetta s. Francesco 8; Tel 0436/3131, Fax 0436/3235; 8:30am-12:20pm/3:30-6:30pm; info-cortina@apt-dolomiti-cortina.it, www.apt-dolomiti-cortina.it)* has printed material for anything you'll need to know in the region—such as maps of all the slopes and lifts. They can't help with hotel reservations.

Public Transportation Your **ski pass** will get you a free ride on any **city bus.** Tickets are also available at newsstands or in the bus station. Most buses stop at **Piazza Roma,** in front of the Church. For a taxi, call **Autogite** *(Piazza Roma; Tel 0436/2839).*

Health and Emergency health emergency: *118;* Alpine rescue: *043/62943.* The hospital, **Ospedale Specializzato Ortopedico** *(Via Stadio; Tel 0436/883-111),* specializes in...broken bones.

Pharmacies To get a prescription filled, head to **Farmacia Internazionale** *(Corso Italia 151; Tel 0436/2223; 9am-12:30pm/3:30-7:30pm).*

Telephone **Phone cards** are available in the bus station bar, or at any newsstand. **Pay phones** are in front of the post office.

Bus Lines Out of the City All buses leave from the **bus station** on Piazza le Stazione. Schedules and fares are available at station information. There's regular bus service to the **train station** in Calalzo, about 32km (20 miles) from Cortina.

Bike Rental You can rent some wheels at **No Limit** [see *great outdoors,* above].

Postal The **post office** *(Largo Poste 18/a; Tel 0436/862-011; 8:10am-6:00pm Mon-Fri, 8:10am-1:30pm Sat)* also changes money and cashes traveler's checks.

Internet See *wired,* above.

AMPEZZO VALLEY SKIING

The incredible amount of snow, as well as the steep, narrow, tree-lined slopes here, can terrify even experienced skiers. Known for the diversity of its slopes, with 140km of runs and 50 lifts, the Ampezzo Valley offers some of the best skiing in the Dolomites. The lure of the slopes, along with the charm and nightlife of nearby **Cortina d'Ampezzo** [see above], make it a favorite European resort for travelers from all over the world. Ampezzo offers more options for beginners and intermediates than for expert skiers, but there are plenty of steep, white-knuckle drops to remind you that you're still alive, if that's the kind of nut you are. And if you're here in the summer, you can hike, mountain bike, raft, kayak, and go canyoning to your heart's content [see *great outdoors* in **Cortina d'Ampezzo,** above, for details].

For the most part, each of the slopes is operated by a different company, but they're all connected by one of two ski-passes: **Dolomiti Superski,** which connects over 1,200km of runs in the Dolomite Mountains, and the **Skipass di Valle,** which covers the Valley alone. All passes can be purchased, logically enough, at **SkiPass** *(Via del Castello 33; Tel 0436/862-171; 8:30am-12:30pm/3:30-7:30pm Mon-Sat, 8:30am-12:30pm/5-7:30pm Sun; info@dolomitisuperski.com, www.dolomitisuperski.com; V, MC),* located behind Cortina's bus station. Resorts are sprinkled throughout the valley, which surrounds Cortina on all sides. **Socrepes** and **Tofana** are favorites on the west side of the valley, while **Faloria** is the darling of the east side. Each of the resorts has more than one run, which often connect with runs from other resorts. With a Skipass, you won't have to worry about who operates which slope, because you've already paid for all of them.

Runs (*pistes,* if you wanna sound European) here are much narrower than what you'll find in the U.S.—someone should really see about moving those trees a bit further out on each side. They're part of the joy of Alpine skiing, but it might not feel so joyous when you're wrapped around a Douglas fir. One word of warning: The difficulty-range of runs here goes from easy to *way* hard in a heartbeat. Don't assume that just because you conquered the baby slope at Socrepes, you're ready for the killer runs at Tofana.

Nestled at the foot of the slopes, **Socrepes** *(Via Lacedel 1; Tel/Fax 0436/867-570; Bus 3, 3qa, or 3b to Socrepes; V, MC)* is a good choice for beginners, and one of the easiest ski centers to reach from the town center. It's pronounced "SO-crep-ehss." The scene is very relaxed: Music blasts from an outdoor sound system, and there are lots of beginners, skiing families, and Italian grandmas in full-length minks dozing in lounge chairs at the bottom of the slopes (please don't run over anyone's grandma). Snow machines help even things out when Mother Nature gets a little stingy with her stash. Ski and snowboard **rentals** are available [see *need to know,* below], as are lessons (around 70,000L an hour, depending on size of group and how many hours you need). Lifts go to the nearby slopes that end here—Socrepes and **Redoncé,** both intermediate runs—and continue up to the beginner runs, **Duca D'Aosta** and **Pomedes.**

The runs at the top of **Tofana,** also on the west side of the valley, get more intense. Two intermediate runs go through scary wooded areas, and the precipitous **Col Drucié A,** is for experts only. You can also take the absolutely terrifying expert run, **Forcella Rossa.** Brave men and women have been known to break into tears at the top of this one. You'll notice that most people here are either Austrian or crazy (or both). If you're not feeling brave or crazy, stay in the cable car hut and take the last leg to the top of Tofana, where there's a magnificent view and a pretty tasty *rifugio* restaurant [see *need to know,* below].

In the sometimes stodgy world of Ampezzo Valley skiing, **Faloria** *(Monte di Faloria; Tel 0436/2737; Last car 5:30pm Feb-Mar; 5pm Apr-Jan; 80,000L half-pension, 70,000L per person in two-six person dorm; V, MC, AE)* on the east side of the valley, is the ski area with the tongue stud. Far from participating in Cortina's usual unprovoked suspicion of shredders, Faloria built a snowboard park just a 10-minute walk downhill from the main lodge, with three jumps, and plans for a half-pipe. The owners blast alternative music at the bottom of the two runs that end here, and there's a cocktail bar where you could grab a beer without stopping your run, at least in theory (don't try it—making change could be a problem). The vibe here is much more laid-back—maybe it's because the majority of the runs are easy at some point, so folks can take things a little less seriously. This can mean "poseur," or it can mean "relaxed," depending on your point of view. A lot of ski bums make the *rifugio* [see *need to know,* below] their home for the season, and it's definitely a cool place to hang out late in the evening.

Lifts go up to **Tondi** (2,362m), with intermediate run **Tondi Normale** and expert run **Canalone Franchetti,** or the **Stratondi,** which starts as an expert run and becomes an intermediate one on its way back to the *rifugio.*

need to know

Hours and Days Open High season here starts in December and runs until Easter. *Avoid* Christmas and Easter weeks, and the last two weeks in February—Italian holidays when the whole country decides to go skiing. **Cable cars** shut down around 5:30pm, depending on weather; always check on your way up. Many slopes have **night skiing** available, but how are you gonna get home?

Directions and Transportation All roads to these mountains pass though **Cortina.** Take **Bus 3, 3qa, or 3b** from Piazza Roma in **Cortina** to get to Socrepes. For Tofana, take **Bus 8 or 8a** to the **Funivia Freccia nel Cielo** *(Tel 0436/5052; 9am-5pm daily, closed in low season; 30,000-45,000L round-trip, included with ski pass)* cable car. You can go up one, two, or three legs. For Faloria, take the **Faloria cable car** from behind the bus station. All bus, lift, and cable car transport is free with a valid **Skipass;** if you spend the night, remember to get one for at least two days.

Rental In Cortina, try **snow service** *(Via 29 Maggio 11; Tel/Fax 0436/866-635; 8:30am-7:30pm daily; snowservice@sunrise.it; Skis 25,000L per day, boots 9,000L per day; V, MC, DC),* near **Largo Poste,** or No Limits *(Piazzetta San Francesco 2; Tel 0436/2503; 8:30am-7:30pm* *daily; V, MC),* in the piazza across from the main tourist office. On the Socrepes side of the valley, try, well, **Socrepes** (skis with boots 32,000-44,000L per day, snowboards 30,000-40,000L per day, boots 10,000-20,000L extra). Multi-day rentals can be stored at the shop free of charge.

Eats Even if you have no intention of skiing down the steep Tofanes mountain, no trip to Cortina should be without a ride up the cable car to enjoy the views. Stop off at **Rifugio Ravalles** *(Cablecar Tofana di Mezzo, at the top of the second stop; Tel 0436/3461; 9am-4:30pm daily, Dec-Apr, Jul-Sep; No credit cards)* for a bite to eat. This beautiful restaurant, clinging to the side of the mountain, offers 360-degree views and decent, local dishes at good prices. The cafeteria line is full of outfitted skiers, gearing up for the ride of their lives with a bowl full of goulash (20,000L) and a *speck*-and-cheese panini (smoked ham sandwich, 5,000L). Head for a booth by the window to watch skiers on their winding descent. The food's not the best, but the view is.

In addition to beds for the night, **Faloria** [see *crashing,* below] offers a self-service restaurant, with pastas and soups from 10,000-13,000L, and main dishes from 15,000-20,000L.

Crashing Most everyone goes back down with the last cable car, usually at 5:30pm or so. But a great way to beat the high prices in Cortina, and to make sure that you hit the slopes early, is to stay at a *rifugio* (refuge, or mountain lodge). Full lists of *rifugi* can be obtained from Cortina's **tourist office** [see **Cortina D'Ampezzo,** above]. Accommodations run from truly hut-like to the level of the best youth hostels. Make sure you bring something to keep your throat from getting too dry after the refuge stops serving, and something to read in case conversation with your fellow lodgers dries up. It can be a long night on the mountainside.

Refugio Faloria *(Monte di Faloria; Tel 0436/2737; last car 5:30pm Feb-Mar, 5pm Apr-Jan; 80,000L half-pension, 70,000L per person dorm; V, MC, AE)* is perhaps the best-looking of the overnight refuges, with its wood walls and new pine furniture. The 33 beds are divided into two-, three-, and four-bed rooms; 10 rooms in all. Every one has a great view of the mountain or the valley below. Giorgio, the owner, looks like a stocky Anthony Hopkins, and can often be found at the bar, holding court with some friends. Beers are 6,000L, but they stop serving at 10pm, unless Giorgio's in a particularly good mood.

friuli-venezia giulia

friuli-Venezia Giulia has everything except tourists. You can really get off the beaten path and dig *la dolce vita* with the locals. **Trieste** is the epicenter of activity; the urban student population gives it a hip edge, an athletic spirit, and a dizzy nightlife that makes it a natural home base. But there's plenty to do in other parts of the region as well. After cafe-hopping, night-clubbing, rock-climbing, and swimming in Trieste, try sipping famous local wines at the *osterias* in **Udine** or wandering the winding city streets in beautifully preserved **Cividale di Friuli.** Or get *way* off the beaten path and hike hundreds of trails in the lush **Natisone Valley.**

Fruili-Venezia Giulia has been a crossroads of Europe since Roman times at least. Even the name is a history lesson: Fruili is a shortening of *"Forum Julii,"* which is what Julius Caesar named Cividale del Fruili when he founded it in 50 BC, and *"Venezia Giulia"* was the Venetian name for that portion of the Republic's hinterland. The conquering Romans came from the south and built good roads, which kinda backfired because they ended up making it that much easier for northerners to invade the territory. The Lombards came through first; their evolution from barbarian hordes to medieval princes and patriarchs can be seen in a tour of Cividale's ancient buildings, sacred spaces, and museums. Attila the Hun also stopped by on his way to Rome, though he left nothing but ashes and legends in his path. In the 1400s, Udine and its environs were folded into the Venetian Republic, and the main piazza of the city was turned into a little bit of mainland Venice. Venetian governors and church patriarchs ruled the area for hundreds of years, cultivating Baroque architects and artists. The Venetians bowed out as Napoleon came roaring in, building a few statues before leaving for death and glory elsewhere, creating a power vacuum willingly filled by the Austro-Hungarian Empire of the Hapsburgs, who gave Trieste a Viennese make-over.

Modern history has followed the same cycle of destruction and renewal. When locals talk about "the war," they mean World War I, when the Italian-Austrian front ran through the vineyards and hills of Fruili, and the Italian Alpine troops *(Gli Alpini)* became a national symbol of tenacity. This was also where Hemingway and other Lost Generation combatants got wounded and disillusioned. World War II was no better for the region: Udine was bombed senseless, and Trieste was disputed by so many nations that the Allied Armies ran it until the 1950s, when the

Friuli-Venezia Giulia

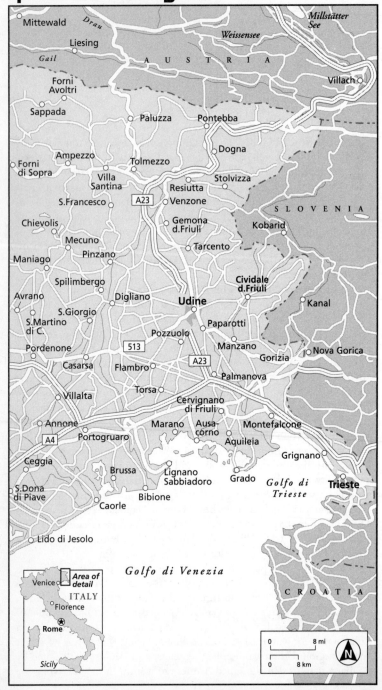

Mittewald
Drau
Liesing
Weissensee
Millstätter See
Gail
A U S T R I A
Villach
Forni Avoltri
Sappada
Paluzza
Pontebba
Dogna
Ampezzo
Tolmezzo
Forni di Sopra
Villa Santina
Resiutta
Stolvizza
S.Francesco
A23
Venzone
S L O V E N I A
Chievolis
Gemona d.Friuli
Kobarid
Mecuno
Pinzano
Tarcento
Maniago
Spilimbergo
Digliano
Udine
Cividale d.Friuli
Avrano
Kanal
S.Giorgio
Paparotti
S.Martino di C.
Pozzuolo
Pordenone
513
Manzano
Nova Gorica
Casarsa
Flambro
A23
Gorizia
Villalta
Torsa
Palmanova
Annone
Cervignano di Friuli
A4
Portogruaro
Marano
Ausa-corno
Montefalcone
Ceggia
Aquileia
Brussa
Grignano
Lignano Sabbiadoro
Grado
Golfo di Trieste
Trieste
S.Dona di Piave
Bibione
Caorle
Lido di Jesolo

Golfo di Venezia

Venice
Area of detail
ITALY
Florence
Rome
Sicily

C R O A T I A

| 0 | | 8 mi |
| 0 | | 8 km |

N

wheeling and dealing between Yugoslavia and Italy resulted in Trieste joining a country it barely knew.

All these names and dates make a difference in the region today, which has either become a poster-child for diversity or has severe multiple personality disorder, depending on your point of view. In the area around Udine and Cividale—"Fruili" proper—older folks still speak a language called *Furlan,* which has German and Slavic traces. Around Trieste, the area known more often as "Giulia," no one speaks of or cares about this fading cultural tradition —people around Trieste speak either Italian or Slavic languages (predominantly Slovan). What it means to be both Italian and *a Triestino* in a city that has only been part of the country for half a century is a huge local debate currently being exploited by the neo-Fascist, anti-Slav "Italian First" movement.

Thankfully, culture wars end at the stomach. The cuisines around Udine and Cividale are most famous for the wonderful wines of the *Colli Orientali* (eastern hills). People eat *frico,* an awesome fried Montasio cheese wedge, and proscuitto San Daniele, cured ham that is the rival of the proscuitto di Parma, for antipasti. And there's cabbage everywhere—from the non-fermented *krauti* that accompanies sausages and pork, to the spicy *gulash.* Eating and drinking in Trieste is epitomized by the cafe culture, which sprang to life 300 years ago when Trieste became a base for coffee bean imports, roasting, and export. Triestini meals are divided between quick stops at buffets and so-fresh it's-still-wiggling seafood. *Fritti misti,* which can contain anything from calamari to shrimp to sardines, each fried in its own batter, is a local specialty that shouldn't be missed.

getting around the region

Getting around Friuli Venezia-Giulia, like getting around most of Italy, is best done by train. Between the beach sports, hiking and climbing, the cultural sights, and the vibrant nightlife you can easily spend five days in **Trieste.** But two very busy days—one at the beach and one in the city—will do. If coming from Venice or points west, **Udine** (90 minutes from Venice) is your natural first stop, and though you really need two days to see it all, one day is plenty.

With only two hotels, **Cividale** is typically a daytrip, but with some planning ahead you can score a room and spend the night. You can only get to Cividale, which is serviced by a local railway company, by going through Udine. The charge is 4,300L for a one-way trip; trains leave every 20 minutes, 6am-8pm. Be aware that Eurail and Interrail passes do *not* work between Udine and Cividale. Udine to Trieste is an easy trip as well, with over 20-trains making the two-hour trip everyday. From Trieste, international trains run to all the Balkan capitals, included the highly recommended Ljubljana, Slovenia (a three-hour trip because of border crossing). With its huge college student population, tons of bars and clubs, and the cheapest drinks this side of the Adriatic, it's been dubbed the New Prague.

Travel Times

	Udine	Cividale
Trieste	1:30	2:00
Udine	-	:15

hardcore politics

Second only to, perhaps, Mussolini on the list of infamous figures in Italian politics, Ilona Staller (a.k.a. Cicciolina)—a well-known porn star—was in 1987 elected to Parliament as a member of the Radical Party. Celebrated less for legislative tenacity and more for her insistence on flashing her boobs at fans and political colleagues alike, Cicciolina, a representative from Lazio, became an enormous celebrity, making headlines in Italy and abroad as the first (surprise, surprise) porn star elected to a political position. The Hungarian born star of such startling pieces of cinema verde as *Porno Poker* and *Atomic Orgy* brought to her position the kind of noble and intrepid political platform one would expect from an MP who's name translates, roughly to "Little Cuddly One": an end to all hunger, disease, and violence—oh yeah, and complete, unadulterated sexual liberation! Get down! She was in office for five years and remains something of a novel, if not distinguished, advocate for issues regarding free speech and sexual freedom. She became wife and muse to wacky American artist Jeff Koons in 1991; the two later divorced and underwent a bitter custody battle (try being the judge of that one). Cicciolina currently lives in Rome. If you want to, uh, "learn more" about Cicciolina, she runs an official website at ***www.ciccolina.com.*** It's, ahem, very informative....

TRIESTE

Feel like devouring sushi with old skool club kids accompanied by French jazz, raging at an S&M-style house party hosted by pastry-chefs? Or would you rather play Dungeons & Dragons with patchouli-scented dread-heads? Hit Trieste. It's one of Italy's best-kept secrets (to use a very tourist brochure-y phrase). Most travelers bypass it completely because it's hidden in the extreme northeast corner of Italy, but the remote setting and cool, eclectic mix of subcultures make it an unforgettable stop.

Trieste's strategic location in the hills on the Adriatic Sea made it an irresistible prize for several great and lesser powers: Venice, Austria, Italy, and Yugoslavia have each left architectural and artistic footprints in the hillside and surf. Today, the city's proximity to Slovenia and Austria make it a multicultural crossroads, with a unique ethnic blend that shows up in everything from food and music to decor. Trieste definitely has a cosmopolitan vibe that you won't find in the more heavily touristed Venice or Milan. You'll love the sophisticated cafe culture and the swirl of hip nightlife.

In many ways, Trieste dominates the region commercially, but as a recent addition it has about as much in common with the rest of the Friuli as Manhattan does with upstate New York. This is not to compare Italy's second largest port with the excitement of the Big Apple—Trieste is Italy's insurance capital (yawn) and it has the highest per-capita number of retirees (double-yawn). Its rep as a senior center has given local kids a major chip on their shoulder about the local scene, which is actually very creative and happening, fueled by a full-force, year-round student population. There's a lively Ska scene, and the local DJs go for the witty and

trieste bars clubs and culture zoo

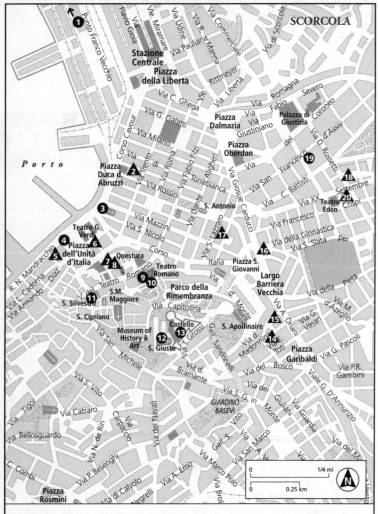

BARS/CLUBS ▲
Bounty Pub **15**
Caffeteria del Borgo **8**
Cibo Matto **2**
Clover Pub **5**
Juice **14**
Mandracchio **6**
Macaki **20**
Naima Jazz Café **18**
Pub Trend **16**
Public House **17**
Sangre de Uva **7**

CULTURE ZOO ●
Antiquarium **10**
Basilica di San Silvestro **11**
Castello di San Giusto **13**
Cathedral di San Giusto **12**
Miramare Castle and Park **1**
Piazza dell' Unitá D'Italia **4**
Sinagoga di via San Francenso **19**
Teatro Romano **9**
Tempio di San Nicoló dei Greci **3**

unique, rather than the latest pop/dance schlock. Trieste is also just about the only city in the region where Vespas are chromed-out babe-magnets instead of just your basic transportation.

The only word for Trieste's population (around 300,000) is diverse. Many people have Slavic first or last names, *strudel* appears on almost every menu, *gulash* is widely available, and people worship at Catholic and Greek Orthodox cathedrals, Swiss Waldenesan churches, and synagogues. Trieste even has an American football team. Of course, where you find great diversity, you also find the opportunity for the usual reactionary nimrods to get some attention. The neo-fascist MSI party does quite well here, and there's even an anti-Slav party. These clowns often team up for "Italian First" and "Italian Trieste" campaigns.

But don't judge everyone by the actions of a few vocal, local crackpots; by and large the Triestini are more liberal and carefree than most northern Italians, and they enjoy their rep for being a little bit different. With the beauty of the mountain and sea views, and the mildness of the Adriatic weather, the Triestini all seem to agree that life is meant to be enjoyed, even if "we are all a little crazy," as one local told us. Hang around awhile, and you may start to welcome a little of that craziness.

neighborhoods

Trieste is spread out and confusing, but you'll do okay if you orient yourself with a few good landmarks: The Adriatic, and the ports that line it, are on the west. The train station and **Piazza Oberdan**—a good place to catch buses and trams, most of which stop here—are at the northern end of town. From here, **Corso Cavour** angles out southwest and eventually along the water—it's a good route into town. From the station, it's about a fifteen-minute walk to most sights.

The first neighborhood to the south of Piazza Oberdan is the **Borgo Teresano,** or **Città Nuova,** which is thankfully laid out in an easy-to-navigate grid pattern. There's lots to do in the Borgo—it's where you'll find most of the budget hotels, restaurants, and some bars. **Corso Italia,** which marks the southern end of the Borgo, runs from **Piazza Goldoni** in the east to the monumental **Piazza dell'Unitá d'Italia,** which opens up to the harbor in the west.

Piazza dell'Unitá d'Italia is Trieste's front porch: Everyone in town passes through here eventually, lingering in the open space and cool sea breeze. This is where the best sidewalk life and often-terrific open-air entertainment is found. Twisty medieval streets spread out southwest of here. Further south of these streets is the **old Jewish ghetto,** which also has some great bars and watering holes. East of the ghetto is **Capitoline Hill (Collina Capolitana),** which stretches east to Via Carducci. On this hill, you'll find the **Teatro Romano,** lots of winding streets, some beautiful public gardens, and at the top, the **Castello di San Giusto** and **Cathedrale San Giusto** [see *culture zoo,* below, for both]. **Via Madonnina,** which branches southeast off Carducci, is the site of some cool bars.

12 hours in trieste

Soaking up as much of Trisetini life as you can in 12 hours is a challenge, but we think you're up to it.

1. **Take the tram.** For the best views of the city and the gulf, take the hair-raising ride up to Opicina and back [see *great outdoors,* below].

2. **Fight the crowds at Buffet Gilda.** Your prize is a hunka meat sandwich [see *eats,* below].

3. **Stop by Sgt. Pepper to find out where the party is.** While you're there, pick up a seven-inch; make a mental note to buy a turntable when you get home [see *stuff,* below].

4. **Grab a cup o' joe:** Order yourself a *capo in b* at one of Trieste's historical cafes—go for Café Tomaseo or Tergesteo [see *cafe scene,* below].

5. **Watch the sun set up at Capitoline Hill.** Sit on a fallen 2,000-year-old column, between the church and the castle, pop open a bottle of vino and enjoy *il tramonte.*

6. **Try for a reservation at All' Antica Ghiacceretta.** Don't feel bad if they don't give you a table; you won't be the first tourist turned away from Trieste's most popular fish-fry, and you won't be the last.

7. **Bus it to Miramare.** Walk down to the castle and stroll around the exotic gardens [see *culture zoo,* below].

8. **Grub for Free.** It's back to the cafes for the *aperativo* hour.

9. **Chill out at Juice.** They have the coolest crowd, the best brews, and the best bullpen of DJs [see *bar scene,* below].

10. **Skank to the rock-steady at Cibo Matto.** Is it a restaurant or a club? Don't worry about it, just get up and dance [see *club scene,* below].

11. **Hang out in Piazza dell'Unita d'Italia.** Don't leave until you see at least two different people pass by twice. Now you're a local!

12. **Go to All' Antica Ghiacceretta again.** Camp out in the doorway until they give you a table.

There are a few places of note just outside of the central city. Running east off Via Carducci are **Viale XX Settembre** and **Via Cesare Battisti,** the heart of Trieste's student life. Late night jazz clubs and all-out discos are hidden behind nondescript storefronts. Three blocks south of Via XX Settembre is the hospital, **Ospedale Maggiore,** the center of a funky residential neighborhood spotted with some of the best food stores in town, and a few more budget hotels.

If you follow the coastline north from the train station, you'll come across **la Barcolana** [see *great outdoors,* below]. The youth hostel [see *crashing,* below], and **Castello Miramare** [see *culture zoo,* below] are also up in this direction. The Bus 36 from Piazza Oberdan will get you there if you don't want to make the trek on foot. If the concrete beach isn't doing it for you, you can take the steep tram-ride from Piazza Oberdan straight up to the **Opicina** neighborhood for stunning mountain views [see *by foot,* below].

hanging out

Trieste has plenty of options for general loafing, the best being the harborside walk-of-life that extends from Piazza dell'Unitá d'Italia, past the Canale Grande, and up to the "beach" at La Barcolana. This stretch is known for its cafes and as the best place to meet up with just about anyone, young or old, tourist or Triestini.

cafe scene

The local cafes are a major cultural institution and a source of local pride. Trieste's young professionals head straight from work to **Antico Caffe Torinese** *(Corso Italia 2; Tel 040/632-689; Bus 11, 17, 25, 28 to Piazza della Borsa; 8am-9pm daily; 3-10,000L wine by the class, 1,400L cappuc-*

COffEE TalK

Cafe talk in Trieste is a language unknown to anyone but the locals. This port town has been the hotbed of the coffee trade since the 17th century, so they're at least a century or two ahead of the rest of the world in terms of cafe culture. Coffee drinks come in a dizzying array of preparations, many of them unknown to Starbuck's, and each seems to have its own special glass. To be a self-actualized cafe-goer, you need to know exactly what you want and how to ask for it, so take a moment to browse this primer for beginners:

Nero: basically an espresso. It can be ordered *lungo,* in a tall glass.

Gocciato: Often abbreviated as simply *goccio,* this is a *nero* with a dash of foamed milk.

Capo: A shot of espresso with heated milk, topped with a dollop of whipped cream. To have it in a glass, ask for *a capo in b.*

cino; No credit cards) one of the city's oldest, most fabled cafes, located across from the stock exchange. Businessmen stop over for a quick whiskey, while their wives and girlfriends more often opt for white wine and Campari spritzers. Here the gender roles are as fixed as the decor, which was designed by famous ship architect Debelli, who wrapped the bar in brass, draped the walls in wood, and hung an oversized crystal chandelier from the ceiling. The wines come from all over the world, with unusual-for-Italy bottles from South Africa and New Zealand. The music is a cool mix of American and international pop, and the *aperitivo* spread includes such exotic fare as guacamole and chips.

Another favorite among locals and tourists alike is the beautiful, classic **Caffe Tomaseo** *(Riva III Novembre 5, on Piazza Tomaseo; Tel 040/362-666, Fax 040/372-5623; Bus 6 to Piazzà dell'Unità d'Italia; 7:30am-11pm daily; www.caffetommaseo.com/index.html; V, MC, AE, DC)*, situated right on the water, just west of Piazza dell'Unità d'Italia. Since 1830, this cafe has been welcoming wayward travelers in need of a fresh cup o' joe. A change of ownership and total renovation in 1997 has turned this icon and old haunt of Joyce into a bit of a country club. Stick to the coffee and the generous array of finger foods—the food is pricey and dull. Both the outside tables and the air-conditioned terrarium hop from noon till about 7pm.

On Piazza Borsa, hidden in an old galleria-cum-shopping mall across from the Verdi theater, is the outrageously beautiful **Caffe Tergesteo** *(Piazza della Borsa 15; Tel 040/365-812; Bus 11, 17, 25, 28 to Piazza della Borsa; 7:30am-8:30pm Tue-Sat; No credit cards)*. Since 1863, the Triestini have taken time out to sit down and enjoy their coffee in the Viennese splendor of this cafe, which doubles as a candy shop. Munch on some *torrone* or homemade *paste* as you sip your *capo*, surrounded by marble reliefs and classical flourishes. The front room offers great people-watching.

If you're inexperienced at ordering coffee in Trieste, you should get some practice before attempting **Crèmcaffe** *(Piazza Goldoni 10; Tel 040/636-555; Bus A-D 1,5 9, 10, 15, 16, 18, 19, 26 to Piazza Goldoni; 9am-9pm daily; 900-2,500L cafe; No credit cards)*, located on the northwest side of Piazza Goldoni. Try one of the other cafes first, just to get used to how the locals do it. Then march over to this institutional looking place, swing open the doors, stand in line at the cash register, and pay for what you *think* you want to drink (you can get coffee prepared any way you want—the sign over the cash register recommends about thirty different blends). Muscle up to the bar—even the gentle-looking grandmas will shove you out of the way if you let them—and hand your ticket to one of the bartenders in the white caps. Yes, that is a conveyer belt where the staff will put your empty cup to zip it to the dishwashers—this place, one of Trieste's oldest coffee roasters, runs like a well-oiled machine. People usually drink and run (there's admittedly not much ambiance to make you want to linger), but you should stick around at least long enough to let some of the place's history soak in.

Gelateria Zampoli (*Piazza Cavana 6; Tel 040/306-00-03; Bus 24 to Via Diaz; 8:30am-9:30pm; No credit cards*), in the old ghetto, is one of those homemade *gelaterias* you'll dream about when you get home. Hot-shot Italian guys with slicked-back hair lounge on their Vespas out front, and seem to forget about flirting, cat-calling, and looking cool as they lick their way to the bottom of the best cone in town. It's well worth the 3-5,000L you'll pay. The airy *semifreddo* (semi-frozen gelato) is good stuff, too.

bar scene

Put on your walking shoes. Trieste has tons of late-night entertainment, but it's spread all over town. Most of the local favorites, college hangouts, and disco bars are around Via Madonnina and Via Settembre XX, while fancier, night-on-the-town venues are closer to the water. They all share a lax attitude—none enforce a dress code. But most locals are fashion hounds, so baggy pants and sneakers will really only feel at home in alterno establishments like Juice and Caffé Borgo. Bars, clubs, cafes, restaurants all blend together, Triestini-style—the best DJ party is in a pastry shop, there's a Ska-fest in an after-hours restaurant, and the best place for music often offers nowhere to dance. For a complete listing of bands and DJ nights, pick up *NETWORK*, a free monthly, from the tourist office [see *need to know*, below].

The same folks that hang at Caffe Torinese move on to the Jewish ghetto's **Sangre de Uva** (*Via delle Beccherie 1; Tel 040/347-82-81; Bus 11, 17, 25, 28 to Piazza della Borsa; 5pm-2am Mon-Sat; No cover; No credit cards*) as the night continues. Velvet curtains, brick arches, and candlelight set the scene in this long, narrow *enoteca* (wine bar), where scenesters nonchalantly bob their heads to the smooth sounds of '60s super-French singer Serge Gainsbourg. Wine drinkers perch on the comfy stools along the wooden bar and order up one of the over 110 wines by the glass (*2-8,000L*)—they're listed on the enormous blackboard hanging

ragazzo incontra ragazza

Trieste sits at a cultural crossroads, but it's still Italy, which makes it a good place to practice your conjugations in the language of love. The **Canale Grande,** with its Venetian views and pedestrian bridge, is the local pick-up joint. Women in groups of two to 20 walk past guys leaning against decked-out Vespas, who pull out their smokes, smooth out their jackets, and *stare.* It seems inevitable that irresistible force and immovable object will collide with the introduction of that age-old request *"Puo darmi un accendino?"* ("Got a light?").

outside the front door, so take a look before heading in. A small deli-case on one end of the bar is filled with great, inexpensive bruschetta (3-10,000L). If you want some of the cheese, salami, or prosciutto, make sure you ask the cost first—some items are surprisingly expensive.

The medieval weaponry and chain-mail shirts hanging on the walls should be the tip-off that you've stumbled onto **Pub Trend** (*Largo Sanforio 1; Tel 040/772-337; Bus A-D 1,5 9, 10, 15, 16, 18, 19, 26 to Piazza Goldoni; Noon-2:30pm/7pm-2am Mon-Sat; No cover; No credit cards*). It's run by the local chapter of the Society of Creative Anachronisms. Before your inner dork-meter goes haywire, consider this: the beers on tap are mostly terrific Belgian brews (7-8,000L pint), the wines are local, and the vibe is extremely *tranquilo*. There's something very new-age about this place. Maybe it's the noodly jazz that bounces around the candle-lit room, but more likely it's the surprisingly friendly mix of people who sit at the gold-tiled tables for hours on end, from intellectuals in wire-rim glasses to patchouli-scented dread-heads to teenagers obsessed with twenty-sided-dice. Flee if you start to wonder why you stopped playing D&D (you stopped because you got your driver's license). It's located just off Piazza Goldoni.

Slap up some maps of the British Isles, scribble some Gaelic on the walls, put Guinness on tap, and suddenly you have what the Italians call a pub. It's a noble attempt, but **Clover Pub** (*Via Diaz 3; Tel 040/366-154; Noon-2:30pm/4:30pm-2am; No cover; No credit cards*) is still more Italian than Irish, with Italian music, more people drinking wine and cocktails than beer, and the kind of communal exuberance that would make James Joyce turn on his heel at the door. But you didn't come to Italy looking for Irish pubs anyway, did you? (Lordy, we hope not.) Filled with both locals and visitors, the Clover is right in the heart of town, a few steps from Piazza dell'Unitá d'Italia and the water. Resist the over-priced hamburger and salad menu and stick to the Guinness (6-8,000L), which is about the only thing Irish about the place.

Trieste's only jazz club, **Naima Jazz Café** (*Via Rossetti 6; Tel 040/662-686; Bus 22 to Via Ginnastica; 7:30pm-2am, closed Monday; No cover; No credit cards*), is a great addition to the up-and-coming theater district around Via XX Settembre. The owner seems to be the most popular kid in town, working the room like a hostess from the Old South, greeting newcomers, stopping to chat with friends on the cushy leather banquettes, and rushing over to help out the busy bartender. Paintings and photographs hang on the red walls under crumbling medieval arches; exhibits change monthly. Come here for soft jazz, 30 wines by the glass (3-8,000L), and inexpensive beers on tap (6,000L).

Sip wine in oversized glasses (5,000L) and rub shoulders with the local hipsters at the little **Juice** (*Via Madonnina 10; Tel 040/760-03-41; Bus 18, 20, 23, 34, 40, to Largo Barriera; 8:30-3:30am daily; Closed Sunday; No cover; V, MC, DC*). There's crummy furniture and a makeshift DJ booth is set up amid the crowded tables in the front room—nothing fancy (whew!). Abstract art hangs next to a blackboard with the evening's sandwich offerings (6,000L). The music is creative and varied, with special theme nights ranging from French jazz to trance and old skool hip-hop. Stop in on Mondays for the popular sushi night, when you can get a multi-course meal for 50,000L.

Location, Location, Location. That's the appeal at the pretty and civilized **Bounty Pub** (*Via Pondares 6; Tel 040/762-952; Bus 18, 20, 23, 34, 40, to Largo Barriera; 7pm-3am Tue-Sun; No cover; V, MC*), situated right around the corner from trendy Via Madonnina. Nautical equipment and lots of brass adorn the cozy rooms that wind around the bar. College kids and couples slouch around big, spacious booths, and business-types sip from the large selection of whiskeys (8-10,000L).

Macaki (*Via XX Settembre 39/A; Tel 040/367-272; Bus 22 to Via Ginnastica; 10pm-late daily; www.macaki.com; info@macaki.com; No cover; No credit cards*) is what happens when an ultra-hip restaurant realizes that its purpose in life is to make people dance. This sprawling space is covered head to toe in broken-glass mosaics and art-nouveau collages, casting an arty vibe. Call ahead to reserve one of the tables that wrap around the sunken dance floor. Every night has a different theme: There are Latin grooves on Mondays, and students meet other internationals and dance to commercial pop and retro favorites on Thursday's *Erasmus night*. Every now and then, there's even live music.

club scene

By day, elegant *pasticceria* **Caffeteria del Borgo** (*Via Malcanton 6, Tel 040/774-512; Bus 11, 17, 25, 28 to Piazza della Borsa; 9:30pm-2 or 3am daily; No cover; No credit cards*) serves up the most sumptuous desserts in Trieste. At night, the lights dim and a DJ sets up behind the glass pastry counter for one kickin' house party. The over-the-top red velvet decor, a wrought-iron staircase that wraps its way upward around the room, suggests a turn-of-the century bordello run by pastry chefs. Thursday's theme nights—from French lounge music to S&M-inspired shows—are as

rules of the game

Maybe it's the thousands of university students, or the ships that dock here for a few days at a time, unleashing primal urges that refuse to go unsatisfied (not to mention drunken exploits all over town), but Trieste is an anything-goes kind of place. Feel free to dive right in and debauch. But beware: The city has more than its fair share of cops, and though drinking on the streets is generally okay, other suspicious activities can get you in serious trouble. Bar and club owners like their crowds lively, but most of the heavily frequented places, like **Macaki** and **Juice,** have zero tolerance when it comes to drugs.

varied and outrageous as the locals that congregate here. Live music is featured whenever there's a band that can line fans up around the corner. If you're not already tempted, the 9:30-10:30pm happy hour, with half-off drinks (regularly priced 6-12,000L) should push you over the edge. It's southeast of Piazza dell'Unitá d'Italia, in the ghetto.

If you ever wondered what it would be like to run a nightclub with your mother, check out **Cibo Matto** *(Via Macchiavelli 3; No phone; Bus 8 to Corso Cavour; 7:30pm-late, closed Mondays; 5-7,000L beer pint, 8-10,000L cocktail; No cover; No credit cards)*, one of the coolest, most down-to-earth spots in town (and no, it's not named for the band). The platinum-haired proprietor, proud mama of the music manager/chef, can be seen sipping wine, chastising overzealous *ragazzi,* and encouraging the DJ to turn the music up. Sleek-suited mods mingle with crusty old fisherman as two of the town's most-loved DJs spin a nightly mix of early-eighties, Ska, indie, and funk. Sometimes you get the sense that Fabrizio, the twenty-something apple of his mother's eye, would rather be running one of the coolest clubs in town with *anyone* else, or would at least like to change the decor of this traditional red-and-white checkered tablecloth pasta joint—it looks like the last place you'd expect to thrive as a late night destination. But mom or no mom, this place parties harder and stays open later than anywhere else in the town center.

In contrast, **Mandracchio** *(Passo di Piazza 1; Tel 040/366292; Bus 11, 17, 25, 28 to Piazza della Borsa; 11pm-late Wed-Sun; Cover varies, usually 10-20,000L; No credit cards)* is *exactly* what you'd expect from a typical Italian nightclub. This plush, eighties-style disco-pub has long since given up on the latest trends—the music is only slightly more interesting than the top-5 Italian dance hits, but far from artsy or alternative. But it is right smack dab in the center of town, and if you're feeling like speaking English, there will be plenty of tourists to keep you company. Beers run about 6-8,000L, cocktails 8-12,000L.

ARTS SCENE

Trieste's cultural diversity and vibrant student life conspire to create a small but always compelling art scene. Many bars, like **Naima Jazz** and **Juice** [see *bar scene,* above], double as exhibit space showcasing local talent.

▶▶VISUAL ARTS
Lipanjepuntin Artecontemporanea *(Via Diaz 4; Tel 040/308-099, Fax 040/308-287; Bus 24 to Via Diaz; 11am-7:30pm Tue-Sat or by appointment; lipuarte@tin.it, www.lipanjepuntin.com; V, MC)* specializes in cutting-edge video, computer, and installation art. Featured artists include notable locals, Europeans, and international celebrities like Robert Longo and David Byrne.

▶▶PERFORMING ARTS
Built in 1801, **Teatro Verdi** *(Piazza Verdi 1; Tel 040/672-25-00, Fax 040/672-22-49; Bus 11, 17, 25, 28 to Piazza della Borsa; Shows begin at 6pm; 15-220,000L depending on seat and show; info@teatroverdi-trieste,*

www.teatroverdi-trieste.com; V, MC) is the pride and joy of Trieste's many music-lovers. The same greats who designed La Fenice in Venice and La Scala in Milan had a hand in the plans. The productions, strictly classic opera, are as grand as the building itself.

Cinema Edera *(Piazza Martiri di Belfiore 2; Tel 0422/300-224; 6-10:15pm; 8,000L, 5,000L student)* has mainly Hollywood films in *lingua originale* (subtitled, not dubbed) on Thursdays.

CULTURE ZOO

Most of the museums in Trieste are missable. The more interesting things to see are the buildings themselves, not necessarily what's inside them. And be ready to walk a lot, because the stuff you'll want to look at is spread out, just like the after-dark scene.

The one concentration of buildings is on Collina Capitolina, the large hill looking down over the city center that was the heart of Roman and medieval Trieste. Basilica di San Silvestro, the Cathedral di San Giusto, the Castello di San Giusto, and the Teatro Romano are all on its winding streets. The view you get from the top of the hill, though, is the best reason to make the climb—apart from the Cathedral, the other structures fall into the "might as well go in, since we're up here" category. The best place to begin your trek up the hill is at the end of Via Del Teatro Romano, closest to Piazza Unitá. From here, climb the stairs to Santa Maria Maggiore and San Silvestro, then follow the winding street up.

Piazza dell'Unitá D'Italia: This piazza on the port was modeled after the Austro-Hungarian conquerors' capital city, Vienna. The neo-classical buildings have recently been restored to their original blinding white, and the square itself has had its broad flagstones re-layed. If you look inside the main arch of the Municipo building, you can see a drawing

THE JOYCE OF TRIESTE

The years James Joyce spent in Trieste (1904-1915, and again, from 1919-1920) were some of his most productive—it must have been all the caffeine. He finished both *Dubliners* and *Portrait of the Artist as a Young Man* here, and started scribbling the first few chapters of *Ulysses* too. Joyce fans may enjoy a stroll past some of his early haunts, such as the **Berlitz School** *(Via San Nicolò 32, first floor)*, where he toiled away teaching English, or the **Dreher restaurant** *(Piazza della Borsa)*, where he's remembered eating his meals. The tourist office [see *need to know*, below] offers a free walking tour and map called *Joyce Itineraries.*

of what the medieval Italianate piazza looked like before the Hungarians sent in their wrecking crew.

Cathedral di San Giusto *(Piazza Cattedrale 1; Tel 040/309-666; 9am-noon/2:30-6:30pm Mon-Sat, 2:30-6pm Sun; Free):* Once the home of the church Patriarchs, who considered themselves the equal of the Pope in Rome, this is still the main religious site in town. The exterior features lopsided Romanesque architecture and a big Gothic window; inside, there are Roman mosaics on the floor. On either side of the altar, with its modern mosaics in the cupola, are half-domed side altars with Byzantine mosaics. The left aisle of the church is also eclectic, with Renaissance oil paintings on canvas displayed next to large marble Baroque altarpieces.

Castello di San Giusto *(Piazza Cattedrale 3; Tel 040/313-636; 9am-7pm Tue-Sun, Oct-Mar, 9am-7pm Tue-Sun, Apr-Sep; 2,000L; No credit cards):* Dominating the skyline of Capitoline Hill, this castle was built as a barracks and lookout by the Venetians, and enlarged and restored many times in the 16th-17th centuries. There's a city-run museum with weapons from the 13th-19th centuries, furniture paintings, and tapestries inside, but it's missable, unless you're a crossbow nut. Stick with the striking view of the exterior.

Teatro Romano *(Via Teatro Romano):* This theater was built in the first century, when Tergesto, as the city was then known, was an obscure yet prosperous provincial town. Its hillside location recalls the Roman Theater in Verona—if you've already seen that, this one's not worth much more than a glance down as you descend the hill after seeing San Giusto. Otherwise, you may enjoy walking around the weathered stone stage and seats, soaking up the atmosphere where gladiators battled and ancient actors emoted. But Trieste doesn't make it easy. To visit the teatro, you have to first check out the **Antiquarium** *(Via Donata, just up the hill from the theater; Tel 040/43631; Bus 11, 17, 25, 28 to Piazza della Borsa; 10am-noon Thu only, call at other times; Free),* the remains of a first-century house just up the hill from the theater—they'll let you in to the Teatro. The antiquarium itself is for serious Roman fanatics only.

Basilica di San Silvestro *(Piazzetta S. Silvestro 1; Tel 040/632-770; 10am-noon Thur, Fri, other times call; Free):* Standing beside Santa Maria Maggiore is a rarity in Catholic-dominated Italy: a Protestant church. The Romanesque building stands on what has been a religious site since at least 313 A.D..

Tempio di San Nicoló dei Greci *(Riva Tre Novembre; Tel 040/368-320 or 040/635-614; Bus 6 to Piazzà Unità d'Italia; 9am-noon/5-8pm daily, closed Thu, winter hours vary; Free):* This neoclassical Greek Orthodox Church built in 1784 is definitely worth a peek. Its bright blue domes, Byzantine-style mosaics, and silver icons would look more at home in Thrace than in Trieste.

Sinagoga di Via San Francenso *(Via S. Francesco 19; Tel 040/371-466; Bus 35 to Via Battisti; 4:40-8pm Mon; Free):* This gorgeous domed and arched building, in the Borgo Teresano, is one of the biggest and most important remaining synagogues in Europe. The stark Syrian-influenced design makes for a solemn visit.

Museo della Risiera di San Sabbia *(Ratto della Pileria 43; Tel 040/826-202 custodian, 040/308-686 offices; Bus 10 to San Sabba; 9am-1pm Tue-Sun, open 'til 6pm, Apr 1-May 15 and Nov 1-11, closed Mon; Free):* The only concentration camp in Italy, the San Sabbia Rice Factory Museum is a chilling reminder of the hatred that sent a once multicultural region spiraling first into slave labor, then the Holocaust, and, most recently, Balkan ethnic cleansing. It's just as unsettling trying to ask directions to this place—even people in the neighborhood seem eager to ignore its existence.

Miramare Castle and Park *(Viale Miramare; Tel 040/224-143, Fax 040/224-220; Bus 36 from Piazza Oberdan to Miramare; Castle 9am-7pm daily, last entry 6:30pm; Park 9am-5pm, Nov-Feb; 9am-6pm Mar, Oct; 9am-7pm Apr-Sep; 8,000L castle admission; No credit cards):* Austrian Emperor Franz-Josef funded construction of this white fairytale-like castle in 1854 as a present for his brother Archduke Maximilian. Max later ran off to Mexico in 1864 and set himself up as Emperor—he never bothered asking the Mexicans' permission, which got him shot three years later. His wife, "Empress" Charlotte, was driven insane by the experience, and returned to this castle. Today you can wander through the happy couple's bedroom and throne-room, and in July and August take in the Maximilian and Charlotte sound and light show! (Curb your enthusiasm.) The park is the real reason to come here—it covers 22 hectares and features tropical plants, a butterfly garden, statuary, and numerous fountains. It's a great place to lose yourself for a couple of hours.

great outdoors

Trieste offers the best of both worlds: that hoppin' nightlife *plus* an impressive natural setting with tons of outdoors activities for those who are still standing come morning. Local outdoor fanatics have loosely organized themselves into clubs and are more than happy to let visitors join in.

With all of these seaside cliffs and mountain outcroppings overlooking the water, it's obvious why some of Italy's best climbers hail from Trieste. One of the most popular spots for climbing is on the path between **Opicina** and the village of Prosecco [see *by foot*, below]; you'll see the climbers hanging from the precipices. Alternately, you can take bus 46, 44, 42, or 39 north from the train station to Prosecco, about a 20-minute ride. Get off at the center of this blink-and-you-miss-it town, and walk east on Via San Nazario until you see the climbers on your left. The **C.A.I Alpina Delle Giulie** *(Via Donota 2; Tel 040/630-464; Bus 11, 17, 25, 28 to Piazza della Borsa)* club can help you plan a day of climbing, from rental to reservations, and may even offer to take you out on one of their excursions. For more one-on-one instruction, guide **Aldo Michelini** *(Via dei Mirissa 24/1; Tel 040/395-447; Rates vary)* gives lessons on everything from rock climbing to alpine skiing.

by foot

One of the highlights of visiting Trieste is just that—high. To get the best view of the **Gulf of Trieste,** go to Piazza Oberdan and wait for tram #2. This tram has been making the steep climb up to Opicina since 1902, crossing neighborhoods built on a 45-degree angle, and vineyards planted on terraced plots. Hop off when you see the mysterious monolith—this is the Obelisk stop. Linger a moment to take in the view, and observe the path map on the sign next to this tall sculpture, which can't be too important, since no one seems to know much about it. There's only one path from here, with woods on a steep incline to the right, and sweeping views of the water below. You'll be sharing your walk with everyone from elderly couples strolling hand in hand, to young moms pushing baby carriages. About 15 minutes later, the path will turn to pavement, and you'll notice a few brave souls navigating the jagged architecture of the rock outcropping to the right. Yes, that is **Miramare** sitting along the waterway down below, but you can't get there from here. Now you have to decide whether to proceed straight into the little town of Prosecco, where you can take Bus 39, 42, 44 or 46 back to the station, or turn around and walk all the way back.

The tranquil ripples of the Gulf of Trieste are perfect for kayaking and canoeing. For rentals and outings, contact the local club, **F.I.C.K Canoa e Kayak** (Piazza della Borsa 7; Tel 040/365-832; Bus 11, 17, 25, 28 to Piazza della Borsa). **Surf Club Trieste** (Viale Miramare 31/C; Tel 040/425-14-45; Bus 36 from Piazza Oberdan to Miramare; surftrieste@tiscalinet.it, www.surftrieste.it; Hours and rates vary;) isn't just a club for action sports aficionados, it's also a school and store where you can buy and rent equipment.

You'd think that with Trieste's weather, views, and good roads, you'd be dodging mountain bikers left and right. Truth is, finding a place to rent a bike is damn near impossible. Even the friendly folks at the tourist office draw a blank when asked for shops that are in the business of noleggiare bici. One thing's for sure: the members of **Ulisse Gruppo cicloturisti e ciclisti urbani di Trieste** (Via del Sale 4/B; Tel 0328/364-22-22; Bus 24 to Via Diaz; 5:30-8pm Tue; ulisse@retecivica.trieste.it) are fanatical about their sport. They print an extremely detailed guide to the best bike paths in the area, called Itinerari Cicloturistici, which you can pick up for free at the tourist office [see need to know, below]. Warning: The tram up to Opicina is the only one in the city where you're allowed to bring your wheels along.

You can take a swim in the **Golfo de Trieste** at **la Barcolana,** a wide strip of concrete that extends north from the harbor-side walk and stretches toward **Miramare,** the seaside suburb of Trieste. It serves as both beach and boardwalk in the summer months (yep, a concrete "beach"—the Riviera this ain't). If you're tired of all the cat calls at the sceney la Barcolana, try the **Piscina Coperta Bianchi** *(Riva T. Gulli 3; Tel 040/303-386; Bus 10 to Piazza Venezia; 7-9am/noon-3pm Mon-Fri, 7am-2pm Sat, 9am-1pm Sun; 10,000L; No credit cards),* a covered swimming pool right on the waterfront, 10 minutes south of Piazza dell'Unità d'Italia, where you can cool off without having to fend off gawkers.

The local skaters are responsible for a new **skate park** beside the Lloyd's Insurance office tower. Take Bus 16 to the "Supermercato PAM" stop and look for the two six-foot quarter-pipes. Skaters are there pretty much every afternoon. You can also find skaters in Piazza Oberdan, hurling themselves down the stairs and across the cement.

STUFF

There are plenty of places along Piazza della Borsa to buy stylish duds without having to fork over the usual tourist mark-up. Otherwise, you'll see the standard collections of stores you'd see in any tourist town: CD shops that double as hipster hangouts, intellectual bookshops, and sports shops.

▶▶BOUND

Libreria Minerva *(Via San Nicolo 20; Tel 040/369-340364; Bus 5, 17, 24, 28 30 to Via Roma; 9am-1pm/4-8pm; V, MC),* in the Borgo Teresano, has paperback classics, newer literature, and pulp fiction in English from 10 to 22,000L.

▶▶TUNES

The owner of **Sgt. Pepper** *(Via San Nicolo 24/A; Bus 5, 17, 24, 28 30 to Via Roma; 10am-1pm/4-8pm Mon-Sat; granganga@tin.it; No credit cards),* the coolest CD store in the Borgo, prides himself on supplying local DJs and civilians alike with the latest in foreign music, especially whatever's happening in London. This little shop has ample selections of drum 'n' bass, electronica, nu jazz, dub, reggae, Ska, indie rock, punk, and '60s and '70s re-issues. He also spins at **Caffeteria del Borgo** [see *bar scene,* above] at least once a week.

▶▶DUDS

Half Pipe Alternative Sports *(Via Diaz 1; Tel 040/362-459; Bus 24 to Via Diaz; 9am-12:30pm/3:30-5:30pm; V, MC),* south of Piazza dell'Unità d'Italia, bills itself as the clothing store for "all extreme sports." You can get cool ski and snowboard wear here, as well as skate duds, and...Fred Perry tennis shirts? What's extreme about that?

▶▶HOW BAZAAR

On the last weekend of each month, Trieste breaks out the old and sells it to its newest fans at the **Antiquarian Market** *(Via della Beccherie; Tel 040/367-530).* Visitors from all over the region come to score bargains from the 50 or so venders who line up along the streets, hawking everything from old pottery to vintage books.

EATS

It's not unheard of to see spaghetti, *gulash,* and *krauti* all offered on the same menu here in ethnically mixed Trieste. An outstanding array of seafood comes into the port daily, and most restaurants sell you your fish while it's practically still wiggling. The battered and fried *fritti misti* shouldn't be missed; it comes to the table as a heaping pile of calamari, shrimp, anchovies, sardines, olives, mushrooms, and artichokes.

What stands out most about eating out in Trieste isn't just what you eat, but how you eat it. The buffet experience is big here. Occupying what looks like a typical Italian bar, a buffet can always be recognized by the shoulder-to-shoulder, stand-up crowds inside. Boiled meats, known as *bolliti,* are sliced into sandwiches, while cheeses, cured hams, and salami are offered by the plate, and wines are poured straight from the barrel.

▶▶CHEAP

For a quick bite, head to **Pizza al Pezzo** *(Via Cavana 1; Tel 040/306-080; Bus 24 to Via Diaz; 11:30am-11pm Mon-Sat, closed Sun; 2,500-3,000L per slice; No credit cards),* the tiny storefront just off the main artery of the old part of town, Via Diaz. It's just a counter with pre-made square slices, a register, and a list of prices, but the food isn't bad. You could also do the all-American thing and grab a hot dog and a fountain Coke. Don't worry, the oblivious teen at the counter chatting with friends will notice you. Eventually.

The pizzas at **Pizzaria Barattolo** *(Piazza San Antonio 2; Tel 040/631-480; Bus A-D 1,5 9, 10, 15, 16, 18, 19, 26 to Piazza Goldoni; 8:30-1am daily; 9-14,000L pizza; V, MC),* along the Canale Grande, are the best in town. Chewy crust, rich sauce, and gooey mozzarella cheese coalesce in a pseudo-gourmet pie so good you won't even mind how long you had to wait for a table. Smaller than your average Italian pie, but heaped with super-fresh toppings, it's still more than enough for a meal. If you're still hungry, order a classic pasta dish or a large salad.

▶▶DO-ABLE

The packed, ever-popular **Buffet Gilda** *(Via Valdirivo 20; Tel 040/364-554; Bus 5, 17, 24, 28 30 to Via Roma; 8am-8pm Mon-Sat; 9,000L per*

TO MARKET

From *bolliti* to prosciutto to cheese, all the usual sandwich makings are available cheap, cheap, cheap, at Trieste's bustling **food market** *(Via Carducci 36; 8am-2pm Mon, 8am-3pm/4-7pm Tue-Sat, closed Sun).*

entree, 4,000L panini; 1,000L seating charge; No credit cards), in the Borgo Teresano, is not for novices. You won't see any English on the menu outside, nor will you hear any spoken inside, so consider your options carefully before negotiating for some elbow-room. If you're willing to eat a *bollito* meat sandwich standing up, walk right into the little fluorescent-lit space and bark out your order to the guys in aprons behind the bar. If you'd rather take a seat, you'll pay a 1,000L-per-person cover charge, but will also have more choices available. The *pasta e fagioli* is comfort in a bowl, and the fried sardines and calamari are out of this world. The house salads are huge, and the bread that accompanies your meal is practically a meal in itself. Don't worry if the elderly waitresses in nurse's uniforms give you attitude—they're like that to everybody.

Located just down the block from the international stock exchange, century-old **Da Bepi Buffet** *(Via Cassa di Risparmio 3; Tel 040/366-858; Bus 11, 17, 25, 28 to Piazza della Borsa; 10am-10:30pm Mon-Sat; Closed Jul 15-Aug 8; 4-4,500L panini; No credit cards)* has perfected boiled meats to an art. They're also accustomed to English-speaking travelers, and make an effort to make you feel at home. Specify whether you want a table or not as you walk in. If you don't, go up to the meat table on the right side of the bar, and point to whatever gets your mouth watering. If you score one of the few tables alongside the buffet, prepare to be jostled by elbows, handbags, and small children.

On the eastern side of the Borgo, **Da Giovanni Buffet** *(Via S. Lazzaro 14b; Tel 040/639-396; Bus A-D 1,5 9, 10, 15, 16, 18, 19, 26 to Piazza Goldoni; 8am-3pm/4:30-9pm Mon-Sat; 3,000L per plate; No credit cards)* is the most sophisticated of the buffet bunch. The dark wood and copper decor is both modern and cozy, and the elevated dining room offers some distance from the hectic feeding frenzy. All offerings are listed on the huge circular sign to the left of the front door; the choices are more varied than what you'll find at Gilda and Bepo, for about the same price. Order one of the five wines drawn from the wooden casks (1,200-2,000L per glass), then point to one of the many salamis, sausages, prosciuttos, or cheeses served up for around 3,000L per plate. For heartier fare, get a table.

If you can't stomach one more serving of *bollito misto* (no more tongue, please!), the Tyrolean cuisine at **Hansel and Gretel** *(Via Nordio 20; Tel 040/662-607; Bus A-D 1,5 9, 10, 15, 16, 18, 19, 26 to Piazza Goldoni; 11am-3pm/7:30-10:30pm Wed-Mon, closed Tue; 12-20,000L per entree; V, MC, DC)* is a refreshing change. This cheery little restaurant off Via Ginnastica has blue and yellow gingham tablecloths and wicker baskets on the six little tables off the large, knotty pine bar. Tyrolean classics like speck *canederli* in brown butter and *gulash* are offered up alongside dishes like baked brie with bilberry sauce, pasta with cod and asparagus, and grilled meat and fish. You can't go wrong with a half-liter of fruity house white or red for 6,000L.

Finding **All'Antica Ghiacceretta** *(Via dei Fornelli 2; Tel 040/305-614; Bus 11, 17, 25, 28 to Piazza della Borsa; Noon-2:30pm/7-9:30pm*

Trieste eats and crashing

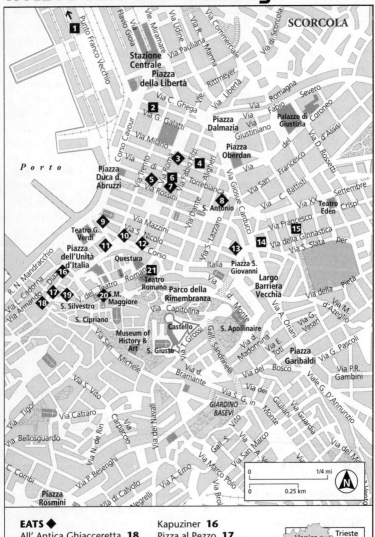

EATS ◆
All' Antica Ghiacceretta **18**
Antico Panada **5**
Antico Caffe Torinese **12**
Buffet Gilda **3**
Caffe Tergesteo **11**
Caffe Tomaseo **9**
Crèmcaffe **13**
Da Bepi Buffet **10**
Da Giovanni Buffet **8**
Gelateria Zampoli **19**
Hansel and Gretel **20**

Kapuziner **16**
Pizza al Pezzo **17**
Pizzaria Barattolo **7**

CRASHING ■
Albergo Brioni **14**
Città di Parenzo **21**
Hotel Alabarda **4**
Hotel Istria **15**
Marina **2**
Nuovo Albergo Centro **6**
Ostello Tegeste **1**

Mon-Sat, closed Sun; Entrees 15-20,000L; No credit cards), tucked away just south of the Piazza dell'Unità d'Italia, is the easy part. But getting a reservation at this little place, Trieste's most sought-after restaurant, takes persistence, luck, or any indication that you refuse to leave town without trying their famous *spaghetti al vongole,* which may score points with the hyper-energetic owner. At first glance you may wonder why such a dingy place is so highly regarded (save your trip to the bathroom until *after* you've eaten), but you'll understand when you get your food. There's no menu, just a verbal barrage of dishes like *calamari fritti, fritti misti,* and pastas with fish. Grilled fish is the house specialty—if you don't know your *dorado* from your *tonno,* the owner will kindly point to the corresponding illustration on the movable easel. A word from the wise: though we all know now that it's okay to drink red wine with fish, il Signore still doesn't like it. Order the house white, and he'll probably bring you a *limoncello* with dessert.

▶▶SPLURGE

Antico Panada *(Via Rossini 8/D; Tel 040/347-62-86; Bus 8 to Corso Cavour; 11am-2:30pm/6:30-11pm; 18-25,000L per entree; V, MC)* is where gussied-up Triestini go when they want to have a good meal—the 1920s-style mural on the wall depicting a feast of gorgeous people chowing down might as well be a mirror. The lights are dim, the ceilings are high, and plush fabric is draped over the walls. Try to get a table in the crowded loft, which gives diners a view of the activity below. A large, open kitchen turns out local dishes from the Veneto, with an emphasis on traditional Umbrian pastas like *stringotti* with almonds—and, of course, an amazing, enormous *fritti misti* for two. Make sure to take a spin on the dessert and cordial cart—the intense infusions of anise, cinnamon, and vanilla steeped in potent liqueur will have your senses reeling.

crashing

Good news: Trieste has some terrific, recently restored cheapies for the sophisticated backpacker, a palace with accommodations plusher than the White House, and a nice range in between. So everyone can look forward to a little bit of relative luxury when they bed down for the night.

▶▶CHEAP

Ostello Tegeste *(Via Miramare 331; Tel/Fax 040/224-102; Bus 36 to Miramare stop; Reception open noon-midnight; Closed last three weeks in Jan; 22,000L dorm, no private baths, breakfast included; Midnight curfew; No credit cards)* is right on La Barlona, the site of much fun-in-the-sun frolic, so book way in advance if you come in the summer. It's a typical cheery hostel with big dorm rooms, bread and coffee for breakfast, and the usual annoying hostel rules. There are also a lot of extras—a cool roof terrace, bikes to rent, and outdoor activity classes. IYH membership is required—if you don't have it already you'll have to cough up an extra 6,000L for a stamp.

    Hotel Alabarda *(Valdrivo 22; Tel 040/630-269, Fax 040/639-284; Bus 30 from the station to Via Roma; hotelalabarda@hotelalabarda.it,*

wired

Internet connections in Trieste are light. You can get online at **Sport Net Center** *(Piazza dello Squero Vecchio 1/C; Tel 040/322-08-61, Fax 040/322-52-13; 8:30am-12:30pm/3-7pm Mon-Fri; gilleri@sportnetcenter.it, www.sportnetcenter.it; 12,000L per hour, 300L per page to print; No credit cards)*, but you may have to make a reservation, since there are just three computers. The quarters are a bit cramped, the connection is DSL, and the location, just off the Piazza dell'Unità, is central. Some hotels, like **Hotel Alabarda** [see *crashing,* below] offer a terminal or two for your browsing pleasure, but other than that, you may have to revel in your electronic isolation for awhile.

You can get local info on the web at *trieste.com/tourism/2parole_ing/2parolehp_ing.html.*

www.hotelalabarda.it; 70,000L single, 80,000/115,000L double w/bath; V, MC, AE), situated in the middle of the Borgo Teresano, knows what travelers want. Someday, all budget hotels and hostels will be like this: phones and TVs in most rooms, new Danish-modern furniture, Internet access *(5,000L per hour),* no curfew, and video poker. That's right, video poker—you can even win a free room, sodas, Internet time, and other goodies. It's an easy walk from the train station: straight across Piazza Libertà and down Via Ghega. Via Rome is the second right, then Via Valdirivo is the fourth left. Or take the bus.

Hmm, maybe all budget hotels and hostels are like this already, at least in Trieste: **Nuovo Albergo Centro** *(Via Roma 33; Tel 040/347-87-90, Fax 040/347-52-58; Bus 30 from the station to Via Roma; 50,000L single, 75,000L double, no private baths; V, MC),* just two blocks down from Alabarda, is just as good a value. The English-speaking owners offer 18 beautiful rooms, all with TVs and phones. This place seems too stylish to be so cheap: all the wood is polished and new, and the towels, curtains, and bedspreads tasteful. The bathrooms, located down the hall, feature shiny new facilities and bright blue tile. Throw in the IKEA-esque furniture and promise of Internet access, and you'll never want to leave. Reservations are definitely recommended.

▶▶**DO-ABLE**

You're about to enter the twilight zone of major renovation: **Hotel Istria** *(Via Timeus 5; Tel 040/371-343, Fax 040/371-343; Bus A-D 1,5 9, 10, 15, 16, 18, 19, 26 to Piazza Goldoni; 65-90,000L single, 85-120,000L double, all w/private bath; No credit cards),* near the Ospedale Maggiore, is stuck somewhere in between fancy and shabby, with fresh rooms and hallways outshining the worn-out lobby and stairs. One double without a bath can be yours for 85,000L, but otherwise, the amenities (new furniture, TV, telephone) are comparable to those of places listed above, but at higher prices. Make sure you get a room in back, because the scooter-noise per minute ratio is high.

Owned by the brother of the proprietor of the nearby Istria, the **Albergo Brioni** *(Via Ginnastica 2; Tel and Fax 040/772-942; Bus A-D 1,5 9, 10, 15, 16, 18, 19, 26 to Piazza Goldoni; 65-90,000L single, 85-120,000L double, all w/private baths; No credit cards)* is much homier, with more of a family feel. All in all, the effect is that of a little-old Italian couple's apartment opened to the public. The rooms are big, the comforters mismatched, and the clientele student-y.

The sweet family who runs **Centrale** *(Via Ponchielli 1; Tel 040/639-482, Fax 040/370-677; 60-75,000L single w/out bath, 90,000L single w/bath, 100,000L double w/out bath, 125,000L double w/ bath, 7,000L breakfast; V, AE)* will greet you like a long-lost cousin. The 20 rooms have a homey, slightly upscale feel, with pretty, institutional furniture, TVs, phones, and plenty of space. There's a nice sitting room with comfy couches, and a cheery breakfast room where you can take your first cappuccino of the day. It couldn't be in a better location—just one block north of the street that's made for strolling, Via Ponchielli.

It looks like a splurge, and feels like a splurge, but **Città di Parenzo** *(Via degli Artisti 8; Tel 040/631-133, Fax 040/367-510; 95,000L single w/out bath, 115,000L single w/bath, 130,000L double w/out bath, 160,000L double w/bath; No credit cards)* doesn't cost what most splurges cost. The sitting rooms and lobby are elegant, with antique furniture and plenty of space, and each of the 35 rooms has air conditioning and satellite TV. Best of all, it's off Corso Italia, behind the Teatro Romano, right in the center of all the sights.

Just a few blocks south of the train station and a few blocks north of the Borgo is **Marina** *(Via Galatti 14; Tel and Fax 040/369-298; 45,000L single, 80,000L double, 100,000L double w/bath; No credit cards)*, a budget hotel with a lot of heart and soul. The elderly woman who runs it loves travelers and makes an effort to help you enjoy your stay. The sitting rooms and hallways are filled with travel guides and books in English that others have left behind, but the showpiece is the aquarium that holds her baby turtles. Rooms are bare basic, with nothing but the bed, sheets, and a small table. It smells a little musty when you first walk in, but everything's very clean.

need to know

Currency Exchange There's an **ATM** in the train station, and tons of **banks** around Piazza Borsa.

Tourist Information The **tourist office** *(Riva Tre Novembre 9; 040/347-83-12, Fax 040/347-83-20; Bus 6 to Piazzà dell'Unità d'Italia; 9am-5pm Mon-Sat)* is near Caffe Tomaseo. English is spoken and fliers are distributed, but they won't be able to help you book a room. There's a smaller version with extended hours *(9am-8:30pm* *daily)* in the train station, on the left as you leave the platform and enter the ticketing hall.

Public Transportation The **bus station** is on Piazza Oberdan. Tickets are available at *tabacchi* shops for 1,500L; maps and schedules can be picked up at the tourist office [see above]. Don't forget that you're supposed to stamp the tickets as you get on the bus yourself. The tram up to Opicina leaves every 20 minutes from Piazza Oberdan. You can catch a **taxi** *(Tel 0422/400-152)* at the train station. **Radiotaxis** *(Tel 040/54533 or 040/54920)* are available 24 hours—don't forget that you pay for their trip to pick you up, too.

Health and Emergency Emergency: *118;* Police: *Tel 0422/37901.* The local hospital is **Ospedale Maggiore** *(Tel 040/399-23-37),* east of the city center.

Pharmacies Both **Al Cedro** *(Piazza Oberdan 2; Tel 040/364-928 or 040/365-556)* and **Al Cammello** *(Viale XX Settembre 4; Tel 040/371-377 or 040/371-323)* have the rotating schedule of 24-hour pharmacies posted on their doors.

Telephone Phone cards are available in 5,000L or 10,000L increments at newsstands or tabacchi.

Airports Direct flights to Rome, Milan, Genoa, Naples, Munich, and London are available from **Ronchi dei Legionari International Airport** *(Via Aquilea, Ronchi dei Legionari; Tel 0481/773-232; www.aeroporto.fvg.it).* An airport shuttle bus *(15,000L)* leaves from Piazza Libertá; it's about 31 kilometers away.

Trains The main station, **Trieste Centrale** *(Piazza Libertá 8; Tel 040/452-80-87)* is no more than a 15-minute walk from anywhere you want to go in town. With baggage lockers, a small tourist office, and a bar with awesome sandwiches, it's one of the better stations you'll come across.

Bus Lines Out of the City Domestic service and links with Slovenia and Croatia are available from the **bus station** *(Piazza della Libertá 11; Tel 040/425-001),* located across from the train station.

Boats Adriatica di Navigazione/Agenzia Agemar *(Piazza Duce degli Abruzzi 1/A; Tel 040/363-222 or 040/363-737)* sails to Greece, Albania, Slovenia and Croatia, as well as Italian destinations like Grado and Venice.

Postal Mail missives from the **post office** *(Piazza Verdi 2; Tel 040/368-208, Fax 040/368-208; 8:10am-2:05pm Mon-Fri, 8:10am-12:50pm Sat).*

Internet See *wired,* above.

everywhere else

udine

As you make your way to Udine, you may find yourself wishing for the ugly to stop. The city suffered badly from bombings in WWII, and nasty new constructions are mixed in with the great old buildings. But the cool buildings gradually increase in density as you get closer to the center of the old town. And when you discover gorgeous Piazza Libertá, one of the most beautiful Renaissance squares in all of Italy, you'll be glad you kept on going. This is Main Street, Italy.

Make no mistake: Udine (the region's capital) is not a tourist town as much as a functioning city, with a university (Università degli Studi di Udine) that keeps its nightlife going. This ain't Florence or Milan, but there's enough to see—including Baroque masterpieces by Giambatista Tiepolo (1696-1770) and Italy's best modern art museum—that you won't feel guilty about sticking around for the bar-hopping. The city is below most of the tourists' radar, so there are no crowds, long lines, or tacky tourist traps. Come to Udine because it's both fun to say (OO-din-ay!), and a bit off the beaten path without being a backwards little turnip-mining village or something.

Outside of the sizable student population, the Udinese are not as likely as Romans or Florentines to speak English. But those who can communicate with you, and even many who can't, are genuinely interested in talking to travelers who decide to give Udine a try. They especially want to find out why you would come to a little-known town like this—just being here at all makes you very cool in their eyes.

Udine's strategic location accounts for its successive waves of conquerors, as well as the artistic, culinary and linguistic signatures they left behind. There are a few Roman traces here (all in museums), and Holy Roman Empire buildings, plus a story that Attila and his Huns built a hill in the center of town. Venice took over in 1420, building the showpiece piazza. Later, the Hapsburgs of the Austro-Hungarian Empire put up a statue or two and left a taste for German and Slavic foods in their wake.

udine bars clubs and culture zoo

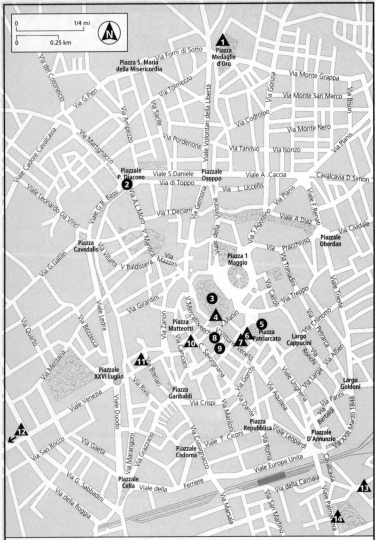

BARS/CLUBS ▲
Arcigay Nuovi Passi **13**
Bar Poscolle **11**
Café Pinocchio **7**
I Piombi **4**
No Fun **14**
Pane e Vino San Daniele **10**
Password **12**
Pilutti's Pub **1**
Taverna dell'Angelo **6**

CULTURE ZOO ●
Castello **3**
Galleria d'Arte Moderna **2**
Il Duomo di Santa
  Maria Annunziata **9**
Museum of Sacred Art
  and Tiepolo Gallery **5**
Piazza Libertà **8**

six things to talk to a local about

1. **Calcio (soccer).** The people of Udine love their team with a passion notable even for soccer-mad Italy. They even sell CDs of the favorite stadium chants. The Udinese soccer team was at the top of the Italian A league for the first part of 2000; in a sport where big, wealthy cites like Milan and Turin dominate, this is like the Detroit Tigers regularly beating up on the Mets and the Braves. Warning: this conversation may be more than you bargained for.

2. **Recovery from the 1976 earthquake.** It was bad. The death toll was enormous. But within 10 years, Udine and the rest of Fruili has been rebuilt. People here are immensely proud of that, but unfortunately some of them use it as a chance to dog the south of Italy. It's a good idea to mention your uncle in Naples before asking about recovery from the earthquake.

3. **Furlan language.** Bumper stickers and T-shirts bespeak the community's pride in the local Furlan language. Of course, TV and other modern ills are speeding its demise. Everyone seems to have a great-uncle who speaks it, and an opinion on its relative merits.

4. **Trieste.** Good rivalries always make for lively conversation. While Udine is really the political capital, its better-known rival dominates the region's commerce and culture. This fact, along with their differences in dialect and culture, causes friction between them.

5. **Ecologic Sundays.** Now this is a cool idea. Once a month, the city government shuts off the center of town to all cars. In order to balance out people's frustrations, it offers free ice cream, free entrance to museums and public pools, and "crazy bikes" for the kiddies. Natch, some of the more car-happy Udinese find the whole thing annoying, but some people will complain about anything. See what they think.

6. **Gli Alpini.** As of 2000, ignorant tourists will no longer be able to chuckle at the uniforms of these Italian servicemen—which can include feathered caps, green knickers, and wool capes. This once elite and respected league has been disbanded—is this a good or a bad thing?

neighborhoods and hanging out

The train station is a 15-minute walk south of the large, rectangular city center, which is still marked by ancient city walls in places. The **Castello** dominates the landscape from **Castello Hill,** exactly in the center of town. The hill is just northeast of **Piazza Libertà** [see *culture zoo,* below], the central square. **Piazza Marconi,** to the north, is lined with cafes. All of Udine's finest boutiques, food stores, and galleries—essentially, all the culture that's fit to print—are housed inside the city walls. The only other area where you might spend some time is the traffic-nightmare **Piazzale Celli,** to the west of the train station, where several budget hotels are grouped.

The Udinese are known for their elegant, very civilized approach to public socializing. To look at them you'd think they were all dressed up for a party, but really, it's just for the daily ritual of the post-work *passegiata:* they begin the stroll at Piazza Libertá and continue along the winding streets that radiate outward. **Via Mercatovecchio** is an especially good place to cafe-hop during this time; **Piazza Matteotti,** one block east, is another prime location. Meanwhile, in addition to its small cafe and great views, **Castello Hill** is the nightly hangout of choice for nine out of ten of Udine's juvenile delinquents.

cafe scene

Reigning on the west-side of Piazza Libertá, the art-deco **Caffe Contarena** *(Via Cavour 1; Tel 0432/512-741; Bus 1, 3, C to Via Mercatovecchio; 9am-11pm daily; No credit cards)* is a sight to be seen—and the place to *be seen,* come *aperitivo* hour. It satisfies the overflowing crowd with coffee, drinks, pastries, and a generous spread of chips, olives, and other free snacks. Even if you don't feel like rubbing shoulders and sharing cocktails (10,000L) with Udine's upper-crust, who chain smoke at the green marble and mahogany wood bar, at least stop in to check out the recently restored mosaics in the sprawling main room. The jazz-aficionado owner arranges live music every week, and the walls function as one of Udine's hipper galleries, with exhibits changing monthly.

The rival **Caffe Ottelio** *(Piazza Matteotti 11/A; Tel 0432/507-441; Bus 1, 3, C to Via Mercatovecchio; 8-2am Tue-Sat; No credit cards)* is located in just as advantageous a spot, in a faded, frescoed palazzo just off the Piazza. The interior of this enormous cafe is slick and new, the timbered ceiling contrasting with the ultra-modern air duct art. Outside, wicker chairs spill out onto the piazza's cobblestones—this is the place to watch the sunset, to meet local kids who pass out flyers on the night's events, and to catch up on those postcards home over a cappuccino (1,700L) or a beer (6-8,000L). Unless you're willing to spend the extra 20 percent waiter-service tax, head up to the bar, pay the cashier first, and scream out your order to the bartender like everyone else.

Prepare to spend some time up at **Casa Delle Contadinanza** *(Castello di Udine; Tel 0432/297-068; Bus 1, 3, C to Via Mercatovecchio;*

9:30am-6pm daily; No credit cards), the medieval palace just next to the castle on the hill, which has become a makeshift cafe and wine bar. Despite the painted crests of 15th-century royal families and the imposing fireplace, it has the temporary feel of someone selling fake Rolexes on the street. There's a folding table with a bunch of bottles of wine (3,000L by the glass), a big prosciutto ham, a portable espresso maker, and a fun, relaxing vibe. When you've had your fill, you can stumble out onto the castle lawn, which gives a 360-degree view of the city and the mountains that wrap around it.

bar, club and live music scene

Udine is one of the better cities for beer-drinking in Italy, especially in the fall, winter, and spring, when the students are in town full-force (only a few stick around for the summers). The very drinkable and very Italian *Birra Moretti* has been brewed here since 1859. *Birra Fruilana,* or *chiara,* is a light lager, while the *Doppiomalto,* or *rossa,* is a malty bock. There's not much in the way of clubbing—at least, not anywhere you can get to without a car and a designated driver.

Although the tiny, modern **Pane e Vino San Daniele** *(Piazzetta Lionello 12; Tel 0432/299-934; Bus 1, 3, C to Via Mercatovecchio/Piazza Libertá; 11am-12:30pm/7:30pm-3am daily; No credit cards)* is named for the plates of San Daniele ham it serves up, the bar is better known for its scene. A hipster crowd drinks cocktails (10,000L) in the narrow dimly-lit space or at the stand-up tables out front, and has been known to shake a leg or two when the music's turned up. There are DJs every night playing electronica, and the live music on Thursdays is free.

It's a 20-minute walk (or 5-minute bus ride) north from the center to get to **Pilutti's Pub** *(P. le Chiavris 67; Bus 2, 3 to Chiavris; Tel 0432/480-573; 10am-3pm/6pm-3am Tue-Sat; No credit cards),* just down Viale Volontari della Libertá, but it may be worth the effort to see an Italian

festivals and events

Friuli Doc *(October 4-7; Tel 0432/295-972; friulidoc @comune.udine.it,http://www.comune.udine.it/fdoc2000/fdoc.htm):* Doc is the viticulture certification that grapes have come from a specific area. This wine festival is a much larger, more sophisticated version of the village harvest festival. The center of town is closed to traffic and Fruilian wines, San Daniele ham, Monstasio cheese, and other local products are on display. Street entertainers roam everywhere, modern banners *(Bivate Coke!)* and medieval flags hang from the buildings. There is also, of course, much imbibing.

biker-bar. OK, so there aren't so many hogs out front, but the rowdy crowd makes up in enthusiasm what it lacks in steel. The big main room is decorated with beer signs and some Harley regalia; other than that, it's as basic as it gets. On weekends, the crowd spills over into the small piazza out front—actually, it's more of an intersection than a piazza, in keeping with the good ole 'merican feel of the place. Don't let the owner's handlebar mustache intimidate you, he's friendly and speaks some English.

Velvet Underground flows from the speakers, Guinness from the taps, and a sulky solemnity drapes over the smoky **Bar Poscolle** *(43 Via Poscolle; Tel 0432/044-020; Bus 4 to Poscolle; 8pm-3am daily; 7-8,000L beer pint; No credit cards),* providing exhausted travelers with some quiet anonymity for a spell. Follow Udine's pierced population to this laid-back dive west of Piazza della Libertá after midnight, and make sure to wear black. It's one of your only options for a jukebox that features something other than Italy's latest and greatest. Unfortunately, the daytime crowd is everything that the nighthawks aren't: think slicked-back teenaged boys and giggly girls who blast over-played Italian dance hits. You have been warned.

You may think nobody drinks in Udine's city center, until you step into **I Piombi** *(Via Manin 12; Tel 0432/506-168; Bus 7 to Via Manin 1, 3, C to Via Mercatovecchio; 11am-3pm/5pm-1:30am Tue-Thu, 11am-3pm/5pm-2am Fri, 11am-2pm/6pm-3am Sat, 11am-2pm/5pm-1am Sun; No credit cards)* and realize that it houses half of the bar-goers in town. Look for the street-level entrance south of Castello Hill and east of Piazza Libertá, but don't be led astray by the quaint, forty-something crowd sipping wine from oversized glasses upstairs. Make a beeline for the stairs to the left and head down into the chaos that is Piombi: a labyrinth that goes on forever, room after tiny, crowded room, all the way under the hill. Extremely dated murals of black jazz musicians shout out in one room, while piles of old kegs teeter in alcoves, and curtains of smoke fill the air. College students smoke, drink, and plot revolution by the bar, where eight kinds of beers are poured on tap (6-8,000L) and teens prowl around the big tables in the smaller rooms. The only travelers here (that would be you) stick out a little bit. But if you want to experience a real Italian scene, this place must not be missed.

Slightly more stylish drinking takes place at the pretty bar on the corner just south of I Piombi, **Taverna dell'Angelo** *(Via Lovaria 3/D; Tel 0432/507-752; Bus 7 to Piazza Patriarcato; 11:30am-3pm/5:30pm-late Mon-Sat; No credit cards).* Despite the tartan and dark wood pervading this two-story bar, it's not the typical Italian interpretation of a British Isles pub. Baroque angels and devils stare down from above as whiskeys (4-15,000L) and dark beers (5,000L-7,000L) are served up to an intellectual twenty and thirty-something crowd.

The only real club accessible to central Udine is **Password** *(Via le Venezia 464; Tel 0432/233-435 and 0348/651-11-81; Bus 4, C to Password; 11:30am-late Thur-Sun; Cover varies between free and 20,000L),* on the southwestern outskirts of town, a five-minute taxi-ride away (it will cost you somewhere between 10 and 15,000L—they start the meter from wherever they are when you call). The vibe is young and very MTV Europe, huge and commercial. Some of the theme nights are creative; others, like "Goldy's American Circus," which involves both male and female strippers, are just lame.

arts scene

Udine's social scene is much more happening than its contemporary arts scene. Alternative types talk of *la vita culturale* in Trieste and Ljubljana with wistful looks in their eyes. Someday....

▶▶VISUAL ARTS

There are few places other than **Caffe Contarena** [see *bar, club, and live music scene,* above] to check out fresh, contemporary art. But **Galleria Plurima** *(Via Erasmo Valvason 11; Tel and Fax 0432/502-236; Bus 1, 3, C to Via Mercatovecchio; 9am-12:30pm/2:30-6pm; V, MC),* northwest of Piazza Libertá, has done a great job of discovering local talent, both in painting and installation art.

▶▶PERFORMING ARTS

On the east side of the city center, **Teatro Nuovo Giovanni da Udine** *(Via Trento 4; Tel 0432/248-418 or 0432/248-419, Fax 0432/248-420; Bus 4 or 8, ask for Via Trento; 10am-12:30pm/4-7pm Tue-Sat, 4-7pm Mon, 75 minutes before show on Sundays and holidays; giovannidaudine@ comune.udine.it; 20-40,000L most seats; V, MC)* is home to classical theater and opera, American cheese *(Seven Brides for Seven Brothers),* and cooler fare like David Hare and Woody Allen plays. The theater is in one of the most avant-garde buildings in Italy, but the plays are almost all in Italian. The musical offerings may be of more interest: classical, some jazz, and the occasional pop star who has faded into an icon (like Joe Jackson).

The centrally located **Cinema Centrale** *(Via Poscolle 8/B; Tel 0432/504-240; Bus 4 to Poscolle; 3-9:30pm showtimes; 12,000L; No credit cards)* occasionally shows films in *lingua originale* (subtitled, not dubbed). This is a rare find in Italy, so if you're here for a long trip, take the opportunity to see movie stars speaking in English on the big screen. The schedule out front will be clearly marked, since Italians (like Americans) don't want to see a subtitled movie by mistake.

gay scene

New York or San Francisco it's not, but most of Udine's nightspots are gay-friendly, due to the liberal influence of the university. There's also a gay support group with regular meetings and a hotline, **Arcigay Nuovi Passi** *(Via Pradamano 8; Tel 0432/523-838; Bus 5 or 6 to Via le Palmanova; 8-11pm Wed; http://www.gay.it/arcigay/udine/index.htm; Free with membership; No credit cards).* It's a members-only organization, but this rule is not strictly enforced for foreigners. On Monday nights at 9pm members meet at the nearby club, **No Fun** *(Via le Palmanova 42; Tel 0432/523-154; Bus 5 or 6 to Via le Palmanova; Free with Arci NA or*

ArciGay membership; No credit cards) for a social in their downstairs bar. Beers are 6,000L and ArciGay has a small booth set up with information about their current activities.

CULTUrE ZOO

When it comes to culture, Udine has a little (not a lot) for everyone—enough to occupy a long day (or two restful, hung-over ones) of sight-seeing. Castello Hill and the exteriors of the buildings around Piazza Libertá are the best of what's here. Lovers of Baroque art and architecture will dig the interiors of most of the churches and the many works of painter Tiepolo. There are some early Renaissance fresco cycles scattered about as well, though nothing like what you'll see in Tuscany or Ferrara. The modern art museum is one of the best in Italy (which is admittedly not known for its modern art museums).

Piazza Libertà *(Bus 1, 3, C to Mercatovecchio/Piazza Libertá):* This split-level piazza is the most impressive site in the city, more proof that the best things in life are free. As you scurry about Udine's other attractions, you can't help but check out "the most beautiful Venetian square on dry land" in detail because it's in the middle of everything. The pink-and-white **Loggia del Lionello,** a Gothic town hall that dates back to 1442, looks like it was just plucked out of St. Mark's Square in Venice. It's a great place to beat the heat, but there's nothing inside except the municipal boardroom—go in for a peek and the guard on duty will happily kick you out. The steps in front of this loggia lead to the raised portion of the Renaissance-style **Loggia di San Giovanni,** a colonnaded gallery topped by a bell tower from which two Moorish figures strike the hour. If you're still not getting the whole Venice connection, there's also a column topped by a winged lion. The two burly statues by the steps are of **Hercules and Cacus,** who the locals call "Florean and Venturin." (Apparently this is funny to the Udinese.) No one knows why their twiddlers have been broken off—maybe someone thought that was funny, too. Other examples of high-concept humor are the nearby **Statue of Peace,** donated by the conquering Austrians in 1819, and the 17th-century **Statue of Justice,** which stands where criminals used to be executed.

Castello *(Piazzale del Castello; Tel 0432/502-872, 501-824 or 271-591, Fax 0432/501-681; Bus 1, 3, C to Mercatovecchio/Piazza Libertá; 9:30am-12:30pm/3-8pm Tues-Sat, 9:30am-12:30pm Sun, Mon; 10,000L, free Sun; No credit cards):* The ramp to the left (when you're looking at it face-on) of the Loggia di San Giovanni leads to the curved portico of the **Arco Bollani,** designed by Palladio, which opens onto the ramps and staircases running up Castello hill. The hill itself was supposedly built by Attila's men, who transported dirt in their helmets so that the head Hun could have a high enough vantage point to watch nearby Aquileia burn (guess who set the fire). The Castello is more of a palace, rebuilt by the local Venetian Governor after a 1511 earthquake. The church up here, **Chiesa della Santa Maria del Castello,** is the oldest religious structure in town. The timber-ceilinged building with its 13th-century frescoes is a departure from the rest of the city's Baroque ostentation.

Il Duomo di Santa Maria Annunziata *(Piazza Duomo; Tel 0432/506-830; Bus 1, 3, C to Mercatovecchio/Piazza Libertá, 8 to Duomo; 7am-12:30pm/3:30-7pm daily; Free):* Just what you where hoping for: a big, Baroque cathedral on a cross-shaped plan, with three airy naves and all the 18th-century trimmings. How original! Of special interest are Tiepolo's singing angels (in the first chapel on the right—look up), and the chapel at the base of the campanile, which Vitale da Bologna frescoed with the life of Saint Nick (minus the red suit and toys for tots) in 1349. Ask the sacristan in the Duomo to open the small **Oratorio della Puritá** *(Via S. Francesco; 7am-12noon/3:30-7pm daily; Free)* just outside the cathedral. It contains an altarpiece and frescoed ceiling by Tiepolo that many consider his masterpiece. A tip to the man who lets you in is not unheard of.

Museum of Sacred Art and Tiepolo Gallery (Galleria degli Ospiti)/Palazzo Arcivescovile *(Piazza Patriarcato 1; Bus 7 to Piazza Patriarcato; 10am-noon/3:30-6:30pm Wed-Sun; 7,000L):* The former palace of the various bishops, archbishops, and patriarchs who once ruled the Church, the Palazzo Arcivescovile today houses Udine's greatest art treasures. It's less than a five-minute walk southeast of Castello Hill. The Museum of Sacred Art on the first floor is a collection of 13th-18th century wooden sculptures. In the second-floor Galleria degli Ospiti, you'll find Tiepolo's Old Testament fresco cycle: *Fall of the Rebel Angels, Rachel Hiding the Idols,* and the *Judgment of Solomon,* are recognized to be among his most outstanding works.

Galleria d'Arte Moderna *(Pizzale Paolo Diacono, 22 or Via Ampezzo 2; Tel 0432/295-891, Fax 0432/504-219; Bus 5 to Pizzale Dicono; 9:30am-12:30pm/3-6pm Mon-Sat, 9:30am-12:30pm Sun and holidays, closed Mon; gamud@comune.udine.it, www.comune.udine.it/gam/astaldi/astaldi.htm; 4,000L, free Sun and holidays; No credit cards):* This museum is a great break from all things Baroque, with works by de Chirico, Modigliani, Fausto Pirandello, Giorgio Morandi, and foreign big-shots like Picasso, de Kooning, Braque, and Chagall. There are also cool exhibits on modern architecture and local industrial design. Ah, smell the 20th-century iconoclasm! You'll find it on the busy Piazzale Diacono, just northeast of the city center.

CITY SPORTS

The city's public pool, **Piscina Comunale Palamostre** *(Via Ampezzo 4; Tel 0432/26967; Bus 4 to Piazzale Diacono; 1-3pm/6:30-8:30pm daily, Covered pool, 1-7pm daily, uncovered pool; 8,000L; No credit cards)* is an OK place for a dip, but make sure there aren't any classes scheduled before you pay to get in, otherwise you may find yourself beached. Bathing suits are, of course, required—guys may have to explain that not all suits are Speedos. It's just off Piazzale Diacono, northeast of the city center.

See **Natisone Valley,** below, for ways to really get out into the wilds in this area.

STUFF

Udine isn't really a shopping town, although there are a surprising number of home-furnishing stores with cool window displays and overpriced stock. (How are you going to get that sofa into your backpack, anyway?) Stick to the essentials: CDs and books to read on the train.

▶▶BOUND

The family-run **Libreria Moderna Udinese** *(Via Cavour 13; Tel 0432/504-284, Fax 0432/503-358; Bus 1, 3, C to Via Mercatovecchio; 9:30am-12:30pm/3-7:30pm daily; V, MC)* has shelves all the way up to the ceiling, mainly stocked with textbooks. But there's also a relatively inexpensive English section, with the kind of classic lit Italian students learning the lingo might want to read. It's on the main drag, heading west from Piazza Libertá.

▶▶TUNES

The only thing natural about **Natural Sound Deejay Store** *(Via Porta Nouva 12; Tel 0432/508-586, Fax 0432/506-66-66; Bus 1, 3, C to Via Mercatovecchio; 9:3am-12:30pm/3:30-7:30pm Tue-Sat; www.naturalsound.it; No credit cards)* is the inclination to stock up on all the music you've been dancing to in those crazy Italian clubs. This little place under the Castello is the place to do it. For more than a decade Renato Pontoni has been supplying DJs from all over Italy with LPs, mixes, compilations, and even consultation. There's a sound box in the back of the store, and a table with fliers from all the region's clubs. If you need to know *anything* about the local (or not so local) club scene, ask Renato. He still spins at a club way outside of town.

EATS

Get ready to feast. For a town of its size, Udine has more than its fair share of inexpensive eateries serving up great local food. The typical Udinese menu is a crossroads of cuisines: whether it's the vegetarian bean and barley soup known as *orzo e fagioli,* the hearty *brovado* with sausage and turnips, or the phyllo-wraped *gubana* fruitcake, there's something for everyone. Enjoy the Friulian specialties while you can—you'll find yourself dreaming about the cheesy-fried goodness called *frico* long after you've returned home. The Udinese are proud of the seven D.O.C wine regions that surround them, so make sure to order some vino with your meal. Refosco, Cabernet, and Merlot are some of the most popular, but try the Verduzzo, the Ramandolo, or the pricey Scioppettino that the Udinese drink on special occasions.

▶▶CHEAP

Every town has its pizza-slice places, but few are as loved as Udine's **King's Pizza** *(Via Poscolle; Bus 4 to Poscolle; 9:15am-3pm/4pm-2am daily; 2-4,000L slice; No credit cards),* the crowded take-away and delivery spot in the heart of town. Its location across the street from **Bar Poscolle** [see *bar, club, and live music scene,* above] makes it a great place to take the edge off around midnight. Stop in for a late-night slice, and you may learn where all the cool kids are heading next.

Sbarco dei Pirati *(Riva Bartolini 12; Tel 0432/21-330; Bus 1, 3, C to Piazza Marconi; Noon-2:30pm/7-9:30pm Mon-Sat, front bar stays open in middle of day; 8-12,000L per entree; No credit cards)* is one of the wackiest places in town. The front bar is covered top to bottom with both pirate paraphernalia and tokens of Friulian pride: Skulls and cross bones share space with signs in the Furlan dialect and local pottery. It looks and sounds like a theme restaurant until you notice the authentic local specialties, the low prices, and yes, that *is* a pig's head on the counter. The Lerussi family makes their own sausages and salamis—everyone from old men to young couples stop in for a slice of this or a sliver of that, served over bread. Just point to the hunk of pork that best catches your fancy and they'll slice it up for 1-2,000L. More serious eating goes on in the packed side-room, which is decorated like a Mexican fiesta. Try the *frico, orzo e fagioli,* and amazing drunken *gubana* dessert.

▶▶DO-ABLE

Don't think twice about giving the nondescript **Il Ristorantino** *(Via Bertaldi 25/A; Tel 0432/504-545; Bus 7 to Piazzale D'Annuzio; 10:30am-3pm/6:30pm-midnight Mon-Sat; 12-14,000L per entree; V, MC)* a try. The dining room is a big, harshly lit white space, but Signore Sinigaglia's culinary finesse more than makes up for what's lacking in ambience. He does all the cooking from scratch, while his sweet, English-speaking twenty-something daughter keeps things running smoothly. The homemade pork sausage *musetto* over fresh *krauti,* or *pappardelle alla cacciatore* (pasta with tender, pulled venison and wild mushrooms), are awesome, and the light, typical fried dough *crespoli* with powdered sugar are to die for with a glass of *limoncello* at the end of your meal. It's about a 15-minute walk south from the center toward the train station.

For a lesson in Udinese cuisine, head to popular osteria **Al Vecchio Stallo** *(Via Viola 7; Tel 0432/21296; Bus 4 to Poscolle; 11am-2pm/5-11pm Mon-Sat; 10-12,000L per entree; No credit cards)* and let the three brothers who run the place order for you. The setting is pleasant enough—a crowded room, with old, wooden tables and windows overlooking a garden. But the food—incredible and cheap—is the real draw. *Frico,* the artery-clogging fried Montasio cheese dish, comes with some of the best polenta in Italy. Also be sure to try the *gnocchi al suino,* delicious dumplings filled with prunes and cinnamon, and the *gabana bagnata,* an intense cake of raisins, pignoli, and amaretto. To find this out-of-the-way place, take Via Cavour west from Piazza Libertá until it turns into Via Poscolle. Take the next right on Via Magrini; Via Viola will be the first left.

People walking along the busy Via Poscolle, west of Piazza Libertá, make pit stops at the cozy **Enoteca della Speziaria** *(Via Poscolle 13; Tel 0432/505-061; Bus 4 to Poscolle; 11:30am-2:30pm/6-10pm Mon-Sat, closed Sunday; 7-10,000L for snacks; 2-10,000L wine by the glass; No credit cards)* all day long, throwing back a glass of wine and a few gorgonzola bruschettas and moving on. You may want to linger—this wine bar has more than 40 wines available by the glass, and it's the only place where you'll be able to try expensive specialties like Ramandorla or Verduzza

udine eats and crashing

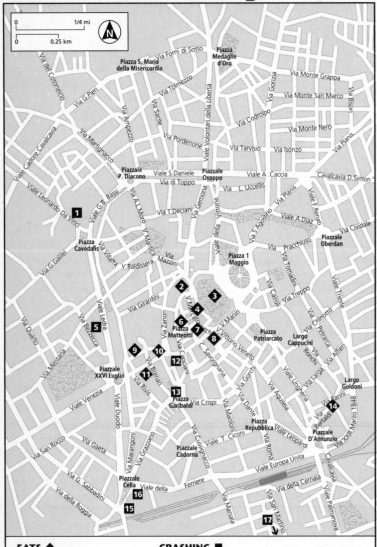

0   1/4 mi
0   0.25 km

Via del Cotoneccio
Via G. Pieri
Piazza S. Maria
della Misericordia
Via Forni di Sotto
Piazza
Medaglie
d'Oro
Via Monte Grappa
Via Ampezzo
Via Tolmezzo
Via Sacile
Via Pordenone
Viale Volontari della Libertà
Via Monte San Marco
Via Gorizia
Via Codrolpo
Via Martignacco
Via Monte Nero
Via Tarvisio
Via Isonzo
Via Bison
Via Planis
Viale Cadore Cavalcavia
Piazzale
P. Diacono
Viale S.Daniele
Via di Toppo
Piazzale
Osoppo
Viale A. Caccia
Via L. Uccellis
Cavalcavia D.Simon
Viale Leonardo Da Vinci
Via G. B. Bassi
Via A.L.Moro
Via T.Deciani
Via Gemona
Via della Vittoria
Via S. Agostino
Via A. Diaz
Viale F.Renati
Viale Cividale
Via Planis

1

Piazza
Cavedalis
Via Villalta
V. Manlica
Via Mazzini
V.Baldissera
Piazza 1
Maggio
Via Pracchiuso
Piazzale
Oberdan
Via G. Galilei
Via Girardini
Via Cairoli
Via Tomadini
Viale Trieste

2
V.Mercatovecchio
3
4
6
Piazza
Matteotti
V. Vittorio Veneto
7
8
Piazza
Patriarcato
Largo
Cappucini
Via Chinotto
Via Pettoraca
Via Rondhi

Via Ledra
Via Bazecca
5
Via Zanon
Via Cicogna
C.Savorgnana
Via Alfieri
Via Larga

Via Quarto
Via Mentana
9 **10**
12
Piazzale
XXVI Luglio
Via Brenari
11
Via Rivis
13
Piazza
Garibaldi
Via Crispi
Via Gorchi
Via Dante
Viale Ungheria
Via Aquileia
Largo
Goldoni
14
Via Martini
Via Bertaldi

Viale Venezia
Viale Duodo
Via Manzoni
Piazza
Repubblica
Viale Leopardi
Via Roma
Piazzale
D'Annunzio
Via XXIII Marzo 1848

Via San Rocco
Via Gaeta
Via Marangoni
Via Grazzano
Piazzale
Cadorna
Via T. Ciconi
Via Cussignacco

Viale Europa Unita

Via G. Sabbadini
Via della Roggia
Piazzale
Cella
16
15
Viale della
Ferriere
Via Marsala
Via della Cernaia
Via San Martino
Viale Palmanova
Cavalcavia
17

EATS ◆
Al Vecchio Stallo **9**
Caffe Contarena **8**
Caffe Ottelio **6**
Casa Delle Contadinanza **3**
Enoteca della Speziaria **10**
Il Ristorantino **14**
King's Pizza **11**
Locanda Medievale **4**
Osteria alle Volte **7**
Sbarco dei Pirati **2**

CRASHING ■
Al Vecchio Tram **13**
Alle Due Palme **1**
Astoria Hotel Italia **12**
Da Brando **16**
Hotel Friuli **5**
Pensione Al Fari **17**
Quo Vadis **15**

Venice ○ ○ Udine
Florence ○ ITALY
Rome ★

without having to buy a whole bottle. Keep your distance from the decidedly grumpy owner, who busies himself with slicing salami and cheese. The friendly, English-speaking Finnish *sommelier* (a waiter in charge of the wine service) has come here to study wine, and will be happy to teach you a thing or two.

If you go on one date in Udine, make it the romantic little three-tiered **Locanda medievale** *(Via Sottomonte 42; Tel 0432/505-881; Bus 1, 3, C to Via Mercatovecchio; 11am-3pm/6-11pm daily; 12-18,000L per entree, cover 2,000L; V, MC)*. No more than 30 people can fit in this tiny, elegant timbered restaurant, where dinner can last for hours. Young, stylish couples engage in hushed conversation at the candle-lit tables over the likes of ravioli with truffled brie and porcini mushrooms, and local wines like the velvety Scioppettino. The bartender is one of the friendliest and most generous in town. It's located on the street just below the Castello—hang a right on the stairs as you're walking down.

▶▶**SPLURGE**

The unremarkable outside of **Osteria alle Volte** *(Via Mercerie 6; Tel 0432/502-800; Bus 1, 3, C to Via Mercatovecchio; Noon-2:30pm/7-10:30pm Mon-Sat; 20-30,000L per entree; V, MC)* disguises the fine dining going on in the 13th-century cellar downstairs. Walk past the crowds nibbling on little plates of prosciutto and sipping glasses of wine and turn left down the stairs, where owner Claudio Trincio will greet you with a seasonally changing menu. Try the duck breast pappardelle, and finish up with the most insanely rich chocolate cake you've ever tasted. Wines are all regional—just make sure to ask Trincio himself, and not one of the 14-year-old waitresses, for a recommendation. It's located on the first street to the left as you walk north from Piazza Libertá.

crashing

Damn, no hostels—but hey, that means no curfews either. There are some decent, affordable places in Udine, but you have to book far in advance, because they're often occupied by seasonal workers for months at a time. There's a big sign outside the train station with a lodging map, but it's not necessarily up to date. Many of the hotels are located on the busy Piazzale Cella, just outside the city walls. It's a 15-minute walk west down Viale Europa Unita (which becomes Viale Delle Ferriere) from the train station; keep an eye on the killer traffic.

▶▶**CHEAP**

Insert whatever tired Marlon Brando imitation you like here ("I coulda been a contendah..."). **Da Brando** *(Piazzale Cella 16; Tel 0432/502-837; Bus 3, C to Piazzale Cella; 30,000L single, 60,000L double, none with bath; V, MC, AE)* is as basic as it gets. The same hoarsely shouted arguments between the crusty staff and the crusty regulars in the old man restaurant/bar downstairs have been going on for years. The 15 rooms upstairs are sometimes noisy (from the traffic in the piazza, as well as the aforementioned crusty old men). Sinks are inside the room, but the bathrooms down the hall. Still, at this price, it's hard to beat. It's about halfway down Piazzale Cella.

Run by enthusiastic new management, **Pensione Al Fari** *(Via V. Melegnano 41; Tel 0432/520-732, Fax 0432/520-732; Walk from the station, Buses 1-11 from center back to station; 52,000L single, 72,000L double, no private baths; No credit cards)* offers very clean, classic back-packer digs at a good price. There's a common room with a bar where you can have a quick drink, or watch soccer on TV with the staff. It's not far from the station, but in the opposite direction from the center of town (south). To get here, you have to walk under a dark graffitied underpass to the left of the train station, which may creep you out a bit. But once you continue on down the quiet residential street, you'll see there's nothing to worry about in this neighborhood, other than a couple of barking dogs, safely behind fences. When you get to Via San Martino, take a right on Via Melegnano; the pensione is 100 meters down on your left. It's not a bad walk back into town, once you've gotten rid of your bags.

Al Vecchio Tram *(Via Brenari 32, Tel 0432/502-516, Bus 24 to Piazza Garibaldi; 35,000L single, 55,000L double, no private baths; No credit cards)*, located just off Piazza Garibaldi, is a typical dark, poky one-star run by La Signora with an iron fist. It's a bit rundown—the signs of age are unmistakable—but it's right in the center of town, and an easy bus ride from the station. Plus it's cheap, cheap, cheap.

▶▶DO-ABLE

Comfortable, and very clean, **Quo Vadis** *(Piazzale Cella 28; Tel 0432/21091, Fax 0432/21092; Bus 3, C to Piazzale Cella; 70,000L single, 110,000L double, 140,000L triple, all w/private baths; V, MC)* offers the best balance of price and quality on the Piazzale Cella. The automatic doors and Victoria Gotti-chic room furniture are a little much, but the TV, phone and great showers in the rooms are a treat. It's not air-conditioned, but you'll keep your cool in the Mediterranean way because of the thick walls and tile floors. The annex *(dipendenza)* across the street allows you greater privacy, since you get your own key. (Sneaky groups may find this a real cost-saver, but there are only single beds, so you'll have to draw straws for the floor.)

Alle Due Palme *(Viale Leonardo Da Vinci 5; Tel 0432/481-807, Fax 0432/480-213; Bus 4 to Piazzale Diacono; 65,000L single, 100,000L double, private baths available, breakfast included; V, MC)* is a bit northeast of the center of town, which puts it *really* far from the train station. Still, it has friendly, professional management, and three-star comforts (phones, TVs and private bathrooms). Be warned that since the buses stop running at midnight, the walk home from anywhere south of the castle is a bear.

▶▶SPLURGE

Hotel Friuli *(Viale Ledra 24; Tel 0432/234-351, Fax 0432/234-606; Bus 10 to Piazza XXVI Luglio; fruili@hotelfruili.udine.it; 90-105,000L single, 145-180,000L double, 180-245,000L suite/triple, all w/private baths; V, MC, AE, DC)* is a big, modern building on the western edge of the city center, no more than a 10-minute walk from Piazza Libertá. It's primarily a businessperson's way-station, but the sleek nineties neo-deco design feels current, and the amenities are impeccable, with first-rate room service, laundry service, and satellite TV all at your disposal. Best of all, the Fruili's low seasons are weekends and summertime, when the business folk aren't there—and you are. This is a great chance to pamper yourself. Keep in mind that that breakfast is not included and the lowest prices are for more than one night's stay. To get here, walk north on Viale Ledra until you see the Agip gas station sign.

With the same ownership as Hotel Friuli, the four-star **Astoria Hotel Italia** *(Piazza XX Settembre 24; Bus 2, 5, 6, 10, 11 to Via Poscolle; Tel 0432/505-091, Fax 0432/509-070; www.hotelastoria. udine.it, astoria astoria @hotelastoria.udine.it; 140,000-210,000L single, 190-280,000L double, all w/private bath ; V, MC, AE)* is one step up, the undisputed best in town. It's the kind of place where the bellboys wear little pillbox hats and make a point of carrying your luggage for you. The rooms are small, but exquisite, featuring antiques, fine linen, and classy stationary. Free Internet access and printing are available downstairs. The good news is their low season is on the weekends and in the summertime, with the best values being on the weekends for more than one night. It's also the most centrally located hotel in town—palaces tended to be built in the middle of things. Take Via Cavour west from Piazza Libertá, and make a left on Via Canciani. The hotel will be on your right across from the big piazza.

need to know

Currency Exchange There's an **ATM** at Banca San Paolo, on the right as you exit the train station. The **post office** also cashes American Express Traveler's checks.

Tourist Information On the huge, uninteresting piazza opposite Castello Hill, the **tourist office** *(Piazza Primo Maggio 7; Tel 0432/295-972, Fax 0432/5040743; 9am-1pm/3-5pm Mon-Fri)* dishes out maps, walking tour brochures, and directions in English, but they haven't gotten used to the whole "tourism is good" thing yet. They don't book rooms, but they do close right on time, which can be a problem if your train arrives after 5pm. You can find Udine on the web at ***www.emmeti.it/Welcome/Friuli/Udine/index.uk.html.***

Public Transportation The **city bus station** *(Via B. Stringher 14; Tel 0432/503-045 or 0432/502-526)* is located across Viale Europa Unita from the train station. Tickets are available at tabacchi stores for 1,500L. You're supposed to stamp them yourself as you board. Remember that buses stop running at midnight; if you're doing any late-night carousing, you'll be hoofing it.

Health and Emergency Emergency: *118;* Local Police: *112;* Fire *115.* The 24-hour hospital, **Azienda Ospedaliera Santa Maria della Misericordia** *(Piazza S. M. della Misericordia 15; Tel 0432/552-361)* is north of the town center.

Pharmacies Farmacia BELTRAME *(Piazza della Libertà 9; Tel 0432/502-877; 9am-7pm Mon-Sat)* is the most centrally located pill-pusher in town. Check the rotating schedule on the front door to see which city pharmacy is open 24-hours.

Telephone Phone cards available at tabacchi shops, which are spread evenly throughout town. Public phones are at the train station.

Trains The **train station** *(Viale Europa Unita 40; Tel 1478/88088; 7am-9pm daily)* is south of town. It's a 15-minute walk to the center of town. You can also take Buses 1, 3, and C to Via Mercato Vecchia, just north of Piazza Libertà. Trains from Udine will carry you to Trieste and Venice, but not points north.

Bus Lines Out of the City Out-of-town buses, run by **Autoservizi FVG,** leave from the **bus station** *(Viale Europa Unita 31; Tel 0432/504-012 0432/508-762),* which is across from the train station.

Postal The **post office** *(Via Vittorio Veneto 42; Tel 0432/223-111; 8:30am-6pm Mon-Sat)* is on the main street running south from Piazza Libertá.

Cividale del friuli

Visiting Cividale del Friuli is like entering a time warp. You can walk from one end of this sleepy little town to the other in just a few minutes without ever seeing a modern structure or a car. What you will find is a well-preserved medieval center is reminiscent of a Tuscan or Umbrian hill village, terrific low-priced restaurants, cozy little bars, and a decent number of low-key late-night spots. Unfortunately, you may have to miss this late night action to catch the last train back to Udine—accommodations are scarce and expensive, with only two hotels in the city limits.

This place goes way back. Founded in 50 B.C. by Julius Caesar, who called it *Forum Julii,* it thrived as a market town. The name "Fruili" is a kind of shortening, like "SoHo" and "frogurt." Cividale del Friuli didn't really flourish until after Rome fell, and the Lombards made it the eastern outpost of their kingdoms. In the late Middle Ages, it was absorbed by the Holy Roman Empire, which built most of the buildings you'll admire when strolling through town. That empire gave way to the Austro-Hungarians, then there were the Italians, a couple of world wars, and here we are.

While a day trip will give you enough time to see the several museums, restored buildings, and historical sights, Cividale has enough atmosphere, personality, and natural beauty to last you for days. The Eastern Hills *(Colli Orientali)* are known for their world-class grapes and wines. The hiking in the Colli is also first-rate [see **Natisone Valley,** below]; many of the paths are actually medieval walking routes. Using Cividale as a base for a jaunt into the hills is actually a great way to spend more time in town and save cash, since there are a couple of affordable *rifugi* (lodges) just a bus ride and short hike away. You won't find many American tourists here, but lots of Austrians descend every summer, especially for **Mittlefest** [see *festivals and events,* below].

The real pleasure of a visit to Cividale is following the locals on their cafe-hopping strolls. Udine, just 15-minutes away by train, may be where the locals work and shop, but Cividale is where they live, and they come home to play. You'll see a lot of lounging around in bars and *enotecas,* and socializing in the piazzas.

neighborhoods

There's really only one neighborhood here: the time-warped **historic center,** which is the main reason to come. No buses, no cars, no scooters (not legally, anyway)—just lots of cafes and bars lining the narrow, twisty streets. The old center is confined by city walls on the north and south, by the river on the east, and by **Viale Libertà,** a big four-lane street, on the west. It's bisected by a main East-West drag, called **Via Carlo Alberto** at the western end, **Corso Mazzini** in the middle and **Corso Paolino d'Aquileia** at the eastern end, where it opens onto the **Ponte Del Diavolo** ("Devil's Bridge") [see *culture zoo,* below]. Across the bridge is the **Borgo di Ponte,** a small neighborhood where you'll find a bit of choice nightlife. An odd fact: City planners must have been so thrilled to ban cars from the center, they didn't really think of where else to put them. After all, people gotta get to work from the 'burbs *somehow.* As a result, several of the potentially beautiful piazzas at the edges of the no-traffic zone have

festivals and events

Mittlefest *(July 20-29; Tel 0432/730-793, Fax 0432/701-099; mittelfest@regione.fvg.it, http://www.regione.fvg.it/mitielfest2000/2000.htm):* Inaugurated in 1991 with major support from dozens of national governments, this annual week-long festival of prose, music, dance, ballet, puppets, and cinema celebrates the historical connection of Central European countries that was lost during the days of the Iron Curtain. There's always a theme promoting the idea of interdependence, like *The Salt Roads* (2001), or *The Silk Road.* These days, Mittlefest is getting really big, and Cividale deserves all the recognition it gets for having the foresight to reach eastward back before Prague was cooler than Paris.

Broadsword Mass *(January 6):* This ancient ritual mass is performed at the Duomo in celebration of Epiphany. A 14-century Patriarch's broadsword, helmet, and Bible are used in a haunting ceremony that recalls the investiture of new Patriarchs by the local clergy. People spend all year making their outfits for the medieval costume procession that follows. Trust us, it's much cooler than "Wherefore art thou, Taco Stand Man?" at a Renaissance Fair.

cividale bars clubs and culture zoo

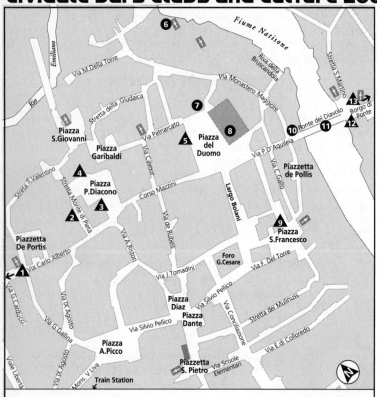

BARS/CLUBS ▲

Al San Daniele **1**
Café Longobardo **3**
Caffe Ai Petrarchi **5**
Coffee Store **12**
Deghejo **13**
Il Santo e il Lupo **9**
L'Enoteca Elefante **4**
Old Tony Bistro **2**

CULTURE ZOO ●

Celtic Caves (Ipogeo Celtico) **10**
The Devil's Bridge **11**
Duomo and Christian Museum **8**
Lombard Temple **6**
National Archeological Museum **7**

been turned into parking lots (boo! hiss!) and the streets where vehicles are legal are filled with cars scrambling to get the last parking space.

hanging out

The central, non-parking, **Piazza Paolo Diacono** is the central meeting place in town, as well as the best bet for some serious loafing. It's here that you'll find the venerable **Caffe Longobardo** [see *bar, club, and live music scene*, below] and some other cafes and wine bars. The whole center of town, though, is like an open-air hangout—it's too small to get lost in, but aimless wandering will always pay off with a Kodak moment or a place to stop for a drink while you rest your dogs.

bar, club, and live music scene

Locals say that there are over 100 bars in the tiny historic center of Cividale—of course, they consider places where old men get pastries and espressos "bars." But whaddaya want in a town of only 11,413—Studio 54? If you're willing to downshift and enjoy life in a slower lane, there's a lot to do in this little burg.

The beautiful, Art-Deco inspired **Caffe Longobardo** *(Piazza Paolo Diacono 2; Tel 0432/730-260; 7-2am daily; No cover; No credit cards)* is not only located in the heart of town, it *is* the heart of town. Cividalians stop in this historic meeting place a few times a day, first for the extra-large cappuccino (1,500L), and later, for the generous free grub during the *aperitivo* hour, from 7 to 9:30pm, when drinks are discounted from the normal 6-10,000L. Gorgeous *paste* (pastries), like almond paste-filled prunes and chocolate treats, are available from the glass cases anytime of the day. Take a seat in one of the wicker chairs, or lean up against the marble counters and enjoy.

Some bars are known for their beer, some for their wine. The brightly lit, euro-sleek **Al San Daniele** *(Via Carlo Alberto 51; Tel 0432/703-009; 8am-11pm Thu-Tue; No cover; No credit cards),* on the west side of the center, is known for its ham. Expert prosciutto tasters believe that Italy's finest salt-cured hams hail from San Daniele, a town about 45 minutes from Cividale, and this great-looking little bar is the perfect place to taste it for yourself. Sate your mid-afternoon appetite with some of the sweet, soft ham, sliced by hand and served with chubby breadsticks for 10,000L a person. Add Fresh Montasio cheese (4,000L/person), a few glasses of the inexpensive local wines (prices are scribbled on blackboards, none more than 5,000L a glass) and you may skip dinner altogether.

Caffe Ai Petrarchi *(Piazza Duomo 9/10; Tel 0432/701-180; 7am-8pm Mon-Sat; No cover; No credit cards)* is right beside the Duomo, and right in front of the piazza-turned-parking lot that most native residents use as their garage. So around 6pm or 7pm, when folks are getting off work and thirsty for a quick one before heading home, this modern little cafe is packed to the brim. Young women sip campari and wine spritzers as the men down *chiara media* (pints of lager, 6,000L).

"Bistro" isn't really the right word for **Old Tony Bistro** *(Monte di Pietà 9; Tel 0432/731-791; 7:30-3am Tue-Sun; No cover; No credit cards)*. In fact, this smoky, loud neighborhood haunt in the west of the center is pretty much a dive bar. If you're looking for a civilized evening, go somewhere else. You'll catch a lot of stares from the kids playing electronic darts for even having the guts to walk in. Don't worry; they usually warm up as the evening goes on. And of course, if there's a soccer match on, nobody will even look away from the TV. The bartender is the most popular girl in town (at 6,000L for a pint for beer, you can understand why), and come late night, things get a little rowdy.

Il Santo e il Lupo *(Corte San Francesco 4; Tel 0432/732-928; 7-2am Mon-Sat; No cover; No credit cards)* is friendly and hip, if a little spendy, and it's in a great location on a big piazza on the east side of the center. The crowd is young and, as you might expect in a small town, fairly cliquish, but if you make the attempt, you'll likely find them eager to talk. What makes the place hip are its decor—an odd blend of mod bright yellow walls, stone columns, and medieval torch holders—and its drink list, which includes 25 kinds of whiskey (6-12,000L), 20 kinds of rum (4-15,000L) and a handful of cocktails (8,000-12,000L), as well as the usual beers (8,000L, 9,000L for Guinness). If you need a bite, sandwiches are 6,000L, pizzas are 12,000L, and more substantial dishes (roast beef plate, anyone?) are 12-15,000L.

There's a brass elephant hanging outside **L'Enoteca Elefante** *(Piazza Paolo Diacono 21; Tel 0432/700-966; 10am-3pm/5-11pm Tue-Sun; No cover; No credit cards)*—your first clue that this isn't your typical Italian wine bar. Sure, it has the requisite oversized photographs of the old town, the ceramic plates, and people noshing on cheese and sausage using huge wine barrels as bar tables. So what's different? This place is part of the Italian association *Le Donne dei Vini,* or "the Women of Wine," and you'll only find women behind the bar. It's a great place to come and learn about the impressive local wines from the Eastern Hills without any macho wine guy asking you to sniff the cork. Keep an eye out for the chalkboard with a small number of featured wines by the glass (3-6,000L).

Just over the Devil's Bridge from the center of town is the oddly-named **Coffee Store** *(Borge di Ponte 2; Tel 0432/731-693; 6pm-3am, closed Mon; 7,000L beer pint; No cover; No credit cards)*. It has no coffee, but what it does have is great river views, a laid-back atmosphere, live music, and an inoffensive Americana theme. The large, antique painted wooden signs are a welcome departure from the cheesy Bud Lite neon of many "American-style" places in Italy. Mixed drinks are 6-8,000L, and the Thursday night rock band and Sunday solo singer play mainly covers.

The recently opened **Deghejo** *(Borgo di Ponte via Ghiarottini; Tel 0432/701-070; 9-3am Thur-Sun; No credit cards)*, otherwise known as "molto music bar," is Cividale's only example of the disco-pub hybrid. Don't worry about dress codes or cover charges here—there aren't any. The chill atmosphere in the big, orange and blue Ikea-inspired room is matched by hot DJs from Udine and Trieste, who spin a mix of commercial tunes and electronica. By 11pm, the place is packed with college kids and twenty-somethings cutting loose. Sunday nights bring live rock bands, and the popular Latin night, held on a different night each week, offers a free dance instructor and enough mojitos to help you get your groove on. For the moment, drinks are cheaper than most places *(5-6,000L for large beers; 6-8,000L for cocktails).* The only drawback is that it's a little hard to find. Cross the Ponte Del Diavolo. The Zarutti Restaurant will be on your left, on Borgo di Ponte. When you reach it, backtrack a few steps to the street before it, and hang a right into the alley. The bar is behind the restaurant. Look for the bouncer wearing what appears to be a zoot suit.

arts scene

To say the local gallery scene is not as fresh as it used to be is an understatement. Cividale stopped being a hotbed of the arts when the Holy Roman Empire faded and the Venetians took over. However, there are a few local artists exhibiting in city-owned buildings.

▶▶VISUAL ARTS

The work at **ARTESTRUTTURA** *(Via S. Giorgio 19/A; Tel/Fax 0432/730-551; 9am-12:30pm/3:30-6pm; No credit cards),* west of the city center, tends to be updated "painterly" expressionism. Many of the local painters and sculptors tucked away in the areas between Cividale and Udine exhibit here, but there's no explosive scene to latch onto.

▶▶PERFORMING ARTS

Teatro Communale "Adelaide Ristori" *(Via A. Ristori; Tel 0432/731-353; Box office 6-8pm, tickets also available by phone; 17-28,000L depending on show; V, MC)* presents complete seasons of Italian dramas, and foreign plays by writers as diverse as Woody Allen and Oscar Wilde, as well as opera and Broadway musical reviews. Everything's in Italian, except for the occasional Andrew Lloyd Webber tribute.

culture zoo

Everyone from the Romans and the Lombards to the Holy Roman and Austro-Hungarian Empires and the Devil himself passed through Cividale in its heyday, and they all left good stuff behind for us to look at. (Well, maybe not the Austrians...they mainly just blew stuff up.)

Ipogeo Celtico/Celtic Caves *(Monastero Maggiore 6, ask at Bar All'Ipogeo, corso Paolina d'Aquileia; Tel 0432/701-211; No regular hours usually 8am-sunset; Free):* If you break your leg climbing down the steep stairs to the main room of this K-shaped system of caves, don't blame us. This cool site, on the west side of the Ponte Del Diavolo, is run with the sort of laxness you would never find in more litigious countries. The nice people at the bar All'Ipogeo, around the corner from the caves, will let you in if they're not too busy (they don't make any money off this, so be sure to buy an espresso or something). This complex is thought to have been an ancient Celtic burial ground, and later a Roman prison. There are niches and benches carved in the walls, as well as two crude masks that appear to be screaming. Oh, and did we mention the zombies? (Kidding!)

National Archeological Museum *(Piazza Duomo 13; Tel 0432/700-700; 8:30am-7pm Tue-Sun, 9am-2pm Mon; 4,000L admission; No credit cards):* Housed in the Palladio-designed Palazzo dei Provveditori (Superintendents' Palace), behind the Duomo, this museum is filled with cool dead stuff. There are Roman, Byzantine, Medieval, and Romanesque tombstones from Fruili and Slovenia's Dalmatian coast, as well as an impressive collection of medieval stone carvings of mythical monsters. The second floor is devoted to the Lombard conquerors of the region, with gold coins, silver religious artifacts, jewelry, armor, and a duke's tomb and burial wear.

Lombard Temple *(Borgo Brossana; Tel 0432/700-867; 9:30am-12:30pm/3-5pm Mon-Fri, 9:30am-12:30pm/2:30-6pm Sat-Sun Oct-Mar, 9:30am-12:30pm/3-6:30pm Mon-Fri, 9:30am-1pm/3-7:30pm Sat-Sun Apr-Sep; 4,000L admission; No credit cards):* This small medieval chapel, along the river north of the Duomo, contains some famous 8th-century frescoes and stucco work. Renaissance snobs will find the painting primitive, but will be more impressed by the intricately inlaid 15th-century choir stalls. Above the grapevine arch on the western wall, the frescoed procession of virgins and martyrs is regarded as one of the triumphs of medieval art; travelers who've seen the mosaics in Ravenna will find it strangely familiar.

Duomo *(Piazza Del Duomo 5; Tel 0432/731-144; 9:30am-12:30pm/3-5pm daily, Nov-Feb, 9:30am-12pm/3-7pm Apr-Oct, closed Sat, Sun mornings; Free):* Begun in 1450, this cathedral seems pretty sterile inside compared to others in Italy. But it's worth seeing for the *Pala del Patriarca Pellegrino,* an exquisite silver altarpiece depicting the enthroned Virgin and Child. The angels Michael and Gabriel and three floors of little saints on either side make quite a standing ovation.

Duomo Christian Museum *(Piazza Del Duomo 5; Tel 0432/731-144; 9:30am-12:30pm/3-6pm daily, Nov-Mar, 9:30am-12pm/3-7pm Apr-Oct, closed Sat, Sun mornings; Free):* This little museum inside the Duomo contains relics of the local Patriarchs who moved here from Trieste and considered themselves the equal of the Pope in Rome. Other *ooh*-and-*ahh*-ables include an 8th-century carved altar and marble baptistery, as well as an 11th-century throne.

The Devil's Bridge: Local legends maintain that His Satanic Handiness himself built this bridge, which connects Via D'Aquileia with the Borgo di Ponte, in exchange for the first soul to cross it. In some versions, he only placed the huge rock that supports the two arches; in others, he had his mom (the Devil has a mom?) bring the rock in her apron, and he built the rest. However it happened, the crafty citizens sent a dog (or a cat, say the dog-lovers) across the bridge, cheating the Devil out of his fee. Old Lucifer got his revenge in 1917 when the Italian Army blew up the bridge to try and hold off the advancing Austrians, who, turns out, had already crossed the river anyway! It was rebuilt in 1918. A stairway at the end of the bridge leads down to water level, where riverside picnics are popular.

the great outdoors

Cividale has tons to offer the athletically-bent nature lover. The gorgeous and green **Natisone Valley** [see below] to the east of town has long been a favorite destination for Italian, German, and Austrian hikers, but it's still a virtual secret from the rest of the world. Most travelers make Cividale their home base, take just a small backpack to stay overnight in the *refugi* (small hut-style accommodations on the trails), and return to town the next day.

▶▶STUFF

There's not much shopping to be done in Cividale. You can buy local wines almost anywhere, and a few Lombard-related trinkets at the museums. If you're interested in browsing, most of the stores are located on the main drag (Carlo Alberto/Corso Mazzini/Via Aquileia).

▶▶BOUND

In the southwestern part of the center is **La Libreria** *(Via Manzoni 3; Tel 0432/730-090; 9am-12:30pm/3pm-7pm daily, winter, 9am-12:30pm/ 3:30-7:30 daily, summer; No credit cards),* a bookstore with a small collection of English classics for 10,000L each and newer fiction for 27,000L each. The large selection of travel guides in Italian either means that the Cividalians go on a lot of trips, or that some people in town dreaming of moving away.

eats

When Italians direct you to a favorite restaurant, nine times out of ten, they'll describe it by saying, *"Si manga bene, e si spende poco"* ("One eats well and spends little"). This is the highest praise possible in Italy, and it could apply to the entire town of Cividale del Fruili. The local cuisine isn't the classic Italian cooking of Emiglia-Romagna or the heavily Austrian fare of the rest of the north, but something unique. Many of the restaurants are centered around an open hearth, called a *fogolar furlan,* which functions as both a cooking instrument and a scene-setter. Most of the local stick-to-yer-ribs fare is comprised of roasted meats—rabbit, venison, chicken, pork—no one can escape the *fogolar.* Other local specialties to look for are doughy, fragrantly spiced *cialzons,* a cross between

TO MARKET

If your budget is so tight that you can't even afford Cividale's cheap eats, try the **Super-Coop Supermarket** *(13-17 Via Adelaide; 8:30am-12:45pm/3:30-7pm daily; No credit cards).*

cividale eats and crashing

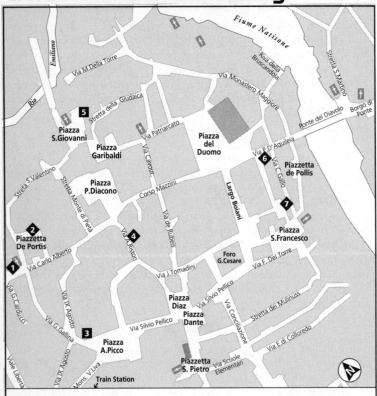

EATS ◆
Al Fortino **1**
Mandi Mandi Pizza al Taglio **6**
O'Scugnizzo **2**
Ristorante Al Monastero **4**
Trattoria Dominissini **7**

CRASHING ■
Hotel Roma **3**
Locanda al Pomo d'Oro **5**

gnocchi and ravioli, and the sweetly seasoned *gnocchi di suisine,* dough balls filled with plums, cinnamon, and other herbs.

▶▶CHEAP

The bench outside of **Mandi Mandi Pizza al Taglio** *(Via Paolino d'Aquileia 8; No phone; 8am-1:30pm/6:15-8pm daily; 2-3,000L per slice; No credit cards),* the little takeaway joint right before the bridge, is always occupied. And for good reason—the pizza is super-cheap. While stuffing your face with that piping hot slice, just be sure to keep an eye on the traffic. The one-lane bridge and speeding driver combo is a deadly accident just waiting to happen, and no pizza, no matter how good, is worth that.

Located on a tiny street off Via Carlo Alberto is **O'Scugnizzo** *(Piazzetta de Portis 8; Tel 0432/700-693; 11am-2:30pm/6-10:30pm Tue-Sun; 7-12,000L per entree; No credit cards),* your typical fluorescent-lit, family-run home-style trattoria. The adorable Vuolo family serves up great pizzas at really low prices (9,000L), and their seafood menu, with fried calamari and roasted fish, is equally delicious. Even the blue walls are cheery, with delicate ladybug murals. Daddy Vuolo tosses the pizza, Momma Vuolo works the register, and Baby Voulo waits tables. Consider yourself Goldilocks.

▶▶DO-ABLE

Everyone from businesspeople on the go to vacationing families to starry-eyed couples eats well cheaply at the classy **Al Fortino** *(Via Carlo Alberto 46; Tel 0432/731-217, Fax 0432/731-192; 11:30am-3pm/6:30-11pm daily, closed Mon-Tue nights; 15-20,000L per entree; V, MC, DC),* on the west side of the town center. For the past 15 years, this beautiful restaurant has been grilling up lamb, venison, and wild boar *(cinghiale)* right over the open fireplace in the center of the room. The *primi piatti,* or first courses, are uniformly awesome. If you can't decide on just one, order the last menu item, a sampler plate of three of the best: homemade *tagliatelle* with fresh roasted artichoke hearts and ham, *crespelle* (crepes) filled with goose liver and truffle pate in a rich béchamel sauce, and pumpkin *gnocchi* in butter and poppyseed sauce. All this for 13,000L? This may be the cheapest evening of fine dining you'll ever have.

It's a little bit pricier, but the home-style food served up at the tiny, underground **Trattoria Dominissini** *(Via Jacopo Stellini 18; Tel 0432/733-763; 9:30am-3:30pm/6:30-11pm Tue-Sun; 13-18,000L per entree; No credit cards)* is well worth it. The oversized wooden tables are packed nightly with folks who've come to feast on *gnochetti all'erbe* (tiny potato dumplings with fresh herbs) and heaping plates of *calamari fritti* (fried squid). It's just north of the Piazza San Francesco, near Il Santo e Il Lupo [see *bar, club, and live music scene,* above].

In a tiny town filled with great restaurants, **Ristorante Al Monastero** *(Via Ristori 11; Tel 0432/700-808; Noon-2pm/7-10pm Tue-Sat, noon-2pm Sun; 10,000L per entree; Cover 3,000L; V, MC, DC)* (aka **La Taverna di Bacco**) is a must. Detailed wood molding and old-fashioned tile floors make this homey spot, a minute's walk south of

Piazza Diacono, seem much older than its 11 years. The chef gives classic dishes an inventive spin without charging a fortune for the fresh ingredients and intricate preparations—nothing costs more than 10,000L. Delicately cured lamb comes with arugala and apples that have been steeped in balsamic vinegar. *Cialzon* pasta arrives as three large ravioli in a smoked ricotta and cinnamon-spiked cream sauce. The *farona* (pheasant) is served over wilted radicchio with a honey truffle sauce. Bottles of local wine are a mere 15,000L—if you can't finish, they eyeball the bottle and deduct 3,000L for each glass that's left. Try to get one of the tables in the little walled courtyard out back in the warm months.

crashing

The good, cheap food in Cividale is the happy-face news. The sad-face news is the scarce, expensive lodging. Before planning anything more than a day trip, make sure to call ahead and find a place to stay. The only really affordable options are a bus ride and a hike away, up at one of the hillside *refugi,* or lodges. The tourist information office [see *need to know,* below] has a short list of townspeople who rent rooms in private homes, but the prices are not what we'd call cheap. To keep from being stuck in town with nowhere to lay your weary bones, keep in mind that the last train to Udine leaves around 8pm.

▶▶CHEAP

If you have time to go the scenic (and cheap) route, you can try **Rifugio Solarie,** just 25 kilometers from Cividale, and accessible by bus and a brisk hike. **Rifugio Pelizzo** is another possibility, although it's a bus ride and an even lengthier two-hour hike [see **Natisone Valley,** below, for both]. If you've come here to get back to nature anyway, one of these little places out in the wild is definitely the way to go.

▶▶DO-ABLE

The Picotti family has run the **Locanda al Pomo d'Oro** *(Piazza S.Giovanni 20; Tel and Fax 0432/731-489; 80,000L single, 120,000L double, breakfast included; No credit cards)* for 60 years in this 12th-century hostel. You'd think that in all that time, someone would have opened a second affordable hotel, but you'd be wrong. There are only 13 rooms and one mini-apartment here, so book *way* in advance. You may not feel like you're getting your money's worth, but at least there's free breakfast.

▶▶SPLURGE

Located at the edge of the historic center of town, just a short walk from the train station is **Hotel Roma** *(Piazza Pico; Tel 0432/731-871, Fax 0432/701-033; 95,000L single, 140,000L double, all w/private bath; 15,000L breakfast; V, MC, AE),* the only other hotel in town. The good news is that all the rooms are comfortable and new, in a Holiday Inn kind of way. Minibars are well-stocked, TVs are satellite-enhanced, and the tile bathrooms and blow dryers will leave you squeaky clean and impeccably coifed. As you can probably guess, the bad news comes when it's time to pay....

need to know

Currency Exchange The **Banca Populare di Cividale** *(Piazza Duomo 8; Tel 0432/707-111; 9am-12:30pm/2:30pm-5pm)* is right in the heart of town, and has an **ATM.**

Tourist Information The super-friendly **tourist office** *(Corso Paolino d'Aquileia 10; Tel 0432/731-461, Fax 0432/731-398; 8am-12:30pm/3:30-6:00pm daily; www.regione.fvg.it/turismo/civadale/welcome.htm, a.r.p.t.cividale@regione.fvg.it)* will help you with planning hiking trips, excursions into Slovenia, and even booking rooms in local homes. It's just on the west end of the Ponte Del Diavolo.

Public Transportation No cars are allowed in the city center, so there are no buses either. But you were planning on walking anyway, right?

Health and Emergency Emergency: *118;* National Police (**Carabinieri**): *112;* Fire: *115.* The **Polizia Municipale** is on Piazza Diaz *(Tel 0432/731-819);* the local hospital, **Ospidale Civile** *(Piazza Ospidale; Tel 0432/7081)* is logically located on the street named for it.

Pharmacies Farmacia Fontana *(Corso G. Mazzini 22, Tel 0432/731-163; 9am-12:30pm/2:30pm-7pm Mon-Fri),* east of Piazza Diacono, rotates with the other local pharmacies for round-the-clock service. A schedule is posted on the door with the number for each night's 24-hour pharmacy.

Telephone Phone cards are available at newsstands as usual. Reliable public phones can be found in Piazza Del Duomo.

Trains Cividale is one of the few Italian towns that the normal FS (Ferrovia del Stato) railroad does not serve. The **local train service** *(Tel 0432/731-032)* goes to Udine every 20 minutes, at a cost of 4,300L. Don't forget that the last train to Udine leaves at 8pm. The **train station** is just southwest of the town center. Don't plan on leaving packs at the station during a day hike; there is no baggage deposit.

Bus Lines Out of the City The **bus station** is across the street from the train station on Via Marconi. Buses to smaller towns, like Savogna and Drenchia, run twice a day. Schedules are available at the station and the tourist office [see above].

Postal Unleash all your clever postcard quips ("The weather is here; wish you were beautiful") on an unsuspecting world at the **post office** *(Largo Boiani 31; 8:30am-6pm Mon-Sat).*

Internet There's not a single public PC in town, much less an Internet connection. You'll live. Cividale does have a website, though: *www.regione.fvg.it/benvenuti/civeng/welcome.htm.*

natisone valley

A hike through the gorgeous, green Natisone Valley—which comprises some 170 square kilometers east of Cividale and stretches to the Slovenian border—is a must for nature-lovers, hikers, and anyone else who wants to get a little alone time. It's long been a favorite destination for Italian, German, and Austrian hikers-in-the-know, but its green paths spotted with wildflowers, winding roads up and over mountain peaks, and wide vistas are still a virtual secret from the rest of the world. With hundreds of trails, paths, and roads carving through the rolling hills and mountain peaks, passing through tiny towns and hilltop villages, there's something for everyone—from WWI history buffs tracing the footsteps of Italian soldiers on old WWI mule paths (which have been rebuilt and are well sign-posted) to Teva-wearing college kids out for an adrenaline-inducing climb through the pristine landscape. Yet you'll rarely pass another hiker as you wander this largely undiscovered valley. The locals you meet along the way will seem thrilled to have visitors—asking for directions can quickly lead to a guided tour, followed by recommendations for other routes, and possibly an invite to dinner.

Most travelers make Cividale de Fruli their home base, taking just a small backpack to stay overnight in the *rifugi,* rustic yet comfortable accommodations situated along the trails, and return to town the next day. Enjoy having the paths to yourself while you still can. Start your exploration at Cividale's tourist office [see *need to know,* below], where you can purchase your most useful hiking tool—the *Valli Del Natisone Cividale del Friuli Cata Topographica 1:25,000,* a map published by the Comunità Montana Valli del Natisone. Every path is clearly labeled with level of difficulty, elevation, *rifugi,* and even buildings and houses. Then ask for the bus schedule, which changes each season—you should take the bus to the village or road closest to the area you want to hike around. One of the most popular hikes is 736a, up to the super-popular and comfy **Rifugio Escursionistica "G. Pelizzo"** [see *need to know,* below].

If you have any questions about how to get there, call ahead. These guys are helpful, if you happen to speak Italian. If you don't, the sweet woman at the tourist office is happy to put her excellent English to good use.

The 6,166-kilometer **Sentiero di Italia,** indicated on the map as SI, cuts through a wide range of terrain, offering sweeping, uncluttered views. North of Refugio Pelizzo, it leads to Palestra di Roccia, a rock face that's great for climbing. It crosses creeks, goes through small towns, and winds its way down mountains and through fields blanketed in green. There are hundreds of paths to choose from—some are better known for the flowers and foliage, others for their views, and still others, for the steep ascent. One disclaimer: hiking is not walking, hotshot. Carry lots of water, wear good shoes, and have some high-protein snacks with you. For the most part, these are easy hikes, but should be treated seriously—don't attempt them without the map.

need to know

Tourist Information Cividale's **tourist office** *(Corso Paolino d'Aquileia 10, Cividale; Tel 0432/731-461, Fax 0432/731-398; 8am-12:30pm/3:30-6:00pm daily)* offers all of the necessary maps and guides you might need for your excursion, including the invaluable *Valli Del Natisone Cividale del Friuli Cata Topographica 1:25,000.* The **C.A.I. Club Alpino Italiano Sezione "Monte Nero"** *(Via Carraria in Cividale; http://canin.sci.uniud.it/%7Erighini/cai.html)* plans group excursions into the hills—ask for a current itinerary at the tourist office. You can also check out ***http://www.vallidelnatisone.it/files/comuni.htm*** for information and maps of the Natisone Valley and its towns.

Directions and Transporation Bus schedules are available at the station in Cividale, as well as the tourist office. Take the bus to the village or street closest to the area you want to hike around. Generally, they leave two or three times a day from the Cividale bus station, and drop you off on the side of the road, next to the hiking paths.

Eats The *rifugi* provide all the sustenance you'll need, from hot meals, to snack-to-packs, to wine and beer in the evenings. As you're hiking, you can also stop to shop in the tiny markets of small towns like Drenchia and Savogna.

Crashing For the past 25 years, **rifugio escursionistica: "G. Pelizzo"** *(Monte Matajur, 1320m; Tel 0432/714-041; Open Apr 1-Nov 15; isadec@libero.it, www.rifugi.it; 23,000L per bed, 30,000L w/linen and towels, 60,000L complete pension; No credit cards),* has functioned as a destination as much as a stop-over. It's run by the most knowing, outdoorsy couple you'll ever meet, in an old house renovated to sooth the souls of wayward travelers. Everything about this place is worth the trip: the fireplace in the living room, the flower garden, the homemade *grappas* offered before you go to bed. The food is also top notch—homemade gnocchi, dense rustic breads, served with excellent local wines. To get here, take the Masseris-Savogna-Cividale Bus from the station in Cividale, and get off four stops after Savogna at Masseris. It's a two-hour hike from there, walking along the easy 736a path.

25 kilometers from Cividale, and just a hop-skip-and-a-jump to the Slovenian border, is the newer **Solaire Rifugio** *(Casoni Saolair, 940m; Tel 0368/371-02-09; Open year round; 25,000L per bed; No credit cards).* Lightweights, this one's for you. Just take the bus from the station (it leaves Cividale twice daily) to Drenchia. Once there, you can either walk to the *rifugio* via the main road through town, or hike up trail 746. If you don't see the signs, ask someone. This place offers stunning views, great food, and a well-stocked bar. When you're ready to come back to civilization, just remember that only two buses a day leave for Cividale, at the same time you were dropped off the day before.

campania

Centuries ago, sirens crooned off the shores of Campania to lure Odysseus into the sea with their song. Today, not that much has changed. This part of southern Italy still tempts travelers—but with good wine, good food, and good times rather than some magic ditty. Spend most of your time in Campania on the **Amalfi Coast,** the southernmost slice of the region and one of the most dramatic coastlines in the world. Forget about educational trips to the museum or guided tours that go on and on—in most of these little towns, it's all about doing as little as possible for as long as you want. A typical Amalfi Coast regimen entails lazing the morning away on the beach or a boat, venturing inland for an afternoon espresso on a cobblestone piazza, and relishing a leisurely dinner of fresh octopus followed by lemon *profiteroles,* washed down with bottles of local wine. Morning will arrive before you know it, when you're partying under the stars in smoky outdoor discos. It's no wonder that victims of *amore* insist that Campania is an aphrodisiac, although the free-flowing *vino* and a susceptibility to foreign accents must be equally to blame for all those sins of passion. In the ancient and medieval world, the small port towns along the Amalfi Coast were once great hubs of the Mediterranean. Arabs, Spaniards, Africans, and others visited these towns, the result of which is a hodgepodge of architectural styles that can best be observed in the great cathedrals of **Amalfi** and **Ravello.** The towns lost their prominence around the 11th century; after floods destroyed Amalfi, Venice and Genoa became the new ports of call.

Campania's economy is radically different from that of the prosperous north; you won't run into many factories here, as most people make their living from farms or hotels. Traveling through major cities such as **Naples** is cheap compared to adventuring in the Gucci-clad north, although the touristy hot spots tend to be ritzy and expensive. If you eat and drink where the locals do, prices are as little as a third of what they are in Rome. (Important note: While in Naples, you'll get more bang for your buck, but you'll also want to keep a close eye on your cash. Tourists and high crime rates plus unemployment equal a pickpocket's paradise.) While we don't recommend you spend too much time in grimy Naples, it's a good launching pad to the south's more desirable destinations. It's the gateway to the hedonistic (and super-pricey) isle of **Capri,** and to **Ischia,** the *isola verde,* where you can soak in the famed thermal springs.

campania

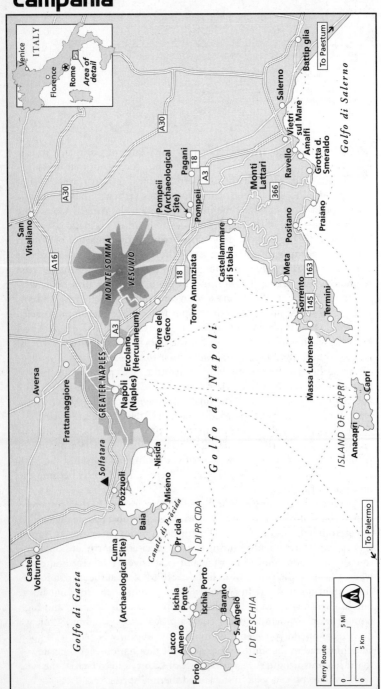

From Naples you can also hop a bus that will take you along the perilous seaside Amalfi Drive, which will deposit you in the seriously charming hillside towns of Amalfi and Ravello. Getting there is part of the fun. As you career around the hairpin turns on the high roads—wondering whether this will be the end of your short time on earth—you'll catch breathtaking glimpses of the bright, cerulean sea and steep hillsides draped in vineyards and lemon groves below you. The nightlife of the Amalfi Coast can be hit or miss, since the crowd here tends to be older, and some towns don't even have a bar. (And, since most youth have to leave the area and find jobs elsewhere, there aren't a huge number of *local* youth here either.) **Positano** has some hip bars, and you can find hard-core discos in the super-touristy party town of **Sorrento.** Ischia offers the best of both worlds, with a few discos, some bars, and great hotels and beaches.

The only trouble with the Amalfi Coast is that it's a little on the expensive side, especially when it comes to places to crash. It wasn't always this way: During the 1950s, starving artists and writers found that they could live very, very cheaply in modest bungalows. But eventually the wealthy art patrons caught on and started building villas. Then tourists started coming south, hotel rates skyrocketed, and massive development followed. On the plus side, there's a lot more to do now and the services for travelers are much better.

Getting around the region

The best time to tour the islands and small towns of the Amalfi Coast is April through October. Otherwise, you'll find that many hotels, restaurants, and shops will be closed. Crowds are heaviest in July and August, when Italians are on month-long holiday. Travel within this region is very easy. Many tourists become nomads for a few weeks as they travel up and down the coast. Buses, trains (not along the coast), and ferries run frequently and rarely sell out (though they're usually packed full), stations are clearly marked and easy to get to, tickets can be purchased right before take-off time.

A great itinerary for the Amalfi Coast would be to: Start at **Naples,** and take a hydrofoil (45 minutes) to **Ischia** or **Capri.** Come back to Naples, and hop on a 2-hour bus ride to **Amalfi** for an afternoon or a day. From Amalfi you can catch a local bus to **Ravello,** a short 15 minutes away. After a few days in this quiet haven, you'll be ready to move on to the livelier **Positano,** another 30-minute bus ride away. And from Positano it's another 30-minute bus ride to Amalfi's resort capital, **Sorrento.** From Sorrento, you could easily take a ferry (45 minutes) out for another visit to Capri or Ischia. However, you might want to stay overnight in Sorrento while visiting these pricey isles. Each of these towns can be covered in a day easily. For those traveling at a more relaxed pace, you might want to plan two or three nights in each location. You can also base yourself in one town, and make day trips of the others.

TraVEL TIMES

All times by train unless otherwise marked:
* Bus
** Ferry
*** Hydrofoil
(asterisks in parentheses denote
that part of the trip is by train,
part by other mode of transport)

	Pompeii	Amalfi	Ravello	Positano
Naples	:30*	2:00*	1:30(*)	:45**
Pompeii	-	1:50(*)	2:00	1:15(*)
Amalfi	1:50(*)	-	:20*	:35*
Ravello	2:00	:20*	-	:30*
Positano	1:15(*)	:35*	:30*	-
Sorrento	:35	1:15*	1:00	:40*
Isle of Capri	1:25(***)	1:00**	1:10*	:40**

Sorrento	Isle of Capri	Ischia
1:00	1:00***	1:00***
:35	1:25(**)	1:15(***)
1:15*	1:00**	1:00***
1:00	1:10*	1:20(*,***)
:40*	:40**	1:15***
-	:50**	:45***
:50**	-	:40***

naples

Score a fake Louis Vuitton bag, check out the awesome archaeological museum, and fuel up on what will possibly be the best pizza you ever had in Naples, the birthplace of this major culinary miracle. Just keep an eye on your Rolex and a firm grip on your wallet because this ain't Kansas. Between the nimble-footed pickpockets and the purse-snatching scooter riders, you'll have to keep your wits about you. Many people are unpleasantly shocked when they first land in Naples. It's extremely polluted, there's lots of traffic, and if you're a woman, the lecherous butt-pinching locals can easily ruin your day. Some of the youth hostels here are on par with Third World refugee camps. Unemployment rates are high, as is crime. Economic disparity is also evident: Gleaming, futuristic Japanese-designed skyscrapers loom over dilapidated 18th century buildings and Mussolini-era cookie-cutter apartment complexes. While some people love Naples' gritty flavor, many think it's a cesspool and try to exit ASAP or bypass it altogether. But it's usually a mandatory stop to get to the Amalfi coast, so you may get stuck there temporarily, even if it's just for a couple of hours. The nightlife isn't anything to write home about, but there are some cool places to blow off steam.

The best part of Naples is its essential diversity, thanks in part to the industrial ships that dock here from all ports of call, be it Africa, China, or elsewhere. Over the years, Naples has embraced, been conquered by, and absorbed many cultures, which today give the city its spark and flavor. Large populations of legal and not-so-legal refugees have moved here for economic or political reasons—or out of pure wanderlust. Leaving the Stazione Centrale on Piazza Garibaldi, you're just as likely to hear *"Salaam Alaikum," "Ni hao ma,"* or *"Nokia?!? Nokia?!?"* as *"Boungiorno!"* It's like you've entered the United Nations of street hawkers, a sometimes unexpected welcome to this city, which is considered the gateway to Southern Italy.

Despite the influx of diverse cultures, though, the people of Naples have remained almost stereotypically Neapolitan. The cab drivers are crooks and they really do yell "Mama mia!" The women look like Sophia Loren. And bodies in garbage bags—presumably victims of the latest Mafia hit—float around the Bay of Naples like so many dead fish. Although some of the locals make their living by fleecing tourists, most of them are harmless and genuinely sociable.

neighborhoods and hanging out

At first glance, Naples seems like a *huge* city. Once you get inside however, it's really not. Almost all visitors will arrive via train at **Stazione Centrale,** right on **Piazza Garibaldi.** The area within a five-block radius of the train station is a good place to find a cheap hotel, although most people prefer to stay somewhere in **Santa Lucia,** the swank (i.e. safe) part of the city. Santa Lucia is a hair-raising 30-minute walk through traffic and crowds from the train station, so unless you want to brave the confusing bus system, it's best to get there via cab (competition is stiff in the Naples taxi biz, so the prices are pretty reasonable). And once you get to Santa Lucia, walking is definitely the best way to get around. On the water, this historic district is filled with beautiful old buildings painted pink, yellow, and green. Here you'll find the city's ritziest hotels, the main port of **Molo Beverello** (where the hydrofoils leave for Capri and Ischia), and the SITA bus station. The rest of Naples is not heavily visited, and many neighborhoods are dilapidated residential areas that you'll probably want to skip.

All the important piazzas, museums, and other sites are in or within walking distance of Santa Lucia. **Piazza Trento e Trieste,** about a block inland (to the east) of Molo Beverello, is where you can find the entrance to **Galleria Umberto I,** on **Via San Carlos.** This massive glass and iron building houses several indoor cafes and stores selling postcards and film. The main shopping street, **Via Roma** (which is actually called **Via Toledo** in this part of town), runs north out of Trento e Trieste. About a ten-minute walk up Roma will bring you to **Piazza Dante,** another popular square, where Roma turns into **Via Enrico Pessina** and leads you further north to the **National Archaeological Museum** [see *culture zoo,* below], one of the best in the world and Naples' star attraction.

If you're planning on staying in Santa Lucia, the best form of transportation is walking.

The social center of Naples for tourists and locals alike is Galleria Umberto I. You'll find Naples' youth in the city's outdoor piazzas, where most of them seem to congregate with their posses, their cell phones, and their scooters. There's a naval school right on the marina, so you'll find plenty of hanging out in that area as well.

naples bars clubs and culture zoo

BARS/CLUBS ▲
Chez Moi **3**
Madison Street **4**
Piazza di Spagna **1**
Riot **7**
Tongue **2**

CULTURE ZOO ●
Duomo **8**
Museo Archeologico **6**
Nazionale (National
Archaeological Musuem
Museo Nazionale **5**
di Capodimonte

Take a bite out of crime

Naples is known for taking first place in certain cultural categories: It has the best pizza, history, art, *and* it's home to the most-skilled pick-pocketing force in the world. One would almost think the city was bewitched: Rolexes slide off wrists, wallets vanish into thin air, and passports (hot merchandise in this people-moving city) soon have someone else's face on them. Nobody in Naples is immune to petty thievery, and happy-go-lucky young tourists are prime targets. The following list of helpful hints may look like a paranoid manifesto, but unfortunately it's justifiable.

1. Get a money belt that you can wear under your clothing. Yes, you'll feel like a dork, but after the inevitable encounter with a troupe of hissing gypsies, you'll be glad you did.
2. Make Xerox copies of your passport and keep them someplace where your passport is not. It's also a good idea to have the copies notarized in your home country. This will give them a convincing and official look and ensure exit out of the country in case your passport gets lost or stolen.
3. Keep valuables that don't fit in your money belt in the bowels of your luggage—put anything in outside pockets without locks and you are practically handing it over. Get small combination locks for zippers and clasps.
4. Wear a bag that slings over your shoulder and across your body. When walking down the sidewalk, wear the bag facing the buildings, not the street. This is conventional Neapolitan wisdom.
5. "Take the camera and run" is blood sport in Naples. When asking strangers to take photos of you, never ask a single person, particularly a male. Your best option is a pack of teenage girls.
6. Razor-bladers. No, they are not people who ride around on the faddish scooters from Japan; they're scooter-riding predators who will slash your bag straps, grab your bag, and scooter off, and they prowl all over Naples and Rome. To resist falling prey, try to get a bag with heavy leather straps and walk close to the buildings, not on the edge of the streets.
7. Be particularly careful when the train doors are about to shut. This is prime time for thieves to grab your bag from the platform, leaving you trapped in the train car heading to your next destination.
8. Beware of people razor-blading the bottom of your backpack or back pocket and helping themselves to your property.

club and live music scene

Naples knows that it's the last call for clubs before travelers move on to the relatively quiet coast, and its nightclubs charge *lira grande* accordingly. All the discos are thick with cigarette smoke, and the only prerequisite to meeting someone is that you have a pulse. As an out-of-towner, you'll probably be in the minority—which is not necessarily a bad thing—wherever you choose to party, since clubs are generally packed with local youth.

To mingle with Naples' classier jet-set, or if you just want to go dancing *without* hundreds of sweaty bodies grinding against you, *voulez-vous dansez a* **Chez Moi** *(Via del Parco Margherita 13; Tel 081/407-526; 10pm-4am Fri, Sat; Cover 25,000L; No credit cards),* in the western end of Santa Lucia. This blue and green colored nightclub occasionally has a live cabaret act, but always ends the night in disco. Guests tether themselves to tables at first, then venture onto the dance floor as the night wears on. Dress code is chic. It's easy to get in, and things really get going around 11pm.

For a younger, more down-to-earth and pungent party crowd, try **Madison Street** *(Via Sgambati 47; Tel 081/546-65-66; 10pm-3am Tue, Thu-Sat, 8pm-2am Sun; Cover 15,000-30,000L),* Naples' biggest disco. There are several bars on the vast and solidly packed dance floor, as well as large screens that play music videos.

A similar crowd hangs out at **Piazza di Spagna** *(Via Petrarca 101; Tel 081/575-48-82; Opens at 10pm Fri-Sun, Sep-July; Cover 15,000-20,000L),* a multilevel bar and disco that's packed with Italians and Americans.

Gay action can be found at the cheekily named **Tongue** *(Via Manzoni 207; Tel 081/769-08-00; 9pm-3am Sat, Sun; Cover 15,000-25,000L; No credit cards).* Like most gay clubs in Italy, this one tosses up a salad of gays, straights, and anything in between, all dancing to *musica commerciale.* Things start happening around midnight and keep going until people start going home, usually around 4am.

Jazz aficionados can sample the local scene at **Riot** *(Via San Biagio 38; Tel 081/552-32-31; 10:30am-3am Thu-Tue; No credit cards),* where the booze flows freely and the crowd gets about as lively as the music happens to be that night. Dress is hip and flashy.

culture zoo

You could argue that Naples itself is one big, swarming culture zoo....But if you're looking for actual museums, these two very cool ones will fit the bill.

Museo Archeologico Nazionale (National Archaeological Musuem) *(Piazza Museo Nazionale 18-19; Tel 081/440-166; Metro to Piazza Cavour; 9am-2pm Wed-Mon; 12,000L adults, 18 and under free):* Dating back to the 16th century, the building that houses this collection is an attraction in itself. Inside, you'll find one of the finest assemblages of archeological artifacts in the world—if you're planning on going out to nearby Pompeii [see below], stop here first and see what was taken away. Check out the famed nude statues of Armodio and Aristogone on the ground floor.

Museo Nazionale di Capodimonte *(Palazzo Capodimonte, Parco di Capodimonte, off Amedeo di Savoia, Via Milano 2; Tel 081/744-13-07; 10am-7pm Tue-Sat, 9am-2pm Sun; 14,000L):* If you prefer art to artifacts, don't worry—Naples has you covered as well. Stroll through this 18th-century royal palace and you'll find works by Masaccio, Michelangelo, Bellini, Correggio, Caravaggio, Titian, and El Greco. The gallery's most important room is filled with religious Renaissance art by the masters—*Adoration of the Child* by Luca Signorelli, a panel by Raphael, and *Madonna and Child with Angels* by Botticelli, to name just a few. And did you know that Italy is a great place to check out some Flemish art? The museum has a room dedicated to the Dutch masters and has Pieter Brueghel's *Blind Men* and *Misanthrope* on display. The museum is in the middle of Capodimonte Park, high above the city in the Capidimonte district.

CITY SPORTS

Jonesin' for a good workout? You may have to let that one go while you're in Naples. Neapolitans aren't exactly sports fanatics, and betting on a soccer game is about as close as they come to exercise. If you really, really need to stretch your legs, the area along the waterfront in Santa Lucia seems to be the only spot for daring joggers. But keep in mind that running outdoors in Naples' black pollution is probably about as good for your lungs as smoking a pack of unfiltered cigarettes. It may be easier to just make like the natives and go dancing.

STUFF

Hopefully you won't be in Naples long enough to do any major retail therapy before you head to the coast. It's no great loss, anyhow, since the local stores aren't really anything special. But what you don't want to miss are the really great fakes you can get from tourist vendors in the main tourist piazzas. Naples has the world's best fake Louis Vuitton, Gucci, or JP Tod bags (with real leather interiors and fake serial numbers). This stuff looks and feels like the real thing, and costs very little. Scavenge the floors and corners of the main tourist piazzas (like the main tourist shopping center, **Galleria Umberto I**) to find them. If you see something you like, go with the impulse and buy it right away: Vendors are constantly on the move to avoid crackdowns, and if they even think they smell *la polizia,* they'll bundle up their portable boutiques and be gone in a flash.

EATS

Naples' culinary claim to fame is that it's the birthplace of pizza. You can probably be a happy camper just sticking with that as a temporary diet.

naples eats and crashing

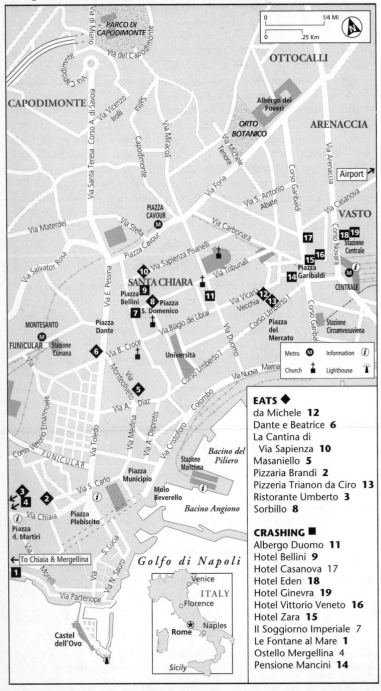

EATS ◆
da Michele **12**
Dante e Beatrice **6**
La Cantina di
  Via Sapienza **10**
Masaniello **5**
Pizzaria Brandi **2**
Pizzeria Trianon da Ciro **13**
Ristorante Umberto **3**
Sorbillo **8**

CRASHING ■
Albergo Duomo **11**
Hotel Bellini **9**
Hotel Casanova **17**
Hotel Eden **18**
Hotel Ginevra **19**
Hotel Vittorio Veneto **16**
Hotel Zara **15**
Il Soggiorno Imperiale **7**
Le Fontane al Mare **1**
Ostello Mergellina **4**
Pensione Mancini **14**

Neapolitan pizza has a thin crispy crust, and you can choose a variety of toppings. Go for the four cheese (with blue cheese) or sausage and onion (thinly sliced sweet onions and crumbled spicy sausage). Like everywhere else in Italy, espresso and Italian cookies, available at espresso bars all over the city, are dietary staples.

▶▶**CHEAP**

The pizza in Naples is *never* bad, but two of the best are the tiny (only five tables) **Sorbillo** *(Via Tribunali 35; No phone; Closed Sun)* in Spaccanapoli, and **da Michele** *(Via Cesare Sersale 1; Tel 081/553-92-04; Closed Sun)* off Corso Umberto near the train station.

If you want to trust the critics, go to **Pizzeria Trianon da Ciro** *(Via Pietro Colletta 42/44/46; Tel 081/553-94-28; 10am-4:30pm/6:30pm-midnight daily, Closed Sun lunch; Pizza 5,500-12,500L; V, MC).* It's considered by many (including *The New York Times*) to have the best pizza in Naples.

And you can't leave Naples without sampling pizza *Margherita* at its birthplace, **Pizzaria Brandi** *(Salita Santa Anna di Palazzo; Tel 081/416-928; www.brandi.it; Noon-3pm/6:30pm-midnight Tue-Sun; Avg 18,000L per entree; V, MC, AE),* near Piazza Plebescito. The old-style cuisine is served up in a space that seats about 200 (mostly tourists). There are all kinds of specialties, including *pasta frutti di mare* (pasta with fruits of the sea), but it's best to stick to the pies.

So you've gorged on pounds of pizza and need to take a breather? You can get typical Neapolitan pastas and meat dishes at **La Cantina di Via Sapienza** *(Via Sapienza 40/41; Tel 081/45-90-78; Noon-4pm Mon-Sat; No credit cards),* a popular spot with young locals. *Primi* courses are an incredible 4,000-5,000L, but they only serve lunch.

▶▶**DO-ABLE**

Dante e Beatrice *(Piazza Dante 44-45; Tel 081/549-94-38; 1:30-4pm/8pm-midnight Thu-Tue; Avg 25,000L per entree; No credit cards)* has become as famous as the romantic tragedies of its namesake. Serving up hearty Neapolitan cuisine in a simple Italian trattoria-style space for low prices, it can't be beat. Try the lasagne, the seafood salad, or both. You can't get hard alcohol here, but there's plenty of wine and beer. Waiters are friendly, but they're not the most attentive. It's located near the archaeo-logical museum.

In central Naples in the Santa Chiara area is **Masaniello** *(Via Don-nalbina 28; Tel 081/552-88-63; 11:30-3pm Mon-Sat; Avg 22,000L per entree; V, MC, DC, AE),* named after the leader of a people's revolution who was king for a day in 1647. The waiters here know the menu by heart—which is good, since there are no paper menus handy. Feel free to go back into the kitchen to consult with the chef if you're not feeling fully committed (really!). Dishes like linguine with Neapolitan clams and cheese are based on handed-down recipes, probably from the time of Masaniello himself. You can get wine here, but no hard booze.

Ristorante Umberto *(Via Alabardieri 30-31; Tel 081/418-555; Tram to Piazza Vittoria; Noon-3:30pm/7:30pm-midnight Tue-Sun, Closed Aug 2-27; 6,000-10,000L pizza, 3,500-18,000L first courses, 8,500-*

21,000L second courses; V, MC, AE, DC) gives you sit-down service in a classy atmosphere at trattoria prices. The white walls are hung with antique mirrors and prints, and the waiters are dressed in waistcoats. Start with the *pasta e lenticchie* (pasta with lentils), and follow it with the *impepata di cozze* (spicy mussel stew). This place is always swarming with locals, who know a good thing when they see it. If you just want a quick pie, head to the pizzeria in the rear.

crashing

With great islands and Amalfian towns less than an hour away, there's really no good reason to stay overnight in Naples. Most of the hotels here are either way too funky or way too expensive. However there are two main neighborhoods to crash in: right around the train station, or right by the water in Santa Lucia. The hotels near the train stations are cheap but creepy, while the ones in Santa Lucia are expensive but convenient to the port, bus station, and cultural activities. There also are a few decent places in the Spaccanapoli district west of the train station.

▶▶CHEAP

Situated off the far end of Piazza Garibaldi from the station, **Pensione Mancini** *(Piazza Mancini 33; Tel 081/553-67-31; Fax 081/554-66-25; 28,000L dorm bed, 65,000L double, 75,000L w/ private bath, breakfast included; No credit cards)* is a haven for backpackers making day trips to other towns in the area. The staff speaks fluent English, among other languages. Some rooms come with private baths.

A few blocks farther from the station you'll find **Hotel Zara** *(Via Firenze 81; Tel 081/287-125; Fax 081/268-287; www.hotelzara.3000.it; 40,000L single, 70,000L double)*, which is quieter and more spacious than most hotels nearby.

Il Soggiorno Imperiale *(Piazza Miraglia 386, 3rd Floor; Tel 081/459-347; 35,000L single, 60,000L double; No credit cards)* offers tidy and secure budget accommodations in a great area of town, near Piazza Dante in the heart of Spaccanapoli. It's much nicer than staying among the prostitutes and pickpockets around the station, although you'll have to share a bathroom.

Hotel Casanova *(Via Venezia 2; Tel 081/268-287; Fax 081/269-792; 40,000L single, 55,000L w/ bath, 70,000L double, 85,000L w/ bath; V, MC, AE)* offers the best of both worlds: It's far enough from Piazza Garibaldi that it's relatively secure and quiet, but close enough that you won't have any trouble making your morning train. Some rooms have private bathrooms.

Ostello Mergellina *(Salita della Grotta 23; Tel 081/761-23-46; Fax 081/761-23-91; Metro to Mergellina; 24,000L dorm bed; No credit cards)* is Naples' youth hostel and could be likened to a UN refugee camp. There's no TV or telephone in the lounge, you have to share the bathroom, and it's as crowded as a tin of sardines. Thankfully there's no curfew, so you're free to go out dancing till dawn, then return when you're too exhausted to be bothered by the drawbacks.

Hotel Eden *(Corso Novara 9; Tel 081/285-344; Fax 081/285-690; 42,000L single, 72,000L double; No credit cards)* is *the* standard budget hotel in Naples. It's only one block from the train station; just turn right as you leave the front entrance of the station, and you're practically there. The 45 rooms come with TVs, telephones, and private baths. The crowd is young, continental, and blissfully unaware of impending back problems. It's a clean place, but very basic. Reservations are recommended.

▶▶DO-ABLE
The family-run **Hotel Ginevra** *(Via Genova 116; Tel 081/283-210; Fax 081/554-17-57; 45,000L singles, 70,000L double, 90,000L w/ bath; V, MC, AE)* is a few blocks from the train station and has 15 quiet rooms, some with private baths. The staff speaks English.

Located in the *"centro centro"* near Piazza San Gaetano, **Hotel Bellini** *(Via San Paolo 44; Tel 081/456-996; Fax 081/292-256; 90,000L single, 130,000L double)* is one of Napoli's best budget hotels. All rooms have private bath, TV, phone, and fridge. The owner is very friendly and helpful.

Hotel Vittorio Veneto *(Via Milano 96; Tel/Fax 081/201-539; 60-70,000L single w/o bath; 80-100,000L double w/o bath; 110-120,000 double with bath; No credit cards)* is nothing to write home about, but it won't take too much out of your wallet. It's in the sketchy part of town near the station.

Set on the first floor of an 18th-century palazzo in the heart of Spaccanapoli, **Albergo Duomo** *(Via Duomo 228; Tel 081/265-988; 70,000L single, 110,000L double; No credit cards)* offers nine cool, clean, blue and white-tiled rooms with immaculate bathrooms.

Le Fontane al Mare *(Via Niccolo Tommaseo 14, 4th Floor; Tel 081/764-38-11; Fax 081/764-34-70; 90,000L single, 100,000L w/ bath, 114,000L double, 144,000L w/ bath; V, MC, AE)* is on the waterfront and has clean, comfortable rooms with a clear view of Capri. Some rooms come with private baths.

need to know

Currency Exchange All major hotels have currency exchange. There are also exchanges at the two main rail terminals, **Stazione Centrale** at Piazza Garibaldi, and **Stazione Mergellina** at Piazza Piedigrotta.

Tourist Information You can pick up info at **Ente Provinciale per il Turismo** *(Piazza dei Martiri 58; Tel 081/405-311; Bus 15, Tram 1; 8:30am-1pm Mon-Sat)*. There are other offices that stay open until 7pm at **Stazione Centrale** *(Piazza Garibaldi; Tel 081/268-779)*, at **Stazione Mergellina** *(Piazza Piedigrotta; Tel 081/761-21-02)*, and at the **Capodichino Airport** *(Tel 081/780-57-61)*. While they won't make reservations for you, they can provide a list of hotels. There are also representatives loitering around the tourist office at the train station who will take you directly to their hotel or hostel free of charge.

Public Transportation There is an orange **bus and tram system,** but it can be a little confusing to navigate. Stops are not clearly marked, but they are *all over* the city: Just look for accumulating crowds. The **Metropolitana** is a better option. It will take you all over the city, and there are underground stations at Stazione Centrale and Stazione Mergellina so you can hop on the metro as soon as you land here. The metro, buses, and trams all use the same tickets. A 90-minute unlimited ticket costs 1,500L, and a full-day pass is 5,000L. They can be bought at most tobacco shops near a station. Trams 1 and 4 run from Stazione Centrale to the port (where you can catch boats to Capri and Ischia). Taxis are also a good way of getting around; there are literally hundreds of them, and it's easy to flag one down wherever you go. The drivers will compete hard for your business, but make sure you agree on a price before you hop in, as Neapolitan cabbies are renowned for their creative pricing.

American Express There is an American Express branch at **Every Tours** *(Piazza Municipio 5; Tel 081/551-85-64; Metro to Garibaldi; 9am-1:30pm/3:30-6:30pm Mon-Sat).*

Health and Emergency Emergency: *113;* Police: *112.* There are several **Guarda Medicale Permanente** throughout town, and you can call **113** for directions.

Pharmacies Farmacia Helvethia *(Piazza Garibaldi 11; Tel 081/554-88-94; Metro to Garibaldi)* is near Stazione Centrale.

Telephone The city code for naples is *081.*

Airports Domestic flights from Rome and other major Italian cities land at **Aeroporto di Capodichino** *(Via Umberto Maddalena; Tel 081/789-63-85),* 6km north of the city. A city bus, **ATAN Bus 14** *(1,500L)* will take you from the airport to Piazza Garibaldi in front of the train station.

Trains Most travelers reach Naples by train. The ride between Rome and Naples is especially beautiful. The train from Rome costs 20,000L. From Milan, it costs 70,000L. The city has two centrally located rail terminals: **Stazione Centrale** on Piazza Garibaldi, and **Stazione Mergellina** on Piazza Piedigrotta. For rail information, call 147/888-088, toll free in Italy.

Bus Lines Out of the City SITA buses *(081/552-21-76)* will get you to where you want to go on the Amalfi Coast.

Boats Tirrenia Lines *(Molo Angionio, Stazione Marritima; Tel 147/899-000)* provides hydrofoil and ferry service between Naples and Palermo. A one-way armchair ticket costs 60,000L; it's 90,000L for a first-class cabin.

Laundry To wash your dirty duds, head to **Bolle Blu** *(62 Corso Navara, three blocks from Piazza Garibaldi; Tel 889/427-14; 8:30am-8pm Mon-Sat; Prices vary).*

Postal The main **post office** is on Piazza G. Matteotti *(Tel 081/551-14-56; Metro to Monte Santo; 8:15am-7:20pm Mon-Sat).*

everywhere else

pompeii

There are two things you need to know about the ruins of Pompeii: 1) you shouldn't miss them, and 2) nobody else does, so you'll have to put up with huge crowds. But it's totally worth it—where else in the world can you see an entire city frozen in stone? (Well, *frozen* is probably the wrong word, since they were actually solidified by fire, but you get the idea.) Pompeii was covered under a deep layer of solidified volcanic ash and pumice stone in 79 A.D., when Mount Vesuvius erupted and buried the prosperous resort town and many of its inhabitants while they slept.

The ruins lay undiscovered for 16 centuries, until the architect Domenico Fontana accidentally unearthed them. Today, this city of ruins is one of southern Italy's most magnetic attractions, drawing hordes of people who want to get a glimpse of what daily life was like more than 20 centuries ago.

The ruins of Pompeii are extensive (remember, this was once a bustling metropolis), so don't underestimate the time you'll need to spend exploring. Four hours is just enough for a cursory tour. It's a good idea to get there at about 8:45am, 15 minutes before the site opens, to get in before the cruise-ship crowd. Also, in the summer the sun is *hot* on the black ash, so avoid a visit at high noon if you'd rather not be burned to a crisp. If you need to cool off, there's a string of fresh OJ stands by the park entrance. You may want to bring your own snack or lunch, since the nearest cafe (serving calzone, pizza, etc.) is at the train station, a half-hour away.

Get a guide brochure and a map at the entrance to help you navigate the ruins. The finest restored villa of Pompeii is the **House of Vettii,** with its intricate dining room fresco of cupids and a charming painting of Priapus resting his giant phallus on a pair of scales. There are plenty of other R-rated sights: Ogle the skeletons in public baths at the Forum in the center of town, or check out the nearby brothel (Lupanare) where johns could request their desired erotic activities by pointing to a position painted on the wall—just like ordering off a menu!

Keep your eye open for the architectural remnants that show what everyday life was like 2,000 years ago, such as the stepping-stones that were used to circumnavigate the canals of garbage or the ovens that are still standing in the ancient bread factory.

The most memorable—and disturbing—site is the *Garden of the Fugitives,* a peaceful olive garden on the edge of town where lifelike children were turned into stone by the volcanic ash. They are curled up in the fetal position, and you can actually see the expressions of horror on their faces.

need to know

Contact Information For more information about the ruins, call 081/861-07-44.

Hours and Days Open You can tackle the ruins from 9am to one hour before sunset daily.

Cost The entrance fee is 16,000L.

Directions and Transportation Reaching Pompeii is *very* easy. Just hop on the **Circumvesuviana Railway** from either Naples (at Stazione Centrale Piazza Garibaldi) or Sorrento (at Circumvesuviana terminal in the center of town). It's about a 30-minute ride from either station. If you are taking the train from Naples, be certain to take the Naples-Sorrento train and get off at the **Pompeii/Scavi** stop (*scavi* means ruins). If you take the Naples-Pompeii train, it will take you to the *town* of Pompeii, not the ruins.

Eats The best place to grab a bite at a decent price here in this petrified playground is **Zi Caterina** *(Via Roma 20; Tel 081/850-7447; Noon-10:30pm daily; Avg. entrees 15,000-32,000L; V, MC, AE, DC),* in the center of town near the basilica. There are two big dining rooms, but the place still always seem to be filled—call ahead and make a reservation if you think of it. The antipasto table is piled with tasty, fresh seafood, and the chef's special—rigatoni with tomato and prociutto—is just plain good.

amalfi

One of the most beautiful towns along the coast, Amalfi is a real gem. Great food, even better wine, strings of outdoor cafes, cool buildings, and a sandy beach make it a great place to hang for an afternoon or two. Though there's not much wild adventure after dark, there's no better place in Italy to catch some rays alongside local teens without having to deal with hordes of young international backpackers. The youth scene is essentially local and laid back.

But Amalfi wasn't always a resort town. Between the 9th and 11th centuries, it was right up there with Genoa and Venice as one of the most powerful maritime cities, a big-time trading hub that served Africa, the Middle East, and Europe. Mediterranean sailors followed its maritime code, the *Tavole Amalfitane,* for centuries. The legacy of this trading empire is a unique hybrid of Romanesque, Moorish, and Byzantine architecture. One of the greatest examples of the "Romanesque-Amalfitian" style is the town's colorful centerpiece, the **Cathedral of Amalfi** [see *culture zoo,* below].

Now that it's reincarnated as a beach resort, Amalfi's biggest bonus is that there's not much to do any more. People come just to hang out, and the laid-back locals are friendly to tourists. The young Italian visitors soak up the sun, middle-aged Americans gorge on gelato, and Germans drink German beer. The social hub for all this action is the **Piazza Duomo,** whose central feature is a magnificent statue of St. Andrew. At the base of the icon, water flows from stone-carved breasts—it's a popular spot to collect drinking water.

Young folks here are mostly Italian, either locals or vacationing Northerners ready to crash out on the sand for a few days. Foreign tourists are mostly on the far side of 35, which could explain the lack of bars and clubs. The only exception is the small 24-hour bar at the **Hotel Marina Riviera** [see *crashing,* below]. Otherwise, what generally passes for nightlife is dinner in a restaurant, where people linger over wine and limoncello until midnight, then go home and crash.

Amalfi is a small, groovy town that you can walk through in about ten minutes. From the bus station, where you'll probably arrive, the beach is in front of you, and the Piazza Duomo, where the cathedral is located, is behind you, amid a smattering of restaurants and sandwich shops.

It's a cool place to visit, but too small and pricey for an extended stay. Make it a long afternoon, or a temporary launching pad for visiting even more expensive neighbor towns such as Ravello.

culture zoo

Amalfian life is definitely lazy-centric; you'll probably want to peel yourself off your beach towels long enough to go see the cathedral. For museums, music festivals, and other cultural diversions, head up the road to Ravello.

Il Duomo (The Cathedral of St. Andrew) *(Piazza del Duomo; Tel 081/871-059; 7:30am-7pm daily; Free admission):* Just behind the bus station's parking lot on the left side of the piazza, Il Duomo is hard to miss, with its distinctive black-and-white mosaic facade. The cathedral dates from the 11th century, though what you see today had been rebuilt. It's bronze doors were made in Constantinople, and the Romanesque bell tower was added in the 13th century. The interior features hauntingly beautiful Moorish vaults and peeling frescoes. The crypt is home to the sacred remains of Saint Andrew, except for the front of his head, which is kept elsewhere.

the great outdoors

The beach and the deep blue Thyrrenian Sea are Amalfi's playground and it's claim to fame. The public (free) beach that lines the harbor is a popular spot to spend the day.

Three miles from Amalfi is the eerie **Emerald Grotto** *(Take boat from Amalfi dock; 9am-4pm daily; 14,000L entry included in boat fare),* a cavern known for its special lighting effect. The cavern chamber is filled with stalactites and stalagmites, and the cavern walls glow green from the reflections off the water. It's a worthwhile trip, but only when the sun is out (otherwise you don't get the glow). If you don't catch the direct boat from Amalfi's dock, you can take a SITA bus (traveling toward Amalfi from Positano), then take the elevator down, where a boat takes you into the cave.

EATS

Amalfi may be your first introduction to "Amalfian" cuisine, which is served up and down the southern coast of Italy. Unlike traditional Campania cuisine, it's heavy on seafood and relies on fresh ingredients—organic herbs and locally grown lemons—for its flavor. You won't find this delicious style of food anywhere else in the country, so you might as well enjoy it while you're here. Be sure to try smoked mozzarella wrapped in fresh lemon leaves, and seafood salad—a melange of squid and shrimp that's served in a sauce worthy of sopping up. You can gorge on all kinds of typical Italian desserts here, but the local delicacies are citrus-based: lemon *profiteroles* (pastries filled with lemon cream) and *crostata,* a marmalade-filled tart. You'll probably be tempted to sample some, since the crisp scent of lemons blows through town from the lemon groves in the hills.

▶▶CHEAP

For cheap eats, head for the harbor. The best deal for panini, coffee, and pastries can be found at the shops in front of the bus station. Their prosciutto and mozzarella sandwiches are as good as anything that you'd pay twice as much for in the touristy cafes. Get your quick gelato fix at **Porto Salvo Gelateria** *(Porto Salvo; Tel 089/871-655; 10am-8:30pm).*

▶▶DO-ABLE

For a taste of authentic Campania-style cooking, hit **La Caravella-Amalfi** *(Via Matteo Camera 12; Tel 089/871-029; 12:30-3pm/7:30-11pm daily; 20,000L per entree; V, MC, AE, DC),* where reservations are required (it's that good). The emphasis here is on fish, which you can order in a ragout, as soup, baked in salt, or fried. For dessert? Anything with lemon.

▶▶SPLURGE

If you have to fast all day to be able to afford **Da Gemma's** *(Via Fra Gerardo Sassi 9; Tel 089/871-345; 12:45-2pm/7:45-10:30pm Thu-Tue, closed Jan; 20,000-50,000L per entree; V, MC, AE, DC),* rest assured that your penance will be rewarded. The restaurant's on the second story of a stone building across from the cathedral; request a table on the balcony so you can enjoy your meal amid a curtain of bougainvillea and mimosa flowers. Specialties include the fresh seafood salad and ravioli. For dessert, don't miss the *crostata* or the lemon *profiteroles. Si,* the prices and the calories are a little high, but you didn't come all the way to Italy to miss out on *this!*

crashing

There are no really cheap hotels in Amalfi, period. In fact, there aren't many hotels at all. But there are a couple of beachside digs where you can crash without totally busting your budget. You can pick up a list of places at the tourist office.

▶▶DO-ABLE

How much do you think you should be paying to stay in a 13th-century building that's filled with Victorian antiques and just a few steps from the sea? The management at **Hotel Lidomare** *(Largo Duchi Piccolomini 9; Tel 089/871-332; Fax 089/871-394; 90,000-100,000L double; AE, V, MC)* doesn't think it should be very much. This cozy hotel is clean and simple, and one of the best deals on the Amalfi Coast. Air-conditioning, TV, and private bathrooms are included. Breakfast is an extra 10,000L. Double rooms only; no singles available.

   Hotel Marina Riviera *(Via Comite 9; Tel 089/872-934; Fax 089/871-024; 220,000-260,000L double, AC/TV, breakfast included; AE, MC, V; Closed Oct 31-Mar 1)* is about 150 steps from the beach, directly on the road at the foot of the mountain. There's a small bar that's open 24 hours a day, and a decent restaurant called Eolo below the hotel. Rooms are spacious and clean, with hairdryers. Some have balconies.

need to know

Currency Exchange There is no currency exchange in Amalfi, so make sure to bring your lira (or your credit cards) with you when you come.

Tourist Information The **tourist office** *(Corso delle Repubbliche Marinare 19-21; Tel 081-871-059; 8am-2pm Mon-Fri, 8am-noon Sat)* is on the main drag. They have a list of hotels, but they can't make reservations for you. You can also pick up information about the cathedral and the Green Grotto here.

Public Transportation There's no public transportation system in Amalfi. Let those boots do the walking!

Health and Emergency Emergency: *113;* Police: *112.*

Bus Lines Out of the City There are no trains to Amalfi. The closest train stop is in Naples, where you can hop on a **SITA** bus *(Piazza Municipio; Tel 081-552-21-76)* in Santa Lucia. SITA buses run from Naples several times a day, and every two hours from Sorrento, costing 4,000L one way. There are also SITA buses from Positano that cost 2,000L one way. The drive along the Amalfi coast is thrilling. The bus driver curls around hairpin turns and plunges without warning into pitch-black mountain tunnels lit by twirling colored lights. This was, no doubt, the inspiration for Space Mountain.

ravello

To soak in some classical tunes and enjoy awesome views of the sea, head to Ravello. This is *the* cultural center of the Amalfi Coast, especially during the summer, when the world's greatest musicians come here to perform at its world-renowned music festival, held in the gardens of **Villa Rufolo** [see *culture zoo,* below] on a perch that hangs over the sea.

A longtime mecca for writers—Henrik Ibsen, D.H. Lawrence, Virginia Woolf, Graham Greene, Tennessee Williams, and André Gide, to name a few—Ravello has since become a posh playground for the wealthy. Now only *rich* literati, such as famed resident Gore Vidal, can afford to live amongst Ravello's ritzy villas and to mix and mingle with its celebrity visitors.

The crowd in Ravello is overwhelmingly comprised of middle-aged Americans. When they arrive and find that even the native toddlers are dressed better than they are, they immediately rush to Ravello's chic shops to remedy the situation. After that, you can see them teetering through the cobblestone streets in their new stiletto mules. The youth delegation is practically non-existent except for a few upper-crust honeymoon couples, but there are a few ubiquitous German backpacker chicks to balance the scales. It's really a shame that more young people don't congregate in Ravello, because it's definitely *the* choice location along the Amalfi Coast. The atmosphere is lush and beautiful, almost like one of those romantic-looking European perfume ads with cobblestone streets, draping vines, fragrant flowers, and flickering lamps. People here are so attractive they can chain-smoke cigarettes and show no wear; older guests are classy without being snobs; streets open onto lush parks where pay phones are conveniently nestled amidst the greenery. And the sea views are to die for, some of the most awesome in all of Italy.

Ravello is not for the wild-at-heart—unless what you're wild about is classical music. There is no bar or club scene and the only live music you're going to get is the annual classical music festival. Make this a day trip from Amalfi unless you're in town for the fest.

neighborhoods and hanging out

If you arrive in Ravello by bus (as you most likely will), the SITA bus will deposit you in a small parking lot on the side of the mountain, just before a large tunnel. Follow the crowds and walk through this tunnel to reach **Piazza del Duomo,** the center of Ravello. If there are any folks hanging out in town, they'll likely be here. The cathedral will be on your right, the mountain on your left. Straight ahead, a main path leads to the end of the town, and just past the cathedral, still on the right, a series of cobblestone stairs lead up to Ravello's second thoroughfare, **Via San Giovanni del Toro.** Directly to your immediate left, on the southern edge of the square, is a well-marked path leading to **Villa Rufolo** and **Villa Cimbrone** [see *culture zoo,* below, for both]. On the piazza itself are a scattering of cafes, *gelaterias,* a popular antique store, and the post office.

There's no public transportation in Ravello, but you won't need it—you can walk across town in about five minutes. The longest stroll is to Villa Cimbrone, which takes about 20 minutes.

CULTURE ZOO

In addition to its annual July music festival (you can pick up a concert schedule at the tourist office), Ravello also has some great old villas. The

festivals and events

Ravello's **summer music festival** is one of its' main attractions. Each year, the world's finest musicians gather in this mountaintop paradise to perform evening concerts of chamber music. Even if classical tunes aren't your bag, you might be turned around hearing them live while stretched out on the lawn of the Villa Rufolo, looking out at the sparkling blue sea...The programs and guests vary each year. Tickets are available at the tourist office [see *need to know*, below] and start at $24.

ornate cathedral is extremely unusual for such a small town, but like Amalfi, Ravello was once a major municipality.

Villa Cimbrone *(Via Santa Chiara 26; Tel 089/857-459; 9am-7pm daily):* This villa is famous for its breathtaking Belvedere, a massive portico from which one can admire what Ravello citizen Gore Vidal claims is "the most beautiful view in the world." Others who have stayed here include D.H. Lawrence (he supposedly wrote parts of *Lady Chatterly's Lover* here) and Greta Garbo with her lover, Leopold Stowkowski. To get to the villa, follow the sign-posted footpath from Piazza del Duomo. Atop vine-draped hills, the 15-minute walk along the stone wall is quite breathtaking (literally and figuratively). Once you reach the 15th-century villa, an attendant can show you around the cloisters, chapels, and gardens. Most people bring newspapers or picnic foods and sprawl out in the peaceful garden.

Villa Rufolo *(Piazza del Duomo; Tel 089/857-657; 9am-8pm daily, closes at 6pm in the winter; 5,000L):* The inspiration for Richard Wagner's magical garden of Klingsor in the second act of *Parsifal,* this villa is now home to an annual Wagner festival that takes place here every July [see *festivals and events,* below]. Boccaccio, too, was so moved by the place that it's the background for some of his writings. This gorgeous villa is right off the Piazza del Duomo––check it out and see if it inspires you, as well.

Duomo and Campanile *(Piazza del Duomo; Duomo hours 8am-7pm daily; Museum hours 9am-1pm/3-7pm daily Apr-Oct; Free Duomo admission, 2,000L museum admission):* Founded in 1806, the cathedral's key attraction is its pulpit, decorated in Byzantine mosaics and supported by columns resting on six white marble lions. To the left of the altar is the Chapel of San Pantaleone, the patron saint of Ravello, where his "unleakable" blood is said to be kept in a vessel. Local conventional wisdom has it that the San Pantaleone's blood liquefies every year on his festival day, July 27. A museum of religious artifacts is in the crypt. The mosaics in the pulpit are worth a look-see.

CITY SPORTS

Ravello is an amazing place for a jog. For a real cardio challenge, head up the stairs on Via R. Wagner (on the left of the cathedral in Piazza del Duomo), take a left onto Via S. Giovanni del Toro, take a pit stop for a breathtaking view at the Belvedere Principessa di Piemonte gardens, and continue all the way down until you reach the end of the village. You'll find your way back no problem.

STUFF

For such a classy little village, it's surprising to discover that even Ravello isn't immune to trinket hawking, and certain stretches are as tacky as Wal-mart. Stores specialize in typical Amalfi Coast souvenirs such as *limon-cello*—a lurid lemon liquor, and ceramics. The prices are really high here, but if you need to pick up a knickknack or two, you'll find plenty along Via Roma and on the short pathway to Villa Rufolo.

If you're looking for something special, Giorgo, the owner of **Camo** *(Piazza del Duomo 9; Tel 089/857-461; 8am-6pm daily; V, MC, AE)* can help you pick out a cameo carved from coral, or you can design one together; expect to drop anywhere from a few to a thousand dollars.

Ceramu *(Via Roma 66; Tel 089/858-181; 9am-1pm, 3-7pm Mon-Sat; AE, V, MC)* can be found on the road to Villa Cimbrone. They have great ceramics here, and will ship them anywhere in the world.

EATS

For superior self-serve eats in Ravello, hit the fresh fruit stands along **Via Roma,** the central street off of **Piazza del Duomo.** Also on Via Roma (which turns into Via del Ospedale) there are small specialty shops that sell cheese, wine, and cookies. Most hotels offer breakfast and dinner.

A picnic is a great idea in Ravello. There are plenty of benches, and the **Villa Cimbrone** [see *culture zoo,* above] has a beautiful garden with chairs where lots of people bring their own food. Some cheese, bread, and fruit will cost around $2-2.50 US, a bargain compared to the tourist cafes. Local specialties include good Amalfian wine and wine from nearby Ischia.

▶▶CHEAP

Agonize over which of the four kinds of spaghetti you'll order at **Ris-torante Garden** *(Via Boccacio 4; Tel 089/857-226; Noon-3pm/7:30-10pm daily, Apr-Sept, Noon-3pm/7:30-10pm, Wed-Mon, Nov-Mar; 15,000-24,000L per entree; AE, MC, V),* which offers huge meals at small prices. Jackie O. used to frequent this family-owned terrace restaurant, so it gets its style points there. The antipasto table should have a warning sign on it, because it's nearly impossible not to fill up on the crispy shrimp and savory grilled vegetables.

▶▶DO-ABLE

Cumpa' Cosimo *(Via Roma 44-46; Tel 089/857-156; Noon-3:45pm/6:30-10pm daily; 15,000-45,000L per entree; AE, DC, V, MC)* is a place for coming together. Tourists mix with locals, and it's not unusual to catch a glimpse of Gore Vidal at this neighborhood favorite. You can mix and match seven sauces with seven different kinds of pasta, but remember that's only the first course—there's also such Campanian staples as herbed lamb, fish fry, and fish soup. The atmosphere is casual family style.

Bring a shovel to **Salvatore** *(Via della Repubbliche 2; Tel 089/857-227; Noon-3:30/6:30-11pm daily; 22,000-45,000L per entree; AE, V, MC)*—you're going to need it to dig through the generous portions. The huge portions and relaxed, casual atmosphere draws an even mix of tourists and locals.

crashing

Don't worry about staying in the "cool part of town," because there isn't one. The entire town is really beautiful. But crashing can be a problem because options are limited. There aren't really any cheap hotels in town, and the few that are doable (and they're at the high end of do-able...) fill up quickly, especially during the summer. You're better off staying in Amalfi, where the prices are way cheaper *and* you're by the beach. If you do plan to overnight it in Ravello, make reservations in advance, via telephone or fax, and ask them to fax you a confirmation.

▶▶DO-ABLE

Ristorante Garden *(Via Boccacio 4; Tel 089/857-226; 110,000-130,000L double, breakfast included; AE, V, MC)* forgot to add *albergo* to its name, but it isn't only a marvelous place to eat, it's also one of the best deals in town to crash, drawing the young set and budget-conscious elders too. The clean doubles come with private bathrooms (no TV or air-conditioning) and a communal terrace with a view.

Just off Piazza del Duomo and up a steep stone staircase is **Albergo Toro** *(Viale Wagner 3; Tel and Fax 089/857-211; 90,000L per person, 180,000L double w/breakfast; AE, MC, V)*, a quaint villa balanced on the hillside with nine double rooms with private bathrooms. Toro also offers breakfasting guests a rustic atmosphere under a flower-filled trellis. The scene is a mixed crowd, although guests tend to be older here.

Villa Amore *(Via del Fusco; Tel and Fax 089/857-135; 110,000L double; AE, MC, V)* is a charming pension on the edge of town. Its somewhat remote location makes it the perfect place for romance or escaping the crowds. Plain double rooms come with private bathrooms but no TV. The crowd here is another mix of older and younger. Reservations are recommended.

need to know

Currency Exchange There is no currency exchange available in Ravello, so bring your lira with you when you come.

Tourist Information Soggiorno e Turismo *(Piazza del Duomo 1; Tel 089/857-096; Fax 089/857-977; 8am-8pm Mon-Sat, May-Sept, 8am-7pm Oct-Apr)* is in the main square. They can't make hotel reservations for you, but they do have a hotel and restaurant guide, maps, and a music schedule.

Health and Emergency Emergency: *113;* Police: *112.* The nearest hospital is in Naples, but most hotels have doctors on staff for emergencies.

Pharmacies There's a pharmacia *(Piazza del Duomo 5; 10am-1pm/4pm-8pm daily)* at Piazza del Duomo 5.

Bus Lines Out of the City The only way to reach Ravello is by car or by bus from Amalfi's harbor; It's a 15-minute drive. Unless you are on heavy doses of anti-anxiety meds and can drive a stick-shift backwards in bumper to bumper congestion around 30-degree turns six inches from the edge of a perilous cliffside, driving is not recommended.

If you are coming from Naples, the **SITA** bus *(Piazza Municipio; Tel 081-552-21-76)* to Ravello (via Amalfi) leaves several times throughout the day. You can also take the SITA bus direct from Amalfi *(Piazza Flavio Gioia; Tel 089/871-009).*

Postal The **poste e telegrafi** *(Tel 089/858-161; 8:30am-1pm/3-6:30pm)* is at Piazza del Duomo 3.

POSITANO

Positano is a bohemian artists' town that has been "discovered" (sort of like Columbus "discovered" America). With its snaking streets, blossom-draped villas, and flickering lamps, Positano looks like a quaint storybook village. But what was once a hidden artists' colony is now a totally commercialized resort for rich people, many of whom neither know nor care about art unless they can wear it. The cheap bars and cafes, artists' shops, bare feet, and tranquility have given way to shops that cater to the Gold Card set on vacation. Jean-Paul Gaultier and Moschino are *de rigeur.* A store called Manhattan Chic sells canvas mail carrier bags for $85, which is a bargain compared to the other boutiques. It used to be that you could rent a room for 500L a night. Now you could easily pay 500,000L.

But the flocks continue to descend upon Positano to soak up the charm and beauty that used to inspire working artists. Nestled into the hillside, the Moorish buildings and melon-colored villas are illuminated by the flickering glow of hanging lamps. The road that wraps around the mountainside is dotted with cafes, so you can enjoy a meal at any altitude. By the mouth of the sea is the city's tight interior, which hosts a lively *kasbah*-like market where vendors selling leather and jewelry crowd the narrow streets. And while your hotel room might cost a bundle, the panoramic views are priceless.

There are no grand tourist attractions in Positano. You can walk across it in 10 minutes, and it's about as high as it is wide. The landscape is craggy and *steep,* with one narrow main road called **Via Pasitea,** which snakes all the way from the bottom to the top of the town in a zigzag pattern. To mix and mingle with other young'ns, try hitting the beach, **Buca di Bacco** [see *bar and club scene,* below], or the center of town near the beach, where there's a cluster of restaurants and shops. You'll probably have a conversation with an elder or two: Even though navigating hills like these requires top physical fitness, there are a whole lot of seniors strolling around.

bar and club scene

Positano's nightlife is 95 percent tourists and 5 percent young locals who work in the hotels. Things start up at about 11pm and go on until 4 or 5 in the morning.

If you've got the urge to shake your bon-bon, **Bucca di Bacco** *(Via Rampa Teglia 8; Tel 089/875-699; No cover; AE, DC, MC, V)* is where you need to go. On Friday and Saturday nights this beachside restaurant/bar converts into a raging Latin disco with no cover charge. Things start to heat up around 11pm, and the dancing goes on until dawn.

The hottest new music, dance moves, and fashion trends collide with old world tradition at **L'Africaana** *(Vettica Maggiore, Praiano; Tel 089/874-042; Closes at 10pm daily Jun-Aug, Fri, Sat only May-Sep),* where the bizarre ritual that goes nightly isn't even a gimmick: When you return to the homeland, you can brag to your friends that you went to a blasting bar and disco where fishermen show up halfway through the night and dredge a sinkhole by the dance floor to pull up fish. Don't ask us why— call it local tradition. Technically, L'Africaana is in Praiano, about two miles from Positano proper, but it's worth the schlep. You can reach Praiano by boat or by foot.

To be part of a more sophisticated and sedate crowd that likes to get boozed up with class, sashay on over to **Music on the Rocks** *(Spiaggia Grande; Tel 089/875-874),* an appealing piano bar. It's definitely not anything like the raucous gay show-tune piano bars in Greenwich Village, where a guy in a business suit could suddenly rise up from his bar stool to belt out a fabulous impersonation of Barbara Streisand, but it's kind of fun if your idea of singing along is more like tinkling the ice cubes against your cocktail glass.

Perhaps the most stylish bar is at **Hotel Poseidon** [see *crashing,* below] where guests from L.A. to London (and sometimes even from Italy) convene in the eclectically-decorated living room next to the bar or the adjoining outdoor terrace. The hotel hosts hip events in this space, and the walls display original art for sale. Oh, and there's an open-arms policy for dogs! The hotel is on Via Pasitea, the main road that winds around Positano, almost at the end of the road at the top of the hill. It's a low, white structure that can be seen from almost anywhere on the hill.

STUFF

It's hard *not* to shop in Positano. Unfortunately it's also hard not to spend a fortune doing it in the main stores. Stick with the street vendors, who sell inexpensive North African jewelry, the latest trends, and handmade leather sandals. Indoors, the pricey shops sell all the standard fashion stuff: silk scarves, Chanel bathing suits, and the latest Moschino jeans. But check the labels if you're buying ceramics—some geographically creative shop owners consider China to be local. Hot bargain tip: A good time to shop is in October, because the stores are getting ready to close for the winter and everything is on sale.

La Myricae *(71 Piazza Mulini; Tel 089/875-882)* is at the foot of town and sells exquisite, hard-to-find antique jewelry. Prices vary dramatically.

For uniquely shaped colored glass bottles and vases, head to **Cafiero** *(171 Via Cristoforo Columbo; Tel 089/875-838)*.

EATS

The food in Positano is very similar to what you'll find in Amalfi and Ravello. However, Positano seems to cater to a more prosperous jet-set—lobster pops up on menus more often here. Restaurants are pricey, but it's possible to grab a slice of pizza or cone of gelato on the street.

▶▶CHEAP

Directly across from the Hotel Poseidon (on the main road, Via Pasitea, at the top of the hill) there's a supermarket where you can pick up a few things (fruit, wine, cheese, bread, and cookies) for a light and delicious lunch. This is a very popular lunch option for lots of visitors, since usually you're stuffed (not to mention bankrupt) from the previous night's four-course meal. A meal for one shouldn't cost more than 10,000L. Don't forget to pack a knife and a corkscrew!

Serving up classic southern Italian cooking, **Da Adolfo** *(Via Laurito, Localita Laurito; Tel 089/875-022; 10am-6pm daily late Jun-Sept, 10am-6pm daily, Sat 8pm-midnight July-Aug; 11,000-24,000L per entree; No credit cards)* defies logic: It's baffling that such an amazing place to eat is so inexpensive. There are two ways of reaching Da Adolfo. If you feel like torturing yourself, you can try walking, but that involves scaling 450 steps from the highway, and that's not really Positano style. Luckily, owners Sergio and Amanda provide a motorboat (marked by a red fish painted on the side) that will whisk you from Positano's main dock to their beachside restaurant. Unsurprisingly, the emphasis is on seafood, with specials like mozzarella wrapped in lemon leaves and spaghetti with clam sauce. The boat leaves every 30 minutes between 10am and 1pm, and 4pm to whenever the last customer has left the beach (usually sometime between 6:30 and 8 pm). Extra bonus: This is one of the few beaches in Southern Italy that has a libertine attitude toward toplessness.

▶▶DO-ABLE

Bucca di Bacco *(Via Rampa Teglia 8; Tel 089/875-699; 12:30-3:30pm, 8-11pm daily; 35,000-55,000L per entree; AE, DC, MC, V)* is one of Positano's most popular multipurpose venues for disco, crashing, and eating. Right on the beach, this multi-dimensional bar-restaurant-disco-hotel has a great spread of fresh seafood and fruits, as well as some pasta classics on hand.

One of Positano's more famous restaurants, **Chez Black** *(Via del Brigantino 19-20; Tel 089/875-036; 12:30-3pm/7:30-11pm daily, closed Jan 7-Feb 7, reservations required in summer; Avg 16,000-35,000L per entree; AE, DC, MC, V)* serves up what is probably the world's best seafood soup. While seafood is their specialty, they also offer a variety of chicken, veal, and beef entrees. The wood and brass interior is decorated to re-create the feeling of a fancy yacht—one that's well stocked with local wines. Reservations are recommended. You'll find Chez Black on a street just off the beach, at the bottom of town.

crashing

When it comes to lodging, *che vergogna* (what a shame). The only thing that's cheap in Positano is possibly you. There are one or two cheap places to stay in town, but what passes for do-able often runs around $100 for a double room, and splurges start around $150.

▶▶CHEAP

You'll find rare refuge from the high prices at the charming **Ostello Brikette** *(Via G. Marconi 358; Tel and Fax 089/875-857; brikette @syrene.it; 35,000L dorm room, 40,000L single, 100,000L double, break-fast included; Lockout 11:30am-5pm; No credit cards)*, which has a stunning view from its terraces. Let Anna and Anna, the charming women who run the place, welcome you to Positano in true Italian hospitable style. There's Internet access for guests, and some rooms come with private baths.

▶▶DO-ABLE

The next most affordable thing in town is **Casa Guadagno** *(Via Fornillo 26; Tel 089/875-042, Fax 089/811-407; Minibus to Fornillo; 70,000L single, 110,000L double, breakfast included; V, MC)*, a family-run spot on the west end of town, just five minutes up from the beach. The rooms are simple and pretty, and some even come with painted tile floors and mini-terraces that look out over the sea. The only drawback is that some of the bathrooms (pri-vate, not shared) are in need of an overhaul, but at least they're clean.

▶▶SPLURGE

While there are many other lovely expensive hotels, **Hotel Poseidon** *(Via Pasitea 148; Tel 089/811-111; Fax 089/875-833; www.starnet.it/poseidon, poseidon@starnet.it; 330,00-410,000L double, 550,000-720,000L suite; AE, DC, MC, V)* is probably where you'll get the most bang for your buck. Once a family home, this groovy hotel welcomes dogs and people alike, serves up some great food on a flower-draped terrace, and has the first and only gym in Positano. It's filled with comfy "living rooms" where you can read the newspapers in all the languages of the world, or pull out an Oprah Book Club selection from the hotel library. At night, the bar is one of the most popular spots in Positano. With its funky decor and terrace, it offers one of the best evening views of the village, and the mixed drinks aren't bad either. All units are air-conditioned and come with TVs, telephones, and private bathrooms. Breakfast is included. Only double rooms are available. The hotel is on Via Pasitea at the top of the hill.

need to know

Currency Exchange If you're using traveler's checks, it's a good idea to change your currency before you reach Positano—the only place you you can trade currency at major hotel desks. There are, of course **ATMs** up and down the main streets.

Tourist Information Get the skinny on local events at the **tourist office** (*Via del Saracino 4; Tel 089/875-067; Mon-Fri 8:30am-2pm; Sat 8:30-noon Jun-Sep*). Sorry—they don't do hotel reservations here.

Public Transportation There is an orange "interior" **bus** that travels up and down the hill. Tickets are 1,500L and can be purchased at the tobacco shop at the top of the hill, across from the SITA bus station.

Health and Emergency Emergency: *113;* Police: *112.*

Bus Lines Out of the City You can come in and out of Positano by **SITA buses** from either Sorrento or Amalfi. Buses run frequently throughout the day and it's about a 30-minute drive from either direction. For information, call 089/871-016.

SORRENTO

If you're craving some action after the string of laid-back villages along the Amalfi Coast, you'll definitely get some satisfaction in Sorrento, the last stop before Sicily. You can dance in a cave, clear your e-mail account of all those junky forwards you've been accumulating, and gracefully drink yourself sick in a smoky pub.

Of course, it may take a little while to get acclimated after your dreamy coastal escape. Sorrento is so crowded you might have to wait more than 20 minutes for your pizza to arrive, and you could hit at least 15 hotels before you find a room, all for a 10 percent markup. In the summer's high season (July and August), streets are nearly impenetrable thanks to all the cruise ship refugees on parade. And after the healthful lemon-leaf scents of those tiny Amalfi towns, it is *just* a bit of a shock to emerge into a loud polluted city that hasn't yet tried to control its heavy traffic with modern conveniences such as traffic lights. But that's Italy, and that's Sorrento.

Traffic jams and pickpockets aside, Sorrento is also a beautiful city. Called the "City of the Sirens" by the Romans, it's known as *the* legendary den of the muses from Greek mythology. Perched right on the Bay of Naples, against a backdrop of lush green mountains, the paradise setting has lured visitors since ancient times. Celebrities and wealthier patrons rent out the hilltop villas, middle-class tourists cram into the strips of hotels, and impoverished backpackers go *au naturel* in the hilltop camping grounds.

No matter how disparate their financial backgrounds, or from what continent on earth they hail from, all of Sorrento's callers seem to have one thing in common. Like pilgrims on a mission to Mecca, everyone has come here to worship, but in this case their god is Bacchus, the ancient Roman god of wine (and apparently *limoncello* and beer pints too). You'll know you've reached the party capital of the Amalfi Coast when you encounter a taxi driver who's perfumed in imitation CK1 cologne, is wearing all black, and tries to sell you a bit of cocaine. Brits, Germans, and North Americans crowd the city, and if you walk into one of the many English-style pubs for a few pints of beer, you'll swear you're on the Jersey shore of England; most of the clientele will likely hail from there. While at times it feels like 90 percent of Sorrento's population are tourists, the locals you do meet are extremely friendly, and some of them speak fluent English.

The best place to get news on events is at the tourist office. Also, posters for concerts and ballets are plastered all over city walls.

neighborhoods

Most people come into Sorrento via train from Naples or on the SITA bus, both of which stop at the **Stazione Centrale** (central station), which is right off **Via Corso Italia,** the central vein of the city. Luckily, most everything is in walking distance from the train station. The stretch of Corso Italia to the west of the station is where you want to be—it's lined with hotels, shops, cafes, and side streets that splinter off into small piazzas. The main hub is **Piazza Tasso,** the big square about a two-minute walk west of the station. Continue on past Tasso and Corso Italia will take you right by the marina and eventually up the mountain to four-star hotels, exquisite villas, and, ironically enough, the local campground.

There is no need for public transportation in Sorrento. For more lackadaisical travelers, a bus travels between the top of the mountain and the center of the city. Circulating taxis are in abundance as well.

bar, club, and live music scene

In Sorrento, many clubs, bars, and live music venues are all rolled up into one. A perfect example of this is **The Merry Monk Guinness Pub** *(Via Capo 4 before Piazza Veniero; Tel 081/18-77-24-09; 11:30-2am daily; 7-8,000L beer; No credit cards),* in the west section of town, where you can find live music, a nightly disco with music from the past four decades, televised soccer games, an Internet point, and haute cuisine pub grub. (Try the veal and chicken sandwiches; they're delicious.) Blues bands perform live on Tuesday evening, while Wednesday and Thursdays are reserved for the Latins.

You'll run into a similar scene at **Bar dei Fiori** *(Piazza A. Lauro 47-48; Tel 081/878-27-28; 11:30-2am daily),* which hosts live music nightly—could be rock, pop, or jazz, depending on the night. Treat yourself to one of their sophisticated desserts, such as the almond mousse or the chocolate Caprese cake. During the day it's bright and cheery, and it's pretty crowded at nights, with a mixed international crowd that pulls in people of all ages.

Chaplin's Pub *(Corso Italia 18; Tel 081/807-25-51; 4pm-2am daily; 6,000L beer; No credit cards),* located on the main avenue, is a great place to check your e-mails while you're downing a pint. Rates are 10,000L an

sorrento bars club and culture zoo

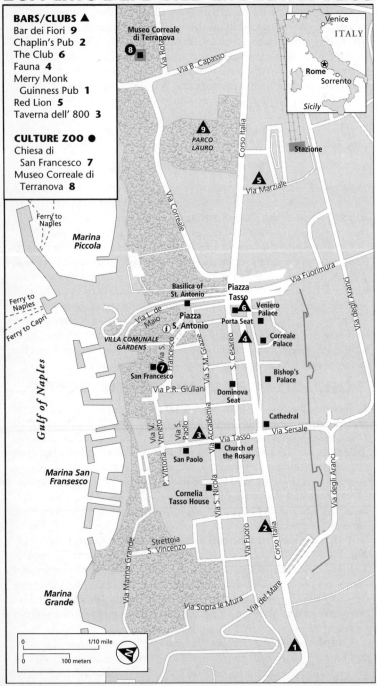

BARS/CLUBS ▲
Bar dei Fiori **9**
Chaplin's Pub **2**
The Club **6**
Fauna **4**
Merry Monk
  Guinness Pub **1**
Red Lion **5**
Taverna dell' 800 **3**

CULTURE ZOO ●
Chiesa di
  San Francesco **7**
Museo Correale di
  Terranova **8**

Museo Correale
di Terranova

Venice
ITALY
Rome
Sorrento
Sicily

Via Rota
Via B. Capasso
Corso Italia
Stazione

PARCO
LAURO

Via Correale

Via Marziale

Via Fuorimura

Ferry to
Naples
Marina
Piccola

Ferry to
Naples
Ferry to Capri

VILLA COMUNALE
GARDENS

Gulf of Naples

San Francesco

Via L. de
Maio
Via S. Francesco

Basilica of
St. Antonio
Piazza
S. Antonio

Piazza
Tasso
Veniero
Palace
Porta Seat
Correale
Palace

Via S.M. Grazie
S. Cesareo

Bishop's
Palace

Via P.R. Giuliani
Dominova
Seat

Cathedral
Via Sersale

Via degli Aranci

Via V.
Veneto
Via S.
Paolo
P. Vittoria
San Paolo

Via Accademia

Via Tasso
Church of
the Rosary

Marina San
Fransesco

Cornelia
Tasso House

Via S. Nicola

Via Fuoro

Via degli Aranci

Strettoia
S. Vincenzo

Marina
Grande

Via Marina Grande

Via Sopra le Mura
Via del Mare
Corso Italia

1/10 mile

0   100 meters

wired

To check your e-mails, head for the **Merry Monk Guinness Pub** *(Via Capo 4; Before Piazza Veniero; Tel 081/187-72-409; 11:30-2am daily)* or the **BluBlu.it Internet Café** *(Via Fuorimura, 20/d; Tel/Fax 081/807-48-54; 8am-noon/4-8pm daily).* Sorrento is on the web at ***www.sorrentoinfo.com/index–en.asp.***

hour, there's a jukebox, and you can choose from mixed drinks as well as a variety of European beers. Any time is a good time to come to this dark, wood-paneled bar. The crowd is mixed, from 18 and up.

Sorrento's staple beer garden, the **Red Lion** *(Via Marziale 25; No phone; 11:30-2am daily; No credit cards)* may not be the classiest joint in town, but thanks to its pizza and pint of beer deals, it's one of the cheapest. A young party crowd that includes a lot of young Brits and Germans packs into this place nightly. You find the Lion just south of the train station.

A dark tavern illuminated by flickering candles, **Taverna dell' 800** *(Via dell'Accademia 29; Tel 081/878-59-70; Tue-Sun 8am-4:30am; No cover; Avg 10,000L per drink; No credit cards)* is one of the most glorious places to spend a night in Sorrento. From 9pm to midnight a lively piano and guitar duet entertains, and you can chow on some inexpensive, home-style food while you're listening to them play. The tavern is in the center of town, a few blocks west of Piazza S. Antonio.

There are two hard-core discos catering to a young crowd in Sorrento. At **Fauna** *(Piazza Tasso; Tel 081/878-10-21; From 8pm-4 or 5am; No cover; No credit cards),* traditional folk-dancers break onto the disco scene à la Ricky Martin and Jennifer Lopez for brief interims throughout the night. It's bizarre but amusing, and most important, gives you just the break you needed to get that next drink.

At **The Club** *(Piazza Tasso; Tel 081/878-40-52; Cover 30,000L; No credit cards),* where the cover charge includes your first drink, the clientele tends to wear lots of makeup and not many clothes. To find Fauna and The Club, just look for the large signs on either side of the Piazza Tasso and follow the stairs down. It's open as long as it has guests—usually 'til around 4 or 5 in the morning.

CULTURE ZOO

Sorrento's cultural side is often shamefully ignored, but the church and museum described below are beautiful, peaceful refuges. So pick your sorry self up off the bar floor and learn something!

Chiesa di San Francesco *(Via San Francesco; Tel 081/878-12-69; 9am-6pm daily; Free):* Between Piazza San Antonio and the Marina San

Francesco, this convent dates back to the 14th century. These days the convent is an art school that hosts exhibits in July and September. Chill out in the peaceful flower-filled garden, or check out the concert schedule posted on the church entrance: Jazz and classical music is performed nightly in the outdoor atrium starting at 9pm, with admission between 18,000 and 25,000L.

Museo Correale di Terranova *(Via Correale; Tel 081/878-18-46; 9am-12:30pm/5-7pm Mon, Wed-Sat, 9am-12:30pm Sun Apr-Sep, 9-11:30am/3-5pm Mon, Wed-Sat, 9-11:30am Sun off-season; 8,000L):* Sorrento's best museum, this former palace is filled with ancient sculptures and Italian art and antiques. It also has a spectacular garden you can stroll through. It's a worthwhile stop if you're into this kind of thing, and the gardens are pretty.

The great outdoors

Like much of the Amalfi Coast, Sorrento's beaches are small and rocky. In fact, some of them are man-made cement piers that extend into the water for sunbathers to soak up some rays from their rented chaise lounges. The best beach is **Punta del Capo,** where there are real sand and real half-naked bodies to appreciate. To reach Punta del Capo, travel west down **Corso Italia** past the center of town until it becomes **Via del Capo,** which will take you straight to the waves at its north end.

What Sorrento lacks in beach, it makes up for in greenery. Hikers and nature lovers will be psyched about the lush and hilly area outside of town, ideal for trekking and camping [see *crashing,* below]. You can pick up a map of well-marked trails at the tourist office [see *need to know,* below].

STUFF

Sorrento is known as a center of traditional handicrafts, and the town specializes in producing wood-carved furniture, lace, and leather. Pottery is a local craft as well, but beware: not all pieces for sale labeled "local" really are.

The gelato stands, winding cobblestone alleyways, scents of roasted chestnuts, and unobtrusive vendors along **Piazza Tasso** and **Via San Cesareo,** and the main shopping areas, make for a shopping experience that's actually relaxing. Street vendors hawk good-quality leather goods like wallets and slippers for fair prices.

The wares at **Cuomo's Lucky Store** *(Piazza Antica; Mura 2-7; Tel 081/878-56-49; 8:30am-1pm/4-8pm daily; MC, V)* might not necessarily appeal to *Hanging Out* readers, but any guide of Sorrento would be incomplete without at least mentioning this store, which is practically a historical landmark. Cuomo's showcases a large selection of hand-carved wooden furniture and antique porcelains alongside affordable handicrafts such as wooden game boards and pottery.

Just west of Piazza Tasso, **Coin** *(Via San Cesareo 39; Tel 081/807-17-47; 10am-1pm/4-8pm daily; V, MC)* is Italy's answer to T.J. Maxx, offering trendy clothes at decent prices (around 40,000L for a shirt; 25,000L for a scarf).

eats

Many of Sorrento's restaurants are indistinguishable. Lined up like dominoes along the main causeways, most serve an array of pastas and pizzas, with a standard list of wine and desserts. You'll probably be satisfied wherever you go, but the ones below deserve to be singled out.

▶▶CHEAP

La Favorita-O'Parrucchiano *(Corso Italia 71; Tel 081/878-13-21; Noon-3:30pm/7-11:30pm daily; 14,000-25,000L per entree; MC, V)* draws you in with its well-deserved name, and is conveniently located on the main drag. Its tavern-esque atmosphere flows out to an outdoor terrace/garden in the back. La Favorita cooks up local pasta dishes as well as the catch of the day.

For the original maccheroni and cheese, get over to **Taverna dell' 800** *(Via dell'Accademia 29; Tel 081/878-59-70; 8am-4:30am Tue-Sun; Avg 14,000L per entree; AE, DC, V, MC).* They serve up generous quantities of creamy pastas, plus standard bar sandwiches like fried veal and chicken. Miraculously, this place is closed less than four hours a day, so you can come here for your morning espresso or your late night beer. It's in the center of town, near Corso Italia.

▶▶DO-ABLE

If you're in the mood for romance—or just some good food—**Ristorante La Lanterna** *(Via San Cesareo 23/25; Tel 081/878-13-55; Fax 081/807-25-25; Noon-5pm/9pm-midnight, closed Wed; 30,000-60,000L per entree; AE, DC, MC, V),* located in the city's historical district, is an ideal spot to sample classic southern Italian specialties such as seafood salad and linguine with clam sauce. You can sit in a backyard garden or out in front overlooking a dimly lit cobblestone street. Make sure you save room for the mountainous tiramisu.

▶▶SPLURGE

One of the most famous restaurants of Southern Italy is **Don Alfonso** *(Piazza Sant'Agata, 6 mi. south of Sorrento; Take the blue-and-white SITA bus marked Sant'Agata from the piazza in front of Sorrento's railway station; Tel 081/878-00-26; 12:30-2:30pm/8-10:30pm Wed-Sun; 40,000-42,000L per entree, 110,000-150,000L set menu; Reservations recommended; AE, DC, MC, V),* 1,200 feet above the sea in the tiny prefecture of Sant'Agata, not far from Sorrento's borders. Don't let the faux Pompeian architecture distract you from the primary reason you came here: the extraordinary dishes made from fruits, vegetables, chickens provided by a local organic family farm. Don Alfonso is a member of the prestigious Relais & Chateau, and its wine cellar has won many awards. Eating here is a treat to your senses, and the food is as healthy as it is delicious. Try the vegetable-stuffed calamari, even if you think you don't like squid.

crashing

You'd be mad to come here in the summer without a reservation, especially in August, when hordes of Europeans descend on Sorrento. Lately,

sorrento eats and crashing

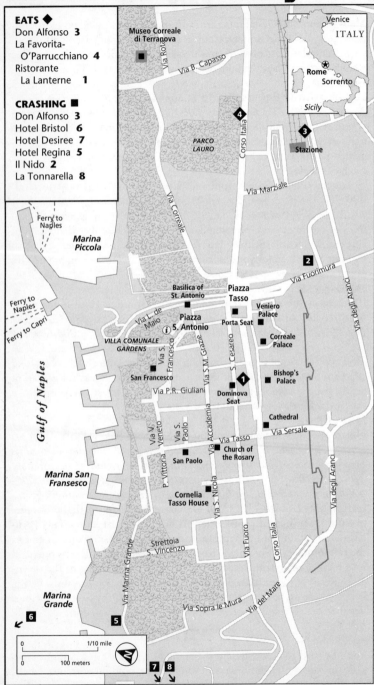

EATS ◆
Don Alfonso **3**
La Favorita-
 O'Parrucchiano **4**
Ristorante
 La Lanterne **1**

CRASHING ■
Don Alfonso **3**
Hotel Bristol **6**
Hotel Desiree **7**
Hotel Regina **5**
Il Nido **2**
La Tonnarella **8**

ITALY
Venice
Rome
Sorrento
Sicily

Museo Correale
di Terranova

Via Rota
Via B. Capasso
Corso Italia
Stazione
PARCO
LAURO
Via Marziale
Via Correale

Ferry to
Naples
Marina
Piccola

Ferry to
Naples
Ferry to Capri

Via Fuorimura

Basilica of
St. Antonio
Piazza
Tasso
Veniero
Palace
Via L. de
Maio
Piazza
S. Antonio
Porta Seat
Correale
Palace
VILLA COMUNALE
GARDENS
Via S.M. Grazie
S. Cesareo
Via degli Aranci

Via S.
Francesco
San Francesco
Via P.R. Giuliani
Dominova
Seat
Bishop's
Palace

Gulf of Naples

Via V.
Veneto
Via S.
Paolo
Via Accademia
Via Tasso
Cathedral
Via Sersale

P. Vittoria
San Paolo
Church of
the Rosary

Marina San
Fransesco

Via S. Nicola
Cornelia
Tasso House
Via Fuoro
Corso Italia
Via degli Aranci

Via Marina Grande
Strettoia
S. Vincenzo
Marina
Grande

Via Sopra le Mura
Via del Mare

6
5

0   1/10 mile
0   100 meters

7 **8**

more hotels have been posting web sites, so it's possible to make reservations online.

▶▶CHEAP

The cheapest option in town is actually free! You'll need to have your own gear, but you can camp for no cost at all in the **campground** to the west of town. To reach the site, follow Corso Italia (which turns into Via del Capo out here) west past the center of town, cross the bridge, and head right up into the hills (about a 15 minute walk). The campsite is clearly marked by signs right at the top of the hill just past the bridge on your right; look for the small store that supplies toiletries and simple foods. For more information, check with the tourist office [see *need to know*, below].

Il Nido *(Via Nastro Verde 62; Tel 081/878-27-66; Fax 081/807-33-04; 80,000L single, 130,000L double, 150,000L triple, 180,000L quad; V, MC)* is about five minutes from the center of town. Its most captivating asset: views of the Gulf of Naples. The fact that each room is fully loaded with a bathroom, telephone, satellite TV, and fridge doesn't hurt either. For breakfast (which is included), you can enjoy croissants and coffee while looking out at the sea. This is a fantastic deal, especially if you are traveling in a group.

A basic but pretty hotel that's just off the main road to the beach, **La Tonnarella** *(Via Capo 31; Tel 081/878-11-53; Fax 081/878-21-69; 170,000L double; MC, V)* is pleasant because it's removed from the town's main drag. The views are terrific. The double rooms have telephones and bathrooms, and breakfast is included.

Another option is the neighboring **Hotel Desiree** *(Via del Capo 31B; Tel and Fax 081/878-15-63; 120,000L double; Closed Nov-Dec 15 and Jan 10-Mar 8; No credit cards)*, perched on the cliffs overlooking the Gulf of Naples just outside the center of town. Rooms are simple and pleasant, with private bath and TVs, and breakfast is included. The crowd is very middle-aged European, but it's a good deal considering its convenient location and its private beach, accessible via elevator.

▶▶DO-ABLE

Don Alfonso *(Piazza Sant'Agata, 6 mi. south of Sorrento; Tel 081/878-00-26; Take the blue-and-white SITA bus marked Sant'Agata from the piazza in front of Sorrento's railway station; 200,000L 4-person suite; AE, DC, MC, V)*, the famous restaurant, offers three rental suites. Two have kitchens (though God knows why anyone would want to use them while staying at Don Alfonso). So round-up some friends and enjoy the air-conditioning, telephone, television, and organic breakfast.

Hotel Regina *(Via Marina Grande; Tel 081/878-27-22; Fax 081/878-27-21; www.belmaretravel.com, info@belmaretravel.com; Closed Nov 15-Feb 15; 280,000L double; AE, DC, MC, V)* is a cute, mid-sized hotel where different rooms come with different features. Some are air-conditioned, others are not; some have balconies, others don't. But all of the medium-sized simple rooms are attractive, with tile floors, private bath, telephones, and televisions. The restaurant is quite good; breakfast and one meal are included.

▶▶SPLURGE

Hotel Bristol *(Via del Capo 22; Tel 081/878-45-22; Fax 081/87-19-10; www.acampora.it/bristol, bristal@acampora.it; 280,000-360,000L double; AE, MC, V)* is a modern hotel that offers old-fashioned service. As soon as you enter, someone will rush up to you, relieve you of your luggage, and usher you out to a flower-filled terrace where you'll be offered a Campari. This 135-unit bastion on the hill is an old sorrento standard. The crowd is mixed, but tends to be older. All rooms are doubles and equipped with full bathrooms, TVs, and television. Breakfast is included.

need to know

Currency Exchange There are several currency exchange offices along **Corso Italia,** but shop around because commission rates vary enough to make a big difference if you're changing a large wad of cash. One reliable exchange booth is just outside the Sorrento train station. Exit through the bottom stairs; as you leave the station, the booth is on your left.

Tourist Information The **tourist office** *(Tel 081/07-40-33; 8am-6pm Mon-Sat)* is at Via di Maio 35. They don't make hotel reservations for you, but they do have a list of local hotels.

Public Transportation Sorrento has a public bus system, but it's erratic at best. There is a very infrequent orange public bus that runs from the top of the mountain to the bottom of the hill, stopping at the main bus station at **Piazza Tasso,** where there's also a **taxi line.** Your best transportation, however, will be your own two feet.

Health and Emergency Emergency: *113;* Police: *112.* The **Ospedale Santa Maria della Misericordia** *(Tel 081/53-311-11)* is on Corso Italia.

Trains Sorrento is served by Italy's handy, high-speed express train, the **Ferrovia Circumvesuviana,** which leaves from the underground **Stazione Centrale** in Naples. In can also be picked up at Pompeii. The name of the train station in Sorrento is also **Stazione Centrale.** There is no information number, but a train schedule is posted at the station.

Bus Lines Out of the City The **SITA buses** *(Tel 089/871-016)* come in from Amalfi via Positano and stop at Sorrento's train station.

Boats It is possible to take a boat from Sorrento to the Marina Grande in Capri. Ferries and hydrofoils dock off of Piazzo Tasso (signs to the marina are posted everywhere) several times a day. You can catch a ferry run by **Linee Marittime Veloci** *(Tel 081/878-14-30)* or **Caremar** *(Tel 081/807-30-77)* for 8,000L. Hydrofoils are run by **Alilauro** *(Tel 081/807-30-24)* for 18,000L.

Laundry You can wash your dirty duds at **Terlizzi** *(Corso Italia 30; Tel 081/878-11-85).*

Internet See *wired,* above.

The isle of capri

Ready to trip out on the prospect of $7 beers, $40 breakfasts, and sweaters that cost as much as your airfare to Italy? Look no further than the Isle of Capri. It's a fun day trip if you like anthropological studies on the spending habits of the rich and the famous, but if being around such inflated prices is just going to make you feel deprived, you may want to skip it altogether.

Originally, Capri was a hot spot because of its rep as an isle of love, not money. Frank Sinatra sang of his undying—and unfulfilled—love for a married woman beneath blue Italian sky of *bella* Capri. And centuries before that, pleasure-seeking Emperor Tiberius, who ruled the Roman Empire from Capri in 27-37 A.D., didn't know the meaning of the word "unfulfilled." He satiated himself with young girls (and boys) to alleviate his insomnia.

Today, Capri is less about *amore* and more about rubbing shoulders with fabulously wealthy socialites. It's a weird mix of curious onlookers, cruise-ship patrons on shore leave, Japanese tour groups, and celebrities who've come to rejuvenate at the popular **Capri Beauty Farm** [see *modification,* below].

Shoestring-budget travelers often need to return to the mainland for the night, but that's okay because Capri isn't that much fun once you've seen your share of face-peeled stars with boob jobs. The streets are jammed with tourists, the crowd is definitely over 30, and it's boring at night. The main form of excitement, aside from star sightings, seems to be spending money at discount designer stores. Sadly, Capri has become a floating outlet mall.

neighborhoods and hanging out

You can reach Capri by hydrofoil or ferry from Naples or Sorrento. The boats dock at **Marina Grande,** a super-high-priced tourist marina (but it's probably just chump change for the many yacht owners who dock there). For maps and other info, there's a tourist office right at the dock. Be warned—it's a looong walk from the ferry docks up to town—your best bet is to take the funicular [see *need to know,* below].

wired

Before you hit the isle, try checking out *www.caprigap.com* or *www.capri.it* for more info.

You can check your e-mail at **Capri Graphic** *(Via Listieri 17; Tel 081/837-52-12; 9:30am-1pm/4-8:30pm Mon-Sat; 5,000L per quarter-hour).*

ISLE OF CAPRI bars and clubs

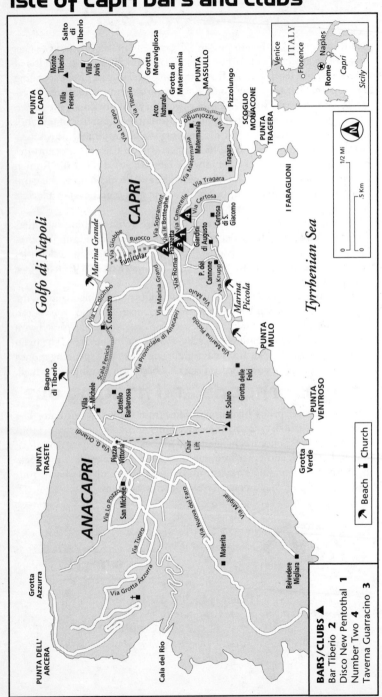

BARS/CLUBS ▲
Bar Tiberio **2**
Disco New Pentothal **1**
Number Two **4**
Taverna Guarracino **3**

🏹 Beach   ✝ Church

There are two main communities on the island: the hopping **Capri** and the remote and secluded **Anacapri**. Because it's so small, you can pretty much walk everywhere, although slackers can take the bus between Capri and Anacapri if the 20-minute walk is too much work. Buses leave as they fill up, which is fairly frequently, and the ride takes about three minutes.

The "heart" of the island is the **Piazza Umberto I** in Capri, a small square that resembles a courtyard. Surrounding the square are a clock tower, some municipal offices, and a mixture of chic stores and cafes. A series of narrow, winding medieval streets extend out from here. The piazza is probably the best place to meet people, or at least get in some serious people watching, anyway.

bar and club scene

Capri's clubs aren't the best place in Italy to hook up with the hip youth of the world, but at least you don't have to pay too often to get in. That's a major switch from the rest of the island's cash-draining venues. And the scene can actually be sort of fun if you like the idea of mixing it up with a wide variety of ages and nationalities.

If you just want to grab a beer or a cocktail, the bar at the **Capri Palace** [see *crashing*, below] is killer. Mix and mingle with the young, rich couples lounging around the indoor and outdoor bar while you ogle the place, which resembles a Moorish palace.

The number-one disco on Capri is called **Number Two** *(Via Camerelle 1; Tel 081/837-70-78; 11pm-4am daily; 15,000-20,000L cover; No credit cards)*. Another is **Disco New Pentothal** *(Via Vittorio Emmanuele 45; Tel 081/837-67-93; 11pm-4am daily; Cover 15,000-20,000L; No credit cards)*. The party at both of these places doesn't get started until around 11pm, and doesn't stop until the crowd does. Expect a mix of local guys and foreign gals getting down to cheesy disco music. The coolest thing: *Everyone* dances.

For a more refined boozing experience without the deluge of human bodies, you can try **Taverna Guarracino** *(Via Castello 7; Tel 081/83-71-05-14; 10am-2am daily; $5US beer; AE, MC, V)* off Piazza Umberto for beer and wine. **Bar Tiberio** *(Piazza Umberto 1; Tel 081/837-02-68; 10am-2am daily; $5-7US drinks; AE, MC, V)* is another good neighborhood joint where you can linger until the sun comes up. Both bars have the classic Italian decor: glass sandwich and dessert cases inside, iron tables outside. Most people stay outside for people watching. The crowd is definitely older, sedate, and classy. A good time to go is right before or after dinner.

modification

Don't be confused by the name; the **Capri Beauty Farm** *(Via Capodimonte 2B, Anacapri, inside the Capri Palace Hotel; Tel 081/837-38-00; Fax 081/837-31-91; 8:30am-7pm daily; AE, MC, V)* caters to beautiful people, not beautiful heifers. From getting a massage to getting wrapped in seaweed and saran wrap to waxing your unmentionables, this is the place to go. Rates are actually pretty reasonable, relatively speaking (a massage is about $50 US), and you just might get a chance to say hi to Julia, Mariah, or one of their famous friends in the dressing room. It's at the top of Anacapri in a massive white building behind the bus station.

THE GREAT OUTDOORS

The eerie **Blue Grotto** *(Marina Grande; No phone; 8:30am-4:30pm; 23,000L round-trip boat ride, 10,000L entrance fee; No credit cards)* is one of Capri's best and most clamored-about attractions. On a sunny day, it's well worth the hassle. Basically, it's a cavern where the sun's rays enter from an opening under the water to create a light effect that turns the cavern a fluorescent blue.

To reach the grotto, take a boat from Marina Grande (it's right near the ferry under a big sign that says "Blue Grotto"; you can't miss it), and then you transfer to a smaller rowboat at the entrance of the cave.

While this is a worthwhile jaunt, be warned that it will have its obnoxious elements—you'll never feel more like a tourist in your life. The rowboat guides work for tips, and some of them sing or play instruments, supposedly to enhance the romantic element of the grotto. A lot of them will sing halfheartedly, just going through the motions to get tips. It's enough to make you feel a little dirty...but you simply can't come to Capri and not see the Blue Grotto. So suck it up.

Swimming and sunning is always an option, although given the island's jagged rocky shores and mountainous terrain, nobody should visit Capri for its beaches. Most unflappable beach bunnies visit **Bagni Nettuno** *(Via Grotta Azzurra 46; Tel 081/837-13-62; 9am-sunset; 15,000L entrance fee)*, where the entrance fee includes a cabana, a towel, and a deck chair.

STUFF

Capri is a shopper's paradise and a bargain-hunter's nightmare. The medieval quarter around the Piazza Umberto I has more jewelry shops than grocery stores, but a sweater from Bottega Veneta could easily cost as much as your airplane ticket to Italy. Yet there are some specialty stores unique to Capri that are worth a visit.

Join the rest of the tourists queuing up for the perfume-making demonstrations at **Carthusia-Profumi de Capri** *(Via Camerelle 10; Tel 081/837-03-68; 10am-1pm/4pm-8pm daily)*, a store that has its own perfume factory on the island and creates its scents from local flowers. You can watch a demonstration to learn how the perfume's made, and even buy your own bottle if you wish. (Unlike the rest of Capri wares, it's affordable: about 40,000L for an 8-oz. bottle.) Scented soaps and candles are also sold here.

Another homegrown Capri concoction is *limoncello,* a bright yellow liquor that contains alcohol, sugar, water, herbs, and lemon zest. The local Canali family invented *limoncello,* and now it's marketed worldwide. For a free sample of this naughty lemonade, or if you are inspired to purchase some, stop by **Limoncello di Capri** *(Via Roma 79; Tel*

081/837-04-87; 10am-1pm/4-8pm daily; AE, MC, V) in Capri, or in Anacapri *(Via Capodimonte 27; Tel 081/837-29-27; 1am-1pm/4-8pm daily; AE, MC, V).*

eaTs

The native Caprese diet is rich in seafood, fresh cheese, and vegetables. But recipes from all over Italy (and the world) have been imported to appease tourists expecting a *Bolognese* sauce or perhaps a heavy lasagna. Capri is also one of the few places in Italy that offers "tourist food," such as deep-fried frozen chicken nuggets, "American-style" hamburgers, and Spanish omelets.

The most famous local dish is the simple Caprese salad: fresh mozzarella, fresh tomatoes, and fresh basil. Other specialties include special squid dishes, whether it's stuffed with vegetables or battered and fried.

Capri has some great food. Watch out for the *really* touristy cafes, like the ones lining the marina, for high prices and lower quality eats. Even if you're only visiting for the day, eating in Capri will be your biggest expense.

▶▶CHEAP

A short walk through the narrow streets off Piazza Umberto I will bring you to **CasaNova** *(Via Le Botteghe 46; Tel 081/837-76-42; Noon-3pm/7-11pm daily, Mar-Nov; 15,000-40,000L per entree; AE, DC, MC, V).* Walking in here is like walking into a family kitchen, only it's a family that happens to have the world's greatest Italian wine collection and can cook much better than the average clan. The homemade pasta (try the ravioli) and seafood are awesome, especially at these prices.

If you find yourself hankering for something besides seafood and pasta, **La Cantinella di Capri** *(Viale Matteotti 8; Tel 081/837-06-16; 12:20-3pm/7:30pm-12:30am Tue-Sun; 18,000-30,000L per entree; AE, DC, MC, V)* is *the* place to eat French food on Capri. The fact that the restaurant is in a circa-1750 villa is an added bonus. It's in the Giardini Augusto, not far from Piazza Umberto I.

For fresh fried squid and pizzas that start at 6,000L, drop by **La Cisterna** *(Via Madre Serafina 5; Tel 081/837-56-20; Noon-3:30pm/7pm-midnight Fri-Wed; 12,000-22,000L per entree; AE, DC, MC, V),* just off Piazza Umberto I. It's run by two brothers, Francesco and Salvatore, who know how to make *good* food.

▶▶DO-ABLE

Located in Anacapri, **La Rondinella** *(Via G. Orlandi 245; Tel 081/837-12-23; Noon-3pm/7pm-midnight; 16,000-28,000L per entree; AE, DC, MC, V)* offers succulent Southern Italian cooking. Classic pasta and seafood dishes (lasagne, Bolognese, spaghetti with clam sauce) are served in an old-fashioned atmosphere (white tablecloths, wooden chairs, and candles).

Ai Faraglioni *(Via Camerelle 75; Tel 081/837-0320; Main courses 18,000-35,000L; Noon-3pm/7:30-11:30pm daily; Closed Nov-mid Mar; V, MC, AE, DC)* is a popular restaurant that puts its tables out on the

Isle of capri eats and crashing

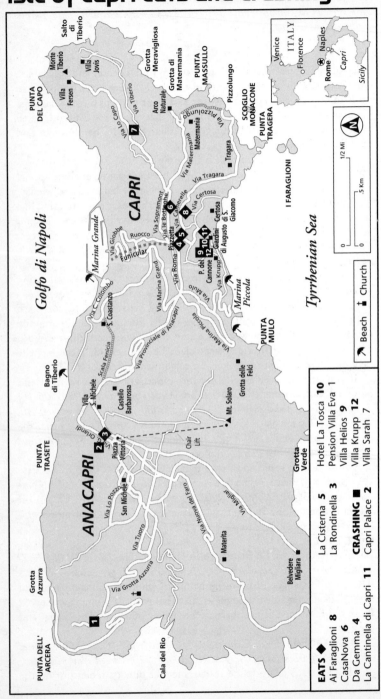

street when the weather is nice. Specialties include linguine with lobster, seafood crepes, fisherman's risotto, and meat dishes such as pappardelle with rabbit.

To get to **Da Gemma** *(Via Madre Serafina 6; Tel 081/837-04-61; Noon-3pm, 7pm-midnight daily; 15,000-28,000L main courses; V, MC, AE, DC)*, enter the vaulted tunnel beginning at Piazza Umberto I and wind your way through dark underground passages. The cuisine includes authentic versions of Caprese favorites, with an emphasis on seafood and pizzas. In warm weather, they expand to an open-air terrace with sweeping views of the Gulf of Napoli.

##▶▶SPLURGE

The legendary **da Paolino** *(Via Palazzo a Mare 11; Tel 081/837-61-02; 8-11pm daily, June-Sept; 25,000-40,000L per entree; AE, DC, MC, V)* wins in the "Most Likely to Spot a Celebrity" category. Owner Paolino transformed what used to be a hangout for locals in the sixties into a beautiful garden restaurant surrounded by lemon trees. Today, Paolino's sons Vittorino and Lino carry on their father's mission. Celebrities mingle with neighborhood folks to sample Caprese cuisine. Past guests include Dianne Furstenberg, Ferragamo, Tom Cruise, Mimi Rogers, John Belushi, and George Hamilton.

crashing

If money is an issue, Capri is best as a day trip (almost all budget travelers skip out before night falls). The hotels here will bleed you, and many moderately expensive hotels are actually quite dumpy, crawling with cockroaches and without hot water. Save your money. What you'd pay for a "cheap" hotel here will get you a room in a really cool splurge hotel back on the mainland.

##▶▶CHEAP

A quaint boarding house that caters to a younger crowd, **Pension Villa Eva** *(Via La Fabbrica, 8; Tel 081/837-20-40; villaevacapri@hotmail.com; 60,000L single room w/out bathroom, 70,000-90,000L single w/bathroom, 130,000-150,000L double w/bathroom; MC, V)* is 10 minutes from the center of Anacapri and three minutes from the bus stop that connects to the main tourist and seaside spots on the island. It's located along the road that leads to the Blue Grotto. No curfew.

Villa Helios *(Via Croce 4; Tel 081/837-02-40; Fax 081/837-02-40; villahelios@capri.it; 110,000-120,000L single, 160,000-180,000L double, 180,000-200,000L triple, 210,000-250,000L quadruple; MC, V)* is a boarding house affiliated with the Italian Social Tourism Center and is therefore qualified to host only members of this organization. You can become a member directly at the villa, which is under non-profit management. It's not especially charming, but it's cheap for Capri, and the profits go to Catholic rest homes. Most rooms are doubles and have a view and new furnishings. A television is in the entrace hall. Villa Helios is centrally located, only five minutes away from Piazza Umberto I. If you come during peak season (May 15 to September 30), prices are slightly higher.

Just past Piazzetta Dalla in Capri, **Hotel La Tosca** *(Via Dalmazio Birago 5; Tel and Fax 081/837-09-89; 65,000L single, 120,000-160,000L double; MC, V)* is a small, tranquil hotel with panoramic views, a friendly staff, and quiet guests. Rooms have private bathrooms and telephones, but no TVs.

▶▶SPLURGE

With its private garden and stunning views, **Villa Sarah** *(Via Tiberio 3A; Tel 081/837-78-17; Fax 081/837-72-15; www.villasarah.it, info@villasarh.it; 180,000-220,000L single, 280,000-320,000L double, 430,000L triple, 450,000L quad; V, MC AE)* feels like its in its own little world. Though far removed from the day-trippers from Napoli, it's only a short (though steep) walk from the main square. One of the island's best values (all it lacks is a pool), it's often booked solid in summer, so call ahead.

The Gorky and Lenin crowd once partied at **Villa Krupp** *(Via Matteotti 12; Tel 081/837-03-62, Fax 081/837-64-89; 190,000-250,000L doubles; MC, V)* in Anacapri, though unfortunately, not at socialist prices. Rates are still reasonable for this terrace-filled villa that's part home, part pension. The double rooms vary in size and you pay accordingly. Rooms all have private bathrooms.

need to know

Currency Exchange There are money exchange offices at **Marina Grande** and **Piazza Umberto I.** In addition, most stores accept traveler's checks, the bigger hotels offer exchange, and there are **ATMs** on the main streets in Capri. Or you can try the official **exchange agency** *(33 Via Roma; Tel 081/837-07-85; 10am-1pm/4-6:30pm).*

Tourist Information Pick up local info and maps at the **tourist board office** *(Piazza Umberto I 19; Tel 081/837-06-86; 8:30am-8:30pm Mon-Sat, 8:30am-2:30pm Sunday).* They will give you names and numbers of hotels if you call in advance, but they won't make reservations for you.

Public Transportation Capri is a very small island, and you can walk everywhere. If you're feeling lazy, however, you can take the bus that runs between Capri and Anacapri. You can catch the bus at **Via Acquaviva 2** *(Tel 081/837-04-20)* in Capri, or at **Staiano Autotrasporti** *(Via Filietto 13; Tel 081/837-24-22)* in Anacapri.

Health and Emergency Emergency: *113;* Police: *112.* The local hospital is **Ospedale Capilupi** *(Via Provinciale, Anacapri; Tel 081/838-12-05).*

Boats To reach Capri, you must come by **boat,** which will dock at the **Marina Grande.** Unfortunately, this is a serious hike away from town. Fortunately, there's a **funicular** *(every 10 minutes 6:30am-midnight in the the summer; 1,700L)* that runs up to Piazza Umberto to save your aching feet.

Most guests come from Naples, but it is possible to come from Sorrento as well. The hydrofoil leaves from Naples' Molo Beverello several times daily. A one-way trip costs 18,000L and takes 45 minutes.

You can also take the ferry, which is cheaper (12,000L) and takes 1-1/2hours. For ferry and hydrofoil schedules, call 081/551-38-82 in Naples.

If you are coming from Sorrento, you can leave by ferry or hydrofoil from the dock off Piazzo Tasso (signs to the marina are posted everywhere) to catch a ferry run by **Linee Marittime Veloci** *(Tel 081/878-14-30)* or **Caremar** *(Tel 081/807-30-77)* for 8,000L. **Alilauro** *(Tel 081/807-30-24)* runs the hydrofoils.

Bike/Moped Rental License or not, you can rent an electric scooter for 25,000L a day from **Electric Scooter** *(Via Roma 68; Tel 081/837-58-63; 9am-10pm daily; Electric scooters 15,000L per hour; AE, MC, V).*

Postal The main **post office** *(Tel 081/837-72-40; 8:30am-7:20pm Mon-Fri, 8:30am-1pm Sat)* is at Via Roma 50.

Internet See *wired,* above.

ISCHIA

Laze in the sun, soak your backpack-weary muscles in a rejuvenating thermal hot spring, or catch a classical concert in a bombed-out castle in green and beautiful Ischia. This hip little island attracts a real mix of visitors—from movie stars and royalty to everyday folks. It's not as exorbitantly priced as its sister island Capri (or as pretty, unfortunately), it's very relaxing, and even if you do end up dropping a wad of cash, at least you'll feel like you're getting your money's worth. Producer Anthony Minghella chose it as a location for *The Talented Mr. Ripley,* the movie based on Patricia Highsmith's novel about rich American slackers enjoying the Amalfi Coast in the 1950s, and when you get here, you'll know why. The cafe-paneled stone streets and striped canopy awnings just couldn't be more perfect or untouched.

In Ischia the wine glasses are bottomless, the Internet is a dirty little secret kept only among hotel managers, and a lifetime of stress can be shed in a single day spent at the **thermal baths** [see *the great outdoors,* below]. The buffalo cheese is from Naples, the wine is made right on the island, and all of the men wear Speedos. Beyond these charms, Ischia's primary appeal is that it has managed to escape the American pop culture invasion. Throughout the cities of the south, Britney Spears blares from microtaxis. Step off the train in Naples' Stazione Centrale, and you'll find yourself assaulted by the blinding lights of a monstrous McDonald's. On the trains, American brethren trade *People* magazine like it's a black market commodity. If this *isn't* why you came to Italy, get fleeced on a taxi ride to Molo Beverello and hop the next hydrofoil to Ischia.

"Real" Italian authenticity aside, Ischia is hardly a place where grandmothers slave all day over tomato sauce. Rather, it's the spa and relaxation capital of Italy, known for its many hot springs, which are believed to be therapeutic. The 18-square-mile island is divided into five communities along the coasts—**Ischia Porto, Forio, Lacco Ameno, Casamicciola Terme, Serrera Fontana,** and **Barano d'Ischia**—and sprinkled with hot springs and perfect sand beaches. Ischia Porto is the main town, where the boats from Naples arrive, and it's definitely where the action is. Crammed with hotels and kitschy seaside shops, it also has a marina where young islanders (most of whom work at the hotels) like to hang on the weekends. If you can afford it, stay here.

bar and club scene

Nightlife is really a misnomer here, since people don't even emerge until midnight and things start hopping around 2am. If this sounds late, just remind yourself that you didn't start dinner until 10:30. Ischia Porto is where you'll find the party. If you just want to grab a beer and chill for an hour or two, try the cafes, since there are no real "pubs" here, just little wine bars.

On a cobblestone street overlooking the Castello Aragonese, **Oh per Bacco!** *(Via Luigi Mazzella 20; Tel 081/991-354; 10am-3:30pm/6pm-2am Thu-Mon, Nov-Apr; V, MC)* is a reference to the Roman god of wine, and it couldn't be a more appropriate name for this classy and charming wine bar. Let Luciana educate you on champagne and pepper jellies, as well as which of her special cheeses, which you should try with which of her special wines. You can enjoy a fine glass of vino here for about 12,000L, or less (or more), depending on what you choose. After an evening here, you'll never want to return home.

Moon Light *(Via Luigi Lavitrano 35, Forio D'Ischia; Tel 081/507-11-45; www.nonsolocabaret.ischia.it; 10:30pm-4am Fri-Sat; No cover; No credit cards)* is Ischia's raciest club. If you want to be picked up, this is the place to go. Dress as you like, but be prepared to dance to DJ'd '80s and '90s disco. The best way to get here is by taxi.

The most hoppin' club on the island is **Il Valentino** *(Piazzetta dei Pini in Ischia Porto; 10:30pm-4am Fri, Sat; 20,000L)*. They advertise the hottest DJs and they like to play hits from the '70s and '80s, as well as the rhythms of the moment. The "club" is actually an outdoor piazza in the middle of Ischia Porto, and is marked by an archway that bears its name.

About a three-minute walk from the marina, **Jane** *(Pagoda Beach, Ischia Porto, Via Iasolino; Tel 081/993-296; 11:30pm-4am daily, Jul-Aug; Cover 20-35,000L)* is the "alternative" disco for the Darias of the island. If you're looking for some potent cocktails and good music from the '70s, '80s, and '90s, minus the Eurotrash, then head to Pagoda Beach in Ischia Porto. This outdoor disco also features Latin beats, played to a crowd of young (20-24ish), longhaired patrons.

arts scene

▶▶**PERFORMING ARTS**
The **Castello Aragonese** *(Castello Aragonese; Tel 081/992-834; Open at 9:30 am daily, closed Nov-Feb; 10,000L entrance fee; 12,000L concert)* is

a *stunning* venue for classical music. Concerts take place in the cathedral section of a fortress that was hollowed out by bombs, so that today you can enjoy music under the stars (while concert-goers can smoke cigarettes to their heart's content). Many world-class musicians tour the Amalfi Coast during the summers, although the venue is sometimes a surprise for them—the piano is actually an electric synthesizer. Mind you, this was a fortress designed to keep invaders out and it was built very, very high, so you'll have to climb many, many steps to the top. You can pick up a concert schedule at the castle.

If you're in the mood to hear some real piano in yet another celestial setting, the recital hall at **La Mortella** *(Via F. Calise 35 80075, Forio; Tel 081/986-220; 9am-7pm daily; 20,000L performance; No credit cards)* in Forio hosts performances by young musical talent, many from the prestigious music school in Naples, San Pietro a Majella. Bring those clapping hands: Susana Walton, the hostess of the concert series, will ask you to be exceedingly generous with your applause, since this is often a first performance for these young stars.

CULTURE ZOO

Castello Aragonese [see *arts scene,* above]: Connected to Ponte Ischia by a rock footbridge, this fortress perches on an isolated rock surrounded by the sea. It used to be the home of the famous poetess Vittoria Colonna, who invited her buddies—including Michelangelo and Boccacio—to live with her on the island. During World War II, the Italians hid their dynamite supplies in the cathedral of the fortress, thinking that their enemies would never bomb a historical cathedral. But they thought wrong: Today the cathedral rests atop the fortress in dramatic ruins, a stunning open-air backdrop for the castle's summer classical music concerts.

THE GREAT OUTDOORS

First touted by Virgil and Homer, the **thermal springs** of Ischia have been famous for centuries. Renowned for their healing properties, they're believed to cure everything from psoriasis and slipped discs to impotence. Today, you can choose from several hot spring parks perched on Ischia's dramatic cliffsides. Each park has many pools (some up to 20) that are kept at different temperatures, and they also have Roman saunas, thermal mud treatments, and massages. To enter the parks and use the pools the cost is about 12,000L, but the special treatments, such as hydromassage, are more costly. However, it's still pretty do-able, and some of the parks even include private beaches. Plan on making a day of it or two if you can. The parks have decent, moderately priced restaurants, but you'll see a lot of picnickers too. Be warned: many of the baths are filled with elderly German tourists in shower caps—you should head to the **Sorgeto** springs, on the opposite side of the island from Ischia Porto. They're the most remote and, hence, most relaxing. You can get there by boat-taxi from Sant'Angelo.

All parks are accessible by bus, microtaxi, or scooter. Plan on biking only if you're in Olympic condition—you'll be peddling up some of the island's steepest heights.

Two of the best large public parks that are not attached to private hotels are **Parco Termale Castiglione** (*Via Castiglione 36, 80074 Casamicciola Terme; Tel 081/982-551; 9am-7pm daily; No credit cards*) and **Giardini Poseidon Terme** (*00075 Forio d'Ischia; Tel 081/907-122; 9am-7pm daily; No credit cards*), both of which can be reached by the local bus from Ponto Ischia. Prices vary by treatment: You can enter the park for free, take a dip for as little as 5,000L, or drop about 50,000L on a massage or special pool.

William Walton, one of Britain's most important contemporary composers, lived on Ischia from 1949 to 1983, until he died at the age of 80. **La Mortella** [see *arts scene,* above] is the magnificent garden, just recently opened to the public, that he and his wife Susana built on the hill of Zaro, a corner of the island. The garden is in a volcanic quarry, and was originally designed so that Walton could seek solace and inspiration to compose his music. Susana imported seeds of her favorite flowers from all over the world, including Indonesia and Australia. The result is an incomparable garden, one of the most exceptional and diverse in all of the world.

While the garden is an attraction in itself, there's also a recital hall that hosts performances by young musical talent, many from the prestigious music school in Naples.

The best beach on the island, with the highest concentration of younger travelers, is on the **Sant'Angelo** settlement. The village is connected to "mainland" Ischia via a 30-foot lava and sand isthmus. You can reach Sant'Angelo by bus from Porto Ischia. Beaches dot the island, however, and can also be found not far from the port.

EATS

Surprisingly, Ischia is slim pickings when it comes to free-standing restaurants. Fortunately most hotels include breakfast and dinner with accommodations, and not even the harshest critic could complain about their fare.

▶▶CHEAP
La Romantica (*Via Marina 46; Tel 081/997-345; Noon-3pm/7pm-midnight daily, closed Wed Nov-Mar; 13,000-25,000L per entree; AE, DC, MC, V*) certainly lives up to its name, though it's an enjoyable place to eat even if you're not playing footsie under the table. Situated near the docks in Forio, the restaurant serves up seafood so fresh that you really can imagine it hopping out of the sea and onto your plate. Order from a menu that includes prawns and seafood salad made with lobster, squid, and shrimp. You can choose between indoor and outdoor seating.

Don't be fooled by the name—although they do serve great pizza, **Ristorante Pizzeria La Beccaccio** (*Via Cava Scialicco Strada Borlonica Lacco Fori; Tel 081/994-510; Noon-3pm/7:30-11:00pm daily*) also considers gnocchi, seafood risotto, and pineapple sorbet specialties of the house. Don't expect much from the decor, though: It's your basic cafeteria-style setting, seating a faithful clientele of large tourist families. The pizzeria is in the very small community of Lacco Fori.

▶▶DO-ABLE

With probably the biggest antipasto spread in the continent and a dessert platter that will put you into insulin shock, **Hotel Il Moresco** *(Via Emanuele Gianturco 16, Ischia Porto; Tel 080/981-355; Avg 50,000 per entree; AE, MC, V)* deserves an honorable mention in the eats category for its superior Mediterranean restaurant. Don't be intimidated by the classy atmosphere: Everyone is here for some serious eating, and the waiters just want you to enjoy. That in mind, no meal here would be complete without a bottle of local white wine. Graze at the mondo antipasto platter, but just remember to save some room: The menu has more than 30 different dishes, from shrimp puffs to grilled squid, and it's also loaded with desserts. Try the chocolate Caprese cake or the crepes Suzette, or go all out and order the dessert buffet. The hotel is on the main thoroughfare of Via Emanuele Gianturco and is accessible from the port; ask any cabbie or local for directions if you lose your way.

▶▶SPLURGE

Ristorante Damiano *(Via Nuova Circumvallazione 270; Tel 081/983-032; 8pm-midnight daily; 30,000-60,000L per entree; MC, V)* is about a mile away from the main harbor. This is a place for true Italian communality, as you'll discover when you're seated at a group table with 10 complete strangers...who will become your closest friends by the end of the night. Damiano hopes his guests like seafood—the menu's primary component—but just in case they don't, he offers other traditional Italian alternatives too.

crashing

Ischia's hotels are a little pricey, but some include use of their thermal spas and two meals a day. If the prices are still too high, remember that Ischia can be made into a day trip from Sorrento or Positano. If you really want to stay here, *you must book well in advance*—hotels get a 95 to 100 percent occupancy rate in the high season.

▶▶CHEAP

The cheapest hotels in Ischia are the bare-bones one-star hotels that offer small, clean rooms without television and with or without private bathrooms. Upon landing, check the tourism office for an extensive list. Two places to try are **Albergo Macri** *(Via Iasolino 96; Tel 081/992-603; 40-55,000L single, 80-105,000L double, 120-140,000L triple)* or **Pensione Il Crostolo** *(Via Cossa 48; Tel 081/991-094; 60-70,000L per person)*, both in Ischia Porto.

▶▶DO-ABLE

You'll get the most bang for your buck at **Hotel La Villarosa** *(Via Giacinto Gigante 5, 80077, Ischia Porto; Tel 081/991-316; Fax 081/992-425; Closed Nov-Mar; 250,000-340,000L double; AE, DC, MC)*, within walking distance of the harbor. This informal antique-filled pension is loaded with charm, from the terra-cotta tiles to the French-country windows to the friendly staff. Rooms are all doubles and come with private bathrooms and TVs, plus breakfast.

need to know

Currency Exchange The best place to exchange money is at the **exchange booth** *(9am-noon/2-5pm daily)* on the small plaza where you get off the ferry. You can also change money at major hotels, or grab lira from the many **ATMs** on the main streets of Ischia Porto.

Tourist Information You'll find the **Soggiorno e Turismo** *(Corsa Vittorio Colonna 116; Tel 081/507-42-11; 9am-noon/2-5pm)* in Ponto d'Ischia, where you can pick up maps and hotel listings (they won't book rooms for you, though). English is spoken, but not fluently.

Public Transportation A **public bus** circumvents the island and stops at all of the major thermal springs parks and towns. A one-way ticket costs 1,500L and can be purchased at the freestanding ticket booth at the marina. You can catch the bus there too: Just look for the signs and accumulating crowds. Buses can be very crowded, but it beats hoofing it up those mondo hills.

Health and Emergency Emergency: *113;* Police: *112.*

Boats Hydrofoils and ferries depart from both of Naples' ports, **Molo Beverello** and **Mergelina Pier.** Transit by **hydrofoil** takes 40 minutes and costs 20,000L. The **ferry** takes one hour and 20 minutes and costs 9,800L. There are two companies that run the ferries and hydrofoils: **Caremar** *(Tel 081/551-38-82 in Naples or 081/991-781 in Ischia)* and **Linea Lauro** *(Tel 081/552-28-38 in Naples or 081/837-75-77 in Ischia).*

Bike/Moped Rental If you can ride a bike, you can drive a scooter. At 20,000L a day, it's a fun way to get around and feel like a real Italian without smoking or wearing super-tight clothes. Look for rental shops near the port; one is **Del Franco** *(133 Via del Luca; Tel 081/984-818; 8am-10pm daily; $18US/day; No credit cards).*

SICILY

SICILY

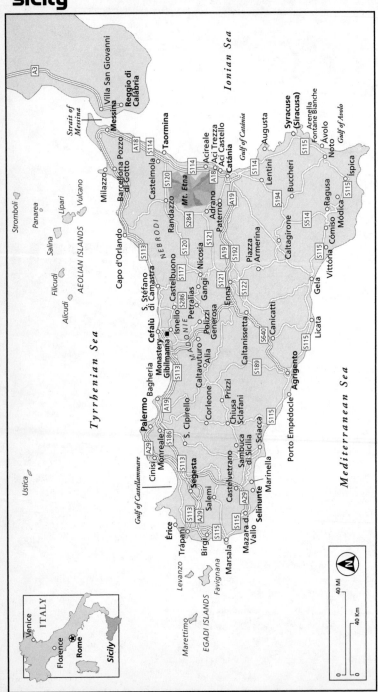

from massive old ruins to gritty cities with attitude, Sicily is a world apart from Italy. As you cross the 2.5-mile strait that divides this island from the pointy boot of Italy, you'll feel like you're crossing the border into an entirely different country. Say *ciao* to the craggy terrain of Calabria—Sicily is all about sand and palm trees, ostriches lazing in the hills, and huge ruins. Smoke hisses and curls out of volcanic isles and sun worshippers lounge naked on black rocks that trim white beaches. Even though it's an island, you'll find plenty of variety in Sicily. If you want to tie one on, hook up with the hair-gelled club kids in **Palermo,** a racy, tough city rich in history and culture. The people here have more spark than people anywhere else in Italy, and the cathedral and creepy catacombs are truly awesome. On the opposite end of the spectrum, you can imagine Greeks laying out libations to the gods at **Valley of the Temples** will lull you into a trance as. The nearby town of **Agrigento** is not a high point, but it's got plenty of good *trattorias* where you can fuel up before you hit the valley.

On the other side of the island is the jet-setting **Taormina,** perched above the beaches on a steep cliff, the astounding ruins of **Siracusa,** and **Mt. Etna**—a 10,800-foot volcano that could blow again any day now (it last erupted in 1992).

One of the best things about Sicily is the people. Sicilians talk with their hands as much as their mouths, drive like dyslexic road warriors, and chain-smoke American cigarettes as if lung cancer were just another American conspiracy theory. They are also *the* friendliest people in the world: If you ask for directions, they'll probably insist on walking you there. Or, if it's a long distance, they'll *drive* you there—even in the middle of a petrol strike—and then invite you over for dinner for some of Mom's home cooking. Sicilians really are that nice.

If this contradicts your *Godfather*-implanted notions of Mafia dons spinning around in armor-plated Alfa Romeos on their way to a "surgical cleansing," it should. While it's true that 10 years ago Sicily was riddled with crime, police crackdowns have cleaned up the streets a lot. Today, the Mafia boasts a reputation for having made the laudable transition into white-collar crime, making the island a safer place for tourists to invade.

But its history of crime has left Sicily one of the poorest regions of Italy. That's good (cheap) for you, but bad for them. Among other things,

art + architecture

The art and architecture of Sicily reflect the island's past succession of conquerors. It's a mélange that's best observed in Palermo, where Norman churches, Spanish Baroque facades, rouge Arab domes, and Byzantine cathedrals coexist peacefully. Palermo's most beautiful art can be found on the walls and in the pulpits of its many churches and cathedrals.

Modern architecture is rare, and most construction efforts are put into refurbishment. One exception is the medieval town of Agrigento. The town suffered great losses during World War II bombings, and the old buildings were replaced with unattractive low-rise apartment buildings, a testament to the local cement industry.

Luckily, Agrigento's *ancient* architecture was spared and remains a feast for the eyes. Architecture students—and a whole lot of other people, too—flock here to gawk at some of the most spectacular ruins of the ancient Greek world. Vases, icons, and replicas of the Greek gods that were excavated from the site can be viewed in the nearby museum.

it means there aren't a whole lot of young people around to help out at home, because they tend to go abroad to work for higher wages during the winter. But they do come home to party all summer long.

Millions of years ago Sicily was actually attached to Africa, not Europe, and it's been conquered over and over again since the Ice Age. Normans, Arabs, Greeks, and Spaniards have all staked their claim here at some point. If America is the melting pot that never melted, then Sicily is the melting pot where everybody got together and shagged. Sicilians are gorgeous—the sample population is evidence of Darwin's survival-of-the-fittest theory. You'll see people with blonde hair and green eyes from the Normans, sharp features from the Greeks, and thick curls from the Arabs.

From food to music to architecture, Arab culture resonates through modern Sicilian life. Rumor has it that Arab men are possessed by a bloodthirsty desire for women; maybe that's why their Sicilian descendants are so saucy. It's a dangerous combo, because when you swirl this baser nature with Italian refinement, you've got a very suave bunch of gents. Ladies, beware: Sicilian men are seduction acrobats. They approach without hesitation, employing tactics that elevate pick-up artistry to a completely new level. But they hold strict equal opportunity policies, so keep in mind those sweet nothings you're hearing may have been used before...and probably will be used again.

Fashion turns to fash-*off* on the fanny-pack- and sandal-sock-saturated Amalfi Coast, but resurfaces in Sicily. Here, the central theme of young women's fashion is lavender land: on eyelids, on snakeskin jackets, on boots, on hip-huggers, on finger- and toenails, and on just about anything else that can be colored purple. A typical look is a tiny denim jacket with lavender hip-huggers, heavy eye makeup, and nude lips. Pants are so tight they must need Astroglide to get them on and off. Guys also go for the Silver Spoons painted-on denim look. (Fashion statement or too much lasagna?)

With designer names like Ferragamo emblazoned across their clothes, chic Sicilian women actually pay hundreds of dollars to be walking advertisements. Luckily for poor souls who can't afford the whole name, they can buy just the initials, on bags and scarves with LV or CD logos stamped all over them.

Italy is the birthplace of some of our greatest cultural gods. Michelangelo gave us *David;* Dante *The Inferno;* and Prada rediscovered sling-back mules. But all of those offerings pale in comparison to the gift from Sicily's bakers: cannoli. The world owes a debt of gratitude to Sicily for their culinary creation, and there is no better place to sample it than in Sicily itself. Deep-fried dough stuffed with sweetened ricotta cheese and sprinkled with powdered sugar, big or small, pistachio or chocolate chip, cannoli is the perfect Sunday breakfast, lunch, or dinner when all the stores and restaurants are closed but the bakeries stay open.

At any decent seafood joint in Sicily, you'll point to your meal while it's still swimming in a bucket five minutes before it lands on your plate. Favorites include octopus and calamari, but the true Sicilian spe-shi-ali-tee is spaghetti with sea urchins. Slice the prickly black spheres in half, drizzle with lemon juice, and dig out their salty orange interiors for an unforgettable meal.

Sicily is not as tourist season-sensitive as the Amalfi Coast. It tends to be a little warmer than mainland Italy, and it's not uncomfortable to travel later into the fall or earlier into spring. Also, with the exception of perhaps a few Mt. Etna-related tourist operations, things are pretty much open all year. However, it's undeniable that Sicily is most beautiful while it's in bloom, which would be spring, summer, and early fall.

getting around

The aquatic gateway to Sicily is **Palermo.** Hydrofoil from **Naples** is the speediest and most comfortable way to travel from mainland Italy to Sicily. They depart every evening, and you can buy your ticket the same day at a ticket booth in the port. The hydrofoil takes about 7 hours.

Once you arrive on the island, getting around is a breeze. The buses and trains go everywhere, and they're reliable. All major towns have train stations, and bus stations are always located not far from, if not directly in front of, the train station. Just be sure to check whether your train is running express before you get on it. Trains and buses run less frequently on Sundays.

A great itinerary for Sicily would be to sail into **Palermo,** and crash there for a few days—two nights and three days is more than enough. Then you can take a scenic train ride two hours south to **Agrigento.** Spend a day or two checking out the Valley of the Temples. Then strike out for the eastern end of the island, where you'll have to rely on buses to get between **Taormina, Siracusa,** and **Mount Etna.** Sicily can be very quiet compared to the rest of Italy, and some people might get bored with a long stay, but architecture buffs will have to be dragged away kicking and screaming.

TRAVEL TIMES

All times by train unless otherwise marked: * By bus	Palermo	Agrigento	Siracusa	Mount Etna
Palermo	-	2:00	5:00	4:00
Agrigento	2:00	-	5:15	4:00
Siracusa	5:00	5:15	-	4:30*
Taormina	7:00	7:15	2:00*	2:30*

palermo

Dig into an eight-course lunch, check out the catacombs with their creepy corpses, wander past Moorish cathedrals and palm trees into Spanish-style courtyards, or just enjoy the overall grit-and-grime of the formerly grandiose Palermo. Once a great port city filled with Arabs, then Normans, then Greeks, then Spaniards, then Romans, among others, Palermo now lies in withering disrepair, with sagging roofs, broken windows, abandoned homes. After all those polished porticos you've seen in Northern Italy, the shabbiness can be downright refreshing. And despite the city's super bad rep, it's not all that dodgy anymore. A decade ago you couldn't walk down the street without suspecting that even the nuns were going to pick your pockets, but 10 years of aggressive anticrime campaigns have made Palermo much safer.

The youth of Palermo—if you get a chance to meet them—are pretty wild, but Palermo's population is an aging one, and many young adults have left home to seek work elsewhere. The people who are still around, though, are fantastic. You will never get a snobby salesperson in a store, and most everyone is friendly. Just a warning: English is rarely uttered here, so this would be a good place to brush up on your Italian.

Generally, Palermo is easy to navigate. The municipal bus system (look for the orange bus) stops at all the major tourist spots, but you can also walk pretty much anywhere you want to go. Pick up a copy of *Un Mese a Palermo* at the tourist office [see *need to know*, below] for info on cultural events and goings-on-about-town. There *is* life after midnight, but Sicily is resolutely Catholic, and for the most part, respectable girls don't go out to bars. For hanging out and meeting other travelers, the

PALERMO

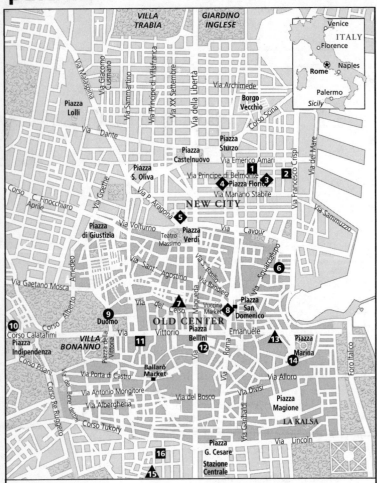

BARS/CLUBS ▲
Candelei **7**
Dancing Club **15**
Exit **13**

CULTURE ZOO ●
Catacombs of the Capuchins **10**
Il Duomo **9**
Oratory of the Rosary of St. Cita **6**
Palazzo Mirto **14**
San Cataldo **12**

EATS ◆
Caffe Mazzara **5**
Shanghai **8**
I Peccatucci di Mamma Andres **3**
Il Mirto e la Rosa **4**

CRASHING ■
Hotel Regina **11**
Hotel Sausele **16**
Petit **1**
Principe di Belmonte **2**

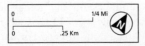

SILVIO MEETS ANTONETTA

Sicilian Guy to Random Female Stranger #1:
You are so bee-yuu-tee-ful, caro. I want to kees you all over and make love with you for-eever. (He caresses her cheek.)

Random Female Stranger: Uh, didn't I meet you just three minutes ago? I don't think so. Get lost.

(One minute later). Sicilian Guy to Random Female Stranger #2, who is standing next to Random Female Stranger #1:
You are so bee-yuu-tee-ful, caro. I want to kees you all over and make love with you for-eever. (He caresses her cheek.)

When it comes to dating, Sicilian guys are heavy on the drama, skimpy on sincerity. As a foreign woman, you'll be an instant target: Unless he's armed with an engagement ring, a Sicilian guy is *not* going to hit it with any Sicilian women. From the cradle to the grave, Italian women are fed lines about their beauty and the preservation of chastity. But all this rejection has made Sicilian guys pretty darn resilient, because if you turn them down, instead of sulking, they'll just try again...or try someone else. They're *try-sexual*, you could say.

cafes in and around the train station are your best bet. Though there are a few cheesy-but-fun clubs, there isn't really a bar scene to speak of. It takes about a day to do the highlights, perhaps two.

CLUB SCENE

There's not a huge club scene here, but Palermo's city and suburban club kids alike party where they can. Everyone's friendly and dressed to impress, but not intimidate.

Check your e-mails when you're not dancing to the pop music at **Candelei** *(Via Candelei 65; Tel 091/327-151; 8pm-4am Fri-Sun; 20,000L cover; No credit cards).* This is Palermo's biggest dance club, and it's usually packed with young people (18-30), almost all of them locals. When we were here, ripped jeans and gobs of hair gel were all the rage. The club is large, but it's still packed, especially on the weekends. Mixed drinks are available for about 10,000L, and rock bands play live here from time to time.

The cleverly named, dark 'n' smoky **Dancing Club** *(Viale Piemonte 16; Tel 091/348-917; 10:30pm-dawn, Wed-Sun; 15,000L including drink; No credit cards)* is in the city's commercial center. The crowd here isn't as hip as Candelei's: It's kind of Eurotrashy. The best time to hit the club is around midnight. The crowd is almost all local, and they're here to rock out to DJ'd disco music.

five things to talk to a local about

1. **The Mafia.** If you want to get a good laugh out of a local, say something like "So, does the Mafia really exist?" Sicilians think it's hilarious that Scorcese pilgrims land here expecting cement-block shoes and polished hearses, when reality smacks of pickpockets and battered Citroens!

2. **Mangia!** If you're looking to secure an invitation to a free, four-hour, eight-course lunch, start chatting about sausages, sambucca, and Sicilian hospitality. Chances are you'll be unbuttoning your pants by 2 o'clock Sunday.

3. **Dating.** Sicilian men love to rag on American men, especially when it comes to comparing their dating prowess. (Convo overheard: "Is that a dead corpse over there on the beach?" "No, it's an American man, I just made love to him.") They'll go on to tell you that despite being so bad at it, all American guys want is sex, but that *they* have a genuine love for women, coupled with an innate gift for pleasure.

4. **Brooklyn, baby.** The Dodgers, Bamonte's Restaurant, Lorimer Street. Almost everyone you meet will have a brother, niece, or second cousin thrice times removed living in a *Prizzi's Honor* refugee encampment by the bridge.

5. **The economy, stupid!** Sicily's woeful economy has coerced much of its motivated youth population to migrate north or to America, leaving behind a brigade of bereft parents with Sony Walkmans and a collection of postcards.

For gay dancing and drinks, enter **Exit** *(Piazza Francesco; Tel 0347/800-74-88),* where you can spend the night getting your groove on outdoors.

CULTURE ZOO

The most interesting attraction in Palermo is totally macabre: The Catacombs. Other cultural activities are church- and architecture-centric.

Catacombs of the Capuchins *(Piazza Cappuccuni 1; Tel 091/212-117; Tours 9am-noon/3-5:30pm Mon-Sat, closed holidays; 2,000L):* Even the gang from *Ghostbusters* would have trouble dealing with this creepy site on the outskirts of Palermo. Before hanging their corpses from hooks in these underground tunnels, 19th century Sicilians treated them with a preservative...and boy, did it work. The lifelike skeletons were buried more than 100 years ago, when family members would pop by for Sunday visits. There is a hallway for monks and another for children. Be prepared to be spooked—these guys look better at their age than a lot of "surgically enhanced" society ladies do now. From Piazza dell'Indipendenza, take Bus 327 to Via Cappuccini. With a map, it's also possible to walk here.

Palazzo Mirto *(Via Mirto 2; Tel 091/616-47-51; 9am-1pm/3-7pm Mon-Fri; 4,000L):* To see how the gentry lived in the early 20th century, check out this old palazzo. If you have a fetish for old houses, it's worth seeing.

San Cataldo *(Piazza Bellini 3; No phone; 9am-4pm Mon-Fri, 8am-1pm Sat, 9am-1pm Sun; Free):* This church, a symbolic landmark, is famous for its bulbous bright red domes. It was formerly the headquarters of the Knights of the Holy Sepulchre.

Oratory of the Rosary of St. Cita *(Via Valverde 3; Tel 091/332-779; 3-5pm Mon-Fri; Free):* This is a trove of artistic masterpieces. It took more than two decades for Giocomo Serpetto to paint his mischievous cherubs on the walls, and they spring to life even today, climbing onto window frames and peeing on the painted flowers. There are also some famous religious scenes (such as the flagellation of Jesus in the Garden at Gethsemane) that date back some 400 years. It's located just a few blocks south of Corso Vittorio Emmanuele.

Il Duomo *(Piazza di Cattedrale, Corso Vittorio Emanuele; Tel 091/443-376; 7am-7pm daily, Apr-Oct; 7am-noon/4-6pm daily, Nov-Mar; Free):* The mother of all cathedrals, Il Duomo is a striking example how East met West on the southernmost island of Italy. A few blocks east of the archeological museum, it was built in the 12th century on the foundation of a basilica that the Arabs had converted into a mosque, and a Gothic porch was added in the 15th century. Inside there are some royal tombs.

RULES OF THE GAME

While there are probably drugs in Palermo's nightclubs, the rules here are the same as anywhere: If you use them and get caught, you'll be busted. Rules are more lax as far as drinking is concerned. If you're stumbling around drunk, the cops are more likely to laugh at you than to arrest you.

Tourists here drink more than the natives do. While there is the ever-present bottle of wine on the table, keep in mind that the natives have been building up a tolerance since birth. But that's not to say they don't partake in vice—Sicilians smoke a hell of a lot, and like everything else they do in life, they try to get the most out of it. They don't seem to be the least bit perturbed by the disproportionate number of the population who talk through a hole in the neck. If a Sicilian's offered a pansy Marlboro Light, they'll say "Grazie mille" with a nicotine-stained smile just before tearing off the filter off.

by foot

Take a stroll through Palermo's battered **La Kalsa** district, where modern-day Sicilian life intersects with history. This section of the old port city used to be a ritzy neighborhood. These days, its nocturnal inhabitants can be slightly less than savory.

To reach La Kalsa, begin at the Quatro Canti di Citta and walk eastward along Corso Vittorio Emanuele, which is locally known as "Il Corso." Cross over Via Roma, then turn right onto Via Paternostro and walk until you reach the 13th-century San Francesco d'Assisi, on Piazza San Francesco d'Assisi.

From Piazza San Francesco d'Assisi, follow Via Merlo to **Palazzo Mirto** [see *culture zoo,* above] for a celebrity crib tour from the early 20th century.

Continue on Via Merlo to Piazza Marina, where you'll find a spectacular garden at the Villa Garibaldi in the center of the square. The historic 14th-century Palazzo Chiaramonte is on the southeast corner of the square, and a Renaissance church takes over the remaining three corners.

EATS

One thing you'll probably notice soon after you arrive is that the streets of Palermo are filled with the aroma of roasting chestnuts, a popular snack that's sold on street corners. The food in general is delicious and cheap.

▶▶CHEAP

The food at **Shanghai** *(Vicolo Mezzani 34; Tel 091/589-702; 8am-11pm daily; Average entree 10,000L; No credit cards)* is as fresh as you can get—since it's right at the end of the market, it fries, broils, and sautees up whatever's being sold that day, mainly *"pesce, pesce, pesce"* (lots of fish) prepared Italian style. (Don't let the name mislead you; this is not an Asian-style restaurant!) Situated high on a balcony overlooking a grungy piazza, Shanghai rules when it comes to good, cheap food in an authentic atmosphere. Hardly any tourists will venture in here, perhaps because of the misleading name and the less-than-sparkling facade, but you'll be glad you did.

Caffe Mazzara *(Via Generale Magliocco 15; Tel 091/321-443; 7:30am-11pm, Sun-Fri, 7:30am-midnight, Sat; Average entree 10,000L; V, MC)* supplies everything you'll need to satisfy your culinary vices in one stylish location, from Sicilian wines to sinful desserts to deep black espresso. Come here on a Sunday when everything else is closed. You can also dine Sicilian style, taking all night if you like, in the adjacent restaurant.

From the almond tarts to the marzipan, Mamma Andrea's legendary pastry skills have clearly been passed down in the family genes at **I Peccatucci di Mamma Andres** *(Via Principe di Scordia 67; Tel 091/334-835; 8:30am-1pm/4-7:30pm daily; No credit cards)*, near the port. You'll find more kinds of cookies than you would in an American grocery megastore—and they were all baked this morning. There are also more elaborate desserts involving a potentially addictive combo of candied fruits and cream. You can easily get your sweets fix here for a few thousand lire.

In the north of town, near Piazza Florio, the cheery **Il Mirto e la Rosa** *(Via Principe di Granatelli 30; Tel 091/324-353; 12:30-3pm/8-11pm daily; Avg. entree 8,000L)* is a great bargain, serving up traditional pastas (including vegetarian options) and tasty pizzas to a mix of locals and tourists.

crashing

Anywhere in Palermo is a good place to crash. Neighborhoods are not really distinct, and most everything is in walking distance. High-end accommodations can be very, very expensive, but moderate places are not too hard to find. The tourist office can help you with a list of hotels, but you'll have to make the reservations yourself.

▶▶CHEAP

Smack dab in the center of the city, the cozy **Hotel Regina** *(C. Vittorio Emanuele 316; Tel 091/611-42-16; 30,000L single, 55,000L double; No credit cards)* is an old budget traveler's standard. Rooms are shabby-chic-charming, and the crowd is young. There's a kitchen for guests to use, but no TVs or phones in the rooms. Reservations are always a good idea. The rooms are a little worn, but clean and cozy (small), with private bathrooms.

Albergo Cavour *(Via Alessandro Manzoni 11; Tel/Fax 091/616-27-59; 55,000L double w/o bathroom, 70,000L double w/bathroom; No credit*

---

down and out

If your cash flow is sputtering, don't feel alone—so are many Sicilians', and *they* never seem to be at a loss for fun things to do! Stroll through **La Kalsa** [see *by foot,* above], or pop into **I Peccatucci di Mamma Andrea** [see *eats,* above] for high-calorie, low-priced native confections. For a free dose of culture, you can tour the church of **San Cataldo** or the **Oratory of the Rosary of St. Cita** [see *culture zoo,* above, for both] which might sound dull, but is a gallery of art in itself.

fashion

Sicilian style is more laid-back than in the northern fashion medians such as Rome, Milan, or Florence, but Sicily is still Italy, which means Sicilians know how to dress. Sicily is a bit more rugged and casual, and sneakers are actually *in* here, instead of items to be pointed at through gales of laughter. However, the rest of your sportswear ensemble may be considered wildly inappropriate.

If you're a woman, avoid donning jogging shorts at all costs: It seems they're considered to be *really slutty.* Apparently only prostitutes go jogging in the morning here, since the kind of reaction you'll solicit as you run by will make you feel like you're, well, *soliciting.*

cards) is a small and clean hotel with functional but decent double rooms, catering to a diverse crowd from all walks of life. It's north of town off Via Cavour.

On the slightly higher end of cheap is **Petit** *(Via Principe di Belmonte 84; Tel 091/323-616, Fax 091/581-156, fax lines only open 9am-1pm/3:30-7:30pm Mon-Fri and 9am-1pm Sat [they get their faxes at a nearby copy shop]; 35,000L single w/o bathroom, 50,000L single w/bathroom, 65,000L double w/bathroom; AE),* a tiny (did you get that from the name?) hotel with tiny rooms on the main drag. This is basic at its most basic, but the owners and staff are very sweet and welcoming and the location is great. One little quirk (besides those weird fax hours): You can only pay by credit card between 9:30am and 7:30pm—cash only at any other time.

▶▶DO-ABLE

Principe di Belmonte *(Via Principe di Belmonte 25; Tel 091/331-065, Fax 091/611-32-42; 40,000L single w/o bathroom, 70,000L single w/bathroom, 91,000L double w/o bathroom, 100,000L suite)* rides the fence between cheap and do-able, depending on how many are in a room and if you feel the need to have a bathroom to yourself. Rooms are a good size and clean enough to please the biggest neat-freak, plus almost all of them have TV and a private balcony. One word of warning: The hot water heater doesn't seem up to the task of providing for a whole hotel, so you might want to shower early....

If you're running low on cash and need to start putting things on plastic, the Swiss-run **Hotel Sausele** *(Via Vincenzo Errant 12; Tel 091/616-13-08, Fax 091/616-75-25; 95,000L single, 155,000L double; Breakfast included; www.hotelsausele.it; AE, DC, MC, V)* near Stazione Centrale is a good place to go. The small, basic rooms come with private baths and telephones, and some rooms even have private balconies. Reservations are recommended, especially around Easter and in September.

need to know

Currency Exchange Currency exchange booths are hard to find in Palermo. **Banks** are open Monday to Friday from 8:20am to 1:20pm. There are **ATMs** up and down Via Roma and Via Maqueda.

Tourist Information There are tourist offices at the train station, and at **Azienda Autonoma Turismo** *(Piazza Castelnuovo 34; Tel 091/591-583-847; 8:30am-2pm/2:30-6pm Mon-Fri, 8:30am-2pm Sat)*. They will provide maps, a list of hotels, and cultural performances, but they won't make hotel reservations for you.

Public Transportation There is a municipal bus in Palermo, but you may have to wait awhile before one shows up at your stop. Tickets *(1,500L per ride, 5,000L day-pass)* are available at most *tabacchi*. The main bus terminal is in front of the train station. A good way to get around is by taxi, which you can easily hail from the street, but most of the time it's just easier to walk.

American Express There are Amex services at **G. Ruggieri and Figli** *(Via Enrico Amari 38-40; Tel 091/587-144; 9am-1pm/4-7pm Mon-Fri; 9am-1pm Sat; ruggieri{agenziaruggieri.it)*.

Health and Emergency Police: *112;* Emergency: *113.* The hospital is **Policlinico Universitario** *(Via del Vespro 129; Tel 091/655-11-11)*.

Pharmacy Lo Cascio *(Via Roma 1; Tel 091/616-21-17; 24 hours Mon-Fri, 8pm-9am Sat, Sun)* is near the train station.

Airports If you fly in from Rome or Naples, you'll land at **Cinisi-Punta Raisi** *(Tel 1478/656-41)*. It's cheapest to catch a bus into Palermo, which leaves you at Villa Castelnuovo (4,500L). A taxi will be at least 65,000L. The trip takes 30 minutes without traffic.

Trains Trains arrive at **Stazione Centrale** *(Piazza Cesare, in the eastern section of town)*.

festivals and events

From June through September you can catch some opera and ballet at the outdoor summer festival at **Villa Castelnuovo,** a seaside outdoor theater that's about a 20-minute walk from the city center. The tourist office will have information about the classical music, jazz, opera, and ballet performances scheduled there.

In July, there is **U Fistinu,** a commemoration in fireworks and lights for St. Rosalia, the patron of Palermo.

Bus Lines Out of the City Bus lines that tour around Sicily are located outside the Stazione Centrale. **Cuffaro** *(Via Paulo Balsomo 13; Tel 091/616-15-10)* offers bus service to Agrigento.

Boats You can reach Palermo via ferry (a very popular way of traveling) from Naples's port, Molo Beverello. The ferry runs once a day and is operated by **Tirrenia Lines** *(Molo Angionio, Stazione Marritima; Tel 147/899-000; 60,000L one-way armchair ticket; 90,000L first-class cabin).* The trip takes 8 hours and runs overnight. It's also possible to come from Cagliari in Sardinia. The two companies that operate from Palermo are **Tirrenia** *(On the waterfront; Tel 091/333-300)* and **Siremar** *(09 Via Francesco Crispi 118; Tel 1/690-25-55).*

Postal The **post office** *(322 Via Roma; Tel 091/160; 8:15am-7:30pm Mon-Sat)* is on Via Roma.

Internet The nightclub **Candelei** [see *club scene,* above] doubles as an Internet bar. You can get up-to-date local info on the web at *http://sicilia.indettaglio.it/eng/turismo/pa/turismopa.html.*

everywhere else

agrigento

Agrigento is sleepy and small and its cobblestoned streets are quiet by midnight, but you're not here for the town, really. You're here for the very cool ruins outside of town. If you're into old temples and really huge pillars, then you have to check out the famous **Valley of the Temples** [see *culture zoo,* below]. Strewn about the valley for miles in every direction, these amazing old buildings were built about a zillion years ago (okay, in the 5th-6th century B.C., if you want to be exact about it). People came here for centuries to worship and contemplate the gods, and today they still come, although it's more to ogle these massive man-made creations than to make libations to Zeus. At night the gargantuan Doric temples are illuminated, creating a stunning contrast against the pitch-black sky.

Party central Agrigento ain't: It's basically a quiet, mid-sized, middle-class town of cobblestoned streets winding around outdoor cafes, palms trees, and seascapes. There aren't any bars, not a lot of tourists, and not very many young people...but you will see a lot of old folks loitering around! There's a large African and Chinese population here, and locals are friendly and welcoming, although most don't speak English.

Besides the temples, the other big thing here is almonds, a local crop that's celebrated in an annual **Almond Blossom Festival** [see *festivals and events,* below] and in traditional dishes like *torte mandorle,* an almond dessert torte that's baked with locally grown almonds.

You can get everywhere you need to go in Agrigento by foot, although you'll probably want to catch a bus to the ruins (they're a thirty-minute walk outside of town). The one main road, **Via Atenea,** is lined with chain stores such as Benetton, discount perfume shops, and simple *trattorias,* a good place to hang out and meet other tourists. You can get info about the ruins and hotels at the tourist office; just don't forget to bring your phrasebook, since nobody here speaks English.

fEStivALS and EVENTS

The **Almond Blossom Festival** takes place in Agrigento during the first two weeks of February. This folk festival includes song, dance, and fireworks. The best way to celebrate? Tasting the traditional dishes, of course.

CULTURE ZOO

Besides the temples, which definitely merit a visit, Agrigento is also home to a pretty cool museum where you can look at more relics up close.

Valley of the Temples *(2 km from the train station; Bus 1 or 2; 8:30am-sunset daily; 4,000L):* The most visited site in Agrigento, this valley holds the monumental ruins of the mythical city of Akragas, a Greek-Sicilian town that was known to be flamboyantly rich and opulent, and was once called "the most beautiful town of mortals." The Greeks first built the city in the 6th century B.C.; later, in 210 B.C., the town fell when the Greeks succumbed to the Romans. The best-preserved building is the Concorde, a quadrilateral Doric temple built five centuries before Christ. In the southeastern part of the valley sits the temple of Juno, which has 36 columns remaining. A stone statue of Hercules also rests horizontally, and there's also a temple for the Greek divinities Castor and Pollux. Behind the valley are aromatic almond, pistachio, and olive groves that you can roam around in. If you want to hire a guide, you'll find plenty (at least one of whom will speak English) loitering at the entrance. You can also buy a guidebook that explains some of the sites.

The Regional Archeological Museum (Museo Regionale Archeologico) *(Near San Nicola, on Contrada San Nicola; Bus 8, 9, 10, or 11; Tel 0922/240-15-65; 8am-1pm daily; 8,000L):* The exhibits here are mostly vases that were excavated from the temples. The museum's star attraction is a sculpture of the head of the god Telamon, from the Templi di Giove.

EATS

Walking around all these big old buildings will probably make you hungry, so check out the **Roadside Tourist Café** *(No phone; 8am-sunset; No credit cards)* across the road from the Valley of the Temples entrance. It sells sandwiches, *gelati,* pizza, and coffee. In town, the main street of Via Atenea is lined with simple, authentic *trattorias.* Local specialties are pretty much the same as you'll find throughout Sicily. If you're here in the summer, you'll have opportunity aplenty to sample to town's *torte mandorle,* an almond tart with a buttery cookie-like crust that's covered in a sweet paste made of crushed almonds and sugar. Almond cookies are another main attraction.

▶▶**CHEAP**

Adjacent to the Hotel Concordia off Via Atenea, **La Fourchette** *(Hotel Concordia, Via San Francesco 11; Tel 0922/596-266; 10,000L per average entree; No credit cards)* serves up simple pasta dishes, like a hearty *Bolognese,* that are so, so cheap and so, so good. The grandmotherly owner/chef will try to feed you as much as she can, and she'll look positively damaged when you tell her you're too stuffed to eat another bite. The dim, no-frills interior is packed with young visitors who come for the huge, huge servings. Wine is available.

While it's no more American than any other restaurant in town, **Manhattan Trattoria** *(Salita M. degli Angeli 9; Tel 0922/209-911; 11am-4pm/7pm-1am Mon-Sat; 15,000L per average entree; No credit cards)* is a cozy *trattoria* with friendly wait staff and a wide selection of food at a moderate price, including lasagna and at least eight kinds of pizza. You'll find the *trattoria* up a few stairs at the eastern end of Via Atenea.

La Corte begli Cfizi Ristorante Pizzeria *(Via Atenea, Cortile Conta; Tel 0922/200-52; 1:00-3:30pm/7:30-11pm Mon-Sat; 15,000L per average entree; V, MC)* has all sorts of terrific pizzas for cheap. They also have pastas and, of course, fresh seafood. Their calamari salad and rocket (bitter green) pizza is tops. Enjoy it all in a sunny, tree-filled garden up a wide staircase off Via Atenea.

crashing

Agrigento's hotels are all within walking distance of the train station, and most of them are off Via Atenea. If you want to do some comparison shopping, you can get a list of hotels from the tourist office in the train station. Reservations are probably not necessary, but they never hurt.

▶▶**CHEAP**

Hotel Concordia *(V.S. Francesco 11; Tel 0922/596-266; 30,000L single, 60,000L double, 10,000L extra for private bathroom; No credit cards)* is a large hotel just off Via Atenea accommodating impoverished students

wired

The popularity of **Sport Net Centre di Stanzani Enzo** *(Via Imera 263; Tel 92/252-00-84; 10am-2pm/4-8pm daily; 5,000L for 30 minutes)* stems from its online sports betting business, but the nice managers have realized that the recent influx of e-mail addicted travelers are good business too. ***www.bestofsicily.com/agrigento.htm*** will give you all kinds of local info.

and budget travelers from nations near and far. It's an ideal place to park your bags while you're out and about, although cramped (i.e., bed-sized) rooms and paper-thin walls don't make it a place to while away your leisure time. The staff is friendly and hilarious. Some rooms come with private bathrooms, but you'll have to shell out an extra 10,000L. We highly recommend the Concordia: It's a good place to meet other kids, with tons of college travelers, and cleaner than many a hostel we've stayed in. The owners are friendly, and it's easy to find.

A run-down but do-able hotel that comes highly recommended by the locals is **Hotel Belvedere** *(Via San Vito 20; Tel/Fax 0922/200-51; 45,000L single w/o bath, 65,000L w/bath; 98,000L double w/bath; 147,00L triple w/bath; MC, V)*. It's a bit more glam than the hostel-style Hotel Concordia (read: no dorm beds), more of a proper hotel catering to a mixed international crowd of college students and young couples. You'll find it off the far end of Via Atenea. The hotel has a garden, and some rooms have views. You can get your own bathroom but you'll have to pay extra.

need to know

Currency Exchange There are no currency exchange booths in Agrigento, so bring your lira and your credit cards with you when you come.

Tourist Information Ufficio Informazioni Assistenza Turist *(Via Battista 13; Tel 0922/492-111; 9am-2pm Mon-Fri, June-Aug)* has a very good map highlighting local hotels and restaurants and also supplies brochures to the Valley of the Temples. On the down side, the people working here don't speak English, and they won't make hotel reservations for you. There's also another tourist information office on the ground floor of the train station, where a map of cheap hotels is available.

Public Transportation Getting around Agrigento by foot is a breeze, and hopping a municipal bus to the temples is easy as pie: The bus leaves from in front of the train station and goes to the Valley of the Temples frequently. Tickets are available at the train station bar and cost 1,500L. Buses run as quickly as they fill up, so expect anywhere from a 10- to 30-minute wait.

Health and Emergency Emergency: *113;* Police: *112.* The **Ospedale Civile San Giovanni di Dio** *(Tel 0922/492-111)* is on Via San Giovanni XXII.

Pharmacies Bato Fontaelle *(Via Atenea 285)* is open 24 hours.

Trains Trains arrive at **Piazza Marconi** *(Tel 1498/880-88)* in the center of town. Several trains make the scenic trip here from Palermo each day.

Bus Lines Out of the City Bus lines out of town can be picked up at **Piazza Roselli,** *(Tel 0922/596-490)* one block uphill from the train station. There is a ticket booth stall there.

Postal The **post office** *(8:10am-1:20pm Mon-Sat)* is on Piazza Vittorio Emmanuel.

Internet See *wired,* above.

siracusa

Thanks to its heroic past, Siracusa (aka Syracuse) boasts one of the best collections of historical ruins and archeological artifacts in all the world—this place could give Athens a run for its money. *Wonder* at the ingenuity of the Greek Theater! *Gasp* as the "Ear of Dionysus" steals away your whispers! *Marvel* at the aesthetic wonder that is the Duomo! Settled in 733 B.C. by Corinthians (those are Greeks to you) attracted to the island's excellent natural ports, became the cultural and political nexus of ancient Sicily. How powerful was it? It dared to challenge the mighty Roman Empire. It lost terribly, of course, was sacked of its riches and art, and got it's greatest thinker, Archimedes, killed—but the point is that it tried!

Whatever you do, just know that Siracusa is no Bologna. You can find a place to party here if you really wanted to, but once you're finished exploring you're probably better off relaxing in a cafe and enjoying the subtle beauty and laid-back spell of this ancient spot.

neighborhoods

Most of what you'll want to see here can be found in one of two locations: The island of **Ortigia,** the cultural core of the city's illustrious past, and the **Archaeological Park,** the formal bastion of Siracusian ruins and archeological wonders. The two sites are opposite on another and are separated by the town proper, which is a jumble of ancient structures and fairly unattractive quasi-urban sprawl. Ortigia is easily accessible from the centrally located train station: simply follow **Corso Umberto,** the main street, east to **Ponte Nuovo,** which brings you straight on to the island. Give yourself at least half a day out here to see the sights [see *culture zoo,* below] and wander aimlessly through the winding streets. Take a load off at **Piazza del Duomo,** on the southwestern end of the island right off **Via Cavour,** Ortigia's main drag.

Once back on the mainland your best bets for transportation out to the Archaeological Park are the bus, which you can catch on **Piazza Pancali** at **Largo XXV Luglio,** or a cab *(0931/697-35)*. You can hoof it if you want, but Siracusa is sweltering in the summer and doing the whole thing on foot might prove to be taxing. The Park is accessible via **Viale Paolo Orsi.**

culture zoo

The mile-long island of **Ortigia** is an archaeological site in and of itself. Do yourself a favor: come here and walk around for an hour or two, stopping in the main square for a coffee. It's one of the most genuine monuments to the past anywhere in Europe. Known as *Città Vecchia,* the old city shows off such structural wonders as the Duomo, the remnants of the Temple of Apollo, the 13th century Palazzo Bellomo and the Galleria Regionale.

Duomo *(Piazza del Duomo; No phone; 8am-noon/4-7pm daily; Free admission):* What began as a Greek temple in the 5th century B.C. has exchanged hands several times through the years, and has the architectural diversity to prove it. It was converted into a basillica by those pushy Christians in the 7th century, then spruced up with Baroque stylings in the 18th century, yet maintains it's original classical form.

Galleria Regionale *(Via Capodieci 14; Tel 0931/69-617; 9am-1:30pm Mon-Sat, 9am-12:30pm Sun; Admission 8,000L)* which contains a fine collection of medieval and Renaissance sculptures. There's also a collection of 18th and 19th century jewelry and textiles. You'll definitely want to check out the *Deposition of S. Lucia,* Caravaggio's 1608 masterwork. Galleria Regionale is housed in the lovely **Palazzo Bellomo,** which sports a beautiful Gothic staircase.

Archeological Park of Neapolis (Zona Archaeologica) *(Via Augusto, at intersection with Corso Gelone and Viale Teocrito; Tel 0931/66-206; 9am-6pm daily Apr-Oct, 9am-3pm daily Nov-Mar; Admission 8,000L):* The majority of classical ruins that remain in Siracusa are contained within this compact site, which you can see in about two hours.

You'll surely want to check out **Latomia del Pardiso,** an ancient quarry now planted with a fragrant jungle of oranges and lemon trees. In the back wall is a narrow cavern that Caravaggio dubbed the "Ear of Dionysius" thanks to its startling acoustics. You can stand at one end of the cavern and hear a whisper spoken at the other. It was believed that Dionysus, Siracusa's most notorious despot, used the cave as a prison, taking advantage of the acoustics to spy on his captives.

Even though you may have peeped several others like it in the course of your travels, the **Greek Theater** is an essential stop. At 455 ft. in diameter, it is one of the largest remaining structures of its kind in the world. The theater's 42 rows were carved from natural stone and could seat upwards of 15,000 eager theatergoers.

The **Roman Amphitheater,** although not quite as architecturally astounding, was built for the purposes of staging grandiose sea-battles that required the periodic flooding of the structure. It was also home to gladiator warfare of Oscar-winning caliber.

Museo Archologico Paolo Orsi *(Vle Teocrito 66; Tel 0931/464-022; Call for times, they vary; Admission 8,000L):* It's just what you'd expect from Siracusa: one of the most important collections of historical artifacts in Sicily, if not all of Italy. The museum features Roman, Greek, and pre-Christian relics, providing an all-encompassing view of Sicily's rich heritage.

EATS

You don't have to pay a lot for that meal, but you might if you don't shop carefully—Siracusa dining tends to run a bit steep. Here are a couple sure bets.

Spaghetteria Do Scogghiu *(V.D. Scina 11; No phone; Avg. entree 10,000L)* is really about as cheap as they come, and perpetually jam-packed with hungry people from all over. Scogghiu serves mix 'n' match pastas and sauces in an à la carte, cafeteria fashion. You can get steak and fish dishes, but they're really not worth it when compared to the massive pasta dishes. The communal seating adds to the stuff-your-face fun.

La Foglia *(V. Capodieci 29; Tel 0931-66-233; Noon-3pm/7pm-midnight Tue-Sun; Entrees 6,000-8,000L; No credit cards)* runs a tasty, partially vegetarian kitchen. The owner of the joint reads you the menu when you've been seated, and it usually contains dishes like ravioli with *ale verdure* (with mixed vegetables) or *burro e salvia* (butter and sage) and salads with *verdure alla griglia* (eggplant, zucchini, mushrooms and other grilled veggies). All the vegetable, fish, and breads are picked, caught, or baked fresh daily, and it shows.

crashing

Aretusa *(V Francesco Crispi 75; Tel 0931/24-211, Fax 0931/24-211; 40,000L single with bath, 70,000 double with bath)* is Siracusa's lone budget option. It's rudimentary in every way, yet clean and comfortable. The location, unfortunately, leaves something to be desired—it's a bit of walk from anything happening. Nonetheless, nine times out of ten this place is gonna have room and, frankly, you could do a lot worse.

Want to step things up a notch or two? Check in to **Gran Bretagna** *(Via Savois 21; Tel 0931/68-765, Fax 0931/462-169; Closed mid-Nov to early Dec; 54,000-64,000L single, 88,000-100,000L double, breakfast included; V, MC, AE, DC).* This immaculate family-run hotel is located right on Ortigia itself—cool, huh? Take a room upstairs if you want a private bath, or stay on the ground floor if you're interested in more spacious quarters. Some of the rooms have frescoes on the walls and ceilings, and Room 8 is the pimp-daddy, with a spiral staircase leading up to a little terrace—call ahead to reserve.

need to know

Currency Exchange Most **banks** and **ATMs** are located in one of two places **Corso Umberto** or **Corso Gelone.**

Travel Information For quick tips on the park and Ortigia try the **main office** *(V.S. Sebastiano 45; Tel 0931/67-710, Fax 0931/67-803; 8am-7pm Mon-Sat, 9am-1pm Sunday).* There is also an office in Ortigia *(V. Maestranza 33)* and a **kiosk** at the entrance to the park. None will make hotel reservations for you.

Health and Emergency Emergency: *0931/685-55.* The **hospital** *(Via Testaferatal)* is just south of the park.

Trains and Buses Trains run to Noto, Palermo, Catania and Messina everyday from the **station** on the mainland. For information call *0931/67-964.* There are two main bus lines in town: **AST** *(Piazza della Posta; 0931/462-711)* and **SAIS** *(Riva Nazario Sauro; 0931/66-710).*

Postal The **post office** *(Piazza Della Posta; 8:30-6:30pm Mon-Fri, till 1pm on Saturday)* is just over the bridge in Ortigia.

Taormina

With gorgeous beaches that dare you not to relax, a long history of on-holiday decadence, and the monolithic Mount Etna looming on the horizon, Taormina remains one of the preeminent spots on the island to indulge your inner tourist.

A relatively tranquil town during most of the year, come summer Taormina erupts with travelers from all over the globe, from the jet-set to the fanny-pack set. Although there are noticeable doses of Hollywood chic and hipster trendiness, Taormina is, at heart, just a good old fashioned place to relax and enjoy. It's managed to hold on to a whole bunch of its charm despite all the package tours, with grandiose-yet-dilapidated mansions and tiny, curving medieval streets lined with tiny old buildings. We wouldn't recommend staying here too long, though—all those tourists have jacked up the prices considerably, and this place is now a bonafide Resort Town with a capital "R". And if you're here in the high season (June through August), it's near-impossible to find a place to stay. Come for a day or two, hit the beaches, wander around town, day-trip out to **Mount Etna** [see below], then head back to more affordable environs.

neighborhoods and hanging out

Taormina teeters on the edge of a cliff that offers amazing views of the regal Ionia Sea, in the shadow of the portentous mass of rock that is Mount Etna—all in all, a pretty dramatic setting. The train station is downhill from the town center, a 15-minute bus ride away. If you come in by bus, you'll be let out at the station just outside the **Messina gate,** the main entrance to the town.

The main drag is the east-west running **Corso Umberto I,** which in the summer is shoulder-to-shoulder with tourists window-shopping and checkin' out the scene. The east end of Corso Umberto I is anchored by **Palazzo Corvaja,** a fine example of 14th century craftsmanship, all limestone walls and black-and-white lava trim. The nearby **Via Teatro Greco** will lead you to Taormina's only major cultural site, the **Greek Theater** [see, *culture zoo,* below]—don't worry, you'll find it, there are signs pointing you in the right direction about every ten feet or so. The town centers around **Piazza IX Aprile,** which was built as a terrace and offers literally breathtaking views of the sea. Now the area is lined with quaint but pricey cafes, caricature artists, and the like. Pass beneath the 12th-century clock tower and you'll eventually end up in the town's medieval section and **Piazza del Duomo,** home to one of the town's quirkier landmarks [see *culture zoo,* below].

the beach

Keep in mind the Taormina is positioned on a cliff, so to actually get to the beach, you have to traverse down the cliff to the sea via the **cable car** *(30L)* that leaves from **Via Pirandello** every 15 minutes. There's a local bus that runs down to the water too, but we think the cable car is much more fun.

The most popular (read: crowded) beach is **Lido Mazzarò,** which is lined with an ample selection of bars, restaurants, and water-sport outfitters. You can rent a beach umbrella and chair here for around 11,000L.

To the right (as you're facing the water) of Mazzarò, past the Capo Sant'Andrea headland, is the region's prettiest cove, where twin crescents of beach sweep from a sand pit out to the tiny **Isola Bella** islet. Although you can walk out to it from the cable car, it's much more fun to paddle a boat (15,000L/an hour) from Mazzarò around Capo Sant'Andrea.

The long, wide beaches of **Spisone** and **Letojanni** are north of Mazzarò. They're fairly overdeveloped, but are, at least, less crowded than the other large beach resort, **Giardini,** located south of Isola Bella.

bars and clubs

Taormina has a thriving nightlife centered on one key question, "So, what is there to do when you're, like, done on the beach?" Ah, yes—drink! All of the nightspots are located on the little alleys they call streets that plunge downhill from Corso Umberto I.

Rumor has it Tennessee Williams used to hang out at the **Caffe Wunderbar** *(Piazza IX Aprile; Tel 0942/625-302; 8:30am-2:30am daily, closed Tue Nov-Feb),* a nice place to get your evening going. You can see why the Southern gentleman would feel at home here: The pseudo-Victorian decor—complete with chandeliers and cushy armchairs—makes you feel just classy enough, and the gleaming wooden bar is well-stocked. You may want to avoid the arbor-covered outdoor area if you're especially sauced—it sits awfully close to the edge of the cliff.

You can start to feel like you're in an over-produced music video after a few hours at **Club Septimo** *(Via San Pancrazio 50; Tel 0942/625-522; 9pm till late).* Hyperactive strobe lights carreen off the big Roman columns (reproductions, natch) that frame a sweeping view of the town and the sea, and somebody's gone a little overboard with the blacklights. Roll with it, baby—you're one of the fabulous people here.

Tout Va *(70 Via Pirandello; Tel 0942/23-824; 9pm till late; 30,000L cover includes one drink)* is pound for pound the most happening club in town in the summer. You certainly couldn't call it inconspicuous—it's an open-air venue, and the young, vivacious crowd gets rowdier as the night goes on. You can hear it long before you see it. The DJs spin pumpin' club and house tracks to keep everyone dancing. Be sure to stop and catch your breath at least once so you can check out the incredible views. It's name appropriately translates to "everything goes."

Although not a bar or club in the dark-and-smoky sense of the word, the **Public Gardens** is one of the better places to unwind with a cool refreshment. There's an actual bar tucked away in this flower-filled garden overlooking the sea. Order drinks, take in the view, watch the clouds, and sip your blues away (though how you could possibly have the blues in this town is beyond us).

CULTURE ZOO

Taormina is definitely more of a hit-the-beach/hit-the-bar kind of town; however, there are a few important sites worth having a look at.

In Piazza del Duomo, the center of the city's medieval quarter, sits one of the loveliest monuments in Taormina: A 17th century **fountain** topped off by a statue of a bizarre two-legged centaur. This uniquely insignificant figure of Greek mythology has become the adopted mascot of the island. It'll only take a few minutes to check out—you won't even realize you've done something cultural.

Greek Amphitheater *(Via Teatro Greco; Tel 0942/23-220; 9am-2 hours before sunset daily; Admission 5,000L):* This spot dates back to the Hellenistic period (that's the 3rd century B.C for you non-history majors). It switched hands when the Romans came to town in the 2nd century A.D., and again when Arabs invaded in the 10th century. The current remains date from the rebuilding that was done when the Romans had control. The site features a museum containing artifacts from the classical and early Christian periods. Besides it value in antiquity, it also offers a picturesque view of Mt. Etna and the coast.

EATS

You can stretch your budget in this costly town by grabbing picnic supplies at the **Standa Supermarket** *(Via Apollo Arcageta; 8:30am-1pm/5-9pm Mon-Sat)* just up the block from the post office. Watch out for the cute little markets along Corso Umberto—they may look like little mom-n-pop groceries, but fussy gourmet food and inflated price tags lurk within.

▶▶CHEAP

Across the street from the Public Gardens sits the tiny **Al Giardino** *(Via Bagnoli Croci 84; Tel 0942/23-453; Noon-2:30pm/7:30-11pm daily June-Sep, Fri-Wed only Oct-May, closed Nov; First courses 8,000-10,000L, second courses 8,000-17,000L; V, MC).* The inexpensive pasta and meat dishes at this cafe are prepared with TLC by owner Sebatiano Puglia—try his luscious spaghetti alla carbonara, or the *paglia e feino alla bolognese,* green and yellow pasta with a meat sauce. The *involtini alla rusticana* (cheese-stuffed veal grilled on skewers with lemon slices and Sicilian sausages) is the second course you've got to try. Call ahead and make a reservation for one of the dozen or so tables out front on the patio under the flower-heavy awning.

▶▶DO-ABLE

You'll be stunned when you see how reasonable your tab is for the excellent food at **Ristorante Luraleo** *(Via Bagnoli Croce 27; Tel 092-24-279; Noon-3pm/7-11pm June-Sep, closed Wed Oct-May; Avg. entree 20,000L; V, MC, DC).* Dig in to the homemade macaroni with tomato, eggplant, and basil, or order up the house specialty: salmon risotto with pistachios. Everything is made that much more elegant when consumed on the endlessly pretty terrace, complete with pastel tablecloths and vine-covered arbor. But don't be too disappointed if you have to sit inside; the cozy candle-lit rustic dining room has those über-Italian tiles on the walls and decorative wine racks scattered around—plus you're closer to the awesome antipasto table.

▶▶**SPLURGE**

If you're gonna spend the big bucks for a meal you'll remember, you might as well do it right. The height of class in Taormina is the tiny 10-table **Maffei's** *(Via San Domenico de Guzman; Tel 0942-240-55; Noon-3pm, 7pm-Midnight daily; Avg. entrees 35,000-40,000L; V, MC, AE).* Word on the street is that they serve the best fish in town, hands down. Maffei's will prepare the catch of the day precisely as you've requested— if you're stuck for inspiration, we'd suggest the *alla messinese,* which means braised with tomatoes, olives, and capers. The *fritto misto* (deep fried calamari, shrimp, swordfish, and sea bream) is made with high quality olive oil, so it's light and crispy, not the soggy grease-fest it can turn out to be at other resturants. The deserts, like crepes flambé stuffed with fresh cream, are equally delicious.

crashing

Let us make this perfectly clear: This is not the town for budget travelers— no hotels come anywhere near cheap. And though it seems like every other building you pass is a hotel, you have to reserve far in advance in the summer months. Plan ahead, suck it up and pay more than you would in most other towns, and spend just one night here, and you'll be okay.

Staying at the cozy little **Villa Gaia** *(Via Fazzello 34; Tel 0942-23-185, Fax 0942-23-185; 55,000 single, 100,000 double, all rooms with bath; V, MC)* in the heart of town is like living at home, except you won't recognize your parents and you'll be in Italy. The beds are just on this side of saggy, but almost all rooms have a terrace or balcony. If you're lucky enough to score room 5 you'll even catch a glimpse of Mt. Etna and the sea. You get a nice breakfast every morning (included in the price) served in a little garden shaded by mandarin orange and grapefruit trees. *Bella!*

Although **Villa Nettuno** *(Via Pirandello 33; 0942-23-797, Fax 0942-23-797; 70,000L single, 110,000L double, all rooms with bath; V, MC Jul-Aug, cash only Sep-Jun)* may have a bit of wear and tear around the edges, the delicate hints of 19th-century Taormina class make up for it. In an excellent location, right between the bus station and the town gate and across from the cable car to the beach, this family home became a hotel in 1953. With a statued garden, an antique-filled salon, tidy rooms, and a view of the coast, Villa Nettuno makes for an excellent place to crash.

need to know

Currency Exchange You can find **ATMs** and **currency exchange depots** all along Corso Umberto I.

Tourist Information The **tourist office** *(Plaza Corvaja; Tel 094/23-243; 8am-2pm/4-7pm Mon-Fri, 9am-1pm/4-7pm Sat)* can help you with questions concerning where to stay, where to eat, and how to get where you want to go. They can also hook you up with info about beach equipment rentals and such. Check out ***www.taormina.it*** for up-to-date info.

Health & Emergency The hospital in town, **Ospedale San Vincenzo** *(Tel 0942/53-745),* is on Piazza San Vincenzo. Call the hospital number for an ambulance.

Trains The **Taormina-Giardini train station** is below the town near the beach, about a mile away from the city center. There are about a dozen trains daily to Siracusa, and three a day to Naples. Buses (2,500L) run every 15-30 minutes from 9am to 9pm from the station up to the village. You can also take the train to nearby Messina and take the 1-1/2 hour bus ride to Taormina (5,000L).

Buses The bus station sits just outside the main gate to the town; you can buy tickets at the small booth *(Tel 0942/625-301)* here. There are two buses daily (none on Sunday) to Siracusa, and hourly runs to Catania, where you can catch a bus to Mount Etna.

Postal The main **post office** is located on Piazza Sant' Antonio, just off the main Corso Umberto I.

MOUNT ETNA

Ask Sicilians about Mount Etna (elevation 10,800 feet) and they'll just shrug their shoulders and say something like "You know, it's just a volcano." But for those of us who don't live with Europe's tallest volcano looming over our backyards, Mount Etna can be pretty intimidating, especially considering that it's still alive and kickin'. In the last century alone, there were three eruptions, in 1928, 1971, and 1992. From a distance, it's hard to believe it's still rumblin'—on the outside it's covered with rocks (which are actually solidified lava) and is speckled with snow and ice at higher elevations. On the eastern edge of Sicily, it's a doable day trip from either Taormina or Siracusa [see above for both].

Tourists who want to explore Mount Etna usually do so from the security of a train that circumnavigates the volcano in about a five-hour tour, called, appropriately enough, the *Circumetnea* train (15,000L). It leaves from Stazione Borgo, the train station in **Catania,** the town at the foot of the Mount [see *need to know,* below]. A more adventurous route is via the daily 8:30am bus, which also leaves from Stazione Borgo, that takes you to **Rifugio Sapienza,** the starting point for all points upward. From here you can hike up the **Torre de Filosofo** (Philosopher's Tower), a popular trail that will bring you to 2,920 meters and takes about five hours round-trip. It's a difficult trek, but a good way to see (and smell) Etna's smoky, sulfurous craters. Really daring hikers can keep going from the Torre de Filosofo to the actual craters; tack on another two hours for that. Of course, if you're a complete slacker, you can take a cable car *(9am-4pm*

respect the volcano

Warning: Before attempting to climb Mount Etna, always get the latest advisory. This is an active volcano, and in 1992, 11 brazen tourists died during an eruption. In fact, you could call the mountain a work-in-progress, since the height of its summit changes with each eruption—not a reassuring thought to have when you're walking on it. So before you pack it up to the top, swing by one of the tourist offices in Catania for maps, hiking instructions, and an advisory and update on current conditions.

daily; 16,000L) instead: It runs from the bus parking lot, and it'll reduce hours of huffing and puffing to a 30-minute ride.

need to know

Contact Information To get more information about visiting Mount Etna, contact the **Parco Regionale dell'Etna** *(Via Etnea 107, Nicolosi; Tel 095/914-588, Fax 095/914-738)* or the base camp of **Grande Albergo del Parco** *(Contrada Serra La Nave, Ragalna; Tel 095/911-500).* You can also contact the regional tourist information office **AAPIT (Azienda Autonoma Provinciale Incremento Turistico)** *(Via Cimarosa; Tel 095/730-62-33; 9am-7pm daily).* There is also an office at the train station in Catania *(Via Caronda 350; Tel 095/730-62-55; 9am-7pm Mon-Sat).*

Directions and Transportation Most major buses and train lines run to Catania. **SAIS Trasporti Buses** *(Tel 095/537-261)* runs several buses daily from Taormina. There are also three trains a day from Palermo and two each day from Agrigento, and they end up at **Stazione Borgo** *(Via Caronda 350; Tel 0922/932-181).*

Health and Emergency In event of emergency, call **Alpine Aid Etna North** *(Tel 095/643-300)* or **Alpine Aid Etna South** *(Tel 095/914-141).*

Eats There're no snack shacks once you hit the mountain, so don't forget to bring food if you're planning on being up there for a while. There are some good sources in Catania if you want to pack a picnic before leaving town. There's an open-air market every morning (except Sundays) in Piazza Stesicoro in the center of town. There are also tons of grocery stores. One particularly grand supermarket is **SMA** *(Tel 095/381-317).*

Crashing Catania isn't the greatest place to stay in the world. It's notorious for crime, and the town itself isn't remarkable—it's much nicer to stay in Taormina. However, if you do decide to stay over and want to stick close to the mount, **Pensione Rubens** *(Via Etnea 196; Tel 095/317-073, Fax 095/932-181; 60,000L single, 85,000L doubles, shared baths; AE, DC, MC, V)* has clean, basic rooms. The central location is incredibly convenient, but it can get a little noisy in the summers and in the early morning, when people are getting ready to catch that 8:30am bus.

Another option is the **Pensione Ferrare** *(Via Umberto 66 off Via Etnea; Tel 095/316-000, Fax 095/313-060; 49,000L single w/o bath, w/bath 62,000L; 75,000L double w/o bath, w/bath 94,000L; No credit cards)*, a well-furnished old palazzo that's a step up from your average pension. As with Pensione Rubens, the location is ideal, but again the trade-off is the early-morning disruption. Near Piazza Umberto.

planning your trip

This chapter is devoted to the where, when, and how of your trip—the advance planning required to get it together and take it on the road. Because you may not know exactly where in Italy you want to go or what surrounds the major city you want to see, we begin with a quick rundown on the various regions.

The Regions in Brief

Italy is about the size of the state of Arizona in the U.S., but the long coastline and the large islands of Sicily and Sardinia make it feel much bigger. Even though it shares borders with four other countries—France on the northwest, Switzerland and Austria on the north, and Slovenia (formerly part of Yugoslavia) on the east—Italy is surrounded mostly by the sea.

In terms of its identity as a country, Italy was a late bloomer; its 20 regions weren't united under a central government until 1870. But the culture of each of those regions has flourished since antiquity (i.e., forever as we know it). No other country on the planet still has as many major physical remnants of its ancient heritage as does Italy, from Rome's Colosseum to Sicily's Greek ruins. But ruins aren't the only vestiges of Italy's rich history. Even today, you can visit two prevailing reminders of the Italian people's notorious refusal to be pigeonholed into a central political system (it's no secret that anarchists have thrived here): the **State of Vatican City** and the **Republic of San Marino** remain sovereign states that are not ruled by the Italian government. Vatican City's 109 acres were established in 1929 by an agreement between Pope Pius XI and Benito Mussolini, acting as head of the Italian government; the agreement also gave Roman Catholicism special status in Italy. The pope is the head of the State of Vatican City, which has its own legal system and post office. The Republic of San Marino, with a capital of the same name, strides atop the slopes of Mt. Titano, 14 miles (23km) from Rimini. It's small and completely surrounded by Italy, so it still exists only by the grace of Italy.

ROME & LAZIO The region of Lazio is dominated by Rome, capital of both the ancient empire and the modern nation of Italy. The scene in modern Rome is everything you imagined it would be: Vespas whizzing past the Colosseum, portrait painters on the Spanish Steps, and the pope waving to massive crowds in Vatican City. But there's much more to the Lazio region than Rome (other than, of course, the city's non-stop nightlife, which is unmatched anywhere else in Italy). What makes the rest of Lazio—which stretches from the Apennine Mountains to the Tyrrhenian Sea—such a great place to visit is completely unknown to most tourists: beaches, lakes, and miles of pristine hiking paths in the hills. And within this incredibly scenic environment, there are beautiful little medieval towns like Viterbo, where the laid-back scene is ideal for curing a hangover or taking a break between megadoses of Rome's deep party scene.

UMBRIA Smack dab in the center of Italy, little-known Umbria is graced with good looks and lots of personality. Its wild nightlife and cultural scene that revolves around its capital, Perugia, rivals those of Italy's largest cities. Its wild landscape is lush and green, with rolling hills, sunflower fields, olive groves, vineyards, and remarkably well-preserved medieval towns like Assisi. Yet the lack of tour buses and camera-clickers leaves these ancient treasures just for you. The whole area is also a major outdoor playground. Regional parks such as Mount Subasio have thousands of kilometers of marked paths for hiking, cross-country skiing, and cycling.

FLORENCE & TUSCANY Tuscany is one of the most culturally and politically influential provinces. Its sun-warmed vineyards and towering cypresses inspired Renaissance artists, whose works now draw tourists to Florence like ants to a picnic. So find a way to put up with the teeming hordes long enough to get up close to Michelangelo's *David,* check out the Donatello bronzes, the Botticelli smiles, and all the other preeminent treasures. Then escape to the nearby Tuscan hill towns, Lucca, Pisa, and especially Siena, Florence's great historical rival with an inner core that appears to be caught in a time warp. As a final treat, visit San Gimignano (northwest of Siena) and its medieval "skyscrapers."

ABBRUZZO & LE MARCHE If you're looking for nightlife here, you're out of luck. With the exception of Urbino's college crowd, youth culture takes a back seat to "real Italy," the one that doesn't exist to accommodate tourists. Abbruzzo and Le Marche are on the Adriatic sea, along the eastern coast of Italy. Much of Le Marche is rural, hilly, unspoiled countryside with olive groves, poppy fields, and ancient towns. Abbruzzo is dominated by the Apennine mountain range, and the sparse population is relatively poor. There are many isolated villages and medieval walled towns, like Sulmona, but most of the region is a vast, untamed wilderness.

MILAN & LOMBARDY Flat, fertile, prosperous, and politically conservative, Lombardy is dominated by Milan, like Lazio is dominated by Rome. Nowhere on earth are people more chic than in Milan. Style just oozes from their pores, and they know it. Even outside of the city, the resort towns of the northern lake regions aren't just outdoorsy, they're fashionably rustic. But don't let the whole Milanese I'm-too-sexy-for-my-shirt thing give you an inferiority complex; they may know how to dress, but they're clueless when it comes to partying. The nightlife there is totally mediocre. So once you've been there and done that, get on out to the northern lake region, where Lago Maggiore, Lago di Como, Lago di Orta, and Lago di Garda are a refreshing break from Milan's urban ego-trip. These little lakeside towns offer tourists pleasures from the tacky (Sirmione is a tourist trap in the best sense of the word) to the sublime (Isola Bella is awesome). You can indulge in every form of outdoor adventure from intense windsurfing to alpine rock-climbing or a 255m bungee jump off a dam.

GENOA & THE ITALIAN RIVIERA A much-needed pit stop for any backpacker looking to unwind from the city-to-city Eurorail frenzy, Liguria is essentially the Italian Riviera. It's famous for its beautiful sandy beaches and aqua-blue sea of towns along the Mediterranean, including the villages of La Spezia and Finale Ligure. Each beach town has its fair share of bars, discos, and cafes, all filled with thirsty backpackers and aspiring skinny-dippers looking for the right liquid to quench their particular thirsts. The international social scene—on and off the beach—makes for a hoppin' time from May to September, when the party rages all along the Ligurian coast. Backpackers and other tourists swarm beautiful coastal villages of Cinque Terra (Rio Maggiore, Manarola, Corniglia, Vernazza, and Monterosso al Mar) in search of authentic Italy, but most of the towns have lost a lot of their simple Italian charm in the process of becoming tourist destinations.

PIEDMONT & VALLE D'AOSTA Set at the foot of the mighty Alps, Piedmont is a diverse region known for its tall mountains, culinary genius, and cultural wealth. It's a backpacker's patradise, with 11 national parks plus a lively urban capital, Turin. The region also has some of Italy's best climbing, whitewater rafting, parasailing, hiking, and skiing. With gigantic mountains to the north and its rolling farmland to the south, Piedmont is a great place to chill, whether that means exploring a small cobblestone village like Asti for a day, or planning a week of skiing in the Valle di Susa. The county's largest national park, Parco di Gran Paradiso, flows into the Piedmont region from Valle d'Aosta. If hiking through glacial mountains, snowboarding five-mile trails through knee-deep powder, or trekking through pine forests amidst giant mountainous valleys is your *stilo,* this is your valley. Join the rest of the snow-happy tourists who flock to the wealthy mountain towns of Courmayeur, La Palud, Valpelline, and Aosta for skiing, hiking, or perhaps a bit of boutique shopping.

BOLOGNA & EMILIA-ROMAGNA The great food, major art and music scenes, and hyper-expensive sports cars will make you drool. And you can bet the folks in this regions aren't going home early after dinner—the nightlife, especially in Bologna, goes on till morning and it can really rock. Eat the incredibly delicious food in Parma and Modena, then burn it off dancing until morning in the nightclubs and underground music spots in Bologna. Check out the glittering gold mosaics in Ravenna, catch some rays at Marina di Ravenna's sun-drenched beaches, and indulge in the glitzy nightlife in Rimini. Then redeem yourself for your sins of excess by making your last stop San Marino—one of the smallest independent republics in the world—where a hike up awesome Mount Titano will be a veritable religious experience (and much more fun than going to confession).

VENICE & VENETO News flash: Venice isn't the only city in Italy that's full of romantic canals. The romantic allure of the Bridge of Sighs and the nightlife in Venice draws backpackers to Venice like rows of ants marching to a picnic, but don't get stuck in this one city. The rest of the Veneto region, which stretches east to the Adriatic and north to the snowy peaks of the Dolomites, offers many diverse thrills without the shoulder-to-shoulder hordes of tourists at every turn. The Venetian Republic's former strongholds—Reviso, Verona, Vicenza, and Padova—all have those cool winding canals and are also rich with *La Serenissima's* former glory, complete with architectural gems and artistic monuments. And each has its own unique kind of fun, from Vicenza's live music venues and Padova's college hangouts to Cortina's adrenalin-rush slopes and quiet hiking trails.

TRENTINO-ALTO ADIGE There are three things you should know before arriving in Trentino-Alto Adige: The natural beauty will knock your socks off, you'll definitely get your adrenaline pumping on the slopes, and technically, you're not in Italy anymore. The country's northernmost region, Trentino-Alto Adige flanks the Eastern Alps, known as the Dolomites. Its incredible mountain peaks, rushing rivers, and rolling valleys are so lush your new mantra will be "green." It's just two hours from Milano and Venezia, but most American tourists skip it entirely—bad for them, good for you. But these mountains aren't just eye candy.

You *will* go skiing. Or snowboarding. Or hiking. And you won't have to stress over what to wear on the slopes; the ski scene here is much more easygoing than its pretentious counterpart in Cortina, a valley or two away. People here appreciate individuality: Trentino-Alto Adige is an autonomous state that can make its own laws and govern itself any way it wants. The area is made up of two distinct regions—the northern, heavily Austrian Alto Adige and the southern, predominantly Italian Trentino—which were fused together only after WWII, and granted autonomy in 1948.

FRIULI-VENEZIA GIULIA Friuli-Venezia Giulia has everything except tourists. It's a great place to visit because you can get off the beaten path and dig *la dolce vita* with the locals. Trieste is the epicenter of activity. The urban student population gives it a hip edge, an athletic spirit, and a dizzy nightlife that makes it a natural home base for exploration. But there's plenty to do in other parts of the region as well. After cafe-hopping, nightclubbing, rock-climbing, and swimming in Trieste, try sipping famous local wines at the *osterias* in Udine or wandering the winding city streets in beautifully preserved Cividale di Friuli. Or trip out on your own and hike the lush Natisone Valley's hundreds of trails.

NAPLES & CAMPANIA More than any other region, Campania reverberates with the memories of the ancient Romans, who loved the area for its strong sunlight, fertile soil, and bubbling sulfurous springs. It manages to incorporate the gritty anarchy of Naples with the elegant beauty of Capri and the Amalfi Coast. While we don't recommend you spend much time in grimy Naples, it's a good launching pad to the south's more desirable destinations. It's the gateway to the hedonistic (and super pricey) isle of Capri, and to Ischia, the *isola verde,* where you can soak in the famed thermal springs. From Naples you can also hop a bus that will take you along the perilous seaside Amalfi Drive, which will deposit you in the seriously charming hillside towns of Amalfi and Ravello. While you're on the coast, forget about educational trips to the museum or guided tours that go on and on. With most of these little towns, it's all about doing as little as possible for as long as you want. (Oh, and you can party till dawn in the local discos.)

SICILY As you cross the 2.5-mile strait that divides Sicily from the pointy boot of Italy, you'll feel like you're crossing the border into an entirely different country. It's an island wonderland of sand and palm trees, ostriches lazing in the hills, and huge ruins. Smoke hisses and curls out of volcanic isles and sun worshippers lounge naked on black rocks that trim white beaches. Even though it's an island, you'll find plenty of variety in Sicily. If you want to tie one on, hook up with the hair-gelled club kids in Palermo, a racy, gritty city rich in history and culture. The people here have more spark than anywhere else in Italy, and the cathedral and creepy catacombs are truly awesome. On the opposite end of the spectrum, the Valley of the

Temples will lull you into a trance as you imagine Greeks laying out libations to the gods. Nearby Agrigento is not a high point, but it's got plenty of good *trattorias* where you can fuel up before you hit the valley. You may also want to include a side trip to Mt. Etna—a 10,800-foot volcano that could blow again any day now (it last erupted in 1992).

TUNISIA A short ferry ride from Italy's Sicilian shore will take you several worlds away from anything you'll encounter in Europe. If you've ever dreamed of riding a camel across the Sahara desert (or at least getting your photo snapped on top of one) you really should include Tunisia in your travel plans. Check out the awesome desert, fierce desert markets, shimmering white mosques, sandy beaches, and smoky teahouses filled with guys smoking *chi-cha* (water pipes). You can even stay in a movie-set "cave hotel" where Luke Skywalker once hung out with Darth, Leia, and the rest of the gang while making *Star Wars*. A modern Muslim country that gained its independence from France in 1956 with the election of president Habib Bourguiba, Tunisia is a country of extreme contrasts: The largest desert in the world is the backyard to some of the most beautiful beaches on the planet. Visit both. The Coral Coast offers the usual surf 'n' turf diversions and your pick of budget or five-star hotels, while time really does stand still in the Sahara, where the few signs of the modern world are occasional Land Cruisers shuttling tourists, and makeshift gas stations (a few plastic bottles of Kool-Aid-colored fuel under an umbrella). Along the coast you can take your pick from developed but still-nice tourist towns like Tabarka or the island of Djerba, a tourist Mecca and famous May getaway for Jewish pilgrims. Inland, you can set up camp in Tozeur, the Sahara's unofficial capital city with all of three streets, and explore from there the cliff dwellings near Tatouine, the lonely desert outpost of Tazmerza, or Luke Skywalker's old digs in Matmata.

VISITOR INFORMATION

For information before you go, contact the **Italian Government Tourist Board.**

In the United States: 630 Fifth Ave., Suite 1565, New York, NY 10111 (Tel 212/245-4822; Fax 212/586-9249); 500 N. Michigan Ave., Suite 2240, Chicago, IL 60611 (Tel 312/644-09-90; Fax 312/644-30-19); 12400 Wilshire Blvd., Suite 550, Los Angeles, CA 90025 (Tel 310/820-0098; Fax 310/820-6367).

In Canada: 1 place Ville-Marie, Suite 1914, Montreal, PQ H3B 2C3 (Tel 514/866-7667; Fax 514/392-1429).

In the United Kingdom: 1 Princes St., London W1R 8AY (Tel 020/74-08-1254; Fax 020/74-93-6695).

You can also write directly (in English or Italian) to the provincial or local tourist boards of the areas you plan to visit. Provincial tourist boards (Ente Provinciale per il Turismo) operate in the principal towns of the provinces. Local tourist boards (Azienda Autonoma di Soggiorno e Turismo) operate in all places of tourist interest; you can get a list from the Italian National Tourist Office. If you are in Italy and need to get information, call the toll-free number (only within Italy, Tel 800/117-700). If you are calling from another country, dial Tel 06/87-70-00-01. The service is available daily from 8am to 11pm in five languages, dispensing information concerning transportation, health assistance, events, museums, safety, hotels, information points, and tourist assistance.

On the web, the Italian National Tourist Board sponsors the site www.italiantourism.com or www.enit.it.

entry requirements and customs

ENTRY REQUIREMENTS U.S., Canadian, U.K., Irish, Australian, and New Zealand citizens with a valid passport don't need a visa to enter Italy if they don't expect to stay more than 90 days and don't expect to work there. If after entering Italy you find you want to stay more than 90 days, you can apply for a permit for an extra 90 days, which as a rule is granted immediately. Go to the nearest *questura* (police headquarters) or to your home country's consulate. If your passport is lost or stolen, head to your consulate as soon as possible for a replacement.

WHAT YOU CAN BRING INTO ITALY Foreign visitors can bring along most items for personal use duty-free, including fishing tackle, a pair of skis, two tennis racquets, a baby carriage, two hand cameras with 10 rolls of film, and 200 cigarettes or a quantity of cigars or pipe tobacco not exceeding 250 grams (0.05 oz.). There are strict limits on importing alcoholic beverages. However, for alcohol bought tax-paid, limits are much more liberal than in other countries of the European Union.

There are no restrictions on the amount of foreign currency you can bring into Italy, though you should declare the amount. Your declaration proves to the Italian Customs office that the currency came from outside the country, and therefore you can take out the same amount or less. Italian currency taken into or out of Italy may not exceed 200,000L in denominations of 50,000L or lower.

WHAT YOU CAN BRING HOME Check with your country's Customs or Foreign Affairs department for the latest guidelines—including information on items that you are not allowed to bring into your home country—just before you leave home, since regulations frequently change.

Returning U.S. citizens who've been away for 48 hours or more are allowed to bring back, once every 30 days, $400 worth of merchandise duty-free. You'll be charged a flat rate of 10% duty on the next $1,000 worth of purchases. Be sure to have your receipts handy. On gifts, the duty-free limit is $100. You can't bring fresh foodstuffs into the United States; canned foods, however, are allowed. For more information, contact the **U.S. Customs Service,** 1301 Constitution Ave. (P.O. Box 7407), Washington, D.C. 20044 (Tel 202/927-6724; www.customs.ustreas.gov/travel/travel.htm), and request the free pamphlet *Know Before You Go.*

U.K. citizens should contact HM Customs & Excise Passenger Enquiries (Tel 0181/910-3744; www.open.gov.uk).

For a clear summary of Canadian rules, visit the comprehensive Web site of the **Canada Customs and Revenue Agency** at www.ccraadrc.gc.ca.

Citizens of Australia should request the helpful Australian Customs brochure *Know Before You Go,* (Tel 1-300/363-263 from within Australia, or 61-2/62-75-66-66 from abroad). For additional information, go online at www.dfat.gov.au and click on "hints for Australian travellers."

For New Zealand customs information, contact the **New Zealand Customs Service** (Tel 09/359-6655), or go online at www.customs.govt.nz.

money honey

THE ITALIAN LIRA The basic unit of Italian currency is the lira (plural: lire), which you'll see abbreviated as L. Coins are issued in denominations of 10L, 20L, 50L, 100L, 200L, 500L, and 1,000L, and bills come in denominations of 1,000L, 2,000L, 5,000L, 10,000L, 50,000L, 100,000L, and 500,000L. Coins for 50L and 100L come in two sizes each (the newer ones both around the size of a dime). The most common coins are the 200L and 500L ones, and the most common bills are the 1,000L, 5,000L, and 10,000L.

With the arrival of the euro, things will change considerably. Until then, interbank exchange rates are established daily and listed in most international newspapers. To get a transaction as close to this rate as possible, pay for as much as possible with credit cards. ATMs and bank cards offer close to the same rate, plus an added-on fee for cash transaction.

WHAT'S UP WITH THE EURO? The euro, the new single European currency, became the official currency of Italy and 10 other participating countries on January 1, 1999. You may run into prices quoted in euros here and there, but it's not universally used yet.

Although the euro technically took effect in 1999—at which time the exchange rates of participating countries were locked in together and are now fluctuating against the dollar in sync—this change applies mostly to financial transactions between banks and businesses in Europe. The Italian lira remains the only currency in Italy for cash transactions. That is, until December 21, 2001, when more and more businesses will start posting their prices in euros alongside those in Italian lira, which will continue to exist (you'll already see some stores listing euro prices). Currently the euro can be used in noncash transactions, such as checks and credit cards.

On January 1, 2002, euro banknotes and coins will be introduced. Over a maximum 6-month transition period, Italian lira banknotes and coins will be withdrawn from circulation and the euro will become the official currency of Italy. The symbol of the euro is a stylized *E:* . Its official abbreviation is "EUR."

For more details on the euro, check out www.europa.eu.int/euro.

EXCHANGING MONEY Exchange rates are more favorable at the point of arrival. Nevertheless, it's often helpful to exchange at least some money before going abroad (standing in line at the *cambio* [exchange bureau] in the Milan or Rome airport may make you miss the next bus leaving for downtown). Check with any of your local American Express or Thomas Cook offices or major banks. Or order Italian lire in advance from the following: **American Express** (Tel 800/221-72-82; cardholders only), **Thomas Cook** (Tel 800/223 73-73), or **International Currency Express** (Tel 888/842-08-80).

It's best to exchange currency or traveler's checks at a bank, not a *cambio*, hotel, or shop. Currency and traveler's checks (for which you'll receive a better rate than cash) can be changed at all principal airports and at some travel agencies, such as American Express and Thomas Cook. Note the rates and ask about commission fees; it can sometimes pay to shop around and ask the right questions.

TRAVELER'S CHECKS Traveler's checks once were the only sound alternative to traveling with dangerously large amounts of cash—they were as reliable as currency, unlike personal checks, but could be replaced if lost or stolen, unlike cash. But these days, traveler's checks seem less necessary because most larger cities have 24-hour ATMs, allowing you to withdraw small amounts of cash as needed. Many banks, however, impose a fee every time you use a card at an ATM in a different city or bank. If you plan to withdraw money every day, you might be better off with traveler's checks—provided you don't mind showing an ID every time you want to cash a check.

You can get traveler's checks at almost any bank. **American Express** offers checks in denominations of $10, $20, $50, $100, $500, and $1,000. You'll pay a service charge ranging from 1 to 4%. You can also get American Express traveler's checks over the phone by (Tel 800/221-7282 or 800/721-9768; you can also purchase checks online at www.american express.com. AMEX gold or platinum cardholders can avoid paying the fee by ordering over the telephone; platinum cardholders can also purchase checks fee-free in person at AMEX Travel Service locations (check the website for the office nearest you). American Automobile Association members can obtain checks fee-free at most AAA offices.

Visa offers traveler's checks at Citibank branches and other financial institutions nationwide (Tel 800/227-6811). **MasterCard** also offers traveler's checks through Thomas Cook Currency Services (Tel 800/223-9920).

If you carry traveler's checks, be sure to keep a record of their serial numbers (separately from the checks, of course), so that you're ensured a refund in case they're lost or stolen.

ATMs ATMs are linked to a national network that most likely includes your bank at home. Both the **Cirrus** (Tel 800/424-7787; www.master-card.com/atm) and the **Plus** (Tel 800/843-7587; www.visa.com) networks have automated ATM locators listing the banks in Italy that'll accept your card. Or just search out any machine with your network's symbol emblazoned on it.

You can also get a cash advance through Visa or MasterCard (contact the issuing bank to enable this feature and get a PIN), but note that the credit card company will begin charging you interest immediately and many have begun assessing a fee every time. American Express card cash advances are usually available only from AMEX offices.

Important note: Make sure the PINs on your bankcards and credit cards will work in Italy. You'll need a four-digit code (six digits won't work), so if you have a six-digit code you'll have to go into your bank and get a new PIN for your trip. If you're unsure about this, contact Cirrus or Plus (above). Be sure to check the daily withdrawal limit at the same time.

CREDIT CARDS Credit cards are invaluable when traveling—a safe way to carry money and a convenient record of all your expenses. You can also withdraw cash advances from your cards at any bank (though you'll start paying hefty interest the moment you receive the cash and you won't receive frequent-flyer miles on an airline credit card). At most banks, you don't even need to go to a teller; you can get a cash advance at an ATM with your PIN.

Note, however, that many banks, including Chase and Citibank, have begun to charge a 2% service fee for transactions in a foreign currency (3% or a minimum of $5 on cash advances).

Almost every credit card company has an emergency toll-free number you can call if your wallet or purse is stolen. They may be able to wire you a cash advance off your credit card immediately, and in many places, they can deliver an emergency card in a day or two. The issuing bank's number is usually on the back of the credit card (which doesn't help you much if the card was stolen). A toll-free **information directory** (Tel 800/555-1212) will provide the number for you. Emergency numbers: **Citicorp Visa** (Tel 800/336-8472); American Express (Tel 800/221-7282); **MasterCard** (Tel 800/307-7309).

when to go

April to June and late September to October are the best months for touring Italy—temperatures are usually mild and the crowds aren't quite so intense. Starting in mid-June, the summer rush really picks up, and from July to mid-September the country teems with visitors. August is the worst month: Not only does it get uncomfortably hot, muggy, and crowded, but the entire country goes on vacation at least from August 15 to the end of the month—and a good percentage of Italians take off the entire month. Many hotels, restaurants, and shops are closed (except at the spas, beaches, and islands, which are where 70% of the Italians head to). From late October to Easter, most attractions go on shorter winter hours or are closed for renovation. Many hotels and restaurants take a month or two off between November and February, spa and beach destinations become padlocked ghost towns, and it can get much colder than you'd expect (it may even snow).

High season on most airlines' routes to Rome usually stretches from June to the beginning of September. This is the most expensive and most crowded time to travel. Shoulder season is from April to May, early September to October, and December 15 to 24. Low season is November 1 to December 14 and December 25 to March 31.

WEATHER It's warm all over Italy in summer; it can be very hot in the south, especially inland. The hottest temperatures begin in Rome in May, often lasting until sometime in October. Winters in the north of Italy are cold, with rain and snow, but in the south the weather is warm all year, averaging 50 degrees (Fahrenheit) in winter.

For the most part, it's drier in Italy than in North America, so high temperatures don't seem as bad since the humidity is lower. In Rome, Naples, and the south, temperatures can stay in the 90s for days, but nights are most often comfortably cooler.

The average high temperatures in Rome are 82 degrees in June, 87 degrees in July, and 86 degrees in August; the average lows are 63 degrees in June and 67 degrees in July and August.

In Venice, the average high temperatures are 76 degrees in June, 81 degrees in July, and 80 degrees in August; the average lows are 63 degrees in June, 66 degrees in July, and 65 degrees in August.

ɪTaLy caLendar of evenTs

HOLIDAYS Offices and shops in Italy are closed on the following national holidays: January 1 (New Year's Day), Easter Monday, April 25 (Liberation Day), May 1 (Labor Day), August 15 (Assumption of the Virgin), November 1 (All Saints' Day), December 8 (Feast of the Immaculate Conception), December 25 (Christmas Day), and December 26 (Santo Stefano).

Closings are also observed in the following cities on feast days honoring their patron saints: Venice, April 25 (St. Mark); Florence, Genoa, and Turin, June 24 (St. John the Baptist); Rome, June 29 (Sts. Peter and Paul); Palermo, July 15 (St. Rosalia); Naples, September 19 (St. Gennaro); Bologna, October 4 (St. Petronio); Cagliari, October 30 (St. Saturnino); Trieste, November 3 (St. Giusto); Bari, December 6 (St. Nicola); and Milan, December 7 (St. Ambrose).

TICKETS FOR EVENTS For major events in which tickets should be procured well before arriving, check with **Edwards & Edwards** in the United States (Tel 800/223-6108).

JANUARY

Carnevale, Piazza Navona, Rome. This festival marks the last day of the children's market and lasts until dawn of the following day. Usually January 4–5.

Epiphany celebrations, nationwide. All cities, towns, and villages in Italy stage Roman Catholic Epiphany observances. One of the most festive celebrations is the Epiphany Fair at Rome's Piazza Navona. Usually January 5-6.

Festa di Sant'Agnese, Sant'Agnese Fuori le Mura, Rome. During this ancient ceremony two lambs are blessed and shorn, and their wool is used later for palliums (Roman Catholic vestments). Usually January 17.

Festival della Canzone Italiana (Festival of Italian Popular Song), San Remo, the Italian Riviera. At this 3-day festival, major artists perform the latest Italian song releases. Late January.

Foire de Saint Ours, Aosta, Valle d'Aosta. Observing a tradition that has existed for 10 centuries, artisans from the mountain valleys display their wares—often made of wood, lace, wool, or wrought iron—created during the long winter. Late January.

FEBRUARY

Almond Blossom Festival, Agrigento, Sicily. This folk festival includes song, dance, costumes, and fireworks. First half of February.

Carnevale, Venice. At this riotous time, theatrical presentations and masked balls take place throughout Venice and on the islands in the lagoon. The balls are by invitation only (except the Doge's Ball), but the street events and fireworks are open to everyone. Contact the Venice Tourist Office, San Marco, Giardinetti Reali, Palazzo Selva, 30124 Venezia (Tel 041/522-6356). The week before Ash Wednesday, the beginning of Lent.

MARCH

Festa di Santa Francesca Romana, Piazzae del Colosseo near Santa Francesco Romana in the Roman Forum. A blessing of cars is performed at this festival. Usually March 9.

Festa di San Giuseppe, the Trionfale Quarter, north of the Vatican, Rome. The heavily decorated statue of the saint is brought out at a fair with food stalls, concerts, and sporting events. Usually March 19.

APRIL

Holy Week observances, nationwide. Processions and age-old ceremonies—some from pagan days, some from the Middle Ages—are staged. The most notable procession is led by the pope, passing the Colosseum and the Roman Forum up to Palatine Hill; a torchlit parade caps the observance. Sicily's observances are also noteworthy. Beginning 4 days before Easter Sunday; sometimes at the end of March but often in April.

Easter Sunday (Pasqua), Piazza di San Pietro, Rome. In an event broadcast around the world, the pope gives his blessing from the balcony of St. Peter's.

Scoppio del Carro (Explosion of the Cart), Florence. At this ancient observance, a cart laden with flowers and fireworks is drawn by three white oxen to the Duomo, where at the noon mass a mechanical dove detonates it from the altar. Easter Sunday.

Festa della Primavera, Rome. The Spanish Steps are decked out with banks of azaleas and other flowers; later, orchestral and choral concerts are presented in Trinità dei Monti. Dates vary.

MAY

Maggio Musicale Fiorentino (Musical May Florentine), Florence. Italy's oldest and most prestigious music festival emphasizes music from the 14th to the 20th century but also presents ballet and opera. Some concerts and ballets are presented free in Piazza della Signoria; ticketed events (concerts 35,000L to 110,000L/$17.50 to $55; operas 45,000L to 200,000L/$22.50 to $100; ballet 25,000L to 55,000L/$12.50 to $27.50) are held at the Teatro Comunale, Via Solferino 15, or the Teatro della Pergola, Via della Pergola 18. For schedules and tickets, contact the Maggio Musicale Fiorentino/Teatro Comunale, Corso Italia 15, 50123 Firenze (Tel 055/27-791 or 055/211-158). Late April to beginning of July.

Concorso Ippico Internazionale (International Horse Show), Piazza di Siena in the Villa Borghese, Rome. Usually May 1-10, but the dates can vary.

Corso dei Ceri (Race of the Candles), Gubbio, Umbria. In this centuries-old ceremony celebrating the feast day of St. Ubaldo, the town's patron saint, 1,000-pound 30-foot wooden "candles" (*ceri*) are raced through the streets of this perfectly preserved medieval hill town. May 15.

JUNE

San Ranieri, Pisa, Tuscany. The town honors its patron saint with candlelit parades, followed the next day by eight rower teams competing in 16th-century costumes. June 16.

Festival di Ravenna, Ravenna, Emilia-Romagna. This summer festival of international renown draws world-class classical performers. A wide range of performances are staged, including operas, ballets, theater presentations, symphonic music concerts, solo and chamber pieces, oratorios, and sacred music. Tickets start at 25,000L ($12.50), and reservations are needed for the most popular events (Tel 0544/213-895 (Fax 0544/215-840; e-mail: ra.festival@netgate.it). Mid-June to July.

Calcio in Costume (Ancient Football Match in Costume), Florence. This is a revival of a raucous 16th-century football match, pitting four teams, in medieval costumes, against one another. There are four matches, usually culminating around June 24, feast day of San Giovanni.

Festival di Spoleto, Spoleto, Umbria. Dating from 1958, this festival was the artistic creation of maestro and world-class composer Gian Carlo Menotti, who continues to be very visible and still presides over the event. International performers convene for 3 weeks of dance, drama, opera, concerts, and art exhibits in this Umbrian hill town north of Rome. The main focus is to highlight music composed from 1300 to 1799. For tickets and details, contact the Spoleto Festival, Piazza Duomo 8, 06049 Spoleto (Tel 0743/220-320 or 0743/45-028; Fax 0743/220-321). For further information, call 167/565-600 (toll-free in Italy only) or 0743/44-700; www.spoletofestival.net. June 28-July 14.

Gioco del Ponte, Pisa, Tuscany. Teams in Renaissance costume take part in a much-contested tug-of-war on the Ponte di Mezzo, which spans the Arno River. Last Sunday in June.

Festa di San Pietro, St. Peter's Basilica, Rome. This most significant Roman religious festival is observed with solemn rites. Usually around June 29.

Son et Lumière, Rome. The Roman Forum and Tivoli areas are dramatically lit at night. Early June to end of September.

Shakespearean Festival, Verona, the Veneto. Ballet, drama, and jazz performances are included in this festival of the Bard, with a few performances in English. June to September.

Biennale d'Arte (International Exposition of Modern Art), Venice. One of the most famous art events in Europe takes place during alternate odd-numbered years. June to October.

JULY

Il Palio, Piazza del Campo, Siena, Tuscany. Palio fever grips this Tuscan hill town for a wild and exciting horse race from the Middle Ages. Pageantry, costumes, and the celebrations of the victorious *contrada* (sort of a neighborhood social club) mark the spectacle. It's a "no rules" event: Even a horse without a rider can win the race. For details, contact the Azienda di Promozione Turistica, Piazza del Campo 56, 53100 Siena (Tel 0577/280-551). July 2 and August 16.

World Pride, Rome. In 2001 Rome hosted the first-ever World Pride gathering. The gay and lesbian extravaganza included art exhibits, performances, and cultural and political events, culminating in a mass demonstration in downtown Rome. For comprehensive information, call (Tel 06/541-3985) or visit www.mariomieli.it or www.interpride.org.

Arena di Verona (Arena Outdoor Opera Season), Verona, the Veneto. Culture buffs flock to the 20,000-seat Roman amphitheater, one of the world's best preserved. Early July to mid-August.

Festa di Nolantri, Rome. Trastevere, the most colorful quarter, becomes a gigantic outdoor restaurant, with tables lining the streets and merrymakers and musicians providing the entertainment. After reaching the quarter, find the first empty table and try to get a waiter—but keep a close eye on your valuables. For details, contact the **Ente Provinciale per il Turismo,** Via Parigi 11, 00185 Roma (Tel 06/4889-92-53 or 06/4889-92-55). Mid-July.

Umbria Jazz, Perugia, Umbria. The Umbrian region hosts the country's (and one of Europe's) top jazz festivals, featuring world-class artists. Mid- to late July.

Festa del Redentore (Feast of the Redeemer), Venice. This festival marks the lifting of the plague in July 1578, with fireworks, pilgrimages, and boating on the lagoon. Third Saturday and Sunday in July.

Festival Internazionale di Musica Antica, Urbino, the Marches. A cultural extravaganza, as international performers converge on Raphael's birthplace. It's the most important Renaissance and Baroque music festival in Italy. For details, contact the Azienda di Promozione Turistica, Piazza del Rinascinento 1, 61029 Urbino (Tel 0722/26-13). Ten days in late July (usually July 18 to July 28).

AUGUST

Festa delle Catene, San Pietro in Vincoli, Rome. The relics of St. Peter's captivity go on display in this church. August 1.

Torre del Lago Puccini, near Lucca, Tuscany. Puccini operas are performed in this Tuscan lakeside town's open-air theater, near the celebrated composer's former summertime villa. Throughout August.

Rossini Opera Festival, Pesaro, Italian Riviera. The world's top *bel canto* specialists perform Rossini's operas and choral works at this popular festival. Mid-August to late September.

Venice International Film Festival, Venice. Ranking after Cannes, this festival brings together stars, directors, producers, and filmmakers from all over the world. Films are shown more or less constantly between 9am and 3am in various areas of the Palazzo del Cinema on the Lido. Although many of the seats are reserved for international jury members, the public can attend virtually whenever they want, pending available seats. For information, contact the Venice Film Festival, c/o the La Biennale office, Ca' Giustinian, Calle del Ridotto 1364A, 30124 Venezia. Call (Tel 041/521-8838) for details on how to acquire tickets, or check out www.labiennale.com. August 30–September 9.

SEPTEMBER

Regata Storica, the Grand Canal, Venice. Here's a maritime spectacular—many gondolas participate in the canal procession, though gondolas don't race in the regatta itself. First Sunday in September.

Giostra del Saracino (Joust of the Saracen), Arezzo, Tuscany. A colorful procession in full historical regalia precedes the tilting contest of the 13th century, with knights in armor in the town's main piazza. First Sunday in September.

Partita a Scacchi con Personnagi Viventi (Living Chess Game), Marostica, the Veneto. This chess game is played in the town square by living chess pieces in period costume. The second Saturday/Sunday of September during even-numbered years.

Sagra dell'Uva, Basilica of Maxentius, the Roman Forum, Rome. At this harvest festival, musicians in ancient costumes entertain and grapes are sold at reduced prices. Dates vary, usually early September.

OCTOBER

Sagra del Tartufo, Alba, Piedmont. This festival honors the expensive truffle in Alba, Italy's truffle capital, with contests, truffle-hound competitions, and tastings of this ugly but very expensive and delectable fungus. For details, contact the Azienda di Promozione Turistica, Piazza Medford 3, 12051 Alba (Tel 0173/35-833). October 7-29.

DECEMBER

La Scala Opera Season, Teatro alla Scala, Milan. At the most famous opera house of them all, the season opens on December 7, the feast day of Milan's patron St. Ambrogio, and runs into July. Even though opening-night tickets are close to impossible to get, it's worth a try; call Tel 02/807-041) for information or 02/809-126 for reservations.

Christmas Blessing of the Pope, Piazza di San Pietro, Rome. Delivered at noon from the balcony of St. Peter's Basilica, the pope's words are broadcast around the world. December 25.

health & insurance

STAYING HEALTHY If you worry about getting sick away from home, you may want to consider medical travel insurance (see "Insurance," below). In most cases, however, your existing health plan will provide all the coverage you need. Be sure to carry your identification card in your wallet.

If you suffer from a chronic illness, consult your doctor before your departure. For conditions like epilepsy, diabetes, or heart problems, wear a Medic Alert Identification Tag (Tel 800/ID-ALERT; www.medicalert.org), which will immediately alert doctors to your condition and give them access to your records through Medic Alert's 24-hour hotline.

Pack prescription medications in your carry-on luggage. Carry written prescriptions in generic, not brand-name form, and dispense all prescription medications from their original labeled vials. If you wear contact lenses, pack an extra pair in case you lose one.

Contact the **International Association for Medical Assistance to Travelers** (Tel 716/754-4883 or 416/652-0137; www.sentex.net/iamat). This organization offers tips on travel and health concerns in the countries you'll be visiting, and lists many local English-speaking doctors (Tel 519/836-0102 in Canada).

INSURANCE There are three kinds of travel insurance: trip-cancellation, medical, and lost-luggage coverage. Trip-cancellation insurance is a good idea if you have paid a large portion of your vacation expenses up front (say, by purchasing a package deal). Make sure you buy it from an outside vendor, though, not from your tour operator; you don't want to put all your eggs in one basket.

Rule number one: Check your existing policies before you buy any additional coverage you may not need.

Your existing health insurance should cover you if you get sick while on vacation—though if you belong to an HMO, you should check to see whether you are fully covered when away from home. For independent travel health-insurance providers, see below.

Your homeowner's or renter's insurance should cover stolen luggage. The airlines are responsible for only a very limited amount if they lose your luggage on an overseas flight, so if you plan to carry anything really valuable, keep it in your carry-on bag.

The differences between travel assistance and insurance are often blurred, but, in general, the former offers on-the-spot assistance and 24-hour hotlines (mostly oriented toward medical problems), whereas the latter reimburses you for travel problems (medical, travel, or otherwise) after you have filed the paperwork. The coverage you should consider will depend on how much protection is already contained in your existing health insurance or other policies. Some credit and charge card companies may insure you against travel accidents if you buy plane, train, or bus tickets with their cards. Before purchasing additional insurance, read your policies and agreements carefully. Call your insurers or credit card companies if you have any questions.

If you do require additional insurance, try one of the companies listed below. But don't pay for more than you need. If you need only trip-cancellation insurance, don't purchase coverage for lost or stolen property, which should be covered by your homeowner's or renter's policy. Trip-cancellation insurance costs approximately 6 to 8% of the total value of your vacation.

Among the reputable issuers of travel insurance are Access America (Tel 800/284-8300; www.accessamerica.com) and **Travel Guard International** (Tel 800/826-1300; www.travel-guard.com). One company specializing in accident and medical care is **Travel Assistance International** (Worldwide Assistance Services; Tel 800/821-2828 or 202/828-5894).

TiPS for Travelers with Special needs

FOR STUDENTS The best resource for students is the **Council on International Educational Exchange (CIEE).** It can set you up with an ID card (see below), and its travel branch, **Council Travel Service (CTS),** 205 E. 42nd St., New York, NY 10017 (Tel 800/226-8624 in the United States to find your local branch, or 212/822-2700; www.counciltravel.com), is the world's biggest student travel agency operation. It can get you discounts on plane tickets, rail passes, and the like. Ask them for a list of CTS offices in major cities, so you can keep the discounts flowing (and aid lines open) as you travel.

From CIEE you can obtain the $18 **International Student Identity Card (ISIC),** the only officially acceptable form of student ID, good for cut rates on rail passes, plane tickets, and other discounts. It also provides you with basic health and life insurance and a 24-hour help line. If you're no longer a student but are still under 26, you can get a **GO 25 card** from the same people; it'll get you the insurance and some of the discounts (but not student admission prices in museums). CTS also sells Eurail passes and YHA (Youth Hostel Association) passes and can book hostel or hotel accommodations.

CTS's U.K. office is at 28A Poland St. (Oxford Circus), London WIV 3DB (Tel 020/7437-7767); the Italy office is at Via Genova 16, 00184 Roma (Tel 06-46-791). In Canada, Travel CUTS, 200 Ronson St., Suite 320, Toronto, ONT M9W 5Z9 (Tel 800/667-2887 or 416/614-2887; www.travelcuts.com), offers similar services. **Usit Campus,** 52 Grosvenor Gardens, London SW1W 0AG (Tel 020/77-30-34-02; www.campus travel.co.uk), opposite Victoria Station, is Britain's leading specialist in student and youth travel.

FOR GAYS & LESBIANS Since 1861, Italy has had liberal legislation regarding homosexuality, but that doesn't mean it has always been looked on favorably in a Catholic country. Homosexuality is much more accepted in the north than in the south, especially in Sicily, though Taormina has long been a gay mecca. However, all major towns and cities have an active gay life, especially Florence, Rome, and Milan, which considers itself the "gay capital" of Italy and is the headquarters of **ARCI Gay,** the country's leading gay organization with branches throughout Italy. Capri is the gay resort of Italy, rivaled only by the gay beaches of Venice.

As a companion to this guide, you may want to pick up *Frommer's Gay & Lesbian Europe,* with helpful chapters on Rome, Florence, Venice, and Milan.

If you want help planning your trip, the **International Gay & Lesbian Travel Association** (IGLTA; (Tel 800/448-8550 or 954/776-2626; www.iglta.org) can link you with the appropriate gay-friendly service organization or tour specialist. With around 1,200 members, it offers quarterly newsletters, marketing mailings, and a membership directory that's updated quarterly. Members are kept informed of gay and gay-friendly hoteliers, tour operators, and airline and cruise-line representatives.

Out and About (Tel 800/929-2268 or 212/645-6922; www.outand about.com) has been hailed for its "straight" reporting about gay travel. It offers a monthly newsletter packed with good information on the global gay and lesbian scene, and its website features links to gay and lesbian tour operators and other gay-themed travel links. *Out and About's* guide-books are available at most major bookstores and through **A Different Light Bookstore,** 151 W. 19th St. (Tel 800/343-4002 or 212/989-4850; www.adlbooks.com).

Other general-type U.S. gay and lesbian travel agencies include **Family Abroad** (Tel 800/999-5500 or 212/459-1800) and **Above and Beyond Tours** (Tel 800/397-2681). In the United Kingdom, try **Alternative Holidays** (Tel 020/77-01-70-40; Fax 020/77-08-56-68; e-mail info@alternativeholidays.com).

FOR TRAVELERS WITH DISABILITIES Laws in Italy have compelled rail stations, airports, hotels, and most restaurants to follow a stricter set of regulations about wheelchair accessibility to rest rooms, ticket counters, and the like. Even museums and other attractions have conformed to the regulations, which mimic many of those presently in effect in the United States. Always call ahead to check on the accessibility in hotels, restaurants, and sights you wish to visit.

With overcrowded streets, more than 400 bridges, and difficult-to-board *vaporetti,* Venice has never been accused of being too user-friendly for those with disabilities. Nevertheless, some improvements have been made. The Venice tourist office distributes a free map called *Veneziaper-tutti* ("Venice for All"), illustrating what parts of the city are accessible and listing accessible churches, monuments, gardens, public offices, hotels, and rest rooms. According to various announcements, Venice in the future will pay even more attention to this issue, possibly adding retractable ramps operated by magnetic cards.

Moss Rehab ResourceNet (www.mossresourcenet.org) is a great source for information, tips, and resources relating to accessible travel. You'll find links to a number of travel agents who specialize in planning trips for disabled travelers here and through **Access-Able Travel Source** (www.access-able.com), another excellent online source. You'll also find rclay and voice numbers for hotels, airlines, and car-rental companies on Access-Able's user-friendly site, as well as links to accessible accommodations, attractions, transportation, tours, local medical resources and equipment repairers, and much more.

You can join the **Society for the Advancement of Travelers with Handicaps (SATH),** 347 Fifth Ave., Suite 610, New York, NY 10016 (Tel 212/447-7284; Fax 212/725-8253; www.sath.org), to gain access to their vast network of connections in the travel industry. They provide information sheets on destinations and referrals to tour operators who specialize in travelers with disabilities. Their quarterly magazine, *Open World,* is full of good information and resources.

A World of Options, a 658-page book of resources for disabled travelers, covers everything from biking trips to scuba outfitters. It costs $35 ($30 for members) and is available from **Mobility International USA** (Tel 541/343-1284, voice and TDD; www.miusa.org). Annual membership for Mobility International is $35, which includes their quarterly newsletter, "Over the Rainbow."

You may also want to join a tour catering to travelers with disabilities. One of the best operators is **Flying Wheels Travel** (Tel 800/535-6790; www.flyingwheels.com), offering various escorted tours and cruises, with an emphasis on sports, as well as private tours in minivans with lifts. Other reputable operators are **Accessible Journeys** (Tel 800/TINGLES or 610/521-0339; www.disabilitytravel.com), for slow walkers and wheelchair travelers; **The Guided Tour** (Tel 215/782-1370); and **Directions Unlimited** (Tel 800/533-5343).

For British travelers, the **Royal Association for Disability and Rehabilitation (RADAR),** Unit 12, City Forum, 250 City Rd., London EC1V 8AF (Tel 020/72-50-32-22), publishes three holiday "fact packs" for £2 each or £5 for all three. The first provides general info, including planning and booking a holiday, insurance, and finances; the second outlines transportation available when going abroad and equipment for rent; the third deals with specialized accommodations. Another good resource is the **Holiday Care Service,** Imperial Building, 2nd Floor, Victoria Road, Horley, Surrey RH6 7PZ (Tel 01293/774-535; Fax 01293/784-647), a national charity advising on accessible accommodations for the elderly and persons with disabilities. Annual membership is £30.

getting there from north america

Most airlines divide their year into roughly seasonal slots, with the lowest fares between November 1 and March 13. Shoulder season (October and mid-March to mid-June) is only slightly more expensive, and can be a great time to visit, unless you plan to bake on the beaches, in which case you'll probably want to go during midsummmer—the hottest, most expensive, and definitely most crowded season.

Fares to Italy are constantly changing, but you can expect to pay somewhere in the range of $400 to $800 for a direct round-trip ticket from New York to Rome in coach class.

Flying time to Rome from New York, Newark, and Boston is 8 hours, from Chicago 10 hours, and from Los Angeles 12½ hours. Flying time to Milan from New York, Newark, and Boston is 8 hours, from Chicago 9¼ hours, and from Los Angeles 11½ hours.

American Airlines (Tel 800/433-7300; www.aa.com) offers daily nonstop flights to Rome from Chicago's O'Hare, with flights from all parts of American's vast network making connections into Chicago.

United (Tel 800/538-2929; www.ual.com) has service to Milan only from Dulles in Washington, D.C.

US Airways (Tel 800/428-4322; www.usairways.com) offers one flight daily to Rome out of Philadelphia (you can connect through Philly from most major U.S. cities).

Continental (Tel 800/525-0280; www.flycontinental.com) flies twice daily to Rome from its hub in Newark.

Canadian Airlines International (Tel 800/426-7000; www.cdnair.ca) flies daily from Toronto to Rome. Two of the flights are nonstop; the others touch down en route in Montreal, depending on the schedule.

British Airways (Tel 800/AIRWAYS; www.british-airways.com), **Virgin Atlantic Airways** (Tel 800/862-8621; www.fly.virgin.com), **Air France** (Tel 800/237-2747; www.airfrance.com), **Northwest/KLM** (Tel 800/374-7747; www.klm.nl), and **Lufthansa** (Tel 800/645-3880; www.lufthansa-usa.com) offer some attractive deals for anyone interested in combining a trip to Italy with a stopover in, say, Britain, Paris, Amsterdam, or Germany.

Alitalia (Tel 800/223-5730 in the United States, 514/842-8241 in Canada; www.alitalia.it/english/index.html) is the Italian national airline, with nonstop flights to Rome from different North American cities, including New York (JFK), Newark, Boston, Chicago, and Miami. Nonstop flights into Milan are from New York (JFK), Newark, and Los Angeles. From Milan or Rome, Alitalia can easily book connecting domestic flights if your final destination is elsewhere in Italy. Alitalia participates in the frequent-flyer programs of other airlines, including Continental and US Airways.

FLYING FOR LESS: TIPS FOR GETTING THE BEST AIRFARES

Take advantage of APEX fares. Advance-purchase booking, or APEX, fares are often the key to getting the lowest fare. You generally must be willing to make your plans and buy your tickets as far ahead as possible: The 21-day APEX is seconded only by the 14-day APEX, with a stay in Italy of 7 to 30 days. Since the number of seats allocated to APEX fares is sometimes less than 25% of plane capacity, the early bird gets the low-cost seat. There's often a surcharge for flying on a weekend, and cancellation and refund policies can be strict.

Watch for sales. You'll almost never see sales during July and August or the Thanksgiving or Christmas seasons, but at other times you can get great deals. In the last couple of years, there have been amazing deals on winter flights to Rome. If you already hold a ticket when a sale breaks, it may pay to exchange it, even if you incur a $50 to $75 penalty charge. Note, however, that the lowest-priced fares are often nonrefundable, require advance purchase of 1 to 3 weeks and a certain length of stay, and carry penalties for changing dates of travel. So, when you're quoted a fare, make sure you know exactly what the restrictions are before you commit.

If your schedule is flexible, ask if you can secure a cheaper fare by staying an extra day or by flying midweek. (Many airlines won't volunteer this information.)

Consolidators, also known as bucket shops, are a good place to find low fares, often below even the airlines' discounted rates. There's nothing shady about the reliable ones—basically, they're just big travel agents who get discounts for buying in bulk and pass some of the savings on to you. Before you pay, however, ask for a confirmation number from the consolidator and then call the airline itself to confirm your seat. Be prepared to book your ticket with a different consolidator—there are many to choose from—if the airline can't confirm your reservation. Also be aware that consolidator tickets are usually nonrefundable or come with stiff cancellation penalties.

We've gotten great deals on many occasions from **Cheap Tickets** (Tel 800/377-1000; www.cheaptickets.com). **Council Travel** (Tel 800/226-8624; www.counciltravel.com) and **STA Travel** (Tel 800/ 781-4040; www.sta.travel.com) cater especially to young travelers, but their bargain-basement prices are available to people of all ages. Other reliable consolidators include Lowestfare.com (Tel 888/278-8830; www.lowestfare.com); 1-800/AIRFARE (www.1800airfare.com); **Cheap Seats** (Tel 800/451-7200; www.cheapseatstravel.com); and **1-800/FLY-CHEAP** (www.fly cheap.com).

Search the **Internet** for cheap fares—though it's still best to compare your findings with the research of a dedicated travel agent, if you're lucky enough to have one, especially when you're booking more than just a flight. A few of the better-respected virtual travel agents are **Travelocity** (www.travelocity.com) and **Microsoft Expedia** (www.expedia.com).

Smarter Living (www.smarterliving.com) is a good source for great last-minute deals. Take a moment to register, and every week you'll get an e-mail summarizing the discount fares available from your departure city. The site also features concise lists of links to hotel, car rental, and other hot travel deals.

getting there from the uk and the continent

BY PLANE

Operated by the **European Travel Network,** www.discount-tickets.com is a great online source for regular and discounted airfares to destinations around the world. You can also use this site to compare rates and book accommodations, car rentals, and tours. Click on "Special Offers" for the latest package deals. Students should also try **Campus Travel** (Tel 0171/730-2101; www.usitcampus.co.uk).

British newspapers are always full of classified ads touting slashed fares to Italy. One good source is *Time Out.* London's *Evening Standard* has a daily travel section, and the Sunday editions of almost any newspaper will run many ads. Although competition is fierce, one well-recommended company that consolidates bulk ticket purchases and then passes the savings on to its consumers is **Trailfinders** (Tel 020/79-37-54-00 in London). It offers access to tickets on such carriers as SAS, British Airways, and KLM.

CEEFAX, a British TV information service included on many home and hotel TVs, runs details of package holidays and flights to Italy and beyond. Just switch to your CEEFAX channel and you'll find a menu of listings that includes travel information.

Both **British Airways** (Tel 0345/222-111 in the U.K.; www.british airways.com) and **Alitalia** (Tel 020/76-02-71-11; www.alitalia.it/eng lish/index.html) have frequent flights from London's Heathrow to Rome, Milan, Venice, Pisa (the gateway to Florence), and Naples. Flying time from London to these cities is from 2 to 3 hours. British Airways also has one direct flight a day from Manchester to Rome.

BY TRAIN

If you plan to travel heavily on the European rails, pick up the latest copy of the *Thomas Cook European Timetable of Railroads.* This 500-plus-page timetable accurately documents all of Europe's mainline passenger rail services. It's available from **Forsyth Travel Library,** 226 Westchester Ave., White Plains, NY 10604 (Tel 800/367-7984; www.forsyth.com), for $27.95 (plus $4.95 shipping in the U.S. and $5.95 in Canada), or at travel specialty stores like **Rand McNally,** 150 E. 52nd St., New York, NY 10022 (Tel 212/758-7488).

New electric trains have made travel between France and Italy faster and more comfortable than ever before. **France's TGVs** travel at speeds of up to 185 miles per hour and have cut travel time between Paris and Turin from 7 to 5.5 hours and between Paris and Milan from 7.5 to 6.75 hours. **Italy's ETRs** travel at speeds of up to 145 miles per hour and currently run between Milan and Lyon (5 hours), with a stop in Turin.

EURAILPASS Many travelers to Europe take advantage of one of the greatest travel bargains, the **Eurailpass,** which permits unlimited first-class rail travel in any country in western Europe (except the British Isles) and Hungary in eastern Europe. Oddly, it doesn't include travel on the rail lines of Sardinia, which are organized independently of the rail lines of the rest of Italy.

The advantages are tempting: There are no tickets; simply show the pass to the ticket collector and then settle back to enjoy the scenery. Seat reservations are required on some trains. Many of the trains have couchettes (sleeping cars), for which an extra fee is charged. Obviously, the 2- or 3-month traveler gets the greatest economic advantages. To obtain full advantage of a 15-day or 1-month pass, you'd have to spend a great deal of time on the train.

Eurailpass holders are entitled to considerable reductions on certain buses and ferries, as well. You'll get a 20% reduction on second-class accommodations from certain companies operating ferries between Naples and Palermo or for crossings to Sardinia and Malta.

If you're under 26, you can buy a **Eurail Youthpass,** entitling you to unlimited second-class travel for $388 for 15 days, $499 for 21 days, $623 for 1 month, $882 for 2 months, and $1,089 for 3 months. Over 26 it's $554 for 15 days, $718 for 21 days, $890 for 1 month, $1,260 for 2 months, and $1,558 for 3 months.

The **Eurail Saverpass,** valid all over Europe for first class only, offers discounted 15-day travel for groups of three or more people traveling together April to September or two people traveling together October to March. The price is $470 for 15 days, $610 for 21 days, $756 for 1 month, $1,072 for 2 months, and $1,324 for 3 months.

The **Eurail Youth Flexipass,** for travelers under 26, is valid in first class and offers the same privileges as the Eurailpass. However, it provides a number of individual travel days you can use over a much longer period of consecutive days. That makes it possible to stay in one city and yet not lose a single day of travel. It allows 10 days of travel within 2 months for $458 and 15 days of travel within 2 months for $599. Over 26, there aremtwo kinds of **Eurail Flexipass:** 10 days of travel in 2 months for $654 and 15 days of travel in 2 months for $862.

EUROPASS The adult **Europass** is more limited than the Eurailpass but may offer better value for visitors traveling over a smaller area. It's good for 2 months and allows 5 days of rail travel within three to five European countries (Italy, France, Germany, Switzerland, and Spain) with contiguous borders. For individual travelers over 26, 5 days of travel costs $348 in first class, $233 in second; 6 days of travel $368 in first class, $253 in second; 8 days of travel $448 in first class, $313 in second; 10 days of travel, $528 in first class, $363 in second; and 15 days of travel $728 in first class, $513 in second. Under 26, **Europass Youth** is good only for second-class travel, but the fares are 35% to 55% off those quoted above. Unlike the adult Europass, there's no discount for a companion.

WHERE TO BUY RAIL PASSES In North America, you can buy these passes from travel agents or rail agents in major cities like New York, Montréal, and Los Angeles. Eurailpasses are also available from the North American offices of CIT Tours (see "Getting Around Italy," below) or through **Rail Europe** (Tel 800/438-72-45; www.raileurope.com). No matter what everyone tells you, you can buy Eurailpasses in Europe as well as in America (at the major train stations), but they're more expensive. Rail Europe can also give you information on the rail/drive versions of the passes.

For details on the rail passes available in the United Kingdom, stop in at or contact the **International Rail Centre,** Victoria Station, London SW1V 1JZ (Tel **0990/848-848**). The staff can help you find the best option for the trip you're planning. Some of the most popular are the Inter-Rail and Under 26 passes, entitling you to unlimited second-class travel in 26 European countries.

UNDER 26 TICKETS These tickets allow you to move leisurely from London to Rome, with as many stopovers en route as you want, using a different route southbound (through Belgium, Luxembourg, and Switzerland) from the return route northbound (exclusively through France). All travel must be completed within 1 month of the departure date. Under 26 tickets from London to Rome cost from £133 for the most direct route or from £209 for a roundabout route through the south of France.

BY CAR
If you're already on the Continent, particularly in a neighboring country such as France or Austria, you may want to drive to Italy. However, you should make arrangements in advance with your car-rental company.

It's also possible to drive from London to Rome, a distance of 1,124 miles (1,810km), via Calais/Boulogne/Dunkirk, or 1,085 miles (1,747km) via Oostende/Zeebrugge, not counting channel crossings by Hovercraft, ferry, or the Chunnel. Milan is some 400 miles (644km) closer to Britain than is Rome. If you cross over from England and arrive at one of the continental ports, you still face a 24-hour drive. Most drivers play it safe and budget 3 days for the journey.

Most of the roads from western Europe leading into Italy are toll-free, with some notable exceptions. If you use the Swiss superhighway network, you'll have to buy a special tax sticker at the frontier. You'll also pay to go through the St. Gotthard Tunnel into Italy. Crossings from France can be through the Mont Blanc Tunnel, for which you'll pay, or you can leave the French Riviera at Menton and drive directly into Italy along the Italian Riviera toward San Remo.

If you don't want to drive such distances, ask a travel agent to book you on a Motorail arrangement where the train carries your car. This service, however, is good only to Milan, as there are no car and sleeper expresses running the 400 miles (644km) south to Rome.

GETTING AROUND ITALY

BY PLANE
Italy's domestic air network on **Alitalia** (Tel **800/223-57-30** in the United States, or 020/76-02-71-11 in the U.K.; www.alitalia.it/english/index.html)

is one of the largest and most complete in Europe. There are some 40 airports serviced regularly from Rome, and most flights are under an hour. Fares vary, but some discounts are available. Tickets are discounted 50% for passengers 2 to 11 years old; for passengers 12 to 22, there's a youth fare. And anyone can get a 30% reduction by taking domestic flights departing at night.

BY TRAIN

Trains provide a medium-priced means of transport, even if you don't buy the Eurailpass or one of the special Italian Railway tickets (below). As a rule of thumb, second-class travel usually costs about two-thirds the price of an equivalent first-class trip. A couchette (a private fold-down bed in a communal cabin) requires a supplement above the price of first-class travel. In a land where mamma and bambini are highly valued, children 4 to 11 receive a discount of 50% off the adult fare, and children 3 and under travel free with their parents.

An **Italian Railpass** (known in Italy as a BTLC Pass) allows non-Italian citizens to ride as much as they like on Italy's entire rail network. Buy the pass in the United States or at main train stations in Italy, have it validated the first time you use it at any rail station, and ride as frequently as you like within the time validity. An 8-day pass is $273 first class and $182 second, a 15-day pass $341 first class and $228 second, a 21-day pass $396 first class and $264 second, and a 30-day pass $478 first class and $318 second. All passes have a $15 issuing fee per class.

With the Italian Railpass and each of the other special passes, a supplement must be paid to ride on certain rapid trains, designated ETR-450 or Pendolino trains. The rail systems of Sardinia are administered by a separate entity and aren't included in the Railpass or any of the other passes.

Another option is the **Italian Flexirail Card,** which entitles you to a predetermined number of days of travel on any rail line in a certain time period. It's ideal for passengers who plan in advance to spend several days sightseeing before boarding a train for another city. A pass giving 4 possible travel days out of a block of 1 month is $216 first class and $144 second, a pass for 8 travel days stretched over a 1-month period $302 first class and $202 second, and a pass for 12 travel days within 1 month $389 first class and $259 second.

You can buy these passes from any travel agent or by phone (Tel 800/248-7245; 800/EURAIL or 800/EUROSTAR).

BY BUS

Italy has an extensive and intricate bus network, covering all regions. However, because rail travel is inexpensive, the bus isn't the preferred method of travel. Besides, drivers seem to go on strike every 2 weeks.

One of the leading bus operators is **SITA,** Viale del Cadorna 105, Florence (Tel 055/47-821). SITA buses serve most parts of the country, especially the central belt, including Tuscany, but not the far frontiers. Among the largest of the other companies, with special emphasis in the north and central tiers, is **Autostradale,** Piazzale Castello, Milan (Tel 02/801-161).

Lazzi, Via Mercadante 2, Florence (Tel 055/363-041), goes through Tuscany, including Siena, and much of central Italy.

Where these nationwide services leave off, local bus companies operate in most regions, particularly in the hill sections and the Alpine regions where rail travel isn't possible.

BY CAR

U.S. and Canadian drivers don't need an International Driver's License to drive a rented car in Italy. However, if driving a private car, they need such a license.

You can apply for an International Driver's License at any **American Automobile Association (AAA)** branch. You must be at least 18 and have two 2-by-2-inch photos and a photocopy of your U.S. driver's license with your AAA application form. The actual fee for the license can vary, depending on where it's issued. To find the AAA office nearest you, check the local phone directory or contact **AAA national headquarters** (Tel 800/222-4357 or 407/444-4240; www.aaa.com) or the **Canadian Automobile Association** (Tel 613/247-0117). Remember that an International Driver's License is valid only if physically accompanied by your original driver's license and only if signed on the back. The **Automobile Club d'Italia (ACI),** Via Marsala 8, 00185 Roma (Tel 06/49-98-23-89), is open Monday to Friday 8am to 2pm. The ACI's 24-hour **Information and Assistance Center (CAT)** is at Via Magenta 5, 00185 Roma (Tel 06-4477). Both offices are near the main rail station (Stazione Termini).

CAR RENTALS Many of the most charming landscapes in Italy lie away from the main cities, far away from the train stations. For that, and for sheer convenience and freedom, renting a car is usually the best way to explore the country. But you have to be a pretty aggressive and alert driver who won't be fazed by super-high speeds on the autostrada or by narrow streets in the cities and towns. Italian drivers have truly earned their reputation as bad but daring.

However, the legalities and contractual obligations of renting a car in Italy (where accident and theft rates are very high) are a little complicated. To rent a car here, a driver must have nerves of steel, a sense of humor, a valid driver's license, and a valid passport and (in most cases) be over 25. Insurance on all vehicles is compulsory, though any reputable rental firm will arrange it in advance before you're even given the keys.

The three major rental companies in Italy are **Avis** (Tel 800/331-2112; www.avis.com), **Budget** (Tel 800/527-0700; www.budgetrentacar.com), and **Hertz** (Tel 800/654-3131; www.hertz.com). U.S.-based companies specializing in European car rentals are **Auto Europe** (Tel 800/223-5555; www.autoeurope.com), **Europe by Car** (Tel 800/223-1516, 800/252-9401 in California, or 212/581-3040 in New York; www.europebycar.com), and **Kemwel** (Tel 800/678-0678; www.kemwel.com).

In some cases, slight discounts are offered to members of the American Automobile Association (AAA) or the American Association of Retired Persons (AARP). Be sure to ask.

Each company offers a collision-damage waiver (CDW) at $15 to $25 per day (depending on the car's value). Some companies include CDWs in the prices they quote; others don't. This extra protection will cover all or part of the repair-related costs if you have an accident. (In some cases, even if you buy the CDW, you'll pay $200 to $300 per accident. Ask questions before you sign.) If you don't have CDW and have an accident, you'll usually pay for all damages, up to the car's replacement cost. Because most newcomers aren't familiar with local driving customs and conditions, we highly recommend you buy the CDW. (But first check your existing auto insurance and also see what's available through your credit cards. Note that credit cards may cover collision but will usually not cover liability.) In addition, because of Italy's rising theft rate, all three of the major U.S.-based companies offer theft and break-in protection policies (Avis and Budget require it). For pickups at most Italian airports, all three companies must impose a 10% government tax. To avoid that charge, consider picking up your car at an inner-city location. There's also an unavoidable 19% government tax, though more and more companies are including this in the rates they quote.

GASOLINE Gasoline (*benzina*) is expensive in Italy. Be prepared for sticker shock every time you fill up even a medium-sized car with (*super benzina*) which has the octane rating appropriate for most of the cars you'll be able to rent. It's priced throughout the country at around 1,900L (95 cents) per liter (about 7,000L/$3.50 per gallon). Gas stations on the autostrade are open 24 hours, but on regular roads gas stations are rarely open on Sunday, many close from noon to 3pm for lunch, and most shut down after 7pm. Make sure the pump registers zero before an attendant starts refilling your tank. A popular scam, particularly in the south, is to fill your tank before resetting the meter, so you pay not only your bill but the charges run up by the previous motorist.

DRIVING RULES The Italian Highway Code follows the Geneva Convention, and Italy uses international road signs. Driving is on the right, passing on the left. Violators of the highway code are fined; serious violations may also be punished by imprisonment. In cities and towns, the speed limit is 50 kilometers per hour (kmph), or 31 miles per hour (mph). For all cars and motor vehicles on main roads and local roads, the limit is 90 kmph, or 56mph For the autostrade (national express highways), the limit is 130 kmph, or 81mph Use the left lane only for passing. If a driver zooms up behind you on the autostrade with his or her lights on, that's your sign to get out of the way! Use of seat belts is compulsory.

ROAD MAPS The best touring maps are published by the **Automobile Club d'Italia (ACI)** and the **Italian Touring Club,** or you can buy the maps of the **Carta Automobilistica d'Italia,** covering Italy in two maps on a scale of 1:800,000 (1cm = 8km). These two maps should fulfill the needs of most motorists.

All maps mentioned above are sold at newsstands and at all major bookstores in Italy, especially those with travel departments. Many travel bookstores in the United States also carry them. If U.S. outlets don't have these maps, they often offer **Michelin's red map of Italy** (no. 988), on a scale of 1:1,000,000 (1cm = 10km).

BREAKDOWNS & ASSISTANCE In case of car breakdown or for any tourist information, foreign motorists can call for help (Tel 116) nationwide. For road information, itineraries, and all sorts of travel assistance, call ACI's information center located near the Automobile Club d'Italia (Tel 06-4477). Both services operate 24 hours.

dining tips

For a quick bite, go to a bar. Although bars in Italy do serve alcohol, they function mainly as cafes. Prices have a split personality: *al banco* is standing at the bar, while *a tavola* means sitting at a table where you'll be waited on and charged two to four times as much. In bars you can find *panini* sandwiches on various rolls and *tramezzini* (giant triangles of white-bread sandwiches with the crusts cut off). These both run 2,000 to 6,000L ($1 to $3) and are traditionally put in a kind of tiny press to flatten and toast them so the crust is crispy and the filling hot and gooey; microwaves have unfortunately invaded and are everywhere, turning panini into something resembling a soggy hot tissue.

Pizza a taglio or *pizza rustica* indicates a place where you can order pizza by the slice—though Florence is infamous for serving some of Italy's worst pizza this way. Florentines fare somewhat better at *pizzerie,* casual sit-down restaurants that cook large, round pizzas with very thin crusts in woodburning ovens. A *tavola calda* (literally "hot table") serves ready-made hot foods you can take away or eat at one of the few small tables often available. The food is usually very good, and you can get away with a full meal at a *tavola calda* for well under 25,000L ($12.50). A *rosticceria* is the same type of place, and you'll see chickens roasting on a spit in the window.

A full-fledged restaurant will go by the name *osteria, trattoria,* or *ristorante.* Once upon a time, these terms meant something—*osterie* were basic places where you could get a plate of spaghetti and a glass of wine; *trattorie* were casual places serving full meals of filling peasant fare; and *ristoranti* were fancier places, with waiters in bow ties, printed menus, wine lists, and hefty prices. Nowadays, fancy restaurants often go by the name of *trattoria* to cash in on the associated charm factor, trendy spots use *osteria* to show they're hip, and simple inexpensive places sometimes tack on *ristorante* to ennoble themselves.

The *pane e coperto* (bread and cover) is a 1,500 to 5,000L ($.75 to $2.50) cover charge that you must pay at most restaurants for the mere privilege of sitting at the table. Most Italians eat a leisurely full meal—appetizer and first and second courses—at lunch and dinner and will expect you to do the same, or at least a first and second course. To request the bill, ask *"Il conto, per favore"* (eel *con* -toh, pore fah-*vohr* -ay). A tip of

15% is usually included in the bill these days, but if you're unsure, ask *"È incluso il servizio?"* (ay een-*cloo*-soh eel sair-*vee*-tsoh?).

You'll find at many restaurants, especially larger ones and in cities, a *menu turistico* (tourist's menu), costing from 15,000 to 50,000L ($7.50 to $25), sometimes called *menu del giorno* menu of the day). This set-price menu usually covers all meal incidentals—including table wine, cover charge, and 15% service charge—along with a first course (*primo*) and second course (*secondo*), but it almost always offers an abbreviated selection of pretty bland dishes: spaghetti in tomato sauce and slices of pork. Sometimes a better choice is a *menu à prezzo fisso* (fixed-price menu). It usually doesn't include wine but sometimes covers the service and *coperto* and often offers a wider selection of better dishes, occasionally house specialties and local foods. Ordering a la carte, however, offers you the best chance for a memorable meal. Even better, forego the menu entirely and put yourself in the capable hands of your waiter.

The *enoteca* wine bar is a growing, popular marriage of a wine bar and an *osteria,* where you can sit and order from a host of local and regional wines by the glass (usually 2,500 to 8,000L/$1.50 to $4.70) while snacking on finger foods (and usually a number of simple first course possibilities) that reflect the region's fare. Relaxed and full of ambience and good wine, these are great spots for light and inexpensive lunches—perfect to educate your palate and recharge your batteries.

fast facts

AMERICAN EXPRESS Offices are found in Rome at Piazza di Spagna 38 (Tel 06/67-641), in Florence on Via Dante Alighieri (Tel 055/50-981), in Venice at San Marco 1471 (Tel 041/520-08-44), and in Milan at Via Brera 3 (Tel 02/7200-36-93). See individual city listings.

BUSINESS HOURS Regular business hours are generally Monday to Friday 9am (sometimes 9:30am) to 1 and 3:30pm (sometimes 4) to 7 or 7:30pm. In July and August, offices may not open in the afternoon until 4:30 or 5pm. Banks are open Monday to Friday 8:30am to 1 or 1:30pm and 2 or 2:30 to 4pm and closed all day Saturday, Sunday, and national holidays. The *riposo* (midafternoon closing) is often observed in Rome, Naples, and most southern cities; however, in Milan and other northern and central cities the custom has been abolished by some merchants. Most shops are closed on Sunday, except for certain tourist-oriented stores that are now permitted to remain open on Sunday during the high season. If you're in Italy in summer and the heat is intense, we suggest that you, too, learn the custom of the *riposo.*

DRUGSTORES At every drugstore *(farmacia)* there's a list of those that are open at night and on Sunday.

ELECTRICITY The electricity in Italy varies considerably. It's usually alternating current (AC), varying from 42 to 50 cycles. The voltage can be anywhere from 115 to 220. It's recommended that any visitor carrying electrical appliances obtain a transformer. Check the exact local current at the hotel where you're staying. Plugs have prongs that are round, not flat; therefore, an adapter plug is also needed.

EMBASSIES/CONSULATES In case of an emergency, embassies have a 24-hour referral service.

The **U.S. Embassy** is in Rome at Via Vittorio Veneto 119A (Tel 06/46-741; Fax 06/488-26-72). **U.S. consulates** are in Florence at Lungarno Amerigo Vespucci 38 (Tel 055/239-82-76; Fax 055/284-088) and in Milan at Via Principe Amedeo 2–10 (Tel 02/29-03-51-41). There's also a consulate in Naples on Piazza della Repubblica 1 (Tel 081/583-81-11). The consulate in Genoa is at Via Dante 2 (Tel 010/58-44-92). The **Canadian Consulate** and passport service is in Rome at Via Zara 30 (Tel 06/445-981). The **Canadian Embassy** in Rome is at Via G. B. de Rossi 27 (Tel 06/445-981; Fax 06/445-98-750).

The **U.K. Embassy** is in Rome at Via XX Settembre 80A (Tel 06/482-54-41; Fax 06/487-33-24). The **U.K. Consulate** in Florence is at Lungarno Corsini 2 (Tel 055/284-133; Fax 055/219-112). The Consulate General in Naples is at Via Francesco Crispi 122 (Tel 081/663-511; Fax 081/761-37-20). In Milan, contact the office at Via San Paolo 7 (Tel 02/723-001).

The **Australian Embassy** is in Rome at Via Alessandria 215 (Tel 06/852-721; Fax 06/852-723-00). The **Australian Consulate** is in Rome at Corso Trieste 25 (Tel 06/852-721).

The **New Zealand Embassy** is in Rome at Via Zara 28 (Tel 06/441-71-71; Fax 06/440-29-84). The **Irish Embassy** in Rome is at Piazza di Campitelli 3 (Tel 06/697-912; Fax 06/679-23-54).

EMERGENCIES Dial **113** for ambulance, police, or fire. In case of a breakdown on an Italian road, dial **116** at the nearest telephone box; the nearest Automobile Club of Italy (ACI) will be notified to come to your aid.

LEGAL AID The consulate of your country is the place to turn for legal aid, though offices can't interfere in the Italian legal process. They can, however, inform you of your rights and provide a list of attorneys. You'll have to pay for the attorney out of your pocket—there's no free legal assistance. If you're arrested for a drug offense, about all the consulate will do is notify a lawyer about your case and perhaps inform your family.

LIQUOR LAWS There's no legal drinking age for buying or ordering alcohol. Wine with meals has been a normal part of family life for hundreds of years in Italy. Children are exposed to wine at an early age, and consumption of alcohol isn't anything out of the ordinary. Alcohol is sold day and night throughout the year, since there's almost no restriction on the sale of wine or liquor in Italy.

MAIL Mail delivery in Italy is notoriously bad. Your family and friends back home may receive your postcards in 1 week, or it might take 2 weeks (sometimes longer). Postcards, aerogrammes, and letters weighing up to 20 grams sent to the United States and Canada cost 1,300L (65 cents), to the United Kingdom and Ireland 800L (40 cents), and to Australia and New Zealand 1,400L (70 cents). You can buy stamps at all post offices and at *tabacchi* (tobacco) stores.

NEWSPAPERS/MAGAZINES In major cities, it's possible to find the *International Herald Tribune* or *USA Today* as well as other English-language newspapers and magazines, including *Time* and *Newsweek,* at hotels and news kiosks. The *Rome Daily American* is published in English.

POLICE Dial **113,** the all-purpose number for police emergency assistance in Italy.

RESTROOMS All airport and rail stations, of course, have rest rooms, often with attendants, who expect to be tipped. Bars, nightclubs, restaurants, cafes, gas stations, and all hotels have facilities as well. Public toilets are also found near many of the major sights. Usually they're designated as *WC* (water closet) or *donne* (women) or *uomini* (men). The most confusing designation is *signori* (gentlemen) and *signore* (ladies), so watch that final *i* and *e!* Many public toilets charge a small fee or employ an attendant who expects a tip, so always keep a few 200L and 500L coins on hand. It's also a good idea to carry some tissues in your pocket or purse—they often come in handy.

SAFETY The most common menace, especially in large cities, particularly Rome, is the plague of pickpockets and roving gangs of Gypsy children who virtually surround you, distract you in all the confusion, and steal your purse or wallet. Never leave valuables in a car and never travel with your car unlocked. A U.S. State Department travel advisory warns that every car (whether parked, stopped at a traffic light, or even moving) can be a potential target for armed robbery.

TAXES As a member of the European Union, Italy imposes a **value-added tax** called **IVA** in Italy) on most goods and services. The tax that most affects visitors is the one imposed on hotel rates, which ranges from 9% in first- and second-class hotels to 19% in deluxe hotels.

   Non-EU (European Union) citizens are entitled to a refund of the IVA if they spend more than 300,000L ($150) at any one store, before tax. To claim your refund, request an invoice from the cashier at the store and take it to the Customs office (*dogana*) at the airport to have it stamped before you leave. *Note:* If you're going to another EU country before flying home, have it stamped at the airport Customs office of the last EU country you'll be in (for example, if you're flying home via Britain, have your Italian invoices stamped in London). Once back home, mail the stamped invoice (keep a photocopy for your records) back to the original vendor within 90 days of the purchase. The vendor will, sooner or later, send you a refund of the tax you paid at the time of your original purchase. Reputable stores view this as a matter of ordinary paperwork and are businesslike about it. Less honorable stores might lose your dossier. It pays to deal with established vendors on large purchases. You can also request that the refund be credited to the credit card with which you made the purchase; this is usually a faster procedure.

Many shops are now part of the **"Tax Free for Tourists"** network (look for the sticker in the window). Stores participating in this network issue a check along with your invoice at the time of purchase. After you have the invoice stamped at Customs, you can redeem the check for cash directly at the Tax Free booth in the airport (in Rome, it's past Customs; in Milan's airports the booth is inside the Duty Free shop) or mail it back in the envelope provided within 60 days.

TELEPHONE A local phone call in Italy costs around 220L (10 cents). Public phones accept coins, precharged phone cards (*scheda* or *carta telefonica*), or both. You can buy a *carta telefonica* at any *tabacchi* (tobacconists; most display a sign with a white *T* on a brown background) in increments of 5,000L ($2.50), 10,000L ($5), and 15,000L ($7.50). To make a call, pick up the receiver and insert 200L or your card (break off the corner first). Most phones have a digital display that'll tell you how much money you've inserted (or how much is left on the card). Dial the number, and don't forget to take the card with you after you hang up.

CALLING ITALY To call Italy from the United States, dial the international prefix, 011; then Italy's country code, 39; then the city code (for example, 06 for Rome and 055 for Florence), which is now built into every number; then the actual phone number.

Note that numbers in Italy range from four to eight digits in length. Even when you're calling within the same city, you must dial that city's area code—including the zero. A Roman calling another Rome number must dial 06 before the local number.

To call from one city code to another, dial the city code, complete with initial zero, then the number. To dial direct internationally, dial 00, then the country code, the area code, and the number. Country codes are as follows: the United States and Canada 1, the United Kingdom 44, Ireland 353, Australia 61, New Zealand 64. Make international calls from a public phone if possible, because hotels almost invariably charge ridiculously inflated rates for direct dial, but bring plenty of *schede* to feed the phone. Calls dialed directly are billed on the basis of the call's duration only. A reduced rate is applied 11pm to 8am on Monday to Saturday and all day Sunday. Direct-dial calls from the United States to Italy are much cheaper, so arrange for whomever to call you at your hotel.

Italy has recently introduced a series of **international phone cards** (*scheda telefonica internazionale*) for calling overseas. They come in increments of 50 (12,500L/$6.25), 100 (25,000L/$12.50), 200 (50,000L/$25), and 400 (100,000L/$50) *unita* (units), and they're usually available at tabacchi and bars. Each *unita* is worth 250L (15 cents) of phone time; it costs 5 *unita* (1,250L/65 cents) per minute to call within Europe or to the United States or Canada and 12 *unita* (3,000L/$1.50) per minute to call Australia or New Zealand. You don't insert this card into the phone; merely dial **1740,** then *2 (star 2), for instructions in English when prompted.

To ring the free **national telephone information** (in Italian) in Italy, dial **12.** International information is available at 176 but costs 1,200L (60 cents) a pop.

To make **collect or calling card calls,** drop in 200L (10 cents) or insert your card, dial one of the numbers below, and an American operator will shortly come on to assist you (as Italy has yet to discover the joys of the Touch-Tone phone, you'll have to wait for the operator to come on). The following calling-card numbers work all over Italy: **AT&T 172-1011, MCI 172-1022, Sprint 172-1877.** To make collect calls to a country besides the United States, dial **170** (free), and practice your Italian counting in order to relay the number to the Italian operator. Tell him or her you want it *a carico del destinatario.*

Don't count on all Italian phones having Touch-Tone service. You may not be able to access your voice mail or answering machine if you call home from Italy.

TIME In terms of standard time zones, Italy is 6 hours ahead of eastern standard time in the United States. Daylight saving time goes into effect in Italy each year from the end of March to the end of September.

TIPPING This custom is practiced with flair in Italy—many people depend on tips for their livelihoods.

In **hotels,** the service charge of 15% to 19% is already added to a bill. In addition, it's customary to tip the chambermaid 1,000L (50 cents) per day; the doorman (for calling a cab) 1,000L (50 cents); and the bellhop or porter 3,000 to 5,000L ($1.50 to $2.50) for carrying your bags to your room. A concierge expects about 15% of his or her bill, as well as tips for extra services performed, which could include help with long-distance calls. In expensive hotels these lire amounts are often doubled.

In **restaurants and cafes,** 15% is usually added to your bill to cover most charges. If you're not sure whether this has been done, ask *"E incluso il servizio?"* (ay een-*cloo-* soh eel sair-*vee-* tsoh?). An additional tip isn't expected, but it's nice to leave the equivalent of an extra couple of dollars if you've been pleased with the service. Checkroom attendants expect 1,500L (75 cents), and washroom attendants should get 500 to 700L (25 cents to 35 cents). Restaurants are required by law to give customers official receipts.

Taxi drivers expect at least 15% of the fare.

WATER Most Italians take mineral water with their meals; however, tap water is safe everywhere, as are public drinking fountains. Unsafe sources will be marked *acqua non potabile.* If tap water comes out cloudy, it's only the calcium or other minerals inherent in a water supply that often comes untreated from fresh springs.

ITALY ONLINE

This is not a comprehensive list, but a discriminating selection to get you started. Recognition is given to sites based on their content value and ease of use. Inclusion here is not paid for—unlike some website rankings, which are based on payment. Finally, remember this is a press-time snapshot of leading websites; some undoubtedly will have evolved, changed, or moved by the time you read this.

TRAVEL-PLANNING WEB SITES

by Lynne Bairstow

WHY BOOK ONLINE?

Online agencies have come a long way over the past few years, now providing tips for finding the best fare, and giving you suggested dates or times to travel that yield the lowest price if your plans are at all flexible. Other sites even allow you to establish the price you're willing to pay, and they check the airlines' willingness to accept it. However, in some cases, these sites may not always yield the best price. Unlike a travel agent, for example, they may not have access to charter flights offered by wholesalers.

Online booking sites aren't the only places to reserve airline tickets—all major airlines have their own websites and often offer incentives (bonus frequent-flyer miles or Net-only discounts, for example) when you buy online or buy an e-ticket.

The best of the travel planning sites are now highly personalized; they store your seating preferences, meal preferences, tentative itineraries, and credit-card information, allowing you to quickly plan trips or check agendas.

In many cases, booking your trip online can be better than working with a travel agent. It gives you the widest variety of choices, control, and the 24-hour convenience of planning your trip when you choose. All you need is some time—and often a little patience—and you're likely to find the fun of online travel research will greatly enhance your trip.

WHO SHOULD BOOK ONLINE?

Online booking is best for travelers who want to know as much as possible about their travel options, for those who have flexibility in their travel dates, and for bargain hunters.

One of the biggest successes in online travel for both passengers and airlines is the offer of last-minute specials, such as American Airlines' weekend deals or other Internet-only fares that must be purchased online. Another advantage is that you can cash in on incentives for booking online, such as rebates or bonus frequent-flyer miles.

Business and other frequent travelers also have found numerous benefits in online booking, as the advances in mobile technology provide them with the ability to check flight status, change plans, or get specific directions from hand-held computing devices, mobile phones, and pagers. Some sites will even e-mail or page a passenger if their flight is delayed.

Online booking is increasingly able to accommodate complex itineraries, even for international travel. The pace of evolution on the Net is rapid, so you'll probably find additional features and advancements by the time you visit these sites. The future holds ever-increasing personalization and customization for online travelers.

TRAVEL-PLANNING & BOOKING SITES

The following sites offer domestic and international flight, hotel, and rental car bookings, plus news, destination information, and deals on cruises and vacation packages. Free (one-time) registration is required for booking.

Expedia. *expedia.com*
Expedia is known as the fastest and, most flexible online travel planner for booking flights, hotels, and rental cars. It offers several ways of obtaining the best possible fares: Flight Price Matcher service allows your preferred airline to match an available fare with a competitor; a comprehensive Fare Compare area shows the differences in fare categories and airlines; and Fare Calendar helps you plan your trip around the best possible fares. Its main limitation is that like many online databases, Expedia focuses on the major airlines and hotel chains, so don't expect to find too many budget airlines or one-of-a-kind B&Bs here.

Personalized features allow you to store your itineraries and receive weekly fare reports on favorite cities. You can also check on the status of flight arrivals and departures, and through MileageMinder, track all of your frequent-flyer accounts.

Expedia also offers packages, cruises, and information on specialized travel (like casino destinations, and adventure, ski, and golf travel). There are also special features for travelers accessing information on mobile devices.

Note: In early 2000, Expedia bought travelscape.com and vacationspot.com, and incorporated these sites into expedia.com.

Travelocity and Preview Travel. *www.travelocity.com; www.preview-travel.com*

Travelocity uses the SABRE system to offer reservations and tickets for more than 400 airlines; you can also reserve and purchase from more than 45,000 hotels and 50 car-rental companies. An exclusive feature of the SABRE system is their Low Fare Search Engine, which automatically searches for the three lowest-priced itineraries based on a traveler's criteria. Last-minute deals and consolidator fares are included in the search. If you book with Travelocity, you can select specific seats for your flights with online seat maps, and also view diagrams of the most popular commercial aircraft. Their hotel finder provides street-level location maps and photos of selected hotels.

Travelocity features an inviting interface for booking trips, though the wealth of graphics involved can make the site somewhat slow to load, and any adjustment in your parameters means you'll need to completely start over.

This site also has some very cool tools. With the Fare Watcher e-mail feature, you can select up to five routes for which you'll receive e-mail notices when the fare changes by $25 or more. If you own an alphanumeric pager with national access that can receive e-mail, Travelocity's Flight Paging can alert you if your flight is delayed. You can also access real-time departure and arrival information on any flight within the SABRE system.

Note to AOL Users: You can book flights, hotels, rental cars and cruises on AOL at keyword: Travel. The booking software is provided by Travelocity/Preview Travel and is similar to the Internet site. Use the AOL "Travelers Advantage" program to earn a 5% rebate on flights, hotel rooms, and car rentals.

TRIP.com. *www.trip.com*

TRIP.com began as a site geared for business travelers, but its innovative features and highly personalized approach have broadened its appeal to leisure travelers as well. It is the leading travel site for those using mobile devices to access Internet travel information.

TRIP.com provides the average and lowest fare for the route requested, in addition to the current available fare. An on-site "newsstand" features breaking news on airfare sales and other travel specials. Among its most popular features are Flight TRACKER and intelliTRIP. Flight TRACKER allows users to track any commercial flight en route to its destination anywhere in the U.S., while accessing real-time FAA-based flight monitoring data. IntelliTRIP allows you to identify the best airline, hotel, and rental-car fares in less than 90 seconds.

In addition, TRIP.com offers e-mail notification of flight delays, plus city resource guides, currency converters, and a weekly e-mail newsletter of fare updates, travel tips, and traveler forums.

Yahoo Travel. *www.travel.yahoo.com*
Yahoo is currently the most popular of the Internet information portals, and its travel site is a comprehensive mix of online booking, daily travel news, and destination information. Their Best Fares area offers what it promises, and provides feedback on refining your search if you have flexibility in travel dates or times. There is also an active section of Message Boards for discussions on travel in general, and to specific destinations.

ONLINE BARGAINS
There's nothing airlines hate more than flying with lots of empty seats. The Net has enabled airlines to offer last-minute bargains to entice travelers to fill those seats. Most of these are announced on Tuesday or Wednesday and are valid for travel the following weekend, but some can be booked weeks or months in advance. You can sign up for weekly e-mail alerts at the airlines' own sites (see the box below listing the airlines' Web addresses) or check sites that compile lists of these bargains, such as Smarter Living or WebFlyer (see below). To make it easier, visit a site that will round up all the deals and send them in one convenient weekly e-mail.

1travel.com. *www.1travel.com*
Here you'll find deals on domestic and international flights and hotels. 1travel.com's Saving Alert compiles last-minute air deals so you don't have to scroll through multiple e-mail alerts. A feature called "Drive a little using low-fare airlines" helps map out strategies for using alternate airports to find lower fares. And Farebeater searches a database that includes published fares, consolidator bargains, and special deals exclusive to 1travel.com. *Note:* The travel agencies listed by 1travel.com have paid for placement.

Bid for Travel. *www.bidfortravel.com*
Bid for Travel is another of the travel auction sites, similar to Priceline (see below), which are growing in popularity. In addition to airfares, Internet users can place a bid for vacation packages and hotels.

Cheap Tickets. *www.cheaptickets.com*
Cheap Tickets has exclusive deals that aren't available through more mainstream channels. One caveat about the Cheap Tickets site is that it will offer fare quotes for a route, and later show this fare is not valid for your

ITALY ONLINE 895

dates of travel—most other websites, such as Expedia, consider your dates of travel before showing what fares are available. Despite its problems, Cheap Tickets can be worth the effort because its fares can be lower than those offered by its competitors.

LastMinuteTravel.com. *www.lastminutetravel.com*
Suppliers with excess inventory come to this online agency to distribute unsold airline seats, hotel rooms, cruises, and vacation packages. It's got great deals, but an excess of advertisements and slow-loading graphics.

Moment's Notice. *www.moments-notice.com*
As the name suggests, Moment's Notice specializes in last-minute vacation deals. You can browse for free, but if you want to purchase a trip you have to join Moment's Notice, which costs $25.

SkyAuction.com. *www.skyauction.com*
An auction site with categories for airfare, travel deals, hotels, and much more.

Smarter Living. *www.smarterliving.com*
Best known for its e-mail dispatch of weekend deals on 20 airlines, Smarter Living also keeps you posted about last-minute bargains.

Travelzoo.com. *www.travelzoo.com*
At this Internet portal, more than 150 travel companies post special deals. It features a Top 20 list of the best deals on the site, selected by its editorial staff each Wednesday night. This list is also available via an e-mailing list, free to those who sign up.

WebFlyer. *www.webflyer.com*
WebFlyer is a comprehensive online resource for frequent flyers and also has an excellent listing of last-minute air deals. Click on "Deal Watch" for a round-up of weekend deals on flights, hotels, and rental cars from domestic and international suppliers.

ONLINE TRAVELER'S TOOLBOX
Exchange Rates. *www.x-rates.com*
See what your dollar, or pound, is worth in Italian lire.

Foreign Languages for Travelers. *www.travlang.com*
Learn basic terms in more than 70 languages and click on any underlined phrase to hear what it sounds like. (*Note:* Free audio software and speakers are required.) They also offer hotel and airline finders with excellent prices and a simple system to get the listings you are looking for.

InnSite. *www.innsite.com*
Listings for inns and B&Bs around the globe (even a "floating hotel"—a six-cabin barge—moored on Paris's Quai Henri IV.) Find an inn at

your destination, have a look at images of the rooms, check prices and availability, and then send e-mail to the innkeeper if you have further questions. This is an extensive directory of bed and breakfast inns, but only includes listings if the proprietor submitted one. (*Note:* It's free to get an inn listed.) The descriptions are written by the innkeepers, and many link to the inns' own websites.

ismap.com. *www.ismap.com*
Locate almost any address in Italy with this neat interactive map that identifies nearby points of interest with icons that link to sites with more information.

Planning a shopping spree and wondering what you're allowed to bring home? Check the latest regulations at these thorough sites.

U.S. Customs Service Traveler Information. *www.customs.ustreas.gov/travel/index.htm.*
HM Customs & Excise Passenger Enquiries. *www.open.gov.uk.*
Canada Customs and Revenue Agency. *www.ccra-adrc.gc.ca.*
Australian Customs. *www.dfat.gov.au*
New Zealand Customs Service. *www.customs.govt.nz*

Visa ATM Locator. *www.visa.com/pd/atm/*
MasterCard ATM Locator. *www.mastercard.com/atm*
Find ATMs in hundreds of cities around the world. Both include maps for some locations and both list airport ATM locations, some with maps.
The Weather Channel. *www.weather.com*
Weather forecasts for cities around the world.

Top Web Sites for Italy

Updated by Matthew Garcia

Many of the following sites give users the option of using English or Italian. Although some will initially come up in Italian, you can follow the icons for English versions. If the location of the English version isn't evident at first, scroll down to find an American or British flag.

The major problem with websites that cover Italy (and many other destinations) is updating—or the lack thereof. Many people think that websites must be more up-to-date than guidebooks, but so far that's definitely not true. One way to check on how stale the information might be is to use a search engine that tells you when each site was updated—I like AltaVista for this, but there are others. If you run across a description or listing of an establishment or event that you know will make or break your trip, *always* double-check that information; call ahead before you block out time for an activity or destination that might turn out to be closed.

COUNTRY GUIDES
Dolce Vita. *www.dolcevita.com*
The self-proclaimed "insider's guide to Italy" is all about style—as it pertains to fashion, cuisine, design, and travel. A scrolling bulletin at the site shares factoids, survey results, and other bits of Italian news,

and the events section brims with major performing arts, music, and museum happenings. While clearly driven by consumers and advertisers, Dolce Vita is a good place to stay current on trends in modern Italian culture.

In Italy Online. *www.initaly.com*
This extensive site helps you find all sorts of accommodations (including country villas, historic homes, and gay-friendly hotels) and includes tips on shopping, dining, driving, and viewing works of art. In Italy Online has an information-packed section dedicated to each region of Italy, plus a section on books and movies to help enjoy the Italian experience at home. Join the mailing list for monthly updates.

Italian Tourist Web Guide. *www.itwg.com*
Need help planning your travel schedule? Be sure to check out the Italian Tourist Web Guide, which each month recommends new itineraries for art lovers, nature buffs, wine enthusiasts, and other Italiophiles. The site features a searchable directory of accommodations, transportation tips, and city-specific lists of restaurants and attractions.

Italy Hotel Reservation. *www.italyhotel.com*
With close to 10,000 listings solely for Italy, this functional site is an ideal place to research and reserve lodgings.

Italy in a Flash. *www.italyflash.com*
This site offers hotel information, railway and airline schedules, the latest exchange rates, weather, and current news.

ItalyTour.com. www.italytour.com
Search ItalyTour.com for all things Italian. This vast directory covers arts, culture, business, tours, entertainment, restaurants, lodging, real estate, news and media, shopping, sports, transportation, and major Italian cities. It's not the most excitingly designed site, but it does include photo collections and videos in the Panorama section.

Travel Europe: Italy. www.traveleurope.it
Take a look at the travel packages highlighted in this guide, or do some travel planning of your own by clicking on one of the many cities and regions on the map of Italy at the top. Although there's some discussion of art and history, most of the site is taken up by hotel information. You can also book online if you wish.

Travel.org: Italy. *www.travel.org/italy.html*
Stroll region-by-region through Italy with help from this directory, or cut to the chase by getting a rundown on food, lodging, nightlife, currency, and language. This site links to countless Italy resources, both in English and in Italian.

Wandering Italy. www.wandering.com
Amid lyrical travel stories of language mishaps and cobblestone streets, penned by an international brood of tourists, Wandering Italy takes you on virtual reality tours of spots such as the village of Marciana Marina and the Piazza San Marco. This site's slide shows reveal views of stunning scenery and artwork from more than 25 of Italy's cities.

THE AMALFI COAST & CAPRI

Amalfi and the Amalfi Coast. *www.starnet.it/italy/incostam.htm*
While promoting the lemon liqueur and stained glass produced on the Amalfi Coast, this site provides a map and a photo-illustrated historical overview of each of the region's little cities and villages. Hotel and restaurant links lead to simple ads. If you're inclined to learn something on your vacation, check out the cooking school.

Capri Online. *www.caprionline.com* or *www.capri.it*
This site glistens with enticing photographs of beaches and beautiful scenery, and descriptions of seafood dishes and luxury lodgings. A profile showcases a local artist and his miniature ceramic replica of Capri. On the practical side, you can look through the directory of hotels, ranked by stars, or download free travel brochures and maps.

APULIA

Welcome to Apulia. *www.inmedia.it/Puglia/eng*
Make reservations online to stay in a three- to five-star hotel in the heel of Italy's boot. Take a virtual tour through the castles of the Adriatic Valley, the Trulli district, or view the nature and archeology of the Upper Murgia.

BOLOGNA

Gambero Rosso: Bologna. *www.gamberorosso.it/e/bologna/bologna.asp*
Get the inside scoop on Bolognan cuisine from Gambero Rosso's decidedly particular critics, who steer you away from the tourist traps and toward eateries that capture Bologna's culinary history. The site's writers are equally selective in their hotel recommendations.

Information About Bologna. *archiginnasio.dsnet.it/engl—bologna.html*
Although this site doesn't score a lot of points for design, it does provide the travel staples: hotel and restaurant reviews, museum hours and prices, bookstore and theater directories, and, whenever possible, links. A bonus: essays and poems by an American student smitten with Bologna. A drawback: lack of recent updates make it unreliable for current event planning.

FLORENCE

Firenze by Net. *www.mega.it/florence*

Firenze Net *english.firenze.net*
Both of these Italy-based websites provide English translations and good general information on Florence.

Informacitta. *www.informacitta.net*
This site is an excellent little guide to each month's events, exhibits, concerts, and theater.

Florence Information. *www.firenze.turismo.toscana.it*
This is the official tourist office site for Florence; was originally only in Italian but an English version is in the works, so check it out to see if the English version is up and running. There's a wealth of up-to-date information (events, museums, practical details) on Florence and Tuscany, including a searchable "hotels" form that allows you to specify amenities, categories, and the like; the site responds by spitting out a list of where you can get contact info and see current room rates.

Florence Online. *www.fionline.it/wel—eng.html*
Use the tourism section of this Florence site to book a hotel room, consult a map, or plan a day of sightseeing followed by a night on the town.

Florence and The Divine Comedy. *english.firenze.net/dante*
See Florence through the eyes of the immortal poet, Dante. While a narrator reads passages written by the famous author, you can see photos of key Florence spots mentioned in *The Divine Comedy* and learn about the history of each place. You can also find a helpful directory of Florentine museums, monuments, and tour guides.

Florence by Net. *www.florence.ala.it*
Most of the attractions listed within this site are ranked—hotels by luxury, restaurants by price, and museums by importance. You'll also find links to Florence's concert listings, weather reports, business information, and Internet facilities.

Your Way to Florence. *www.arca.net/florence.htm*
If you're going to Florence to see the magnificent works of art housed there, first take a peek at this site, a combined tour guide and Florence art history lesson that includes a glossary of art terms such as "altar frontal" (no, this doesn't refer to Michelangelo's *David*). The site provides hotel reviews and city news as well.

THE ITALIAN RIVIERA
Liguria. *www.emmeti.it/welcome/liguria/index.uk.html*
This guide to the the Italian Riviera encompasses Genova, Savona, Imperia, and La Spezia. The hotel sections include information on room rates, amenities, and locations and offer online booking.

MILAN
Milan International Home Page. *www.milanoin.it/index—eng.asp*
After taking an online tour through the museums, monuments, parks, libraries, exhibits, shops, and fairs of Italy's fashion capital, search for a restaurant by ethnicity or for a hotel by neighborhood. Although this

site's seemingly random mix of Italian and English is a bit confusing, and can make navigating difficult, the sheer volume of information, combined with helpful icons, makes it a worthwhile stop.

Milan City Center Map and Guide. *www.citylightsnews.com/ztmimp1.htm*
A big map shows the location of each of Milan's highlights as well as hotels by Brera (a sponsor). Click on the name of an attraction for a description and photo. Visit the links page for guides to arts, entertainment, government, schools, sports, business, news, and, of course, shopping.

Milan Malpensa Airport. *www.airwise.com/airports/europe/MXP/*
It would be hard to get lost in the airport in Milan after visiting this site, which provides an extensive overview of the terminal along with information on airlines, ground transportation to and from Malpensa, car rentals, parking, and airport hotels.

NAPLES
Naples in Virtual Reality. *ww2.webcomp.com/virtuale/us/napoli/movie.htm*
This site will give you a good idea of what you can see in Napoli. The virtual reality tour shows the Piazza del Plebiscito, Il Maschio Angioino, the Galleria Umberto, and other great artifacts. It's almost like being there.

POMPEII
Pompeii Forum Project. *pompeii.virginia.edu*
The University of Virginia and the National Endowment for the Humanities explore urban history and design in an unearthed Pompeii. Their site is full of cool photos, educational information, and even some virtual reality segments and video clips.

ROME
Nerone: The Insider's Guide. *www.nerone.cc*
Get tips on everything from museums to Roman public toilets. Check the site's events menu to see which arts and entertainment highlights will coincide with your visit to the Eternal City. Sort through archives of the Nerone newspaper as well.

Roma Online. *www.romaonline.net/eng*
This online tourist guide has pictures, QuickTime video, and virtual renderings of Roman monuments and sights around the city. There is also information on getting around, enjoying the city's parks, sports, and shopping.

Rome Guide. *www.romeguide.it*
Click on the British flag for the English version of this site, which is so chockful of information you'll need a pickax to excavate it. Each click of

the mouse reveals multiple new layers of tourist information, extending beyond the typical hotel/restaurant listings and into ecotourism opportunities, walking tours, nightclubs, airfares, and other specifics. One unique feature is the ability to search for upcoming cultural events by venue.

Time Out Rome. *www.timeout.co.uk*
Download the latest issue of *Time Out Rome,* which offers a great up-to-date listing of events and exhibits.

Traveling with Ed and Julie. *www.twenj.com/romevisit.htm*
Seasoned travelers advise first-timers on what to do when in Rome. Musing romantically about the ancient city, the pair will guide you to hotels, restaurants, excursions, quiet spots, tips on seeing Rome with kids, and, of course, attractions such as the Vatican and the Colosseum.

Vatican: The Holy See. *www.vatican.va*
The official site of the Vatican offers audio and video programs in multiple languages to accompany profiles of all the popes, the Vatican museum, the Roman Curia, and the Vatican library.

SICILY
Sicily For Tourists. *www.sicily.infcom.it*
Follow this site's ready-made itineraries to see the many treasures lurking in Palermo in the form of parks, cathedrals, great works of art, and nightlife. This site also has information about Sicilian culture, events, transportation, lodging, public services, and businesses. Note that the events calendar does not seem to be regularly updated.

TURIN
Tourism in Turin. *www.comune.torino.it/turismo*
Thumb through this vast Italian-language guide for the history of Turin and its symbols, cuisine, monuments, leisure activities, and academic centers. For a sample of the city's visual pleasures, check out the online photo gallery or virtual postcard rack.

TUSCANY
See also "Florence," above.

Chianti Doc Marketplace. *www.chianti-doc.com*
Taste a bit of Chianti's flavor at this site before traveling to the famous wine region. Take a quick online course in grape producing and Chianti Classico wines. You can also peek at Alitalia flight schedules and get information on booking vacation rentals in Chianti or Sienna.

Farm Holidays in Tuscany. *www.toscana.agriturismo.net*
Book your accommodations at this site if you'd like to stay on a Tuscan farm
or at a rural bed-and-breakfast after traipsing through Tuscany countryside
wineries. To help win you over, the site presents a photo-filled virtual tour of
the province's cities, villages, and lovely landscapes.

Florence Bike Pages. *www.abeline.it/fbp.htm*
If you want to bike around Tuscany on your own, head for this helpful
site. You'll find bike maps of Florence and Tuscany, instructions on how
to bike solo, and information on bike supplements for the trains (many
trains have a cargo car for bikes; on train schedules look for a bike icon
that designates these trains).

The Heart of Tuscany. *www.nautilus-mp.com/tuscany/indexing.htm*
For each of five major art towns in Tuscany, this site provides a historical
overview, photographs, maps, and a shopping guide. You'll find information on a range of accommodations, including historic residences,
farmhouses, vacation rentals, and hotels, some of which take reservations online. More useful for its overview of the area than for updated
information.

Know it All: Know Tuscany. *www.knowital.com*
As the name suggests, this travel guide does seem to know it all about
lodging, dining, and Tuscan wines. Set up everything from an agri-tourism
stay at a Lucca vineyard estate to a romp through the tourist sites of Pisa.
You'll even get some useful facts about weather, mosquitoes, and computer modems.

Pisa Online. *www.pisaonline.it/e-default.htm*
Once you've seen the tower, stick around to check out Pisa's art galleries,
restaurants, shops, pubs, discos, golf courses, and hotels—with guidance
from this site.

Tourism in Tuscany. *www.turismo.toscana.it*
This is the official site for Tuscany, with an English-language version
available. There are suggested itineraries, plus information on accommodations, dining, spas, festivals, and the artistic heritage of the region.
You'll also find links to every provincial tourist office site.

THE VENETO & THE DOLOMITES
Dolomiti Web. *www.dolomiti.it/eng*
This site is organized seasonally so that you can check out winter sports,
spring fairs, and fall harvesting. Look through electronic postcards of the
mountainous terrain. Make hotel reservations online.

Verona: City of Art and History. *www.intesys.it/tour/eng/verona.html*
Don't let the Montagues and Capulets bog you down; there's a lot more
to do in Verona than reenact the scene at Juliet's balcony. For suggestions,
peruse some itineraries here, where tours are based on historic themes

such as Roman Verona, Verona as a city state, Austrian Verona, and the city's churches and monasteries. And if you must see the balcony, there's a Shakespeare tour as well.

VENICE
Carnival of Venice. *www.carnivalofvenice.com/uk*
Experience today's carnival celebration of the city of gondolas or explore past carnivals, dating back to the year 1268, in the mask-filled historic section of this online guide to one of Italy's most grand annual events. Travelers also can find information about transportation, city services, and other Venice basics.

Venice World. *www.veniceworld.com*
Modeled after a standard American web directory, this site lists links to Venice's accommodations, centers for the arts, nightclubs, restaurants, sporting events, travel agencies, Internet service providers, transportation, schools, newspapers, and so forth.

Venezia Net. *www.doge.it*
Learn about the history of one of Europe's most heavily trodden tourist spots. Take virtual tours of the Doges' Palace and the Piazza San Marco. Skim through directories of hotels and travel agencies. Find out when you can catch the Carnival celebration or the Venice Film Festival.

GETTING AROUND
CIT Tours *www.cittours.com*
This tour company specializes in trips to Italy. Even if you're not interested in one of their group tours, you can buy all kinds of European rail passes online on this site, from Eurailpasses to passes that are specifically for the Italian railway system. The Italian Flexirail Card, in particular, entitles holders to a predetermined number of days on any rail line of Italy within a certain period. It must be purchased before you arrive in Italy, making CIT Tours a valuable contact.

Rail Europe. *www.raileurope.com*
Rail Europe lets you buy Eurail, Europass, and Brit Rail railroad passes online, as well as rail and drive packages and point-to-point travel in 35 European countries. Even if you don't want a rail pass, the site offers invaluable first- and second-class fare and schedule information for the most popular European rail routes.

Rail Pass Express. *www.eurail.com*
A good source for Eurail pass information, purchasing, and deals.

Autostrade S.P.A. *www.autostrade.it*
This site is a valuable resource for anyone brave enough to drive in Italy. The interactive Motorway Map helps you plan your route and prepare

for the toll booths you'll encounter along the way. The site also offers traffic forecasts, safety tips, and lists of service stations.

Subway Navigator. *http://metro.ratp.fr:10001/bin/cities/english*
An amazing site with detailed subway route maps for Milan and Palermo and dozens of other cities around the world. Select a city and enter your departure and arrival points. Subway Navigator maps out your route and tells you how long the trip should take. It will even show your route on a subway map.

hostel appendix

The source for all hostel listings and hostel-resource information below was the website for the Italian Youth Hostel Association, a member of the International Youth Hostel Federation: ***www.hostels-aig.org.*** The International Youth Hostel Association boasts 5,000,000 members, providing access to 5,000 youth hostels throughout the world. If you don't have a membership, you'll need to purchase one upon arrival at a particualr hostel or at the **AIG Head Office** *(Via Cavour 44, 00184 Rome, Tel 06/487-11-52, Fax 06/488-04-92)*. It works this way: you buy six stamps that are attached to your membership card. They cost 5,000L each, and each stamp allows you to spend one night in a hostel at the normal nightly rate. As soon as you use all six stamps on your card, you've proven yourself and are considered to be a full Hostelling International member. Members enjoy the ability to find affordable lodging at any affiliated hostel in the world, as well as a variety of special discounts and services. These often include reduced fares on rail travel, car rental, entrance to select museums and other cultural sites, and many other benefits.

HOW TO BOOK A HOSTEL

Once you have a membership, you can book a room at any of the Italian Youth Hostels, and pay with your credit card or with Western Union, on the phone or over the internet. Go to the Italian Hostel Association website, ***www.hostels-aig.org,*** and click on the map to choose your Youth Hostel. Each one has a form that will permit you to ask for availability during the period that you need lodging.

You can also book through the **IBN (International Booking Network),** a computerized and centralized booking service in IYHF's head office in London. This service will link you to any hostel in the world that has joined this network. This booking service, which is currently available at seven locations in Italy, costs the equivalent of $2U.S. and allows you to book up to nine guests up to six months in advance of your arrival. The IBN network covers major destinations in Europe, Australia, New Zealand, Canada, USA, and Japan.

ABETONE
Tuscany
Renzo Bizzarri
S.S. dell'Abetone
51021 ABETONE PT
Tel: 0573/60-117
Fax: 0573/606-656
E-mail: baicchienrico@freedomland.it
Open: Dec 1-Mar 30, June 15-Sep 30
Beds: 64

ACQUASPARTA
Umbria
San Francesco Youth Hostel
Via di San Francesco 1
05021 ACQUASPARTA TR
Tel: 0744/943-167
Fax: 0744/944-168
E-mail: info@ostellosanfrancesco.it
Open: all year
Desk Hours: 7-10am/3:30-11:30pm
Beds: 120

AGEROLA
Campania
Beata Solitudo Youth Hostel
Piazza G.Avitabile
80051 AGEROLA S.L. NA
Tel: 081/802-50-48
Fax: 081/802-50-48
E-mail: paolog@ptn.pandora.it
Open: Jan 1- Sep 14, Oct 1- Dec 31
Desk Hours: 7-10am/3:30-11:30pm
Beds: 16

AGROPOLI-PAESTUM
Campania
La Lanterna Youth Hostel
Via Lanterna 8, Loc. San Marco
84043 AGROPOLI SA
Tel: 0974/838-364
Fax: 0974/838-364
E-mail: lanterna@cilento.it
Open: Mar 15-Oct 30

Desk Hours: 7-10am/3:30-11:30pm
Beds: 56

ALESSANDRIA
Piemonte
Santa Maria di Castello
Piazza Santa Maria di Castello 14
15100 ALESSANDRIA AL
Tel: 0131/288-187
Fax: 0131/220-280
E-mail: serenity.2000@libero.it
Open: all year
Desk Hours: 7-10am/3:30-11:30pm
Beds: 70

ALGHERO
Sardinia
Ostello dei Giuliani
Via Zara 1
07040 ALGHERO Fertilia SS
Tel: 079/930-353-930015
Fax: 079/930-353
E-mail: ostellodeigiuliani@tiscalinet.it
Open: all year
Desk Hours: 7-10am/noon-
  2:30pm/3:30pm-midnight
Beds: 50

AMELIA
Umbria
Giustiniani Youth Hostel
Piazza Matteotti
05022 AMELIA TR
Tel: 0744/978-673
Fax: 0744/983-025
E-mail: n/a
Open: Mar 1-Dec 31
Desk Hours: 7-10:30am/3:30-midnight
Beds: 60

ANCONA
Marche
Ancona Youth Hostel
Via Lamaticci

60126 Ancona AN
Tel: 071/42-257
Fax: 071/42-257
E-mail: n/a
Open: all year
Desk Hours: 7am-noon/3:30-midnight
Beds: 56

ARGENTA-CAMPOTTO
Emilia Romagna
Ostello di Campotto Y.H.
Via Cardinala 27
44010 CAMPOTTO DI ARGENTA FE
Tel: 0532/808-035
Fax: 0532/808-035
E-mail: n/a
Open: Mar 1- Oct 31
Desk Hours: 7-10am/5-11:30pm
Beds: 52

ARPY-MORGEX
Valle d'Aosta
Valdigne- M. Blanc Y.H.
Loc.tà Arpy
11017 MORGEX AO
Tel: 0165/841-684 (010/247-18-26)
Fax: 0165/841-684 (010/246-93-61)
E-mail: yh.arpy@tin.it
Open: Jan 1-Apr 8, June 17-Sep 2
Desk Hours: 7-10am/3:30-11:30pm
Beds: 130 summer, 70 winter

ASCOLI PICENO
Marche
Ostello de' Longobardi Youth Hostel
Via Soderini 26
Palazzetto Longobardo
63100 ASCOLI PICENO AP
Tel: 0736/261-862
Fax: 0736/259-191
E-mail: n/a
Open: all year
Desk Hours: 7am-midnight
Beds: 30

ASIAGO
Veneto
Ekar
Via Ekar 2/5
36012 ASIAGO VI
Tel: 0424/455-138
Fax: 0424/455-138

E-mail: ostelloechar@tiscalinet.it
Open: Jan 1-Feb 28, May 20 -Sep 10,
   Dec 1-Dec 31
Desk Hours: 7am-11pm
Beds: 130

ASSISI
Umbria
Ostello della Pace Youth Hostel
Via di Valecchie 177
06081 ASSISI PG
Tel: 075/816-767
Fax: 075/816-767
E-mail: n/a
Open: Jan 1-Sep 1, Mar 1-Dec 31
Desk Hours: 7-10am/3:30-11:30pm
Beds: 66

BAGNACAVALLO
Emilia-Romagna
*Antico Convento di San Francesco Youth
Hostel*
Via Cadorna
48012 BAGNACAVALLO RA
Tel: 0545/60-622
Fax: 0545/937-228
E-mail: info@ostellosanfrancesco.com
Open: all year
Desk Hours: 7-10am/3pm-midnight
Beds: 90

BARI
Puglia
Ostello del Sole Youth Hostel
S.S. 16 Adriatica 78
70126 BARI BA
Tel: 080/549-11-75
Fax: 080/549-12-02
E-mail: n/a
Desk Hours: 7-10:30am/
   3:30-11:30pm
Beds: 30

BERGAMO
Lombardia
Nuovo Ostello di Bergamo Youth Hostel
Via Galileo Ferraris 1
24123 BERGAMO BG
Tel: 035/361-724 — 343-038
Fax: 035/361-724
E-mail: hostelbg@spm.it
Open: all year

Desk Hours: 7am-midnight
Beds: 84

BERGOLO
Piemonte
Le Langhe Youth Hostel
Via Roma 22
12070 BERGOLO CN
Tel: 0173/87-222
Fax: 0173/87-222
E-mail: n/a
Open: Mar 1-Oct 31
Desk Hours: 7-10am/
    3:30-11:30pm
Beds: 34

BIONAZ
Valle d'Aosta
Ostello per la Gioventù
La Batise
Loc.tà Capoluogo
11010 BIONAZ AO
Tel: 0165/730-105
Fax: 0165/730-214
Open all year
Desk Hours: 7-10am/3-11:30pm
Beds: 38

BOLOGNA
Emilia-Romagna
Due Torri — San Sisto 2 Youth Hostel
Via Viadagola 5, San Sisto
40127 BOLOGNA BO
Tel: 051/501-810
Fax: 051/501-810
E-mail: n/a
Open: Jan 20-Dec 19
Desk Hours: 7am-noon/3:30pm-mid-
    night
Beds: 75

BOLOGNA
Emilia-Romagna
San Sisto Youth Hostel
Via Viadagola 14
40127 BOLOGNA BO
Tel: 051/501-810
Fax: 051/501-810
E-mail: n/a
Open: all year
Desk Hours: 7-10am/3:30-11:30pm

BOMBA
Abruzzo
Isola Verde Youth Hostel
Via Lago
66042 BOMBA CH
Tel: 0872/860-475 — 860-568
Fax: 0872/860-450
E-mail: isolverd@tin.it
Open: all year
Desk Hours: 7am-midnight
Beds: 28

BOSA MARINA
Sardinia
Malaspina Youth Hostel
Via Sardegna 1
08013 BOSA MARINA NU
Tel: 0785/375-009
Fax: 0785/375-009
E-mail: n/a
Open: all year
Desk Hours: 7am-1pm/3:30pm-midnight
Beds: 48

CASTEL DEL GIUDICE
Molise
La Castellana Youth Hostel
Via Fontana Vecchia 1
86080 CASTEL DEL GIUDICE IS
Tel: 0865/946-222
Fax: 0865/946-222
E-mail: n/a
Open: all year
Desk Hours: 7am-midnight
Beds: 60

CASTELFIORENTINO
Tuscany
Castelfiorentino Y.H.
Viale Roosvelt 26
50051 CASTELFIORENTINO FI
Tel: 0571/64-002
Fax: 0571/64-002
Open: all year
Desk Hours: 7-10am/3:30-11:30
Beds: 84

CASTELLANETA MARINA
Puglia
Villini Paradiso Youth Hostel
Via Zond 2

74010 Castellaneta Marina TA
Tel: 099/843-32-00
Fax: 099/843-00-46
E-mail: n/a
Open: all year, reservation required Aug 1-31
Desk Hours: 24 hours
Beds: 100

CASTELSARDO
Sardinia
Golfo dell'Asinara Youth Hostel
Via Sardegna 1
Località Lu-Bagnu
07031 CASTELSARDO SS
Tel: 079/474-031 — 587-008
Fax: 079/587-142
E-mail: ostello.asinara@tiscalinet.it,
Open: May 1-Sep 30, Easter; reserved groups all year round
Desk Hours: 7am-midnight
Beds: 110

CASTROREALE
Sicilia
Ostello delle Aquile Y.H.
Salita Federico II d'Aragona
98053 CASTROREALE ME
Tel: 090/974-63-98
Fax: 090/974-64-46
E-mail: n/a
Open: Apr 1-Oct 31
Desk Hours: 7-10am/3:30-11:30pm
Beds: 24

CAVA DE' TIRRENI
Campania
Borgo Scacciaventi Y.H.
Piazza San Francesco 1
84013 CAVA DE' TIRRENI SA
Tel: 089/466-631
Fax: 089/466-631
E-mail: n/a
Open: Apr 1- Sep 30
Desk Hours: 7-10am/3:30pm-12:30am
Beds: 140

CHIAVARI CAMPING
Liguria
Camping Al mare
Via Preli 30

16043 CHIAVARI GE
Tel: 0185/304-633
Fax: 0185/304-633
E-mail: n/a
Open: Apr 1- Oct 31

COLLEONGO
Abruzzo
Collelongo Youth Hostel
Via Nasaline
67050 COLLELONGO AQ
Tel: Collelongo Municipality 0863/ 948-113
Fax: 0863/948-317
E-mail: n/a
Desk Hours: 7-10am/3:30-11:30pm
Beds: 55

COLLESCIPOLI TERNI
Umbria
Ostello dei Garibaldini Youth Hostel
Corso dei Garibaldini 61,
05033 COLLESCIPOLI TR
Tel: 0744/800-467
Fax: 0744/800-467
E-mail: n/a
Open: all year
Desk Hours: 7-10am/3:30-11:30pm
Beds: 37

COMO
Lombardia
Villa Olmo Youth Hostel
Via Bellinzona 2
22100 COMO CO
Tel: 031/573-800
Fax: 031/573-800
E-mail: ostellocomo@tin.it
Open: Mar 1-Nov 30
Desk Hours: 7-10am/3:30-11:30pm
Beds: 76

CORREGGIO
Emilia Romagna
La Rocchetta Youth Hostel
Corso Cavour 19
42015 CORREGGIO RE
Tel: 0522/632-361
Fax: 0522/632-361
E-mail: ostello-correggio@hotmail.com
Open: Apr 1-Oct 31

Desk Hours: 7-10am/3:30-11:30pm
Beds: 25

CORTONA
Tuscany
San Marco Youth Hostel
Via Maffei 57
52044 CORTONA AR
Tel: 0575/601-392 — 601-765
Fax: 0575/601-392
E-mail: ostellocortona@libero.it
Open: Mar 15-Oct 15
Desk Hours: 7-10am/3:30-midnight
Beds: 80

DOMASO
Lombardia
La Vespa Youth Hostel
Via Case Sparse 12
22013 DOMASO CO
Tel: 0344/97-449
Fax: 0344/97-575
E-mail: ostellolavespa@lombardiacom.it
Open: Apr 1-Oct 31
Desk Hours: 8am-midnight
Beds: 25

ERICE-TRAPANI
Sicily
G. Amodeo Youth Hostel
Strada Provinciale Trapani-Erice
RAGANZILI-ERICE TP
Tel: 0923/552-964
Fax: 0923/552-964
E-mail: scral.erice-touring@libero.it
Open: Oct 15- Mar 31, Apr 1- Oct 14
Desk Hours: 7:30-10am/3:30-11pm
Beds: 52

ETROUBLES
Valle d'Aosta
Dortoir Echevennoz
Loc.tà Echevennoz
11014 ETROUBLES AO
Tel: 0165/78-225
Fax: n/a
E-mail: n/a
Open: for reserved groups all
 year round
Desk Hours: 7am-11:30pm
Beds: 11

FERRARA
Emilia-Romagna
Estense Youth Hostel
Corso Biagio Rossetti 24
44100 FERRARA FE
Tel: 0532/204-227
Fax: 0522/204-227
E-mail: n/a
Open: all year
Desk Hours: 7-9am/3:30-11:30pm
Beds: 84

FINALE LIGURE
Liguria
Castello Vuillermin Youth Hostel
Via G. Caviglia 46
17024 FINALE MARINA SV
Tel: 019/690-515 — 0347/241-46-83
Fax: 019/690-515
E-mail: hostelfinaleligure@libero.it
Open: Mar 15-Oct 15
Desk Hours: 7-10am/3:30-11:30pm
Beds: 69

FLORENCE
Tuscany
Europa-Villa Camerata Youth Hostel
Viale Augusto Righi 2/4
50137 FIRENZE FI
Tel: 055/601-451
Fax: 055/610-300
Open: all year
Desk Hours: 7am-midnight
Beds: 322

FLORENCE
Tuscany
Ostello del Carmine Youth Hostel
Via del Leone 35
50124 FIRENZE FI
Tel: 055/291-974
Fax: 055/610-300
Open: Mar 15-Oct 31
Desk Hours: 7am-midnight

FLORENCE CAMPING
Tuscany
Camping Villa Camerata
Viale Augusto Righi 2/4
50137 FIRENZE FI
Tel: 055/601-451

Fax: 055/610-300
Open: all year

FOLIGNO
Umbria
Pierantoni Youth Hostel
Via Pierantoni 23
06034 FOLIGNO PG
Tel: 0742/342-566
Fax: 0742/343-559
E-mail: folhostel@tiscalinet.it
Open: all year
Desk Hours: 7am-midnight
Beds: 203

GENOVA
Liguria
Genova Youth Hostel
Via Costanzi 120n
16136 GENOVA GE
Tel: 010/242-24-57
Fax: 010/242-24-57
E-Mail *hostelge@iol.it*
Open: 2/1- 12/19
Desk Hours: 7-11:30am/3:30pm-midnight
Beds number 213

GUASTALLA
Emilia Romagna
Quadrio Michelotti Youth Hostel
Via Lido Po 11
40126 GUASTALLA RE
Tel: 0522/219-287
Fax: 0522/839-228
E-mail: lunetia@tin.it
Open: Apr 1-Oct 15
Desk Hours: 7-10am/3:30-11:30pm
Beds: 25

ISCHIA
Campania
Il Gabbiano Youth Hostel
 S.S. Forio-Panza 162
80075 FORIO D'ISCHIA NA
Tel: 081/909-422
Fax: 081/909-422
E-mail: n/a
Open: Apr 1-Sep 30
Desk Hours: 7-12:30am
Beds: 100

ISOLA POLVESE
Umbria
Il Poggio Youth Hostel
Isola Polvese, Lago Trasimeno
06060 San Feliciano PG
Tel: 075/965-95-50
Fax: 075/965-95-51
E-mail: ostelloilpoggio@libero.it
Open: Mar 1 Oct 31 for individuals, all
    year for reserved groups
Desk Hours: 7-10am/
    3:30-11:30pm
Beds: 66

LORETO
Marche
Loreto Youth Hostel
Via Aldo Moro 46
60025 LORETO AN
Tel: 071/750-10-26
Fax: 071/750-10-26
E-mail: n/a
Open: all year
Desk Hours: n/a
Beds: 230

LUCCA
Tuscany
San Frediano Youth Hostel
Via della Cavallerizza 12
55100 LUCCA LUTel:
    0583/469-957
Fax: 0583/461-007
E-mail: n/a
Open: all year
Desk Hours: 7-10am/3:30-11:30
Beds: 148

MARINA DI MASSA E CARRARA
Tuscany
Ostello Apuano
V.le delle Pinete 237
Partaccia, I
54037 MARINA DI MASSA E
    CARRARA — PARTACCIA — MS
Tel: 0585/780-034
Fax: 0585/774-266 — 74-858
E-mail: ostelloapuano@hotmail.com
Open: Mar 16-Sep 30
Beds: 200

MENAGGIO
Lombardia
La Primula Youth Hostel
Via IV Novembre 86
22017 MENAGGIO CO
Tel: 0344/32-356
Fax: 0344/31-677
E-mail: menaggiohostel@mclink.it
Open: Mar 15- Nov 5
Desk Hours: 7-10am/4-11pm
Beds: 50

MILAN
Lombardia
Piero Rotta Youth Hostel
Via Martino Bassi 2,(entrance from Via
 Salmoiraghi 1)
20148 MILANO MI
Tel: 02/39-26-70-95
Fax: 02/33-00-01-91
Open: Jan 13-Dec 23
Desk Hours: 7-9:30am/3:30-11:30pm
Beds: 380

MIRA
Veneto
Ostello di Mira
 Via Giare 169
30030 GIARE DI MIRA VE
Tel: 041/567-92-03
Fax: 041/567-64-57
E-mail: ostellomira.venezia@tin.it,
Open: Mar 1-Sep 1
Desk Hours: 7-10am/3:30-11:30pm
Beds: 56

MODENA
Emilia Romagna
San Filippo Neri Youth Hostel
Via Santa Orsola
41100 MODENA
Tel: 059/234-598
Fax: 059/234-598
E-mail: hostelmodena@hotmail.com
Open: all year
Desk Hours: 24 hours
Beds: 80

MONTAGNANA
Veneto
Rocca degli Alberi Youth Hostel
Castello degli Alberi

35044 MONTAGNANA PD
Tel: 0429/81-076 — 049/807-02-66
Fax: 0429/81-076 — 049/807-02-66
Open: Apr 1-Oct 15
Desk Hours: 7-10am/3-11:30pm
Beds: 48

NAPLES
Campania
Mergellina Youth Hostel
Salita della Grottaa
Piedigrotta 2380122 NAPOLI NA
Tel: 081/761-23-46 — 761-12-15
Fax: 081/761-23-91
E-mail: n/a
Open: all year
Desk Hours: 6:30-12:30am
Beds: 200

NICOLOSI
Sicily
Etna Youth Hostel
Via della Quercia 7
95030 NICOLOSI CT
Tel: 095/791-46-86
Fax: 095/791-47-01
E-mail: etnahostel@hotmail.com
Open: all year
Desk Hours: 7am-1pm/ 3-11pm
Beds: 70

NOTO
Sicily
Il Castello Youth Hostel
Via Fratelli Bandiera
96017 NOTO SR
Tel: 0931/571-534
Fax: 0931/571-534
E-mail: ostellodinoto@tin.it
Open: all year
Desk Hours: 7am-midnight
Beds: 68

PADOVA
Veneto
Città di Padova Youth Hostel
Via Aleardo Aleardi 30
35122 PADOVA PD
Tel: 049/875-22-19
Fax: 049/654-210
E-mail: pdyhtl@tin.it
Open: Jan 7-Dec 24

Desk Hours: 7-10am/2:30-11pm;Sat,
Sun 7-10am/2-11pm
Beds: 112

PARMA
Emilia Romagna
Cittadella Youth Hostel
Parco Cittadella 5
43100 PARMA PR
Tel: 0521/961-434
Fax: n/a
E-mail: n/a
Open: Apr 1-Oct 31
Desk Hours: 6:30-10am/3:30-11:30pm
Beds: 50

PERUGIA
Umbria
M. Spagnoli Youth Hostel
Via Cortonese 4
06100 PERUGIA Pian di Massiano PG
Tel: 075/501-13-66
Fax: 075/502-68-05
E-mail: perugiahostel@pg.technet.it
Open: all year
Desk Hours: n/a

PERUGIA
Umbria
Torri Baldelli Mombelli Youth Hostel
Via Manicomi
06077 PERUGIA Ponte Felcino
Tel: 075/501-13-66
Fax: 075/502-68-05
E-mail: perugiahostel@pg.technet.it
Desk Hours: 7am-midnight

POMPEI
Campania
Casa del Pellegrino Youth Hostel
Via Duca d'Aosta
80045 POMPEI NA
Tel: 081/761-23-46
Fax: 081/761-23-91
E-mail: n/a
Desk Hours: 7-10am/3:30-11:30pm
Beds: 90

PRATO
Tuscany
Villa Fiorelli Youth Hostel
Parco di Galceti

59100 PRATO PO
Tel: 0574/697-611
Fax: 0574/697-62-56
E-mail: n/a
Open: all year
Desk Hours: 7-10am/3:30-11:30pm
Beds: 52

RAVENNA
Emilia Romagna
Dante Youth Hostel
Via Aurelio Nicolodi 12
48100 RAVENNA RA
Tel: 0544/421-164
Fax: 0544/421-164
E-mail: hostelravenna@hotmail.com
Open: all year
Desk Hours: 7am-noon/2-11:30pm
Beds: 140

REGGIO EMILIA
Emilia Romagna
Basilica della Ghiara Youth Hostel
Via Guasco
42100 REGGIO EMILIA RE
Tel: 0522/454-795
Fax: 051/224-913
E-mail: n/a
Open: all year
Desk Hours: 7-10am/3:30-11:30pm
Beds: 100

RIVA DEL GARDA
Trentino Alto Adige
Benacus
Piazza Cavour 10
38066 RIVA DEL GARDA TN
Tel: 0464/554-911
Fax: 0464/559-966
E-mail: ostelloriva@anthesi.com
Open: Apr 1-Oct 31
Desk Hours: 7-9am/3pm-midnight
Beds: 67

RIVAMONTE AGORDINO
Veneto
Imperina
Loc.tà Le Miniere
32020 Rivamonte Agordino BL
Tel: 0437/62-451, info:
0437/62-099
Fax: 0437/643-301

Open: Apr 1-Sep 30
Desk Hours: 7-10am/3:30-11:30pm
Beds: 44

ROME
Lazio
Foro Italico-A.F.Pessina Youth Hostel
Viale delle Olimpiadi 61
00194 ROMA RM
Tel: 06/323-62-67
Fax: 06/324-26-13
E-mail: n/a
Open: all year
Desk Hours: 7am-midnight
Beds: 334

ROVERETO
Trentino Alto Adige
Città di Rovereto
Via delle Scuole 16/18
38068 ROVERETO TN
Tel: 0464/433-707
Fax: 0464/424-137
E-mail: youthostrov@tqs.it
Open: Jan 1- Feb 2, Feb 25- Dec 31
Desk Hours: 7am-midnight
Beds: 90

SALERNO
Campania
Ave Gratia Plena Youth Hostel
Via dei Canali
84100 SALERNO SA
Tel: 089/790-251
Fax: 089/405-792
Open: all year
Desk Hours: 7-10am/3:30pm-12:30am
Beds: 150

SAN LAZZARO DI SAVENA
Emilia Romagna
Centro Europa Uno Y.H.
Via Emilia 297, Cicogna
40068 SAN LAZZARO DI
  SAVENA BO
Tel: 051/625-83-52
Fax: 051/625-52-39
E-mail: n/a
Open: all year
Desk Hours: 24 hours
Beds: 42

SANTA SOFIA
Emilia Romagna
Santa Sofia Youth Hostel
Piazza Matteotti
47018 SANTA SOFIA FO
Tel: 0543/970-014
Fax: n/a
E-mail: n/a
Open: all year
Desk Hours: 7-10am/
  3:30pm-midnight
Beds: 26

SAN VITO AL TAGLIAMENTO
Friuli Venezia Giulia
Ostello Europa
Via Amalteo 39
33078 SAN VITO AL TAGLIA-
  MENTO PN
Tel: 0434/876-898
Fax: 0434/877-156
E-mail: wwwbat@tin.it
Open: all year
Desk Hours: 7-10am/3-11:30pm
Beds: 35

SAVONA
Liguria
Fortezza del Priamar Youth Hostel
C.so Mazzini
17100 SAVONA SV
Tel: 019/812-653
Fax: 019/812-653
E-mail: priamarhostel@iol.it
Open: Jan 15- Oct 15
Desk Hours: 7-10am/
3:30-11:30pm
Beds: 60

SAVONA
Liguria
Villa De Franceschini Y.H.
Via alla Strà 29, Conca Verde
17100 SAVONA SV
Tel: 019/263-222
Fax: 019/263-222
E-mail: concaverdehostel@iol.it
Open: Mar 15-Oct 15
Desk Hours: 7-10am/
  4pm-midnight
Beds: 244

SOVERIA MANNELLI
Calabria
La Pineta Youth Hostel
Bivio Bonacci
88049 SOVERIA MANNELLI CZ
Tel: 0968/666-079, — 0349/636-00-
31, — 0339/638-92-24
Fax: 0968/666-079
E-mail: n/a
Open: all year
Desk Hours: 7-10am/
3:30-11:30pm
Beds: 52

SPERLONGA
Lazio
Marina degliu Ulivi Y.H.
Contrada Fiorelle
04029 SPERLONGA LT
Tel: 0771/549-296
Fax: 0771/549-296
E-mail: n/a
Desk Hours: 7-10am/
3:30pm-midnight
Beds: 60

TAORMINA
Sicily
Ulisse Youth Hostel
Vico San Francesco di Paola 9
98039 TAORMINA ME
Tel: 0942/23-193
Fax: 0942/23-193
E-mail: n/a
Open: Jan 10-Dec 31
Desk Hours: 7:30am-noon/
3:30pm-midnight
Beds: 28

TAVARNELLE VAL DI PESA
Tuscany
Ostello del Chianti
Via Roma 137
50028 TAVARNELLE VAL
DI PESA FI
Tel: 055/805-02-65
Fax: 055/806-50-39
Open: Mar 15-Oct 31
Desk Hours: 7-10am/
3:30-midnight
Beds: 82

TERMINILLO
Lazio
Ostello della Neve Youth Hostel
Anello di Campoforogna
02017 TERMINILLO RI
Tel: 0746/261-169
Fax: 0746/261-169
Open: Dec 1-May 15, June 15-Aug 1
Desk Hours: 7am-midnight
Beds: 120

TORRICELLA LAGO TRASIMENO
Umbria
Torricella Youth Hostel
Via del Lavoro 10
06060 TORRICELLA S.Feliciano di
Magione PG
Tel: 075/843-508
Fax: 075/843-508
E-mail: n/a
Open: Mar 1-Oct 31; reservation
required Jul 7-Aug 31
Desk Hours: 7am-1pm/3pm-midnight
Beds: 88

TRIESTE
Friuli Venezia Giulia
Tergeste Youth Hostel
Viale Miramare 331
34136 TRIESTE TS
Tel: 040/224-102
Fax: 040/224-102
E-mail: n/a Open: all year
Desk Hours: 7-10am/Noon-midnight
Beds: 74

TURIN
Piemonte
Torino Youth Hostel
Via Alby 1
10131 TORINO TO
Tel: 011/660-29-39
Fax: 011/660-44-45
E-mail: hostelto@tin.it
Open: Feb 1-Dec 17
Beds: 76

VENICE
Veneto
Venezia Youth Hostel
Fondamenta Zitelle 86, Giudecca

30123 VENEZIA VE
Tel: 041/523-82-11
Fax: 041/523-56-89
E-mail: vehostel@tin.it
Open: Dec 27- Dec 31, Jan 1-Dec 11
Desk Hours: 7am-midnight
Beds: 260

VERBANIA
Piemonte
Verbania Youth Hostel
Via alle Rose 7
28048 Verbania VB
Tel: 0323/501-648
Fax: 0323/507-877
E-mail: n/a
Open: Jan 1-6, Mar 1-Oct 3,
 Dec 5-Dec 31
Desk Hours7-10am/3:30-midnight
Beds: 72

VERONA
Veneto
Villa Francescatti
Salita Fontana del Ferro 15
37129 VERONA VR
Tel: 045/590-360
Fax: 045/800-91-27

Open: all year
Desk Hours: 7am-11:30pm
Beds: 120

VICENZA
Veneto
Olimpico
Viale Giuriolo 9
36100 VICENZA VI
Tel: 0444/540-222
Fax: 0444/547-762
Open: all year
Desk Hours: 7:30-9:30am/3:30-
 11:30pm
Beds: 85

VILLA VALLELONGA
Abruzzo
Tre Confini Youth Hostel
Via Aia Canale
67050 Villavallelonga AQ
Tel: 0863/949-406
Fax: 0863/949-406
E-mail: treconfini@hotmail.com
Open: Apr 1-Sep 30, Dec 1-Feb 29
Desk Hours: 7am-11pm
Beds: 48

glossary

No one expects Americans to arrive in Italy with a perfect command of the Italian language, but it is amazing how much goodwill you can create for yourself by trying even a word or two of Italian when you communicate with locals. Learn a few numbers, basic greetings, and—above all—the life raft, *Parla inglese?* (Do you speak English?). As it turns out, many people do speak a passable English and will be happy to use it, especially if you demonstrate the basic courtesy of at least attempting to greet them in their language. So don't be bashful, but do remember to keep it simple—if you ask questions in Italian, you're likely to get answers in Italian.

BASICS

English	Italian	Pronunciation
Thank you	**Grazie**	*graht*-tzee-yey
You're welcome	**Prego**	*prey*-go
Please	**Per favore**	pehr fah-*vohr*-eh
Yes	**Sì**	see
No	**No**	noh
Good morning or Good day	**Buongiorno**	bwohn-*djor*-noh
Good evening	**Buona sera**	*Bwohn*-ah *say*-rah
Good night	**Buona notte**	*Bwohn*-ah *noht*-tay
How are you?	**Come sta?**	*koh*-may *stah*
Very well	**Molto bene**	*mohl*-toh *behn*-ney
Goodbye	**Arrivederci**	ahr-ree-vah-*deh*-chee
Excuse me (to get attention)	**Scusi**	*skoo*-zee
Excuse me (to get past someone)	**Permesso**	pehr-*mehs*-soh

getting around

Where is ?	Dovè ?	doh-*vey*
The station	la stazione	lah stat-tzee-*oh*-neh
A hotel	un albergo	oon ahl-*behr*-goh
A restaurant	un ristorante	oon reest-ohr-*ahnt*-eh
The bathroom	il bagno	eel *bahn*-nyoh
To the right	A destra	ah *dehy*-stra
To the left	A sinistra	ah see-*nees*-tra
Straight ahead	Avanti (or sempre diritto)	ahv-*vahn*-tee (*sehm*-pray dee-*reet*-toh)
Paying the bill		
How much is it?	Quanto costa?	*kwan*-toh *coh*-sta?
The check, please	Il conto, per favore	eel kon-toh *pehr* fah-*vohr*-eh
Days and times		
When?	Quando?	*kwan*-doh
Yesterday	Ieri	ee-*yehr*-ree
Today	Oggi	*oh*-jee
Tomorrow	Domani	doh-*mah*-nee
Breakfast	Prima colazione	*pree*-mah coh-laht-tzee-*ohn*-ay
Lunch	Pranzo	*prahn*-zoh
Dinner	Cena	*chay*-nah
What time is it?	Che ore sono?	kay *or*-ay *soh*-noh
Monday	Lunedí	loo-nay-*dee*
Tuesday	Martedí	mart-ay-*dee*
Wednesday	Mercoledí	mehr-cohl-ay-*dee*
Thursday	Giovedí	joh-vay-*dee*
Friday	Venerdí	ven-nehr-*dee*
Saturday	Sabato	*sah*-bah-toh
Sunday	Domenica	doh-*mehn*-nee-kah

NUMBERS

1	uno (*oo*-noh)
2	due (*doo*-ay)
3	tre (tray)
4	quattro (*kwah*-troh)
5	cinque (*cheen*-kway)
6	sei (say)
7	sette (*set*-tay)
8	otto (*oh*-toh)
9	nove (*noh*-vay)
10	dieci (dee-*ay*-chee)
11	undici (*oon*-dee-chee)
20	venti (*vehn*-tee)
21	ventuno (vehn-*toon*-oh)

22	**venti due** (*vehn*-tee *doo*-ay)	
30	**trenta** (*trayn*-tah)	
40	**quaranta** (kwah-*rahn*-tah)	
50	**cinquanta** (cheen-*kwan*-tah)	
60	**sessanta** (sehs-*sahn*-tah)	
70	**settanta** (seht-*tahn*-tah)	
80	**ottanta** (oht-*tahn*-tah)	
90	**novanta** (noh-*vahnt*-tah)	
100	**cento** (*chen*-toh)	
1,000	**mille** (*mee*-lay)	
5,000	**cinque milla** (*chen*-kway *mee*-lah)	
10,000	**dieci milla** (dee-*ay*-chee mee-*lah*)	

READING A MENU

Abbacchio	Roast haunch or shoulder of lamb baked and served in a casserole and sometimes flavored with anchovies.
Agnolotti	A crescent-shaped pasta shell stuffed with a mix of chopped meat, spices, vegetables, and cheese; when prepared in rectangular versions, the same combination of ingredients is identified as **ravioli.**
Amaretti	Crunchy, sweet almond-flavored macaroons.
Anguilla alla veneziana	Eel cooked in a sauce made from tuna and lemon.
Antipasti	Succulent tidbits served at the beginning of a meal (before the pasta), whose ingredients might include slices of cured meats, seafood (especially shellfish), and cooked and seasoned vegetables.
Aragosta	Lobster.
Arrosto	Roasted meat.
Baccalà	Dried and salted codfish.
Bagna cauda	Hot and well-seasoned sauce, heavily flavored with anchovies, designed for dipping raw vegetables; literally translated as "hot bath."
Bistecca alla fiorentina	Florentine-style steaks, coated before grilling with olive oil, pepper, lemon juice, salt and parsley.
Bocconcini	Veal layered with ham and cheese, then fried.
Bollito misto	Assorted boiled meats served on a single platter.
Braciola	Pork chop.
Bresaola	Air-dried spiced beef.
Bruschetta	Toasted bread, heavily slathered with olive oil and garlic and often topped with tomatoes.
Bucatini	Coarsely textured hollow spaghetti.
Busecca alla Milanese	Tripe (beef stomach) flavored with herbs and vegetables.
Cacciucco ali livornese	Seafood stew.
Calzone	Pizza dough rolled with the chef's choice of sausage, tomatoes, cheese, and so on, and then baked into a kind of savory turnover.

Cannelloni	Tubular dough stuffed with meat, cheese, or vegetables and then baked in a creamy white sauce.
Cappellacci alla ferrarese	Pasta stuffed with pumpkin.
Cappelletti	Small ravioli ("little hats") stuffed with meat or cheese.
Carciofi	Artichokes.
Carpaccio	Thin slices of raw cured beef, sometimes in a piquant sauce.
Cassatta alla siciliana	A richly caloric dessert combining layers of sponge cake, sweetened ricotta cheese, and candied fruit, bound together with chocolate butter cream icing.
Cervello al burro nero	Brains in black-butter sauce.
Cima alla genovese	Baked fillet of veal rolled into a tube-shaped package containing eggs, mushrooms, and sausage.
Coppa	Cured morsels of pork fillet encased in sausage skins, served in slices.
Costoletta alla milanese	Veal cutlet dredged in bread crumbs, fried, and sometimes flavored with cheese.
Cozze	Mussels.
Fagioli	White beans.
Fave	Fava beans.
Fegato alla veneziana	Thinly sliced calves' liver fried with salt, pepper, and onions.
Foccacia	Ideally, concocted from potato-based dough left to rise slowly for several hours, then garnished with tomato sauce, garlic, basil, salt, and pepper and drizzled with olive oil; similar to a deep-dish pizza most popular in the deep south, especially Bari.
Fontina	Rich cow's-milk cheese.
Frittata	Italian omelette.
Fritto misto	A deep-fried medley of whatever small fish, shellfish, and squid are available in the marketplace that day.
Fusilli	Spiral-shaped pasta.
Gelato (produzione propria)	Ice cream (homemade).
Gnocchi	Dumplings usually made from potatoes (*gnocchi alla patate*) or from semolina (*gnocchi alla romana*), often stuffed with combinations of cheese, spinach, vegetables, or whatever combinations strike the chef's fancy.
Gorgonzola	One of the most famous blue-veined cheeses of Europe— strong, creamy, and aromatic.
Granita	Flavored ice, usually with lemon or coffee.
Insalata di frutti di mare	Seafood salad (usually including shrimp and squid) garnished with pickles, lemon, olives, and spices.
Involtini	Thinly sliced beef, veal, or pork that is rolled, stuffed, and fried.
Minestrone	A rich and savory vegetable soup usually sprinkled with grated parmigiano and studded with noodles.
Mortadella	Mild pork sausage, fashioned into large cylinders and served sliced; the original lunchmeat bologna (because its most famous center of production is Bologna).

Mozzarella	A nonfermented cheese, made from the fresh milk of a buffalo (or, if unavailable, from a cow), boiled and then kneaded into a rounded ball, served fresh.
Mozzarella con pomodori (also "caprese")	Fresh tomatoes with fresh mozzarella, basil, pepper, and olive oil.
Nervetti	A northern Italian antipasto made from chewy pieces of calves' foot or shin.
Osso buco	Beef or veal knuckle slowly braised until the cartilage is tender and then served with a highly flavored sauce.
Pancetta	Herb-flavored pork belly, rolled into a cylinder and sliced—the Italian bacon.
Panettone	Sweet yellow-colored bread baked in the form of a brioche.
Panna	Heavy cream.
Pansotti	Pasta stuffed with greens, herbs, and cheeses, usually served with a walnut sauce.
Pappardelle alle lepre	Pasta with rabbit sauce.
Parmigiano	Parmesan, a hard and salty yellow cheese usually grated over pastas and soups but also eaten alone; also known as *granna*. The best is *parmigiano reggiano*.
Peperoni	Green, yellow, or red sweet peppers (not to be confused with pepperoni).
Pesci al cartoccio	Fish baked in a parchment envelope with onions, parsley, and herbs.
Pesto	A flavorful green sauce made from basil leaves, cheese, garlic, marjoram, and (if available) pine nuts.
Piccata al marsala	Thin escalope of veal braised in a pungent sauce flavored with marsala wine.
Piselli al prosciutto	Peas with strips of ham.
Pizza	Specific varieties include *capricciosa* (its ingredients can vary widely depending on the chef's culinary vision and the ingredients at hand), *margherita* (with tomato sauce, cheese, fresh basil, and memories of the first queen of Italy, Marguerite di Savoia, in whose honor it was first made by a Neapolitan chef), *napoletana* (with ham, capers, tomatoes, oregano, cheese, and the distinctive taste of anchovies), *quatro stagione* (translated as "four seasons" because of the array of fresh vegetables in it; it also contains ham and bacon), and *siciliana* (with black olives, capers, and cheese).
Pizzaiola	A process whereby something (usually a beefsteak) is covered in a tomato-and-oregano sauce.
Polenta	Thick porridge or mush made from cornmeal flour.
Polenta de uccelli	Assorted small birds roasted on a spit and served with polenta.
Polenta e coniglio	Rabbit stew served with polenta.
Polla alla cacciatore	Chicken with tomatoes and mushrooms cooked in wine.
Pollo all diavola	Highly spiced grilled chicken.
Ragù	Meat sauce.

Ricotta	A soft bland cheese made from cow's or sheep's milk.
Risotto	Italian rice.
Risotto alla milanese	Rice with saffron and wine.
Salsa verde	"Green sauce," made from capers, anchovies, lemon juice and/or vinegar, and parsley.
Saltimbocca	Veal scallop layered with prosciutto and sage; its name literally translates as "jump in your mouth," a reference to its tart and savory flavor.
Salvia	Sage.
Scaloppina alla Valdostana	Escalope of veal stuffed with cheese and ham.
Scaloppine	Thin slices of veal coated in flour and sautéed in butter.
Semifreddo	A frozen dessert; usually ice cream with sponge cake.
Seppia	Cuttlefish (a kind of squid); its black ink is used for flavoring in certain sauces for pasta and also in risotto dishes.
Sogliola	Sole.
Spaghetti	A long, round, thin pasta, variously served: *alla bolognese* (with ground meat, mushrooms, peppers, and so on), *alla carbonara* (with bacon, black pepper, and eggs), *al pomodoro* (with tomato sauce), *al sugo/ragù* (with meat sauce), and *alle vongole* (with clam sauce).
Spiedini	Pieces of meat grilled on a skewer over an open flame.
Strangolaprete	Small nuggets of pasta, usually served with sauce; the name is literally translated as "priest-choker."
Stufato	Beef braised in white wine with vegetables.
Tagliatelle	Flat egg noodles.
Tiramisu	Richly caloric dessert containing layers of triple-cream cheeses and rum-soaked sponge cake.
Tonno	Tuna.
Tortelli	Pasta dumplings stuffed with ricotta and greens.
Tortellini	Rings of dough stuffed with minced and seasoned meat and served either in soups or as a full-fledged pasta covered with sauce.
Trenette	Thin noodles served with pesto sauce and potatoes.
Trippe alla fiorentina	Beef tripe (stomach).
Vermicelli	Very thin spaghetti.
Vitello tonnato	Cold sliced veal covered with tuna-fish sauce.
Zabaglione/zabaione	Egg yolks whipped into the consistency of a custard, flavored with marsala, and served warm as a dessert.
Zampone	Pig's trotter stuffed with spicy seasoned port, boiled and sliced.
Zuccotto	A liqueur-soaked sponge cake, molded into a dome and layered with chocolate, nuts, and whipped cream.
Zuppa inglese	Sponge cake soaked in custard architectural terms

ARCHITECTURAL TERMS

Ambone	A pulpit, either serpentine or simple in form, erected in an Italian church.

Apse	The half-rounded extension behind the main altar of a church; Christian tradition dictates that it be placed at the eastern end of an Italian church, the side closest to Jerusalem.
Atrium	A courtyard, open to the sky, in an ancient Roman house; the term also applies to the courtyard nearest the entranceway of an early Christian church.
Baldacchino (also ciborium)	A columned stone canopy, usually placed above the altar of a church; spelled in English, *baldachin* or *baldaquin*.
Baptistry	A separate building or a separate area in a church where the rite of baptism is held.
Basilica	Any rectangular public building, usually divided into three aisles by rows of columns. In ancient Rome, this architectural form was frequently used for places of public assembly and law courts; later, Roman Christians adapted the form for many of their early churches.
Caldarium	The steam room of a Roman bath.
Campanile	A bell tower, often detached, of a church.
Capital	The top of a column, often carved and usually categorized into one of three orders: Doric, Ionic, or Corinthian.
Castrum	A carefully planned Roman military camp, whose rectangular form, straight streets, and systems of fortified gates quickly became standardized throughout the Empire. Modern cities that began as Roman camps and still more or less maintain their original forms include Chester (England), Barcelona (Spain), and such Italian cities as Lucca, Aosta, Como, Brescia, Florence, and Ancona.
Cavea	The curved row of seats in a classical theater; the most prevalent shape was that of a semicircle.
Cella	The sanctuary, or most sacred interior section, of a Roman pagan temple.
Chancel	Section of a church containing the altar.
Cornice	The decorative flange defining the uppermost part of a classical or neoclassical facade.
Cortile	Courtyard or cloisters ringed with a gallery of arches or lintels set atop columns.
Crypt	The main burial place in a church, usually below the choir.
Cupola	A dome.
Duomo	Cathedral.
Forum	The main square and principal gathering place of any Roman town, usually adorned with the city's most important temples and civic buildings.
Grotesques	Carved and painted faces, deliberately ugly, used by everyone from the Etruscans to the architects of the Renaissance; they're especially amusing when set into fountains.

Hyypogeium	Subterranean burial chambers, usually of pre-Christian origins.
Loggia	Roofed balcony or gallery.
Lozenge	An elongated four-sided figure that, along with stripes, was one of the distinctive signs of the architecture of Pisa.
Narthex	The anteroom, or enclosed porch, of a Christian church.
Nave	The largest and longest section of a church, usually devoted to sheltering and/or seating worshipers and often divided by aisles.
Palazzo	A palace or other important building.
Piano Nobile	The main floor of a palazzo (sometimes the second floor).
Pietra Dura	Richly ornate assemblage of semiprecious stones mounted on a flat decorative surface, perfected during the 1600s in Florence.
Pieve	A parish church.
Portico	A porch, usually crafted from wood or stone.
Pulvin	A four-sided stone serving as a substitute for the capital of a column, often decoratively carved, sometimes into biblical scenes.
Putti	Plaster cherubs whose chubby forms often decorate the interiors of baroque chapels and churches.
Stucco	Colored plaster composed of sand, powdered marble, water, and lime, either molded into statuary or applied in a thin concretelike layer to the exterior of a building.
Telamone	Structural column carved into a standing male form; female versions are called *caryatids*.
Thermae	Roman baths.
Transenna	Stone (usually marble) screen separating the altar area from the rest of an early Christian church.
Travertine	The stone from which ancient and Renaissance Rome was built; it's known for its hardness, light coloring, and tendency to be pitted or flecked with black.
Tympanum	The half-rounded space above the portal of a church, usually showcasing a sculpture within this semicircular area.